FIFTH EDITION

BUSINESS MARKETING MANAGEMENT

An Organizational Approach

TEXT AND CASES

Robert W. Haas, Ph.D.

San Diego State University

PWS-KENT Publishing Company   Boston

PWS–KENT
Publishing Company

Sponsoring Editor: Al Bruckner
Production Editor: Patricia Adams
Interior Designer: Catherine Johnson
Cover Designer: Julia Gecha
Cover Image: Thomas Lochray/The Image Bank
Manufacturing Coordinator: Lisa M. Flanagan
Typesetter: G & S Typesetters
Cover Printer: Henry N. Sawyer Co., Inc.
Printer/Binder: Arcata Graphics/Halliday

PWS-KENT Publishing Company is a division of Wadsworth, Inc.

Printed in the United States of America.

3   4   5   6   7   8—97   96   95   94   93

Library of Congress Cataloging-in-Publication Data

Haas, Robert W.
    Business marketing management : an organizational approach /
Robert W. Haas.—5th ed.
    p.   cm.—(The Kent series in marketing)
Rev. ed. of: Industrial marketing management. © 1989.
Includes bibliographical references and index.
ISBN 0-534-92976-1
1. Industrial marketing—Management.   2. Industrial marketing—Management—Case studies.   I. Haas, Robert W.   Industrial marketing management.   II. Title.   III. Series.
HF5415.13.H2713   1992   91-42284
658.8—dc20   CIP

This book is printed on recycled, acid-free paper.

Contents

• •

PART TWO
. . . .

ORGANIZATIONAL CUSTOMERS AND MARKET BEHAVIOR

4

Demand Estimation and Sales Forecasting in Business Markets 100

5

Purchasing and Materials Management 133

6

Organizational Buying Behavior 169

7

Strategic Alliances and Partnering Relationships in Business Marketing   206

PART THREE
. . . .

THE BUSINESS MARKETING PROCESS: SEGMENTATION, PLANNING, STRATEGY, AND INTELLIGENCE GATHERING

8

The Standard Industrial Classification (SIC) System   242

9

Segmentation in Business Markets   277

10

Planning Business Marketing Strategy   303

PART FOUR
. . . .

THE BUSINESS MARKETING MIX

12

13

14

Physical Distribution Strategy in Business Marketing 467

15

Promotional Strategy in Business Marketing—Personal Selling 500

16

Promotional Strategy in Business Marketing—Advertising and Sales Promotion 541

17

Pricing Strategy in Business Marketing 593

PART FIVE
. . . .

BUSINESS MARKETING PERFORMANCE: CONTROL AND EVALUATION

18

Business Marketing Control and Evaluation 646

PART SIX
. . . .

CASES

Preface

• •

Now in its fifth edition, this text was first published in 1976. The title of this edition has been changed from *Industrial Marketing Management* to *Business Marketing Management* to better reflect the more contemporary nature of marketing to organizations. In many circles today, the term *business marketing* has supplanted the term *industrial marketing*. The change in title reflects that movement.

This edition involves more than a change in title, however. Although the basic format of the previous editions is maintained, significant changes have been added. There is a greatly expanded coverage of the environment in which business marketing takes place. In addition, a separate chapter (Chapter 5) on purchasing has been added to develop a better understanding of the importance of this activity, and a new Chapter 7 covers strategic alliances, partnerships, and networks that are becoming critically important in contemporary business marketing. Expanded coverage of service marketing has been added to Chapter 12, and Chapter 17 now includes coverage of pricing in JIT (Just-in-Time) situations. There are 25 cases at the end of the text (Part Six), 10 of which are new to this edition. Finally, although this text concentrates primarily on U.S. business marketing, global implications are greatly expanded. Collectively these changes have the effect of updating the text and bringing it more in line with current happenings in business marketing.

The basic philosophy of previous editions remains unchanged. Primary em-advancing from marketing principles courses to business marketing courses.

I wish to thank all those who contributed to the writing of this edition. Particular thanks go to Professor Wesley Johnston of Georgia State University whose insight and advice helped to define the new directions taken in this edition. Professor Johnston made significant contributions to the new chapters covering the environment, purchasing, and strategic alliances. I also wish to specially thank Professors W. E. Patton III and Ronald King of Appalachian State University and Professor Hubert D. Hennessey of Babson College for their excellent cases that have added greatly to this edition. Special thanks are also extended to all of the authors who contributed cases included in this edition. Finally, thanks are given to those who reviewed this text. I feel fortunate to have had such qualified and constructive reviewers as Vaughan Judd of Auburn University, Jakki Mohr of the University of Colorado, and Marti Rhea of the University of North Texas.

My sincerest hope is that this new edition will continue to help further the study of business marketing and contribute to a better understanding of this vital area of the overall marketing discipline.

Robert W. Haas
Ramona, California

CASE CONTRIBUTORS

Robert H. Collins, Hilton Distinguished Professor of Marketing, University of Nevada, Las Vegas, "Medical Electronic Instruments."

C. Merle Crawford, Graduate School of Business Administration, The University of Michigan, "DOW—IRMA."

Harold W. Fox, former Professor of Marketing, Pan American University and Seminar Leader, "Gypsum Wallboard Corporation."

John L. Graham, Professor of Marketing, University of California, Irvine, "Bolter Turbines, Inc."

Hubert D. Hennessey, Associate Professor of Marketing, Babson College, "Milford Glove Company."

Hubert D. Hennessey, Associate Professor of Marketing, Babson College, **Larry Isaacson,** Professor of Marketing, Babson College, and **Linda Block,** Associate Professor of Marketing, Bentley College, "Prime Plastics, Inc."

Hubert D. Hennessey, Associate Professor of Marketing, Babson College, and **Barbara Kalunian,** Babson College, "Royal Corporation."

Ronald H. King, Professor of Marketing, and **W. E. Patton III,** Professor of Marketing, both of Appalachian State University, "Carolina Jam & Jelly (A)," "Carolina Jam & Jelly (B)," "Bay City Steam Fittings, Inc.," "General Supply Company," and "Superior Equipment Company."

G. Dean Kortge, Associate Professor of Marketing, and **Patrick A. Okonkwo,** Associate Professor of Marketing, both of Central Michigan University, "Great Lakes Building Products Company."

Carla S. Lallatin, President, Lallatin & Associates, Rego Park, New York, "ABC Computer Corporation."

John MacFie, Graduate Assistant, San Diego State University, "Southwest Paper, Inc."

Jakki Mohr, Assistant Professor of Marketing, University of Colorado at Boulder, and **Kenneth Manning,** Doctoral Student, University of South Carolina, "Wind Technology."

Charles O'Neal, Professor of Marketing, University of Evansville, "Electrotech, Inc."

Linda Rochford, Assistant Professor of Marketing, San Diego State University, "Veber Chemical Corporation."

Steven Turtletaub, Graduate Assistant, San Diego State University, "City of Brookings."

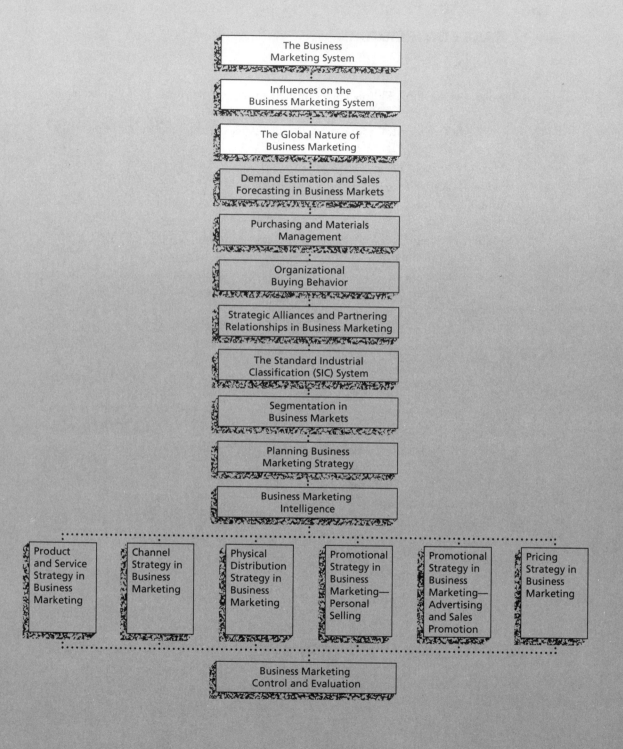

The Business
Marketing System

Influences on the
Business Marketing System

The Global Nature of
Business Marketing

Demand Estimation and Sales
Forecasting in Business Markets

Purchasing and Materials
Management

Organizational
Buying Behavior

Strategic Alliances and Partnering
Relationships in Business Marketing

The Standard Industrial
Classification (SIC) System

Segmentation in
Business Markets

Planning Business
Marketing Strategy

Business Marketing
Intelligence

Product
and Service
Strategy in
Business
Marketing

Channel
Strategy in
Business
Marketing

Physical
Distribution
Strategy in
Business
Marketing

Promotional
Strategy in
Business
Marketing—
Personal
Selling

Promotional
Strategy in
Business
Marketing—
Advertising
and Sales
Promotion

Pricing
Strategy in
Business
Marketing

Business Marketing
Control and Evaluation

Understanding the Business Marketing Environment

1

The Business Marketing System

•••

Business marketing is that area of marketing that addresses organizational customers and prospects who buy goods and services necessary to the operation of their own businesses or organizations. As such, business marketing does not include marketing to final consumers who buy goods and services for personal consumption. For many years, this area of overall marketing was seen as mechanical and unimaginative and was slighted in the marketing literature. Today, however, indications are that business marketing is a dynamic, growing, and vibrant component of the overall marketing discipline.

The term **business marketing** has evolved from what historically has been known as **industrial marketing.** For years, the latter term was used to describe all marketing activities designed to attract customers other than personal consumers. In fact, the previous editions of this text were titled *Industrial Marketing Management*. In recent years, however, there has been a trend toward use of the terms **business marketing** or **business-to-business marketing** rather than industrial marketing. To illustrate, the trade publication *Industrial Marketing* changed its name to *Business Marketing*. To many, industrial marketing suggests marketing only to rust-belt heavy-manufacturing type industries and thus seems antiquated. Regardless of which terms are used, this area of marketing concentrates on organizational customers whether they are in heavy industry or otherwise. Thus, as will be developed, business marketing includes marketing to private business and commercial organizations, reseller organizations, governmental organizations, and institutional organizations. Viewed in this manner, business marketing involves marketing activities aimed at organizations of any type, but it does not include marketing primarily designed to attract final personal consumers.

As regards the term *business-to-business marketing*, it does not seem appropriate and thus will not be used in this text. To illustrate, a defense contractor

Business Marketing Is Big Business

One of the main points of differentiation between business and consumer marketing is the size and magnitude of business marketing orders and transactions. A few examples will help show just how big business marketing actually is and illustrate the challenges that face business marketers.

Boeing Company's 747-400 airliner, the firm's long-range version of the jumbo jet, sells for approximately $150 million. This plane has the advantage of being able to fly nonstop to Asia from either the United States or Europe, making it very popular with Asian air carriers. In mid-1991, Boeing had 412 such aircraft on order or in service, 54 percent of them for Asian and Pacific airlines. A plane ordered from Boeing at that time could not be delivered before 1997. Those 412 aircraft, with an average price of $150 million each, had a total value of about $62 billion, which is big-time marketing in any league.

Cubic Corporation's Automatic Revenue Collection Group was awarded a $43 million contract to install an automatic toll-collection system on the 320-mile Florida turnpike, which connects Orlando to Miami. Described as the largest toll-collection contract ever awarded in the United States, the system will service 300 freeway lanes that are expected to handle more than 125 million vehicles per year. The system will speed up the flow of traffic and improve the accuracy of fare collection.

Rohr Industries, Inc., entered into a contract with Europe's Airbus Industrie to provide engine components for 800 A320 and A321 aircraft. Rohr would provide nacelle systems to Airbus, including fan cowls, thrust reversers, exhaust nozzles and cones, inlets, and pylons. Under the terms of the contract, Rohr would realize sales of approximately $1 billion starting in 1992 and extending into the late 1990s. For Rohr, this was the second largest contract it had entered into in 1990, having also signed a $1 billion contract to supply nacelles for McDonnell–Douglas's MD-90 airliner.

A rather unique example of business marketing took place during the 1991 Desert Storm war in the Middle East. When they were notified that troops at Fort Stewart, Georgia, were being sent to Saudi Arabia, officials at the military base sent an order to K-Mart in nearby Hinesville, Georgia, for more than 24,000 items, including 2,400 cans of bug spray, 5,550 bottles of skin lotion, 5,550 tubes of lip balm, 5,500 containers of foot powder, and 5,550 bottles of suntan lotion. These goods were shipped to Fort Stewart from K-Mart's regional warehouse in Atlanta. In addition, the store was asked to help the military find sources for 174,000 gallons of bottled water. While not a conventional business marketing transaction, this example clearly shows the magnitude of orders in business markets.

These examples may be exceptional in size, but they are typical of what takes place in business marketing. Marketing effectively in such situations requires close attention to detail and a real commitment to quality service. These examples illustrate clearly that business marketing is different from traditional consumer marketing.

Source: Adapted from various editions of the *San Diego Union.*

selling products or services to a government agency, such as the Department of Defense (DOD), is not really representative of a true business-to-business situation. Similarly, selling to not-for-profit institutions also does not constitute true business-to-business marketing. Thus, this text will use the term *business marketing* to denote marketing to all types of organizations, whether they are true businesses or not.

This book is written primarily for use in courses in business or industrial marketing and assumes that the reader has a sound understanding of basic marketing principles. The basic format is traditional in that the text identifies the corporate or top-level marketing responsibilities that make up a strategic marketing plan, such as market segmentation and buyer behavior, and the functional-level marketing activities, such as pricing, product planning, promotion, and physical distribution. The intent of this book is to use the base of marketing principles and from it build a sound understanding of how those same principles apply to the specific area of business marketing.

A DEFINITION OF MARKETING

In 1985, the American Marketing Association updated its 1960 definition of marketing. *Marketing* is now defined as "the process of planning and executing the conception, pricing, promotion, and distribution of ideas, goods, and services to create exchanges that satisfy individual and organizational objectives."[1] This revised definition assumes that marketing involves individuals within an organization who develop products and/or services that satisfy the needs and wants of customers in whatever markets may be involved to the mutual benefit of both buyers and sellers. It implies that marketing is a process that takes place before products and services are produced and continues even after the sale. Since this new definition is used in many marketing principles textbooks, its use is continued in this text.

A DEFINITION OF BUSINESS MARKETING

As has been stated, business marketing involves the performance of those marketing activities directed toward organizational customers rather than toward consumers who buy goods and services for personal consumption. Business customers are usually organizations and may be public or private, end-users or re-sellers, domestic or multinational. For example, privately owned factories, mills, shops, and other such manufacturers would be considered business customers. So would wholesalers, retailers, and other such resellers buying goods and services in the operation of business. Similarly, governmental agencies, boards, and commissions at all levels (federal, state, county, and municipal) also qualify as business customers. In addition, not-for-profit institutions such as colleges and universities, hospitals, churches, and the like are also seen as business customers.

There is marketing to organizations that does not fit under the subject of business marketing. Retailers and wholesalers are, of course, organizations that buy many goods and services for resale to their consumer market customers. For example, a large grocery chain buys canned fruit and vegetables from a producer such as Del Monte strictly for resale. Similarly, a grocery wholesaler may purchase these same consumer goods from Del Monte for resale to smaller grocery retailers who purchase for the purpose of providing them to their customers. Such transactions are not considered to be business marketing ones in that the goods and services that are bought and sold are designed and intended for consumer markets. In such cases, the resellers are actually **channel intermediaries** in consumer marketing and are not considered customers in business marketing. This distinction is important because it marks where business marketing ends and consumer marketing begins. Organizational customers in business markets purchase goods and services to use either directly or indirectly in the operation of business. Resellers, such as retailers and wholesalers, are considered elements in the business marketing system when they are purchasing cleaning equipment, fixtures, shelving and other storage facilities, displays, office supplies, checkout counters, shopping carts, theft prevention and security systems, sprinkler systems, and other goods and services that are necessary to the operation of their businesses, but not when the goods and services purchased are intended solely for resale. In summary, reseller organizations typically operate in both consumer and business markets, but this text is concerned only with the latter.

Viewed from these perspectives, the revised American Marketing Association definition is flexible enough to apply to the topic of business marketing. All that is needed is to adapt the definition's process to organizational rather than ultimate consumer customers and prospects. The basis for defining business marketing lies in the understanding of the organizational customer rather than in the products or services involved. Goods and services are "want satisfiers" and as such must fulfill the wants, needs, and expectations of selected target customers if the supplying companies are to survive and succeed. This fact is true for both the business market and the consumer market. There are, however, some big differences in the rationale behind buying motives in the two markets, and the basic structures of the two markets contrast sharply. This book focuses on those differences and how they affect marketing strategy development and decision making. Table 1.1 provides some examples of the diverse nature of business marketing.

From here on, the term *business marketing* refers to marketing activities

TABLE 1.1   **Examples of the Diverse Nature of Business Marketing**

Supplier	Products or Services Offered	Customer
Machine tool manufacturer	Machine tools used in production processes	Machine shops, mills, manufacturers
Insurance company	Pension plans, employee insurance programs	Organizations providing such coverage
Earth-moving equipment manufacturer	Bulldozers, backhoes, graders	Local governments maintaining roads
Aircraft manufacturer	Military aircraft	U.S. Department of Defense
Office/school equipment manufacturer	Desks, tables, chairs, file cabinets	School systems, colleges, and universities
Materials handling equipment manufacturer	Forklifts, conveyors, cranes, pallets	Warehouses, wholesalers, distributors, manufacturing plants
Electronics manufacturer	Electronic cash registers	Retailers of all types
Pharmaceutical company	Drugs for medicinal purposes	Hospitals, clinics, physicians' offices
Advertising agency	Advertising services	Business organizations lacking own advertising capabilities
Sporting goods manufacturer	Baseballs, bats, gloves	Professional teams, schools, sporting goods wholesalers and retailers
Publisher	University textbooks	University book stores
Protection service company	Guards, guard dogs, electronic protection devices	Businesses and other organizations requiring protection
Commercial laundry service company	Laundry services	Hospitals, hotels and motels, nursing homes

that are intended to acquire and sell goods and services to organizations to be used directly or indirectly in their own operations. These organizations may be public or private, end-user or reseller, domestic or multinational.

BUSINESS MARKETING MANAGEMENT

The following definition is appropriate for describing the marketing management function in business marketing:

> Marketing management is the analysis, planning, implementation, and control of programs designed to create, build, and maintain mutually beneficial exchanges and relationships with target markets for the purpose of achieving organizational objectives.[2]

This definition implies a managerial perspective: Someone within the marketing organization is responsible for the marketing process taking place in an effective and economical manner. That someone is typically the **chief marketing officer.** This person may hold any one of a number of titles, including vice president of marketing, director of marketing, and marketing manager. Figure 1.1

FIGURE 1.1   Titles of Chief Marketing Officers in Business Marketing Firms

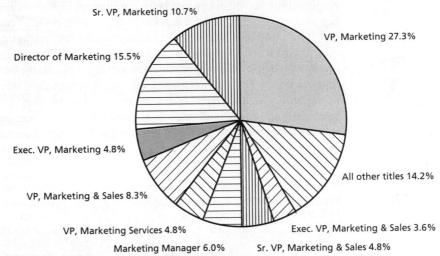

Sr. VP, Marketing 10.7%

Director of Marketing 15.5%

VP, Marketing 27.3%

Exec. VP, Marketing 4.8%

All other titles 14.2%

VP, Marketing & Sales 8.3%

VP, Marketing Services 4.8%

Exec. VP, Marketing & Sales 3.6%

Marketing Manager 6.0%   Sr. VP, Marketing & Sales 4.8%

Source: Reprinted by permission from *Chief Marketing Executive* (Chicago: Heidrick & Struggles, Inc., 1988), 3.

% of respondents citing each title

shows the many titles held by chief marketing officers in business marketing firms. This text will use the title *business marketing manager*. Regardless of the title, this person's task is one of managing change in the marketplace to the mutual benefit of the marketing organization and its customers.

Marketing management refers to the managing of subordinates in the completion of those marketing programs and activities necessary to achieve the organization's marketing objectives. Such management involves implementing required marketing activities through the efforts of others inside, and often outside, the organization. Although the main focus of this text is at the marketing manager level, it should be understood that many marketing activities are performed by other functional managers in the marketing department. To illustrate, many business marketing companies employ product managers who are responsible for new product planning, product research, and product service. Advertising managers, if used, are responsible for corporate and product advertising decisions. Sales managers recruit and train salespeople and manage the company's field sales force. These functional managers typically report to the marketing manager, who is ultimately responsible for the marketing plan.

In a detailed study of the areas of responsibility of business marketing managers, Heidrick and Struggles, Inc., found that there is no uniform set of activities for which the manager is responsible that is common to all business marketing companies. Moreover, the areas of responsibility may differ depending on the size of the company involved. Table 1.2 shows the findings of this study. Analysis of the table does reveal, however, that certain activities are usually the responsibility of business marketing managers. These include determining strategy and tactics, identifying markets, and setting policies and objectives.

The table also shows that accountability for marketing activities often occurs at two levels in the business marketing firm. These are the top management level, which may be responsible for setting objectives, policies, and planning, and the functional management level, which might then be responsible for developing and executing parts of the overall marketing plan. For example, while the marketing manager is ultimately responsible for pricing, he or she usually does not have the direct task of recommending, setting, and administering prices.

TABLE 1.2 **Primary Marketing Tasks of Chief Marketing Executives in Business Marketing Firms**

Marketing Task	Average of All Business Marketing Firms	Business Marketing Firms by Size of Sales		
		$2B or More	$1–$1.9B	Under $1B
Determine strategy and tactics	74.1%	86.8%	68.4%	58.3%
Identify markets for present and new products/services	60.5%	55.3%	78.9%	54.2%
Set policies and objectives	51.9%	57.9%	36.8%	54.2%
Execute plans	27.2%	31.6%	21.1%	25.0%
Measure market shares of company and competitors	18.5%	21.1%	15.8%	16.7%
Prepare long-range plans	17.3%	15.8%	10.5%	25.0%
Manpower training and development	14.8%	13.2%	15.8%	16.7%
Prepare short-run plans in functional areas	9.9%	7.9%	5.3%	16.7%
Provide customer services	4.9%	2.6%	5.3%	8.3%
Forecast sales	7.4%	5.3%	10.5%	8.3%
Recommend product and package specifications	3.7%	2.6%	5.3%	4.2%
Select channels of distribution	6.2%	0.0%	15.8%	8.3%
Recommend, set, and administer prices	3.7%	0.0%	10.5%	4.2%
Other tasks	1.2%	2.6%	0.0%	0.0%

Source: Reprinted by permission from *Chief Marketing Executive* (Chicago: Heidrick & Struggles, Inc., 1988), 11.

This can be seen in the table, where only 3.7 percent of the chief marketing executives surveyed performed this task. The same may be said for functional short-run planning, providing services, sales forecasting, selecting channels, and determining product and service specifications. These tasks are often performed by the functional managers in the marketing area such as product managers, sales managers, distribution managers, etc., or they may even be performed by people in areas outside the marketing department. For example, providing customer service may be the responsibility of the firm's service department. Viewed from this perspective, then, the term marketing management involves efforts of people both inside and outside the marketing department.

As stated, marketing decisions are made at two levels. This text focuses more on the top marketing management level than on management in the individual functional areas. As the definition at the beginning of this section suggests, the term *marketing management* is derived from the recognition that business marketing firms plan marketing activities, execute the planned activities, and then control the results to evaluate the plan and its execution.

WHO ARE BUSINESS CUSTOMERS?

Within the definition of business marketing previously developed, business customers are organizations rather than individual consumers or households buying goods and services for personal consumption. From here on, business customers are defined as organizations buying goods and services for use, either directly or indirectly, in their own operations. Business customers can be classified into four sometimes overlapping groups:

1. **Business and commercial organizations** are private organizations that buy goods and services to use either directly or indirectly in producing the goods and services that they in turn market to their customers. An example might be a manufacturer that purchases production equipment.

2. **Reseller organizations** are private commercial organizations such as retailers and wholesalers that buy goods and sometimes services that are directly or indirectly necessary to the operation of business. An example might be a retailer such as Sears & Roebuck or K-Mart that purchases lighting fixtures, display equipment, computerized point-of-purchase machines, and so forth.

3. **Governmental organizations** are governmental entities operating at the federal, state, or local level that purchase goods and services in order to provide necessary services for their constituents. An example might be a water district that purchases water purification equipment to better serve those in its district.

4. **Institutional organizations** are organizations that do not fall into the commercial, reseller, or governmental classifications but that may be large purchasers of goods and services. An example may be a private university that purchases computers for student use in its computer laboratories.

A more detailed look at each of these classifications follows.

Business and Commercial Organizations

Many private business and commercial organizations purchase goods and services that they use either directly or indirectly in the operation of their businesses. The products and services they buy either produce or become part of other goods and services or in some other way facilitate the operation of the organization itself. Basically, these types of organizational customers may be classified as either original equipment manufacturers (OEMs) or user customers.

Original Equipment Manufacturers The **original equipment manufacturer,** more commonly referred to as the OEM, is a commercial customer that buys products and sometimes services to incorporate into the products that it, in turn, produces and sells either into business or consumer markets. Thus, an electronics company that sells component parts such as transistors to a manufacturer of television sets would consider the television firm an OEM customer. The important point to realize with this type of customer is that the product of the business marketer (the transistor) ends up in the product of the customer (the television set). The purchased product becomes an integral part of the final customer's product. Typically, the term OEM refers to the customer of a producer of **business products.** There are times, however, when **business services** may be involved. For example, a manufacturer of electronic testing equipment may contract to provide service on a customer's machines. The customer may view this service as a part of the product purchased, and if so, the contracted service is being provided to an OEM customer.

User Customers A second type of commercial enterprise customer is known as the user. In the business market, this term refers to those organizations that purchase goods and/or services for use in producing other goods and/or services, which are then sold into the business or consumer market or both. Examples of user customers are manufacturing companies that purchase lathes, drilling machines, gear-cutting machines, punching and shearing machines, bending and forming machines, and other, similar pieces of machinery that are used in their production processes.

User customers also purchase supplies and services, the consumption of which is necessary for the production of their own goods and services. For example, a manufacturer will purchase grease and oil to keep its equipment maintained and operating in peak condition. These lubricants are necessary in the normal operation of any manufacturing business. Similarly, the manufacturer may contract for janitorial services that are also necessary in normal operation. In contrast to the OEM, products and services purchased by user customers do not become part of the business customer's final product. The user customer buys the product or service and uses it, directly or indirectly, to produce the product or service that it, in turn, sells to its customers.

It is important to realize that customers of this commercial classification system are not exclusively OEMs or users. To illustrate, a fabricating plant may be an OEM customer when purchasing component parts from some suppliers;

however, the machinery that the company purchases for its production line simultaneously qualifies it as a user customer to the suppliers of such machinery. This situation means that the same company can be an OEM and a user at the same time, but normally not for the same supplier! As may be expected, it is of critical importance that any business marketing manager knows whether customers are OEMs or users. If proper classification is not known, the marketing manager can hardly market effectively, as the manager will be completely ignorant of the differences in buying motivations predominant with each type of customer. An OEM does not purchase for the same reasons as does a user customer. And of course, OEMs and users do not normally buy the same products.

Reseller Organizations

Many business marketing firms market their products and/or services to reseller organizations such as retailers and wholesalers. While these organizational customers are themselves often in the consumer market, they are still business marketing customers. As organizations, they buy goods and services, often in a manner similar to original equipment manufacturers and user customers. As stated, although resellers are operating in the consumer market, they are often considered elements of the **business marketing system.**

Retailers   U.S. retailers constitute a large market for many business marketers. In 1990, there were over one million retailers operating in the United States. Table 1.3 shows the basic types of retailers in terms of both number of establishments and sales. For many producers of business goods and services, retailers

TABLE 1.3   Basic Types of U.S. Retailers by Number of Establishments and Retail Sales Volume

Type	Number of Establishments (1,000s)	Annual Sales in Current Dollars ($ billions)
Business materials & garden supplies	69.6	$ 88.9
General merchandise stores	36.0	183.8
Food stores	187.4	331.9
Auto dealers & service stations	201.6	369.0
Apparel & accessory stores	141.8	82.0
Furniture & home furnishings	101.4	93.0
Miscellaneous retail stores *	327.2	480.6
Total	1,065.0	$1,629.2

Source: U.S. Department of Commerce, *Statistical Abstract of the United States* (Washington, DC: U.S. Government Printing Office, January 1990), 771–772.

* Includes drug, liquor, sporting goods, stationery, gifts, mail order, and florist retailers.

constitute a major market. A producer of floor display units, for example, may sell its products almost entirely to retail organizations.

Wholesalers   There are approximately 470,000 wholesalers operating in the United States. Table 1.4 shows that total sales by wholesalers exceed $1,580 billion annually, implying another large market for producers of many business goods and services. To illustrate, producers of material handling equipment such as shelving, pallets, fork lifts, etc., will probably view wholesaler organizations as a prime target market for their products.

Governmental Organizations

Business customers of the government variety can range from the smallest township or village in the United States to the Department of Defense. All levels of government comprise what is considered to be the largest single market for goods and services in the world.[3] Great variations occur among governmental

---

TABLE 1.4   Basic Types of Merchant Wholesalers by Sales Volume

Type	Annual Sales in Current Dollars ($ billions)
Durable Goods:	$ 782.8
Motor vehicles	$ 164.0
Furniture	28.0
Lumber/construction materials	55.7
Sporting goods	24.5
Metals	69.0
Electrical goods	104.1
Hardware, plumbing, heating equipment	47.0
Machinery, equipment & supplies	209.2
Miscellaneous durables	81.3
Nondurable Goods:	$ 805.6
Paper	$ 51.7
Drugs	36.5
Apparel	50.2
Groceries	223.9
Farm products/raw materials	126.0
Chemicals	34.8
Petroleum	127.5
Beer/wine	43.7
Miscellaneous nondurables	111.3
Total	$1,588.4

Source: U.S. Department of Commerce, *Statistical Abstract of the United States* (Washington, DC: U.S. Government Printing Office, January 1990), 780.

customers in their buying patterns, purchasing procedures, and buying volume, but basically they all fit into the general classification of governmental customers. Broadly defined, government customers fall into three basic classifications: (1) local, (2) state, and (3) federal.

Local Government   There are four main types of local government organizations: (1) municipalities, (2) townships, (3) special districts, and (4) counties. A brief analysis of each may provide an understanding of the local government market.

Municipalities   There are approximately 19,000 municipalities in the United States. Their major expenses typically are made in such areas as streets and highways, municipally owned water supply systems, solid waste disposal, police and fire protection, wastewater treatment, and parks and recreation.

Townships   In addition to the 19,000 municipal governments, there are about 16,700 townships in the United States. Townships differ from municipalities in that they are established to serve defined geographical areas, whereas municipalities are set up to serve specific population concentrations in defined areas. In all other respects, the township market is similar to the municipal market. Major expenses of townships are typically in such areas as streets and highways, police and fire protection, wastewater treatment, solid waste disposal, and water supply systems.

Special Districts   There are also about 28,500 special districts in the United States. Most of these are established to provide specific functions, and in that sense, they differ from municipalities and townships. Major expenditures of special districts are in such areas as water supply systems, preservation of natural resources, wastewater treatment, and fire protection.

Counties   Finally, there are 3,041 counties in the United States. Of this total, 323 are metropolitan in nature, and their expenditures alone account for more than half of all county government expenditures. This division between metropolitan and rural counties indicates great variation in purchase volumes and in buying practices. County government expenditures are typically in such areas as streets and highways, police protection, preservation of natural resources, parks and recreation, solid waste disposal, wastewater treatment, and fire protection.

Collectively, these four classifications compose a local government market of about 62,000 separate buying units. Purchases in 1990 by these buying units was estimated to be $223 billion, of which an estimated 90 percent will be accounted for by only 17 percent of the buying units. This indicates that some local governments are very large customers, whereas others are very small.

State Government   The nation's 50 states are also customers for many marketing firms. Their major expenditures often are made in such areas as education, highways, hospitals and institutions, police and correctional facilities, and miscellaneous areas such as water, airports, and community redevelopment projects. Purchases of goods and services by the nation's 50 states in 1990 was estimated to be $148 billion.

Federal Government The U.S. federal government is also a large buyer of goods and services. In 1990, various federal government buying units purchased $436 billion of goods and services. "The federal government alone buys more goods and services than any other government, business, industry or organization in the world."[4]

Federal government buying units can be classified into civilian and military sectors. The civilian sector consists of the following: (1) departments such as the U.S. Department of Agriculture, (2) administrations such as the General Services Administration, (3) agencies such as the Federal Aviation Agency, (4) boards such as the Civil Aeronautics Board, (5) commissions such as the Federal Communications Commission, (6) executive offices such as the Bureau of the Budget, and (7) other independent establishments such as the National Science Foundation.

The federal military sector includes the Defense Supply Agency and the departments of the army, navy, and air force. The Defense Supply Agency was created in 1961 to centralize buying among the three branches of the armed services as much as possible, but considerable buying is still performed by the individual service branches.

In total, the purchasing needs of the federal government are basically the following: (1) consumer office supplies and general housekeeping products needed to run the many paper-based U.S. agencies; (2) items bought from the standard product lines of American industry such as computers, automobiles, and furniture; and (3) nonstandard products and services needed for unique activities of the federal government, including specialized armaments for the military, customized Social Security studies, and innovative laboratory equipment for cancer research.[5]

The total government market is big and diverse, and it accounts for about 38 percent of the nation's total gross national product. Breaking down this market reveals that about 54 percent of all government purchases are made by federal government buying units, 28 percent by local governments, and 18 percent by state governments. Figure 1.2 illustrates the breakdown of purchases by governmental customers based on 1990 purchases. The products and services purchased often differ appreciably by the type of government involved. For example, the federal government spends a large amount on defense contracts, whereas state and local governments spend large amounts on education and public welfare. In summary, all six levels of government (municipal, township, county, special district, state, and federal) make up the largest market for goods and services in the world.[6] Figure 1.3 shows annual purchases by all six levels between 1986 and 1990. Total purchases by all six levels are expected to increase by 13.3 percent between 1990 and 1993.[7]

FIGURE 1.2   **Breakdown of Purchases by Governmental Customers Based on 1990 Purchases (in billions of current dollars)**

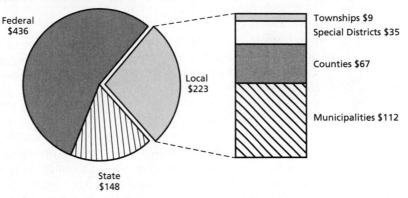

Source: Adapted from *Introduction to the Government Market: Local, State, and Federal,* 3d ed. (Cleveland: Government Product News, 1987), 7, 12.

FIGURE 1.3   **Annual Purchases of Governmental Customers from 1986 to 1990 (in billions of current dollars)**

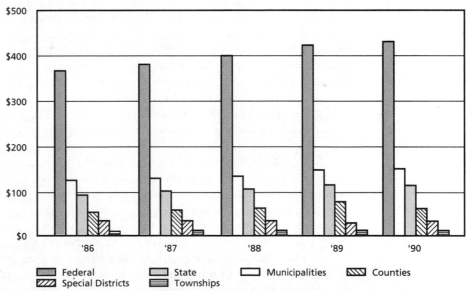

Source: Adapted from *Introduction to the Government Market: Local, State, and Federal,* 3d ed. (Cleveland: Government Product News, 1987), 7, 12.

Institutional Organizations

The institutional market includes all those customers of the organizational variety that do not fall into commercial or governmental classifications. Examples of institutional customers are schools, colleges and universities, churches, hospitals, nursing homes, sanitariums, rest homes, medical clinics, trade schools, and nonprofit foundations. As can be seen by these examples, institutional customers can be public or private. A company can market products to both state universities and private universities, to both public and parochial schools, to both private and government-sponsored vocational schools, and so on. From the business marketing manager's point of view, the difference is not so much whether the institution is public or private, but rather how each institution purchases its goods and services. For example, a multicampus state university with autonomous purchasing authority on each of its campuses may be marketed to in the same manner as any private university; but a multicampus state university with centralized buying for all its campuses may more properly be considered a governmental customer. The point to remember is that institutions do not fall into a clear-cut classification but are a hybrid of government and private organizations that must be considered on an individual basis according to their purchasing practices and policies.

Determining the size of the institutional market is not an easy task but all evidence points to it being large. As stated before, some elements of this market, such as a county hospital or a local school system, fall into governmental areas. Expenditures here are included in the governmental statistics previously cited. Other elements of this same market, such as health maintenance organizations (HMOs), are essentially commercial organizations and are included in that previously discussed section. The third element of the institutional market has been called the third sector or the nonprofit sector.[8] This group includes all nonprofit associations and nongovernmental community service agencies at the national, regional, or local levels. One study of this third sector estimated that it is comprised of approximately six million organizations and spends about $250 billion annually on purchases of goods and services.[9] Thus, the total institutional market is quite large and constitutes an important target market for many producers of business goods and services.

Although all four general types of organizational customers are dissimilar in many respects, they generally are considered to compose business markets because they all purchase goods and/or services to use directly or indirectly in providing goods and/or services to their own customers. Thus, they all differ from ultimate consumers in that they purchase goods and services only to satisfy directly or indirectly the demands of their own customers.

In addition, they are often remarkably similar in their purchasing behavior. A hospital may buy in much the same manner as does a manufacturer, and at times, they may both be purchasing the same products from the same suppliers. This text concentrates on all three types of organizational customers, showing similarities and differences where appropriate.

CLASSIFICATIONS OF BUSINESS PRODUCTS AND SERVICES

Although many types of goods and services can be sold into business markets, they generally fall into one of seven general classifications: (1) heavy equipment, (2) light or accessory equipment, (3) supplies, (4) component parts, (5) raw materials, (6) processed materials, and (7) business services. An analysis of each follows. The purpose of classification is to help identify those variables in each category that may subsequently affect marketing planning. In reading each category, notice that purchasing motives may differ from category to category, which, in turn, means that marketing strategy and tactics will change from category to category.

Heavy Equipment

The heavy equipment classification of business products includes metal-cutting machine tools (lathes, boring mills, drilling machines, gear-cutting machines, grinders, and polishers), metal-forming machines (punching and shearing machines; hydraulic, mechanical, and forging presses; and forging machines), fork-lifts, overhead cranes, blast furnaces, electrical drive systems, trucks, mainframe and microcomputers, industrial robots, and other such heavy capital goods. Figure 1.4 provides an example of this product classification. The product illustrated is an industrial robot that can be used for a wide variety of process applications such as arc welding, inspection, materials handling, drilling, routing, grinding, and polishing.

Heavy equipment products are basically capital goods, and as such, their purchasers are normally user customers. Sometimes, however, a fabricator may purchase several pieces of heavy equipment, integrate them into one package, and then sell this package to a user customer. In this case, the first purchaser would actually be an OEM customer. Generally, heavy equipment can be purchased outright or it can be leased by user customers. Each approach has its own marketing merits, of which the marketing manager should be aware. When capital equipment is purchased, it is treated as an asset by the purchasing firm and depreciated for tax purposes. Such an approach cannot be taken with some other types of business products.

Light Equipment

The light equipment classification of business products includes portable power tools such as drills, saws, sanders, polishers, and routers; measuring instruments; typewriters and word processors; calculators; and other, similar products. Figure 1.5 illustrates a line of cutter products that may be classified as light equipment in the business market. Although the market for light equipment is normally comprised of user customers, transaction values are considerably lower than those seen with heavy equipment, and the products purchased are

FIGURE 1.4   **Example of a Heavy Equipment Business Product: An Industrial Robot for Process Applications**

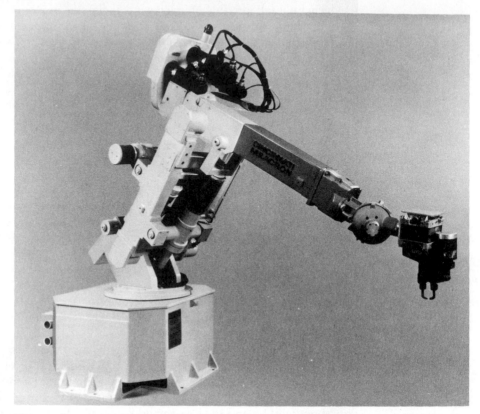

Photograph courtesy of Industrial Robot Division of Cincinnati Milacron, Cincinnati, OH

not permanently affixed to the buyer's physical plant as is heavy equipment. Light equipment may also be purchased outright or leased by the business customer. When purchased, it can be treated by the customer as an asset and depreciated for tax purposes.

Supplies

The supplies classification of business products includes any products that are used up or consumed by the purchasing company in some aspect of its operation. Examples are cleaning compounds, office supplies, and the like. Sometimes called MRO (maintenance, repair, and operating or overhaul) products, this classification can be further divided into those three areas. For example, maintenance supplies can include paints, nails, light bulbs, cleaning compounds,

FIGURE 1.5   **Examples of Light Equipment Business Products**

Photograph courtesy of H. K. Porter, Inc., Somerville, MA

brooms, window-cleaning equipment, and other such items. Repair items can include nuts, bolts, washers, fasteners, small tools, and other such products used to repair equipment. Operating supplies may be lubricating oils and greases, grinding compounds, typing paper, ink, paper clips, computer diskettes, and similar items. The essential characteristic of this product classification is that the product purchased is used up by the customer organization, either directly or indirectly, in the normal operation of its business. Such products are considered expense items and are not depreciated by the customer for tax purposes.

Business customers of such supplies are normally user customers. Figure 1.6 illustrates the product line of a producer of brushes used in the business market. These brushes may be purchased as either maintenance, repair, or operating items, depending on their use by the customer.

Component Parts

The component parts classification of business products includes all those purchased products included in the final product of an organizational customer. Examples of this classification are switches, transistors, motors, gears, nuts, bolts, and screws. Figure 1.7 illustrates motors typically purchased as component parts in the business market.

When sold to organizational customers such as manufacturers that use them in their final products, component parts are marketed as OEM products. Switches bought by a manufacturer of television sets are a good example. Such products are also sold to industrial distributors for resale to other distributors or to OEM customers. At other times, component parts are sold for replacement purposes as MRO items. To illustrate, a manufacturer may purchase replacement motors for those worn out in production equipment. In this case, the motor is being purchased as a repair item. In addition, component parts are sometimes purchased for replacement purposes in what is sometimes called the aftermarket. For example, in Figure 1.7, Baldor Electric Company markets its motors as OEM products to manufacturers that produce products requiring electrical motors such as commercial dishwashers. However, Baldor may also market its motors as replacements in machines used in restaurants, hotels, or military dining halls. Thus, component parts often have a number of distinctly different markets.

Raw Materials

The raw materials classification of business products includes all those products generated by the extractive industries that, in turn, sell those products to their customers with little or no alteration. Examples of this classification are coal, iron ore, bauxite, gypsum, crude oil, fish and other seafood, lumber, field crops, copper, lead and zinc ores, tungsten ores, and other such similar products. These products may at times be marketed as either user or OEM products. An example

FIGURE 1.6   Examples of Consumable Supply Business Products

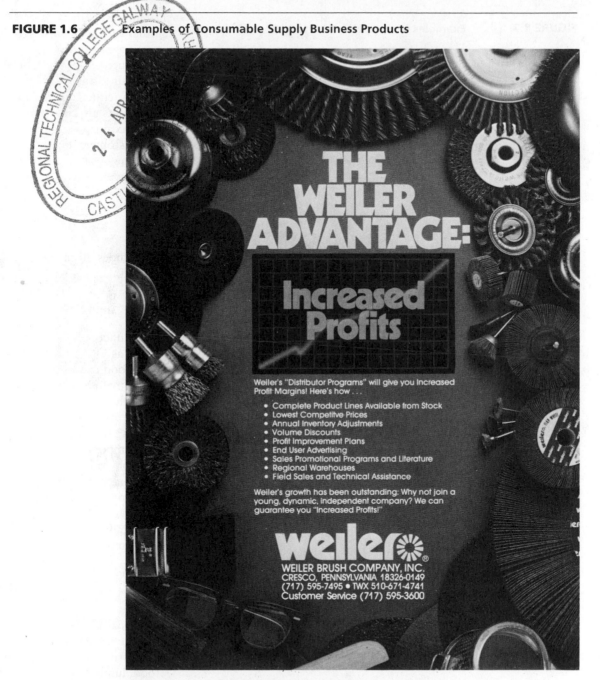

Photograph courtesy of Weiler Brush Company, Inc., Cresco, PA

FIGURE 1.7   Examples of Component Parts Business Products

We may not have the answer to the energy shortage, but we have over 1,500 answers to high power costs.

Less than a decade ago the average price for electricity was a mere 1¢ per kilowatt hour. But look at it today. The average is already more than four times higher—seven or eight times in many areas. And there's no relief in sight.

That's why it makes such good sense to specify Baldor motors—the only manufacturer of energy-efficient motors with a complete range of sizes and types. Designed to cut power usage in just about any application you have in mind.

C-face, explosion-proof, motors for use in hostile environments, closed coupled pump motors, brake motors, open and TEFC—you name it. In all, more than 1,500 sizes and types—and more on the drawing board.

As the chart shows, there's

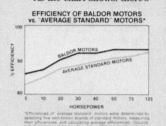

a big difference in efficiency between Baldor and "average standard" motors.* Enough to reduce operating costs substantially. And unlike other manufacturers' energy-efficient models, our motors are not premium priced.

Want more information about savings possible with energy-efficient Baldor motors? And a simple method of comparing motors head-to-head on the basis of initial cost, operating costs and pay-back? Write BALDOR, Fort Smith, Arkansas 72902 or call the Baldor District Office nearest you. Just ask for our free Energy Management Pak.

*Efficiencies of "average standard" motors were determined by selecting five well-known brands of standard motors, measuring their efficiencies, and calculating average efficiencies. (Source: U.S. Department of Energy, November 1980 report, "Classification and Evaluation of Electric Motors and Pumps," Table 3-3.)

© 1982, BALDOR

Photograph courtesy of Baldor Electric Company, Fort Smith, AK

of the former is the purchase of coal by a manufacturer for heating purposes. An example of the latter is the purchase by a seafood processor of tuna from the fishing industry.

Processed Materials

The processed materials classification of business products includes all types of processed materials not considered component parts. Typical of the products in this classification are steel plate, chemicals, glass, coke, sheet metal, plastics, cold-finished steel bars, leather, asphalt, plywood, and other, similar products. Figure 1.8 illustrates processed materials products produced by the steel industry for its customers. In most cases, processed materials are marketed to OEM customers, but this rule is not hard and fast. A steel producer purchasing coke may well be considered a user customer rather than an OEM customer. In addition, processed materials may also be sold to distributors who, in turn, resell to the OEM or to the user market. A good example of the latter are steel service centers that purchase various types of steel products and then process them to customers' specifications.

Business Services

Not all business marketing companies are involved with marketing physical, tangible products. Many service companies also operate in the business markets, and their numbers increase annually. Business services are used by organizational customers for three basic reasons.[10] First, service organizations often offer a specialization that would be difficult to have in-house. For example, manufacturers may contract with service companies to repair and maintain production equipment because they either lack the ability themselves or cannot economically justify the cost of hiring competent service people full-time. Second, service organizations permit the customer to keep up-to-date with rapidly changing areas outside its areas of expertise. To illustrate, the manufacturer may utilize a repair service because repair technology is changing so fast that the manufacturer feels it cannot keep up-to-date. Third, use of service organizations permits some customers to be more flexible in that their fixed costs are reduced. For example, business customers often use the services of an outside marketing research firm rather than undertake the costs of a full-time, in-house department. Because of these factors, a wide range of business services is offered to the market. Table 1.5 illustrates some basic services classifications commonly found in business markets. As can be seen, these categories differ considerably in terms of cost, complexity, and sophistication, and they may not be marketed in similar manners.

Buying motives and practices may differ greatly depending on the type of service involved. The contract for janitorial services, for example, may be straightforward and simple, and the decision may be made at a relatively low

FIGURE 1.8 Examples of Processed Materials Business Products

BECAUSE YOU NEED
BETTER WIRE MORE THAN EVER

ATLANTIC MAKES MORE WIRE
BETTER THAN EVER.

You count on having good wire. Plenty of it when you need it. And so do the production lines your purchasing decisions affect. That's why you have to have dependable suppliers who are concerned with product quality. And who are concerned with your business enough to be committed to expansion and growth.

At Atlantic, we've made the moves that assure you of both. In the midst of one of the most cautious periods in the history of the American steel industry, Atlantic has been moving rapidly ahead. Bringing to completion one of the newest and most modern steel mills in the

United States, increasing our production capability that begins in our own furnaces and rod mill. And at the same time we've added new galvanizing capacity while improving production and quality control capability in existing facilities.

Atlantic can assure you of the manufacturers' wire supply you depend on, uniformly drawn to your specifications in ductility, tensile

strength and finish. And on carriers that fit your requirements.

Contact your Atlantic representative for more information on Dixisteel manufacturers' wire or write A. M. Buckler, Atlantic Steel Wire Products Manager, today for a free brochure.

Atlantic
Steel
COMPANY

Post Office Box 1714/Atlanta, Georgia 30301
Phone 404-875-3441

TABLE 1.5   Examples of Business Services in Business Markets

General Service Classification	Examples of Services
Cleaning/maintenance services	Janitorial services; window cleaning services; linen supply services; industrial launderers; landscaping and gardening services; carpet and upholstery cleaning services
Protection/security services	Detective, guard, and armored car services; watchdog services; security systems and services
Accounting/auditing/bookkeeping services	Accounting services; auditing services; tax services; bookkeeping services; consulting services
Advertising/PR services	Advertising agencies; publicity agencies; public relations agencies; direct-mail advertising services; media buying services; outdoor advertising agencies
Operating/repair services	Equipment repair services; computer maintenance and repair services; auto maintenance and repair services; equipment installation and training services
Personnel services	Employment agencies; temporary help supply services; secretarial services; training services
Consulting services	Management consulting; marketing and market research services; management services; engineering consulting services; facilities support management services
Leasing/rental services	Equipment rental and leasing services; heavy construction equipment rental and leasing services; computer rental and leasing services; vehicle rental and leasing services
Computer services	Programming services; prepackaged software services; computer integrated systems design services; information retrieval services; computer maintenance and repair services
Technical services	Engineering services; architectural services; surveying services; testing laboratories; commercial physical and biological research services
Insurance services	Accident, fire, marine, casualty, liability services; workers' compensation services; retirement and annuity services
Financial services	Credit reporting services; banking services such as loans, lines of credit; pension plan services; collection services
Medical/health care services	Hospital and medical coverage services; dental plan services; nursing and personal care services; physical fitness and therapy services; drug and rehabilitation services
Legal services	Litigation services; labor relations problems services; real estate and tax legal services; advice on merger, acquisition, and dissolution issues; patents, copyrights, and trademark services; advice on contracts, product liability, and consumer protection issues
Distribution services	Trucking services; air freight services; water transportation services; rail transportation services; freight forwarding services; public warehousing services

Source: Adapted from Office of Management and Budget, *Standard Industrial Classification Manual 1987* (Washington, DC: U.S. Government Printing Office, 1987).

level in the purchasing organization. Many times, awards of service contracts of this type are made via a simple bidding process. On the other hand, a contract awarded for engineering services may be quite complex and require considerable negotiation. The decision maker in the customer company may hold a high position in production or engineering. The individual marketing manager whose company offers business services must address such specific requirements when marketing his or her company's services.

Summarizing, business marketing managers must realize the classification or classifications of their products and/or services as they are purchased by customers, because buying motives differ with classifications. Processed materials are not purchased for the same reasons as are component parts. Heavy equipment is not bought in the same manner as is light equipment or auxiliary services. Buyers of component parts for replacement or aftermarket purposes are not motivated by the same considerations as are buyers of identical component parts in the OEM market. Business services may be purchased in a manner different from products, and some services are bought differently than others are. Effective marketing can hardly take place if the marketing manager sees the product being purchased as light equipment when customers perceive it as heavy equipment.

THE BUSINESS MARKETING SYSTEM

Now that you have an understanding of the basic concepts of business marketing and of types of business customers, products, and services, the business marketing system can be explained by viewing its fundamental components. These components are: (1) producers of business goods and services, (2) suppliers to these producers, (3) customers for business goods and services, and (4) channels and channel intermediaries linking the producers and customers. In addition, there are environmental and facilitating forces that affect the relationships among producers, suppliers, customers, and channel intermediaries. Figure 1.9 illustrates the business marketing system by interrelating these four basic components exclusive of the environmental and facilitating forces, which will be covered in detail in Chapter 2. A brief description of the roles played by these four major components may be useful in better understanding the basic system.

Producers of Business Goods and Services

Business goods and services are produced by such organizations as (1) manufacturing plants such as machine tool manufacturers, (2) mill industries such as steel mills and pulp and paper mills, (3) processing plants such as food processors and petroleum refineries, (4) assembly plants such as truck assembly plants, (5) machine shops, (6) fabricating plants such as electronic manufacturers that buy component parts and fabricate finished products from those parts, and (7) service organizations that specialize in the business markets. Organizations such as these produce the goods and services that are purchased by

FIGURE 1.9   The Business Marketing System

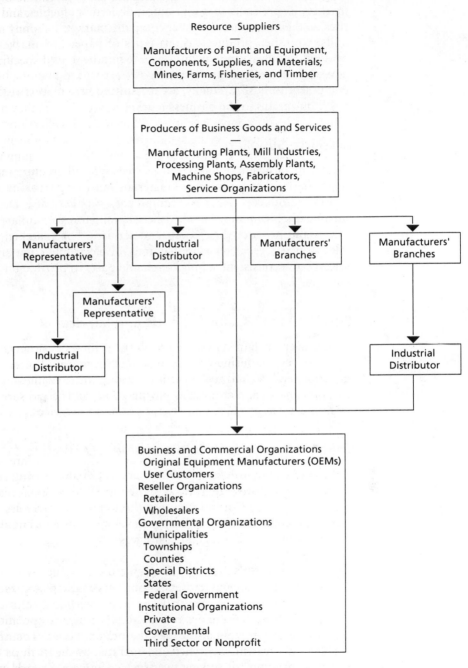

Resource Suppliers
—
Manufacturers of Plant and Equipment, Components, Supplies, and Materials; Mines, Farms, Fisheries, and Timber

Producers of Business Goods and Services
—
Manufacturing Plants, Mill Industries, Processing Plants, Assembly Plants, Machine Shops, Fabricators, Service Organizations

Manufacturers' Representative

Industrial Distributor

Manufacturers' Branches

Manufacturers' Branches

Manufacturers' Representative

Industrial Distributor

Industrial Distributor

Business and Commercial Organizations
  Original Equipment Manufacturers (OEMs)
  User Customers
Reseller Organizations
  Retailers
  Wholesalers
Governmental Organizations
  Municipalities
  Townships
  Counties
  Special Districts
  States
  Federal Government
Institutional Organizations
  Private
  Governmental
  Third Sector or Nonprofit

◄——— Flow of Goods and Services

OEMs, users, resellers, institutions, and governmental agencies. Some examples may help clarify the point. A manufacturer of tires produces OEM tires and markets its products to major automobile manufacturers, who then install the tires on their new cars. A timber company markets its forestry products to paper mills, who then produce various types of paper for use by their customers. A hospital supply company produces equipment and markets its products to government and private hospitals. An aerospace manufacturer markets space equipment to NASA. Finally, an accounting firm markets its payroll services to small businesses in the business market.

Resource Suppliers

Producers of business goods and services typically require materials to produce their offerings, and often these materials must be purchased from other organizations. Producers purchase equipment, supplies, and materials from other manufacturers, mines, farms, fisheries, and forest industry firms to run their plants and produce their goods and services. For example, a manufacturer of television sets relies on manufacturers of electronic components such as transistors for a consistent supply of reliable parts to provide on-time delivery to its customers.

Customers for Business Goods and Services

As has been explained in some detail, the primary customers for business goods and services are business and commercial organizations, reseller organizations, governmental organizations, or institutional organizations. All of these organizations can be characterized as buying goods and services for use either directly or indirectly in producing their own goods and services.

Channel Components in the Business Marketing System

Based on a study of 156 manufacturers, six channels of distribution are dominant in the industrial market, as shown in Figure 1.9. These channels are analyzed in depth later in this text, but the following brief description of common channel components is necessary in developing an understanding of the link between business producers and customers.

The Manufacturer's Branch Manufacturers' branches are wholly owned field operations of the manufacturers in business markets and as such are not independent intermediaries. Nevertheless, they provide intermediary functions by the manufacturer. There are two basic types of this operation. The first is the manufacturer's branch, also called the branch house. The branch house is primarily a field warehouse owned and operated by the manufacturer and placed at strategic locations for serving the firm's customers. Branch houses are basically company-owned warehouses.

The second type is the branch office, which is essentially owned and operated by a manufacturer as a field sales office. In contrast to the branch house, branch offices ordinarily carry no inventory but are strategically located offices from which the company's field sales personnel operate in their respective field territories. At times, branch houses and branch offices may be housed in the same physical facilities, whereas at other times they may be housed independently. In other instances, a manufacturer may elect to use only a branch office for selling purposes and ship directly from the factory, thus performing no inventory function in the field and therefore requiring no branch house. In yet other instances, a manufacturer may use only branch houses to field inventory its product and use manufacturers' representatives to perform the selling function. In any case, the manufacturer's branch, as shown in Figure 1.9, indicates instances in which manufacturers are performing intermediary functions of one type or another or both in the business market.

The Industrial Distributor The industrial distributor is an intermediary that sells the production tools, operating equipment, and maintenance supplies used by all types of organizational customers. Distributors are normally local and independently owned and operated, and they take title to and possession of the goods they handle. They stock goods, thus they perform a field inventory function for the manufacturer. Industrial distributors are analyzed in great depth later in this text. At this point, all that is needed is to understand that they are intermediaries who take title to and stock goods in the business marketplace. They perform a function quite similar in some respects to that performed by wholesalers in the consumer market. As has been described, industrial distributors can be highly specialized or widely diversified in their product-line offerings and in their sales and service capabilities.

The Manufacturers' Representative The manufacturers' representative, also called the manufacturers' agent, is also an independent intermediary, but he or she is quite different from the distributor. Quite common in business markets, the manufacturers' representatives are agents who sell on behalf of manufacturing principals. As such, they take no title to the goods involved, and they often do not even see or handle those goods. Basically, they are independent salespeople who sell on a commission basis for manufacturers, thus eliminating the need for those manufacturers to employ company salespeople. The manufacturers' representatives often represent a number of manufacturers whose products are complementary and not competitive. They are compensated on a commission basis and assigned to sales territories just as company field salespeople are. Simply viewed, they are comparable to company salespeople except that they are independent and usually represent several manufacturing principals. Their basic function as intermediaries in the business marketing system is to sell, but in recent years there has been a trend toward what is called a *stocking representative*. A stocking representative is basically a manufacturers' representative who also carries some field inventory and is a sort of hybrid between a distributor and a manufacturers' representative. In business, this general classification of intermediary may be called the manufacturers' representative, the manufacturers' agent, the manufacturers' rep, or simply the MR. In this text, the term *MR* shall be used in reference to this type of channel intermediary. Later in the text, manufacturers' representatives are analyzed in great depth for their contribution toward effective business marketing.

In addition to the industrial distributor and the manufacturers' representative, such intermediaries as brokers and sales agents may sometimes be found. Overall, these components do not form a significant part of the business marketing system.

THE GLOBAL NATURE OF BUSINESS MARKETING

This text focuses primarily on business marketing in domestic markets in the United States. Major emphasis is placed on business marketing in the United States because the U.S. domestic market is the single largest business market in the world. This should not, however, be interpreted to mean that business marketing is not global in nature. Many U.S. business marketing firms market goods and services to organizational customers in other countries. In some cases, the firms focus exclusively on global markets, while in other cases, they market to both domestic and global customers. Global markets are important in that commercial, reseller, institutional, and governmental organizations in other countries also purchase large quantities of business goods and services. Because of the expanding importance of global markets, this subject will be covered in detail in Chapter 3 to show the global ramifications for the business marketing manager. However, time and space constraints do not permit an in-depth coverage of both domestic and global markets, thus, the major emphasis in this text is on business marketing in U.S. markets. If more information is desired on global marketing, the reader is referred to the many good references that exist in this area of marketing.[11]

BASIC DIFFERENCES BETWEEN BUSINESS AND CONSUMER MARKETING

Another way to gain a better understanding of the business marketing area is to contrast it with consumer marketing. There are major differences, although these are often not understood even by marketing practitioners. For example, one well-known marketing professor states: "Marketing is marketing—there are basic concepts and methods that vary little depending upon the individual situation."[12] This argument holds that marketing is generic and basically does not differ between consumer and business markets. Most practicing business marketing managers would not agree with this contention. A marketing director for a manufacturer of cable television equipment illustrates the other side of the argument by stating: "You can't use (consumer marketing) strategies and techniques in industrial marketing situations. Industrial marketing is really an entirely different type of marketing." [13] The basic premise of this text is that business marketing is indeed different from consumer marketing, and these differences are emphasized throughout this book. At this point, however, it may be worthwhile to create an appreciation of some of these differences. Table 1.6 lists some of the major differences between marketing in the two markets.

Students of business marketing should be made aware that such differences do exist and appreciably impact marketing strategic and tactical decision making. They should become familiar with what is often behind-the-scenes work by salespeople and other marketing personnel on service, product design to individual customer specifications, competitive bidding, and tight segment-by-segment trade advertising. [14] The preceding discussion does not mean to say that business marketing and consumer marketing are derived from two separate sets of concepts and principles. Rather, the applications of these concepts and principles are distinctly different in the two markets—different enough to justify the study of business marketing as a separate emphasis area.

TABLE 1.6　　　　**Major Differences Between Business and Consumer Marketing**

- Customers in the consumer market purchase goods and services for personal consumption, whereas business customers purchase goods and services to produce other goods or services.
- Business marketers sell to organizations, whereas consumer marketers sell to individuals and households.
- The demand for consumer goods and services is direct, whereas the demand for business goods and services is derived.
- The business market involves multiple buying influences in almost all purchases—rarely does a single individual make a buying decision—and committee buying is commonplace.
- Business customers purchase in more formal manners involving specific purchasing policies and procedures and professional buyers.
- The role of specifications is extremely important in business marketing—suppliers not meeting the customer's desired specifications may not be considered by the buyer.
- Product support activities such as service, installation services, technical assistance, spare parts, and so on are crucial in business marketing.
- A much heavier emphasis is placed on personal selling in business marketing than in consumer marketing—there is wide usage of direct sales forces, and channel intermediaries are often selected because of their sales capabilities.
- Physical distribution is extremely important in business markets—late deliveries, stockouts, back orders, and so on can shut down a customer's total business operation.
- Activities that are typically very important in consumer marketing, such as advertising and marketing research, often play minor support roles in business marketing.
- Price often plays a different role in business marketing than in consumer marketing. In some instances, business customers will pay a higher price to ensure delivery, product quality, and service, and prices are often negotiated between buyer and seller. In other instances, however, such as bidding situations, price is all-important.

Referring to Table 1.6, it can be seen that a number of significant differences do exist, and the table is not all inclusive. There are differences in market characteristics, buyers, target markets and segments, marketing research, and individual areas of the marketing mix. These differences are investigated in more detail later in the text, but a brief discussion of some basic differences may be appropriate here. For example, the concept of derived demand basically differentiates the two markets. The business marketing manager cannot focus simply on the organizational customer; he or she must also pay attention to the markets for that customer's products. Although Boeing Corporation sells its aircraft to the airlines, it must also be cognizant of present and future trends in passenger air travel. Thus, as a business marketer, Boeing must also be a consumer marketer. Similarly, mass media advertising campaigns to pull products through consumer channels of distribution are often neither effective nor efficient in business markets. Just-in-time (JIT) buying by business customers such as manufacturers requires different distribution strategies and tactics than are needed to sell to consumers.

There are enough differences between consumer marketing and business marketing to make the job of marketing management in each a separate area of specialization. Companies that sell the same products into consumer and business markets often establish two divisions to handle these differences.

Although there are many similarities, there are also many differences, and this discussion has attempted to outline some of those differences. Any consumer marketing manager moving into business markets must adapt to these differences, since they affect decisions regarding products and services to be offered, prices to be charged, channels to be used, and promotional efforts to be employed.

PLAN OF THE BOOK

This book analyzes marketing management as it applies to the marketing of goods and services to organizational customers in both domestic and global markets. Figure 1.10 illustrates the plan to be followed. Chapter 2 discusses in detail those factors that influence the business marketing system that was developed in this chapter. Chapter 3 then focuses exclusively on the global aspects of business marketing and illustrates the expansive size of business markets. Chapter 4 reviews and analyzes factors to be considered in assessing demand for business goods and services. Chapters 5 and 6 then develop the areas of purchasing and materials management and organizational buying behavior. In Chapter 7, strategic alliances and partnering relationships are explored as they impact on effective business marketing.

Chapter 8 develops an understanding of the Standard Industrial Classification (SIC) system, which is necessary for effective business marketing. Chapters 9, 10, and 11 focus on the managerial areas of business marketing. Chapter 9 is devoted to a discussion of target market determination and market segmentation as it applies to business markets. Chapter 10 analyzes the development of overall

FIGURE 1.10   Flow Plan of the Book

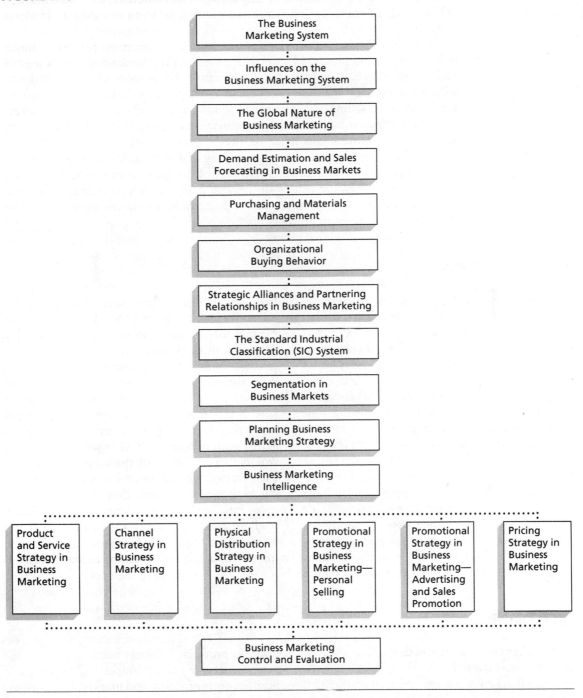

marketing strategy from the marketing manager's perspective. This is followed in Chapter 11 by a discussion of marketing information systems and marketing research as these intelligence areas contribute to more effective business marketing.

Chapters 12 through 17 develop the business marketing mix and address both strategies and tactics. Chapter 12 focuses on the product and service area of marketing, whereas Chapters 13 and 14 cover the areas of channels of distribution and physical distribution as these affect business marketing. Chapter 15 details personal selling and sales management, and Chapter 16 discusses advertising and sales promotion in business markets. Chapter 17 integrates pricing into the business marketing mix.

Finally, Chapter 18 discusses controlling and evaluating the overall marketing strategy and the substrategies and tactical programs in the marketing mix. The text thus brings the reader all the way from an understanding of business marketing to the development, control, and evaluation of marketing strategies and programs specific to business markets.

CHAPTER SUMMARY

This chapter identified what business marketing is and what it is not. The chapter also showed why business marketing should be viewed as different from consumer goods marketing, even though similarities exist between the two. A definition of business marketing was derived by adapting the current American Marketing Association's definition of overall marketing. The topic of business marketing management was explored with emphasis on the various levels of management involved. The main emphasis in the chapter was to explain the business marketing system by focusing on suppliers of business goods and services, customers for those goods and services, and intermediaries operating between suppliers and customers. Types of organizations selling in this system were explored, as were types of organizational customers ranging from private firms to institutions to governmental entities at all levels. The chapter then explained the various types of goods and services that pass through the business marketing system. Although this book primarily emphasizes domestic business marketing, the chapter stressed the importance of international markets to U.S. business marketing firms. Business marketing is much more than consumer marketing with different terms, as some authorities would suggest. Some of the more basic differences between business and consumer marketing were explored to make the point that differences are sufficient to warrant the separate study of business marketing. Finally, the chapter discussed the plan of the book and explained the thrust of each of the chapters that follow.

KEY TERMS

business/commercial organization
business marketing
business marketing system

business product
business service
business-to-business marketing

channel intermediary
chief marketing officer
governmental organization
industrial marketing

institutional organization
marketing management
original equipment manufacturer
reseller organization

QUESTIONS

1. Business marketing is characterized as marketing directed toward organizations, while consumer marketing is characterized by efforts directed toward individuals and households. Do you think this difference is sufficient enough to justify the separate study of business marketing? Explain your answer.
2. Some marketing authorities contend that business marketing is just consumer marketing with different labels. Take a position pro or con on this statement and back up that position.
3. Why is it important that the business marketing manager recognize that for the U.S. manufacturer, focusing only on the domestic market has major shortcomings? Why are global markets so important to the U.S. business marketing firm?
4. Explain why it is not considered business marketing when a power-driven handtool manufacturer, such as Black & Decker, markets products to retailers and/or wholesalers for resale to final consumers.
5. Looking at Table 1.1 in your text, add five examples to the list and then justify each as a valid example of business marketing.
6. Using Figure 1.9 in your text as a reference, develop a model of the consumer marketing system. Then, compare and contrast the two systems.
7. The term *business marketing* has evolved over time to the point where it has supplanted the term *industrial marketing*. Why do you think this is so and what are its marketing implications?
8. Do you believe the marketing of business services is different from the marketing of business products? If so, explain why. If not, also explain why.
9. For many business marketing firms, it is common to serve all four types of organizational customers at the same time. Such firms sell to private organizations, reseller organizations, governmental entities, and institutions at the same time, and sometimes even the identical products are involved. Can you think of any examples of companies in this position?
10. The governmental market in the United States is very large and, with its many levels, also very complex. Explain these levels and then relate how marketing to each level might differ.

NOTES

1. "AMA Board Approves New Marketing Definition," *Collegiate Edition Marketing News* 3 (April 1985): 1.
2. Philip Kotler, *Marketing Management: Analysis, Planning, and Control* (Englewood Cliffs, NJ: Prentice-Hall, 1980), 22.
3. *Selling to the Government Markets: Local, State, & Federal* (Cleveland: Government Product News, 1991), 1.
4. *Selling to the Government Markets: Local, State, & Federal* (Cleveland: Government Product News, 1988), 2.
5. Carlos R. Vest, "As Spectrum of Federal Activities Expands, So Will Government as an Industrial Market," *Marketing News* 13 (April 4, 1980): 17.
6. See note 4 above.
7. *Selling to the Government Markets: Local, State, & Federal* (Cleveland: Government Product News, 1991), 9.

8. Larry C. Giunipero, William Crittenden, and Vicky Crittenden, "Industrial Marketing in Non-Profit Organizations," *Industrial Marketing Management* 19 (1990): 279.

9. Ibid.

10. John M. Rathmell, *Marketing in the Service Center* (Cambridge, MA: Winthrop Publishing, 1974), 5.

11. See Frederick E. Webster, Jr., and Rohit Deshpande, *Analyzing Corporate Cultures in Approaching the Global Marketplace* (Cambridge, MA: Marketing Science Institute, 1990); Edward R. Koepfler, "Strategic Options for Global Market Players," *The Journal of Business Strategy* (July/August 1989): 46–50; John

Young, "Global Competition: The New Reality," *California Management Review* 27 (Spring 1985): 11–25; Kamran Kashani, "Beware the Pitfalls of Global Marketing," *Harvard Business Review* 67 (Sept.–Oct. 1989): 91–98; and J. A. Quelch and E. J. Hoff, "Customizing Global Marketing," *Harvard Business Review* 64 (May–June 1986): 59–68.

12. Diane L. Kastiel, "Why Johnny Can't Market," *Business Marketing* 71 (November 1986): 102.

13. Ibid., 104.

14. J. Barry Mason and Arthur Allaway, "Industry and University Initiatives and the Industrial Marketing Course," *Journal of Marketing Education* (Spring 1986): 2.

SUGGESTED ADDITIONAL READINGS

Carroll, Daniel T. "The Changing Environment for Industrial Marketing." In *Proceedings of 20th Anniversary Conference*, Report No. 82-101. Cambridge, MA: Marketing Science Institute, 1982, 52–58.

Fern, Edward F., and James R. Brown. "The Industrial/Consumer Marketing Dichotomy: A Case of Insufficient Justification." *Journal of Marketing* 48 (Spring 1984): 68–77.

Hlavacek, James D. "Business Schools Need More Industrial Marketing." *Marketing News* 13 (April 4, 1980): 1.

Kastiel, Diane L. "Why Johnny Can't Market." *Business Marketing* 71 (November 1986): 100–105.

Leroux, J. C. "Industrial Marketing." *Journal of International Marketing and Marketing Research* 9 (June 1982): 59–89.

Mason, J. Barry, and Arthur Allaway. "Industry and

University Initiatives and the Industrial Marketing Course." *Journal of Marketing Education* (Spring 1986): 2–10.

Plank, Richard E. "Industrial Marketing Education: Practitioner's View." *Industrial Marketing Management* 11 (1982): 311–315.

Ursic, Michael, and Craig Hegstrom. "The Views of Marketing Recruiters, Alumni and Students About Curriculum and Course Structure." *Journal of Marketing Education* (Summer 1985): 21–27.

Webster, Frederick E., Jr. "Industrial Marketing— An Academic's Perspective on Past, Present, and Future." In *Proceedings of 20th Anniversary Conference*, Report No. 82-101. Cambridge, MA: Marketing Science Institute, 1982, 46–51.

‚2‚

Influences on
the Business
Marketing System

••

In the previous chapter, the business marketing system was outlined and described. This system began with resource suppliers providing materials and services to producers of business goods and services. Types of organizational customers and prospects were then discussed, and producers and customers were tied together by those channels most common in business marketing. Within this system, the business marketing manager makes decisions regarding the selection of target markets and the development of appropriate marketing mixes to attract customers and prospects in those defined markets. But business marketing decisions are not made in a vacuum. Marketing managers are constrained in their decision making by influences that are not always within their control. These influences must be understood and adapted to if intelligent decisions are to be made. This chapter addresses those types of influences that most affect the business marketing system and illustrates their effects on the marketing manager.

There are two major types of influences that act on and shape the activities of participants in the business marketing system: environmental forces and facilitating forces. This chapter will focus on each of these important forces and examine the influences they exert on the overall business marketing system and its components.

TYPES OF MAJOR INFLUENCES IN BUSINESS MARKETING

As previously stated, two major types of influences seem to be most predominant in business marketing. Influences may be caused by both environmental forces and facilitating forces. Before discussion actually begins, a clarification of each is in order.

37

● ●

How Environmental Changes Affect Marketing Practices of Business Marketing Companies

The U.S. commercial aircraft manufacturing industry provides a good example of how environmental changes can affect marketing strategies and tactical programs. Faced with declining domestic demand for airliners, Boeing Company has focused on Asian air carriers as the target market for its 747-400, 767, and forthcoming 777 aircraft.

Asian air carriers are expanding dramatically and it is estimated that Asian air traffic growth is about double that of the United States and Europe. For example, Cathay of Hong Kong served twenty-four cities with but seventeen aircraft in 1980. In 1990, the carrier flew forty-one aircraft to thirty-eight cities. Such growth patterns provided great potential for producers such as Boeing, and the company estimates that Asia and the Pacific alone will constitute a $13.3 billion annual commercial aircraft market by 2001 with only 10 percent of demand due to replacements—the rest will be for expansions.

Conversely, the U.S. market is tapering off. U.S. airlines are dropping cities, merging, or going out of business. Fewer airlines and fewer routes translate to fewer new airplanes. In contrast to the Asian market, more than 30 percent of new aircraft will be for replacement purposes. Thus, it can be seen that while the traditionally large and powerful U.S. commercial aircraft market is declining, the Asian market is expanding rapidly. All this is causing Boeing, as well as McDonnell–Douglas and Airbus Industrie, to focus marketing efforts more heavily on the Asian market, with the effect that the U.S. market now plays less than its traditionally dominant role. The changing environments in the two markets have increased the appeal of one and decreased the appeal of the other.

Source: Adapted from Matt Miller, "Boeing Sees Its Long-Term Fortunes in Satisfying Pacific Rim Market Needs," *San Diego Union* (June 9, 1991), A1–A7.

Environmental Forces

Environmental forces are those that affect business marketing managers but that are noncontrollable by those managers. Thus, the manager must adapt to them rather than try to control them. A company's marketing environment consists of the actors and forces that affect the company's ability to develop and maintain successful transactions and relationships with target market customers.[1] These forces are often classified into the general categories of economic, technological, political and/or legal, competitive, global, and ecological forces. For example, the business marketing firm is constrained by such economic factors as recessions, shortages of materials, inflation, and the like. In addition, changing technology may affect the life cycles of existing products and bring about increased sophistication in marketing techniques. Other factors such as increased global competition, ecological pressures from the Environmental Protection Agency (EPA), and changes in political leadership also affect marketing decisions in business marketing. Thus, an analysis of the marketing implications of such forces is necessary.

Facilitating Forces

In addition to environmental forces, business marketing firms are also constrained by what may be called **facilitating forces.** Facilitating forces occur when the marketer, for one reason or another, deals with organizations that are necessary to the proper operation of the business marketing system but that play roles outside those of resource suppliers, producers, channel intermediaries, and customers. Typical of these facilitating organizations are financial institutions. If a business marketing firm wishes to expand, for example, it will require capital. When such capital is not available internally, the firm may have to turn to a financial institution for assistance. Whether that lender can be convinced to provide the needed financial assistance may be instrumental in the company's decision to expand or not. Similarly, many business marketing firms use public warehouses to store goods, use common carriers to transport them, and rely on other organizations such as advertising agencies, marketing research firms, consulting organizations, purchasing groups, etc., to assist in their marketing strategies and tactical programs. When that happens, these facilitating organizations affect the business marketing system and they must be taken into account by the marketing manager in the development of strategies and programs.

Figure 2.1 illustrates how both the environmental and facilitating forces relate to the business marketing system and therefore to the individual business marketing manager. These forces may affect resource suppliers, producers, channel intermediaries, and customers alike. In this text, the main focus will be at the producer level, but influences on other system components must also be considered by the manager. At this point, it might be helpful to develop a systems perspective to business marketing and then return to discuss the environmental and facilitating forces in detail.

DEVELOPING AN OPEN SYSTEM PERSPECTIVE

The preceding discussion has focused primarily on the overall business marketing system. Now, it becomes useful to examine how the individual business marketing company is influenced by this system. From this viewpoint, the business marketing company can be thought of as an **open marketing system** that is composed of a set of interdependent parts or subsystems (people and departments

FIGURE 2.1   Forces Influencing the Business Marketing System

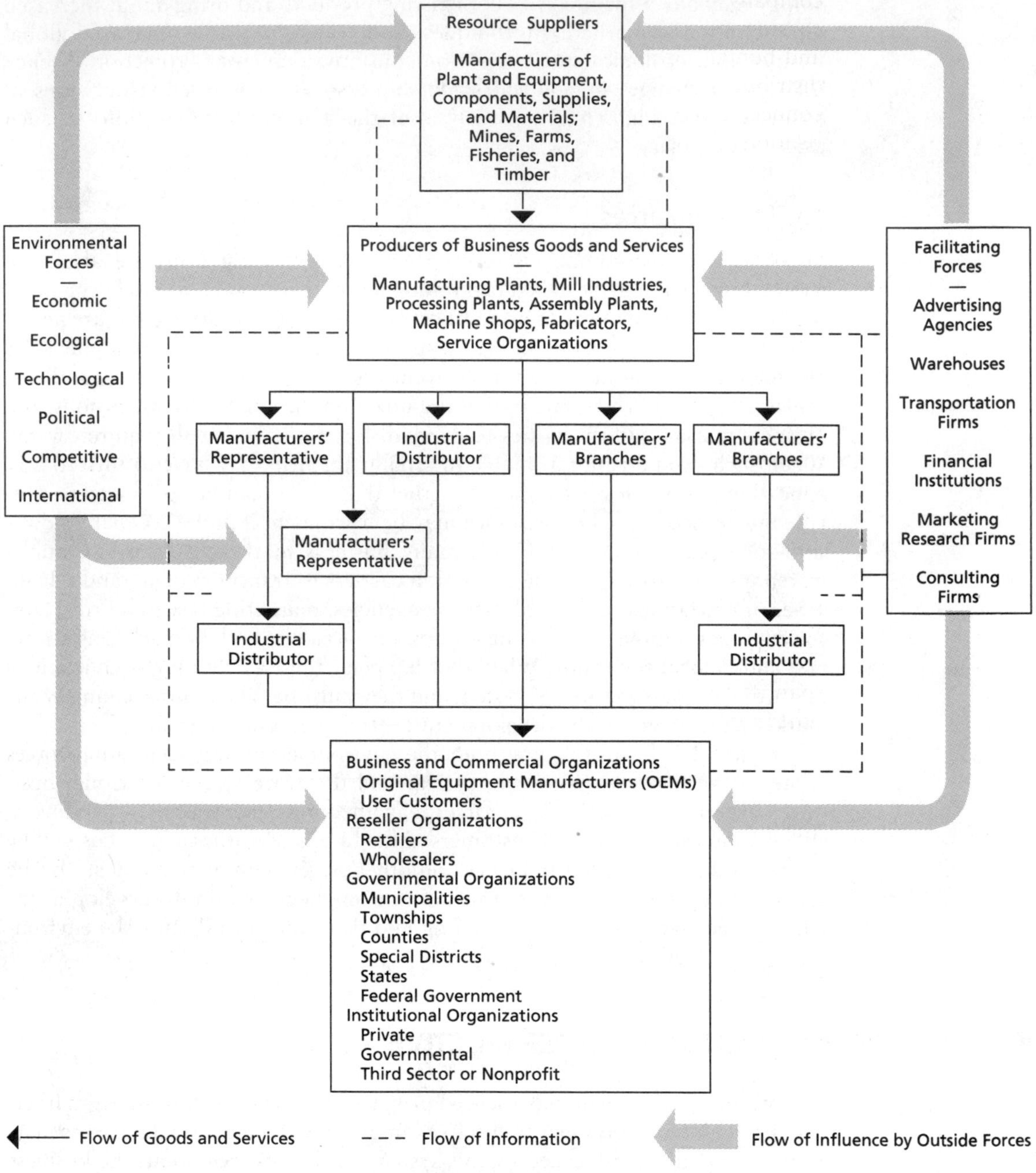

Resource Suppliers
—
Manufacturers of
Plant and Equipment,
Components, Supplies,
and Materials;
Mines, Farms,
Fisheries, and
Timber

Environmental
Forces
—
Economic

Ecological

Technological

Political

Competitive

International

Facilitating
Forces
—
Advertising
Agencies

Warehouses

Transportation
Firms

Financial
Institutions

Marketing
Research Firms

Consulting
Firms

Producers of Business Goods and Services
—
Manufacturing Plants, Mill Industries,
Processing Plants, Assembly Plants,
Machine Shops, Fabricators,
Service Organizations

Manufacturers'
Representative

Industrial
Distributor

Manufacturers'
Branches

Manufacturers'
Branches

Manufacturers'
Representative

Industrial
Distributor

Industrial
Distributor

Business and Commercial Organizations
  Original Equipment Manufacturers (OEMs)
  User Customers
Reseller Organizations
  Retailers
  Wholesalers
Governmental Organizations
  Municipalities
  Townships
  Counties
  Special Districts
  States
  Federal Government
Institutional Organizations
  Private
  Governmental
  Third Sector or Nonprofit

◄─── Flow of Goods and Services   ─ ─ ─ Flow of Information   Flow of Influence by Outside Forces

within the firm) who interact with other components of the system and who are influenced by forces in the external environment. In a typical business marketing company, these subsystems may include departments such as marketing, purchasing, production, engineering, research and development (R&D), logistics, and human resources. These departments must work together to produce and distribute the goods and services required by target market customers, and are connected to each other by communication and other links such as reporting relationships, policies, and procedures.

Each business marketing firm has some degree of structure and is differentiated from its environment by a boundary. In the open system concept, the company exchanges information as well as other inputs and outputs with that environment. Thus, there are three basic functions necessary for a business marketing firm to operate: (1) there must be some type of input; (2) there must be an output; and (3) there must be a process to convert inputs to outputs. Each business marketing firm performs these functions and interacts with other organizations in the overall environment such as suppliers, customers, channel intermediaries, common carriers, and the like. In simple terms, the company takes resources and information from its environment, processes these, and returns them in some different form. Figure 2.2 illustrates this type of conceptual open system.

All business marketers purchase goods and services (inputs) to process into goods and services (outputs) for their customers. The business marketing firm survives only so long as it can perform these basic functions and its outputs are purchased in quantities and prices favorable to the continuation of the cycle. Viewed in this manner, both purchasing and marketing are key subsystems. They have been referred to as boundary spanning positions, which means they span an organization's boundary and interact with individuals, functions, and other subsystems both internal and external to the firm.

FIGURE 2.2 **The Business Marketing Firm as a System**

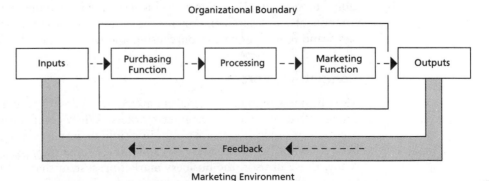

Applying this concept to the workplace, it can be seen that the purchasing, production, and marketing subsystems are interdependent within the marketing firm. This means that the marketing manager cannot simply make decisions regarding new products, product modifications, dropping old products, and so forth without consulting with other departmental managers. For example, if adding a new product would require new production processes and equipment, this has to be coordinated with the production department. Similarly, if adding a new product means finding new suppliers, this has to be coordinated with purchasing. In short, the marketing organization is a system and the marketing department is but one part of this system. The marketing manager must be cognizant of this fact.

Viewing business marketing firms as open systems, or more properly as sets of subsystems, is growing in popularity in business marketing. This has been a result of the widespread use of systems selling, which requires close coordination between departments, and the increasing trend toward strategic alliances or partnerships between business marketing firms. This will be developed in more detail in Chapter 7.

Every sale by one marketing organization is also a purchase by another organization. Thus, companies in the business marketing system are linked with each other in a large network of firms selling to and buying from each other. Now that the systems concept has been developed, it is time to look in more detail at the two major influences that affect the individual marketing firm in the overall business marketing system.

ENVIRONMENTAL INFLUENCES ON BUSINESS MARKETING

As was stated earlier, a company's marketing environment includes all those elements external to the firm that affect the successful marketing of its goods and services to target market customers. This marketing environment is sometimes split into three components: (1) competitive forces; (2) macro-level forces of broad scope such as economic, ecological, technological, political, legal, and global forces; and (3) customers.[2] This section will examine the first two of these components. The third component, customers, will be covered in detail in Chapters 5 and 6, which relate to purchasing and organizational buying behavior.

Competitive Forces

Most business marketing managers are concerned with reacting to competitive changes that occur in their target markets. When competitors introduce new products or services, increase promotion, initiate pricing changes, increase product quality, or better their service capabilities, some response is required. Eventually, those firms in the business marketing system that fail to respond effectively to **competitive forces** cease to exist. See Exhibit 2.1.

EXHIBIT 2.1   The Changing Face of Competition in Business Marketing

In business marketing, the competitive environment is constantly changing and the marketing manager must keep abreast of such changes. This is true even in what might be considered very stable and traditional industries such as the American steel industry, which provides an excellent example of this phenomenon.

Between 1982 and 1985, 20 percent of all U.S. steel companies were operating under bankruptcy proceedings and the industry as a whole lost approximately $11 billion. What had traditionally been a mainstay of the U.S. economy was clearly in trouble. Things had to change—and they did, thanks to infusions of Japanese capital and technology. Today, a leaner, more efficient domestic steel industry earns record profits as a result of sweeping modernization. Today's steel mills are not the same as those in the early 1980s and thus they have changed dramatically as competitors.

Competitors in the domestic steel industry today are often not U.S. firms and their marketing strategies differ from those of the past. Many American steel operations are now joint ventures between American and Japanese owners and their strategies reflect Japanese marketing skills. For example, a joint venture between Inland Steel and Nippon Steel created an entity called I/N Tek and I/N Kote. This partnership operates a steel mill at New Carlisle, Indiana, in which the Japanese invested over $1 billion. There are almost seventy such American and Japanese joint venture steel works now in the United States.

Another change in the industry can be seen in the case of USX Corporation, formerly called U.S. Steel. This firm was once the dominant competitor in the American steel industry. In the 1940s, this company had 340,000 employees and was the largest of all domestic steel producers. Today, the steel manufacturing part of USX has but 20,000 employees and, in 1991, the company was dropped from the Dow Jones Industrial Average. Changes such as these show clearly that this giant steel company is no longer the competitor it once was.

The example of the American steel industry illustrates the changing competitive environment often found in business marketing. Competition cannot be taken for granted and the marketing manager must constantly monitor competitive changes and incorporate them into his or her marketing strategies and tactical programs.

Source: Adapted from various editions of the *San Diego Union.*

Types of Competitors   Determining just who one's competitors are is not always an easy task. Sometimes, a supplier may end up being a competitor. When a make-or-buy situation occurs, a customer may even be a competitor. According to Michael Porter, there are five sources of competition: [3]

1. **Current competitors** are those firms with whom a business marketing firm now competes or has traditionally competed.

2. **New competitors** emerge when new firms enter the market. These may often be unexpected and may possibly be global in nature.

3. **Product substitutes** are products that customers perceive to be substitutes

for existing ones. These substitute products may not be identical to existing products, but customers see them as performing a like or similar enough function.

4. **Customers** in business marketing often only possess the capabilities to produce products they are currently purchasing. In this make-or-buy situation, a customer can thus become a competitor and the marketing manager must recognize this.

5. **Suppliers** may sometimes bypass the business marketing firm and go directly to the user. This may happen when a supplier recognizes that it can service the marketing firm's customers directly by simply bypassing the marketer.

Figure 2.3 illustrates the types of competitors operating in business markets. For the individual marketing manager, these different types of competitors present different challenges. For example, traditional competitors are relatively easy to identify and the manager often has at least a general idea of how they might respond to changes. With new competitors, the manager is at more of a disadvantage. Sometimes he or she doesn't even know the competitor exists or, if so, how the new competitor might react to competitive moves. In the case of **sub-**

FIGURE 2.3   **Sources of Competition in Business Marketing**

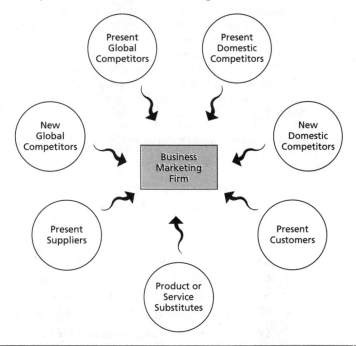

---

stitute products, different firms respond in different manners. Larger firms often do better here because they are more strategically oriented and therefore their intelligence gathering efforts are focused in these directions. In smaller companies, competitive intelligence is sometimes marginal at best and the firms are caught off balance. In the cases of both suppliers and customers, the marketing manager needs to recognize that such situations exist and work toward creating relationships that may alleviate potential problems. For example, if a customer possesses the ability to produce a component part that it now purchases, the manager in the marketing firm needs to convince that customer that purchasing the component has advantages over making the same part in-house. In Chapter 5, this topic of make-or-buy will be discussed in more detail.

Intensity of Competitors   In business marketing, competition takes the form of battling for individual customers and for market share. This battling, which is what marketing is really all about, may take many forms. For example, a competitor may lower its price to attract new customers and increase market share. Or the competitor may initiate a sales and advertising campaign to bring in new customers. Or new products may be introduced to attract new customers. Or customer service and other product support activities may be upgraded to appeal to new customers. How to respond to such moves is the responsibility of the business marketing manager and he or she has the task of developing marketing strategies and tactical programs to bring about successful responses. Later in the text, in Chapters 10 through 17, we will discuss strategy and tactics in detail, but at this point, all that is necessary is to recognize that competition is a major element in the environment and the marketing manager must understand the types of competitors and their relative intensities. The intensity of competition seems to be determined by eight factors: [4]

1. Number of equally balanced competitors: High levels of competition are typical in industries where competitors are relatively equal in terms of size and resources.

2. Industry growth: Competition is often more fierce in mature and other slow-growth industries. Here, increases in market share typically have to be at the expense of competitors who in all probability will not readily give up market share.

3. High fixed or storage costs: When firms face high fixed costs or high storage costs, they are likely to use excess capacity to help overcome such costs. Often this leads to increased price competition when demand softens, thus creating intense competition in the market.

4. Differentiation: In business marketing, customers' specifications often cause products to be almost identical. Typically, this often results in heavy price competition as competitive product offerings are so close.

5. Capacity: A competitor's capacity also affects its intensity. In some industries, capacity additions by manufacturers may only be accomplished in

large increments. When demand is high, producers tend to add capacity. A drop in demand often results in overcapacity, which causes competition to become fierce.

6. Diversity: When competitors are diverse in strategies, origins, personalities, and relationships, judging the form that competition will take is a difficult undertaking. Because of this uncertainty, developing long-term strategy becomes risky. Foreign competitors can also upset long-term equilibriums with respect to how firms compete.

7. High strategic stakes: When competitors place high strategic value on the same product or market opportunity, competition becomes fierce. For all, there is too much at risk. If a firm has such high stakes, it may be willing to sacrifice profits to establish itself competitively. In some international situations, a country may be willing to subsidize firms because of the importance of the industry to the country involved. The eleven-country European consortium that subsidizes Airbus Industrie is an example of how sacrificed profits and government subsidies can affect competition. In this case, the subsidies permitted Airbus to compete more aggressively with Boeing and McDonnell–Douglas for sales worldwide.

8. High exit barriers: In some industries, exit barriers prevent competitors from leaving a market and thus force them to compete more strenuously. Exit barriers are factors that keep companies in business even where profits are low or nonexistent. Such barriers may be economic, strategic, or emotional in nature. For example, the firm may have assets that cannot be used for other endeavors, or the costs required to terminate may be seen as prohibitive. When this happens, competition stiffens.

The above points refer to the intensity of competition among existing competitors. When new competitors enter a mature industry, competition will also increase until the new firm has established an acceptable market share or profit level or is driven out. If the industry is growing rapidly, however, new competitors may find it easier to enter because existing firms may be concentrating more on increasing capacity and growing at an acceptable rate than on preventing competition. An exception to this takes place when entry barriers are high. These barriers may take the form of high capital costs, expensive expertise, and so forth. When this happens, new competitors may be reluctant to enter or may even be unable to do so.

Substitute Products For the business marketing manager, it is important to realize that his or her company competes not only with other firms that produce a like product, but also with firms that produce substitute products. Some examples may help illustrate this point. Producers of concrete compete with petroleum companies for highway contracts because asphalt is seen as an acceptable substitute for concrete in the construction of roadways. Similarly, manufacturers of industrial robots compete with other forms of automation as well as with each other. Public utilities compete with cogeneration firms in the electrical power market. There are all kinds of examples of substitute products competition in business marketing. What this means is that if the price of one solution becomes too high, buying organizations can switch to alternative solutions and technology. This is what is called cross-elasticity of demand, which means that if prices for one product become too high, buyers will substitute. Demand will then fall and prices should moderate. The business marketing manager, therefore, cannot simply focus on present competitors but must be constantly on the alert for substitute products.

Bargaining Powers of Suppliers and Customers   As was discussed briefly earlier in the chapter, suppliers to and buyers from a business marketing firm can also become competitors. Powerful suppliers can squeeze profitability from the firm by raising prices and/or reducing product quality. Buyers can hold profitability down by forcing prices down, bargaining for higher quality, and playing competitors against each other. Table 2.1 provides instances where suppliers and customers may become powerful enough to emerge as competitors. The marketing manager thus needs to assess his or her company's suppliers and customers in this light and not simply assume that all is well. For example, if the firm is selling large volumes of a relatively standardized product to a large customer who has the ability to make the product in-house, the manager had better recognize that the conditions exist for that customer to become an actual competitor.

Formulating Competitive Responses   The point of all this discussion is that competition is a very important element in the marketing environment. Competition can come from present domestic global competitors as well as from new

---

TABLE 2.1	Conditions That Make Suppliers and Customers Powerful in Business Marketing

Suppliers Are Powerful When:	Customers Are Powerful When:
• They are concentrated in number	• They are concentrated in number
• They face few substitutes for their product or service	• They purchase a large percent of the marketing firm's sales
• They have a broad customer base	• They purchase a standard undifferentiated product or service
• Their product or service is very important to the customer	• They face few switching costs
• Their product or service is highly differentiated	• They have the ability to make the product or service themselves rather than buy
• Switching costs for the customer are high	• They are quality insensitive
• They can easily replace the buyer	• They have wide tolerance for variation in quality

domestic and global competitive entries. There is also the area of substitute products to be considered. And finally, both suppliers and customers can become competitors.

Once the business marketing manager assesses these various sources of competition, an effective competitive strategy must be formulated. This is where the areas of strategic market planning, marketing planning, and tactical marketing programs enter the scene. Chapters 10 through 17 will address the manner in which these competitive assessments are integrated into actual marketing planning and decision making.

Macro-Level Forces

In addition to competitive forces in the marketing environment, the business marketing manager must assess what are called **macro-level forces** that affect that environment. These forces—economic, technological, political and/or legal, ecological, and global—affect the entire business marketing system as well as individual firms. Since the marketing manager must operate in an environment containing such forces, it becomes necessary to examine each of them sufficiently to gain an understanding of their impact on decision making in business markets.

Economic Forces   The entire business marketing system and the individual companies within that system operate within a domestic national economy, which in turn is a part of the world economy. Thus, the business marketing manager is influenced by **economic forces** and changes in both the national and world economies. Economic growth or decline, changes in employment, prices, income, and availability of resources, money, and credit all affect the individual marketing manager.

For the business marketing manager, an important point must be understood. As was mentioned in the preceding chapter, the demand for business goods and services is said to be *derived,* which means that it is derived from the demand for other goods and services. For example, assume a tire manufacturer markets its tires to a producer of automobiles. The auto manufacturer's demand for tires is derived from sales of its cars to consumers and other buyers. Thus, when the demand for autos is down, the demand for tires also decreases. The subject of derived demand and its marketing implications is examined in detail in Chapter 4. Here, all that is needed is to recognize that when changes occur in the economy and consumers change their buying habits, the effects on business marketing firms can be dramatic. Many well-planned marketing strategies have failed because of changes in the economy that were either unforeseen or ignored by marketing managers. During recessions, and especially depressions, bankruptcies increase and production slows significantly. As organizational customers attempt to reduce their inventories, demand falls for most types of business goods and services and some purchases may be completely eliminated. In periods of rapid growth, on the other hand, manufacturers have difficulty meeting demand. Capacity may be added and prices for materials and labor may rise.

These periods of growth and decline are often cyclical and comprise what is known as the business cycle. Sometimes, this cycle is stimulated by the government in order to slow down inflation or decrease unemployment. Swings in the economy are important for business marketers to understand because they affect supply and demand for materials and labor, buying power, willingness to buy, and the intensity and nature of competitive behavior. Thus, a brief look at the four basic stages in the business cycle is in order. These stages are prosperity, recession, depression, and recovery.

During prosperity, the economy grows and the business marketing system thrives. Buying power is usually high because unemployment is low and aggregate income is up. New competitors arise to supply the increasing demand for business goods and services. Demand often increases for goods and services that create more efficiency and/or increase productivity. Sales can increase while market shares stay relatively the same because of the increased demand. The major problem for business marketers is keeping up with demand—they may not have the capacity to meet such demand increases. However, the seeds of recession can sometimes be found in prosperity. At the end of a period of prosperity, for example, production bottlenecks and capacity constraints begin to develop. Wages and prices surge, inventories build up, and the Federal Reserve Board tries to control developing inflation with higher interest rates. With these economic brakes applied, the system slows and begins to decline.

In a recession, growth stops and the business marketing system declines. Unemployment rises and total buying power decreases. Business customers become more price sensitive and are willing to spend time and effort searching for the lowest possible prices from suppliers. Those purchases that are not seen as immediately necessary may be postponed or cancelled altogether. For the business marketing manager, these are difficult times. Some marketing plans and programs may need revision. Moreover, it is very difficult to introduce new products or services during a recession because customers typically try to reduce inventories. In addition, organizational customers focus more on price than on value, which creates more intense competition for fewer sales. Business marketing in a recession often involves campaigns to make present and potential customers aware of savings in cost, energy, and manpower and of the benefits of increased productivity. Thus, marketing does not cease during a recession; rather, it focuses on different points than during an era of prosperity. In many business marketing firms, however, there is often a tendency to view marketing expenses as avoidable, or at least postponable, during a recession rather than viewing them as an investment in the future. When this happens, marketing budgets become leaner and the manager may have to be more innovative.

In a recession, the federal government can attempt to stimulate the economy by altering monetary and/or fiscal policies. Monetary policy adjustments might include increasing the money supply in order to increase buying power and/or decreasing interest rates so as to decrease savings, increase spending, and thus increase the demand for goods and services. Changes in fiscal policy might include reducing taxes in order to increase buying and/or using investment tax credits to encourage organizations to spend for plant and equipment. In addition, government spending might be increased, which would help stimulate sales to government markets.

A severe recession can become a depression if the government refuses or is powerless to take steps necessary to ease the downturn. In a depression, unemployment is extremely high, wages are very low, total disposable income is at a minimum, and many companies find it impossible to cope with the limited demand for their goods and services. Since there has not been a true depression in the United States since the 1930s, many believe that the government is capable of avoiding one through its monetary and fiscal policies. The marketing manager must recognize how government uses these policies to avoid depressions and understand what effects these policies can have on business marketing strategies.

In a recovery period, the economy moves from recession back to prosperity. Buying by business customers begins to increase as inventories bottom out, employment rises, and falling prices stabilize and eventually begin to rise. Recoveries can be fast-paced and relatively short, or they can be long and drawn out. The term *business expansion* is used to define that period between a low point in total spending in the U.S. economy and the following high point in total spending. Between 1945 and 1981, the duration of such expansions ranged from a low of twelve months to a high of 106 months; the average of all U.S. expansions has been thirty-three months.[5] In addition, different sectors take off before others and some may never recover. Less competitive industries may move to other countries or they may be replaced by new industries with more modern techniques.

This discussion shows clearly that business marketing is not immune to changes in the economy and the manager must adapt or fail. An excellent example of this can be seen in the case of America West Airlines, once one of the fastest growing U.S. carriers. In 1991, America West suspended lease payments to aircraft suppliers and asked for three-month deferral agreements on its payments. The planes had been leased during a period of prosperity but the carrier could not meet its payments in the recession that followed, citing a slumping economy combined with the rise in fuel prices caused by the Persian Gulf crisis.[6] This example shows that the state of the economy must be an integral part of marketing planning and strategy development, as will be discussed further in Chapters 10 through 17. To accomplish this integration, however, the marketing manager must be able to recognize the various stages in the business cycle and understand the marketing implications of each.

Technological Forces   Technology has been called the most dramatic force in the marketing environment.[7] While this assertion is subject to debate, there is little doubt that **technological forces** have profound effects on the business marketing firm. Technological breakthroughs often have adverse effects on existing products. For example, word processors have replaced typewriters, transistors have replaced vacuum tubes, copy machines have replaced carbon paper, and robotics have replaced more traditional production processes. Today, some of the most exciting research is taking place in biotechnology, solid-state electronics, robotics, and material sciences.[8] All of these fall within the business marketing system, suggesting that technological change is every bit as important in business marketing as it is in consumer marketing.

One way to view the impact of changing technology on business marketing firms is to look at sales of new products. Depending on the industry, anywhere from one-third to three-quarters of the sales of most business marketing firms are accounted for by products that did not exist ten to fifteen years ago. Technological forces affect product offerings in two ways. First, the marketing manager is forced to compete with far more competitive products than ever before. Second, the manager must work toward the development of new products if his or her own firm is to continue to compete effectively. Chapter 12 will examine this topic more completely.

Technological change is typically related to research and development expenditures. Business marketing firms are often big R & D spenders. As can be seen in Table 2.2, the largest R & D spenders are the aerospace, instruments, machinery, and chemicals industries. Research conducted by the Strategic Planning Institute has shown a high correlation between R & D expenditures as a percent of sales and return on investment.[9] All this implies a great emphasis on the importance of technology in business marketing and illustrates the level of effort put forth by business marketing firms to keep abreast. In recent years, there has been a trend toward joint venture or cooperative R & D organizations. A good example of this is the Microelectronics and Computer Technology Corporation,

TABLE 2.2	**Percentage of Sales Spent in Research and Development in Business Markets**
Industry	Total R & D Expenditures as a Percentage of Sales
Iron and steel	1.5%
Nonferrous metals	.8%
Electrical equipment	7.1%
Machinery	5.6%
Aerospace	16.0%
Fabricated metal products	.5%
Instruments	8.7%
Stone, clay, and glass	.8%
Chemicals	4.7%
Paper	.8%
Rubber	1.3%
Petroleum	1.6%
Food	.3%
Textiles	.3%
All manufacturing	3.2%

Source: Reprinted by permission from the 33rd Annual DRI/McGraw-Hill Survey of Research & Development Expenditures, 1988–90.

which is jointly sponsored by twelve companies including Contol Data, RCA, Digital Equipment, Honeywell, and Sperry.[10] This subject is discussed in detail in Chapter 7, but it deserves mention here because it again shows the importance of technology in contemporary business marketing.

Looking ahead to the future, there are many indications of new technological changes that are likely to occur. Scientists around the world are perfecting a new class of motors, sensors, and mechanical devices so small that some would fit into the period at the end of this sentence. Such microscopic machines could have untold medical and industrial applications. The Japanese are developing robots so tiny that they could be used to perform surgery. Scientists at the University of Wisconsin are making metallic gears so small that several could be set on the head of a pin. Tiny mechanical sensors have been developed that can detect pressure, motion, or vibration. Technologies such as these have the potential to completely change some industries if they prove to be successful. Some will never develop but others that cannot even be envisioned now may have profound changes on the business marketing system.[11]

Political and/or Legal Forces Political and legal forces are closely related aspects of the business marketing system, but they are not exactly the same thing and therefore will be discussed separately.

Political Forces **Political forces** at all levels of government affect the business marketing system, but it is the federal government that plays the major role. With respect to that role, two competing views emerge. One view sees government as a positive influence in that it provides rules that industry must operate under; it encourages the best from industry without directly supporting any specific sectors through an industrial policy; it helps all business marketing firms with an even hand through the U.S. Department of Commerce; it guards the environment from pollution; and it provides regulation, where necessary, to ensure fairness and protect various publics of the business system.

An interesting example of the positive influence that can be exerted by the federal government is the Malcolm Baldridge National Quality Award Program. This is an annual award to recognize U.S. companies that excel in quality achievement and quality management. Companies participating in the award process submit applications that include completion of an award examination. Members of the Malcolm Baldridge National Quality Award Board of Examiners review and evaluate all applications. The board is composed of approximately 150 quality experts selected from business, professional and trade organizations, accrediting bodies, universities, and government. The award examination is based on quality excellence criteria, created through a business/government partnership. Such an award is prestigious and is often used to advantage by winners in their promotion. Since the program was created by Public Law 100-17, it serves as an excellent example of how government can stimulate business marketing firms to perform better. An example of this took place in 1990 when an industrial distributor, Wallace Company, Inc., won the coveted award, joining such previous winners as Federal Express, IBM Rochester, and the Cadillac Motor Car Division of General Motors.[12]

Conversely, many see the U.S. political environment as a major contributor to the decline in the competitiveness of American business marketing firms.[13] The U.S. economy is often perceived as suffering from too little investment, productivity, and growth, and too much inflation and government. The following quotation by Jack Kemp seems to summarize this view: "If you tax something, you get less of it. If you subsidize something, you get more of it. The problem with the United States today is that we tax work, savings, thrift, production, and capital; and we subsidize non-work, welfare, and consumption."[14] This view suggests that there is too much government and that there is a close relationship between the growth of government in the United States and poor economic performance. The federal government is accused of taking an increasing percentage of current output and, through ever-higher levels of borrowing and debt, crowding out the productive private sector, thus mortgaging the economy's future. Figure 2.4 and Table 2.3 illustrate the significant milestones in government growth and the shift in the government's allocations from defense to welfare type outlays. The effects of both of these are to remove funds from the business marketing system, the first through taxation and the second by limiting the buying power of a significant sector of the business system.

FIGURE 2.4 Changes in the Federal Government as Reflected in Percent of Gross National Product Spent on National Defense and on Federal Payments to Individuals Between 1960 and 1988

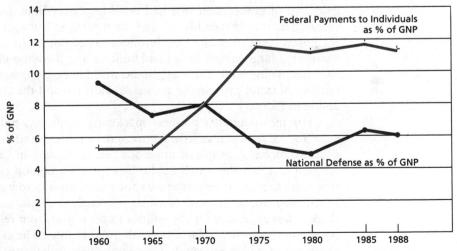

Source: U.S. Department of Commerce, *Statistical Abstract of the United States 1990* (Washington, DC: U.S. Government Printing Office, January 1990), 330, 428.

TABLE 2.3   History of Government Growth in the United States as Reflected in Total Government Spending in Billions of Current Dollars

Year	Total Federal, State, and Local Expenditures	Historical Happening
1789	$ 0.010	Federal government begins
1944	109.947	Spending exceeds $100 billion for first time, 155 years after government established
1965	205.550	Spending exceeds $200 billion, 21 years after reaching $100 billion
1969	308.344	Spending exceeds $300 billion, only 4 years after reaching $200 billion
1975	560.100	Spending exceeds $500 billion, only 6 years after reaching $300 billion
1981	1,070.000	Spending exceeds $1 trillion, only 6 years after reaching $500 billion
1990	896.000	Spending decreases to about $900 billion
1993 *	1,015.000	Spending is again expected to exceed $1 trillion

Source: Adapted from various editions of U.S. Department of Commerce, *Statistical Abstract of the United States* (Washington, DC: U.S. Government Printing Office).

* 1993 projections from *Selling to the Government Markets: Local, State, & Federal* (Cleveland: Government Product News, 1991), 3.

The true overall effect of government varies from industry to industry and changes over time. A good example of this can be seen in what occurred during the Reagan administration. Reagan attempted to reverse some of the perceived problems of government that had developed over time. By lowering taxes, increasing military expenditures, and attempting to cut spending in other areas, the government stimulated the business environment. After a number of years, however, a large budget deficit had built up and the national debt had increased to a threatening level. Excesses also occurred during this period, as revealed by a number of fraud cases in the aerospace industry and the collapse of the savings and loan industry.

For the individual business marketing company, political forces include state and local as well as federal government entities, and these forces take many different forms. A couple of situations that took place in California serve as examples. In 1991, the state's Public Utilities Commission (PUC) adopted tough new rules to make it very expensive for public utilities to buy or make electricity from smog-producing fuels such as oil, coal, and gas. Conversely, the ruling made it less expensive for the utilities to get power from relatively smog-free resources such as wind, solar, and geothermal sources. The expected results of this decision are higher energy bills for consumers, a halt to the building of traditional power plants, a boom in building alternative-fuel power plants, and a rush by large industrial firms to build in-house power plants to avoid higher energy costs.[15] But in another situation that occurred at about this same time, this same Public Utilities Commission permitted one large public utility to lower its rates below those charged by cogeneration operations. This ruling had the effect of making an alternative source of energy (cogeneration) more expensive than the energy produced by the utility via traditional power plants.[16] As a result, a number of cogeneration operations became noncompetitive and lost contracts.

While many industry trade associations and large companies try to influence governments through lobbying activities, political contributions, and promotional efforts to stockholders and the public, many business marketing firms view political forces as beyond their control. Either way, the business marketing manager must be aware of all the government programs that directly and indirectly affect his or her company both positively and negatively. The political environment simply cannot be ignored in business marketing decision making and strategy development.

Legal Forces   Government at all levels can enact legislation that affects the business marketing system and the individual business marketing company. These **legal forces** can range all the way from federal laws enforced by the U.S. Justice Department to enforcement by local zoning boards and commissions. Thus, the individual business marketing manager must be alert to legal requirements at all levels of government.

In the United States, legislation has three basic purposes. The first is to protect companies from each other. These laws are intended to prevent unfair competition and are enforced by the Federal Trade Commission. The second purpose is to protect consumers from unfair business practices. The third purpose is to protect the interests of society against business practices that may adversely affect what is best for society.[17] All three have business marketing implications and the marketing manager needs to be on guard against marketing decisions that could be at odds with any of these three basic purposes.

Listing all the existing laws and regulations that could affect business marketers is a physical impossibility. As was mentioned previously, there are local and state regulations in addition to the federal ones, so the marketing manager has to be aware of what local and/or state laws are also involved. Table 2.4 illustrates some of the major pieces of federal legislation that have business marketing implications. Business marketers have been prosecuted under these laws. Perhaps the best-remembered example took place in 1961 when price fixing charges were brought against twenty-nine firms in the electrical equipment industry resulting in fines amounting to $2 million. The table shows that legislation dropped off in the 1980s. Much of this was due to the Reagan administration's position on deregulation, which relaxed attitudes toward merging and contributed to many of the alliances and partnerships now found in contemporary business marketing. Nevertheless, the legal environment is one that cannot be ignored in any way by the business marketing manager, and the manager typically must rely heavily on his or her legal department to guard against possible infractions at all levels of government.

TABLE 2.4	Federal Legislation Affecting Business Marketing	
Year	Legislation	Purpose
1890	Sherman Antitrust Act	Forbids agreements among suppliers to fix prices, prohibits attempts to monopolize, and outlaws contracts, combinations, or conspiracies in restraint of trade
1914	Federal Trade Commission Act	Established the Federal Trade Commission to investigate and stop unfair methods of competition
1914	Clayton Antitrust Act	Prohibits price discrimination, tying clauses and exclusive dealing, intercorporate holdings, and interlocking directorates where effects substantially lessen competition
1936	Robinson-Patman Act	Amends the Clayton Act by adding phrase, "to injure, destroy, or prevent competition," and defines price discrimination as unlawful, subject to certain defenses
1937	Miller-Tydings Act	Amends the Sherman Act to exempt fair-trade agreements from antitrust prosecution
1938	Wheeler-Lea Act	Prohibits unfair and deceptive acts and practices regardless of whether competition is injured
1950	Antimerger Act	Amends Clayton Act to prevent intercorporate acquisitions that could have a substantially adverse effect on competition
1969	National Environmental Policy Act	Establishes a national policy on the environment and created the Environmental Protection Agency
1974	Sherman Antitrust Act amendments	Makes criminal violations a felony and increased maximum penalty for an individual to a fine of up to $100,000 or up to three years in prison, or both

Ecological Forces   Concerns about the natural environment affect many business marketers. This is particularly true of those business marketing firms that use large amounts of raw materials that are in relatively short supply and those who damage the quality of the natural environment through noise, air, water, and/or solid waste pollution. Many manufacturers, refineries, mills, processors, and so forth are particularly sensitive to these environmental concerns. In many cases, their by-products pollute ground and water areas to the detriment of the entire society. This, in turn, has resulted in both regulation and public reaction by such organizations as the Sierra Club and Friends of the Earth.

Ecological forces affect the business marketing manager in a number of ways. First, the Environmental Protection Agency was created to monitor environmental infractions and the government is therefore often involved. The EPA can levy large fines on firms that pollute the environment and it can also force firms to correct their operations in order to eliminate pollution. Table 2.5 provides some examples of pollution-abatement expenditures in business marketing. In addition, the EPA can force firms to clean up polluted areas, which can be very expensive for the marketing company. Second, the many environmental groups have exerted pressures on business marketers to do a better job of protecting the natural environment. These pressures cannot be ignored because they often influence consumers who in turn can negatively affect business marketers. Perhaps the best-known example of this in business marketing took place with McDonald's, which, under pressure from environmental groups, decided to eliminate its plastic foam boxes and replace them with biodegradable paper products. Exhibit 2.2 provides more insight to this situation. Finally, ecological forces have brought about marketing changes regarding the disposal of wastes, recycling, and the use of nonbiodegradable packaging materials. This, in turn, has led business marketing firms to search for alternative ways to better preserve the natural environment. Thus, ecological forces offer opportunities to business marketers as well as threats to existing products and processes. In fact, concern for the ecology in the United States has fostered totally new industries that are now part of the business marketing system. For example, Chemical Waste Management, Inc., operates sixteen hazardous waste treatment, disposal, and recovery facilities around the United States. All indications are that the deteriorating state of the natural environment will continue to be a major issue facing business marketing companies in the 1990s.[18]

TABLE 2.5   Annual Pollution-Abatement Capital Expenditures and Operating Costs by Selected Industries in Business Marketing in Billions of Current Dollars (1986)

Industry	Capital Expenditures for Pollution Abatement			Gross Operating Costs for Pollution Abatement			
	Air	Water	Solid Waste*	Air	Water	Solid Waste*	Total
Chemicals	197.9	325.5	100.9	646.5	1,301.9	705.9	3,278.6
Electrical machinery	46.6	61.5	16.9	88.3	210.9	231.5	655.7
Fabricated metals	36.6	80.9	18.2	95.6	187.7	219.2	638.2
Machinery except electrical	16.7	25.7	6.3	209.7	128.2	149.1	535.7
Petroleum	273.6	121.5	29.1	123.0	578.0	196.3	1,321.5
Primary metal	102.8	74.6	48.4	968.5	509.4	264.1	1,967.8
Transportation equipment	432.4	81.8	26.8	195.7	269.4	304.9	1,311.0

Source: U.S. Department of Commerce, *Statistical Abstract of the United States 1990* (Washington, DC: U.S. Government Printing Office, January 1990), 208.

* Solid waste includes both hazardous and nonhazardous waste.

EXHIBIT 2.2   How Ecological Forces Affect Business Markets

Pressures from environmental groups can at times influence major business marketing decisions. This was illustrated in a decision announced by McDonald's Corporation in 1990 to stop using plastic foam boxes to package its fast-food offerings as a result of pressure from environmental groups. The decision was made to eliminate the use of the boxes within sixty days, which had disastrous effects on suppliers of the boxes to the giant fast-food chain.

Even though McDonald's management claimed to have scientific proof that the foam packaging was environmentally safe, that same management decided to drop the product. In the words of McDonald's president, "Although some scientific studies indicate that foam packaging is environmentally sound, our customers just don't feel good about it. . . . So, we're changing."

Polystyrene had already been banned by a number of municipalities across the United States, which claimed that the product contributed to landfill problems and was made with chemicals that also harmed the ozone layer. Thus, the pressures on McDonald's were not totally unexpected nor should the incident have surprised suppliers of the plastic foam packaging material.

Reactions to the decision by McDonald's were quite mixed. The Environmental Defense Fund praised the decision and voiced hopes that other fast-food chains would follow. Not surprisingly, the packaging industry saw it differently. The Foodservice & Packaging Institute accused McDonald's of bowing to public pressure that was based on misconceptions and misinformation. The EPA refrained from commenting one way or the other but a spokesperson did state that the agency had no studies to support the claim that foam packaging is environmentally sound.

The results of the pressures, however, show clearly that business marketers cannot simply ignore environmental issues, as the firms that produce the foam packaging found out. On the other hand, McDonald's decision created opportunities for producers of paper and other biodegradable packaging materials.

Source: Adapted from "McDonald's Says Paper Will Replace Foam Boxes," *San Diego Union* (November 2, 1990), E1.

Global Forces   Earlier in this chapter, the point was made that the U.S. business marketing system is part of a larger global or worldwide business marketing system. U.S. business marketing companies no longer market only to domestic organizations, nor do they compete only with other U.S. business marketers. Foreign competition is extremely acute as business marketing firms throughout the world move from relatively insulated domestic markets to worldwide markets. In addition, many U.S. firms have formed and are still forming strategic alliances and partnerships with foreign firms. Thus, **global forces** are stronger than ever before on the business marketing system and on the individual business marketing company. This, in turn, requires that business marketing managers think and act globally in their deliberations and decisions. Figure 2.5 illustrates U.S. imports and exports between 1960 and 1988. As can be seen, imports began to exceed exports in the middle to late 1970s. Since many imports include

FIGURE 2.5   U.S. Imports and Exports Between 1960 and 1988

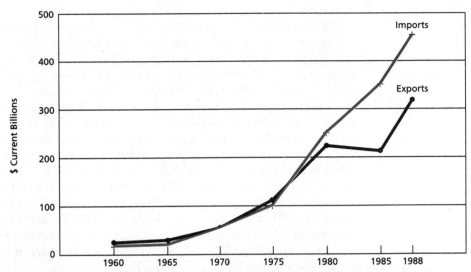

Source: U.S. Department of Commerce, *Statistical Abstract of the United States 1990* (Washington, DC: U.S. Government Printing Office, January 1990), 804.

business goods and services, it can be seen that U.S. firms are facing increased global competition even in domestic markets. Business goods and services account for many exports as well and this, of course, means increased global marketing responsibilities. This area is so important in contemporary business marketing that it will be covered exclusively in Chapter 3, where the major marketing implications resulting from such global operations will be discussed in detail. Here, however, all that is required is a recognition that the U.S. business marketing system is but part of the global system and as such is influenced by what happens in other parts of that global system.

FACILITATING INFLUENCES ON BUSINESS MARKETING

Figure 2.1 shows that, in addition to environmental influences, the business marketing system must interact with a number of facilitating influences. These influences are not unrelated to the environmental influences, but neither are they the same. The business marketing system is affected by facilitating organizations that may or may not be directly involved in the system, but that become involved in various capacities. These facilitating influences often have considerable impact on the making of marketing decisions and, in many cases, the business marketing manager must adapt to them or conform to their constraints. While facilitating influences do not typically draw as much attention as do environmental forces, they are important. Some examples may help to clarify their roles in business marketing.

Facilitating influences occur when organizations other than producers, customers, and channel intermediaries become involved in the business marketing system. For example, many business marketing firms do not own their distribution systems. Rather, they rely on common carriers to transport their goods and on public warehouses to store them. When this happens, these organizations can either positively or negatively affect the performance of the marketing firm. For example, assume that such a marketer is required to deliver a specified amount of goods to a customer at a specified date. As has been discussed already, late deliveries or backorders are anathema in business marketing. If the goods are delivered late or backordered, the marketing firm may lose a good customer. In this case, the marketing firm is dependent on the common carrier and the public warehouse to deliver and release the goods on time. In most cases, this process would work without any hitch but since the manufacturer lacks a certain degree of control over either facilitating organization, their performances can affect the system. The problem might be eliminated if the marketing firm owned the transportation means and the warehouses, but this is very expensive for some firms. Thus, these facilitating organizations exert influences on the system and on the individual company that must be considered in marketing strategy formulation and tactical program development.

Other facilitating influences might be financial institutions that supply needed funds to the system. If, as previously discussed, a business marketing firm wishes to expand to meet increased demand but does not have the financial resources, it may wish to borrow. The ability and willingness to lend affects the system and the individual firm. If outside funding cannot be obtained, the marketing manager may have to revise his or her strategy to adjust to a less than favorable financial picture. Other facilitating organizations that affect the system and firms within that system might be advertising agencies, marketing research organizations, consulting firms, buying groups, and other such operations often used by business marketers. These forces affect behavior in the system and should be considered as part of that system. Throughout this text, many of these forces will be addressed as they apply to more specific areas of the marketing mix. Here, the point is that they are part of the business marketing system and, as such, should be considered carefully by the business marketing manager.

CHAPTER SUMMARY

This chapter has examined those factors that most influence the business marketing system described and outlined in the previous chapter. That system begins with resource suppliers providing materials and services to producers of business goods and services. These producers then market their goods and services to organizational customers through a network of direct and indirect channels of distribution. In this chapter, the focus was on what forces most influence these components of the business marketing system. In addition, the effects of these forces on individual marketing firms and managers were examined.

The business marketing firm was studied using an open system perspective so that the influences might best be understood. Two major types of influences are seen as most important. These are environmental influences and facilitating influences. Environmental influences were analyzed in terms of competitive forces and macro-level forces. The former looked at types of competitors and factors contributing to the intensities of various competitors. The latter examined economic, technological, political and/or legal, ecological, and global forces as these affect the overall system and individual

companies within that system. Finally, the chapter looked at facilitating forces that affect the system and its components. Facilitating forces are typically organizations that are not directly involved in the system but that often become involved in more indirect manners. Examples of such organizations are financial institutions, common carriers, public warehouses, advertising agencies, marketing research firms, buying groups, consultants, and so forth.

The main point of this chapter is that business marketing management does not take place in a vacuum. The individual marketing manager is constrained in his or her decision making by many diverse types of forces. Understanding these forces and the possible roles they may play is fundamental to sound business marketing practice.

KEY TERMS

competitive force
ecological force
economic force
environmental force
facilitating force
global force

legal/political force
macro-level force
open marketing system
substitute product
technological force

QUESTIONS

1. Explain how an organizational buyer of component parts could become a competitor to one of that buyer's present suppliers. What do you see as the major implications for the marketing manager of the supplying company?
2. Why can U.S. business marketing firms no longer focus exclusively on U.S. domestic markets for the marketing of their goods and services?
3. Explain why the business cycle is so important to producers of business goods and services. How should marketing be adapted to each stage of the business cycle?

4. A business marketing company has a policy of curtailing marketing expenditures during periods of recession and postponing them until recovery of the economy takes place. Assess the firm's policy.
5. Why is the federal government such an important factor in the environments of most U.S. business marketing companies? In what ways does the federal government affect decisions in business marketing?
6. McDonald's Corporation's decision to substitute paper for plastic foam in packaging its fast foods took place in the consumer market but

also had major impacts in business markets. Explain why this was so.

7. In terms of adapting to its ecological environment, the business marketing company must be alert to more than just the Environmental Protection Agency (EPA). Explain why an understanding of the EPA alone is not sufficient to compete in business marketing.

8. Marketing is sometimes described as the ability to adapt to change and those firms that are unable or unwilling to adapt often cease to exist. For the individual business marketing manager, adapting involves both marketing intelligence gathering and analysis of the marketing mix.

Explain how each of these may be used to better adapt to environmental forces in the business marketing system.

9. What kinds of factors cause competition to be more or less intense in the environment of a business marketing company? Under what conditions may the marketing manager expect competition to be most difficult? When might it be the least difficult?

10. In business marketing, the statement is often made that decisions cannot be made in a vacuum. Explain what this means and then relate how it applies to a firm's marketing environment.

NOTES

1. Philip Kotler, *Marketing Management: Analysis, Planning, Implementation, & Control*, 7th ed. (Englewood Cliffs, NJ: Prentice-Hall, Inc., 1991), 129.
2. Ibid., 135.
3. See Michael E. Porter, *Competitive Strategy: Techniques for Analyzing Industries and Competitors* (New York: The Free Press, 1980).
4. Ibid.
5. *Cahners Advertising Research Report No. 700.01* (Newton, MA: Cahners Publishing Company, 1984).
6. "America West Halts Payment on Planes," *San Diego Union* (June 7, 1991), C3.
7. Kotler, op. cit., 144.
8. See Charles Panat, *Breakthroughs* (Boston: Houghton Mifflin Company, 1980); and "Technologies for the '80s," *Business Week* (July 6, 1981), 48.
9. Sidney Schoeffler, "Market Position: Build, Hold, or Harvest," *The Pimsletter* 3 (1977): 3.

10. "Four Cities Vie For High-Tech Joint Venture," *Wall Street Journal* (May 12, 1983), 35.
11. "Scientists See Decade of Promise," *San Diego Union* (January 7, 1991), E1.
12. See Christine Forbes, "And the Winner Is . . . ," *Industrial Distribution* 80 (February 1991): 20–23.
13. J. Peter Grace, speech given before the National Frozen Food Convention, San Francisco, California, November 10, 1981.
14. Ibid.
15. Charles W. Ross, "Utilities Using Fossil Fuels Face Soaring Smog Cost," *San Diego Union* (June 6, 1991), D1, D2.
16. Pamela Wilson, "SDG&E Sued Again Over Cogeneration," *San Diego Daily Transcript* (June 13, 1991), A1–A3.
17. Kotler, op. cit., 146.
18. Ibid., 142.

SUGGESTED ADDITIONAL READINGS

Capon, Noel, and Rashi Glazer. *Marketing and Technology: A Strategic Co-Alignment*, Report No. 86-106. Cambridge, MA: Marketing Science Institute, 1986.

Carroll, Daniel T. "The Changing Environment for

Industrial Marketing." *Proceedings of 20th Anniversary Conference*, Report No. 82-101. Cambridge, MA: Marketing Science Institute, 1982, 42–58.

Day, George S., and Robin Wensley. "Assessing Advantage: A Framework for Diagnosing Competitive Superiority." *Journal of Marketing* 52 (April 1988): 1–20.

Demsetz, Harold. "Barriers to Entry." *American Economic Review* 72 (March 1982): 139–152.

Harrigan, Kathryn Rudie. "Barriers to Entry and Competitive Strategies." *Strategic Management Journal* 2 (1981): 395–412.

Haverty, John L. "What Happens When New Competitors Enter an Industry." *Industrial Marketing Management* 20 (1991): 73–80.

Karakaya, Fahri, and Michael J. Stahl. "Barriers to Entry and Market Entry Decisions in Consumer and Industrial Goods Markets." *Journal of Marketing* 53 (April 1989): 80–91.

McFarlan, E. Warren. "Information Technology Changes the Way You Compete." *Harvard Business Review* 62 (May–June 1984): 98–103.

Methe, David T. *Technological Competition in Global Industries*. Westport, CT: Quorum Books, 1990.

Park, C. Whan, and Daniel C. Smith. *Competitors As Sources of Innovative Marketing Strategies*, Report No. 86-109. Cambridge, MA: Marketing Science Institute, 1986.

Porter, Michael E. *Competitive Strategy: Techniques for Analyzing Industries and Competitors*. New York: The Free Press, 1980.

Porter, Michael E. "Technology and Competitive Advantage." *Journal of Business Strategy* 5 (Winter 1985): 60–78.

Webster, Frederick E., Jr. *It's 1990—Do You Know Where Your Marketing Is?*, Report No. 89-123. Cambridge, MA: Marketing Science Institute, 1989.

Werner, Ray O. *Legal and Economic Regulation in Marketing*. Westport, CT: Quorum Books, 1989.

Yip, G. S. *Barriers to Entry: A Corporate Strategy Perspective*. Lexington, MA: D. C. Heath and Company, 1982.

Yip, G. S. "Gateways to Entry." *Harvard Business Review* 60 (September–October, 1982): 85–92.

Young, John. "Global Competition: The New Reality." *California Management Review* 27 (Spring 1985): 11–25.

Zeithami, Carl P., and Valerie A. Zeithami. "Environmental Management: Revising the Marketing Perspective." *Journal of Marketing* 48 (Spring 1984): 46–53.

3

The Global Nature of Business Marketing

● ●

In Chapters 1 and 2, the business marketing system and its environments were examined to show that business marketing decisions take place in light of many surroundings and constraints. In both those chapters, references were made to the changing global nature of U.S. business marketing. The business marketing manager can no longer focus simply on U.S. **domestic markets** in developing strategies and tactical programs, nor can that manager assume that only domestic competitors will be involved. The world is becoming smaller and the economies in individual countries are intertwined into a more global economy. In no area of marketing is this more true than in business marketing. Today's business marketers face **global markets** quite different from those they have served in the past. They face competitors quite different from those faced in past years. And they often become involved in strategic alliances or partnerships with business marketers in other countries. Thus, some form of global perspective is imperative for all U.S. business marketing managers, whether their firms are currently involved in global marketing, contemplating moves in this direction, or trying to avoid global competition.

One point must be made clear here. This is a text devoted to the study of business marketing to organizational customers and its primary emphasis is on the marketing of goods and services to U.S. markets. Even though global aspects pervade all of business marketing, adequate coverage of all of these aspects is a physical impossibility. The problem is that global or multinational marketing is a field in itself. Global marketing is a complex area and is covered in many excellent textbooks that are devoted exclusively to this subject. Therefore, this chapter provides more of an overview of the global nature of business marketing as it affects the practicing business marketing manager. Global marketing will be defined as it applies to business marketing and sources of information on global markets will be examined. Marketing strategy development and mix im-

Business Marketing Is Truly Global Marketing

A global perspective pervades many areas of contemporary business marketing, sometimes to the point that business marketing equals global marketing. Many business marketing firms simply cannot afford to focus solely on domestic markets and global competition is thus their way of life. An excellent illustration of this may be seen in the case of manufacturers of commercial airliners. The following examples point out just how global this area of business marketing has become.

Boeing Company, one of the largest of all commercial aircraft manufacturers, is designing aircraft specifically for such Asian air carriers as Thai Airways International, Cathay Pacific Airways, Singapore Airlines, Japan Airways, and Nippon Airways. At the same time, the company continues to serve its U.S. customers, including United Airlines, which has asked Boeing to look into the possibility of designing a plane capable of carrying 650 passengers, 50 percent more passengers than any existing plane. United is one of Boeing's largest customers and is important to the company, as are all other U.S. carriers, but the demand in Asia and Europe is so great that the company cannot focus only on U.S. carriers, no matter how big or important they may be.

The global character of this manufacturing industry is evidenced in three separate transactions that took place in the same week in June 1991. At that time, a Beverly Hills, California, aircraft leasing firm placed orders for up to fifteen Airbus jets from the European consortium, Airbus Industrie. In the same week, Airbus received orders for up to twenty-four jets from Kuwait Airways. Also that week, Thai Airways International placed firm orders with Boeing for six 777 jetliners and took options on six more. All this business in the same week shows that customers for commercial aircraft exist worldwide and in order to compete, manufacturers must concentrate their marketing efforts globally.

Source: Adapted from various editions of the *San Diego Union.*

plications will also be reviewed and, finally, an examination will be made of changes taking place in the global environment that have business marketing ramifications.

WHAT IS GLOBAL MARKETING?

Global marketing is simply marketing across national boundaries.[1] Applied to business marketing, it is the marketing of goods and services across national boundaries to private, institutional, or governmental organizational customers. For the U.S. business marketing manager, international marketing has three major meanings. First, global marketing means that the manager may be able to market goods and services to other than domestic markets. Second, however, is that competitors from other countries may market their goods and services to U.S. markets. Third, many U.S. business marketers are forming partnerships or strategic alliances with companies in other countries. Since all three have marketing management implications, each will be analyzed. How should products and services be changed for global markets? How should the marketing mix be adjusted to better fit the needs of global customers? What marketing changes may have to be made to adapt to global competitors in U.S. markets? And should the marketing company consider forming partnerships with global companies? This chapter discusses these aspects of global business marketing.

BUSINESS MARKETING AND GLOBAL MARKETS

When the subject of global marketing is discussed, it becomes important to consider the question of how involved is business marketing. If global marketing involves primarily consumer products, then the impacts on business marketers may be minimal. If, however, a major part of global marketing involves business goods and services, then the importance to business marketers becomes more profound.

One way to answer this question is to look at U.S. **exports**—goods and services shipped to customers in other countries. Figure 2.5 showed that annual U.S. exports exceed $300 billion. Table 3.1 examines the ten largest U.S. exporting industries. Analysis of this table reveals that all but one, passenger motor vehicles, involve business rather than consumer marketing. Such products as aircraft, parts, computers, components, chemicals, instruments, resins, and engines are all purchased by organizational customers. This table shows rather conclusively that business marketing plays a major role in global marketing and,

TABLE 3.1	The 10 Largest Exporting Industries in the U.S. in 1988 (in billions of dollars)	
Rank	Industry	Value of Exports
1	Aircraft and spacecraft	$20.3
2	Road vehicle and tractor parts	13.1
3	Office machine parts	12.6
4	Computers	11.6
5	Electronic components & parts	10.4
6	Passenger motor vehicles	9.4
7	Organic chemicals	7.8
8	Measuring instruments	7.4
9	Synthetic resins, rubber and plastic materials	7.3
10	Internal combustion engines	6.2

Source: U.S. Department of Commerce, *U.S. Industrial Outlook 1990* (Washington, DC: U.S. Government Printing Office, January 1990), 17.

thus, the business marketing manager should not simply write off global markets as inconsequential. Global demand for business goods and services may well exceed global demand for consumer products and services.

Figure 3.1 provides another example of the importance of global marketing in some selected business marketing areas. For example, exports by U.S. manufacturers of chemicals total over $32 billion; these same manufacturers compete with almost $20 billion of imports from global competitors. Similarly, U.S. producers of electrical machinery sell over $20 billion of goods to global markets but compete with over $30 billion of imported electrical machinery. The figure shows a similar picture for other U.S. business marketers, which suggests that many American business marketing firms are heavily involved with marketing in other than domestic markets and compete vigorously with foreign competitors in U.S. domestic markets. U.S. government figures show that the countries supplying the largest amount of goods and services to U.S. markets are, in terms of rank, Canada, Japan, Mexico, Germany, and Taiwan.[2]

All of this suggests strongly that U.S. business marketing managers need to have a global orientation in developing marketing strategies and tactical programs. A global marketing perspective is not a luxury but a necessity in contemporary business marketing.

FIGURE 3.1   Ratio of Imports to Exports in Selected Areas of Business Marketing (in billions of 1988 dollars)

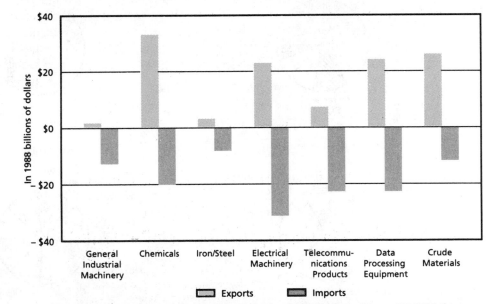

Source: U.S. Department of Commerce, *Statistical Abstract of the United States 1990* (Washington, DC: U.S. Government Printing Office, 1990), 805.

SOURCES OF MAJOR GLOBAL COMPETITION IN U.S. BUSINESS MARKETS

In the previous section, evidence was introduced to show that the main sources of **imports** into the U.S. are Canada, Japan, Mexico, Germany, and Taiwan. For the individual business marketing firm, this general ranking may not hold true. But by analyzing imports of particular products or services, some measure of the competition may be obtained. This analysis provides insight to where major **global competition** may originate and helps to determine the specific firms involved.

Based on an analysis of imports to the United States, Figure 3.2 provides some examples of competitors for U.S. manufacturers of chemicals, telecommunications equipment, general industrial machinery, and electrical machinery. Looking at these individually, some interesting findings arise. In chemicals, for example, the major sources of competition for U.S. producers are Canada, Western Europe, and Japan. But for manufacturers of telecommunications equipment, major global competitors come from Japan, Taiwan, South Korea, and

FIGURE 3.2 Major Global Competitors for Selected Business Products (imports in millions of dollars)

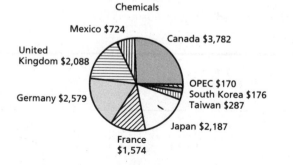

Chemicals

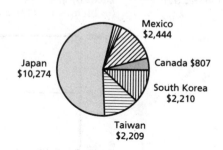

Telecommunications Equipment

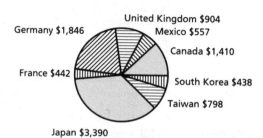

General Industrial Machinery

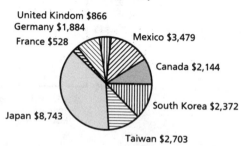

Electrical Machinery

Source: U.S. Department of Commerce, *Statistical Abstract of the United States 1990* (Washington, DC: U.S. Government Printing Office, 1990), 805.

Mexico. As the chart shows, the three Asian countries account for about three-quarters of all imports. In the case of general industrial machinery, major competitors come from Japan, Germany, and Canada. In electrical machinery, major competitors are from Asia, Mexico, and Canada. Based on information from another source, major competitors for business services come from the United Kingdom, Japan, Mexico, Canada, and Germany.[3] Thus, while competitors may differ by product or service, the data suggest that certain countries provide most of the global competitors to U.S. producers of business goods and services. These countries are located in Western Europe (United Kingdom, Germany, and France), North America (Canada and Mexico), and Asia (Japan, Taiwan, and North Korea).

Another way to assess global competitors in U.S. domestic markets is to look at direct foreign investment in this country, with particular emphasis on investment in manufacturing, which involves business marketing. Figure 3.3 outlines direct investment by foreign firms in all areas of the U.S. economy and specifically in manufacturing during the period from 1970 to 1988. This shows clearly that global competitors are actively involved in U.S. markets. In 1970, total foreign investment in U.S. manufacturing totalled about $6.1 billion. By 1988, that figure had increased to $121.4 billion. Where this increased investment is coming from also provides insight to competition. Figure 3.4, based on

FIGURE 3.3   Direct Foreign Investment in the U.S. Between 1970 and 1988 (in millions of dollars)

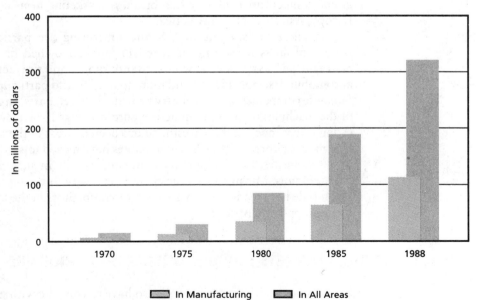

Source: U.S. Department of Commerce, *Statistical Abstract of the United States 1990* (Washington, DC: U.S. Government Printing Office, 1990), 794.

FIGURE 3.4   Foreign Investment in U.S. Manufacturing (in millions of 1988 dollars)

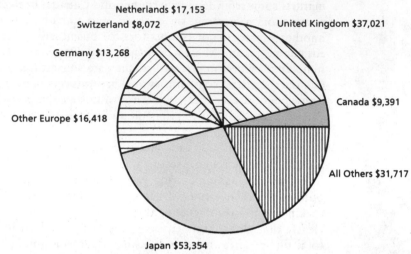

Netherlands $17,153
Switzerland $8,072
Germany $13,268
Other Europe $16,418
United Kingdom $37,021
Canada $9,391
All Others $31,717
Japan $53,354

Source: U.S. Department of Commerce, *Statistical Abstract of the United States 1990* (Washington, DC: U.S. Government Printing Office, 1990), 794.

1988 data, shows Western European countries and Japan as the major investors in U.S. manufacturing, which reinforces the previous argument that the major global competitors for many U.S. business marketing firms come from Western Europe, Asia, and North America.

Japanese investments in U.S. manufacturing are particularly interesting from a business marketing perspective. Japanese-owned plants in the United States include sixty-six steel works, twenty rubber and tire factories, eight major automobile assembly plants, and more than 270 auto parts suppliers. In essence, Japanese companies in this country provide the steel, parts, tires, glass, and some of the machines used to manufacture automobiles.[4] Perhaps what is most interesting is that much of this investment has been in areas of the country vacated by U.S. manufacturers. While U.S. companies have moved to sun belt states or third world countries, the Japanese have invested heavily in such states as Ohio, Indiana, Illinois, Michigan, Kentucky, and Tennessee. Investments of this type and magnitude have made the Japanese major competitors in the U.S. auto manufacturing supply industries.

MAJOR GLOBAL MARKETS FOR U.S. BUSINESS MARKETERS

U.S. business marketing firms will also have to compete with global competitors in other areas of the world outside U.S. domestic markets. According to the U.S. Department of Commerce, the largest export markets for American goods and services are ranked in the following order: Canada, Japan, Mexico, United Kingdom, and Germany.[5] This is interesting because it suggests that the major global markets for many U.S. business goods and services are in the same countries that provide the bulk of imports to this country.

For individual producers of business products and services, however, different patterns occur, as may be seen in Table 3.2, which provides a representative sample of business marketing products and services. Analysis of the table reveals that over one-half of all exports of U.S. manufactured cutting tools are sold to Canadian and Mexican organizational customers, with the bulk going to Can-

TABLE 3.2 Global Demand for Selected Business Products

Product/Industry	Top Five International Markets for Each Product/Industry *					% of Total Export Shipments to Top 5 Markets
Laboratory instruments	Japan (28%)	Germany (16%)	Brazil (8%)	Italy (8%)	Sweden (8%)	68
Pollution control equipment	Japan (18%)	Spain (14%)	Brazil (13%)	Germany (7%)	France (6%)	58
Electrical energy systems	Germany (29%)	Japan (21%)	Spain (12%)	France (10%)	Netherlands (5%)	77
Electronic components	Japan (28%)	Germany (21%)	United Kingdom (11%)	Israel (7%)	France (6%)	73
Business equipment and systems	Japan (18%)	Germany (16%)	United Kingdom (13%)	France (12%)	Australia (8%)	67
Building products and construction equipment	Venezuela (15%)	Brazil (11%)	Japan (10%)	United Kingdom (10%)	Germany (8%)	54
Chemicals	Japan (12%)	Canada (12%)	Mexico (6%)	OPEC (5%)	Taiwan (5%)	40
Aircraft parts	Japan (11%)	United Kingdom (10%)	Canada (7%)	Germany (5%)	South Korea (4%)	37
Instruments	Japan (14%)	Canada (12%)	United Kingdom (9%)	Germany (8%)	France (4%)	47
Metal cutting tools	Canada (44%)	Germany (10%)	Japan (5%)	Mexico (5%)	United Kingdom (5%)	69
All U.S. exports	Canada (21%)	Japan (11%)	United Kingdom (6%)	Mexico (6%)	Germany (4%)	48

Source: Adapted from various issues of *Business America*, *Global Market Surveys*, and *U.S. Industrial Outlook*.

* Percent imported by each country is in parentheses.

ada. But with building products, the two major markets are in Venezuela and Brazil. U.S. manufacturers of instruments find that their markets are relatively evenly spread among Japan, Canada, and Western Europe. Other research indicates the major global markets for business services are in Japan, Canada, the United Kingdom, and Germany.[6] These analyses again support the fact that major global competitors for U.S. business marketing firms originate in Asia, Western Europe, and North America. Thus, all factors considered point to countries in these geographic areas as providing the primary competitors for U.S. producers of business goods and services.

STRATEGIC ALLIANCES AND PARTNERSHIPS

Contemporary business marketing involves more than just competing with global competitors in domestic and global markets. Many U.S. firms are forming what are called **strategic alliances** or **partnerships** with companies from other countries. These are interorganizational cooperative agreements between business marketing companies. While such agreements may also be made with domestic firms, the discussion here will focus on international alliances. Later, in Chapter 7, the whole subject of alliances will be discussed in more detail.

These alliances may take many forms, including **joint ventures, licensing** and distribution agreements, R & D consortia, partnerships, business networks, and other types of cooperative agreements. For many U.S. business marketing firms, such alliances have become standard operating procedure. Table 3.3 provides a number of examples of such agreements and shows that they are fairly common in business marketing. Because they involve agreements with companies in other countries, they have major global implications and selecting the right partner often becomes the responsibility of the marketing manager. Choosing a partner can be risky when only U.S. firms are involved, and it can become even more risky when global partners are considered.

As suggested earlier, there are many reasons behind such alliances. Some are formed to share research and development costs, some may be formed to better facilitate distribution in other countries, some are formed because capital is needed, some are formed to share production expertise or capacity, and some are formed primarily to facilitate penetration into global markets. In addition, some may be formed to reduce the threat of competition. A good example of this is the major alliance between Boeing, Mitsubishi, Kawasaki, and Fuji, which is not without its critics. A Boeing spokesperson called the arrangement a "partnership" and not coproduction. But another Boeing spokesperson stated that, "It's better that they're our partner than working against us. . . . But, eventually they're going to enter the market."[7] Japanese critics complain that Boeing is trying to lessen the role of its Japanese partners, while others believe that, rather than compete head-on with Boeing, the Japanese would rather gradually increase their participation and learn more about the market before actually entering the market as competitors. Whatever the case, this example shows some of

TABLE 3.3	Examples of Global Partnerships Between U.S. and Foreign Firms	
U.S. Partner	Global Partner	Purpose of the Partnership
Ford Motor Company	Volkswagen (Germany)	To build a plant to manufacture various kinds of vehicles in Setubal, Portugal
Boeing Company	Mitsubishi, Kawasaki, Fuji (Japan)	Joint production of Boeing's next generation of commercial aircraft, the 777. Japanese partners will manufacture 20% of the plane
Inland Steel	Nippon Steel (Japan)	Joint venture to operate a steel mill in New Carlisle, Indiana
McDonnell–Douglas	People's Republic of China Government	Joint venture to produce MD-90 jetliners
Merck	Yamanouchi Pharmaceuticals (Japan)	Merck licenses U.S. and European rights to Pepcid, an antiulcer drug, from Yamanouchi
Quidel Corporation	Fujirebio, Inc. (Japan)	Joint development and marketing of a test for detection of gastrointestinal disorders, including cancer
Viagene, Inc.	Green Cross Corporation (Japan)	Development and marketing of an AIDS drug. Green Cross provided funding in exchange for worldwide exclusive license to market the product
General Dynamics	Mitsubishi, Kawasaki, Fuji (Japan)	Joint production of a military fighter aircraft based on the F-16
National Steel	Marubeni (Japan)	Joint venture to operate a plant in Michigan to produce and market steel coils

Source: Adapted from various editions of the *San Diego Union.*

the dangers of strategic global alliances. The marketing manager must be aware of all that is involved before entering into any such agreements or the move could very well prove to be detrimental to his or her company. Since this entire area of alliances and partnerships is so important today in business marketing management, it will be covered in detail in Chapter 7. The discussion here is intended only to show the global ramifications of this trend in business marketing.

STATUS OF GLOBAL MARKETING BY U.S. FIRMS

Despite logical reasons for moving into global markets, there is evidence to conclude that the U.S. share of global markets is not what it could be or should be. Some statistics may help illustrate this point. In 1985, for example, the U.S. trade deficit was $148.5 billion, but exports accounted for only 5.3 percent of the U.S. gross national product. This 5.3 percent figure can be compared to 28 percent for West Germany, 22 percent for Great Britain, and 13.5 percent for Japan.[8] The U.S. Department of Commerce estimates that out of 300,000 American companies, only 30,000 export their goods, although another 18,000 could do so.

Table 3.4 illustrates some examples of the state of involvement of U.S. business marketers in global markets. The table is useful in that it shows that different industries have markedly varying degrees of participation in world markets. For example, 59 percent of the value of shipments of American pulp mills and 26 percent of the value of shipments of domestic synthetic rubber producers are marketed overseas. On the other hand, less than 1 percent of the value of shipments of fiber cans and drums and wood skids and pallets are sent to markets in other countries. The table makes another interesting point. Looking at the leading markets for the U.S. industries on the list, it becomes apparent that for many U.S. managers current global marketing again means marketing in Canada, Mexico, Japan, and Western Europe. This table again points out that a high percentage of exports is made to a small number of countries and also reinforces the argument that U.S. business marketers are not as involved in global marketing as they might be. Exhibit 3.1 shows some examples of where this may be changing.

TABLE 3.4   **Representative Examples of U.S. Industries in Global Markets**

Industry	Value of Shipments ($ millions)	Value of Exports ($ millions)	Percent of Shipments Exported	Leading Markets
Machine tools	$ 6,691	$1,513	22.6%	Mexico, Canada, Japan, China, United Kingdom, Germany
Power transformers	$ 3,779	$ 400	10.6%	Canada, Mexico, United Kingdom
Air and gas compressors	$ 3,360	$ 720	21.4%	Canada, Mexico, United Kingdom, Saudi Arabia, Venezuela
Printing trades machinery	$ 3,597	$ 877	24.4%	Western Europe, Canada
Surgical appliances and supplies	$ 9,315	$1,455	15.6%	Canada, United Kingdom, Germany, Mexico, Japan
Fiber cans, drums, etc.	$ 1,794	$ 11.5	0.6%	Canada, Mexico, United Kingdom
Wood skids and pallets	$ 1,634	$ 134	8.2%	Canada, Mexico, Costa Rica
Synthetic rubber	$ 3,390	$ 899	26.3%	Canada, Brazil, Belgium/Luxembourg, Germany
Tires and inner tubes	$10,953	$ 899	8.2%	Canada, Japan, South Korea
Power-driven hand tools	$ 8,125	$ 449	5.5%	Canada, Italy, Mexico, Japan, Germany
Pulp mills	$ 6,132	$3,645	59.4%	Japan, Germany, Mexico, Italy

Source: Adapted from U.S. Department of Commerce, *U.S. Industrial Outlook 1990* (Washington, DC: U.S. Government Printing Office, January 1990).

EXHIBIT 3.1   U.S. Business Marketers Are Regaining Lost Global Market Shares

Although U.S. business marketing firms as a whole have a long way to go to recoup market share lost to more aggressive Japanese and German competitors, there are some industries that appear to be coming back. Some of the most successful U.S. companies in global markets are manufacturers of such products as heavy construction equipment, diesel engines, computer software, high-speed computers, chemicals, and pharmaceuticals.

One example of such a success story is Xerox Corporation, which had been hurt by low-cost, high-quality Japanese products that had cut into Xerox's domestic sales. Xerox's response was to become more productive. The company streamlined its copier's design and eliminated production-line defects. The result was a reasonably priced copier that regained domestic market share and also penetrated new global markets.

Another example may be found in the American semiconductor industry. In 1990, U.S. producers of semiconductors gained market share at the expense of Japanese competitors for the first time in over ten years. Between 1989 and 1990, the U.S. market share increased from 34.9 percent to 36.5 percent, while the Japanese share decreased from 52.1 percent to 49.5 percent. While these changes are not large, this was the first decrease in Japanese market share since 1982. One of the reasons given for the U.S. gain was that American semiconductor producers were able to sell more microchips in Japan.

The U.S. share of the global microchip market has been eroding for years and thus the 1990 increase was seen as very positive by the industry. In 1979, U.S. microchip manufacturers held 57.9 percent of the world market and the Japanese but 25.8 percent. The 1990 figures, while encouraging, show that U.S. manufacturers still have a way to go to recoup their once large 1979 market share.

These two examples show that U.S. business marketing firms can certainly compete in global markets if they are willing to rethink traditional strategies and develop global perspectives.

Source: Adapted from "U.S. Computer Chip Firms Gain in Market Share," *San Diego Union* (January 3, 1991), E1; and "Competitive Comeback," *San Diego Union* (June 11, 1991), B8.

Why Enter Global Markets?

There are some compelling reasons for American business marketing firms to enter global markets with their goods and services. The basic rationale is simply that private companies, institutions, and government agencies in other countries are often large purchasers of business goods and services. In buying these goods and services, they may well consider U.S. manufacturers just as they do competing manufacturers in other countries. Thus, ignoring global markets may be very shortsighted. More specifically, there are several reasons why U.S. business marketers enter global markets. The following are some of the most frequently cited reasons.

Domestic Market Saturation For some business marketers, traditional U.S. markets have become saturated. There is little untapped potential left, and thus focusing on global markets opens up new opportunities for existing goods and services.

Market and Sales Potential For many business marketers, there is great potential in overseas markets, regardless of the domestic marketing situation. Developing countries have great needs for business goods and services that are required to produce the consumer goods and services desired by their populations. New markets may be emerging overseas at a faster rate than ever before. A good example of this can be seen in the case of Boeing, which is finding that the demand for commercial airliners in Asia is growing at a much faster rate than domestic demand.[9]

Drying Up of Domestic Markets Another reason for exploring global markets is that some U.S. business marketers are no longer competitive domestically and are losing their market shares to overseas competitors. A good example is U.S. purchases of Japanese machine tools, instead of tools made by domestic manufacturers. In 1986, for example, foreign manufacturers made 30 percent of all the machine tools purchased by U.S. firms. They also made 40 percent of all electronics purchased and 50 percent of all the microchips bought by U.S. organizational customers.[10] In some cases, domestic markets have declined for U.S. manufacturers because buyers perceive foreign-made goods as better. To quote the president of a Connecticut industrial distributor, "I have had people tell me that they didn't want to buy American goods because foreign products were less expensive and better in quality."[11] When such a situation arises, seeking global markets to replace lost domestic markets may have benefits.

Quality Image of U.S. Products The products of some U.S. manufacturers have good images overseas, and marketing them globally as well as domestically is quite logical. In Japan, for example, some U.S. industrial products enjoy good reputations for technology and product quality.[12]

Protecting Existing Market Shares Protecting existing domestic market shares from global competitors is a major problem, as noted previously. To protect themselves, some U.S. business marketers move into the countries of origin of these competitors to draw attention away from the U.S. market. More marketing effort in those countries often forces the overseas competitors to increase their marketing efforts to offset their new U.S. competitors.

Life Cycle Stages It is sometimes possible for U.S. business marketers to take products in the later stages of the life cycle in American markets and find earlier life cycle stages in other countries. An example may be seen in reciprocating aircraft engines for such planes as the C-47 transport. There is no OEM market for such products in the United States. Neither is there much of a replacement market, as only a limited number of C-47s still operate in the United States. But in some emerging countries, these planes are still used in great numbers, and the replacement market is considerable.

Other reasons include U.S. government incentives to stimulate exports and favorably affect the U.S. balance of payments. In addition, exchange rates sometimes make U.S. products quite popular with some foreign customers. In total, the preceding reasons provide incentive for American business marketers to consider movements into global markets.

Why Do Business Marketers Not Move into Global Markets?

Looking at the present status of U.S. business marketing firms in global marketing, it is obvious that not many are involved in overseas markets despite all the possible advantages. Some of the major reasons for this lack of involvement are as follows. Many domestic marketing managers believe that the United States is still the single largest market in the world and that concentrating on it is the best way to realize the firm's full potential in that market. Others do not yet seem to realize what global markets have to offer—they do not look past domestic markets. Another important reason is the lack of sound marketing information regarding many global markets. The amount of international information available is limited, when compared to domestic sources. Without adequate information, many marketers are hesitant to move into new markets they do not feel they adequately understand. Still another reason is that cultural differences are seen by some marketers as too formidable—they may not feel they can effectively compete in different cultural settings. Higher costs are also cited by some business marketers as a reason. Overseas competition is difficult when U.S. labor costs are higher and significant distribution costs are encountered. Many business marketing managers may believe they simply cannot be competitive in global markets.

These reasons are all valid, although the trend is toward more, not less, global marketing. Thus, many business marketing managers are coming to view global markets as opportunities rather than threats.

MARKETING INFORMATION ON GLOBAL MARKETS

One of the reasons given by some U.S. business marketers for not entering global markets is that the amount of information available regarding global markets is not as good as that available for domestic markets. While this is true, information on global markets is available if one knows where to find it. Table 3.5 illustrates some of the major sources that may be used by the business marketing manager.

Sources of such information vary considerably. Some of the sources in Table 3.5 are provided by private U.S. organizations such as Dun & Bradstreet, which

TABLE 3.5	Sources of Information on Global Business Markets	
Source	Regions/Areas Covered	Type of Information Provided
Business International	Eastern and Western Europe, Middle East, Latin America, Asia, Africa, Australia	Indicators of percent of growth over past 5 years, degree of concentrated purchasing power, measures of relative size of each national market as a percentage for its region
World of Information	Middle East, Africa, Asia, the Pacific, Latin America, the Caribbean	Annual surveys of general business environment in regions covered
Worldcasts	World, regions of the world, individual countries	Forecasts for 1-, 6-, 10-, and 15-year periods on commodities and industrial products
Global Market Surveys	Limited to top 20–30 best foreign markets	Detailed surveys for given industries such as graphics, computers, medical equipment, industrial equipment
Dun & Bradstreet's *Principal International Businesses*	135 countries of the world	Names, addresses, number of employees, products produced, chief executive officer, up to 6 SIC classifications (4-digit) for each organization; over 144,000 business units classified by 4-digit SIC and alphabetical order
Dun & Bradstreet's International Marketing Services	133 countries of the world	Information similar to *Principal International Businesses* on over 500,000 businesses and subsidiaries
Moody's *International Manual*	5,000 major corporations in 100 countries	Company histories, descriptions of business, financial statistics, management personnel
Europe's 1500 Largest Companies	Europe	Companies by sales, profit, number of employees, country; classified by U.N. International ISIC activity codes
Major Companies of Europe	Europe	Company names, addresses, telephone numbers, executives, principal products/activities, number of employees, sales size; classified by business activity codes 1 to 131
Predicasts's *F & S Index*	Worldwide	Company, product, and industry information from 750 publications; up to 7-digit SIC codes
Survey of Industrials	Canada	Company names, addresses, telephone numbers, product types, key personnel, sales size, and financial statistics
Overseas Business Reports	Worldwide	Monthly reports provide information for marketing to specific countries (e.g., "Marketing in Pakistan," "Marketing in Nigeria")
Foreign Economic Trends	Worldwide	Annual analyses of economic trends in specific countries, implications for U.S. companies
Business America	Worldwide	Published biweekly, provides statistics, success stories by U.S. firms, features on particular markets, trade show announcements

publishes a directory titled *Principal International Businesses* that provides information on possible target market organizations worldwide. Dun & Bradstreet's Marketing Services division also provides information of global nature. Figure 3.5 shows information available regarding a German manufacturer of motor vehicle bodies and exemplifies what is available from this source. Another example is Predicasts's *F & S Index*, which provides information on new products, markets, end users of new products, and so forth on a worldwide basis.

There are also U.S. government sources that provide global information of value to the business marketer. Several U.S. Department of Commerce sources are often useful: *Business America, Overseas Business Reports,* and *Foreign Economic Trends. Overseas Business Reports* can be quite useful once the marketing manager has determined which countries contain target market prospects. These reports contain information pertinent to marketing in those countries, and they refer to channels to be considered, cultural differences, buying

FIGURE 3.5   **Example of Global Information Available from Private Sources in Business Marketing**

This is *International Dun's Market Identifiers*®...Online!

1 Company Name	1 KAHOFER MOTOR GMBH
2 Street Address	2 BAHNHOFPLATZ 150
3 Mailing Address	3 POSTFACH 426
4 City	4 HAMBERG, 5 GERMANY 2000
5 Country	6 (47) (621) 615105
6 Telephone	7 30786
7 Postal Code	8 HAMBERG
8 State/Province	9 CHIEF EXECUTIVE HEINRICH MULLER, GESCHAFTSFUHRER
9 Chief Executive Officer	10 DUNS NUMBER 31-500-0787

11 Standard Industrial Classification (SIC) Codes—primary and up to 5 secondary codes

11 PRIMARY SIC:	3711	12 MOTOR VEHICLE BODIES
SECONDARY SIC:	3714	MOTOR VEHICLE PARTS & ACCESSORIES
SECONDARY SIC:	3519	INTERNAL COMBUSTION ENGINES, NEC
SECONDARY SIC:	5012	WHOLESALE MOTOR VEHICLES
SECONDARY SIC:	5013	WHOLESALE AUTO EQUIPMENT

12 SIC Descriptions

13 Year Business Was Started	13 YEAR STARTED: 1922
14 Number of Employees	14 EMPLOYEES TOTAL: 4,600

15 Gross Annual Sales in local currency & U.S. Dollars	15 SALES (LOCAL CURRENCY): 40,850,300
	SALES (U.S. CURRENCY): 20,020,958

THIS IS:

16 Denotes a Subsidiary of another company	16 A SUBSIDIARY
17 International Trade Indicator	17 AN IMPORTER AND EXPORTER AND AGENT
18 Control (private ownership, public, or government controlled)	18 A GOVERNMENT CONTROLLED COMPANY

19 Parent Company Information (when applicable)	19 PARENT NAME:	GLOBAL MOTORS CORP.
	PARENT DUNS NUMBER:	00-585-6618
	PARENT COUNTRY:	UNITED STATES

Source: Reprinted by permission of Dun's Marketing Services.

practices, and so on. In addition, *Business America* provides articles that feature success stories of U.S. companies in particular overseas markets, announcements of future overseas trade shows, descriptions of individual markets, and similar information.

There are also sources of information available from global sources outside the United States. Two examples in Table 3.5 are *Major Companies of Europe* and *Europe's 1500 Largest Companies*. These sources are published in Europe and contain information specifically on European business markets but they are similar to other sources available in other parts of the world.

Although information is not as readily available on global markets as it is on domestic markets, sources of considerable value exist. Retrieving this information, however, requires that the marketing manager understand what sources are available and then search out these sources. Since the information is provided by so many different sources, integrating it all may be an arduous task. If it is done properly, however, the marketing manager can gain valuable information that will be useful in formulating effective marketing strategies and tactical programs.

MARKETING STRATEGY IN GLOBAL BUSINESS MARKETS

The principles of marketing strategy are the same whether they are applied to consumer or business markets. Similarly, these principles apply whether a business marketing firm is selling to private organizational customers, institutions, or governmental agencies. Mix elements may change in each of these markets, and these are illustrated in the sections that follow.

There are some overall strategy differences, however, when a business marketing company wishes to market its goods and services on an international basis. These differences apply not to specific products or services, channels, promotional efforts, or prices but to the general approach that is taken to address customers in different countries or regions of the world. Several options are available in developing **global marketing strategy,** and these directly affect marketing activities and programs.[13]

Perhaps the simplest strategy approach is exporting, or selling what the company produces into overseas markets. The strategy is based on simply expanding sales into new, global markets. Different channels, promotion, and pricing may be involved, and products may or may not have to be changed. Another strategy option is licensing, which involves selling the right to use some process, trademark, or patent for a fee or royalty to a producer in another country. This strategy is, of course, different, and it involves additional decisions regarding choice of licensee and contract arrangements. Contract manufacturing is another option. Here, the company turns over production to a producer in another country but retains the marketing responsibilities. From a marketing perspective, this method may be similar to exporting, but it involves another company and thus may be more complex. Still another option is management contracting. Applied to marketing, it means that the overseas production facilities are owned and operated by foreign nationals and that the American company provides management skills in the marketing area. Forming strategic alliances is another strategy approach that is sometimes used. As previously described, the marketing company enters into a partnership with an overseas firm. Finally, the marketing company can create a wholly owned subsidiary to operate in a particular country. These six possibilities affect the strategy that may be employed by the company selling business goods and services to global customers.

All of these methods are used to some degree by U.S. business marketing firms, but there are changing patterns. Prior to 1980, the most widely used method was exporting from U.S. plants, followed by joint ventures, overseas production, and licensing. More recently, the trend has been less toward exporting from domestic manufacturing facilities and more toward such strategies as licensing, strategic alliances, overseas production, and third-country exporting.[14] Third-country exporting means that the U.S. business marketer produces goods in a third country such as Mexico for shipment to customers outside the United States.

An individual business marketing manager seldom decides which option or combination of options should be used. Sometimes, particular countries dictate which is acceptable and under what terms. At other times, such decisions are made at the strategic market planning level, and the marketing manager develops a strategy consistent with directions from higher levels of management. Even considering these options, the basic strategy principles apply to the global marketing of business goods and services.

Marketing Strategies Used in Global Marketing

U.S. and foreign companies that are heavily involved in global markets often use differing marketing strategies. Japanese business marketers are among the toughest faced by U.S. firms, and it is interesting to note how marketing strategies differ among Japanese and American firms. A study by the Japan Management Association found that the most important elements in Japanese global marketing strategies were innovative sales channels, systemization of marketing information, and training and development of marketing planners. In the same study, American marketers felt the most important elements were training of first-line salespeople, systemization of marketing information, and development of measurements for advertising and sales promotion. Another interesting comparison in this study was that American marketers were quite concerned about global competitors selling in U.S. domestic markets, but the Japanese respondents did not feel threatened about U.S. competitors in Japanese markets.[15] This study may be important in that Japanese manufacturers are seen as some of the most formidable competitors faced by U.S. business marketers, and overall, the Japanese have been more successful than their American counterparts. Some would argue that U.S. global marketing strategies are not focusing on the proper mix elements, which is related to their lack of success in many overseas markets.

A similar conclusion was drawn by the American Business Conference, an association of 100 high-growth, mid-size U.S. firms that have been successful in their global marketing endeavors. Analyzing the success of its members, ABC found five marketing strategy factors that explain why these companies have been successful. These factors are: (1) they have segmented tighter and found niches in the global markets; (2) they emphasize global marketing as an integral part of their business planning and do not treat it as an afterthought; (3) they do not try to avoid their toughest competitors; (4) they stress product quality, service, and innovation rather than low-cost production; and (5) when production facilities have been moved from the United States, the reason was to be closer to their customers and not due to cost.[16]

These are interesting and meaningful points if a business marketing manager wishes to be successful in global markets. In the current scheme of things, Germany is the world's number one exporter, followed by the United States and Japan. German and Japanese business marketers are big advocates of tighter segmentation. For example, the basic German marketing strategy is to stress product quality and find niches.[17] The Japanese employ a similar strategy. Japanese machine tool producers have designed high-quality small and mid-size machines, and they have directed their marketing toward small and medium-size markets in the United States. Eighty percent of Japan's exported machine tools go to small and mid-size plants in the United States.[18] The typical U.S. marketer is likely to focus on larger customers first, which is a much more difficult way to make inroads in global markets. Thus, marketing strategy has much to do with success or failure in global business markets and marketing mixes in those markets cannot simply be copied from what has worked in domestic markets. A look at how marketing mix elements may change when working in global markets is in order.

GLOBAL CONSIDERATIONS IN PRODUCT STRATEGY

Involvement in global markets has had profound implications on business marketers' product and service strategies. Product policies and procedures for many business marketers have changed considerably because of their moves away from domestic markets to diverse global markets. Interestingly, this was not always true. Some of the first products to be sold into global markets were business products designed for U.S. customers that could also be marketed overseas. Typical of these were agricultural machinery and mining equipment. These types of products were relatively insensitive to cultural and environmental differences and could easily be sold with little change in specifications.[19] Today, global sales are not quite so simple, and it is worthwhile to look at some of those factors that should be considered in the product strategy area.

Specifications

One of the most easily understood factors in product strategy for global markets is that product and/or service specifications often must change from country to country. Many U.S. business marketers find that they simply cannot take products designed to meet domestic specifications and export these to foreign customers. In fact, a major complaint by Japanese buyers is that American companies are reluctant to customize their products for the Japanese market.[20] Specifications often must be altered to fit special needs and requirements based on national considerations.

A few examples may help. A manufacturer of industrial waste disposers was forced to change the electrical specifications on its basic models to accommodate differences in electrical power available in different countries. Although its machines using 115 volt, 60 cycle, 1 phase electricity could be sold anywhere in the United States, they had to be installed with different, often specially wound, motors and switches to be sold in many European and Asian countries.

Solar Turbines produces a gas turbine-driven compressor set configured for use in the United States that compresses gas and sends it down a pipeline, which then distributes the gas to homes, industries, and other users. The product could not be marketed overseas in Germany and other Western European countries under its domestic specifications because legal codes differ in Europe and the United States. The U.S. code permits explosion-proof boxes, so that if an explosion is to occur, it will be contained in the box and will not spread to the rest of the plant. European codes do not relate to explosion-proof boxing but follow a system called Eurocable, which is designed to prevent any explosion in the first place. Therefore, product specifications had to be changed according to law and were not subject to negotiation. Solar had two options: (1) ship relatively stripped models overseas and purchase and install necessary controls locally or (2) hire the expertise to complete the job to Eurocable specifications in the United States before shipping overseas. Both options were used, because some countries required local content in what is purchased (that is, option 1), and other countries permitted the second option.[21] Specifications changes such as these are commonplace in global markets with all types of organizational customers.

Research and Development

As business marketing becomes more global, R & D is becoming a global process for more and more American companies, as well as for Japanese and European producers. Companies establish research centers in other countries to keep abreast of worldwide technological changes. This change is then adapted for use by the manufacturer. A good example is Data General Corporation's Japanese research center. Originally, it existed to adapt the company's computers for use by Japanese customers. It now has expanded into an operation to provide assistance to the company in worldwide product development. From this research center's input, the company was able to transfer Japanese technology in its digital watch industry to Data General's portable computers.[22] As markets become more global and differences between national markets begin to break down, more companies are looking at international R&D as a necessary element in their product strategies.

Product Support Activities

Global markets sometimes require different product support activities than those found in domestic markets. For example, warranties sometimes must differ when customers are in distant countries. It is more difficult for some companies to send service representatives to a customer in Ankara, Turkey, than to Roanoke, Virginia. Thus, some changes may have to be made in warranty coverages to accommodate customers in both locations. Similarly, stocking of replacement parts, service centers, technical assistance, and emergency service often cause major changes when applied to global markets.

New Competitors

As American marketers expand into global markets, they encounter new competitors, and as business marketing becomes more global, they face new competitors even in their domestic markets. This influx of competitors creates numerous new considerations for the marketing manager. First, it requires more analysis in terms of competing products and services. Second, these new competitors may employ new and different tactics that may be hard to counter. A good example exists in the case of the Japanese and German power tool producers who completed warranty and routine repairs within 72 hours, whereas many U.S. manufacturers required two to four weeks.[23] Third, many global competitors operate with much lower cost structures, which makes it hard for the U.S. producer to compete effectively. Finally, the American marketing manager may find it impossible to compete in some global markets without changing to accommodate required national content in products or services themselves or their support activities. Whatever the circumstances, these new competitors affect product strategy in many ways neither previously considered nor encountered.

Licensing

A new process is involved for those U.S. business marketing companies electing to enter international markets via the licensing option. The marketing manager has to be especially careful in selecting national companies that will have the right to produce the company's products. In some ways, the problem is similar to that of selecting distributors in the domestic market. If the licensed company does not operate in a manner compatible with the U.S. company's desires, a particular country's market can be lost to competitors. This case is also somewhat true of companies electing to enter global markets through contract manufacturing, management contracting, joint venturing, or other forms of partnering. Product strategy decisions are involved that perhaps were never considered previously.

GLOBAL CONSIDERATIONS IN CHANNEL STRATEGY

Business marketing companies involved in global markets have had to develop channels of distribution to accommodate those markets. Channel strategy in global markets is dependent on the approach used by the company to enter such markets. For example, the channel arrangements of a company choosing merely to export its products to customers in another country may differ from one choosing to set up a wholly owned subsidiary. Similarly, channels may differ between setting up such a subsidiary and partnering with a company in that country. Still, the basic elements in channel strategy for global markets are the same as they are for the domestic market, although they may have to be adapted to global constraints.

Figure 3.6 illustrates channels of distribution commonly found in global business marketing. Ignoring again the direct channel implications because they are addressed in the following section, attention here focuses on forms of indirect channels. Intermediaries in channels in global business marketing are quite similar to those found in domestic markets, but there are some interesting variations. Typical channel components in global channels include resident buyers in the United States, manufacturers' representatives, industrial distributors, and international trading companies.

Resident Buyers in the United States

Many global organizational customers, channel intermediaries, and governmental customers establish resident buying offices in the United States for the express purpose of buying American goods and services. In this channel, the transaction is made in the United States to an intermediary for shipment to global customers.

Manufacturers' Representatives

Many manufacturers' representatives operate in global business markets and buy at the request of overseas customers. These MRs are similar to those described in Chapter 1. They may be American businesses that have contacts in other countries and are used to reach global customers because of these contacts, or they may be foreign MRs that have contacts in global markets. Some domestic MR firms, sometimes referred to as manufacturers' export agents, con-

FIGURE 3.6   Structure of Channels in Global Business Markets

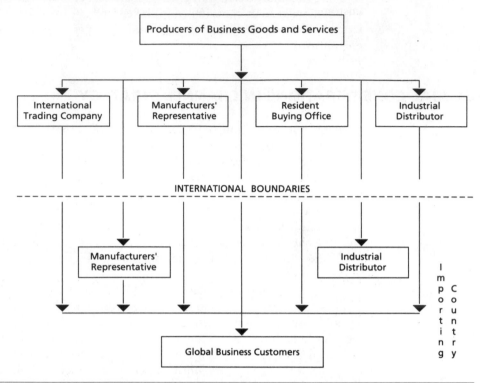

centrate on customers in just a few countries and become specialized in market coverage in that way. These global reps play basically the same roles as MRs do in domestic marketing.

Industrial Distributors

Many industrial distributors are also involved in business marketing at the global level. Some U.S. distributors, called export merchants, buy U.S. goods and either ship them overseas to customers or assume the marketing functions for manufacturers through their own sales forces or intermediary contacts. In addition, many U.S. business marketing firms sell goods to foreign distributors, who then resell to organizational customers in those countries in which they operate. Again, these distributors are similar to those described in Chapter 1.

International Trading Companies

Some U.S. business marketers reach global markets through importing and exporting firms that often have worldwide buying and selling operations. These firms, known as **international trading companies,** buy from many manufacturers, consolidate the products, and distribute them on a global basis. Since they have many international contacts, their use offers access to organizational customers that may be unknown or inaccessible to the marketing company.

Developing channel strategy for global markets often requires knowledge and use of intermediaries who specialize in some manner in that area. But the process of establishing channel objectives, assessing alternatives, setting up arrangements with channel components, and controlling and evaluating remains basically the same as it is in domestic marketing.

GLOBAL SALES CONSIDERATIONS IN PROMOTIONAL STRATEGY

Probably no element in the business marketing mix is affected by global considerations more than personal selling. This area is an especially difficult one for the business marketing company selling in global markets. The problem is caused by the fact that the salesperson personally is involved in environments often quite different from those encountered in the United States. In making sales presentations to buyers and buying influences in other countries, the field sales representative must consider differences in languages, cultural values, social customs and taboos, religion, and even aesthetic factors such as color, brand name, trademark, and configuration of the product itself. If these factors are not understood or are somehow misinterpreted, a complete breakdown in communication can occur.

Personal selling is a culture-bound activity because of the face-to-face contact between salesperson and buyer. Some examples are useful in illustrating the potential problems.[24] In the Middle East and Latin America, when people talk, they stand much closer together than they do in the United States, and the salesperson should refrain from a natural reaction to back off. French buyers consider the use of first names in sales presentations offensive and do not say "thanks" in response to praise. A salesperson who speaks too loudly may be perceived as angry by Chinese buyers. In some German-speaking countries, a salesperson who smiles while shaking hands with prospects may be considered too affectionate. In Germany, it is also a mistake for a salesperson to reach across a customer's desk to shake his or her hand—proper etiquette calls for the customer to walk around the desk and greet a visitor. In Japan, buyers insist on long, drawn-out sales cycles that involve many layers of management and prolonged negotiation. A salesperson attempting to make a quick sale with an aggressive approach is usually not successful.[25]

Another factor to consider in global sales is the high cost of such selling. McGraw-Hill Research Department determined the cost of a European sales call to be significantly higher than the cost of a domestic sales call. In addition, this same research found it takes an average of six calls to close a sale in Western Europe, compared to about four in the United States.[26]

Because of the costs and cultural differences, many U.S. manufacturers use manufacturers' representatives, distributors, and international trading companies, as was discussed previously. By turning to these sales intermediaries, the cost and cultural difficulties may be reduced. When these intermediaries cannot be used and personal selling is required, the marketing manager often is forced to choose between assigning American salespeople and teaching them the cultural differences or hiring salespeople of the nationality of the country involved. For many business marketing companies, the latter approach has been successful. Overall, sales management for direct selling involves the same principles in both domestic and global markets. The difference lies in multinational constraints that must be integrated into those principles.

GLOBAL ADVERTISING AND SALES PROMOTION CONSIDERATIONS IN PROMOTIONAL STRATEGY

The same basic advertising and sales promotion concepts apply for those firms involved in global markets as for those involved in domestic markets. Nevertheless, some important constraints and differences must be taken into consideration.

In the area of advertising media, there is a wealth of data to aid the business marketing manager in the United States. The same amount of information is simply not available in many international markets, which makes media decisions more difficult. Some countries have trade journals, but circulation figures are often quite suspect and available information is just not as definitive as it is in the United States. In some of the less-developed countries, advertising media are highly limited. To bypass these types of problems, some U.S. business marketing companies select advertising agencies that operate branches in countries targeted for marketing efforts. These agencies often have the best information possible on media in particular countries, and they can be of great help in putting together business advertising campaigns.

Direct mail is as applicable a medium in global business marketing as it is in domestic marketing. Referring to Table 3.5, it can be seen that organizations such as Dun & Bradstreet can provide data cards and mailing lists for potential customers in other countries. Such data permit the use of the direct-mail medium in global markets.

Advertising themes or appeals can also be a problem. The natural tendency for many U.S. business marketing managers is to translate domestic advertisements directly into other languages for use in other countries. This practice can be quite dangerous if the translator is not well aware of the idioms and dialects that may be involved. When these are ignored, what appear to be straightforward translations often convey a totally different message to global buyers and buying influences.

Other factors are also involved. For example, the use of comparative advertisements is frowned on in many countries. Similarly, many countries, especially in Western Europe, emphasize their national identities. Advertisements by U.S. marketers should reflect such interests. Advertising copy should also reflect cultural differences among countries. For example, the meaning of colors can change from country to country as can that of numbers, shapes, and symbols. These cultural differences often make it impossible simply to translate U.S. advertisements into Japanese, French, or German. Because of these difficulties, many U.S. business marketing companies use advertising agencies already familiar with important cultural characteristics in target market countries.

Catalogs are still a plausible medium in the area of sales promotion, but they sometimes require considerable thought in translation, especially when different codes, electrical specifications, and other such factors are involved. At other times, standard U.S. versions can be used without any repercussions, since English is close to a universally accepted language and product use is fairly standardized. Trade shows are big promotional media in many regions of the world. They often afford the U.S. business marketing manager excellent representation in other countries, particularly in parts of Asia and Europe.

In summary, while global marketing does not require a different basic approach to promotional strategy, it does require some adaptation to the principles that apply to domestic advertising and sales promotion.

GLOBAL CONSIDERATIONS IN PRICING STRATEGY

For the business marketing manager whose firm is actively involved in global markets, pricing offers some special challenges. The same concepts apply to international as well as domestic markets, but modifications often must be made. There are some rather obvious factors to consider, such as currency differences, tariffs, export credit terms, special taxes that exist in some countries, and international shipping costs. These factors complicate the pricing area, but they do not change the basic approach to pricing of business goods and services.

One factor that often affects pricing in global markets is exchange rate fluctuations, which do not occur in domestic marketing. For example, when the British pound sterling increases in value relative to the U.S. dollar, American goods become cheaper in the United Kingdom. Exchange rate fluctuations are especially bothersome to business marketing managers who attempt to negotiate long-term contracts with global customers. In determining prices appropriate for customers in different countries, the marketing manager should be well aware of possible exchange rate fluctuations in every country involved.

Another consideration in pricing in global markets concerns situations in which foreign distributors are used. Typically, it is difficult for U.S. manufacturers to exert control over their distributors in other countries in terms of final prices to organizational customers. Thus, prices sometimes vary considerably for the same product in the same country when multiple intermediaries are used.

U.S. business marketing firms frequently price the same products differently for global customers than they do for domestic customers. The FOB factory prices are often lower on products to be exported than on products for U.S. customers for several reasons. First, there is often lower buying power in some foreign markets, which in turn requires lower prices to compete. Second, in many overseas markets, U.S. business marketing firms face strong competition and are forced to lower prices to compete effectively. Third, since additional factors such as tariffs and international shipping costs must be added to the FOB price, many marketers lower the latter price to keep competitive.[27] These points exemplify the types of considerations that need to be integrated into the pricing strategy by marketing managers whose firms are involved with global customers.

THE CHANGING GLOBAL ENVIRONMENT

The 1990s promise to be a period in which major changes in global business marketing will take place. Some of these changes started in the 1980s and are continuing, while others are in the process of development and still others are in the inception stage. Since these changes will profoundly affect U.S. business marketing firms, they need to be addressed. While it is not within the scope of this text to examine all possible changes, three appear to have the most impact and will be discussed here. These are the changes taking place in Eastern Europe, the continuing development of the European Economic Community (EEC) in Western Europe, and the negotiations beginning on the North America Free Trade Pact between the United States, Canada, and Mexico. Since these three phenomena will contribute heavily toward changes in global business marketing, they are singled out for discussion.

The Economic Decentralization of Eastern Europe

When the Berlin Wall came down in late 1989, it signalled the beginning of what is now referred to as the economic decentralization of the countries of Eastern Europe. This decentralization opened up countries such as Poland, Hungary, Romania, Bulgaria, Czechoslovakia, and the U.S.S.R. to producers of business goods and services.

According to the U.S. Department of Commerce, these countries have particular needs for many business products and/or services. These include earth-moving equipment, telecommunications equipment, pollution-control equipment, aircraft and aircraft parts, nuclear safety products, energy savings equipment, and medical equipment and technology. With economic revitalization a major thrust in these countries, demand for all types of capital goods will be high, which some believe points toward Eastern Europe as a major business market in the coming years.

At present, however, there are some problems for U.S. business marketing firms that want to penetrate Eastern European markets. These problems mean risk and some U.S. business marketers are skeptical despite the longer-term potential. Some of the major problems are as follows. First, although these countries need business goods and services, many of them lack the financial ability to buy them. In addition, they have little foreign exchange and many of their currencies (the ruble, for example) are not convertible to world money markets. Second, there is much political and economic uncertainty in the area and many countries are seriously disorganized. Also, there is no assurance that further uncertainties will not arise in the future. Some political scientists believe that civil wars are not an impossibility because of all the area's problems. Third, before decentralization, buyers in these countries purchased through **Foreign Trade Organizations (FTOs)**. Now, buyers are free to make purchases on their own but their levels of knowledge and sophistication are understandably lower than those of their counterparts in Western Europe, Asia, or North America. Fourth, some of the Eastern European countries fear that trading with other countries for goods will inhibit the restructuring of their own industries and thus it is difficult for U.S. firms to penetrate these markets. Finally, the existing logistical, communication, and transportation systems in Eastern Europe are archaic by western standards. There is little availability of such basics as telephones, fax machines, copy machines, highways, etc., to facilitate marketing as it is practiced elsewhere in the world. For these reasons, business marketing in the area is risky, difficult, and somewhat dangerous. The feeling of many business marketers, however, is that these are short-term problems and the longer-term potential makes the area a very viable business market for many firms.[28]

A good example of this can be seen in a quote by the CEO of Compaq Computer Corporation of Houston, Texas, who stated, "Eastern Europe and the Soviet Union together represent an even bigger opportunity than Western Europe for microcomputer marketers. . . . Widespread application of computer technology is essential to carry out the management and manufacturing reforms that are at the heart of peristroika."[29] Similarly, marketers of telecommunications equipment and services have also been active in the area. Motorola, for example, completed a large contract to supply Hungary with about 5,000 cellular telephones. Commenting on that contract, a spokesperson for the Cellular Telecommunications Industry Association stated, "It's clear to us that the first big step they need to take is modern communication with an eye toward the business world."[30] Evidently, a number of global business marketing firms feel similarly because a large number of joint ventures have already taken place between Eastern European companies and firms around the world. Table 3.6 shows the number of alliances just between Eastern European companies and western partners—it does not include those with other than western firms. The table provides interesting insight. For one thing, most of the ventures involve business marketing goods and services and thus the area does appear to constitute a major geographic business market. But the participation of U.S. business marketing companies is low compared to that of Western European firms. The major reason given for this relatively low participation rate is that the Eastern European partners cannot exchange their shares of venture profits for U.S. dollars or other hard currency.[31] Whatever the reason, U.S. business marketers, while recognizing the long-term potential, have not been as aggressive as their global competitors in moving into this market.

TABLE 3.6   **Strategic Alliances with Eastern European Companies**

Country	Number of Alliances with Western Partners	Number of Alliances with U.S. Partners	Percent of Western Alliances with U.S. Partners	Major Industries Involved
Bulgaria	60+	10	16.7%	Food processing, chemicals, electronics
Czechoslovakia	32	1	3.1%	Manufacturing
Hungary	600–700	140	20.0+%	Services, light manufacturing
Poland	866	60	6.9%	Food processing, construction
Romania	5	1	20.0%	Data processing, chemicals

Source: Adapted from materials developed by the U.S. Department of Commerce, International Trade Administration, Washington, DC, 1990.

The European Economic Community

Another big change in global business marketing involves the countries of Western Europe. Beginning in the mid-1980s, twelve Western European countries entered into the process of developing a single market in Europe. Termed the **European Economic Community** or **EEC,** it includes Belgium, Denmark, France, Germany, Greece, Ireland, Italy, Luxembourg, the Netherlands, Portugal, Spain, and the United Kingdom. The EEC's basic goals are (1) to improve the productivity and performance of the European community and (2) to provide a strong base for European companies in key industries to compete globally. The EEC will work toward eliminating barriers at national boundaries, harmonizing technical standards, improving European communications, reducing the overhead of doing business within Europe, and ultimately raising the standard of living in the twelve countries.[32] The intended results are that the EEC will permit member countries to compete more aggressively in global markets with U.S. and Japanese competitors. At the same time, the EEC will constitute a single market.

For U.S. business marketing firms, the development of the EEC is extremely important. It has been described as one of the more important forces at work in changing the character of global markets and competition in the decades ahead.[33] This is certainly true for U.S. business marketers who presently export large amounts of goods and services to these twelve countries on an individual basis. Figure 3.7 shows what kinds of goods constitute current sales exceeding $100 billion annually to EEC countries. As can be seen, the majority are business goods and services and thus there are major implications for U.S. business marketers. In more specific terms, U.S.-produced business products in high demand in these countries include aircraft and aircraft parts; aerospace; auto parts; biotechnology; CAD/CAM equipment; computer hardware, software, and peripherals; fiber optics; industrial process controls; laser systems and equipment; health care products; robots and industrial automation systems; telecommunications equipment; and textiles.[34] Stakes are big for U.S. marketers when the single market becomes a reality.

The EEC has also been referred to as EC'92 or simply "1992" because it was originally intended to be operational by 1992. At the time this text was prepared, many doubted that it would be operating by 1992 because of difficulties in resolving differences in a manner that is agreeable to all twelve countries—common standards for laboratories and testing institutes, for example. Indications are that agreement will ultimately be reached among the members and the EEC will become an operational reality, but that may happen well after 1992.

For U.S. business marketing companies, the emergence of the EEC has created uncertainty, even in situations where they have been doing business with individual companies for years. For example, in 1989 the EEC decided that the origin for semiconductors would be determined by the location of the plant where the etching of circuits onto blank silicon wafers takes place. Such a ruling certainly affects U.S. producers of semiconductors if that etching is performed in U.S. plants. Similarly, yet-to-be-determined EEC standards may affect many U.S.-made products. U.S. manufacturers will, of course, have to meet those standards and in some cases will have to submit their products to independent testing and certification by EEC labs and testing institutes.

As in Eastern Europe, the EEC is changing the environment in which U.S. business marketers have been operating. There is such vast potential in the EEC that American firms will compete, and probably compete favorably, once the EEC can agree on standards and other involved factors. In the meantime, U.S.

FIGURE 3.7   **U.S. Sales to European Economic Community (EEC) Countries**

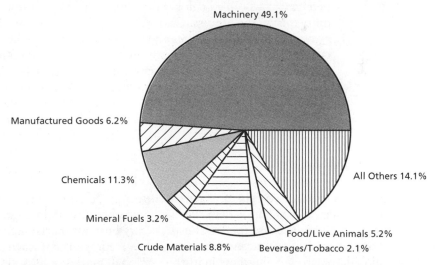

Machinery 49.1%

Manufactured Goods 6.2%

Chemicals 11.3%

Mineral Fuels 3.2%

Crude Materials 8.8%

Beverages/Tobacco 2.1%

Food/Live Animals 5.2%

All Others 14.1%

Total 1990 Sales $100 Billion

Source: Mary Sanders, "EC92: Opportunities and Challenges for U.S. Business," in *U.S. Industrial Outlook 1990* (Washington, DC: U.S. Government Printing Office, January 1990), 31.

firms must continue to market aggressively in the area and not simply wait until the EEC agrees before moving. If they wait, the single market may preclude any penetration whatsoever.

The North America Free Trade Pact

In mid-1991, the United States, Canada, and Mexico embarked on discussions to establish the **North America Free Trade Pact,** which would eliminate barriers to the flow of goods and services among the three countries. For U.S. business marketing firms, such a pact could have profound effects since Canada and Mexico are two of the nation's largest export markets and both are also among the top five suppliers of goods and services to this country. Total population in the three countries is approximately 360 million and their combined annual economic output is about $6 trillion. The purpose of the proposed pact is to enable the three countries to attain the benefits of combined economic strength in dealing with Japan and the European Economic Community in global markets. As stated, the United States has traded extensively with each of the two other countries, and the United States and Canada have had a bilateral trade agreement since 1989. This pact would bring Mexico into the group and encourage trade between Canada and Mexico, which have not historically had strong economic ties with each other. To illustrate, Mexico's trade with the United States approximates $53 billion annually and Canada's trade with the United States is over $160 billion annually, but Canada's trade with Mexico is only about $2 billion.[35]

Because initial talks began as this text was being completed, a detailed discussion of the pact here is not possible and predicting what will happen is difficult. Proponents argue that the pact will help North American countries compete more favorably in global markets with EEC countries and Japan and create more jobs in the process. Critics fear that lower wages in Mexico will draw jobs away from the United States and Canada and work to the detriment of those two countries. The Bush administration has taken a position in favor of the pact, so the prospect of such an agreement cannot be dismissed lightly. If the pact does become a reality, it will certainly affect U.S. business marketers because so many of their sales are to Canadian and Mexican customers. How the pact will change these relationships is yet to be determined.

CHAPTER SUMMARY

This chapter has addressed global factors affecting the business marketing system. Such a discussion is necessary because the U.S. business marketing system is so intertwined with the larger global system. U.S. business marketing firms no longer can focus exclusively on domestic markets, even though these may make up the bulk of their sales. Business marketers are facing different competitors and in different ways because of the global nature of contemporary business marketing. They are encountering new competitors when they move into new global markets, as well as facing new competitors who are entering U.S. markets. In addition, many U.S. business marketing firms are forming strategic alliances or partnerships with global marketing companies. This chapter has attempted to emphasize the need for a more global perspective on the part of U.S. business marketing managers.

Global marketing was defined and its importance to U.S. business marketing companies was examined. Major competitors were analyzed in terms of the U.S. domestic market and in terms of global markets where U.S. firms are most active. The subject of forming strategic alliances with global partners was also examined. The present status of U.S. business marketing companies in global markets was covered and the reluctance of some American marketers to enter global markets was discussed.

The chapter also focused on business marketing information sources available to the marketing manager. Comparisons were made between marketing strategies used by U.S. and global business marketers so that differences and similarities could be seen. Then, the marketing mix areas of product and service, distri-

bution, promotion, and pricing were examined in terms of how they are affected when business marketing companies enter global markets.

The chapter concluded with a discussion of major changes taking place in the global business marketing environment. Particular emphasis was placed on the economic decentralization of Eastern Europe, on the European Economic Community (EEC), and on the North America Free Trade Pact as these may affect business marketing.

This chapter should be considered in the context of the rest of the text. This is not a book on global marketing; rather, it is concerned with business marketing in the United States. The purpose of this chapter is to make the reader aware of the global implications for the business marketing manager as they relate to marketing information gathering, segmentation, planning, strategy development, and tactical program implementation.

KEY TERMS

domestic market
European Economic Community (EEC)
export
foreign trade organization (FTO)
global competition
global market
global marketing
global marketing strategy

global partnership
import
international trading company
joint venture
licensing
North America Free Trade Pact
strategic global alliance

QUESTIONS

1. Some of the first successful U.S. global marketing firms were producers of heavy industrial goods who simply marketed their domestic products in other countries. Today, most U.S. firms that are successful do not use this same approach. How do you explain this change?
2. If a business marketing company moves into new global markets and transfers its best do-

mestic salespeople into those markets, what problems can you see arising?
3. Both German and Japanese marketers have been successful in global markets through the use of what they call "niche" marketing. Explain what this means and then relate why niche marketing is often successful in entering new global markets.

4. When the Berlin Wall came down and opened up Eastern European countries to business marketing firms worldwide, U.S. business marketers were reluctant to jump into this new market. Explain the reasons for this reluctance on the part of American business marketers.

5. Some authorities believe that one of the main reasons that U.S. business marketing firms have not been as successful as they might be in global markets is that they seem to concentrate initially only on large and dominant prospects. How can this contribute to lack of success in global market penetration?

6. As in domestic business markets, manufacturers' representatives and industrial distributors are often used in global markets. Why do you believe these two types of channel intermediaries are so popular in global marketing? If these are not used, what other options are open to the U.S. business marketing manager?

7. One manner of understanding global business marketing is by analyzing the practices of U.S. firms compared to those of firms outside the country. How do Japanese marketing strategies differ from those of their American competitors? Why do you believe Japanese business marketers have been more successful in penetrating American markets than U.S. firms have been in entering Japanese markets?

8. If the North America Free Trade Pact becomes an operational reality, how do you believe U.S. business marketing firms will be affected? What changes in marketing can you see?

9. When the European Economic Community (EEC) becomes an operational reality, many believe it will have profound effects on the marketing practices of U.S. business marketing firms. What changes do you see for companies that currently have customers in the twelve EEC countries? What changes do you see for U.S. firms not currently serving the Western European market?

10. Explain how a business marketing company could have two separate marketing strategies when serving both domestic and global markets. How might these strategies be similar and how might they be different?

NOTES

1. Vern Terpstra, *International Marketing* (Chicago: The Dryden Press, 1978), 5.
2. John Jelacic, "The U.S. Trade Outlook in 1991," *Business America* 112 (April 22, 1991): 7.
3. *U.S. Industrial Outlook 1990* (Washington, DC: U.S. Government Printing Office, January 1990), 14.
4. Martin Kenney and Richard Florida, "Rust Belt Rescuers Are, Yes, Japanese," *San Diego Union* (April 7, 1991), C7.
5. Jelacic, op. cit.
6. *U.S. Industrial Outlook 1990,* op. cit.
7. Matt Miller, "Boeing Sees Its Long-Term Fortunes in Satisfying Pacific Rim Market Needs," *San Diego Union* (June 9, 1991), I1.
8. Joachim Schafer, "Exhibiting at a German Trade Show," *Agency Sales Magazine* 17 (May 1987): 42.
9. Miller, op. cit., I7.
10. Edward W. Cundiff and Marye T. Hilger, *Marketing in the International Environment,* 2d ed. (Englewood Cliffs, NJ: Prentice-Hall, 1988), 4.
11. A. H. Krieg, "Why Some U.S. Made Products Don't Sell in the U.S.," *Industrial Distributions* 74 (February 1985): 57.
12. *Industrial Marketing in Japan* (Tokyo: Japan External Trade Organization, 1978), 40.
13. See E. Jerome McCarthy and William D. Perrault, Jr., *Basic Marketing,* 8th ed. (Homewood, IL: Richard D. Irwin, 1984), 691–693.
14. See John K. Ryans and Lori Mitchell, "The Changing Face of American Foreign Trade," *Business Marketing* 71 (January 1986): 49–67.
15. "Japan vs. America: Same Goal, Different Tactics," *Sales & Marketing Management* 130 (October 1986): 116.
16. Tom Peters, "Here Are the ABCs of Not Whining, But Winning Foreign Markets," *San Diego Union* (January 4, 1988), E1–E2.
17. Ibid.
18. Tom Peters, "How U.S. Surrendered Lead in Machine Tools Market to Japan," *San Diego Union* (August 10, 1986), E1.
19. McCarthy and Perrault, op. cit.

20. Daniel C. Brown, "Fiddling While Export Markets Burn," *Business Marketing* 70 (January 1985): 4.
21. Letter of May 13, 1985, from William S. Bishop, manager of sales service, Solar Turbines, San Diego, CA.
22. See Paul Ingrassia, "Industry Is Shopping Abroad for Good Ideas to Apply to Products," *Wall Street Journal* (April 29, 1985), 1, 14.
23. Y. D. Scholar, "Faster Delivery Seen as Edge for Foreign Power Tools," *Industrial Distribution* 74 (February 1984): 45.
24. William F. Schoell, *Marketing*, 2d ed. (Boston: Allyn & Bacon, 1985), 695.
25. "Innocents at Home Send Trainers Abroad," *Sales & Marketing Management* 131 (April 1987): 22.
26. Schoell, op. cit., 696.
27. Ibid.
28. Kate Bertrand, "Marketers Rush to be First on the Bloc," *Business Marketing* 75 (October 1990): 22.
29. Ibid., 21.
30. Ibid., 22.
31. Ibid.
32. John F. Magee, "EC '92," *Marketplace: The ISBM Review* (Spring 1990): 1.
33. Ibid.
34. Mary Sanders, "EC92: Opportunities and Challenges for U.S. Business," in *U.S. Industrial Outlook 1990* (Washington, DC: U.S. Government Printing Office, January 1990), 29–30.
35. "Talks on North America Free Trade Pact Begin," *San Diego Union* (June 13, 1991), A1.

SUGGESTED ADDITIONAL READINGS

Dawson, Leslie M., and Jean Larson Pyle. "New Focus of U.S. Industrial Firms in the Pacific Basin." *Industrial Marketing Management* 20 (1991): 1–8.

"Drastic New Strategies to Keep U.S. Multinationals Competitive." *Business Week* (October 8, 1984), 168–172.

Jain, Subhash C. *Export Strategy*. Westport, CT: Quorum Books, 1989.

Kaikati, Jack. "Opportunities for Smaller U.S. Industrial Firms in Europe." *Industrial Marketing Management* 20 (1991): 339–348.

Kashani, Kamran. "Beware the Pitfalls of Global Marketing." *Harvard Business Review* 67 (September–October 1989): 91–98.

Klein, Saul, Gary L. Frazier, and Victor J. Roth. "A Transaction Cost Analysis Model of Channel Integration in International Markets." *Journal of Marketing Research* 27 (May 1990): 196–208.

Locke, William W. "The Fatal Flaw: Hidden Cultural Differences." *Business Marketing* 71 (April 1986): 65–76.

Magee, John F. "1992: Moves Americans Must Make." *Harvard Business Review* 67 (May–June 1989): 78–84.

Magee, John F. "EC '92." *Marketplace: The ISBM Review* (Spring 1990): 1–5.

Ohmae, Kenichi. "The Global Logic of Strategic Alliances." *Harvard Business Review* 67 (March–April 1989): 143–154.

Onkvisit, Sak, and John Shaw. "An Examination of the International Product Life Cycle and Its Application Within Marketing." *Columbia Journal of World Business* 18 (Fall 1983): 73–79.

Ostmeier, Hanns. *Standardizing International Entry, Positioning, and Distribution Strategies*. Cambridge, MA: Marketing Science Institute, 1986.

"Pinpointing Export Markets." *Business America* 10 (August 3, 1987): 2–11.

Porter, Michael E. *The Competitive Advantage of Nations*. New York: The Free Press, 1990.

Samli, A. Coskun, Dhruv Grewal, and Sanjeev K. Mathur. "International Industrial Buyer Behavior: An Exploration and a Proposed Model." *Journal of the Academy of Marketing Science* 16 (Summer 1988): 19–29.

Webster, Frederick E., Jr., and Rohit Deshpande. *Analyzing Corporate Cultures in Approaching the Global Marketplace*. Cambridge, MA: Marketing Science Institute, 1990.

Young, John. "Global Competition: The New Reality." *California Management Review* 27 (Spring 1985): 11–25.

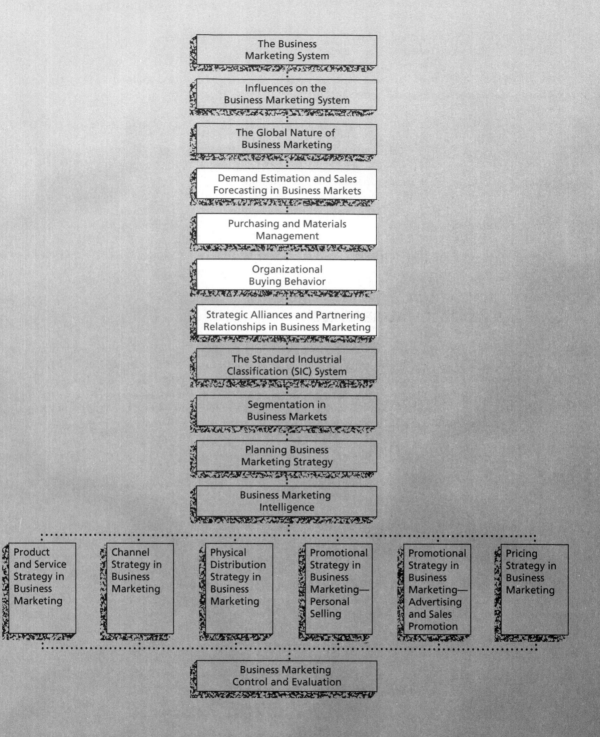

PART TWO

Organizational Customers and Market Behavior

‣4‣

Demand Estimation
and Sales Forecasting
in Business Markets

••

Effective business marketing requires a thorough understanding of demand mechanisms that operate in business markets. Measurement of demand is important because of its relationship to both strategic and marketing planning. Accurate and realistic demand estimates are fundamental requirements for planning. Demand measurement is basic to planning because it describes the potential size of a market and the relative ease or difficulty by which that market can be entered. It is also necessary for any market-share or market-penetration calculations. This chapter examines demand characteristics that are peculiar to business markets and that must be understood by the marketing manager. The chapter begins with a discussion of the total demand for business goods and services so that the magnitude of business markets may be appreciated. Demand factors unique to business markets are then examined, with particular emphasis on market characteristics, product characteristics, derived demand characteristics, and joint demand characteristics. The chapter concludes with a discussion of demand estimation and sales forecasting techniques that have particular applications to business markets.

THE TOTAL DEMAND FOR BUSINESS GOODS AND SERVICES

Estimating the total demand for business goods and services in the United States is relatively difficult. One estimate is that more than half of all manufactured goods are sold into the business markets and that most raw materials are sold directly into these markets.[1] Add to this the amount of goods sold by manufacturers to reseller organizations (wholesalers and retailers) and it can be argued that business marketing accounts for the vast majority of all goods and services

Estimating Demand for a New Product

Sorrento Electronics, a San Diego-based high-tech electronics manufacturer, developed a system for surveying soil contaminated by hazardous and radioactive wastes. This system was capable of determining the amount of contamination in soils as well as verifying remediation activities taken to eliminate such contamination.

Investigating and correcting hazardous and radioactive waste sites was not new at the time of development. Traditionally, such efforts involved removing earth, transporting it to a laboratory, and then analyzing it to determine if contamination was present. All this took time. In concept, Sorrento's new product would accomplish the same thing but on an instantaneous basis. The new product could perform the analysis without ever having to remove soil and transport it, thus saving both time and money.

But before management would move past the conceptual stage, reliable estimates of demand for the new product had to be developed. Management wanted proof that a market existed before it committed any more funds to product development. Determining just how to estimate demand became a high priority and efforts were undertaken to find the best way to accomplish such estimates. Because the product existed in concept only and there were thus no past sales data, such techniques as trend extrapolation, correlation and regression, and direct derivation were eliminated from consideration. Judgmental tech-

niques were also ruled out for a number of reasons. For one, the company had no existing sales force, so estimating demand via the sales force buildup technique was not possible. In addition, no channel components existed and thus distributors could not be used for estimation purposes. Finally, the executive jury technique was also eliminated from consideration because there was an insufficient number of company executives with the necessary experience.

By a process of elimination, a mail survey technique was chosen. It was decided to survey a sample of waste site contractors across the country to gauge their potential demand for the new product because these businesses actually conducted both characterization and remediation services for their customers. Respondents were asked how satisfied they were with their existing systems and how likely they would be to switch to the new concept if such a product became available. Of the 100 respondents to the survey, only 29 percent were very satisfied with their present system, 53 percent were somewhat satisfied, and 18 percent were dissatisfied to some degree. Coupled with this, 43 percent said they were very likely to try the product if it could be priced competitively, 54 percent said they were somewhat likely, and only 2 percent were not likely to try it. If the new product could be priced lower than existing systems, 58 percent claimed they were very likely to try it, 41 percent claimed to be somewhat likely, and none said they were not likely at all. Finally, 59 percent claimed they would use the new product if it completed the job in less time than their existing system, as long as it did not cost more. Based on survey findings, the company was able to determine a reasonably good estimate of the sales potential of the new product concept.

marketed. No single source, however, provides such data on the total domestic and global market for all business goods and services. Data on the size of the institutional market are especially elusive. Still, it is possible to deduce the enormity of the total business market by examining the sizes of some of its components.

For example, it is estimated that the combined government market in the United States (federal, state, and local buying units) purchased approximately $807 billion in goods and services during fiscal year 1990.[2] The federal government accounted for 54 percent of the total purchased, state governments for 18 percent, and local governments for the remaining 28 percent.

There are some other representative indicators. Manufacturers' new net orders exceed $2,660 billion per year; new capital expenditures by manufacturers are in excess of $79 billion annually; and the book value of all manufacturing inventories exceeds $300 billion annually.

Another estimate involves purchases by reseller organizations such as wholesalers and retailers. Annual U.S. retail sales are over $1,600 billion while annual wholesaler sales are slightly under this figure. Since these resellers must purchase goods and services in order to market them, it is clear that this market is also huge.[3]

Finally, the total value of all U.S. shipments and receipts by manufacturers and service organizations is about $4,000 billion.[4] If only half of this is accounted for by business marketing, as is indicated in the first paragraph of this section, it can be seen there is tremendous demand in U.S. business markets alone.

In addition, there are large global markets for many business goods and services. Exports by U.S. manufacturers are approximately $530 billion annually and many of these firms sell their goods and services to business markets in Canada, Germany, Japan, the United Kingdom, Mexico, the Netherlands, and South Korea.[5]

For the individual marketing manager, it is not as important to know the total demand in all business markets as it is to understand the demand in those markets served by the individual company's goods and services. Thus, although trying to estimate the size of all business markets is interesting, it is more of an academic interest than a practical decision-making factor. What may be more important is to understand the demand characteristics that are unique to business marketing.

DEMAND CHARACTERISTICS UNIQUE TO BUSINESS MARKETS

For the business marketing manager, there are demand characteristics that are unique to organizational markets. While some of these also apply to consumer marketing, they have somewhat different implications for business marketing. Others, such as derived demand, are not found in consumer marketing and thus are extremely important in estimating demand. This section will examine some of these characteristics in detail.

Geographic Characteristics

The demand for business goods and services is not spread evenly throughout the United States, nor is it spread evenly across all countries of the world. It is often concentrated in various regions for differing products. The business marketing manager must recognize the important locational demand characteristics for individual goods and/or services as they apply to the domestic U.S. market and to the larger international market. If this fact is not grasped, effort may be expended in areas where little or no demand exists, and effort may be lacking in other areas where demand potential is considerable. This statement is not to imply that a single **geographic demand** factor exists for all business products, but that a number of generalizations are possible. Of the nation's 3,041 counties, 294 are considered major industrial counties when measured by manufacturing employment, a common method for assessing manufacturing concentration. These 294 counties account for an estimated 80 percent of all industrial buying power. According to data provided by *Country Business Patterns,* these 294 counties list 10,000 or more in manufacturing employment and are in addition to other counties that have less than 10,000 in manufacturing employment but that are part of standard metropolitan statistical areas.[6] *Sales & Marketing Management* estimates that the top fifty counties in manufacturing activity account for about 36 percent of all U.S. manufacturing shipments.[7]

Figure 4.1 illustrates manufacturing geographic demand based on several criteria. Analysis of this figure discloses that firms are concentrated in the northeast (New England, Middle Atlantic, and East North Central states), in the southeast (South Atlantic and East South Central states), and the Pacific states. For example, 46 percent of manufacturing plants are located in the northeast; 19 percent are in the southeast; and 16 percent are in the Pacific coast area. Thus, 81 percent of all U.S. manufacturing plants are located in these three general areas. Similar distribution is found for manufacturing employees, value added by manufacturers, and value of manufacturers' shipments.

Overall, the major domestic demand concentrations for business goods and services are located in the northeast, southern, and Pacific coast areas of the United States. Such a summary has general interest in attempting to determine geographic demand, but it may have little meaning to individual marketing managers whose market concentrations do not match this general pattern.

FIGURE 4.1 **The Geographic Distribution of U.S. Manufacturing Plants Based on Selected Criteria**

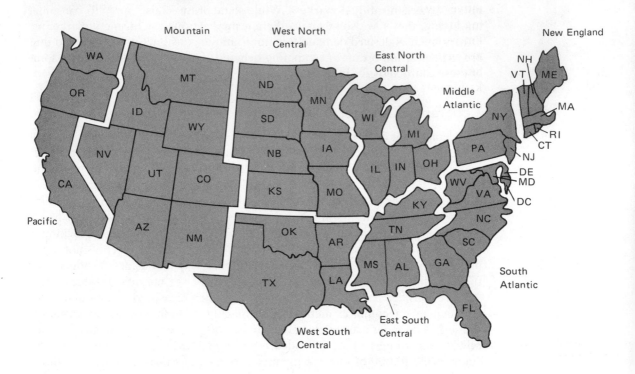

Percent of Nation's Total in Each Region

Region	Number of Manufacturing Plants (%)	Number of Manufacturing Employees (%)	Value Added by Manufacturers (%)	Value of Manufacturers' Shipments (%)
New England	7.2	6.7	6.7	5.5
Middle Atlantic	16.8	14.7	15.4	13.9
East North Central	18.9	22.3	22.9	23.8
West North Central	6.6	6.8	7.3	7.9
South Atlantic	14.5	17.8	15.5	15.1
East South Central	5.3	8.0	6.4	6.6
West South Central	8.5	7.7	8.6	10.6
Mountain	4.5	2.9	3.0	3.0
Pacific	17.7	13.0	14.2	13.4
Total U.S.	100.0	100.0	100.0	100.0

Source: U.S. Department of Commerce, *Statistical Abstract of the United States 1990,* 110th ed. (Washington, DC: U.S. Government Printing Office, 1990), 711.

Note: Columns may not add to 100.0 because of rounding.

Table 4.1 illustrates geographic demand information for a number of selected business products. This table shows clearly that the overall concentrations in the northeast, southeast, and Pacific coast areas are not necessarily representative of the markets for individual products. For example, if a business marketing firm sold products used in the manufacture of alkalis and chlorine, its market would primarily be concentrated in a four-state area—which clearly does not match up with the overall concentration. The same is true, to one degree or another, for every product in the table. In developing marketing plans, the marketing manager must determine the geographic concentration for his or her company's products or services and not be misled by overall concentration figures.

TABLE 4.1   **Domestic Geographic Demand for Selected Business Products**

Product Group	Value of Industry Shipments ($ million)	Number of Establishments	Major Producing Areas
Alkalis and chlorine	1,508	49	Texas, Louisiana, Wyoming, California
Phosphate fertilizers	3,783	91	Florida, Texas, Louisiana, Mississippi
Pharmaceutical preparations	20,543	756	New Jersey, Missouri, New York
Synthetic rubber	3,200	63	Texas, Louisiana
Primary copper	3,761	27	Arizona, Utah, New Mexico
Metal-cutting machine tools	4,400	919	Ohio, Michigan, Illinois
Industrial heating equipment	1,150	327	Ohio, Pennsylvania, Michigan, Illinois
Air and gas compressors	3,540	175	New York, Pennsylvania, Illinois, Ohio, Indiana
Farm machinery	10,590	2,004	Illinois, Wisconsin, Indiana, Missouri, California
Mining machinery	2,635	344	Pennsylvania, Ohio, West Virginia, Virginia, Kentucky
Oil field machinery	10,950	478	Texas, California, Oklahoma, Pennsylvania, Louisiana
Ball and roller bearings	3,550	149	Connecticut, Ohio, South Carolina, Pennsylvania
Turbine generator sets	1,372	15	New York, Pennsylvania, North Carolina
Computing equipment	34,060	932	California, Massachusetts, New York, Minnesota
Motor vehicles	67,700	322	Michigan, Missouri, Ohio

Source: U.S. Department of Commerce, *1983 U.S. Industrial Outlook for 250 Industries with Projections for 1987* (Washington, DC: U.S. Government Printing Office, January 1983).

To illustrate, sales territories cannot be determined without specific knowledge of where present and prospective customers are located.

The information illustrated in Table 4.1 shows the relative ease with which geographic demand data may be obtained. Geographic demand information can be obtained from the *U.S. Census of Manufactures, U.S. Industrial Outlook,* and *Dun's Census of American Business.* Use of sources such as these can provide domestic geographic demand information down to the county level.

As was developed in Chapter 3, understanding geographic demand characteristics is also important for business marketers who operate in global markets. The same type of analysis is required for these markets as for domestic markets. Figure 4.2 shows the geographic global demand for some representative U.S.

FIGURE 4.2 **Global Geographic Demand for Selected Products Based on Total Exports of the Products**

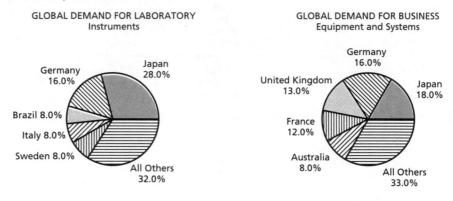

GLOBAL DEMAND FOR LABORATORY
Instruments

Japan 28.0%
Germany 16.0%
Brazil 8.0%
Italy 8.0%
Sweden 8.0%
All Others 32.0%

GLOBAL DEMAND FOR BUSINESS
Equipment and Systems

Germany 16.0%
United Kingdom 13.0%
Japan 18.0%
France 12.0%
Australia 8.0%
All Others 33.0%

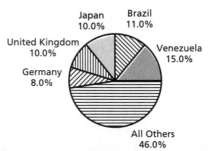

GLOBAL DEMAND FOR BUILDING
Products

Japan 10.0%
Brazil 11.0%
United Kingdom 10.0%
Venezuela 15.0%
Germany 8.0%
All Others 46.0%

Source: Adapted from "World Trade Outlook," *Business America* 8 (March 4, 1985): 5, and various editions of *Global Market Surveys,* International Marketing Information Series, U.S. Department of Commerce.

business marketing firms based on the percent to each country of total U.S. exports of the products involved. As can be seen, this figure shows again that global geographic demand may differ appreciably according to the product involved.

Size and Number Characteristics

Related to the geographic characteristics of market demand is the area that pertains to market size and number of possible organizations in that market. Not only must the geographic distribution of any market be determined, the marketing manager also should know how large a market is and how many organizations comprise that market. In addition, demand estimation involves knowing the sizes of organizations in that market to judge the potentiality of each. It is possible to determine many characteristics about that market in addition to its geographic concentration. Referring to Table 4.1, the number of companies in each product group can be easily determined. For example, the marketing manager whose firm sells products used in the manufacture of alkalis and chlorine finds forty-nine such manufacturers in the United States, and industry shipments of these manufacturers approximate $1.5 billion. Conversely, if a company sells products to pharmaceutical manufacturers, there are 756 such firms in the United States with combined industry shipments of $20.5 billion. By using such sources as the *Census of Manufactures, U.S. Industrial Outlook,* and *Dun's Census of American Business,* a marketing manager can easily determine the size of a market and its number of components.

Concentration Characteristics

In addition to the demand characteristics discussed thus far, other factors that the business marketing manager must consider are whether goods and/or services are being sold into a horizontal or a vertical market and the degree of concentration in that market. A vertical market exists when a company sells its products and/or services to one specific industry, whereas a horizontal market exists when a firm is able to market its goods and/or services to a broad spectrum of industries. For example, the market for manufacturers of blast furnaces is vertical, whereas the market for manufacturers of machine tools may be horizontal. Vertical or horizontal markets may exist for all types of products and services in business markets, and there are degrees of occurrence. An aerospace firm selling only to the U.S. Department of Defense is about as vertical a market as can be found—there is only one buyer for the product.

Concentration refers to the total number of companies or organizations in a market and the percentage of purchases made by the larger, more dominant members. Rarely are all members of a target market equal in purchasing power and market potential. This point can be illustrated by examining some domestic examples. The United States has approximately 300,000 manufacturing plants of all sizes. Only 19 percent have fifty or more employees, the remaining 81 percent are smaller; however, this 19 percent accounts for about 88 percent of all value added by U.S. manufacturing.

This concentration phenomenon exists in specific industries as well as throughout all U.S. manufacturing. Table 4.2 shows that the amount of concentration can vary considerably by industry. For example, although there are 322 establishments in the motor vehicle industry, the four largest firms account for 93 percent of all industry shipments. Conversely, there are 2,462 fabricated structural steel manufacturers in the country, but the four largest account for only 10 percent of all industry shipments. Demand may differ greatly in these two industries because of such great concentration differences.

It is possible to further refine these types of factors. For example, the *Census of Manufactures* shows a total of 2,420 manufacturers of motor vehicle parts and accessories in the United States, which range in size from fewer than four employees to more than 1,000. As shown in Table 4.3, there are only fifty-nine firms with more than 1,000 employees, but these organizations account for a very high percentage of both the total value of shipments and the costs of materials. This is apparent even though information on the twenty largest firms is not included because governmental sources are bound by the nondisclosure rule, which bars information that may disclose the operation of a specific company. Analyses such as this show that the marketing manager cannot simply use total

---

TABLE 4.2   **Examples of Concentration of Demand Using Selected Domestic Target Market Industries**

Industry	Total Number of Establishments in Industry	Percentage of Total Industry Shipments by Largest Four Firms in That Industry
Motor vehicles	322	93
Primary copper	27	87
Alkalis and chlorine	49	66
Ball and roller bearings	149	56
Glass containers	126	54
Air and gas compressors	175	45
Computing equipment	932	44
Mining machinery	344	37
Phosphate fertilizers	91	35
Oil field machinery	478	30
Industrial heating equipment	327	26
Engineering and scientific instruments	786	25
Metal-cutting machine tools	919	22
Fabricated structural steel	2,462	10

Source: U.S. Department of Commerce, *1983 U.S. Industrial Outlook for 250 Industries with Projections for 1987* (Washington, DC: U.S. Government Printing Office, January 1983).

TABLE 4.3   Data Pertaining to Manufacturers of Auto Parts and Accessories
Based on Number of Employees

Number of Employees	Number of Companies with This Number of Employees	Cost of Materials ($ million)	Value of Shipments ($ million)
1–4	589	41.7	78.8
5–9	345	90.9	169.1
10–19	375	183.2	355.3
20–49	395	454.6	852.2
50–99	229	706.8	1,325.7
100–249	248	1,767.4	3,383.7
250–499	120	1,859.0	3,736.9
500–999	60	1,914.6	4,076.9
1,000–2,499	39	11,988.8	22,315.0
2,500+	20	D*	D*
Total	2,420	19,007.0	36,293.6

Source: U.S. Department of Commerce, *1982 Census of Manufactures: General Summary* (Washington, DC: U.S. Government Printing Office, December 1985), 1–86.

* D indicates that data were not included because disclosure could reveal operations of specific companies.

numbers of organizations in a market but must also attempt to break those numbers down into more meaningful categories.

DEMAND RELATED TO PRODUCT CHARACTERISTICS

Demand in business markets also varies depending on the types of products or services being marketed. For example, the demand for processed materials may differ considerably from the demand for capital equipment because of the characteristics of the products themselves. In choosing among possible suppliers, buyers of processed materials are heavily influenced by factors such as specifications, price, and delivery. Thus, price and ability to deliver are major determinants in the demand for these types of products. On the other hand, buyers of heavy or capital equipment may be more influenced by installation assistance, operational training, quality of service, and financing arrangements such as leasing. In selecting one manufacturer's product over another's, these factors constitute major demand determinants. Thus, the marketing manager in a firm that produces processed materials must consider different demand factors than his or her counterpart in a firm manufacturing heavy equipment. In turn, such consideration affects marketing mix elements in such areas as physical distribution, service, sales, and pricing. Pricing may be much more important in processed materials, whereas technical assistance may be more important in capital goods marketing. The following is a partial list of those factors that affect demand for each of the classifications of business products and services. This type of demand analysis is meaningful in that individual marketing managers typically do not market wide ranges of product classifications. For example, the marketing manager in a firm that markets capital equipment typically does not become involved in marketing component parts, raw materials, and so on. Thus, **product demand** is usually focused on those products specific to the marketing company itself.

Heavy Equipment

When organizational customers purchase heavy or major equipment, their ultimate selection of a supplier or suppliers is often influenced by several factors. There often must be strict conformity to the buyer's specifications. If the product deviates even slightly, it may not be considered to meet the specifications. In addition, the choice of one supplier's product over that of another may be dependent on the service capabilities of each supplier as well as the quality and quantity of technical assistance provided at the time of installation. Product warranties also may differentiate competing products, thus increasing the demand for one supplier's products while decreasing the demand for another's similar products. Other factors affecting demand pertain to ease of operation, difficulty or ease of integration of the new product into existing facilities, compatibility of the product with the other equipment used by the buyer, and amount of training required for the buyer's personnel to operate the product properly. Many heavy equipment buyers are further influenced by the energy and manpower requirements of individual competing products. If two drill presses will do the same job, but one uses much less energy than the other, that product may be selected. The supplier's ability to deliver on time is also a factor in the choice. Finally, price and price considerations such as financing and leasing arrangements can play a big part in the buyer's decision-making process.

Light Equipment

The demand for light or accessory equipment products of competing suppliers is also affected by a number of factors, some of which are similar to those affecting the demand for heavy equipment items, such as the supplier's ability to deliver on time, product warranties, service capabilities of the competing suppliers, and price. Since light equipment is often more standardized, is marketed into a wide spectrum of industries, and has specifications that are often more general, other factors differ. For example, provisions for returning defective equipment may be more important than service capabilities, and price discounts such as quantity, cash, and trade discounts are commonplace. In addition, more personal factors often influence the choice of products selected, such as the personal preferences of those who will use the products, past experience with suppliers, and relationships with different sales representatives.

Component Parts

The demand for component parts may be influenced by factors quite different from those affecting the demand for capital equipment, whether heavy or light. One major difference is that heavy and light equipment are sold to user customers, whereas component parts typically are marketed to OEM customers. The impact of this difference on derived demand may be quite important. To illustrate, although ultimate consumers may not know or care what drill press or boring mill was used to produce the products they are buying, they often care a great deal about what component parts are put into those same products. This fact is especially true when the consumer knows, uses, and understands those parts, such as tires on a car and compact disc players on a stereo.

Component parts, by virtue of the derived demand mechanism, have different factors that affect demand than capital goods do. Often, OEM customers choose among competing suppliers of component parts on the basis of the following factors. The products must be in strict conformity to the buyer's specifications even to be considered. Product quality and uniformity must be ensured, and delivery dates must be met—delays on delivery can cause production line shutdowns and incur enormous costs for the customer. Price considerations such as cash, trade, and quantity discounts often influence the decision to buy from one supplier in preference to another. In addition, customers often are influenced by the supplier's ability to produce the quantity of goods that will be required, which means that a supplier who otherwise meets all the criteria may be rejected if a buyer believes that supplier cannot produce enough in a specified period. Specific brands of component parts sometimes are selected because they have ultimate consumer appeal or in some other manner contribute to the marketability of the organizational customer's final product. Finally, the demand for component parts is often influenced by the size of the aftermarket, which was discussed in Chapter 1. This factor generally does not affect the demand for heavy or light equipment.

Processed Materials

The demand for processed materials is also influenced by the OEM market, but it differs in two major ways from the demand for component parts. First, there is usually no replacement market for processed materials. Second, processed materials usually are not used in the same form by the purchasing OEM as component parts are. Normally, processed materials are cut or pressed into required shapes and forms by the OEM after it buys the materials. Thus, derived demand may not be so brand-conscious with processed materials as it is with component parts. In choosing among suppliers of processed materials, organizational buyers are influenced by ability to meet buyer specifications, price and discounts available, certainty of delivery, and quality and uniformity of the materials purchased. Buyers also consider the ability of a supplier to produce the required quantity, the return provisions for defective materials, and the freight differences that may be involved because of the bulk of shipments made.

Supplies

Supplies probably have the simplest demand mechanism of all business goods. Normally, they are standardized products that can be sold to all different types of business customers. Often, there are no specifications involved, and these products are marketed much like many consumer goods. In choosing among possible suppliers, organizational customers often base their purchasing decisions on price and price considerations such as quantity and trade discounts, the ability to deliver on time, and sometimes, the name of the supplier or the brand of product involved.

Raw Materials

In choosing among competing suppliers of raw materials, organizational customers often base their decisions on factors such as standards and grades of materials, the supplier's ability to deliver on time, the supplier's capability to deliver the desired quantity over time, and price. Since shipments are often large and bulky, freight charges may also play a part in the decision.

Business Services

The demand for business services is often influenced by factors that are different from those involved with business goods, because of the intangibility of such services. In addition, such services can be complex (computer software services) or mundane (janitorial services). In choosing among suppliers of such services, organizational customers often weigh such factors as the reputation of the supplier and past experiences with that supplier. Personal references from peers and colleagues in other companies often play a major part, as do references from previous customers of firms producing the services. In addition, personal references of those in the company who must work with the service supplier are often taken into consideration. Finally, the cost of the service and financing arrangements may affect the decision to choose one supplier and not another.

The preceding discussion shows that demand varies according to the type of product or service being marketed. The business marketing manager must fully understand those characteristics of demand peculiar to the particular products or product line of the company. For example, a company selling capital equipment through direct sales to user customers faces a demand situation completely different from that of a firm selling standardized component parts to OEM customers in many different industries.

DERIVED DEMAND CHARACTERISTICS

Derived demand may be the most important point for the business marketing manager to understand. Basically, it is a simple concept, although many people are confused by the term. The term *derived demand* means that business customers, including government and institutions, do not purchase goods and services because of their own personal needs or desires but rather to produce or distribute other goods and/or services for their customers. The use of the word *derived* originates from the business customer's demand for the products and services it purchases, which is derived from the demand of its customers.

Table 4.4 provides some examples of how derived demand occurs in the petrochemical industry. Manufacturers of synthetic fibers sell tire cord to tire manufacturers, who in turn sell tires to the auto industry as OEM products and ultimately to consumers as replacement products. Neither the auto manufacturer nor the individual car owner is purchasing tire cord, but their tire purchases determine the amount of tire cord that is purchased by the tire industry from the synthetic fibers industry. When new car sales are down, auto production drops. Therefore, auto manufacturers need fewer tires, which means that tire sales to the auto industry are down. If replacement purchases of tires by consumers are not enough to offset the decrease in auto production, the tire manufacturers will require less tire cord from their suppliers. Thus, the consumer, in

TABLE 4.4	**The Business Marketing System in Operation Using the Petrochemical Industry as an Example**	
These Petrochemical Inputs	Supply These Industries	To Make These End Products
Plastics	Coatings	Containers
	Construction	Plywood
	Electrical	Paints
	Housewares	Seat covers
	Packaging	Wire coating
	Transportation	Engineering material
Synthetic fibers	Apparel	Clothing
	Carpet	Rugs
	Home furnishings	Upholstery fabrics
	Tire	Tire cord
Solvents	Dry cleaning	Cleaning fluids
	Toilet preparation	Personal care items
	Printing	Inks
Surface active agents	Soap and detergent	Household products
	Mining	Industrial cleaners
		Copper and zinc
Additives	Petroleum refining	Gasoline
	Transportation	Lubricants
Synthetic rubber	Tire	Tires
	Fabricated rubber product	Belting, hose, footwear
Fertilizers and agricultural chemicals	Agriculture	Foodstuffs

Source: U.S. Department of Commerce, *1979 U.S. Industrial Outlook with Projections to 1983 for 200 Industries* (Washington, DC: U.S. Government Printing Office, January 1979), 124.

buying or not buying new automobiles, has an indirect effect on the demand for tire cord. In other words, the demand for tire cord is derived from the consumer demand for new automobiles.

Another simple example may help to explain how derived demand works. Producers of wood panel products such as softwood plywood, hardwood plywood, and particle board sell their products to contractors in the home construction industry. These contractors do not purchase those products for personal consumption but to satisfy the demand of their customers. Thus, when housing starts are depressed, as they were in the early 1980s, the demand for wood panel products is also depressed. Figure 4.3 shows these relationships clearly. The demand for wood panels depends primarily on housing starts and

FIGURE 4.3   **Relationship of Panel Products Quantity Shipments to Housing Starts, 1972–1980**

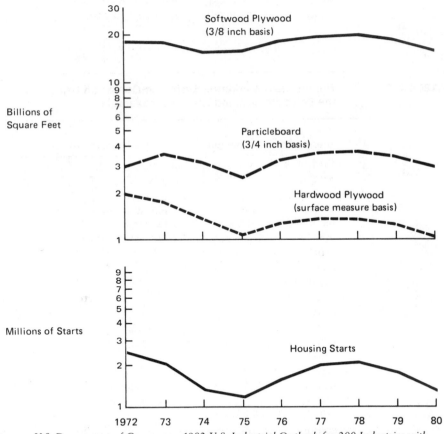

Source: U.S. Department of Commerce, *1982 U.S. Industrial Outlook for 200 Industries with Projections to 1986* (Washington, DC: U.S. Government Printing Office, January 1982), 32.

thus is considered derived. Going a step backward, housing starts are influenced by such factors as interest rates, availability of loanable funds by lenders, and lending policies of financial institutions.

In the actual business world, there are often many levels of derived demand. For example, the demand for cotton is dependent on the demand of the textile industry, which in turn is dependent on the demand of the garment industry, which is ultimately dependent on the demand of the consumer for clothing in general and for cotton products in particular. A shift in the preferences of the consumer from cotton to synthetic fibers, because of less wrinkling or some other such properties, would be felt all the way back to the cotton farmer. And if the switch were drastic enough, some firms could fail, even though they themselves never really came in contact with the ultimate consumer. In other words, even though the ultimate consumer buys no cotton per se, he or she is the driving force behind the production of cotton—the cotton producer's demand is derived from the consumer's demand for fabric preferences. Exhibit 4.1 illustrates this situation as it occurred in the computer disk drive industry.

EXHIBIT 4.1 **Derived Demand in a High-Tech Industry**

Derived demand affects all types of industries, and high-tech suppliers are not immune to its effects. A good example took place in 1984 in the computer disk drive industry. These firms produce disk drives for microcomputer manufacturers such as Apple and IBM. A disk drive spins the magnetic disk, which can be floppy or hard and on which data are stored; in doing so it moves the data between the disk and the computer's processor.

As the demand for personal computers exploded in the early 1980s, the worldwide number of disk drive manufacturers expanded from a handful to more than seventy-five. In 1984, however, the growth in personal computer sales slowed dramatically. This drop brought about a decrease in demand by computer manufacturers for disk drives and an oversupply of disk drive producers. As a result, many suppliers experienced a significant loss in earnings, merged with other companies, or completely dropped out of the market. Those remaining companies enacted stringent cost-cutting efforts that included moving production overseas to obtain cheaper labor and vertical integration moves to acquire component part suppliers. In effect, considerable consolidation took place in the industry because of the effects of derived demand.

Marketing strategies also changed. One industry spokesperson stated, "This year (1985) will not be the year of new-product announcements and big promises. This year will be the year of delivering the products that were already promised, and companies will watch their profit margins carefully, rather than just trying to get more business."

This example illustrates the dangers of derived demand for business suppliers when consumers' demand for a product produced by their customers begins to decline.

Source: Adapted from "Disk Drives Stall in a Glutted U.S. Market," *San Diego Union* (January 20, 1985), I–10.

The Volatility of Derived Demand

Derived demand affects business marketing firms whether they are selling to OEMs, users, or resellers in the private sector, institutional, or governmental markets. Examples using tires and wood panel products have already illustrated the effects on the private sector. With institutional and governmental customers, the effects are similar. For example, a hospital buying medical supplies for its patients is directly affected by its number of patients. If for some reason admissions drop, the hospital does not continue to purchase those supplies as it did previously. Thus, hospital demand is derived from patient demand. Similarly, a municipality's ability to buy required goods or services is derived from its constituents' demand for those services. If a school bond issue is defeated at the polls, the municipality cannot purchase goods or services related to that school. In this case, the municipality's demand for school supplies is derived from the voters' willingness to undertake the project. Thus, all business marketing managers face some aspect of derived demand, and the biggest factor involved is volatility. **Volatility of derived demand** means that relatively small fluctuations in the demand for the products of a business customer can bring about relatively large fluctuations in that customer's demand for goods or services. A classic example occurred during the Great Depression (1929–1932). During that time, the physical production of consumer goods dropped twenty index points from 100 to 80. At the same time, capital spending for equipment dropped sixty-five index points from 100 to 35. A 20 percent drop in the demand for consumer goods was accompanied by a 65 percent drop in purchases of equipment used to produce those same consumer goods. The message for the business marketing manager should be clear. Whereas a consumer marketing firm may be hurt by a 20 percent sales decline, it can survive. But, the company supplying that consumer marketing firm can scarcely hope to absorb an accompanying 65 percent decrease in sales!

Table 4.5 may help to explain the derived demand phenomenon in regard to user customers. Assume that the Premold Corporation produces premolded fiberglass shower stalls, which are sold to contractors for installation into new houses, apartment buildings, and condominiums. To produce these stalls, Premold uses heavy equipment heat presses, each of which is capable of producing 200 stalls per year. Each machine has a ten-year life cycle, and the company replaces 10 percent of its machines each year. Premold purchases the heat presses from the ABC Company. Table 4.5 shows the relationship between Premold's sales of stalls and the sales of the ABC Company supplying Premold.

If it is assumed that the six-year period in the table illustrates years in which 10 percent of the presses will wear out and that no new technological innovations will render the presses obsolete, the table shows the effects of changing consumer market demand on the sales of both Premold and the ABC Company. The volatility of derived demand can easily be seen; in the second year, for example, a 10 percent increase in the consumer demand for shower stalls (from 100,000 to 110,000) brings about a 100 percent increase (from 50 to 100) in the

TABLE 4.5   Derived Demand Example with User Type of Customer

Time Period	Consumer Demand for Premolded Fiberglass Shower Stalls			Number of Machines in Use to Produce the Shower Stalls			Demand for the Machine		
Year	Previous Year	Current Year	Net Change	Previous Year	Current Year	Net Change	Replace-ment	New	Total
1	100,000	100,000	—	500	500	—	50	—	50
2	100,000	110,000	+10,000	500	550	+50	50	50	100
3	110,000	115,000	+5,000	550	575	+25	50	25	75
4	115,000	118,000	+3,000	575	590	+15	50	15	65
5	118,000	100,000	−18,000	590	500	−90	—	−40	−40
6	100,000	100,000	—	500	500	—	10	—	10

Source: Adapted from R. L. Vaile, E. T. Grether, and R. Cox, *Marketing in the American Economy* (New York: Ronald Press, 1952), 16.

demand for the presses to produce those stalls. In the third year, however, the demand for the stalls increases 4.5 percent (from 110,000 to 115,000), but the demand for the presses decreases 25 percent (from 100 to 75). A similar event occurs in the fourth year. In the fifth year, the consumer demand decreases 15.2 percent (from 118,000 to 100,000), but the demand for presses ceases to exist and in fact becomes negative, because Premold has forty more presses than are required to fulfill its demand. Premold can apply its excess machines to the replacement of worn-out machines in the sixth year, which depresses demand for ABC in that year.

With this admittedly oversimplified example, volatility is easy to see and understand. Consumer demand for the shower stalls never fluctuated by more than 12.5 percent, but business demand fluctuated wildly, as much as 400 percent in the sixth year, and sometimes even in inverse relationship to consumer demand as in years 2 and 4.

With OEM customers and resellers, there is fundamentally a one-to-one relationship in the long run although inventories may be affected differently in short-run periods. Assume that an electronics manufacturer produces and supplies switches to a producer of television sets. If the TV manufacturer purchases switches for inventory rather than for immediate use, short-run sales of the switches will fluctuate to a degree greater than the sales of the TV sets.

Inventory levels have an effect because, if TV sales decrease, the customer will use up present inventory stocks first and thus reduce purchase levels. This activity may be illustrated by using the **economic order quantity (EOQ)** concept, which balances the cost of inventory against the cost of ordering, and the average inventory is one-half the order quantity. The EOQ formula determines the exact order quantity at which the annual combined costs of ordering and maintenance are at the lowest point for a given sales volume. The standard formula for EOQ is:[8]

$$EOQ = \sqrt{\frac{2 \times Co \times S}{Cm \times U}}$$

where:

Co = cost per order
Cm = cost of maintenance per year
S = annual sales volume (demand) in units
U = cost per unit

Table 4.6 illustrates how derived demand affects the ordering process of an OEM customer such as the TV manufacturer. Assume in year 1 that this customer buys 2,400 units at a cost of $5 per unit. Ordering costs per order are $20 and maintenance costs are 20 percent of the unit cost per year. Using these data, the table shows that the most economic order size in year 1 is 310 units. Dividing the 2,400 units by 310 shows that the company should purchase 7.7 times in that year and that the average inventory should be 155 units (50 percent of the most economic order size).

The same computations can be used to show how these figures will change according to demand changes in a six-year period. The effects of derived demand can best be seen by comparing year 1 with year 4. Due to decreasing sales of TVs, the TV manufacturer's demand for switches has dropped from 2,400 to 1,800 per year. The customer now buys 6.7 times per year rather than 7.7, and the size of the order is decreased from 310 units to 268. The company making the switches is now making fewer sales and realizing smaller order sizes due to the effects of derived demand.

The falling demand for the customer's product not only leads to less frequent orders from that customer but also to smaller orders. Thus, orders are more expensive to service when they do come—the cost per sales increases. In

---

TABLE 4.6   Derived Demand Example with OEM Type of Customer

Year	Number of Units Demanded	Most Economic Order Size	Number of Times per Year Orders Will Be Placed	Average Inventory
1	2,400	310	7.7	155
2	2,600	322	8.1	161
3	2,200	297	7.4	148
4	1,800	268	6.7	134
5	1,200	219	5.5	110
6	2,400	310	7.7	155

addition, the effects on field sales personnel may be undesirable. For example, if a salesperson is paid on a straight commission basis, decreasing customer demand means fewer and smaller sales and therefore decreasing commissions. Continued decreases in customer demand can contribute to higher sales turnover, which also increases costs.

Not all OEM customers buy in this manner. In recent years, there has been a trend toward **just-in-time (JIT)** buying. Under this concept, the customer expects the supplier to deliver the exact quantity required at the precise time needed. JIT is defined as a manufacturing system in which the parts that are needed to complete the finished products are to arrive at the assembly site as they are needed. Under this concept, the customer maintains no inventory and expects the supplier to deliver to its requirements. In effect, inventories are now held by the supplier instead of by the customer. Demand will differ depending on whether the customer is purchasing on an EOQ or JIT basis. An example will help explain the difference.

Table 4.7 illustrates the situation of an OEM customer operating under the EOQ concept. This customer will demand 360 units over the next twelve weeks. There is a one-week lead time on orders and the reorder point occurs when the customer's inventory drops to thirty units. At the beginning of the twelve-week period, the customer has 140 units in current inventory and its economic order quantity is computed to be 150 units. The table illustrates the customer's use pattern over the twelve weeks. As can be seen, the customer plans to use the product in only seven of the twelve weeks, i.e., eighty in week two, forty in week three, and so on. Given the previously discussed constraints, this customer will place orders in the third and eighth weeks for 150 units to be delivered in weeks four and nine. Thus, the demand here will be for 300 units in the twelve-week period with 150 to be delivered in the fourth week and the other 150 in the ninth week.

Table 4.8 shows what happens to demand if this same customer uses the JIT

TABLE 4.7 **Demand Situation Under the EOQ System**

Week	1	2	3	4	5	6	7	8	9	10	11	12
Demand	0	80	40	0	50	30	0	70	0	50	0	40
Receipts	0	0	0	150	0	0	0	0	150	0	0	0
Inventory[a]	140	60	20[b]	170	120	90	90	20[b]	170	120	120	80
Order	0	0	150	0	0	0	0	150	0	0	0	0

Source: Reprinted by permission from Dillard B. Tinsley and Joseph G. Ormsby, "Improving Marketing with DRP," *Industrial Marketing Management* 17 (1988): 349. © 1988 Elsevier Science Publishing Co., Inc.

[a] End-of-week inventory.

[b] Inventory levels dropped below order point of 30, so EOQ of 150 placed.

TABLE 4.8		Demand Situation Under the JIT System										
Week	1	2	3	4	5	6	7	8	9	10	11	12
Demand	0	80	40	0	50	30	0	70	0	50	0	40
Receipts	0	0	0	0	30	30	0	70	0	50	0	40
Inventory[a]	140	60	20	20	0	0	0	0	0	0	0	0
Order	0	0	0	30	30	0	70	0	50	0	40	0

Source: Reprinted by permission from Dillard B. Tinsley and Joseph G. Ormsby, "Improving Marketing with DRP," *Industrial Marketing Management* 17 (1988):349. © 1988 Elsevier Science Publishing Co., Inc.

[a] End-of-week inventory.

concept. In this case, the supplier will ship only enough units to meet the customer's immediate demand. This demand is determined by considering the one-week lead time necessary to deliver the product. Looking at the table, it can be seen that the customer's use has not changed—it still will use eighty in week two, forty in week three, and so on. In addition, the customer still has 140 units on hand at the beginning of the twelve-week period and those will be used up first. After this, the supplier is expected to deliver the required number of units at the time needed by the customer. Table 4.8 shows clearly how demand will change over the same twelve-week period. As can be seen, the customer will now order 30, 30, 70, 50, and 40 units in weeks 4, 5, 7, 9, and 11 for delivery in the following weeks. Demand now changes to five deliveries, rather than two, in the twelve-week period with much smaller order sizes each time. This example shows that demand for an OEM customer may differ considerably depending on the buying system used, even though the actual use of the purchased items has not changed at all.

Derived demand has tremendous implications for the business marketing manager and will be referred to extensively throughout this text. The concept serves to impress on the marketing manager that he or she cannot let business customers succeed or fail on their own (see the user and OEM examples just discussed). Derived demand also reminds the marketing manager that simply serving business customers may not be enough. When customer sales start to decline, the natural tendency might be to counter with increased advertising, sales campaigns, and perhaps even price decreases to the business customers. But none of these actions would have any effect if the root cause of declining customer sales was due to derived demand. If the demand for customers' products was falling because their customers were buying less, heavy advertising would have little, if any, effect. The manager may have to be involved with stimulating demand in the marketplace of his or her business customers so that desired levels of derived demand are maintained. A good example may be seen in Boeing Corporation's advertising that extolled the merits of air travel over other forms. These ads stressed comfort, reduction of traveling time, and arriving fresh as advantages of air travel over other modes such as driving. With such an approach,

Boeing attempted to stimulate air travel and thus positively affect the airlines' demand for new and replacement aircraft. Thus, the business marketing manager must be consumer oriented, even though the company does not market directly into the consumer market.

JOINT DEMAND CHARACTERISTICS

Joint demand is another demand characteristic that must be understood by the business marketing manager. Joint demand occurs when the demand for one product depends on that product's being used in conjunction with another product or products. In such a situation, the products are demanded jointly, or they may not be demanded at all. For example, to produce pig iron, a producer requires both coke and iron ore. If, for some reason, the producer cannot obtain coke, it will not continue to purchase iron ore in the same quantities. Without coke, the firm has no need to keep buying iron ore—thus the two products share a joint demand.

Joint demand is common in business markets, especially with OEM customers. A fabricator purchasing 200 to 300 component parts for assembly into a finished product has a joint demand for all these components. Often for lack of a single component, no matter how large or small, the final product cannot be assembled. Therefore, purchases of all other products may be curtailed, at least in the short run, if the fabricator has delivery problems with any suppliers. A good example occurred in the auto industry, when strikes at A. O. Smith Corporation and at Briggs & Stratton Corporation, both suppliers of critical auto parts, caused production cutbacks at General Motors and Chrysler.[9] These production cutbacks in turn caused depressed sales of other GM and Chrysler suppliers because of the joint demand aspect.

Demand can also be affected in joint demand situations whenever the purchasing company changes specifications on a component, because previously purchased components may not be compatible with the new specifications. In these instances, the joint relationship may be dissolved, and the demand for many components may disappear if they do not fit the new specification.

Joint demand can also occur with user customers. For example, if a manufacturer is currently using a particular brand of machine in its production process, other pieces of peripheral equipment must be compatible with that machine if the production line is to function effectively. If the manufacturer replaces the brand with an updated version or switches to another brand and the replacement machine is not compatible with the existing peripheral equipment, the demand for the latter may be depressed and even eliminated because the joint relationship is dissolved. New pieces of peripheral equipment would have to be purchased that would be compatible with the new machine, thus creating an entirely new series of joint relationships.

Still another aspect of joint demand can be seen in the product lines of many business marketing firms. Customers often prefer to buy complete product lines from one manufacturer rather than purchase individual products from different manufacturers. If a manager has a gap in an otherwise complete product line, the business customer may buy none of the company's products and, in fact, purchase from a competitor who can supply the entire product line desired. In this case, the products in the product line are demanded jointly or in conjunction with one another: The individual products do not have individual demand; they are demanded jointly with the other products in the line.

These examples show that joint demand is common in business marketing and may take various forms. There is a tendency to view joint demand as a variation of derived demand, but such a perspective is not correct. Derived demand relates to the customer's marketplace, whereas joint demand relates to other suppliers. Since each type of demand relates to a different phenomenon, both types of demand can and do occur simultaneously. The business marketing manager typically must adapt to both.

With joint demand, the astute business marketing manager must be aware of any such joint relationships with the products or services offered by the company. The stability and reliability of other suppliers is critical, inasmuch as company demand can be affected if anything happens to these other suppliers. For example, if another supplier suffers a long strike and cannot deliver its products to the customer, the manager's firm is also affected. Thus, other suppliers should be analyzed in terms of reliability, competence, stability, and other such factors. The marketing manager must be aware of any conditions regarding other suppliers that can have detrimental effects on the demand for his or her company's products or services. When problems are foreseen, the marketing challenge is to alert the customer so that demand decreases may be averted or avoided.

TYPES OF DEMAND ESTIMATES

There is no universally accepted definition of what constitutes demand estimating. There are specific types of estimates of demand and each is somewhat different. For the business marketing manager, several types are very important and should be clearly understood. This section explores those types that are most useful to the marketing manager. Table 4.9 summarizes these and explains the meaning of each type.

These are basic types of demand estimates used in business marketing to estimate demand from a number of perspectives. Two important distinctions are made here. First, the word "market" implies estimates related to the entire industry, while the word "sales" implies estimates related to an individual company within that industry. Second, the word "forecast" refers to expected sales under given marketing plans, while the word "potential" refers to the total sales opportunity available.[10] Viewed in this manner, "potential" involves opportunities while "forecast" involves expectations.

These are reasonably common types of demand estimates. For example, the marketing manager may well wish to estimate the size of a potential market for particular products or lines of products. He or she may also wish to estimate

TABLE 4.9   Types of Demand Estimates Used in Business Marketing

Type	Explanation of Each Type of Demand Estimate
Market potential	The maximum sales of a product or product line that all firms together expect in a specified period of time under all the firms' respective marketing plans
Market forecast	An estimate of the sales of a product or product line that all firms together expect in a specified period of time under all the firms' respective marketing plans
Sales potential	The maximum sales of a product or product line available to an individual firm within a specified period of time
Sales forecast	An estimate of the sales of a product or product line that an individual firm expects in a specified period of time under a given marketing plan

Source: Adapted from Robert W. Haas and Thomas R. Wotruba, *Marketing Management: Concepts, Practices, and Cases* (Plano, TX: Business Publications, Inc., 1983), 100–101.

how much of that total market can be sold by his or her company. How much can the manager expect to sell given his or her marketing plan? While there are other types of demand estimates, these four are the most basic and probably of most value in this discussion.

DEMAND ESTIMATION AND SALES FORECASTING TECHNIQUES

At this point, it may be beneficial to look at how business marketing managers estimate demand and forecast sales in view of what this chapter has discussed thus far. There are a number of techniques commonly used in demand estimating and sales forecasting. In general, these techniques may be classified as objective or subjective and top-down or bottom-up.

An objective technique is based on a numerical relationship between an estimate and other variables that explain that relationship. Examples might be correlation and regression analysis, extrapolation, and direct derivation. A subjective technique introduces personal experience, knowledge, and intuition into the estimation process. An example might be using a company sales force to estimate demand.

A top-down technique starts by analyzing national and/world economies followed by moving down to industries involved and then moving down to the market for the particular company involved. A bottom-up technique starts when a company makes its own estimates from research surveys, sales force opinions, etc. As these examples suggest, objective and subjective techniques integrate with top-down and bottom-up techniques.

There are a number of techniques widely used in business marketing and a discussion of each is in order.

Judgmental Techniques

Judgmental techniques are based on the premise that various groups of people possess sufficient knowledge or insight collectively so that the composite of their views provides a meaningful estimate of demand. These techniques are most often bottom-up and subjective in nature. There are a number of variations used in business marketing.

Sales Force Buildup Here, a manager requests estimates of demand from company field sales personnel. These salespeople, in covering their territories, have insight and may be able to provide reasonably good estimates for their territories. Since direct sales is such a dominant force in business marketing, this technique is widely used. There are, however, drawbacks to be considered. There is often a lack of uniformity among salespeople in both ability and willingness to participate. Some salespeople may purposely underestimate demand to protect themselves against higher sales quotas. Despite such shortcomings, use of this variation is common in business marketing.

Channel Component Buildup When the company markets its products through distributors and/or manufacturers' representatives, demand estimates may be made by these channel intermediaries in much the way described for company salespeople. These organizations are often very knowledgeable and capable of providing useful input. Here too, there may be problems since these are independent organizations who may not have the time to participate or the interest to do so.

Executive Jury This variation may be used when company executives are considered capable of providing useful demand estimates. Executives with considerable experience may be excellent sources of information and using them to estimate demand is common in business marketing. The term "executive" does not refer exclusively to top management, but might include product managers, regional and district sales managers, purchasing managers, production supervisors, and others. Estimates are then derived from the composite of their judgments. This variation may also suffer from the lack of ability or willingness of selected executives to provide meaningful estimates.

Trend Analysis and Extrapolation Techniques

Trend analysis and extrapolation techniques are based on determining demand estimates based on what has happened in the past. They examine historical data to detect trends and patterns that may then be projected into the future. To use these techniques, the marketing manager must determine the existence of a pattern within a series of data.

A relatively simple example may best illustrate how trend analysis and extrapolation may be used to estimate future demand for a company's product.

The marketing manager for an aluminum company wishes to estimate a sales forecast for the firm's aluminum ingots for the coming year using company sales data from previous years. These data are shown in Table 4.10. The manager now wishes to plot these data to determine if a relationship exists. Using time series analysis, the past sales data are plotted and a trend line calculated as shown in Figure 4.4.

Extrapolation or projection of trend, as shown in Figure 4.4, provides the manager with a sales forecast estimate of approximately 82,750,000 units for

TABLE 4.10   Past Company Sales of Aluminum Ingots

Year	Sales in Pounds	Year	Sales in Pounds
1992	88,759,000	1985	60,250,000
1991	79,500,000	1984	58,250,000
1990	69,750,000	1983	43,500,000
1989	63,500,000	1982	47,750,000
1988	70,500,000	1981	40,000,000
1987	54,000,000	1980	36,500,000
1986	55,750,000		

FIGURE 4.4   Time Series Plot of Aluminum Ingot Sales

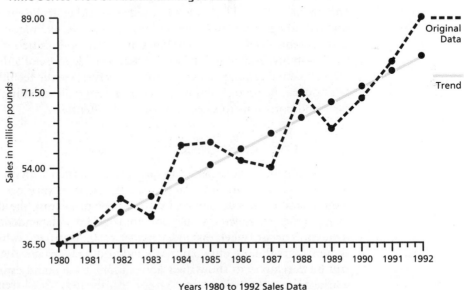

Years 1980 to 1992 Sales Data

the year 1993. There are some limitations in using extrapolation techniques. First, they are based on the premise that what happened in the past determines what will happen in the future. This is often not true. In addition, these techniques are of little use in estimating demand for new products or services where no past data exist. Despite shortcomings, time series analysis is useful when the manager is able to determine a closely fitting mathematical description of the trend.[11]

Survey Techniques

Survey techniques establish demand estimates on the basis of answers supplied by respondents directly replying to a questionnaire. Based on these responses, the results are then projected to the entire market. The assumption with such techniques is that customers and/or prospects can and will provide information about various products or services and their intentions to buy them. Provided there is adequate sampling, data collection and analysis, and questionnaire design, these intentions may then be inferred to the entire population to provide an estimate of potential demand. The opening feature on page 101, "Estimating Demand for a New Product" is an example of this.

Several approaches may be used in implementing the survey technique. They are: (1) personal interviews, (2) telephone interviews, (3) mail surveys, and (4) panel and group interviews. Since estimating demand via the survey technique is a marketing research task and will be covered in detail in Chapter 11, it is not necessary to discuss particulars at this point.

Survey techniques are useful when no historical data exists. They are also used as adjuncts to other estimates based on historical data. For example, survey findings may be used to test the validity of other techniques employed. If the survey findings agree with the findings of another technique, the validity of the latter is reinforced. These techniques are sometimes criticized as lacking predictive reliability. Some hold that they often provide more of a direction of demand than an actual estimate itself. All told, however, survey techniques are very flexible and can be used in almost all types of demand estimating from market forecasts and potentials to sales forecasts and potentials.

Correlation and Regression Techniques

Correlation and regression techniques are concerned with relating demand for a product or service to those factors that cause it to vary over time. These techniques produce a mathematical formula for predicting the dependent variable (demand) given specific values for appropriate independent variables. Simple regression occurs when one independent variable is used, while multiple regression involves the use of two or more independent variables. An example of each will be developed to show their applications to demand estimating in business markets.

Simple Regression   Assume that the manufacturer of auto parts and accessories used by U.S. producers of automobiles wishes to determine the market potential for these products. The marketing manager has accumulated data pertaining to the value of shipments of parts and accessories and unit sales of domestic cars from 1972 to 1987, as shown in Table 4.11. Is there a relationship that can be used to estimate demand?

Using the values in the table, a simple regression ($y = a + bx$) analysis can be conducted. This analysis provides the following equation:

value of shipments = 18,651.47 + (4.48 × car sales)

The manager finds that next year new domestic car sales are forecasted to be 7,135 million. Plugging this figure into the regression formula projects next year's value of shipments of auto parts and accessories to be $50,616 million.

In the simple regression example, only one independent variable was used—unit car sales. In multiple regression, two or more independent variables are employed. A manufacturer of reinforcing bar used in construction wishes to estimate market potential for its products. Table 4.12 illustrates shipments of reinforcing bar and values of construction of private single residences, private multiunit housing, private industrial buildings, and office

---

TABLE 4.11   **Demand Data for Manufacturers of Motor Vehicle Parts and Accessories**

Year	Value of Shipments ($ million)	Domestic Car Unit Sales (in millions)
1972	53,486	9,237
1973	61,468	9,676
1974	54,674	7,454
1975	45,507	7,053
1976	56,588	8,611
1977	64,305	9,106
1978	67,413	6,312
1979	61,017	8,341
1980	44,829	6,581
1981	40,551	6,209
1982	36,293	5,757
1983	43,678	6,795
1984	51,508	7,952
1985	53,040	8,196
1986	54,620	7,850
1987	56,250	7,050

Source: U.S. Department of Commerce, *U.S. Industrial Outlook 1987* (Washington, DC: U.S. Government Printing Office, 1987), 36-2, 36-11.

TABLE 4.12   Demand Data for Manufacturers of Reinforcing Bar

Year	Shipments of Reinforcing Bar (1,000 tons)	Private Single Residences ($ million)	Private Multiunit Residences ($ million)	Industrial Buildings ($ million)	Office Buildings ($ million)
1975	3,666	27,423	6,986	8,018	4,973
1976	3,876	40,049	7,228	7,183	4,763
1977	4,179	55,271	10,478	7,712	5,269
1978	4,704	62,385	13,422	10,994	6,574
1979	5,303	60,790	17,798	14,950	9,461
1980	4,683	45,662	17,476	13,837	13,318
1981	4,371	44,401	18,263	17,030	17,473
1982	4,049	35,663	16,253	17,343	23,049
1983	4,138	72,203	22,447	12,861	20,768
1984	4,315	85,605	28,221	13,745	25,940
1985	4,444	86,123	28,539	15,769	31,580
1986	4,352	102,123	31,038	13,747	28,591
1987	4,308	114,463	25,452	13,707	26,430

buildings. Is there a relationship that can be used to estimate the demand for reinforcing bar?

Using multiple regression analysis, the following regression formula was developed:

$$y = 2,523.76 + .0088x_1 + .0542x_2 + .13298x_3 - .08763x_4$$

where:

x = rebar shipments (in thousands of tons)
x_1 = private single residence construction (in millions of dollars)
x_2 = private multiunit housing construction (in millions of dollars)
x_3 = industrial construction (in millions of dollars)
x_4 = office building construction (in millions of dollars)

This equation produced a multiple correlation coefficient of .93, which resulted in a multiple coefficient of determination of .88. In addition, the F test showed that the results were significant at the .001 level. As a result, the formula may be judged acceptable. Construction forecasts for the next year are found to be as follows:

$120,000 million—private single residences (x_1)
$ 28,000 million—private multiunit residences (x_2)
$ 15,000 million—industrial buildings (x_3)
$ 30,000 million—office buildings (x_4)

By plugging these values into the regression formula, it is estimated that 4,463.16 thousand tons of reinforcing bar will be required.

Correlation and regression techniques have the advantage of being very objective and they produce automatic weightings of factors involved in demand estimation. In addition, they provide statistical reliability, which may be lacking in other techniques. On the negative side, market changes can invalidate an analysis and make an equation obsolete and unreliable. As can be seen, these techniques also require a considerable amount of past data to be used properly. In summary, these techniques have been found very useful in demand estimation in business markets and will continue to be used.

Direct Derivation Techniques

Direct derivation techniques are based on the premise that the demand for certain business products is derived from the demand for other related products. For example, U.S. auto manufacturers, in producing their cars and trucks, consume tons of alloy steel, stainless steel, malleable iron, aluminum, copper and copper alloys, etc. A direct relationship exists between auto industry production and consumption of materials as long as cars continue to be made from the same materials. Thus, if the demand for new autos is known, the demand for copper, stainless steel, and so on may be determined.

An example may help to illustrate this technique. Going back to the reinforcing bar manufacturer, it may be possible to determine the amount of reinforcing bar used in private multiunit residences, etc. For example, material published in various editions of *The Construction Review* provide such information. It is estimated that there is about $7.63 of reinforcing bar per $1,000 of construction of private multiunit family dwellings.[12] If next year's value of this type of construction is estimated to be $28,000 million, then $213,640,000 in reinforcing bar will be required. Given that reinforcing bar is selling at $387 per ton, 552.041 tons of bar will be demanded for this one type of construction alone. If such coefficients as the $7.63 figure can be determined, this technique can be used effectively with all types of construction requiring reinforcing bar.

One other example might be useful. One of the better-known direct derivation techniques is input–output analysis, which focuses on the fact that the sales or output of one industry are the purchases or inputs of other industries. Going back to the auto industry example, sales of steel, aluminum, etc., are purchases by the auto manufacturers. Input–output analysis can show the manager employed by a steel producer the extent to which steel sales will be affected by auto sales. Using the U.S. Department of Commerce national input–output model, it is found that for each dollar's worth of auto output, 8.05 cents of steel will be used directly. In addition, the model shows that, for each dollar of output, 19.55 cents of steel will be used in total (purchased for indirect use by the auto industry for machinery or other purposes, and purchased by supplying industries).[13] Now, if the auto industry projects a $500 million increase in auto sales, this will call for a direct increase in steel sales of $40.2 million, and ultimately a total increase of $97.7 million worth of steel.

Direct derivation is especially useful to business marketers when products are used directly in construction, production, and so forth. These techniques are relatively simple to understand and easy to implement. The major concern is in finding the proper coefficients and monitoring them to determine if they are changing over time.

CHAPTER SUMMARY

This chapter stressed the importance of estimating demand in business marketing. Effective estimation of demand is necessary for marketing planning and strategy development because many marketing planning tools require sound estimates for implementation. This chapter examined in detail those characteristics unique to business marketing. Particular emphasis was placed on geographic characteristics, concentration characteristics, product and service characteristics, and characteristics related to both derived and joint demand. The effects of derived demand were discussed as this characteristic relates to different types of organizational customers. Types of demand estimates in business

marketing were defined with attention paid to market potentials and forecasts and sales potentials and forecasts. Techniques most appropriate for estimating demand and/or forecasting sales in business markets were examined in detail. Particular emphasis was placed on judgmental techniques such as the sales force buildup and executive juries; on trend analysis and extrapolation techniques; on survey techniques; on correlation and regression techniques; and finally on direct derivation techniques. Examples were developed to show how these techniques are especially useful in estimating different types of demand in business markets.

KEY TERMS

correlation and regression technique
derived demand
direct derivation technique
economic order quantity (EOQ)
geographic demand
joint demand
judgmental technique
just-in-time (JIT)

market forecast
market potential
product demand
sales forecast
sales potential
survey technique
trend analysis and extrapolation technique
volatility of derived demand

QUESTIONS

1. It is sometimes argued that joint demand is simply a variation of derived demand. What is your position on this statement? Support your position by using examples.
2. Why is demand estimation such an important factor in business marketing in terms of the de-

velopment of marketing plans and strategies? Explain how effective and accurate demand estimation may lead to better marketing planning and strategy development.
3. Overall, the major concentrations of demand for business goods and services are in the north-

east, southeast, and Pacific regions of the United States. Explain why this may not be too meaningful to the marketing manager of a firm that markets component parts to manufacturers of farm machinery.

4. From the perspective of a business marketing manager, why is the understanding of concentration of demand so important?

5. It is sometimes argued that an estimate of market forecast for a particular product can never equal an estimate of market potential for that same product. Explain why this is so.

6. Assume you are the marketing manager of a business marketing firm that has developed a new product concept and wishes to estimate sales potential for that product. What technique would you employ to develop such an estimate? Justify your choice.

7. Explain why the direct derivation technique would be more useful to business marketers than to consumer marketers in estimating sales potentials.

8. Since personal selling is very important in business marketing, many business marketing firms have extensive sales forces that could be used to estimate various forms of demand via the sales force buildup technique. What do you see as the advantages and disadvantages of using this technique for demand estimation purposes?

9. How does the direct derivation technique differ from correlation and regression techniques when used to estimate demand in business markets? Which do you see as the more useful of the two? Explain your position.

10. Some business marketers are of the opinion that the use of trend analysis and extrapolation techniques to estimate market and sales potentials is risky unless used in conjunction with other forecasting techniques. Explain what this statement means and then state whether you agree or disagree with it. Support your position.

NOTES

1. E. T. Martin, *Core Business Programs: Marketing* (New York: Facts on File Publications, 1983), 63.

2. *Introduction to the Government Market: Local, State, and Federal,* 3d ed. (Cleveland: Government Product News, 1987), 7, 12.

3. U.S. Department of Commerce, *Statistical Abstract of the United States 1990* (Washington, DC: U.S. Government Printing Office, January 1990), 771–772, 780.

4. *Dun's Marketing Services 1990 Business Statistics Report* (Parsippany, NJ: Dun's Marketing Services, 1990), 148.

5. U.S. Department of Commerce, op. cit., 790.

6. Arthur H. Dix, "Industry Moving West, South," *Marketing Insights* 1 (January 23, 1967): 10.

7. "The Top 50 Countries in Manufacturing Shipments," *Sales & Marketing Management* 138 (April 27, 1987): 29.

8. Donald J. Bowersox, *Logistical Management* (New York: Macmillan, 1974), 194.

9. "Car Output Fell 4% Last Month from 1973 Pace," *Wall Street Journal* (September 4, 1974), 2.

10. Robert W. Haas and Thomas R. Wotruba, *Marketing Management: Concepts, Practices, and Cases* (Plano, TX: Business Publications, Inc., 1983), 100–101.

11. See Robert S. Reichard, *Practical Techniques for Sales Forecasting* (New York: McGraw-Hill, 1966), 130–154; and Charles W. Gross and Robin T. Peterson, *Business Forecasting* (Boston: Houghton Mifflin, 1976), 53–79.

12. Joseph T. Finn, "Materials Requirements for Private Multi-Family Housing," *Construction Review* 22 (April 1976): 4–10.

13. "The Input–Output Structure of the U.S. Economy, 1977," *Survey of Current Business* 64 (May 1984): 42, 84.

SUGGESTED ADDITIONAL READINGS

Bishop, William S., John L. Graham, and Michael H. Jones. "Volatility of Derived Demand in Industrial Markets and Its Management Implications." *Journal of Marketing* 48 (Fall 1984): 95–103.

Cox, William E., Jr., and George N. Havens. "Determination of Sales Potentials and Performance for an Industrial Goods Manufacturer." *Journal of Marketing Research* 14 (November 1977): 574–578.

Ehrlich, Isaac. "The Derived Demand for Advertising: A Theoretical and Empirical Approach." *American Economic Review* 72 (June 1982): 366.

Hurwood, David L., Elliott S. Grossman, and Earl L. Bailey. *Sales Forecasting*. New York: The Conference Board, Inc., 1978.

Martin, Warren S., and Al Barcus. "A Multiattribute Model for Evaluating Industrial Customers' Potential." *Interfaces* 10 (June 1980): 40–44.

Piersol, Robert J. "Accuracy of Estimating Markets for Industrial Products by Size of Consuming Industries." *Journal of Marketing Research* 5 (May 1968): 147–154.

Ranard, Elliot D. "Use of Input/Output Concepts in Sales Forecasting." *Journal of Marketing Research* 9 (February 1972): 53–58.

Rosenberg, Richard D. "Forecasting Derived Demand in Commercial Construction." *Industrial Marketing Management* 11 (February 1982): 39–46.

Rudelius, William, Raymond W. Willis, and Steven W. Hartley. "Forecasting for Firms Selling Projects of Jobs 'To Order'." *Industrial Marketing Management* 15 (1986): 147–155.

Scott, Jerome E., and Stephen K. Keiser. "Forecasting Acceptance of New Industrial Products with Judgment Modeling." *Journal of Marketing* 48 (Spring 1984): 54–67.

Shapiro, Stanley J., and Jean-Charles Chebat. "Appraising the Market for New Industrial Products." In *Marketing Management: Readings in Operational Effectiveness*. New York: Harper & Row, 1974.

Thomas, Robert J. "Forecasting New Product Market Potential." *Journal of Product Innovative Management* 4 (1987): 109–119.

5

Purchasing and Materials Management

∙∙∙

In business markets, most organizational customers and prospects have some type of department devoted to **purchasing,** the buying of needed goods and services. Personnel who work in such departments are commonly referred to as purchasing professionals. These are people whose primary responsibilities involve working with present and prospective suppliers. Many business marketers view purchasing professionals as gatekeepers who fulfill administrative functions but who often have little influence over the final purchase decision. The following quotation probably summarizes their feelings:

> The typical buyer is a man past middle-life, sparse, wrinkled, intelligent, cold, passive, noncommittal with eyes like a codfish, polite in contact, but at the same time, unresponsive, cool, calm, and damnably composed as a concrete post or a plaster of paris cat; a human petrification with a heart of feldspar and without charm; or the friendly germ, minus bowels, passions, or a sense of humor. Happily, they never reproduce, and all of them finally go to hell.[1]

While the purchasing professional's primary objective still is to contain purchasing input costs, the methods of achieving this objective have changed dramatically over the past decades. It is thus necessary to update the traditional view of purchasing managers and their responsibilities. The purchasing department still negotiates for the lowest prices and carefully selects suppliers based on their ability to perform. However, many companies view their purchasing departments as "outside manufacturing managers." In this role, they are expected to train, develop, and build relationships with selected suppliers in order to decrease the costs of poor quality and untimely deliveries. Rather than being primarily clerical, the purchasing manager's job is changing to a role in top management with a potential path to the CEO's suite.[2] For this and other reasons, it behooves business marketers to better understand the purchasing and materials

A Typical Day for the Purchasing Professional in Business Markets

8:00 AM   Buyer arrives at work and reviews daily schedule; notes a lunch meeting with a salesperson from a new supplier; begins work on revising a supplier contract.

8:30 AM   Receives a frantic call from the plant foreman that a scheduled shipment of parts did not arrive; calls vendor to begin tracking down the parts.

9:00 AM   Foreman calls back to inform buyer that the plant will have to shut down at noon if the parts are not in the plant by 11:30 AM.

10:00 AM   After numerous phone calls to the warehouse, plant manager, and logistics department, another process is substituted to keep the plant operational until the purchased parts can be located; finally, the supplier's salesperson calls to say that a new shipment will be delivered by 11:00 AM.

10:30 AM   Buyer returns to work on the supplier contract revisions and asks secretary to take messages on all phone calls except emergencies.

11:00 AM   Calls plant manager to see if parts have arrived; they have and plant can continue its normal manufacturing process; calls supplier salesperson to thank him for his help and asks if original shipment has been found; salesperson informs buyer that the original shipment was mislabeled and was about to be sent elsewhere when a shipping clerk noticed that the part count was incorrect; during the following investigation, the mistake was discovered and they were able to ship the originally ordered parts.

12:00 PM   New vendor salesperson arrives; buyer and salesperson talk over lunch about company's needs and the vendor-development program; buyer wants to investigate other sources of this product before placing an order.

1:00 PM   Attends meeting with information systems department to discuss the EDI implementation program; primary concern discussed is how to encourage the firm's smaller suppliers to link their EDI systems with the firm's.

2:00 PM   Meets with product development team to spec out parts costs and potential suppliers.

3:30 PM   Meets with strategic planning people to discuss economic forecasts and corporate global strategies.

5:00 PM   Buyer completes draft of contract revisions and leaves for the day.

| **EXHIBIT 5.1** | The Changing Role of Purchasing in U.S. Organizations |

Many U.S. organizations are recognizing the importance of effective and efficient purchasing performance and they are increasing the role of their purchasing departments. This increased role can be seen in the number and level of new responsibilities taken on by purchasing departments in the United States in the past decade. A study of 297 U.S. organizations found the following functions had been *newly assigned* since 1980. These are: (1) personnel travel, now performed by 14 percent of the surveyed firms; (2) traffic and/or transportation, 13 percent; (3) countertrade—offset planning/execution, 12 percent; and (4) strategic planning, 9 percent. Prior to 1980, these departments had not participated in such activities.

In addition, the survey found another set of functions in which purchasing's responsibilities had *increased* since 1980. These included: (1) strategic planning, up 43 percent; (2) providing economic forecasts, up 41 percent; (3) buying capital equipment, up 37 percent; (4) product development, up 31 percent; (5) new product evaluation, up 26 percent; (6) traffic and transportation, up 23 percent; (7) personnel travel, up 16 percent; (8) countertrade—offset planning/execution, up 15 percent; and (9) cash flow planning, up 13 percent.

This study shows clearly that purchasing professionals today are involved in many activities other than simply buying goods and services. They are now responsible for new tasks never before undertaken by purchasing departments and they are becoming more and more involved in other tasks at the same time. This, in turn, suggests that business marketing managers will have to deal with new and different kinds of purchasing professionals in the future.

Source: Adapted from Harold E. Fearon, *Purchasing Organizational Relationships* (Tempe, AZ: Center for Advanced Purchasing Studies, 1988), 16.

management functions of their organizational customers. Exhibit 5.1 explains how these functions are changing in contemporary business markets. As the exhibit shows, there are changes taking place in both the tasks of purchasing personnel and their responsibilities.

THE PURCHASING PROFESSIONAL

The job titles of **purchasing professionals** range from purchasing agent, purchasing manager, director of purchasing, vice president of purchasing, buyer, senior buyer, procurement manager, procurement officer, and materials procurement manager. These titles vary from firm to firm, and the jobs are not equal in rank, status, or compensation. For example, a buyer usually has the responsibility for purchasing specific products. The vice president of purchasing normally oversees the purchasing department, setting policy without performing day-to-day buying.

The average buyer wants most to purchase the best products and services at reasonable prices, so that he or she contributes to improvements in company profits. He or she also seeks to affect company profits by negotiating effectively with suppliers and looking constantly for opportunities for cost reductions. Typically, buyers like longer-term contracts that offer better price protection. Table 5.1 lists factors that are seen as most important to purchasing professionals in their dealings with present and prospective suppliers. Like all people, buyers have their gripes. The average buyer abhors late deliveries, price instability, and material shortages. Within his or her organization, the typical purchasing professional does not like requisitions submitted with insufficient lead times, people who circumvent the purchasing department in their buying, and product specification, quantity, or date revisions. The feature at the beginning of this chapter describes a typical day for the purchasing professional in business markets and provides insight to the various tasks and responsibilities of a person in this position.

PURCHASING DEPARTMENTS

As discussed in the chapter introduction, **purchasing departments** typically handle buying goods and services for their organizations. These departments can vary widely in size and sophistication. In smaller companies (fewer than twenty employees), purchasing is often a part-time responsibility held by someone such as an office manager or owner/manager. In mid-size firms (twenty to 100 employees), formal purchasing departments are common but they may be small, sometimes with only one or two people. In larger companies (100+ employees), large purchasing departments employing specialized purchasing professionals may exist. In megacompanies (with thousands of employees), purchasing functions are often decentralized and managed via computer systems, with factory-based purchasing agents specializing in products or location-specific buying.

TABLE 5.1	**Factors Seen as Most Important to Purchasing Professionals in Dealing with Suppliers of a Standard Business Product**

1. Supplier regularly meets quality specifications.
2. Supplier advises buyer of potential trouble.
3. Supplier is honest in dealing with buyer.
4. Supplier provides products during times of shortages.
5. Supplier is willing to cooperate in the face of unforseen difficulties.
6. Supplier delivers when promised.
7. Supplier provides needed information when requested by buyers.
8. Supplier is helpful in emergency situations.

Source: Standley D. Sibley, "How Interfacing Departments Rate Vendors," *National Purchasing Review* 5 (August–September–October 1980): 11. Reprinted by permission of the National Association of Purchasing Management.

Differences in the size and sophistication of purchasing departments affect how business marketers offer their products and/or services. In the small firms, the purchasing person is not usually a specialist, implying a need for educational marketing. In the mid-size companies, the purchasing people specialize in buying but their knowledge may be spread over many different types of products. In the larger companies, individual buyers are often highly specialized and very knowledgeable. Marketing to these types of purchasing professionals requires an equally specialized knowledge on the part of the business marketing firm.

PURCHASING OBJECTIVES

Increasing domestic and international competition has prompted many U.S. companies to implement management methods to ensure delivery of the right quality product at the right time for the right price. An emphasis on looking at the product or service from the customer's perspective has also led to an increased focus on suppliers.

This concern over suppliers has prompted changes in purchasing operations. In the past, purchasing was often conducted through arm's length negotiations with a large number of suppliers in order to achieve the lowest possible price. While purchasing still attempts to contain input costs, total cost estimates now include factors such as quality, transportation, factory delays, and production planning. The systems, skills, and strategies to contain these costs now attempt to actively manage fewer supplier relationships in order to optimize product quality and delivery as well as to obtain the lowest prices. Figure 5.1 shows this trend toward fewer but more reliable suppliers. Since many U.S. manufacturers have moved to just-in-time (JIT), the supplier base for companies has been reduced by 37 percent. Some examples include Xerox, which cancelled 4,700 suppliers in a single year, Ford Motor Company, which has reduced its supplier base by more than 40 percent since 1980, and Pemco, which reduced its number of suppliers from 500 to 300, and had plans to again reduce this number to 200.[3] There is clearly a trend toward fewer but better suppliers, which has great implications for business marketing.

New systems combined with fewer supplier relationships create more formal links between buyers and suppliers. This will be addressed in some detail in Chapter 7, but it still should be discussed here. In this emerging environment, not only does the business marketer need to address all buying center relationships but business marketing today often means achieving supplier certification, creating early dialogue with product design teams, setting up EDI links, and managing inventory flows and delivery to provide products and services when the buyer needs them. According to management experts, purchasing functions (those largely performed by the purchasing department) will play a key role if U.S. business marketers are to regain their competitive advantage. The remainder of this chapter will examine the key elements of purchasing's changing strategies, skills, and systems.

FIGURE 5.1   The Trend Toward Fewer but More Carefully Selected Suppliers

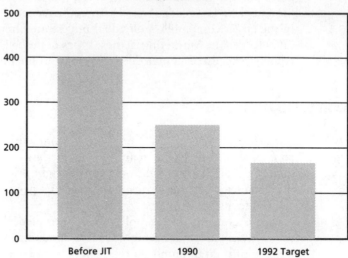

AVERAGE NUMBER OF PRODUCTION
Suppliers Per Plant

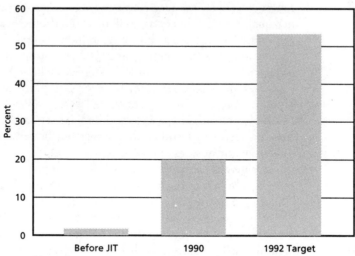

PERCENTAGE OF SUPPLIERS
Certified by Buying Firms

Source: Reprinted by permission from Ernest Raia, "JIT Delivery: Redefining 'On-Time'," *Purchasing* 109 (September 13, 1990): 69.

PURCHASING STRATEGIES

Business marketers can gain an advantage by determining each customer's or prospect's strategic purchasing direction and then planning the marketing approach accordingly. In its enhanced role as manager of "outside manufacturing," purchasing has taken on a new strategic role in many businesses. Leenders, Fearon, and England have divided **purchasing strategies** into five major categories: (1) assured supply, (2) cost reduction, (3) supply support, (4) environmental change, and (5) competitive edge.[4] A look at each of these is in order.

Assured Supply

These strategies estimate changes in both demand and supply and extract guarantees from suppliers in exchange for guaranteed order levels. In essence, such a strategy is aimed at assuring receipt of purchases in exchange for a commitment to the supplier regarding future purchases. Organizations that employ this strategy will seek out suppliers who are seen as capable of delivering required quantities on time regardless of almost any unforeseen situations. Supply must be assured or the customer will search out new suppliers.

Cost Reduction

Cost reduction strategies are designed to reduce the total cost of acquisition and operation. Changes in the environment or in technology force the customer to seek out alternatives that can reduce its overall operating costs through changes in materials purchased, sources used, and purchasing methods. This involves more than looking simply at invoice prices. Organizations that use this purchasing strategy may look closely at any other events that may involve cost. For example, Rockwell's Defense Electronics Group identifies what it calls "overt identifiable money costs" in its dealings with suppliers.[5] Any event that costs Rockwell money, such as late deliveries, defects to be returned, etc., is costed out and considered as part of the total cost of doing business with a supplier. Organizations with such a strategy are constantly monitoring the performance of present suppliers and seeking lower costs when possible.

Supply Support

Supply support strategies are created to enable buyer and seller to share information and capabilities. For example, better communication systems (typically computerized) facilitate the timely notification of order changes and assure that vendor inventory and production goals are consistent with the buying firm's needs. Strategies to improve relations between buyer and seller may be necessary to improve the communication needed to assure better and/or more consistent product quality and service. JIT customers often employ such a purchasing strategy.

Environmental Change

These strategies attempt to anticipate and recognize shifts in the total environment due to economic circumstances, organizational changes, personnel changes, changes in governmental regulations and controls, or systems availability. The object of the buying organization is to respond to these changes to the long-term advantage of the buying organization. For example, McDonald's made the decision to purchase paper rather than styrofoam cups, plates, etc., and then developed an ecologically oriented promotional campaign to publicize its good intentions to the public.

Competitive Edge

Competitive edge purchasing strategies attempt to exploit market opportunities and organizational strengths to give the buying organization a significant competitive advantage. An organization may want to purchase leading-edge products in order to further develop its own desired image as an industry leader. A good example of this can be seen in the case of Intel, which is building an image of its own product quality (see Exhibit 5.2). This objective also becomes part of the organization's purchasing strategy with the result that the company seeks out quality parts suppliers and works closely with them to develop closer relationships.[6]

Because the purchasing organization operates in political, cultural, economic, and physical environments, it is only logical that such factors will affect buying behavior. In addition, there are often other influences at work, including government regulations, product liability risks, environmental protection concerns, waste disposal factors, and ethical considerations. Thus, these strategies are not normally mutually exclusive but rather often complement one another. For the business marketing manager, this means that he or she must determine which strategy is being used when a customer or prospect buys or considers buying company products and/or services. Communicating a cost reduction theme may have little appeal if a business customer is following an assured supply strategy.

STAGES OF DEVELOPMENT OF PURCHASING ORGANIZATIONS

Purchasing organizations often give clues to their strategic directions by the types of approaches they use. A study of 140 purchasing departments in the United States and Canada found that organizational customers may be categorized into four types based on the stage of development of the department in terms of form and function.[7] At each stage, purchasing plays a different role in planning and management philosophy, which should be understood by the business marketing manager. Because most organizations pass through a sequence of phases in their planning and management philosophies, it is feasible that the business marketer could be dealing with customers and prospects at any one of these stages.[8] The four stages found in the study are as follows.

Basic Financial Planning

In this stage, the purchasing department is viewed as providing a service within the organization. Its purpose is to minimize cost against budgetary norms and cost is restricted to cash or out-of-pocket costs. The department in this stage is generally reactive. It processes requisitions, bids, writes purchase orders, and the like. Products bought are often limited to MRO items, office equipment, etc., and most of the problems faced by the department are process-oriented. These are organizations that still rely primarily on purchasing strategies that maintain relatively high inventory levels—those that use EOQ buying procedures, employ arm's length bidding from suppliers, use many supplier sources to achieve competitive pricing, and emphasize inspection rather than developing quality through integrated value analysis. In short, the strategy of customers or prospects in this stage is to purchase as they have for years.

Forecast-Based Planning

At this stage, there is a tendency to call the function "purchasing" and not "buying." There is a strong emphasis placed on forecasting and price/cost variance responsibilities. The purchasing function is expanded from cost minimization to include more cost reduction and cost avoidance activities. The focus is still reactive, but there is some involvement in the development of purchasing plans that are compatible with corporate planning. Basically, the department strives to manage the buying function and make the process more efficient. In addition to purchasing MRO supplies and equipment, the department may also purchase raw materials. Personnel are required to have managerial and forecasting skills in addition to clerical skills. Purchasing here is becoming more complicated.

Externally Oriented Planning

At this stage, purchasing functions broaden and may include responsibilities for inventories, transportation, and outsourcing. The department's purpose is to support lines of business and make positive contributions through value analysis. Departmental plans are integrated with the plans of the rest of the organization. The purchasing cycle is designed to fit the product cycle of the business. The department often has a full range of commodity responsibilities that may extend to managing relations with suppliers. Purchasing systems are structured to pursue profit-seeking ventures through sales of company materials, scrap and other surplus items, and hedging. The basic focus of the department is on supply-chain management and positioning itself to contribute to the organization's defined lines of business.

Strategic Management

In this stage, the purchasing department is involved in the broader concept of supply management. Anything that involves inbound materials or service needs is now included in its responsibilities. Purchasing functions as an equal member of an organizational team responsible for product development and overall business results. Purchasing here takes an extremely proactive stance and provides strong input to corporate planning. Some people in the purchasing department may do little or no actual purchasing but rather act as liaisons in supply relationships between departments in the organization and between the organization and its suppliers. The department thus coordinates supply relationships. Personnel are very knowledgeable about supply management and may well control the choice of suppliers or change the products and materials purchased to be more in line with market opportunities. The department may be very involved with decisions made in such areas as product development and marketing and function as a partner with other departments. Its decisions tend to be viewed as total business decisions rather than just purchasing ones.

Table 5.2 illustrates how a business customer's purchasing emphases can change according to the phase involved. As the table shows, purchasing departments at each phase have different responsibilities and different needs. This in turn means the business marketing manager should know which phase a customer or prospect is in before developing any marketing or sales strategy. It would be a major mistake to develop a strategy for a prospect in the basic financial planning phase only to find later that it is really in the strategic management phase. For example, with a customer in phase I, the buying firm may well be using EOQ buying procedures and employing arm's length bidding from suppliers. In addition, the customer may use many different suppliers and emphasize inspection of purchased products rather than development of quality via value analysis. Here, the marketing manager should consider offering a form of value analysis and upgrading systems technology, which could help solidify an ongoing relationship with the purchasing organization.

With a customer in phase IV, however, the buying organization's purchasing department is involved in much more than just purchasing goods and services. This means that marketing involves much more than just selling the same. Suppliers to such a customer may be included in the firm's supplier council and may well be consulted at the initial design of the customer's product or service, as is illustrated in Exhibit 5.2 in the case of Intel. In such a situation, the business marketer must meet the buying organization's criteria for supersupplier status and then work quickly to enact whatever changes are necessary to adapt to these criteria. If existing relationships with other suppliers preclude the marketing manager's company from being a supplier, the approach might be to attempt to create relationships with the prospect's product development team and work backward to create a relationship with purchasing. Such an approach might give the business marketer an opportunity to gain access to quality partner company business.

TABLE 5.2 Purchasing Emphases Throughout Range of Strategic Settings

Purchasing Attributes	Phase I Basic Financial Planning	Phase II Forecast-based Planning	Phase III Externally Oriented Planning	Phase IV Strategic Management
Concept of the field	Buying	Purchasing	Procurement	Supply
Concept of "strategy"	Better price on next buy	Maintain favorable price/cost variances	Support line of business	Entrepreneurial team member
Expectations	Minimization of costs	Cost minimization Cost avoidance Cost reduction Purchase for quality	Contributions through Value analysis Value engineering	Involved in product development and line-of-business management Line-of-business results
Management approach	Reactive	Reactive but plan for future	Fit department in with plans of rest of firm	Positive, proactive
Major activities	Process requisitions into purchase orders and contracts	Management of the buying function Make process efficient	Fit buying cycle to the line-of-business product cycle	Manage commercial relationships for the firm Source for long term
Range of products	MRO items Office goods	Raw materials MRO items Office goods	Capital goods Raw materials MRO items Office goods Outsourcing management	Suggest source firms to purchase Suggest product changes in line with market opportunities and future constraints
Budgetary approach	Cost center	Cost center Planning for future	Supply-chain management Shape future of department for line-of-business or SBU	True supply management Partner in change
Management style	Clerical/reactive	Managerial Forecasting	Managerial Planning	Team member
Key personal skills	Task oriented	Some management	Managerial Strong interpersonal Strong analytical	Purchasing decisions are business decisions
Concerns	Conformance to norms Process problems	Basic managerial issues Concern with power regarding scope, backdoor buying, headcount, centralization, etc.	Supply-chain management	Shape of function not important, results and output are the keys

Source: Reprinted by permission from Virginia T. Freeman and Joseph L. Cavinato, *Fitting Purchasing to the Strategic Firm: Frameworks, Processes, and Values,* Report 1-1989 (University Park, PA: Institute for the Study of Business Markets, The Pennsylvania University, 1989), 15.

EXHIBIT 5.2   **Monitoring Supplier Performance in Business Markets**

Intel is one company that strives to develop its own product quality through its suppliers. To do this, the company relies on developing its suppliers into world-class status. Monitoring their performances becomes an integral part of Intel's overall product quality objective. Using a scoring system, Intel audits each of its suppliers on a monthly basis. Suppliers are rated on a scale of 1 to 5 on a number of criteria with a 1 being a fair supplier, 2 being a good supplier, 3 being a better supplier, 4 being an excellent supplier, and 5 being a supersupplier. A total score of between 90 and 100 is considered evidence of successful performance but a score of between 80 and 89 signals that some type of corrective action is needed fast. Those suppliers that receive high ratings are rewarded with larger shares of Intel's business. In fact, top-rated suppliers are guaranteed at least 55 percent of Intel purchases of the product or products involved.

To better control its supply, Intel trains its suppliers in the latest quality management and purchasing procedures. This keeps the vendors on top of the latest developments in their product areas and contributes to the quality of the products received by Intel. At times, Intel makes capital investments in equipment for its key suppliers to help support the company's future plans. According to the vice president of administration and materials at Intel, "The magic of getting a good supplier is in recognizing that you have a commitment to not just helping him be a good supplier, but also to clearing the way for him to continue to improve—and there are different levels to that depending on the size and sophistication of your suppliers."

Source: Adapted from J. William Semich and Somerby Dowst, "How to Push Your Everyday Supplier into World Class Status," *Purchasing* 101 (August 17, 1989): 76.

CONTEMPORARY PURCHASING PRACTICES AND SKILLS

Contemporary purchasing involves a number of practices of importance to the business marketer. These practices in turn require a number of purchasing skills that should be understood by business marketing personnel. These skills may be classified as traditional or contemporary. Traditional purchasing skills include identifying many sources of supply, arranging supplier bids for jobs, developing hard negotiation styles, deciding whether to make or buy a needed product, maintaining paper requisition files to control purchasing functions, and estimating future inventory needs. For years, purchasing professionals have developed the skills necessary to perform these tasks and they will probably continue to do so.

But, as has been discussed, additional skills are necessary today for purchasing professionals to adequately perform their jobs. These skills include database management and information systems knowledge, value analysis, defining the purchasing company's quality expectations, evaluating vendors' abilities to manufacture and deliver specified quality products on time, managing outside vendors to encourage quality-oriented cultures, and undertaking market analysis to determine fair pricing standards and new efficiency improvements that can reduce costs and/or increase productivity.[9] Because some of these newer skills have profound marketing implications, it is necessary to look at them in more detail.

Meeting Quality Expectations Via Purchasing

Product quality has become perhaps the major goal of many U.S. and international organizations. Much of the literature on quality assumes that high quality is desirable as an end in itself. Yet, quality in organizational purchasing is determined by the reconciliation of two inseparable considerations: (1) the technical considerations of suitability and (2) the economic considerations of cost and availability. These two considerations form the basis of discussions and negotiations between customers and manufacturers, between various departments of the manufacturing company, and between suppliers and purchasers.

In the case of a manufacturing customer, the design engineering department generally determines the suitability of production materials. Engineering works closely with both production and marketing people in such determinations. Many manufacturers now include certified suppliers and customers in design discussions, which in turn influences the definition of quality for a particular product.

The purchasing department reviews the economic considerations related to the derived quality requirements. Once the technical specifications have been made, purchasing is responsible for finding the most cost-effective source. In many companies, purchasing assumes both the technical and the economic responsibility for nontechnical materials such as office supplies, janitorial supplies, etc. More organizations are now including a representative from purchasing at the beginning of the product design stage to assist in developing the most cost-effective specifications early in the process. This rarely happened in traditional purchasing.

In addition to determining the most suitable product at the most economic price, quality considerations include identifying appropriate services performed by a supplier and determining acceptable levels of defects in shipped products. The traditional purchasing management perspective was that the quality–cost curve was similar to the economic order quantity curve, or broadly U-shaped. Figure 5.2 shows that under this notion, purchasing was content to live with a relatively high defect level, because it was assumed that attempting to substantially reduce defect levels would significantly increase costs.

Because of contributions by Deming, Juran, and others, however, a new perspective on achieving quality has emerged.[10] This view of quality argues that every defect is expensive and prevention or avoidance of defects actually lowers costs. Figure 5.3 conceptualizes this approach. Therefore, many business marketing customers today focus more on preventing defects through statistical sampling and other test methods at the beginning of the process to reduce production variabilities. This, of course, can only be accomplished through close purchaser–supplier relationships and a top management commitment to zero-defects—from production of the raw materials through the final product processes.

FIGURE 5.2   Traditional View of Purchasing Management Regarding
the Quality/Cost Trade-Off

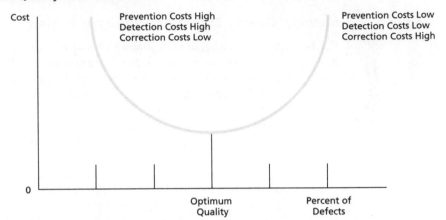

Source: Adapted from Michael R. Leenders, Harold E. Fearon, and Wilber B. England, *Purchasing and Materials Management,* 9th ed. (Homewood, IL: Irwin, 1989), 142.

Prior to this focus on the cost of poor quality, purchasers were willing to pay more for higher-quality products or services. This was based on a recognition of the benefits to purchasing organizations of higher-quality goods, but it was also assumed that the supplier might have to incur higher costs to achieve better quality. If quality is "inspected in" after production, it would indeed create higher costs. Deming argues, and the Japanese manufacturers have proven, that quality should result from making it right the first time. When this is accomplished, the result is a lower-cost solution. Therefore, it is not unreasonable for a purchaser and marketer to work together to achieve both improved quality and lower costs! One contrast drawn between U.S. and Japanese manufacturers is that the former will accept minimum levels of defects from a supplier (such as 5 percent) while the latter will accept none. Thus suggests strongly that making it right the first time is certainly possible.

Historically, many of purchasing's policies and procedures have been based on the assumption that competition is at the heart of the buyer–seller relationship. This notion of competition fosters the belief that sellers remain sharp only if they fear that another supplier can take away sales to a particular purchaser, which is possible only when purchasers assume that it is inexpensive to switch suppliers and that multiple sourcing gives the purchaser both supply security and control over suppliers.

The emergence of quality as a prime purchasing criterion challenges this traditional competitive view in favor of a more cooperative one. The current cooperative approach argues that finding and developing a high-quality supplier is expensive. This is especially true when continuous quality improvements are

FIGURE 5.3   Contemporary View of Purchasing Management Regarding
the Quality/Cost Trade-Off

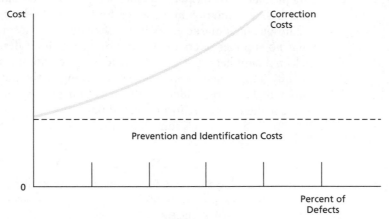

Source: Adapted from Michael R. Leenders, Harold E. Fearon, and Wilber B. England, *Purchasing and Materials Management*, 9th ed. (Homewood, IL: Irwin, 1989), 143.

expected. In fact, this job requires extensive work by various experts in the purchasing organization, along with their appropriate counterparts in the selling organization, to achieve continuing quality improvements. Under these circumstances, it is not realistic to use multiple sources for the same end-item, to switch suppliers frequently, or to take offers to sell based only on the bid price. On the other hand, single sourcing makes many purchasing professionals nervous. What are the repercussions to a buyer when he or she has made a decision to go with a single supplier and then that supplier does not deliver on time?

The idea of sharing key organizational information with suppliers to facilitate better planning, designing, and servicing of the purchaser's requirements also makes procurement experts whose skills were honed under the competitiveness philosophy uneasy. The transition to a more cooperative relationship between buyer and seller based on specific definitions and measurements of quality must be managed skillfully by the business marketer in order to place his or her firm at the forefront of potential quality partnerships with buying organizations. This is no easy task and requires more than just promises—the business marketing manager must have the capabilities in production, engineering, and distribution to make such a relationship work.

Negotiation

One way for a business marketing firm to encourage a purchasing customer toward the opening of communication channels is to change its **negotiation** strategy. As contemporary purchasing departments themselves learn new negotiation techniques, business marketers can assist buyers by negotiating offers under a new negotiation strategy that focuses on building relationships and solving problems. As more companies selectively weed out suppliers and focus their purchasing primarily on those vendors that provide the highest-quality product, many business marketers will be left without customers. As companies realize that no supplier offers the quality and price level desired by purchasers, a few selected suppliers will be chosen to receive training in how to better manage quality improvements and deliver according to the purchasers' specifications. In order to favorably influence the selection process, marketers need to become more skilled in newer forms of negotiation.

Table 5.3 outlines some basic principles of negotiation that may be useful in

---

TABLE 5.3   Principles of Negotiation Used in Business Marketing

PROBLEM Positional Bargaining: Which Game Should You Play?		SOLUTION Change the Game—Negotiate on the Merits
Soft	Hard	Principled
Participants are friends.	Participants are adversaries.	Participants are problem-solvers.
The goal is agreement.	The goal is victory.	The goal is a wise outcome reached efficiently and amicably.
Make concessions to cultivate the relationship.	Demand concessions as a condition of the relationship.	**Separate the people from the problem.**
Be soft on the people and the problem.	Be hard on the problem and the people.	Be soft on the people, hard on the problem.
Trust others.	Distrust others.	Proceed independent of trust.
Change your position easily.	Dig in to your position.	**Focus on interests, not positions.**
Make offers.	Make threats.	Explore interests.
Disclose your bottom line.	Mislead as to your bottom line.	Avoid having a bottom line.
Accept one-sided losses to reach agreement.	Demand one-sided gains as the price of agreement.	**Invent options for mutual gain.**
Search for the single answer: the one *they* will accept.	Search for the single answer: the one *you* will accept.	Develop multiple options to choose from; decide later.
Insist on agreement.	Insist on your position.	Insist on using objective criteria.
Try to avoid a contest of will.	Try to win a contest of will.	Try to reach a result based on standards independent of will.
Yield to pressure.	Apply pressure.	Reason and be open to reasons; yield to principle, not pressure.

Source: Getting to Yes, by Roger Fisher and William Ury. Copyright © 1988 by Roger Fisher and William Ury. Reprinted by permission of Houghton Mifflin Co. All rights reserved.

this area. Once negotiations become less "hard" to more "principled," a business marketer can influence his or her level of involvement with customers' decisions. The table describes a method of negotiation that allows a dialogue about mutual interests to begin. While many business customers want to offer better-quality products or services themselves, they do not know how to get better-quality parts and supplies at fair prices from their suppliers. Purchasing departments are slowly moving to accomplish this via such concepts as quality partnerships and other kinds of links with suppliers. Many purchasing professionals learned a different approach to the marketplace, however, and are reluctant or unable to implement such a different philosophy. For business marketers, the early institution of top quality control methods and "principled" forms of negotiation should influence their ability to compete with other suppliers and win a place on a purchaser's short list of approved suppliers.

Value Analysis

Although a relatively old concept (it was developed during the 1940s by General Electric's L. D. Miles), **value analysis** is still useful for today's purchasing professional.[11] It provides another way for business marketers to become involved in their customers' product selection processes. Value analysis compares the function performed by a purchased item with its cost in order to find a lower-cost alternative. Often the buyers make purchasing decisions under a great deal of time pressure. In addition, technology and manufacturing methods change fairly rapidly. In many instances, a customer buys a higher-priced item than is necessary. Value analysis reviews product functions and cost after these initial decisions have been made.

According to a study by *Purchasing* magazine, the purposes of value analysis are to (1) reduce costs, cited by 92 percent of respondents; (2) improve quality, 80 percent; (3) encourage supplier involvement, 49 percent; (4) encourage creative teamwork within the buying company, 40 percent; (5) better satisfy users' needs, 33 percent; and (6) meet new marketing objectives, 26 percent.[12] Exhibit 5.3 outlines an approach used by purchasing personnel in business markets to implement this value analysis concept.

In some organizations, a form of value analysis called value engineering is performed during the design phase, which takes place before production purchases are actually made. If suppliers are included in these design discussions, they can contribute to lower-cost yet functionally effective materials. While design stage value engineering often provides the most efficient way to do the job, time pressures often make this impossible. Therefore, value analysis presents a fruitful area for purchase cost reduction as well as an opportunity for business marketers to provide lower-cost solutions to their customers. Indications are that the trend will continue toward newer and more sophisticated approaches to value analysis. This in turn means that the business marketing manager must become more knowledgeable on this subject.

EXHIBIT 5.3   Procedure for Performing Value Analysis

Value analysis involves the reviewing of present product specifications as set by the using departments to eliminate unneeded cost factors and/or improve products. A relatively common procedure that is often used includes the following steps being taken by an organization's purchasing and related departments. First, a relatively high-cost or high-volume purchase item is selected for value analysis. Second, the purchasing department finds out how the item is used and what is expected of it by the using department. Third, a series of questions are asked and answered. Typical questions might be: Does the use of the item contribute value? Can the item be eliminated? Is its cost proportionate to its usefulness? If the item is not standard, can a standard item be substituted? Is there a similar item in inventory that might be used? Does the item's specifications exceed what is needed? Are all the features of the item required? Can you make the item cheaper yourself? Have suppliers been asked for suggestions on how to reduce its cost? Will another supplier provide the needed item for less? And is anyone else buying it for less? Questions such as these are answered by either the purchasing department or using departments, or both. Fourth, a decision is made regarding continuing to use the item or seeking a replacement. Fifth, if the present item from the existing supplier proves to be the best purchase, the procedure is finished. If this is not the case, however, purchasing may recommend that changes be made in the item purchased or the supplier providing it.

Source: Adapted from Michael R. Leenders, Harold E. Fearon, and Wilbur B. England, *Purchasing and Materials Management,* 9th ed. (Homewood, IL: Irwin, 1989).

Vendor Analysis

Vendor analysis is the evaluation of supplier performance by a purchasing organization. As stronger links form between buyers and fewer suppliers, an organization's ability to analyze, select, and evaluate vendors becomes more important. As has been discussed, higher interdependency involves greater risks for purchasing personnel, especially when one link in the chain does not perform as expected. Traditional vendor analysis can be divided into two areas: (1) evaluating the performances of current vendors and (2) assessing the strengths and weaknesses of new or untried vendors. Most purchasing departments still perform these two functions, but some have added a third, that of assessing current vendors in terms of their quality potential, which ultimately leads to certification in some form or manner as a quality supplying partner.

Previously, purchasing evaluation of existing vendors involved assessing their negotiation and sales skills more than following up on product quality and delivery promises. Now, because of more sophisticated computer capabilities, many purchasing departments are able to track deliveries and follow up on production promises made by a particular vendor in order to fully evaluate the potential for long-term contracts. Additionally, more buying organizations now look at their own internal strengths and weaknesses with an eye toward developing closer relationships with suppliers who have complementary strengths.

An example may help to understand how vendor analysis works and show its implications for suppliers. Assume that a customer now purchases a particular component part from three different suppliers but wishes to streamline its buying and reduce the number of suppliers. Based on their own experiences, company buyers and buying influences have agreed on six factors as being critical in selecting among possible suppliers. These factors are product quality, average delivery time, delivery time variability, price, willingness to supply rush orders, and returns policy. Using these six factors, each of the three present suppliers is evaluated based on experiences over the past three years. Buyers and buying influences assign weights to each of the factors to reflect its relative importance in the buying process. Table 5.4 illustrates how each of the three suppliers are evaluated based on the six weighted factors. When the respective supplier ratings are multiplied by the assigned weights, an evaluation of each vendor may be made. This process shows that Supplier C is rated highest (6.45), followed by Supplier B (6.10), and then by Supplier A (5.80). If a decision is made to buy only from one source, Supplier C would be selected. If, however, the decision is made to reduce to two suppliers, then Supplier A would be eliminated from consideration.

Notice that none of the three could really be considered a poor supplier of the needed part. This is logical in that all three have been current suppliers over the past three years, which explains why all were rated 7 on product quality. Vendor analysis such as this is possible because business customers are now able to track supplier performances and thus have little difficulty in evaluating their suppliers in such a manner. For the marketing manager, it is imperative that he or she know the criteria used by each present and prospective customer and develop marketing strategies to accommodate those criteria. In this example, the marketing manager for Supplier A may well have underestimated the importance to the customer of average delivery time and delivery time variability, with the result being the loss of a customer.

In analyzing a new supplier, an organization looks at the vendor's financial and managerial capabilities, its technical and engineering abilities, and its manufacturing strengths. These are commonly assessed by a team composed of rep-

TABLE 5.4 Vendor Analysis Using a Weight/Rate Approach

Factor	Weight	Supplier A	Supplier B	Supplier C
Product quality	.30	7	7	7
Average delivery time	.25	5	6	6
Delivery time variability	.10	6	7	7
Price	.15	5	6	5
Rush orders	.10	4	4	7
Returns policy	.10	7	5	7

Rating code: 7 = Very Satisfactory Performance; 1 = Very Unsatisfactory Performance.

resentatives of the firm's purchasing, engineering, manufacturing, and finance departments. A small order may then be placed to test the supplier's capabilities.

Financial strength might be assessed through financial rating services or credit evaluations. Typically, a detailed analysis of the prospective vendor's structures, policies, procedures, and organizational culture assists the purchaser in determining managerial strengths. In a typical approach used by organizations in business markets, the following might take place. Engineering evaluates the potential supplier's technical and engineering strengths. The supplier's manufacturing strengths are assessed through plant visits by the purchasing company's personnel. Additionally, purchasing companies look at such things as geographic location, capacity in relation to the present level of business, and relation to other purchasers who may be competitors.

Analyzing Existing Suppliers for Partnership Status

When a purchasing company wishes to evaluate existing suppliers to determine which might be considered for **partnership status,** a formal analysis similar to the analysis of untried vendors is often performed for existing vendors. The difference lies in the informal information that is available to a purchaser after working with a supplier. Interdepartmental teamwork can uncover a great deal of information about a supplier's sales force, delivery habits, and product quality. Since a purchasing organization is attempting to weed out either unproductive or costly relationships, extremely high standards are expected of partnership status suppliers. Of course the level of these standards depends on the level of standards within the purchasing company for its own operations.

Vendor Performance Evaluation

Ongoing and regular performance evaluations are important considerations in overall vendor analysis. The daily personal contact between users and purchasers in small organizations often provides informal feedback on supplier performance. This in turn steers the supplier–purchaser relationship toward either mutual satisfaction or complete severance. In larger organizations, such evaluations tend to be more formal and require feedback from a number of involved departments. A simple vendor rating system evaluates performance based on price, delivery, quality, and service. Table 5.5 provides an example of one vendor's point rating system. Note that this company uses four factors (quality, delivery, price, and service), weights those factors by importance, measures performance, and then develops an overall rating. In the table, the vendor receives a rating of 92.9 out of a possible 100 points, which indicates a relatively strong rating by the buying organization.

Those purchasing organizations that are committed to improving their performances in their markets will look closely at a supplier's defect percentage, percent of improvement, percent of reduction in manufacturing cycle, and percent of reduction in costs. To facilitate an understanding of poor supplier perfor-

TABLE 5.5   Example of a Vendor Rating System in Business Markets

Factor	Weight	How Measured	Vendor Performance Past 12 Months	Rating
Quality	40	1% defective subtracts 5%	0.8% defective	$\dfrac{40(100 - (0.8 \times 5))}{100} = 38.4$
Delivery	30	1 day late subtracts 1%	average 3 days late	$\dfrac{30(100 - (3 \times 1))}{100} = 29.1$
Price	20	$\dfrac{\text{lowest price paid}}{\text{price charged}}$	$\dfrac{\$46}{\$50}$	$\dfrac{20\left(\dfrac{46}{50} \times 100\right)}{100} = 18.4$
Service	10	good = 100% fair = 70% poor = 40%	fair = 70%	$\dfrac{10(70)}{(100)} = 7.0$
Total Points	100		Vendor Rating	92.9

Source: Reprinted by permission from Michael R. Leenders, Harold E. Fearon, and Wilbur B. England, *Purchasing and Materials Management,* 9th ed. (Homewood, IL: Irwin, 1989), 246.

mance, a buying organization seeking to develop suppliers into world-class or partner status might conduct a supplier survey to determine areas of dissatisfaction on the part of the supplier. Once these areas are identified, a partner-seeking purchaser will work to resolve disputes that reduce both quality and productivity.

A good example of this is the Supplier Rating and Incentive Program (SRIP) developed by Rockwell International Corporation's Defense Electronics Group.[13] In this system, Rockwell identifies "events" that result in buyer overt actions or overt identifiable money costs. These include source inspection rejection, paperwork rejection, receiving inspection rejection, rework at Rockwell, returns to suppliers, issuance of corrective action letters, interim undershipments, early receipts, overshipments, and late shipments. Rockwell then assigns man-hours per each event and multiplies them by their hourly manufacturing costs. For example, the firm found it cost $275 to return something to a supplier, $120 for a late shipment, etc. Using this system, Rockwell analyzed each supplier's past twelve-month performance and developed a Supplier Performance Index (SPI) for each. This SPI permits the firm to determine each supplier's true cost of nonquality. This system has enough merit that it has been adopted by many other organizations, including Motorola, Hamilton Standard, Honeywell, Ford Aerospace, General Dynamics, Hughes Aircraft, Litton Data Systems, Sunstrand, Simmons Precision, and Northrup.

As this discussion has shown, vendor analysis has become very sophisticated in business markets and business marketers cannot ignore it in their marketing strategies. Mistakes can haunt the marketing manager for years in the future, as the following quote illustrates: "The purchasing manager knows exactly what he purchased from you last year, and the year before, what he paid for it, and also how long you took to deliver it."[14] As business markets move more and more to JIT and reduce their number of suppliers, it should be apparent that vendor analysis will play a major part in determining who becomes a supplying partner and who will no longer be used.

Purchasing Systems

In business markets, purchasing organizations that are trying to develop partnering relationships with select suppliers rely heavily on relationship building and systems development. Many of the links between buyer and seller take the form of quality partnerships or strategic alliances. These subjects will be covered in more detail in Chapter 7. Here, the systems that make the new links possible will be examined. In efforts to market products to more selective organizational purchasers, the ability to link systems may be the competitive advantage that allows one supplier to edge out all others and end up on the customer's preferred vendor list. One of the first places an organization looks to improve its purchasing and **materials management** function is at systems that closely track inventory.

Inventory Management   **Inventory management** in many organizations today has become a concentrated effort to reduce warehoused inventory levels, to better estimate production needs, and to increase the frequency of deliveries. Combined with these are efforts to reduce set-up time, improve just-in-time (JIT) systems, reduce order costs, and install electronic data interchanges (EDI).

In organizations in business markets, inventories exist for many purposes including:

1. To provide and maintain good customer service.
2. To smooth the flow of goods through the production process.
3. To provide protection against the uncertainties of supply and demand.
4. To obtain reasonable utilization of people and equipment.

Very simply, for every item carried in inventory, the costs of having it must be less than the cost of not having it. The main types of inventory costs are: (1) carrying, holding, or possession costs; (2) ordering or purchase costs; (3) setup costs; (4) stockout costs; and (5) price variation costs.[15]

As was introduced in Chapter 4, manufacturers in business markets may use either a **materials requirement planning (MRP)** model or an economic order quantity (EOQ) model for determining reorder timing and amounts. Building on what was developed in the preceding chapter, MRP differs from the EOQ-type system in a number of important ways, which are summarized below:[16]

MRP system	*EOQ-type system*
Product/component-oriented	Part-oriented (every item)
Dependent (derived) demand	Independent demand
Discrete/lumpy demand	Continuous item demand

No lead time	Continuous lead time
Time-phased order signal	Reorder point signal
Future production base	Historical demand base
Forecast end-items only	Forecast all items
Quantity- and time-based	Quantity-based
Safety stock for end-items	Safety stock for all items

These factors illustrate basic differences between the two inventory management systems. For example, when inventory stock of an item runs low enough to reach a reorder point, it is replenished under the EOQ approach. Under an MRP system, however, items are replenished only when they are needed as determined by the master production schedule. EOQ models, based on historical usage, provide high customer service while optimizing the balance between setup and carrying costs. MRP systems, in contrast, support the activities of manufacturing or maintenance by ordering parts based on forecasts and customer orders.

The tight control required by MRP requires more centralized purchasing and storing functions as well as highly accurate purchasing records. The on-time delivery required by MRP demands a high level of cooperation from suppliers. Purchasers have begun to educate their suppliers and evaluate suppliers' systems based on their ability to deliver under a highly fluctuating demand curve.

The integrating and forward-looking nature of MRP creates more specialization in the purchasing department. This specialization is based on finished product line outputs rather than on the raw material inputs of an EOQ system. For the business marketer, this requires an understanding of end products sold by customers as well as his or her own company's input products.

Just-in-Time (JIT)

The topic of just-in-time or JIT was also introduced in the previous chapter but it will be discussed here from a purchasing perspective. In contrast to MRP, Japanese manufacturers have developed their own means of achieving many of the goals of MRP—reduced inventories, high service coverage, and low manufacturing lead time. They have accomplished this through the use of just-in-time (JIT) production methods. JIT production means that components and raw materials arrive at a work center exactly as they are needed, which greatly reduces work-in-process inventory. The goals of JIT production are similar to those of MRP—providing the right part at the right place at the right time—but the ways of achieving these goals are radically different. Whereas MRP is computer-based, JIT is industrial engineering-based.

JIT is ideal for production systems with a relatively small product line produced repetitively with reasonably level loading. It is, however, not a good technique for job shops with many nonstandard products or for manufacturers of wide product lines. In these cases, EOQ and MRP are probably better techniques, but there are many JIT features that are good practice in any operation.

JIT depends heavily on workers and suppliers to deliver exceptionally high-quality products, processes, and parts. Responsibility for quality rests with the marketer of the products purchased and not with the buyer's quality control department. Thus, purchasers will reject marginally unacceptable items and will visit a supplier's plant frequently to check quality on the production line for themselves. In addition, workers rather than inspectors actually control the production process quality.

The use of JIT has grown in the United States since 1980 when the auto industry began to implement the concept. A survey of 400 companies revealed that nearly 65 percent were either using JIT or planning to adopt it.[17] Another study of JIT implementation in the United States looked at 131 companies and found that 108, or 82 percent, were using JIT, and another 10 percent were considering using it.[18] As Figure 5.4 shows, indications are that this concept will continue to grow in use by manufacturers in business markets.

JIT has some important marketing ramifications that will be developed in Chapter 14, which covers physical distribution strategies in marketing. Here, however, certain points are important. Marketing to customers who use JIT or

FIGURE 5.4   **Changes in JIT Shipments Between 1988 and 1995**

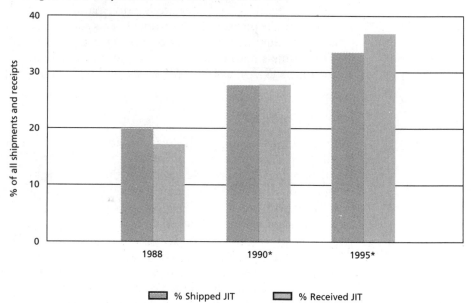

* Projected figures for 1990 and 1995.

Source: Reprinted by permission from Bernard J. LaLonde, Martha C. Cooper, and Thomas G. Noordwier, *Customer Service: A Management Perspective* (Oak Brook, IL: Council of Logistics Management, 1988), Question III.C.1.

MRP systems requires efficient and up-to-date physical distribution systems. In addition, the concept forces much closer relationships between the business marketing firm and the customer. For example, to meet a customer's production schedule requires that the marketing company understand and adapt to that schedule.

In actuality, use of JIT should lead to better relationships in the marketplace. It offers many opportunities for buyer and seller to cooperate with each other. Exhibit 5.4 illustrates this in the case of Caterpillar, which actually trains its suppliers in what it calls its Quality Institute. On the other hand, JIT firms tolerate few, if any, delays to maintain straight rebuy orders. Late deliveries, backorders, and stockorders are simply not acceptable. In addition, JIT requires that existing price structures be analyzed. More inventory and quality risks are downstreamed to suppliers. Unless a business marketing firm is able to manage a similarly based inventory management system, its costs will increase more rapidly than its prices. The business marketer cannot pass on large increases in distribution and inventory costs to a customer and price as it did before the buyer switched to JIT. This point will be developed in more detail in Chapter 14.

EXHIBIT 5.4   **Integrating Suppliers into the Buying Firm's JIT System**

Much of the push toward JIT delivery and EDI information link-ups leave suppliers uninspired. The requirements of faster information and delivery flows shift much of the risk onto suppliers who are required to perform within a shorter time frame with much higher-quality merchandise. While the economic climate and moves by many purchasers toward downsized supplier lists should encourage suppliers to strengthen ties to larger purchasers, sometimes the pace and level of technological changes are hard for suppliers to keep up with.

Many companies are offering support for their key suppliers through training programs. Caterpillar's Quality Institute is one example of a supplier training program. As part of Caterpillar's supplier certification program, a team from Caterpillar's purchasing, quality, engineering, and manufacturing departments assesses and monitors suppliers' quality improvement plans. In order to remain certified, suppliers must obtain training in the areas identified by the Caterpillar team. While the supplier may choose where to obtain the training, Caterpillar offers a full array of courses as well as a training seminar for supplier representatives to learn to train other supplier personnel.

Classes began more than eleven years ago as part of an internal training program. Statistical applications courses are at the core of the program. The seminars give participants tools to diagnose, correct, and implement continuous quality improvement programs at their own companies. The courses give suppliers the skills to compete in the world of JIT and EDI, where quality and process control can make or break a company.

Source: Adapted from Shirley Cayer, "Welcome to Caterpillar's Quality Institute," *Purchasing* 102 (August 16, 1990): 81–84.

Electronic Data Interchange (EDI)

One way for the business marketing firm to assist in the formation of more integrated relations with buyers is to develop the capability to provide direct electronic transmission of data and standard business forms. This allows the marketer and the customer to both obtain and provide much more timely and accurate information. It also facilitates greater administrative efficiency by reducing paperwork and raises the quality of decisions. The system commonly used for such communication is **electronic data interchange,** or EDI, which is defined as "the exchange of computer data between two or more companies." [19]

With the direct communications linkups to a supplier available through EDI, a buyer can obtain price quotes, determine availability of items in stock, transmit a purchase order, obtain follow-up information, provide information to the supplier about changes in purchase requirements brought on by schedule revisions, obtain service information, and send letters and memos. All of these tasks can be accomplished instantly, which serves to show why EDI is becoming the preferred way of communicating between customer and marketer in business markets. Figure 5.5 illustrates the increase in EDI use in business markets. Thus, the business marketing manager must become familiar with the use of EDI in rapidly changing manufacturer markets.

FIGURE 5.5 **Percent of Orders Transmitted EDI Between 1988 and 1995**

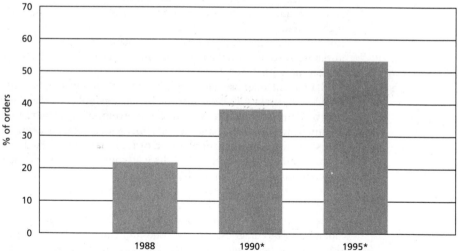

Source: Reprinted by permission from Bernard J. LaLonde, Martha C. Cooper, and Thomas G. Noordwier, *Customer Service: A Management Perspective* (Oak Brook, IL: Council of Logistics Management, 1988), Question III.C.1.

* Projected figures for 1990 and 1995.

An early and thorough guide to implementing EDI systems between buying and selling organizations in business markets claims that EDI makes five specific contributions to a customer's procurement strategy: (1) it will reduce paperwork; (2) it will reduce the need for personnel who do work that can be performed by EDI; (3) it will foster development of integrated and improved procurement and material management systems; (4) it will enhance the buying organization's capabilities and thus reduce total costs of doing business; and (5) it will provide a vehicle to integrate operations of both marketer and customer in their supply and manufacturing systems.[20] Exhibit 5.5 shows how J. C. Penney uses EDI in working with its many suppliers.

EXHIBIT 5.5   **Using Electronic Data Interchange (EDI) to Communicate with Suppliers**

Large retailers like J. C. Penney are paving the way for EDI and manufacturers are close behind. There are now more than 9,000 firms using EDI in the United States and that number is expected to double annually through 1993.

J. C. Penney is using EDI to tie together their quick response philosophy of merchandise buying, which expedites purchasing of retail goods. EDI allows buyers at J. C. Penney to buy more precisely with a better handle on what customers like and dislike. EDI sends orders to suppliers the day after they are created, compared to mailing a paper order, which could take up to ten days. EDI provides an advance-ship notice that lists what inventory the manufacturer has available. This gives stores the ability to compare advance-ship notices against their purchase orders to determine when and how much of the delivery to expect.

Ideally, point-of-sales (POS) data, including styles, colors, and sizes, feed into J. C. Penney's central systems. When inventory reaches a predetermined level, an electronic reorder purchase order is automatically triggered. The orders are available to suppliers the next day. This way, the manufacturer can determine (and notify his raw materials supplier via EDI) which styles, colors, and sizes are in demand and which are not. When suppliers have a limited quantity of goods available for shipment, the order that arrives first is filled first, so retailers who order with EDI will have the edge over competitors who do not.

By the end of 1990, J. C. Penney planned to have 1,000 of its 5,000 active suppliers on EDI. As of March 1990, about 300 suppliers were transmitting or receiving at least one transaction via EDI. According to William L. Lane, manager of electronic data interchange for J. C. Penney, "Our goal is to get 95 percent of our suppliers up and using EDI, but I'd prefer 100 percent." Major suppliers such as Levi Strauss, Fieldcrest, Totes, Cannon, Vanity Fair, Samsonite, and Mattel are leading the way in EDI usage.

In addition, J. C. Penney is supplied by many smaller regional and seasonal suppliers. Most of these may never implement EDI and may not need to if their product is especially unique with proven demand. If two companies offer similar lines and one participates in EDI while the other does not, J. C. Penney's buyers will be inclined to choose the EDI-active supplier.

Source: Adapted from Susan Zimmerman, "Sold on EDI," *Purchasing* 102 (May 17, 1990): 86–87.

Transportation Systems

Under JIT, not only is order information being relayed more quickly but products are being delivered in smaller shipments, more often, and at specific times. This was discussed in the preceding chapter and illustrated in Tables 4.7 and 4.8. Transportation decisions thus become more complex as the number of shipments increases and accurate delivery time becomes vital. This in turn means that transportation decisions are crucial to how well a business marketer meets customer expectations. This topic will also be covered in detail in Chapter 14, but it is useful here to understand the importance of transportation systems from the buyer's point of view.

Often, the buyer will wish to specify how purchased items are to be shipped. This is the buyer's legal right if the purchase has been made under any FOB origin terms such as FOB origin or FOB origin freight prepaid and charged back. If the purchaser has received superior past service from a particular carrier, that carrier is often the preferable means of shipment. Or if a carrier has been particularly helpful in assisting the shipper in the past, it may be preferred. As might be expected, many buyers are most concerned that the carrier used meet its delivery promises and provide the service without damaging the goods. Thus, buyers will often require that the marketing firm ship via a certain carrier or that a certain carrier should not be used.

Information Systems

In order to facilitate the changes taking place in U.S. manufacturing, purchasing departments are relying heavily on new information systems that go beyond simply organizing paperflow and order processing to managing information about raw materials markets and vendors. Purchasing procedures are established by business customers and prospects basically to process inputs of information from outside the purchasing function and to produce outputs of information needed by departments and other functional areas within the organization as well as institutions outside the purchasing firm. A good example of this can be seen in the system developed by the Hydrokinetix company of Drifting, Pennsylvania. The company uses an integrated manufacturing and accounting software package that allows it to track vendor performance as well as inventory, production, and costs. In an environment where production is keyed to the lowest inventory levels possible, timely delivery of raw materials from vendors is crucial. With the system, the required shipping date is entered on each purchase order, and the actual date the order is received at Hydrokinetix is posted in the system. This system also tracks the quality of material delivered by suppliers and allows the company to review a historical analysis of consistently high-quality deliveries. Using this approach, Hydrokinetix is able to track vendor performances as well as inventory, production, and costs.[21]

Few business functions have the breadth of contacts both within the organization and with the external environment that the well-operated purchasing department has. Purchasing receives information from planning, sales (forecasting), budgeting, accounting, legal, engineering, production, inventory control, quality control, and new products. As Figure 5.6 shows, purchasing also sends information to top management, engineering, product development, marketing,

FIGURE 5.6   Information Flows to and from the Purchasing Department

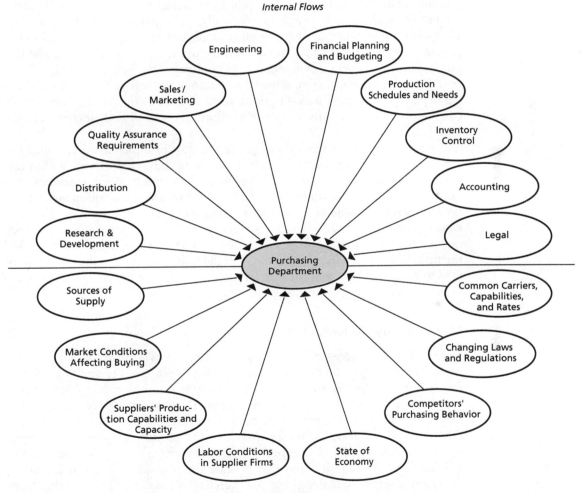

Source: Adapted from Michael R. Leenders, Harold E. Fearon, and Wilbur B. England, *Purchasing and Materials Management,* 9th ed. (Homewood, IL: Irwin, 1989), 105, 109.

production, legal, finance, and accounting. Thus, it can be seen that purchasing is constantly communicating information to and receiving it from many different sources. This implies a need for an effective communication system if all this information is to pass smoothly and quickly.

An efficiently operated purchasing department is one of the firm's major points of contact with the external world. Information obtained includes general market conditions, sources of supply, suppliers' capacity, production rates, labor conditions, pricing, transportation availability and rates, and product information. Using an up-to-date information system allows a purchaser to organize this information flow to better manage the purchasing process as well as relationships with outside suppliers. Typically, principal sources of vendor information are supplier catalogs (both printed and microfilm), trade journals, advertisements, vendor and commodity directories, sales presentations, and the purchasing department's own records. In contemporary business markets, current database, materials management, and accounting software permit purchasing departments quicker access to more accurate information on vendors, which can then be used to monitor suppliers' performance as well as their current capabilities and prices.

As purchasing departments organize the flow of information and make it available to other departments, their influence on buying decisions within the organization will likely increase. This means that the business marketer will need to focus more time and effort on its production and distribution qualities in order to positively influence purchasing's image of the marketing firm. The purchasing department may be much more inclined to use a supplier whose product quality and delivery capabilities are appreciated by the using departments within the firm. This will be discussed in detail in the following chapter, but it is important to recognize here that the purchasing department is but one element in an organization's buying of needed goods and services.

Make-or-Buy Considerations

The marketing manager in business markets often faces a constraint not faced by consumer marketers. Some organizational customers have the ability to manufacture a needed product instead of purchasing that same product from outside suppliers. This decision is called the customer's **make-or-buy** decision, and it may occur at different stages in the buying process. For example, the organization may find that there are no suppliers who can produce to their specifications or who are interested in doing so. Purchasing departments may also find that the bids received are too high and that making the product in-house is a feasible alternative. When these things happen, purchasing may end up not buying from any supplier, which means that the marketing company that is attempting to sell finds itself in the usual situation of having to compete with the prospective customer.

Typically, the prospective purchasing company computes the cost of producing the product in-house. The purchasing department then compares this cost with the costs of buying from outside suppliers. Normally, five costs are involved in manufacturing the product: (1) direct materials costs, (2) factory supplies costs, (3) direct labor costs, (4) indirect labor costs, and (5) factory overhead costs.[22] If the cost of making a product is cheaper than the cost of buying it, the buying company ends the buying process.

Although lower cost may be the major reason why organizations in business markets make rather than buy, it is not the only one. Other reasons include utilizing excess plant capacity, assuring control over supply, protecting trade secrets, and broadening the base for overhead absorption.[23] Despite these reasons, however, the use of outside suppliers is increasing in most business markets. A *Purchasing* magazine survey found that organizational buyers are more likely to use outside suppliers than to produce themselves because of high domestic labor costs, uncertainty of availability of key components, inventory restraints, and concerns over product quality.[24]

The marketing implications of the make-or-buy decision are many. To illustrate, the marketer must be able to determine the customer's cost to produce in order to price effectively. Additionally, any promotional efforts must communicate the benefits of buying and the problems involved in manufacturing in-house. If the business marketing manager is unable to convince a prospect to buy rather than make, the result may be the loss of a customer.

THE IMPORTANCE OF THE PURCHASING PROFESSIONAL TO THE BUSINESS MARKETER

Whether or not the purchasing department has a great deal or only a small amount of influence on the customer organization's buying decisions, the purchasing professional is important to the business marketer for many reasons. In many instances, the purchasing professional may have actual line authority to purchase goods and services. When this happens, he or she must be considered as very important and cannot be ignored by any marketing firm. In other cases, the purchasing professional may not have the authority to determine what will or will not be purchased, but he or she may be able to select the supplier. One study found that 56 percent of all requisitions received by purchasing departments do not specify the manufacturer.[25] This means that the buyer is in a position to determine which particular supplier should get the order. Table 5.6 shows how often this happens in different industries. As can be seen, there is some variance according to product type but the table also shows that high percentages of requisitions from using departments are sent to purchasing without a particular supplier being named. This, of course, means that the purchasing department may well select the supplier to be used. When this happens, the business marketer must view the purchasing professional as very important. Table

TABLE 5.6   Selected Characteristics Related to Purchasing in Business Markets

Product Type	# of Monthly Requisitions Received by Purchasing	% of Requisitions Received by Purchasing Where Manufacturer's Name Is Suggested	Mean Number of Manufacturers on Approved Source List
Materials	13.0	24.1%	5.0
Power transmission	6.9	45.5%	3.4
Mechanical components	11.7	31.7%	4.2
Electrical components	8.1	47.6%	3.3
Hydraulic & pneumatic components	4.0	55.8%	3.4
Production supplies	6.6	49.5%	3.3
Plant & MRO equipment	3.8	42.1%	3.4
Packaging & marketing materials	8.3	45.4%	2.7
Safety & health products	4.6	45.1%	3.1
Office equipment	3.7	46.4%	3.0
Materials handling	.6	47.1%	4.6
Miscellaneous	2.2	57.3%	3.1

Source: Reprinted by permission from *Cahners Advertising Research Report,* Nos. 551.1A, 551.3A, 551.4A (Boston: Cahners Publishing Company, 1984).

5.6 shows another reason why purchasing is important to the business marketing firm. Many buying organizations have an approved source list of suppliers and the purchasing department often plays a major role in developing such a list. In addition, the purchasing professional may make recommendations to other departments regarding which brands might be purchased or excluded from consideration in the purchase decision. In other cases, the purchasing professional may be the only person who is accessible to the marketer. This is often true in the case of new prospects. At still other times, the buyer may refer the marketer or the field salesperson to others within the buying organization who will actually make the decision. Finally, in many organizations today the marketer must work with the purchasing department to set up and maintain a partnering relationship between buyer and seller. The business marketer must understand how customers and prospects purchase goods and services and a thorough understanding of the organization's purchasing function is a logical first step. Many times, the buying organization prepares a guide to aid present and potential suppliers in better understanding how its purchasing function works. Exhibit 5.6 provides an example of such a guide and shows purchasing's involvement at Hewlett–Packard Company. Guides such as these may be very useful to business marketing firms and provide a start to better understanding how particular organizations buy their goods and services.

EXHIBIT 5.6   Information Available on How Purchasing Departments Operate in Business Markets

Hewlett–Packard Company publishes a supplier's information guide entitled "Selling to Hewlett–Packard Company." This guide, which the company provides to present and prospective suppliers, provides information that gives insight to the company's purchasing processes and procedures. This information can be used by business marketing firms to more effectively market their goods and services to Hewlett–Packard.

Each Hewlett–Packard product division functions independently. For example, production buyers have the responsibility for buying HP part-numbered components and they also manage the inventory levels of such components. Requisition buyers purchase all special or non-part-numbered items such as maintenance supplies, services, etc. Subcontract buyers place subcontracts for fabrication, machining assembly, and other process operations when such are used. In addition, most divisions have material engineering departments that are responsible for reviewing all suppliers before they are added to the firm's approved supplier lists. Finally, the company also has a central staff, called corporate materials management, that works with the divisions in (1) developing and maintaining policies, standards, and documentation of purchased goods and services; (2) negotiating and maintaining companywide contracts for commonly used products or services; and (3) developing policies and objectives concerning supplier relations. Corporate materials management serves as the focal point for coordinating activities between Hewlett–Packard and its suppliers. This type of information, which is exclusively published for and made available to present and prospective suppliers, is most useful to the business marketing manager in learning more about the manner in which this particular firm purchases goods and services. With this type of information, the marketer can better develop and implement strategy for marketing to the firm.

Source: Adapted from *Selling to Hewlett–Packard Company* (Palo Alto, CA: Hewlett–Packard Company, 1980), 3.

CHAPTER SUMMARY

This chapter has focused on the purchasing professionals and departments in organizational customers and prospects. The role of purchasing in organizational buying was explored and the objectives and strategies of purchasing departments were examined. Five major strategies were reviewed; they can be categorized as assured supply, cost reduction, supply support, environmental change, and competitive edge. Stages in the development of purchasing departments were also analyzed for their effects on business marketing firms. The chapter then looked at specific areas of purchasing responsibilities and actions such as negotiation, value analysis, and vendor analysis. The manners in which these take place were reviewed for their possible implications for the business marketing manager. Purchasing systems in use in business markets were then examined. These included inventory management, just-in-time (JIT), electronic data interchange (EDI), transportation systems, information systems, and make-or-buy situations. Finally, the importance of the purchasing professional to the business marketer was explored in terms of better understanding how organizations in business markets purchase needed goods and services. The following chapter will discuss organizational buying behavior in detail and help illustrate how purchasing fits into this process.

KEY TERMS

electronic data interchange (EDI)
inventory management
make-or-buy
materials management
materials requirement planning (MRP)
negotiation
partnership status

purchasing
purchasing department
purchasing professional
purchasing strategy
value analysis
vendor analysis

QUESTIONS

1. Why have purchasing departments begun to downsize supplier lists? How do you believe that smaller inventories and smaller lists of approved suppliers will be detrimental to business marketing firms?

2. How would a firm's marketing approach to a customer whose purchasing function is in the basic financial planning stage differ from its approach to another customer in the strategic planning stage of purchasing?

3. Why should the business marketer consider the purchasing professional as such an instrumental part of business marketing strategy and tactics?

4. Explain why there is a tendency on the part of some business marketing managers and field salespeople to look at purchasing people simply as gatekeepers? Why is this a dangerous view in contemporary business marketing?

5. Some business marketing customers use vendor analysis to determine the capabilities of prospective suppliers both for purchasing individual goods or services and for certifying some suppliers as "quality supplying partners." Explain how the vendor analysis process would differ in these two situations.

6. In contemporary business markets, there is a tendency in many organizations to view their purchasing departments as "outside manufacturing managers." Explain what this statement means and then relate its meaning to the business marketing manager.

7. Purchasing functions in business markets traditionally focused on buying the goods and services needed by other departments within an organization. In recent years, however, the functions of purchasing have changed dramatically. What changes have taken place and how do they affect the business marketing firm?

8. Assume that an existing customer is switching from buying on an EOQ basis to purchasing for a JIT situation. How would the purchasing function change and how would this affect the marketing manager in the firm now supplying this customer?

9. Explain the difference between vendor analysis and value analysis and then show how each affects marketing strategy and tactics in business markets.

10. At one time, relationships between business marketing firms and customer purchasing departments were considered by many to be adversarial. Today, these relationships are often more in the form of partnerships between the two. Explain what factors have brought about such a change and then relate what all this means to the business marketing manager.

NOTES

1. Charles A. Koepke, *Plant Production Control,* 3d ed. (New York: Wiley, 1961), 60.
2. *The Kiplinger Washington Letter* (August 30, 1985), 3.
3. See Ernest Raia, "JIT Delivery: Redefining 'On-Time'," *Purchasing* 109 (September 13, 1990): 64–76.
4. Michael R. Leenders, Harold E. Fearon, and Wilbur B. England, *Purchasing and Materials Management,* 9th ed. (Homewood, IL: Irwin, 1989), 618.
5. Tom Stundza, "Can Supplier Ratings Be Standardized?" *Purchasing* 109 (November 8, 1990): 60.
6. J. William Semich and Somerby Dowst, "How to Push Your Everyday Suppliers into World Class Status," *Purchasing* 101 (August 17, 1989): 76.
7. See Virginia T. Freeman and Joseph L. Cavinato, "Positioning Purchasing," *Marketplace: The ISBM Review* (Fall 1989): 1–4.
8. See Frederick W. Gluck, Stephen P. Kaufman, and Stephen Walleck, "Strategic Management for Competitive Advantage," *Harvard Business Review* 58 (July–August 1980): 154–161.
9. Anne Millen, "How Effective Is Purchasing?" *Purchasing* 102 (October 25, 1990): 58.
10. See Joseph M. Juran, *Juran on Planning for Quality* (New York: Free Press, 1988); W. Edward Deming, *Out of the Crisis: Quality, Productivity and Competitive Position* (Cambridge, MA: MIT Center for Advanced Engineering Study, 1986); W. E. Deming, P. B. Crosby, J. M. Juran, and A. V. Feigenbaum, "Preaching of Quality Gurus: Do It Right the First Time," *Electronic Business* 15 (October 16, 1989): 88–89.
11. Donald W. Dobler, Lamar Lee, Jr., and David N. Burt, *Purchasing and Materials Management,* 4th ed. (New York: McGraw-Hill, 1984), 310.
12. Somerby Dowst, "VA '86: Buyers Say VA Is More Important Than Ever," *Purchasing* 105 (June 26, 1986): 67.
13. Stundza, op. cit.
14. Milt Ellenbogen, "The Changing Face of Purchasing," *Industrial Distribution* 75 (September 1986): 36.
15. See Dobler, Lee, and Burt, op. cit.
16. R. J. Tersine, *Principles of Inventory and Materials Management* (New York: Elsevier Science Publishing, 1983), 311.
17. Albert F. Celley, William H. Cless, Arthur W. Smith, and Mark A. Vonderembse, "Implementation of JIT in the United States," *Journal of Purchasing and Materials Management* 22 (Winter 1986): 13.
18. Ibid.
19. Daniel J. Biby, "EDI Software: Do You Have What You Need?" *Transportation & Distribution* (April 1990): 22.
20. Robert M. Monczka and Joseph R. Carter, *Electronic Data Interchange: Managing Implementation in a Purchasing Environment* (East Lansing, MI: Graduate School of Business Administration, Michigan State University, 1987), 3–4.
21. John Shaughnessy, "Tracking Vendor Performance Along with Inventory," *Automation* (June 1990): 52–53.
22. Robert W. Haas and Thomas R. Wotruba, "Marketing Strategy in a Make-or-Buy Situation," *Industrial Marketing Management* 5 (June 1976): 65–76.
23. See George Risley, *Modern Industrial Marketing* (New York: McGraw-Hill, 1972), 83–84.
24. "Industrial Newsletter," *Sales & Marketing Management* 135 (July 1987): 38.
25. Arch G. Woodside and Daniel L. Sherrell, "New Replacement Part Buying," *Industrial Marketing Management* 9 (April 1980): 128.

SUGGESTED ADDITIONAL READINGS

Ellenbogen, Milt. "The Changing Face of Purchasing." *Industrial Distribution* 75 (September 1986): 36–40.

Farrell, Paul V. "Purchasing Into the '90s . . . and Beyond." *Purchasing World* (January 1990): 27–29.

Fearon, Harold E. *Purchasing Organizational Relationships.* Tempe, AZ: Center for Advanced Purchasing Studies, 1988.

Fiorentino, Patrick. "Buying in a Zero Defects Environment." *Purchasing World* (November 1989): 32–33.

Freeman, Virginia T., and Joseph L. Cavinato. "Positioning Purchasing." *Marketplace: The ISBM Review* (Fall 1989): 1–4.

Giunipero, Larry, and Gary Zenz. "Impact of Purchasing Trends on Industrial Marketers." *Industrial Marketing Management* 11 (1982): 17–23.

Gordon, Jay. "The Purchasing Manager in the 1990's." *Purchasing* 101 (January 1989): 46, 48.

Hahn, Chan K., Kyoo H. Kim, and Jong S. Kim. "Costs of Competition: Implications for Purchasing Strategy." *Journal of Purchasing and Materials Management* 22 (Fall 1986): 2–7.

Hahn, Chan K., Charles A. Watts, and Kee Young Kim. "The Supplier Development Program: A Conceptual Model." *Journal of Purchasing and Materials Management* 26 (Spring 1990): 2–7.

Heide, Jan B., and George John. "Alliances in Industrial Purchasing: The Determinants of Joint Action in Buyer–Seller Relationships." *Journal of Marketing Research* 27 (February 1990): 24–36.

Henke, John W., Jr., and William R. D. Martin. "Developing a Procurement Training Program." *Journal of Purchasing and Materials Management* 25 (Summer 1989): 26–34.

Leenders, Michael R., Harold J. Fearon, and Wilber B. England. *Purchasing and Materials Management,* 9th ed. Homewood, IL: Richard D. Irwin, 1989.

Modic, Stanley J. "This Is the Time: Value Analysis Evolves into Value Management." *Purchasing World* (February 1990): 32–38.

Morgan, James P., and Susan Zimmerman. "Status Report: Building World-Class Supplier Relationships." *Purchasing* 102 (August 16, 1990): 62–77.

O'Neal, Charles R. "JIT Procurement and Relationship Marketing." *Industrial Marketing Management* 18 (1989): 55–63.

Semich, J. William, and Somerby Dowst. "How to Push Your Everyday Supplier into World Class Status." *Purchasing* 101 (August 17, 1989): 74–80.

Shaughnessy, John. "Tracking Vendor Performance Along with Inventory." *Automation* (June 1990): 52–53.

Woodside, Arch G., and Niran Vyas. *Industrial Purchasing Strategies.* Lexington, MA: Lexington Books, 1987.

6

Organizational Buying Behavior

••

The preceding chapter detailed the many roles played by purchasing professionals and departments in the buying of goods and services by their organizations. This should not be construed to mean, however, that an understanding of purchasing and materials management in business markets is sufficient to fully appreciate what is involved when an organization buys goods or services. In most cases, the purchasing department does not directly use those goods and services even though it has responsibility for buying them. Many other departments may be involved, and these typically influence both the goods and services bought as well as the choice of suppliers. This means that the business marketing manager cannot simply focus his or her efforts on purchasing departments. Rather, the manager must develop an understanding of all that is entailed within a prospect organization both before and after the purchasing department is involved. As this suggests, organizational behavior is complex and adequately understanding what is involved is a prime responsibility of the business marketing manager. Without such an understanding, the marketing manager cannot develop effective marketing strategies and tactical programs. In addition, buying typically differs from organization to organization even when they buy similar products or services for similar reasons. The task, therefore, for the business marketer is to develop an approach for determining what is involved in organizational buying and then apply this approach to individual situations. Organizational buying is not simply the action someone takes; rather, it is the outcome of interactions between purchasing professionals, users of the products and services, others within the organization who may in one way or another influence what is being purchased, and suppliers. Viewed in this manner, buying is rarely an action in and of itself. More likely, organizational buying is a problem-solving stream of behaviors and those involved are differentiated by their function and position in that stream.[1] The business marketing manager

169

How Do Organizations Buy Goods and Services?

For the business marketing manager, determining how organizations actually buy goods and services and identifying who is involved in such buying are major marketing tasks. Insight to these issues can be gained from a survey entitled "A Survey of Industrial Buying," which was conducted by Business Marketing Research. This survey was based on responses from a large sample of subscribers to the trade publication *Industrial Equipment News*.

Some major findings of the survey can provide some understanding of the buying behavior of organizations in business markets. First, there is a growing trend toward team buying decisions involving more interdepartmental participation. Overall, an average of five buying influences are involved in such purchase decisions; this increases to six in organizations employing over 500. Buying organizations typically investigate an average of four suppliers when deciding to buy and then invite three of the four to submit proposals. In addition, the survey found that buying organizations now base their purchasing decisions on more product criteria than in the past. For example, buyers of non-capital-equipment products considered safety, product durability, and compatibility with existing production processes as the most important buying criteria. Thus, organizations buy in a manner that involves considerable group interaction and members of such groups seek rather precise product attributes when they buy or specify to buy. And, even though the movement to JIT is resulting in more single sourcing, the study indicates that organizations initiate contact with a number of potential suppliers before deciding which they will actually use.

Source: Adapted from Kate Bertrand, "Survey Finds Many 'Critical' Buying Criteria," *Business Marketing* 71 (April 1986): 30–31.

must understand that stream and know who is involved in each and every prospect and customer. While this would seem to be an almost impossible undertaking, it can be done and is being done.

This chapter builds on the previous one, expanding the focus beyond the purchasing and materials management function. To accomplish this, a review will be undertaken of models of organizational buying behavior. The emphasis will then be placed on understanding the organizational buying process itself—the process typically used by organizations in their buying of goods and services. Then, those personnel involved in that process will be analyzed. This will include a discussion of buying influences and buying centers and their impacts on organizational buying. Finally, the buying motives of those involved in the process will be examined. The chapter thus focuses primarily on how organizations buy, who is involved in that buying, and what are they seeking. These understandings will then provide a basis for much of what takes place in the chapters that follow.

MODELS OF ORGANIZATIONAL BUYING BEHAVIOR

The buying of goods and services by organizations is complex and difficult to analyze. Over the years, many models have been developed in attempts to explain **organizational buying behavior.** Critics complain, however, that little progress has been made in defining organizational buying behavior despite considerable research efforts.[2] There is concern that many of the models that have been developed lack replication—they have not been repeated to determine their durability over time.[3] In addition, many models have been developed on the basis of relatively small and possibly even nonrepresentative samples.[4] Nevertheless, a brief look at some of these models is in order because they are true attempts to better understand organizational buying, which is of paramount importance to the business marketing manager. These models fall into three basic classifications: task models, nontask models, and complex or joint models. Table 6.1 summarizes some of the better known models of each type.

Task models attempt to explain organizational buying behavior by focusing on variables that can be directly related to the purchasing decisions themselves. One of the most commonly used variables is price, and several task models use price as their base. For example, the Minimum Price Model assumes that the buyer has reasonably perfect knowledge of all buying choices available and simply buys the product or service from the supplier that offers the lowest price. The Reciprocal Buying Model explains buying behavior on the basis of reciprocity or trade relations between buyer and seller. These models are rather simplistic, and they typically ignore the personal characteristics of people involved, the interaction of these people, and the organizational structure.

TABLE 6.1 Summary of Models of Organizational Buying Behavior

Type of Model	Description	Examples
Task models	Task models attempt to explain organizational buying behavior by focusing on variables directly related to purchasing decisions	Minimum Price Model, Lowest Total Cost Model, Rational Buyer Model, Materials Management Model, Reciprocal Buying Model, Constrained Choice Model
Nontask models	Nontask models bring the human element into the organizational buying process and introduce noneconomic variables	Ego Enhancement Model, Perceived Risk Model, Dyadic Interaction Model, Lateral Relationship Model, Buying Influences Model, Diffusion Process Model
Complex or joint models	Complex or joint models consider more than a single variable or set of variables and may combine task and nontask models to better understand organizational buying	Decision Process Model, Competitive Activity (COMPACT) Model, Buygrid Model, Sheth Industrial Buyer Behavior Model, Webster and Wind Organizational Buying Behavior Model, Problem Solving Stream Model, Buyer's Decision Framing Process Model, Participation and Influence Model

Nontask models introduce the human element into organized business buying. They add noneconomic elements to the buying process. For example, the Dyadic Interaction Model focuses on the interaction between the buyer and the supplier's salesperson. The Diffusion Process Model views the buying company in light of its receptivity or lack of it in terms of buying new products and services. This model places the organization in the diffusion process by defining it as an innovator, early adopter, early majority, or laggard type of organization. The model then attempts to explain buying behavior based on where a particular organization is in this diffusion process. Nontask models focus heavily on the human element involved. The weakness of these models is that they focus on specific phenomena to the exclusion of everything else. To illustrate, cannot a buyer in a Dyadic Interaction Model also attempt to avert risk? Cannot that buyer also be one of many buying influences in a buying organization?

Complex or joint models attempt to consider more than a single variable or set of variables. Typically, they combine various task and nontask models to understand organizational buying behavior better. For example, the Buygrid Model was developed as a result of study by the Marketing Science Institute, which determined that the organizational buying process could be described by an eight-stage model. This model integrates eight buyphases with three buyclass situations—new task, modified rebuy, and straight rebuy. Since this model is one of the best known and most widely accepted, it is developed in detail later in the chapter.

These basic types of organizational buying behavior models are shown only to illustrate the research that has taken place in this area. If more information is desired, many sources can be consulted.[5] Understanding the manner in which organizations purchase goods and services is complex, and as can be seen, no single model sufficiently describes the process. Table 6.2 examines the many models and describes how each fits into current research based on various focuses within the organization.

Discussion of these models is worthwhile in that it points out variables that may be used to advantage by the marketing manager in business markets. At the same time, however, it should be recognized that these models clearly show a lack of general direction in the study of organizational buying behavior. In addition, many of them are highly descriptive in character and of limited use to the practicing business marketing manager. Nevertheless, they have contributed to research efforts in the area of organizational behavior.[6] Later in this chapter, we will examine some of the more recent contributions to this important area of business marketing.

The tasks for the business marketing manager, as well as the field salesperson, are then to: (1) determine the process by which organizations buy goods and services; (2) discover who in the customer organizations participates in this process and at what stage each becomes involved; (3) find out what each of those people is seeking from the purchase—what the buying motives are; and (4) discover what factors affect the interaction of participants in the process. Once these things are known and understood, the business marketing manager is in a

TABLE 6.2   Models of Business Buying Behavior Classified by Area of Research and Focus

Area of Research	Focus Is On	Specific Models Fitting into These Areas of Research
Individual correlates	Individual differences among organizational buyers and their impact on decision-making process	Constrained Choice Model, Ego Enhancement Model, Perceived Risk Model, Dyadic Interaction Model, Decision Process Model, Sheth Industrial Buyer Behavior Model, Webster & Wind Organizational Buying Behavior Model
Organizational correlates	Impact of organizational characteristics on organizational buyers' decision-making process	Lateral Relationships Model, Buying Influences Model, COMPACT Model, Decision Process Model, Webster & Wind Organizational Buying Behavior Model
Situation correlates	Distinct types of purchase situations that affect business buyers' decision processes	Decision Process Model, Webster & Wind Organizational Buying Behavior Model
Marketing communications	Impact of specific marketing communications efforts such as direct mail, trade shows, and press releases	Decision Process Model, Sheth Industrial Buyer Behavior Model
Decision-making processes	Buying decisions based on either the ultimate choice or outcome of a decision and/or on the sequential process or steps involved in buying products or services within a given decision or dynamic changes in the process	Minimum Price Model, Lowest Total Cost Model, Rational Buyer Model, Buying Influences Model, Diffusion Process Model, Decision Process Model, Sheth Industrial Buyer Behavior Model
Types of decisions	How and why organizations make various choices entailed in the purchasing function with emphasis on the types of decisions being made	Materials Management Model, Reciprocal Buying Model, Constrained Choice Model, Buygrid Model, Decision Process Model
Evaluation of buying tasks	Evaluating the buying task on a qualitative or quantitative basis	Buygrid Model

position to segment markets and develop and implement marketing strategies and tactical programs. Thus, an analysis of each of these factors is needed.

THE ORGANIZATIONAL BUYING PROCESS

Although there is no single format dictating how organizations actually purchase goods and services, a relatively standard process is followed in most situations. Figure 6.1 outlines the standard **organizational buying process**. Following through the figure, the standard buying process may be traced. For example, a department discovers or anticipates a problem in its operation that it believes

FIGURE 6.1   Conceptual Model of the Organizational Buying Process

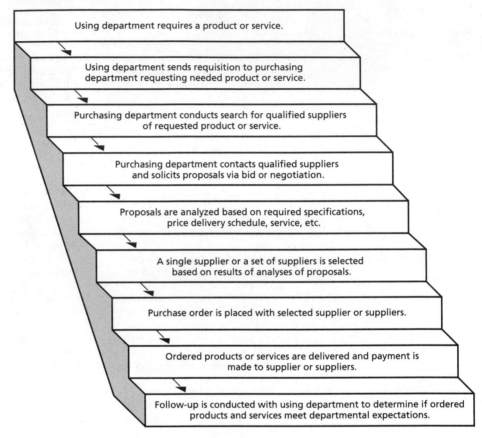

Using department requires a product or service.

Using department sends requisition to purchasing department requesting needed product or service.

Purchasing department conducts search for qualified suppliers of requested product or service.

Purchasing department contacts qualified suppliers and solicits proposals via bid or negotiation.

Proposals are analyzed based on required specifications, price delivery schedule, service, etc.

A single supplier or a set of suppliers is selected based on results of analyses of proposals.

Purchase order is placed with selected supplier or suppliers.

Ordered products or services are delivered and payment is made to supplier or suppliers.

Follow-up is conducted with using department to determine if ordered products and services meet departmental expectations.

may be solved by buying a certain product or service. The department head then draws up a requisition form describing the specifications of the product or service desired. He or she sends the requisition to the company's purchasing department. Based on the specifications required, the purchasing department searches for qualified sources of supply. When these sources are determined, proposals based on the specifications are solicited, received, and analyzed for such factors as price, delivery, and service. Proposal prices may be compared with the cost of producing the product in-house in a make-or-buy decision. If prices are too high compared to the cost of creating the product or service, the buying process may be terminated. If buying seems more feasible than making, the process continues. After proposals are analyzed, a supplier or a number of suppliers are selected. The purchase order is then placed, and copies of the purchase order are sent to the originating department, accounting, credit, and any other departments involved. After the product is shipped, received, and used, a follow-up with the originating department is conducted to determine how well the purchased product meets the needs of the using department. Although there may be variations in this process, this example typifies how business goods and services are purchased.

The model in Figure 6.1 typifies the manner in which organizational customers enact transactional purchases in that it reflects a single purchase, but the process also applies to longer-term or JIT purchases. As discussed in the preceding chapter, when organizations seek out suppliers for long-term buying relationships, they typically buy something from them first to test the process. When this happens, the process in Figure 6.1 certainly applies. However, once a decision is made to create a partnering relationship with a supplier, the process does not apply to each and every order. Thus, while JIT buying differs from transactional buying, the same process is still involved, although with modifications.

There are variations in the process that should be understood because they have marketing implications. For example, originating departments may or may not stipulate the specifications desired and they may or may not designate particular suppliers. In some cases, the using department knows exactly what it wants to purchase in terms of product or service specifications and it makes this known to the purchasing department in its requisition. In other cases, the desired product or service may be so generic that specifications are not needed. In addition, using departments sometimes stipulate which particular supplier's brand they want; in other cases they do not. As stated in the preceding chapter, 56 percent of all departmental requisitions do not specify the manufacturer.[7] Whatever happens, it affects the search for suppliers later in the process. A good example of this may be seen in the case of a particular hospital. Whenever a requisition from a physician recommends a specific brand or supplier, there may be no search for other possible suppliers because the purchasing department may be reluctant to choose a supplier other than the one the physician wanted. This logic may not apply, however, to requisitions received from department heads wanting to buy supplies, materials, etc. In these cases, purchasing may actively seek out suppliers.

Another variation in the process occurs where purchasing contacts possible suppliers. In some instances formal bids are requested, while in others a negotiating process takes place involving many meetings between supplier salespeople and purchasing personnel. Still another variation may take place when the buying organization finds no acceptable suppliers and decides to make the needed products rather than attempt to buy them. When this happens, the process essentially stops. Yet another variation occurs in the selection of suppliers. In some situations, the buying organization seeks to have a number of suppliers and will not sole source. In others, such as JIT situations, the move is toward the selection of one supplier only. As was discussed in Chapter 5, there is a movement toward more single sourcing, which also affects the buying process. Finally, the last step in the process is much more sophisticated today because of the widespread use of vendor analysis and value analysis by customers in business markets. All these variations of the basic model do not detract from the usefulness of Figure 6.1 in explaining how organizations buy goods and services. Rather, they show that while the buying process is relatively standardized, there are enough differences in individual practices to warrant researching the process used by each and every customer or prospect.

This basic process also is used by institutional and most governmental customers. Hospitals, for example, purchase goods and services in much the same manner, once the authorization to buy has been obtained. Most school systems and local governments use variations of this process. Figure 6.2 illustrates the buying process typically used by many state and local governmental customers. The figure shows how a product is purchased and how the using department, purchasing department, and suppliers are involved in the process. Although there are some variations, it can be seen that the process is quite similar to that outlined in Figure 6.1.

The process is somewhat similar for federal government purchases such as in the Department of Defense (DOD). Here, an agency component such as the Strategic Air Command (SAC) desires a new product or wishes to upgrade an existing product with new technology. SAC submits a mission need statement for approval at a higher level within the DOD. If approval is obtained and budgeting authority is granted, alternative products are considered and a preferred supplier is selected. Except for the first few steps, the process is similar to that found in civilian industry.[8] Figure 6.3 illustrates the buying process used by customers in federal government markets. The same process occurs in most instances of organizational buying in other countries, although differing national regulations may cause some variations. For example, one study compared the buying processes in Canada and Hungary using components, equipment, and materials. While the study found differences in who was involved in the process and the level of influence exerted by those involved, the whole buying process for all three categories of products was handled in a similar fashion in both countries.[9] All this supports the argument that the organizational buying process is relatively standardized in most areas of business marketing.

Marketing Implications in the Buying Process

The real importance of the buying process to the business marketing manager is that it shows how customers make a purchasing decision and what must be done if the company's product or service is to be considered and ultimately purchased. Two considerations are vital. First, the manager must recognize that such a process exists for every organizational customer. Second, the manager must involve the company's marketing efforts in the process as early as possible if it is to be considered as a supplier of the required product or service. As will be developed throughout this text, the marketing firm has a better chance of getting the order if its salespeople are involved in the first step of the process than if they become involved later in the process. The reason is not difficult to understand. If the marketing manager or the company salesperson or both can become involved in

FIGURE 6.2

The Buying Process Used by State and Local Governmental Customers

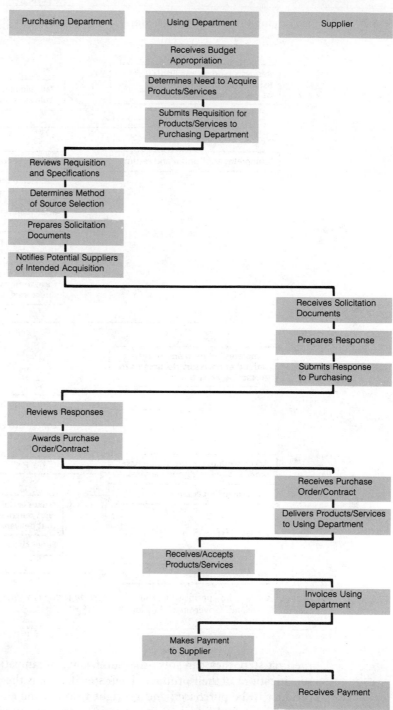

Source: Reprinted by permission of Lallatin & Associates from Carla S. Lallatin, "Sales Opportunities in State and Local Government Markets," *Agency Sales Magazine* 17 (February 1987):52.

FIGURE 6.3   The Buying Process Used in Federal Government Markets

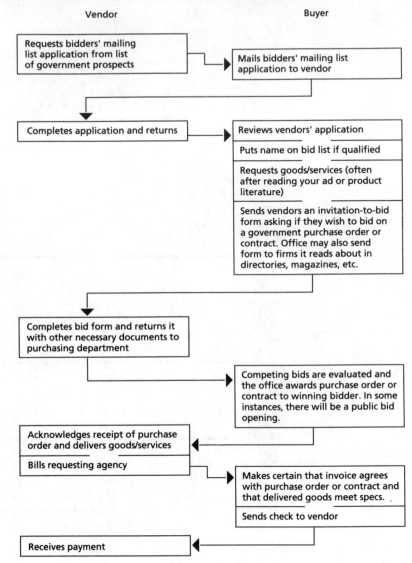

Source: Reprinted by permission from *Introduction to the Government Market: Local, State, and Federal* (Cleveland: Government Product News, 1990), 17.

the first step, they can solve the purchasing organization's problem around the specifications of their product. Their specifications then become the basis for the product to be purchased and go right through the entire process. Unless competitors can duplicate these specifications, they may not be considered, although, of course, they may convince the buying firm to change specifications later. In most cases, however, there is an edge to be gained from becoming involved early in the process at the point at which specifications are established.

Another way in which the marketing manager should view the purchasing process of customer firms is in relation to the types of purchases being made. To illustrate, what is the difference in the process if the company is purchasing a new product for the first time as opposed to the company's purchasing on a repeat basis? These questions are important to the marketing manager because they affect the marketing strategies and tactics to be employed in each case. What is needed now is an approach that facilitates this thinking.

The Buygrid Analytical Framework

The preceding paragraphs have explained the process by which organizations purchase goods and services. The expansion of this process to include buyphases and buyclasses has come to be known as the **buygrid analytical framework,** or Buygrid Model. Of all the models of organizational buying behavior that have been developed, the buygrid has been the most enduring. It has been described as ". . . one of the most useful analytical tools for both academicians and practitioners interested in organizational buying behavior."[10] The buygrid's main contribution is its theory of buyclasses, which illustrate a typology of buying situations. Practitioners are interested in various types of purchasing categories because situations differ in terms of the marketing effort required.[11] Table 6.3 illustrates the Buygrid Model. As can be seen, the model combines stages in the buying process (buyphases) with types of buying situations (buyclasses), which allows for a better understanding of the marketing implications than would be provided by looking solely at the stages in the process.

Purchases are classified into three basic types: (1) new task purchases, where the buying firm is buying a new product for the first time to accomplish a new task, solve a new problem, and so forth; (2) straight rebuy purchases, where the buying firm simply buys on a repeat basis those products it has always bought; and (3) modified rebuy purchases, where, for one reason or another, the purchasing company modifies a purchase the second or third time through or modifies a straight rebuy purchase, looking for lower price, better service, better delivery, or some other such factor. New task and straight rebuy situations are easy to understand, but the modified rebuy situations confuse many marketing managers. Some examples may help.

Starting in the 1970s and extending into the 1990s, shortages of materials and rising prices are the two most pressing problems facing business purchasers, according to the National Association of Purchasing Management.[12] The effect has been to force professional buyers to review what had traditionally been straight rebuy situations, seeking better prices and adequate supplies. Modified rebuys often occur when buyers are faced with new problems or constraints and seek other sources of supply to adapt. Other actions taken by buyers at one time or another that have led to modified rebuy situations include the development of

TABLE 6.3   The Buygrid Analytic Framework for Organizational Buying Situations

	Buyclasses		
	New Task	Modified Rebuy	Straight Rebuy
1. Anticipation or recognition of a problem (need) and a general solution			
2. Determination of characteristics and quantity of needed item			
3. Description of characteristics and quantity of needed item			
4. Search for and qualification of potential sources			
5. Acquisition and analysis of proposals			
6. Evaluation of proposals and selection of supplier(s)			
7. Selection of an order routine			
8. Performance feedback and evaluation			

Source: Reprinted by permission from Patrick J. Robinson, Charles W. Faris, and Yoram Wind, *Understanding the Industrial Buyer*, vol. 3 (Cambridge, MA: Marketing Science Institute, November 1967), 3.

1. The most complex buying situations occur in the upper left portion of the buygrid matrix, when the largest number of decision makers and buying influences are involved. Thus, a new task in its initial phase of problem recognition generally represents the greatest difficulty for management.

2. Clearly, a new task may entail policy questions and special studies, whereas a modified rebuy may be more routine, and a straight rebuy essentially automatic.

3. As buyphases are completed, moving from phase 1 through phase 8, the process of "creeping commitment" occurs, and there is diminishing likelihood of new vendors gaining access to the buying situation.

long-term supply contracts, the use of reverse selling to persuade suppliers to do business with the buyer, the use of "reverse" and "time reciprocity," the expansion of inventories, and the entertaining and courting of selected supplier salespeople.[13]

Modified rebuys also occur when an organizational customer moves to JIT buying. As was discussed in detail in the preceding chapter, more and more U.S. manufacturers are moving to JIT. As was also discussed, such a move typically entails a reduction in the number of suppliers. This has modified rebuy implications. Assume, for example, that an organization now buys from three suppliers the same basic product on a straight rebuy basis. If the organization moves to JIT, perhaps only one of the three will be retained, which involves a switch from a straight rebuy situation to a form of modified rebuy.

With reference to Table 6.3, when a product is purchased for the first time, all eight buyphases or steps in the buying process are important, but the first few phases are critical. If the salesperson can point out the problem to the originating department and then solve that problem around the specifications of his or her products, it is difficult for a competing salesperson to get those specifications changed at a later stage in the process. Most effective business salespersons and marketing managers understand this concept and attempt to get their products specified as the solution to the buyer's problem. They then follow their customer through each stage of its buying process to make sure nothing goes wrong. This follow-through is necessary because it is a new experience for the buyer, and a great deal of communication must occur between purchaser and seller. New task purchases are important to the marketing manager because, if properly handled, they can lead to repeat purchases and ultimately to straight rebuy situations, which are ideal marketing conditions.

Again with reference to Table 6.3, a straight rebuy situation would be handled quite differently. The early stages of the process are probably of little importance because buyers are purchasing products they are familiar with and feel that they know most of what they need to know. The major emphasis for the business marketing manager should be placed in the latter stages of the process, since the purchaser is only concerned with getting the products when needed, in the required quantity, and up to specifications. The real danger to the marketing manager in straight rebuy situations is a tendency to become complacent and take customers for granted, thus not paying them enough attention. In these circumstances, the marketing manager may be unwittingly setting up a modified rebuy situation if deliveries are late or service is poor or some other such mishap occurs to irritate customers.

Straight rebuys can be looked at from two points of view. With the company's straight rebuy customers, the marketing manager should pay close attention to phases 7 and 8 to make sure no opportunities are created for competing firms to come in and take them over. With the competitors' straight rebuy customers, the marketing manager should be examining the process for areas of dissatisfaction or unrest to switch them to modified rebuys and create sales opportunities. Satisfied straight rebuy situations are almost the ideal in business marketing when they involve the firm's own customers. When they involve competitors' customers, straight rebuying by satisfied customers probably creates the single most difficult task in the areas of business selling and marketing.

In modified rebuy situations, emphasis on the buyphases differs from the other two instances. The early phases as well as the latter phases are important. Organizational buyers must be convinced to look elsewhere if modified situations are to be created. The business marketing manager and company field salespeople must then provide information that encourages the buyer to switch. Once this is accomplished, the marketing job involves ensuring that all goes right and that the customer is not irritated by any problems or delays. Again, the job of the marketing manager in the modified rebuy situation is to change it to a straight rebuy situation.

The Buygrid Model has been described as the most widely accepted model of the organizational buying process.[14] The Buygrid Model also provides the marketer with a clean and easy-to-use approach to understanding the organizational buying process. It is a tool that may be used to advantage by the marketing manager in analyzing customers and then assessing where marketing emphasis should be placed within the process.

Despite its popularity, the Buygrid Model is not without criticism. Critics are primarily concerned with its handling of the buyclasses. For example, one concern is that the buyclass variable is overemphasized and has never been empirically justified. Critics contend that although the buyclasses may be useful in explaining the general importance of a purchasing decision, they should not be used to infer other buyer behavior concepts such as their influence on purchases.[15] Another study found that the Buygrid Model better represents the purchases of some products than it does others. For example, it was found that the process was quite representative of the buying process for an informational process system, but less so for the purchase of replacement office furniture.[16] Even with such criticisms, however, the Buygrid Model provides a useful framework for understanding the organizational buying process and recognizing where marketing emphasis might be placed within that process.

MULTIPLE BUYING INFLUENCES

Although the purchasing process found in the buying practices of businesses and other organizations may be relatively standardized, each probably differs in regard to which people and positions are involved. Two firms may be in the same industry, have the same Standard Industrial Classification (SIC) designation, and need the same equipment, sometimes even buying from the same supplier. Both may follow the same basic buying process, yet the people who influence the purchase and their respective positions can differ in each firm. They may differ both in personality and in accountability. Understanding who is involved in each customer firm is a vital consideration in business marketing. Usually, many individuals influence the decision.[17] "The Purchasing Manager, the Chief Engineer, the Plant Engineer, and the Controller—these are just a few of the people you can expect to meet, if you are selling high ticket industrial products or even high volume, low cost products."[18] Thus, the business marketing manager and the field salespeople must discover who in each target market organization influences the decision to buy. Once these people are known, marketing approaches can be directed specifically toward them through personal selling, distribution, and advertising. If these people are not known, it is virtually impossible to communicate with them, although they will continue to make decisions and buy those products they know and prefer.

In short, effective marketing requires a knowledge of who in each customer organization has an effect on products and services that are purchased. These people or positions are known as **buying influences**. Their importance may be seen in the following quotation: "We have to admit that those of us who are into or who observe the selling/marketing scene are awed by the colossal clout the 'buying influence' has on the budgets, the time and effort of those who market and sell industrial products."[19]

Because the purchasing of goods and services affects virtually every other function of the organization and because other departments use or are affected by what is bought, it is only logical that the using departments may in some way influence what is purchased. Table 6.4 illustrates departmental involvement in the purchasing of component parts by chemical plants. This table is useful in that it depicts the influence of various departments at different stages of the buying process. For example, the purchasing department is influential in such tasks as searching out suppliers and deciding which supplier gets the order. The design and development engineering and research departments are the most influential, however, when product specifications and characteristics are determined. Similarly, the purchasing department is most likely to initiate the purchase of parts to take advantage of any price differentials, whereas the design and development engineering and production engineering departments are most likely to initiate such a purchase because of design changes in existing products.

In summary, buying influences are those personnel within the purchasing organization who in one way or the other actually have an influence on what is or is not purchased. Because, as has been stated, there is rarely one such person involved, most business marketing firms face **multiple buying influences.** In other words, several people in the purchasing firm have the power, either formally or informally, to influence the decision being made. A good definition of a buying influence is anyone within the purchasing firm who not only has the power to make a decision in favor of the product involved but who also may be able to cast a negative vote for that product. Thus, buying influences can be positive or negative, and there can be any number of influences involved, depending on the product and the buying firm.

Buying influences may also be described by the roles they play in the buying process. The most common roles are as follows: [20]

> Initiators—buying influences who first recognize or anticipate a problem that may be solved by buying a good or service
>
> Gatekeepers—buying influences who control information and/or access to decision makers
>
> Influencers—buying influences who have some positive or negative input into what is to be bought
>
> Deciders—buying influences who actually say yes or no to a contemplated purchase
>
> Purchasers—buying influences who process the paperwork and place the order
>
> Users—buying influences who ultimately use the product or service

A simple example may help to understand these roles. Assume a machine shop purchases a drill press for its manufacturing process. The **initiator** is a foreman or department head. The **gatekeepers** are receptionists or secretaries for various executives involved, such as the purchasing agent or production superintendent. The influencers are employees who operate such machines, quality assurance personnel, or maintenance engineers. The **decider** is the production superintendent who makes the final decision. The **purchaser** is the purchasing

TABLE 6.4 Departmental Involvement in Tasks in the Buying Process of Chemical Firms Purchasing Component Parts

Buying Task	Overall Corporate Policy and Planning	Operations and Administration	Design and Development Engineering	Production Engineering	Research	Finance	Sales	Purchasing	All Others
Who is most likely to initiate a project leading toward the purchase of component parts to									
1. Take advantage of a price differential?	11.0%	9.6%	4.1%	5.5%	1.4%	—	—	53.4%	1.4%
2. Take advantage of innovation in component design?	9.6%	9.6%	19.2%	17.8%	15.1%	1.4%	—	11.0%	4.1%
3. Accommodate a change in the design of an existing product?	9.6%	13.7%	21.9%	21.9%	8.2%	1.4%	1.4%	8.2%	4.1%
4. Accommodate a change in the production process?	9.6%	15.1%	15.1%	27.4%	8.2%	—	—	8.2%	2.7%

5. Incorporate into a new product? Who surveys alternatives and determines kind (not make) of component parts to be used?	13.7%	11.0%	15.1%	6.8%	20.5%	—	5.5%	11.0%	4.1%
Who determines specifications and characteristics to be met by the component parts?	8.2%	9.6%	20.5%	11.0%	11.0%	1.4%	1.4%	24.7%	1.4%
Who surveys available makes of the specified component parts and chooses suppliers from whom to invite bids?	8.2%	11.0%	20.5%	15.1%	17.8%	1.4%	1.4%	6.8%	2.7%
Who evaluates submitted component parts for accord with specifications?	9.6%	9.6%	8.2%	0.8%	2.7%	—	1.4%	47.9%	1.4%
Who decides which supplier gets the order?	8.2%	12.3%	17.8%	17.8%	16.4%	1.4%	—	12.3%	6.8%
	9.6%	9.6%	5.5%	5.5%	1.4%	1.4%	—	50.7%	1.4%

Source: Adapted by permission of the publisher from Robert A. Erickson and Andrew C. Gross, "Generalized Industrial Buying: A Longitudinal Study," *Industrial Marketing Management* 9 (July 1980):257. Copyright © 1980 by Elsevier Science Publishing Company, Inc.

Note: Dash indicates no departmental involvement in the buying task involved.

agent who actually places the order, and the **users** are the employee operatives who run the machines. Although this example is grossly oversimplified, it shows clearly how various buying influences can play different roles in the buying process.

It is also important to realize that such buying influences may be formal, informal, or both, depending on the individual customer firm. To illustrate, a manufacturer's decision to purchase a new drill press may be influenced in some instances by the machinist who actually operates the unit. There appears to be a trend in this direction. Blue- and white-collar workers are becoming integral parts of the decision-making process, not in the traditional labor union sense but in improving productivity. This trend impinges directly on the kinds of tools, machines, and services that are purchased by the companies. Workers are gaining voices in decision making on the shop floor, even in designing and rearranging plants.[21]

Buying influences exist for institutional and governmental customers as well. They affect purchasing in the same manner as in private firms, in that they influence the products and services being bought. In hospitals, for example, typical buying influences include administrators, purchasing agents, business managers, central service directors, pharmacists, dietary supervisors, maintenance chiefs, and laundry supervisors. In addition, practicing physicians, radiologists, pathologists, and anesthesiologists often influence what is bought. Who becomes involved depends on the product or service being purchased, but buying influences are almost always encountered.

Two main buying influences affect purchasing by churches: the clergy and the lay leaders who serve on boards and committees that do the actual buying and specifying of equipment and supplies. Buying influences in school systems typically include school board members at the policy level, superintendents and business managers at the administrative level, and specialists (maintenance, audio/visual, food service, and transportation) at the product/supplier selection level. Similarly, local government purchasing also involves buying influences. A typical U.S. city with a population of 50,000 has a management team of a city manager or mayor, a purchasing agent or a city clerk, and a consulting engineer, as well as engineering influences such as a parks superintendent, a water and light superintendent, a sewage treatment superintendent, and a street and refuse superintendent. These people interact with and consult each other in buying situations. Buying influences are simply a fact of life in organizational buying, whether the organization is private, institutional, or governmental in nature. They exist and play the same roles in buying by international organizations as they do in U.S. buying units.

The Number of Buying Influences

The actual number of buying influences for any product or service differs among purchasing organizations. These differences are often caused by such factors as size of the buying organization, breadth of use of the product being purchased, dollar value of the purchase, technical competence of the company's purchasing department, and how technical the product or service is. For example, when the product or service is to be used by many different departments, the number of buying influences normally increases. Similarly, the more expensive the purchase, the more likely the number of buying influences is to increase. On the other side, as the product becomes more sophisticated, fewer people in the company may understand it, and the number of buying influences may decrease. Similarly, companies with sophisticated purchasing departments may rely heavily on those departments, thus reducing the number of others who may be involved. However, there are few rules, and the number of buying influences can range from a single person to over twenty. Some examples may illustrate this point.

A study of 908 subscribers to *Industrial Equipment News* magazine, representing a broad spectrum of industries, found that an average of five people investigate each possible purchase. In larger companies having 500 or more employees, an average of six people were involved in the investigation. These buying influences investigated the products of an average of four suppliers and invited three of the four to submit proposals.[22]

A *Purchasing Magazine* survey of 603 chemical industry purchasing executives disclosed that in only 13 percent of the cases, the purchasing agent alone chose the source of supply for the purchased products. In 10 percent of the cases, buying influences other than the purchasing agent chose the source of supply. In the remaining 77 percent, the purchasing department and other departments agreed on the approved sources of supply, and then the purchasing department selected the particular supplier. In this survey, the average number of buying influences involved in the purchase of bulk chemicals was five, but the range ran from one to over fifty in a few cases.[23]

Viewed in terms of the type of transaction, the number of buying influences may also vary. For example, a *Business Week* study showed that an average of 3.5 buying influences are involved in a typical nonrepetitive type of purchase, and this number increased to 4.4 persons when such purchases were repetitive in nature.[24] *Factory* magazine determined that 11.9 buying influences, not including purchasing personnel, are involved in the average industrial purchase.[25]

An in-depth study of the purchasing practices in a typical pulp and paper mill disclosed that forty persons in that mill could influence the purchase of chemical products, twenty-six persons could influence the decision to buy instrumentation equipment, and forty-five persons could influence the decision to purchase stock of paper preparation or conversion equipment.[26] Conversely, a manufacturer of office equipment found that four buying influences are typically involved in the purchase of its equipment: the office manager, the comptroller, the supervisor of the customer's billing department that would actually use the equipment, and the purchasing agent.[27]

In the local government market, six buying influences commonly were found when municipal customers purchased highway hardware and materials (culvert pipe, street signs, traffic controls, and guard rails). These were individual board members, city engineers, directors or superintendents of public works, mayors, city managers, and engineers within traffic departments.

These examples make the point that organizational purchasing involves many people in many positions. Business marketing involves discovering these people and their purchasing motivations. Although the task is difficult, there is no alternative, and this fact is recognized by every successful business marketing manager and field salesperson. Table 6.5 illustrates some examples of typi-

TABLE 6.5   **Examples of Buying Influences and How They May Affect Organizational Purchasing Decisions and Marketing Strategy**

Buying Influence	Effects on Buying	Appropriate Marketing Strategy
Purchasing agent, buyer	Handles requisitions from the plant, maintains personal library of supplier's catalogs. Does some discretionary purchasing, especially when delivery is critical. Usually honors sources recommended by key plant personnel.	See them regularly. Keep them informed if you see others in the plant. Keep them supplied with new product and price information. Offer them a benefit on every call. Allow them to pave the way to other buying influences in the plant.
Production manager, general foreman	Usually confined to specific production operations such as assembly, finishing. Can describe specific problems in detail.	Sell brand superiority, depth of your inventory, delivery, and your potential for contributing to productivity of production people and equipment. Leave catalog, put him on general mailing list. Call only when you have a real constructive offering.
Plant controller, head bookkeeper	With purchasing department, interested in terms of sale or systems contract.	Be fully prepared with terms stated simply. Come armed with benefits offered over and above those of terms to impress him with value added.
Director or vice president of engineering	Concerned with product or process improvements. Generally involved with future changes, seldom with immediate needs. Searches continually for new, improved products. Relies heavily on library of suppliers. Also relies heavily on technical aid from vendors. Strong influence on OEM and MRO product type and brand selection.	Responds favorably to outside help in the form of new, potentially useful data and technical counsel. Offer him your complete catalog. Offer him technical capabilities via your own experts. Personally introduce new, improved products regularly. Put him on your general mailing list and keep him supplied with your latest complete catalog.
Plant manager, general manager, vice president of operations, vice president of manufacturing	Key buying influence on larger plant expenditures. May direct vendors to key personnel and problem areas in the plants.	Receptive to constructive information. Often easier to reach than floor personnel. Contact periodically if possible with your management, to demonstrate your interest in serving, to sell your firm's capabilities, and to probe prospect's problems and plans. Keep him informed on important product breakthroughs.

Source: "Finding the Real Buying Influence," *Industrial Distribution* 67 (June 1977): 36, 37, 39. Reprinted with permission.

EXHIBIT 6.1   **Determining Buying Influences in Organizational Customers and Prospects**

Determining just who in an organizational customer or prospect is a buying influence is often a difficult and tedious task, but such determinations must be made if the business marketing firm is to be able to sell to that organization. The purchasing organizations themselves are often helpful in providing this information through their buying guides, which are publications distributed to present and prospective vendors. An example of this may be seen in American Cyanamid's buying guide entitled "Selling to American Cyanamid."

The booklet informs suppliers that the purchase of any new item is usually decided on by several groups of people working together. Depending on whether the item is a chemical, a piece of equipment, or a construction contract, different groups will be involved—rarely will the decision be made by one individual or even one group of people. Regardless of the item involved, the supplier must recognize that four major buying influences will almost always be involved. These are: product research, process development, project engineering, and purchasing. The booklet then explains in some detail the responsibilities of each of these four types of influences. Then, the guide outlines seventeen steps that are involved in the development, design, construction, and improvement of a process and shows where each of the four influences are active in those seventeen steps.

Information such as this is invaluable in that it provides insight to how the company buys goods and services, who is involved in that buying, and where they become involved. Accumulating information such as this permits the business marketing manager to develop strategies and tactical programs to reach those buying influences who are most important to the manager.

Source: Adapted from *Selling to American Cyanamid* (New York: Reinhold Publishing Corporation, 1975).

cal buying influences and shows how they may affect organizational purchasing decisions and subsequent marketing strategy as a result of their effects on buying. Also see Exhibit 6.1 above.

Key Buying Influences

Complicating the multiple buying influence phenomenon is what is commonly referred to as the **key buying influence,** which basically means that all customer buying influences are not equal in the power they can exert. Some have more influence than others, even though they all have some influence on the product being purchased. The key buying influences are those who for some reason are able to sway other influences to their way of thinking, sometimes by design and sometimes without even realizing it. For example, ten buying influences may be involved in the purchase of a piece of equipment, but perhaps two or three are able to influence the others. Obviously, the ability to pick out the key buying influences and sell them on the product in question is an integral part of business marketing. Equally obvious is the fact that this task is not an easy one to accomplish.

Few rules apply to finding the key buying influences, but experience and diligence seem to be the major factors in locating them. Generally, it is the field salesperson who ferrets out such information, but the marketing manager can also exert concentrated efforts to locate the key buying influences through marketing research. To quote the marketing vice president of FMC's Link Belt Division, "the guy who's good at locating the key buying influence has an innate curiosity and drive to get at the bottom of things."[28] Again, it is important for the business marketing manager to realize that key buying influences exist in almost every case and to alert company personnel, especially the field salespeople, to the need to discover these people in each customer firm. It is then up to the field salespeople to listen and observe in every buying situation encountered, so as to determine who is most influential in the purchases made. Following such discoveries, records should be kept so that such knowledge is not lost when a salesperson quits, dies, or retires. Locating key buying influences is a tough job that requires constant attention, because customer firm personnel change jobs, retire, are promoted, and so on. When these things happen, buying influences are shuffled, and purchasing decisions often change. Thus, keeping track of key buying influences is a constant job if the manager is to continue to market effectively to customer firms.

Recent research has indicated that the concept of key buying influences may be related to interpersonal relationships between buying influences. Later in the chapter, we will focus on the interpersonal factors that may help facilitate a better understanding of the behavior of key buying influences. At this point, however, all that is necessary is to understand that key buying influences do exist and are of paramount importance to the business marketer.

The Buying Center

As has been developed, business marketers need to determine the process by which organizations buy goods and services. They then need to determine who in the buying organization will be involved and at what stages of the process this involvement will take place. One approach to this integration is through what is known as the **buying center** concept. In its simplest form, the concept is another way of looking at buying influences. Those people in buying organizations who are related to the purchasing process (buying influences) are members of what can be termed a buying center.[29] A buying center is composed of a number of buying influences who interact at a particular stage of the buying process.

Typically, there is not a single buying center involved in the purchase of a good or service. Rather, a number of such centers may be involved at different stages in the buying process, and the membership of these centers varies considerably depending on requirements at each stage. For example, a buying center might be operational in the first stage of the process, such as where a department recognizes a need. This particular center might be composed of a machine operator, a foreman, the department head, or other personnel involved in the department. Collectively, this center may determine what is to be purchased, the specifications that will be required, the quantity needed, the date to be delivered, etc. Once these factors are decided on and a requisition sent to purchasing, the buying center may cease to function. After the requisition is received by the purchasing department, another buying center may evolve. This second center, however, has different responsibilities than the first. For example, the search for suppliers of the needed product might require input from the purchasing agent, the department head, the controller, and possibly representatives from quality assurance, production engineering, maintenance engineering, and so forth. These buying influences comprise the second buying center. Then, once suppliers are selected, the job of this particular center may be completed. These examples show that buying centers may be conceptual rather than formal. They exist and they function in quite effective and efficient manners but never show up on an organization chart. This discussion also shows that a particular buying influence may be part of more than one buying center, even in the same purchase. In addition, that person's role can differ in each center. He or she might be a gatekeeper in one center, an influencer in another, and a purchaser in still another.

Figure 6.4 illustrates the flow diagram of organizational buying behavior for paper mill disc refinery plates. Analysis of this diagram shows that five buying centers are involved in the total purchasing process. Each performs a different function, since each is involved in a different decision phase. Memberships of the five centers are as follow:[30]

Buying center A: mill manager, purchasing agent, machine foreman, machine operator

Buying center B: machine foreman, quality control, purchasing agent

Buying center C: mill manager, purchasing agent, machine foreman

Buying center D: purchasing agent, machine foreman, quality control

Buying center E: purchasing agent, mill foreman

This example shows the usefulness of the buying center concept. It provides a vehicle for integrating the buying influences into the buying process, and it permits both the marketing manager and the field salesperson an objective perspective. Yet, implementation of this important but abstract concept has been slow.[31] Difficulties in its implementation in actual marketing decisions stem from (1) identifying the number of buying centers and their memberships, (2) identifying the decision-making process in each center, (3) recognizing that buying centers change from product to product, (4) understanding the dynamics and power relationships in each center, and (5) realizing the informal nature of most buying centers (often, buying centers are not recognized as such by the purchasing firm). Despite such limitations, the concept may be a useful tool in segmenting markets and better understanding organizational buying.

FIGURE 6.4   Buying Centers in the Organizational Purchasing Process

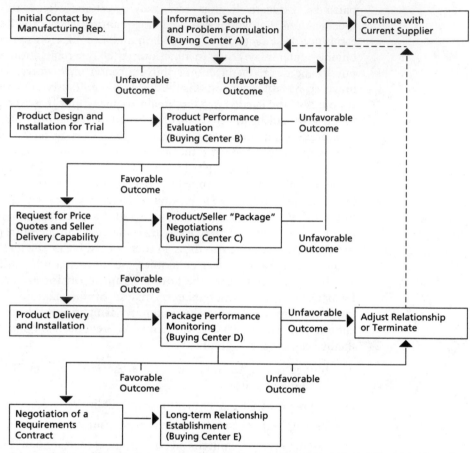

Source: Reprinted by permission of the publisher from Arch G. Woodside and Daniel L. Sherrell, "New Replacement Parts Buying," *Industrial Marketing Management* 9 (April 1980):129. Copyright © 1980 by Elsevier Science Publishing Company, Inc.

UNDERSTANDING BUYING MOTIVATIONS

For the business marketer, it is generally not sufficient to know only the buying process used by an organizational customer and those buying influences who may be involved in that process. The purchasing motivations of those buying influences must also be sought out and addressed in a marketing strategy. For instance, assume that a drill press is being marketed to a manufacturing customer for use in the customer's production line. The main buying influences are located and found to be the purchasing agent, the foreman of the using department, the production supervisor, and the comptroller. Although each is interested in the same product—the drill press—they may not all be looking for the same things in that drill press. The purchasing agent may make the decision among suppliers on the basis of price and certainty of delivery; the foreman may be choosing on the basis of ease of operation for the workers; the supervisor may make a decision on the basis of how well the drill press integrates into the entire production process; and the comptroller may choose on the basis of return on investment, labor-saving reductions, or some other such financial factors.

The point: Although all four people are buying influences for the same product, their **buying motivations** differ, and unless the business marketing manager and the field salesperson address themselves to these differences, they may not communicate well with the buying influences. If they are talking to the purchasing agent about ease of operation when that is not at all the basis of his or her decision, their marketing messages will have little effect. Of course, the marketing manager must address the motivations of the key buying influences if that manager is to sell the company's products or services. Thus, the business marketing manager must analyze the buying influences once they are defined and located. In the actual business world, this procedure takes time, but effective field salespeople are masters at the art. Through repeat calls and conversations and by keeping their eyes and ears open, they find out who in each customer firm is influenced by what, who is interested in what, and so forth. They then make a concentrated effort to discover what motivates each buying influence for their company's products or services. Exhibit 6.2 illustrates factors that motivate buying influences in various departments in their selection of suppliers.

Another factor involved is that individual buying influences in a customer firm often do not understand or appreciate the motivations of peer buying influences. To illustrate, if the product involved is a relatively inexpensive maintenance supply such as a cleaner, lubricant, or adhesive, the purchasing agent may be highly motivated by price, delivery, and product availability. But, the maintenance staff may be more concerned about which brand is more easily used, leaves less oily residue, and has a lower frequency of required cleaning. It is possible that neither buying influence appreciates the other's motives in selecting a supplier and brand. What may be significant to one may be unimportant or not even apparent to another. Of course, this fact complicates the task of determining the motivations involved.

Decision Criteria in Organizational Buying

One approach toward understanding the motivations of buying influences is to look at the decision criteria used. Organizational buying decisions often reflect five types of criteria. These criteria are likely to operate in every buying situation except for the most minor purchases:[32]

EXHIBIT 6.2   **Ranking of Factors Motivating Buying Influences in Various Departments in Selecting Suppliers of a Standard Industrial Product**

Accounting Department:

1. Offers volume discounts.
2. Regularly meets quality specifications.
3. Is honest in dealing.
3. Answers all communications promptly.
5. Has competitive prices.
5. Handles product rejections fairly.
5. Provides needed information when requested (such as bids).

Production Control Department:

1. Can deliver quickly in an emergency.
2. Ships products when wanted (for example, moves up and/or pushes back deliveries if necessary).
3. Regularly meets quality specifications.
4. Willing to cooperate in the face of unforeseen difficulties.
4. Helpful in emergency situations.

Purchasing Department:

1. Regularly meets quality specifications.
2. Advises of potential trouble.
2. Is honest in dealing.
2. Provides products during times of shortages.
5. Willing to cooperate in the face of unforeseen difficulties.
5. Delivers when promised.
5. Provides needed information when requested (such as bids).
5. Helpful in emergency situations.

Manufacturing Engineering Department:

1. Delivers when promised.
2. Is honest in dealing.
2. Provides products during times of shortages.
4. Regularly meets quality specifications.
5. Can deliver quickly in an emergency.

Quality Control Department:

1. Regularly meets quality specifications.
2. Is honest in dealing.
3. Allows credit for scrap or rework.
3. Provides products during times of shortages.
5. Has a low percentage of rejects.

EXHIBIT 6.2   Continued

Special Machinery Engineering Department:

1. Provides products during times of shortages.
2. Regularly meets quality specifications.
3. Has a low percentage of rejects.
4. Delivers when promised.
5. Is honest in dealing.

Tool Design Department:

1. Is honest in dealing.
2. Has technical ability and knowledge.
2. Handles product rejections fairly.
2. Allows credit for scrap or rework.
2. Invoices correctly.
2. Provides products during times of shortages.
2. Answers all communications promptly.

Source: Stanley D. Sibley, "How Interfacing Departments Rate Vendors," *National Purchasing Review* 5 (August–September–October 1980):11. Reprinted by permission of the National Association of Purchasing Management.

Note: Duplicate numbers indicate ties in rankings. A standard product was defined as having three or more of the following characteristics: (1) low unit cost; (2) little additional information required; (3) few people involved in the purchase; (4) short commitment (1 year or less) to the product; and (5) little or no supplier modification of the product needed before use.

1. *Performance criteria*—how well will the product or service do the job?

2. *Economic criteria*—what costs will be associated with buying and using the product or service?

3. *Integrative criteria*—will the supplier go beyond minimal actions in meeting the customer's expectations?

4. *Adaptive criteria*—how certain is the buying influence that the supplier will produce and deliver to specifications?

5. *Legalistic criteria*—what legal or policy considerations must be kept in mind when buying the product or service?

One study of purchasing agents found that although buyers profess to use all five criteria, the economic and performance criteria receive the most weight depending on product sophistication and application. As products become less standardized, economic factors decrease in importance, and performance criteria become more important. Adaptive criteria were found to be important for all types of products, whereas integrative criteria were generally less important.[33]

Applying these criteria to examples of buying influences may help to show how motives are determined. For example, purchasing agents in general have been described as being concerned primarily with product quality, service, the reputation of the selling company and its products, and cost effectiveness.[34] Viewed as a group, the motivations of purchasing agents may be based on economic, adaptive, and performance factors in that order. Other studies, however, show that purchasing agents in different industries are motivated by different factors. A study conducted by *Purchasing* magazine of 3,000 randomly selected readers asked those sampled what information they most needed before choosing a prime supplier. The top five factors cited by metal buyers were (1) product quality, (2) on-time delivery, (3) supplier responsiveness and flexibility, (4) price, and (5) availability and service. Electronics buyers cited (1) product quality, (2, 3) a tie between on-time delivery and price, (4) availability, and (5) service. Buyers of office products and systems, however, cited (1) product quality, (2) product performance, (3) on-time delivery, (4) price, and (5) information about sales and service.[35] Viewed in terms of the decision criteria, it can be seen that metals buyers are highly motivated by adaptive factors. Office products buyers, on the other hand, appear to be motivated more by performance factors.

The motivations of other buying influences may differ. Design engineers have the basic responsibility for designing new products. They are concerned with methods of manufacturing products and components that will go into the newly designed units.[36] These buying influences may be motivated by performance, adaptive, and economic factors. Table 6.6 illustrates the results of a study of what motivates design engineers in selecting suppliers of electronic components. Manufacturing engineers, on the other hand, have the responsibility for overall plant engineering. Their jobs may include installing a new, efficient heating or air-conditioning system or spray booth and analyzing the efficiencies of proposed new manufacturing equipment.[37] Buying influences of this type may be more heavily motivated by performance and integrative factors.

The motives of buying influences in institutional customers are remarkably close to those of such influences in private organizations, because many hospitals, schools, churches, and other institutional customers function in the same manner as private business firms do. This point is somewhat true of governmental buying influences as well, but a major difference is often encountered. Buying influences in many government agencies are highly motivated by the "lowest ultimate cost" concept, which often means that rational motivations take preference over more emotional motivations. Decisions may be made more on the basis of price and overall lowest cost than on personal preferences.

Many of the same motives exist in customers in international markets. For example, a study of South African buyers of high-technology laboratory instruments found those buyers were motivated by the following factors in this order: (1) technical service provided, (2) perceived product reliability, (3) after-sales support, (4) supplier's reputation, (5) ease of maintenance, (6) ease of operation,

TABLE 6.6   Factors Found to Influence Design Engineers in Selecting Suppliers of Electronic Components

Factor	Percent Believing Each Factor as Important in the Supplier Selection Process
Technical assistance capabilities of supplier	56.4%
Price	52.3%
Supplier's reliability	50.0%
Supplier's ability to deliver required quantities on time	38.6%
Past experience with supplier	36.2%
Compatibility of supplier's product with other purchased products and equipment	23.2%
Supplier's ability to show examples of other applications	15.8%
All other factors, including specifications, product reliability, and second sourcing	4.0%

Source: Reprinted by permission from Cahners Publishing Company, *Cahners Advertising Research Report*, No. 740.6A (Boston: Cahners Publishing Company, 1982).

Note: Responses exceed 100% because many respondents provided multiple answers.

(7) price, (8) confidence in the sales representative, and (9) product flexibility.[38] This ranking appears to be logical in terms of what may be expected of American buyers, and it indicates that international buying motives may be quite similar to those found in U.S. markets. There are differences, however, that may be due to cultural or national implications depending on the country involved. For example, buying influences in many foreign countries may be motivated by such factors as the degree of commitment the U.S. firm is making toward a long-run presence in the country involved. Foreign firms are reluctant to buy from a supplier that may not be there in the future. Similarly, many foreign buying influences want to buy from people they know and trust. They may believe American marketers expect too much too fast and may refuse to buy for that reason. Other buying influences may believe U.S. manufacturers do not customize their products for particular international markets but rather attempt to sell leftover or excess products made for U.S. domestic customers. Still others require that U.S. firms have additional local content, such as licensing, before they will consider an American supplier. Since such motives vary greatly from country to country, companies selling to international customers have a more complex task of understanding motivations of buying influences. The same principles apply, however, to all business markets, whether domestic or international. Buying influences need to be determined, understood, and addressed in a manner that facilitates effective communication.

DETERMINING THE RELATIVE IMPORTANCE OF BUYING INFLUENCES

Earlier in this chapter, the topic of key buying influences was introduced. Key buying influences are those who are able in one way or another to influence other buying influences to their way of thinking. This section will examine why some buying influences are more influential than others. This is an important area for the marketing manager, because for effective business marketing to occur, the marketing firm must determine who the key buying influences are and then must communicate with them. If this does not happen, these people will still influence others in the buying organization but not to the advantage of the marketer. Thus, some discussion of factors that determine key buying influences is beneficial.

Why some buying influences are more influential than others is a complex phenomenon. Why, for example, is one buying influence influenced by another when the reverse is not true? Why does one buying influence have more credibility than another? Why is one listened to attentively while another is not? If the business marketer can determine what characteristics differentiate key buying influences from the others, it may be possible to then identify them and focus marketing efforts on them. As stated, this is a complex and difficult area to understand, but recent research has delved into it and it is worthy of discussion here. Unfortunately, there is not much agreement in the research regarding which characteristics differentiate and which do not. Individual studies differ considerably in their methodologies and results but most focus in one way or another on two sets of categories. The first concerns the buying influence's department and formal position in the buying organization. The second pertains to the social environment in which the buying influence interacts with others in a buying center. A look at some of the studies helps to better understand the relative importance of different buying influences in the buying process.

A study of 186 purchases by Canadian organizations looked at the involvement of different types of buying influences at various stages of the buying process in purchases of components, materials, and equipment.[39] Table 6.7 illustrates the relative importance of purchasing, design and development engineering, production engineering, research, and operations and administration in terms of their involvement in determining specifications and in selecting suppliers. The table shows quite clearly that the importance of some buying influences changes appreciably in the two tasks. For example, purchasing played a rather minor role in determining specifications for equipment, but played a significant role in selecting the supplier. Similarly, research played a strong role in determining specifications of materials to be purchased, but had a very small role in selecting the supplier. And, while research played the major role in determining specifications of materials, this was not the case in the buying of equipment. While this study was not very sophisticated, it does a good job of showing that the relative influence of buying influences is often determined by their department. In other words, a purchasing buying influence may be much more influen-

TABLE 6.7   Relative Importance of Selected Buying Influences at Different Stages in the Buying Process

Who Determines Specifications?

Product Type	Purchasing	Design and Development Engineering	Production Engineering	Research	Operations and Administration
Materials	16.8%	27.6%	27.0%	51.9%	14.1%
Components	19.3%	37.3%	46.0%	31.7%	19.3%
Equipment	8.3%	39.2%	61.3%	9.4%	27.6%

Who Selects Supplier?

Product Type	Purchasing	Design and Development Engineering	Production Engineering	Research	Operations and Administration
Materials	88.5%	4.9%	10.9%	7.1%	16.4%
Components	86.1%	9.1%	16.4%	4.8%	14.5%
Equipment	70.9%	15.4%	33.0%	1.6%	26.9%

Source: Adapted from Peter Banting, Jozsef Beracs, and Andrew Gross, "The Industrial Buying Process in Capitalist and Socialist Countries," *Industrial Marketing Management* 20 (1991): 109–111.

tial in selecting suppliers than in determining what the specifications of the product should be. This study focused exclusively on departmental involvement and did not include any social ramifications.

Another study expanded on this by looking at the buying influence's influence in terms of what it called the formal structure and the network structure. The former included the buying influence's formal rank and departmental membership, while the latter included centrality, distance from the dominant reference group, and distance from the organizational boundary.[40] This study found that a buying influence's influence is derived from the formal organization structure as well as from the network structure. Formal rank and departmental membership are very important, as is centrality—the level of involvement in the networking relationship. In other words, buying influences derive influence from the structural position they occupy within the buying system. Thus, key buying influences might be identified as those who are (1) close to the organizational boundary, (2) central to the workflow, (3) active in communication across departments, and (4) linked directly to senior managers. In addition, their importance is also determined by their level in the hierarchy and departmental membership.[41]

Another study was based on the premise that relative influence is based on the level of communication participation of a buying influence within the center.[42] Before one buying influence can influence another, he or she must communicate information that is received by the other buying influences involved. In this study, three constructs were involved: (1) the novelty of the purchase—the lack of buying experience; (2) complexity—the amount of information needed; and (3) importance—the perceived impact of the purchase on the organization. Four types of buying influences were analyzed: purchasing, plant management, engineering, and operations. In the purchase of a piece of sophisticated capital equipment, the study showed that plant management and engineering were more influential than either purchasing or operations. Plant managers offered more communication than operations personnel at the alternative evaluation stage; more than all other three types at the choice stage; and more than both purchasing and operations throughout the entire buying process. Engineering personnel offered more communication than operations during the evaluation of alternatives stage, and more than purchasing throughout the entire process; and engineering had more influence than both purchasing and operations throughout the process. Thus, the study findings suggest that the novelty of a purchase and its importance to the buying company can serve to predict the relative importance of different buying influences at different stages of the process.

Yet another research effort looked at the effects of contingency variables on relationships between types of power and manifest influence.[43] Manifest influence refers to changes in the purchase-decision-related opinions and behavior of buying center members resulting from an individual's participation in a buying center. Seven types of power were considered: reward, coercive, referent, legitimate, expert, information, and departmental. Reward and coercive power were then combined into what was called reinforcement power, which was defined as the ability to mediate positive and negative reinforcements. These types of power were then related to a number of moderator or contingency variables: (1) the size of the buying center; (2) the degree to which buying influences in a center were familiar with each other; (3) the viscidity or extent to which the buying influences worked together as a team; (4) the perceived risk of the purchasing decision as seen by the buying influences; (5) the time pressure involved in making the decision; and (6) the amount of effort expended by a buying influence to influence the purchasing decision. The study found expert power to be the most important determinant of manifest influence, followed by reinforcement power. Expert power appears to be related strongly to manifest influence in buying centers that are large, viscid, and not under time pressures when not accompanied by strong influence attempts. In contrast, reinforcement power relates strongly to manifest influence when accompanied by strong influence efforts and in centers that are small, not very viscid, and under time pressures. Referent, informal legitimate, and information power were found not to play major roles in most circumstances.[44]

This discussion shows clearly that there is no universally accepted approach to determining the relative power of different buying influences. At the same time, it also shows that research efforts are underway to better understand how one buying influence influences another. The research indicates that it is possible to determine which buying influences should be considered key in a particular buying center. Modifications of these basic research approaches could be undertaken by the business marketing manager to apply to individual customers in a target market. While the cited studies are only a few of the many that have been conducted, there is evidence to conclude that determining the relative influence exerted by individual buying influences is possible and can be done if the manager is willing to work at it.

CHAPTER SUMMARY

This chapter, along with the preceding one, examined those areas of organizational buying behavior most relevant to the business marketing manager. Organizational buying is complex and a discipline in itself. Thus, this chapter has not attempted to cover fully all aspects of organizational buying behavior. Rather, the focus has been on those areas of buying behavior that are of particular concern to the business marketing manager.

The discussion covered the process by which organizations typically buy goods and services. Special emphasis was placed on understanding the Marketing Science Institute Buygrid Model, as this model is probably the most accepted one of the organizational buying process. Buyphases and buyclasses of the model were examined and marketing implications were discussed. Business marketing cannot effectively take place until the buying process is understood and integrated into overall marketing strategy. Understanding the buying process, however, is not sufficient.

The chapter then explored the area of multiple buying influences, who are those people in the customer organization involved in the purchasing process. Different types of buying influences were explained, and their roles in the buy-

ing process were defined. Buying centers were analyzed as they relate to purchasing decision making. The importance of knowing the relevant buying influences cannot be overstated. Business marketing strategies must reach the appropriate buying influences if favorable outcomes are to be accomplished. Product specifications, channels of distribution, advertising media and messages, price, and sales techniques must all consider the buying influences to be reached. The motives of the buying influences are greatly involved in the buying process. Motives were discussed as they relate to different types of buying influences.

The chapter concluded with a discussion of current research pertaining to the understanding of the relative influence exerted by different buying influences in the buying process. The amount of influence exerted by a buying influence is typically related to his or her position in the formal structure, as well as to the social environment in which the person operates. Research efforts were examined that indicate that the determination of relative influence can be accomplished. The next chapter will extend the areas of purchasing and buying behavior by investigating strategic alliances and partnerships as they exist in business markets.

KEY TERMS

buygrid analytical framework
buying center
buying influence

buying motivation
decider
gatekeeper

initiator
key buying influence
multiple buying influences
organizational buying behavior

organizational buying process
purchaser
user

QUESTIONS

1. Explain how multiple buying influences affect the marketing strategy and tactics used by a business marketing company. What are the relationships between multiple buying influences and the marketing mix?

2. Explain why the purchasing agent in a buying organization should always be considered as a key buying influence unless proven to be otherwise.

3. In a new task buying situation, most business marketing managers believe that it is important to become involved early in the process if effective marketing is to take place. Explain what this statement means and then develop the advantages of early involvement and the disadvantages of later involvement.

4. In your opinion, are there more buying influences involved in a new task or straight rebuy situation? Explain the reasons for your position and then relate the marketing implications.

5. Review of the literature reveals that there has not been a single best approach to the study of organizational buying behavior. What factors do you believe are responsible for this? What factors prevent the development of a universal model of organizational buying behavior?

6. Using the example of a manufacturer purchasing a line of metal forming machines for its production line, determine the most likely buying influences for those machines in terms of: (a) initiators, (b) gatekeepers, (c) influencers, (d) deciders, (e) purchasers, and (f) users.

7. Using the buying influences determined in the previous question, show where they fit into each buyphase of the Buygrid Model. Show where each buying influence may become involved in the buying process.

8. Explain why the key buying influence concept is so important in business marketing. What do you see as the problems involved in identifying key buying influences in particular organizations?

9. A major study found that buying influences differ from buying organization to buying organization even when the same product is being purchased. In addition, that same study found that buying influences can change from purchase to purchase of the same product by the same organization. Explain what these findings mean to the business marketing manager.

10. Explain how a business marketing manager could use the buying center concept to marketing advantage. What are the major contributions of this concept to business marketing?

NOTES

1. Herbert F. Brown and Roger W. Brucker, "Charting the Industrial Buying Stream," *Industrial Marketing Management* 19 (1990): 55.

2. Peter Banting, Jozsef Beracs, and Andrew Gross, "The Industrial Buying Process in Capitalist and Socialist Countries," *Industrial Marketing Management* 20 (1991): 105.

3. Ibid.

4. See R. J. Thomas and Yoram Wind, "Conceptual and Methodological Issues in Organizational Buying Behavior," *European Journal of Marketing* 14 (1980): 239–263.

5. See Patrick J. Robinson, Charles W. Faris, and Yoram Wind, *Industrial Buying Behavior and*

Creative Marketing (Boston: Allyn & Bacon, 1967); Thomas V. Bonoma, Gerald Zaltman, and Wesley J. Johnston, *Industrial Buying Behavior* (Cambridge, MA: Marketing Science Institute, 1977); Rowland T. Moriarty and Morton Galper, *Organizational Buying Behavior: A State-of-the-Art Review and Conceptualization* (Cambridge, MA: Marketing Science Institute, 1978).

6. Daniel H. McQuiston, "Novelty, Complexity, and Importance as Causal Determinants of Industrial Buying Behavior," *Journal of Marketing* 53 (April 1989): 66.

7. Arch G. Woodside and Daniel L. Sherrell, "New Replacement Part Buying," *Industrial Marketing Management* 9 (1980): 128.

8. See Ronald S. Schill, "Buying Process in the U.S. Department of Defense," *Industrial Marketing Management* 9 (1980): 291–298.

9. Banting, Beracs, and Gross, op. cit., 112.

10. Rowland Moriarty, *Industrial Buying Behavior* (Lexington, MA: Lexington Books, 1983), 29.

11. McQuiston, op. cit., 67.

12. "Market Newsletter," *Chemical Week* 114 (April 10, 1974): 23.

13. Alan J. Dubinsky and Thomas N. Ingram, "Salespeople View Buyer Behavior," *Journal of Purchasing and Materials Management* 18 (Fall 1982): 6.

14. Morry Ghingold, "Testing the 'Buygrid' Buying Process Model," *Journal of Purchasing and Materials Management* 22 (Winter 1986): 30.

15. See Joseph A. Bellizzi and Phillip McVey, "How Valid Is the Buy-Grid Model?" *Industrial Marketing Management* 12 (1983): 57–62.

16. Ghingold, op. cit., 36.

17. Moriarty and Galper, op. cit., 18.

18. "They're Ganging Up on You," *Agency Sales Magazine* 15 (July 1985): 9.

19. George Berkwitt, "The Real Buying Influence," *Industrial Distribution* 72 (January 1982): 37.

20. Thomas V. Bonoma, "Major Sales: Who Really Does the Buying?" *Harvard Business Review* 60 (May–June 1982): 113.

21. Berkwitt, op. cit.

22. Kate Bertrand, "Survey Finds Many 'Critical' Buying Criteria," *Business Marketing* 71 (April 1986): 30.

23. *Purchasing Magazine Readers Have Something to Tell You about Chemicals*, Report Number 10-A (New York: *Purchasing*, 1965), 7–8.

24. Murray Harding, "Who Really Makes the Purchasing Decision?" *Industrial Distribution* 51 (September 1966): 76.

25. Mary Rita O'Rourke, James M. Shea, and William M. Solley, "Survey Shows Need for Increased Sales Calls, Advertising and Updated Mailing Lists to Reach Buying Influences," *Industrial Marketing* 58 (April 1973): 38.

26. Ibid.

27. Henry Holtzman, "Selling the Right Man," *Agency Sales Magazine* 11 (September 1981): 8.

28. Steve Blickstein, "How to Find the Key Buying Influence," *Sales & Marketing Management* 107 (September 20, 1971): 52.

29. Robinson, Faris, and Wind, op. cit., 101.

30. Arch G. Woodside and Daniel L. Sherrell, "New Replacement Parts Buying," *Industrial Marketing Management* 9 (April 1980): 128.

31. Gary L. Lilien and M. Anthony Wong, "An Exploratory Investigation of the Structure of the Buying Center in the Metalworking Industry," *Journal of Marketing Research* 21 (February 1984): 1.

32. Donald R. Lehmann and John O'Shaughnessy, "Decision Criteria Used in Buying Different Categories of Products," *Journal of Purchasing and Materials Management* 18 (Spring 1982): 10.

33. Ibid.

34. Holtzman, op. cit.

35. John F. O'Connor, "What Your Peers Really Want to Know About Suppliers," *Purchasing* 96 (May 10, 1984): 57.

36. William H. Krause, "How to Sell to Engineers," *Agency Sales Magazine* 14 (April 1984): 18.

37. Ibid.

38. Russell Abratt, "Industrial Buying in High-Tech Markets," *Industrial Marketing Management* 15 (1986): 296.

39. Banting, Beracs, and Gross, op. cit., 1, 5, 113.

40. See John R. Ronchetto, Jr., Michael D. Hutt, and Peter H. Reingen, "Embedded Influence Patterns in Organizational Buying Systems," *Journal of Marketing* 53 (October 1989): 51–62.

41. Ibid., 59.

42. McQuiston, op. cit., 66–79.

43. See Ajay Kohli, "Determinants of Influence in Organizational Buying: A Contingency Approach," *Journal of Marketing* 53 (July 1989): 50–65.

44. Ibid., 61.

SUGGESTED ADDITIONAL READINGS

Anderson, Erin, Wujin Chu, and Barton Weitz. "Industrial Purchasing: An Empirical Exploration of the Buyclass Framework." *Journal of Marketing* 51 (July 1987): 71–86.

Anderson, Paul F., and Terry M. Chambers. "A Reward/Measurement Model of Organizational Buying Behavior." *Journal of Marketing* 49 (Spring 1985): 7–23.

Banting, Peter, Jozsef Beracs, and Andrew Gross. "The Industrial Buying Process in Capitalist and Socialist Countries." *Industrial Marketing Management* 20 (1991): 105–113.

Bellizzi, Joseph A., and Phillip McVey. "How Valid Is the Buy-Grid Model?" *Industrial Marketing Management* 12 (1983): 57–62.

Berkowitz, Marvin. "New Product Adoption by the Buying Organization: Who Are the Real Influencers?" *Industrial Marketing Management* 15 (1986): 33–43.

Bonoma, Thomas V. "Major Sales: Who Really Does the Buying?" *Harvard Business Review* 60 (May–June 1982): 111–119.

Brown, Herbert E., and Roger W. Brucker. "Charting the Industrial Buying Stream." *Industrial Marketing Management* 19 (1990): 55–61.

Crow, Lowell E., Richard W. Olshavsky, and John O. Summers. "Industrial Buyers' Choice Strategies: A Protocol Analysis." *Journal of Marketing Research* 17 (February 1980): 33–44.

Ghingold, Morry. "Testing the 'Buygrid' Buying Process Model." *Journal of Purchasing and Materials Management* 22 (Winter 1986): 30–36.

Jackson, Donald W., Janet K. Keith, and Richard K. Burdick. "Purchasing Agents' Perceptions of Industrial Buying Center Influence." *Journal of Marketing* 48 (Fall 1984): 75–83.

Johnston, Wesley J., and Thomas V. Bonoma. "The Buying Center: Structure and Interaction Patterns." *Journal of Marketing* 45 (Summer 1981): 143–156.

Kohli, Ajay. "Determinants of Influence in Organizational Buying: A Contingency Approach." *Journal of Marketing* 53 (July 1989): 50–65.

Kohli, Ajay K., and Gerald Zaltman. "Measuring Multiple Buying Influences," *Industrial Marketing Management* 17 (August 1988): 197–204.

LeBlanc, Ronald P. "Insights Into Organizational Buying." *Journal of Business & Industrial Marketing* 2 (Spring 1987): 5–10.

Lynn, Susan A. "Identifying Buying Influences for a Professional Service: Implications for Marketing Efforts." *Industrial Marketing Management* 16 (1987): 119–130.

Martin, James H., James M. Daley, and Henry B. Burdg. "Buying Influences and Perceptions of Transportation Services." *Industrial Marketing Management* 17 (1988): 305–314.

McQuiston, Daniel H. "Novelty, Complexity, and Importance as Causal Determinants of Industrial Buyer Behavior." *Journal of Marketing* 53 (April 1989): 66–79.

Moriarty, Rowland T. *Industrial Buying Behavior.* Lexington, MA: Lexington Books, 1983.

Qualls, William J., and Christopher P. Puto. "Organizational Climate and Decision Framing: An Integrated Approach to Analyzing Industrial Buying Decisions." *Journal of Marketing Research* 26 (May 1989): 179–192.

Reese, Richard M., and Louis H. Stone. "Participation in the Buying Process: A Vendor's Perspective." *Journal of Business & Industrial Marketing* 2 (Winter 1987): 51–60.

Robinson, Patrick J., Charles W. Faris, and Yoram Wind. *Industrial Buying and Creative Marketing.* Boston: Allyn & Bacon, 1967.

Ronchetto, John R., Jr., Michael D. Hutt, and Peter H. Reingen. "Embedded Influence Patterns in Organizational Buying Systems." *Journal of Marketing* 53 (October 1989): 51–62.

Salmond, Deborah. *Business Buying Behavior.* Cambridge, MA: Marketing Science Institute, 1988.

Silk, Alvin J., and Manohar U. Kalwani. "Measuring Influence in Organizational Purchase Decisions." *Journal of Marketing Research* 19 (May 1982): 165–181.

Thomas, Robert J. "Bases of Power in Organizational Buying Decisions." *Industrial Marketing Management* 13 (1984): 209–217.

7

Strategic Alliances and Partnering Relationships in Business Marketing

••

Strategic alliances or partnering relationships come in all shapes and sizes in business marketing. Beyond **mergers** and acquisitions, there is a whole world of joint ventures, **cross-licensing** and **cross-distribution** agreements, research and development consortia, quality partnerships, business networks, and other forms of cooperative agreements. Alliances may be between manufacturers, between manufacturers and customers, between manufacturers and suppliers, and between manufacturers and channel intermediaries. Table 7.1 illustrates a sample of such agreements. These types of interorganizational cooperative agreements have become standard operating procedures in the past decade for many U.S. and other business marketing firms. The ability to create and maintain these relationships has become an important skill in contemporary business marketing.

In some industries, there were more joint domestic ventures announced in a single year in the 1980s than there were in the previous fifteen to twenty years combined.[1] Such cooperative interorganizational relationships have been part of the business marketing environment for some time, particularly in countries other than the United States. For example, Japanese companies such as Mitsubishi, Mitsui, Sumitomo, Dai-Ichi Kangin, Fuyo, Sanwa, and others have used such arrangements very successfully. In addition, companies preparing for entry into the European Economic Community (EEC) have also brought business marketing relationships into prominence.

This chapter will focus on such partnerships and alliances as they affect the contemporary business marketing manager. Types of alliances will be discussed and analyzed for their roles in business marketing planning and strategy development.

Creating Working Partnerships with Industrial Distributors

In business marketing, where manufacturers use channel intermediaries such as industrial distributors or manufacturers' representatives, relationships between marketer and channel components have historically been at arm's length or even adversarial in some instances. Creating partnering relationships with those intermediaries has become more common in today's business markets.

A good example of this is the case of Lyon Metal Products of Aurora, Illinois. Management at Lyon believes very strongly that distribution is a crucial marketing element and the firm works diligently to create better relationships with its distributors. To quote the company's president, "The idea is to show our distributor that we understand what his problems are, and that if he commits to us exclusively, we will do everything possible to create a successful partnership."

To accomplish this end, the company developed a four-part program that includes (1) more favorable freight allowances, (2) a "no hassle" claims policy, (3) a revised inventory exchange program, and (4) a lifetime warranty on all new products. More specifically, these were implemented as follows.

For any order exceeding $1,200, the company pays the freight, which means the distributor no longer has to take the time and effort to compute freight charges for its customers. Under its new claims policy, any distributor or drop-shipped customer who receives damaged goods can have them replaced within ten days and Lyon will take the responsibility of handling damages and claims with carriers. Finally, the company provides an inventory exchange program for those distributors who elect not to stock directly competitive lines. Under this program, Lyon will annually swap slow-moving products held by distributors for faster-moving products of equal value providing the goods swapped are current stock items in original cartons. With this program, the company is protecting its partnering distributors from being stuck with unwanted inventory.

Summarizing the entire package, the president of Lyon states, "In the future, our greatest commitment is going to be to those distributors who demonstrate the greatest commitment to us. It's as simple as that." This example illustrates clearly the present trend toward fostering better relations with channel components in business markets. Through such relationships, both manufacturer and distributor gain. The distributor gains protection from the manufacturer against unwanted problems or contingencies and the manufacturer gains from increased service and loyalty by a more satisfied distributor. This is the essence of any successful partnering relationship in business marketing.

Source: Adapted from "Lyon Metal Pays the Freight," *Industrial Distribution* 79 (August 1990): 10.

TABLE 7.1   Examples of Networks and Strategic Alliances in Business Marketing

---

- Merck wants to be alone, but with lots of friends. Instead of looking to merge, Merck created a network of alliances with DuPont, ICI Americas, Johnson & Johnson, and with start-up biotechnical companies such as Imulogic Pharmaceutical Corporation and Repligen Corporation.

- Citibank, American Airlines, and MCI join to maximize marketing efforts. By sharing information and customer data, these companies hope to increase customer loyalty and cross-market to credit-worthy customers.

- At Mazda's plant in Hiroshima, Japan, cars with Ford labels come off production lines every few minutes. These and other multinational companies such as General Motors and Toyota, Mitsubishi Motors and Chrysler, and Volvo and Renault have developed strategic alliances of various types to deal with international marketing and manufacturing of products.

- MIPS bases an entire corporate strategy on alliances with other high-tech companies. Through a turnaround strategy, MIPS Computer Systems developed manufacturing, customer, R & D, and marketing alliances with key high-technology companies.

- U.S. and Japanese steel manufacturers have formed manufacturing partnerships. Via joint ventures, a number of U.S. and Japanese steel companies have joined forces in the United States to compete more effectively. These partnerships include Inland Steel and Nippon Steel; ARMCO and Kawasaki Steel; LTV Corporation and Sumitomo Metal; and USX Corporation and Kobe Steel.

- U.S. industrial distributors have developed alliances in the form of marketing groups. In such industries as safety equipment, plumbing and heating supplies, industrial supplies, and specialty tools and fasteners, distributors have joined together to form new organizations called marketing groups.

- Major forest products producers join together to protect the environment. Major U.S. producers of forest products have combined efforts to form the American Forest Council for the purpose of better balancing demand for paper and wood products with environmental concerns.

- Texas Instruments, Canon, Hewlett–Packard, and the Singapore Economic Development Board are partners in a joint venture named TECH Semiconductor Pte. Ltd. to build a $330 million microcomputer chip plant in Singapore to become operational in 1993.

WHY STRATEGIC ALLIANCES HAVE BECOME POPULAR

Traditionally, business marketing managers, particularly those in the United States, have emphasized efficiency and price. In cases where interorganizational relationships were cooperative and successful, the reason was more likely due to strong personal relations between key managers in each company rather than because of company policy or strategy. As product quality has become more and more a key competitive advantage, however, forging stronger links with customers, suppliers, channel intermediaries, and even competitors has become more widespread and better managed.

A number of reasons account for the increased use of business marketing alliances as a key strategic tool, including (1) more intense global competition, (2) the success of foreign-made products and services, particularly those from Japan and Germany, (3) rising costs of R & D, (4) shorter times required to market new products, (5) the growth of megacompanies through mergers and acquisitions, (6) the desire of U.S. business marketing firms to manufacture and market in foreign countries, and (7) the search for more cost-effective growth strategies during times of rising stock prices.

Strategic alliances allow business marketing managers to utilize the strengths of other companies without a long-term financial investment in the firm. For example, joining a **R & D consortium** gives the marketing manager access to the joint talents of the consortium at less cost than investing directly in his or her own company's R & D capabilities. In addition, such alliances provide some other real benefits to the business marketer. These include facilitating entry into foreign markets and blocking and co-opting competitors. Alliances also allow the firm to spread both risk and cost while leveraging economies of scale and to access new research developments. Finally, they facilitate the forging of links with customers, suppliers, channel intermediaries, and even competitors, which in turn may improve productivity and eventually product quality itself.

While strategic alliances provide a way to gain intangible assets without making a long-term investment in tangible assets, this does not mean that they are without cost. On the contrary, such alliances and other forms of interorganizational networks require a new level of commitment by the partners. This commitment often relies on rather old-fashioned concepts such as trust, reliability, and keeping promises. Exhibit 7.1 provides an example of this type of commitment, or, rather, a lack of it, and shows that strategic alliances do not reduce the need for sound marketing practices but rather are based on them. This point will be developed in detail later in the chapter.

TYPES OF STRATEGIC ALLIANCES

There is no single type of strategic alliance used in business marketing. Rather, there are a number of different types, which should be understood by the marketing manager because each has different marketing implications. Research reveals that alliances are often categorized according to ownership ties, purpose, or interdependence intensity. Perhaps the most thorough grouping was developed by Kanter, who identifies three basic types of alliances: (1) service alliances, (2) opportunistic alliances, and (3) stakeholder alliances.[2]

Service Alliances

Service alliances occur when organizations with a similar need, often in the same industry, band together to create a new entity to fill the common need. A good example can be seen in the case of major U.S. forest products companies joining together to form the American Forest Council. The purpose of this alliance was

| **EXHIBIT 7.1** | **Importance of Strategic Alliances in Business Marketing** |

Intel, the world's largest manufacturer of microprocessor chips, was under pressure from its customers to improve its product quality. The problem was an important one in that this pressure came from such large customers as Ford, IBM, and AT&T. Intel management knew that its product quality would never be any better than its supplier base. Since the company used so-called "world-class" suppliers, management felt it had to determine why Intel was not receiving the expected level of service from its suppliers.

The problem can be summarized in the following quote by a vice president of administration and materials at Intel:

Our Japanese competitors were getting near perfect quality, near perfect on-time delivery, and near perfect service from their suppliers—rather our suppliers since many supply Intel as well. Not getting that kind of service, we called in Kyocera [Intel's number-one supplier] for an explanation.

Kyocera's management was embarrassed, not by the question, but by the answer they knew they had to give. Management stayed up all night to find a subtle way to tell Intel why they were not receiving the same level of service as their Japanese competitors. Kyocera answered Intel's question in the form of a riddle, which stated, "To Kyocera, the customer is always king, but reliable kings have reliable servants." It took Intel management almost a full year to understand the message of the riddle.

When a Japanese company places an order, its suppliers can take that order to the bank—there will be no changes, cancellations, or other such surprises. Commitment and predictability are the rule when dealing with suppliers and cooperation is a must. The latter is at the root of all strategic alliances and is necessary to develop top-quality products. There has to be commitment and predictability from both the supplier and purchaser.

This example shows clearly the importance of such alliances. Intel may well have been a very large customer but its purchases may have been based more on a commodity approach than on a partnership approach. Since Kyocera had the latter with its Japanese customers, it could afford to provide them with better service than it provided to Intel. For Intel, the message was clear: It had to focus more on creating the same type of relationship with its major supplier rather than depending solely on its purchase volume to obtain the service it desired. The important point here, from a marketing perspective, is that Intel's failure to understand the importance of such supplier–purchaser relationships was negatively affecting its product quality, which constitutes a major problem in business marketing.

Source: Adapted from J. W. Semich and S. Dowst, "How to Push Your Everyday Supplier into World Class Status," *Purchasing* 107 (August 17, 1989): 74–78; and "Intel Focuses on the Customer," *Electronic Business* 16 (March 19, 1990): 74+.

to show the public that the industry is concerned with protecting the environment. By banding together, members could balance the needs of wood and paper products manufacturers with ecological concerns. Other examples include industry research consortia, marketing groups, the Independent Grocers of America (IGA), and large companies combining funds to extend insurance coverage to areas not covered by existing insurers. In all these cases, firms in the same industry combine their efforts for a common purpose, either because the service provided by the alliance is too costly or too difficult for a single organization to provide for itself or because the service cannot be purchased on the open market. The resulting new organization is then jointly controlled by the member organizations. The limited purpose of the consortium, resource pooling, and large-scale efforts combined with low interdependence makes this type of alliance particularly attractive in new technology development. Exhibit 7.2 illustrates such a consortium within the U.S. semiconductor industry. The purpose of the consortium, a partnership of fourteen U.S. manufacturers called Sematech, is to help its members better compete with Japanese manufacturers.

Consortia are stronger versions of the traditional trade associations. The latter have existed for years and are composed of companies in the same industry that join together to conduct research or take other action at the industry level. One difference is that membership in a consortium is generally more restricted—not everyone in the industry is necessarily invited to join. In addition, membership costs are usually higher. Finally, the consortium has much more strategy significance than does the trade association. Exhibit 7.3 provides an easily understood example of a service alliance in business marketing. The common

---

EXHIBIT 7.2   **Example of a Research and Development (R & D) Consortium in Business Marketing**

In August 1987, fourteen companies who were competitors in the U.S. semiconductor industry formed a partnership that they titled Sematech. The purpose of this ambitious partnership was to provide the U.S. semiconductor industry with the domestic capability to compete in world markets. Firms participating in Sematech were AMD, AT&T, Digital Equipment, Harris, Hewlett–Packard, Intel, IBM, LSI Logic, Micron, Motorola, National Semiconductor, NCR, Rockwell, and Texas Instruments.

The formation of Sematech was a direct response to the entry of Japanese and other foreign firms into the U.S. market through direct competition or purchase. According to a Sematech spokesperson, "Many critical links in the industry supply chain are now dominated by foreign concerns. Sixty-two U.S. equipment and materials suppliers have disappeared during the last 2½ years." To strengthen U.S. competitiveness against the foreign intruders, Sematech focused its resources on providing information and tools to suppliers to help develop stronger links between materials suppliers and purchasers based in the United States. The organization has worked to develop management techniques to encourage shared R & D costs, supplier–purchaser quality partnerships, and a cooperative culture within the U.S. semiconductor industry to bring about overall quality improvements.

This consortium is representative of what is happening in many U.S. industries because of increased foreign competitors. The concept is interesting because it fosters communication and cooperation among U.S. competitors to better protect themselves as an industry against strong foreign competitors. In essence, it is a "united we stand, divided we fall" strategy against a common threat.

Source: Adapted from "Letter to the American Semiconductor Industry," *Partnering for Total Quality* (Austin, TX: Sematech, June 15, 1990).

EXHIBIT 7.3   **Service Alliances in Business Marketing Using Marketing Groups**

An interesting type of service alliance found in contemporary business marketing is what is called the marketing group. Marketing groups have developed in recent years among distributors of industrial supplies, safety equipment, plumbing and heating supplies, and specialty tools and fasteners. Basically, the marketing group is an alliance of organizations, in this case distributors, who band together to remain competitive and viable businesses.

An example of a business marketing group is The Evergreen Marketing Group which began in early 1989 with an alliance of ten specialty tools and fasteners distributors. Ultimately, the group is expected to be composed of sixty-five carefully selected distributors across the United States. Also in 1989, the group signed agreements with twelve national suppliers of specialty tools and fasteners.

To join the alliance, individual distributors must (1) have at least $4 million in sales; (2) be a privately held company whose main business is in the distribution of construction and industrial supplies; (3) have an active stocking warehouse; and (4) agree to make no changes in ownership without the approval of Evergreen's board of directors. Suppliers must buy 25 percent of their costs of goods sold from Evergreen's approved vendor list.

Both suppliers and distributors profit from the alliance. Manufacturers enjoy the written commitment of a number of distributors to purchase their products. Distributors gain because they receive an allowance that permits them to remain competitive. They receive this allowance because of larger volume levels and marketing services offered. The marketing group, in essence, is a vehicle for creating closer relationships between manufacturers and distributors. Thus, the marketing group is an alliance of organizations who join together and form a new organization that acts on their behalf in fostering closer relationships with selected suppliers in the market.

Source: Adapted from "Another Marketing Group Formed," *Industrial Distribution* 78 (July 1989): 7.

need is the requirement to effectively compete in a changing market environment. Of the three basic types of alliances, service alliances or consortia involve the lowest degree of joint commitment. In some cases, this low level can cause member companies to withhold their best people and ideas for competitive reasons.

Opportunistic Alliances

Opportunistic alliances are formed where organizations see an opportunity to gain an immediate, although perhaps temporary, competitive advantage through the alliance. Such an alliance often opens up possibilities that might not have existed for either of the partners acting alone. Once the present opportunity is exploited, it may be unclear to either or both parties whether there is any basis for the relationship to continue. Exhibit 7.4 provides a good illustration of this type of alliance. As can be seen, through the use of alliances, Merck was able to gain access to both new markets and new technologies by this approach.

EXHIBIT 7.4   **Using Opportunistic Alliances in Business Marketing Strategies**

The use of opportunistic alliances in business marketing can be seen in the case of Merck, a major U.S. drug manufacturer. Faced with a changing environment caused by rising development costs, generic sales, and steep price increases, many pharmaceutical firms merged to better compete. Merck, however, chose the path of forming alliances to gain access to new markets and new technologies. By forming strategic alliances with both large firms such as DuPont and small biotechnical firms such as Imulogic Pharmaceutical Corporation, Merck believed it could better adapt to the changing market conditions. Some of the alliances undertaken by Merck in the 1980s include the following.

In 1983, the company obtained the U.S. and European rights to Pepcid (an antiulcer drug) from Japan's Yamanouchi Pharmaceutical. In 1984, Merck then bought a majority stake in Banyu Pharmaceutical of Japan. Then in 1986, the firm joined with ICI Americas to comarket an antihypertensive drug called Zestril by ICI and Prinivil by Merck. In 1989, Merck entered into a 50–50 joint venture with Johnson & Johnson to acquire, develop, and market over-the-counter drugs. In that same year, it joined with DuPont to develop compounds for high blood pressure and heart disease for comarketing rights. Also in 1989, Merck agreed to swap Mylanta antacid and other over-the-counter products to ICI Americas for the antidepressant drug, Elavil.

This example clearly shows the roles that strategic alliances can play in developing overall marketing and mix strategies in business markets. In contemporary business marketing, such alliances have become far more common than in the past.

Source: Adapted from Joseph Weber and Emily T. Smith, "Merck Wants to Be Alone but with Lots of Friends," *Business Week* (October 23, 1989), 62.

A joint venture is a generic example of the opportunistic alliance. Here, partners gain expertise from each other, which allows them to move more quickly toward their business goals. Examples may be found in the construction industry where different types of contractors form a joint venture to develop and construct a major operation. Often the partners trade technology expertise for market expertise—one member possesses the necessary technological skills and the other has the marketing know-how. Such an alliance may become vulnerable to dissolution as each partner gains competence by learning from the other. In the case just illustrated, the partner possessing the technological skills may no longer need the other firm if the former learns enough to develop its own marketing skills.

Stakeholder Alliances

Preexisting interdependence between stakeholders involved in different stages of the value-creation chain allow the formation of what can be called **stakeholder alliances.** Stakeholders are those groups on which a business marketing firm depends—those that can help it achieve its goals or frustrate its attempts. Typical of such groups are suppliers, customers, channel intermediaries, facilitating intermediaries, and even employees. A look at some of these is in order.

Suppliers Historically, some business marketers have had only arm's length relationships with their suppliers. They bought what they needed, in the quantity needed, and in the time required, and that was about the extent of the relationship until the next purchase. Today, such relationships often do not produce sufficient motivation for suppliers to invest in technology to improve quality or to manage the growing complexities of just-in-time (JIT) inventory. At the same time, the business marketing manager faces international competitors who force him or her to reduce costs and improve quality in order to survive. Many companies have used purchaser–supplier partnerships to improve quality. They have accomplished this by drastically reducing the number of suppliers and improving support and training for the remaining suppliers. This subject was discussed in some length in previous chapters and it will be developed again in Chapter 14.

Customers For most business marketers, there have always been strategic advantages to staying close to customers. This is particularly true where a business marketing firm serves a number of large influential OEM or user customers. For years, business marketers have used national accounts to serve such customers. Not only does close cooperation with customers provide good sales results, it can also provide timely knowledge of customers' changing requirements as well as access to innovations. Many innovation-conscious high-technology business marketing companies create formal ties with customers through user councils, invitations for customers to consult on R & D projects, joint promotions, and joint development projects. Through the use of national accounts, relationships with large key customers are often administered so that true **partnering relationships** are developed. Again, JIT has had the effect of requiring closer coordination and cooperation between business marketing firms and their customers.

Channel Intermediaries Chapter 1 contained a discussion of how common indirect channels are in business marketing. Many business marketing firms use industrial distributors and/or manufacturers' representatives in their channels of distribution. Creating relationships or alliances with such intermediaries works to the advantage of both manufacturer and intermediary. Referring back to the vignette at the beginning of this chapter, it can be seen how Lyon Metal Company set up and maintained closer relationships with its distributors to increase its marketing effectiveness. Both John Deere and Caterpillar use distributors in their channels and both work diligently at selecting the best intermediaries they can find and then creating close relationships with them to facilitate better service for their customers.[3] In contemporary business marketing, close relationships with channel intermediaries is a must. Chapter 13 will focus on the means of accomplishing such channel relationships.

Facilitating Intermediaries In similar fashion, many business marketing firms rely heavily on such organizations as common carriers, warehouses, financial institutions, consulting firms, advertising agencies, and leasing organizations. Again, creating alliances with these types of organizations is just intelligent marketing and is necessary to provide adequate service to target market customers. If, for example, a business marketer ships by air freight, it makes good marketing sense to move toward creating closer relationships with the carriers used most.

Employee Organizations   In many business marketing companies, union–management alliances are emerging, particularly in industries that are undergoing rapid change, because it helps encourage innovation. By collaborating in work rule or job condition changes, companies can improve their competitiveness. Examples can be found in such industries as telecommunications, auto, steel, and air transportation. While such alliances are typically outside the authority of the marketing manager, they do indirectly affect marketing offerings and are thus important.

Ties among stakeholders represent some of the closest of the three different types of alliances. Stakeholder partners often have a long history of interaction with one another and may even involve overlapping systems or cultures, such as when an American manufacturer uses an overseas distributor. While these alliances may be the most durable over time, there can be friction when power imbalances or shifts occur. Thus, the business marketing manager must not become complacent regarding such relationships but must work diligently at maintaining them. Maintaining stakeholder alliances is just as important, if not more so, as creating them in the first place.

ALLIANCE LINKAGES

It is now time to look at the links that hold the various alliances or partnerships together. What types of connections exist to create or maintain such relationships? Figure 7.1 illustrates six types of links that have been found to be most common.[4] These are: (1) technical, (2) logistical, (3) informational, (4) social, (5) economic, and (6) legal. Table 7.2 provides examples of each of these links.

FIGURE 7.1   **Strategic Alliance or Trading Partner Linkage Levels**

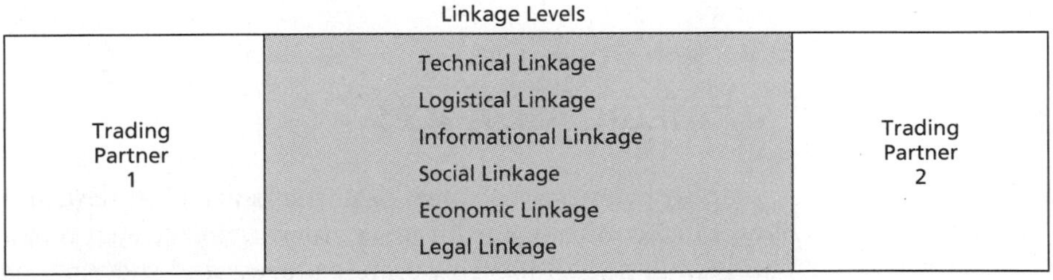

Linkage Levels

Trading Partner 1	Technical Linkage Logistical Linkage Informational Linkage Social Linkage Economic Linkage Legal Linkage	Trading Partner 2

TABLE 7.2	Linkages Found in Strategic Alliances in Business Marketing
Linkage	Example
Technical	Two companies have made mutual technical adaptations in product specifications, product design, production methods, or business practices.
Logistical	Two companies have coordinated the sequential activities in a production process through an exchange of information or adaptations in distribution and/or delivery mechanisms.
Informational	Two companies exchange information about each other's structure, processes, strengths and weaknesses, problems and opportunities.
Social	Two companies form an alliance based on contacts between people in their respective organizations. As people in each organization get to know each other and build up mutual trust, strong social ties can develop and tie the two firms together.
Economic	Two companies invest in each other's business through minority shareholder interests, developing a joint venture marketing project, extending credit for longer periods of time, or taking economic risks on behalf of the other. Mutual benefits may create ties between companies.
Legal	Two companies enact contracts that form the basis of the relationship.

Source: Adapted from L. Mattson, "An Application of a Network Approach to Marketing," paper presented at the Workshop on Alternative Paradigms in Marketing, University of Rhode Island, May 13–14, 1983, as quoted in Lars-Erik Gadde and Bruce Grant, "Quasi-integration, Supplier Networks and Technological Cooperation in the Automotive Industry," *Proceedings of the International Research Seminar on Industrial Marketing*, August 29–31, 1984, Stockholm School of Economics.

Some additional examples may help to understand how these **alliance linkages** operate in business markets. R & D consortia are forms of alliances based on technical links. A JIT customer providing production schedules to a supplier via electronic data interchange (EDI) is based on an informational link. A contract between a manufacturer and a manufacturers' representative is an example of an alliance based on legal linkages. It should be recognized that these links are not necessarily substitutes for each other but in fact often complement one another. Each of these links may be part of forming an alliance to begin with and the strength of each will then determine the nature of controls needed on the alliance.

CONTROLS ON STRATEGIC ALLIANCES

To survive over time, alliances or partnerships require **strategic alliance controls.** Power and control mechanisms in interorganizational relationships vary significantly with social and corporate cultures, and they may well differ according to the country involved. To illustrate, alliances in the United States have been primarily opportunistic joint ventures or outright acquisitions relying on contracts or organizational authority for controls. In this country, success models emphasize equilibrium between partners. Japanese alliances are different, however, and rely heavily on strong social norms. In Europe, forces to maintain interorganizational relationships rely more on historical longevity. European alliances are based primarily on a high level of job stability and the length of time that relationships have existed. European alliances place more emphasis on cooperation and information sharing than do those in Japan. Table 7.3 summarizes some key elements from these three major industrialized cultures that affect how interorganizational relationships are formed and maintained. Because it has been found that family interactions often parallel and influence other organizational structures, this table offers a comparison of differing family and value systems within each culture and their effects on organizational relationships. In each culture, those forces that create loose or tight family relationships, open or closed communications patterns, and the myths that embody cultural values, seem to have an impact on organizational relationships. While this text focuses primarily on U.S. business marketers, it may be worthwhile to show how strategic alliances in this country differ from those

TABLE 7.3   **Key Elements Affecting the Formation and Maintenance of Interorganizational Relationships in the Three Major Industrialized Cultures**

| Element | *Major Industrialized Cultures* | | |
	Japan	United States	Europe
Family structure	Authoritarian	Supportive/loose	Authoritarian/supportive
Communication	Closed	Open	Open
Values	Family's honor	Individual achievement	Tradition and history
Myths	Working hard brings honor to family and protects them against powerful forces	Teenage boy runs away from home, becoming successful and wealthy. Returns home only to visit	Young person, educated abroad, returns to work in home town of family business
Strains	Resentment of authority and closed system; unsure how to create a more open system	Desire to reduce glorification of self, increase cooperation, without treading on others' territory	Looking toward future requires lessening influence of particular nationalities
Alliances based on	Tight structure; informal controls; protection through social ties	Mutual economic benefit and opportunism; formal controls; loose structure	Long-standing personal relationships or historical connections; formal controls

found in Japan and Europe. Many U.S. business marketers may become involved with organizations in those cultures and an understanding of what affects relationships with those organizations will be useful.

Japan

Japan's success in product innovation and cost-saving production methods is due to a number of factors, including such well-known management techniques as "quality circles," JIT delivery procedures, and heavy quality and cost control at the initial production stages. These techniques are accomplished through a production system composed of subcontractors. Each subcontractor makes only a small portion of a product. This portion is then delivered to the next company, which bundles parts into components and delivers to the next company in the chain. These small subcontractors, from which are required low-cost, high-quality, JIT production, make up more than 99 percent of Japanese industry.[5] Most are family-owned businesses and 75 percent of them are capitalized under $70,000.[6]

Only 1 percent of all companies in Japan are capitalized over $700,000.[7] Such well-known companies as Mitsubishi, Matsushita, Toshiba, Hitachi, etc., consider themselves the *daimyo* (supreme power) in Japan's industrial world. Small companies that feed production into the larger companies' networks do so in exchange for their freedom to sell their products and services elsewhere. Their loyalty and obedience is taken for granted. While some of the large companies may hold minority interests and cross directorships in their larger suppliers, most of the control of Japanese alliances is based on cultural deference to authority rather than on legal contractual agreements as in the United States.[8]

In addition to this type of supplier–purchaser network, groups of daimyo band together under strong leaders to further their common competitive goals. These types of interorganizational networks are called *keiretsu*. Usually, keiretsu center around a main bank, which provides financing, information, and organization for the group. The group personality makes a strong mark on its members and purchasing links are so strong that even the type of beer purchased for a business function reveals keiretsu loyalties. Once again, it is the Japanese need to honor and submit to the authority of the "family head" that creates strong cultural ties without formal contractual arrangements.

While this system has enabled Japan to become the world's bankers with its large trade surplus, there are strains on the system. As Japanese business marketing firms move into other countries and foreign companies move into Japan, dissatisfaction with a closed, authoritarian system may well push the system toward change. If small or medium-size family-owned businesses could obtain a fairer, more competitive delivery arrangement from foreign-owned companies, they might venture from under the wing of their daimyo.[9] Then again, the protection available to small companies within a network might outweigh the benefits of price independence found in selling to more than one manufacturer. Figure 7.2 illustrates the bases of Japanese alliances and networks.

FIGURE 7.2   Bases of Japanese Alliances and Networks

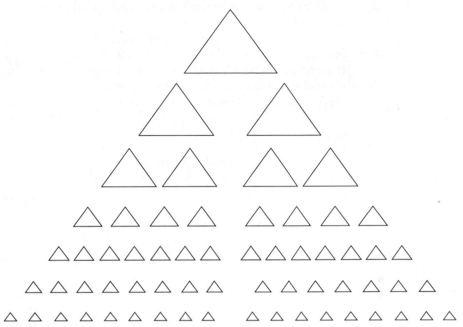

Note: Japanese alliance structures and business networks can be depicted as a series of pyramids with smaller companies part of a larger company's group and larger companies part of an even larger group. Ties are informal but the structure is tight. Much of the controls are based on social connections and expectations.

United States

The U.S. economic fabric is based on freedom rather than authority—free trade, open markets, creating and allowing free competition, free choice, and freedom of labor movement. This emphasis on free and open markets was particularly compelling when U.S. manufacturing led the world in price and quality. Then, each individual company's goal was to become the strongest. Interorganizational relationships were based on exploiting weaker opponents either through price, negotiated terms, or by **acquisition.** At the expense of the total U.S. economy, companies strove to develop portfolios of divergent businesses intent on dominating every aspect of their market. Bigger was better! The basic philosophy was as follows: [10]

> Good fences make good corporations, the traditional management assumptions could read. If you don't own it, if it hasn't been branded with your market, you don't control it, and it might hurt you. What you own is "inside" the fence; everything else is "outside" to be treated as a potential enemy or adversary unless brought under your domination.

As the U.S. economy has weakened in comparison to those in other industrialized countries, there has been more emphasis on joining efforts to gain international clout and improve market position, as in the case of Sematech, which was formed to counter strong overseas competitors that were eroding the U.S. semiconductor industry's markets (see Exhibit 7.2). Much of the U.S. based literature describing alliances emphasizes maintaining a power equilibrium between partners and generating trust. This focus results from a weakened U.S. economic position and the ingrained opportunistic bent of U.S. alliances. Figure 7.3 conceptualizes the change taking place in the United States.

Europe

The difference in control mechanisms between European and U.S. networks are more subtle than those between Western and Japanese systems. Western-based systems rely more heavily on contractual links and opportunistic goals than do

---

FIGURE 7.3   Changes in the U.S. Economy Reflecting Increased Use of Networks and Alliances

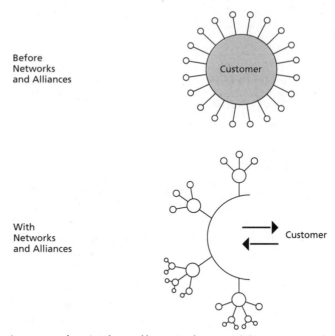

Before
Networks
and Alliances

With
Networks
and Alliances

Note: U.S. businesses are changing from self-contained units with business networks based primarily on opportunistic and adversarial relations to a structure that seeks and gives information to the customer. Businesses in the U.S. are now more likely to work with fewer suppliers who combine processes and components from other smaller shops. Because the U.S. ties are looser and structures are more formal, U.S. alliances resemble a group of free-floating but connected molecules.

Japanese-based networks. The difference between U.S. and European networks, however, lies in the nature of relationships. Social ties form a strong link in Japanese systems but a relatively weak one in the United States. European systems fall somewhere in between.

One study of British, German, and Swedish business marketing firms investigated the factors that create strong interorganizational relationships between purchasers and suppliers.[11] Testing five propositions, the study found that strong relationships form around mutual business practice adaptation and information sharing, rather than on one-sided adaptations as a result of uneven power distribution. The study also found that relationships in domestic markets are stronger than those in foreign markets and that longer relationships create stability, which in turn facilitates mutual adaptation and information exchange.

In Europe, there is less geographic and job mobility than in the United States. This helps to create longer and more stable relationships, at least within a particular country's market. These more stable relationships in turn foster greater emphasis on cooperation and mutual gain in European networks than in U.S. networks. Figure 7.4 illustrates the makeup of European alliances. However, environmental factors such as the rising cost of wages, development costs,

FIGURE 7.4   **Bases of European Strategic Alliances in Business Marketing**

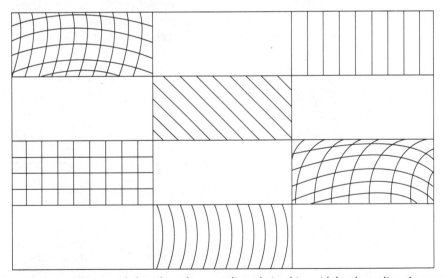

Note: European alliances rely heavily on long-standing relationships with local suppliers. In many instances, companies and towns have the same name. The close, durable relationships based on geographical proximity create an atmosphere of cooperation in which companies are aware of their connection to a particular location. In this sense, European business networks resemble a patchwork quilt in which each geographic area is woven together by economic and social ties but is slightly separate from the networks in other political or geographic areas.

absence of manpower, shorter development, EEC 1992, and globalization are threatening the stability of existing European alliances. In the future, these factors will require new mechanisms to control relationships outside of domestic groups.[12]

In summary, strategic alliances are formed as a response to highly uncertain environments in which business marketing firms often lack information regarding and/or access to markets, technology, resources, and production expertise.[13] Generally, formal controls are less effective in highly uncertain environments. Therefore, informal controls such as social ties, cultural values, norms, and corporate history are often more effective in controlling behavior in strategic alliances. At the same time, as environments become more competitively hostile, more formal controls are likely to be used.[14] Such controls, which specify outputs, tend to be short-term and emphasize financially based measures. This emphasis on short-term results undermines efforts to build trust and therefore can adversely affect the long-term effectiveness of such alliances.

When alliances are formed within similar cultures, the chances of success are much higher because of the use of informal controls. Yet much of the motivation for forming alliances today is based on gaining access to technology, knowledge, or markets in other countries. This poses a slightly different yet parallel strategic and marketing dilemma for business marketing firms in each of the three major industrial cultures described. For the individual marketing manager, this means the approach to creating alliances may have to differ significantly for the three cultures. This may be difficult but it is not impossible. Table 7.4 shows that a number of U.S. and Japanese steel producers have been able to work out the difficulties and form successful strategic alliances.

TABLE 7.4   **Examples of Strategic Alliances Between U.S. and Japanese Steel Manufacturers**

Joint Venture Name	U.S. Partner	Japanese Partner	Manufacturing Locations
I/N Tek and I/N Kote	Inland Steel	Nippon Steel	New Carlisle, IN
National Steel	National Intergroup	NKK	Encorse, MI; Granite, IL; Portage, IN
—	ARMCO	Kawasaki Steel	Middleton, OH
California Steel	CVRD (Brazil)	Kawasaki Steel	Fontana, CA
Lorain Works and Aztec Coating	USX Corporation	Kobe Steel	Lorain, OH
LSE I and LSE II	LTV Corporation	Sumitomo Metal	Cleveland, OH; Columbus, OH
Wheeling–Nisshin	Wheeling–Pittsburgh	Nisshin Steel	Follansbee, WV
ProCoil	National Steel	Marubeni	Detroit, MI

Source: Adapted from Martin Kenney and Richard Florida, "Rust Belt Rescuers Are, Yes, Japanese," *San Diego Union* (April 7, 1991), C7.

SUCCESSFUL STRATEGIC ALLIANCES

As has been discussed, strategic alliances are formed for a variety of reasons. In addition, they often depend on strong social ties, which vary in each culture. Thus, there is no well-defined body of research on what specifically defines or creates a successful strategic alliance. Much of the current literature describes how or why particular business marketing companies have successfully joined forces with various other organizations. From these cases, a set of criteria for judging the success or failure of an alliance may be derived. They also suggest a theory about the conditions necessary for creating successful alliances.

Measures of Success of Strategic Alliances

There are a number of measures that may be used to judge the success or failure of strategic alliances:

First, does the alliance meet its stated objectives for both parties? Second, does the alliance improve dynamic innovation in each company? And third, do both parties point to successes or does one partner feel exploited by the alliance?[15] Fisher and Brown of the Harvard Negotiation project have studied what constitutes good relationships.[16] The following quotation summarizes their concept of a good relationship:[17]

> Competing and changing interests create problems. The working relationship we need is one that produces a solution that satisfies the competing interests as well as possible, with little waste, in a way that appears legitimate in the eyes of each of the parties. The solution should also be durable and efficiently reached. A robust relationship should be able to produce such outcomes in the face of differences in values, perceptions, and interests. It should be able to cope successfully with times when I disapprove of something you did and when we both feel anger rather than affection. It should be strong enough to keep the problem-solving process going even if we develop conflicting views about the relationship itself.

In business marketing, creating and maintaining strategic alliances depends on building ongoing relationships that can manage disagreements in the face of cultural, perceptual, and value differences. If these things cannot be done, the alliance will erode in value over time and eventually cease to exist.

Elements Contributing to Successful Alliances

What makes a successful alliance? For the business marketing manager contemplating an alliance, there appear to be four basic elements required of a successful one: (1) choosing the right partner, (2) creating a cooperative process, (3) creating an accountability structure, and (4) observing and controlling bargaining positions. Since these are crucial to the formation of alliances that work, it is worthwhile to look at each in some detail.

Choosing the Right Partner The right partner usually has something unique to contribute to the venture or alliance. After the manager has determined his or her own company's core capabilities, the search may be made for a partner possessing slightly different, but complementary, core capabilities. These differences provide new information for both parties, which adds to their respective knowledge bases. The information shared is usually something that is not readily available in the market involved. Figure 7.5 illustrates the concept of core capabilities applied to an alliance or partnering relationship.

A good example of this can be seen in the case of NEC, which entered into

FIGURE 7.5   **Concept of Core Capabilities Applied to an Alliance or Partnering Relationship**

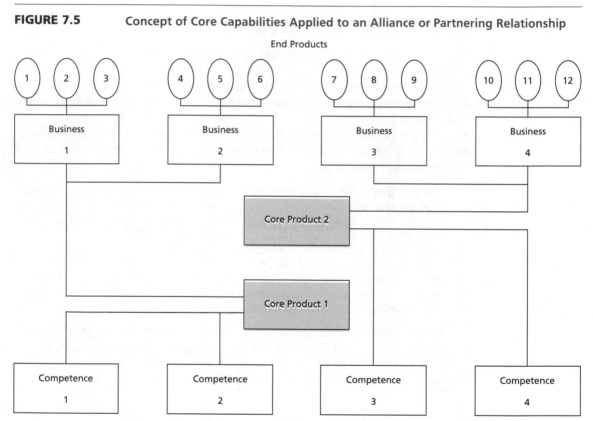

Source: Adapted from C. K. Prahalad and Gary Hamel, "The Core Competence of the Corporation," *Harvard Business Review* 68 (May–June 1990): 79–91.

Note: Prahalad and Hamel describe the diversified corporation as a large tree. The trunk and major limbs are core products; the smaller branches are business units; the leaves, flowers, and fruit are end products. The root system that provides nourishment, sustenance, and stability is the core competence. Looking only at the corporation's end products does not reveal the strengths of the corporation, just as looking only at a tree's leaves does not reveal the strong root system.

a number of alliances in the 1980s to learn and absorb the skills of other companies. Early in the 1970s, the company articulated a strategic intent to develop competencies in communications and computer equipment and established alliances designed to obtain access to technology. It then transferred that knowledge to its own managers. This strategy enabled NEC to increase sales between 1980 and 1988 by 476 percent. This can be compared to the record of a major competitor, GTE, which saw sales increase during the same period by only 65 percent.[18]

Identifying each company's core competencies and core products results in developing a straightforward strategic plan. Sharing long-term strategic plans with potential partners allows each marketing manager to determine if long-term mutual benefits are possible. A good fit of strategic plans enables companies to more easily share information at all levels, and good communication throughout each organization helps ensure that both partners gain strategic skills and knowledge from each other. Open communication is not possible with partners who may contemplate a competitive strategy at some point in the future. Thus, the business marketing manager must recognize the importance of effective communication with prospective partners if a solid relationship is to ensue.

One of the most thorough studies of strategic alliances to date was undertaken by Kathryn Rudie Harrigan.[19] In that study, 895 strategic alliances in twenty-three industries during the years 1924 to 1985 were tested for the influence of firm asymmetries on venture duration and success. Duration was measured by how long the venture lasted and success was measured by field interviews and delphi-method questionnaires to determine whether the participants judged the venture a success. Only if both partners indicated a successful alliance did the study record the alliance as mutually satisfying.

According to this study, significant asymmetries among sponsoring firms generally help stabilize a venturing relationship because one partner needs what the other can supply. But these same imbalances may be harmful to venturing success because heterogeneity intensifies differences in how partners value their venture's activities. If an alliance can be formed with organizations that have closely related markets, products, technology, or culture, as well as similar levels of venturing experience and asset size, the alliance will probably not only last longer but will also be more likely to be judged a success by both participants.

While the Harrigan study looks at alliances that have a sponsoring partner in a variety of countries, 93.4 percent of the ventures had at least one of the sponsoring firms based in the United States and 57.1 percent of the ventures were sponsored by two U.S. based firms. Harrigan found that more joint ventures between firms of differing national origins are now occurring than ever in the past. The study does not address whether differences in national origin assist in or detract from successful alliance formation. Harrigan suspects, based on comments made by managers interviewed, that venture success depends more on corporate cultural homogeneity than on symmetry in national origins.

Other observers of strategic alliances have noticed the ease and benefit of creating cooperative interorganizational relationships when both partners are based in close geographic proximity to each other.[20] For example, many of the strategic alliances being formed in the United States are with high-technology firms (based in or near San Jose, California) or automobile industry companies (based in or near Detroit, Michigan). Exhibit 7.5 provides a number of examples of Silicon Valley joint ventures and shows clearly that physical proximity may encourage the formation of such alliances. Similarly, Japan's entire economy, which is based on various types of strategic alliances, is also located in a small geographic area. This suggests that many alliances are formed with partners who are in close physical proximity, but it would be a mistake if the manager concluded that closeness is an absolute must for a successful alliance. Table 7.4 illustrated this quite clearly in the cases of a number of alliances formed between U.S. and Japanese steel manufacturers.

The European "Interaction School" of business marketing behavior advances a theory based on business relationship networks instead of traditional market or hierarchical theories. This school of thought has its origin in the Stockholm School of Economics, the University of Uppsala, the University of Stockholm, and other Swedish and European universities. This theory originated in an area where geography, manufacturing plant location, and political boundaries have kept local **business networks** closely tied to each other through close geographic proximity.[21]

For the business marketing manager, then, the process of selecting the right partner involves a clear understanding of what factors contribute to successful and enduring relationships. As the previous paragraphs have shown, these factors may differ by nation but are based on mutual benefit, sound communication, and closely related markets, products, technologies, and cultures. In addition, the manager should also seek out prospective partners with similar levels of venturing experience and asset size. When these factors are of a positive nature, research suggests the alliance has a better chance of proving successful to both partners.

Figure 7.6 illustrates a working model of those elements involved in a successful partnership between a manufacturer and an industrial distributor. As can be seen, relative dependence on each other and communicating trust and cooperation are key elements if such a partnering relationship is to be successful.

Creating a Cooperative Process   A variety of sources, particularly those actually involved in managing strategic alliances, identify cooperation between partners as a key element of successful alliances. This is only logical in that any adversity between partners has the potential to destroy any such relationship. This section describes in more detail an approach that the marketing manager may consider for building cooperative relationships. This approach offers some general points mentioned by managers in companies that enjoy successful strategic alliances.

Open, informal communication based on mutual trust appears to be one

EXHIBIT 7.5   Examples of Joint Ventures in the Silicon Valley

Novellus Systems, Inc., is a semiconductor equipment manufacturer. By relying on partners for all but a few key modules in the production process, Novellus managed to ship $51 million worth of equipment with only seven production workers. This gives Novellus incredible productivity figures of $380,000 in sales per employee. The company is able to accomplish this through partnerships with qualified and Novellus-trained vendors. Novellus returns the favor by supporting its vendors with engineering help, financial assistance, and continued training.

Altera, a maker of programmable logic devices (PLDs), accomplished close to $60 million in sales. Altera's PLDs are widely considered state of the art, but the company has no chip-production facility of its own. Instead, it has long-term manufacturing agreements with such companies as Intel, Texas Instruments, and Cypress. The manufacturers, in turn, get the right to make and sell some of Altera's innovative devices for their own accounts.

Cypress Semiconductor, a company with revenues for 1990 over $200 million, introduced fifty-six new chips and chip subsystems in 1989 alone. Cypress invests resources in its leading-edge manufacturing capability and relies on its other companies to provide additional new products through second sourcing. An example of this is the Cypress–Altera relationship. Altera purchased equity in a Cypress subsidiary that runs the company's most up-to-date fabrication facility. As a minority owner, Altera gets a guaranteed fraction of the fab's output at cost plus, along with full access to the information it needs to determine what cost really is. Cypress, which already has the rights to produce and sell some of Altera's products, gets a sizable cash investment, plus the ability to run its plant at closer to capacity, lowering production costs.

MIPS Computer Systems developed a powerful new microprocessor called the RISC chip but was unable to turn this innovation into a profitable company. As the venture capital funds evaporated, the board of directors hired Robert Miller, an industry veteran from Data General Corporation. After trying to raise more capital, Miller met with executives of Kubota Ltd., a major Japanese tractor and industrial company. Kubota was a financial backer of Ardent Computer Corporation which was one of MIPS's first customers. Since Ardent's graphics supercomputers relied on RISC chips, Kubota was very interested in the technology and commercial potential. Kubota paid MIPS $25 million for the rights to sell MIPS products in Japan. In addition, it agreed to build a $100 million plant for MIPS in Japan. MIPS had pioneered the RISC chips but lacked the marketing know-how. On the strength of its alliances with Kubota and others and its on-going technological innovation, MIPS was able to achieve a large share of the RISC-processor market.

Source: Adapted from Steve Kaufman, "Sharing the Wealth," *Business Month* (September 1989); and John Case, "Intimate Relations," *INC.* (August 1990).

of the most commonly mentioned attributes of a cooperative relationship. The marketing manager in each partnering firm needs to respect his or her counterpart and have open lines of communication operating. This is true for all types of alliances, but the type of information flow can differ when the alliance is with a potential or current competitor. Generally, to facilitate problem solving, both

FIGURE 7.6 Model of Manufacturer and Industrial Distributor Working Partnerships

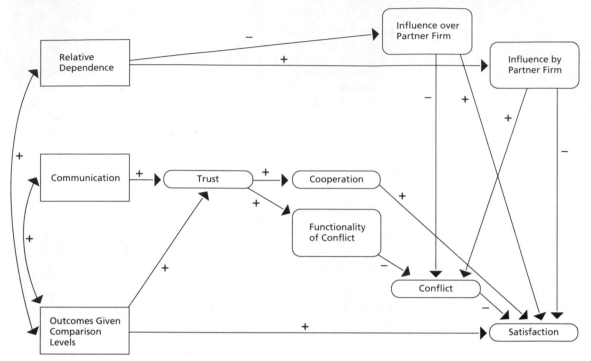

Source: Reprinted by permission from James C. Anderson and James A. Narus, "A Model of Distributor Firm and Manufacturer Firm Working Partnerships," *Journal of Marketing* 54 (January 1990):44. Published by the American Marketing Association.

parties contribute relevant information to the process. The term *relevant* is important in that the information shared must be relevant to both parties, which takes some managerial time and effort.

An example of the kind of information exchange necessary to making an alliance work can be seen in a case study of the long-term development of the relationship between Volvo, the Swedish auto manufacturer, and Olofstrom, one of its parts suppliers. This relationship began in 1926 and ended in 1969 when Volvo acquired Olofstrom. In the early stages, Assar Gabrielsson, managing director of Volvo, and Karl Granfors, chief engineer of Olofstrom, were negotiating a supply contract. The contract gave Olofstrom an exclusive right to deliver pressed parts to bodies, chassis and motor components on three conditions: a) the quality should be on a level with the American standard; b) the deliveries should be on time; and, c) the prices should be lower than those of any potential competitor.

While these conditions implied that it was not truly an exclusive agreement, the trusting relationship between Granfors and Gabrielsson made this type of arrangement work. According to Granfors, this trust level derived from an episode during a negotiation when Gabrielsson tried to read Granfors calculations. Instead of trying to cover up the figures, Granfors handed the calculations to Gabrielsson. This gesture of confidence was the beginning of a lifelong, trusting relationship even though Granfors may never have realized it at the time.[22]

In addition to open and trusting communication, there should be a clear definition of roles and operating areas for each partner. These should then be integrated into a specific plan of action and formalized in a cooperative contract. To some, the concept of a cooperative relationship may seem the opposite of legal contracts, but this does not have to be the case. Most business marketing relationships suffer when expectations and rewards are not clearly laid out. This seems to be particularly true of relationships between manufacturers and channel intermediaries. The cooperation and trust built into relationships allow businesses to move beyond what was expected at the beginning and continue innovating and forming new ventures together. But trust cannot simply be assumed—it is only possible through slow steps toward meeting and slightly exceeding each partner's clear expectations.

Creating an Accountability Structure   Once strategic plans are exchanged, a partner chosen, and a contract agreed to, someone must be responsible for making sure the relationship thrives. While this should be the responsibility of the entire organization, it typically is championed by one person in each organization who is dedicated to making the alliance work. This person may differ by firm but it could be argued that since many alliances are essentially marketing ones, the most logical person to assume this responsibility should be the marketing manager. This person should be responsible for monitoring the perceptions of each organization and determining how the relationship can be improved. Just as in all areas of marketing, change is always taking place and the marketing manager's responsibilities should include constant monitoring of changes that could affect the relationship.

This does not mean to imply that the marketing manager must always carry out this responsibility in person. These responsibilities may often be delegated to others. For example, national account supervisors are used in many business marketing firms to maintain such relationships. Similarly, others in the marketing company may also be delegated to monitor specific relationships. Regardless of who is involved, the person negotiating a supplier contract or bidding on a job should have the authority and ability to make promises that the company can and will keep. This requires internal dynamics that give negotiators the ability to guarantee the actions of their organizations. If this is not done, it may be very difficult to develop the level of trust required to form and maintain a successful alliance.

Related to the above idea, companies must have an ability to provide commitment and predictability in areas crucial to their partner's success. Internal cooperation is necessary to marshall a company's resources to be able to effectively form, manage, and learn from strategic alliances. In other words, until a company masters basic quality management techniques, strategic alliances are out of the question. The entire company must become enthusiastic about making the best product it can as well as continually learning to do better. Only then should a search for an alliance partner truly begin.

Observing and Controlling Bargaining Position Fully understanding one's own company's bargaining position is one of the strongest control mechanisms in developing and maintaining strategic alliances. Bargaining positions are based on knowledge of the other party's interests, long-term strategy, and possible options.

Negotiations based on positions are typically not as effective as negotiations based on mutually agreeable outcomes. But knowledge of bargaining positions gives each party an insight into the propensity of a partner to cooperate. This in turn makes it easier to develop and meet realistic expectations. Generally, equalized bargaining positions are more likely to promote continued joint venture status while unequal bargaining positions are more likely to lead to acquisition or exploitation. For example, a relationship between a manufacturer and an industrial distributor will probably flourish and grow when both parties gain from the alliance. It is much more likely to disintegrate, however, when one party gains at the expense of the other because the former is more powerful than the latter.

Table 7.5 provides an illustration of how power, position, and motivation to cooperate affect joint ventures and strategic alliances. The table shows how bargaining position evaluation may be used to determine the stance of two firms considering a joint venture.

When bargaining positions are about equal, this may require allowing one party to be "in charge."[23] For many business marketing managers, this is not easy. Giving up control may be difficult when a manager is used to being rewarded for how well he or she controls short-term results. But giving up control in one instance may be a way to gain more overall control of the total situation. Accurately evaluating both parties' capabilities, needs, and visions can help determine which party should take the leadership role. Both parties must understand that this "leadership" position relies on agreement about goals and methods of achieving goals that optimize the benefits of joining an alliance. If neither marketing manager will permit the other to be "in charge," it should be obvious that the alliance is in trouble.

One way to evaluate the level of cooperation versus dominance in a potential partnership, particularly in buyer–supplier partnerships, comes from the European "Interaction School."[24] From the perspective of the supplier, such factors as intensity of interaction between supplier and purchaser during identification, development, selection, and implementation phases of industrial systems, and which party dominates activities and interaction, can shed light on whether a

TABLE 7.5   Using Bargaining Power to Evaluate Potential Alliances

Position of:		Hypothesized Action	
Firm A	Firm B	Firm A	Firm B
Needs new technology for next generation of products	Has proprietary knowledge related to needed technology, but no contact with the new market		
1. Established in target market		Cooperate	Cooperate
2. Weak in target market		Cooperate	Will not venture
3. Strongly entrenched in a narrow segment of target market		Will not venture	Cooperate
Only unaffiliated seller in the target market	Recently developed a new product that is successful in its traditional market. Now Firm B wants entry into a different, highly volatile target market	Cooperate	Cooperate
	1. Several other potential venture partners for entering target market exist	Cooperate	Drive a hard bargain with Firm A or another seller
	2. Affiliated with Firm A's major customer	Must cooperate	Cooperate
	3. Has resources and history to become a major competitor of Firm A in target market	Will not venture	Cooperate only on its own terms

Source: Adapted from Kathryn Rudie Harrigan and William H. Newman, "Bases of Interorganization Cooperation: Propensity, Power, Persistence," *Journal of Management Studies* (July 1990).

good fit exists between the parties. Table 7.6 lists supplier–purchaser interaction strategies in increasing order of intensity and complexity. The table shows three main types of interactions as distinguished by Jan Vollering of the Netherlands' Delft School of Management:[25]

Type I. All phases of the process executed by the supplier or the customer.

Type II. Supplier takes over execution after completion of the previous phase by the customer.

Type III. Intensive interaction of supplier and customer in problem solving and/or implementation.

TABLE 7.6   Interaction Strategies for Suppliers and Purchasers

Type	Role of Supplier	Activities and Interaction
I	Supplier of components	Domination of customer in all phases
I	Total package supplier	Domination of supplier in all phases
II	Executer	Supplier executes implementation of solution of the customer
II	Problem solver	Supplier composes the solution of the problem identified by the customer
III	Joint problem solving	Supplier and customer have intense interaction during the development phase
III	Joint problem solving and implementation	Supplier and customer develop and implement jointly by intense interaction
III	Total cooperation	Supplier and customer interact intensely in all phases of the process

Source: Jan B. Vollering, "Interaction Strategies for Marketing Development of Industrial Systems," *Proceedings of the International Research Seminar on Industrial Marketing,* August 29–31, 1984, Stockholm School of Economics.

According to Vollering's model, the supplier's and purchaser's preferences for an interaction strategy can be mapped on the following grid to determine where the dominance and intensity expectations lie.

Supplier Interaction Preference

		Customer Dominated	Intense Interaction	Supplier Dominated
Customer Interaction Preference	Customer Dominated	!!	??	No agreement
	Intense Interaction	??	!!	??
	Supplier Dominated	No action	??	!!

If there are compatible expectations, the fit between the two firms is good (indicated with a !!). If expectations differ (indicated with a ??), interactions are unstable. When both supplier and customer prefer to dominate all interactions, there is no agreement. When both supplier and customer prefer to let the other dominate, no action is taken.

Once an alliance is formed, bargaining positions typically change through information transfers and an ability to learn and adapt. Strong alliances occur when both parties strive to make the most out of the alliance by optimizing the benefits of the alliance. Optimizing benefits means that both partners maximize their gains from the alliance without minimizing the other party's benefits. This is possible when both companies exhibit (1) a managerial willingness to learn, (2) an ability to control the pace of information transfer, and (3) a determination to exploit newly acquired skills to reduce fixed costs.[26]

This ability (or inability) of the business marketing manager to learn and adapt to another company is often cited as a prime reason for alliance success or failure. As an alliance creates new opportunities or there are changes in the competitive landscape, some managers are able to adapt and extract value from the alliance, which greatly improves their bargaining position. If the managers of both companies in the alliance are able to extract value, combined improvements keep bargaining positions close to status quo. According to C. K. Prahalad, U.S. firms have not fared well in joint ventures with foreign partners, in part because of a difficulty in learning from their partners. The improved capacity of the marketing manager to learn and absorb comes from communicating the purpose of alliances to operating-level employees and supporting an organizational structure that defines employees' roles in an alliance.

STRATEGIC ALLIANCES AND THE MARKETING MANAGER

Chapter 3 discussed in detail the concept that global competition is increasing for U.S. business marketing companies. This chapter has focused on strategic alliances as useful ways to improve a firm's competence. Given these two premises, how can business marketing managers develop marketing strategies in such an environment?

Business marketing in an environment with increasingly dense "webs" of business-to-business relationships requires some new marketing skills in addition to applying more traditional skills in new ways. The marketing concepts of positioning and segmenting become even more important in business marketing as networks and alliances grow. In addition, marketing information systems will have to include more thorough sourcing and more systematic data organization. For example, these systems will have to be capable of assessing other firms' internal structures, styles, and cultures. Finally, some individual or some department will have to be responsible for business relationships. In many business marketing firms, the most logical choice is the marketing department because of its external orientation. But this may cause problems when the marketing personnel involved seek short-term gains, which is often the case. These shortcomings must be overcome with a strategic view of long-term relationship management if the marketing manager is to take responsibility for managing strategic alliances. This may be a difficult undertaking for a marketing manager as evidence suggests that many existing business marketing relationships in the United States are adversarial or arm's length in nature. These will have to be changed if strategic alliances are to succeed, and breaking old habits is sometimes hard.

Perhaps the first step is for the manager to assess his or her own company's unique contributions to the market, core competencies, and relative size and leadership abilities. Chapters 10 and 11 will discuss such analyses in some depth but it should be understood here that the firm must determine what it has to contribute to an alliance before one is created. Then the manager should attempt to determine similar characteristics in other firms selling to the same target market customers. This approach provides a basis for targeting the most likely partners based on realistic assumptions of the company's skills and an assessment of the target market.

Since social ties have been found to be such strong forces within strategic alliances, the marketing manager must work at building and maintaining such relationships. In many ways, marketing to prospective partners is not much different from marketing to prospective customers. At the same time, the marketing manager must create opportunities for both of the organizations involved. This is the primary marketing tool used to market within strategic alliances and other business marketing networks. Many authorities believe that most relationship building takes place in the negotiation process. Thus, negotiating with prospective or present suppliers, customers, channel intermediaries, employees, etc., provides possibilities for developing partnering relationships and the manager must take advantage of such opportunities. According to experts in negotiation, there are certain guidelines that if followed may facilitate the creation of the desired relationships. These guidelines are as follows: [27]

1. Be rational. Even if your counterpart is acting emotionally, balance emotions with reason.

2. Be understanding. Even if your counterpart misunderstands you, try to understand him or her.

3. Communicate. Even if he or she is not listening, consult with your counterpart before deciding on matters that concern him or her.

4. Be reliable. Even if your counterpart is trying to deceive, neither trust nor deceive him or her—be reliable.

5. Avoid coercion. Even if your counterpart is trying to coerce you, neither yield to the coercion nor try to coerce him or her—be open to persuasion and try to persuade.

6. Be accepting. Even if your counterpart rejects you and your concerns as unworthy of consideration, accept him or her as worthy of your consideration, care about him or her, and be open to learning from him or her.

These are general guidelines to follow in negotiating with prospective partners. Exhibit 7.6 provides tips that are considered by both manufacturers and manufacturers' representatives to be important in the creation and maintenance of successful partnering relationships. But effective business marketing is more than just negotiating. There must be positions to negotiate from and this is where traditional marketing skills are valuable. For the marketing manager whose company enjoys high-quality products or services, cost-effective distribution capabilities, sound sales personnel, good promotional skills, and effective

EXHIBIT 7.6   Tips for Creating Closer Relationships Between Manufacturers and Manufacturers' Representatives

Creating and maintaining relationships with manufacturers' representatives is a primary responsibility of many business marketing managers. A panel of manufacturers and manufacturers' representatives were queried by *Agency Sales Magazine* to determine what factors were most important in creating closer relationships between the two. The following were seen as crucial in developing and maintaining such relationships:

1. Effort. To make such a relationship work, both parties must exert the effort necessary to build a solid, long-lasting relationship. Work at creating close personal relationships as well as close business relationships.

2. Honesty. Both parties must be totally honest with each other even when it may not be to the advantage of one or both of the partners.

3. Work together. Both parties must be willing to work together on all matters of concern and work out amicable solutions (for good or bad) for those matters. Teamwork is the key.

4. Communicate. For such a relationship to work, both parties must regularly communicate with each other those things that are necessary to continue the relationship.

5. Commitment. Both parties must have a solid commitment toward the relationship. Each partner must recognize that the other has as much commitment as it does toward creating and maintaining the relationship. Providing support to each other may be vital to exhibiting such commitment.

6. Details. Pay attention to details. Lack of attention to details by one partner is an aggravation to the other partner and could ultimately cause the dissolution of the relationship even though the individual disparities may not be of much consequence if taken separately.

7. Promptness. Both parties should be prompt in their dealings with one another. Deliver on promises made and deliver as promptly as possible. In a true partnership, serving one another in a prompt and efficient manner is only logical.

In summary, doing these things builds trust and confidence in the relationship. Each partner must have unwavering trust and confidence in the other if the relationship is to flourish. The surveyed panel believed the above factors are necessary to develop the level of trust and confidence on both sides that is required to maintain a manufacturer–manufacturers' representative relationship over time.

Source: Adapted from "How Manufacturers and Agents Build Solid Relationships," *Agency Sales Magazine* 19 (September 1989): 31–37.

pricing, negotiating with prospective partners becomes easier. In addition, the ability to segment markets properly and serve them effectively also contributes. Thus, it can be seen that searching out and creating strategic relationships is very much part of the marketing manager's responsibilities in business marketing.

CHAPTER SUMMARY

Strategic alliances are business relationships formed with key suppliers, customers, competitiors, stakeholders, or other related businesses such as channel intermediaries. These alliances provide the business marketing manager with another way to obtain and develop expertise in a market, technology, or system of production method that is not readily available through other means. Because of the speed at which new products are being brought to market and increased international competition, many business marketers have turned to strategic alliances as an essential part of marketing strategy and planning. This is particularly true of companies that are facing increased competition and/or rapid changes in technology. Strategic alliances have become commonplace in such industries as automobiles, communications, computers, electronic components, financial services, pharmaceuticals, medical products, and heavy machinery.

Strategic alliances depend on the social ties and relationships developed between people at all levels in each partner company. Differences in national cultures also require different approaches and structures. The chapter has developed the differences in strategic alliances in the U.S., Japanese, and European cultures and focused on marketing to such differences. This is important because misunderstandings of the differences may be a distinct hindrance to the creation of a successful strategic alliance. The importance of negotiation in creating the best opportunity for each partner was stressed, as were the vital roles played by cooperation and trust in the creation and maintenance of such alliances. A format was developed to better facilitate the formation of successful alliances, and choosing the right partner, creating a cooperative process, creating an accountability structure, and observing and controlling a bargaining position were discussed. The chapter then concluded with a discussion of the business marketing manager's responsibilities in the creation and maintenance of successful strategic alliances.

KEY TERMS

acquisition
alliance linkage
business network
cross distribution
cross licensing
merger
opportunistic alliance

partnering relationship
quality partnership
research and development consortium
service alliance
stakeholder alliance
strategic alliance
strategic alliance control

QUESTIONS

1. For the business marketer, what do you see as the major benefits and costs of joining a strategic alliance?
2. Assume that you are the marketing manager in a small biotechnology firm that wants to turn its research into a marketable product. What type of business would you want to partner with? How would you structure an alliance that gives

you access to market and product development skills without giving up your proprietary innovation?

3. In the situation outlined in the previous question, what type of alliance would you recommend? Would you recommend a joint venture, licensing, quality partnership, or some other arrangement? Provide an argument for your choice.

4. If you were the marketing manager in a firm producing glass, how would you begin to develop stronger ties with an auto parts manufacturer in order to create a quality partnering relationship with that manufacturer? What actions would you recommend?

5. You are the marketing manager of a computer manufacturer and you are approached by your counterpart in an international competitor to jointly market your products in their markets. What information would you want in order to determine whether to consider the offer?

6. In the situation outlined in the previous question, how would you structure an alliance that would minimize the potential of future competitive problems?

7. What are the advantages of open and informal communication between alliance partners? What

are some ways one organization can communicate its goals for an alliance to all levels of employees and open communication lines between the partnering organizations without fearing that proprietary or competitive advantage is given away through an exchange of information?

8. Explain why the business marketing manager should consider creating strategic alliances with key customers. What are the advantages and disadvantages of this approach to marketing to important business customers?

9. Explain why the business marketing manager should consider creating strategic alliances with the firm's channel intermediaries such as industrial distributors or manufacturers' representatives? What kinds of factors are important in creating and maintaining solid partnering relationships with key intermediaries?

10. Looking at strategic alliances and partnering relationships in the context of the entire marketing mix, explain the roles played by such relationships in all areas of the marketing mix. In other words, how does the creation of strategic alliances affect the types of decisions made in the product/service, distribution, promotion, and pricing areas of marketing?

NOTES

1. Rosabeth Moss Kanter, "Becoming PALs: Pooling, Allying, and Linking Across Companies," *Academy of Management Executive* (August 1989): 183.
2. Ibid., 183–193.
3. Allan J. Magrath, "Differentiating Yourself Via Distribution," *Sales & Marketing Management* 130 (March 1991): 57.
4. L. Mattson, "An Application of a Network Approach to Marketing," paper presented at the Workshop on Alternative Paradigms in Marketing, University of Rhode Island, May 13–14, 1983, as quoted in Lars-Erik Gadde and Bruce Grant, "Quasi-integration, Supplier Networks and Technological Cooperation in the Automobile Industry," *Proceedings of the International Research Seminar on Industrial Mar-*

keting, August 29–31, 1984, Stockholm School of Economics.
5. Kuniyasu Sakai, "The Feudal World of Japanese Manufacturing," *Harvard Business Review* 68 (November–December 1990): 40.
6. Ibid.
7. Ibid.
8. William J. Holstein, James Treece, Stan Crock, and Larry Armstrong, "Mighty Mitsubishi Is on the Move," *Business Week* (September 24, 1990), 99.
9. Sakai, op. cit., 48.
10. Ibid.
11. Nazeem Seyed Mohamed, "Industrial Marketing in Europe—An Interaction Approach," *Working Paper Series 6,* Department of Business Studies, Uppsala University, 1989.

12. Henrik Brandes and Johan Lilliecreutz, "Structural Changes in Networks," *Research Developments in International Industrial Marketing and Purchasing: Proceedings of the 6th Annual I.M.P. Conference,* 1990, vol. 1, 287.

13. Robert E. Spekman and David T. Wilson, "Managing Strategic Partnerships: Toward an Understanding of Control Mechanisms and Their Impact on Partnership Formation and Maintenance," *Research Developments in International Industrial Marketing and Purchasing: Proceedings of the 6th Annual I.M.P. Conference,* 1990, vol. 2, 1000–1016.

14. Ibid., 1007.

15. F. A. Johne, "Functional and Dysfunctional Structures for Product Innovation," *Proceedings of the International Research Seminar on Industrial Marketing,* August 29–31, 1984, Stockholm School of Economics.

16. See Roger Fisher and Scott Brown, *Getting Together: Building Relationships As We Negotiate* (New York: Penguin Books, 1988).

17. Ibid., 8–9.

18. C. K. Prahalad and Gary Hamel, "The Core Competence of the Corporation," *Harvard Business Review* 68 (May–June 1990):79.

19. K. R. Harrigan, "Strategic Alliances and Partner Asymmetries," *Management International Review* (Special Issue 1988):53–71.

20. Jan Glete, "High Technology and Industrial Networks: Some Notes on the Cooperation Between Swedish High Technology Industries and Their Customers," *Proceedings of the International Research Seminar on Industrial Marketing,* August 29–31, 1984, Stockholm School of Economics.

21. See Hakan Hakansson, ed., *International Marketing and Purchasing of Industrial Goods: An Interaction Approach* (Chichester: John Wiley, 1982).

22. Nils Kinch, "The Long-Term Development of a Supplier–Buyer Relation: The Case of the Olofstrom–Volvo Relationship," first draft paper presented at the International Research Seminar on Industrial Marketing, August 29–31, 1984, Stockholm School of Economics.

23. See George Weimer, Bernie Knill, Stanley J. Modic, and Caren Potter, "Integrated Manufacturing VI—Successful Strategic Alliances: Making Strategic Alliances Work," *CAE* 7, no. 11 (November 1988).

24. Leigh Bruce, "Strained Alliances," *International Management* (London, May 1990), 28–34, and "Perils of Cross-border Alliances," *International Management* (London, May 1990).

25. Jan B. Vollering, "Interaction Strategies for Marketing Development of Industrial Systems," *Proceedings of the International Research Seminar on Industrial Marketing,* August 29–31, 1984, Stockholm School of Economics.

26. R. G. Bertodo, "The Strategic Alliance: Automotive Paradigm for the 1990's," *International Journal of Technology Management* 5, no. 4 (Switzerland, 1990).

27. Fisher and Brown, op. cit., 38.

SUGGESTED ADDITIONAL READINGS

Achrol, Ravi S., Lisa K. Scheer, and Louis W. Stern. *Designing Successful Transorganizational Marketing Alliances.* Cambridge, MA: Marketing Science Institute, 1990.

Anderson, James C., and James A. Narus. "A Model of Distributor Firm and Manufacturer Firm Working Partnerships." *Journal of Marketing* 54 (January 1990):42–58.

Baranson, Jack. "Transnational Strategic Alliances: Why, What, Where, and How." *Multinational Business* (UK) (Summer 1990):54–61.

Barber, Norman F. "Linking Trading Partners: More Than Just Technical Connectivity." *EDI World* 1 (January 1991):31–34.

Devlin, Godfrey, and Ian Biggs. "Partners in the Strategic Quick-Step." *Accountancy* (UK) (November 1989):144–146.

DeYoung, H. Garret, and Dwight B. Davis. "Strategic Alliances: Piecing Together Successful World-Class Partnerships." *Electronic Business* (May 28, 1990):32–40.

Dwyer, F. Robert, Paul Schurr, and Sejo Oh. "Developing Buyer–Seller Relationships." *Journal of Marketing* 51 (April 1987): 11–27.

Ford, David. "The Development of Buyer–Seller Relationships in Industrial Markets." *European Journal of Marketing* 14 (May–June 1980): 339–353.

Frazier, Gary L., and Raymond C. Rody. "The Use of Influence Strategies in Interfirm Relationships in Industrial Product Channels." *Journal of Marketing* 55 (January 1991): 52–69.

Frazier, Gary L., Robert E. Spekman, and Charles R. O'Neal. "Just-in-Time Exchange Relationships in Industrial Markets." *Journal of Marketing* 52 (October 1988): 52–67.

Gross, Thomas, and John Neuman. "Strategic Alliances Vital in Global Marketing." *Marketing News* 22 (June 19, 1989): 1–2.

Jackson, L. P., and J. B. Wilcox. "Building Customer Relationships That Last." *Harvard Business Review* 63 (November–December 1985): 120–128.

Lascelles, D. M., and B. G. Dale. "The Buyer–Seller Relationship in Total Quality Management." *Journal of Purchasing and Materials Management* 25 (Summer 1989): 10–19.

Lorange, Peter, and Johan Roos. "Why Some Strategic Alliances Succeed and Others Fail." *Journal of Business Strategy* (January–February 1991): 25–30.

Lynch, Robert P. "Building Alliances to Penetrate European Markets." *Journal of Business Strategy* (March–April 1990): 4–8.

Noordewier, Thomas G., George John, and John R. Nevin. "Performance Outcomes of Purchasing Arrangements in Industrial Buyer–Vendor Relationships." *Journal of Marketing* 54 (October 1990): 80–93.

Ohmae, Kenichi. "The Global Logic of Strategic Alliances." *Harvard Business Review* 67 (March 1989): 143–154.

Ross, William T. *Managing Marketing Channel Relationships.* Cambridge, MA: Marketing Science Institute, 1985.

Spekman, Robert E., and Wesley Johnston. "Relationship Management: Managing the Selling and Buying Interface." *Journal of Business Research* (December 1986): 519–533.

Spekman, Robert E., and Kirti Sawhney. *Toward a Conceptual Understanding of the Antecedents of Strategic Alliances.* Cambridge, MA: Marketing Science Institute, 1990.

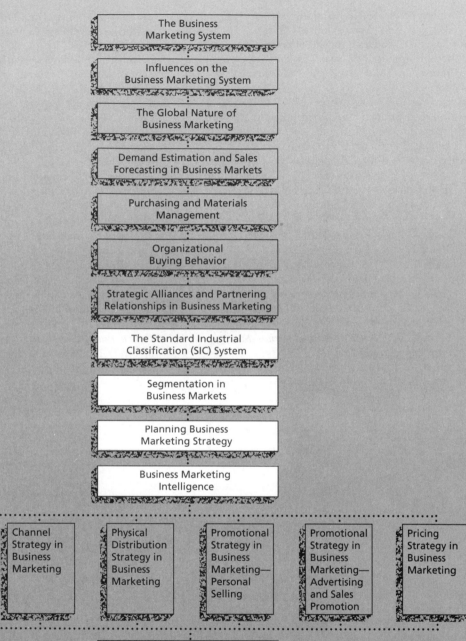

The Business
Marketing System

Influences on the
Business Marketing System

The Global Nature of
Business Marketing

Demand Estimation and Sales
Forecasting in Business Markets

Purchasing and Materials
Management

Organizational
Buying Behavior

Strategic Alliances and Partnering
Relationships in Business Marketing

The Standard Industrial
Classification (SIC) System

Segmentation in
Business Markets

Planning Business
Marketing Strategy

Business Marketing
Intelligence

Product
and Service
Strategy in
Business
Marketing

Channel
Strategy in
Business
Marketing

Physical
Distribution
Strategy in
Business
Marketing

Promotional
Strategy in
Business
Marketing—
Personal
Selling

Promotional
Strategy in
Business
Marketing—
Advertising
and Sales
Promotion

Pricing
Strategy in
Business
Marketing

Business Marketing
Control and Evaluation

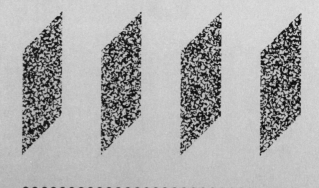

The Business Marketing Process: Segmentation, Planning, Strategy, and Intelligence Gathering

8

The Standard Industrial Classification (SIC) System

• •

From the discussion thus far, it is apparent that business marketing, in focusing on various types of organizational markets, requires an approach that will provide information on customers and prospects in these markets. Fortunately, a very useful tool already exists that facilitates such a search, the **Standard Industrial Classification system,** commonly referred to as SIC. The SIC system is especially useful in that it classifies all types of organizations according to basic four-digit U.S. government **Standard Industrial Classification codes.** The SIC system is the standard that underlies all establishment-based federal economic statistics classified by industry. The classification covers the entire field of economic activities and defines industries in accordance with the composition and structure of the economy.[1] This chapter explains the SIC system and outlines its strengths and weaknesses for business marketing purposes. Additional sources of SIC-related information are examined, and specific marketing uses are developed as these apply to business marketing decision making.

WHAT IS THE SIC SYSTEM?

Standardization of the United States Government Industrial Classification was originated in the mid-1930s by the federal government to provide macro-oriented statistical aggregation of significant economic activity. The purpose of this aggregation was to allow government agencies to perform their functions in a more effective manner.[2] The responsibility for determining SIC codes lies with the Statistical Policy Office, a department of the Office of Management and Budget.

242

Use of the Standard Industrial Classification (SIC) System in Business Marketing

Terramarine Bioresearch, Inc., a small (less than twenty-five employees) high-tech biochemical firm located in San Diego County, California, was founded by a number of biochemists who wanted to find commercial applications for their biochemical expertise. Management decided to concentrate its efforts on producing diagnostic reagent chemicals that would be sold to manufacturers of medical testing apparatus, such as instruments used in blood testing, etc. The idea was that Terramarine could become a subcontractor to the large instrument manufacturers. But success was slow in coming. After five years, the company had but two customers, both of whom had called on Terramarine thinking the company was a possible customer only to find it to be a supplier. Purchases by these two customers had kept the firm in existence but little more. Then management learned of the SIC system.

After recognizing that SIC could contribute to future marketing activities, Terramarine used Dun & Bradstreet's *Million Dollar Directory* and Standard and Poor's *Poor's Register* to find what SIC number was assigned to its two customers. Because this was before the 1987 revision of the *SIC Manual,* the number was found to be SIC 3811 for both. Then, using the *Census of Manufactures* and *U.S. Industrial Outlook,* it was discovered that approximately 1,200 firms in the United States were classified by this code. From those same sources and Sales & Marketing Management's *Survey of In-dustrial and Commercial Buying Power,* the company was also able to determine where these firms were located. At that time, however, further analysis revealed that not all SIC 3811 firms produced medical testing apparatus. Included in this code were manufacturers of aeronautical, nautical, measuring, and other such testing equipment. Thus, some method of selecting the appropriate SIC 3811 firms had to be devised. This was accomplished by looking up individual 3811 firms in the *Million Dollar Directory,* the *Poor's Register,* and industrial directories in states where concentrations were already known to exist. The result was the discovery of about 400 SIC 3811 firms that were true prospects for Terramarine's expertise—they were known to produce instruments that required diagnostic reagent chemicals of one type or another. Through the directories, the company found names, addresses, telephone numbers, names of key executives, etc., for these prospects. Using this list, the company passed on the information to its salespeople in the field. It also sent direct mail pieces to each prospect and called the larger prospects to arrange for possible sales calls. The end result of this very economical program was that the company discovered prospects previously unknown and built its marketing programs to attract these same prospects. Thus, use of the SIC system facilitated the development of a more focused and cost-effective marketing plan.

SIC is a uniform numbering system for classifying establishments in the United States according to the economic activity engaged in by those establishments. These establishments may be private businesses, institutions, or government agencies; they are classified by economic activity and compiled in the *Standard Industrial Classification Manual.* This manual, which is published periodically, was most recently revised in 1987, replacing the 1972 manual and its 1977 supplement.

The 1987 **Standard Industrial Classification revision** takes into account technological and institutional changes that have occurred in the U.S. economy and attempts to improve industry detail, coverage, and definitions. The revision resulted in an increase of industries for services, wholesale trade, and manufacturing. Table 8.1 shows some examples of new industry groups created by the 1987 manual. In addition, some industries were deleted and were merged into

TABLE 8.1	**Examples of New Industry Groups Created by the 1987 SIC Manual Revision**
SIC	Description of the New Industry Group
3571	Electronic Computers
3572	Computer Storage Devices
3575	Computer Terminals
3577	Computer Peripheral Equipment
3695	Recording Media (Blank Disks)
7371	Computer Programming Services
7372	Prepackaged Software
7373	Computer Integrated Systems Design
7374	Computer Processing & Data Preparation Services
7375	Information Retrieval Services
7376	Computer Facilities Management Services
7377	Computer Rental & Leasing
7378	Computer Maintenance & Repair
7379	Computer Related Services, n.e.c.*
7291	Tax Return Preparation Services
7334	Photocopying & Duplicating Services
7382	Security Systems Services
7841	Video Tape Rental
7991	Physical Fitness Facilities
8082	Home Health Care Services
8741	Management Services
7842	Management Consulting Services
8743	Public Relations Services
8748	Business Consulting Services, n.e.c.*

Source: Office of Management and Budget, *Standard Industrial Classification Manual 1987* (Washington, DC: U.S. Government Printing Office, 1987).

*not elsewhere classified

other industries, and new industries were created by subdividing or restructuring existing industries. An appendix in the 1987 manual illustrates all changes made since the 1972 manual and the 1977 supplement.

The basis of the SIC manual is relatively easy to understand. The U.S. economy is divided into eleven divisions, including one for nonclassifiable establishments. Within each division, major industry groups are classified by two-digit numbers. Table 8.2 illustrates the basis of the SIC system: the eleven divisions and the major industry groups within each division. For example, all manufacturing firms are in division D, and two-digit numbers from 20 to 39 indicate major manufacturing industries. All manufacturers of textile mill products are included in SIC 22, whereas SIC 25 includes all manufacturers of furniture and fixtures, and SIC 37 includes all manufacturers of transportation equipment. As can be seen, the two-digit SIC numbers describe major or basic industries. These major industries can be further subdivided into three-, four-, five-, and seven-digit SIC numbers.

Within each major two-digit SIC industry group, industry subgroups are defined by a third digit, and detailed industries are defined by a fourth digit. These additional digits form the basis of the four-digit SIC system found in the *Standard Industrial Classification Manual*—the longer the number, the more detailed is the industry being defined. It is also possible to supplement the four-digit SIC numbers with five- and seven-digit SIC numbers provided by the *Census of Manufactures* and other, similar census sources covering mining, construction, and selected services. Table 8.3 shows the breakdown of the SIC system by different classifications carried out to a seven-digit number.

Figure 8.1 expands Table 8.3 to show the detailed breakdown possible. As the figure shows, the seven-digit SIC numbers are quite specific and provide good business market segmentation criteria. For example, note that SIC 3441121 defines fabricated structural metal for buildings—iron and steel—for sale to other industrial companies. SIC 3441122 defines the same products, but for sale to commercial rather than industrial customers, and SIC 3441127 defines these same products for sale to public utilities. In this case, the seven-digit SIC numbers provide market data not available through the four-digit SIC numbers provided by the *Standard Industrial Classification Manual.*

This discussion shows that the business marketing manager can access an existing classification system for marketing purposes. Organizations of every type, including government agencies, are already classified by SIC codes. When the manager can determine enough about present and potential customers to classify them into SIC number designations of a four-digit minimum, that manager has taken a major step toward locating such customers, determining their sizes, and determining sales and market potentials. Because SIC codes provide access to a wealth of data pertaining to organizational customers in both domestic and international markets, they are widely used in business markets. The existing four-digit SIC code is used by most, if not all, major business marketers.[3]

TABLE 8.2   The Standard Industrial Classification (SIC) System

Division	Industries Classified	Division	Industries Classified
A	*Agriculture, forestry, and fishing*		Major Group 35. Industrial and commercial machinery and computer equipment
	Major Group 01. Agricultural production—crops		Major Group 36. Electronic and other electrical equipment and components, except computer equipment
	Major Group 02. Agriculture production livestock and animal specialties		Major Group 37. Transportation equipment
	Major Group 07. Agriculture services		Major Group 38. Measuring, analyzing, and controlling instruments; photographic, medical, and optical goods; watches and clocks
	Major Group 08. Forestry		Major Group 39. Miscellaneous manufacturing industries
	Major Group 09. Fishing, hunting, and trapping		
B	*Mining*	*E*	*Transportation, communications, electric, gas, and sanitary services*
	Major Group 10. Metal mining		Major Group 40. Railroad transportation
	Major Group 12. Coal mining		Major Group 41. Local and suburban transit and interurban highway passenger transportation
	Major Group 13. Oil and gas extraction		Major Group 42. Motor freight transportation and warehousing
	Major Group 14. Mining and quarrying of non-metallic minerals, except fuels		Major Group 43. United States Postal Service
C	*Construction*		Major Group 44. Water transportation
	Major Group 15. Building construction—general contractors and operative builders		Major Group 45. Transportation by air
	Major Group 16. Heavy construction other than building construction—contractors		Major Group 46. Pipelines, except natural gas
	Major Group 17. Construction—special trade contractors		Major Group 47. Transportation services
D	*Manufacturing*		Major Group 48. Communications
	Major Group 20. Food and kindred products		Major Group 49. Electric, gas, and sanitary services
	Major Group 21. Tobacco products	*F*	*Wholesale trade*
	Major Group 22. Textile mill products		Major Group 50. Wholesale trade—durable goods
	Major Group 23. Apparel and other finished products made from fabrics and similar materials		Major Group 51. Wholesale trade—nondurable goods
	Major Group 24. Lumber and wood products, except furniture	*G*	*Retail trade*
	Major Group 25. Furniture and fixtures		Major Group 52. Building materials, hardware, garden supply, and mobile home dealers
	Major Group 26. Paper and allied products		Major Group 53. General merchandise stores
	Major Group 27. Printing, publishing, and allied industries		Major Group 54. Food stores
	Major Group 28. Chemicals and allied products		Major Group 55. Automotive dealers and gasoline service stations
	Major Group 29. Petroleum refining and related industries		Major Group 56. Apparel and accessory stores
	Major Group 30. Rubber and miscellaneous plastics products		Major Group 57. Home furniture, furnishings, and equipment stores
	Major Group 31. Leather and leather products		Major Group 58. Eating and drinking places
	Major Group 32. Stone, clay, glass, and concrete products		Major Group 59. Miscellaneous retail
	Major Group 33. Primary metal industries		
	Major Group 34. Fabricated metal products, except machinery and transportation equipment		

TABLE 8.2   Continued

Division	Industries Classified	Division	Industries Classified
H	*Finance, insurance, and real estate*		Major Group 83. Social services
	Major Group 60. Depository institutions		Major Group 84. Museums, art galleries, and botanical and zoological gardens
	Major Group 61. Nondepository credit institutions		Major Group 86. Membership organizations
	Major Group 62. Security and commodity brokers, dealers, exchanges, and services		Major Group 87. Engineering, accounting, research, management, and related services
	Major Group 63. Insurance carriers		Major Group 88. Private households
	Major Group 64. Insurance agents, brokers, and service		Major Group 89. Miscellaneous services
	Major Group 65. Real estate	*J*	*Public administration*
	Major Group 67. Holding and other investment offices		Major Group 91. Executive, legislative, and general government, except finance
I	*Services*		Major Group 92. Justice, public order, and safety
	Major Group 70. Hotels, rooming houses, camps, and other lodging places		Major Group 93. Public finance, taxation, and monetary policy
	Major Group 72. Personal services		Major Group 94. Administration of human resources programs
	Major Group 73. Business services		Major Group 95. Administration of environmental quality and housing programs
	Major Group 75. Automotive repair, services, and parking		Major Group 96. Administration of economic programs
	Major Group 76. Miscellaneous repair services		Major Group 97. National security and international affairs
	Major Group 78. Motion pictures		
	Major Group 79. Amusement and recreation services	*K*	*Nonclassifiable establishments*
	Major Group 80. Health services		Major Group 99. Nonclassifiable establishments
	Major Group 81. Legal services		
	Major Group 82. Educational services		

Source: Office of Management and Budget, *Standard Industrial Classification Manual 1987* (Washington, DC: U.S. Government Printing Office, 1987), 7–9.

TABLE 8.3   Breakdown of the Standard Industrial Classification System

Classification	SIC Number	Description
Division	D	Manufacturing
Major group	34	Manufacturers of fabricated metal products
Industry subgroup	344	Manufacturers of fabricated structural metal products
Detailed industry	3441	Manufacturers of fabricated structural metal
Manufactured products	34411	Manufacturers of fabricated structural metal for buildings
Manufactured products	3441121	Manufacturers of fabricated structural metal for buildings—iron and steel (for sale to other companies): industrial

Source: Adapted from Office of Management and Budget, *Standard Industrial Classification Manual 1987* (Washington, DC: U.S. Government Printing Office, 1987); U.S. Bureau of the Census, *1982 Census of Manufactures: Fabricated Structural Metal Products* (Washington, DC: U.S. Government Printing Office, 1984).

FIGURE 8.1 Breakdown of the Standard Industrial Classification System. Example: Manufacturers of Fabricated Metal Products

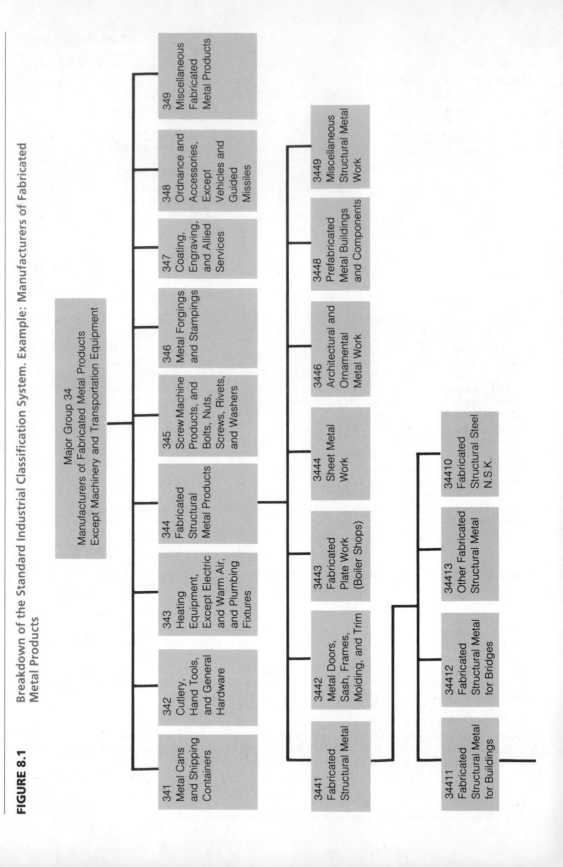

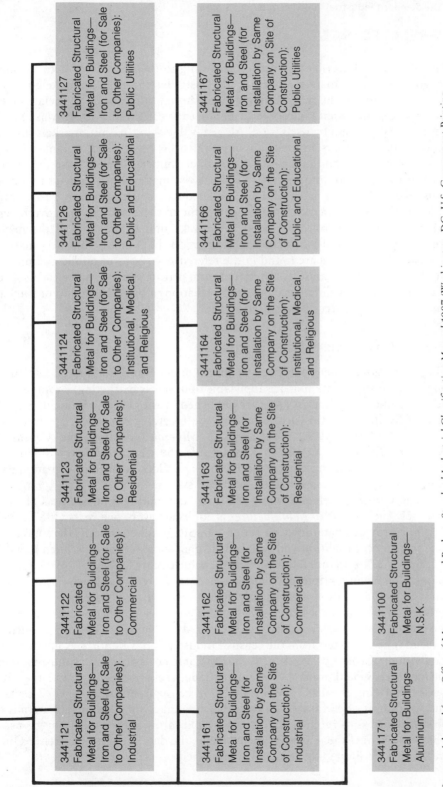

Source: Adapted from Office of Management and Budget, *Standard Industrial Classification Manual 1987* (Washington, DC: U.S. Government Printing Office, 1987); and U.S. Bureau of the Census, *1982 Census of Manufactures: Fabricated Structural Metal Products* (Washington, DC: U.S. Government Printing Office, 1984).

SOURCES OF SIC-RELATED DATA

The SIC manual classifies industries according to their economic activity only; it provides no information other than the basic classification. To make good use of the SIC system, the marketing manager should know what SIC-related data sources exist and what kinds of information each can offer. Without this knowledge, the SIC system by itself is of little real value—but with it, markets may be segmented, customers located, buying influences determined, volume of purchases discovered, and other such factors determined. The SIC system permits access to a wealth of information that otherwise may be quite difficult to locate. This section discusses many of the SIC-related data sources that are easily available to the business marketing manager. Some of these sources are governmental; others are in private business. Table 8.4 summarizes some of the major sources of SIC-related information pertaining to the domestic business market. Many of these sources are found in the reference sections of public and university libraries. Others must be purchased from private sources. Since each source provides somewhat different types of information, a brief discussion of some of the more useful sources is warranted.

Federal Government Data Sources

The federal government publishes an almost unbelievable amount of data based on the SIC system, data that are applicable to business marketing. Examples can be seen in the many censuses that are published by the U.S. Department of Commerce. To illustrate, this department of the federal government produces the *Census of Manufactures,* the *Census of Mineral Industries,* the *Census of Wholesale Trade,* the *Census of Retail Trade,* the *Census of Selected Services,* and the *Census of Construction.* Each census provides detailed information particular to its own coverage based on the SIC system.

The *Census of Manufactures* illustrates the marketing usefulness of these censuses. The *Census of Manufactures* is published every five years (1982, 1987, etc.) and provides data down to seven-digit SIC number codes. This source details industry information and can provide data such as that illustrated in Table 8.5 for SIC 3714 (manufacturers of motor vehicle parts and accessories). If these manufacturers are prime customers, the data show 2,420 such firms in the United States and, more significantly, fifty-nine companies with over 1,000 employees. In addition, these fifty-nine large companies comprise 59.5 percent of the buying power in this industry, as measured by "value added."[4] Data such as these may be extracted from the census's Industry Series Reports. A major problem with the *Census of Manufactures* is that it is not as current as most marketing managers would prefer—the data are updated every five years, with the 1987 census replacing the 1982 census, the 1982 census replacing the 1977 census, and so forth. It often takes a considerable amount of time for these materials to be distributed into reference areas, such as libraries, where they may be used. Thus, by the time the materials are available, the data are not as current as they were when the individual census was published.

TABLE 8.4 Sources of Data on Domestic Business Markets Based on SIC

Source	How Often Published	Number of Digits of SIC Information	Type of Data Contained
U.S. Census of Manufactures, Mineral Industries, Wholesale Trade, Retail Trade, Selected Services, Construction	Every 5 years: 1967, 1972, 1977, 1982, 1987, etc.	2-, 3-, 4-, 5-, and 7-digit data	Detailed industry information by time periods, area, product classes
U.S. Survey of Manufactures	Years other than when census is published	2-, 3-, 4-, and 5-digit data	Data similar to that in census of manufactures but less detailed
U.S. Industrial Outlook	Annually	3-, 4-, and 5-digit data	Number of companies, where concentrated, past industry trends, projected trends
County Business Patterns	Annually	2-, 3-, and 4-digit data	Number of employees, taxable payrolls, total reporting units by state and county
Dun & Bradstreet's Annual Business Statistics Reports	Not published—computerized data bank	4-digit data	Number of establishments, number of large establishments, value of goods produced or distributed, or services rendered for total U.S. and by state and county
Private industrial directories (e.g., Standard and Poor's Register, Dun & Bradstreet's Million Dollar Directory)	Annually	4-digit data	Company names, addresses, primary and secondary SICs, products produced, sales volumes, names of key executives
State/county/municipality directories (e.g., MacRae's State Industrial Directories, Harris Publishing)	Varies—some annually, some every 2 years	4-digit data	Company names, addresses, primary and secondary SICs, products produced, sales volumes, names of key executives
Predicasts's "Basebook" and "Forecasts"	Quarterly, also in computerized data banks	7-digit data	Short- and long-term forecasts by SIC, article abstracts, market size measurements, time series data, annual growth rates, and data sources
Dun's Census of American Business	Annually	4-digit data	Number of companies, by employee size, by sales volume, by state and county
Databases (e.g., Dun & Bradstreet's "Market Identifiers," Trinet, Inc., Electronic Yellow Pages, Market Statistics, Thomas Marketing Information Center, American Business Directories)	Not published—computerized data bank	4- and 5-digit data	Company names, addresses, SICs, sales volumes, products produced, number of employees, names of key executives, market share, estimated consumption of products/services, more detailed company data on request
Mailing list companies (e.g., National Business Lists, R. L. Polk, Thomas, Ed Burnett, American Business Lists, Inc.)	Not published—computerized data bank	4- and 5-digit data	Labels, printouts, diskettes, tapes—company names and addresses, more detailed company data on request

Source: Adapted from Robert W. Haas, "SIC System and Related Data for More Effective Market Research," *Industrial Marketing Management* 6 (1977):431.

TABLE 8.5 Types of SIC Data Available from U.S. *Census of Manufactures* Using SIC 3714 Motor Vehicle Parts and Accessories as an Example

Establishment Size (# Employees)	Number of Establishments	Number of Employees (1,000)	Value Added by Manufacture ($ Million)	Cost of Materials ($ Million)	Value of Shipments ($ Million)	New Capital Expenditures ($ Million)
1–4	589	1.1	37.4	41.7	78.8	5.8
5–9	345	2.3	78.1	90.0	169.1	9.9
10–19	375	5.2	170.5	183.2	355.3	14.6
20–49	395	12.2	392.5	454.6	852.2	39.1
50–99	229	15.7	619.6	706.8	1,325.7	60.7
100–249	248	40.0	1,586.3	1,767.4	3,383.3	97.0
250–499	120	42.3	1,767.0	1,859.0	3,736.9	133.9
500–999	60	40.0	2,134.6	1,914.6	4,076.9	115.1
1,000+	59	162.6	9,978.6	11,988.8	22,315.0	1,315.5
Total	2,420	321.4	16,764.6	19,006.1	36,293.2	1,791.6

5-Digit SIC	Description	Number of Establishments	Number of Employees (1,000)	Value Added by Manufacture ($ Million)	Cost of Materials ($ Million)	Value of Shipments ($ Million)	New Capital Expenditures ($ Million)
37142	Gasoline engines	179	58.2	3,183.2	4,244.5	7,512.6	580.7
37143	Rebuilt parts	203	15.7	519.6	478.1	993.0	22.0
37144	Filters	34	11.7	501.9	481.5	986.8	18.1
37145	Exhaust system parts	63	14.4	874.3	906.5	1,799.5	43.1
37146	Drive train components	126	70.8	4,142.3	5,252.3	9,609.6	498.5
37147	Motor vehicle wheels	32	7.5	302.4	419.0	731.0	37.2
37148	Brake parts/assemblies	64	17.3	840.6	1,144.3	2,044.4	60.9

Source: Compiled from U.S. Department of Commerce, 1982 *Census of Manufactures: Motor Vehicles and Equipment* (Washington, DC: U.S. Government Printing Office, March 1985), 37A-12, 13.

Despite their limitations, the *Census of Manufactures* and the other economic censuses are useful sources of SIC-related data pertaining to business markets. There is also an *Annual Survey of Manufactures,* which is conducted for those years not covered by the *Census of Manufactures*. Although the *Survey of Manufactures* does not have the depth of coverage of the *Census of Manufactures,* it can be used in conjunction with the latter for updating purposes.

Another good source of data is the U.S. Department of Commerce's *U.S. Industrial Outlook*. This book is published annually, is classified according to four- and five-digit SIC numbers, and contains projections that are useful to the marketing manager. Table 8.6 illustrates the types of information this valuable government source can provide once markets are defined in SIC numbers. If the metal-cutting machine tools market (SIC 3541) is the desired market, it can now be seen that there are over 900 potential customers, of which 612 are small. In addition, the four largest companies account for over one-fifth of all industry shipments.

The industrial marketing manager may also consider the use of *County Business Patterns* as a source of data on business markets, especially when information is desired by county. With this source, it is possible to determine by the

TABLE 8.6   SIC-Based Data Available from Federal Government Sources

Metal-Cutting Machine Tools		Metal-Forming Machine Tools	
SIC code: 3541		SIC code: 3542	
Industry Data:		*Industry Data:*	
Value of industry shipments ($ millions)	2,100	Value of industry shipments ($ millions)	800
Value added ($ millions)	1,385	Value added ($ millions)	490
Total employment (in thousands)	45.0	Total employment (in thousands)	16.5
Total number of establishments	919	Total number of establishments	426
Number of establishments with less than 20 employees	612	Number of establishments with less than 20 employees	263
Percent of industry shipments accounted for by 4 largest companies	22	Percent of industry shipments accounted for by 4 largest companies	18
Major producing states accounting for largest percent of industry shipments		Major producing states accounting for largest percent of industry shipments	
Ohio (22%)		Illinois (24%)	
Michigan (20%)		Ohio (23%)	
Illinois (10%)		Michigan (10%)	
Product Data:		*Product Data:*	
Value of product shipments ($ millions)	1,950	Value of product shipments ($ millions)	775
Value of exports ($ millions)	400	Value of exports ($ millions)	250
Value of imports ($ millions)	900	Value of imports ($ millions)	290
Exports as a percent of shipments	20.5	Exports as a percent of shipments	32.2
Imports as a percent of new supply	31.5	Imports as a percent of new supply	27.2
Imports as a percent of apparent consumption	36.7	Imports as a percent of apparent consumption	35.6

Source: Compiled from various issues of *U.S. Industrial Outlook,* 1984–1987.

basic four-digit SIC code the number of firms in a particular county and the number of employees for each company. In addition to these federal government sources, state and county governments sometimes provide data pertaining to business concentrations in their areas in **state/county business directories.**

Nongovernment Data Sources

Private sources also provide useful SIC-related information. Some of the best-known sources are as follows.

The "Survey of Industrial & Commercial Buying Power" From 1974 to 1988, *Sales & Marketing Management* magazine published annual surveys of domestic industrial and commercial purchasing power that provided information based on four-digit SIC numbers by state and county. The surveys showed the total number of establishments classified by SIC for each county. In addition, they showed how many of the establishments were large (100 or more employees), total shipments from all county establishments, the county's percentage of all U.S. shipments or receipts, and the percentage of county shipments accounted for by the large establishments. In 1988, *Sales & Marketing Management* discontinued publishing this source.

Beginning in 1990, however, Dun's Marketing Services began providing the same data under the title of *Dun's Marketing Services 1990 Business Statistics Report.* Although the information was not published, it could be purchased from Dun & Bradstreet. For example, the survey might show that in San Diego County, California, there are thirty-nine establishments classified by SIC code 3571 (manufacturers of electronic computers). Of these thirty-nine, five have 100 or more employees and thus are considered large. Total shipments by the thirty-nine firms was $457.9 million in 1990, which accounts for about 1.6 percent of all U.S. shipments by firms in this SIC designation. Seventy percent of the $457.9 million in shipments was accounted for by the five large firms.[5] As can be seen, this is an especially useful source for determining the number of prospects by SIC code, county, and size, and it also permits the manager to locate those counties where the greatest number of prospects are located.

While *Sales & Marketing Management* magazine no longer publishes the previously discussed survey, it does still publish a similar source that uses the same format but reports data only on a national basis. It shows by four-digit SIC code the total number of U.S. establishments, the number that are large (100 or more employees), employment, shipments or receipts, and the percentage accounted for by large establishments.[6] For the business marketing manager, the "Survey of Industrial & Commercial Buying Power" was a valuable marketing tool and its adoption by Dun & Bradstreet should guarantee its continued use.

Private Business Directories A number of privately printed directories also provide information on individual companies by SIC code designations. Thus, once a marketing manager has determined the appropriate four-digit SIC code for prospective customers, it is possible to find information on all companies classified by that code number. Typically, these directories provide information such as company name, address, primary and secondary SIC codes, products produced, sales volumes, number of employees, and names of key executives. Some directories are national in scope, others are for states and even counties. A brief look at each is in order.

Some of the best known national directories are *Standard & Poor's Register of Corporations, Directors & Executives,* and Dun & Bradstreet's *Million Dollar Directory.* The latter, for example, provides basic information on approximately 160,000 companies with assets of $500,000 or more and contains three separate volumes, each with alphabetical, SIC, and geographical indexes.

State industrial directories are available from a number of sources. Each state has its own directory, and some examples are the *California Manufacturers Register, Connecticut State Industrial Directory,* and *Illinois Manufacturers Directory.* Figure 8.2 illustrates a number of these state directories. State directories include listings with companies listed alphabetically, by city and town, product, key executives, SIC codes, number of employees, ZIP codes, telephone numbers, and other such information. Figure 8.3 shows the type of information available from these directories. State directories can be useful when customers or prospects are known to be concentrated in certain states. In addition, such directories include small firms as well as large within the state involved.

Mailing List Companies   Some companies specialize in providing mailing lists and other information based on SIC code designations. Most of these firms provide information on four- and five-digit SIC codes. Some of the better known **mailing list companies** are National Business Lists, R. L. Polk, Ed Burnett Consultants, and American Business Directories, Inc. These companies can provide mailing labels based on SIC codes for all listings in their files. For example, Burnett's file for SIC 3541 (manufacturers of metal-cutting tools) contains 4,230 companies classified by this code. In addition to mailing labels and mailing lists, these companies can also provide magnetic tapes and diskettes based on SIC codes. These sources are useful in that they can provide names of companies in a relatively cheap and efficient manner. Some mailing list companies also provide on-line database services.

Database Services   A number of companies provide database services classified by SIC code to business marketers. Since they do not all provide the same types of services, it is worthwhile to look at some of them as illustrative of information that may be gathered from these sources. Figure 8.4 shows the offerings of one such database company, Harris Publishing Information Services. Trinet, Inc., through its Data Base product line, can provide the name, address, telephone number, SIC code, and employment data on almost every business location in the United States. *Iron Age* magazine has compiled a special six-digit SIC database on over 46,000 plant locations of companies in the domestic metalworking industry. Dun's Marketing Services, a company of The Dun & Bradstreet Corporation, provides a number of on-line information services and direct response services, all classified by SIC code. Figure 8.5 shows the type of infor-

FIGURE 8.2   Illustrations of State Industrial Directories

Source: Reprinted by permission of Manufacturers' News, Inc., Chicago, IL.

FIGURE 8.3

Type of Information Available from State Industrial Directories

Rockford—(cont.)

Sales—$1Mil
Mfg. plant—12,000 sq. ft.
Distrib.—Regional
Year established—1974

J C MILLING CO., INC.
988 Industrial Ct. (61111-7512)
Telephone—(815) 654-1070
FAX—(815) 654-2094
Pres.—John Czaczkowski
Secy.-Treas.—Helen
  Czaczkowski
GM—Steven Harmon
*Cutting tools, fixtures &
  prototypes*
SIC—3599
Employs—25
Sales—$500,000-$1Mil
Mfg. plant—4,000 sq. ft.
Distrib.—Local
Year established—1975
Privately owned corporation

J & D SIGNS
9207 Segunda Ln. (61111)
Telephone—(815) 633-2416
Owner—Jack Houck
Redwood signs
SIC—3993
Employs—1
Sales—under $500,000 (est)
Distrib.—Local

J INDUSTRIES INC.
7576 Forest Hills Rd. (61111-
3304)
Telephone—(815) 654-0055
FAX—(815) 654-9679
Pres., Sales & Mktg. Mgr.—Jeff
  Foster
*Looseleaf binders & menu
  covers*
Brand name—*J-Hyde Line*
SIC—2782
Employs—8
Sales—under $500,000
Mfg. plant—5,000 sq. ft.
Distrib.—National
Year established—1977
Privately owned corporation

J & L ENGINEERING
5055 28th Ave. (61109-1718)
Telephone—(815) 226-8844
Owner—John W. Uhlar
General machining job shop
SIC—3599
Employs—5
Sales—under $500,000 (est)
Mfg. plant—3,000 sq. ft.
Distrib.—Local
Year established—1973
AKA: Uhlar, Inc.

J & M PLATING
1711 Seminary St. (61104-5148)
Telephone—(815) 964-4975
FAX—(815) 964-4979
Pres.—Joe Morris
Sales & Mktg. Mgr.—Mark
  Morris
Pur. Agt.—Ron Roling
Zinc & phosphate plating
SIC—3471
Employs—50
Sales—$1Mil-$5Mil
Distrib.—National
Privately owned corporation

JACKSON SCREW CO.
Div. of Rockford Bolt & Steel Co.
6483 Falcon Rd. (61109-9998)
Telephone—(815) 874-2467
FAX—(815) 874-6261
Pres.—Michael Rosman
V.-P., GM—Dan Anderson
Cont.—Doug Carter
Engr.—Don Gahlbeck
Sales Mgr.—Tom Hendryx
Pur. Agt.—Al Kent
Screws & rivets

SIC—3452
Employs—75
Sales—$5Mil-$10Mil (est)
Mfg. plant—45,000 sq. ft.
Distrib.—Regional
Year established—1950
Computer—IBM System 36 RPG
  II

JAEGER SAW CUTTER
1005-7 5th Ave. (61104-1301)
Telephone—(815) 963-0313
Owner—Franklin Jaeger
*Carbide cutters & blade
  sharpeners*
SIC—3425
Employs—4
Sales—$130,000
Mfg. plant—2,500 sq. ft.
Distrib.—Regional
Year established—1941
Sole ownership

JANAR TOOL CO.
4729 Hydraulic Rd. (61109-2617)
Telephone—(815) 874-9488
FAX—(815) 874-4782
Pres.—H. James Patterson
V.-P., Secy.—Carl Chandler
*NC jig mills, precision machining,
  fixtures & tooling*
SIC—3544
Employs—41
Sales—$1Mil-$5Mil (est)
Mfg. plant—33,000 sq. ft.
Distrib.—Regional
Computer—IBM System 36

JANE'S STAINED GLASS
3422 Lansdale Dr. (61111)
Telephone—(815) 654-8576
Owner—Jane Rapp
*Residential, commercial &
  ornamental stained glass*
SIC—3211
Employs—1
Sales—under $500,000 (est)
Distrib.—Local
Year established—1987

**JEFCO SCREW MACHINE
PRODUCTS, INC.**
6203 Material Ave. (61111)
Mail addr: P.O. Box 2625,
  Rockford (61132-9998)
Telephone—(815) 282-2000
FAX—(815) 282-1328
Pres.—Bruce Mayer
Secy.-Treas., Pur. Agt.—Wilbert
  Mayer
Prodn. Control Mgr.—Theron
  Short
Sales Rep.—Donald Whitchurch
Screw machine products
SIC—3451
Employs—20
Sales—$867,000
Mfg. plant—6,850 sq. ft.
Distrib.—National
Year established—1960
Privately owned corporation

JERHEN INDUSTRIES INC.
5295 28th Ave. (61109-1722)
Telephone—(815) 397-0400
FAX—(815) 397-0710
Pres.—Roger Jerie
V.-P.—Tom Henderson
General machining job shop
SIC—3599
Employs—15
Sales—$500,000-$1Mil (est)
Distrib.—Regional
Year established—1983

JOAQUIN'S TORTILLAS
1325 7th St. (61102-9998)
Telephone—(815) 963-2211
Ptnr.—Robert Campos
Ptnr.—Linda Campos
*Corn & flour tortillas, nachos &
  Mexican bread*
SIC—2099

Employs—4
Sales—under $500,000 (est)
Distrib.—Regional
Year established—1982
Computer—IBM

JOHNSON ENTERPRISES, INC.
220 N. 4th St. (61107-4017)
Telephone—(815) 968-7557
Illinois—(800) 892-2983
National—(800) 435-6950
FAX—(815) 968-0363
Pres.—Arthur L. Johnson
V.-P., GM—Donald Stenger
V.-P., Sales & Mktg.—Walter
  Schoonover
Prodn. Mgr.—Terry Lewis
Pur. Agt.—Brandy Schoonover
Plt. Mgr.—Eugene Adamski
Draft beer dispensing equipment
Brand name—*Beer Sphere*
SIC—3585
Employs—60
Sales—$12Mil
Mfg. plant—20,000 sq. ft.
Distrib.—National
Year established—1962
Privately owned corporation
Computer—IBM System 34 RPG
  II

JOHNSON-OSTIC MFG.
3485 Brick Dr., P.O. Box 6143
  (61125-6143)
Telephone—(815) 874-2826
Pres., Pur. Agt.—Dennis
  Johnson
V.-P.—Al Ostic
Tool & die job shop
SIC—3544
Employs—7
Sales—under $500,000 (est)
Distrib.—Regional
Year established—1982

JOHNSON PRESS, INC., H. C.
Div. of Johnson Group, The
2801 Eastrock Dr., P.O. Box
  5566 (61125-5566)
Telephone—(815) 397-0800
FAX—(815) 397-1304
Pres.—Dale H. Johnson
CEO—Dennis W. Johnson
V.-P., Admn.—Rod Peterson
Sales Mgr.—Gene Toepfer
Mktg. Mgr.—Tonya Meister
Pur. Agt.—Dave Klang
Off. Mgr.—Pam Ingrassia
Plt. Mgr.—Bill Didier
*Commercial printing, color
  separations, typesetting &
  binding*
SIC—2759
Employs—60
Sales—$5Mil-$10Mil
Mfg. plant—30,000 sq. ft.
Distrib.—Regional
Year established—1957
Privately owned corporation
Parent co.—Johnson Group, The
  5214 28th Ave., Rockford
  (61109)

K D SERVICE CO., INC.
1904 7th St. (61104)
Telephone—(815) 965-7800
Pres.—Bradley Carlson
Lock making machines
SIC—3599
Employs—8
Sales—under $500,000 (est)
Distrib.—National
Year established—1985

K & D TOOLING
3019 Wallin Ave. (61101-3447)
Telephone—(815) 963-0668
Pres.—Tim Kampmeier
Plastic injection molds & tools
SIC—3544
Employs—8

Sales—under $500,000 (est)
Distrib.—Local
Year established—1979

K-KAP TOPPER MFG.
4412 W. State St. (61102-1341)
Telephone—(815) 965-8801
Owner—Kevin L. Paulson
Aluminum framed truck tops
SIC—3714
Employs—2
Sales—under $500,000 (est)
Distrib.—Local
Year established—1976

**K & M SCREW MACHINE
PRODUCTS INC.**
5604 Pike Rd. (61111-4711)
Telephone—(815) 877-9579
FAX—(815) 877-0892
Pres.—Wallace Kardell
V.-P., Pur.—Ken Moeller
Secy.-Treas.—Robert Kardell
Sales & Mktg. Mgr.—Kirk
  Moeller
Plt. Mgr.—Earl Trotter
*Screw machine products,
  hydraulic components, CNC
  machines & precision grinding*
SIC—3451
Employs—49
Sales—$1Mil-$5Mil
Mfg. plant—29,000 sq. ft.
Distrib.—Regional
Year established—1976
Privately owned corporation

K W, INC.
2007 Clinton (61103)
Mail addr: P.O. Box 5, Rockford
  (61105-0005)
Telephone—(815) 963-8383
Chrm.—James W. Wolf
Die cast toys
SIC—3944
Employs—15
Sales—$500,000-$1Mil
Mfg. plant—20,000 sq. ft.
Distrib.—International
Year established—1980
Privately owned corporation

[NEW ENTRY]
KADIA CORP.
4848 Stenstrom Rd. (61109)
Telephone—(815) 874-4799
Ex. V.-P.—C. R. Van Sickle
Tooling & deburring
SIC—3541
Employs—2
Sales—under $500,000 (est)
Distrib.—International; Importer
Year established—1962

KADON SCREW MACHINE CO.
832 Roosevelt Rd. (61109-2025)
Telephone—(815) 397-5306
FAX—(815) 397-7630
CEO—James Franklin
Pres.—Jeffrey Franklin
Off. Mgr.—Sue Bollinger
Screw machine products
SIC—3451
Employs—20
Sales—$900,000
Mfg. plant—7,500 sq. ft.
Distrib.—National
Privately owned corporation

**KANNEBERG CUSTOM
KITCHENS**
11122 N. 2nd St. (61111-1408)
Telephone—(815) 654-1110
Owner—Roger Kanneberg
GM—Fred Cook
Kitchen & bath cabinets
SIC—2511
Employs—3
Sales—under $500,000 (est)
Mfg. plant—4,200 sq. ft.
Distrib.—Local
Year established—1968

Source: Reprinted by permission of Manufacturers' News, Inc., Chicago, IL.

FIGURE 8.4   Example of Types of Services Available from Database Companies

Expanding Your Business Profitably is as Easy as 1-2-3 with Harris Information Services

A Division of Harris Publishing Company

- *Identify New Prospects*
- *Qualify Sales Leads*
- *Estimate New Market Potential*
- *Optimize Sales Travel Time*

1. STATE INDUSTRIAL DIRECTORIES

Organized Geographically, Alphabetically, by Product Classification and by SIC Code.

2. DIRECTORY ON DISKETTE

Our in-depth database combined with flexible, easy-to-use search software.

3. CUSTOM LIST SERVICES

- Magnetic Tapes
- Mailing Labels
- 3 x 5 Sales Lead Cards
- Custom Diskettes

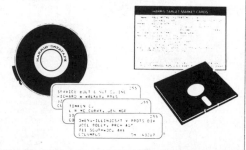

For more information, contact Customer Service
1-800-888-5900

Harris Publishing Information Services

™   2057 Aurora Road • Twinsburg, Ohio 44087 • FAX: 216-425-7150

Source: Reprinted by permission of Harris Publishing Information Services.

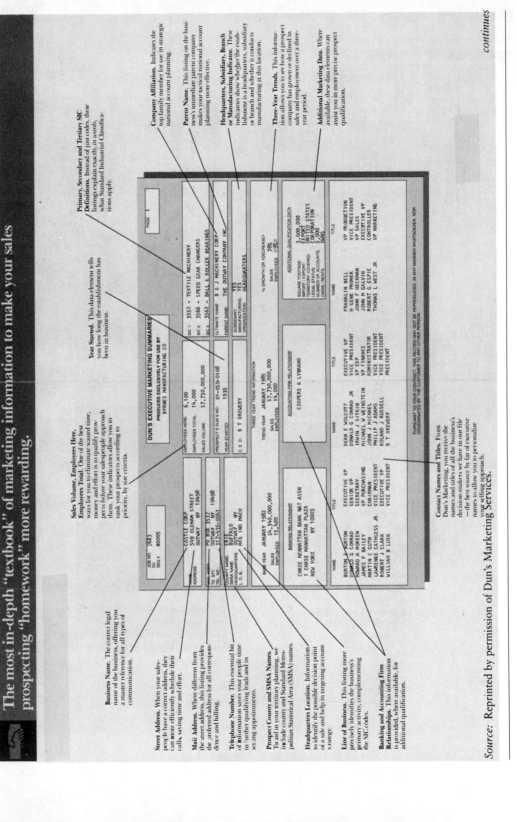

Source: Reprinted by permission of Dun's Marketing Services.

continues

FIGURE 8.5 Continued

This is the *Million Dollar Directory*®...Online!

1 Company Name

2 Secondary Trade Name

3 Address (includes mailing address if different)

4 City, State, Zip Code (of mailing address)

5 Telephone Number

6 County Name

7 Standard Metropolitan Statistical Area (SMSA) Code and Name

8 Line of Business (supplied by the establishment)

9 Standard Industrial Classification (SIC) Codes—primary and up to 5 secondary codes

10 SIC Descriptions

11 Year Business Was Established

12 Gross Annual Sales

13 Number of Employees at the establishment (Employees Here) and 14 of the organization of which the establishment is part (Employees Total)

15 Denotes a Manufacturing Operation at this location

16 Denotes the Establishment is a Headquarters Location. (Or single location)

17 Denotes Establishment Is the Subsidiary of another company

18 Legal Status (corporation or partnership or proprietorship)

19 Denotes the Establishment Imports And/Or Exports its products or services.

20 Publicly or Privately Held

21 Ticker Symbol used on the stock exchanges

22 Stock Exchange(s) where the company shares are traded

23 Principal Bank

24 Principal Accounting Firm

25 Principal Law Firm

26 DUNS Number of the Establishment

27 DUNS Number of the Parent Location

28 Parent Company Name

---

1 FRH CORP.
2 TELECOM
3 29 ECHELON PLAZA
   BOX 425   FDR STN
4 NEW YORK, NY 10007
5 PHONE: 212-482-1221
6 NEW YORK COUNTY   7 SMSA: 406 (NEW YORK, NY)

8 BUSINESS: MNFR, SALE, DISTRIBUTION, LEASE & SERVICING OF & RESEARCH RELATING TO ELECTRONIC PRODUCTS INCLUDING TELEVISION RECEIVERS, HOME VIDEO CASSETTE RECORDERS, VIDEO DISC PLAYERS & DISCS, RECORDS & RECORDED TAPES, COLOR TELEVISION PICTURE TUBES

9 PRIMARY SIC:	3651	10 RADIO, TV RECEIV SETS
SECONDARY SIC:	3652	PHONOGRAPH RECORDS
SECONDARY SIC:	3661	TEL. TELG APPARATUS
SECONDARY SIC:	3662	RADIO & TV COMM'N EQP
SECONDARY SIC:	3671	ELEC TUBE, RECEIV TYP
SECONDARY SIC:	4833	TV BROADCASTING

11 YEAR STARTED: 1929
12 SALES: $8,000,000,000
13 EMPLOYEES HERE: 495
14 EMPLOYEES TOTAL: 133,000

THIS IS:
15 A MANUFACTURING LOCATION
16 A HEADQUARTERS LOCATION (OR A SINGLE LOCATION)
17 A SUBSIDIARY
18 A CORPORATION (OR A PARTNERSHIP OR A PROPRIETORSHIP)
19 AN IMPORTER AND EXPORTER (OR AN IMPORTER OR AN EXPORTER)
20 A PUBLIC COMPANY

TICKER SYMBOL:	21 FRH
STOCK EXCHANGES:	22 BSE, CIN, MSE, NYS, PBS, PCS
BANK:	23 BANKERS TR CO., NEW YORK
ACCOUNTING FIRM:	24 TOUCHE ROSS & CO., NEW YORK
LAW FIRM:	25 CAHILL GORDON & REIMNELL, NEW YORK

DUNS NUMBER:	26 00-214-6272	
PARENT DUNS:	27 00-416-7846	28 FRH CORPORATION
CORPORATE FAMILY DUNS:	29 00-131-7254	30 RCA CORPORATION

31 CHAIRMAN:	PODMOLIK, EUGENE F/CH BD*
PRESIDENT:	MURPHY, VALERIAN F/PR CHIEF EX OFCR*
CORPORATE SECRETARY:	LASIG, WILLIAM P/SEC
TREASURER:	ALEXANDER, KENNETH H/VP TR
INTERNATIONAL:	TWITTY, LAWRENCE M/EX VP*
PERSONNEL:	CODACOVI, CHARLES/VP
ADVERTISING:	GROSS, EDWARD/*
SALES:	YEAKER, KENNETH/VP
MARKETING:	STACKHOUSE, LAWRENCE M/EX VP*
OPERATIONS:	LASSIG, THOMAS R/VP
FINANCE:	VALLELY, KENNETH H/VP TR
CONTROLLER:	SWAIM, WILLIAM J III/COMP
ENGINEERING:	LYNCH, LAWRENCE T/VP
PURCHASING:	DEROSA, WILLIAM/*
EXECUTIVE VICE PRESIDENT:	DOTEN, EDWARD M/EX VP*
OTHER DIRECTORS:	ALLATA, PETER J/*

29 DUNS Number of the Ultimate Company of the Corporate Family

30 Ultimate Company Name

31 Principal Executives
*Asterisk after executive name denotes director

Dun's Marketing Services

D&B a company of The Dun & Bradstreet Corporation

All illustrative data are fictitious.
OMD 0684

SOURCE: Reprinted by permission of Dun's Marketing Services.

mation available from this source. Through Dialog Information Services, it is possible to access Dun's *Million Dollar Directory* on an on-line basis. Another useful **database source** is Predicasts, whose Predicasts Terminal System (PTS) offers a wide variety of on-line data. Predicasts uses a two- to seven-digit SIC system and provides information such as forecasts, time series data, annual reports abstracts, and article abstracts from businesses and trade press sources. American Business Directories, Inc., has a database of over 13 million business listings covering over 1,100 different types of businesses classified by five-digit SIC codes. This company compiles its database from over 4,800 *Yellow Page* phone directories and provides on-line information with its "Instant Yellow Page Service." With a personal computer, a modem, and a subscription to this service, the marketing manager can retrieve SIC information instantly, twenty-four hours per day. Providing on-line SIC information has become big business, and these are only a few of the many sources that provide such services to business marketers.

LIMITATIONS OF THE SIC SYSTEM

Although quite useful, the SIC system is not perfect when viewed from a marketing management perspective. It should be remembered that the system was never designed for this purpose; thus, deficiencies may be expected in the basic four-digit SIC system. The current SIC system ignores marketing needs and is basically a convenience device for the study of American industry by government and private economists. "Any business usage is simply a ride-along." [7] The marketing manager should recognize the system's limitations when using it for marketing purposes. A discussion of some of the major limitations is in order.

One of the major complaints pertains to the four-digit U.S. government SIC coding structure that is covered in the SIC manual. Many practicing marketing professionals believe the four-digit code is too broad and not specific enough for marketing purposes. As industries become more specialized, this problem will increase. For some marketing managers, four-digit SIC codes are sufficient to describe their markets, whereas others find that four-digit codes simply include more industries than those desired. [8]

Another limitation is that the four-digit SIC system, as designed by the government, may omit some basic industries. For example, the 1987 SIC manual does not include any of the following: direct response advertising agencies, telemarketing service bureaus, and list suppliers. [9] Thus, for some business marketers, it may be impossible to determine an appropriate four-digit SIC code for present and prospective markets from the SIC manual.

Still another problem with the SIC manual is its revision schedule. As stated earlier, the 1987 manual replaced the 1972 manual and its 1977 amendments. Between 1977 and 1987, many changes took place, and it is questionable whether the SIC system in those years truly reflected fundamental changes in the

U.S. economy. If it takes another ten years to revise the system again, this problem will continue to exist. The same may occur with other government sources that are published over longer time periods. The *Census of Manufactures* is a case in point. It is published every five years, but it usually takes two or three more years to get into libraries. Thus, its data may not be as current as desired.

There are often discrepancies between government and private sources when the same SIC codes are involved. For example, the *Census of Manufactures* and *Dun's Business Statistics Report* may not agree on how many firms are in a particular SIC designation, because different reporting practices are used when multiproduct establishments are involved. Government practice is to assign the total output to a single, four-digit SIC industry, whereas most private sources assign primary and secondary SIC codes when multiple products are involved. Thus, government sources sometimes overstate primary SIC data and understate secondary SIC information.

Another discrepancy may occur when data are produced at the local level. Government sources are bound by the **nondisclosure rule** that bars information that may disclose the operation of a specific company. If a large company dominates a county's statistics, it cannot be listed because that would reveal the company's business operations. Therefore, that firm's shipments or receipts can be excluded, which results in an understatement.[10] Private sources are not bound in the same manner, and thus data reporting may show significant differences.

Despite such limitations, SIC is a valued tool in business marketing, and most marketing managers are able to adapt to its shortcomings. The Standard Industrial Classification code has been and will continue to be a critical tool for efficient, effective business marketing, regardless of the many weaknesses and deficiencies of the four-digit U.S. government SIC coding structure.[11]

EXPANSIONS OF THE BASIC FOUR-DIGIT SIC CODES

The preceding section indicated that a major shortcoming of the four-digit SIC system is that its level is too broad for marketing purposes. Because of this situation, many private sources have developed their own expansions of the codes and are able to provide more detailed data. Some examples may help in understanding how these expansions work.

A common type of **Standard Industrial Classification expansion** is that of developing five-digit codes with the fifth digit often being a letter, rather than a number. Table 8.7 illustrates one such example, breaking SIC 3079 into sixteen five-digit codes. Thus if a manager were interested only in manufacturers of plastic molding, information on these firms could be obtained using SIC 3079A, and all other SIC 3079 firms would be excluded—overcoming the limitation of the four-digit code being too broad. However, these five-digit expansions may not be uniform from all sources. For example, although Burnett's SIC 3079A designates plastics molders, the code for these manufacturers may be different else-

TABLE 8.7   Expansion of Basic Four-Digit SIC Code to Five-Digit SIC Codes

SIC Code	Description	Number of Firms
3079	Plastic products manufacturers—miscellaneous	21,070
3079A	Plastics molders	4,100
3079B	Fiberglass fabricators	2,080
3079C	Plastics fabricating finishing	2,360
3079D	Plastics foam	640
3079E	Plastics laminates	860
3079F	Plastics rods, tubes, sheets	1,530
3079G	Plastics—vacuum forming	750
3079H	Plastics—extruders	690
3079J	Cellophane and cellulose	60
3079K	Plastics—fabrics and film	420
3079L	Closures—industrial protective	20
3079M	Identification cards	230
3079N	Plastic products ornamental	10
3079O	Polyethylene materials and products	360
3079P	Boxes—plastic	130
3079Q	Glass substitutes	20

Source: Reprinted by permission from *Sales Leads Prospects List* (Englewood Cliffs, NJ: Ed Burnett Consultants, 1987), 36.

where (the fifth digit may not be an *A*). Thus, each source's revised codes must be clarified.[12]

Iron Age has developed its own six-digit SIC coding system for the U.S. metalworking industry. This system also builds on the basic four-digit SIC codes but adds two additional digits. To illustrate, SIC 3541 designates manufacturers of metal cutting machine tools. The *Iron Age* system breaks this code down into SIC 354111 (boring and broaching machines), SIC 354121 (drilling machines), SIC 354131 (gear cutters and finishing machines), and so forth. Table 8.8 illustrates a more complete expansion of SIC 3541. By this expansion, this source is able to offer more detailed data to its customers.

Predicasts has expanded out to seven-digit SIC designations; Table 8.9 illustrates this expansion. Again, the system builds on the basic four-digit SIC structure but permits the retrieval of much more specific information by the marketing manager. This expansion system permits Predicasts to cover about 20,000 categories, as opposed to approximately 1,000 four-digit SIC categories.[13]

Finally, Dun & Bradstreet Corporation's Marketing Services division has introduced an expansion named the SIC + 2 + 2 concept, which it calls a two-level hierarchical expansion. Table 8.10 illustrates this system by again using SIC 3541 (manufacturers of metal cutting machine tools) as an example. As can be seen, SIC 3541 + 01 + 00 is the code for manufacturers of drilling and boring

TABLE 8.8   Expansion of Basic Four-Digit SIC Code to Six-Digit SIC Codes

SIC Code	Description
3541	Machine tools, metal cutting
354111	Boring and broaching machines
354121	Drilling machines
354131	Gear cutters and finishing machines
354141	Grinding and polishing machinery
354145	Sawing and cutting machines
354151	Lathes
354161	Milling machines
354169	Special cutting machine tools
354180	Other machine tools, n.e.c.
354191	Parts for metal cutting machine tools
354194	Rebuilt metal cutting machine tools

Source: Reprinted by permission from Robert W. Haas, "SIC—A Marketing Tool in Transition," *Business* 40 (April–June 1990):19.

TABLE 8.9   Expansion of Basic Four-Digit SIC Code to Seven-Digit SIC Codes

SIC Code	Description
36	Electrical and electronic equipment
367	Electronic components
3674	Semiconductor devices
36741	Integrated and hybrid circuits
367411	Integrated circuits
3674111	Very-high-speed integrated circuits
3674112	Gate array integrated circuits
3674113	Conventional circuits

Source: New Product Announcements (Cleveland: Predicasts, 1987), 2.

machines; SIC 3541 + 01 + 01 designates manufacturers of boring mills; and so forth. As with the expansions by the other sources, this permits Dun & Bradstreet to provide more specific data to its customers.

Variations and expansions of the basic four-digit SIC system codes offer more specific information to business marketing managers. Use of those sources providing extended codes allows the manager to overcome many of the limitations inherent in the basic structure. Given the adherence of the federal government to the four-digit SIC codes, it is likely that such expansions will continue to occur in the private sector as information sources attempt to offer more precise data to their customers.

For the business marketing manager, there may be a down side to all these expansions. The various sources that are expanding the four-digit system in order to offer more precise data to their customers are doing so independent of each other; and thus, different expansion codes are sometimes being assigned to the same products. Table 8.11 clearly illustrates the problem. Turret lathes, for example, are assigned six different expansion codes by six different data sources, although it should be noted that the first four digits are the same. For the business marketing manager, this may mean having to pay more attention when using the sources in conjunction with each other so that inconsistencies will not arise.

TABLE 8.10   **Expansion of Basic Four-Digit SIC Code to Eight-Digit SIC Codes**

SIC Code	Description
3541	Machine tools, metal cutting
35410100	Drilling and boring mills
35410101	Boring mills
35410102	Broaching machines
35410103	Countersinking machines
35410104	Cylinder reboring machines
35410105	Drill presses
35410106	Drilling machine tools (metal cutting)
35410107	Jig boring and grinding machines
35410108	Reaming machines
35410109	Vertical turning and boring machines (metal cutting)

Source: Reprinted by permission from Robert W. Haas, "SIC—A Marketing Tool in Transition," *Business* 40 (April–June 1990):20.

TABLE 8.11   **Examples of Differing SIC Code Designations Assigned to the Same Products by Various Data Sources**

Data Source	Jig Broaching Machines	Turret Lathes	Radial Drilling Machines	Gear Hobbers
1987 SIC Manual	3541	3541	3541	3541
Iron Age	354111	354151	354121	354131
Dun & Bradstreet	35410107	35410403	35410106	35419905
Predicasts	354117	354155	354123	354131
U.S. Census of Manufactures	3541172	3541554	3541233	3541312
Ed Burnett Consultants	3541C	3541A	3541D	n/a
American Business Lists	3541C	3541D	3541C	3566A

Source: Reprinted by permission from Robert W. Haas, "SIC—A Marketing Tool in Transition," *Business* 40 (April–June 1990):20.

DETERMINING APPROPRIATE SIC CODES

To use the SIC system and the many SIC-related sources to advantage, the marketing manager should develop some means of determining which numbers are appropriate. Such a task is not always easy, but in most cases it can be done with quite beneficial results. There are a number of approaches to determining appropriate SIC codes—some are quite simple, others are complex. A discussion of these approaches may be useful in better understanding how a manager may accomplish this task.

Perhaps the simplest and most expedient approach is to classify existing customers by their appropriate SIC designations. Any other organizations with similar SIC codes can be considered prospective customers. For example, say a small California producer of diagnostic reagent chemicals discovered its only two customers were both manufacturers of medical instruments. Looking up the listings for these customers in Dun's *Million Dollar Directory,* the SIC code of 3811 was found to classify both firms. Again using the same directory, the firm discovered over 400 other such manufacturers in the United States. Subsequent marketing programs were directed toward these prospective customers. Classification of existing customers seems an obvious first step in determining SIC codes if this activity has never been tried.

For new companies with no present customers or existing firms moving into new markets, classifying existing customers is not possible. In such cases, there are many options to consider. For example, research may be conducted on competitors to determine who their customers are. This task may be accomplished by marketing research or by requesting field salespeople to provide such information from their respective sales territories. When names of companies are discovered, their SIC codes can be determined by looking up their listings.

Some managers seek references regarding prospective customers. For example, field salespeople, industrial distributors, manufacturers' representatives, and suppliers may be asked to provide names of organizations they believe can use the firm's products or services. These firms can then be classified into appropriate SIC codes in the same manner previously described.

SIC codes may also be determined from sales leads obtained from various sources. A few examples may help to show how this activity may be accomplished. Business marketing firms participating in trade shows typically have sign-up sheets at company exhibits. Visitors at exhibits may be requested to provide their names and their company names so that the exhibiting firm may send this information to field salespeople. It is possible to look up the listings for each company and determine SIC codes. Similarly, advertisements in trade publications typically have "800" phone numbers or request cards so readers may request additional information. These leads, if qualified and found to be legitimate, can also be classified into SIC designations.

Many trade associations also provide information that can be translated to SIC numbers for possible segmentation. For example, the Valve Manufacturers Association projected that 97.4 percent of all domestic industrial valve shipments would be made to fourteen basic industries, with almost 60 percent of total shipments going to the petroleum production, chemical, water and sewage, and petroleum refining industries. Leads such as these are quite useful in determining possible leads for conversion to SIC numbers.

More complex approaches are possible and include using data available from the various government censuses such as the *Census of Manufactures,* which includes a table showing what materials are consumed by four-digit SIC industries. For example, it is possible to determine what materials are used by the steel industry in its production processes and in what proportions these materials are consumed. In this manner, the manager can determine which industries consume large amounts of the materials produced by the marketing company's industry. These large consuming industries are then candidates for conversion into SIC-based market segments.

Input–output analysis may be used by some business marketing managers to determine SIC codes. Such analysis is based on the relatively simple concept that the sales, or outputs, of one industry are the purchases, or inputs, of other industries. This concept may be useful in that it may reveal which industries or markets are purchasing the products of the manager's industry.

National input–output models are published by the Commerce Department's Office of Business Economics, and upgraded versions appear periodically in issues of the *Survey of Current Business,* a monthly periodical that is published by the U.S. Department of Commerce. Although regional and even local input–output models may occasionally be found, references here will be to the national model of the Office of Business Economics, because it is most readily accessible to most marketing managers.

The Office of Business Economics input–output table covers eighty-three basic industries in a grid, or matrix. Each horizontal row shows how an industry's sales (output) is distributed among its customer industries. Because each sale is a purchase, each vertical column shows how an industry's purchases (input) is a percentage of the supplier's output. A second table, which converts the percentages to dollars, shows the value of the flow of goods and services between industries. In essence, this second table indicates an industry's potential in sales to other industries.

Table 8.12 shows a portion of the basic input–output grid. Selling industries are on the vertical axis, and buying industries are on the horizontal axis. Figures shown are in millions of dollars, asterisks indicate figures less than $500,000, and dashes indicate that data were unavailable. Where row 1 meets column 6, it means that industry 1 sold $124 million in goods or services to industry 6. Conversely, industry 6 purchased $124 million of goods or services from industry 1.

This same pattern exists in the Office of Business Economics input–output table for eighty-three basic industries. To understand the value of this type of analysis, assume that the marketing manager in a company in industry 1 is seeking new customers. After finding that industry 1 correctly describes his or her company's industry, the manager can follow row 1 across the eighty-three columns in the grid. Where large figures are found, target market industries can be located. In Table 8.12, for example, industries 1 and 6 appear to be good prospects, whereas other industries appear much less likely prospects. Input–output

TABLE 8.12   Data Available in the Basic Input–Output Matrix

		Industries as Buyers						
		Electrical Lighting and Wiring Equipment	Radio, Television, and Communications Equipment	Electrical Components and Accessories	Miscellaneous Electrical Machinery, Equipment, and Supplies	Motor Vehicles and Equipment	Aircraft and Parts	Other Transportation Equipment
		[1]	[2]	[3]	[4]	[5]	[6]	[7]
Wooden Containers	[1]	150	17	36	26	28	124	—
Chemicals and Selected Materials	[2]	21	—	*	19	7	28	6
Plastics and Synthetic Materials	[3]	—	41	261	98	—	3	*
Primary Iron and Steel Manufacturing	[4]	6	4	—	11	109	17	—
Engines and Turbines	[5]	14	4	—	*	61	43	7
Glass and Glass Products	[6]	77	16	4	—	77	16	12
Paperboard Containers and Boxes	[7]	10	23	20	6	*	*	—

Industries as Sellers (row-group label, left side)

Notes: Figures are in millions of dollars.
Asterisks denote figures less than $500,000.
Dashes indicate data not available.

analysis has thus permitted the marketing manager to identify industries that are big purchasers of the output of the selling industry of which his or her company is a part. Comparisons can be made between company sales and industry sales to the same consuming industries to see if customers are being missed by the company. Used in this manner, input–output analysis can be helpful in determining prospects for conversion into SIC-based market segments.

Because input–output numbers do not provide access to information in the manner of SIC codes, they must be converted to SIC numbers. This conversion is sometimes a rather difficult undertaking when specific industries are involved, but at other times it is relatively easy. The federal government has prepared materials that help the marketing manager convert the input–output numbers to the appropriate SIC numbers.[14] For example, a manufacturer of steel springs may use input–output analysis to determine which industries use such products and in what quantities. After such analysis and subsequent conversion to SIC numbers, the data in Figure 8.6 are achieved.

FIGURE 8.6   Consumption of Steel Springs by Four-Digit SIC Industries ($ millions)

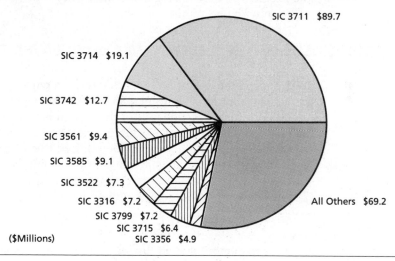

SIC	Consuming Industry	Percent of Total Consumption
3711	Motor vehicles	37.0
3714	Motor vehicle parts & accessories	7.9
3742	Railroad and street cars	5.2
3561	Pumps and compressors	3.9
3585	Refrigeration machinery	3.8
3522	Farm machinery	3.0
3316	Cold finishing of steel shapes	3.0
3799	Transportation equipment, n.e.c.*	3.0
3715	Truck trailers	2.6
3356	Nonferrous rolling & drawing, n.e.c.*	2.0
All Others†		28.6

Notes: *Not elsewhere classified.

†Composed of twenty-four separate SIC consuming industries, none of which consumes 2 percent of the output of steel springs.

Input–output analysis is a useful tool for some business marketing managers because it provides an objective and practical way to determine customers by examining consuming industries. Other managers may find that the tables are not current enough to reflect contemporary happenings, and still others find input–output industry designations too broad to be useful.

Business marketing managers may also use consultants to help determine appropriate SIC codes. For example, on request, Dun's Marketing Services can provide this type of assistance. The Trinet database can be used to determine the estimated consumption of hundreds of business products and services for 400,000 locations with twenty or more employees.

In this manner, the marketing manager may determine firms that consume the output of the marketing firm's industry in terms of SIC designations. These are but examples to show how the practicing marketing manager may approach the problem of determining SIC codes. They may be used separately or in conjunction with one another.

MARKETING USES OF THE SIC SYSTEM AND RELATED DATA

In the opening paragraph of this chapter, reference was made to the SIC system as a useful tool for the business marketing manager. Throughout this chapter, suggestions for marketing uses of the system have been made, and the information provided from the many sources available has been described. In the following chapters, the SIC system will be referred to consistently as it affects various areas of marketing decision making. At this point, however, it may be beneficial to look at some general uses of the system in business marketing.

Table 8.13 outlines some common uses of the SIC system and related infor-

---

TABLE 8.13   Business Marketing Uses of the SIC System and Related Data Sources

- Developing a marketing information system (MIS)
- Defining and segmenting target markets
- Determining market and sales potentials
- Identifying and locating prospective customers
- Planning sales territories and sales quotas
- Designing marketing research projects
- Building direct-mail lists for advertising
- Determining names and positions of buying influences
- Developing leads for field sales personnel
- Identifying competitors
- Identifying and locating prospective channel intermediaries
- Selecting trade publications for advertising
- Facilitating physical distribution decisions such as warehouse size and location
- Measuring market share and market penetration
- Measuring advertising effectiveness

mation for marketing purposes. Most business marketing managers are probably quite capable of using the system to accomplish the tasks outlined in the table. To illustrate, a discussion of a number of examples may help make the desired point.

The first marketing use outlined in the table is developing a marketing information system, which is a basic marketing task for any marketing manager. Figure 8.7 illustrates how this task may be accomplished using the sources that have been described in this chapter. After determining the appropriate SIC code, the manager can determine industry data such as number of firms, geographic locations, value of shipments, number of employees, and so forth by using the sources illustrated. Information can then be obtained to show where industry firms are concentrated using such sources as the *U.S. Industrial Outlook* and *Dun's Census of American Business*. After that, additional information can be obtained on individual companies within the industry by using directories, databases, mailing list companies, and other sources. Table 8.14 summarizes the possible applications to marketing of many of the sources previously discussed.

Reading down the list in Table 8.13, many examples can help illustrate the uses of SIC. A large southern California public utility was interested in measuring electric and gas consumption by type of commercial customer. A program was designed to classify every commercial meter by a four-digit SIC code. The company used the SIC system as the basis for customer classification and then measured consumption in this manner.

A major midwestern university conducted seminars on the liabilities and problems associated with asbestos in schools and hospital buildings. The university used direct mail to reach schools and hospitals on a nationwide basis. Via the use of four-digit SIC codes (8211 and 8062), the university was able to develop an effective mailing list for its advertising.[15]

Another example was the California contracting firm that specialized in municipal wastewater treatment plants and wished to expand from that market into waste water treatment for commercial firms such as canners and other processing plants. By determining the appropriate SIC codes for types of businesses that generated waste water, the contractor was able to locate prospective customers that it then targeted in its marketing programs. This same company also produced cogeneration equipment and targeted industries that produced high levels of steam or excess heat in their production processes. By converting these businesses to SIC codes, new prospects were located and addressed by company marketing efforts using sales calls and direct-mail promotions.

Many trade publications can provide readership characteristics based on four-digit SIC codes. If a marketing manager is interested in reaching purchasing agents in a specific four-digit SIC industry, it is often possible to determine which purchasing journals will have the highest circulation or readership characteristics in this industry. In this manner, the most effective trade journals may be selected for the advertising program. These are but a few of the many uses possible when the SIC system is used in an effective manner.

FIGURE 8.7   Model for Developing an Information File on Business Customers

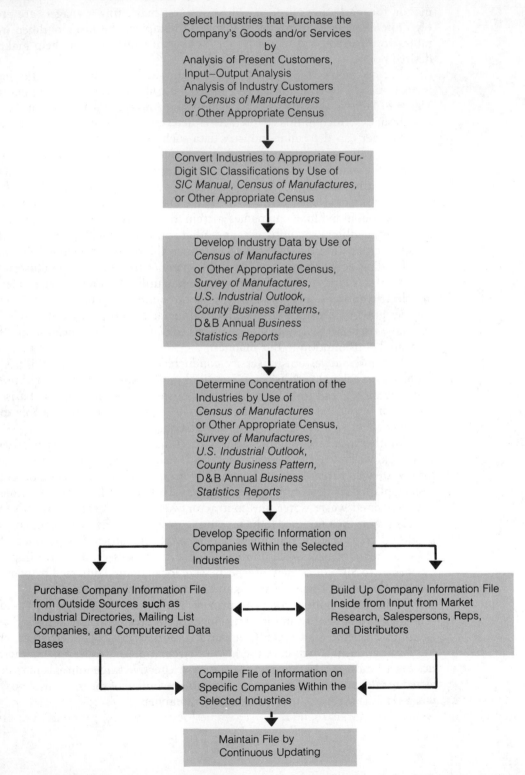

TABLE 8.14   Marketing Applications of SIC-Related Sources

SIC Source	Possible Applications to Marketing
SIC Manual	Determining target markets/segments in terms of SIC codes.
U.S. Census of Manufactures, Mineral Industries, Wholesale Trade, Retail Trade, Selected Services, Construction	Determining market size, growth, areas of geographic concentration, number of firms.
U.S. Industrial Outlook	Determining number of firms, areas of geographic concentration, past industry trends, projected industry forecasts.
Dun & Bradstreet's *Annual Business Statistics Reports*	Determining number of firms by county, number of large firms, value of shipments for total United States and by state and county.
County Business Patterns	Determining number of firms by county, number of employees.
Dun's *Census of American Business*	Determining number of firms by employee size, by sales volume, and by state and county.
Predicasts	Short-term and long-term forecasts by SIC per article abstracts; determining market size, annual growth rates.
Private business directories, such as *Million Dollar Directory, Poor's Register*	Determining company names, addresses, secondary SIC codes, products produced, sales volumes, and names of key executives; on a national basis.
State/county business directories	Similar to private business directories but on individual state and county basis.
Databases, such as Dun & Bradstreet, Trinet, Thomas	Determining company names, addresses, sales volumes, products, number of employees, names of key executives, market share, consumption of products or services.
Mailing list companies	Determining company names, addresses on labels, printouts, diskettes, tapes.

Source: Reprinted by permission from Robert W. Haas, "SIC—A Marketing Tool in Transition," *Business* 40 (April–June 1990): 16.

CHAPTER SUMMARY

This chapter discussed the Standard Industrial Classification (SIC) system and its applications to business marketing. The basic four-digit system of the U.S. government's Office of Management and Budget was described in detail. Discussion then focused on using the SIC system for business marketing purposes. Particular attention was paid to sources of marketing information that are based on SIC: federal government sources such as the censuses, and other useful publications such as *U.S. Industrial Outlook* and *County Business Patterns*. Private sources were also discussed. These include those publications, directories, mailing lists, and databases that are based on the SIC system. Examples of the types of information each can provide were illustrated. The chapter then reviewed the limitations of the SIC system and analyzed expansions of the basic four-digit system now being produced. Methods of determining specific SIC codes were discussed and the chapter concluded with a discussion of the business marketing uses of the SIC system itself and the many SIC-related information sources.

KEY TERMS

Census of Manufactures
database source
input–output
mailing list company
nondisclosure rule
private business directory

Standard Industrial Classification (SIC) code
Standard Industrial Classification expansion
Standard Industrial Classification Manual
Standard Industrial Classification revision
Standard Industrial Classification (SIC) system
state/county business directory

QUESTIONS

1. How many reasons can you list to show why an understanding of the SIC system should be necessary in effective business marketing management? Why is the SIC system especially relevant to business marketing?

2. Some business marketing managers claim that they are unable to use the SIC system in any effective manner because the *SIC Manual* does not provide enough information to apply to practical decision-making situations. Take a position on this statement and back up your position.

3. The U.S. government expands the basic four-digit SIC code to seven-digit codes. Explain how this expansion works and then show how it differs from the Dun & Bradstreet eight-digit code expansion system.

4. Using Table 8.5 in the text, show how the business marketing manager might use the information shown for the purpose of determining target markets and segments.

5. For business marketing purposes, the basic OMB four-digit SIC codes have a number of limitations that must be considered by the marketing manager in using the system for marketing purposes. What are these limitations and how can the manager work around them?

6. Look at Figure 8.3 in the text and explain how you would use the information contained in this figure to more effectively develop marketing strategy and programs. What information do you see as most useful and how would you use it if you were a business marketing manager?

7. Assume that you are a business marketing manager whose company wishes to move into the reseller market with products that you have traditionally marketed to OEM and user markets. How would you use the SIC system to develop a better understanding of the reseller market? What sources would you recommend be used?

8. Assume that you are a business marketing manager whose company wishes to switch from company-owned warehouses to private industrial distributors. How can you use SIC to help you find prospective distributors for your products? What sources would you recommend be used to accomplish this task?

9. You are in charge of advertising for a business marketing company that wishes to expand into totally new business markets. Your task is to contact prospects in these new markets by direct mail promotion to purchasing agents in prospective customer firms. How can you use the

SIC system to develop an approach to accomplish this task? What sources would you use?

10. In theory, the user of input–output analysis to uncover leads for conversion into SIC codes sounds impressive. Actual implementation of this approach, however, may be much harder. Explain why input–output is a good approach but sometimes a difficult one to implement.

NOTES

1. *Standard Industrial Classification Manual 1987* (Washington, DC: Office of Management and Budget, 1987), 3.
2. Jerry Reisberg, "An Expanded SIC Code: Let's Do It Ourselves," *Direct Marketing* 50 (October 1987): 150.
3. Ibid., 148.
4. Adapted from *Marketing to Manufacturing Industries* (Boston: Cahners Publishing Company, 1977), 15.
5. *Dun's Marketing Services 1990 Business Statistics Report* (Parsippany, NJ: Dun's Marketing Services, 1990), 16.
6. "Data Supplement: U.S. Totals for 4-Digit SIC Industries," *Sales & Marketing Management* 138 (June 1990): 138–148.
7. Ira Belth, "The SIC Code Needs Therapy," *Business Marketing* 69 (August 1984): 50.
8. Reisberg, op. cit., 148.
9. Arnold Fishman, "The Census According to GARP," *Direct Marketing* 50 (October 1987): 140.
10. "SIC: The System Explained," *Sales & Marketing Management* 138 (April 27, 1987): 36.
11. Reisberg, op. cit., 148.
12. See Robert W. Haas, "SIC—A Marketing Tool in Transition," *Business* 40 (April–June 1990): 15–22.
13. Belth, op. cit., 52.
14. Reisberg, op. cit., 148.
15. For more examples, see Patrick J. Robinson, Charles L. Hinkle, and Edward Bloom, *Standard Industrial Classification for Effective Marketing Analysis* (Philadelphia: Marketing Science Institute, 1967), 9–21.

SUGGESTED ADDITIONAL READINGS

Anderson, Kenneth A. "Using SIC Codes to Strengthen Your Company's Market Position." *Industrial Marketing* 64 (June 1979): 60–62.

Barr, Joel J. "SIC: A Basic Tool for the Marketer." *Industrial Marketing* 54 (August 1969): 52–79.

Belth, Ira. "The SIC Code Needs Therapy." *Business Marketing* 69 (August 1984): 50–52.

"Data Supplement: U.S. Totals for 4-Digit SIC Industries." *Sales & Marketing Management* 138 (June 1990): 138–148.

Eisenhart, Tom. "Business List Industry Readies Pinpoint Accuracy." *Business Marketing* 73 (February 1988): 78–88.

Fishman, Arnold. "The Census According to GARP." *Direct Marketing* 50 (October 1987): 140.

Haas, Robert W. "Locating Industrial Customers." *Atlanta Economic Review* 26 (September–October 1976): 9–14.

——. "SIC—A Marketing Tool in Transition." *Business* 40 (April–June 1990): 15–22.

——. "SIC System and Related Data for More Effective Market Research." *Industrial Marketing Management* 6 (1977): 429–435.

——. "Sources of SIC Related Data for More Effective Marketing." *Industrial Marketing* 62 (May 1977): 32–42.

——. "Using Government Data Sources for More Effective Analysis of Business Markets." *Agency Sales* 20 (January 1990): 41–46.

Henderson, Russell H. "Relating Company Markets to SIC." *Journal of Marketing* 27 (April 1963): 42–45.

Kern, R. "SIC System on the Mend (OMB)." *Sales & Marketing Management* 136 (May 1986): 20.

"Profiles and Targets: SIC Is My Copilot." *Sales & Marketing Management* 132 (April 23, 1984): 25–28.

Reisberg, Jerry. "An Expanded SIC Code: Let's Do It Ourselves!" *Direct Marketing* 50 (October 1987): 148–151.

Robinson, Patrick J., Charles L. Hinkle, and Edward Bloom. *Standard Industrial Classification for Effective Marketing Analysis.* Philadelphia: Marketing Science Institute, 1967.

"SIC Revision (1987)." *Monthly Labor Review* 109 (November 1987): 2.

"SIC Revisions Disappoint Marketers." *Direct Marketing* 49 (February 1987): 72ff.

"SIC: The System Explained." *Sales & Marketing Management* 138 (April 27, 1987): 36.

Using SICs for Profit. Boston: Cahners Publishing Company, 1977.

9

Segmentation in Business Markets

●●

Marketers, both business and consumer, have long recognized that markets are not made up of customers and prospects with identical needs and wants.[1] A business marketing company may sell its products or services to hundreds of organizations within the same basic industry. All may be purchasing those products or services for essentially the same purpose—to use directly or indirectly in the operation of their own organizations. However, the needs and wants of the buying influences in those organizations are not necessarily the same, nor are the buying processes or even the cultures of the organizations involved. In addition, no single marketing mix will necessarily appeal to all organizations within a market. It is much more likely that the market is composed of subgroups or segments that differ in some manner. Thus, separate marketing mixes may be required. The ability to segment business markets is a key factor in determining effective marketing strategy. This chapter provides the foundation for the discussion of strategy that follows in Chapter 10. In addition, this chapter builds on the material developed in the preceding chapters by applying it to the segmentation process. The concept of marketing segmentation will be developed with an emphasis on its necessity in business marketing. The bases used to segment business markets will be examined, and discussion will focus on approaches used by business marketing managers to segment markets. The development of the market segment decision-making process will also be described. Finally, an assessment of the present status of segmentation in business markets will be undertaken. The purpose of this chapter is to create an understanding of the importance of sound segmentation to effective marketing strategy. In today's complex business markets, segmentation is not a luxury—it is a basic necessity.

•••

Segmenting a Business Market

McNichols Company is a specialty metal products distributor based in Tampa, Florida. As part of its promotional strategy, the company traditionally mailed approximately two million catalogs per year to both present customers and prospects in the sheet metal work industry, SIC 3444. For McNichols, it was concluded that the SIC 3444 target market was too broad and needed further segmentation in order to reduce waste in both producing and distributing its catalogs.

The firm's director of marketing used Dun & Bradstreet's SIC + 2 + 2 system to break up the SIC 3444 market into more manageable segments. Dun's system divides SIC 3444 into 45 different SIC + 2 + 2 classifications. By analyzing these segments by past company sales, McNichols was able to eliminate 50 percent of its previous catalog mailings to segments that had never produced any sales. This permitted more optimum distribution of the costly catalogs to customers and true prospects rather than mass mailings to all SIC 3444 firms.

For McNichols, a number of benefits were achieved by the new segmentation process. First, catalog mailings were reduced by 20 percent in the first year, saving the company over $100,000. Second, the SIC + 2 + 2 segmentation approach permitted the company to eliminate previously unidentified marginal segments. Third, the company could now test segments never previously identified under the four-digit SIC 3444 system. All this permitted the company to distribute its catalogs in a more cost-effective manner. Excess catalogs no longer used in marginal segments could be redirected toward more promising segments. By adopting this refined form of SIC segmentation, McNichols believes it will ultimately be able to reduce total catalog mailings by 40 percent and yet still get the same return. This example clearly shows the use of tighter segmentation to develop a more cost-effective approach to business marketing strategy.

Source: Adapted from Tom Eisenhart, "Segmenting with Precision," *Business Marketing* 74 (September 1989): 60–61.

WHAT IS MARKET SEGMENTATION?

A market segment is defined as "a group of present or potential customers with some common characteristic which is relevant in explaining and predicting their response to supplier's marketing stimuli."[2] In its simplest form, the term **market segmentation** means taking a heterogeneous total market and dividing it into a number of smaller homogeneous subgroups or segments. Exactly what common characteristics should be used in segmenting is a topic of considerable discussion—there is no single best characteristic to use in segmenting business markets. Rather, there are many different suggested characteristics, and each has its own advocates and critics. These characteristics are discussed in depth later in the chapter.

Market segmentation is the process of breaking total markets into more manageable segments. The question of how best to perform this process has become a major business marketing topic in recent years.[3] There are two components to the **market segmentation process:** market segmentation analysis and market segmentation strategy. The components differ in the following manner. Market segmentation analysis seeks to define segments most appropriate for future marketing efforts. This analysis involves the determination of which segment or segments are to be addressed. On the other hand, market segmentation strategy seeks to direct marketing efforts at previously defined segments on the basis of needs or some other characteristics.[4] The logical sequence is for analysis to precede strategy. The marketing manager must first determine the segments before he or she can direct marketing efforts toward them. This chapter primarily discusses the analysis component of market segmentation, although some strategy examples are also provided. Chapter 10 then incorporates the strategy component into the marketing planning process. The following quotation emphasizes the logic of this sequence: "The most important decisions in planning marketing strategy are those related to the choice of a market or markets to serve. All else follows."[5]

WHY SEGMENT BUSINESS MARKETS?

Market segmentation is a difficult and complex undertaking in business markets. If true, why bother to do it? The recognition of the need for segmentation in business marketing is not new. "Industrial product markets are highly heterogeneous, complex, and often hard to reach because of the multitude of products and uses as well as a great diversity among customers."[6] This statement provides an overall explanation of why segmentation is vital in business marketing. Customers and prospects in a market are rarely the same in terms of buying goods and services. Within a market, there may be distinct differences in purchasing policies, processes, and procedures. In addition, different buying influences and buying centers are typically found, and buying motives can differ considerably from organization to organization. The business marketing manager who is able to determine such differences and classify customers and prospects into similar groupings is usually able to develop more effective marketing strategies to serve those differences. Thus, segmentation is usually necessary because it leads to more efficient and effective marketing.

As well, there are other reasons for segmenting business markets. Many business marketing companies in basic industries are finding their traditional markets declining in size and potential. At the same time, they are facing increased foreign competition. For many such firms, the shift has been toward more specialized products that, in turn, require more specialized markets. Tighter segmentation of existing and new markets has often been necessary to carve out market niches. This trend is likely to continue, and as it does, the value of segmentation becomes even more pronounced and apparent.

Properly accomplished, market segmentation is market driven, which means that bases used to segment markets are relevant to the needs and wants of buyers and buying influences. Segmentation often leads to more satisfied customers, which in turn leads to better, long-term relationships between buyers and sellers. Thus, segmentation is necessary to implement the marketing concept more effectively.

Finally, another reason for the growing importance of segmentation is the increased emphasis by U.S. business marketers on global markets. As more and more American business marketing companies move into global markets, they find that blanket marketing strategies are not effective. Too many factors differ among target market countries, and segmentation may be the most logical way to address such differences. Reasons such as these account for the growing importance of market segmentation in business marketing, and indications are that it will become even more important in the future.

BASES USED TO SEGMENT BUSINESS MARKETS

In segmenting business markets, the primary problem faced by the marketing manager is to identify the best variables to use in such segmentation.[7] As in consumer markets, many bases may be used. Table 9.1 illustrates different **market segmentation bases** used by business marketers to segment markets. Analysis of the table reveals that these range from quite simple to quite complex. For example, segmentation on the basis of geographic characteristics is a relatively easy undertaking, whereas segmentation based on buying processes and benefits may be much more difficult. The simpler characteristics (geographic and demographic) are sometimes called supplier driven. Segments are defined on the basis of what can be identified by and what is accessible to the supplier. The more complex characteristics (benefit and buying needs) are termed customer driven, which means that segmentation works conceptually from the customer backward toward the vendor.[8] Typically, the customer-driven and supplier-driven characteristics are used in some sort of unified framework, as they are not mutually exclusive. For example, the manager may wish to segment by size of customer firm and by region of the country and then refine segments according to customer benefits or needs.

Early attempts to segment business markets focused almost exclusively on the uses of geographic and demographic bases. Such characteristics as geographic location and company size were easy to use, data were easily available, and some homogeneity was created. The problem was, and still is, that the use of these bases by themselves provide little information regarding buyer behavior. Later attempts incorporated these supplier-driven criteria with the use of buyer and organizational criteria such as segmenting on the basis of purchasing process and buying influences involved in that process.[9] By combining the behavioral characteristics with demographic and geographic variables, it was possible to expand segmentation to include purchase motives in the process. More re-

TABLE 9.1 Bases of Segmentation Used in Business Markets

Segmentation Base	Examples of This Segmentation Base
Geographic characteristics	Domestic/international markets Country Region of the country State and/or county Standard metropolitan statistical area (SMSA) Census tract ZIP code

Demographic characteristics	Standard industrial classification (SIC)
	Input–output classification
	Company size in terms of
	  Number of employees
	  Sales volume
	  Annual purchases
	  Average order size
	  Value added by manufacturing

Organizational purchasing characteristics	Purchasing policies Purchasing procedures Buying process used Composition of buying center Buying influences involved Average order size Frequency of purchases Buyer inventory requirements Just-in-Time vs. EOQ
Buyer/buying influence personal characteristics	Personality Attitudes Lifestyle Self-image Risk tolerance Decision-making style Cognitive style
Supplier/customer relationship/other characteristics	Present, past, or nonuser Heavy, medium, or light user Single source or multiple source user Reciprocal relationships Product benefits Partnering vs. nonpartnering relationships National accounts

cently, the emphasis has been placed on **benefit segmentation,** which identifies the major benefits sought by organizational buyers and buying influences. Advocates argue that benefit segmentation provides more effective insight into the structure of the market and opportunities for repositioning and new entrants.[10]

This range then represents the spectrum of segmentation bases used in business markets. At this point, it may be beneficial to illustrate how some of these characteristics may be used in market segmentation analysis.

Geographic Characteristics

Segmentation on the basis of geographic variables is widely used in business markets. Using region of the country as a demographic characteristic is common. This supplier-driven criterion assumes homogeneity in the form of geographic region, which may have little or nothing to do with explaining or predicting buyer behavior. Because two customer companies are located in the same region of the country does not mean they are otherwise similar. Still, **geographic segmentation** is popular for strategy purposes, since it can be related to market and sales potential estimates, to determining sales territories and quotas, and to locating distribution outlets. In addition, it is a relatively easy analysis to perform. An example may help in understanding this form of segmentation.

A company produces products used by U.S. meat-packing plants (SIC 2011). Using the *Census of Manufactures,* the marketing manager determines that this market consists of 1,780 companies. Figure 9.1 illustrates the geographic distribution of these firms by region of the country. As can be seen, meat-packing plants are not evenly distributed throughout the United States; over 50 percent are located in the East North Central, West North Central, and West South Central regions. Instead of directing marketing efforts at the entire U.S. market, the manager may elect to concentrate efforts only in the East North Central, West North Central, and West South Central segments. Such a strategy may mean completely ignoring the other segments. Although geographic segmentation alone is quite elementary, because buying motives are not addressed, it is not without merit when not used as the sole criterion. Selecting certain segments and ignoring others may be a good way to allocate marketing resources. Regional segments can be further refined to individual states and even counties within those states using the SIC system, as explained in Chapter 8. Geographic segmentation is relatively easy to implement, which explains why it is such a popular method in business marketing.

Figure 9.2 illustrates the use of geographic segmentation applied to global markets. A manufacturer of electrical energy systems has analyzed U.S. shipments of such products to determine possible segments and finds the information shown in the figure. The marketing manager now realizes that 77 percent of all U.S. shipments of such systems are imported by five countries. He or she may now wish to segment the total market and address marketing efforts only to a select few segments. For example, the decision might be made to focus on Germany, France, Spain, and the Netherlands because of their close proximity to each other. This proximity could well simplify sales and distribution problems and the company could still reach 56 percent of the global market.

FIGURE 9.1   Segmentation of the Meat-Packing Market (SIC 2011)
Using Geographic Characteristics

Source: Compiled from U.S. Department of Commerce, *1982 Census of Manufactures: Meat Products* (Washington, DC: U.S. Government Printing Office, March 1985), 20A-7.

Region of Country	Percent of Total Plants
New England	.7%
Middle Atlantic	8.6%
South Atlantic	12.1%
East North Central	20.9%
East South Central	9.3%
West North Central	18.4%
West South Central	15.3%
Mountain	7.5%
Pacific	7.2%
Total market	100.0%

Demographic Characteristics

Another widely used approach is **demographic segmentation,** or segmenting on the basis of demographic variables such as company size or SIC designation. Figure 9.3 provides an example of using number of employees as a segmentation variable in the truck manufacturing market (SIC 3713). Number of employees is often used as an indicator of company size, and thus it is a likely segmentation

FIGURE 9.2   Segmentation of the Global Market for Electrical Energy Systems Based on Percent of Total U.S. Export Shipments Imported by Each Segment

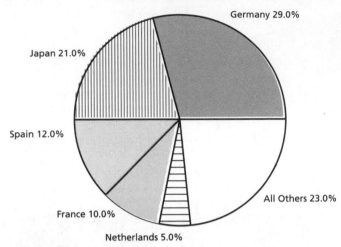

Source: Adapted from "World Trade Outlook," *Business America* 8 (March 4, 1985): 5, and various editions of *Global Market Surveys,* International Marketing Information Series, U.S. Department of Commerce.

characteristic. Figure 9.3a illustrates the size of eight number-of-employee segments in terms of percentage of total firms. For example, only 8 percent of the 681 firms in this market have 100 or more employees. Figures 9.3b and 9.3c, however, show that firms with 100+ employees account for 63 percent of the industry's value of shipments and 60 percent of materials purchased by all firms in the market. Instead of trying to market to all 681 companies in the market, the marketing manager may choose to focus on the 8 percent of prospects in segments F, G, and H. This strategy seems a good one, since the firms in those three segments have the most employees, have the highest values of shipments, and use the greatest percent of materials in the market. This type of segmentation is useful in that it may help determine the potential of the segments involved, which in turn helps to allocate marketing resources.

Segmentation by SIC occurs when the marketing manager tries to determine segments within SIC industry designations. An example is the market composed of manufacturers of motor vehicle parts and accessories that are classified by SIC 3714. Assume a seller of grease, oils, and fluids wishes to sell its products to manufacturers of new auto parts and accessories. The products are used in those automotive parts requiring lubricants. Figure 9.4 illustrates five-digit product classes within the basic 3714 industry and shows nine segments in this market. Not all of these segments use lubricants (for example, firms in segments 37144 [filter manufacturers] and 37145 [exhaust systems]). The marketing manager

FIGURE 9.3 Segmentation of the Truck Manufacturing Market (SIC 3713) Using Demographic Characteristics

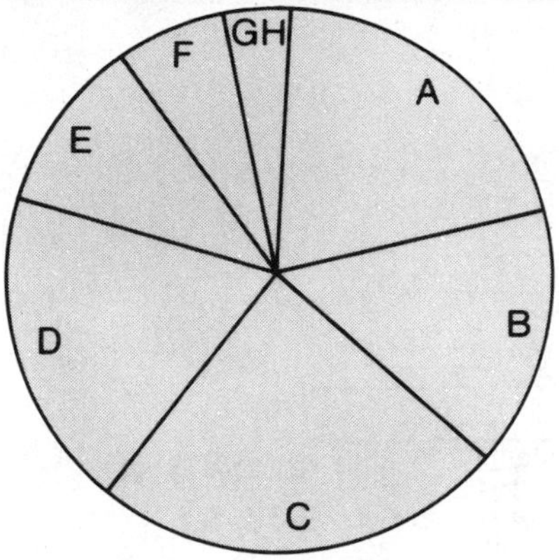

Segmentation by Number of Employees

Ⓐ = 1 to 4 Employees	21%
Ⓑ = 5 to 9 Employees	17%
Ⓒ = 10 to 19 Employees	21%
Ⓓ = 20 to 49 Employees	21%
Ⓔ = 50 to 99 Employees	11%
Ⓕ = 100 to 249 Employees	5%
Ⓖ = 250 to 499 Employees	2%
Ⓗ = 500+ Employees	1%

(a)

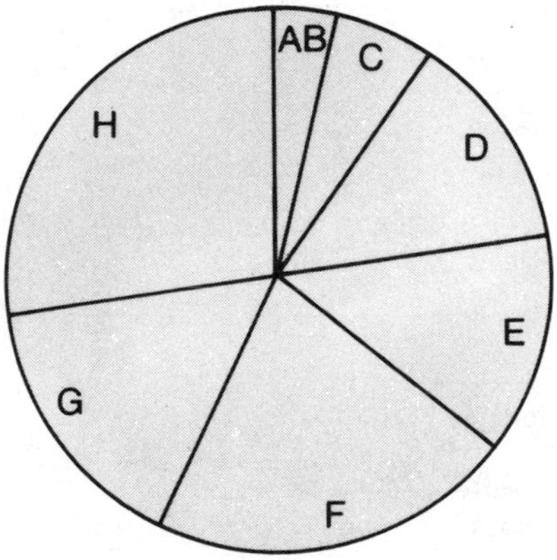

Segmentation by Value of Shipments

Ⓐ = 1 to 4 Employees	1%
Ⓑ = 5 to 9 Employees	2%
Ⓒ = 10 to 19 Employees	5%
Ⓓ = 20 to 49 Employees	14%
Ⓔ = 50 to 99 Employees	15%
Ⓕ = 100 to 249 Employees	19%
Ⓖ = 250 to 499 Employees	17%
Ⓗ = 500+ Employees	27%

(b)

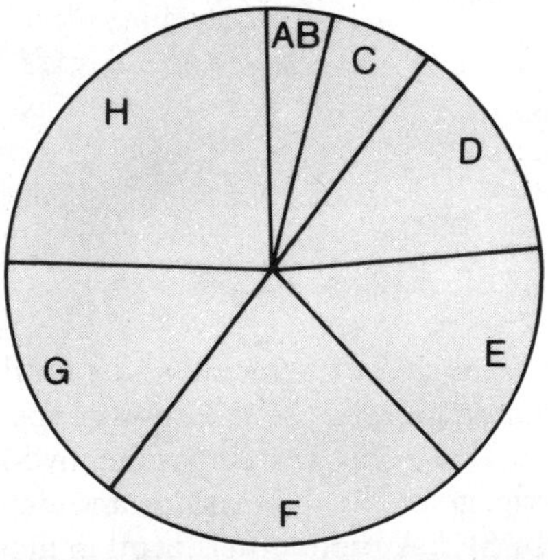

Segmentation by Costs of Materials

Ⓐ = 1 to 4 Employees	1%
Ⓑ = 5 to 9 Employees	2%
Ⓒ = 10 to 19 Employees	6%
Ⓓ = 20 to 49 Employees	15%
Ⓔ = 50 to 99 Employees	17%
Ⓕ = 100 to 249 Employees	19%
Ⓖ = 250 to 499 Employees	17%
Ⓗ = 500+ Employees	24%

(c)

Source: Compiled from U.S. Department of Commerce, *1982 Census of Manufactures: Motor Vehicles and Equipment* (Washington, DC: U.S. Government Printing Office, March 1985), 37A-12.

FIGURE 9.4   Market Segmentation by SIC Using SIC 3714 as an Example
(\$ millions value of shipments)

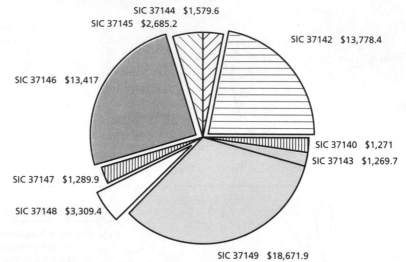

SIC 37144 \$1,579.6
SIC 37145 \$2,685.2
SIC 37142 \$13,778.4
SIC 37146 \$13,417
SIC 37140 \$1,271
SIC 37143 \$1,269.7
SIC 37147 \$1,289.9
SIC 37148 \$3,309.4
SIC 37149 \$18,671.9

Source: U.S. Department of Commerce, *1986 Annual Survey of Manufactures: Value of Product Shipments* (Washington, DC: U.S. Government Printing Office, April 1988), 2–29.

SIC	Description
37142	Gas engines
37143	Rebuilt parts
37144	Filters
37145	Exhaust systems
37146	Drive trains
37147	Wheels
37148	Brake parts
37149	All others, n.e.c.
37140	Parts, n.s.k.

will logically wish to focus marketing efforts on those segments in which lubricants are involved (such as 37142 [engine manufacturers], 37146 [power train components], and 37148 [brake assemblies]). Thus, only certain segments out of the total 3714 market are selected. Knowledge of the SIC system and data sources permits relatively easy segmentation by SIC. As with other forms of geographic and demographic segmentation, homogeneity exists because of similar SIC designations, but this similarity may help little in explaining or predicting buyer behavior.

Another example of segmenting by SIC may be seen in the case of a Kansas City, Missouri, manufacturer of commercial office space systems.[11] The firm directed its promotion toward dealers who worked with contractors and classified them by the appropriate four-digit code. But the code was too broad to allow the company to differentiate between different types of dealers. Using the Dun & Bradstreet SIC + 2 + 2 system, the firm could break the market down further in terms of whether the dealers worked with plaster, drywall, or relocater walls. Once this was accomplished, the firm could concentrate its promotional efforts on those dealers who worked with relocators rather than promote to all types of dealers.

Buying Process Characteristics

Another segmentation variable is the organizational buying process. Target market customers with similar buying processes may be considered a market segment. This method of segmentation is a more complex way of segmenting than the previous geographic and demographic examples, but if properly performed, it does relate more closely to buyer behavior.

There are not many examples of **buying process segmentation** in the marketing literature, but one approach has been to segment business markets on the basis of functional involvement in phases of the purchasing decision process.[12] In the following example, a segmentation process was used that (1) defined similar organizations in terms of the participants involved, (2) identified groups of organizations that exhibited similar buying processes, and (3) described segments in terms of the pattern of involvement in purchasing process categories of individuals identified as participants in the buying decision stages. Using the industrial cooling industry, interviews were conducted with potential customers, with the result that five major buying phases were identified, and seven buying influences were isolated. Table 9.2 shows the decision matrix used with the phases and buying influences. Decision matrix analysis revealed four market segments, which are shown in Table 9.3. These four segments composed 12 percent, 31 percent, 32 percent, and 25 percent respectively of the total market. Firms in segment 4 tended to be small, satisfied with their present systems, with a medium percentage of plants requiring air conditioning, and saw great consequences if the system was less economical than anticipated. Firms in segment 2 were large, not highly satisfied with their present systems, with a small percentage of plants requiring air conditioning, and saw little consequences if the system was less economical than anticipated. As can be seen, this form of segmentation combines demographic characteristics such as company size and number of plants with customer satisfaction regarding existing systems and anticipated economic or reliability consequences. Buyer behavior is better understood here, which is what effective segmentation is supposed to achieve. Given segments such as the four revealed, it is now possible to direct different marketing efforts toward the individual segments.

TABLE 9.2   Decision Matrix for Segmenting Cooling Industry by Using Criteria of Buying Process and Buying Influences

| | | Decision Phases | | | | |
	Decision Participants	1 Evaluation of A/C Needs, Specification of System Requirements	2 Preliminary A/C Budget Approval	3 Search for Alternatives, Preparation of a Bid List	4 Equipment and Manufacturer Evaluation*	5 Equipment and Manufacturer Selection
Company Personnel	Production and maintenance engineers	%	%	%	%	%
	Plant or factory managers	%	%	%	%	%
	Financial controller or accountant	%	%	%	%	%
	Procurement or purchasing department personnel	%	%	%	%	%
	Top management	%	%	%	%	%
External Personnel	HVAC/engineering firm	%	%	%	%	%
	Architects and building contractors	%	%	%	%	%
	A/C equipment manufacturers	%			%	%
	Column total	100%	100%	100%	100%	100%

Source: Reprinted by permission of the publisher from Jean-Marie Choffray and Gary L. Lilien, "Industrial Market Segmentation by the Structure of the Buying Process," *Industrial Marketing Management* 9 (1980):334. Copyright © 1980 by Elsevier Science Publishing Company, Inc.

* Decision phase 4 generally involves evaluation of all alternative A/C systems that meet company needs, while decision phase 5 involves only the alternatives (generally 2–3) retained for final selection.

TABLE 9.3   Descriptions of Segments of the Cooling Industry Market

	Segment 1	Segment 2	Segment 3	Segment 4
Satisfaction with current A/C system	Medium High	Low	Medium Low	High
Consequence if A/C system is less economical than projected	Medium High	Low	Medium Low	High
Consequence if A/C system is less reliable than projected	Medium High	Low	High	Medium Low
Company size	Medium	Large	Large	Small
Percentage of plant area requiring A/C	Medium Large	Small	Large	Medium
Number of separate plants	Medium Large	Small	Large	Medium Small

Source: Reprinted by permission of the publisher from Jean-Marie Choffray and Gary L. Lilien, "Industrial Market Segmentation by the Structure of the Buying Process," *Industrial Marketing Management* 9 (1980): 336. Copyright © 1980 by Elsevier Science Publishing Company, Inc.

Benefits Characteristics

As was stated earlier, one of the latest trends in business marketing has been to segment markets using product benefits rather than customer characteristics.[13] Target market firms perceiving similar benefits in a specific product or service may be viewed as being in the same segment. Homogeneity is created by the similar benefits. Benefit segmentation is not new in consumer marketing, but its application to business markets is quite recent.

Again, an example may help illustrate how this type of segmentation works. A processor of resins wanted to market tactifiers into the specialty chemical market.[14] Research indicated six product variables affected buyers' choices of brand: softening point, viscosity, color stability, starting color, tack, and price. Also important were four supplier variables: product range, service support, geographic coverage, and reputation for reliability. Analysis revealed twelve market segments, which are shown as clusters A–L in Table 9.4. Company management then decided that only seven of the twelve were viable segments. Of those seven, four were considered most attractive—segments C, G, J, and K. It was then decided that marketing efforts would be directed toward only these four segments, which accounted for 54 percent of the total tactifier market.

Subsequent marketing strategies differed in the four targeted segments. In segments G and J, the company marketed me-too products with reductions in price. In segments C and K, emphasis was placed not on lower price but on improved technical product characteristics and product support. This example shows the value of benefit segmentation. When properly performed, it permits the marketing manager to understand differences related to buyer behavior and then to focus on those benefits seen as most important by buyers and buying influences.

TABLE 9.4 Characteristics and Attractiveness of Alternative Product Benefits Segments

Features	Clusters											
	A	B	C	D	E	F	G	H	I	J	K	L
No. of brands	10	9	8	7	2	12	4	4	2	10	4	4
Softening point	91	109	96	151	92.5	122	90	97.5	90	109	80	110
Viscosity	8	8	9	8	7	6	6	4	9	7	14	4
Color stability	102	126	95	51	100	70	77	90	200	92	130	500
Start color	8	9	7.5	11	8	8	7	3	4	8	9	.5
Tack	2	2	2	2	1	1	1	2	2	2	1	1
Price	9.8	9.7	6.6	8.0	7.7	9.1	9.2	14.3	9.1	12.3	6.5	14.3
Range	16	20	10	18	2	10	30	17	7.5	55	36	21
Service	2	2	2.6	2	2	2	4	1.5	2.5	4	2.5	4
Coverage	2	2	2.6	2	3	2	4	2	2.5	4	3	4
Reputation	2	2	2	2	1	3	3	2	2	3	2	3
Attractiveness:												
Size ($M)	2.4	1.8	4.2	3.2	5.0	4.0	10.1	0.8	4.2	10.4	8.1	7.4
Growth (% per annum)	3	5	7	12	15	8	10	8	4	14	13	10
Competitive strength	W	S	M	S	M	S	S	W	W	S	M	S
Capability fit	M	S	S	W	W	W	S	S	M	S	S	M

Source: Reprinted from Peter Doyle and John Saunders, "Market Segmentation and Positioning in Specialized Industrial Markets," *Journal of Marketing 49* (Spring 1985): 30. Published by the American Marketing Association.

Note: S = strong, M = medium, W = weak

Product Characteristics

Somewhat similar to benefit segmentation is **product feature segmentation,** or segmenting by product characteristics or features, often called attributes. Segmenting by those attributes that most determine purchasing behavior has been found useful in business marketing. This is based on the assumption that buyers view products as bundles of attributes and those attributes differ in their contribution to product evaluation and choice. While a particular product may have many attributes, not all affect purchasing decisions to the same degree. Those attributes that directly influence choice are called determinant.[15] Segmentation based on determinant product attributes can be applied to business marketing situations.[16] An example may help to explain how this type of segmentation works.

Manufacturers of residential siding might be interested in better serving their contractor market. The demand for siding is derived from the demand for housing and remodeling, but the siding is typically purchased and installed by some type of contractor. Initial analysis revealed four types of contractors in the market: (1) contractors who build single-unit dwellings, (2) contractors who build multiunit dwellings, (3) siding contractors, and (4) remodeling contractors. Do all four see the same types of product attributes as important in buying siding? Are these four really segments or are they all basically the same as regards the purchasing of siding?

A study was conducted of 406 contractors who were requested to rate twenty-three product characteristics or attributes.[17] Of the twenty-three, only seven were found to be determinant: (1) high-status or quality image, (2) competitive price, (3) dent or impact resistance, (4) beautiful appearance, (5) structural strength, (6) low or easy maintenance, and (7) weather resistance. Of these seven, beautiful appearance, high-status image, and weather resistance were found to be the most important. The remaining four, while also determinant, were less important.

For the marketing manager, the question still remains whether the four types of contractors are segments. Table 9.5 shows how each type of contractor ranked the seven determinant attributes. As can be seen, there are some obvious differences. For example, single- and multidwelling contractors rated high-status image first, but remodeling contractors ranked it third, and siding contractors ranked it fifth. Using rank correlation analysis, the following correlation matrix can be derived:

	Single	Multi	Siding	Remodeling
Single	1.00			
Multi	.89*	1.00		
Siding	.18	.18	1.00	
Remodeling	.57	.54	.86	1.00

*Significant at .05 level.

TABLE 9.5   Rankings of Importance of Determinant Attributes by Four Types of Contractors

Determinant Attribute	Single-Dwelling Contractors [N = 130]	Multidwelling Contractors [N = 81]	Siding Contractors [N = 86]	Remodeling Contractors [N = 109]
High-status or quality image	1	1	5	3
Competitive price	4	3	7	7
Resistance to dents or impacts	7	6	3	4
Beautiful appearance	2	2	2	1
Structural strength or rigidity	6	7	6	5.5 *
Low or easy maintenance	5	5	4	5.5 *
Weather resistance	3	4	1	2

Source: Adapted from Steven A. Sinclair and Edward C. Stalling, "How to Identify Differences Between Market Segments with Attribute Analysis," *Industrial Marketing Management* 19 (1990): 34, 37.

* Denotes tie for 5th ranking.

The only significant correlation was found between single- and multiunit dwelling contractors, which suggests they may not compose separate segments. But the analysis clearly shows that these two are not the same as siding and remodeling contractors and the latter are not the same as each other. Thus, there appears to be three distinct segments in the contractor market. Such analysis strongly suggests that product attributes can be used to segment business markets. The rankings shown in Table 9.5 appear to reinforce this conclusion. The market is not homogeneous. For the business marketing manager, it would be a mistake to stress price in the same way in all three segments. Similarly, pushing a high-status or quality image might work well in the single- and multidwelling segment, but it may not have the same impact in the other two. And ads stressing impact resistance would probably appeal more to siding and remodeling contractors than to the others. This discussion illustrates the marketing applications of segmenting by product characteristics or attributes.

APPROACHES USED TO SEGMENT BUSINESS MARKETS

There are two basic **market segmentation approaches** a business marketer can use. In the first, segmentation in business markets may be viewed in terms of a two-stage process.[18] In the first stage, customers are segmented by geographic, demographic, organizational buying, and other such observable characteristics. This stage is the process of **macrosegmentation**—segmentation between or among organizations. Homogeneity is attempted based on rather basic and easily obtained characteristics such as geographic location or number of employees. The second stage, **microsegmentation,** involves segmenting within the organization as opposed to between organizations. Microsegmentation attempts to find similarities between decision-making units in terms of buying processes used, buying influences involved, and the buyer's motivations and decision-making styles. This second stage uses characteristics more difficult to obtain and often involves the use of detailed marketing research efforts and an effective marketing information system. The total process proceeds from macrosegmentation to microsegmentation and results in an integration of the two stages.

An updated version of this two-stage segmentation process has been called **nested segmentation,** or the nested approach.[19] This approach examines five general segmentation criteria in a nested hierarchy: (1) demographics (for example, industry, company size, and location), (2) operating variables (for example, users or nonusers and operating, financial, and technical capabilities), (3) customer purchasing approaches (for example, purchasing policies, centralized or decentralized purchasing), (4) situational factors (for example, product applications, urgency of the order, and size of order), and (5) personal characteristics (for example, buying motivations, individual perceptions, and risk-management strategies). Using the nested approach, the manager first focuses on the more general, easily observed characteristics and then moves to the more specific, subtle ones.

An example may help to explain how such segmentation occurs. Assume a marketing manager elects to direct marketing efforts toward manufacturers of engineering, laboratory, and scientific instruments. However, the manager may be interested in only those firms in the Middle Atlantic and East North Central regions of the country. In addition, the manager may wish to focus on larger firms and thus uses number of employees as a segmentation variable. Only companies with more than 100 employees are desired. These companies may then be segmented by their purchasing policies such as buying local, decentralized buying, and present customer/noncustomer status. Segmentation thus far has been in the first stage, and customers are similar in terms of industry designation, geographic location, size, and basic buying characteristics.

At this point, the manager may still question whether segmentation has been sufficient to break the market into groups that behave similarly. Since no behavioral segmentation has yet taken place, the manager may move into the second stage of the process. Customers and prospects may now be segmented based on the personal characteristics of those involved in the buying process. In some plants, the key buyers and buying influences may be classified as conservative and fearful. In others, they may be innovative and willing to take risks. Homogeneity is now refined, using more complex characteristics such as personalities and decision-making styles. The two stages are now integrated to the point at which segmentation provides groups of customers and prospects who will respond similarly to the manager's marketing efforts.

THE SEGMENTATION DECISION PROCESS

For the marketing manager, segmenting business markets is a process that proceeds from macrosegmentation to microsegmentation and results in an integration of the two stages. In determining which segments to serve, the manager first should understand that such a process exists, and then he or she should comprehend how to use that process. Figure 9.5 illustrates the process used in making segmentation decisions. This process can be described in a step-by-step fashion.

In step 1, the marketing manager must determine which macrosegmentation variables are desired. For example, the manager may wish to segment on the basis of geographic location, customer size, size of purchases, frequency of purchases, present or potential customer, heavy users versus light users, or any other such easily obtained characteristics. Of course, this step can combine any number of such macrosegmentation variables. It is the logical first step, and it should be accomplished prior to considering microsegmentation variables.

Step 2 involves the selection of microsegmentation variables that may be described as buying attributes, which may relate to differences among the macrosegments. For example, the manager may wish to use types of buying influences to differentiate between large and small business segments. If he or she feels that number and types of buying influences change according to company size, this

FIGURE 9.5   **Flow Chart of the Business Market Segmentation Decision Process**

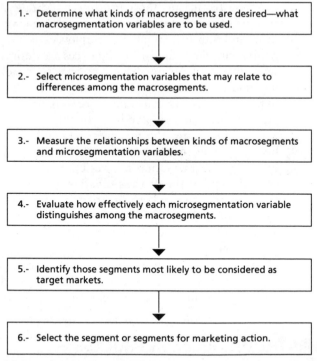

Source: Adapted from Robert W. Haas and Thomas R. Wotruba, *Marketing Management: Concepts, Practice and Cases* (Plano, TX: Business Publications, 1983), 187.

factor may be a logical microsegmentation variable. The buying process and benefits examples illustrated earlier in the chapter are also illustrative of this selection of microsegmentation variables.

Once the manager has determined both those macrosegmentation and microsegmentation variables considered to be most relevant, he or she should attempt to measure the relationships between them. Suppose, for example, the marketing manager is using macrosegmentation variables of company size in terms of number of employees and geographic area of the country. The manager is also interested in such microsegmentation variables as the buying process, benefits sought, and number and type of buying influences involved in that process. What is lacking, however, is the knowledge of which of the microvariables best define segment differences. This step (step 3) typically requires the kind of research study illustrated earlier in both the buying process and benefits examples. Once data are collected, analyses must be undertaken to determine the segmentation relationships. For example, this analysis may show high correlation coefficients between size of purchase order and type of buying process, indicating that the buying process may be a sound segmentation variable. In such measurement, techniques such as cross-tabulation, correlation analysis, factor analysis, or cluster analysis may be considered.[20]

It may be useful to show how this measurement may be accomplished using the cross-tabulation technique. Assume that a marketing manager may wish to distinguish between large and small corporate customers and prospects and thinks that benefits may be the microsegmentation variable that will provide such a distinction. A survey is conducted of an equal number of large and small firms (determined by number of employees), and it reveals the information shown in situation A in Table 9.6. A perfect microsegmentation variable is one that differentiates "perfectly" between the macrosegments. Situation A shows that benefits are a poor segmentation variable in that they do not differentiate at all between large firms (100+ employees) and small firms (under 100 employees). If situation A is the result of the survey, the marketing manager will reject benefits as a microsegmentation variable.

However, if the results of the survey are as shown in situation B in the table, benefits are a perfect microsegmentation variable. Situation B reveals that all firms in the survey that have under 100 employees are in the reliability segment, and those with 100+ employees are in the service segment. In this situation, the benefits microsegmentation variable perfectly differentiates between large and small customers and prospects.

Neither situation A nor situation B is probably realistic in terms of what typically is found in surveys. Situation C is more likely to be encountered. In this situation, it appears that smaller firms (under 100 employees) are more likely to be interested in service, and larger firms (100+ employees) are more likely to be concerned with product reliability. In this situation, 70 percent of the respondents are correctly classified (35 percent in smaller firms want service, 35 percent in larger firms are interested in reliability). The remaining 30 percent do not fit the pattern and are not useful in this segmentation scheme. In situation C, the

TABLE 9.6   **Measuring the Relationship Between Macrosegmentation and Microsegmentation Variables Using Cross-Tabulation Method**

Situation A

		Size of Firm		
		Under 100 Employees	100+ Employees	Total
Benefits	Product reliability Quality and	25%	25%	50%
	speed of service	25%	25%	50%
		50%	50%	100%

Situation B

		Size of Firm		
		Under 100 Employees	100+ Employees	Total
Benefits	Product reliability Quality and	50%	0%	50%
	speed of service	0%	50%	50%
		50%	50%	100%

Situation C

		Size of Firm		
		Under 100 Employees	100+ Employees	Total
Benefits	Product reliability Quality and	15%	35%	50%
	speed of service	35%	15%	50%
		50%	50%	100%

Source: Adapted from Robert W. Haas and Thomas R. Wotruba, *Marketing Management: Concepts, Practice and Cases* (Plano, TX: Business Publications, 1983), 193.

manager may still decide to use benefits as the microsegmentation variable, feeling that it explains enough of the differences between large and small firms.

Step 4 is concerned with the statistical effectiveness of the macrosegmentation variables selected. The variables selected in step 2 and measured in step 3 are compared to determine which appear best. For example, size of purchase order as a microsegmentation variable and the relationships among size and buying process, benefits sought, and number and type of buying influences involved are now compared. If no relationship is found, for example, between size of order and number and type of buying influences, the latter variable may be deleted from consideration. On the other hand, if relationships are found between size of order and both buying process and benefits sought, both of these variables remain included as possible segment variables.

The marketing manager now knows from the previous steps which segment alternatives are statistically meaningful. In step 5, the task is to profile the segments, as was done in the discussion of segmentation using the industrial cooling industry. In that example, each of the four segments was profiled in terms of company size, number of separate plants, satisfaction with current air-conditioning system, percentage of plants requiring air conditioning, and per-ceived consequences of economics and reliability (see Table 9.3). This step in-volves developing a qualitative comparison of the characteristics found in each microsegment.[21]

The last step (step 6) in the process is to select those segments to address in the company's marketing efforts. If any of the remaining segments are seen as too small or not profitable, these may be eliminated. For the others, the manager must decide which to use and which to disregard. In making these types of seg-mentation decisions, the marketing manager may consider such factors as com-petitor strengths and weaknesses in each segment, financial resources available, production capacity, physical distribution capabilities, service abilities, and sales constraints. For example, if production capacity is limited, the manager may not be able to serve all feasible segments. Similarly, if financial resources are scarce, some viable segments may have to be eliminated because the company cannot afford to serve them effectively. Accomplishment of this step is actually the first step in market segmentation strategy.

Whether the manager uses the two-stage macrosegmentation and micro-segmentation approach or the nested approach, the process is consistent. Using either approach brings about the integration of macrosegmentation and micro-segmentation variables in a manner that is both feasible and managerially useful.

THE STATUS OF SEGMENTATION IN BUSINESS MARKETING

Although it is generally conceded that segmentation is as appropriate for busi-ness marketers as it is for consumer marketers, there is considerable evidence to conclude that the former have been slow to appreciate the concept. In cases in which segmentation has taken place in business markets, the emphasis has been mainly on the use of macrosegmentation variables. Practicing marketing man-agers have not fully realized the utility of the microsegmentation approach.[22] A number of reasons may help explain the lack of use of such an important mar-keting concept by business marketers.

One major reason is that the marketing literature is surprisingly devoid of practical examples of segmentation and positioning applied to business markets. Marketing managers desiring to develop practical and effective segmentation will find little help in academic research.[23] Another related problem is that those few models found in the literature are quite complex and difficult to implement by the practicing marketing manager. Thus, these models are often disregarded by managers who will not accept what they do not understand.[24] For practicing marketing managers to embrace the segmentation concept, they need to find both models specific to business markets and ones they are capable of implementing. Most segmentation techniques in the marketing literature have been developed for consumer markets, and they often do not lend themselves well to business marketing.

Another often cited reason for the lack of use of segmentation is that business markets are characterized by more complex buying processes and by interrelated buying influences and buying centers. In addition, many business products and services are used for many different reasons. These factors combine to create a complicated situation for determining segmentation variables. Reasons such as the preceding may or may not be technically correct, but so long as enough marketing managers believe them, they will continue to contribute to slow acceptance.

This does not mean, however, that attempts to better segment business markets are not being investigated or developed. There is evidence to conclude that the segmenting of business markets is becoming more sophisticated. Some examples may help to illustrate this trend.

One approach investigated segmenting organizational customers by the nature of their corporate cultures.[25] This approach is based on the premise that an organization's corporate culture influences what is and what is not purchased. Based on research conducted, three corporate culture segments were discovered: (1) happy doers, (2) middle-of-the-roaders, and (3) satisfaction seekers. Happy doers are characterized as being most interested in a smooth operation, satisfied with present suppliers, and more motivated by logic than emotion. Satisfaction seekers are very customer-oriented and frequently dissatisfied with present suppliers, and evaluate suppliers in very formal manners—they are quite willing to switch from one supplier to another. Organizations in the middle-of-the-road segment are characterized as being willing to work with multiple suppliers, selecting suppliers according to a predetermined model, making decisions after long study of the issues, and, frequently, conducting formal evaluations of supplier performances. This is an interesting approach in that it focuses on the organization itself and not just on individuals within it. If corporate culture does actually affect selection of suppliers, etc., then this type of segmentation may well lead to more practical and useful segmentation of business markets.

There are also some indications that consumer market psychographic segmentation models, such as lifestyle, are beginning to slowly filter into business marketing. A Kansas City advertising firm has developed CUBE (Comprehensive Understanding of Buyer Environment), a framework it has used successfully in segmenting and tracking consumer buying groups. It is now developing a pilot program to study the application of CUBE to the health insurance, building, and agricultural chemical industries.[26] If such attempts to apply consumer marketing models to business markets succeed, more and more such approaches may find use in business marketing.

Another exploratory study focused on buying center purchase responsibilities as a basis for segmenting business markets.[27] By analyzing buying centers, differences were revealed between organizations with "overlapping" versus "position-dominant" patterns of purchase responsibility. Organizations with distinctly defined patterns of purchase responsibility correlated with organizational position are said to be position-dominant, while others have more overlapping patterns. Comparing the two segments, it was determined that organizations in the overlapping segment had the following characteristics: they (1) were smaller in size, (2) had higher organizational performance, (3) had buying centers with lower education levels, (4) had buying centers with a greater number of external professional affiliations, and (5) had buying centers with a greater proportion of male participants. As stated, this was an exploratory study and the authors state that "the findings cannot be generalized beyond the sample due to nonresponse and geographical limitations."[28] Still, the example is indicative of the inroads being made to upgrade the level of market segmentation in business marketing.

In summary, although market segmentation is necessary for effective marketing strategy, many business marketing managers may yet fail to recognize the value of this concept until better business market segmentation techniques are developed. What is needed to increase the use of segmentation in business markets is a methodology that recognizes the complexity of the organizational purchasing decision, incorporates it in its measurement procedure, and provides criteria for classifications of buying organizations.[29] At this time, unfortunately, such a universal methodology has yet to be developed despite advances such as those previously discussed. Until that happens, business marketing practitioners will continue to rely on the simpler forms of macrosegmentation that are now widely used.

CHAPTER SUMMARY

This chapter emphasized the need for market segmentation in the development of effective business marketing strategy. Strategy cannot take place until specific target markets have been delineated, which involves breaking total markets into segments. In addition, the chapter focused on segmentation analysis as it occurs in business markets and its relation to segmentation strategy.

The concept of market segmentation was defined as the process of breaking total markets into more manageable subgroups or segments. This process is divided into the two components of segmentation analysis and segmentation strategy. Segmentation analysis seeks to define those segments most appropriate for the com-pany's marketing efforts; segmentation strategy seeks to direct those efforts at the defined segments. This chapter explored the analysis aspect of segmentation (the strategy aspect is covered in Chapter 10).

Reasons why market segmentation is needed were discussed, with emphasis on the managerial implications. The bases most used to segment business markets were examined, ranging from the simpler to the more complex. Examples were provided to show how geographic, demographic, buying process, product benefit, and product attribute criteria can be used to segment business markets.

A model was developed for use in segmentation in business marketing. Finally, the present status of segmentation was examined as it exists in business marketing. Examples were shown to illustrate recent developments in segmenting business markets and they suggest that major advancements are likely to occur in the near future in this very important area of marketing.

KEY TERMS

benefit segmentation
buying process segmentation
demographic segmentation
geographic segmentation
macrosegmentation
market segmentation

market segmentation approach
market segmentation base
market segmentation process
microsegmentation
nested segmentation
product feature segmentation

QUESTIONS

1. Why is it necessary to segment business markets? What is to be gained from the segmentation of such markets?
2. It has been stated that market segmentation is market segmentation whether it be in consumer or business markets. Do you agree or disagree with this statement? Back up your position.
3. Based on what you have learned from previous marketing courses you have taken, compare and contrast segmentation in consumer and business markets.
4. Explain the relationship between "segmentation analysis" and "segmentation strategy." How do these two terms differ? How do they relate to each other?
5. What is meant by the two-stage process of segmentation as it is practiced in business marketing? Why are both stages necessary for effective segmentation?
6. What is the difference between segmenting business markets on the basis of demographic and geographic variables, and developing average customer profiles using the same demographic and geographic variables?

7. It is often argued that market segmentation is a process. Explain that process and then show how it can be applied to business marketing.
8. In recent years, the trend in business marketing has been to become more sophisticated and rely less on the more basic demographic and geographic bases. Explain what this statement means and provide examples to prove it is true.
9. For a number of reasons, many practicing business marketing managers still fail to appreciate the value of segmentation or are unable to implement it even if they do appreciate it. What reasons account for this behavior? What will have to take place before segmentation in business markets catches up to segmentation in consumer markets?
10. Some argue that segmentation in business marketing is more difficult than it is in consumer marketing because the former deals with marketing to organizations while the latter is concerned with serving individuals and households. Why should this make it more difficult to segment business markets?

NOTES

1. Fred W. Winter, "Market Segmentation: A Tactical Approach," *Business Horizons* 37 (February 1984): 57.

2. Yoram Wind and Richard N. Cardozo, "Industrial Market Segmentation," *Industrial Marketing Management* 3 (1974): 153.

3. Cornelis A. de Kluyver and David B. Whitlark, "Benefit Segmentation for Industrial Products," *Industrial Marketing Management* 15 (1986): 273.

4. Henry Assael, *Marketing Management Strategy and Action* (Boston: PWS-KENT, 1985), 224.

5. See Raymond E. Corey, "Key Options in Market Selection and Product Planning," *Harvard Business Review* 53 (September–October 1975): 119–128.

6. De Kluyver and Whitlark, op. cit.

7. Benson P. Shapiro and Thomas V. Bonoma, "How to Segment Industrial Markets," *Harvard Business Review* 62 (May–June 1984): 104.

8. Thomas V. Bonoma and Benson P. Shapiro, "Evaluating Market Segmentation Approaches," *Industrial Marketing Management* 13 (1984): 258.

9. Shapiro and Bonoma, op. cit.

10. Peter Doyle and John Saunders, "Market Segmentation and Positioning in Specialized Industrial Markets," *Journal of Marketing* 49 (Spring 1985): 25.

11. Tom Eisenhart, "Segmenting with Precision," *Business Marketing* 74 (September 1989): 61.

12. See Jean-Marie Choffray and Gary L. Lilien, "Industrial Marketing Segmentation by the Structure of the Purchasing Process," *Industrial Marketing Management* 9 (1980): 331–342.

13. Doyle and Saunders, op. cit.

14. Ibid., 24–32.

15. See James H. Myers and Mark I. Alpert, "Determinant Buying Attitudes: Meaning and Measurement," *Journal of Marketing* 32 (October 1968): 18–20.

16. See Rowland T. Moriarty and David J. Reibstein, "Benefit Segmentation in Industrial Markets," *Journal of Business Research* 14 (December 1986): 463–486.

17. Steven A. Sinclair and Edward C. Stalling, "How to Identify Differences Between Market Segments with Attribute Analysis," *Industrial Marketing Management* 19 (1990): 31–40.

18. See Wind and Cardozo, op. cit., 153–166.

19. See Shapiro and Bonoma, op. cit., 104–110; and Bonoma and Shapiro, *Segmenting the Industrial Market* (Lexington, MA: D. C. Heath & Company, 1983).

20. See Robert W. Haas and Thomas R. Wotruba, *Marketing Management: Concepts, Practice, and Cases* (Plano, TX: Business Publications, Inc., 1983), 191–197.

21. Choffray and Lilien, op. cit., 336.

22. Camille P. Schuster and Charles D. Bodkin, "Market Segmentation Practices of Exporting Companies," *Industrial Marketing Management* 16 (1987): 96.

23. Doyle and Saunders, op. cit., 24–25.

24. John D. C. Little, "Decision Support Systems for Marketing Managers," *Journal of Marketing* 43 (Summer 1979): 9–27.

25. Tom Eisenhart, "Segmenting Markets by Corporate Culture," *Business Marketing* 73 (July 1988): 50–51.

26. "Spotting Those Rising Stars," *Business Marketing* 73 (July 1989): 54.

27. See Robert J. Thomas, "Industrial Market Segmentation on Buying Center Purchase Responsibilities," *Journal of the Academy of Marketing Science* 17 (Summer 1989): 243–252.

28. Ibid., 249.

29. Choffray and Lilien, op. cit., 332.

SUGGESTED ADDITIONAL READINGS

Bonoma, Thomas V., and Benson P. Shapiro. "Evaluating Market Segmentation Approaches." *Industrial Marketing Management* 13 (1984): 257–268.

———. *Industrial Market Segmentation: A Nested Approach.* Cambridge, MA: Marketing Science Institute, 1983.

———. *Segmenting the Industrial Market.* Lexington, MA: D. C. Heath & Company, 1983.

Cheron, E. J., and E. J. Kleinschmidt. "A Review of Industrial Market Segmentation Research and a Proposal for an Integrated Segmentation Framework." *International Journal of Research in Marketing* 2 (1985): 101–115.

Choffray, Jean-Marie, and Gary L. Lilien. "Industrial Market Segmentation by the Structure of the Purchasing Process." *Industrial Marketing Management* 9 (1980): 331–342.

De Kluyver, Cornelis A., and David B. Whitlark. "Benefit Segmentation for Industrial Products." *Industrial Marketing Management* 15 (1986): 273–286.

Devine, Hugh J., Jr., and John Morton. "How Does the Market Really See Your Product?" *Business Marketing* 69 (July 1984): 70–79, 131.

Doyle, Peter, and John Saunders. "Market Segmentation and Positioning in Specialized Industrial Markets." *Journal of Marketing* 49 (Spring 1985): 24–32.

Eisenhart, Tom. "Segmenting with Precision." *Business Marketing* 74 (September 1989): 60–61.

Morton, John. "How to Spot the Really Important Prospects." *Business Marketing* 75 (January 1990): 62–67.

Plank, Richard E. "A Critical Review of Industrial Market Segmentation." *Industrial Marketing Management* 14 (1985): 79–91.

Shapiro, Benson P., and Thomas V. Bonoma. "How to Segment Industrial Markets." *Harvard Business Review* 62 (May–June 1984): 104–110.

Sinclair, Steven A., and Edward C. Stalling. "How to Identify Differences Between Market Segments With Attribute Analysis." *Industrial Marketing Management* 19 (1990): 31–40.

Spekman, Robert E. "Segmenting Buyers in Different Types of Organizations." *Industrial Marketing Management* 10 (1981): 43–48.

Sutters, Peter A. "Measures Exist for Segmenting Industrial Markets." *Marketing News* 17 (April 1, 1983): 11.

Thomas, Robert J. "Industrial Market Segmentation on Buying Center Purchase Responsibilities." *Journal of the Academy of Marketing Science* 17 (Summer 1989): 243–252.

Wilson, R. D. "Segmentation and Communication in the Industrial Marketplace." *Journal of Business Research* 14 (December 1986): 487–500.

Wind, Yoram, and Richard N. Cardozo. "Industrial Market Segmentation." *Industrial Marketing Management* 3 (1974): 153–166.

Wind, Yoram, Thomas S. Robertson, and Cynthia Fraser. "Industrial Product Diffusion by Market Segment." *Industrial Marketing Management* 11 (1982): 1–8.

10

Planning Business Marketing Strategy

• •

Marketing planning and strategy development is one of the major responsibilities of business marketing managers. Determining target markets and then developing and implementing marketing mixes to address those markets is the essence of marketing management. A study of chief marketing executives in business marketing firms conducted by the Heidrick and Struggles consulting firm found that determining strategy and tactics was the number one responsibility of these executives. This was followed by identifying markets, setting policies and objectives, and executing marketing plans.[1] Another study conducted by the Conference Board found over 60 percent of surveyed marketing managers in business marketing firms were responsible for creating their firms' marketing planning efforts.[2] These studies clearly show that most business marketing managers are heavily involved in the marketing planning process for their firms. Products and services have to be developed to meet target market needs. These products and services must then be effectively distributed, promoted, and priced so that they are accessible to those who want them. Determining the proper mix and integrating all mix activities constitutes the area of planning and strategy development. Markets are identified and segmented when necessary, objectives are set for each target market, strategies are developed and executed through mix activity programs, and the results are then controlled and evaluated.

This chapter builds on the concept of segmentation, which was developed in the preceding chapter. It also establishes the parameters for the more specific marketing mix chapters that follow. This chapter sets the tone for the rest of the text in that it details the overall area of marketing planning and strategy development. Then, the specific mix chapters that follow may be integrated into the overall process developed in this chapter. This chapter first develops the concept of strategy and introduces the area of strategic market planning. It then looks in detail at the marketing planning process and focuses on each element in such

Marketing Strategy in a Business Marketing Environment

Genentech, Inc., produces a drug called Tissue Plasminogen Activator, commonly known as TPA. TPA is a fast-acting agent that clears blood clots that cause heart attacks and has the ability to dissolve clots within thirty minutes. Its main competitors are Streptokinase, which is produced by the German company Hoechst, and Eminase, which is manufactured by SmithKline Beecham. Genentech spent more than $150 million to develop TPA and first-year sales of $180 million seemingly justified the investment.

TPA was priced at $2,200 a dose, which was higher than that charged by either of the two competitors: Eminase was priced at $1,700 a dose while Streptokinase sold at only $200 a dose. Despite the large price differential, TPA proved most competitive in that it was believed to be 50 percent more effective than Streptokinase. Thus, Genentech found itself with a price eleven times higher than that of its major competitor, but TPA's product advantages supported that higher price.

In 1989, however, a large European study called GISSI-II showed that TPA was no more effective than Streptokinase. Given the great price differential, this study was seen as a major blow to TPA sales. But another study by two U.S. cardiologists found that TPA worked the best so long as the drug heperin was administered at the same time. Heperin is an inexpensive coagulant that keeps arteries open after TPA first clears up the clots. The different results in the two studies were caused by the fact that

doctors in the United States administer heperin at the same time as TPA, while the practice in Europe is to administer heperin twelve hours later. Streptokinase is not dependent on heperin and thus is not influenced by the drug as TPA is. Genentech knew that the GISSI-II findings would be presented at the 1990 annual American College of Cardiology meeting, which would be attended by thousands of cardiologists. The company had to develop a marketing strategy to offset the GISSI-II study's impact and to use the American study to advantage.

In late 1989, the company had its 278 sales reps call on 7,000 doctors to explain the heperin connection and show how the GISSI-II findings might be irrelevant. In January 1990, the company also provided hospital pharmacies extensions in time to pay for TPA. This encouraged them to stock up on TPA, which afforded Genentech protection against its two competitors. In addition, the two U.S. researchers addressed the American College of Cardiology meeting, in a symposium sponsored by Genentech, and explained the critical importance of heperin. This presentation was made immediately after that of the European researchers who had conducted the GISSI-II study.

The entire strategy was based on quick and responsive action to changes in the environment—the European and American studies. Then, by careful decisions made in the promotion and distribution areas, Genentech was able to counter the GISSI-II findings and capitalize on the

American findings. The price of TPA was kept at $2,200 a dose and the product remained virtually unchanged except for the simultaneous administration of heperin. This strategy permitted Genen- tech to repel a strong competitive effort and maintain its share of the market.

Source: Adapted from Joan O'C. Hamilton, "Genentech: A Textbook Case of Medical Marketing," *Business Week* (August 13, 1990): 96–97.

planning. The marketing plan is discussed and tools are introduced that may be used by the marketing manager to aid in more effective planning and strategy development in business markets. This is an important chapter in that it provides the framework for discussing the more specific mix strategies and tactics in the product or service, distribution, promotion, and pricing areas. Sound planning facilitates the necessary integration of these mix activities so that marketing efforts are effectively directed and controlled.

THE MEANING OF STRATEGY

The word **strategy** is of Greek derivation and originally was applied to military endeavors. From a contemporary business perspective, the term is defined as "an organized statement of broad tasks and/or areas of activities necessary to achieve an objective."[3] This definition implies action—defining goals or objectives, then undertaking activities to achieve those goals or objectives. Applied to marketing, strategy is the general approach taken to achieve predetermined objectives in defined markets and segments. Follow-up action programs are the tactics to carry out the strategy and achieve those objectives.

STRATEGIC MARKET PLANNING

Today's business marketing manager may be involved in planning at several levels within an organization. Two types of normal planning activities most affect the manager: strategic market planning and marketing planning. Although they sound similar, they do not mean the same thing and should be clarified to prevent misuse. **Strategic market planning** is defined as the managerial process of developing and maintaining a strategic fit between the organization and its marketing opportunities.[4] This type of planning involves the entire organization and is typically the responsibility of top management rather than an activity manager such as the marketing manager.[5] Strategic market planning assesses market opportunities and company capabilities in developing a total strategic approach to a marketplace. The end product of strategic market planning is a strategic market plan that attempts to determine how a company should be defined, what its mission should be, what marketing, manufacturing, research and development, and other functional activities should be stressed, and how funds should be allotted.[6] Figure 10.1 illustrates the strategic market planning process and shows how marketing planning is only one element in this process, just as are production planning, financial planning, manpower planning, and logistics planning.

Another way of understanding this relationship is to consider those components that determine overall business profitability. The Strategic Planning Institute cites the three major components as (1) strategic factors such as relative product quality, relative market share, investment intensity, growth of the market served, and vertical integration; (2) operating effectiveness such as effectiveness of labor use, effectiveness of market strategy, and effectiveness of working capital usage; and (3) transitory factors such as the business cycle, weather conditions, labor union relations problems, and technological problems or breakthroughs.[7] Analysis of these three components shows that marketing is heavily involved in some elements, marginally involved in some, and uninvolved in others. For example, the marketing manager may be directly responsible for markets selected, partially responsible for product quality, and uninvolved in working capital usage. Viewed in this manner, the relationship between strategic market planning and marketing planning may be better appreciated. The former involves all the strategies in the corporate or business plan, whereas the latter relates to the marketing mix elements.

FIGURE 10.1   **The Strategic Market Planning Process**

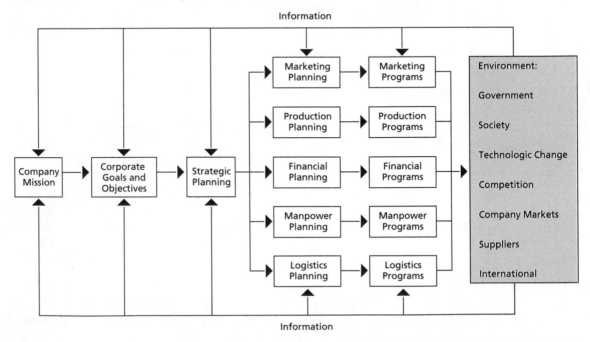

MARKETING PLANNING

Marketing planning involves the selection of a marketing strategy and the tactics to implement it to reach a defined set of goals.[8] Marketing planning differs from strategic market planning in three ways: (1) strategic market planning focuses on long-term directions and goals, whereas marketing planning usually involves shorter-term horizons, often one year; (2) marketing planning is usually the direct responsibility of the marketing manager, whereas top management is responsible for strategic market planning; and (3) marketing planning tends to detail line-by-line budget items and tactical approaches, whereas strategic market planning is concerned with the rationale, not the details, used in marketing planning.[9] The strategic market plan gives the manager a direction for marketing planning. Indeed, it has been stated that business marketing firms need to adopt a strategic marketing perspective that integrates the strategic orientation of corporate planning with the tactical orientation of marketing planning.[10]

Figure 10.2 shows the close relationship between strategic market planning

FIGURE 10.2 The Relationship Between Strategic Planning and Marketing Planning

Source: Reprinted by permission from *Business Magazine,* "Strategic Planning and the Marketing Process," by Philip Kotler (May–June 1980).

and marketing planning. Corporate mission, goals and objectives, growth strategy, and business portfolio plan impact target market selection and subsequent marketing strategy development. This relationship is important because it shows the marketing manager that strategy to achieve marketing objectives must be integrated with strategies of other managers such as the production manager and comptroller. Marketing planning and strategy formulation do not take place in a vacuum—they must be tied to other functional strategies if overall corporate success is to be achieved. When a business marketing firm adopts a strategic market planning approach, marketing thinking is broadened in three ways: (1) laterally, by strengthening its role of integrated planning across product markets and functional areas; (2) vertically, by accounting for corporate- and business-level strategies and financial performance aspects of decisions; and (3) dynamically, by focusing on strategic adaptation to changing environments.[11]

This relationship may also be found in the previously cited Conference Board study of business marketing firms. That study found that about 50 percent of the surveyed producers of business products directly tied their marketing plans to their firms' strategic market plans. This increased to about 63 percent for producers of business services.[12]

Since this text is devoted to marketing management in business markets, the focus here will be on marketing planning and not strategic market planning. For more information on the latter, the reader is referred to the many fine texts that specifically cover the topic of strategic market planning in more detail. From here on, discussion will focus primarily on the marketing planning process as it exists in business marketing.

THE MARKETING PLANNING PROCESS

The marketing planning process consists of analyzing marketing opportunities, researching and selecting target markets, designing marketing strategies, planning marketing programs, and controlling the marketing effort.[13] This definition illustrates clearly the comprehensive nature of the process. It begins with a situational analysis and continues all the way to actual control and evaluation of the strategies and tactical programs implemented. Given that marketing is basically the ability to adapt to change and that markets are constantly changing, the marketing planning process is never-ending—to be effective it must operate on a continuous basis. Figure 10.3 illustrates the concept of this planning process. As can be seen, the figure provides a visual representation of what is developed in the definition that begins this section. Although the process can be described in linear fashion, it is more appropriate to think of it as a circular flow as the figure shows.[14] As one marketing director of a glass manufacturer states, "it's a . . . priority-setting, weeding-out process that is ongoing."[15]

Figure 10.4 illustrates the marketing planning process of a large chemical corporation. Analysis of the figure reveals that it follows quite closely the conceptual model illustrated in Figure 10.3. The company defines a number of target

FIGURE 10.3   Flowmodel of the Marketing Planning Process

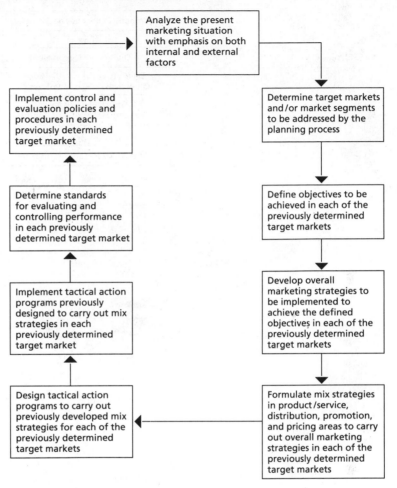

markets, conducts a situation and environment analysis in each, and then sets objectives to be reached in each market. It then determines appropriate strategies and action programs to carry out those strategies. The process then concludes with a control and review procedure.

Figures 10.3 and 10.4 suggest that business marketing firms use relatively standard approaches in their marketing planning processes. This being the case, it is now worthwhile to develop in some detail each step in the flowmodel in Figure 10.3. In this way, a better understanding of the entire marketing planning process may be developed.

FIGURE 10.4   The Marketing Planning Process at a Large Chemical Corporation

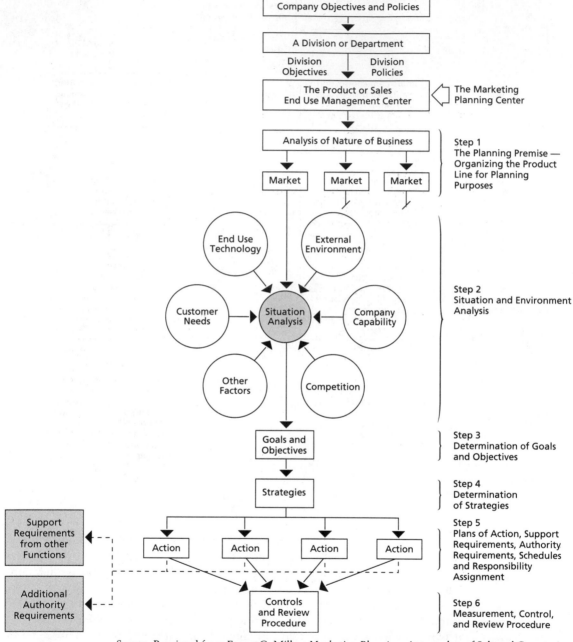

Source: Reprinted from Ernest C. Miller, *Marketing Planning: Approaches of Selected Companies*, Research Study No. 81 (New York: American Management Association, 1967), 60. Copyright © Industrial Research & Decision, Inc.

Analysis of the Present Marketing Situation

The first step in any marketing planning process should be a sound analysis of the present marketing situation. Effective marketing planning requires marketing information. The **situation analysis** is the information-gathering phase of the planning process—it is basically the cornerstone of the process. Objectives cannot be determined prior to an assessment of where the company stands in its present total marketing environment. No marketing manager can project future market positions if he or she does not know where the company presently stands. In conducting a situation analysis, the business marketing manager needs to view the company in terms of both its external and internal environments. Since these two parts of the analysis are different, each should be approached separately.

External Analysis   As was developed in Chapter 2, external information gathering involves the manager learning as much as possible about the market or markets in which the company plans to compete. Major categories to be investigated include (1) environmental factors that might be involved, (2) market conditions, (3) customers, (4) noncustomers, (5) channels, and (6) competitors.[16] Table 10.1 provides some examples of information that may be desired in each category, and Table 10.2 illustrates one approach used to analyze competitors.

TABLE 10.1	External Information Gathering in the Situation Analysis
Major Categories	**Types of Information Sought**
Environmental factors	Economic conditions such as recession, inflation, unemployment, interest rates, and capital availability; social changes taking place; governmental policies and regulations; costs and availability of required materials, manpower, energy, etc.; and environmental policies and regulations
Market conditions	Market needs, size, growth, and geographic location; market potentials and forecasts; market shares; market segments
Present or prospective customers	Buying influences involved; buying processes used; size of purchases; rates of product use; purchasing policies and procedures; buying centers; motives of buying influences
Channels	Present channel relationships; channel options; motivations of channel intermediaries; requirements of channel intermediaries; costs of channel options; physical distribution characteristics of channel intermediaries; legal aspects of using channel intermediaries
Competitors	Number and location of primary and secondary competitors; market shares held by competitors; competitive strengths and weaknesses in terms of products/services, pricing, distribution, sales, advertising and sales promotion, production capacity and capabilities; R & D, engineering, purchasing, etc., capabilities

Source: Adapted from Robert W. Haas and Thomas R. Wotruba, *Marketing Management* (Plano, TX: Business Publications, Inc., 1983), 288.

TABLE 10.2   Approach Used to Analyze Strengths and Weaknesses of Competitors in Business Marketing

Competitive Dimensions			Us	Competitors			Comments on Data
				A	B	C	
	Market size	Growth per year		Market share			
1. Product Position							
Line 1	$15MM	0%	65%	20%	10%	5%	1. Not subject to share gain, manage for cash.
2	$30MM	10%	25%	40%	15%	20%	2. Subject to share gain, A most vulnerable, B, C less so.
3	$20MM	15%	10%	25%	30%	35%	3. Subject to share gain, A, B, C equally vulnerable. Substantial unfilled need for a new product.
2. Pricing Strategy							
H = Price for margin	Line 1		C	C	C	H	B and C will be easiest to take share away from on price, and it will be least expensive to maintain share taken away. A is more competitive, will require larger price differentials to gain and maintain share, and it is therefore more costly to take share away.
C = Price with market	2		C	L	C	C	
L = Price leader or very aggressive	3		C	L	C	C	
3. New Product Policy							
L = Leader	Line 1		L	L	F	F	Expect new products first from A, monitor market carefully to identify what they're working on—expect A to imitate earliest any new products introduced.
F = Follower	2		F	L	F	F	
	3		L	L	L	F	
4. Overall Marketing Strength							
No. representatives	Line 1		5	10	15	15	A strongest and equal to us. B and C vulnerable to more intensive selling effort offered by us.
No. distributors	2		40	35	30	30	
No. salesmen	3		25	20	10	7	
5. Geographic Strength							
No. salesmen and reps territory	E		9	7	7	6	We may be weak in district G and should consider adding salesmen, otherwise are equal or superior to competition.
	F		7	7	6	6	
	G		5	8	7	6	
	H		9	8	6	4	

6. *Distributor Strength*

No. distributors

territory				
E	12	10	8	7
F	10	9	7	8
G	10	9	7	7
H	8	7	6	6

A approximately equal in strength. *B* and *C* weaker and definitely vulnerable.

7. *Delivery Norm (Weeks)*

Product				
1	6	6	4	7
2	6	3	4	4
3	6	6	7	9

Delivery improvements necessary in 1, 2 to be competitive. Improvement beyond competitive levels will not gain share. Improvement in line 3 will gain advantage against *A*, *B*, and *C* according to sales force survey.

8. *Penetration by Account Size %*

$ Market—all products

40 Large	40%	30%	15%	15%
15 Medium	15%	30%	25%	30%
10 Small	10%	30%	20%	40%
$65MM				

We're weak in medium and small accounts, need program to improve penetration and coverage there.

9. *Probable Reaction to:*

• Lower price

A—Immediate retaliation, continued price reduction to gain share back.
B, C—Weaker response. Will try to hold large accounts.

Cost in taking share away from *A* on price will be high. *B* and *C* more vulnerable.

• New product

A—Will immediately match new product offering.
C—May match immediately.
B—Eventually match.

B and to some extent *C* vulnerable to new product offering.

• Increased sales coverage

A—Will match.
B, C—Some increase.

B and *C* vulnerable in some measure to sales coverage, particularly if a new product is launched.

Key Strategic Conclusions

1. *Product Policy:* Focus on lines 2 and 3 where gain is possible by increased penetration and growth with the market and product modification for product 3.
2. *Competitive Strategy:* Focus on taking share away from *B* and *C*, who are vulnerable to lower pricing and a new product innovation requested by salesmen. Selectively take business away from competitor *A*—only up to the point where expensive price retaliation is expected.
3. *Marketing Strategy:* Add three salesmen to territory G and one to F to build strength against key targets—*B* and *C*. Shift call pattern and develop mktg. programs for medium to small accounts where penetration is poor. Develop distributor promotion program to capitalize on advantage over *B* and *C*.
4. *Service:* Invest in capacity to lower delivery time in product 2 to level competitive with *B* and *C*. Maintain competitive standards in other lines.

Source: Reprinted by permission from C. Davis Fogg, "Planning Gains in Market Share," *Journal of Marketing* 38 (January 1974):35, published by the American Marketing Association.

Internal Analysis Internal information gathering involves the manager learning about the capabilities of his or her company to compete in a market. This is a necessary part of the planning process since many people in many departments may be involved in carrying out marketing strategies and action programs. The manager must assess the company's own strengths and weaknesses as these relate to marketing efforts. General categories to be investigated include (1) financial resources and capabilities, (2) operating facilities, (3) competitive strengths and weaknesses, (4) environmental assumptions held by company personnel, (5) forecasts and projections, and (6) organizational characteristics.[17] Table 10.3 illustrates examples of information pertinent to each category.

The adage that marketing decisions should be made on the basis of marketing facts provides the foundation for the situation analysis. In turn, the situation analysis provides the basis for the establishment of objectives and the determination of practical and realistic marketing strategies and tactical action programs. Since the marketing planning process is a continuous one, a sound situation analysis is imperative if the manager is to keep abreast of changes taking place inside and outside his or her company.

It should be understood that implementing an effective situation analysis is not an easy task. As the previous discussion indicates, there are many areas of concern that should be investigated. This takes considerable time, money, and effort and is not accomplished overnight. This will be developed in more detail

---

TABLE 10.3   Internal Information Gathering in the Situation Analysis

Major Categories	Types of Information Sought
Financial resources & capabilities	Net earnings; cash flow position; profits by SBUs, products, product lines; credit restrictions; financial ratios; receivables; inventories; payables; borrowing capabilities
Operating facilities	Plant production capacity; manufacturing abilities; purchasing capabilities; engineering and R & D capabilities; service capabilities; quality assurance abilities; inventory levels
Competitive strengths and weaknesses	Assessment of competitive capabilities in terms of production and technical capabilities; marketing capabilities; distribution capabilities; and mix elements
Environmental assumptions	Understanding of attitudes of management regarding material shortages; technological changes; social changes; governmental and economic changes; labor changes
Organizational factors	Corporate mission; corporate goals and objectives; corporate growth strategies; anticipated organizational changes; corporate climate; power centers; power struggles; organizational strengths and weaknesses
Forecasts and projections	Sales forecasts by products and markets; market share projections; sales potential projections; financial budgets and forecasts; production and manpower projections

Source: Adapted from Robert W. Haas and Thomas R. Wotruba, *Marketing Management* (Plano, TX: Business Publications, Inc., 1983), 286.

in Chapter 11, which covers both the marketing information system (MIS) and formal marketing research. Both of these may be instrumental in organizing and implementing a successful situation analysis. Regardless of the degree of difficulty, the situation analysis is a necessary part of the marketing planning process and must be designed and implemented with care if that process is to be reliable and managerially useful.

Determination of Target Markets

Following the situation analysis, markets must be selected and segmented if necessary. First, though, some terminology should be clarified, since the term *market* has many meanings. A market is an aggregate of organizations that presently purchase or potentially can purchase a particular product or service for direct or indirect use in its operations. For an aggregate to be truly a market, four factors are required: (1) the organizations must need the product or service, (2) the organizations must have the ability to purchase, (3) the organizations must be willing to purchase, and (4) there must be authority to purchase.[18] Thus, any group of organizations does not necessarily compose a market. The marketing manager must first determine which aggregates are true markets and which are not. It makes little sense to develop a marketing strategy to reach organizational customers who do not have the need for, willingness, or ability to buy specific products or services. For example, the manager may find that many machine shops across the United States can use industrial robots. Further analysis, however, may show that the smaller ones cannot afford to buy such expensive products. Thus, true markets must first be determined.

Typically, these markets must then be segmented, since all customers and prospects within those markets will not have identical needs and wants. Chapter 9 developed the concept of segmentation in detail. The marketing manager at this point determines which segments in those markets offer the greatest potential for the company's marketing efforts. Using macrosegmentation and microsegmentation variables, the marketing manager selects the segments to address in the marketing plan. Chapter 9 outlined how this task may be accomplished. The selected segments are then defined as **target markets.** Once segmentation is accomplished, target market customers can then be identified and located using the SIC system (see Chapter 8).

After target markets have been identified and segmented and customer organizations are known, the marketing manager needs to objectively appraise what resistance will be encountered and what difficulties will have to be overcome in marketing to these customers. The fact that potential market targets exist is not enough. The manager must realize that competitors also will be examining these markets and that penetrating these markets will not be easy. Thus, the manager should try to define the areas of difficulty that will be encountered in the attempt to penetrate those markets. The company's capabilities of overcoming these difficulties must be objectively evaluated if effective marketing is to take place. This step underscores the importance of a sound situation analysis. Ideally, these assessments should be performed before products are produced and should take place for each product in each market segment. In addition, these assessments should be viewed by the marketing manager as "go–no go" situations.

To illustrate, if the potential is not sufficient to support the costs involved, the target market might not be entered, and perhaps the product should be dropped from consideration. Similarly, if the manager's firm does not have the financial, technical, or managerial capabilities to overcome anticipated competition and buyer resistances, then the decision to market the product might be abandoned. In other words, when the assessments of target market potential, resistances and difficulties, and the company's capabilities are favorable, it is a "go" situation. When any or all of these same assessments are unfavorable, it may well be a "no go" situation, and other marketing opportunities should be sought. The major point in this step is that the identification of a market target means much more than just the definition and location of that target—it also means an objective assessment of the company's ability to penetrate that target.

Some examples may help in better understanding what takes place at this step in the marketing planning process. In Chapter 9, an example was given in the case of a processor of resins that wanted to market tactifiers to the specialty chemical market. That company found the market to be composed of twelve separate benefit segments (shown in Table 9.4). In this example, management decided that only seven of the twelve segments could be considered worthy of pursuing. Further analysis found that only four of the seven were considered really attractive for the firm. Thus, the company decided to focus its marketing efforts on these four segments, which incidentally accounted for 54 percent of the total tactifier market.

Another example of target market selection can be seen in the case of AT&T's Data Systems Group. Its strategy was to think smaller in terms of target markets. To accomplish this, the company focused its marketing efforts on such markets as telemarketing, airline reservations, lodging, government, and finance.[19] Instead of trying to be all things to all people, AT&T segmented the market and then focused its efforts on those segments that it believed to offer the most promising returns.

Definition of Marketing Objectives

If the "go" decision is reached, the marketing manager must set specific, realistic objectives that are to be achieved. In addition to being specific and realistic, these objectives must be consistent with overall corporate goals and objectives, and they must be capable of measurement. If the objectives cannot be measured, the marketing manager will never know if the strategy accomplished its intention. And if accomplishment cannot be known, corrective action can hardly be taken. The establishment of **marketing objectives,** then, involves determining goals that reflect corporate philosophies, objectives, and market capacities in such categories as illustrated in Table 10.4.

Corporate goals and objectives compose the overall business directions the company plans to take. Because many companies are complex organizations, no

TABLE 10.4   **Examples of Marketing Objectives in Business Markets**

Type of Objective	Illustration
Sales volume—by product, market, customer type, or time	Company wishes to attain $60,000 in sales of product A in market A during fiscal year 1995, or 60,000 units of product B in market B during fiscal year 1995.
Market share	Company wishes to attain a 30 percent share of market A with product A during fiscal year 1995.
Sales growth rate	Company wishes to attain a 10 percent growth rate in sales in market A with product A over previous year's sales.
Market penetration	Company wishes to attain 20 percent of the total market potential in market A with product A during fiscal year 1995.
Profitability or return on investment (ROI)	Company desires to attain a 12 percent ROI after taxes on product A in market A during the life cycle of the product.
Social responsibility	Company wishes to be seen as a good corporate citizen in its immediate community.
Company image	Company wishes to be seen as a reliable supplier of good, quality products.
Innovation	Company wishes to be seen as on the cutting edge of new technological breakthroughs in its industry.

single set of objectives can represent the entire company and its personnel. Therefore, top management often formulates statements of the company's general mission and its specific aims. Top management then requires the various departments within the company to define their own more specific objectives within the constraints of the overall corporate or business objectives. Typical examples, taken from a list of corporate objectives of a large business marketing corporation, are "maximize revenue," "continue to be a good corporate citizen," and "stay one step ahead of competitors through a thorough understanding of the market and customer needs." Corporate objectives generally are quite broad and relate to many functions of the company, not just to marketing. In addition, some corporate objectives relate to the marketing function, and some do not. It is important that the manager know the company's overall business or corporate objectives well enough to ensure that the marketing objectives are consistent with the general corporate direction.

Again, the value of sound thinking when conducting the situation analysis and the market assessments becomes apparent. If the marketing manager has not made an objective effort to determine where the company is now, that manager can hardly define realistic future objectives.

An example may again help to illustrate types of objectives sought by business marketing firms. A producer of air pollution control equipment had the following five marketing objectives: (1) become a recognized leader in the development and application of air pollution control equipment in the United States; (2) attain a 30 percent share of the U.S. market for air pollution control equipment; (3) increase the percentage of value added/cost of sales to 60 percent; (4) achieve an ROI of 20 percent; and (5) attain 20 percent of annual sales volume from international markets.[20] As can be seen, this company focused primarily on image, market share, and profitability in its objectives.

Evidence suggests that business marketing firms are becoming much more specific in their setting of objectives.[21] In past years, many marketing objectives were set only to provide general senses of direction. Today, the necessity that objectives be specific and measurable is much more the norm since these same objectives are often used as control and evaluation criteria later in the marketing planning process.

Development of Overall Marketing Strategies

At this point in the process, the business marketing manager has conducted his or her situation analysis, determined target markets, and defined objectives to be attained in each of those markets. The next step is to develop strategies that will facilitate the attainment of the predetermined objectives.

Marketing strategy comprises the broad principles by which the manager expects to achieve business and marketing objectives in a target market. It consists of basic decisions on marketing expenditures, marketing mix, and marketing allocation.[22] Table 10.5 illustrates a hypothetical strategy statement for a producer of component parts used by instrument manufacturers. As the table

---

TABLE 10.5   **Example of a Marketing Strategy Statement in Business Marketing**

Target market	Companies in SIC 3811 with 100+ employees in Northeast, Southeast, and Pacific Coast areas of the U.S.
Positioning	The most reliable supplier of high-quality component parts used by firms in SIC 3811
Product line	Continue to offer a complete line of components required by the target market and expand our product line by adding two new components
Price	Premium pricing based on our high-quality products and our ability to deliver
Distribution	Direct to larger JIT customers; use regional industrial distributors to smaller customers
Sales	Develop a national account system to serve all larger JIT customers; continue to use company sales force to sell to distributors; establish inside sales force to support both of above
Advertising	Trade journal advertising aimed at purchasing agents in SIC 3811 target market directed toward nonusers in market; direct mail campaign to purchasing agents in nonusing prospects
Sales promotion	Attend three major trade shows in electronics industry; develop new POP materials for distributors; update catalog to include new products
Research & development	Concentrate primarily on the development of the two new components to be added to the product line
Marketing intelligence	Conduct focus group interviews with selected distributors to determine specifications for the two new products under consideration; require salespeople to request similar information from both distributors and users

Source: Adapted from Philip Kotler, *Marketing Management*, 7th ed. (Englewood Cliffs, NJ: Prentice-Hall, Inc., 1991), 78.

shows, this strategy consists of broad principles involving the target market, image desired, marketing mix to be used, research and development, and marketing intelligence. Such a statement outlines the direction the company plans to follow and serves as a reference for action programs to be developed and implemented later. It should be noted that this statement comprises strategy for one target market—there may be other strategies developed for addressing other target markets. Exhibit 10.1 shows the marketing strategy used by a manufacturer of gaskets to focus on major U.S. auto manufacturers. Here again, the strategy outlines the approach that will be taken to achieve objectives in the particular market and provides direction for the marketing programs necessary to carry out the strategy.

APPROACHES TO STRATEGY

There is no single best approach to the determination of marketing strategy to be used by the business marketer. Rather, there are many different approaches that might be employed. At this point, it may be worthwhile to discuss some of the more basic approaches and illustrate how they relate to business marketing.

EXHIBIT 10.1   Marketing Strategy of a Supplier to the Auto Industry

---

The Detroit Gasket Company is a supplier of gaskets to the nation's major auto manufacturers. With its plant located in Newport, Tennessee, Detroit Gasket is over 600 miles from the city of Detroit where most of its customers are located.

The company produces over 59 million gaskets a year for its auto producing customers. Product managers at Detroit Gasket are responsible for determining the gasket specifications that are based on the various types of engines produced by the auto manufacturers. Those same product managers must also determine the appropriate number of each type of gasket to be produced.

Detroit Gasket's market information comes from (1) feedback from the company's field sales representatives who call on the customer firms and (2) analysis of auto industry trends and new engine developments undertaken by auto manufacturers.

The company uses field sales representatives in the Detroit area who call on buyers and other buying influences. Once a sale is made, gaskets are shipped by rail or truck directly to the customer's plant from inventories that are maintained to provide required quantities as needed.

Contracts are awarded by competitive bid. Detroit Gasket bases its bid prices on its costs, on the estimated demand for the product or products involved, and on the actions company management believes competitors will take. Despite its distance from Detroit, through its bidding process the company is able to provide gaskets cheaper than the auto manufacturers could make them and cheaper than customers could buy them from competitors who are closer to Detroit.

Source: Adapted from David W. Cravens, Gerald E. Hills, and Robert D. Woodruff, *Marketing Decision Making: Concepts and Strategy* (Homewood, IL: Richard D. Irwin, 1980), 5.

Perhaps the most basic approach is that of determining strategy from the perspective of products and markets.[23] For example, a business marketing firm has existing products and/or services that it sells to present target market customers. The manager may elect to develop a strategy to increase sales to present customers or be directed by those in the company responsible for strategic market planning to find new markets for existing products or services, or do both.

Figure 10.5 illustrates the basic approaches that can be used, individually or collectively. Each cell in the figure calls for a different strategy approach. In a market penetration strategy, the manager attempts to increase sales of existing products and/or services to customers in present markets. In a market development strategy, the manager attempts to find new markets and customers for existing products and/or services. In a product development strategy, the focus is placed on developing new products and/or services for customers in present markets. In a diversification strategy, marketing is emphasizing both new products and/or services and new markets. An individual marketing manager may employ any or all of these strategy approaches simultaneously and may change any of them as the situation dictates.

Some examples may help. Reynolds Metals used a market penetration strategy to sell more aluminum to the American auto industry. The strategy approach was to (1) demonstrate to the auto industry the structural advantages of aluminum over steel, (2) show the auto industry how aluminum could be used, and (3) stress to the auto industry the improved gasoline mileage and decreased shipping costs due to lowered auto weight.[24] Copperweld, a producer of alloy steel and tubing products, found its traditional automotive and farm equipment markets depressed in the early 1980s. The company reacted to this depressed demand by employing a product development strategy and a diversification strategy.[25] In the product development strategy, the company found that the auto industry's downsizing of cars resulted in a demand for improved lighter tubing to replace solid-steel components. In the diversification strategy, Copperweld switched from the production of unfinished to finished tubing for energy market producers, because increased drilling and exploration brought about the demand for high-quality tubing.

FIGURE 10.5   **Product/Market Strategy Matrix**

Products / Markets	Existing products	New products
Present markets	Market penetration strategy	Product development strategy
New markets	Market development strategy	Diversification strategy

Another commonly used approach to determining marketing strategy relates to a company's position within an industry and its market share. For example, the strategy employed by the dominant firm in an industry with a relatively large market share may differ appreciably from that of a market challenger in that same market. The dominant firm may elect to expand the total market or it may focus primarily on defending or expanding its market share.[26] If it chooses the former strategy, the firm may attempt to find new users for the product, find new uses for the product, or get more use out of existing products. If, however, the firm elects to defend its market share against competitors, it then may choose from six different defensive strategy positions: (1) position defense, (2) flanking defense, (3) preemptive defense, (4) counteroffensive defense, (5) mobile defense, and (6) contraction defense.[27] In a position defense, the firm concentrates entirely on protecting its existing market holdings. In a flanking position, it continues to protect its existing market position but at the same time initiates a flanking maneuver to draw off the competitor. In a preemptive position, the company strikes at the competitor before it can strike. In the counteraction position, the firm reacts to the competitor's attack with a counterattack of its own to throw the competitor off balance. A mobile defensive position implies that the firm will expand its domain over new territories that will later be used as future centers for an offensive strategy. The expansion stretches the competitor thinner and thus protects the dominant firm. The contraction defense means that the firm recognizes that it cannot protect its entire market position and thus it reduces the areas it will strive to protect.

Marketing strategies for challengers in the market will differ considerably from those of the market leader. For example, a challenger might elect to attack the market leader, to attack firms in the industry that are more in its own position, or to attack smaller regional firms. The strategy here would be to increase market share at the expense of different types of competitors. A good example of this can be seen in the case of German machine tools manufacturers, which moved into the U.S. market by attacking smaller competitors first and then ultimately moved up to the point where they confronted and outmaneuvered the large U.S. manufacturers. In developing such strategies, the marketing firm may again elect to use a number of attack strategy options. These include: (1) frontal attack, (2) flank attack, (3) encirclement attack, (4) bypass attack, and (5) guerilla attack.[28] In a frontal attack, the marketer goes head to head with targeted competitors—strength against strength. In a flank attack, he or she attempts to focus more on the competitors' weak areas. In an encirclement attack, the approach is to initiate several offensives on several fronts at the same time, which forces competitors to react in a number of areas simultaneously. A bypass attack means the marketer actually bypasses competitors and attacks easier markets, and the guerilla attack involves conducting small intermittent attacks at competitors in different areas.

The challenger, however, may elect not to confront competitors but rather to just follow them in some manner. Here, such strategies as cloning, imitating, or adapting may be involved. A number of personal computer manufacturers have developed successful marketing strategies simply by cloning the IBM models. Whichever is chosen, it should be obvious that each strategy requires different action programs, activities, etc. Selection of the appropriate marketing strategy position is imperative before any mix strategies can then be developed.

Another interesting approach to strategy has been proposed by Michael Porter, who suggests that competitors within a particular industry can pursue different strategies at the same time.[29] Since each may be operating according to different objectives, opportunities, and resources, there is no single best strategy. Porter further states that there are three generic approaches to strategy development: (1) overall cost leadership, (2) differentiation, and (3) focus. With the cost leadership, the firm's strategy is to attain the lowest cost of production and marketing and thus compete favorably on price. With differentiation, the strategy is to focus on superior performance in terms of some highly valued customer benefits. With focus, the strategy is to address narrow market segments or niches. Porter's point is that within an industry different competitors will select different approaches. This means that some competitors' strategies will emphasize cost leadership, others' will stress differentiation, while still others' will choose the focus approach. Those competitors that address the same markets with the same approaches make up a strategic group. This means that there may actually be three sets of competitors, each using a different strategy. Within each strategy, the firms developing and implementing the best programs will be more likely to succeed. For example, if there are four competitors stressing cost, the firm that is able to develop the lowest cost should do the best. The same goes for leaders in the differentiation and focus strategies. Carried to its logical conclusion, this means that a number of competitors in a given market could be successful because they are using different marketing strategies. There is, of course, a fourth option here. The firm could elect not to use any of Porter's three strategies but rather pursue a less clear approach by combining all three. Porter found that these actually fare the worst, however. For example, International Harvester had difficult times because it did not stand out in terms of lowest cost, highest perceived value, or as best serving a segment.[30]

Neither time nor space permits an exhaustive discussion of strategy in this text. If the reader desires more complete coverage, several texts are available. At this point, the message is that marketing mix strategies cannot be developed until overall strategy positions are determined. This section has shown some of the more common approaches to determining those positions.

FORMULATE MARKETING MIX STRATEGIES

Once overall marketing strategies have been determined, the marketing manager now needs to consider what individual mix strategies will be required to carry out the overall strategy. The **marketing mix** is a set of marketing tools that a firm uses to pursue its marketing objectives in its target markets.[31] If a particular firm wishes to pursue a strategy of entering a target market now held by competitors, what should that firm's mix strategies be in terms of products and/or services, distribution, promotion, and pricing? A study of forty firms that pursued such a strategy found their mix strategies were characterized by such factors as (1) producing higher-quality products, (2) offering superior service, (3) marketing a narrow product line, (4) charging higher prices, (5) lowering expenses in sales and advertising, and (6) using the same channels as competitors.[32]

Determining mix strategies is a complicated process and becomes even more complicated when multiple target markets are involved. Product strategy considers such factors as additions to, deletions from, and modifications to existing products and services, in addition to product support activities such as warranties, service, and the like. Distribution strategy involves determining those channels to be used and physical distribution systems to be employed. Promotion strategy considers the proper combination of personal selling, advertising, and sales promotion to communicate desired messages to target market buying influences. Pricing strategy involves formulating list prices, discounts from those list prices, rebates, special deals, handling of transportation charges, and other such price considerations. In addition, an information gathering strategy may also be employed to better understand the markets involved. All of these mix strategies are then integrated to bring about the accomplishment of the overall strategy previously decided upon.

Table 10.6 illustrates mix strategies of microcomputer manufacturers to

TABLE 10.6   **Elements of Marketing Strategies Used by Large and Small Manufacturers in the Minicomputer Industry to Sell to OEM and User Markets**

Elements	Companies Selling to OEMs		Companies Selling to Users	
	Large Firms	Small Firms	Large Firms	Small Firms
Target markets	Several medium to large companies	Limited number of companies	Several large end users	Limited number of small users
Competitors	Other large minicomputer manufacturers	Digital Equipment Company (DEC)	International Business Machines (IBM)	Other small minicomputer manufacturers
Product emphasis	Reliability price/ performance	Reliability	Compatibility with mainframes Software	Customized product
Price	Outright sale Discounts Competitors' prices No unbundling of software prices	Outright sale Discounts Fixed cost plus margin No unbundling of software prices	Outright sale Discounts Competitors' prices Software prices unbundled	Outright sale Discounts Fixed cost plus margin No unbundling of software prices
Distribution	Direct	Direct	Direct	Distributors
Personal selling	High use	Minimal use	High use	Minimal use
Mass media	No	No	Low	No

Source: Reprinted by permission of the publisher from Sushila Rao and Samuel Rabino, "Product-Market Strategies in the Minicomputer Industry," *Industrial Marketing Management* 9 (October 1980): 329. Copyright © 1980 by Elsevier Science Publishing Company, Inc.

reach large and small customers in both OEM and user markets. Reference to this table shows different mix strategies. For example, strategies directed toward small user customers involved customized products, price discounts, use of industrial distributors to sell products with minimal use of direct sales, and no mass media. In contrast, strategies aimed at large OEMs involved products stressing reliability and performance, price discounts, use of a personal selling direct channel, no use of channel intermediaries, and no mass media advertising.

Note that mix elements differ by target market and by size of company in many instances. For example, large firms selling to large user customers stress mainframe compatibility in their product strategies, and small firms selling to small user customers stress customized products. Distribution channels also differ: Companies selling to small user customers tend to use distributors, and the others tend to sell direct. Pricing objectives also differ: Large suppliers are more competitor-oriented in their pricing, and small suppliers tend to focus more on fixed cost plus margin. On the other hand, many mix activities are similar, such as the use of price discounts and the lack of mass media promotion. According to those who conducted the survey, mix elements differed more in terms of the target markets and segments sought than in supplier size.[33]

The determination of mix strategies is an important step in the marketing planning process for a number of reasons. First, such mix strategies are necessary to carry out overall strategy positions and achieve objectives in target markets. Second, the mix strategies are necessary before any tactical action programs can be developed. Viewed in these ways, the mix strategies provide direction for the rest of the process.

DESIGN TACTICAL ACTION PROGRAMS

The previous two steps in the planning process addressed the broad marketing thrusts to be used in achieving the predetermined objectives. Each mix element now must be carried out and this involves the designing of **tactical action programs**—programs that contain all the individual activities necessary to put the strategies into action. More specifically, these programs must be designed to answer a number of basic questions: *What* will be done? *When* will it be done? *Who* will do it? And, *how much* will it cost?[34] If any strategy is to be successful, questions such as these must be answered and that is the purpose of the tactical programs.

Table 10.7 is useful in understanding what is involved at this step. In this example, the target market has been identified, objectives set, and overall and mix strategies determined. Now, the manager must decide what specific activities will be necessary to implement those strategies. Table 10.7 shows the activities that have been determined to be necessary and how long each activity is expected to take. For example, a number of advertising activities must be undertaken, including developing a preliminary advertising program, developing an advertising plan, selecting advertising media, and implementing trade advertis-

TABLE 10.7 Typical Activities to Be Performed in Marketing Planning

Activity Number	Activity Description	Time Estimate (Weeks)
1–2	Initial screening and management approval	2
2–3	Research and development technical evaluation	6
2–4	Marketing suggestions	1
3–5	Development of preliminary specifications	2
5–6	Estimate of competitive reactions	2
5–7	Estimate of manufacturing costs	2
5–8	Estimate of advertising, sales, and distribution costs	2
6–9	Estimate of market demand	1
7–9	Preliminary price setting	1
8–9	Profit analysis	3
9–10	Management evaluation	1
10–11	Engineering tests	6
10–12	Preliminary package design	4
10–13	Selection of brand name	2
11–15	Check of product safety	2
12–15	Package design testing	2
13–14	Preliminary advertising program	4
14–15	Development of sales plans	3
15–16	Management evaluation	1
16–17	Product introduction decision	3
17–18	Development of advertising plan	4
17–19	Appointment of sales manager	3
17–20	Establishment of distributor network	4
17–21	Acquisition of production equipment	10
18–22	Selection of advertising media	3
19–23	Hiring and training of sales force	6
20–24	Training of distributors' salespeople	3
21–25	Hiring of production workers	3
21–26	Installation of production equipment	3
22–29	Implementation of trade advertising	3
23–29	Assigning of sales force to territories	2
24–29	Selling to distributors	4
25–27	Training of production workers	2
26–27	Acquisition of materials inventory	3
27–28	Initial production run	3
28–29	Shipping to distributors	4
29–30	Introducing new product to market	4

ing. These activities are necessary to carry out the predetermined advertising strategy. Similarly, sales activities include developing sales plans, hiring and training a sales force, training distributor salespeople, assigning salespeople to territories, and selling to distributors. These activities are needed to carry out the sales strategy. Action programs contain all those activities necessary to implement and carry out previously designed strategies.

IMPLEMENT TACTICAL ACTION PROGRAMS

Once tactical programs have been designed they must be implemented. At this stage in the process, the marketing manager needs to address the actual conducting of those activities seen as necessary to carry out strategy. Proper implementation depends on the coordination of required activities, the motivation of personnel who perform those activities, and effective communication within the marketing organization.[35] In implementing the programs, it is the marketing manager's responsibility to bring about the coordination, motivation, and communication that best carries out predetermined strategy and attains marketing objectives.

To properly implement previously designed program activities, a number of steps should be taken. First, the time required to perform each activity must be estimated. Second, the activities must be arranged in a logical sequence. Some activities cannot be started until other activities are completed and scheduling must thus consider these constraints. Third, individual activities must be combined into programs. Fourth, dates should be established for the start and completion of each required activity. Fifth, responsibility has to be assigned for activities required to carry out a program. Sixth, program costs and budgets should be determined. Finally, program progress should be monitored so that changes can be made where necessary.

In this program implementation stage, many business marketing managers have used forms of network analysis such as Programmed Evaluation Review Technique (PERT) and Critical Path Analysis (CPA) to integrate substrategy activities on a time and sequence basis. Both PERT and CPA can be applied to the scheduling of marketing activities in the overall strategy. With each method, a sequence of required activities is developed to carry out the desired strategy. Time schedules then are worked out for each activity involved. The two methods differ regarding time estimates of the activities. The time frames are known in CPA and are based on experience, research, and so forth. Activity times are not known with the same certainty in PERT and are more likely to be probabilistic. Typically, PERT networks use three time estimates for the completion of each activity: (1) optimistic, (2) most likely, and (3) pessimistic. From these three estimates, an expected time frame is derived as follows:

$$t_e = \frac{t_o + 4t_m + t_p}{6}$$

where

t_o = optimistic time

t_m = most likely time

t_p = pessimistic time

An example may help. Assume that a preliminary advertising program must be developed in a marketing strategy. Assume also that the company's advertising manager has never developed such a program before and estimates that the soonest it can be accomplished is two weeks, the latest six weeks, and the most likely time four weeks. Using the formula, an expected time can be estimated as follows:

$$t_e = \frac{2 + 4(4) + 6}{6} = \frac{24}{6} = 4 \text{ weeks}$$

Once activities have been placed in proper sequence and time frames assigned to each activity, the results are placed in a network. Table 10.7 illustrated activities that may be found in a typical marketing plan or strategy. These activities have been placed in a logical sequence, and time estimates have been derived. Figure 10.6 shows these same activities plotted in a network analysis. As the figure illustrates, several paths of activities are involved. The marketing manager now needs to plot the "critical path" through all of these activities, which is defined as that path of activities that will take the longest to complete. All other activities are planned around this critical path. In this way, the business marketing manager can ensure that all activities in the strategy or plan occur when they are supposed to and in the correct sequence. When all of a strategy's activities are planned around the critical path, coordination of many diverse activities is possible. The critical path may be seen in Figure 10.6, and definition of the specific activities that make it up can be found by comparing Figure 10.6 with Table 10.7. In this case, the length of the critical path is fifty-six weeks. This example shows why such tools as PERT and CPA are useful to business marketing managers when scheduling those activities necessary to carry out a desired marketing strategy.

FIGURE 10.6   Use of the Critical Path Method to Schedule Activities in a Marketing Plan

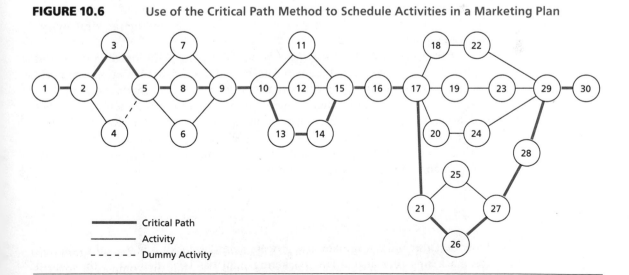

DETERMINE STANDARDS FOR CONTROL AND EVALUATION

This step in the marketing planning process involves the determination of measures of criteria to control and evaluate performance in each target market. Are programs achieving desired objectives? Are strategies appropriate for achieving the objectives? Are objectives realistic and attainable? If these are not being accomplished, why are they not and what needs to be done to correct any problems? Questions such as these should be addressed in the latter stages of the process. To do this, however, the manager first needs to develop those criteria most appropriate for effective **control** and **evaluation.** Useful criteria include (1) the predetermined objectives in the strategy, (2) historical trends in performance, (3) the industry average in performance, (4) budget considerations, (5) industry ratios, and (6) adherence to predetermined time schedules.

Chapter 18 will discuss control and evaluation in some detail so not much more is required here. The point is that control and evaluation is necessary in any effective marketing planning process and the marketing manager must determine which criteria he or she wishes to use.

IMPLEMENT CONTROL AND EVALUATION PROCEDURES

Once measurement criteria are defined, questions such as the following must be considered for each area of the strategy. Who is responsible for each area of the strategy? What routine control reports should be required, and from whom? How often and when should such control checks be made? How much deviation from criteria standards will be permitted, and for how long? If unacceptable deviation occurs, how can the cause be pinpointed? Who is responsible for overall control and evaluation of the marketing strategy? Are the plans and substrategies properly coordinated among all areas of the marketing mix? How are the results of each period's evaluation to be used in the marketing strategy for the coming period?

Chapter 18 will also focus heavily on the implementation of control and evaluation procedures, so there is no need to discuss it here. Determining and implementing control and evaluation are the final stages in the marketing planning process as it was outlined in Figure 10.3. Accomplishing these stages does not, however, mean that marketing planning ceases at this step. Rather, what is learned from control and evaluation then becomes part of a revised situation analysis, and the entire process continues. It is important to recall that the marketing planning process is a continuous one.

THE MARKETING PLAN

Now that the marketing planning process is understood, it is logical to discuss the marketing plan itself. The **marketing plan** has been defined as the central instrument for directing and controlling the marketing effort.[36] It has also been described as an arranged structure to guide the marketing planning process.[37] Thus, the marketing plan is the formal written documentation of the previously discussed marketing planning process. It commits to paper the entire process of marketing planning and thus becomes the tangible result of such planning.

Characteristics of Business Marketing Plans

A comprehensive study conducted by The Conference Board provides good insight to characteristics of marketing plans in business marketing. According to the findings of this study, business marketing plans may be characterized by the following: [38]

1. The marketing manager is typically the one responsible for preparing the marketing plan.

2. The marketing plan is typically used as a guide to action and not an absolute document to be followed.

3. Almost one-half of all marketing plans in business markets are one-year plans, but about one-quarter are from three- to five-year plans.

4. The typical business marketing plan is thirty pages long, but more than one-quarter exceed fifty pages.

Contents of Business Marketing Plans

As stated, the marketing plan is the written documentation of the marketing planning process. Thus, its contents should match what is covered in the marketing planning process. The Industrial Products Division of the Goodyear Tire and Rubber Company defines its annual marketing plan as a document that sets forth goals and action programs required to achieve those goals for a twelve-month period. The essential ingredients of its marketing plan include a situation analysis; development of strategy; action assignments; and management endorsement.[39] This example shows clearly the close relationship between the planning process and the formal written marketing plan. While there is no single best way to write a marketing plan, all successful plans include the same elements discussed in the planning process: (1) a situation analysis to determine where the company stands in the marketplace, (2) a statement of marketing objectives to be achieved, (3) a development of strategies to achieve those objectives, (4) a determination of programs necessary to carry out those strategies, and (5) a control and evaluation process to measure performance and make necessary corrections. In a well-conceived plan, what is learned in the control and evaluation process becomes part of the situation analysis, so that the plan is continuous.

What Makes a Good Marketing Plan? As was stated earlier in the chapter, no single marketing plan is correct for all companies. The best marketing plans, however, have the following characteristics in common: [40]

1. The plan is specific; the details of the plan must be precise enough for implementation and control.

2. The plan is measurable; the results of the plan must be measurable or its effectiveness or ineffectiveness cannot be determined.

3. The plan includes a specific time frame or time frames.

4. The plan is flexible enough to be adapted to unforeseen changes; a plan that is too rigid is unrealistic and valueless if conditions change.

5. The plan includes accountability; the responsibility and authority for each phase of the plan must be communicated to those who will be held responsible for performance.

A marketing plan that is fuzzy, full of generalities, timeless, and loaded with marketing clichés typically fails or is never followed, which is tantamount to failure. In developing the formal marketing plan, the marketing manager should ensure that his or her plan includes the preceding characteristics.

Not all marketing plans succeed. In the view of marketing planners at the Industrial Products Division of Goodyear Tire and Rubber Company, marketing plans fail for the following reasons: (1) lack of real planning involved, (2) inadequate situation analysis, (3) plans are prepared without support of those who are expected to implement them, (4) unrealistic goals or objectives, (5) plans are not adequately "sold" within the marketing company after being prepared, and (6) unanticipated circumstances.[41] This discussion suggests a need to give considerable attention to the writing of the marketing plan if it is to be successful. It is also necessary to realize that a marketing plan is not simply followed by all just because it is written—it must be communicated throughout the entire marketing organization so that it is accepted and properly implemented.

In summary, the marketing plan is the instrument to be used by the marketing manager in directing his or her company's total marketing efforts. As has been developed, the plan is the written result of the marketing planning process and it provides guidance for all involved. In business marketing, the marketing plan is seen as a very vital marketing tool and all indications are that it will become even more important in the future.[42] Finally, to be useful the plan has to be activated—it cannot be merely a document. To quote a marketing manager in an electrical equipment manufacturing firm, "You can't put together a plan, put it up on the shelf, and go run your business. It has to be the type of document that you can pull out and use all the time."[43]

MARKETING PLANNING TOOLS

As has been developed in this chapter, marketing planning is a complex and arduous undertaking for the business marketing manager. This suggests that the manager could well use some aids or tools to help in the process of marketing planning. While such tools are not substitutes for the overall planning process, they are instruments that might contribute to more effective planning and strategy determination. While many tools exist, this discussion will focus on four in particular because of their easy applications to business marketing. These are:

(1) matrix modeling, (2) the Boston Consulting Group's "Growth–Share Matrix," (3) the General Electric Strategic Business Planning Grid, and (4) the PIMS (Profit Impact of Market Strategies) program. Some of these are strategic tools, but with some adaptation they can be applied to the business marketing arena. Where this is the case, it will be pointed out in the discussion. Since each tool contributes in its own way, a brief discussion of each may be beneficial.

Matrix Modeling

The use of matrix models has proven beneficial for many business marketing managers in implementing marketing plans and strategies. Simply defined, a *matrix model* is a rectangular array of mathematical elements.[44] Applied to business marketing, this type of model may be used to form a grid or matrix to understand the relationships between markets to be reached and products or services to be marketed. Table 10.8 illustrates a basic matrix in which the horizontal axis lists customers and/or prospects to be reached, and the vertical axis lists products and/or services for a manufacturer of farm machinery. Note that customers and prospects have been segmented by SIC numbers.

At this point, the manager needs to input meaningful data in the cells of the matrix. One approach is to examine industry sales, company sales, and company market share over time. Table 10.9 shows this type of analysis in the cell in which farm tractors and distributors interrelate. Industry data may be obtained from various SIC sources, trade associations, trade publications, research reports, and the like. Company data may be obtained from past sales records and sales forecasts. The cell analysis shows the manager that in the SIC 5083 market for farm tractors, industry sales and company sales are increasing, but market share is decreasing. Thus, the company is not keeping pace with others in the industry, and marketing action may be required. This type of analysis is then applied to every cell in the basic matrix, and each cell is judged to be favorable or unfavorable in terms of industry and company sales trends. A favorable cell may be one in which both sales trends are up and market share is increasing. An unfavorable cell may be one in which industry sales are up, company sales are down, and market share is dropping.

Once the individual cells have been analyzed and judged, these assessments are plugged into the basic matrix. An example may help to show how this procedure is done. Assume that (1) *Up* indicates a favorable cell analysis—industry sales and company sales are rising, and the company's market share is increasing; (2) *Down* indicates an unfavorable cell analysis—company sales are not keeping up with industry sales, and the market share is decreasing; and (3) *NC* indicates no change or a static cell analysis, in which the company's performance approximates industry performance, and its market share is relatively unchanged. Assume now that such cell analyses as those illustrated in Table 10.9 have been conducted, that the cells in the basic matrix have been evaluated in terms of favorable, unfavorable, or static situations, and that these findings are then plugged into the basic matrix with the results shown in Table 10.10.

TABLE 10.8   Basic Matrix of a Manufacturer of Farm Machinery SIC 3522

Product Mix	SIC 0112 Cotton Growers	SIC 0113 Cash Grain Growers	SIC 0114 Tobacco Growers	SIC 0119 Field Crops	SIC 3522 Manufac-turers of Farm Ma-chinery and Equipment	SIC 5083 Wholesale Distributors of Farm Ma-chinery and Equipment	SIC 5252 Farm Equipment Dealers	All Other Markets
Farm tractors								
Balers								
Combines								
Harvesting machines								
Mowers								

Source: Adapted from William J. E. Crissy and Robert M. Kaplan, "Matrix Models for Marketing Planning," *MSU Business Topics* 11 (Summer 1963): 53. Reprinted by permission of the author and the publisher, Division of Research, Graduate School of Business Administration, Michigan State University.

TABLE 10.9 Segment Analysis

| | | SIC 5083 Wholesale Distributors of Farm Machinery and Equipment | | | |
		Past Market $ (199X)	Present Market $ (199X)	Potential Market $ (199X)	Trend
Farm Tractors	Industry sales	$35,754,000	$50,325,000	$62,250,000	Up
	Company sales	$ 6,274,000	$ 7,369,000	$ 8,004,000	Up
	Company share of market	17.5%	14.6%	12.9%	Down

TABLE 10.10 Situations Arising from Matrix Analysis

Situation A: Customer/Prospect Mix

Product Mix	SIC 0112 Cotton Growers	SIC 0113 Cash Grain Growers	SIC 0114 Tobacco Growers	SIC 0119 Field Crops	SIC 3522 Manufacturers of Farm Machinery and Equipment
Farm tractors	Up	Down	Up	NC	Up
Balers	Up	NC	Up	Up	NC
Combines	Up	Down	NC	Up	Up
Harvesting machines	Up	Down	Up	Up	Up
Mowers	Up	Down	Up	Up	NC

Situation B: Customer/Prospect Mix

Product Mix	SIC 0112 Cotton Growers	SIC 0113 Cash Grain Growers	SIC 0114 Tobacco Growers	SIC 0119 Field Crops	SIC 3522 Manufacturers of Farm Machinery and Equipment
Farm tractors	Up	NC	Up	Up	Up
Balers	Down	Down	NC	Down	Down
Combines	Up	Up	Up	NC	Up
Harvesting machines	NC	Up	Up	Up	NC
Mowers	Up	Up	NC	Up	Up

Situation C: Customer/Prospect Mix

Product Mix	SIC 0112 Cotton Growers	SIC 0113 Cash Grain Growers	SIC 0114 Tobacco Growers	SIC 0119 Field Crops	SIC 3522 Manufacturers of Farm Machinery and Equipment
Farm tractors	Up	Up	Down	NC	Up
Balers	Up	Down	NC	Up	Up
Combines	Up	Up	Up	NC	Up
Harvesting machines	NC	Up	Up	Up	NC
Mowers	Up	NC	Up	Up	Up

In situation A, there is a definite customer problem, as the cell analyses reveal an unfavorable picture only for cash grain growers. The analysis is unfavorable in four of the five cells in the basic matrix that relate to this type of customer. The problem does not appear to be product-oriented but more likely is due to poor marketing in some manner to cash grain growers.

Situation B presents a different picture. Here, a distinct product problem is in evidence, as the trend is definitely unfavorable for balers but not for the other products. This problem also cannot be traced to any particular classification of customer.

A completely different phenomenon is observed in situation C, as no specific product or customer problem can be identified. Balers are down with cash grain growers, and farm tractors are down with tobacco growers, whereas all other cells appear favorable on the basis of this analysis.

In the implementation of these types of matrix analyses, there is no telling what combinations will occur, but there is also no doubt that by using such analyses, the marketing manager knows much more than would be known without them. For example, what corrective action would the marketing manager take in situation A to alleviate the problems with the cash grain grower market? What action would be taken to correct the product problem found in situation B? Marketing strategy will differ according to what is discovered in the matrix analysis. This is the real value of such matrices—they do not solve marketing problems in and of themselves. They give marketing direction to the manager, and thus their contribution to business marketing planning and strategy formulation is invaluable, especially in the situation analysis stage of the marketing planning process. In the three situations illustrated in Table 10.10, the marketing manager would apply a different marketing strategy to correct what is wrong in each; thus, the basic strategy hinges on what is revealed by the matrix analysis.

Matrix modeling is usually appropriate in both domestic and international business markets, primarily because of the types of products produced and the relatively small number of market segments often found. As shown, the marketing manager can integrate data from SIC sources into the matrix, which provides industry figures with which to compare company figures. This type of model is also extremely flexible and will accommodate any type of organizational market. Private enterprise commercial firms, institutions, governmental agencies, and international customer types can all be used in the model. Essentially, the model permits the business marketing manager to compare his or her company's performance over time with that of the industry and, in doing so, generates both company and industry life cycles for each product in each market. These life cycles can then be used for strategy directions.

The BCG Growth–Share Matrix

Another useful marketing planning tool was developed by the Boston Consulting Group (BCG) and involves the development of strategies based on relative market share and the growth rate of the market involved. In using the BCG matrix, which was originally designed as a strategic planning concept, the business marketing firm creates strategic business units (SBUs) or profit centers and then develops specific strategies for each as if they were unrelated entities. The matrix, illustrated in Figure 10.7, consists of four categories:

1. Stars, which are high growth–high market share business units. Stars are often users of cash, which is needed to finance their growth. They ultimately may become major cash producers for the company, but they currently require cash from other sources to support their growth.

FIGURE 10.7   Boston Consulting Group's Growth–Share Matrix

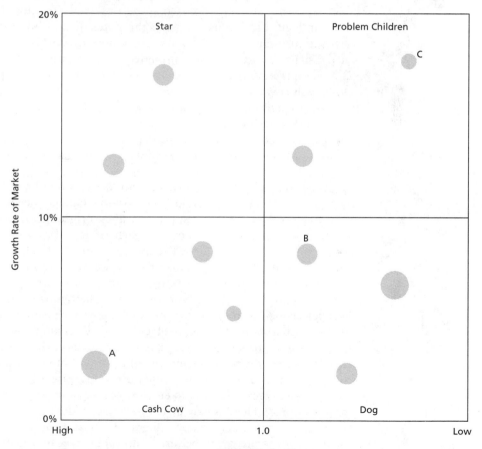

Source: Adapted from Bruce D. Henderson, *The Experience Curve Reviewed. IV. The Growth Share Matrix of the Product Portfolio* (Boston: Boston Consulting Group, 1973), Perspectives no. 135.

2. Dogs, which are low growth–low share business units. Since dogs have low shares of slow growing markets, they are unlikely ever to be major cash producers.

3. Cash cows, which are low growth–high share business units. Cash cows are the major cash contributors that the company uses to finance other areas of the business.

4. Problem children, which are also called question marks and wildcats and are high growth–low share business units. They typically require considerable cash to maintain or increase and are major cash users in a company. The marketing manager must decide whether they should be given the cash required, downplayed, or even phased out.

Once the business units have been fitted into the matrix, insight into possible marketing strategy moves may be observed. To illustrate, the company shown in Figure 10.7 can now assess the status of each business unit and decide what actions may be taken. Four strategy options exist: (1) build—increase the market share even though it may mean draining short-term earnings to do so; (2) hold—preserve the market share, which is often an appropriate strategy for strong cash cows; (3) harvest—increase short-term earnings even though it will be at the expense of long-term effects; and (4) divest—drop the business unit and use the money elsewhere. Harvesting may be an appropriate strategy move for weak cash cows, problem children, and dogs; divestment is a common strategy move for dogs and problem children when the company involved cannot finance growth.

The concept of the BCG matrix is not difficult to adapt to business marketing planning and strategy development. All the manager needs to do is to classify individual products or services, product lines, or groups of products into strategic business units, which means that each is viewed as a profit center. For example, Figure 10.7 might depict ten separate products marketed by a business marketing firm. Here, the manager has placed each product in the matrix based on its market share and the market growth rate as shown in the figure. The question now is what strategy is best for each of the ten products? In this case, the manager may elect to employ a "hold" strategy for product A, which is a large cash cow. This strategy might involve the use of a strong position defense to discourage competitors from attempting to take market share. In the case of product B, however, the manager may want to use a "build" strategy and initiate a frontal attack on a competitor in an effort to increase market share. With product C, the manager may want to employ a "divest" strategy and simply drop the product entirely. Here, it may be felt that the product cannot be made competitive or that competitors are not vulnerable. These examples show how previous discussions of strategy can be fitted into the matrix in a manner that helps the manager in his or her marketing planning efforts. While the BCG matrix has its critics, it appears that the concept still provides a useful approach to marketing planning in business markets.

General Electric Strategic Business Planning Grid

Yet another useful marketing strategy tool is the General Electric Strategic Business Planning Grid, sometimes called the General Electric Spotlight Strategy.[45] Figure 10.8 illustrates the basic nine-cell grid developed by General Electric in conjunction with McKinsey & Company. This grid is more detailed than the BCG growth–share matrix. The vertical axis is labeled "industry attractiveness." This term is described as an evaluation of the attractiveness of whatever

FIGURE 10.8   General Electric Strategic Business Planning Grid

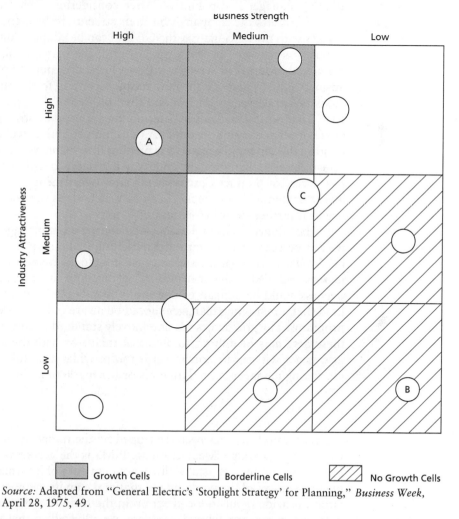

Source: Adapted from "General Electric's 'Stoplight Strategy' for Planning," *Business Week,* April 28, 1975, 49.

market is under consideration. It is made up of such factors as (1) size of the market, (2) growth rate of the market, (3) amount and intensity of competition to be faced, (4) cyclical and/or seasonal fluctuations in the market, (5) profit margins, and (6) social needs. Using these criteria, the marketing manager develops an assessment that reflects market phenomena. Industry attractiveness is then judged to be high, medium, or low.

The horizontal axis is labeled "business strength," and it describes the strengths and weaknesses of the individual company involved in that market. Here, the manager considers such factors as (1) the firm's relative market share, (2) the quality of the product(s) offered, (3) price competitiveness, (4) company sales capabilities, (5) the quantity and quality of market information possessed, and (6) managerial capabilities. After considering such factors, the manager then determines the company's business strength to be high, medium, or low.

As with the BCG matrix, the GE grid can be adapted to marketing planning in business markets. In using the GE grid, the manager also needs to classify individual products or services, product lines, or groups of products as strategic business units. These are then evaluated according to the business strength and industry attractiveness criteria and then plotted in the grid as shown in Figure 10.8. That positioning aids in determining appropriate strategy for each product or service. For example, product A rates high in both categories, which suggests a "growth" strategy. Conversely, product B is perceived as rating low in both categories and, therefore, the company may elect to divest itself of this product. In the case of product C, which falls into a borderline cell, the picture is much less clear than with products A and B, which alerts the manager to the possible need for further study before taking action.

The GE grid is useful because it encourages the manager to fit subjective as well as objective factors into the marketing planning process. However, it may be simpler in concept than it is to use in actual situations because some of the factors included under the headings of business strength and industry attractiveness could be difficult to develop. On the other hand, these factors are the kind that a marketing manager should be aware of before developing plans and programs. The grid makes use of relatively standard marketing data even though these data may be difficult to obtain at times. As with the BCG matrix, the GE grid is not without its critics, but it too provides a useful tool for the business marketing manager in preparing his or her marketing planning efforts.

The PIMS Program

Another useful tool has been developed by the nonprofit Strategic Planning Institute of Cambridge, Massachusetts. PIMS is the acronym for Profit Impact of Marketing Strategy. Basically, PIMS is a data pool of information on the marketing experiences of those companies that make up its membership. Member companies provide input to the program in the form of information on their products and/or product lines. These data are adjusted so that individual company information is not revealed, analyzed, and conclusions drawn. The computer then processes this information and shows marketing strategy decisions that are best for an individual company based on what other, similar companies have done in the past. The central premise of the program is that business situations generally behave in a regular and predictable fashion. This premise implies that business situations can be studied in an empirical and scientific manner and that strategy formulation can become an applied science. In essence, the PIMS program replaces guesswork and speculation in strategy formulation with objective decision criteria based on past experience.

Over 250 member companies support the program, and more than 2,000 business units have been analyzed since 1972, when the program was moved from the General Electric Company, where it originated, to the Harvard Business School. In 1975, it was moved to its present location in Cambridge, Massachusetts.

Basic PIMS Marketing Strategy Findings   A company does not have to be a member of the program for an individual marketing manager to benefit from the program's findings. Much has been written on PIMS that can be applied directly by the business marketing manager to his or her own strategy situations.[46] The basic PIMS findings are most informative and provide considerable help in intelligent marketing planning and strategy formulation. Since the PIMS program is, however, an overall business or corporate strategy tool, parts of it apply to marketing strategy and other parts are more applicable to other areas of strategy formulation. In view of this fact, our discussion here focuses primarily on those aspects of strategy that are the marketing manager's direct responsibility. Some of the more meaningful marketing findings follow.

Market Share   Share of market (both absolute and relative to the three largest competitors) has a positive impact on both profit and net cash flow. Figure 10.9 shows that companies achieving larger market shares are generally more profitable than their counterparts with smaller market shares. This situation is due to such factors as (1) economies of scale enjoyed in working capital, research and development (R & D), marketing, and other areas; (2) economies of cumulative volume, which reduce unit costs; (3) buyers fearful of the wrong buying decision who tend to favor larger suppliers; and (4) the larger market share companies, which often enjoy greater bargaining power over customers and suppliers.[47]

Market Growth   Growth of the market served may be an important consideration in marketing strategy formulation. According to PIMS, market growth is generally favorable to dollar measures of profit but indifferent to percentage increases and negative to measures of cash flow. Thus, the marketing manager must know if the company's markets are expanding, stabilizing, or contracting, because such movements may have direct effects on company profits.

Quality of Products/Services Offered   The PIMS program has determined that product/service quality, which it defines as customers' evaluation of the com-

FIGURE 10.9 Relationship Between Market Share and Return on Investment (ROI)

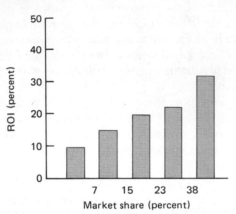
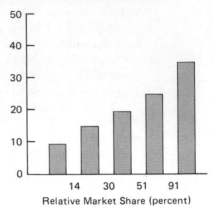

Source: Sidney Schoeffler, "Market Position: Build, Hold, or Harvest," *The Pimsletter* 3 (1977): 2, 3. Reprinted by permission.

pany's products/services compared with those of competitors, generally has a positive effect on profit. Table 10.11 illustrates this relationship between product quality and profitability. The PIMS program has found that product quality is extremely important and is an essential element in the marketing mix. High product quality can even offset a weak market-share position.

New Products The PIMS findings reveal that new product introductions can help attain a competitive edge and higher profitability when conditions are correct. A high level of new product activity usually has a positive impact on market share, but short-term ROI is likely to suffer. This decrease in ROI may be lessened when a firm enjoys high product quality, a broad product line, and a strong market share. The PIMS program advises companies with a narrow product line, low product quality, low market share, or high marketing costs to introduce new products carefully.[48]

Product Pricing The PIMS program considers a low price as one that is less than those of competitors, whereas a high price involves a meaningful price premium compared with those of competitors. PIMS findings show increases in market share and ROI based on product quality and relative price. High product quality results in higher gains in market share regardless of pricing. Lower pricing permits product quality to be translated into greater gains in market share and ROI.

Brand Awareness Research by PIMS has also shown that market share is connected to brand awareness and profitability. Increased brand awareness can lead

TABLE 10.11   Product Quality and ROI by Type of Business

Type of Business	Average ROI				
	Lowest Quality	Below Average Quality	Average Quality	Above Average Quality	Highest Quality
Capital goods	10%	8%	13%	20%	21%
Raw materials	13%	21%	21%	21%	35%
Components	12%	20%	20%	22%	36%
Supplies	16%	13%	19%	25%	36%

Source: Reprinted by permission from Robert D. Buzzell, "Product Quality," *The Pimsletter* 4 (1978):5.

to an improved potential for market share, which in turn leads to a better potential for a higher return on investment. The sequence may be depicted as follows: previous level of brand awareness + changes in brand awareness = current level of brand awareness × conversion rate of brand awareness into market share = level of achieved market share, which then influences ROI or profitability.

This sequence does not automatically lead to success. Its success or failure depends on two things: (1) how positive the changes in brand awareness are and (2) how effective the conversion rate of brand awareness to market share is. Regarding these two factors, PIMS found the following. First, to effect changes in awareness, it may be necessary to spend more than "par" in marketing and promotional efforts. Second, conversion depends on product quality, breadth of product line compared with that of competitors, and tactical efforts to differentiate the company and its products. Failure to differentiate the firm from competitors in terms of direct costs, prices, product-line breadth, or advertising levels has resulted in low success rates in converting awareness to market share.[49]

Marketing Expenditures   Companies that require large marketing expenditures relative to their sales are generally not very profitable. High marketing expenditures for low-quality products have adversely affected profitability. Many companies have used heavy marketing and promotional activities to offset low product quality, but the PIMS findings suggest such a strategy is not wise. Putting big money into a program to shore up weak products is seen as potentially unprofitable.

Research and Development   Extensive R & D programs used to build up a marketing strategy have a positive effect only if a company already enjoys a strong market share position. The PIMS analysis has found that a company with a weak market position should copy competitors' products rather than invent new products through heavy R & D expenditures. In such a company, a minimal R & D program has been found to be most effective. Another PIMS finding is that R & D spending reaches a point of diminishing return in ROI. Profits of weak market share companies suffer when R & D expenditures exceed 3 percent of sales.[50]

Vertical Integration Another interesting PIMS finding is that vertical integration actions, such as making needed parts rather than buying them and operating company-owned distribution rather than using independent industrial distributors, favorably affect financial performance only when markets are mature and stable. Such moves when markets are rapidly growing, declining, or otherwise changing have negative effects on profit. This finding has direct application to the business marketing manager's channels and physical distribution strategies.

Using PIMS in the Marketing Planning Process The preceding discussion suggests that the PIMS findings have applications in the design and implementation of marketing plans. These findings may be used to aid in decisions made in such areas as product, promotion, distribution, and pricing. Perhaps the best way to illustrate this is through an example. Exhibit 10.2 provides an example of the application of PIMS materials to the marketing planning process in the case of a manufacturer of machine tools.

For its members, PIMS offers three reports for each business or product analyzed: (1) the Par Report specifies the ROI that is normal or par for each business and also identifies factors that cause high or low performance; (2) the Strategic Sensitivity Report tests several strategic moves the business could make and indicates possible short-run and long-run consequences; and (3) the Optimum Strategy Report shows those strategic moves that would provide the best results in terms of factors such as ROI, discounted cash flow, and short-term earnings. In terms of accuracy, PIMS estimates that it can approximate results within three to five points of after-tax return on investment for most businesses (90 percent) over a three- to five-year period.[51] This suggests that planning in business marketing need not be based on guesswork, but may also be derived from objective data such as that provided by PIMS.

As with the other planning tools discussed, PIMS has its critics. There are concerns over the PIMS sampling techniques, data collection methods, and statistical analysis procedures, and its heavy emphasis on ROI. In addition, the subjectivity of perceived product quality is troublesome to many. In contrast to the PIMS, other studies have found numerous cases of successful low market share companies.[52] One study of business marketing firms found forty low market share businesses that achieved pretax ROIs of 20 percent or more, which would seem to conflict with the PIMS findings.[53] Despite the criticism, PIMS still provides a useful tool for the business marketing manager in that its findings provide directions that otherwise might not be appreciated. Used with proper caution, PIMS can be used to develop more realistic marketing plans. As with all of the tools discussed here, the manager must recognize that they do not replace

EXHIBIT 10.2   Using PIMS Materials in Marketing Planning

Assume that a manufacturer of machine tools has a weak number 3 position in terms of market share: It has 10 percent compared with its two major competitors' respective 15 percent and 25 percent. The company's products are high-quality and are sold for a premium. Currently, the company spends only 2 percent of sales on R & D to keep pace with competitors, and about 4 percent to 5 percent of sales is spent on marketing. The company's marketing manager is contemplating a move toward a major marketing program to increase its market share. What strategy decisions should the manager make?

The manager may opt to boost R & D spending to develop new products and increase the market share in that manner. The PIMS experience warns against this strategy because of the company's relatively small market share: The company probably does not have sufficient resources to develop the type of product that is needed to hurdle the stronger competition. Even if it did, there is nothing to prevent the stronger competitors from copying the new product and marketing it more heavily than the smaller company could afford to do.

The manager also may consider launching a major sales and advertising campaign to increase the market share. Again, the PIMS experience discourages such a strategy. Even though the company enjoys high product quality, a heavy marketing campaign would backfire because the advantages enjoyed by the larger competitors probably could not be overcome by the weaker company's promotion. It could be quite dangerous for the smaller company to spend so much in marketing a single endeavor.

What PIMS would recommend is that the manager focus strategy on the company's high product quality, which is its greatest marketing strength. Rather than investing heavily in R & D to improve quality, the manager should tighten up quality control standards for the existing products, build minor improvements into these products, and work on strengthening customer relationships with faster delivery, assurances of delivery, service, technical assistance, and the like. In essence, PIMS would advise the manager that the best way for a weak competitor to strengthen a market position is to become a good follower and concentrate on more specific, although probably narrower, target markets.

Source: Adapted from Paula Smith, "Unique Tool for Marketers: PIMS," *Dun's Review* 108 (October 1976): 95–106.

marketing planning and decision making but rather are simply aids that may be used to accomplish more effective planning in business markets.

CHAPTER SUMMARY

This chapter discussed marketing strategy and planning and expanded on the topic of segmentation strategy described in Chapter 9. The chapter defined marketing strategy and how it relates to strategic market planning, sometimes called business planning or corporate planning. Marketing planning and strategy development is one of the major tasks of the marketing manager, and the process is a complex one in that all areas of the marketing mix must be integrated and coordinated.

The marketing planning process involves defining target markets, establishing objectives in those markets, developing overall marketing strategy, implementing that strategy via tactical mix programs, and controlling and evaluating the results. The chapter emphasized the necessity of this integration through a well-organized process. Sound marketing planning should allow the marketing manager to avoid what is termed the "law of unintended consequences." Integration of the marketing mix through an overall marketing plan should ensure that decisions made in one area of marketing, such as advertising, do not cause major problems in another area, such as distribution.

The chapter has focused on the process of marketing planning and the development of the marketing plan, the written documentation of the process. In addition, it introduced tools that may be used by the business marketing manager in such planning efforts. These included matrix modeling, the Boston Consulting Group's growth–share matrix, the General Electric Strategic Business Planning Grid, and contributions from the PIMS program.

Finally, this chapter serves as the foundation for the rest of the text. Chapter 11 covers the subject of marketing intelligence, which dovetails into the situation analysis stage of the marketing planning process. Chapters 12 through 17 will discuss the mix areas of product and service, distribution, promotion, and pricing as each fits into the overall marketing planning process. Chapter 18 will then cover in detail the subjects of control and evaluation as these relate to the same planning process.

KEY TERMS

control
diversification strategy
evaluation
market development strategy
market penetration strategy
marketing mix
marketing objective
marketing plan

marketing planning
product development strategy
situation analysis
strategic market planning
strategy
tactical action program
target market

QUESTIONS

1. Explain the relationship between market segmentation and marketing planning. How does this relationship correspond to segmentation analysis and segmentation strategy?

2. Some business marketers are of the opinion that marketing planning is something they do before they start to make decisions and take action and that whether they planned or not, the actions they take and the decisions they make are the same. What is your position on this statement?

3. What do you see as the relationship between strategic market planning and marketing planning? From a managerial perspective, what are the differences between these two types of planning?

4. Why are matrix models such as the one developed in this chapter appropriate for developing marketing strategy for business goods and services?

5. What is PERT and why is a technique such as

PERT useful in developing and implementing marketing plans in business markets? What other techniques may be used in addition to PERT?

6. What are the differences and similarities between the BCG growth–share matrix and the General Electric Strategic Business Planning Grid? Which one do you believe provides the better planning tool for the business marketing manager?

7. Explain how a business marketing company could employ market penetration, market development, product development, and diversification strategies all at the same time. If this situation occurred, how might the marketing mix change among the four strategies?

8. What major benefits do you believe are gained by the marketing manager in a business marketing firm who takes the time and effort to develop a comprehensive marketing plan? What risks does the manager take by developing such a plan?

9. Explain the relationship between the marketing plan and tactical programs developed in the functional areas of product, distribution, promotion, and price. What is the marketing manager's involvement in both the marketing plan and the tactical mix programs?

10. Explain how the business marketing manager may use the BCG growth–share matrix to make more effective decisions in the marketing mix areas. How may he or she use the GE Strategic Business Planning Grid to do the same?

NOTES

1. *Chief Marketing Executive* (Chicago: Heidrick and Struggles, 1988), 11.

2. Howard Sutton, *The Marketing Plan in the 1990s,* Report No. 951 (New York: The Conference Board, 1990), 16.

3. *A Guide to Marketing Strategy,* Report No. 23 (Princeton, NJ: Marketing Communications Research Center, 1974).

4. Philip Kotler, "Strategic Planning and the Marketing Process," *Business* 30 (May–June 1980): 4.

5. Richard F. Vancil, "Strategy Formulation in Complex Organizations," *Sloan Management Review* 17 (Winter 1976): 7–8.

6. Derek F. Abell and John S. Hammond, *Strategic Market Planning* (Englewood Cliffs, NJ: Prentice-Hall, 1979), 9–10.

7. Ben Branch, "Above-Par or Below-Par: Profitability," *The Pimsletter* 26 (1981): 5.

8. Various other definitions and descriptions are found in David S. Hopkins, *The Short-Term Marketing Plan,* Report No. 565 (New York: The Conference Board, 1972).

9. Ron Paul, "Organizing for Marketing Planning," *Sales & Marketing Management* 124 (December 7, 1981): 37.

10. "Linking Marketing and Corporate Planning," *Marketing Science Institute Research Briefs* (Cambridge, MA: Marketing Science Institute, September 1982), 3.

11. See H. Igor Ansoff, "Strategies for Diversification," *Harvard Business Review* 35 (September–October 1957): 113–124.

12. Sutton, op. cit., 11.

13. Philip Kotler, *Marketing Management: Analysis, Planning, Implementation, & Control,* 7th ed. (Englewood Cliffs, NJ: Prentice-Hall, Inc., 1991), 63.

14. Sutton, op. cit., 9.

15. Ibid., 11.

16. Paul, op. cit., 38.

17. Ibid.

18. Kotler, *Marketing Management,* op. cit.

19. Peter Coy and Goeff Lewis, "How AT&T Learned to Act Like a Computer Company," *Business Week,* January 22, 1990: 68–69.

20. Rochelle O'Connor, "Guides for Strategic Divisional Planning," *Industrial Marketing Management* 6 (1977): 74.

21. Sutton, op. cit., 23.

22. Kotler, *Marketing Management,* op. cit., 68.

23. William M. Pride and O. C. Ferrell, *Marketing: Basic Concepts and Decisions,* 4th ed. (Boston: Houghton Mifflin, 1985), 34.

24. Gay S. Miller, "Displacing Steel," *The Wall Street Journal,* June 13, 1977, 1.

25. "Copperweld Forges New Steel Markets," *Sales & Marketing Management* 125 (January 18, 1982):23–24.
26. Kotler, *Marketing Management,* op. cit., 378–381.
27. Ibid.
28. Ibid., 388–391.
29. See Michael E. Porter, *Competitive Strategy: Techniques for Analyzing Industries & Competition* (New York: Free Press, 1980).
30. Kotler, *Marketing Management,* op. cit., 55.
31. Ralph Biggadike, *Entering New Markets: Strategies and Performance* (Cambridge, MA: Marketing Science Institute, September 1977), 12–20.
32. Kotler, *Marketing Management,* op. cit., 68.
33. "25 Generalities to Ruin a Marketing Plan," *Sales & Marketing Management* 114 (January 1, 1971):20.
34. Kotler, *Marketing Management,* op. cit., 78.
35. William M. Pride and O. C. Ferrell, *Marketing: Basic Concepts and Decisions,* 2d ed. (Boston: Houghton Mifflin, 1980), 51.
36. Kotler, *Marketing Management,* op. cit., 62.
37. Roman G. Hiebing, Jr., and Scott W. Cooper, *The Successful Marketing Plan* (Lincolnwood, IL: NTC Business Books, 1991), 1.
38. Sutton, op. cit., 39.
39. Ibid.
40. See William J. E. Crissy and Robert M. Kaplan, "Matrix Models for Marketing Planning," *MSU Business Topics* 11 (Summer 1963): 48–66; William J. E. Crissy and Frank M. Mossman, "Matrix Models for Marketing Planning: An Update and Expansion," *MSU Business Topics* 25 (Autumn 1977): 17–26; and Lee H. Mathews, "Stock What You Can Sell by Using Product/Customer Matrix," *Marketing News* 13 (May 30, 1980): 4–5.
41. Sutton, op. cit., 39.
42. Sutton, op. cit., 27.
43. Sutton, op. cit., 9.
44. "Nine Basic Findings of Business Strategy," *The Pimsletter* 1 (November 1, 1977): 1.
45. See "General Electric's 'Stoplight Strategy' for Planning," *Business Week,* April 28, 1975, 49.
46. Bradley T. Gale, "Planning for Profit," *Planning Review* 6 (January 1978): 30.
47. Richard Morrison and Donald Tavel, "New Products and Market Position," *The Pimsletter* 28 (1982): 8.
48. See William L. Burke and Ruth G. Newman, "Brand Awareness and Profitability," *The Pimsletter* 24 (1980): 1–11.
49. Paula Smith, "Unique Tool for Marketers: PIMS," *Dun's Review* 108 (October 1976): 95–106.
50. Mark J. Chussil, "How Much to Spend on R & D," *The Pimsletter* 13 (1978): 1.
51. See Sidney Schoeffler, Robert D. Buzzell, and Donald F. Heany, "Impact of Strategic Planning on Profit Performance," *Harvard Business Review* 52 (March–April 1974): 137–45; and Robert D. Buzzell, Bradley T. Gale, and Ralph M. Sultan, "Market Share: A Key to Profitability," *Harvard Business Review* 53 (January–February 1975): 97–106.
52. Richard G. Hamermesh, M. J. Anderson, Jr., and J. E. Harris, "Strategies for Low Market Share Businesses," *Harvard Business Review* 56 (May–June 1978): 95–102.
53. Carolyn Y. Woo and Arnold C. Cooper, "The Surprising Case for Low Market Share," *Harvard Business Review* 60 (November–December 1982): 106–113.

SUGGESTED ADDITIONAL READINGS

Bailey, Earl L. *Marketing Strategies,* Report No. 629. New York: The Conference Board, Inc., 1974.
Choffray, Jean-Marie, and Gary L. Lilien. *Marketing Planning for New Industrial Products.* New York: John Wiley & Sons, 1980.

Glazer, Rashi. *Marketing and the Changing Information Environment: Implications for Strategy, Structure, and the Marketing Mix,* Report No. 89-108. Cambridge, MA: Marketing Science Institute, 1989.

Haeckel, Stephen H. *Business Strategies in an Information Environment*, Report No. 90-119. Cambridge, MA: Marketing Science Institute, 1990.

Hiebing, Roman G., Jr., and Scott W. Cooper. *The Successful Marketing Plan*. Lincolnwood, IL: NTC Business Books, 1991.

Hopkins, David S. *The Marketing Plan,* Report No. 801. New York: The Conference Board, Inc., 1981.

Kastiel, Diane. "Building an Integrated Marketing Strategy." *Business Marketing* 72 (August 1987): 47–52.

Kotler, Philip, and Paul N. Bloom. "Strategies for High Market-Share Companies." *Harvard Business Review* 53 (November–December, 1975): 63–72.

Lehman, Donald R., and Russell S. Winer. *Analysis for Marketing Planning,* 2d ed. Homewood, IL: Irwin, 1991.

O'Connor, Rochelle. "Guides for Strategic Divisional Planning." *Industrial Marketing Management* 6 (1977): 61–82.

"Planning the Marketing Plan." *Sales & Marketing Management* 124 (December 7, 1981): 54–55.

Porter, Michael E. *Competitive Strategy: Techniques for Analyzing Industries & Competition*. New York: Free Press, 1980.

———. *Competitive Advantage*. New York: Free Press, 1985.

Schanck, J. Thomas. "Strategic Planning for Industrial Products." *Industrial Marketing Management* 8 (1979): 257–263.

Sutton, Howard. *The Marketing Plan in the 1990s,* Report No. 951. New York: The Conference Board, Inc., 1990.

Wiersema, Frederik D. *Strategic Marketing and the Product Life Cycle,* Report No. 82-103. Cambridge, MA: Marketing Science Institute, 1982.

'11'

Business Marketing Intelligence

••

Marketing decisions cannot be made without the benefit of relevant and accurate information. This applies to the areas of market segmentation and marketing planning, as covered in the preceding two chapters. In both chapters, the emphasis was placed on the need for valid and reliable information. It is virtually impossible to segment business markets without sufficient knowledge of the market environment. Whether segmentation is based on geographic, demographic, buying process, benefit, or product characteristics, it cannot be performed effectively unless current, accurate, and relevant information is obtained. Benefit segmentation, for example, requires a thorough understanding of what benefits are important to buyers in different segments. Segmentation by product attributes requires a thorough understanding of which attributes are important to buyers and buying influences.

Similarly, the first step in any realistic marketing planning process involves an analysis of the current marketing situation. This means information gathering must take place before markets are selected, objectives are set, strategies are developed, and tactical plans are implemented. This same logic applies to decision making in the marketing mix areas of product and service, distribution, promotion, and price. Functional managers, such as product managers, sales managers, etc., require input from the market to develop realistic strategies and programs. For example, product managers cannot determine product specifications without some input from the market; advertising managers require information regarding the wants, needs, and expectations of the buying influences involved to be able to determine which media and copy to use; and pricing managers can hardly set realistic prices without knowing the value of the products or services to present and potential customers.

Providing these various types of information to those who will use them is

Using Marketing Research in a Business Marketing Environment

Sonoco Products Company is a Hartsville, South Carolina, manufacturer of industrial and consumer packaging supplies. The company conducts regular surveys of its customers to keep pace with changes taking place and to ensure that its products continue to meet customer needs. Through this research, Sonoco is able to determine what is needed to improve product quality as well as gain an understanding of its market position relative to the customer's perception of what constitutes an ideal supplier. The company's many divisions conduct such research projects about every two or three years just to make certain that customer needs are being met and that marketing plans are on target.

These surveys follow a five-step process. First, key executives at Sonoco conduct workshops to determine what product quality attributes are to be associated with the product in the survey. An average of ten to twelve attributes are typical. Second, customers and prospects are selected for inclusion in the survey. Third, personal visits are scheduled with personnel in those customers and prospects who are willing to participate. Interviewees are typically in engineering, purchasing, plant management, and sometimes corporate management. Interviews take, on the average, from forty-five to ninety minutes. Fourth, after completion of the interviews, a preliminary qualitative and quantitative analysis is performed, data are reviewed, and conclusions are drawn. Fifth, a final report is developed and an action plan is designed based on the survey findings.

The results of such surveys may be seen in the following examples. One division found that a major customer wanted more innovation and packaging ideas to help it differentiate its own products in the market. Sonoco improved package print quality so that the packages would appear more vibrant on the store shelf. The company also developed a reclosable cap for the package and a new plunger system for easier product dispensing.

Another study revealed that a key customer wanted quicker deliveries to reduce its own inventories. Even though current deliveries were on time, the survey disclosed a need for improved service. Sonoco and the customer then worked together to determine how best to reduce lead times and implement just-in-time delivery. The result was that delivery time was cut in half and both Sonoco and the customer were able to hold less inventory.

These examples show the value of marketing research in business marketing. By surveying customers and prospects, Sonoco Products Company is able to better focus its efforts on better serving the needs in the marketplace. Without such input, the company might be at a loss to truly understand what its markets seek and expect.

Source: Adapted from Robert Kearns, "Is Everybody Happy?" *Business Marketing* 74 (December 1989): 30–36.

the task of the intelligence-gathering process. If the business marketing manager is to develop realistic and effective marketing plans, the basic building block is accurate and pertinent information.[1]

This chapter examines the information-gathering process as it exists in business marketing. While it may be argued that intelligence gathering is the same whether in consumer markets or business markets, this chapter focuses on the peculiarities of business marketing and stresses the differences between business and consumer marketing. Emphases are placed on the marketing information system (MIS) and marketing research as both relate to intelligence gathering in business markets.

MARKETING INTELLIGENCE

Marketing intelligence refers to information that can be used by the marketing manager to enhance the competitive position of the company. This broad definition can include almost any information that can help the marketing manager make more effective decisions in market segmentation, overall marketing strategy formulation and marketing planning, and the marketing substrategies of product, promotion, channels, and price. Such information can vary from distributors' complaints about packaging to data provided by the company's own accounting department regarding increasing costs of raw materials. Therefore, marketing intelligence can be internal (obtained from within the marketing firm) and external (obtained outside the firm).

Internal Marketing Intelligence

Internal marketing intelligence can be any type of useful information obtained from such sources within the company as (1) production, (2) production control, (3) purchasing, (4) quality control, (5) research and development, (6) credit, (7) accounting, (8) data processing, (9) personnel, (10) logistics and shipping, and (11) the legal department. Examples of internal marketing intelligence include reports by the production department of production capabilities that must be considered in sales forecasting, cost analysis data provided by the company's accounting department, credit ratings of potential customers supplied by the company's credit department, estimates of engineering capabilities supplied by the firm's engineering department, and cash flow data provided by the comptroller's office. All of these can be termed forms of marketing intelligence, for they can affect marketing decisions being made by the marketing manager. To illustrate, adding new products to the company's product line to fill a market demand may make little sense if the company lacks production, engineering, or financial capabilities. Therefore, any internally generated bits of information that pertain to such capabilities are useful to the manager and should be considered marketing intelligence.

External Marketing Intelligence

External marketing intelligence can be any type of useful information obtained from sources outside the company, such as (1) company salespeople in the field, (2) manufacturers' representatives, if used, (3) distributors, if used, (4) formal marketing research projects, (5) customers, (6) analysis of competitors, (7) trade shows, (8) trade journal publications, (9) trade associations, (10) government publications, (11) private sources providing SIC-related and other marketing data, and (12) outside consultants retained by the company. Examples of external marketing intelligence include customer or channel intermediary complaints about products or services, service parts, and so on; feedback from sales personnel or manufacturers' representatives regarding customer preferences or buying habits; information obtained from trade publications and trade associations and other such sources of secondary data; analysis of competitive reactions; and any forms of formal marketing research surveys, studies, and reports. Adding new products to the company's product line is foolish if customer buying habits and preferences, competitive reactions, and so forth are ignored or overlooked.

As can be seen, marketing intelligence sources are as varied as the types of information sought. Many sources of marketing intelligence are open to the business marketing manager, but no marketing manager can simply start collecting information from all possible sources on the pretense that sooner or later it will all have some marketing application. Such a haphazard collection of information rarely contributes to more effective decision making because the bits and pieces may never interrelate. The collection of marketing intelligence must be selective and deliberate if it is to be used to advantage. It should be selective in terms of the specific objectives in the marketing plan and in choosing those sources of intelligence most likely to produce valid information. In other words, the marketing manager ideally should refer to the specific objectives in the marketing plan and attempt to define the types of information that will best help to achieve those objectives. The manager should analyze all of the various sources that can provide such information, in full or in part, and choose those sources that offer the best material. The marketing manager should then develop some form of MIS to ensure the flow of desired information.

Basically, marketing intelligence plays the same role in business marketing that it does in consumer marketing. It is the basis of all sound marketing strategies and marketing plans. What differs, however, are the types of information desired and the types of sources available in each market.

THE MARKETING INFORMATION SYSTEM

Figure 11.1 illustrates the conceptual framework of the **marketing information system (MIS)** as applied to a company in business markets. The rationale behind this model can be described as follows. The company collects information continuously regarding its marketplace from a variety of sources, such as those

FIGURE 11.1   Model of the Business Marketing Information System (MIS)

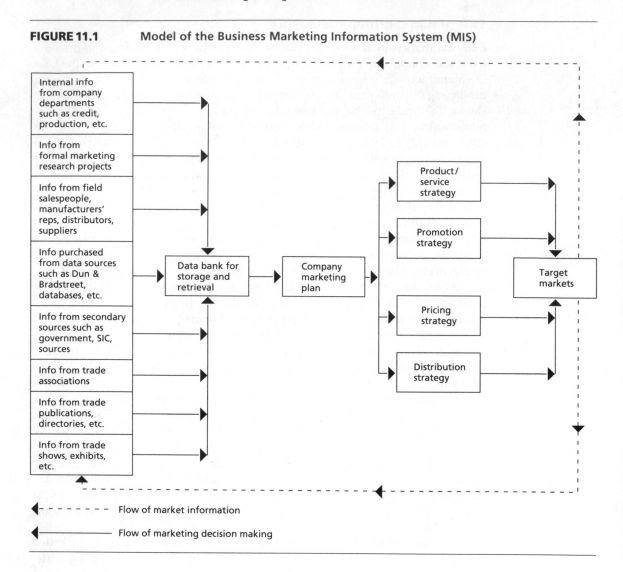

shown in the figure. Some of this information is primary in nature and some of it is secondary; some of it is internal and some is external. The marketing department then classifies this information, using that which is needed immediately and storing other data that are known to have future marketing applications. This information is then fed directly, as needed, into the company's formal marketing plan and becomes an integral part of the firm's overall marketing strategy. Finally, the data that have been collected are used as an input into the products and services to be offered, the prices to be charged, the promotional methods to be used, and the distribution changes to be enacted. Once such decisions have been made, the process begins again in terms of customer reaction to the decisions that have been made and competitive reactions to those decisions. Because the MIS never ceases to collect monitoring data from the marketplace, it provides the marketing manager with the continuous flow of marketing intelligence required for intelligent decision making.

In its simplest form, the concept of the MIS is to provide reliable market data on a continuous basis—data that can be incorporated into marketing decision making wherever possible to prevent decisions being made based on rumor or speculation. Properly implemented, the MIS enables the business marketing manager to make more effective decisions in overall marketing strategy and in respective substrategies. The logic of the MIS is hard to refute: If the target market has the ultimate ability to accept or reject a product or service, an advertising campaign, or whatever (which it does), then it is imperative that attitudes, opinions, impressions, and feelings in the target market be considered before the decision is made. Making business marketing decisions without input from the marketplace appears illogical and dangerous, considering the degree of competition faced by most U.S. business marketing firms. The MIS is intended to provide information about customer problems and dissatisfactions, channel intermediary concerns, competitive moves, and so forth before crisis situations are reached. If properly formulated, the MIS can be preventive as well as curative for the practicing business marketing manager.

Using this definition, the concept differs appreciably from what is commonly called marketing research, although marketing research certainly must be considered a part of the MIS. The MIS is an attempt to collect, analyze, and distribute market data continuously to those who will use it, whereas marketing research normally attempts to collect data that pertain to individual problems encountered at periodic or irregular intervals. To collect data through marketing research on a continuous basis involves tremendous costs in terms of time, money, and manpower, yet such a commitment is precisely what is required to make intelligent marketing decisions in the face of a constantly changing business marketplace. Such circumstances require continuous data, which has resulted in an increasing reliance on the MIS as a source of such market data.

One of the basic functions of the MIS is to get the right data to the right people at the right time. If this task is not accomplished, it is questionable whether the MIS is managerially useful. Thus, the properly formulated MIS can provide data from the system on both regular and irregular bases. Executives can obtain data from the MIS irregularly when they have decisions to make. In addition, a sound MIS can typically provide different types of reports and other data on regularized and predetermined schedules.

An Example of a Business Marketing Information System in Operation

An example may help to underscore the marketing importance of the MIS. University Mechanical and Engineering Contractors of San Diego, California, is the nation's seventh-largest mechanical contractor. The company designs, makes, and installs plumbing, industrial and process piping, instrumentation, heating, ventilation, air-conditioning systems, and fire protection networks. Its markets are primarily major construction projects in such areas as high-rise office buildings, commercial complexes, manufacturing and processing plants, wastewater treatment plants, and nuclear generating plants. Although the company does perform residential work, its primary marketing emphasis is in the industrial market.

Management at University Mechanical learned early on that to succeed in this market environment, the company could not merely wait for bid lists to be published on a specific job and then submit a bid in competition with many other bidders. Under such a situation, a contract award became basically a price war, and the company was seen as but one of many possible vendors. In addition, this process of obtaining jobs meant conforming to job specifications determined without the company's input, which meant that potential customers determined the job specifications and University Mechanical was forced to adapt its capabilities and resources to these if the company wanted the job. Often, this adaptation meant doing a job that used University Mechanical's expertise inefficiently and sometimes resulted in a less efficient job for the customer. In short, straight bid work often put the company at a definite disadvantage in the marketplace.

To overcome such disadvantages, management began to market its engineering and construction management capabilities as well as its traditional construction abilities. It was felt that the company had the expertise and talent to help customers more than it had been doing with straight bid work. To do so, however, University Mechanical had to be involved with any construction project early in its development, which meant it must be constantly attuned to events in its markets. Some form of marketing information system was required to turn up leads early enough so that action could be taken. This switch was a considerable change from past practice and involved some redefinition of company goals, policies, and priorities. The MIS developed by the company is shown in Figure 11.2.

The purpose of the system was threefold: (1) to provide top management with information on all upcoming projects, (2) to provide and facilitate direction from top management to field sales engineers, and (3) to assist the sales engineers in keeping track of major projects in their territories in a systematic way. The system is ongoing and provides market data on a continuous basis, which is, of course, one of the primary functions of any good MIS.

How the University Mechanical MIS Works

To understand better how this MIS works and how it contributes to more effective marketing, a description of activities, following the flowchart depicted in Figure 11.2, is useful. The company's marketing manager is directly responsible for implementing the MIS and keeping it operational. This manager regularly follows the appropriate published secondary sources of potential future jobs. Typical lead sources include (1) *National Building News' Weekly Construction Preview,* which provides advance news reports on leading construction projects in the United States and Canada; (2) Herb Ireland's *Sales Prospector,* which

FIGURE 11.2   Example of a Business Marketing Information System (MIS)

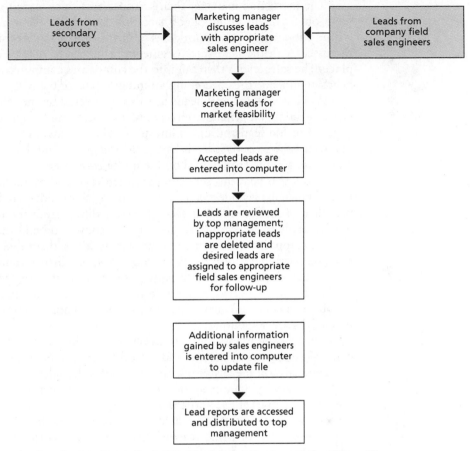

Courtesy of University Mechanical and Engineering Contractors, San Diego, CA.

provides advance reporting of industrial, commercial, and institutional construction on a monthly basis with both regional and national coverage; (3) bid listings, such as those put out by the *Dodge Green Sheet, Engineering News Record,* the *Journal of Daily Commerce,* and other such trade news sources; (4) trade journals in their respective markets, which often report news items regarding new plant construction plans, relocations, and so forth; and (5) newspapers in the major cities in the company's market areas. The purpose of this intensive, almost daily, search of secondary information sources is to uncover information on upcoming jobs as early as possible. Typically, these leads provide such information as the type of job (commercial, industrial, or federal), a job description, the dollar value of the project, the status of the project (that is, if the project is only proposed, or if architects, engineers, or construction firms have already been selected), the target date of the project, and the name of the owner, the architect, and the structural engineer, if they have been appointed.[2]

The marketing manager then screens these sales leads to conform to company objectives in terms of job size, job type, and so forth. Those leads not within the criteria are discarded. The leads that pass this initial screening are discussed with the field sales engineers in whose territories the jobs will take place. The sales lead is then put into the company's computer with the sales engineer's comments, thus becoming an integral part of the MIS.

As Figure 11.2 shows, leads are also uncovered by the sales engineers in the field. In calling on general contractors, architects, and engineers, the sales engineers also find leads on upcoming jobs. These leads are screened in the same manner as the secondary leads by the sales engineer and the marketing manager, and those accepted are placed on file in the computer.

Leads that pass this screening are then reviewed by top management. This review normally is undertaken by the company's president and its executive vice president of marketing. This second review differs from the initial screening in that all leads to be considered are already known to be in the proper markets, but the company may not be able to act on all of them due to conflicting job schedules, staffing problems, labor shortages, or other internal factors. This review is based more on the company's ability to perform a specific job at a particular time in a specific locale than on a rejection or acceptance of the type of job. In essence, this review sets priorities on available potential jobs so that the better jobs are sought first.

The leads that pass this second review are then assigned to the appropriate field sales engineer by a sales lead record form. The field sales engineer receives the lead, calls on the customer, and completes the sales lead form to the best of his or her ability. One copy of the form is then returned to the executive vice president of marketing, and the sales engineer keeps another copy in a sales project notebook, which is a field reference for possible follow-up. Unless the job is discarded for some reason, the sales lead record becomes the sales engineer's field record for sales efforts. The returned copy is then input into the company's computer, updating the previous file, and is accessed for top management, so that management is always aware of the status of each job under consideration.

This University Mechanical system provides a good example of a business MIS. Through its use, the company has current information on all jobs in all its markets at all times. This information gives the company much more control over its markets in terms of jobs to be sought, marketing priority of those jobs, materials required, labor required, and financing. This system has enabled the company to obtain more work on a more profitable, negotiated bid basis rather than on a lower profit, straight bid basis. Because the MIS allows University Mechanical quicker access to possible jobs, the company also has been able to move into more lucrative design and construction management jobs. In this company, the MIS plays a key role in all marketing strategies and programs.

A complete MIS should be designed to incorporate those types of information necessary to give the marketing manager the ability to compete in an effective manner. Individual marketing information systems vary according to manager preferences, but some information areas are central to any MIS. These areas may be classified as shown in Table 11.1, which also illustrates types of sources commonly used to obtain the needed information. Development of such a comprehensive MIS provides the marketing manager with such advantages as (1) greater profitability based on market segments, (2) reduced marketing expenses and tighter cost control, (3) quicker recognition of forces and events affecting sales and profits, (4) documented decision support for strategic and tactical planning, (5) improved distribution efficiencies, (6) improved marketing performance control and evaluation, (7) greater accuracy in forecasting and budgeting, and (8) a strategy planning database that permits faster and more accurate evaluation of options.[3]

TABLE 11.1   Informational Areas in the Marketing Information System (MIS)

Informational Areas	Types of Information to Include	Information Sources
Market information	Target market characteristics such as size and growth rates, seasonal and cyclical trends, entry barriers, geographic distribution, number of firms	SIC-related sources, trade associations, trade journals, marketing research, outside marketing consultants
Competitor information	Number and location of competitors, competitor strengths and weaknesses in terms of products, channels, distribution, sales, advertising, and pricing	SIC-related sources, trade journals, trade shows, field salespeople, suppliers, intermediaries, marketing research
Buyer information	Purchasing policies, processes, buying centers, buying influences, buyer motives in present and prospective customers	Marketing research, field salespeople, channel intermediaries, marketing consultants
Economic information	Interest rates, exchange rates, balance of payments, gross national product, inflation, unemployment	Government publications, trade journals, business publications
Internal nonmarketing information	Production capacity, R & D capabilities, engineering capabilities, financial situation, purchasing capabilities, top-management perspectives, corporate goals and mission	Production, engineering, R & D, purchasing, finance department records, and related information
Internal marketing information	Product quality, product lines, service, and product support; channels and distribution abilities; sales force size and competence, advertising and sales promotion effectiveness, and pricing competitiveness	Product manager, sales manager, field salespeople, distribution manager, advertising manager, sales and marketing records
Derived demand information	Size and growth rates of business customers' target markets, preferences and buyer motivations in those markets	Business customers, marketing research and consultants
External organizations' information	Capabilities of suppliers, distributors, manufacturers' representatives, warehouses, freight forwarders, transportation companies, financial intermediary institutions used	Records of organizations' references from their customers, marketing research, past company records such as sales, purchasing, inventory

Making the MIS Operational

In concept, the MIS is relatively simple, as the preceding sections have indicated. Information is collected, analyzed, and distributed to those responsible for making marketing decisions. Making the MIS operational, however, can be a very difficult undertaking and requires considerable time and effort. No matter how sound in concept, the MIS cannot function unless properly implemented. A discussion is in order regarding ways to make the MIS function effectively.

Secondary Data If secondary data are to be used in the MIS, the manager must determine which sources to use and then organize a method for collecting the required information. For example, if an MIS is to provide information on a regular basis from trade publications, government publications, or other SIC-related sources, someone has to do it. Some firms will employ a clipping service to search out and find appropriate materials for input to the MIS. In other companies, there may be someone in the marketing department with this responsibility. Whichever, the manager must see to it that his or her organization provides for the personnel to provide this service.

Field Market Data If information is desired from field salespeople, manufacturers' reps, or distributors, the manager must also devise ways to make this happen. These are all good sources of information from the market in that all are in the field and see things firsthand. But, they do not always recognize the need for information, nor do they always want to take the time to obtain it. For example, company salespeople often have reservations about using their time to obtain information for input to the MIS even though it might help them in the long run. Taking time to search out information means spending less time selling and possibly losing income. If the marketing manager wishes to use his or her company salespeople in the MIS, the compensation plan must be designed to encourage and not hinder participation. Salespeople sometimes see using time in this manner as a waste. For example, Cutler-Hammer at one time required all its field salespeople to fill out very detailed reports following each sales call. These reports were seen almost as an imposition on the salesperson's time. In addition, many salespeople never saw any results after reports were sent in. As a consequence, they did not give the reports their best efforts (some even claimed to fudge them) with the result that their input was much less valuable than thought by management. If salespeople are expected to contribute to the MIS, the manager must make certain they are rewarded in some way for this contribution.

Manufacturers' representatives and distributors also are good sources of information, but are not necessarily interested in being used to gather information for manufacturers. With reps, who are paid on a commission basis, the lost sales because of time spent collecting information mean a loss of income. Many reps will not do this no matter how strongly they feel about the manufacturer. Similarly, distributors have problems with such requests. Many distributors handle large number of products and they simply do not have the time to gather information for their suppliers. This does not mean that reps and distributors cannot be used in the MIS, but rather that the marketing manager must provide incentives for these channel intermediaries if they are expected to contribute to the MIS.

Internal Company Data As has been discussed, a good MIS should also include information from internal company departments such as production, purchasing, logistics, accounting, credit, and so forth. Again, desired information from such sources will not occur unless the marketing manager makes it apparent to department heads that it is in their interest to contribute. Effective marketing requires up-to-date information from other departments and this information should be input to the MIS. Close communication with other department heads is necessary. For example, any problems with production scheduling or meeting delivery dates should immediately be known by the marketing manager. Close relationships with other departments should ensure that this type of information is passed on immediately.

These are but examples of what may be required to effectively implement the MIS in a business marketing firm. The MIS can be a very valuable marketing tool if all who are expected to contribute will do so. It is the job of the marketing manager to take steps to see that this happens. If it does not, the MIS will not really be an information system at all.

MARKETING RESEARCH IN BUSINESS MARKETS

Marketing research is defined as "the systematic gathering, recording, and analyzing of data about problems relating to the marketing of goods and services."[4] If this definition is compared with that given earlier for marketing intelligence, it is apparent that the two are not the same. Marketing research is more confined in scope and is generally considered part of overall marketing intelligence. Marketing research frequently is classified as a subsystem of a marketing information system; its primary activity is organized on a project basis to deal with specific problems and opportunities.[5] Moreover, marketing research normally involves projects of a single or nonrepetitive nature, whereas marketing intelligence gathering is more of a continuous process. In addition, marketing research is conducted to build a database for individual marketing problems such as those in the product, promotion, pricing, or channel areas. Marketing intelligence is broader and may encompass many problems simultaneously. A general principle is that marketing research should be tied to a specific concern, such as product introduction, understanding of buyer behavior, or new markets. Viewed in its proper perspective, formal marketing research should be considered as one input into a local marketing information system that is designed to collect marketplace data, as was illustrated in Figure 11.1.

The definition of marketing research applies to both consumer and business markets. Perhaps the addition of the word *business* to the definition is all that is required to derive an acceptable definition of business marketing research. Thus, business marketing research is defined as the systematic gathering, recording, and analyzing of data about problems relating to the marketing of goods and services to organizational markets. Marketing research uses the scientific method to find solutions to problems involving organizational customers. In other words, it means using objective study techniques to collect relevant data and analyze the gathered information. This explanation implies that marketing research is marketing research whether it is in consumer or business markets and that there are probably more similarities than differences between the two types. It has been argued that a well-trained, competent **marketing researcher** can switch from a consumer marketing firm to business marketing company, although that marketing researcher probably will not be truly effective until he or she becomes acquainted with the unique aspects of the industry or industries involved. There are differences between the two markets, however, and it often takes considerable time and effort to adapt to these differences. For example, a marketing researcher for Procter & Gamble may not move to American Cyanamid without first attaining a knowledge of the chemical industry and the organizational behavior of organizations in American Cyanamid's marketplace.

THE MARKETING RESEARCH PROCESS

The **marketing research process** is a relatively standard one and applies to both business and consumer marketing. This process may be seen in Figure 11.3. For the business marketer, the steps in this process are the same as those used in consumer marketing, although applications may differ appreciably. These differences will be covered in detail but a brief explanation of what goes on in each step of this process is worthwhile.

Define the Research Problem

The first step is the determination of what problem exists that can possibly be solved by research. Such problems may involve overall strategic marketing areas such as market potential, market growth, geographic distribution of the market, and other considerations. However, problems may also arise from the functional mix areas. For example, an advertising manager may not know how certain ads are perceived by target market customers. A product manager may have a problem with new product acceptance in a target market. A pricing manager may need information on customer value before prices can be determined. Regardless of the source, the problem must be defined before any research can take place. In addition, the problem must be defined specifically enough so that the researcher is fully aware of the problem involved.

Develop the Research Hypothesis

A **research hypothesis** is a reasonable guess or assumption about the problem defined.[6] For example, a distribution manager may believe that large target market customers prefer to buy directly from the manufacturer, whereas smaller

FIGURE 11.3   The Marketing Research Process

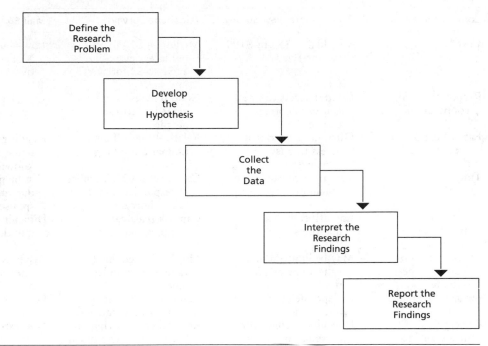

customers prefer to buy from distributors. As information is gathered, this hypothesis may be tested and either accepted or rejected. Marketing research studies often contain many hypotheses, and the research findings are then used to accept or reject them. The results are the major findings of the research.

Collect the Data

Once the problem is defined and the hypothesis determined, the next step is to collect the data, which may either be primary or secondary. **Primary data** are collected directly from survey respondents; **secondary data** are those compiled elsewhere but that have application to the problem. In business markets, primary data are typically collected in three ways: (1) use of surveys—personal interviews, telephone, and mail; (2) observation—recording the behavior of respondents by observing actions; and (3) experimentation—developing a controlled situation whereby the problem is tested and evaluated. All three types of **data collection** can be used in business marketing research, but the survey method appears to be used most widely.[7] Table 11.2 outlines the pros and cons of personal, telephone, and mail surveys as these apply to business marketing research.

In addition to primary data, business marketing researchers are big users of secondary data. Such data are often quite accessible in business markets because

TABLE 11.2   Comparison of the Three Basic Survey Methods in Business Marketing Research

Comparison Factors	Personal Interview Surveys	Telephone Surveys	Mail Surveys
Cost *	Very high—$50 to $100 per interview	Medium—$20 to $30 per interview; as low as $2 to $3 for WATS line surveys	Low—approximately $5 per completed questionnaire
Respondent cooperation	Good if access can be gained to correct people	Good if access can be gained to correct people	Can be good if questionnaire well developed
Ease of conducting survey	Often difficult to gain access to busy influences	Relatively easy if questionnaire not long	Easy if respondent's name and position known
Time	Very time-consuming to obtain many responses	Can cover a large number of respondents in a fairly short time	Can be time-consuming due to wait for responses in mail
Complexity of information to be obtained	Can ask complex questions	Can ask reasonably complex questions	Difficult to ask complex questions
Amount of information to be obtained	May be limited due to value of respondent's time	May be limited due to value of respondent's time	Depends on respondent's interest and willingness to respond
Biggest advantage	In-depth detailed information	Can reach many respondents at moderate cost	Low cost and no interviewer bias
Biggest disadvantage	Difficulty of conducting personal interviews with busy buying influences	Reluctance of buying influences to spend much time on phone answering questions	Nonresponse problems caused by those who do not respond

* Based on *Cahners Research Services No. 900A* (Newton, MA: Cahners Publishing Company, 1986), 3.

of the SIC system and its many related data sources, both public and private. Chapter 8 developed this area in detail, and uses of such sources as the *Census of Manufactures, Predicasts,* and *U.S. Industrial Outlook* should be recalled. In addition, trade associations, trade journals, databases, and outside research organizations often provide useful secondary data.

Interpret the Research Findings

After data have been collected, they must be analyzed and interpreted. Data typically are tabulated according to categorical classifications such as company size, geographic location, and so on. They are then cross-tabulated if desired. Following tabulation, analysis takes place to determine how responses are distributed and how they vary from "the average." Interpretation of research results is one of the prime contributions of the marketing research specialist—the ability to interpret findings correctly is extremely important and often requires considerable expertise.

Report the Research Findings

The final step in the research process is the preparation of a report by the marketing researcher and submission of this report to the marketing manager or functional manager involved. For example, if the research project is conducted to determine problems involved with the acceptance of a new product in a target market, the research report should be prepared for the product manager. That report typically includes tables, analysis, and recommendations developed by the researcher. The importance of defining the problem precisely can now be seen. If the problem is clearly defined by the product manager, the researcher should be able to prepare a report that directly relates to the manager's concerns. In most cases, the manager is not compelled to follow the researcher's recommendations, but he or she should view them as another input in the decision-making process. Research reports have been criticized by practicing marketing managers, who complain that researchers are often infatuated with statistical techniques and sometimes fit problems to techniques rather than vice versa. In addition, they believe researchers disdain simple studies in favor of more complex and more challenging ones.[8] It is important that the research reports made to line marketing managers be both correct and practical if good use is to be made of the findings.

BUSINESS MARKETING RESEARCH—A CASE STUDY

An example may help to illustrate the marketing research process as applied by a business marketing firm.[9] Loctite Corporation is a manufacturer of industrial sealants and adhesives. In the company's target markets, mechanical engineers were seen as the key buying influences. The company was interested in learning more about these key buying influences that could be applied to decisions made in the marketing mix. The research problem faced was that there was an inadequate understanding of those buying influences that are crucial to the marketing of Loctite's products. The hypothesis that was developed was based on the assumption that three types of mechanical engineers were influential enough to be researched: design, maintenance, and production engineers.

Loctite used an outside research agency to conduct in-depth interviews with samples of design, maintenance, and production engineers drawn from target market companies. Using the survey method, data were collected from the selected respondents.

The interpretation of the research findings showed that the hypothesis was correct—the three types of buying influences were not similar in their self-images or in their perceptions. For example, design engineers were found to be risk avoiders even though they considered themselves to be innovators, futuristic types, and problem solvers. They felt pressured to be right and were fearful of making wrong decisions. They saw a risk of failure in being innovative and believed a problem implied that they had a problem.

Plant engineers, on the other hand, considered themselves to be unsung company heroes—they were the fixers who kept things running with creative and expedient solutions to MRO problems. The third type, the production engineers, were found to feel the pressures for performance to be "today-oriented," and they were concerned about making mistakes that would have large financial repercussions for the companies or their jobs. The research clearly showed that differences existed among the three types of key buying influences.

The research findings were then reported to Loctite's advertising department so that advertisements could be created that would most effectively communicate with each type of buying influence. For example, ads directed toward design engineers employed tables, pictures, and cutaway diagrams to explain specifically how particular products worked—the research had disclosed that these buying influences liked to see charts, diagrams, and graphs in advertisements. Ads aimed at the plant engineers employed photographs stressing the merits of pipe sealants used to lock threaded pipes together compared with the more common use of tape for such purposes. These ads were designed to overcome fears that the sealant would permanently lock the pieces together and to show that the sealant, unlike tape, would not leak. This example shows how Loctite used the marketing research process to better understand its key buying influences, and to develop advertisements more attuned to the customer's needs.

UNIQUE CHARACTERISTICS OF BUSINESS MARKETING RESEARCH

As has been developed, the basic objectives, process, and principles of marketing research are basically the same in both business and consumer marketing. This does not mean, however, that there are not differences of some importance. There are characteristics unique to researching business markets. Some authorities believe that these characteristics make business marketing research substantially different and more demanding than research conducted on consumer goods and services.[10]

One point to keep in mind concerns the difference between business and consumer markets. In Chapter 1, it was learned that business markets are composed of organizational customers while consumer markets consist of individuals and households. This basic difference is important to understand when discussing the subject of marketing research. The consumer marketing researcher is researching individuals and households, while the business marketing researcher is researching people within organizations. This does not mean that a business marketing firm would never research consumer markets; it simply means that when this is performed it is closer to consumer marketing research than to business marketing research. This basic differentiation is at the root of many of the following characteristics that are unique to business marketing research. The following sections look at some of the unique characteristics of business marketing research based on the basic difference between the two markets.

Differences Between Business and Consumer Marketing Research

Organizational Buying Behavior Whereas the consumer marketing researcher deals with individual consumers and households, the business marketing researcher is concerned with business, institutional, and governmental organizations. Therefore, to perform the job effectively, the researcher must understand the behavior of the organizations involved in terms of formal and informal buying influences, purchasing processes, key buying influences, budget considerations governing buying, corporate purchasing policies, and so on. As may be suspected, this understanding involves a knowledge of factors not normally considered by the consumer marketing researcher in surveying the ultimate consumer.

Multiple Buying Influences Buying influences are much more complex in business markets than in consumer markets. This statement does not mean to imply that buying influences do not exist in the consumer market; they do, and sometimes they exert great influence over what is purchased by the household. Everyone is familiar with the child influencing his or her mother to buy a certain brand of breakfast cereal. In the consumer market, however, the number of buying influences for a product is normally small, and the buying motives are relatively easy to determine. For the business marketing researcher, a thorough knowledge of buying influences, both in general in the industry involved and in particular with specific firms in that industry, is imperative if the researcher is to collect valid and representative data. If the business marketing researcher does not reach those influences who can and will affect buying decisions in their respective firms, the research is basically worthless. The researcher must know who influences the buying decisions and how to reach those individuals. In addition, their interests must be known well enough to communicate with them in the research design.

Derived Demand For the most part, the consumer marketing researcher is concerned only with the direct consumer demand for the products or services produced by the researcher's company. For example, a consumer goods manufacturer typically conducts its marketing research on present and potential buyers of its products. The business marketing researcher, however, is concerned with both direct and derived demand estimation. Hence, a business marketing researcher must be able to read two sets of customer demands accurately.[11] To illustrate, marketing research at Boeing should consider both the direct demand from airlines for aircraft and the demand of air travelers who use those airlines for travel purposes. If air travel is projected to decrease, this fact will affect the airline's demand for specific types of aircraft. Viewed from this perspective, the business marketing researcher often ends up researching both organizational and ultimate customers.

Technical Knowledge The business marketing researcher typically must be more technically oriented than his or her consumer marketing counterpart. Often, the researcher must obtain data pertaining to exotic metals, electronics, and nuclear physics from technically trained respondents such as engineers, purchasing agents, production and production control personnel, and quality assurance specialists. If the researcher does not understand the pertinent technology and principles, data collection may be superficial or irrelevant. If reports are to be read by technical people within the company, the researcher must know enough to write using technical language and terminology. It is generally possible to team the marketing researcher with technically oriented counterparts such as in-house engineers to ensure the desired level of technical validity, but the main point here is that business marketing research often requires a higher level of technical sophistication than consumer marketing research does. This sophistication is required not so much because of increased product complexity as it is because of the backgrounds of people with whom the researcher must work, both as respondents to survey efforts and as recipients of reports once the survey work is completed. Ideally, the business marketing researcher may have need of an engineering or production background in addition to marketing research training.

Budgetary Constraints Business marketing firms typically have lower marketing research budgets than their consumer marketing counterparts. For example, an American Marketing Association study disclosed that business marketing firms spend less than consumer marketing firms for marketing research in every size classification. The mean budget for consumer marketing firms was $1,899,000, whereas the mean budget for business marketing firms was only $379,000.[12] Table 11.3 shows the relatively low percentage of sales spent on marketing research by business marketing firms. Using the 0.3 percent average, a firm with $1 million in sales would spend but $3,000 in marketing research.

Lower budgets result in different research practices than those found in consumer firms with larger research budgets. For example, business marketing firms are less likely to conduct costly national surveys using personal or phone interviews. They are more likely to use their own sales representatives in field surveys with buying influences than to pay for outside interviewers. In addition, since business marketing firms appear to rely heavily on their marketing information systems, they are likely to rely more on secondary data sources than on primary research efforts by the survey method. By relying more on the MIS and their field sales representatives, many business marketing companies believe they do not require the large research budgets often found in consumer marketing.

Sampling Because business and consumer market structures differ appreciably, sampling differences are involved in researching the two markets. In consumer markets, where large numbers of customers are involved, sampling is widely used to reduce costs in time, effort, and money. In business markets, however, there are often relatively few customers involved, and a census rather than

TABLE 11.3   Percentage of Sales Spent in Marketing Research in Selected Business Markets

Industry	Market Research Expenditures as a Percentage of Sales
Furniture and fixtures	0.03%
Chemicals and allied products	1.1
Fabricated metal products	0.1
Machinery, except electrical	0.4
Electronic computing equipment	1.2
Electrical and electronic equipment	0.2
Transportation equipment	0.3
Instruments and related products	0.2
All reporting industries	0.3

Source: Reprinted by permission from *Laboratory of Advertising Performance Report No. 8015.8* (New York: McGraw-Hill Research Department, 1985).

Note: Marketing research costs include salaries, direct expenses, administrative overhead, and interviewer and computer-related expenses.

a sample may be common. To illustrate, at one time nine companies made 100 percent of all piston-type fire extinguishers. Obviously, a random sample drawn from a population of nine makes little sense. For any manufacturer producing parts for such extinguishers, a research effort would have to include all nine customer firms and not just a selected few customers, no matter how sophisticated the selection process. This example is rather extreme, but many business marketing firms market their goods and services to a relatively small number of customers; thus the point does apply.

When sampling is used, it is often judgmental rather than random. In other instances in which business products are sold into horizontal markets, large customer segments may exist and sampling will occur. Of course, if the business marketing researcher is interested in obtaining derived demand data, he or she may use the same sampling techniques as those used by consumer marketing counterparts. In general, however, these sampling differences exist between the two markets.

Data Sources   Both primary and secondary data sources often are quite different in consumer and business markets. The consumer marketing researcher who is accustomed to using census data and other sources such as *Sales & Marketing Management's* "Survey of Buying Power" will find these sources quite inappropriate if he or she switches to business markets. A new set of sources is required. The researcher is now forced to rely on the SIC system and its many related data sources, such as were detailed in Chapter 8. Until that researcher learns to use sources such as the *Census of Manufactures, U.S. Industrial Outlook,* and other previously discussed sources, it is unlikely that he or she will be able to provide adequate secondary data.

This difference becomes even more pronounced when institutional or governmental markets are involved. In these markets, data sources often focus on very narrow markets and are not always easily found. To illustrate, information available on hospitals is not obtained from the same sources as are data on school systems. Similarly, information available on local government markets does not always come from the same sources that supply federal government buying information. The Federal Procurement Data Center, for example, provides useful information on all federal contracts over $10,000. From this center, reports are available that break down such contracts according to governmental department or agency, type of purchases made, and the leading contractors.[13] Unfortunately, this source cannot be used for similar information on state, county, or municipal markets, although other sources can provide these data. Thus, the business marketing researcher often has to search out specific sources depending on the type of market information desired.

There are also research organizations that specialize in business markets. Some conduct research activities for clients in both business and consumer markets, and others focus primarily on organizational customers. An example of the former is McGraw-Hill Research, which conducts primary research on buying influences, market size, new products, and competitive position. An example of the latter is McFarlane & Company, which promotes itself as a business marketing specialist. Some concentrate on domestic markets; others focus on research capabilities in international markets. Figure 11.4 illustrates a research firm that specializes in business markets.

Learning the data sources necessary for business marketing is not a major problem, but it is a basic difference and often involves expending considerable time and effort to learn the data sources.

Many other differences exist, but these appear to be the most significant. Table 11.4 provides a comparative analysis of some of the major differences between consumer and business marketing research. As the table indicates, some differences are significant enough to affect performance if they are not recognized and adapted to.

Similarities Between Business and Consumer Marketing Research

The preceding section has shown that there are indeed unique characteristics of business marketing research. It would be a mistake, however, to conclude that business and consumer marketing research are more different than they are similar. In spite of the differences, the skills required to prepare a study design, develop a questionnaire, establish processing specifications, instruct interviewers, and analyze gathered data are basic for any marketing research project, whether it is in business or consumer markets. Regardless of which market is involved, many similarities exist:[14]

1. The overall administration, design execution, and analysis of survey research tend to follow the same basic rules and procedures.

FIGURE 11.4   Example of a Business Marketing Research Organization

Cost-Effective Industrial Marketing Information

A new concept in determining market share, position and potential.

- Inexpensive
- Rich in Market Over-View
- Furnishes Market Share of Specific Product Groupings
- Furnishes Target Account Potential
- Includes Information on Even Smallest Accounts

Write or call for free brochure. No obligation.

BASIC DISTRIBUTOR-MARKETED PRODUCT GROUPS COVERED IN THE IMI SYSTEM
(Partial List Only—Additional Groups on Request)

Abrasives • Drills • Saw Blades • Hand Tools • Files • Power Tools • Cutting Tools • Pipe • Valves • Cylinders • Belts • Sprockets • Hoists • Conveyors • Shelving • Hose • Motors • Safety Equipment • Coolants • Paint • Adhesives • Fasteners • Bearings • Petroleum Products • Instrumentation • **Over 150 Different Groups!**

INDUSTRIAL MARKET INFORMATION, INC.
1313 5th St. S.E., Suite 111A, Minneapolis, MN 55414 (612) 379-3939

Source: Reprinted by permission of *Industrial Market Information, Inc.*

2. The research study addresses the problem and the information needed in a valid and reliable manner.

3. The data processing procedures are similar.

4. The analysis of data requires the same type of skill and knowledge.

5. The marketing researcher in both markets is a problem solver and marketing consultant.

6. The researcher's tools of the trade are the application of valid and reliable research techniques to uncover information that aids in problem solving and helps create a better business solution.

TABLE 11.4   Consumer Versus Business Marketing Research: What Are the Differences?

	Consumer	Business
Universe/population	Large. Dependent on category under investigation but usually unlimited. 72.5 million U.S. households and 215 million persons.	Small. Fairly limited in total population and even more so if within a defined industry or SIC category.
Respondent accessibility	Fairly easy. Can interview at home, on the telephone, or by mail techniques.	Difficult. Usually only during working hours at plant, office, or on the road. Respondent is usually preoccupied with other priorities.
Respondent cooperation	Over the years has become more and more difficult, yet millions of consumers have never been interviewed.	A major concern. Due to the small population the industrial respondent is being over-researched. The purchaser and decision makers in an industrial firm are the buyers of a variety of products and services, from office supplies to heavy equipment.
Sample size	Can usually be drawn as large as required for statistical confidence since the population is in the hundreds of millions.	Usually much smaller than consumer sample, yet the statistical confidence is equal due to the relationship of the sample to the total population.
Respondent definitions	Usually fairly simple. Those aware of a category or brand, users of a category or brand, demographic criteria. The ultimate purchaser is also a user for most consumer products and services.	Somewhat more difficult. The user and the purchasing decision maker in most cases are not the same. Factory workers who use heavy equipment and secretaries who use typewriters are the users and, no doubt, best able to evaluate these products and services. However, they tend not to be the ultimate purchasers and in many cases do not have any influence on the decision-making process.
Interviewers	Can usually be easily trained. They are also consumers and tend to be somewhat familiar with the area under investigation for most categories.	Difficult to find good executive interviewers. At least a working knowledge of the product class or subject being surveyed is essential. Preferably more than just a working knowledge.
Study costs	Key dictators of cost are sample size and incidence. Lower incidence usage categories (for example, users of soft-moist dog food or powdered breakfast beverages) or demographic or behavioral screening criteria (attend a movie at least once a month, over 65 years of age, and do not have direct deposit of Social Security payments) can up costs considerably.	Relative to consumer research, the critical elements resulting in significantly higher per-interview costs are the lower incidence levels, the difficulties in locating the "right" respondent (that is, the purchase decision maker), and securing cooperation (time and concentration of effort) for the interview itself.

Source: Reprinted by permission from Martin Katz, "Use Same Theory, Skills for Consumer, Industrial Marketing Research," *Marketing News* 12 (January 12, 1979):16. Published by the American Marketing Association.

These aspects do not change simply because a study is in a business or consumer market; they are the fundamentals of sound marketing research.

AREAS OF MAJOR BUSINESS MARKETING RESEARCH ACTIVITIES

Almost any area of marketing can be researched. This statement is as true for business marketing as it is for consumer marketing, but there are indications that business marketers do not place emphasis in the same manner as consumer marketers do. Table 11.5 illustrates some differences as revealed in the American Marketing Association's "Survey of Marketing Research." This survey is conducted every five years, and it includes respondents from both consumer and business markets. Analysis of the table reveals those areas most frequently researched by business marketing firms.

It is of interest to note that business marketers are heavily into research activities that relate to short- and long-range forecasting, analysis of business trends, measurement of market potentials, market share analysis, determination of market characteristics, pricing analysis, and sales analysis. Over 90 percent of the respondents conducted these types of research activities. The AMA survey does not state whether these activities were conducted using primary or secondary data, but many of them lend themselves to the latter. As was developed in Chapter 8, the SIC system and its related data sources lend themselves easily to such research. For example, forecasting, trend analysis, market potentials, and market shares can be determined using secondary data. Thus, it is likely that business marketers are big users of secondary data in their research endeavors.

On the other hand, there is evidence of relatively low use of some of the newer research activities that require primary research. For example, there is limited use of advertising research, despite the fact that almost all business marketing firms advertise in one form or another. With the exception of ad effectiveness studies, only about one-half of the respondents measured such advertising areas as copy, media, and competitor analysis. Similarly, business marketers were not much involved in corporate responsibility research activities such as "right to know" studies, ecological impact studies, and social values studies.

Viewing business marketing research from the perspective of the marketing mix, some interesting observations can be made. Although the survey shows that business marketers are light researchers in advertising and sales promotion, there is evidence that they conduct significant research in such mix areas as product, pricing, distribution channels, physical distribution, and sales. Business marketing research appears to focus on the necessary but less glamorous marketing areas. In summary, however, business marketing research does cover those basic areas necessary for effective strategic planning: (1) product/market mix, (2) competitive analysis, and (3) distribution channels and buying factors.[15]

Figures 11.5 and 11.6 provide examples of marketing research in business marketing. The questionnaire illustrated in Figure 11.5 was developed to help

TABLE 11.5   Marketing Research Activities Conducted by Consumer and Business
Marketing Firms

	Percent Performing Each Activity	
Type of Research Activity	Consumer Companies (*n* = 143)	Business Companies (*n* = 124)
Advertising Research		
Motivation research	61	29
Copy research	78	55
Media research	72	57
Studies of ad effectiveness	86	67
Studies of competitive ad effectiveness	73	54
Business Economics and Corporate Research		
Short-range forecasting	97	98
Long-range forecasting	96	94
Studies of business trends	90	99
Pricing studies	91	90
Plant and warehouse location studies	71	78
Acquisition studies	81	89
Export and international studies	69	82
Management information system	89	90
Operations research	71	68
Internal company employees	73	80
Corporate Responsibility Research		
Consumers' "right to know" studies	21	12
Ecological impact studies	37	35
Studies of legal constraints on advertising and promotion	58	46
Social values and policies studies	47	29
Product Research		
New product acceptance and potential	89	73
Competitive product studies	97	92
Testing of existing product studies	98	86
Packaging research	91	61
Sales and Market Research		
Measurement of market potentials	99	99
Market share analysis	99	98
Determination of market characteristics	99	99
Sales analysis	98	99
Establishment of sales quotas and territories	93	95
Distribution channel studies	89	83
Test market store audits	88	36
Consumer panel operations	87	31
Sales compensation studies	83	73
Promotional studies of premiums, coupons, sampling, deals, and so on	82	36

Source: Adapted from Dik W. Twedt, ed., *1983 Survey of Marketing Research* (Chicago: American Marketing Association, 1984), 41, 43. Published by the American Marketing Association.

FIGURE 11.5   **Example of Business Marketing Research in the Distribution Area of the Marketing Mix**

MODERN MATERIALS HANDLING

Dear Materials Handling Professional:

May we have your valuable assistance in: market for **conveying equipment**? The stu vital to our understanding of this market.

Your respose is totally confidential; only enclosed a postage-paid reply envelope fo

Thank you in advance for your help. Perha filling out the survey.

BS/dlv-b875

1. Does your company use **conveying e**
   ┄ Yes   ┄ No
2. Is your company **planning** on purchas
   ┄ Yes   ┄ No
2A. If NO, is your company **considering** t
   ┄ Yes   ┄ No
If your company does not use or is not proceed to Question 5 A and B on the ne
3. Please check the facility for which you **equipment**.
   ┄ Warehouse   ┄ Shippin
4. For the following **conveying equipmer** next 18 months. Also check your reas

   Purchase plans in the next 18 month:
   Overhead Conveyors (Continuous) Up to 500 lb. Capacity
   Overhead Conveyors (Continuous) Ov 500 lb. Capacity
   Overhead Power & Free Conveyors Up to 500 lb. Capacity
   Overhead Power & Free Conveyors Over 500 lb. Capacity
   Hand Push Trolley Conveyors
   None of the above

Please answer the following questions for each piece of equipment shown at the right.

	Wheel Loader	Wheel Tractor
1. Please check the equipment your company uses at this location.	┄	┄
1A. How many of each does your company use at this location?	_____ (# Units)	_____ (# Units)
1B. What attachments are your machines equipped with? (Ex.: buckets, forks, quick couplers, booms, blades, etc.)	_____	_____
1C. What is your equipment used for?		
Bulk material handling	☐	┄
Finished goods handling	☐	┄
Utility work	☐	┄
2. Is your company planning to acquire any of these vehicles within the next 18 months?		
Yes	☐	┄
No	☐	┄

If YES . . .

2A.	Wheel Loader	Wheel Tractor
How many units will you purchase new?	_____	_____
How many units will you purchase used?	_____	_____
How many units will you short-term rent?	_____	_____
How many units will you rent/purchase?	_____	_____
How many units will you lease/purchase?	_____ (# Units)	_____ (# Units)

3. Does your company service its own equipment or does it contract outside servicing?
   ☐ In-house servicing   ☐ Outside servicing

4. Does your company use lift trucks in addition to mobile powered yard equipment?
   ☐ Yes   ☐ No

4A. In the operation of your manufacturing or non-manufacturing facilities, what type of power do you use?
   ☐ Prime Power   ☐ Standby Power   ☐ Both

Source: Reprinted by permission from *Cahners Research Services* (Newton, MA: Cahners Publishing Company, 1986), p. 5.

FIGURE 11.6   **Example of Business Marketing Research in the Product Area of the Marketing Mix**

EDN

A CAHNERS PUBLICATION • CAHNERS BUILDING, 275 WASHINGTON ST., NEWTON, MA 02158-1630 • TELEPHONE (617) 964-3030

Dear Reader:

In an effort to determine y
I am asking for your assist

Since we have selected only
participate in the study, y
complete and reliable. Pl
be treated anonymously and
We've included a postage-pa

Your cooperation is earnest

IS/mds-E911

1. Do you use threaded inserts?   [ ] Yes   [ ] No
   Do you specify them?   [ ] Yes   [ ] No
   Do you let your subcontractors supply them?   [ ] Yes   [ ] No

2. Do you use Self Tapping/Self Threading inserts? [ ] Yes [ ] No

3. What makes of these inserts have you bought in the past year?

   _____

4. Four brands of Self Tapping/Self Threading inserts are listed below. If
   you did not purchase from these companies, please check the reason(s)
   why:

COMPANY NAME TRADE NAME	CEM/SELF TAPPING INSERTS	GROOVE PIN TAP-LOK	HELICOIL TAPSERT	TRIDAIR SPEEDSERTS
Doesn't meet requirements of my application.............	[ ]	[ ]	[ ]	[ ]
Have not heard of company or product....................	[ ]	[ ]	[ ]	[ ]
Brand is unsatisfactory/ poor quality.................	[ ]	[ ]	[ ]	[ ]
Too high quality..............	[ ]	[ ]	[ ]	[ ]
Price.........................	[ ]	[ ]	[ ]	[ ]
Delivery......................	[ ]	[ ]	[ ]	[ ]
Reliability....................	[ ]	[ ]	[ ]	[ ]
High installed cost, special tooling, equipment....	[ ]	[ ]	[ ]	[ ]
No salesperson has called/ poor service.................	[ ]	[ ]	[ ]	[ ]
No local distribution.........	[ ]	[ ]	[ ]	[ ]

5. Approximate annual volume of threaded inserts:

   Quantity _____

   Dollars _____

THANK YOU VERY MUCH!

Source: Reprinted by permission from *Cahners Research Services* (Newton, MA: Cahners Publishing Company, 1986), p. 8.

the business marketer determine the best markets for his or her products. Respondents were first asked if their company used conveying equipment. They were then asked if their company was planning on buying such equipment or considering the purchase, what kinds of facilities the equipment would be used in, purchasing plans over the next eighteen months in regard to particular types of conveying equipment, etc. The purpose of the study was to determine the market potential for conveying equipment as seen by materials handling professionals in business organizations.

Figure 11.6 was developed to be used in a brand preference or awareness study to tell the business marketer how his or her product stands in the market. As the figure shows, the questionnaire attempted to determine the use of self-tapping/self-threading inserts and to determine how the company's products were rated by respondents on the basis of a number of criteria such as price, product quality, delivery, availability, etc.

PROFILE OF THE BUSINESS MARKETING RESEARCHER

The average business marketing researcher is well educated and technically competent. Studies indicate an above-average amount of education in this area: As high as 77 percent possess more than a bachelor's degree, 31 percent have a master's degree, and 17 percent have a doctorate.[16] The average researcher is well experienced in the research area, and in most cases, the present job is not the only such job held, which indicates that he or she has worked elsewhere in the marketing research area. Most research efforts are conducted for the company's sales department, primarily in the area of marketing analysis, or for the product development department. The researcher can, however, be involved in many types of field research studies. The marketing research manager reports to the marketing manager, and he or she must be able to communicate with field sales personnel, plant and production engineers, production personnel, purchasing agents, and other such technically oriented individuals. As can be seen in Figure 11.7, business marketing companies expect their marketing research managers to have good research and solid technical backgrounds with heavy job responsibilities in the product and market analysis areas.

The help-wanted advertisement in the figure implies that the business marketing researcher must have qualifications quite different from those required of his or her consumer marketing counterpart. If it is kept in mind that the business marketing researcher reports to the marketing manager and that areas of research are often determined by the latter, it can be seen that a good, technically competent marketing researcher can offer invaluable aid to the decision-making process. On the other hand, a business marketing researcher who does not possess the required research and technical background can well ruin the marketing manager with information that is not valid, not representative, or both.

FIGURE 11.7　　　Want Ad for a Business Marketing Research Manager

---

SEEKING A MARKETING RESEARCH EXECUTIVE

We are looking for a person to:

1. Establish and head a marketing research department.

2. Find new markets for existing products.

3. Identify new products for present markets.

A BS degree in Engineering and a Master's degree in Business, plus a minimum of six to eight years practical experience in the industrial field of market research would be a good background for the individual we are seeking. He or she must be experienced in instrumentation and the controls field.

This is an excellent income opportunity for that person with proper qualifications and a proven track record as a solid marketing research manager.

We are a dynamic growth company in Central Massachusetts. Please reply directly, including resume in confidence to Box Number C-1267.

THE STATUS OF MARKETING RESEARCH IN BUSINESS MARKETS

Determining the status of marketing research in business markets is an elusive task, for there is no single reference or universally accepted source. Indications are that marketing research originated in consumer marketing and is slowly finding its place in business marketing. There is, however, a lack of agreement even on this point. For example, one authority states the following:

> In the past decade or so, the techniques and personnel from consumer marketing research have found their ways into the industrial giants, where staffs and budgets have been dedicated to market analysis, new products research, copy testing, focus group sessions, and other marketing research applications commonly associated with consumer research.[17]

Another authority claims that of the three types of primary data studies (survey, observational, and experimental), only the survey method has been found acceptable in business markets. Observational and experimental methods are rarely used in business marketing research. This authority believes that the observational methods, especially panels and audits, are largely inapplicable, whereas the experimental methods are too costly and complex and often do not fit into business marketing situations.[18]

Reconciling such diverse claims is difficult and makes it hard to summarize the present status of marketing research in business marketing. Studies, however, shed light on this topic. Based on these, a number of conclusions may be drawn.

A large number of business marketing companies have formal **marketing research departments.** The previously described American Marketing Association study (see Table 11.5) found 78 percent of surveyed business marketing companies had such departments, although 19 percent had only one person assigned to them. Larger companies are much more likely to have such a department. Of surveyed firms with sales exceeding $100 million, 75 percent had formal marketing research departments. Of firms with sales under $5 million, however, only 9 percent had such departments.[19]

Marketing research budgets are much smaller in business marketing companies than in consumer marketing firms. As discussed on page 366, the American Marketing Association study found that the mean budget of business marketing firms was $379,000, compared with $1,899,000 for consumer marketing firms. Business marketing companies were found to spend approximately 0.3 percent of sales in marketing research.[20]

Business marketing researchers rely heavily on secondary data in their research efforts. This statement may be due to lower research budgets and the availability of excellent, low-cost, SIC-related information from governmental and private sources.

Primary data in business marketing research typically are collected using survey methods and are used to supplement secondary data to understand customers' buying behavior.[21] Business marketing researchers appear to turn to primary data collection when they find available secondary data are incomplete or unavailable. Personal interviews and nonstructured, nondisguised interviews of a limited number of respondents constitute the most prevalent survey approaches.[22] Interviews such as these are often conducted by company sales representatives and may not even be considered marketing research by the companies involved. The use of phone and mail surveys is also quite common. One study of sixty-eight business marketing companies found 75 percent used personal interviews, 74 percent used phone surveys, and 69 percent used mail surveys.[23] Primary data collection by **focus groups,** panels, and audits is not conducted by most business marketing firms, but there are indications that focus groups are being used by more and more business marketing firms.[24] See Exhibit 11.1.

Outside research organizations are used less by business marketers than by their consumer counterparts. The American Marketing Association study found only 24 percent of business marketing companies used outside services, compared with 49 percent of consumer marketing firms.[25]

Business marketing researchers appear to lag behind consumer researchers

---

EXHIBIT 11.1   Use of Focus Groups in Business Marketing Research

---

Beckman Instruments, a southern California manufacturer of precision instruments, used focus group interviews to generate ideas and designs for a new line of process control equipment. Beckman brought together forty-six engineers from firms that used process control equipment at a cost of cocktails plus $40 for expenses. Sessions were held after work hours to ensure three hours of uninterrupted participation by the engineers. Participants were first asked to complete a thirty- to forty-five-minute questionnaire on the process control equipment field. The remainder of each session was then spent in a tape-recorded discussion of process control equipment. Using a third-party moderator, Beckman was able to avoid being associated with the focus groups, which the company believed fostered more openness among the participating engineers. From these focus groups, Beckman obtained several useful new product ideas that were then incorporated into the new product. These included the use of a different type of process printing device, process control equipment that was more convertible to computer control, and a larger window for viewing measurement scales. The addition of these new product attributes differentiated Beckman's new product from those of competitors.

Source: Adapted from "Beckman Gets Customers to Design Its Products," *Business Week* (August 17, 1974), 52, 54.

in research analysis. This statement is especially true regarding the use of more recent and sophisticated research analysis techniques, such as analysis of variance, factor analysis, cluster analysis, multidimensional scaling, discriminant analysis, and canonical analysis.[26] Many of these techniques have their roots in the behavioral sciences and have not yet been found useful by many business marketing researchers. This lack of use may be due to an unawareness of a particular technique or a mistrust of its use as a business marketing tool.

Business marketing researchers also seem to lag behind their consumer marketing counterparts in the use of **measurement techniques** such as semantic differential, projective psychological techniques, Likert scaling, multidimensional scaling, Thurstone scaling, and the Q-sort technique.[27] The reasons that account for this lower use probably are quite similar to those that account for the lower use of analysis techniques: unawareness, mistrust, or both.

Marketing research seems to be becoming more accepted as a normal part of business marketing management.[28] At the same time, business marketing research is considerably behind consumer marketing research in terms of research techniques used. In addition, research in business markets appears to be much less formal than it is in consumer markets.

In summary, although marketing research is making inroads in business marketing, a disturbingly large portion of the work remains trivially descriptive, unnecessarily repetitive of earlier work, based on small, unrepresentative samples and overly simple assumptions, and naively unaware of real-world complexity.[29] In short, business marketing research has a long way to go to catch up with its consumer marketing counterpart. Indications are, however, that as business marketing becomes more sophisticated, it will become more and more dependent on marketing research.

CHAPTER SUMMARY

Effective marketing management requires relevant and accurate information. Business marketing managers must recognize that seeking information is a vital task and marketing research and intelligence cannot be treated as a sporadic or optional activity. Contemporary business marketing requires better information, which in turn requires adequate marketing information systems and marketing research. This chapter has developed an understanding of both of these tools as they apply specifically to business marketing.

Marketing intelligence was defined and both internal and external marketing intelligence were examined. The concept of the marketing information system (MIS) was developed with emphasis placed on the informational areas commonly found in business marketing information systems. The benefits of using such systems were then reviewed.

Marketing research was then defined and the marketing research process was outlined. Marketing research was then described as it is applied to business marketing situations. Comparisons were made between marketing research in business and consumer markets and differences examined in terms of their managerial implications. Areas of major business marketing research activities were discussed and the status of marketing research in business marketing was examined.

Business marketing companies use both marketing information systems and marketing research in collecting data to be used in marketing decision making. There are indications that the former may be used more than the latter. Business marketing companies typically have smaller research budgets, smaller research departments, and often seem to rely more on secondary data and their MIS's in their data collection efforts. Despite the second-class citizenship of marketing research in business marketing, there are indications that it is gaining in popularity and in use as informational needs become more pressing. This does not mean, however, that the MIS will decrease in use but rather that both the MIS and marketing research will increase in sophistication and effectiveness in business marketing.

KEY TERMS

data collection
external marketing intelligence
focus group
internal marketing intelligence
marketing information system (MIS)
marketing intelligence
marketing research
marketing research department

marketing research process
marketing researcher
measurement technique
outside research organization
primary data
research hypothesis
secondary data

QUESTIONS

1. Explain the fundamental differences between the marketing information system and marketing research as each apply to business marketing.
2. Explain why a business marketing research project's findings must be both valid and reliable if the marketing manager is to make decisions based on those findings. How does validity and reliability affect the outcome of the marketing research project's findings?
3. Critics of business marketing research argue that it is about ten years behind marketing research in consumer marketing and therefore it must be of much less importance in business marketing than it is in consumer marketing. Take a position on this statement.
4. What do you see as the real advantages of using an MIS in business marketing? What do you see as the major disadvantages?
5. For a marketing information system to work effectively, it must be orderly and have a design. Explain what this means and then explain what happens if an MIS lacks order and design.
6. Why is it necessary to have both internal and external data inputs in an effective marketing information system? What happens to the MIS if either is lacking?
7. Why do you believe marketing research budgets are so much smaller in business marketing than in consumer marketing? Given that the budgets are smaller, what does this mean to the business marketing researcher?
8. The following quotation is taken from the marketing literature: "The time when we put old salesman, Charlie, into the marketing research group because he can't do much harm there, has to be at an end." What does this statement mean? Why is it more true today than it ever was?
9. Of the three types of primary data studies (survey, observational, and experimental), some authorities argue that only the survey method has real application to business markets. Take a position on this statement and back up that position.
10. What do you see as the major roles of the marketing researcher in business marketing? How does the marketing researcher, for example, contribute to the effectiveness of the marketing manager? Provide specific examples to explain these roles.

NOTES

1. Donald E. Sommers, "Industrial Marketing Research Helps Develop Product/Market Strategies," *Industrial Marketing Management* 12 (1983): 2.
2. Ibid.
3. Van Mayros and Dennis J. Dolan, "Hefting the Data Load: How to Design the MIS that Works for You," *Business Marketing* 73 (March 1980): 47.
4. Committee on Definitions (compilers), *Marketing Definitions: A Glossary of Marketing Terms* (Chicago: American Marketing Association, 1960).
5. William E. Cox, Jr., *Industrial Marketing Research* (New York: Ronald Press, 1979), 3.
6. William M. Pride and O. C. Ferrell, *Marketing:*
Basic Concepts and Decisions, 4th ed. (Boston: Houghton Mifflin, 1985), 116.
7. Bruce J. Walker, Wayne Kirchmann, and Jeffrey S. Conant, "A Method to Improve Response to Industrial Mail Surveys," *Industrial Marketing Management* 16 (1987): 305.
8. Joseph H. Rabin, "Top Executives Have Low Opinion of Marketing Research, Marketers' Role in Strategic Planning," *Marketing News* 12 (October 16, 1981): 3.
9. See Bob Donath, "What Loctite Learned with Psychological Insights," *Business Marketing* 69 (July 1984): 100–134.
10. Benjamin D. Sackmary, "9 Guidelines for Industrial Marketing Research," *Marketing News* 15 (January 6, 1984): 3.

11. Rohit Deshpande and Gerald Zaltman, "A Comparison of Factors Affecting Use of Marketing Information in Consumer and Industrial Firms," *Journal of Marketing Research* 24 (February 1987): 115.

12. Dik W. Twedt, ed., *1983 Survey of Marketing Research* (Chicago: American Marketing Association, 1983), 28.

13. "Government Purchasing Data Being Resold by Private Researchers," *Marketing News* 19 (April 26, 1985): 11.

14. Ibid.

15. Sommers, op. cit.

16. "Who Is the Marketing Researcher? Is There a Chance He'll Become Company President?" *Marketing Insights* 4 (March 20, 1974): 4.

17. "Government Purchasing Data Being Resold by Private Researchers," op. cit.

18. Cox, op. cit., 420.

19. Twedt, op. cit.

20. See *Laboratory of Advertising Performance Report No. 8015.8* (New York: McGraw-Hill Research Department, 1985).

21. Twedt, op. cit., 428.

22. Ibid.

23. Barnett A. Greenberg, Jac L. Goldstucker, and Danny N. Bellenger, "What Research Techniques Are Used by Marketing Researchers in Business?" *Journal of Marketing* 41 (April 1977): 64.

24. See Robert C. Inglis, "In-Depth Data: Using Focus Groups to Study Industrial Markets," *Business Marketing* 72 (November 1987): 78–82.

25. Twedt, op. cit., 28.

26. William S. Penn, Jr., "Problem Formulation in Industrial Marketing Research," *Industrial Marketing Management* 7 (1978): 402.

27. Greenberg, Goldstucker, and Bellenger, op. cit.

28. Penn, op. cit.

29. Frederick E. Webster, Jr., "Management Science in Industrial Marketing," *Journal of Marketing* 42 (January 1978): 21.

SUGGESTED ADDITIONAL READINGS

Cox, William E., Jr. *Industrial Marketing Research.* New York: Ronald Press, 1979.

Deshpande, Rohit, and Gerald Zaltman. "A Comparison of Factors Affecting the Use of Marketing Information in Consumer and Industrial Firms." *Journal of Marketing Research* 24 (February 1987): 114–118.

Fram, Eugene H. "How Focus Groups Unlock Market Intelligence." *Business Marketing* 70 (December 1985): 80–82.

Grabowski, Donald P. "Building an Effective Competitive Intelligence System." *Journal of Business & Industrial Marketing* 2 (Winter 1987): 39–44.

Gross, Irwin. "Why All of Industry Needs Research." *Business Marketing* 72 (April 1987): 112–115.

Inglis, Robert C. "In-Depth Data: Using Focus Groups to Study Industrial Markets." *Business Marketing* 72 (November 1987): 78–82.

Krigman, Alan. *Researching Industrial Markets.* Research Triangle Park, NC: Instrument Society of America, 1984.

London, Sandra J., and Curt J. Dommeyer. "Increasing Response to Industrial Mail Surveys." *Industrial Marketing Management* 19 (1990): 235–241.

Mayros, Van, and Dennis J. Dolan. "Hefting the Data Load: How to Design the MIS that Works for You." *Business Marketing* 73 (March 1988): 47–69.

More, Roger A. "Timing of Market Research in New Industrial Product Situations." *Journal of Marketing* 48 (Fall 1984): 84–94.

Samli, A. Coskun, and John T. Metzer. "An Industrial Analysis Market Information System." *Industrial Marketing Management* 9 (1980): 237–245.

Soares, Eric J. *Cost-Effective Marketing Research.* Westport, CT: Quorum Books, 1988.

Zinkhan, George M., and Betsy D. Gelb. "Competitive Intelligence Practices of Industrial Marketers." *Industrial Marketing Management* 14 (1985): 269–275.

The Business
Marketing System

Influences on the
Business Marketing System

The Global Nature of
Business Marketing

Demand Estimation and Sales
Forecasting in Business Markets

Purchasing and Materials
Management

Organizational
Buying Behavior

Strategic Alliances and Partnering
Relationships in Business Marketing

The Standard Industrial
Classification (SIC) System

Segmentation in
Business Markets

Planning Business
Marketing Strategy

Business Marketing
Intelligence

Product
and Service
Strategy in
Business
Marketing

Channel
Strategy in
Business
Marketing

Physical
Distribution
Strategy in
Business
Marketing

Promotional
Strategy in
Business
Marketing—
Personal
Selling

Promotional
Strategy in
Business
Marketing—
Advertising
and Sales
Promotion

Pricing
Strategy in
Business
Marketing

Business Marketing
Control and Evaluation

PART FOUR

The Business Marketing Mix

′12′

Product and Service Strategy in Business Marketing

•••

The lifeblood of any successful business marketing company involves the continuous development and introduction of quality products and/or services that meet customer needs and achieve company objectives. This typically involves providing target markets with differentiated products and/or services—differentiated according to what the markets perceive as important and what is profitable to the marketer. Determining which products and/or services to offer and when to offer them is a marketing responsibility that requires close coordination with other departments such as research and development, engineering, and production. There must be coordinated efforts between all these departments to ensure that a steady flow of products and services does take place, whether they are developed internally or acquired through partnering relationships with other producers.

This chapter focuses specifically on the product and service area of the marketing mix as it relates to business marketing, with particular emphasis on the development of new products and services. The product and service area is the first area of the mix to be considered and thus sets up the following chapters, which will be devoted to distribution, promotion, and pricing of those products and services. The applications of both products and services to business markets are explored and business product/service strategy is defined. Then, comparisons between consumer and business product strategies are explored. The importance of planning in this vital area of marketing is discussed and reasons for the success and failure of business products and services are examined. The chapter then proposes a format for the development of new business products and/or services and their introduction to the marketplace. Product support activities are examined as they relate to business products, and pure business services are also discussed. The chapter concludes with a discussion of product management options used in business marketing.

Example of New Product Planning in Business Marketing

Boeing Corporation foresaw the need for a replacement product for its 727 airliner. In developing this replacement, the company's goal was to produce concepts and technology for a "next generation" airplane. In addition, it wanted to develop an airplane that would be smaller than the competition's Airbus A300 but have a longer range. Beyond these things, the company was unsure of how it should proceed. Since the cost of the effort would be about $1.5 billion, Boeing could ill afford to make a mistake with the new product. Its complex product planning process involved the following steps.

Boeing worked closely with its airline customers, having them review nine different airplane concepts and inviting their design teams on site to make certain the basic design concept met their requirements.

The firm completed the development of all new technologies in the early stages of the R & D process. When the final product was specified, there was nothing untested aboard the plane.

Boeing made extensive use of CAD/CAM to improve design quality, cut prototype development time, and reduce costs of later design changes.

The final product of this product planning process was the Boeing 767, which was designed to meet market requirements and provide leading-edge technology advantages to the user. The 767 was introduced to the market a full eight months ahead of Airbus's 310, even though both firms announced their new products within days of each other. In this case, the extensive time and effort put into product development paid off for Boeing by giving it an edge over its major competitor.

Source: Adapted from Edward G. Krubasik, "Customize Your Product Development," *Harvard Business Review* 66 (November–December, 1988): 46–52.

WHAT IS A BUSINESS PRODUCT?

From a marketing perspective, a **product** is everything that is considered inclusive of the satisfactions and utilities that the buyer obtains in the purchase.[1] For example, a manufacturing customer may wish to purchase a drill press for its production process. But that customer may also want the seller to install the drill press, train customer employees in the most efficient use of the product, and warrant its performance. In this situation, it can be seen that what is inclusive of the satisfactions and utilities purchased involves much more than just the physical product, the drill press. Thus, a product is any object, **service,** or combination of the two, offered by the producer to organizational markets. A business marketer could offer only products, only services, or some combination of the two.

Types of Business Products and Services

Chapter 1 discussed the types of products and services that exist in business marketing. It will be recalled that business products were classified in the following manner: (1) heavy equipment, (2) light equipment, (3) supplies, (4) component parts, (5) raw materials, and (6) processed materials. In addition, types of business services were also examined. These classifications form the basis of discussion in this chapter, although some variations will be examined for their product management applications.

Table 12.1 provides a useful framework for viewing the product/service area of the marketing mix. As can be seen, the decision first has to be made whether the marketing firm should produce and market exclusively products, exclusively services, or combine the two into a package that meets target market needs. Then, the decision has to be made whether the product/service offering should be a **customized product/service** or a **standardized product/service.** For example, an aerospace contractor that wants to market to the Department of Defense may have to totally customize its product to meet the very rigid specifi-

TABLE 12.1   Framework for Viewing the Product/Service Area of the Marketing Mix

Range of Customization/Standardization

	Totally Customized	Relatively Customized	Relatively Standardized	Totally Standardized
Product	Product is produced to meet specs determined by one particular customer or prospect	Product is produced to meet specs determined appropriate for whole market, and not just a single customer or prospect	Product is produced to meet the requirements of a variety of markets with minor modifications where necessary	Product is produced to meet the general requirements of a wide spectrum of markets
Service	Service is developed to meet the specific needs of one particular customer or prospect	Service is developed to meet the unique needs of a whole market, and not just a single customer or prospect	Service is developed to meet the requirements of a variety of markets with minor modifications where necessary	Service is developed to meet the general requirements of a wide spectrum of markets
Product & Service	Product and accompanying service are developed to meet the specific needs of one particular customer or prospect	Product and accompanying service are developed to meet the unique needs of a whole market, and not just a single customer or prospect	Product and accompanying service are developed to meet the requirements of a variety of markets with minor modifications where necessary	Product and accompanying service are developed to meet the general requirements of a wide spectrum of markets

cations of the customer. In this situation, the customer decides what the product will be and the supplier's product must meet those requirements or it will not be considered. On the other end of the spectrum, a producer of computer paper used by many different types of organizational customers may produce a very standardized product—one that easily meets the needs of many different customers or prospects. As the table shows, there are also variations between these custom and standard poles.

Some examples may help to better understand these variations. A producer of building materials that finds that its products will have to meet industry codes in order to be accepted is an example of a relatively customized product. A software company that provides packaged accounting programs that may be used by almost any type of business is an example of totally standardized service. A manufacturer of industrial robots used in production processes that also provides maintenance contracts might be an example of a relatively customized product and service. It is, of course, possible to market more than one type of product and/or service at the same time. For example, Toledo Kitchen Machines, a producer of commercial kitchen equipment, sold basically the same equipment in totally customized, relatively customized, relatively standardized, and totally standardized versions to completely different markets all at the same time. Thus, it can be seen that a business marketer may elect to market only products, only services, or combinations of the two and these may be sold in customized or standardized forms depending on requirements of organizational markets.

BUSINESS PRODUCT STRATEGY

Business product and/or service strategy involves such matters as determining a company's basic product policies, establishing specific product objectives that are consistent with previously defined marketing objectives, determining which types of products and/or services are to be manufactured and marketed, and establishing product lines. Once these decisions have been made, tactical programs are implemented to carry out the predetermined strategy. These programs often include determining specific products and/or services to be produced, developing their specifications, establishing brand names and trademarks, determining adequate packaging, and considering specific **product support** services such as warranties, technical assistance, and postsale servicing. Viewed from an overall perspective, **product strategy** ranges all the way from broad product policies to specific grades, models, and sizes to be produced and specific services to be performed.

Thus, the marketing manager is responsible for the following areas of product and/or service planning and strategy in business markets:

1. Establishing product and/or service policies.
2. Setting product and/or service objectives.

3. Searching out new product and/or service additions, including those acquired by mergers or other partnering relationships.

4. Determining product and/or service specifications.

5. Introducing new products and/or services.

6. Modifying existing products and/or services.

7. Dropping old products and/or services.

8. Maintaining the product and/or service line.

9. Packaging the products.

10. Providing the necessary technical assistance and presale and postsale product support activities necessary to meet the requirements of business customers and prospects.

An important point must be made here. The product area of business marketing must not be viewed as a given or uncontrollable element in the marketing mix. The manager must remember that the marketplace is the fundamental reason for the existence of any product or service. Once the product or service fails to fulfill a need in the marketplace, its sales will decline and its marketability may be finished. Far too many business marketing managers and product managers have a tendency to see business marketing as those activities that take place in distribution, promotion, and pricing *after* the product or service has been developed. This thinking is faulty and involves a product rather than a market orientation. The manager must always remember that intelligent product strategy is dependent on good market input, just as are the other three marketing substrategies of channels, promotion, and price.

A good example of this market-driven orientation in product strategy can be found in Black & Decker's Professional Products Division's move into a line of industrial lubricants and chemical products developed for professional equipment. Black & Decker is a well-known manufacturer of power tools, and the addition of the lubricant chemical line of products represented a major change in product strategy. The reason for this change was explained by a company spokesperson, who stated, "We found that professional user interest is shifting from hardware store products to premium, high-performance lubricants. We are committed to growth in both the base power tool accessory business plus entering new business opportunities which offer high growth potential. When proper fits are found, we are moving quickly to seize the opportunities." [2]

Differences Between Business and Consumer Product and/or Service Strategies

Product strategy by definition is basically the same in both consumer and business markets, although practices may differ considerably because of the characteristics of the products and the customers involved. Table 12.2 illustrates some of the basic differences that may be found between producers of consumer goods and producers of business goods. As can be seen, service plays an important role

TABLE 12.2   Comparison of Product and/or Service Strategy Factors
in the Consumer and Business Markets

Factor	Consumer Markets	Business Markets
Importance of product area in marketing mix	Important but can at times be overshadowed by price or promotion	Very important, at times more important than any other single mix element
Demand	Product designed for satisfaction of direct consumer demand	Product must consider derived and joint demand in addition to direct demand
Buyer/user of the product and/or service	Buyer and user often the same person	Buyer and user often not the same person or in same department
Specifications	More general even with large products	Product often designed to business customers' specifications
Product and/or service life cycles	Often short due to fads, fashion, changing consumer expectations	Often longer, especially for traditional business products, but shorter for high-tech products
Product support activities	Important in some large consumer products but nonexistent in many others	Often critical as many business customers include support in buying specifications
Packaging	Both protective and promotional	Primarily protective with minimal promotional packaging
Aesthetic characteristics such as color and shape	Often essential to product success	Usually not important with majority of products
Failure rate of new products	Often high; estimates are as high as 80% or more	Lower, rates of 30%–40% are common
Importance of marketing research	Often a major factor in new product and/or service development	Usually not that dominant a factor in new product and/or service development

in industrial marketing, especially presale service. Organizational customers consider technical assistance and other presale support activities as important aspects of product strategy. Product support activities such as customer employee training, installation, mobile repair units, and loaner equipment often permit a business marketer to differentiate product offerings from those of competitors.

Although exceptions can be found, product life cycles appear to be longer in business markets than in consumer markets. Even with derived demand, most business products and services enjoy longer life cycles than their consumer counterparts, where fads and fashion are often so important.

Specifications often play a different role in business marketing. Although specifications are involved in the production and distribution of all products, their importance seems greater in business markets. Most consumers do not buy based on specifications, whereas most organizational customers do. This fact is true of commodity products and services as well as specialty ones. In addition, many business market specialty products are manufactured precisely to customers' specifications, as was discussed earlier.

The failure rates of new business products appear to be lower than those recorded for consumer products. Studies have shown that failure rates in some consumer markets exceed 80 percent, whereas similar studies in business markets show such rates to be between 30 percent and 40 percent. This difference may be because business marketers often have fewer customers and may understand their needs better. As well, it may also occur because business marketers traditionally have paid a lot of attention to the product area in developing their marketing mixes.

Market research seems to play a lesser role in business markets than in consumer markets, especially in the more technical industries. The reasons for this difference are many, but generally products in such industries are developed by inhouse engineering and R & D departments, which possess the technical sophistication necessary to develop such products but often do not believe the same level of customer sophistication exists for these products.

Another difference is in the area of product packaging. Business product packaging is generally more of a protective nature than of a promotional nature, although the latter has become quite popular in off-the-shelf OEM products sold through industrial distributors and goods sold to wholesalers and retailers.

Other differences between product strategy in the two markets arise at times in this chapter, with the point being that business marketing product strategy decisions differ from those found in the consumer market even though the basic principles are similar. As has already been shown, product characteristics and the characteristics of business customers almost of necessity dictate a different approach to the products sold into business markets.

THE IMPORTANCE OF PRODUCT PLANNING

With few exceptions, sound product and service planning are essential to continued success in business markets. Referring to the discussion of marketing strategy in Chapter 10, four options exist: (1) a market penetration strategy—seeking more customers in present markets for existing products and services; (2) a product development strategy—developing new products and services for present markets; (3) a market development strategy—finding new markets for existing products and services; and (4) a diversification strategy—developing new products and services for new markets. These options are directly related to product and/or service strategy in one manner or another. For example, new products can be developed within a company through research and development activities, or new products can be acquired through mergers and acquisitions of other producers.

By examining these four strategy options, it can be seen that **product planning** is an essential element in effective marketing management. Unless the marketing manager can generate a stream of successful **new products or services** over time, the potential of his or her company is limited. Few business marketing companies can exist permanently by selling only existing products or services to present or new customers. With market saturation and relatively high rates of technical product obsolescence, it becomes virtually impossible to succeed with only market penetration or market development strategies. In addition, acquisition typically cannot be counted on as a single source of new products or services. Antitrust problems, the reluctance of companies to be absorbed, and image differences of merged companies hamper this approach. Thus, product planning is imperative for most business marketing companies' continued successes. It should be recognized, however, that new product development does not usually mean completely new inventions but rather improvements of existing products and services. Thus, invention and acquisition are not likely to become the major sources of new products. Most business products are created through an evolutionary process of change and adaptation in response to the needs and opportunities of the marketplace.[3]

Thus, to be successful, the business marketing manager must recognize the need for new products and/or services in the marketing strategy. Naturally, the manager should continue to expand the customer base for existing products and services and pursue strategic alliances and partnerships as was covered in Chapter 7 if they are consistent with overall marketing and product objectives. However, somewhere in the product strategy and the marketing plan, the manager must emphasize new product development. Failing to do so may be tantamount to marketing disaster; thus, product planning is critically important to the business marketing manager.

Although all these points appear to be common sense, in actual business markets they often are overlooked, as marketing managers become obsessed with marketing their present products and services and are not prepared to replace those when demand decreases or ceases to exist. In other words, they are often caught unaware by competitive moves. As a result, marketing managers are often placed on the defensive in their strategy, which is not where any aggressive marketing manager wishes to be.

Product planning is especially important in business marketing for the reasons explained in the following sections.

Increased Competition

Because of increased domestic and global competition, today's organizational buyers have more choice in their purchasing. New materials, new processes, new technologies, and new sources of supply place great strain on the business marketing manager as regards product and/or service strategy. Depending on the industry, anywhere from one-third to three-quarters of the sales of most business firms are accounted for by products or services that did not exist ten to fifteen years ago. These changes place great responsibility on the marketing manager and those responsible for product planning to keep the company contemporary. The move toward global markets by business marketers has increased competitive pressures on U.S. business marketing managers. American producers of business goods and services compete with foreign producers in both the U.S. market and international markets.

Derived Demand

Derived demand forces the marketing manager to pay close attention to product and/or service planning. In an era in which ultimate consumer wants and needs are changing faster than ever before, this situation has profound effects on the demand for business goods and services used to produce goods sold into the consumer market. The business marketing manager cannot be complacent about the product line, even if business customers seemingly are satisfied.

Increased Purchasing Sophistication

As was developed in Chapter 5, purchasing professionals and other buying influences are becoming increasingly sophisticated in their buying. Product quality and performance are judged harshly by professionals using vendor analysis, value analysis, and the latest computer methods. For example, suppliers undergo extensive analysis in regard to the performance of their products; thus defects and other nonperformances become part of a continuous record system. With such detailed analyses, product planning is essential if the products and/or services delivered are to meet buyer expectations. Movements toward just-in-time purchasing by organizational customers have also exerted pressure on marketing managers to increase their product and/or service planning. One of the ramifications of JIT is that customers substantially reduce their numbers of suppliers and create close relationships with those they keep.[4] Given the importance of product quality in business markets, it is logical to conclude that such buyers will eliminate those present suppliers with questionable product or service planning.

Labor-Saving Requirements

American industry is quite sensitive to rising labor intensity and costs. In their purchasing, organizational customers are constantly seeking labor savings in equipment and materials. Purchases are viewed with this point in mind, and customers will switch to competitors' products or services for labor-saving reasons, even if they otherwise are reasonably satisfied with their present ones. This demand for labor savings by business customers has placed great stress on product planning, especially in firms selling to user customers.

Energy-Saving Requirements

Since the mid-1970s, the United States has been experiencing energy crises in the form of decreased energy availability and increased costs of available energy. Business customers are constantly looking for products and services that reduce energy consumption in their operating processes. Studies have shown that organizational buyers and buying influences are quite interested in such factors as economy of operation and cost savings in operation.[5] Product planning must accommodate these buying pattern changes if the manager is to continue to sell products to such customers.

Costs of Business Product Failures

Considerable cost is involved in a business **product failure.** A new product may mean a new plant, new equipment, new materials, and new labor, all of which must be covered even if the new product fails. Convair Aerospace Division of General Dynamics lost more than $450 million in the failures of its 880 and 990 jetliners.[6] Eaton Corporation spent thirteen years developing its airbag business for the auto industry and lost $20 million in the venture.[7] Exxon lost $15 million trying to produce electric motor controls.[8] The high costs of product failures have placed great emphasis on product planning in business markets.

Failure Rate of Business Products

New business products are risky and subject to failure. A number of studies found that about 30 percent to 40 percent of all new business products fail.[9] Adding this fatality rate to the high costs of product failure should impress on the marketing manager the need for careful and effective product planning.

Reasons such as these clearly illustrate why effective product and/or service planning is crucial in business marketing. Recognizing the strategic importance of new products and services, business marketing firms are consciously developing new product and service strategies as a key facet of their overall corporate plans.[10]

Another indicator of the importance of product and service planning can be seen in the Marketing Science Institute's "Top Ten Research Issues for 1990–1992." This organization sees improving processes for developing new products and services as the fourth most important research issue because of compressed life cycles, rapid technological change, and accelerated new product introduction by global competitors.[11]

Now that the importance of effective product and/or service planning has been established, it may be worthwhile to look at the reasons why new products and services fail in business markets. Then a process will be developed for introducing new products and services into business markets—a process that will address the reasons for failure.

SUCCESS AND FAILURE OF BUSINESS PRODUCTS AND SERVICES

If business marketing firms are to survive and prosper, marketing managers must become astute in selecting new product and service winners and effective in managing the new product process from idea to launch.[12] Investigating successes and failures is imperative if product management is to be effective. Many of the factors separating winners from losers are within the control of the firm.[13] Analysis is necessary if the marketing manager is to learn from experience—to emphasize those factors found relevant to product and service success and to avoid those determined to be related to failure. A number of studies provide insight into both types of factors. It may be beneficial to look at the results of some of these studies and understand the product planning implications.

Factors Influencing New Product Success

What factors seem to affect new product success in a positive manner? If these factors can be isolated, then the marketing manager can concentrate on them when marketing new products or services. A successful product is often defined as one that meets management's objectives. Why is it that some products meet their objectives and others do not?

A study of 200 new business products (successes and failures) introduced by some 100 companies revealed three major factors that differentiated winners from losers. These factors were (1) superiority of the new product, (2) strong market orientation and marketing proficiency, and (3) superior technological and production capabilities.[14] Superiority of the product meant superiority over competing products in terms of better meeting customer needs, unique features not found in competitive offerings, high quality, the product's ability to perform unique tasks, innovativeness, and lower cost to the customer. Strong marketing was characterized by good research prior to product development, good understanding of the market, strong marketing and distribution efforts, and guidance by knowledgeable marketing people. Superior technological and production capabilities implied that the company had a strong and compatible engineering and production base for the new product. These characteristics were found in the product successes that were studied but they were not found with failures.

Another study of new products introduced by business marketing companies in Australia revealed the major determinants of success to be the following: (1) new product synergy with existing company marketing skills, (2) new product synergy with existing company technical and manufacturing skills, (3) high product quality, (4) product offered significant user benefits, (5) appropriate target marketing and pricing, and (6) good distribution channel support.[15] Synergy referred to the fit between the product and company capabilities. For example, if a new product could easily be sold by existing company salespeople, the success rate might be higher than if new salespeople had to be hired and trained to sell the product. Similarly, if the new product were compatible with existing technical skills, the product had a better chance of success than if those skills had to be learned.

Still another research project found three dimensions of new product success: (1) financial performance, (2) market impact, and (3) opportunity window.[16] The financial performance dimension included relative profits and sales of the product, profit level, payback period, and the meeting of sales and profit objectives. Market impact was comprised of the impact of the product in both foreign and domestic markets in terms of market shares. Opportunity window involved the degree to which the new product opened up opportunities in terms of other products or market areas. Within each of these dimensions, components were found that were highly correlated with new product success. Some of the major components were well-defined customer needs before the product launch, product was seen as superior to competitive products, high-quality product, strong fit between the product and the company's technical abilities, clearly defined target market, and the product's ability to perform unique tasks for the customer.

Looking at all three studies, it appears that certain factors positively affect new product and service success. As may be suspected, high-quality offerings are more likely to succeed than lower-quality products in business markets. If the product or service is perceived as superior to competitive offerings by customers in the target market, it is more likely to succeed. The product that better meets customer needs and offers benefits not found in competitive products stands a better chance of succeeding. In addition, the better the fit between the new product and the company's technical and marketing expertise, the more likely the product will succeed. Finally, new product success is enhanced when competent and skillful marketing personnel direct the product launch. These factors reinforce the PIMS contention that high product quality is the key to marketing success. The factors also reemphasize the value of a sound marketing information system that provides valid and reliable data pertinent to product and service needs in the market.

Factors Influencing New Product Failure

Just as it is useful to analyze new product successes, it is also of value to look critically at failures. The most common definition of a product or service failure is one that fails to meet its objectives. As stated earlier, the failure rate of business products is between 30 percent and 40 percent. In other words, about one of every three new business products introduced ends in failure. However, the fact that twice as many succeed as fail is considered better than the average in the consumer market. Still, a failure rate of one in three may be too high when the costs of a business product failure are considered. A look at the causes of business product failure is in order.

A study of 114 Canadian business product failures found four general reasons for such failures: (1) sales fell below expectations, (2) profit margins fell below expectations, (3) development costs exceeded expectations, and (4) investment exceeded expectations.[17] Of the four, failure to meet sales objectives was the most cited of the general reasons, followed by failure to meet profit objectives, high development costs, and higher investment required than anticipated. Looking past the general reasons, the study detailed those factors most likely to contribute to new product failure. These factors are (1) competition was tougher than anticipated, (2) market size was less than estimated, (3) product price was too high, (4) product had design or technical problems, (5) marketing efforts were misdirected in terms of target markets or buying influences, (6) product had no competitive advantages, (7) product did not meet customer specifications, and (8) insufficient marketing efforts. Also see Exhibit 12.1.

The previously mentioned study of new Australian business products found somewhat similar reasons for explaining product failures.[18] These factors were

(1) market was too competitive, (2) insufficient market information prior to the launch, (3) product was not new or different to the market, (4) product offered no real benefits over competing products, (5) inadequate sales efforts, and (6) inadequate promotion and advertising.

These studies when viewed collectively indicate that most reasons for new product or service failure are marketing reasons—not production or technical reasons. In both studies, failures appear to be caused by some manner of poor marketing rather than poor production, R & D, or engineering. The studies show that product failures can be analyzed, causes discovered, and action taken to avoid them in the future.

EXHIBIT 12.1   **Anatomy of a Business Product's Demise—The Case of U.S. Industrial Robots**

Probably no business product caught the imagination of business marketers in the United States to the degree that industrial robots did. Robotics was expected to supply the competitive edge for U.S. manufacturers against foreign competitors. In addition, their use would re-employ blue-collar workers and raise up depressed rust belt communities with training centers and recharged industries. Industry expectations were that 100,000 robots would be in operation by 1990 in a business worth $1 billion in annual sales.

When 1990 came and went, however, these rosy predictions had not materialized. Only 38,000 robots were in use in the United States and 1989 sales were only $500 million. General Motors, the largest U.S. user of such robots, had 8,000 in use, compared to the 20,000 it expected to be using by 1990. Many U.S. manufacturers who had pioneered the product were no longer in the business or had been taken over by foreign competitors. Cincinnati Milicron, once the largest U.S. manufacturer of robots, sold its line to a subsidiary of Asea Brown Boveri, AG, of Zurich, Switzerland, after three straight years of losing money or breaking even.

What went wrong? What would cause such a promising industry to fail? There are a number of reasons that collectively caused the collapse: (1) U.S. manufacturers expected large sales in a short period of time and were not as patient as their Japanese competitors. They expected immediate returns, which was not feasible with the selling of expensive robotics systems; (2) U.S. manufacturers failed to realize that robots could not do everything that people could; (3) they failed to understand that a customer's entire manufacturing process often had to be redesigned to make the robots profitable; and (4) they focused too heavily on the U.S. auto industry and thus became entangled in the decline of that industry. When the auto industry took a dive and firms cut back on their capital expenditures, robot sales were affected.

The result of all this is that while the robotics market is expected to continue to expand, it will be dominated by foreign firms, particularly Japanese producers. Only a handful of small U.S. manufacturers survived and they focused primarily on specific applications. Thus, it can be seen that the failure of U.S. producers to maintain market share in an industry they actually pioneered was due to some basic market errors—too narrow a market, too short a time frame, a lack of understanding of the impact of their products on customer requirements, and strong foreign competitors.

Source: Adapted from Stephen Franklin, "U.S. Dreams for Robotics Turn from Boom to Rust," *San Diego Union*, October 28, 1990, I1, I12.

Examples of Business Product Failures

Examples of business product failures may add substance to this discussion. One of the best-known failures was Corfam, a synthetic leather substitute developed by DuPont. DuPont spent some thirteen years in the laboratory trying to develop a synthetic material that could serve as a substitute for leather in the making of shoes. Corfam was removed from the market in 1970, seven or eight years after its introduction. Three reasons accounted for the product's demise: (1) a domestic shoe market flooded by foreign-made leather shoes priced lower than those made of Corfam, (2) increased domestic competition, and (3) an overall slump in retail shoe sales in the country.[19] The company was estimated to have spent millions of dollars on Corfam up to the time it was withdrawn from the marketplace. It is interesting to note that this failure follows the same lines as the Canadian study: Corfam's failure was due to an overestimation of market size and an underestimation of competition.

After spending thirteen years and $20 million, Eaton Corporation dropped out of the business of providing airbags to the automotive industry. The decision to drop the product was prompted by three factors.[20] First, most automakers fought the passive restraint ruling of the U.S. Department of Transportation, which caused a governmental delay in enforcing the requirement. Second, public doubts were created about the effectiveness of such airbag safety devices. Third, Eaton came to believe that when passive safety restraints were required, auto manufacturers would opt for automatic seat belts rather than airbags.

Exxon suffered a product failure with its alternating current synthesizer, a product that enabled the amount of electricity used by electric motors to be reduced when work loads varied. The target market was comprised of industrial firms using electric motors to power pumps, fans, and conveyor systems. Competitors already offered similar products at prices ranging from $200 to $350 per motor horsepower. Exxon planned to price its new product at $50 per motor horsepower and thereby segment the market on the basis of price. After spending $15 million in R & D, buying Reliance Electric to produce the product, and initiating a promotional campaign while the product was still in the laboratory, the company dropped the idea of marketing the product. Exxon was unable to rectify reliability and cost problems brought about when the company attempted to move into large-scale production.[21]

Factors Influencing New Service Success

What factors seem to affect success in new business services and are these different from those that positively affect new products? Until recently, there was little research conducted on the success and failure of new business services but a study of 150 successes and 126 failures has shed some light on this subject.[22] This study revealed that success factors for new services are not that different from those for new products. Some of the major success factors are: (1) the marketing company has a strong marketing orientation and has a sound understanding of customer needs; (2) the service is innovative and provides customers with superior quality; (3) the service is unique in the eyes of customers; (4) the service matches the firm's expert capabilities and reputation; and (5) there is a high growth rate in the market. These factors suggest that sound marketing practices have a definite effect on new service success, just as with business products.

Factors Influencing New Service Failures

The previously mentioned study also looked at business service failures and found a number of factors that relate to such failure. Again, many of these factors are similar to those relative to new product failure. Some common contributors to failure are: (1) lack of clearly defined markets; (2) lack of a formal new service development process; (3) lack of effective internal communication within the marketing company and lack of involvement of front-line personnel in the development process; (4) lack of testing in the marketplace before market entry; (5) too much reliance on independent intermediaries to perform the service; (6) lack of control of costs; and (7) inability to maintain a competitive edge when new competition emerges. In addition, since services are different from physical products in terms of tangibility, heterogeneity, simultaneity, and perishability, other factors were also involved. For example, new services are likely to fail when they are so abstract that potential customers have difficulty understanding them. In addition, they may fail when customers can't evaluate their quality because of the heterogeneity. Finally, services may fail when their demands vary appreciably because, unlike products, they cannot be stored for future use. Thus, it appears that new business services fail for many of the same reasons that products do but they may also be affected by other factors because of the basic differences between services and products that relate to heterogeneity, intangibility, simultaneity, and perishability.

This discussion of successes and failures of new business products and services emphasizes the importance of sound planning, whether products or services are involved. It is now time to discuss the new product/service planning process as it applies to business marketing.

THE PLANNING PROCESS FOR NEW PRODUCTS OR SERVICES

With product and service failure rates of between 30 percent and 40 percent and the high cost of failure, a company cannot simply produce and market all new product or service suggestions it receives. A formal **new product/service planning process** should be employed so that new ideas are handled systematically and effectively. Typically, there is no shortage of such suggestions in business marketing. They may come from company salespeople, engineering personnel, production people, suppliers, channel intermediaries, business partners, purchasing agents, and top management. Unless these ideas are handled efficiently, they can be overwhelming. On the other hand, such suggestions cannot simply be dismissed out of hand because some may have good potential. The new product or service planning process attempts to address both of these concerns. It should allow the ruling out of infeasible ideas early in the process and yet permit the most efficient allocation of resources to those ideas with potential. The end result of such a process is that those products and services that finally reach the market have the best chance of becoming successful.

Figure 12.1 illustrates the steps in the conceptual new product or service planning model. This model outlines clearly the logical sequence of activities that should occur between soliciting new ideas and actual introduction in the market. As the figure shows, the following steps are involved:

Idea generation. The purpose of **idea generation** is to generate a steady and reliable flow of new product or service ideas that may then be considered for possible adoption.

Basic screening. The purpose of **basic screening** is to develop and implement an objective and orderly assessment of new product or service ideas

FIGURE 12.1   **The New Product/Service Planning Process**

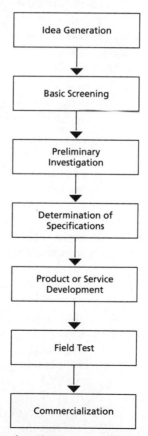

Source: Adapted from "Flow of Product Planning in an Industrial Products Company," *Sales Forecasting* (New York: The Conference Board, Inc., 1978), 170.

so as not to discard good ideas or to spend inordinate amounts of time, effort, and money on ideas with little or no chance of commercial success.

Preliminary investigation. The purpose of this step is to explore in more depth those ideas that have been found worthy of further consideration following the basic screening. This step applies only to those ideas that pass the screening step.

Determination of specifications. The purpose of this step is to determine a detailed and precise definition of the characteristics desired in the new product or service by customers and prospects.

Product or service development. The purpose of this step is to produce and laboratory test a prototype of the product based on the specifications determined in the previous step. In the case of services, this involves the determination of what will need to be offered to meet the predetermined specifications.

Field test. The purpose of a **field test** is to produce a limited number of products and operate them under actual conditions so as to test product performance and customer reactions so that changes may be made if necessary. In the case of services, this involves actually performing the services for a limited number of present or potential customers to also determine what, if any, changes need to be made.

Commercialization. The purpose of this step is to introduce to the market the new product or service that will meet customer and prospect expectations and provide sufficient quantities to meet demand.

The sequence of activities involved in Figure 12.1 typically are viewed in a "go–no go" manner since the model is basically a filtering out system. For example, a new product idea may be dropped in the screening stage because it is inconsistent with corporate objectives, or a product idea may pass the screening stage but be discarded if specifications cannot be determined. A product idea might be thrown out later in the process because it fails in the field test step. Those products or services that pass successfully through the sequence are those that are thought to have the best chances of success. Through the use of a process such as this, the business marketing firm attempts to weed out those products or services that are most likely to fail.

One other point should be understood here. The new product or service planning process rarely involves only marketing. In the case of a new product idea, such departments as production, engineering, and research and development are typically involved closely since they must ultimately engineer and manufacture the actual product under consideration. In the case of a new service idea, close coordination will be required with company personnel who will be involved in carrying it out. Rarely, if ever, is the new product or service planning process the exclusive domain of the business marketer.

Figure 12.2 illustrates the new product planning process for a producer of industrial products. Upon analysis, it can be seen that this figure is really an elaboration of the basic process that was shown in Figure 12.1. This figure also shows

FIGURE 12.2   Flow of Product Planning in an Industrial Products Company

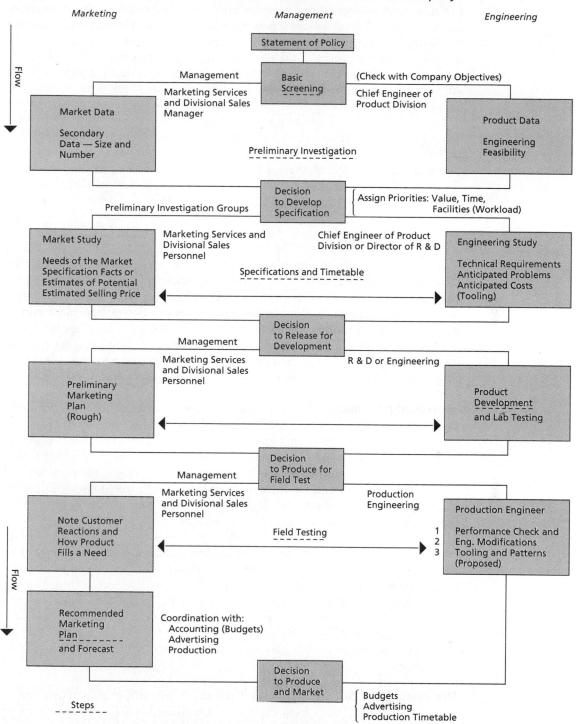

Source: Reprinted by permission from The Conference Board, *Sales Forecasting* (New York: The Conference Board, Inc., 1978), 170.

the close relationship needed between marketing and engineering, production, and research and development if new product success is to be achieved. Both the marketing and technical personnel have responsibilities in new product planning at each step in the process. In the field testing step, for example, these different responsibilities are easily seen. Marketing's task is to note customer reactions with the new product while the technical departments check performance and engineering modifications. The result of such integration in the process is that products that are finally released to the market must have passed the close scrutiny of both marketing and technical personnel and should have a high likelihood of succeeding. Since, as has been discussed, about two of every three new business products succeed, there is reason to believe that the process does work. Since this planning process is so vital to the success of new products and services, a more detailed coverage of each step is in order.

Idea Generation

As Figure 12.1 shows, the entire new product or service planning process is dependent on a steady flow of ideas. Without a sufficient number of ideas for possible products or services, the process will grind to a halt. Thus, developing methods to encourage the submission of ideas is a primary task for the business marketing manager. Ideas should flow to the firm not by chance but by design and from those sources most likely to offer substantive ideas. This means that the marketing manager must first decide which sources to tap for new ideas, and then determine how best to get those same sources to cooperate.

Sources of New Ideas   There are many possible sources of new product ideas, some internal and others external.[23] Figure 12.3 illustrates some commonly used sources in business marketing. Internally, new product or service ideas could be sought from research and development, salespeople, telemarketing, top management, and other employees within the company. For example, the research and development department, by virtue of its pure research role, may well develop ideas for possible products. Similarly, field salespeople may see opportunities that could be filled with new products or services.

Externally, a large number of possible sources exist. Customers and prospects, suppliers, channel intermediaries, trading partners, competitors, and independent inventors all could, in one way or another, offer possible ideas for new products or services. In addition, ideas might also be discovered from reading trade publications, attending trade shows, belonging to trade associations, conducting marketing research surveys, and contacting government agencies, such as the U.S. patent office. Using an organized approach to obtain ideas from all these types of sources, a business marketing manager could develop a base to draw from.

Stimulating the Sources to Submit Ideas   While the sources illustrated in Figure 12.3 are probably most capable of supplying ideas for new products or services, that does not mean that they will do so! For example, customers may

FIGURE 12.3   Sources of New Business Product or Service Ideas for Input to the Screening Process

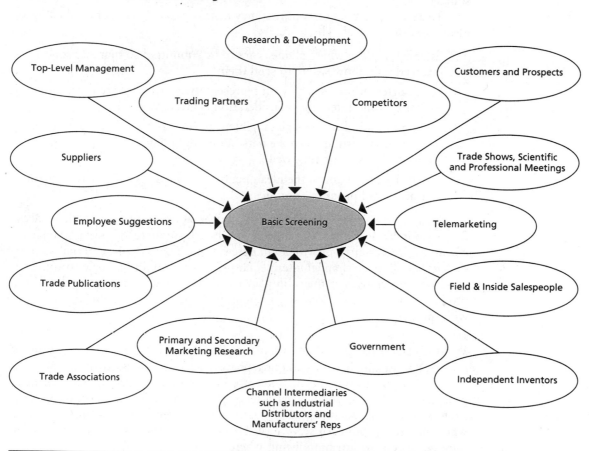

have ideas about what products or services a supplier might offer but they may never take the time or effort to communicate these to the supplier. Similarly, an industrial distributor may also have good ideas but may never be asked or, if asked, may either refuse to cooperate or simply ignore the request. Even with internal sources, there is typically no assurance that employees will offer such ideas if there is no incentive to do so. There has to be a receptive corporate climate within the marketing firm if new ideas are to be attracted. There are four conditions necessary to create such a climate: (1) management must have an expressed need for ideas as a requisite for growth; (2) contributors must believe that their suggestions will not be rejected before being thoroughly thought through; (3) management must be willing to consider all ideas; and (4) contributors must be recognized for their efforts.[24] If these factors are missing, potential contributors will not submit ideas because they will not feel it is worth the effort.

Thus, it can be seen that part of a successful idea generation program involves the manager truly wanting such ideas and communicating this to the various sources.

There are a number of steps that may be taken to help encourage the flow of ideas from the sources. These are:[25]

1. Establish a place where all ideas are to be submitted so that everyone involved will know where to send them.

2. Set up orientation sessions with representatives from different departments so that full and integrated consideration is given to all ideas.

3. Respond to all ideas in some tangible way such as by phone, in writing, by a personal visit, etc., so the person offering the idea knows it has been received and is being reviewed.

4. Credit the originator of the idea openly if the idea does ultimately end up in a successful product or service.

Finally, some form of incentive should be considered to help elicit ideas. Employee incentives include cash, contests, or corporate recognition, so internal incentives are easier to provide than external incentives. With external sources such as suppliers or channel intermediaries, efforts should be made to convince these organizations that they too gain when the marketing firm develops new products and services. Contests, recognition, and awards might also be used with these types of sources.

Methods Used to Solicit New Ideas   Soliciting ideas from the diverse sources is basically an intelligence-gathering process as was discussed in Chapter 11. Some of the more common methods used to find new ideas include: (1) focus groups with selected suppliers, customers, prospects, etc.; (2) brainstorming sessions with top management, employees, etc.; (3) reverse brainstorming sessions where negative product or service attributes provoke discussion on new ideas or improvements; (4) attribute listing where the existing attributes of a new idea are discussed by respondents and modified until a new combination of attributes emerges; (5) forced relationships where new product ideas are discussed in pairs by selected respondents, thus deriving even more ideas from the comparison; and (6) problem inventory analyses where customers, prospects, etc., are asked to discuss the problems of a general product or service category and then make suggestions regarding the solution of these problems.[26] Through the use of methods such as these, selected sources are encouraged to supply ideas for new products or services that then pass on to the screening step of the overall process.

Basic Screening

The screening of new product or service proposals is the first critical evaluation in the new product process. It is the initial decision to commit, or not to commit, resources to a new project. Screening involves an objective and orderly assessment of new product or service ideas, as no company wants to throw out good ideas, nor does it want to spend inordinate amounts of time, money, and effort on ideas that never materialize into commercial successes. The magnitude of this problem may be seen in an example. International Minerals and Chemical Corporation found that 540 new product ideas resulted in one commercial success. After screening the 540 ideas, only ninety were considered appropriate. Of these, only nine showed good laboratory evaluation tests, and only one of those nine finally was successful.[27] The real contribution of the screening process in this case was to eliminate the 450 product ideas that were unworthy of real consideration, so that time and resources could be allocated to those that were.

One approach to screening consists of four elements: (1) developing a list of criteria (factors thought to be relevant to the company considering the launch of a new product or service) against which the screening will take place, (2) weighting the importance of each criterion, (3) developing descriptive statements to be used with each criterion to illustrate the range from optimal to worst-case situations, and (4) determining a rating scale so that each criterion can be rated.[28]

Exhibit 12.2 provides an example of this approach to screening. Based on the weightings assigned to the five criteria and the ratings given on each by the marketer, the analysis indicates that product idea 4 is seen as most promising, followed by ideas 1, 5, 3, and 2. If all five product ideas exceed minimum screening requirements and the company can only pick one, product idea 4 should be selected. However, changing of the weightings can bring about a different decision. This simple approach is often seen as beneficial in that it provides a basis for ranking new ideas in an organized fashion.

No single set of criteria is universally used to screen new product or service ideas in business markets. Studies have shown different results in terms of what marketing managers believe to be important in such screening processes. For example, one study found marketability, durability, productive ability, and potential to be the major screening criteria.[29] Another found marketability, product/company fit, and market opportunity to be basic screening criteria.[30] A more recent study found four criteria to be dominant: (1) financial potential—expected ROI, rapid sales growth, market growth, and high expected market share; (2) corporate synergy—compatibility of product or service idea with firm's present business, resources, abilities, and general fit of firm in the market involved; (3) technical synergy—compatibility of idea with firm's engineering/design resources, known production processes, and production facilities; and (4) differential advantage—product or service idea would make firm first in market, would have clear advantages over competitors, would develop a high-quality product or service, and so on.[31] Although the study results differ somewhat, there is also considerable agreement, and the following criteria are commonly used.

Company and marketing objectives and goals. Perhaps the most basic criterion used in screening involves the compatibility of the new idea with the mission, goals, and objectives of the firm itself. Product or service ideas that are inconsistent with a desired corporate image, incompatible with the corporate mission, or in contrast with overall company objectives

---

EXHIBIT 12.2   **Screening of New Business Products**

ABC Engineering Company is considering five new product ideas and wishes to rank these ideas in its screening process. The company uses the following criteria and weights them in the following manner:

CRITERION	WEIGHTING OF IMPORTANCE (%)
1. Market size and growth potential	40
2. Consistency with corporate objectives	10
3. Ability to match competitors' strengths	20
4. Ability to sell and service customers	15
5. Ability to engineer and manufacture product	15
Total	100

The company uses the following rating system for each of the five new product ideas under consideration: 5 = excellent, 4 = good, 3 = average, 2 = fair, 1 = poor. Management rates each of the five new products on each of the criteria as follows:

NEW PRODUCT IDEA NUMBER	CRITERIA					TOTAL WEIGHTED POINTS
	1	2	3	4	5	
1	5	4	5	3	4	21
2	2	2	3	2	1	10
3	4	3	4	3	3	17
4	5	5	5	4	5	24
5	3	3	5	4	4	19

---

are typically screened out early. In addition, companies usually have product or service objectives and will screen out ideas not consistent with those objectives. Screening by objectives ties the decision into the strategic market plan at an early stage. An example may help to show what is involved. The objectives of a steel company for its new products were that (1) sales would exceed $1 million annually within three years of introduction, (2) incremental profits would amount to 7 percent after taxes, and (3) incremental net return on investment would be 20 percent.[32] This company probably would discard new product ideas judged incapable of reaching these objectives.

Market and sales potential. New product or service ideas are typically screened on the basis of potential. Screening questions here include the following. What is the estimated market size and growth? What are the expected sales in that market? Who are the potential users and what is their buying behavior? What is the expected life cycle of the product or service? What are the size and frequency of purchases? Who are the expected competitors and what are their strengths and weaknesses? What support activities may be required? Such screening attempts to judge the potential profitability of the proposed idea.

Company capabilities. Even if a product or service idea is consistent with objectives and shows good potential, the manager should analyze the company's ability to produce and market it. The potential may exist, but perhaps not for the manager's company. Screening questions here include the following. Will the technical resources be available to produce and market it? Can those resources be applied to this project? Will new manu-facturing or distribution facilities be required? Will new channels of distri-bution have to be developed? Will present customers buy the product, or will the company have to reach completely new customers? Can existing company salespeople effectively sell the product or service? Are present service facilities sufficient to market it? These questions force the marketer to consider the compatibility of the product idea with the present capabili-ties of the company.

Contribution of the product or service. Even when the idea looks good based on the preceding factors, the company may still be better off not producing and marketing it because of negative effects on the firm's other product or service offerings or in other areas of the company. To illustrate, what is to be gained if the company adds a new product that is consistent with objectives, has market potential, and can be economically produced, if that product has adverse effects on other good products in the com-pany's product line?

Appropriate screening questions here include the following. What effect will the new product have on the existing product line? Does it fill a gap in an otherwise incomplete line, or does it compete with a present product in that line? Does it increase the marketability of other products in the line? How will the product affect the image of the present products? Does the product help utilize excess plant capacity? Will the product com-pete with products of present customers? Will it give company salespeople a more competitive product offering? What contribution to profit should the new product make to the firm? These kinds of questions are necessary in that they compel the marketer to think about the *potential* contribution of the proposed product.

From a marketing perspective, this type of basic screening makes good sense. These questions should be answered sooner or later. The logic of looking at them prior to producing a product or service is wiser than allowing the market-place to answer them after introduction. One study found the majority of new idea rejections in the screening stage were those in which (1) a major develop-ment cost was required, (2) the technology was new to the company, (3) a new group of potential buyers was involved, (4) unfamiliar selling and service tasks were involved, (5) product life cycles were expected to be short, (6) the market showed great fluctuations in demand, (7) competitors had major advantages, and (8) the risk to buyers was seen as high.[33]

Screening is a necessary but difficult undertaking. At the screening stage, relatively little reliable information is available on the idea's market, costs, and the investment involved.[34] Without screening, however, time and effort may be directed toward ideas that have little, if any, chance of ever becoming successful products. Without appropriate screening, the cost of product or service management increases, and its effectiveness decreases.

Preliminary Investigation

Those product or service ideas that have successfully passed the basic screening step now become candidates for more thorough research. The task here is to perform a more extensive analysis of an idea before attempting to determine specifications. This is necessary because the basic screening step is really intended to rule out ideas of little or no potential rather than examine them in great detail. Thus, the preliminary investigation stage is a logical extension of the screening process but it applies specifically to those ideas that are still considered worthy of more consideration.

In this step, a number of important questions have to be answered in sufficient detail for a decision to be made whether to develop specifications. These questions include: What specific target markets can be identified? How large are these markets and are they increasing, decreasing, or remaining static? How many potential customers exist in these target markets and what are the characteristics of these customers? Is the product or service idea really new in these target markets or merely a refinement of an existing product or service? Where are these target markets located? How do customers in these markets buy in terms of size of purchases, frequency of purchases, etc.? What buying influences will have to be reached if the firm is to successfully penetrate each market? What competitors will be encountered in these markets and how firmly entrenched are they? What length of product or service life cycles might be anticipated? What kinds of costs will be involved? Questions such as these require answers before any further commitment to the idea is made. Answering such questions is a marketing responsibility and requires considerable time and effort. But, as has been developed, this step applies only to those ideas that have survived the basic screening, which typically implies the numbers are much smaller. The logic of this step is easy to understand. No business marketing manager wants to commit time, effort, and resources to a new product or service idea only to find later that there is no clearly defined market, or that the market is too small to justify the expense, or that competition is so strongly entrenched that the new product or service has no real chance of adoption. This step in the process is designed to further rule out ideas that would cause difficulty in later marketing efforts. This may be seen in the previously discussed case of Minnesota Minerals and Chemical Corporation. It will be recalled that ninety ideas out of the original 540 survived the basic planning step. The preliminary investigation step then reduced these ninety to only nine ideas considered worthy of further consideration.

Those new product or service ideas that survive this preliminary investigation step are then passed on to the next step, where specifications will be determined.

Determination of Specifications

Figure 12.1 shows the decision to develop specifications as an important step in new product or service development. Specifications may be defined as a detailed, precise presentation of those characteristics desired in the product or service. They should be described in the clearest and most technically accurate manner, so that all involved parties know exactly what is required. In summary, specifications spell out the exact form the new product or service will take. The specifications for a new business product may include its height, width, depth, weight, color, tolerances, electrical or other power characteristics, packaging, component parts, legal requirements, and operating characteristics. Figure 12.4 illustrates the specifications of a relatively standard business product.

The importance of specifications in business marketing cannot be overemphasized, as many buyers and buying influences purchase primarily on the basis of specifications. If the supplier's product specifications do not meet the buyer's requirements, the product is not even considered. In addition, if precise product specifications are not developed, the marketing firm's engineering and production departments cannot produce the product under consideration. As well, the purchasing department cannot be expected to buy the proper materials.

Figure 12.2 illustrates the close association among marketing and engineering and production in determining specifications. Market input is necessary so that the new product meets customer requirements and competes favorably in the market. Technical input is also necessary so that those types of requirements are met. If either side dominates, a poor performing or unprofitable new product may result. For example, if the marketing manager has sole responsibility for determining specifications, the product may well meet customer and competitive requirements, but the company may not be able to produce such a product at a profit. On the other hand, if the engineering manager exclusively determines specifications, the product may not meet the needs in the marketplace.

In the case of business services, there are still specifications even though services are considered to be intangible as opposed to products. What is the buyer purchasing and what does he or she expect from the service provider? The new service should be designed in light of such considerations. Such factors as how long it takes to perform the service, the qualifications of the person who will perform the service, the firm's ability to meet the customer's time requirements, the availability of spare parts, etc., must all be designed into the new service if it is to meet customer expectations. Thus, even though services are intangible and are therefore not manufactured as are products, they still must be designed according to specifications that match target market needs.

Specifications vary by type of product or service and by type of market involved. This can be seen by referring back to Table 12.1, which illustrated types of products and services in business marketing. To illustrate, with a totally customized product, the specifications are designed specifically to meet the requirements of a single customer. The customer may have determined the specifications for the supplier to meet or the customer and supplier may have determined the specs jointly. Regardless, the specifications here are designed for a single cus-

FIGURE 12.4   Specifications of a Business Product

Series 44R

Retainer, Captive Screw
FSC-5304-411
Retainers listed on this page mate with Series 4100 Captive Screws

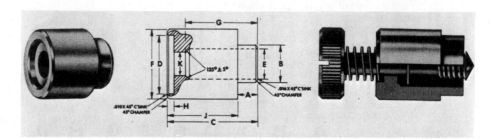

PART NO.	THREAD	PANEL THICKNESS	A ±.005	B +.000 -.003	C ±.010	D +.005 .000	E +.002 -.000	F ±.003	G +.005 -.010	H ±.005	J ±.005	K +.004 -.000
44R01	4-40	.052/.067	.062	.250	.437	.192	.188	.281	.312	.062	.375	.125
44R02	4-40	.084/.099	.093	.250	.437	.192	.188	.281	.312	.062	.344	.125
44R03	4-40	.109/.140	.125	.250	.437	.192	.188	.281	.312	.062	.312	.125
44R04	6-32	.052/.067	.062	.250	.437	.192	.188	.281	.312	.062	.375	.152
44R05	6-32	.084/.099	.093	.250	.437	.192	.188	.281	.312	.062	.344	.152
44R06	6-32	.109/.140	.125	.250	.437	.192	.188	.281	.312	.062	.312	.152
44R07	8-32	.052/.067	.062	.433	.625	.312	.375	.531	.469	.093	.563	.177
44R08	8-32	.084/.099	.093	.433	.625	.312	.375	.531	.469	.093	.532	.177
44R09	8-32	.109/.140	.125	.433	.625	.312	.375	.531	.469	.093	.500	.177
44R10	8-32	.171/.203	.187	.433	.625	.312	.375	.531	.469	.093	.438	.177
44R11	8-32	.234/.265	.250	.433	.625	.312	.375	.531	.469	.093	.375	.177
44R12	10-24	.052/.067	.062	.433	.625	.312	.375	.531	.469	.093	.563	.203
44R13	10-24	.084/.099	.093	.433	.625	.312	.375	.531	.469	.093	.532	.203
44R14	10-24	.109/.140	.125	.433	.625	.312	.375	.531	.469	.093	.500	.203
44R15	10-24	.171/.203	.187	.433	.625	.312	.375	.531	.469	.093	.438	.203
44R16	10-24	.234/.265	.250	.433	.625	.312	.375	.531	.469	.093	.375	.203
44R17	10-32	.052/.067	.062	.433	.625	.312	.375	.501	.469	.093	.563	.203
44R18	10-32	.084/.099	.093	.433	.625	.312	.375	.531	.469	.093	.532	.203
44R19	10-32	.109/.140	.125	.433	.625	.312	.375	.531	.469	.093	.500	.203
44R20	10-32	.171/.203	.187	.433	.625	.312	.375	.531	.469	.093	.438	.203
44R21	10-32	.234/.265	.250	.433	.625	.312	.375	.531	.469	.093	.375	.203
44R22	12-24	.052/.067	.062	.433	.625	.312	.375	.531	.469	.093	.563	.228
44R23	12-24	.084/.099	.093	.433	.625	.312	.375	.531	.469	.093	.532	.228
44R24	12-24	.109/.140	.125	.433	.625	.312	.375	.531	.469	.093	.500	.228
44R25	12-24	.171/.203	.187	.433	.625	.312	.375	.531	.469	.093	.438	.228
44R26	12-24	.234/.265	.250	.433	.625	.312	.375	.531	.469	.093	.375	.228
44R27	1/4-20	.052/.067	.062	.433	.625	.312	.375	.531	.469	.093	.563	.257
44R28	1/4-20	.084/.099	.093	.433	.625	.312	.375	.531	.469	.093	.532	.257
44R29	1/4-20	.109/.140	.125	.433	.625	.312	.375	.531	.469	.093	.500	.257
44R30	1/4-20	.171/.203	.187	.433	.625	.312	.375	.531	.469	.093	.438	.257
44R31	1/4-20	.234/.265	.250	.433	.625	.312	.375	.531	.469	.093	.375	.257
44R32	1/4-28	.052/.067	.062	.433	.625	.312	.375	.531	.469	.093	.563	.257
44R33	1/4-28	.084/.099	.093	.433	.625	.312	.375	.531	.469	.093	.532	.257
44R34	1/4-28	.109/.140	.125	.433	.625	.312	.375	.531	.469	.093	.500	.257
44R35	1/4-28	.171/.203	.187	.433	.625	.312	.375	.531	.469	.093	.438	.257
44R36	1/4-28	.234/.265	.250	.433	.625	.312	.375	.531	.469	.093	.375	.257

UNICORP   291 Cleveland Street • Orange, N.J. 07050 • 201-674-1700

Source: Reprinted by permission of Unicorp (Orange, NJ).

tomer. Figure 12.4 shows the specifications for a relatively standardized product. Here, the manufacturer has determined the specifications and provides a range of products adaptable to the requirements of many different users. In either case, the specifications must meet customer requirements if the products are to gain market acceptance.

In the case of services, the same applies. For example, a software manufacturer designed a software program totally customized to meet the needs of light airplane flying schools. The program has no other applications and is a good example of a totally customized service. It had to be designed to meet the unique needs of this specialized market. On the other hand, there are basic accounting software packages designed to meet the needs of any type of organization that requires accounting assistance. These could be considered totally standardized services and their specifications must meet the general needs of many types of users.

Similarly, the specifications for a particular type of product can change depending on whether the customer is a private organization, an institution, or a government agency. For example, a manufacturer of commercial dishwashing machines found that models sold to restaurants, hotels, and industrial kitchens would not be purchased by many types of institutional and governmental customers, even though all used the machines for the same purpose. Specifications had to be changed to accommodate each customer's different needs, even though the machines were basically the same. Mental institutions required a stainless steel mesh surrounding all motors and switches to protect against accidents. The General Services Administration (GSA) also had its own specifications, which differed appreciably from those of other governmental customers such as the United States Navy and Air Force.

Not all ideas necessarily make it through this step in the process. In some cases, it may be impossible to determine specifications for the product or service idea. When this happens, the idea may be rejected and eliminated from further consideration. An example of this might be where target market needs simply cannot be defined explicitly enough to determine what is needed to meet them. It is also possible that engineering and production cannot determine technical specifications that will meet customer needs. Thus, some ideas may be discarded this late in the process. Those ideas that now possess specifications move on to the next step in the process—product or service development.

Product or Service Development

At this point in the process, the new idea must be converted into an actual product or service. Specifications have been determined and must now be transferred to a product or service that meets those specs. At this step, there are some significant differences between new product ideas and new service ideas. If the idea relates to a product, the technical departments (research and development, engineering, and production) will develop and laboratory test a prototype of the desired product. An actual model of the product will be constructed, tested, and modified by the technical people for the purpose of developing products for field testing. Since the marketing manager is typically not directly involved in the actual development and production of the prototype, his or her primary responsibility is to see that necessary market specifications are followed in the process of making the prototype. Whatever is produced at this step must conform to the previously determined specifications if market success is to be achieved. Confrontations between the marketing and technical people are common here and must be overcome in a manner that does not detract from what target market customers expect and demand.

In the case of business services, no tangible prototype is involved and thus the close coordination with technical departments is not required in the same manner as with products. In fact, some argue that because a service is an intangible, the development phase should be bypassed and a market test conducted before the service is offered to the entire market.[35] This point of view, however, ignores the fact that a service is a deed or performance that must also be produced but in a different manner. Producing a service typically involves assembling and delivering the output of a mix of physical components and mental or physical labor.[36] This assembling takes place at this step in a manner designed to fulfill the previously defined specifications and meet customer demand. Research suggests that involving experts in the creation and planning of the new service and using a detailed "drawing board" approach for new service development is significantly correlated with success.[37]

Once the idea has been converted to a physical product or a conceptual service, it is ready to be test marketed. Again, it should be realized that not all ideas survive this step. For example, engineering and manufacturing may find that they cannot produce a product that will meet desired specifications. Or it may be impossible to assemble the right combination of components and labor to supply a service as needed in the market. However, those ideas that do pass this stage are now ready to be market tested.

Field Test

The products or services that were developed in the previous step are now field tested in some manner to test product or service performance and customer reactions. If there are problems, these are corrected before entry into the total market. The purpose here is to see how the new product or service performs under actual conditions in the target markets.

There are a number of approaches to field testing that are used in business marketing. In the case of products developed for reseller organizations, the new products may be test marketed in selected establishments. In the case of products designed for user customers such as manufacturers, agreements may be made to install the new product in the customer's plant and then let that customer's employees operate it. In that way, performance may be monitored. In situations where light equipment, component parts, etc., are designed for OEM customers, samples may again be used and recipients asked to try them. All of these approaches are intended to get the product into the market on a limited basis so its performance may be monitored and changes made, if necessary, before full market entry.

In the case of business services, formal prelaunch testing of the new service to make necessary adjustments and eliminate bugs is closely linked to getting a competitive edge. In other words, the service is performed free for selected prospects with the intent of finding areas that need improvement. Research has shown that formally testing a new service just before launch not only lowers costs but helps to create a competitively superior service.[38]

Even at this late stage in the process, the products or services may be eliminated if the field testing shows problems that cannot be rectified or that demand does not exist to the extent previously thought. Those, however, that enjoy successful field testing are now ready for the commercialization step.

Commercialization

Once the new idea has passed successfully through the screening and planning process and the decision is made to market it commercially, its introduction must be planned. This period is crucial for the product or service involved, and the introduction must not be allowed to occur haphazardly. It has long been recognized that launching a new product or service is one of the most important and yet hazardous actions in which any firm can engage.[39] One authority claims that there are five requisites for the successful introduction of new business products or services:[40] (1) possessing strategic guidelines for the identification of new ideas, (2) knowing where to look for those ideas, (3) using marketing research and audits effectively, (4) having a sound selection process, and (5) using effective launching tactics. Even if the first four steps are performed correctly, the product or service can still fail if the launching process is faulty.

After the strategy components have been selected for the new product or service, all the activities required to introduce the product and monitor its progress successfully must be coordinated. Launching a new product or service is a complex process. Many people with diverse responsibilities must coordinate their activities to bring the product to the market in the shortest possible time.[41] Chapter 10 discussed PERT and critical path analysis to show their applications to overall marketing planning. These techniques are equally applicable for coordinating the activities involved in introducing new products or services in business markets. Figure 12.5 illustrates the use of critical path analysis to introduce a new gear or sprocket into the industrial OEM market. This new product introduction system is useful in that it (1) outlines and schedules all activities that will be involved; (2) shows the longest time (the critical path) in which the introduction can take place—in this case, the critical path is twenty-two weeks; (3) integrates the responsibilities of marketing, engineering, and manufacturing throughout the entire system; and (4) permits the implementation of the mix required to market the product—the figure shows all activities in product, price, promotion, and channels.

The business marketing manager should realize the importance of such planning in the introduction of new products and services. Tools such as PERT

FIGURE 12.5 Critical Path Method Graph for a Business Product Introduction

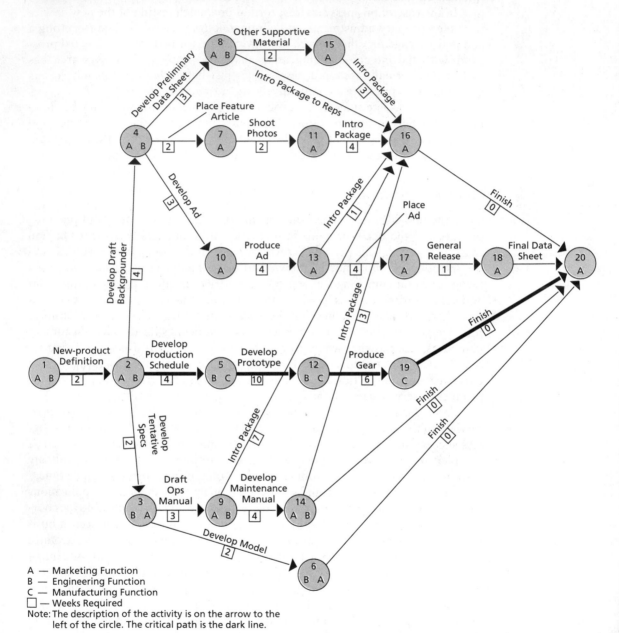

A — Marketing Function
B — Engineering Function
C — Manufacturing Function
☐ — Weeks Required
Note: The description of the activity is on the arrow to the
left of the circle. The critical path is the dark line.

Source: Reprinted by permission from G. A. Marken, "New Product Introduction Schedule Yields Fantastic Results," *Marketing News*, April 15, 1974: 4. Published by the American Marketing Association.

and critical path analysis are very useful in developing an adequate procedure for successful introduction. Nothing should be left to chance in the new product or service introduction process.

The key in introducing new products or services is to increase the chances of success and reduce the chances of failure. As can be seen, the new product or service planning process facilitates that end. Success requires careful attention to the steps in this process and involves both marketing and technical input. Through the use of such a process, the business marketing manager can focus on those factors known to have positive or negative effects on product or service introduction.

Similarly, the process should help to reject those new ideas that would ultimately fail, before they are actually introduced to the market. To illustrate, the preliminary investigation stage should rule out ideas where market sizes are not sufficient or competitors are too firmly entrenched. Similarly, between the marketing and technical people involved, it should be possible to determine whether the idea does or does not have competitive advantages. By combining the reasons for success and failure with a sound planning process, new products or services should stand a better chance of succeeding in the marketplace. This assumption is consistent with the recommendations of a major U.S. consulting firm that reports that those companies that will experience success with new products (1) make a long-term commitment to new product development, (2) make a concentrated effort to develop new product strategy, (3) use their experience to increase new product introduction effectiveness, and (4) establish an organizational environment conducive to achieving new product and corporate objectives.[42]

The process discussed here is an ideal sequence of product or service development decisions but in actuality it may not happen that way for many business products or services. New ideas may be discovered accidentally rather than by design. In addition, other new ideas may simply be by-products of technical research. Such things can and will happen in large and complex firms but when they do, the ideas should be subjected to the previously discussed process just as all other ideas.

An interesting diversion from the ideal took place with Lockheed Corporation's secret "Skunk Works" that created the first U.S. produced jet fighter, the U-2 spyplane, the SR-71 Blackbird, and more than forty other airplanes and spacecraft. The secrecy of the Skunk Works was so great that even the origin of the name was secret, although it was thought to have been derived from the "Li'l Abner" comic strip, which featured a moonshine distillery called the Skonk Works.[43] This was a situation where new products were developed in secret and then later released for development.

PRODUCT SUPPORT

As was discussed earlier in the chapter, business marketing firms may offer a product, a service, or a product and a service. Services that accompany a product are often referred to as product support. When making purchases, business customers often believe they are buying more than the physical item itself; they also have expectations about the level of postpurchase support the product carries with it. Product support can help maximize the customer's aftersale satisfaction and includes such things as assembly and use instructions, roughing-in diagrams, service contracts, warranty programs, replacement parts, technical assistance provided by the marketer, customer employee training, equipment on loan to replace defective products under repair, mobile repair units, providing diagnostic equipment, and location of service facilities close to customers.

Product support applies to all types of business products, although its extent may vary considerably by product type. For example, the amount of product support required to market a piece of high-tech heavy equipment may differ appreciably from that required for a standardized consumable supply item. This variation does not mean that product support is less important with the latter, only that it takes a different form. The purchaser of such a standardized product may be concerned with the ease and speed of replacing defective items. A good example occurred in the power tool industry. Japanese and German manufacturers were able to accomplish warranty and routine repairs within seventy-two hours, whereas many U.S. manufacturers required between two to four weeks.[44] This time difference created a definite reason in the minds of many U.S. industrial distributors for buying from the overseas suppliers.

Product support must be considered a marketing area of responsibility because it affects customer satisfaction with the product being purchased. This satisfaction is necessary for repeat business and a favorable image. The marketer who provides loaner equipment to customers greatly reduces downtime and probably saves the customer thousands of dollars. Such product support activities can differentiate competing products in the minds of buyers and other buying influences. An example illustrates this point. Both Caterpillar Tractor and John Deere employ marketing strategies founded on providing excellent product support. Both concentrate heavily on strengthening their dealers' service capabilities and on upgrading parts availability. Both back these efforts with extensive service staffs and emergency parts ordering systems. In addition, both design equipment to emphasize reliability and serviceability to minimize downtime.[45]

Support should be considered early in the new product planning process. The company's capability to provide the required support and the level of technical assistance necessary should be assessed as early as the screening stage. If a company lacks the ability to support a product, that product should not be introduced unless the desired support activities can be adequately offered. Poorly conceived or implemented support activities can contribute to product failure.

Although product support activities offer additional benefits to customers, they are not without cost to the business marketer. Their use is based on the premise that additional sales and profits will offset the additional costs, which is true when used successfully. Still, the marketing manager should realize those costs involved. An example may help clarify the cost side. Table 12.3 shows the results of a Conference Board study of business product warranty practices. Note that most warranties are for one year or less. Note also the variation in costs. Of all the companies surveyed, 24 percent spent less than 1 percent of sales

TABLE 12.3   Business Product Warranty Characteristics Classified by Type of Product Manufactured

Warranty Servicing Costs as a Percentage of Net Sales	All Companies	Business Equipment	Electrical Equipment	Heating and Refrigeration	Machinery Products	Scientific Equipment and Controls	Mobile Equipment and Controls	All Other Products
Less than 1.0%	24%	23%	20%	21%	33%	23%	21%	30%
1.0–1.9%	37%	26%	38%	41%	33%	21%	54%	38%
2.0–2.9%	20%	26%	20%	24%	22%	16%	17%	16%
3.0–4.9%	11%	20%	20%	10%	13%	16%	2%	7%
5.0–6.9%	4%	3%	—	3%	—	12%	2%	4%
7.0–9.9%	4%	3%	2%	—	2%	12%	4%	1%
10.0% or more	1%	—	—	—	—	—	—	3%
Total*	100%	100%	100%	100%	100%	100%	100%	100%

Length of Extended Warranty Period (in Months)	All Companies	Business Equipment	Electrical Equipment	Heating and Refrigeration	Machinery Products	Scientific Equipment and Controls	Mobile Equipment and Controls	All Other Products
0–12	91%	97%	85%	63%	94%	98%	96%	92%
13–24	3%	3%	11%	—	2%	2%	—	6%
25–36	2%	—	—	7%	2%	—	2%	1%
37–48	2%	—	—	27%	—	—	—	—
49–60	2%	—	4%	3%	4%	—	2%	—
Total*	100%	100%	100%	100%	100%	100%	100%	100%

Source: Reprinted by permission from E. Patrick McGuire, *Industrial Product Warranties: Policies and Practices*, Report No. 800 (New York: The Conference Board, 1980), 7, 13.

Note: *Totals may not equal 100% due to rounding.

on this activity. Twenty percent of companies spent 3 percent or more. Depending on the product, even higher expenditures may be found. In scientific equipment and controls, 40 percent of the companies spent 3 percent or more, and 56 percent spent in excess of 2 percent. Compared with other marketing expenditures, these percentages are relatively high and show the magnitude of product support costs.

Many U.S. business marketing firms do an excellent job of providing product support activities. Exhibit 12.3 shows how important product support activities were to Black & Decker in the introduction of a new product line. On the other hand, many companies do not seem to recognize product support activities as part of marketing strategy.[46] These firms are characterized by a lack of explicit product support strategy, diffused responsibility for such activities, product support activities tacked on as afterthoughts, and focus placed on individual support activities rather than on their integration into a total support function.

PRODUCT MANAGEMENT IN BUSINESS MARKETING

The area of **product management** must be addressed. Throughout the chapter, references have been made to the marketing manager as the decision maker in various product area decisions. In many business marketing companies, market-

---

EXHIBIT 12.3　　Example of the Importance of Product Support Activities in the Introduction of a New Business Product

---

The U.S. Power Tools Group of Black & Decker introduced its new "Master Series" line of industrial power tools in 1987. The line was designed for the industrial and construction markets and was sold exclusively through distributors serving those two target markets. The objective was to serve the industrial and construction markets more effectively with high-performance power tools.

Product specifications included high-powered motors to guarantee maximum operating power and exacting weight, balance, and size specifications to ensure better control, superior handling, and reduced operator fatigue.

Product support activities included free repair service for one year. Black & Decker also guaranteed that any tool needing repair would be serviced within four hours if brought into one of the company's 100+ authorized service centers. If a customer could not wait the four hours, a loaner tool would be provided until the defective tool could be repaired. In addition, Black & Decker established a new policy of 100 percent spare parts availability at the service centers.

To market the new line through the distributors, the company established a separate sales force to serve the two target markets. Regional seminars were held with key distributors to familiarize them with the new line.

Source: Adapted from "B & D's New Line Hailed as Ultimate Power Tool," *Industrial Distribution* 77 (August 1987): 9.

ing aspects of product strategy are the direct responsibility of the marketing manager. In other firms, however, various product management options are used to introduce specialization into the product area of the overall marketing mix. The major product management options are (1) the product manager, (2) new product committees, (3) project teams, and (4) venture teams.[47] Since each of these may be found in business markets, used by itself or used in conjunction with others, a clarification and discussion of each is in order.

The Product Manager

Product managers have evolved over time in business marketing because many marketing managers have found the product area to be so critical and so complex that specialists were required to handle the area adequately. It has even been argued that companies do not really compete in the marketplace—their products or services compete. This reasoning has led to the recognition that because products may well be the determinant of success or failure, the product area is no place for a generalist; thus, specialists, the product managers, have come into prominence. Generally, the product manager is responsible for coordinating company marketing and sales efforts for particular products or services. In this responsibility, the product manager reports to the marketing manager, as does the advertising manager, the sales manager, the marketing research manager, and other such marketing officers. According to several studies, in making decisions, the product manager interacts with buyers, distributors, the sales force, engineers, advertising agencies, product development teams, and marketing research teams. The product manager's responsibilities may include developing and screening ideas, planning new products or services, developing a marketing plan for the products or services, working with sales managers and salespersons on sales strategies, working with advertising managers and advertising agencies on appropriate promotional programs, working with sales promotion people on packaging, working with distribution managers to bring about effective physical distribution of the product, pricing the product, and providing necessary service and technical assistance. Table 12.4 lists the duties and responsibilities of business product managers, as reported by one study.

In short, the product manager takes the product or service from the idea stage to the operational stage in the customer's plant, complete with support activities and performance feedback—"from conception through profitable performance in the marketplace."[48] The product manager is a marketing tactician, much as is the advertising manager, the sales manager, the distribution manager, the sales promotion manager, and the marketing research manager. One major difference, however, is that a company may have any number of product managers, depending on the composition of its product or service line.

Despite the great number of responsibilities carried by the product manager, he or she generally lacks corresponding authority. He or she has the normal responsibilities required of managers but often has little or no authority to carry out those responsibilities and is typically in a staff rather than a line posi-

TABLE 12.4 Duties and Responsibilities of Product Managers in Business Marketing [*n* = 69]

Duty/Responsibility	Percent of Respondents Having This Duty or Responsibility
Oversees product(s) progress	91%
Decides the nature of or initiates changes in ongoing products	70
Initiates product reengineering	67
Determines product deletion	65
Determines product phaseout	65
Determines markets to enter or depart	64
Initiates and controls new product conceptualization	64
Responsible for product profitability	62
Develops and presents product's budget requests	61
Initiates price changes	58
Presents promotional strategy	57
Initiates market research analysis	57
Sets pricing strategy	55
Develops sales goals and objectives	55
Attends product committee	52
Develops product control criteria	45
Has chief responsibility and decides which new products are added	42
Determines product's channel of distribution	39
Chairs product committee	36
Decides the type of promotional mix	35
Controls package changes	25

Source: Reprinted by permission of the publisher from Robert W. Eckles and Timothy J. Novotny, "Industrial Product Managers: Authority and Responsibility," *Industrial Marketing Management* 13 (1984): 73. Copyright © 1984 by Elsevier Science Publishing Company.

Note: Responses exceed 100 percent due to multiple answers.

tion.[49] This situation implies that authority rests with the marketing manager; therefore, whether or not a firm uses a product manager, the basic product principles discussed in this chapter apply to the business marketing manager.

Product managers in business marketing often are considered the equivalent of brand managers in the consumer market. Indeed, their basic responsibilities are quite similar. Regardless of terminology, product management or brand management is a special type of management characterized by involvement with one, and only one, product or service. Efforts of both the product manager and the brand manager are directed toward the management of that single, generally big-budget product.[50]

Despite these basic similarities, a study disclosed some of the following differences between the two: (1) Product managers are generally older, more experienced, and responsible for more products than consumer brand managers; (2) compared with brand managers, product managers interface more with distribution, sales, and customers but less with marketing research, advertising, and advertising agencies; and (3) product managers are less involved with promotion and market research decisions than consumer brand managers, but they are more involved with decisions about pricing and distribution.[51]

The level of product manager use in business marketing may be gauged from the results of a Conference Board study, which found that 85 percent of the companies surveyed had product managers responsible for the managing of existing products, 63 percent had such managers responsible for more than routine product-line modifications, and 43 percent gave product managers responsibility for planning major new products.[52] The results of this study indicate that the product manager concept is popular in business marketing, and business marketing companies using this approach include Union Carbide, Diamond Chain Company, Uniroyal, and Johns Manville.[53]

New Product Committees

Using the new product committee option, decisions are made by a committee whose members are borrowed from other departments within the company. For example, a company may initiate a new product committee whose members are drawn from such departments as production, engineering, purchasing, sales, marketing research, and R & D. Typically, these people are involved in a temporary capacity in various areas of product or service development in addition to performing their normal duties. The basic purpose of such an approach is to ensure representation of involved functional areas in the decision. It encourages representatives of involved departments to work closely together, unencumbered by normal organizational boundaries and constraints.

Although conceptually sound, this approach often has serious implementation drawbacks. Since the committee is temporary in nature, members often lack commitment, responsibilities are often unclear, and functional departments sometimes assign lesser-qualified personnel to serve. For example, there may be little incentive for an engineering department head to assign his or her top engineers to such a temporary appointment, and the engineers involved may be reluctant to serve in such a temporary capacity as it may be inconsistent with career path objectives.

New product committees are less widely used in business marketing than product managers are. The previously cited Conference Board study found that 37 percent of the industrial firms surveyed never used such committees. Of those that did, only 25 percent used them for decision-making purposes. More commonly, they were used primarily for communications and coordination.[54]

It should be understood that the product manager concept and the new product committee can be used in conjunction. The use of one does not preclude the use of the other. Indeed, both are commonly used; the product manager oversees existing products or services and perhaps even serves on a committee devoted to new considerations.

Project Teams

The new product project team is an extension of the new product committee. Responsibility for new products is assigned to a separate unit that may report to top management at the same level as other functional departments. Again, specialists from other departments are assigned to the project team, and a project manager is appointed. Typically, members are appointed to the project team for a longer time and usually see the project through to completion. Members' jobs in the other departments are held open while they serve on the project team. In essence, the project manager is a variation of the product manager. This project team concept has merit in that it permits the communication and coordination of the new product committee but overcomes the temporary status disadvantage of the latter. The concept, however, has its limitations. Truly competent personnel may not be attracted to it, and due to its relative permanency, objectivity is sometimes lost. In addition, by placing new product responsibility in a unit separate from traditional departments, an elitism can develop that can lead to alienation by those other departments. As with the new product committee, its limitations are due more to implementation than to the concept itself.

Project teams are used in business marketing. The Conference Board study found that 65 percent of the industrial firms surveyed used them occasionally, although only 16 percent used them routinely.[55] The project team can, of course, be used in conjunction with other forms of product management.

Venture Teams

The venture team is a newer approach to product management and is an extension of the project team. Typically, it is used to develop a new product or service or a new business that is completely different from the company's present line of business. Its basis is more permanent than the project team's basis. If the venture were to prove feasible, venture group members could become the operating management in a new division or subsidiary created specifically for the venture. Venture teams typically have the following characteristics:[56]

1. The venture team is organizationally separate from the remainder of the company.
2. Its members are recruited from various functional departments within the company.
3. Existing lines of authority within the permanent organization may not apply to the venture team.
4. The venture team manager usually reports to top management and has the authority to make major decisions.
5. The team is free of deadlines and remains together until the task is completed.
6. Freedom from time pressures fosters creativity and innovativeness.

The main advantages of this approach are its specialized members, its permanency, and its decision-making powers. Its disadvantage again lies in the fact that other departments must cooperate by supplying top-quality personnel whom they may not be willing to give up permanently. The Conference Board study found that 42 percent of the industrial firms surveyed had used this approach.[57]

This discussion illustrates the complexity of product management in business marketing. The text also points out how important this area of marketing is—companies are prepared to organize and reorganize, if need be, to manage their product or service offerings better.

CHAPTER SUMMARY

Effective product or service strategy is essential to the future success of business marketing firms. This means producing quality products and services that meet customer needs and compete in the marketplace. This does not happen by chance but requires managerial expertise and attention. With an effective product or service strategy, however, the business marketing company is able to increase the effectiveness of the other elements of the marketing mix— quality products and services that meet customers' needs are easier to sell, distribute, promote, and price.

A quality product or service must possess certain characteristics. First, it must respond to clearly identified customer needs and values. It must also be perceived as superior to competitive offerings and it must be seen as unique or different by customers and prospects. In addition, it often has to solve a previously unsolved or poorly solved problem or offer the customer better value. Finally, it is perceived by customers and prospects as highly synergetic with its supplier's capabilities, skills, reputation, and resources.

Product or service quality has become a national priority. The federal government's Malcolm Baldridge National Quality Awards seek to recognize businesses that excel in the quality of their goods or services. To quote President George Bush, "The improvement of quality in products and the improvement of quality in service—these are national priorities as never before."[58]

To produce this type of quality, the Malcolm Baldridge National Quality Improvement Act of 1987 states, "In order to be successful, quality improvement programs must be management-led and customer-oriented and this may require fundamental changes in the way companies and agencies do business."[59] This chapter has stressed approaches that business marketing firms might consider in producing high-quality products and services.

Types of business products and services were examined and product and service strategy was defined with differences illustrated between business and consumer markets. The importance of planning was then developed. Reasons why new business products and services succeed or fail were then discussed as they apply to the introduction of new products or services. Then, the new product and service planning process was developed in detail so that it can be seen how sound planning can overcome many of the reasons that new products and services fail in the marketplace. This process covered the steps of idea generation, basic screening, preliminary investigation, determination of specifications, product or service development, field testing, and commercialization. The area of product support activities was then developed and, finally, product management options appropriate for business marketing were examined. In summary, the chapter content was developed to show how new products and services can be designed in an orderly, managed fashion to meet the needs of target market customers. Another purpose of the chapter was to demonstrate how product or service strategy is a controllable element in the marketing mix. Through the use of proper product management, sound new product processes, and learning from past experiences, product and service strategy can be improved. If successful, this strategy leads to more satisfied customers, fewer failures, and increased profitability.

KEY TERMS

basic screening
customized product/service
field test
idea generation
new product/service
new product/service planning process
product
product failure

product management
product planning
product strategy
product support
service
specifications
standardized product/service

QUESTIONS

1. Looking at product or service strategy in terms of determining specifications, explain how the concept of multiple buying influences complicates the task of establishing product or service specifications.

2. Unfortunately, some business marketers view the product or service area of the marketing mix as a given rather than a controllable variable. What is incorrect about viewing the product or service component as fixed? What is gained by viewing it as a variable that is controllable at least to some degree?

3. Why is the screening of new product or service ideas so important in the product or service planning process in business marketing?

4. Explain what is meant by product support activities in business marketing. Why are such activities so important in the marketing of many business products?

5. Explain how the use of a new product or service planning process, such as was developed in the chapter, can help increase the chances for success of product or service ideas and decrease the chances of future new product or service failures.

6. It is sometimes argued that new products and services fail for basically the same reason, but because services are different from products, there are other circumstances that help account for new service failure. Explain why this is a valid argument.

7. Explain how a business marketing company may use a product manager, new product committee, and project team at the same time in managing its overall product or service line.

8. In the product or service area of the marketing mix, departments other than marketing are commonly involved. Explain which departments are most often involved and why for both products and services.

9. In business marketing, a product or service may range from being totally customized to being to-

tally standardized. Explain what causes such a wide range and how all this affects the specifications of the product or service involved.

10. Looking at the rest of the marketing mix, explain how a job well done in the product or service strategy area makes it easier to be successful in the other areas of the mix. Conversely, what are the effects on the rest of the mix when the product or service strategy is incomplete, faulty, or both?

NOTES

1. David J. Luck, *Product Policy and Strategy* (Englewood Cliffs, NJ: Prentice-Hall, Inc., 1972), 5.

2. "Black & Decker Offers New Professional Line of Lubricants & Chemicals," *Industrial Distribution* 74 (June 1984): 8.

3. "Eleven Guidelines Help Point the Way for Successful Introduction of New Industrial Products by Marketers," *Marketing News* 16 (April 29, 1983): 8.

4. David T. Wilson, Shirish P. Dant, and Sang-Lin Han, "Buyer–Seller Relationships—Frontline Views," *Marketplace: The ISBM Review* (Fall 1990): 2.

5. "Know Thy Buyer," *Sales Management* 105 (July 22, 1974): 4.

6. *Convair Aerospace Division of General Dynamics: Fiftieth Year Anniversary* (San Diego: Convair Aerospace Division, 1973), 2.

7. "Eaton Is Deflated by Air Bags," *Marketing Executive's Digest* (April 1979): 4.

8. Richard T. Gordon, "Exxon's R & D Flop," *Industrial Marketing* 66 (May 1981): 9.

9. See John R. Rockwell and Marc C. Paraticelli, "New Product Strategy: How the Pros Do It," *Industrial Marketing* 67 (May 1982): 49–60; and Robert G. Cooper, "The Impact of New Product Strategies," *Industrial Marketing Management* 12 (1983): 246.

10. Ibid.

11. "MSI Research Priorities: Mirror for Marketing Concerns," *Marketing Science Institute Review* (Fall 1990): 3.

12. Robert G. Cooper and E. J. Kleinschmidt, "Success Factors in Product Innovation," *Industrial Marketing Management* 16 (1987): 215.

13. Robert G. Cooper, "The Dimensions of Industrial New Product Success and Failure," *Journal of Marketing* 45 (Summer 1979): 93.

14. "Fall '86 Workshop: New Product and Service Planning," *Marketplace: The ISBM Review* (Spring 1987): 1.

15. Peter J. Link, "Keys to New Product Success and Failure," *Industrial Marketing Management* 16 (1987): 111.

16. Cooper and Kleinschmidt, op. cit., 216.

17. Robert G. Cooper, "Why New Industrial Products Fail," *Industrial Marketing Management* 4 (1975): 273.

18. Link, op. cit., 110.

19. Robert D. Hisrich and Michael P. Peters, *Marketing a New Product: Its Planning, Development, and Control* (Menlo Park, CA: The Benjamin/Cummings Publishing Company, 1978), 14.

20. "Eaton Is Deflated by Air Bags," op. cit.

21. Gordon, op. cit.

22. Ulrike de Brentani, "Success and Failure in New Industrial Services," *Journal of Product Innovation Management* 6 (1989): 239–258.

23. Richard T. Hise, *Product/Service Strategy* (New York: Petrocelli/Charter, 1977), 148.

24. James H. Flournoy, "Organizing and Getting New Product Ideas," in A. Edward Spitz, ed., *Product Planning* (Princeton, NJ: Auerbach Publishers, 1972), 148.

25. Ibid., 151.

26. See Hisrich and Peters, op. cit., 57–61.

27. E. Karns and H. T. McGee, "Product Planning Aids Industry," *Iron Age* (November 24, 1960): 93.

28. John I. Coppett and William A. Staples, "Product Profile Analysis: A Tool for Industrial Selling," *Industrial Marketing Management* 9 (1980): 208.

29. See J. T. O'Meara, Jr., "Selecting Profitable Products," *Harvard Business Review* 39 (January–February 1961): 83–89.

30. Robert G. Cooper, "An Empirically Derived

New Product Project Selection Model," *IEEE Transactions on Engineering Management,* EM-28 (1981): 54–61.

31. Robert G. Cooper and Ulrike de Brentani, "Criteria for Screening New Industrial Products," *Industrial Marketing Management* 13 (1984): 149.

32. "Why New Products Fail," *The Conference Board Record* 1 (October 1964): 16.

33. Roger A. More, "Risk Factors in Accepted and Rejected New Industrial Products," *Industrial Marketing Management* 11 (1982): 14.

34. Cooper and de Brentani, op. cit.

35. John M. Rathmell, *Marketing in the Service Sector* (Cambridge, MA: Winthrop Publishers, Inc., 1974), 63.

36. Christopher H. Lovelock, *Services Marketing* (Englewood Cliffs, NJ: Prentice-Hall, Inc., 1984), 480.

37. De Brentani, op. cit., 251.

38. Ibid., 247.

39. Coppett and Staples, op. cit., 209.

40. "Know Thy Buyer," op. cit.

41. *A Guide to Marketing New Industrial Products* (New York: Thomas Publishing Company, 1984), 2.

42. Cooper, "The Dimensions of Industrial New Product Success and Failure," op. cit.

43. "Kelly Johnson, Creator of 'Skunk Works,' Dies," *San Diego Union,* December 22, 1990, A1, A8.

44. Y. D. Scholar, "Faster Delivery Seen as Edge for Foreign Power Tools," *Industrial Distribution* 74 (February 1984): 45.

45. Miland M. Lele and Uday S. Karmarkar, "Good

Product Support Is Smart Marketing," *Harvard Business Review* 61 (November–December 1983): 124.

46. Ibid., 125.

47. David S. Hopkins, *Options in New Product Organization* (New York: The Conference Board, 1974), 50–53.

48. William J. Constandse, "Why New Product Management Fails," *Business Management* 40 (June 1971): 16.

49. Rance Crain, "Profiles of the Product Manager: The Man in the Middle of It All," *Industrial Marketing* 55 (June 1970): 51.

50. "Product Management: Today's Most Demanding Business Job," *MBA Executive* 7 (September 1978): 3.

51. J. Patrick Kelly, and Richard T. Hise, "Industrial and Consumer Product Managers Are Different," *Industrial Marketing Management* 8 (1979): 331.

52. Hopkins, op. cit., 51.

53. See "Has the Product Manager Failed? Or the Folly of Imitation," *Sales Management* 98 (January 1, 1967): 27–66.

54. Hopkins, op. cit., 53.

55. Kelly and Hise, op. cit.

56. Hopkins, op. cit., 52.

57. Constandse, op. cit.

58. See *1990 Application Guidelines: Malcolm Baldridge National Quality Award* (Gaithersburg, MD: U.S. Department of Commerce National Institute of Standards and Technology, 1990).

59. Ibid.

SUGGESTED ADDITIONAL READINGS

A Guide to Marketing New Industrial Products. New York: Thomas Publishing Company, 1983.

Choffray, Jean-Marie, and Gary L. Lilien. "Marketing Planning for New Industrial Products." *Business Marketing* 69 (November 1984): 83–94.

Cooper, Robert G. "The Dimensions of Industrial New Product Success and Failure." *Journal of Marketing* 43 (Summer 1979): 93–103.

———. "The New Product Process: A Decision Guide for Management." *Journal of Marketing Management* 3 (1988): 238–255.

———. "Defining the New Product Strategy." *IEEE: Transactions in Engineering Management,* EM-34 (August 1987): 183–193.

Cooper, Robert G., and Ulrike de Brentani. "Criteria for Screening New Industrial Products." *Industrial Marketing Management* 13 (1984): 149–156.

Cooper, Robert G., and E. J. Kleinschmidt. "Success Factors in Product Innovation." *Industrial Marketing Management* 16 (1987): 215–223.

Cravens, David W., Charles W. Holland, Charles W.

Lamb, Jr., and William C. Moncrief III. "Marketing's Role in Product and Service Quality." *Industrial Marketing Management* 17 (1988): 285–304.

Dawes, P. L., and P. G. Patterson. "The Performance of Industrial and Consumer Product Managers." *Industrial Marketing Management* 17 (1988): 73–84.

De Brentani, Ulrike. "Do Firms Need a Custom Designed New Product Screening Model?" *Journal of Product Innovation Management* 3 (June 1986): 108–119.

––––––. "Success and Failure in New Industrial Services." *Journal of Product Innovation Management* 6 (1989): 239–258.

Hise, Richard T., Larry O'Neal, A. Parasuraman, and James U. McNeal. "Marketing/R & D Interaction in New Product Development: Implications for New Product Success Rates." *Journal of Product Innovation Management* 6 (1990): 142–155.

Hopkins, David S. *New Product Winners and Losers,* Report No. 773. New York: The Conference Board, 1980.

Krubasik, Edward G. "Customize Your Product Development." *Harvard Business Review* 66 (November–December 1988): 46–52.

Lele, Miland M., and Uday S. Karmarkar. "Good Product Support Is Smart Marketing." *Harvard Business Review* 61 (November–December 1983): 124–132.

Link, Peter L. "Keys to New Product Success and Failure." *Industrial Marketing Management* 16 (1987): 109–118.

Lucas, George H., Jr., and Alan J. Bush. "Guidelines for Marketing a New Industrial Product." *Industrial Marketing Management* 13 (1984): 157–161.

Moenaert, Rudy K., and William E. Souder. "An Information Transfer Model for Integrating Marketing and R & D Personnel in New Product Development Projects." *Journal of Product Innovation Management* 7 (1990): 91–107.

Moore, William L. "New Product Development Practices of Industrial Marketers." *Journal of Product Innovation Management* 4 (1987): 6–20.

More, Roger A. "Timing of Market Research in New Industrial Product Situations." *Journal of Marketing* 48 (Fall 1984): 84–94.

Souder, William E. *Managing New Product Innovations.* Lexington, MA: Lexington Books, 1989.

Robinson, William T. "Sources of Market Pioneer Advantages: The Case of Industrial Goods Industries." *Journal of Marketing Research* 25 (February 1988): 87–94.

Wilson, David T., and Morry Ghingold. "Linking R & D to Market Needs." *Industrial Marketing Management* 16 (1987): 207–214.

⸌13⸌

Channel Strategy in
Business Marketing

●●●

For the business marketing manager, the development or acquisition of quality products or services must be accompanied by channels of distribution that deliver those goods and services to target market customers in the quantities required and within the times desired. High-quality products and services cannot be marketed effectively when improper channels are used or when problems occur within proper channels. Establishing and maintaining the channels of distribution that most effectively and economically get the company's product or service mix to target market customers constitute the area of marketing called channel management. This chapter discusses the channel area of the marketing mix as it relates specifically to business markets. Channel strategy is defined and comparisons are made between this type of strategy in business and consumer markets. The chapter examines both direct and indirect channels used in business marketing. Direct channels exist when no independent intermediaries are involved, which means the marketing firm sells directly to its organizational customers. Indirect channels involve the use of independent intermediaries, which are typically industrial distributors and manufacturers' representatives although others may be used at times. Both direct and indirect channels are common in business marketing in both domestic and global markets. The chapter also develops an approach for formulating business channel relationships that are effective and lasting. This chapter is primarily concerned with channels of distribution, not with the physical distribution of products and services within those channels. Physical distribution is covered in detail in the following chapter.

Channel Strategy in Business Marketing

The Information Systems Division of Hyundai Electronics of America formerly functioned primarily as a supplier to IBM and Sun Microsystems, Inc. The division produced and marketed microcomputers for these OEM customers but then expanded its product line to include IBM-compatible AT micros and local area network (LAN) components. After the expansion of its product line, the company's marketing strategy became one of providing low-priced microcomputers to customers through a network of retailing dealers. It focused primarily on dealers who carried one major brand of microcomputer but who were looking for a low-end alternative to round out their product lines.

Moving into this new market, Hyundai first signed agreements with four regional distributors who were then to serve the dealers. This channel failed when the distributors crossed over into one anothers' territories, causing conflict that resulted in the destruction of the channel.

Hyundai then created a direct dealer channel that would bypass the distributors. The company distributed direct to selected dealers in order to avoid the distributor problem. Before moving into this channel, however, Hyundai interviewed dealers across the United States to determine what they saw as shortcomings in their present suppliers. Compiling all these perceived shortcomings, the company then developed a marketing strategy to avoid the same mistakes. Hyundai developed distribution policies and procedures designed to convince the retailer that becoming a Hyundai dealer would mean being a partner with the manufacturer in the distribution process.

Hyundai's initial objective was to have 900 dealers in the United States with an average of three locations per dealer. After one year, 160 dealers with 400 locations had been signed up. This later expanded to 380 selected dealers with about 700 locations nationally. Careful screening and selection by Hyundai management ensured the quality of the dealers in the channel.

In its second year of operation, Hyundai sold 100,000 units and achieved a 5 percent market share. These results were seen as very successful and much of the credit was given to the new channel of distribution. To quote a Hyundai spokesperson, "There's no question that we've established a viable channel."

Source: Adapted from Tom Eisenhart, "Smashing Distribution Barriers," *Business Marketing* 74 (April 1989): 12–16.

BUSINESS CHANNEL STRATEGY

Channel strategy in business marketing involves determining specific channel objectives, choosing what kinds of channel arrangements are to be used, deciding whether or not to use **channel intermediaries,** and determining the types and number of such intermediaries, if used. Once these decisions have been made, tactical programs are implemented to carry out the predetermined strategy. Such programs may include selecting specific intermediaries, developing procedures and arrangements for working with them, determining physical distribution activities to provide goods and services to the intermediaries, and controlling and evaluating their performance. If direct channels are used, many of these tasks become a sales management area of responsibility, which is covered in Chapter 15.

The channel strategy area of business marketing is undergoing turbulent change. For years, it was considered a relatively unchanging and unimaginative part of marketing, and business marketing managers rarely tampered with traditional channels. Although termed "the long neglected side of marketing,"[1] this attitude appears to be changing. The rising cost of personal selling, coupled with the economic forces that are pushing inventory carrying costs and transportation costs higher, points to the need for a careful assessment of the alignment of industrial marketing channels.[2] Such alignment is precisely what is happening— traditional channels are being questioned and replaced. Feeling the strain of high interest rates and inflation, top managements have been demanding greater efficiency from operations. Distribution has been one area in which there is room for improvement, and increased attention has been paid to it. In addition, business marketing firms are seeing that channels can create differential advantages, especially in instances in which competitors' products, prices, and promotional efforts are almost homogeneous.[3] The following quotation summarizes the importance of channel strategy in contemporary business marketing:

> For two decades, product management has dominated marketing strategy. It is not suggested that this will change. Product managers using their planning and analytical techniques will continue to play a crucial role. It is likely, however, that channel management will become a more important concern in the future, particularly if the locus of channel power continues to swing away from the manufacturer.[4]

Another reason why channel strategy is undergoing change is that business markets are undergoing rapid change themselves. As business customers move into new technologies such as CAD, CAM, MRP, and JIT, they demand and expect closer relationships with their suppliers. Many business marketing customers are substantially reducing their numbers of suppliers and creating unusually close partnership relationships with the ones that remain.[5] As this happens, some business marketers have had to move from indirect to direct channels to be able to maintain such close relationships, and those that have continued to use indirect channels have had to be much more selective in their choices of intermediaries. Thus, it can be seen that channel strategy in business marketing is both important and ever-changing, which requires close attention by marketing managers.

Differences Between Business and Consumer Channel Strategies

By definition, channel strategy is channel strategy whether it is in business or consumer markets. However, there are some basic differences between the two markets that affect decision making. Some of these differences may be seen in Table 13.1.

Channels in business markets are typically shorter than those in consumer markets. Based on the dollar volume of sales of business goods and services, it is estimated that about three-fourths are sold directly to the customer with no intermediaries involved. When intermediaries are used, the channels are still

TABLE 13.1   Comparison of Channel Strategy Factors in Consumer and Business Markets

Factor	Consumer Market	Business Market
Importance of channel strategy in marketing mix	Important because many consumers relate retail outlets to product quality and company image	Critical because stockouts, back-orders, and delays cause major and costly delays for many business customers
Channel control	Channels usually dominated by either manufacturers or large retailing organizations	Channels normally dominated by manufacturers, although some industrial distributors sometimes exert control
Length of channels	Often long, passing through many levels of independent intermediaries	Typically short and often direct with no independent intermediaries involved; short even if intermediaries are used
Intermediaries	Many types used (e.g., wholesalers, retailers, jobbers, brokers, agents)	Two types most widely used: industrial distributors and manufacturers' representatives
Amount of goods and services sold through intermediaries	Most products go through intermediaries; estimated that only 5% go direct to customers	Many products go direct, especially those of high unit value; over 75% go direct to customers
Buying customer characteristics	Choice of retailer often emotional and based on image	Choice of intermediaries less emotional and based more on performance
Customer inventory requirements	Often extensive at wholesaler, retailer	Normally extensive, and customers rely on channels
Personal selling	May or may not be important—not so with self-service retailer	Of major importance in business channels, which are fundamentally sales channels
National/major/house accounts	Only with large intermediaries such as retailers and wholesalers	Common with large customers and intermediaries
Strategic partnerships or other relationships	Relationships primarily based on customer loyalty and satisfaction	Partner relationships common between manufacturers and channel intermediaries

comparatively short. Figure 13.1 illustrates the structure of channels in business markets. As can be seen, a channel passing through two intermediaries (the manufacturers' representative and the industrial distributor) is a long channel in business marketing. In the consumer market, a channel of this length may be considered short.

A point of clarification should be made. Figure 13.1 shows the most commonly used channels in business marketing. It should be noted that neither wholesalers nor retailers are shown as channel intermediaries. As was explained in Chapter 1, retailers and wholesalers are customers for some types of business marketing firms. They may well be channel intermediaries in consumer markets, but they are not in business markets. This is why Figure 13.1 shows them as customers and not channel intermediaries.

Business marketing managers often have less choice among channel options than their consumer counterparts. As Figure 13.1 illustrates, six basic channels are most common domestically. Note that these channels are variations of three options—the direct channel, the industrial distributor, and the manufacturers' representative. These options are not true choices in many instances. For example, it is normally not possible to substitute a distributor for a manufacturers' representative, which means that some managers are restricted to the use of one or the other depending on the functions to be performed. Often, the manager has little, if any, choice of channels. Customers may purchase only from traditionally accepted channels, or certain intermediaries will not carry the manager's products.

Because of customer expectations and the complexity of business products and services, there is much greater emphasis on selling, service, and technical assistance in business channels than in consumer channels. Although it is true that intermediaries in the consumer durables market also perform the functions of selling and service, they normally do not do so to the degree that industrial distributors and manufacturers' representatives may have to do in business marketing. In business markets, personal selling, presale and postsale servicing, and technical assistance in setting up operations are prerequisites for effective marketing. As is shown later in this chapter, manufacturers' representatives are basically independent salespeople selling on behalf of their manufacturing principals, and distributors are often chosen on the basis of the capabilities of their field sales forces.

There are indications that business marketing managers believe that an inventory holding service is more important than consumer marketing managers do. This indication is due to the production requirements of many business customers. If a retailer runs out of toothpaste in the consumer market, the customer may suffer an inconvenience, but it is highly unlikely that such a shortage will cause any major consternation. If a distributor or a branch house runs out of OEM component parts, however, that stockout can shut down the production line of a customer, with disastrous marketing effects on the supplier, as most buyers will not tolerate late deliveries of such products. In JIT cases in business markets, customer firms unload incoming shipments directly into the produc-

FIGURE 13.1   Structure of Channels in Business Marketing

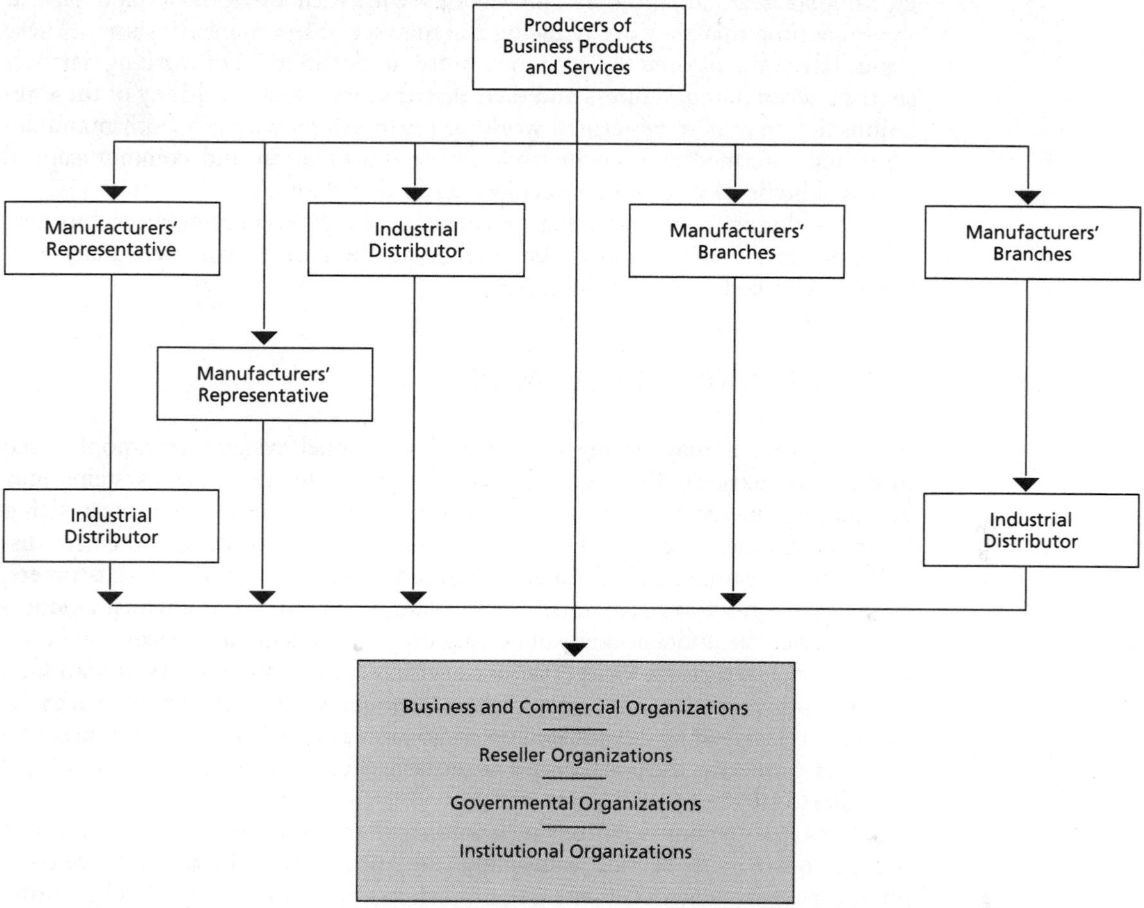

Channel of Distribution	Percent of Unit Sales
Producer–Distributor–Customer	48.7%
Producer–MR–Distributor–Customer	16.8
Producer–Customer	12.7
Producer–Branch–Customer	9.6
Producer–Branch–Distributor–Customer	8.6
Producer–MR–Customer	3.6

tion line to avoid second and third handling of the same products. When this situation occurs, field warehousing and field inventory control become a critical part of the manager's channel strategy.

Another difference between the two markets is that in business marketing, there are often much closer relationships between manufacturers and their channel intermediaries, as was developed in Chapter 7. Many manufacturers are creating strategic alliances or partnerships with their distributors and reps at the same time that they are reducing the number of intermediaries used. These trends have underscored the need for a better understanding of working partnerships between manufacturers and their distributors and reps.[6] Many of these relationships may best be termed working partnerships whereby both manufacturer and intermediary benefit from closer coordination and communication. This will be developed in more detail later in this chapter.

This discussion implies that there are major differences between business and consumer marketing in the channel area. Therefore, a complete analysis of business channel strategy is in order.

ANALYSIS OF BUSINESS CHANNEL SYSTEMS

At this point, it may be useful to describe channel systems commonly used in business markets. Review of Figure 13.1 illustrates that these systems may be analyzed in terms of their channel components. The figure indicates that business channels may be (1) direct to customers, (2) through industrial distributors to customers, (3) through manufacturers' representatives to customers, or (4) through various combinations of distributors and MRs. Thus, business channels may be understood by analyzing these approaches and becoming familiar with the characteristics of each. For example, to use distributors or manufacturers' representatives, it is first necessary to understand what each type of intermediary is and what advantages or disadvantages each offers the marketing manager. Similarly, the positive and negative aspects of the direct channel should be understood.

Use of one channel option, such as direct, does not mean others cannot be used. In business marketing, multiple or dual channels of distribution are common, especially when different target markets are involved. Figure 13.2 shows this quite clearly using the climate control industry as an example. Note that some manufacturers sell their products direct to contractors, consulting engineers, owners/operators, and other manufacturers. These customers could be large and influential and a firm that uses a direct channel to distribute to them will have a closer relationship with such important customers. At the same time, the figure shows that other manufacturers in the industry sell to some of the same types of customers through either industrial distributors, manufacturers' representatives, or both. Actually, a single company could use all three options at the same time. It might use a direct channel to its larger customers, distributors to reach smaller customers, and a manufacturers' representative in global markets.

This same multiple channel concept can also be seen in Table 13.2, which analyzes the sales of some business products direct and through distributors and manufacturers' representatives. The table shows wide variations by product type, but it also shows that few industries seem to use one option exclusively. In

FIGURE 13.2 Marketing Channel System Used by the Climate Control Industry

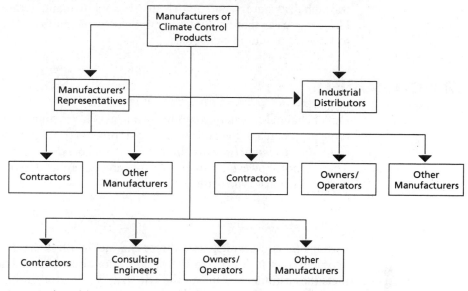

Source: Adapted from *The Changing Markets in the Heating–Cooling Industry* (Birmingham, MI: Air Conditioning, Heating & Refrigeration News, 1975), 3.

TABLE 13.2 Sales Through Business Channels of Selected Business Products

Products	Percent Through Manufacturers' Branches	Percent Through Distributors	Percent Through Manufacturers' Representatives
Electrical apparatus and equipment	46.7%	40.6%	12.7%
Electronic parts and equipment	25.8	38.1	36.0
Industrial machinery and equipment	33.0	52.0	15.1
Industrial supplies	46.0	45.6	8.4
Professional equipment and supplies	23.4	69.4	7.2
Chemicals and allied products	76.4	19.3	4.3
Farm supplies	22.6	72.1	5.2
Paints, varnishes, and supplies	53.1	39.6	7.4
Lumber, plywood, and millwork	24.9	69.3	5.8
Metals service centers and offices	51.1	41.3	7.6
Coal and other minerals and ores	37.4	38.1	24.5
Plumbing and heating equipment and supplies	20.2	64.5	15.3
Commercial machines and equipment	65.8	29.7	4.5
Construction and mining machinery and equipment	27.9	69.8	2.3
Industrial paper	53.8	38.8	7.4

Source: Adapted from U.S. Department of Commerce, *1977 Census of Wholesale Trade*, vol. 1, *Subject Statistics* (Washington, DC: U.S. Government Printing Office, August 1981), 1-6–1-16.

fact, some are very evenly spread over all three. For example, in the distribution of electronic parts and equipment, 26 percent are sold direct, 38 percent are sold through distributors, and 36 percent are sold by manufacturers' representatives. Here, it is clear that manufacturers of electronic parts and equipment are likely to be users of multiple channels.

DIRECT CHANNELS

Direct channels are very common in business marketing, and they account for a large percentage of the dollar value of shipments through business channels. The term *direct channel* means there are no independent intermediaries involved. There is not, however, a single type of direct channel. Clarification is needed to understand each type better.

Field Salespeople

Perhaps the most widely used direct channel involves the use of company salespeople who sell directly to the organizational customer. The salesperson contacts the customer and makes the sale with the goods then shipped directly to the customer either from the factory or from a regional branch location or warehouse. Regional sales offices may or may not be used, but the main point is that company field salespeople constitute the actual channel of distribution. Management of this type of channel is basically sales management. Field salespeople must be recruited, selected, trained, assigned to territories, evaluated, promoted, terminated, and replaced. These activities are usually the responsibility of the sales manager, and they are covered in Chapter 15.

Inside Salespeople

Some business marketing companies use inside or telephone salespeople extensively as a channel of distribution. A Conference Board study of business marketing firms found 25 percent used this channel.[7] This channel is rarely used in an exclusive manner, but it is common as a support for the direct sales channel. For example, inside salespeople may be used with straight rebuy customers in a sales maintenance capacity. This channel is similar in many ways to the field salespeople channel except that contact is made by telephone rather than field sales call. Again, management of an inside sales channel is usually the responsibility of the sales manager and is covered in Chapter 15.

Telemarketing

A newer direct channel used in business markets is via telemarketing direct to present and prospective customers. Telemarketing can be viewed as an expansion of inside sales into newer forms of telecommunication technology such as computer-controlled scripts and computer-to-computer communication between buyer and seller. The previously cited Conference Board study disclosed 10 percent of business firms using this channel.[8] This area also is commonly the responsibility of the sales manager and is covered in Chapter 15.

Catalogs

There are some, but not many, direct business channels in which no personal contact is involved. This channel typically exists with relatively standardized products such as MRO supplies, processed materials, and some component parts. The channel is a relatively simple one, whereby the customer orders directly from a catalog and the goods are then shipped. About 6 percent of respondents in the Conference Board study used this channel.[9] No salesperson or intermediary is involved. As stated, this channel is not widely used in business marketing.

National or Major Accounts

Another form of direct channel often found in business marketing is the national or major account. This type of direct channel may also be called the house, corporate, or key account. Typically involving very large, important customers with which partnerships or alliances are created, the company deals with these customers direct and bypasses any intermediaries. For example, a manufacturer may use a network of industrial distributors to sell to customers across the United States; nonetheless, it does not permit those distributors to sell to national or major accounts. These customers are directly contacted by the manufacturer in some manner. Even when company field salespeople are used, certain customers may be kept as national or major accounts. Companies using this concept typically maintain contact with the customer in one of three manners. Some assign a top executive to the account; others assign a sales specialist to the account; and still others set up a separate sales division to service their national or major accounts. The reasons for this type of channel are better control, more attention paid to larger customer needs, prevention of competitors making inroads, increased efficiency, and reduction in sales costs. Chapter 15 addresses national accounts from the perspective of sales management.

This discussion indicates that the term *direct channel* may have many different meanings. Thus, different options are available in setting up direct channels. The marketing manager should consider these options in developing proper channels. In addition, many of these options can be used simultaneously, which further complicates the direct channel issue.

INDIRECT CHANNELS

While direct channels may account for a large percentage of the dollar value of shipments in business marketing, this does not mean that **indirect channels** are either unimportant or rarely used. Since most business marketing indirect channels use industrial distributors, manufacturers' representatives, or both, a thorough understanding of each of these intermediaries is necessary if the marketing manager is to use them in an effective manner.

The Industrial Distributor

An **industrial distributor** is an independently owned and locally managed operation that buys, stocks, and sells the production tools, operating equipment, and maintenance supplies used by all forms of industry. The distributor is basically a wholesaler that services and sells to business markets as opposed to consumer markets. As classified by *Industrial Distribution* magazine, there are three basic types of industrial distributors: the specialist, the generalist, and the combination house.[10]

> *The specialist.* The **specialist distributor** is the distributor who specializes in such lines as bearings, cutting tools, fasteners, and machine tools. A specialist is defined as a distributorship in which one product category consistently accounts for 50 percent or more of total sales.

> *The generalist.* In contrast with the specialist, the **generalist distributor** is almost like an industrial supermarket, stocking a wide variety of goods and having no specific area of specialization. A general line house is defined as a distributorship in which no one major product category contributes 50 percent or more of total sales.

> *The combination house.* The **combination house distributor** is a type of distributor that handles such other goods as plumbing supplies, hardware, etc., in addition to carrying industrial supplies. Basically, this type is a combination of wholesaler and distributor that operates in both business and consumer markets.

The annual surveys conducted by *Industrial Distribution* magazine reveal a trend toward specialization in the nation's distributors in recent years. This trend has important implications for the business marketing manager, as it means more and more distributors are available for consideration in channels of producers of technically sophisticated products. Producers in such channels previously had to use direct channels to obtain the level of technical expertise required by the marketplace. A continued trend toward specialization can well mean shifts from company salespeople to the use of distributors and their sales personnel.

Sales Through Distributors   It is difficult to determine precisely the usage of industrial distributors in business markets. In some industries they are used extensively, whereas in other industries they are rarely used. On the basis of the dollar value of sales, roughly about 15 percent to 20 percent of all business sales go through industrial distributors. In terms of unit sales, an estimated three-fourths of all business sales pass through distributors. It must be realized that in terms of unit sales, a nut or a washer counts the same as a blast furnace—each is one unit.

Referring back to Table 13.2, the use of industrial distributors in specific industries may be examined. As can be seen, some industries use distributors much more than others. The largest users of these intermediaries are: farm supplies (72.1 percent); construction and mining machinery and equipment (69.8 percent); professional equipment and supplies (69.4 percent); lumber, plywood, and millwork (69.3 percent); plumbing and heating equipment and supplies (64.5 percent); and industrial machinery and equipment (52.0 percent).

Another study of 219 manufacturers in industries between SIC 22 and 37 found that 43.4 percent used industrial distributors in some manner.[11] Summarizing information from these sources, it may be concluded that industrial distributors are commonly used in situations where the following conditions are found:

- The product is relatively standardized.
- The market is composed of many relatively small customers and prospects who may be geographically scattered.
- Purchase orders are relatively small and purchases are made quite frequently.
- Customer lead times for delivery are relatively short.

Profile of the Industrial Distributor   Industrial distributors come in all sizes of operations. Some are huge: Their sales exceed $100 million annually, and their inventories may exceed $3 million. Others are local and small. Still others are of medium size. In terms of numbers, the majority of distributors appear to fall into the medium-sized classification. On the basis of data derived from *Industrial Distribution,* it is possible to construct a profile of the average industrial distributor that may help in better understanding this intermediary and its characteristics. Table 13.3 shows relevant characteristics of distributors, as discovered in *Industrial Distribution*'s annual survey of distributor operations.

If a summary is made from this profile, it can be seen that the industrial distributor is a locally owned and operated intermediary that provides field warehousing, sales, and service capabilities into business markets. As such, this intermediary can be an effective channel component for the marketing manager.

How the Distributor Serves the Marketing Manager   For the marketing manager, the decision to use distributors is based on what is to be gained from their use that might not be achieved from a branch house and company salespeople. Distributors can be used to advantage in a number of ways.

First, distributors offer the marketing manager established sales forces. If it is assumed that the average distributor has three field salespersons and each makes six calls per day, this amount is equal to eighteen field sales calls per distributor used. Multiply this amount by a network of fifty or 100 or 250 distributors, and the full impact can be realized. Using distributors allows the marketing manager to capitalize on the sales capabilities of those distributors.

Second, because distributors are often locally owned and operated, their

TABLE 13.3   Profile of the Industrial Distributor

Type of distributor	50% are specialists; 35% are generalists; and 15% are combination houses
Age of the organization	Average age is 24 years; only 14% started before 1945; more than one-half are 20 years old or less
Ownership	45% are owned by one individual; 33% by members of the same family; and 18% by family and non-family members
Total warehouse space	5,000 square feet for specialists; 8,400 for generalists; 15,000 for combination houses
Median inventory value	$250,000 for specialists; $258,000 for generalists; $200,000 for combination houses
Average inventory turnover	5.6 times for specialists; 5.4 times for generalists; 4.5 times for combination houses
Sales from stock	Approximately two-thirds of all sales from stock
Number of invoices billed annually	Ranges from 4,000 for specialists to 6,000 for generalists
Average invoice value	Ranges from $500 for specialists to $416 for generalists
Collections—Median number of days outstanding	Average is 44 days
Total number of employees	Range from 10 for specialists to 10.5 for generalists to 13.5 for combination houses
Number of salespeople	Approximately 3 outside salespeople and 2 to 3 inside salespeople
Median sales per employee	$170,000 for specialists; $150,000 for generalists; $130,000 for combination houses
Branch locations	64% of specialists and 66% of generalists have no branches; 24% of specialists and 23% of generalists have 1 to 2 branches; 9% of specialists and 6% of generalists have 3 or more branches

Source: Compiled from recent surveys of distributor operations conducted by *Industrial Distribution* magazine.

personnel often know buyers and buying influences on a more personal basis than company salespeople would when coming into the community from outside. In addition, distributors can often provide quicker delivery and service because of their location. Thus, the use of distributors often permits the marketing manager to have local representation in the channel of distribution.

Third, distributors stock goods, which in turn reduces stocks that must be maintained in the field by the marketing manager. Since distributors also have their own warehousing facilities, their use in the distribution channel means that the marketing company does not have to maintain its own buildings, materials-handling equipment, and personnel. The business marketing manager desiring field warehousing and inventory maintenance may find a distributor to be a useful channel component.

Fourth, distributors can also reduce the credit requirements of the business goods manufacturer. In taking title, the distributor extends credit to its customers, thereby relieving the marketing manager of this requirement. Instead of extending credit to many final customers, the marketing company may be involved in credit extension to only a few distributors, who in turn serve those same final customers.

Fifth, some distributors are good sources of local market feedback because of their close proximity to customers. A network of such distributors can be beneficial in a marketing information system. Since distributors are also technically oriented, they are often good sources of technical data.

Finally, the use of distributors often lowers the final costs to customers. Because the distributor breaks bulk and provides inventory and delivery services and personnel, the cost of using this channel is typically lower than using branch houses and company salespeople. In turn, its lower costs can sometimes be passed on to customers in terms of lower prices. A good example can be seen in the case of Ducommun Metals & Supply Company. Ducommun claims it can save customers 37.7 percent if they purchase Ducommun materials as opposed to buying from the manufacturers.[12] In Ducommun's case, the customer saves because costs of inventory possession are shifted to a distributor, Ducommun.

Limitations of Using Industrial Distributors   The preceding section implies so many benefits from using the distributor that a business channel of distribution without this intermediary seems illogical. Yet for many business marketing managers, using distributors may make little sense. They may be impossible to control, and in some cases, they may actually dominate the channel. They may not possess the technical sales or service capabilities to handle sophisticated products. Often, they handle competing products and do not emphasize the marketing manager's products. Their product lines can even have adverse effects on some manufacturers' products. Like many consumer market intermediaries, distributors look for turnover and margin, and they may not accept products that take considerable time to sell and deliver.

In addition, other problems may be encountered when using distributors.[13] If manufacturers keep large customers as national or major accounts, these profitable customers are not available to the distributors, even though the customers may be in the distributors' territories. Thus, national accounts can be a point of conflict between manufacturers and distributors. Another problem is that many distributors are small and not well managed. Therefore, a system of distributors can include both well-run and poorly run companies, making an uneven channel system. A study of distributors revealed that only 22 percent rated themselves as good or better in setting goals and standards.[14] Another major problem with distributors involves inventory levels. Manufacturers typically want their distributors to carry higher inventories than the intermediaries want to carry. For the business marketing company, inventory levels must be large enough to meet customer demands, otherwise stockouts and backorders occur. Since distributors take title, however, they are often reluctant to carry excess inventories, and therefore conflict can often take place. Still another problem is that distributors typically want to carry second lines, which means they carry competitors' products. In this situation, the marketing company may lose sales to competitive products and give up control at the same time. Yet another problem with distributors is fitting them into existing company sales territories. For example, a marketing company may wish to have a distributor in the New England area but may not find any distributors available to serve only this territory. Some may cover only a few of the New England states; others may cover areas wider than New England. Finally, distributors, in being independently owned and managed, may be cantankerous and difficult to control. They may well reject the marketing company's policies and procedures, and they may simply ignore marketing advice provided by the manager. Nonetheless, these problems are not insurmountable if the marketing manager is willing to work at their solution.

By classifying distributors as local, regional, or national, insight may be gained regarding the strengths and weaknesses of each type. Tables 13.4 and 13.5 show how manufacturers and buyers see each type as providing a number of characteristics. Table 13.4 shows that manufacturers rate local distributors low on feedback but fairly high on appreciation of customers' purchasing procedures. Conversely, national distributors are rated reasonably well on feedback but not so well on appreciation of customers' purchasing procedures. Table 13.5 shows how buyers rate distributors as providing a number of various services. Again, distinct differences exist based on type of coverage. For example, local distributors are given the worst possible score for providing engineering assistance, whereas national distributors are rated quite highly on this service.

Viewing distributors in this manner is managerially sound. The tables show

TABLE 13.4 How Manufacturers See Different Types of Distributors as Providing Various Services

As Providing	Local	Regional	National
Marketing services: feedback, market information, and forecasting	2.78	1.83	1.48
Salespeople's knowledge of the industry	2.32	1.86	1.82
Appreciation of technical aspects of customers' projects	1.93	1.63	2.44
Salespeople's knowledge of manufacturers' lines	1.79	1.72	2.48
Local sales promotion	1.89	1.74	2.37
Appreciation of customers' purchasing procedures	1.50	1.88	2.62
Personal integrity: reliability of statements and promises to manufacturers and customers	1.56	1.92	2.52
Frequency of sales contact: depth of penetration	1.63	1.85	2.52
Customer service: quotes and samples	1.71	1.79	2.54

Source: Reprinted by permission from "Grading Distributor Competence," *Industrial Distribution* 66 (May 1976):84.

Note: 1.00 = best possible score; 3.00 = worst possible score.

TABLE 13.5   **How Purchasing Agents See Different Types of Distributors as Providing Various Services**

As Providing	Local	Regional	National
Engineering assistance: before and/or after the order	3.00	1.81	1.19
Appreciation of technical aspects of the project	2.46	1.85	1.69
Inventory reliability	2.32	1.84	1.84
Salespeople's knowledge of the product	2.24	1.82	1.94
Reliability of delivery	2.00	1.94	2.06
Frequency of sales calls	1.94	1.88	2.19
Personal integrity: reliability of promises and information	1.78	1.83	2.39
Appreciation of customers' purchasing procedures	1.69	1.81	2.50
Salespeople's ability to expedite factory action, to obtain factory information	2.33	1.89	1.79
Availability of spares, parts	2.32	1.82	1.79
Fulfillment of partials, backorders	2.21	1.74	2.05
Reliability of delivery commitments	2.06	1.84	2.16

Source: Reprinted by permission from "Grading Distributor Competence," *Industrial Distribution* 66 (May 1976):85.

Note: 1.00 = best possible score; 3.00 = worst possible score.

that the business marketing manager contemplating the use of distributors should look at them not only as specialists or general line types but also as local, regional, or national. The strengths and weaknesses of each type can then be matched against channel objectives to aid in decision making.

Industrial Distributor Trends   The industrial distributor industry appears to be undergoing a number of changes. Despite the fact that most distributors are small, independent businesses, there is a definite trend toward becoming larger and more specialized, as market needs become more sophisticated and specialized. In addition, many mergers and acquisitions are taking place as larger distributors acquire smaller ones. In a report prepared by Arther Anderson, Inc., for the National Association of Wholesalers-Distributors, it was estimated that the number of U.S. distributors could decrease by 25 percent between 1987 and 1995 primarily due to mergers and acquisitions.[15] A survey by *Industrial Distribution* magazine found that 30 percent of surveyed distributors had been approached with an acquisition offer, 33 percent would welcome an acquisition, and 17 percent were actively seeking an acquisition.[16] Indications are that this merger mania will continue as, "Every year more and more family businesses are being acquired by quasi-distributorships, holding companies, with access to capital." [17] All this is happening because the industry is changing so fast that smaller distributors are having difficulty surviving due to economic constraints. The result may be fewer but larger and more sophisticated distributors.

At the same time, another trend is occurring. Small distributors are joining buying groups such as ID One and Evergreen so that they may better compete on price with their larger peers. By such moves and by offering personalized service, there still are niches filled by the smaller distributors.[18]

Another trend is that manufacturers are reducing the number of their distributors so as to control the channel and eliminate marginal intermediaries more effectively. Harnischfeger Corporation reduced its network of 250 small distributors to twenty-two large distributors because it wanted its "distributors to be larger, more professional, and better financed."[19]

Yet another trend is the creation of closer relationships between manufacturers and distributors. These basically are partnership agreements whereby both benefit. Having a partnership with a supplier (or distributor) is a concept rather at odds with the traditional arm's length, almost adversarial, interaction between supplier and intermediary, but it is a concept gaining acceptance on both sides.[20] This subject will be covered in more detail later in the chapter.

The general trend appears to be toward increased use of industrial distributors in business marketing. The Conference Board study cited previously in the chapter found that 54 percent of business marketing firms surveyed currently use industrial distributors and that 30 percent expected to depend more heavily on them in the future.[21] As the costs of personal selling continue to increase, many business marketers have turned to distributors as a way to reduce sales costs without negatively affecting sales productivity. In doing so, many marketers have increased the amount of support given to their distributors. Exhibit 13.1 typifies the approach taken by many business marketing companies in supporting distributors in their channels.

The Manufacturers' Representative

The other intermediary most often found in business marketing is the **manufacturers' representative,** commonly called the manufacturers' rep, or simply the MR. In some markets, these intermediaries are known as manufacturing agents, engineering representatives, and even brokers, although the latter term is technically incorrect. In this section, the term *MR* is used to describe this intermediary. According to the Manufacturers' Agents National Association, a manufacturers' agent or manufacturers' representative is a self-employed salesperson who represents one or more manufacturers on a commission basis.[22] Such independent salespeople sometimes work alone, in partnerships, or in corporations. The organization itself is sometimes called a manufacturer's agency. As used in this text, the term *manufacturers' representative* denotes an individual or an organization, depending on which type is involved. Some MR operations are individuals using their own homes as offices; others are multiperson, multioffice operations that are incorporated and employ large numbers of people. There is great diversity in MR businesses. Although female MRs may be found, most MRs in business markets are male. Unlike the distributor, the MR does not take title and usually does not even take possession of the goods involved. Basically, the MR is an independent salesperson who usually sells within assigned territories and is

EXHIBIT 13.1   **Example of a Business Marketing Company Using Distributors in Its Channel of Distribution**

Bullard Abrasive Products produces a line of industrial abrasive products that it sells through industrial distributors to the welding, industrial, construction, hardware, and rental markets. The company wished to capture a larger share of the abrasive market through a program involving its distributors to create a new level of visibility and activity for Bullard. In addition, the company wanted to increase its presence among distributors not presently carrying Bullard products.

Bullard's approach was to help its distributors promote their strengths. To support its distributors and increase their effectiveness, Bullard designed a full-color product catalog to help distributors easily match specific products with specific applications. The company also redesigned packaging and information sheets for use by the distributors, and it provided point-of-purchase displays that could be customized by the distributors. In addition, the company increased trade advertising to final customers to stimulate demand for the distributors. Finally, Bullard used its company salespeople to work with its distributors rather than selling to end customers. To quote a company spokesperson: "We see our salespeople as being account managers or program managers, as opposed to sales reps."

Bullard's channel strategy was based on the fact that the firm produced high-quality products that were competitively priced. But Bullard saw the need for aiding its distributors in more effectively marketing to the target markets.

Source: Adapted from "Bullard Takes the Offensive in Competitive Abrasives Market," *Industrial Distribution* 77 (August 1987): 52.

compensated on a straight commission basis for those sales. The MR may represent any number of manufacturers in that territory, or closely related territories, whose products are normally complementary rather than competitive. With a line of complementary products from various manufacturers, MRs are often able to supply a complete product line to their customers. Under normal conditions, the MR possesses limited authority with regard to prices and terms of sale. Simply stated, the MR is an independent salesperson and is used by manufacturers in business marketing in lieu of company sales personnel. The MR's basic function is to sell the principal's products in the assigned sales territory.

The average MR probably began in business by working as a salesperson for a manufacturer, a distributor, or another manufacturers' rep, although MRs have come from such areas as purchasing, production, and engineering. After working in the field and building customer contacts for a time, and believing those contacts to be loyal, the MR quit his or her job and started his or her own sales business, continuing to sell to the same customers. The MRs are often thought of as the elite of salespersons, and they are often just that. It takes an excellent salesperson to live on a straight commission form of compensation: If the MR does not sell, he or she does not eat. There is little calling for MRs who are poor salespeople—they simply do not survive in business markets.

It should also be understood that some MRs do carry inventory for their principals and that they ship from that inventory. These MRs are known as **stocking representatives,** and about one-third of the nation's rep firms provide some form of warehousing. The stocking rep is a hybrid form of intermediary. In some cases, the business takes title to the goods stored and is a combination of representative and distributor. In other instances, the rep does not take title but merely provides warehouse space for the principal and thus still functions as a true manufacturers' representative.

Manufacturers' representatives also can be found in various areas of the consumer market, where they often are lumped together with brokers. Their greatest marketing impact, however, seems to be in business markets.

Sales Through Manufacturers' Representatives Estimating the use of manufacturers' representatives in business marketing is difficult but some figures provide insight. There is, however, considerable variance in the studies that have been conducted. For example, the previously discussed Conference Board study found 37 percent of its business marketing respondents used reps in their channels of distribution.[23] Another study of 219 business marketing firms revealed that 56.6 percent used reps in some capacity. These data suggest that the use of manufacturers' representatives is common in business marketing. Some other indicators may be seen by referring to Table 13.2. The table shows that reps are not used to the extent that direct channels or distributors are but there is considerable use in such industries as electronic parts and equipment (36.0 percent), coal and other minerals and ores (24.5 percent), plumbing and heating equipment and supplies (15.3 percent), and industrial machinery and equipment (15.1 percent). Thus, the conclusion is that reps are used in business marketing channels but not to the same extent as are distributors. In summary, the use of reps is most appropriate when the following conditions exist: [24]

- The product is not standard but is closer to made-to-order.
- The product tends toward technical complexity.
- Gross margins are not large.
- The market is composed of relatively few customers that are concentrated geographically and concentrated in a few industries.
- Customers order relatively infrequently and allow fairly long lead times.

Profile of the Manufacturers' Representative Manufacturers' reps come in all forms and differ according to the size of their operations, territories covered, depth and breadth of product lines carried, number of principals represented, commission rates, and their technical and sales capabilities. In spite of these differences, a profile of the average MR can be constructed that may be helpful in better understanding this intermediary. This can be seen in Table 13.6.

Compensation of Manufacturers' Representatives The primary method of compensating MRs is straight **commission** on sales. Commission rates vary considerably from industry to industry and even among reps in the same industry. For example, rates can range from around 5 percent in lumber to over 20 per-

TABLE 13.6   Profile of the Manufacturers' Representative

Type of organization	24% sole proprietorships, 4% partnerships, 57% corporations, 15% Sub-S corporations
Average gross sales	$5,872,027
Average number of years in operation	15.7 years
Average number of states covered	4.9 states
Manufacturers (principals) represented	Average number of principals is 10.4, but wide variances exist
Average time representing a principal	12.5 years
Average number of field salespeople	3.6
Methods of paying field salespeople	30% salary only, 48% salary plus commission, 22% commission only
Commission rates	Average about 7.5%, but as low as 2% and as high as 20%+
Major markets served	57% OEM, 50% distributors, 25% capital equipment in primary markets, 25% capital equipment manufacturing, 12% government, 12% retailers
Types of products sold	All types, from component parts and supplies to technical capital goods; products complementary and not competitive
Marketing activities performed for principals	52% market research, 80% manning trade show booths, 73% sales forecasting, 37% training distributor salespeople, 52% service calls for products sold
Global interests	40% represent foreign manufacturers, 15% sell products overseas, and 20% plan more global business
Warehousing and inventory stocking	Most do not provide warehousing or carry stock, about 31% do provide some level of warehousing, 43% also act as distributors on occasion
Major expenses	25.4% to salaries and commissions to employees, 43.0% to salaries and draws to owners, 31.6% to office, rent, phone, promotion, transportation, insurance, and administrative expenses
Origin of the business	84% were founded by owners, 16% were acquired from previous owners, 4% came about through merger
Background of owner	48% were sales managers, 26% were former salespeople, 5% were former purchasing agents
Average age of owner	51.4 years
Future of the business	34% believe business will cease when owner retires, 40% will sell business to employees, 29% will pass business on to heirs

Source: Compiled from surveys conducted by the Manufacturers' Agents National Association.

cent in medical supplies and services. Because of these wide variations, it is difficult to compute an average income for MRs. According to the Manufacturers' Agents National Association, the average agency rep earns $56,000 per year after taxes.[25]

Some reps (about 20 percent) receive additional fees or commissions from their principals for activities other than selling. These commissions range from 2 percent to 25 percent for such services as stocking orders, invoicing and carrying receivables, stocking and delivering spare parts, installing equipment, training operators in customer firms, and providing engineering design assistance. Some manufacturers pay MRs additional fees for pioneering new products, opening new accounts, and exceeding sales quotas. Manufacturers' representatives are increasingly being compensated for two types of service: (1) commissions on sales and (2) commissions or fees for additional services.

How the Manufacturers' Representative Serves the Marketing Manager
Just as with the industrial distributor, the decision to use manufacturers' representatives in the channel of distribution is dependent on what these intermediaries can offer the marketing manager. The marketing manager typically compares manufacturers' representatives and company salespeople in making such a decision. Manufacturers' representatives may be chosen for a number of reasons.

First, most reps have contacts established in the marketplace, and they can provide immediate entry because of these contacts. The use of a company salesperson in the same territory may involve that person attempting to develop such contacts, which can take considerable time.

Second, since manufacturers' representatives typically represent a number of manufacturers of compatible products, they can carry a broader product line than a company salesperson can. Often, other products in that line contribute to the sale of the marketing manager's products. Figure 13.3 illustrates the line of products carried by a rep who serves the midwestern electrical industry. This rep's products complement each other and contribute to one another's sales—a situation that cannot happen with a company salesperson selling any one of the products by itself.

Third, using manufacturers' representatives can be beneficial when products have seasonal demand. Since reps are compensated by commission, they are paid only when they sell. In addition, because they are independent agents, sales costs such as fringe benefits, travel, lodging, meals, and entertainment are not involved in their use. Thus, it is often more economical to use reps than company salespeople.

Fourth, some sales territories cannot support the costs of full-time salespeople. In such instances, the marketing manager may still wish to have his or her products represented, and those products may require some type of personal selling efforts. The use of manufacturers' representatives permits representation without the high costs of personal sales.

Finally, manufacturers' representatives sometimes represent the only choice for a marketing manager. When a company is financially strained or cannot afford to hire its own salespeople, manufacturers' representatives constitute a source of qualified salespeople. For such a company, the rep offers technical and selling competence at reasonable cost. When reps are highly trained and technically competent, they can provide excellent sales coverage for the business marketing manager.

FIGURE 13.3   Example of the Product Line of a Manufacturers' Representative

 ELECTRICAL JOBBERS EQUIPMENT, INC.

2533 - 24TH AVENUE SOUTH • MINNEAPOLIS, MN 55406 • PHONE AC 612/721-4815

CHUCK HEALY, SR. • TOM BURT • RANDY HUYCK • CHUCK HEALY, JR.   FAX 612-721-4818

☐ **NORTH AMERICAN TRANSFORMER**
(Formerly Federal Pacific Electric Company)
Power transformers for utilities

☐ **GEC Measurements**
Protective Relays, Power Transducers

☐ **GEC Switchgear**
SF6 - Power Circuit Breakers

☐ **ROBINTON PRODUCTS, INC.**
Remote data acquisition for load research, revenue metering, substation monitoring and load management.

☐ **SLACAN**
Pole Line Hardware

☐ **CADWELD**
ERICO PRODUCTS, INC. Cadweld Div.
Exothermically welded connections for computer, telephone, utility grounding systems.

☐ **POWER CONVERSION PRODUCTS, INC.**
Battery chargers and rectifiers

☐  **TCC Trinity Chemical Company, Inc.**
PCB testing for oil, water, soil and swab samples.

☐ **SEMCO DIVISION**
Expansion foam kits for conduit seal and fire barrier.

☐ **Adtech**
Signal conditioners, limit alarms, custom engineered electronics.

☐  **ESTERLINE ANGUS**
Chart recorders, data loggers and power survey equipment.

☐ **SCI**
SOLIDSTATE CONTROLS, INC.
Static uninterruptible power systems.

☐  **POST GLOVER RESISTORS, INC**
Neutral grounding, stamped grid and wound type resistors.

☐ **AERO-MOTIVE MFG. COMPANY**
Cable reels, hose reels, balancers, crane electrification systems.

☐  **P-W INDUSTRIES, INC.**
Cable tray, tubing tray, and KBS sealbags.

☐ **boltswitch**
BOLTSWITCH, INCORPORATED
Bolted Pressure Contact Switches

☐ **Transport Technics**
Modular tool belt, tool pouches and holders.

EERA

To request literature check the box adjacent to the manufacturer and fold with our address showing. Staple and return. (Be sure to include name and address.)

 MANA

Limitations of Using MRs Despite their contributions to a business marketing company, there are serious limitations to using MRs in the channel of distribution. These limitations must be understood by the business marketing manager. The MRs can be difficult to control, and their broad product lines often make it impossible for any one principal to direct efforts to the manager's advantage. If a product requires a great deal of specialized care, the MR may be unwilling to take the time to provide such care. Because of their straight commission form of compensation, it is often difficult to get MRs to furnish market feedback, provide necessary service, and perform other functions that take them away from selling and thus reduce their immediate earning revenue. Generally, the MR prefers to concentrate on large customers and large orders, so if a company has many small firms in its target market, it may be impossible to use MRs to reach those customers. Moreover, because the MR normally provides little, if any, field inventory, this intermediary is of little help when local service or parts are required. In addition, great differences exist in the selling and technical competence of individual manufacturers' reps. They must be carefully screened in terms of the marketing manager's channel objectives. To engage an MR in place of a company salesperson because of reduced selling costs makes little sense if sales produced are disproportionate to the savings in cost. Simply stated, a good rep may be a better choice than an equally good company salesperson, but a poor MR is worthless. Finally, using MRs in the channel makes little marketing sense if the buyers and buying influences in the target market will not buy from them but prefer to purchase directly from the manufacturer.

Manufacturers' Representative Trends As with industrial distributors, there has been a growing trend in the United States toward increased use of manufacturers' representatives in business markets. It is estimated that between 45,000 and 50,000 American manufacturers use this intermediary in addition to foreign suppliers.[26] Forecasts are that reps are likely to become a larger and more important marketing tool in the future.[27] The reasons that account for the increased popularity are similar to those related to the increased use of distributors. The big factor is the increased cost of field sales calls by company salespeople. Since the manufacturers' rep is basically a substitute for the company salesperson, it is likely that this intermediary will grow in popularity as sales costs continue to increase. Alternative channels of distribution are becoming a hot button among business marketers, as changes in the selling environment cast a shadow over the future prospects of direct sales organizations. Nonetheless, the chances of the manufacturers' rep channel completely replacing the direct sales channel are remote because of a number of factors. It is not always possible to find reps capable of selling certain products or to certain markets, and the difficulty in controlling MRs should be overcome. Still, as business marketing managers continue to look for more efficient ways to sell goods and services, the manufacturers' representative will continue to offer a viable channel option. Exhibit 13.2 illustrates how one business marketing firm made the decision to use reps in its channel.

EXHIBIT 13.2   **Example of the Use of Manufacturers' Representatives in the Channel of Distribution of a Business Marketing Company**

The Mechanical Division of Reliance Electric developed a new product called the VAV (variable air volume) fan drive. The product's major application was in reducing energy consumption in air-conditioning systems. The VAV fan drive was designed to meet the market's demand for a reliable, maintenance-free, and cost-effective product. Because of this fact, Reliance management believed the product would be successful if effectively sold and distributed.

Looking at its own sales force and its present distributors, Reliance management believed its present channels would not effectively reach the target markets for the VAV fan drive. Company salespeople sold in channels inappropriate for the product, and they used a different kind of sales presentation and strategy than what was required. Based on these considerations, Reliance management judged the company sales force inappropriate for selling the new product.

Reliance management then decided that a network of manufacturers' representatives could best sell the new product. A careful screening and selection process took place, and representatives were selected in the major metropolitan areas to match the concentration of contractors, the prime customers. A two-phase training program was begun, with company salespeople initially training the new representatives in the field. Later, groups of representatives were brought to a central location for a two-day, more extensive training session.

In addition, Reliance provided the representatives with support tools that included an audiovisual sales presentation program, a comprehensive literature package, and computer software aids. By developing a timely product, marketing through a network of selected, independent representatives already in the field, and supporting these representatives with modern tools and training, Reliance hoped to penetrate the market effectively.

Source: Adapted from "Reliance Relies on Agents to Market Important New Product," *Agency Sales Magazine* 11 (September 1981): 12.

FORMULATING BUSINESS CHANNEL STRATEGY

As we have seen, channel strategy is but one part of overall marketing strategy, and as such, it must be formulated within the context of the company's marketing plan. Constructing channels requires specific target marketing and a sound knowledge of the product or service and its requirements. Unless these aspects are known, it is virtually impossible to construct realistic and effective **channels of distribution.** To attempt to build a channel of distribution without knowing whom it is supposed to reach makes no marketing sense whatsoever. Similarly, trying to pick channel components without knowing the product or its requirements is equally foolish. Thus, developing macromarket and micromarket segments and determining product specifications to fill the needs in those segments seems to be in order. It is necessary to match those products and market segments with appropriate channels of distribution. To accomplish this task, the marketing manager should develop some direction in the channel strategy process. Figure 13.4 outlines a process that may be used to view channel selection decisions in an orderly manner. This process integrates manufacturer objectives, buyer preferences, product characteristics, intermediary characteristics, and competitive characteristics into a comprehensive channel decision-making approach.

FIGURE 13.4   **Channel Strategy Process in Business Marketing**

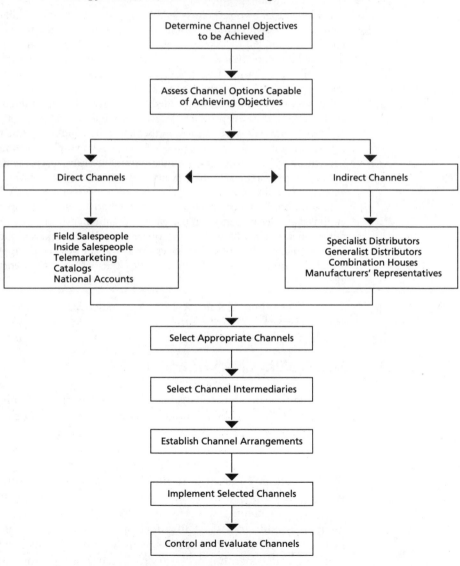

Determining Channel Objectives

Once target markets have been defined and located and product strategy has been formulated, channel objectives should be established. As was developed with product objectives in Chapter 12, channel objectives must be consistent with overall corporate and marketing objectives in the company's marketing plan. Some typical objectives used by business marketing managers in setting up their channels of distribution follow.

Low Cost of Operation   Everything else being equal, business marketing managers strive to reduce costs in their channels, since lower costs allow for higher profitability and lower prices with which to compete in the marketplace. As will be detailed in Chapter 15, the highest cost channel in business marketing is the direct channel in which the company's own salespeople call on the customers. In recent years, many business marketing managers have switched to distributors and manufacturers' representatives who can supply the required sales effort to replace the company's own sales personnel. This switch permits the manager to maintain the required level of sales effort while simultaneously lowering distribution costs and achieving low-cost channel operations. This objective is quite common, although in adopting such an objective, the manager usually relinquishes some control of his or her channel.

Control   It is also quite common to find business marketing managers desiring a high degree of control over their channels of distribution. This wish may come about because the manager feels that the company's policies and strategies are best for its products and does not want individual channel intermediaries deciding otherwise. In other words, the manufacturer wishes to exercise considerable control over the channel of distribution. This objective often leads to direct channels, which may be the most expensive but are also the easiest to control. If the manager's basic objective is **channel control,** he or she must use either a direct channel or one with intermediaries that can be controlled. If such control is not maintained, the chances of achieving the objective are reduced. On the other hand, it must be realized that this objective requires a company that is financially able to support it. Probably most business marketing managers would like to control their channels of distribution, but it is a financial impossibility for many of them.

Strategic Alliances or Partnerships with Intermediaries   As has been stated a number of times, many business marketing firms are seeking to create **partnering relationships** or strategic alliances with their channel intermediaries. There are a couple of valid reasons for such an objective. First, such relationships are more enduring and provide more continuity for manufacturer, intermediary, and customer. There are benefits to the manufacturer, such as the stability of the association. Second, many business marketing managers believe that the manufacturer and intermediary are partners since both have the same goals—building sales and maximizing profits. To quote a spokesperson for Kodak's Business Imaging Systems Division, "The key ingredient in the manufacturer–intermediary relationship is understanding that it's a partnership."[28] This partnership orientation often leads to an objective of creating a closer relationship with channel components.

Sales Effort   As has been emphasized, personal selling plays a great role in business marketing. It also plays a great role in business channels, and many marketing managers have a high degree of sales effort as a basic channel objective. This objective has a number of effects on channels found in business markets. Some companies sell directly because they are unable to find intermediaries who possess the required sales ability. This situation often arises with sophisticated technical products. In such cases, direct channels are not used by choice, but by necessity. In other instances in which intermediaries can be used, distributors and manufacturers' representatives are included in a channel on the basis of their proven sales capabilities.

Service and Technical Assistance   Service, technical assistance, and other product support activities are big factors in business marketing, and they extend into the channel of distribution area. For example, a marketing manager may use a direct channel and provide service facilities because of the inability to find intermediaries with the capabilities or the desires to provide such services. On the other hand, the manager may choose intermediaries, especially industrial distributors, on the basis of their proven service facilities and personnel. In other instances, a marketing manager with this objective may be prohibited from using manufacturers' representatives in the channel because of their reluctance to provide such services or technical assistance.

Market Feedback   Some business marketing managers expect market feedback from their channels of distribution and make this a specific channel objective. When a company has such an objective, it may well lead to channel components being selected on the basis of their willingness to provide such feedback. For example, it would be unrealistic to expect manufacturers' representatives or company salespeople who are compensated on a straight commission basis to take time to search out market information.

Company Image   The company image is often quite important to the business marketing manager, and creation and maintenance of that image often extends into channels of distribution. Customers form impressions of a manufacturer and its products through their dealings with that manufacturer or its intermediaries. Therefore, manufacturers must find intermediaries whose images are consistent with theirs. They may choose distributors and/or manufacturers' representatives on that basis. In fact, a direct channel may be used because sufficient intermediaries with the proper image cannot be located or enlisted by the manufacturer.

The preceding objectives are typical of those found in business marketing.

They are not, however, mutually exclusive in most instances. For example, a company may wish to exert a high degree of control in the market, achieve sales of a specific volume, create an image of an industry leader, and desire high-quality service at the same time through its channels. In such a situation, the marketing manager attempts to develop channels capable of achieving such objectives. First, however, the objectives must be determined for the products and markets involved.

Referring again to Exhibit 13.2, Reliance Electric's channel objectives can be seen when the company moved into a new market with its VAV fan drive. The channel objectives were to penetrate a new target market and control the quality of the sales effort. The exhibit outlines the marketing programs undertaken to accomplish these objectives.

The determination of realistic channel objectives is imperative because these objectives provide direction for the rest of the channel selection process. It is important to realize, however, that in determining such objectives, the marketing manager must also consider customer and possible intermediary objectives, since these may conflict. For example, if the marketing manager desires a high degree of feedback from the channel, the time and effort involved to provide it can be inconsistent with the objectives of some distributors and MRs. Similarly, an objective of high degree of control may be in conflict with customers who prefer to purchase from independent intermediaries. At any rate, the first step is to determine the proper combination of objectives that subsequent channels are to achieve.

Assessing Channel Options

Once channel objectives have been determined, the business marketing manager must review the channel options available. The logical starting point is to view direct versus indirect channels. Many marketing managers probably prefer to use direct channels because they are easier to control, but direct channels are also more expensive. Thus, some companies may prefer to use a direct channel but cannot afford to do so; therefore, they are forced to consider indirect channel options. Of course, both types of channel options may be used at the same time, but such an undertaking requires the same type of decision making. In considering the options, the manager is influenced by factors such as the following. Do customers in the target market prefer to buy direct or through specific types of intermediaries? Will intermediaries carry the company's products? Does the company have the financial resources to support the direct sales channel? Are profit margins sufficient to support a direct channel? Are order sizes estimated to be large or small? How are competitive products sold? Can intermediaries sell and service the products involved? Will the company be able to motivate independent intermediaries if such are used? Armed with the answers to these questions, decisions may be made to employ direct, indirect, or a combination of channels (whereby the company sells direct to some markets and indirect to others).

If the decision is made to sell via direct channels to target market customers, the manager then determines what form of direct channel can best achieve the desired objectives. Should field salespeople or inside salespeople be used, or should a combination be used? Should the company set up national or major accounts? Can telemarketing be used and what should be the role of catalogs? As stated previously, direct channels in business marketing are essentially sales channels, and management of this area is covered in Chapter 15.

If, however, the decision is made to sell via indirect channels, the marketing manager then determines which of those are most appropriate. To illustrate, should distributors, manufacturers' representatives, or both be used in these channels? If distributors make good sense, should they be specialist or general line distributors? What intermediaries can best sell and service the products under consideration? Can distributors sell to some markets and MRs to others? It can now be seen why intermediaries were examined in such great detail in this chapter. Answering questions such as these requires a sound understanding of possible channel components.

A couple of examples may help to illustrate what takes place at this step. The opening feature at the beginning of this chapter discussed the situation of the Information Systems Division of Hyundai Electronics of America. In that case, the company had added products that enabled it to expand from being a supplier to other computer manufacturers to marketing its own computers. This entailed a different channel from its OEM channel. Management looked at options and focused on either using distributors to reach retail dealers or going direct to those dealers. These two possibilities were examined in detail and found to be the most appropriate for reaching the new market. As the feature shows, the final decision was made to use a direct to dealer channel.[29] Another situation took place with Tilt-Lock, Inc., of Hamel, Minnesota. As the company acquired new products, it found that some would not fit their traditional direct sales channel. Looking at other options, they found the use of either industrial distributors or manufacturers' representatives to be the most feasible. After further analysis, it was decided that the most effective channel would be using MRs to reach target market customers. These two examples show how business marketing firms have to assess possible channel options before actually selecting those that are to be used.[30]

In situations in which combinations of direct and indirect channels are more feasible, the same types of questions are involved. Whatever the situation, the manager's task here is to determine which channel options are most feasible and most likely to achieve desired objectives.

Selecting Appropriate Channels

After channel objectives have been determined and channel options assessed, the manager is ready to select the specific channels to be used. Choice is typically made on the basis of factors such as the following. What are the buying practices and preferences of target market customers? What channels are competitors using? What is the unit value of the product and average order size? What is the size or bulk of the product? What are the costs of different channel alternatives? How sophisticated is the product? What is the level of service and technical assistance that will be required? What level of sales effort will be needed to sell the product effectively? What field warehousing will be required and what will be the field inventory requirements?

If only direct channels are selected, implementation of the channel becomes a sales management responsibility. When indirect channels are required, the channel management area becomes more complex. Still, there are only six basic channels commonly used in business markets (see Figure 13.1). Using the figure as reference, there are only three completely indirect channels: distributors to customers, MRs to customers, and MRs to distributors to customers. Note also that company salespeople may also be used to sell to distributors, who then sell to target market customers, which is also a form of indirect channel. From such possible alternatives, the marketing manager selects the channels to be used.

Again, some examples may help illustrate how business marketing firms select their channels. In the previously mentioned Hyundai Electronics situation, the company first selected the distributor to dealer channel because this was more or less the traditional channel. But, it soon found out that distributors cut into one another's territories and the channel came apart. The company then elected to go direct to the dealers. In a somewhat similar situation, Tilt-Lock, Inc., selected manufacturers' representatives over distributors because they found the product involved really wasn't a distributor product.[31] Kodak's Business Imaging Systems Division selected a dual channel of distributors for film products and manufacturers' representatives for the equipment that uses the film.[32] The company had gone through a considerable reduction in direct sales activity, which led to the dual indirect channels.

Selecting Channel Intermediaries

Once prospective channels are selected and types of intermediaries specified, specific MRs or distributors must be chosen and approached in regard to taking on the company's products. If direct channels are used, this step is omitted. The actual recruiting, however, of desired individual intermediaries is quite difficult in many instances, especially when new products are involved. It is often thought that the manufacturer, almost by virtue of being the manufacturer, has the upper hand when it comes to intermediaries and that therefore, the latter come to the manufacturers for their products. In actual business markets, often the opposite is true. Quality distributors and manufacturers' representatives must be sought out, contacted, and persuaded to carry the manufacturers' products. Often, this seeking involves a tough selling job when intermediaries are highly qualified and other manufacturers also want them to carry their products. The business marketing manager is forced to sell such intermediaries on the merit of being associated with the company as opposed to being associated with competitors.

In selecting the particular MRs or distributors to use in the channel of distribution, many business marketers use a relatively standardized selection process such as the following: [33]

1. Locate the candidates to be considered.
2. Screen the candidates to determine which are most desired.
3. Conduct in-depth interviews of those that pass the screening.
4. Select those that are most appropriate.

This is an important step in that the intermediaries that are selected will be the ones that make the channel work or not work. Improper selection may render a conceptually sound channel inoperable and thus care is required. Some examples may be useful in illustrating how business marketing firms actually select particular intermediaries for inclusion in their channels.

As discussed earlier, Kodak's Business Imaging Systems Division used a channel of manufacturers' representatives to sell its film using equipment. In recruiting MRs, Kodak used the following approach, as outlined by a company spokesperson: [34]

> Recruiting agents is not much different from recruiting a top executive. Before you start looking, you have to profile the best agent for the territory. Then, you have to gather information on agencies in the areas that serve your markets. These two steps can be more than intimidating and time consuming for an active manufacturer.

Another good example exists in the case of the Columbia Machine, Inc., company of Vancouver, Washington. This firm uses manufacturers' representatives in its channels. Because the product involved is costly and very technical, Columbia uses a ten-part screening system to qualify and select MRs. Exhibit 13.3 illustrates the criteria used in this screening system. Information such as this may be found by contacting the rep organization itself, present suppliers, and present customers and making personal visits. The same criteria are then used to decide which particular reps are finally selected.

Establishing Channel Arrangements

Once particular channel intermediaries have been recruited and selected, arrangements must be made so both manufacturer and intermediary are clear as to what is expected. Setting up such channel arrangements basically becomes a legal problem, in which responsibilities and rights of both manufacturer and intermediaries are spelled out in a formal contract. These contracts cover such specific points as the following for distributors and manufacturers' representatives.

Industrial Distributors　Arrangements between a manufacturer and an industrial distributor cover areas such as the following. Sales territory or scope of coverage must be agreed on, and FOB points must be designated. Any discounts such as cash, trade, and quantity discounts should be clearly outlined. Provisions for returned goods, consignments, and warranties must be clarified. Cooperative

EXHIBIT 13.3   **Criteria Used by a Business Marketing Firm to Screen and Select Manufacturers' Representatives**

Columbia Machine, Inc., of Vancouver, Washington, is a manufacturer of automatic palletizers and uses manufacturers' reps in its channel of distribution. In recruiting prospective rep agencies, the company uses the following ten-part screening system to qualify and select its rep organizations:

1. How long has the company been in the rep business?
2. What compatible product lines does the rep possess?
3. What are the rep's marketing qualifications?
4. What are the rep's office capabilities? How does it qualify and handle sales leads?
5. What are the references from the rep firm's present customers and principals?
6. What territories does the rep firm cover now for other principals?
7. What do our present reps know about the prospective rep firm?
8. What is the rep firm's mechanical and electrical capabilities?
9. What is the rep firm's ability to handle large or corporate accounts?
10. What is the size of the rep firm in terms of number of people?

Source: Adapted from "Manufacturers Tell How They Found Their Best Agents," *Agency Sales* 41 (September 1989): 27.

advertising arrangements and other promotional aids should be understood by both parties. Required distributor inventory levels must be worked out, and procedures for handling inquiries and quotations should be spelled out. Service and technical assistance required of both parties must also be clarified. Finally, arrangements should include conditions for termination of the distributor agreement, and the rights of both parties after termination must be clear. Arrangements between manufacturer and distributor should be clearly understood by both parties before the channels are implemented.

Manufacturers' Representatives In similar fashion, any arrangements between manufacturer and MR must be clear in regard to the rights and responsibilities of both parties. Contracts here involve the legal agency/principal relationship and spell out those rights and responsibilities. Typically, the following factors are involved. What sales territory is assigned to the MR? What commission rates will be involved and when will they be paid? How will inquiries, quotations, invoices, and collections be handled? What restrictions will be placed on handling competitive products? What sales aids or other support activities will be provided by the manufacturer? If cooperative advertising is involved, what are the conditions? Under what conditions can the MR legally bind the manufacturer? What should be required before either party can terminate the agency/principal arrangement? What rights does each have after termination?

An example of such arrangements may be seen in the case of Lyon Metal Products of Aurora, Illinois, a company selling its products through industrial distributors. Arrangements with the distributors include: (1) Lyon will pay the freight for any order with a list price of $1,200 or more; (2) any distributor receiving damaged goods can have them replaced within ten days by Lyon; and (3) slow-moving inventory purchased by the distributor from Lyon can be exchanged for fast-moving products of equal value once a year.[35] These arrangements were created by Lyon Metal in order to form closer relationships with its distributors, but they are very explicit so that both manufacturer and distributor understand clearly what is involved.

Implementing the Selected Channels

At this stage, the channels selected are made operational. When field inventory is involved, goods are shipped to the intermediaries. Promotional aids such as catalogs, price sheets, specification sheets, and displays are sent to the intermediaries. Sales training by manufacturer personnel may be initiated with intermediary salespeople and other personnel. Company advertising should include reference to appropriate intermediaries, so that customers are aware of the relationship. Inquiries received by the manufacturer are forwarded to those involved, and communication networks are established between manufacturer and intermediaries. In essence, this step involves close coordination between manufacturer and intermediary to facilitate the best possible initial relationship.

This discussion suggests that implementing channels by a business marketing manager cannot be a passive undertaking. If the channel is to operate smoothly and effectively, the manager must take an active role in helping intermediaries. A good example of this may be seen in the case of the previously mentioned Business Imaging Systems Division of Kodak.[36] That company believes that its marketing, sales, advertising, technical, financial, managerial, and operational people must work closely with the firm's manufacturers' representatives. Kodak is actively involved in both training and motivational programs for its reps. Moreover, the company established a Kodak Rep Council comprised of six rep members who meet twice a year for two-day sessions with Kodak product managers and product support people. This is the kind of effort that is required to make a channel operational and functioning in a positive manner.

Controlling and Evaluating the Selected Channels

Once the channels are operational, they should be closely monitored in terms of channel objectives desired and overall company goals. This monitoring is often accomplished through the marketing information system (MIS), and it implies keeping current on channel effectiveness, efficiency, and productivity. Whether channels are direct, indirect, or a combination, it is essential that they be closely monitored in terms of costs, sales, profitability, image, coordination, and overall compatibility among the parties involved. Chapter 18 covers overall control and evaluation, and it includes channels of distribution as well as other marketing mix areas.

Monitoring channel performance is an important consideration even where a great deal of time, effort, and resources have been committed to channel development. Things just don't always work out as envisioned. A good example can be seen in the case of Hyundai Electronics of America, which is discussed at the beginning of this chapter. Its initial channel for its microcomputers involved distributors selling to dealers. But, when implemented, the distributors pirated accounts from one another's territories, which destroyed the credibility of the entire channel. By carefully monitoring, Hyundai was able to discover the problem and correct it by changing the channel.

PARTNER RELATIONSHIPS IN BUSINESS CHANNELS

Throughout the discussion in this chapter, references have been made to the topic of closer relationships between manufacturers and channel intermediaries in business markets. These closer relationships are often thought of as partnerships whereby both manufacturer and intermediary benefit. This area was discussed in a general sense in Chapter 7, but here it is applied specifically to channels. In contemporary business marketing, creating partnerships with industrial distributors and/or manufacturers' representatives is simply good business for marketing managers. It should be understood that such relationships are really not new. Business marketers for years have realized the advantages of working closely with their channel intermediaries. Recently, however, there has been renewed emphasis in the subject and so it should be developed here in more detail.

The manufacturer–intermediary partnership has been defined as "the extent to which there is mutual recognition and understanding that the success of each firm depends in part on the other firm, with each firm consequently taking actions so as to provide a coordinated effort focused on jointly satisfying the requirements of the customer marketplace." [37] As the definition shows, the purpose is mutual success in the market brought about by better coordination between manufacturer and channel intermediary.

Elements in the Manufacturer–Intermediary Relationship

There are a number of elements necessary for this type of working relationship to exist: [38] (1) relative dependence—the degree to which the two are dependent on each other in the channel; (2) influence—the extent to which the two influence each other; (3) conflict—the frequency, intensity, and duration of disagreements; (4) coordination—how well the two work together in the relationship; (5) communication—how well meaningful and timely information is shared; (6) trust—trust that the other firm will perform actions beneficial to both;

(7) cooperation—actions taken by each that contribute to mutual outcomes; and (8) satisfaction—a positive affective state resulting from the appraisal of all aspects of the relationship. For the relationship to prosper, manufacturer and intermediary should recognize the importance of such criteria and work together to make them positive and not negative in nature.

Making the Relationship Work

To make such a relationship work, the following recommendations have been made:[39]

1. Mutually define performance objectives for each partner.
2. Specify the cooperative efforts each firm requires of its partner to attain its objectives.
3. Communicate regularly with each other on progress toward attaining objectives.
4. Review each other's performance.

Performing tasks such as these can lead to trust, which is the basic foundation for the relationship.

For the manufacturer, a number of things should be undertaken to make the relationship work. The manufacturer should be flexible in its dealings with intermediaries—not rigid and unyielding. In addition, the manufacturer should offer assistance to intermediaries and communicate regularly with them. Furthermore, there should be monitoring of intermediary performance so that problems can be corrected quickly. There will always be disagreements—the key is to resolve them quickly. Finally, there should be an expectation of continuity expressed by the manufacturer so that the intermediary realizes the relationship is not temporary in nature. When all this takes place, an element of trust is involved, which as stated before is crucial. Many business marketing firms have established councils with their reps and/or distributors to ensure these principles are followed. These facilitate better communication, coordination, resolution of conflict, and trust.

Perhaps one way to sum up this discussion of relationships is by means of a quote by Kodak's Business Imaging Systems Division's manager of broker and distribution sales. Speaking of Kodak's relationship with its manufacturers' representatives, he stated:[40]

> The key ingredient in the manufacturer–agency relationship is understanding that it's a partnership. The partnership is absolutely essential to this business because we have gone through a considerable reduction in direct sales activity. We have literally assigned large regions of the country to the indirect sales organization. They have become an extension of our marketing arm.

A statement by the president of Lyon Metal Products echoes a similar theme. In discussing his company's relationship with its distributors, he stated,

"The idea is to show our distributor that we understand what his problems are, and if he commits to us exclusively, we will do everything possible to create a successful partnership." [41]

These examples are indicative of what is taking place in contemporary business marketing when manufacturers use manufacturers' reps and/or distributors in their channels of distribution. Through cooperative, rather than adversarial, efforts the manufacturer, the intermediaries, and the customers all benefit.

CHAPTER SUMMARY

Effective and efficient channels of distribution are a must in business marketing. There is little to be gained when high-quality products and services are not accessible to target market customers. Thus, the development of proper channels of distribution has much to do with marketing success. The marketing manager's ability to establish and implement effective channels may be what differentiates one company from another.

This chapter addressed the channel area of the marketing mix. Business channel strategy was defined, and differences were examined between consumer and business marketing strategy. The structure of business channels was reviewed in terms of what channels are most common in business markets. Forms of direct channels were discussed, with emphasis on field salespeople, inside salespeople, telemarketing, catalogs, and national or major accounts. Indirect channel components were examined, with

attention paid to the industrial distributor and the manufacturers' representative. Both of these intermediaries were analyzed in detail in terms of their basic characteristics and the advantages and disadvantages of using them in the marketing strategy. Profiles of both types of intermediaries were developed.

An outline was presented for the development of channel strategy. Stages in this outline included the determination of channel objectives, assessing channel options, selecting appropriate channels, selecting channel intermediaries, establishing channel arrangements, implementing the selected channels, and controlling and evaluating those channels.

Finally, the topic of partner relationships between manufacturer and intermediary was discussed. Elements necessary to implement such a relationship were examined and recommendations given in regard to making the partner relationship work in an effective manner.

KEY TERMS

channel control
channel intermediary
channel of distribution
channel strategy
combination house distributor
commission
direct channel

generalist distributor
indirect channel
industrial distributor
manufacturers' representative
partnering relationship
specialist distributor
stocking representative

QUESTIONS

1. Explain the difference between a manufacturer having an adversarial relationship with its channel intermediaries and having a partner relationship with those same intermediaries.
2. Discuss reasons why a partnership with channel intermediaries is more beneficial to a manufacturer than an adversarial relationship with those same intermediaries.
3. In business marketing, channels of distribution are often considered to be sales channels as well. Thinking in terms of both direct and indirect channels, explain what this statement means.
4. In most cases, industrial distributors and manufacturers' representatives are not good substitutes for each other in business channels. Explain why they are normally not considered as substitutes.
5. It is sometimes argued that every business marketing manager would prefer to use direct channels when possible. If this is a valid argument, why are indirect channels used so frequently?
6. Why are retailers and wholesalers typically not considered to be channel intermediaries in business markets?
7. The manufacturers' representative is sometimes seen as a substitute for a company salesperson. Explain why this is so and then relate factors that influence a business marketing manager to select one over the other. Why may a rep be preferred to a company salesperson and vice versa?
8. The industrial distributor is sometimes seen as a substitute for a company-owned branch operation. Explain why this is so and then relate factors that influence a business marketing manager to select one over the other. Why may a distributor be preferred to a company-owned branch and vice versa?
9. A study cited in the chapter found that trust is one of the most important factors in the manufacturer–intermediary relationship. What does this mean and how does a business marketing manager go about instilling trust in his or her channel intermediaries?
10. When a manufacturer produces products such as portable electric power tools that can be used by both business and consumer customers, how might channels differ between the two markets? Illustrate the channels that might be used to reach each market.

NOTES

1. Philip Mahar, "Distribution: Key to Success," *Industrial Distribution* 71 (December 1981): 29.
2. Michael D. Hutt and Thomas W. Speh, "Realigning Industrial Marketing Channels," *Industrial Marketing Management* 12 (1983): 171.
3. Mahar, op. cit.
4. Peter R. Dickson, "Distributor Portfolio Analysis and the Channel Dependence Matrix: New Techniques for Understanding and Managing the Channel," *Journal of Marketing* 47 (Summer 1983): 43.
5. David T. Wilson, Shirish P. Dant, and Sang-Lin Han, "Buyer–Seller Relationships—Frontline Views," *Marketplace: The ISBM Review* (Fall 1990): 2.
6. James A. Anderson and James A. Narus, "A Model of Distributor Firm and Manufacturer Firm Working Partnerships," *Journal of Marketing* 54 (January 1990): 42.
7. *Rethinking the Company's Selling and Distribution Channels*, Report No. 885 (New York: The Conference Board, 1986), 2.
8. Ibid.
9. Ibid.
10. John G. F. Bonnanzio, "What's Your Share?" *Industrial Distribution* 79 (July 1990): 25.
11. Donald M. Jackson and Michael F. d'Amico, "Products and Markets Served by Distributors and Agents," *Industrial Marketing Management* 18 (1989): 28.
12. *We Could Save You a Few Thousand Bucks* (Cleveland: Steel Service Center Institute, 1972), 2–10.
13. See Frederick E. Webster, Jr., *The Changing*

Role of the Industrial Distributor (Cambridge, MA: Marketing Science Institute, 1975); and "The Supplier Connection," *Industrial Distribution* 73 (June 1984): 30.

14. George M. Fodor, "Reducing the Cost of Sales," *Industrial Distribution* 77 (January 1988): 94.

15. John G. F. Bonnanzio, "Can Mom and Pop Survive?" *Industrial Distribution* 79 (February 1990): 22.

16. Bonnanzio, "What's Your Share?" op. cit., 26.

17. Bonnanzio, "Can Mom and Pop Survive?" op. cit., 19.

18. Ibid., 25.

19. Kate Bertrand, "Manufacturers 'Rethink' Distribution Channels," *Business Marketing* 72 (February 1987): 40.

20. Wilson, Dant, and Han, op. cit., 1.

21. *Rethinking the Company's Selling and Distribution Channels,* op. cit., 2–3.

22. *The Manufacturers' Agent* (Irvine, CA: Manufacturers' Agents National Association, 1983), 3.

23. *Rethinking the Company's Selling and Distribution Channels,* op. cit., 2.

24. Jackson and d'Amico, op. cit., 33.

25. "1990 Profile of the Manufacturers' Sales Agency," *Agency Sales Magazine* 42 (July 1990): 10.

26. See Earl Hitchcock, "What Marketers Love and Hate About Their Manufacturers' Reps," *Sales & Marketing Management* 134 (September 10, 1984): 60–65.

27. See "The Role of the Rep," *Hardware Age* 221 (August 1984): 193–201.

28. "For Kodak, Agents Are Their Business Partners," *Agency Sales Magazine* 42 (June 1990): 4.

29. Tom Eisenhart, "Smashing Distribution Barriers," *Business Marketing* 74 (April 1989): 12–16.

30. "Tilt-Lock Switches to Agents—Increases Sales," *Agency Sales Magazine* 40 (September 1988): 4–9.

31. Ibid., 6.

32. "For Kodak, Agents Are Their Business Partners," op. cit.

33. Harold J. Novick, "Yes, There Is a Perfect Rep," *Business Marketing* 74 (February 1989): 74–75.

34. "For Kodak, Agents Are Their Business Partners," op. cit.

35. "Lyon Metal Pays the Freight," *Industrial Distribution* 79 (August 1990): 10.

36. "For Kodak, Agents Are Their Business Partners," op. cit., 4–7.

37. Anderson and Narus, op. cit.

38. Ibid., 43–46.

39. Ibid., 56.

40. "For Kodak, Agents Are Their Business Partners," op. cit., 4.

41. "Lyon Metal Pays the Freight," op. cit.

SUGGESTED ADDITIONAL READINGS

Anderson, James C., and James A. Narus. "A Model of Distributor Firm and Manufacturer Firm Working Partnerships." *Journal of Marketing* 54 (January 1990): 42–58.

Bellizzi, Joseph A., and Christine Glacken. "Building a More Successful Rep Organization." *Industrial Marketing Management* 15 (1986): 207–213.

DuBois, Lois C., and Roger H. Grace. "The Care and Feeding of Manufacturers' Reps." *Business Marketing* 72 (December 1987): 52–64.

Hlavacek, James D., and Tommy J. McCuiston. "Industrial Distributors—When, Who, and How?" *Harvard Business Review* 61 (January–February 1983): 96–101.

Jackson, Donald M., and Michael F. d'Amico. "Products and Markets Served by Distributors and Agents." *Industrial Marketing Management* 18 (1989): 27–33.

Magrath, Allan J., and Kenneth G. Hardy. *A Strategic Framework for Diagnosing Manufacturer–Reseller Conflict,* Report No. 88-101. Cambridge, MA: Marketing Science Institute, 1988.

——. "Factory Salesmen's Roles with Industrial Distributors." *Industrial Marketing Management* 16 (1987): 163–168.

Narus, James A., and James A. Anderson. "Industrial Distributor Selling: The Roles of Outside and Inside Sales." *Industrial Marketing Management* 15 (1986): 55–62.

——. "Distribution Contributions to Partnerships

with Manufacturers." *Business Horizons* 30 (September–October 1987): 34–42.

_____. "Strengthen Distributor Performance Through Channel Positioning." *Sloan Management Review* 31 (Winter 1988): 31–40.

Noordewier, Thomas G., George John, and John R. Nevin. "Performance Outcomes of Purchasing Arrangements in Industrial Buyer–Vendor Relationships." *Journal of Marketing* 54 (October 1990): 80–93.

Novick, Harold J. "Yes, There Is a Perfect Rep." *Business Marketing* 74 (February 1989): 73–76.

Rethinking the Company's Selling and Distribution Channels, Report No. 885. New York: The Conference Board, 1986.

Ross, William T. *Managing Marketing Channel Relationships,* Report No. 85-106. Cambridge, MA: Marketing Science Institute, 1985.

‚14‚

Physical Distribution Strategy in Business Marketing

• •

Closely related to the area of channel strategy in the marketing mix is the area known as physical distribution. Regardless of the channel or channels selected, the business marketing manager must also manage the physical movement of goods and services through the marketing channels. The proper channels may have been selected to reach defined target markets, but if the goods and services moving through those channels are not reaching customers in the desired time frames or quantities required, the results can lead to marketing disaster. Physical distribution involves the transportation of goods, warehousing, inventory stocks, processing of orders to ship goods from inventory, packaging to protect the goods in storage and transit, and materials-handling equipment. This chapter looks at physical distribution as an element in the total marketing mix as applied to the marketing of business products and services. Physical distribution is first defined and differentiated from the larger area of logistics. Then, components of physical distribution are examined. The physical distribution system is viewed as it exists in business markets and as it relates to channels of distribution. The importance of sound physical distribution management is emphasized. Managerial implications are analyzed as these exist in the basic physical distribution components. The total integrated system of physical distribution is also analyzed. Finally, the chapter explores the effects on physical distribution activities in business marketing when target market customers are involved in just-in-time (JIT) buying and materials requirement planning (MRP). In these instances, physical distribution requirements may be quite different as the business marketing firm is serving relationship rather than transactional type customers.

Physical Distribution in Business Marketing

Union Carbide Corporation produces and delivers packaged gases through regional branches across the United States. These branches are subsidiaries of its Linde Division. Customers are also supplied with supplies that may be used with the gases, such as welding rods. The company ships nitrogen, oxygen, and other gases from central points to its branch locations in large tank cars. In addition, gases in smaller steel cylinders are also shipped to the locations via tractor trailers. Originally, the distributors then delivered the cylinders to their customers by truck.

In the industrial gas business, control of distribution costs is a major competitive factor. Linde, therefore, undertook a change in its physical distribution system to better control such costs.

Initially, its branches were full-service establishments with personnel performing operational, marketing, and administrative duties. Union Carbide's goal was to consolidate its gas filling business. It wanted the branches to distribute the gases to their customers from central sites rather than from the branch. The gases would be delivered to the customer site from the central plants, which would reduce the costs of maintaining inventory, transportation, and fixed facilities in the branches.

This change involved switching the branches from full-service establishments to what Union Carbide called "storefront operations." These storefronts were locations that would take orders, initiate customer contacts, and maintain limited inventories of gas cylinders and spare parts. Storefront operational costs were low because they were limited to the costs of carrying moderate amounts of cylinders and parts. Not all branches, however, were switched to storefronts. The company selected the branches to be changed using sales volume and proximity to the primary market as criteria. The closer a branch was to a central site and the lower its sales volume, the more likely it was to be converted to a storefront operation.

The result of such consolidation was that distribution costs were reduced appreciably with no decrease in customer service. The company claimed that customers still received the same service—products were just delivered from a different location. By better controlling its distribution costs, Union Carbide was able to squeeze large savings out of its storefront operations and at the same time maintain the quality of service required by customers in the target market.

Source: Adapted from Donald B. Rosenfield, "Storefront Distribution for Industrial Products," *Harvard Business Review* 67 (July–August 1989): 44–48.

WHAT IS PHYSICAL DISTRIBUTION?

The term **physical distribution** is often used in marketing to pertain to those activities involved in the physical movement of goods to target market customers. According to the Council of Logistics Management, physical distribution is defined as follows:

. . . A term employed in manufacturing and commerce that describes the broad range of activities concerned with the efficient movement of finished products from the end of the production line to the consumer, and in some cases including the movement of raw materials from the source of supply to the beginning of the production line. These activities include freight transportation, warehousing, material handling, protective packaging, inventory control, plant and warehouse site selection, order processing, market forecasting, and customer service.[1]

This definition includes movement of goods both to the manufacturer and from the manufacturer to the market. When the former is included, the process is often called logistics rather than physical distribution.[2] In this text, the term physical distribution relates only to the movement of goods from the manufacturer to target market customers. The physical movement of goods to the beginning of the production line is not a marketing responsibility. This task is usually undertaken by materials management people. The concern here is with the marketing aspects of physical distribution, and thus focus is placed on the shipment of company products through the selected distribution channels.

Physical Distribution Activities

Transportation. **Transportation** activities involve the selection of the modes of transportation to be used in shipping products to customers. Possible modes include shipping via motor vehicles, rail, air freight, water, and pipeline.

Warehousing. **Warehousing** activities involve the determination to use field warehouses, where to locate those warehouses for optimum impact, and deciding on the sizes of the warehouses.

Inventory control. **Inventory control** activities involve the determination of inventory sizes in the warehouses that will provide customers with what is needed, when it is needed, and in the quantities desired.

Materials handling. **Materials handling** involves the movement and storage of inventory stocks in the warehouses and elsewhere in the physical distribution system. Included are the use of forklifts, conveyors, handlifts, cranes, hoists, motorized handtrucks, and other such equipment used to move and store inventory.

Protective packaging. **Protective packaging** activities involve the protection provided to the product during storage and transportation. Such packaging includes crating, containerization, export packing, package design, and other activities to ensure goods are delivered undamaged.

Order processing. **Order processing** refers to all those activities involved in collecting, checking, and transmitting sales order information.[3] Typical of such activities are order write-ups, credit checking, price verifications, preparing bills of lading, allocation of stocks to orders, actual shipments of goods, and electronic networking between supplier and customer.

Physical distribution management is thus concerned with the integration of the preceding six areas into a complete distribution strategy. The primary objectives of such an overall strategy are to provide customers with the service they require and to do so in the most cost-effective manner. All these areas are covered in detail later in the chapter.

THE PHYSICAL DISTRIBUTION SYSTEM IN BUSINESS MARKETING

Physical distribution exists in both consumer and business markets, but there are differences to consider. In addition, there is also a relationship between physical distribution and the channels of distribution used. Figure 14.1 illustrates the physical distribution system that exists in U.S. business markets whether the

FIGURE 14.1   Physical Distribution in Business Marketing

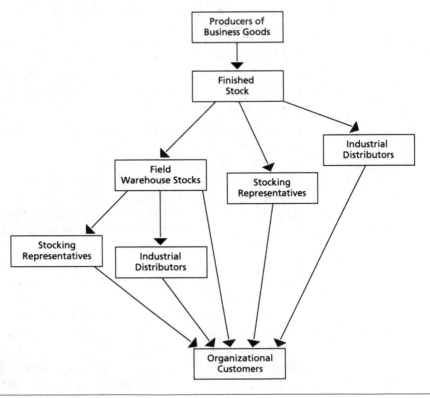

customers are private commercial, institutional, or governmental. Using the figure as a basis for discussion, it is possible to analyze the business marketing physical distribution system.

In Chapter 13, it was shown that six channels of distribution are most common in business marketing (see Figure 13.1). For the marketing manager, the physical distribution implications vary appreciably depending on the channel or channels used. For example, if a business marketer sells direct to a customer such as a national account, the entire responsibility for physical distribution lies with that marketer. Decisions made in transportation, warehouse size and location, inventory control, packaging, materials handling, and order processing are all made by the marketing firm. These areas of decision and responsibility also exist when company salespeople are employed. They usually exist also when manufacturers' representatives are used, although the use of stocking representatives may be an exception.[4] In all these situations, the business marketing manager must design a physical distribution system to provide timely delivery of the desired goods. The total cost of physical distribution is borne by the marketing company, and control is also kept by the company. Thus, the ultimate responsibility for designing and implementing the physical distribution system lies with the business marketing manager.

When industrial distributors are used, however, the physical distribution system changes. Unlike the manufacturers' representative, the industrial distributor is usually an integral part of the physical distribution system. This fact can easily be understood by recalling that distributors typically take title to the goods involved, provide warehousing, maintain inventory stocks, and ship to customers from such inventory. Thus, any business marketing manager who relies on industrial distributors should recognize the benefits and problems associated with their use. For example, since the distributor provides warehousing and maintains inventory stocks, the cost to the business marketing company may be considerably less. On the other hand, if the distributor refuses to carry adequate stocks, has inadequate warehousing space, or is unreliable in delivery, the physical distribution strategy will break down. Chapter 13 revealed that these are major concerns for business marketing managers. Thus, distributors must be carefully screened for physical distribution capabilities as well as for sales and marketing abilities, if an effective system is to be found.

This discussion points out the close interaction between channels of distribution and physical distribution in business marketing. When setting up channels of distribution, the marketing manager needs to determine physical distribution objectives as well as sales and marketing objectives. It should also be recognized that the area of physical distribution must be addressed regardless of what channels are used. The two areas are related and similar in many respects, but each requires its own attention by the business marketing manager. Physical distribution problems differ appreciably depending on the channels used. Exhibit 14.1 illustrates the case of a channel of distribution being affected by changes in physical distribution.

EXHIBIT 14.1   Physical Distribution Problems in Business Channels of Distribution

---

Channels of distribution and physical distribution are closely entwined in business marketing and sometimes what happens in one area greatly affects the other. A classic example can be seen in the case of Dow Corning's Maintenance, Repair and Engineering Industries operation.

Dow Corning used manufacturers' representatives to sell its products to industrial distributors, primarily power transmission houses, for sale to customers. The company had a national network of about 900 distributor locations, which were served by the manufacturers' representatives. Typically, the rep would sell to the distributor and the goods would be shipped directly to the distributor's warehouse. The reps were paid a commission on sales by their distributors and not on their sales to the distributors. In terms of physical distribution, goods flowed from Dow Corning to the distributors to the customers—the reps were not part of the physical distribution process.

But conditions changed over time. Japanese manufacturers were dumping their products into the American market at very low prices just to gain market penetration. When this happened, some manufacturers' reps saw opportunities to carry these products and set up their own warehouses to carry the inventory. This put them in direct competition with their own distributors, who complained loudly to Dow Corning. In essence, the reps had become involved in the physical distribution system as well as in the channel and this caused considerable channel conflict.

Dow Corning could not allow the dual stocking situation to continue and expect to meet its channel objectives. The decision was made to inform all reps that Dow Corning would not retain them if they continued to warehouse competitive products. They had the choice of either discontinuing their warehousing operations or not being renewed by Dow Corning when their agency contracts expired.

As a result of the company's policy, the company lost about one-third of its reps. The two-thirds who remained now work on a nonwarehousing basis. This has alleviated problems with the distributors who had threatened to leave if the reps were allowed to continue to stock competitive items. In the end, the channel arrangement returned to what it was initially—one in which the reps were not part of the company's physical distribution system.

Source: Adapted from "Handling Problems When Agent Warehousing Conflicts with Distributor Operations," *Agency Sales Magazine* 42 (March 1990): 18–20.

THE PHYSICAL DISTRIBUTION PROCESS
IN BUSINESS MARKETING

To help understand physical distribution in business marketing, it may be useful to describe the **physical distribution process**. Figure 14.2 illustrates such a process that starts when the customer places an order with the marketing firm. This order can be mailed directly, through a company salesperson, or through intermediaries such as industrial distributors or manufacturers' representatives. The

FIGURE 14.2   The Physical Distribution Process in Business Marketing

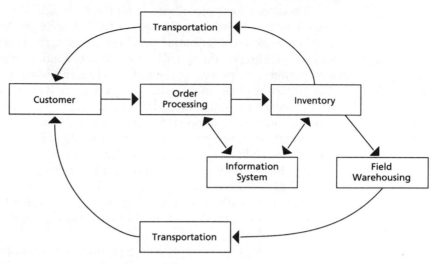

purchase order is received and processed by the marketing company. Processing may include verifications of products ordered, credit checking, price verifications, correct shipping address, and the like. The information system facilitates the order processing task and may even allocate inventory for shipment on the order. After the order passes through the processing step, it is sent to the proper department for shipment to the customer. If stocks are maintained at that company location, goods are shipped to the customer. If that situation is not the case, shipment is made from the field warehouse involved. Some examples may help in seeing how this process may differ depending on the situation.

In situation A, the manufacturer has no field warehouses and ships directly from its plant. The customer places the order, which is processed and shipped direct to the customer. This situation can be seen in the upper path in Figure 14.2.

In situation B, the manufacturer maintains a number of strategically located field warehouses, but purchase orders are sent to company headquarters and not to the individual warehouses. The customer's purchase order is processed and goods are then shipped from the appropriate warehouse.

In situation C, the manufacturer maintains no field warehouses but sells only through authorized distributors. The order is sent to company headquarters, where it is then forwarded to the proper distributor, who processes the order and ships from warehouse stocks.

In situation D, there are no inventory stocks, and the manufacturer builds custom products to buyer specifications. In this case, the order is received and processed, and it is then sent to engineering and production so that work orders may be developed. The product is then produced and shipped directly to the customer.

These four examples illustrate how the physical distribution process takes place in business markets and how it often changes depending on type of product, channels used, and distribution practices. The length of time for this process also varies depending on the situation. One study found a national mean of fourteen days between the placing of the order and receipt of the goods by the customer. The process analyzed in this study involved seven days in the reorder cycle, three days in order processing, three days in transit, and one day in customer receiving when items could be shipped from plant stock. However, the study found a range from a high of fifty-three days to a low of four days. If the items had to be made to order, three additional days were required to issue the manufacturing order, and another thirty days were required for manufacturing—for a total of forty-seven days. The range here was from a low of fifteen days to a high of 120 days.[5] The great variance involved indicates that there is no standard length of time for the process. The same process occurs, but the elements require different amounts of time to complete.

The above discussion applies to transaction situations with business customers. Goods are ordered and shipped as requested by the customer. Where closer relationships are involved between manufacturer and customer, the process is similar but its initiation may be quite different. For example, an electronic linkage may be operating between the two whereby the order is placed electronically on a regular or irregular basis. This order may be part of a much larger relationship and so some steps may be eliminated (verification, credit checking, price verifications, etc.). In such cases, shipment is greatly expedited but the rest of the process is similar. Required products are shipped much as are transactional goods.

THE IMPORTANCE OF PHYSICAL DISTRIBUTION IN BUSINESS MARKETING STRATEGY

How important is physical distribution in business marketing? Is it important enough to be viewed as a major strategy element or should it be seen basically as a support activity for other areas of the marketing mix? In answering these questions, it should be remembered that customers in business marketing are organizations buying products and services in order to better serve their own customers. If the products and services are not available, those customers may very well go elsewhere, and if this happens they may not return. Thus, it could be argued that physical distribution is more important in business marketing than it is in consumer marketing. There are a number of factors that support the argument that physical distribution is indeed a very important element in the business marketing mix. A discussion of these factors in in order.

Cost to the Marketing Company

Physical distribution is a cost that must be managed effectively to control the efficiency of the system used. A national study conducted by the Council of Logistics Management found that U.S. manufacturers spend an average of 20.8 percent of sales on distribution activities.[6] Figure 14.3 illustrates the breakdown of these activities. As can be seen, the most costly elements are transportation, which includes both inbound and outbound, warehousing, and inventory carrying costs. It should also be noted that interest, taxes, and insurance are also significant contributors. **Physical distribution costs** are significant when compared to other marketing costs. McGraw-Hill Research Department research indicates that the average percentage of sales spent in all marketing activities (marketing communications, direct selling, marketing support, and market research) by U.S. business marketing firms is 8.9 percent.[7] Based on such data, it can be argued that physical distribution may constitute the single most expensive element in the marketing mix. If this is so, then physical distribution is important in marketing strategy because its cost alone justifies a high level of attention by the marketing manager. Evidence shows this situation to be true. Another study revealed that about 44 percent of the firms surveyed had reduced physical distribution costs as a percentage of sales compared to the previous year. But 36 percent of those re-

---

FIGURE 14.3   Percent of Sales Spent in Various Physical Distribution Activities

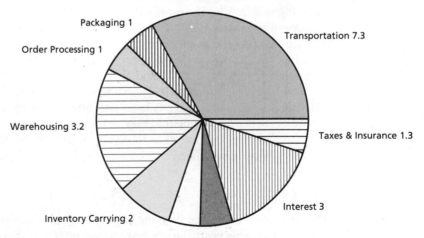

Source: Reprinted by permission from Bernard J. LaLonde, Martha C. Cooper, and Thomas G. Noordewier, *Customer Service: A Management Perspective* (Oak Brook, IL: Council of Logistics Management, 1988), Question III.B.2.

Note: 1990 estimates for all manufacturing.

sponding showed no change, and 20 percent actually increased distribution costs as a percentage of sales.[8]

Importance to the Customer

There is considerable evidence to conclude that physical distribution capabilities are extremely important to organizational buyers and buying influences. A study of purchasing managers randomly selected from regional associations affiliated with the National Association of Purchasing Management revealed that buyers rank physical distribution second only to product quality when selecting suppliers.[9] Physical distribution service was ranked higher than price, meaning that buyers were willing to pay more to a supplier who could ensure delivery when required. The study also showed that buyers would switch suppliers because of poor distribution service. Of those managers surveyed, about one-third claimed they would switch suppliers in the case of a backorder or stockout notice. In addition, one-half indicated that they stopped using suppliers in the preceding two-year period because of inadequate distribution service. Late deliveries and/or incomplete shipments are extremely irritating to organizational buyers. In addition, they cost customers a great deal of money. For example, the cost of downtime for an oil drilling rig is more than $100 per minute, and the downtime on an automotive engine assembly line is estimated at more than $100,000 per hour.[10] The inability to deliver purchased products on time can cause such downtimes, and thus buyers are acutely interested in a supplier's ability to deliver. Any marketing mix element having this much potentially negative impact must be considered important by the marketing manager.

Another reason that physical distribution activities are important to business customers is that inventory carrying costs have been increasing steadily. This has been caused by higher interest rates, and costs such as obsolescence, shrinkage, insurance, storage, and taxes. Because of this, many business customers have attempted to reduce their levels of inventory through the use of JIT, MRP, and DRP. These actions have permitted them to improve service to their customers at the same time that they reduce their inventory carrying costs. When this happens, they become even more dependent on the physical distribution capabilities of their suppliers.[11]

Competitive Advantage

Physical distribution can be quite important to the business marketing manager because a reliable distribution system can offer a vital competitive advantage. The ability to deliver on time when competitors cannot is a big advantage in business markets. **Order cycle time** is the most often cited element of physical distribution service.[12] This cycle time is the elapsed time between the initial placing of the order and the customer's receipt of the order in acceptable condition. When two suppliers are perceived as relatively the same in product quality, price, and selling efforts, the one with the shortest order cycle time may well receive the order. Evidence suggests that an improved physical distribution system can be used to marketing advantage when present service is not what it could be or should be. Table 14.1 shows how a survey of purchasing managers rated physical distribution activities by their suppliers. The bottom line in the table is quite revealing, considering that a "1" is satisfactory and a "7" is unsatisfactory. The lowest ratings given in the table were for average delivery time, delivery time variability, rush service, and order status information. These ratings indicate less than total satisfaction by the respondents. In this same study, respondents claimed that 20 percent of their orders were stockouts or backorders. Another study conducted in the engineering purchasing division of a large communication company disclosed that 67 percent of their deliveries were on time for actual job starts; 16 percent were early; and 11 percent were late.[13]

Table 14.2 illustrates some characteristics of physical distribution as revealed in a national study conducted by the Council of Logistics Management. The table also suggests that opportunities exist for creating competitive advantage by means of physical distribution. This may be seen using the electronics industry as an example. If backorders are involved in 12.8 percent of all orders, and customers have to wait 14.6 days to receive the backordered items, a marketer might be able to improve his or her company's competitive situation by improving on each of those figures. Similarly, if the average order cycle time is seven days, might there not be an advantage to the firm that could reduce this to five days? Studies such as these suggest that physical distribution in business markets may be less than ideal. Thus, physical distribution is important in business marketing because it offers competitive opportunities.

Complementing Other Marketing Mix Elements

Still another reason for the importance of physical distribution in the marketing strategy is its effect on other mix elements. To illustrate, if a company produces what is perceived in the target market as a high-quality product but cannot deliver in a reliable manner, the advantage of high product quality may be wasted. Similarly, failure to deliver on time destroys the credibility of good field salespeople. If a salesperson promises a valued customer delivery by a certain date and the company cannot meet that date because of an ineffective distribution system, the future effectiveness of that salesperson is compromised. Another example may be seen with pricing. If reliable delivery can be assured, it may be possible to price the products higher, even when product quality is similar to that of competitors.

This discussion emphasizes the importance of physical distribution in business marketing. Organizational customers expect and demand reliable delivery from their suppliers, and if they do not receive that reliability, they look elsewhere. Thus, physical distribution activities must be organized and implemented in an effective and efficient manner if they are to contribute to sound marketing

TABLE 14.1 Satisfaction Ratings of Physical Distribution Service (PDS) Variables by Purchasing Managers: Means and Correlations

Variable	Correlations									
	Billing Procedure	Average Delivery Time	Delivery Time Variability	Rush Service	Returns Policy	Order Status Information	Accuracy in Filling Orders	Action on Complaints	Order Methods	Overall PDS
Billing procedure	1.00									
Average delivery time	0.25	1.00								
Delivery time variability	0.25	0.78	1.00							
Rush service	0.14	0.71	0.57	1.00						
Returns policy	0.23	0.37	0.40	0.36	1.00					
Order status information	0.23	0.54	0.55	0.47	0.48	1.00				
Accuracy in filling orders	0.39	0.44	0.44	0.35	0.49	0.41	1.00			
Action on complaints	0.22	0.47	0.43	0.53	0.39	0.57	0.46	1.00		
Order methods	0.44	0.47	0.42	0.35	0.46	0.38	0.48	0.34	1.00	
Overall physical distribution service	0.39	0.76	0.72	0.59	0.44	0.67	0.46	0.56	0.56	1.00
Mean ratings by variable*	1.99	2.94	3.15	2.68	2.21	2.90	2.00	2.35	2.21	2.30

Source: Reprinted by permission from William D. Perreault, Jr., and Frederick A. Russ, "Physical Distribution Service in Industrial Purchase Decisions," *Journal of Marketing* 40 (April 1976): 8. Published by the American Marketing Association.

Note: * Based on a rating scale ranging from (1) satisfactory to (7) unsatisfactory.

TABLE 14.2   Characteristics of Physical Distribution Service

Characteristic	Food	Chemicals	Paper	Electronics	Total Manufacturing
Percent of orders resulting in backorders	1.3%	3.6%	1.6%	12.8%	6.6%
Number of days customer must wait for back-ordered items	4.4	8.1	10.5	14.6	11.0
Average order cycle time in days	5.0	7.0	7.0	7.0	5.0
Percent of all deliveries that are late to customer	3.0%	3.0%	3.0%	5.0%	4.0%
Average length of delay (days)	1.5	3.6	3.7	6.9	4.0
Percent of orders shipped damaged or defective	1.0%	1.3%	1.7%	.9%	1.2%
Percent of shipments resulting in customer complaints	1.7%	2.7%	1.7%	2.0%	2.1%
Average time in days to remedy a complaint after notice received	7.0	8.5	8.4	7.6	8.1

Source: Reprinted by permission from Bernard J. LaLonde, Martha C. Cooper, and Thomas G. Noordewier, *Customer Service: A Management Perspective* (Oak Brook, IL: Council of Logistics Management, 1988), 57–68.

strategy. This can be seen in Exhibit 14.2 where the distribution of replacement parts is involved. With this in mind, the area of physical distribution management is examined.

PHYSICAL DISTRIBUTION MANAGEMENT

As stated earlier, physical distribution management involves the integration of six areas into a complete distribution strategy. Decisions in transportation must be interrelated with decisions in warehousing, inventory control, and other physical distribution areas to meet stated objectives. Effective physical distribution management represents a balance between product delivery capabilities and related cost.[14] Earlier in the chapter, it was disclosed that in many firms, physical distribution is combined with materials management to compose what is known as logistics. The following discussion pertains only to the physical distribution aspect, and this approach appears justified in that physical distribution and materials management remain largely separate focal points of specialized management attention within the enterprise.[15]

EXHIBIT 14.2   The Importance of Physical Distribution in Providing Product Support Services

The importance of physical distribution in the providing of product support services can be seen in the case of Caterpillar, Inc., in getting replacement parts to its customers.

Caterpillar believes replacement parts support to be an integral and important part of its overall marketing strategy. The purpose of parts support is to (1) minimize equipment owning and operating costs, (2) decrease user downtime, and (3) create demand for Caterpillar replacement parts as opposed to competitor parts.

The company's international network consists of fourteen parts departments and nine emergency parts depots in eleven countries. In addition, it has more than 200 independent dealers who operate approximately 1,000 branch stores around the world. This network is organized to provide forty-eight-hour parts availability. If a replacement part is not delivered to the customer within forty-eight hours, the part is provided free of charge.

To provide this type of service, Caterpillar had to develop an efficient and effective physical distribution system. This system had to integrate the parts departments, the emergency parts depots, and the dealers. Stock orders for the dealers are filled on a regular basis by the parts departments. Caterpillar stresses the importance of moving toward a daily cycle with its dealers. About one-third of its dealers are on the one-day delivery cycle with efforts expended to increase this to more dealers. Company objectives are to be able to deliver 93 percent to 95 percent of all dealer orders from parts department stocks and a 94 percent delivery rate was achieved.

From the customer's point of view, everything starts with a request for a replacement part. In most cases, the customer contacts a dealer, and Caterpillar's objective is that 80 percent to 82 percent of all such requests be handled immediately at the dealer level. The actual current fill rate is around 81 percent, which means that in 81 percent of the cases, the part is available to the customer immediately.

For those orders that cannot be filled at a dealer, Caterpillar has installed a computer tracking system that can generate a list of all Caterpillar facilities that have the required part and can ship it. Typically, if a part is not available at a dealer, it can be found in one of the fourteen parts departments or nine emergency parts depots. In such cases, the company objective is to be able to fill from 81 percent to 83 percent of the requests in this manner; the actual fill rate is 83 percent within twenty-four hours.

For the few parts that cannot be located at any facility in the Caterpillar network, the company either manufactures the part or obtains it from another supplier. If it involves a product currently in the product line, the company objective is to deliver 100 percent in five days. For a noncurrent product, this becomes 100 percent in ten days.

Since there are almost 350,000 parts available through the Caterpillar system, it can be seen that supplying needed parts to customers and dealers is an enormous undertaking. It is also an extremely important undertaking since customers will not tolerate the inability to deliver replacement parts when needed and they will ultimately switch to other manufacturers if this happens. This example shows clearly how the physical distribution elements of transportation, warehousing, inventory control, and order processing are integrated into a total system to provide the level of service required.

Source: Adapted by permission from Bernard J. LaLonde, Martha C. Cooper, and Thomas G. Noordewier, *Customer Service: A Management Perspective* (Oak Brook, IL: Council of Logistics Management, 1988), 98–101.

Physical distribution activities are interrelated, and finding the proper mix of those activities is a difficult task. Before they are interrelated, however, there should be a sound understanding of physical distribution objectives.

Physical Distribution Objectives

There are three general goals in designing and implementing a physical distribution system: (1) providing service to customers, (2) minimizing the total integrated cost of providing this service, and (3) realizing profit from accomplishing the other two objectives. Within these rather broad goals, business marketing managers set more specific performance objectives.

Referring back to Table 14.2, it is possible to illustrate some typical physical distribution objectives found in business marketing. These are as follows:

1. Achieve an average order cycle time of so many days.
2. Reduce the percent of orders that result in backorders.
3. When backorders are involved, reduce the number of days involved in shipping backordered items.
4. Reduce the percent of deliveries that are late to customers.
5. Reduce the percent of orders shipped that contain damaged or defective goods.
6. Reduce the number of customer complaints regarding physical distribution activities.
7. When complaints are received, reduce the time taken to remedy them.

These are physical distribution and not channel objectives in that they relate to the actual movement of goods through channels. Business marketing firms typically attempt to achieve objectives such as these. For example, a Chicago electronics manufacturer has three specific customer service objectives: (1) to deliver requested goods to each customer within ten days of receipt of the purchase order, (2) to keep an out-of-stock percentage to less than 10 percent, and (3) to deliver at least 98 percent of all goods in perfect condition.[16]

Cost objectives are often set in terms of percent of sales of distribution costs. A business marketing firm that now spends 10 percent of its sales on physical distribution activities may wish to reduce that figure to 9 percent in the following year without impairing customer service. There is wide acceptance that providing customer service is the main marketing goal of any physical distribution system. If customers cannot be obtained or retained because of physical distribution problems, concerns about costs and profits are meaningless. Yet, determination of objectives is only a start. The marketing manager should then answer such questions as those that follow. What modes of transportation should be used? If field warehouses are required, where should they be located? What inventory levels should be carried in these warehouses? How should orders be placed and processed? What materials-handling equipment is needed? What packaging is required to deliver products in acceptable condition? To answer these questions, an understanding is needed of what constitutes each of the major physical distribution areas.

Transportation

Transportation decisions typically are made at two levels. The manager first needs to determine which mode or modes of transportation should be used to ship goods to customers or to intermediaries. Once that decision is made, a specific carrier or group of carriers must be selected. Transportation is an important element in physical distribution systems in business markets, and decisions often have far-reaching effects.

Five modes of transportation are commonly used in business marketing. Goods may be shipped by rail, motor carrier, air freight, water transport, and in some instances, pipeline. Often, a combination may be used, such as piggyback situations in which truck trailers are transported long distances on railroad flatcars. In choosing one mode over another, the marketing manager typically considers the following factors:

1. Cost of each mode; for example, comparing the cost of shipping by truck with the cost of shipping by rail.

2. Speed of delivery service; it may cost less to ship by rail than by truck, but it may take longer, which may be important if time is of the essence.

3. Reliability of the mode; for example, establishing which modes of transportation cannot deliver on time or in an acceptable manner and which can move the types of products involved. Although a pipeline is an acceptable mode of transportation for some products such as petroleum, it is totally unacceptable for many products.

4. Accessibility of each mode; for example, establishing whether the mode can serve certain customers in geographically remote areas.

5. Ability of the mode to protect goods in shipment.

Costs differ appreciably among the basic transportation modes. One comparison using cost per ton-mile found the following differentials: pipeline $.27, water $.30, railroad $1.43, truck $7.70, and air freight $21.88.[17] These findings indicate that the cost to ship goods via air is about three times the cost to send them by truck and about fifteen times the cost to send them by railroad. Cost, however, should not be used as the only factor. The marketing manager may wish to assess the preceding five factors in terms of products and desired target markets involved, as shown in Table 14.3.

In the table, a rating of "1" indicates the most favorable and "5" the least favorable. In this situation, the manager rules out pipelines because they are considered to be inaccessible. Similarly, water transit is rejected, leaving the manager to decide between truck, rail, and air. The decision now hinges on the importance placed on the five factors previously listed. For example, if speed of

TABLE 14.3   Rating of Transportation Mode Decision Factors

Decision Factor	Railroad	Truck	Waterway	Pipeline	Air
Cost per ton-mile	3	4	2	1	5
Speed of delivery	3	2	4	5	1
Reliability	4	3	5	1	2
Accessibility	2	1	4	5	3
Protection of goods	4	3	5	1	2

Source: Adapted from Donald J. Bowersox, *Logistical Management,* 2d ed. (New York: Macmillan, 1978), 120.

delivery is the major factor, air shipments may be chosen. But if cost is the critical factor, the company may elect to ship via rail. However, if neither of these modes of transportation is easily accessible to the target market, truck transportation may be selected. As mentioned, however, it is possible to combine the major modes by "piggybacking" (truck trailers on railroad cars), "fishybacking" (truck trailers on ships), and "birdybacking" (truck trailers in air carriers).

Once the mode of transportation has been selected, the individual carriers must be chosen. For example, if goods are to be shipped by motor carrier, which carriers should be used? The process is somewhat similar as cost, carrier reliability, accessibility, and capability to provide the desired service again must be considered.

Table 14.4 provides insight to reasons why business marketing firms select particular carriers based on a national study conducted by the Council of Logistics Management. In this study, 332 manufacturers or other shippers were surveyed on this subject and Table 14.4 shows their responses. As can be seen, the five highest ranked factors are: (1) delivery reliability, (2) pick-up reliability, (3) transit time reliability, (4) equipment availability, and (5) speed of transit time. These findings are consistent with what has been discussed thus far. Business marketers are concerned with timeliness and reliability in their carriers.

In addition, customers often specify on their purchase orders specific carriers they want or do not want used. Many organizational customers have relationships with specific carriers and prefer to use them. Others may want to avoid the use of freight forwarders, which are transportation intermediaries who collect small shipments from many shippers, aggregate them, and move them to delivery points. Their function is to obtain lower transportation rates for large shipments. Use of freight forwarders lowers transportation costs, but it often results in slower shipments because the forwarder may have to wait to accrue enough shipments to achieve the lower rates. At other times, customers may prefer freight forwarders because of their lower freight costs. In summary, carriers are selected when the manager feels that they can deliver the goods in an acceptable condition on time for a reasonable charge and that delivery meets customer conditions.

One other point should be made here. The preceding discussion relates to

TABLE 14.4	Factors Seen as Important by Shippers in Selecting a Carrier	
Factor		**Mean Rating of Importance**
Equipment availability		1.96
Availability of specialized equipment		4.30
Condition of equipment		2.58
Opportunity for intermodal shipments		4.74
Reliability of pick-up		1.44
Reliability of delivery		1.31
Reliability of total transit time		1.59
Speed of transit time		2.00
Tracing of shipments		2.13
Response to claims		2.40
Paperwork accuracy		2.15

Source: Reprinted by permission from Bernard J. LaLonde, Martha C. Cooper, and Thomas G. Noordewier, *Customer Service: A Management Perspective* (Oak Brook, IL: Council of Logistics Management, 1988), 74.

Note: 1 = very important; 7 = very unimportant.

public carriers such as airlines, railroads, and trucking companies. Some business marketing firms own their transportation systems, such as truck fleets, because of unacceptable performance by common carriers or a desire for more control by the manufacturer. This system is a high-cost form of transportation, and most business marketers do not take this approach. Nevertheless, this option can be considered when the common carrier approach is found wanting.

Warehousing

Warehousing decisions involve locating warehouses or storage points in the field to best supply and serve customers and/or channel intermediaries. The basic functions performed by warehouses are to receive, hold, and facilitate shipment of goods to customers. Through the use of strategically placed warehouses, a business marketing company can provide better delivery service to customers than can be provided by direct shipments from the plant.

A number of options are available to the business marketing manager in the warehousing area. Some companies own and operate their own warehouses, which are sometimes called branch houses. This high-cost option requires considerable investment, but it permits a high degree of control over inventory levels and shipments. An alternative is the use of public warehouses.[18] Public warehouses are private businesses whose primary activity is to store, receive, and sometimes ship goods on a rental basis. Instead of owning and operating its own warehouse, the company may elect to rent space in a public warehouse. Compared with private warehouses, public warehousing requires no fixed investment, is flexible when demand varies, and involves only variable costs. The choice between a private warehouse and a public warehouse is often based on such factors as the respective costs, the company's financial situation, the degree of control desired, and the size and stability or variability of demand. In recent years, there has been a trend toward the use of public warehouses by business marketing firms because of high interest rates and high real estate costs. These two factors drove up the costs of private warehouses, making the public warehouse a feasible alternative.

Warehousing is closely related to channels used. For example, if a business marketing manager uses direct channels or manufacturers' representatives, warehousing activities are undertaken by the marketer. If distributors are used, however, warehousing is often provided by those distributors. If warehouses are used to serve the distributors, both manufacturer and distributors are involved in warehousing activities, but at two different levels.

The location of warehouses is complex but can be understood by looking at basic decision considerations. There seem to be three approaches to the location of warehouses.[19] The first approach is market-oriented, in which warehouses are located close to target market customers. The second is production-oriented, in which warehouses are located close to the production facility. The third approach is intermediary-oriented, in which warehouses are located somewhere in between the manufacturing plant and the target markets. The purpose of all three approaches is to serve customers better, but each differs in its method. For example, in a market-oriented approach, the size of the warehouse market is dependent on the speed of inventory replenishments to the customer, the average order size, and the cost per ton of local delivery. Warehouses are located based on these factors to ensure the lowest cost and fastest delivery to customers. In the production-oriented approach, the warehouse is intended to serve as a collecting point for products manufactured at different locations. These products are aggregated at the warehouse, and orders are then filled from the collection center. This type of approach facilitates quick shipments and may lower costs to the customer. The intermediary approach is similar to the latter, but the collection center is closer to the customers.

Warehouse location analysis is based on a number of factors including the degree of market concentration. If the target market is concentrated in a limited regional area, the decision is different than if the market is widely scattered over a large geographical area. The location of the production plant is also a factor. If the manufacturing facility is in New Jersey and the market is concentrated in the northeastern United States, the warehouse decision differs from what it would be if the plant were located in California. Another factor pertains to the adequacy of transportation facilities between manufacturing plant and the target market. For example, if cost-effective and reliable transportation is not available, the warehouse decision differs from that if cheap, reliable transportation exists. Unreliable or costly transportation argues for additional warehouses, whereas low-cost, reliable transportation may eliminate the need for warehouses.

If multiple warehouses are used, it is common in business markets to define warehouse territories by the distance of the customer from the warehouse. The cost to the customer should be approximately the same for each warehouse in the system. To create this set-up, business marketers attempt to define equal-cost warehouse territory boundaries by integrating transportation costs to the warehouse, handling costs in each warehouse, and local transportation costs from the warehouse to the customer. Warehouses are located in territories to ensure, as much as possible, that costs and delivery times are uniform throughout the system. If it costs more and/or takes more time for a customer in one territory to obtain goods from a warehouse than it does for a similar customer in another territory, it can be argued that warehouse location is not optimum.

Inventory Control

To prevent **stockouts** and **backorders,** inventory levels in warehouses and distributors must be adequate to supply the needs of customers and intermediaries. Conversely, inventory cannot be kept high simply to protect against these happenings because of the high cost of carrying inventory. Thus, the marketer must balance these two factors by the process of inventory control. Basically, inventory control involves establishing upper and lower limits for inventory levels. The upper level is usually designed to meet the required level of customer service, whereas the lower level is based on how long it takes to replenish stocks. When stocks reach the lower level, new inventory is ordered. An example may be useful in showing how this process occurs.

Assume that a marketing firm operates a private warehouse to supply customers in a particular service area. Those customers purchase approximately 500 units per day, and it takes the marketer fifteen days to replenish stocks. By multiplying the 500 units by fifteen days, a basic stock level of 7,500 units is necessary to service customers. When inventory on hand drops to 7,500 units, the warehouse manager places an order. If demand increases or it takes longer than fifteen days to replenish stocks, the company may be in trouble, because stockouts will be created. Thus, companies typically protect themselves against such happenings by means of a safety stock, which provides a cushion. There is risk in this practice if demand decreases: Inventory levels become too high, which is costly. The manager's task is to balance the cost of overstocking against the risk of stockouts.

The reorder point, as just described, tells the marketer how much to keep on hand and when to reorder. It does not tell how much inventory should be reordered at that point. This decision depends on inventory carrying costs—costs of storage, recordkeeping, handling, insurance, damage, interest, and obsolescence—and order processing costs—the costs of placing an order. Perhaps the most common approach used to balance the cost of inventory against the cost of ordering is the economic order quantity (EOQ) concept. This concept was detailed in Chapter 4 and will not be fully developed here. It should be recalled that EOQ is described by the following formula:

$$EOQ = \sqrt{\frac{2 \times Co \times S}{Cm \times U}}$$

where

Co = cost per order
Cm = cost of maintenance per year
S = annual demand in units
U = cost per unit

In the preceding example, customers purchase 500 products per day over a 250-day work year for a total demand of 125,000 units. Assuming a unit cost of $5.00, an ordering cost of $20.00, and maintenance costs of 20 percent of the unit cost per year, the EOQ value is 2,236 units. Dividing the total demand of 125,000 by the EOQ value of 2,236 means the marketing company must replenish stock fifty-six times per year.

Another aspect of inventory control involves the ability to know inventory levels at any time in warehouses and the production facility. With this information, stocks can be moved from one location to another to avoid stockouts and backorders. An example may be seen in the BPCS (Business Planning and Control System) software program, which is a fully integrated manufacturing, distribution, and financial package.[20] This system provides the user with immediate on-line display of inventory transaction history, location of inventory, and all orders and allocation details per item. Inventory information is immediately available on each item, each warehouse, each location, and each lot, which permits the marketing manager to move stocks easily to avoid delivery problems.

Discussion so far has focused on inventory control for transaction segments in business marketing. Where relationship segments are involved and shipments are made to JIT, MRP, or DRP customers, the EOQ model is not appropriate. Later in the chapter, discussion will focus exclusively on the role of physical distribution with JIT customers and the effects on inventory control will be addressed there.

Order Processing

Order processing refers to all activities involved in collecting, checking, and transmitting sales order information.[21] A typical process for a transaction type order is described as follows.[22] The salesperson or the customer fills out an order form, which is then transmitted to the location where the desired goods are stored. This location may be a main warehouse or field warehouse. Checking the customer's credit, preparing the bill of lading, and carrying out the order constitute order processing. The order is filled from warehouse inventory stock, and the goods are shipped.

Order processing systems in business markets are either manual, automated, or a combination. Some examples may help to understand how each works. A manufacturer of commercial kitchen equipment used a manual system to process the 75 to 100 orders it received each day. Purchase orders were mailed in, or sometimes phoned in and later confirmed, by customers, distributors, or company salespeople to the company's main sales office. Once received, sales order analysts reviewed the orders for completeness in terms of products desired, prices, discounts, shipping addresses, billing addresses, and other such factors. If an order were incomplete in any manner, the originator was contacted for clarification. At the end of the day, orders were reviewed by the sales manager. On the following day, the orders were transcribed onto the standard order form, and copies were sent to the customer, the salesperson in whose territory the order originated, the credit department, the sales department, and either the shipping department or the production control department. If the order pertained to products in inventory, the shipping department was notified. If the product had to be manufactured to the customer's specifications, the production control department scheduled it into the production process. When the order was ready to be shipped, the credit department released it, and shipment was made. In some cases, credit holds were applied because of outstanding balances. Shipment then would not be made until these were rectified by the customer. The process could vary from three days in processing for standard products to thirty days when products had to be produced to buyer specifications.

An example of an automated order processing system can be seen in the previously mentioned BPCS software program. This system permits on-line order entry, inventory availability checking and allocation, customer credit checking and credit holds, release of hold orders, and shipment.[23] With this system, orders can be processed and released for shipment almost instantaneously if goods are in inventory and no credit holds exist.

Comparing these two systems provides insight into the advantages of a good order processing system. As emphasized earlier in this chapter, order cycle time is important to organizational customers. An inefficient order processing system adds time needlessly to the order cycle. On the other hand, an efficient order processing system subtracts time, which can be a competitive advantage. In the two systems just described, minimum order processing time in the manual example was two to three days, whereas minimum time in the automated example could be almost instantaneous after receipt of the purchase order.

What has been described thus far applies primarily to transaction segments. In situations where JIT customers are involved, each and every shipment does not go through such a process. Rather, all shipments may be covered under the relationship agreement between buyer and seller. This topic will also be viewed in more detail later in the chapter.

Materials Handling

Materials handling involves the physical movement of inventory in the warehouses or elsewhere in the total physical distribution system. Included in this area are forklifts, handlifts, conveyors, cranes, hoists, industrial tractors, motorized handtrucks, and other such equipment used to move and store inventory. Also included are the personnel required to perform materials-handling tasks.

Physical distribution management involves decisions regarding which types of equipment are most cost effective. For example, conveyers have been found useful for moving small bulky items, and cranes are more useful when heavy items must be moved. Proper use of equipment also can reduce losses from damage. To illustrate, sloppy work by forklift operations often results in breakage, which costs the marketing company. An effective physical distribution system should be aimed at reducing such costs by selecting proper equipment and training to ensure correct operation of that equipment. For those business marketers using industrial distributors, materials handling is the responsibility of the distributor, and thus is not under the direct control of the marketing manager.

Protective Packaging

Goods to be shipped and stored must be packaged in a manner that protects them in shipment and in the warehouse. This is the protective packaging function. Products that pass through a physical distribution system are often subjected to a number of factors that require considerable thought as to package design. The greater the caution taken ahead of time in package design, the better the chances that damage can be prevented. Two types of damage are most common: that caused by physical elements and that caused by environmental elements. Physical damage is most often caused by vibration, impact, puncture, and compression. Environmental damage is commonly brought about by exposure to inclement weather, temperature, humidity, and other foreign matter such as insects and rodents.[24] Packages must be developed to counter the causes of damage that are most likely to be encountered in transit or storage. In addition, there are other cost considerations in packaging. The greater the degree of standardization in packaging, the lower the long-run costs of packing, filling, ordering, and storage. Well-designed packaging can lead to reductions in cost of the total physical distribution system, which is a basic objective.

THE TOTAL INTEGRATED SYSTEM OF PHYSICAL DISTRIBUTION

Most business marketing firms do not view the six physical distribution areas as separate, but rather as a **total integrated system of physical distribution.** In terms of costs, for example, it is believed less important to minimize the cost of any one component, such as transportation or ordering, than to minimize the total cost.[25] For example, to select water transportation because of its low cost makes little sense if that mode of transportation requires more field warehouses and higher inventory stocks. Similarly, shipping by high-cost air freight may be defensible if the short delivery times allow the marketer to eliminate warehouses or reduce field inventory stocks. These examples mean that physical distribution decisions in business marketing often involve trade-offs, such as transportation costs versus field inventory costs or the costs of field warehousing, or the costs of distribution versus the costs of reduced or inferior service. Trade-offs exist because when a decision is made in one area of physical distribution, it affects other areas, and the resultant costs must be understood. For example, assume a marketing manager makes the decision to increase the number of field warehouses to meet localized demand by customers. In making this decision, transportation costs may decline, but inventory costs and perhaps order processing costs may increase. Should the decision be made? Another example may be when the manager is considering switching from truck transportation to air transportation, which is much more expensive. But air shipments can be guaranteed on a next-day delivery, which eliminates the need for field warehouses and field inventories. Should this decision be made? These two examples illustrate well the need for viewing physical distribution as a network of integrated activities. This network is what is referred to as the total cost concept in physical distribution. The following equation represents this integration: [26]

$$D = T + FW + VW + S$$

where

D = total distribution costs of a proposed system
T = total freight of a proposed system
FW = fixed warehouse costs of a proposed system
VW = variable warehouse costs (including inventory) of a proposed system
S = total cost of lost sales due to delivery delays under a proposed system

This equation, although simple in concept, provides an approach to the integration problem by forcing the manager to consider opportunity costs in the form of lost sales, in addition to out-of-pocket costs in transportation, warehousing, and inventory. Using the equation, the marketing manager would consider the available options and select the system that minimizes total distribution costs. By also including the cost of lost sales, the manager would be selecting the system that best meets customer needs at the lowest price.

An example may help to explain. Assume the marketing manager is undecided about whether to use an industrial distributor, with its accompanying warehousing facilities, or to set up private warehouses to serve its customers. Either way, the product will be the same, and rail shipment will be used. Customer locations and requirements are known, and either option is acceptable to customers. If the distributor is used, fixed and variable warehouse costs will be less than with company-owned warehouses. If the distributor will not maintain required inventory levels or is slow in delivering, however, the costs of lost sales may be high enough to offset the advantages. On the other hand, if the manager can control the distributor and provide desired customer service in that manner, that option may be more logical.

Assume another situation in which the business marketing manager's company owns and operates a number of field warehouses across the country. The manager believes a reduction in the number of these warehouses and their inventory stocks may be worthwhile because of their high cost. But, the reduction in warehouses means that transportation costs to customers will increase, because bulk shipping rates to the warehouses will not remain the same for customers purchasing in smaller volumes. In addition, time of delivery will be increased from one day from the present warehouses to five days from the manufacturer. Before making the decision to close down the warehouses, the manager must consider the effects of increased transportation costs and the longer order cycle to customers. The cost of possible lost sales may well change the manager's decision. Exhibit 14.3 illustrates the total cost concept from an air freight perspective.

Another way to look at integration, as mentioned earlier, is to integrate level of physical distribution service with overall cost. For example, what is the cost of perfect service? How does this differ from the cost of what might be considered acceptable service? In other words, must physical distribution always be perfect regardless of cost, or might it be reduced to an acceptable level with lower cost? For the marketing manager, these are difficult but important questions.

Figure 14.4 illustrates one way to look at this problem. Assume that analysis of the marketplace discloses that the average total order cycle time is five days and the perceived maximum acceptable order cycle time is found to be ten days. In addition, it is found that 4 percent of all vendor shipments are late, and the

---

EXHIBIT 14.3   Changing Patterns in Industrial Distribution

The high interest rates that characterized the economic picture in the early 1980s brought about an interesting change in physical distribution in business markets. Manufacturers of high-technology products found it more economical to ship goods on demand by air freight than to store up inventory in distant warehouses to meet customers' needs. The reason was that the cost of money was so high that companies could not afford to borrow to carry inventory. They found that in shipping by air freight, the savings in reduced inventory more than paid for the extra cost of air transport.

John C. Emery, Jr., chairman and president of the nation's largest air freight forwarder, explained the phenomenon in this way: "Physical distribution is . . . shifting away from the old ways of regional warehouses and trucks to an instant supply cycle."

Emery pointed out that any manufacturer making a product valued in excess of $3 per pound would find air freight a more economical way to supply customers. In his words, "If you have slow moving parts that get obsolete in the warehouse and if you only turn inventory once a year, the thing to do is shrink it back and air ship parts on demand. If you have a high value component and may turn inventory six times a year, it might be better to supply overnight by air cargo on an item worth $20 a pound, rather than carry inventory at 15 percent interest."

Testimony to the validity of Emery's statements was that the company's revenues in 1980 were up 50 percent over those in 1979, and the air cargo industry was expected to increase tenfold in the 1980s.

Source: Adapted from Helen L. Call, "Emery Is Very High on Air Freight," *San Diego Union,* November 14, 1980, D1.

FIGURE 14.4   Composite Service Performance Window

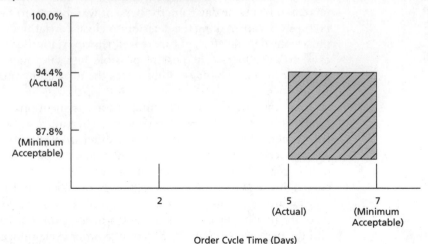

Order Cycle Time (Days)

Source: Reprinted by permission from Bernard J. LaLonde, Martha C. Cooper, and Thomas G. Noordewier, *Customer Service: A Management Perspective* (Oak Brook, IL: Council of Logistics Management, 1988), 43.

average length of delay is four days. Further analysis reveals that the average performance measure for all respondents is 94.4 percent product availability delivered within five days. The minimum acceptable service level is reported as 87.8 percent product availability delivered within seven days.[27] These constraints dictate the performance window outlined in Figure 14.4. This example shows there is flexibility. In this case, the business marketer does not have to achieve 100 percent of orders delivered within five days to be successful. He or she can probably operate quite effectively within the performance window and thus reduce the costs of physical distribution. But costs cannot be reduced to the point that the company cannot perform to the minimum levels outlined in the window.

JUST-IN-TIME IMPLICATIONS FOR PHYSICAL DISTRIBUTION

References have been made throughout this text to the implications of just-in-time buying by organizational customers. Now, attention will focus on JIT and its effects on the area of physical distribution. JIT already has been defined as a manufacturing system in which the parts that are needed to complete the finished products are produced or arrive at the assembly site as they are needed.[28] This section examines the JIT concept and its implications for physical distribution management in business markets.

Serving JIT customers requires the business marketer to provide high-quality, defect-free products on a continuous basis. Since customers do not carry safety stocks of inventory, they rely on their supplier to deliver on time and in the right quantity. Thus, business marketing firms with such customers must possess an efficient and effective physical distribution system to serve the specific needs of those customers. The JIT concept affects physical distribution more than any other area of marketing and thus its effects on physical distribution activities must be examined.

The importance of understanding JIT effects on physical distribution cannot be overstated. JIT is becoming well-entrenched in business markets, both domestic and global, and all indications are that its use will continue to increase. Figure 14.5 illustrates the findings of the previously discussed study conducted by the Council of Logistics Management. This figure shows the percent of all U.S. shipments and receipts by manufacturers that took place in 1988 and projections for the future. As can be seen, in 1988, 20 percent of all shipments were JIT. This was projected to increase to 27.7 percent in 1990 and to 33.2 percent in 1995. Similarly, the percent of all volume received that was JIT was 17.7 percent in 1988 and predicted to reach 27.6 percent in 1990 and 36.3 percent in

FIGURE 14.5   Changes in JIT Shipments Between 1988 and 1995

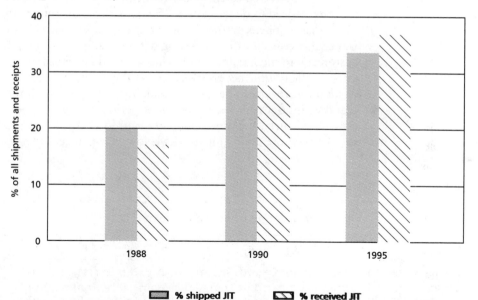

Source: Reprinted by permission from Bernard J. LaLonde, Martha C. Cooper, and Thomas G. Noordewier, *Customer Service: A Management Perspective* (Oak Brook, IL: Council of Logistics Management, 1988), Question III.C.1.

Note: Projected figures for 1990 and 1995.

1995.[29] Another study of 400 business marketing customers found that 65 percent were either using JIT or planning to adopt the concept.[30] These data suggest that JIT is a reality and will continue to grow in importance in managing physical distribution activities in business markets.

How JIT Buying Affects Physical Distribution

To better understand how JIT affects physical distribution activities, an example is useful.[31] Assume a business marketing firm has a customer who presently buys its products on an order point or EOQ system. What will happen if that customer switches to the JIT concept? How will the marketing firm's physical distribution activities be affected?

At present, the customer will demand 360 units over the next twelve weeks for a mean weekly demand of thirty units. There is a one-week lead time on orders and the reorder point occurs when the customer's inventory drops to thirty units. At the beginning of the twelve-week period, the customer has 140 units in current inventory and its economic order quantity is 150 units. Table 14.5 shows the pattern of use of the product over the twelve-week period. As can be seen, the customer plans to use the product in only seven of the weeks, i.e., eighty in week two, forty in week three, etc. Given the above constraints, the customer will place orders for 150 units each in weeks 3 and 8 and these will have to be delivered by the marketer in weeks 4 and 9. Thus, the marketing firm will be required to deliver lots of 150 units twice during the twelve-week period.

What happens if this same customer now switches to the JIT concept? Under this concept, the marketing firm will ship only enough units to meet the customer's immediate demand. This demand is determined by considering the one-week lead time necessary to deliver the product to the customer just in time to meet a forecasted specific demand. Table 14.6 shows how the customer's demand will differ over the twelve-week period. As can be seen, the customer will now order thirty, thirty, seventy, fifty, and forty units in weeks 4, 5, 7, 9, and 11 for delivery the following weeks. Now the marketing firm must deliver five

---

TABLE 14.5   Customer Ordering Under Order Point (EOQ) System

Week	1	2	3	4	5	6	7	8	9	10	11	12
Demand	0	80	40	0	50	30	0	70	0	50	0	40
Receipts	0	0	0	150	0	0	0	0	150	0	0	0
Inventory[b]	140	60	20[a]	170	120	90	90	20[a]	170	120	120	80
Order	0	0	150	0	0	0	0	150	0	0	0	0

Source: Adapted from Dillard B. Tinsley and Joseph G. Ormsby, "Improving Marketing with DRP," *Industrial Marketing Management* 17 (1988):349.

[a] Inventory levels dropped below order point of 30, so EOQ of 150 placed.

[b] End-of-week inventory.

times, rather than two, during the twelve-week period with much smaller order sizes. This example shows clearly why physical distribution activities may often change for JIT situations. Table 14.7 summarizes some of the impacts that JIT purchasing may have on specific physical distribution activities. A brief discus-

TABLE 14.6   Customer Ordering Under Just-in-Time (JIT) System

Week	1	2	3	4	5	6	7	8	9	10	11	12
Demand	0	80	40	0	50	30	0	70	0	50	0	40
Receipts	0	0	0	0	30	30	0	70	0	50	0	40
Inventory[a]	140	60	20	20	0	0	0	0	0	0	0	0
Order	0	0	0	30	30	0	70	0	50	0	40	0

Source: Adapted from Dillard B. Tinsley and Joseph G. Ormsby, "Improving Marketing with DRP," *Industrial Marketing Management* 17 (1988):349.

[a] End-of-week inventory.

TABLE 14.7   Impact of Just-in-Time on Physical Distribution Activities

Activity	Impact
Transportation	Number of shipments may increase while the size of each shipment may decrease; shipments will have to meet varying demand schedules of the customer; may place much more emphasis on trucks to deliver smaller quantities more often
Field warehousing	To serve larger JIT customers, warehouses may have to be located closer to customers to better facilitate the increased number and smaller size of shipments—shipping from larger centralized warehouses may not be effective or feasible; use of public warehouses or distributors may be less than optimal if shipments must be timed to customer delivery requirements
Field inventory control	Field inventory levels of producers may have to be increased as customers reduce their stocks; traditional ordering techniques such as EOQ may become obsolete; adequate field inventory control is vital as customers will not and cannot tolerate stockouts, backorders, and late deliveries; manufacturers will have to control inventory levels thus making industrial distributors more difficult to use
Protective packaging	In some cases, there may be no change as goods will still have to be protected in transit and storage; in other cases, packaging may be changed or even eliminated where delivered products are used directly in production
Materials handling	No major changes are expected as same pieces of equipment, etc., will be involved
Order processing	Order processing will become much more important as supplier and customer become partners; direct-line electronic linkages between the two will be necessary to ensure meeting of customer delivery requirements

sion of the effects on transportation, field warehousing, field inventory control, and order processing may help to better understand which activities are most affected.

Transportation   In terms of transportation, JIT often requires an increased number of deliveries that must be timed to the production schedule of the customer. This can be seen by comparing orders in Tables 14.5 and 14.6. A study of 108 companies using JIT purchasing revealed that 49 percent of them believe the inability of suppliers to deliver to their requirements was still a problem.[32] When customers switch to JIT purchasing, the marketing manager may be forced to reevaluate modes of transportation used and individual carriers. A company that traditionally ships by rail may well have to use trucks to deliver at the times dictated by the JIT customer. In addition, only those trucking companies able and willing to make such accommodation should be considered.

Field Warehousing   The location, size, and type of field warehouses may also have to be reevaluated. With large JIT customers, the manager may have to relocate warehouses to be closer to those customers, so as to be certain transportation time will not detract. When JIT came into vogue in U.S. manufacturing, some farsighted suppliers had anticipated it and purchased property close to large potential customers for location of warehouses. Relocation of warehouses is not necessarily required to deliver to customer requirements if efficient transportation capabilities exist, but JIT typically involves reevaluation of present locations.

Field Inventory Control   Inventory control is critical with JIT customers. Since there are no safety nets on the customer's part, the supplier must have adequate inventories and absolute knowledge of customer requirements. Customers using JIT purchasing cannot and will not tolerate backorders, stockouts, and other such delays. Therefore, the marketing manager should pay special attention to the inventory control issue.

Order Processing   It is in the order processing area that some of the major changes take place. The marketer's order processing system must be capable of integrating inventories and shipments with customer delivery requirements. Typically, electronic linkage between JIT customer and supplier is required, so that the latter knows in advance the delivery requirements of the former. An example may help illustrate the point. General Motors uses the JIT concept with seventy-five of its major suppliers and utilizes an electronic order processing system that works in the following manner. GM's computer transmits the upcoming five days' needs to the suppliers' computers. The suppliers then electronically transmit to GM advance notice of each shipment.[33] By providing suppliers with on-line access to GM's daily material schedules, suppliers are able to ship as required. A business marketing company now using a manual order processing system would be forced to make major changes to attract potential JIT customers.

CHAPTER SUMMARY

Physical distribution strategy involves decision making in terms of transportation of goods, warehousing, field inventory control, protective packaging, materials handling, and order processing. In business markets, physical distribution is often considered one of the essential elements in an effective overall marketing strategy. Organizational buyers and buying influences expect to receive purchased goods on time and in the correct quantities. When this situation does not occur, they are likely to seek other suppliers.

This chapter described the physical distribution area of the marketing mix. Physical distribution was defined and differentiated from the larger area of logistics. Activities involved in physical distribution management were then described, and the importance of the integration of these activities was stressed. The physical distribution system in business marketing was examined in relation to the channels of distribution system in the same market. The process of physical distribution was then analyzed as it applies to the marketing of business goods.

The chapter explored the importance of physical distribution to the business marketing manager with emphasis on costs, meaning to the customer, possible competitive advantages, and complementing the other marketing mix elements. Management of physical distribution was then reviewed in terms of establishing objectives and decisions made in transportation, warehousing, inventory control, order processing, materials handling, and protective packaging. These areas were integrated into the total cost concept to show they interact in an effective, overall distribution strategy. Finally, the chapter looked at the effects of just-in-time purchasing on physical distribution decision making in business marketing.

This chapter is closely related to Chapter 13 on channels of distribution, and it is important to realize that physical distribution decisions are closely entwined with decisions made in the channels area. Regardless of the channels selected, however, an effective and efficient physical distribution system must be designed and implemented by the marketing manager.

KEY TERMS

backorder
inventory control
materials handling
order cycle time
order processing
physical distribution
physical distribution costs

physical distribution process
protective packaging
stockout
total integrated system of physical distribution
transportation
warehousing

QUESTIONS

1. Explain why a physical distribution system designed to service a customer using an order point or EOQ approach to buying would be inadequate if that customer switched to the JIT concept.

2. What do you see as the relationship between physical distribution and channels of distribution in business marketing? How do decisions made in one area affect those made in the other?

3. Physical distribution has been called the "forgotten side" of marketing. What does this statement mean? Do you believe this statement is true in contemporary business marketing?

4. Assume that you are the marketing manager of a company that wishes to differentiate itself from competitors using the area of physical distribution as the focal point. What would you recommend that would create this differential advantage for your company?

5. What is meant when it is claimed there are no safety stocks in a JIT situation and what are the physical distribution implications for the business marketing manager?

6. What is meant by a total integrated system of physical distribution and why is such a system necessary to compete effectively in today's business markets?

7. In looking at the six major activities that comprise the area of physical distribution in business marketing, order processing may appear to be the least important activity. Explain why this is not true in developing an effective physical distribution program in business markets.

8. What is meant by physical distribution management? Explain its role in overall marketing management.

9. It is sometimes argued that physical distribution efforts by U.S. business marketers are less than perfect. Explain why this argument is probably correct and then tell how these shortcomings might be used to advantage by a perceptive business marketing manager.

10. What is the difference between physical distribution and logistics? Explain why physical distribution is typically seen as a marketing area of responsibility while logistics is not.

NOTES

1. Definition used by the Council of Logistics Management, Oak Brook, IL.

2. Donald J. Bowersox, *Logistical Management* (New York: Macmillan, 1974), 1.

3. Thomas C. Kinnear and Kenneth L. Bernhardt, *Principles of Marketing* (Glenview, IL: Scott, Foresman, 1983), 415.

4. See "Handling Warehouse Problems When Agent Warehousing Conflicts with Distributor Operations," *Agency Sales Magazine* 42 (March 1990): 18–20.

5. John F. Magee, *Physical Distribution Systems* (New York: McGraw-Hill, 1967), 10.

6. See Bernard J. LaLonde, Martha C. Cooper, and Thomas G. Noordewier, *Customer Service: A Management Perspective* (Oak Brook, IL: Council of Logistics Management, 1988), Question III.B.2.

7. *Laboratory of Advertising Performance,* Report No. 8015.6 (New York: McGraw-Hill Research Department, 1985).

8. "Distribution Costs Up . . . And Down," *Business Marketing* 71 (September 1986): 54.

9. See William D. Perreault, Jr., and Frederick A. Russ, "Physical Distribution Service in Industrial Purchasing Decisions," *Journal of Marketing* 40 (April 1976): 3–10.

10. James D. Hlavacek and Tommy J. McCuiston, "Industrial Distributors—When, Who, and How?" *Harvard Business Review* 61 (January–February 1983): 97.

11. LaLonde, Cooper, and Noordewier, op. cit., 16.

12. Perreault and Russ, op. cit., 4.

13. Larry C. Giunipero and Edward F. Keiser, "JIT Purchasing in a Non-Manufacturing Environment: A Case Study," *Journal of Purchasing and Materials Management* 23 (Winter 1987): 23.

14. Bowersox, op. cit., 5.

15. Ibid., 7.

16. Kinnear and Bernhardt, op. cit., 409–410.

17. Donald J. Bowersox, *Logistical Management,* 2d ed. (New York: Macmillan, 1978), 120.

18. See "Public Warehouses Can Make Local Stock Available Economically," *Agency Sales Magazine* 42 (March 1990): 33–37.

19. Bowersox (1978), op. cit., 223–225.

20. Milt Ellenbogen, "Modular Business Planning and Control System for Distribution," *Industrial Distribution* 75 (May 1986): 175.

21. Kinnear and Bernhardt, op. cit., 415.

22. Richard H. Ballou, *Basic Business Logistics* (Englewood Cliffs, NJ: Prentice-Hall, 1978), 310.
23. Ellenbogen, op. cit.
24. Bowersox (1978), op. cit., 262–264.
25. Richard E. Trueman, *An Introduction to Quantitative Methods for Decision Making* (New York: Holt, Rinehart & Winston, 1974), 404–405.
26. Philip Kotler, *Marketing Management: Analysis, Planning, and Control* (Englewood Cliffs, NJ: Prentice-Hall, 1980), 453–454.
27. LaLonde, Cooper, and Noordewier, op. cit., 42–43.
28. Giunipero and Keiser, op. cit., 19.

29. "Just-in-Time: The Corporate View," *Industrial Distribution* 75 (May 1986): 83.
30. Kate Bertrand, "The Just-in-Time Mandate," *Business Marketing* 71 (November 1986): 48.
31. See Dillard B. Tinsley and Joseph G. Ormsby, "Improving Marketing with DRP," *Industrial Marketing Management* 17 (1988): 347–354.
32. Albert F. Celley, William H. Clegg, Arthur W. Smith, and Mark A. Vonderembse, "Implementation of JIT in the United States," *Journal of Purchasing and Materials Management* 22 (Winter 1986): 14.
33. "Just-in-Time: The Corporate View," op. cit., 84.

SUGGESTED ADDITIONAL READINGS

Blanding, Warren. *Blanding's Practical Physical Distribution.* New York: Van Nostrand Reinhold, 1987.

Bullen, H. J. "New Competitive Selling Weapon—Physical Distribution Management." *Sales & Marketing Management* 130 (May 8, 1985): 41–42.

Collins, Robert S., and D. Clay Whybark. "Realizing the Potential of Distribution Requirements Planning." *Journal of Business Logistics* 6 (1985): 53–65.

Herron, David P. "Managing Physical Distribution for Profit." *Harvard Business Review* 57 (May–June 1979): 121–132.

LaLonde, Bernard J., Martha C. Cooper, and Thomas G. Noordewier. *Customer Service: A Management Perspective.* Oak Brook, IL: Council of Logistics Management, 1988.

Lambert, D. M., and H. M. Armitage. "Managing Distribution Costs for Better Profit Performance." *Business* 30 (September–October 1980): 46–52.

Lambert, D. M., and J. T. Mentzer. "Is Integrated Physical Distribution Management a Reality?" *Journal of Business Logistics* 1 (1980): 18–27.

Morash, Edward A. "Using Transportation Intermediaries for Industrial Purchasing Decisions." *Journal of Business & Industrial Marketing* 2 (Fall 1987): 15–27.

————. "Customer Service, Channel Separation, and Transportation Intermediaries." *Journal of Business Logistics* 7 (1986): 89–107.

Perreault, William D., Jr., and Frederick A. Russ. "Physical Distribution Service in Industrial Purchasing Decisions." *Journal of Marketing* 40 (April 1976): 3–10.

————. "Physical Distribution Service: A Neglected Aspect of Marketing Management." *MSU Business Topics* 22 (Summer 1974): 38–46.

————. "Quantifying Marketing Trade-Offs in Physical Distribution Policy Decisions." *Decision Sciences* 7 (1976): 186–201.

Rosenfield, Donald B. "Storefront Distribution for Industrial Products." *Harvard Business Review* 67 (July–August 1989): 44–48.

Saipe, Alan B. "Reducing Branch Inventories—The Ordering Kit." *Business Quarterly* 46 (Autumn 1981): 35–40.

Steward, Wendell M. "Physical Distribution: Key to Improved Volume and Profits." *Journal of Marketing* 39 (January 1965): 65–70.

Tinsley, Dillard B., and Joseph G. Ormsby. "Improving Marketing with DRP." *Industrial Marketing Management* 17 (1988): 347–354.

Uhr, Ernest B., Ernest G. Hauck, and John C. Rogers. "Physical Distribution Service." *Journal of Business Logistics* 2 (1981): 158–169.

‚15‚

Promotional Strategy in Business Marketing— Personal Selling

• •

As has been developed thus far, the business marketing manager is ultimately responsible for defining target markets, developing overall marketing strategy and tactics, determining products and services to be marketed, and setting up distribution systems. In addition, those products and services must be promoted to buying influences in the target markets. This promotional area of marketing management is an important aspect of the marketing of business goods and services. In today's markets, it is not sufficient to produce high-quality products and services and hope for customers. The merits of the products and services must be communicated to buyers and other buying influences in present and prospective target market customer firms. The role of promotion in marketing strategy is to communicate with the market to stimulate demand for the company's products and services.

The methods of communication typically used compose the promotional mix. In business marketing, there are four major components of this mix:

Personal selling. Personal selling is an oral presentation in a conversation with one or more prospective purchasers for the purpose of making sales.[1] In business markets, such presentations may be made by field salespeople, inside salespeople, telemarketing personnel, sales teams, and national account representatives.

Advertising. Advertising is any paid form of nonpersonal presentation and promotion of ideas, goods, or services by an identified sponsor.[2] In business marketing, this communication is directed toward present or prospective customers via the use of such media as trade publications and other print media, direct mail, directories, radio, television, and outdoor media.

Sales promotion. Sales promotions are short-term incentives to encourage the purchase or sale of a product or service.[3] In business marketing, this

What Attributes Must the Business Salesperson Possess to Be Successful in the 1990s?

For the business salesperson to be successful in the business marketing environment of the 1990s, that salesperson must possess a number of attributes. These attributes may be classified as his or her (a) eyes, (b) ears, (c) heart, (d) briefcase, (e) legs, and (f) feet. According to the The Forum Corporation, these attributes may be described as follows:

Eyes Successful salespeople have to look at situations from the customer's point of view. They will have to see their customers as partners, not conquests.

Ears The best salespeople will be the best listeners. They will involve their clients in creating solutions.

Heart Honesty is a key to successful selling. Good salespeople will not promise what they cannot deliver.

Briefcase Successful salespeople do their homework. They prepare their plans and presentations *before* they come knocking.

Legs Savvy salespeople will use their influence *within* their companies to help meet their clients' needs.

Feet Fancy footwork and product knowledge will no longer be sufficient. Successful salespeople will have to earn the right to do business with their clients and not just assume that right exists.

For the sales manager in business marketing, the task is to recruit and hire these types of people, giving them assistance where required, motivating them to do their best, and rewarding them so they do not leave to take employment elsewhere.

Source: Adapted from "The Anatomy of a Salesperson in the 1990s" (The Forum Corporation, 1990).

component includes trade shows and expositions, catalogs, point-of-purchase (POP) materials and other intermediary materials, samples, premiums, contests, trading stamps, and other such promotional approaches.

Publicity and public relations. Publicity is anything that appears in the print or broadcast media about a company. It can be initiated by the media in either a positive or negative manner or it can be company initiated such as where the company sends press releases, new product announcements, and the like to the media in the hope that it will be published or aired. Public relations can be described as a set of tools used by the company to create goodwill among all its publics, which may include customers, employees, unions, governmental agencies, communities, and other such entities. As this list suggests, not all areas of public relations are related to marketing. Examples of public relations that do have marketing implications might be press conferences, charitable donations, and tours of facilities.

It is probably safe to say that a good promotional mix usually encompasses some combination of these four components, but this rule is not hard and fast. Some companies have been successful without personal selling, and other firms have succeeded without much emphasis on advertising. Still others have succeeded with no sales promotional activities. Marketing managers have differing opinions about the effectiveness of each component, and market considerations affect the valid use of each. The components of a promotional mix are not important as long as the overall mix communicates effectively with the target audience of buyers and buying influences, convinces them to purchase or take some other desired action, and competes favorably in the marketplace with the promotional mixes of competitors. Naturally, the components of any company's promotional mix should complement, not compete with, each other. If the company's promotional mix does not accomplish these things, then the firm's promotional strategy will be ineffective. The decisions that affect the formulation and implementation of this mix can be termed the **promotional strategy.** As with other substrategies, to be effective promotional strategy must be compatible with the company's objectives and its marketing plan. At the same time, it must be integrated into its product, channel, and pricing substrategies. This is true for both domestic and global business marketing firms, whether their customers are private, institutional, or governmental.

BUSINESS PROMOTIONAL STRATEGY

Promotion in business marketing involves sales managers, advertising managers, and sometimes, sales promotion, publicity, and public relations managers, who head their own departments and report to the marketing manager in their respective specialized areas. The marketing manager must integrate personal selling, advertising, sales promotion, publicity, and public relations into one overall promotional package that is then further integrated into the total marketing strategy with product, channel, and pricing decisions. In view of this division of promotional efforts, no format for overall business promotional strategy will be developed. Instead, formats are developed individually for sales, advertising, sales promotion, and publicity and public relations. This chapter discusses the personal selling area of promotion in business marketing. Chapter 16 covers the areas of advertising, sales promotion, and publicity and public relations.

Difference Between Business and Consumer Promotional Strategies

Business and consumer marketing practices differ sharply in the area of promotion, even though the basic tasks may be the same. To understand these differences—and all of business promotion, for that matter—it is first helpful to understand the tasks involved in promotion in business markets. According to McGraw-Hill's Research Department, there are six basic steps or tasks to be accomplished in promotion: (1) making contact, (2) arousing interest, (3) creating preference, (4) making specific proposals, (5) closing the order, and (6) keeping customers sold.[4] Accomplishing these tasks indicates an effective promotional strategy, whereas failure to do so indicates a lack of effectiveness if the marketing manager has a competitive product and a clear understanding of market targets to be reached.

Keeping the McGraw-Hill tasks in mind, refer to Table 15.1. Some great differences can be observed between the relative importance of promotional mix

TABLE 15.1 **Comparison of Promotional Strategy Factors in the Consumer and Business Markets**

Factor	Consumer Markets	Business Markets
Importance of promotion strategy in marketing mix	Very important; task of promotion to communicate with large number of consumers and households puts emphasis on advertising and sales promotion	Very important; task of promotion to communicate with professional buyers and buying influences puts major emphasis on personal selling
Emphasis on promotional mix elements	Major emphasis often placed on advertising, then sales promotion, then personal selling; task of advertising to pull consumer through entire adoption process	Major emphasis usually placed on personal selling, then sales promotion, then advertising; tasks of advertising and sales promotion to create environment conducive to personal selling
Advertising media	Major media are television, radio, newspapers, magazines, and outdoor	Major media are trade journal publications, direct mail, and industrial/business directories
Sales promotion media	Major media are POP displays, contests, brochures, inserts, demonstrations, samples, and specialty advertising	Major media are catalogs, trade shows, distributor materials, and specialty advertising
Advertising and sales promotion themes	Aimed at ultimate consumers; themes often stress more emotional than rational factors	Aimed at professional buyers and buying influences; themes often stress more rational than emotional factors
Promotional packaging	A major consideration with consumer products marketed through self-service distribution outlets	A minor consideration with most business products but may be useful with some aftermarket products
Promotional budgets	Large, with heavy emphasis on advertising and sales promotion; advertising budgets often exceed 5 percent of sales	Large, with heavy emphasis on sales; advertising budgets often less than 1–2 percent of sales
Sales efforts	Majority of sales efforts carried out by salespeople of wholesalers and retailers, although manufacturers' salespeople call on the intermediaries	Majority of sales efforts carried out by manufacturers' salespeople, although distributors and manufacturers' representatives also sell to customers
Partner relationships	Do not exist in consumer markets in most cases, causing less personal promotion means to be used	Important in many types of business markets and requires close personal promotional efforts to create and maintain

components as seen by consumer and business marketing executives. Personal selling plays a much greater role in business markets; again, the importance of personal contact with organizational buyers and buying influences is emphasized. Mass media, promotional branding, and promotional packaging are used far less in business marketing. Although the use of print media plays a significant role in business promotion, as it does in the consumer area, its use is different: In business markets, media use relies heavily on the trade publication variety.

Table 15.1 shows that business and consumer marketing managers differ in their assessments of which promotional components work best in achieving the McGraw-Hill Research Department's six basic tasks. For example, in the consumer market, using mass advertising and effective promotional packaging, a consumer goods manufacturer can bring the ultimate consumer through the six tasks or steps. For the manufacturer of sophisticated electronic products being sold to engineers, however, such a promotional approach will probably fail. Stated briefly, consumer marketing promotional strategies differ from those found in business marketing primarily because buyer expectations are different and product and service characteristics differ.

There are also other important differences. As stated, media differ in the two markets. Most business advertising is in trade journals and direct-mail media. In addition, business advertising themes or messages are generally less emotional than those found in the consumer market. Sales promotion also differs: The bulk of business sales promotion is in trade shows, catalogs, directories, and specialty advertising items.

These are a few of the general differences, but they are sufficient to make the desired point. There are enough differences between business and consumer promotional strategies to merit an in-depth analysis of each of the components. In these analyses, more specific differences between business and consumer promotional strategies will be developed as they relate to these four areas of promotion.

PERSONAL SELLING IN BUSINESS MARKETS

In the majority of cases, **personal selling** is an important component in the marketing strategies of business marketing managers. This fact is borne out by the large number of direct channels in business marketing. As was discussed in Chapter 13, an estimated three-fourths of all business goods, based on their dollar volume, are marketed without benefit of channel intermediaries. This statistic, in turn, implies the use of company salespeople. As has also been shown, even manufacturers' representatives and distributors are chosen because of their sales capabilities. Table 15.1 emphasizes the great importance business marketing managers place on personal selling.

Personal selling is important to the marketing of business goods and services because conditions in business markets are almost identical to those cited in the classic marketing textbooks as ideal for this form of promotion. To illustrate, there are relatively few customers, and they can be specifically defined and located. The products and services are often complex and expensive, and large dollar volume sales are common. Buyers and buying influences require and demand technical, immediate answers to complex questions before they will purchase, and presale and postsale service and technical assistance are common requirements. Conditions such as these account for the great emphasis on personal selling in business markets. Although exceptions can be found, business goods and services rarely are marketed without benefit of personal selling somewhere along the way, either by company salespeople, distributors' sales personnel, or manufacturers' representatives.

Personal selling is also important because of the importance placed on it by organizational buyers and buying influences. Table 15.2 shows this quite clearly based on a study of 232 buyers of different types of business products. They were asked to rank the importance of various components of the promotional mix when they made a purchasing decision. As can be seen, personal selling was ranked first for all six product types. It is only natural that business marketing managers would rate personal selling as so important when their customers see it in this way.

To discuss adequately the topic of personal selling in business marketing, it is necessary to break the subject into parts. First, the personal selling function will be examined as it is performed by sales representatives in business markets. Then, the chapter will address the topics of the costs involved in personal selling and the management of sales forces in business marketing.

Classifications of Salespersons in Business Marketing

In a general sense, the business salesperson can be broadly defined as a technically oriented person whose primary responsibility is to sell business goods and services to buyers and buying influences in organizational markets. Within

TABLE 15.2 Rankings of Importance of Promotional Elements in Making a Purchase Decision as Seen by Organizational Buyers of Different Types of Products

Promotional Element	Major Capital Goods [N = 39]	Minor Capital Goods [N = 34]	Materials [N = 49]	Component Parts [N = 57]	Supplies [N = 53]
Salespeople	1	1	1	1	1
Technical literature	2	2	2	2	2
Trade shows	3	4	5	5	6
Trade publications	4	3	4	4	4
Sales promotion	5	5	3	3	3
Direct mail	6	6	6	6	5

Source: Adapted by permission from Donald W. Jackson, Janet E. Keith, and Richard K. Burdick, "The Relative Importance of Various Promotional Elements in Different Industrial Purchase Situations," *Journal of Advertising* 16 (1987):30.

this broad definition, however, different variations exist. For example, some salespeople sell direct to end users such as manufacturers, government agencies, and institutional customers such as hospitals, schools, and so forth. Other salespeople in business marketing sell to distributors or other reseller organizations. Table 15.3 shows how these two types compare in use in selected business markets. As the table shows, there are variations among industries. For example, in sales in the electronics industry, almost three-fourths of all salespeople are of the type that sell direct to end users—only one-quarter sell to channel intermediaries. But, salespeople in the foodservice industry are almost evenly split. Looking at the overall average, however, the conclusion may be drawn that about two-thirds of all business salespeople call on organizational customers and prospects that use the goods or services for reasons other than resale. Within this basic grouping, business salespeople may further be classified into the following groups: (1) the sales engineer, (2) the executive salesperson, (3) the business supplies salesperson, (4) the inside salesperson, and (5) the missionary salesperson. A description of each of these types follows.

The Sales Engineer The **sales engineer** is a business salesperson who often has a degree in some area of engineering. This salesperson is highly technically trained and calls on technically oriented personnel such as purchasing agents, plant engineers, product engineers, production supervisors, and maintenance engineers. Products sold are normally of a complex technical nature, and they require technical competence to sell. The sales engineer may be selling to OEMs or users or distributors (in cases in which the latter resell such equipment to the OEMs and users). Simply stated, this type of business salesperson is an engineer who sells.

The Executive Salesperson The **executive salesperson** is a business salesperson who also possesses a high degree of technical competence, but of a different

---

TABLE 15.3 **Percent of Sales Calls by Business Salespeople Direct to the Business Customer and to Distributors**

Industry	Percent Selling Direct to Business Customer	Percent Selling to Distributors
Electronics and computer manufacturing	74%	26%
Nonmanufacturing/services	71%	29%
Foodservice	49%	51%
Building and construction	57%	43%
Manufacturing	62%	38%
Industry average	67%	33%

Source: Reprinted by permission from Cahners Publishing Company, *Cahners Advertising Research Report,* No. 542.7 (Newton, MA: Cahners Publishing Company, 1989).

type than that possessed by the sales engineer. The executive salesperson is a loose term to describe all those people selling products and services to executives in all types of organizations including resellers. Typical of this type are salespeople who sell computer software programs, consulting services, company insurance programs, and advertising to such executives as purchasing directors, comptrollers, personnel managers, production managers, data processing managers, advertising managers, and other such corporate officers. The products and services sold by this type of salesperson are not normally used in the production of goods and services but are required in the operation of the customer's organization.

The Business Supplies Salesperson   The term **business supplies salesperson** is used to describe those people selling into business markets who operate in the field but who cannot be called sales engineers or executive salespersons. The term defines those salespeople who sell relatively standardized business products such as component parts, supplies, raw materials, and processed materials to all types of organizational customers. Often technically oriented and trained, they do not require the engineering background of the sales engineer, although they must have knowledge of their customers' particular needs. Generally, this type of salesperson sells to OEMs rather than user customers, channel intermediaries, or resellers, and although they call on buying influences, they probably deal much more with purchasing agents than sales engineers and executive salespersons do.

The Inside Salesperson   The three types of salespersons previously discussed all operate in the marketplace as field sales personnel. The **inside salesperson** is basically a telephone salesperson, although there are instances of selling by linking computer terminals between suppliers and customers. This latter type of selling may better be defined as part of telemarketing, which is discussed in depth shortly. The inside salesperson sells by telephone from within the manufacturer's or distributor's facilities. Inside salespersons have been very effective in situations in which customer relationships are already established and personal sales calls may no longer be required. The use of salespersons of this type to open new accounts has not been found effective, as buyers usually will not purchase an unknown commodity from an unknown supplier over the telephone. Properly used, the inside salesperson is not a substitute for a field salesperson but rather a complement. Figure 15.1 provides a good example.

Inside salespersons should not be thought of as passive sales types who answer the telephone if it rings. In many companies, they are assigned territories and are responsible for taking care of customers in those territories. Typically, inside salespeople are less expensive to use than field salespeople. They are less expensive to train, and they do not require field selling expenses such as car, travel, meals, lodging, and entertainment.[5] Used effectively, the lower-cost inside salespeople can perform many sales tasks and free the higher-cost field salespeople for the important job of selling. Industrial distributors, for example, average one inside salesperson for every field salesperson.[6] One estimate is that over

FIGURE 15.1   Inside Sales in Business Marketing

Source: Reprinted by permission of Dacor Computer Systems, Bowling Green, OH.

90 percent of the sales of steel distributors are made by inside salespeople.[7] Inside salespeople must be technically trained and capable of solving customer problems over the phone for the concept to work properly.

The Missionary Salesperson   Another type of salesperson found in business marketing is the so-called **missionary salesperson,** who works with customers and channel intermediaries in a consulting or advisory capacity as opposed to selling per se. Sometimes called a factory representative or factory rep, this type is more involved with indirect sales that may accrue from helping a customer with technical assistance, aiding a distributor or reseller with inventory control, training distributor salespeople, training customer employees in the operation of machinery and equipment, and other such similar functions. Basically, this type of salesperson does not sell but can be instrumental in future sales. The factory rep also must possess the technical competence necessary to communicate with knowledgeable buyers and buying influences in all types of organizational customers and prospects.

As can be seen by these classifications, the "average business salesperson" does not really exist. There are a number of types, and their functions and responsibilities differ. It probably can be argued that every company's salespeople are different, even when the products and markets served by those companies are basically the same. For example, an experienced business supplies salesperson differs considerably from a semiexperienced salesperson of the same type by virtue of experience and ability. The sales forces of most companies include experienced, semiexperienced, and training sales personnel whose tasks and responsibilities differ because of ability.

The business salesperson is a marketer in every sense of the word. In the words of one sales manager, the role of the salesperson is

> to analyze his or her territory, know both existing and potential accounts, and understand who are the key buying influences in each company. He or she has to look at the products the prospects turn out, figure what they have to go through to make them, then meet their needs to the best of his or her company's ability.[8]

Because of requirements such as these, it is difficult to find effective business salespeople. An estimated 75 percent of all sales in business markets are accounted for by about 25 percent of all salespeople.[9] The following quotation summarizes the problem: "Few salespeople are capable of doing high-caliber creative selling, cultivative selling, maintenance selling, and information gathering while accounting for product, market, and customer differences in a given territory."[10] This statement implies that only a minority of business salespeople are able to master the stringent requirements for selling in organizational markets.

Trends in Selling in Business Marketing

Several important trends have occurred in business selling in recent years. These trends do not have a common cause. Some relate to the high cost of field selling; others relate to technological breakthroughs that have been applicable to selling in business markets. Still others relate to a changing marketplace and the shortage of competent and efficient field salespeople. The following sections describe some of the major trends.

Increased Use of Sales Teams Team selling often occurs in situations in which customer firms employ committee buying, which is basically a form of team buying. Assume, for example, that a manufacturing customer wishes to buy punching and shearing machines for its production line. Because of the large investment involved, the firm may appoint a committee to decide whose equipment will be purchased. This committee may be comprised of such people as the production supervisor, the purchasing agent, production foremen, the comptroller, a plant engineer, and a quality control expert. Although all these people may be considering the same manufacturer's equipment, they may also be looking for something different in that equipment.

What then is the task of the salesperson trying to sell to all of these buying influences in their specific areas of expertise? The job is almost impossible for one person to perform. What often happens in such cases is that the salesperson is able to call on his or her own company for help; such personnel as an engineer, a financial specialist, and a vice president of marketing come into the field and team-sell the equipment with the salesperson. Together, the **sales team** is able to answer specific questions relating to engineering, financing, installation, production capabilities, service, and other such factors that the salesperson alone may have been incapable of answering.

Expanded Role of Inside Sales Still another trend is the expanded role of the inside, or telephone, salesperson. As has already been developed, inside salespeople are now assuming many of the tasks previously performed by field salespeople, which frees the latter for the critical field sales activities. In addition to actual phone selling, some of these tasks include following up sales made in the field, developing leads for field sales representatives, qualifying sales leads, following up complaints, qualifying new customer credit, making field visits and goodwill calls, reviving inactive accounts, and reviewing or helping customers solve problems.[11] Field salespeople can perform these tasks, but at a much higher cost. For example, McGraw-Hill Research determined the cost of a business sales field call to average $229.70 in 1985.[12] At the same time, a Conference Board study found that a phone call to a business decision maker ran between $21.00 and $25.00.[13] These data suggest that using an inside salesperson for sales support tasks is cheaper and probably more efficient than using a field salesperson to perform those tasks. In many business marketing firms, inside salespeople team with field salespeople to form a tandem that offers increased sales effectiveness at decreased cost. Other firms have even replaced field salespeople with inside types for straight rebuy situations involving standardized and frequently purchased products. This situation is not the rule, however, as field salespeople and inside salespeople usually are not direct substitutes for each other.

There are some compelling reasons for the increased use of inside salespeople by business marketers. One of the most pressing reasons is that as field sales costs continue to rise, marketing managers seek out alternatives, and inside sales cost less than field sales. In addition, inside salespeople are usually easier to control than field salespeople. It typically costs less to recruit and train inside salespeople, and the use of inside sales types can reduce field sales expenses such as travel, meals, and lodging. It is also argued that inside selling can sometimes be more efficient than field selling because neither traveling nor waiting is involved. Finally, many marketing managers have found that they can use inside salespeople to qualify leads for their field sales counterparts, and thus they reduce the actual cost to close a sale. Properly used, inside salespeople can often relieve field salespeople of certain nonselling tasks such as follow-up on orders and tracing shipments, thus permitting those in the field more time to sell to customers and prospects.

Increased Use of Telemarketing Another change in business selling is **telemarketing,** which might be viewed as an extension of inside selling. Telemarketing is defined as a marketing communication system that uses telecommunication technology and trained personnel to conduct planned marketing activities directed at targeted groups of customers.[14] Telemarketing thus covers a wide spectrum, ranging from an inside salesperson using the telephone to call a prospect to a complete telemarketing center with trained personnel using computer technology to facilitate instantaneous responses to questions from customers or prospects. In simple terms, telemarketing includes all forms of telecommunications technology used for selling and sales support functions. Often, telemarketing systems begin with a company using an 800 telephone number in advertisements, thus prompting customer or prospect action.

One of the main objectives of most telemarketing systems is to reduce the number of calls needed to close a sale, rather than making a direct sale.[15] Telemarketing may better be viewed as a sales support tool and not as a substitute for a field salesperson. As with the inside sales concept, telemarketing is a way to reduce the high cost of personal selling and at the same time increase the effectiveness of field salespeople. An example may be useful. Salesnet is a system founded by Dun & Bradstreet and works in this manner. A salesperson with a computer terminal makes calls to prospective customers. Each phone call is guided by a computer-controlled script. The computer anticipates the prospect's objections and questions, and it provides appropriate responses. The process repeats itself until the end of the sales call.[16]

Comprehensive telemarketing systems are more expensive than simply using inside salespeople to handle telephone orders. To make a telemarketing system work, four components are necessary: (1) competent personnel, (2) equipment, which may range from a WATS line to a complete computerized system, (3) an up-to-date customer/prospect list, and (4) promotional support.[17] Considerable cost can be involved, but it can also contribute to increased sales. An average telemarketing operation can increase sales 10 percent to 20 percent, whereas well-run programs frequently double sales volume.[18]

The trend in telemarketing is influenced by its flexibility. Business marketing companies use it for a variety of sales and sales support reasons, such as generating and qualifying leads for field sales representatives, selling marginal accounts, selling products not receiving enough attention by field representatives, informing customers/prospects of new products or services, handling customer complaints and inquiries, measuring advertising effectiveness, and conducting marketing research. Although telemarketing probably will not replace field selling, it appears to be a trend that will continue.

Some examples may help to understand how telemarketing works. The B. F. Goodrich Chemical Group uses a telemarketing center for order taking, customer service, and information dissemination purposes. When customers call, a center specialist brings up the customer's file on a computer screen, records the order, checks inventory, and when necessary, talks with production and shipping to schedule shipment. Field sales personnel are then provided current inventory data and estimated arrival times. High-volume accounts are scheduled for field visits, thus increasing the number and quality of contacts between B. F. Goodrich and its best customers.[19] This example shows telemarketing being used to support field sales. Another example may be found in Industrial Fabricators of Jackson, Tennessee. This company replaced its field sales force of thirty-nine people with an in-house, fourteen-person telemarketing department. With this change, sales of industrial-strength wiping cloths went up 25 percent, and selling costs decreased by 30 percent.[20] This example is somewhat unique in that telemarketing was substituted for field selling.

Increased Use of Microcomputers in Field Sales   In addition to telemarketing systems, a further development involves the use of portable personal computers in the selling process. Today's field salesperson uses a briefcase-size portable microcomputer in the sales presentation, which may be tied to the supplier's mainframe computer or use software programs on diskette. Typical uses are following up on deliveries and shipments, determining inventory availability, projecting customer needs, calculating optimum delivery schedules for customers, bidding, and providing graphics in the presentation.

An example may help to illustrate this trend. At Rockwell International's heavy vehicle components division, sales representatives were given personal computers to help sell automatic slack adjusters. Programs contained the cost data necessary to compute what fleet operators were spending on brake adjustments. These were then compared with the cost of Rockwell's slack adjusters to show the savings to the customer from using their equipment.[21] This trend toward the use of microcomputers has brought about instantaneous answers to customers' questions and problems and has greatly changed field selling in many industries.

Growing Impact of Women in Field Sales   Another important trend in selling in business markets is the impact made by female sales personnel. Not many years ago, women were rare in business selling and many reasons were given why women could not sell business goods and services. In 1967, for example, it was estimated that only 2 percent of all business salespeople were female.[22] In 1974, a survey by the Research Institute of America found that only one of five responding companies employed any saleswomen at all.[23] Studies such as these show that only a few years back women were not dominant factors in business selling.

During the decade of the 1980s, much changed. In 1982, a study by the Dartnell Institute of Financial Research found women to comprise 7.3 percent of all business sales forces.[24] In 1989, Dartnell revised its figure to 27.9 percent.[25] In contemporary business marketing, almost one-third of all salespeople are women although great variations seem to exist among industries. For example, Dartnell's mean of 27.9 percent was computed from industries with low percentages (5.9 percent in chemicals and 7.3 percent in fabricated metals) to industries with high percentages (50.0 percent in communications and 39.4 percent in printing and publishing). Thus, in a relatively short number of years, women have made great inroads and equally great contributions to field selling in business markets.

There is thus a sharp trend toward the use of women in business selling, and a number of reasons account for this movement. First, women have been found to be successful in selling to business customers. The old myth that women cannot perform business selling jobs has been proven false—gender apparently has little effect on the personality qualities necessary for such selling. Second, there are not enough men with the attributes necessary for successful selling. Thus, women comprise the biggest single source of untapped sales talent around. Third, women have become more interested in sales and see it as a good way to higher managerial positions. Fourth, equal opportunity employment requirements have opened up the business sales area to women. The real key, however, to the increased use of women in business selling is that many have been successful, and organizational buyers' attitudes toward buying from women are changing.

A *Journal of Marketing* study looked at how purchasing professionals rated female and male salespersons.[26] In this study, men were rated significantly higher on (1) knowledge of the companies being sold to, (2) product knowledge, (3) provision of technical assistance, and (4) presentation of new ideas to buyers. On the other hand, women were rated significantly higher on (1) being vigorous and having a lot of drive, (2) knowing how to listen, (3) preparing for sales presentations, (4) follow-through on deliveries, (5) personalizing the sales presentation, (6) willingness to expedite rush orders, and (7) not bypassing the purchasing people. Based on this study, it appears that women are capable of effective field selling in business markets and that many buyers do not hold negative feelings regarding their use. Exhibit 15.1 illustrates an example of a successful woman in a business sales position.

Expanded Use of National Accounts Business marketers have long given special sales treatment to their large and important customers. In this regard, the topic of **national accounts** was discussed in Chapter 13. Growing interest in na-

---

EXHIBIT 15.1   Women in Business Sales

Purchasing magazine annually polls its 100,000+ professional buyer readers to honor outstanding field salespeople. Readers are requested to nominate salespeople who they believe exemplify outstanding sales performers.

In one survey, one of the national winners was Wendy Snyder, a field sales representative of the Torrington Company. Snyder, who holds a master's degree in engineering, undertook a two-year training program at Torrington before entering the field.

In addition to possessing a great deal of technical expertise, Snyder possesses the ability to understand customer problems and a willingness to work toward the solution of those problems. Often working closely with a customer's production and quality control engineers, she also monitors the buyers' MRP (materials requirement planning) schedules for the best fit with Torrington's MRP. This diligence has allowed her to make a favorable impression on her customer. In the words of one of her buyers, "We have cut our inventory in half on some very expensive bearings." Her customers see her strongest sales attribute as her willingness to follow through and keep her customers informed. One buyer states that "she never fails to confirm the details of every discussion/session with a letter outlining what was decided."

Source: Adapted from Somerby Dowst, "Super Sellers Get Green Light to Go Extra Mile," *Purchasing* 82 (August 25, 1983): 45–46.

---

tional account marketing reflects fundamental changes in the business marketing environment.[27] As strategic alliances and partnerships are developed between marketers and customers, a higher-level and closer sales relationship is often desired. When a customer is this important, a major concern is how best to serve that customer. Creating and maintaining a national account with this customer is simply smart marketing. There appear to be three ways in which business marketing firms organize their sales functions to service such accounts. In some cases, especially with smaller marketers, a top executive is assigned to the national account. A high-level executive can provide the attention that the account requires in a high-level manner, and customer requests and concerns can be quickly addressed. In addition, the cost may be relatively low in relation to the value of the customer to the firm. Another approach has been to assign sales specialists to important customer accounts, which may mean that some people in the sales force handle national accounts and others do not. Although this approach may provide the specialized attention required, it may also require additional salespeople, and coordination must be achieved between the two types of salespeople when they both are in the same territory. There may also be resentment among salespeople when national accounts are seen as higher quality than the other customers. Yet another method is to create a separate and distinct sales division to sell to the national accounts. This approach has been used in many large business marketing firms such as IBM's National Accounts Division, XEROX, and AT&T. Indications are that the trend toward national accounts will continue in U.S. business markets. A study of manufacturers conducted by the Manufacturers' Agents National Association found that 89 percent of them had regular national accounts.[28]

As stated earlier, the increase in national accounts is being driven by changes in the business marketing environment. As customers move more into JIT buying practices, reduce their number of suppliers, and enter into strategic alliances and partnerships with their suppliers, all indications are that national account marketing will grow even more in the future.

Increased Specialization of Field Sales Forces   Another trend occurring in many areas of business marketing involves the specialization of sales forces. Traditionally, business sales forces have been specialized by (1) classes of customers, (2) types of products sold, (3) geographic territories, or (4) some combination of these factors.[29] These are still the basic forms; the most widely used method is assigning the salesperson to a territory and holding him or her responsible for selling all product lines to all customers within that territory.

Currently, some interesting variations are taking place. For example, some firms have developed a form of functional or task specialization. A good example is the creative and maintenance sales team. This concept works in the following way. The creative member of the team is responsible for finding new customer accounts, calling on them, and initially selling to them. Once this team member acquires a new customer, he or she looks for more new prospects, and the maintenance member of the team takes over the account. Sometimes companies use inside salespersons to perform the maintenance task. The team members work in tandem, and perhaps no team member can perform both prospecting and maintaining as well as the members are able to do collectively.

Another type of specialization is the resident salesperson. This concept has been used in highly technical markets in which large customers are found and technical assistance and training are extremely important to those customers. In this situation, the salesperson is assigned to a customer firm and works in-house exclusively in an advising/consulting capacity with that customer for a specified period. Once the customer is prepared to operate on its own, the salesperson may be transferred to another such customer and performs the same functions. Exhibit 15.2 provides an example of the use of this type of specialized salesperson in business marketing.

Still another approach to specialization in sales forces in business marketing has been to create separate sales efforts for transaction type customers and for relationship type customers. The logic of this type of specialization is based on the premise that selling is quite different in each case. Thus, a company may well use its regular salespeople to call on transaction type customers but may use resident or national account sales personnel to serve relationship type customers.

A good example of the benefits of specialization may be seen in the case of Cabot Wrought Products of Kokomo, Indiana. This company assigned its thirty-five salespeople according to industries they sold to rather than to specific sales

---

EXHIBIT 15.2   **Use of Resident Salespeople in Business Marketing**

Resident salespeople have been used in military markets since the late 1940s. Known in the military market as "tech reps," these people are sales types who go along with the product to the customer's facility and teach customer personnel how to use it. Placement of tech reps on ships and military installations is fairly common practice.

In marketing to the military, the tech rep program is a standard tutorial system where the manufacturer who produces the product helps train the customer who will use the product. Basically, the tech reps are there to provide training and guidance to the customer. They are assigned to the customer by the manufacturer to help its employees use new products they have not previously experienced. In short, the tech rep's responsibility is one of assisting and advising. To quote a Grumman Aerospace Corporation spokesperson, "The tech reps' mandate wherever they are assigned is to assist, advise, and act as consultants to the customer." For firms marketing into this environment, the resident salesperson or tech rep is a valued part of the marketing effort.

Source: Adapted from Kip Cooper, "Companies Send Along 'Tech Reps' to Teach Military How to Use Products," *San Diego Union,* June 9, 1985, E1.

---

territories. Within a given territory, one salesperson sold to the chemical process industry and another concentrated on the electronics industry. The company believed this type of specialization provided better communications with its diverse customers.[30]

This specialization trend has been caused in part by the increased emphasis on segmentation by business marketing companies. For example, firms who sell to private commercial, institutional, and governmental customers sometimes specialize their salespeople accordingly. For example, in selling the same products or services in the same geographic area, a firm may use one salesperson to call on commercial customers and another salesperson to call on hospitals and school systems. Still another salesperson may handle governmental sales. This form of specialization is expensive, but it may be necessary when purchasing policies, procedures, and buying practices differ so drastically that one salesperson cannot effectively sell to all types. Similarly, when a business marketer sells in international markets, specialization by country or even region of the world has merit because of the widely diverse cultural and national implications.

These trends show that field selling in business marketing is changing and becoming more sophisticated. The salesperson of the 1990s must be a business consultant and an advisor to customers. He or she must be systems-oriented and skilled in the areas of finance, human behavior, and communications to identify customer needs and relay them to management.[31] The stage version of the salesperson, the glib, boisterous glad-hander who rides on a shoestring and a spicy story, is gone. The glad-hander has been replaced by a salesperson who is more of a technician who advises his or her company on new products and counsels customers on how to use them.[32]

Profile of the Business Salesperson

Although there is no such thing as an "average business salesperson," a profile of this person can be developed. This profile may be seen in Table 15.4, which is based on information provided by three of the best-known sources of information on business salespeople.

Some clarification is necessary so that data in the table are not taken out of context. It must be remembered that the figures represent averages and thus wide variances are sometimes possible. For example, while the average number of sales calls required to close a sale is 3.8, Dartnell found that this ranged from a low of 3.0 in machinery sales to a high of 5.3 in instruments.[33] Similarly, while Dartnell found that an average of 17.3 percent of all salespeople turn over annually, this ranged from a low of 11.6 percent in rubber and plastics to a high of 35.9 percent in office equipment.[34] This same variance may be seen in Table 15.5 in viewing how salespeople in different industries spend their time. Thus, the profile is both informative and interesting but it must be used with caution. The averages may not represent the situation for individual business marketers.

TABLE 15.4 **Profile of the Average Business Salesperson**

Average age	36.3 years of age
Gender	Three times more likely to be male than female
Education	Has a college degree or at least some college education
Work week	Works approximately forty-five hours per week
Sales calls per day	Between four and five personal sales calls per day and about eight telephone calls to customers and prospects
Length of sales call	Approximately twenty-five minutes
How often the salesperson sees a buying influence	About 2.8 times per year
Number of accounts called on	179 active accounts and 216 prospective accounts for a total of 395 companies contacted annually
Number of sales calls required to close a sale	Approximately four but may vary significantly from industry to industry
Annual sales	Approximately $2 million in sales volume each year
How time is spent	25% in face-to-face selling; 25% in traveling and waiting; 22% on reports, paperwork, and attending sales meetings; 17% in selling customers and prospects on telephone; 8% on service calls; and 3% on all other activities
Turnover rate	About one in five leave their jobs each year either voluntarily or involuntarily
Manner of compensation	Three major methods are straight salary, salary plus commission, and salary plus individual bonus
Training period	Approximately four months

Source: Compiled from materials from Dartnell Corporation, McGraw-Hill Research Department, and *Sales & Marketing Management* magazine.

TABLE 15.5   Industry Breakdown of How Business Salespersons Spend Their Time

Industry	Average Length of Day	Face-to-Face Selling (%)	Selling Customers and Prospects by Telephone (%)	Traveling and Waiting for Interviews (%)	Paperwork and Meetings (%)	Service Calls (%)	Other (%)
Chemicals and allied products	9 hr 4 min	34%	13%	30%	12%	11%	0%
Rubber and miscellaneous plastics products	9 hr 21 min	23%	10%	40%	18%	8%	1%
Fabricated metal products	8 hr 43 min	26%	14%	24%	25%	7%	4%
Machinery, except electrical	8 hr 53 min	27%	16%	29%	20%	6%	2%
Electrical and electronic equipment	8 hr 36 min	18%	26%	15%	30%	9%	2%
Instruments and related products	8 hr 41 min	16%	27%	19%	23%	11%	4%
Wholesale, trade-durable goods	9 hr 29 min	27%	18%	27%	16%	11%	1%
Total	8 hr 49 min	25%	17%	25%	22%	8%	3%

Source: Reprinted by permission from McGraw-Hill Research Department, *Laboratory of Advertising Performance Report*, No. 7023.3 (New York: McGraw-Hill, 1986).

THE COST OF PERSONAL SELLING

Many references have been made thus far to the high cost of personal selling in business markets. For most business marketing companies, personal selling is an area of prime importance to the marketing manager, and components of its cost should be understood. A sound understanding of personal **selling costs** is also valuable in developing the promotional mix, since there are costs of other mix variables and the manager should integrate all of these in terms of cost and effectiveness. For example, the cost of contacting a new prospect through a personal sales call should be compared with the cost of accomplishing this task through a trade journal advertisement, a direct-mail piece, or a trade show. A look at some of the major components of personal selling costs is in order.

The Cost of a Business Sales Call

One important factor is the cost to a company of a sales call. What does it cost a business marketing firm each time one of its field salespeople makes a call? What is the cost whether a sale is made or not? A number of sources provide sales call costs and their data do not always agree, which complicates the issue.

For over thirty years McGraw-Hill Research Department conducted surveys every two years to measure such costs. Since McGraw-Hill's figures were the best known, previous editions of this text used that organization's data. But after publishing its 1987 survey findings, McGraw-Hill ceased these surveys thus making it necessary to use some other source. Similar studies now are conducted by Cahners Publishing Company and these newer data are used in this text. Figure 15.2 illustrates changes in the cost of an average business sales call between 1980 and 1988.

A sales call is defined as "each time a salesperson makes a face-to-face presentation to one or more buyers or prospects."[35] Cahners defines selling costs as "salaries, benefits, commissions, travel and related expenses, and costs of promotional materials and samples taken on the call."[36] Looking at Figure 15.2, it can be seen that these costs are rising dramatically. Cahners estimates its 1988 figure of $240 represents an increase of 22 percent over its 1984 figure and that costs increased 146 percent between 1978 and 1988. These data indicate that personal selling in business marketing is expensive and getting more so. Thus, a careful assessment of the continued use of company sales personnel in a direct channel of distribution is in order. Again, these rising costs have affected many firms, which have switched to manufacturers' representatives and industrial distributors when feasible. This switch helps account for the growth in distributor sales, such as was illustrated in Chapter 13.

The figure of $240 is again an average and variances exist based on the type of product or service involved, on the industry, and on the region of the country. These differences may be seen in Table 15.6. As the table shows, the cost to a company that markets capital equipment ($272.17) is considerably higher than the cost to a producer of parts and supplies ($222.38). This might be expected

FIGURE 15.2   Average Cost of a Sales Call in Business Marketing

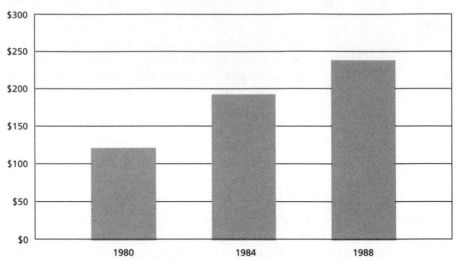

Source: Reprinted by permission from Cahners Publishing Company, *Cahners Advertising Research Report* No. 542.1F (Newton, MA: Cahners Publishing Company, 1989).

because selling capital equipment may be more complex and more demanding than selling supplies, and compensations may reflect this. Similarly, the table shows that costs are not uniform when compared across industries or by region of the country.

In addition, the previously discussed McGraw-Hill Research Department findings found that costs also differ by size of the firm's sales force and channels of distribution.[37] The larger the size of the sales force, the lower the costs. Small companies with fewer than ten salespeople had high costs of personal selling. McGraw-Hill also found that the channel of using only company salespeople was very expensive when compared to companies that sold through both direct channels and channel intermediaries such as distributors or manufacturers' representatives. These variations mean that the $240 figure is not an absolute. Individual marketing managers should compute such costs for their respective companies based on such factors as type of product or service, industry, geographic region, size of the sales force, and channels used.

Another useful way to look at these costs is in terms of the cost to close a sale. The figure of $240 applies whether or not a sale is made. Since only a small minority of sales in business marketing are made with a single sales call, the cost to close a sale is significantly higher. In its research, Cahners found an average of 4.3 calls required to close a sale in business marketing. As Table 15.7 shows, there is variation when classified by industry.

TABLE 15.6   Average Cost of a Business Sales Call Classified by Type of Product or Service Sold, by Selected Industries, and by Region of the Country

Classification	Average Cost of a Business Sales Call
Industry Average	$240.00
By Type of Product/Service Sold:	
Capital equipment	272.17
Durable goods	224.59
Services	251.94
Materials or components	227.98
MRO parts, supplies, or services	222.38
By Industry:	
Electronics and computer manufacturing	255.43
Nonmanufacturing/services	231.37
Foodservice	229.67
Building and construction	242.00
Manufacturing	232.00
By Region of the Country:	
New England	273.75
Mid-Atlantic	257.56
East North Central	236.83
West North Central	250.28
South Atlantic	202.75
East South Central	269.50
West South Central	240.67
Mountain	230.58
Pacific	242.86

Source: Reprinted by permission from Cahners Publishing Company, *Cahners Advertising Research Report,* Nos. 542.2B, 542.21, and 542.9 (Newton, MA: Cahners Publishing Company, 1989).

An example may help clarify the point being made. If the average cost of a business sales call is $240 and it takes 4.3 calls to make a sale, the cost to close that sale is $1,032. This cost may be increased or decreased depending on the individual company's comparable figures. This can be seen by using data in Tables 15.6 and 15.7. For example, the cost to close a sale in the electronics industry would be $1,200.52 ($255.43 × 4.7) and $689.01 in the foodservice industry ($229.67 × 3.0). Judged by any standards, these costs are high, and they are a major problem in business marketing.

The cost to close figures can be used to make another relevant point. If other sales support activities such as telemarketing, inside selling, advertising, catalogs, and trade shows are effective, it may take fewer calls to close a sale, thus decreasing the cost to close a sale. For example, the Trade Show Bureau has

TABLE 15.7	Number of Sales Calls Required to Close a Business Sale in Selected Industries

Industry	Average Number of Calls Required to Close a Sale
Electronics and computer manufacturing	4.7
Nonmanufacturing/services	4.9
Foodservice	3.0
Building and construction	3.2
Manufacturing	4.0
Industry average	4.3

Source: Reprinted by permission from Cahners Publishing Company, *Cahners Advertising Research Report,* No. 542.5A (Newton, MA: Cahners Publishing Company, 1989).

found that it takes about one sales call to close a sale initiated by a trade show contact.[38]

Similarly, using telemarketing or inside sales to qualify leads before they are sent to field sales representatives may also result in reduction of calls needed to close a sale. This topic is addressed in Chapter 16.

In other words, in some industries personal selling costs are reasonable and can be tolerated by the sales manager and the marketing manager. In other industries, however, the cost of personal selling is so high that a company-owned sales force may be an expense that cannot be borne, and other forms of promotion must be studied for possible adoption. It is important to recall that the cost of a personal sales call can differ according to the industry, product or service involved, the channel used, the size of the sales force, and the region of the country.

The Cost of Recruiting and Training a Business Salesperson

Another contributor to the cost of personal selling involves the recruiting and training of sales personnel. Cost estimates vary greatly because of differing practices. For example, some firms only hire experienced salespeople, which means their recruiting and training costs are minimized and immediate sales effectiveness is often achieved. In these instances, higher compensation costs usually are involved. Other firms recruit inexperienced sales trainees and train them by a variety of means. For these firms, recruiting and training costs may be high but initial compensation costs are lower.

Estimates of the total costs of recruiting and training for a business products salesperson range from under $1,000 to over $50,000.[39] The more extensive the training program, the higher is the cost. A survey by *Sales & Marketing Management* found that the average cost of sales training for an industrial products salesperson was $22,500, which included salary, instructional materials, transportation, and living expenses incurred during the training period, instructional staff, outside seminars and courses, and management time spent with a salesperson when it was part of the training budget.[40] This figure is an average, meaning that for some companies, the costs of training are much higher.

A good example exists with pharmaceutical salespeople. A study by McGraw-Hill's Research Department found that the average cost of recruiting, selecting, training, and supervising a pharmaceutical salesperson until productive was $50,200. This figure represents a 23 percent increase from a study conducted two years earlier, which revealed an average cost of $40,823. In those companies surveyed, the costs ranged from a low of under $20,000 to a high of over $100,000, which appears to be fairly typical in business markets.[41]

These figures point toward one thing—it is expensive to search out, select, hire, and train business salespeople. To understand fully the implications of these costs, imagine what it would cost to make a sales force of 50, 100, or 500 salespersons productive in the field. As may be suspected, the costs involved in getting productive salespeople into the field account for much of the shift toward manufacturers' representatives and distributors, where trained salespersons are already available. All indications are that the costs of recruiting and training business salespersons will continue to rise. *Sales & Marketing Management* estimates that these costs will increase an average of 5 percent per year for producers of business goods.[42]

The figures cited here are out-of-pocket costs and do not reflect opportunity losses from salespersons in the field who, although trained, are not yet fully productive and lose sales because of this lack of experience. In some industries, it takes years for a salesperson to make contact with and gain the support of all decision-making buying influences. Until the salesperson is able to do so, his or her company will lose sales. All of these costs place a tremendous burden on the sales manager, and they stress the importance of effective selection of business salespersons.

The Cost of Salesperson Turnover in Business Markets

Adding to the business marketer's problems with the costs involved in recruiting and training salespersons is the turnover of such people once they are trained. **Turnover** refers to those salespeople who either leave of their own accord or are for some reason terminated by their employers. It has been defined as the rate at which salespeople leave the sales force because of separations such as promotions, resignations, retirements, or dismissals.[43] When this happens, there are costs involved that must be considered in the overall cost of personal selling in business marketing. The higher the turnover, the higher the costs involved.

There appear to be four broad categories of turnover: (1) those who leave voluntarily, (2) those who are dismissed from employment, (3) those who are promoted to managerial duties within the company in or out of the sales force, and (4) those who leave for "natural" reasons such as death, illness, disability, or retirement.[44] Much of the research that has been conducted on this subject has been focused on those who leave and those who are dismissed and, for this reason, the term *turnover* does not always refer to all four of the above categories. Exhibit 15.3 illustrates the findings of one study of salesperson turnover in business marketing.

EXHIBIT 15.3   **Salesperson Turnover: Are Those Who Leave Different from Those Who Stay?**

Salesperson turnover continues to intrigue business sales managers. Why do some stay and others leave? Are those who leave different in some manner from those who remain? A study of 201 salespeople from a large American computer manufacturer sheds some interesting light on these questions. In this study, 162 or 80.6 percent remained and thirty-nine or 19.4 percent left to take employment elsewhere. The study looked at each of these groups in terms of three criteria: (1) demographic and individual characteristics, (2) work-related factors, and (3) performance variables.

In terms of demographic characteristics, no significant differences were observed between the two groups. There were no differences in age, marital status, number of dependents, stage in life cycle, or education. In other individual characteristics, no differences were found in experience, average sales, or years in the territory. Differences were found, however, in hours worked per week, feelings toward job security, and rating of the company. Those who stayed worked more hours, felt more job security, and gave the company a higher rating than those who left.

In terms of work-related factors, no differences were found between members of the two groups in terms of role conflict, role ambiguity, or organizational commitment. There also were no differences in terms of satisfaction with customers or coworkers. But there were differences in job satisfaction in terms of satisfaction with management, with compensation, with the work itself, and with promotion opportunities. Those who stayed were much more satisfied with these areas than those who left.

In terms of performance variables, managers were asked to rate members of both groups on such factors as ability to work with others, technical knowledge, sales produced, customer relations, information collected, presentation skills, time management, percent of quota attained, and overall performance. Significant differences were found in all these factors. Those who remained were rated higher by their managers than those who left.

Based on this study, it can be argued that those who leave are different from those who stay. In terms of characteristics expressed by the salespeople themselves, those who leave rate the company lower as a good place to work and think their futures are less secure than those who stay. In addition, they tend to work fewer hours than those who remain. In terms of ratings by their sales managers, those who leave are rated lower than those who stay on all performance measures including sales produced, percent of quota attained, presentation skills, time management, and overall performance. In summary, those who leave appear to be less dedicated to the company, less sure about their future, less satisfied with the job, and lower producers than their counterparts who remain.

Source: Adapted from Edward F. Fern, Ramon A. Avila, and Dhruv Grewal, "Salesforce Turnover: Those Who Left and Those Who Stayed," *Industrial Marketing Management* 18 (1989): 1–9.

When turnover occurs in a sales territory, there are a number of costs involved. These may be summarized as follows: [45]

Separation costs. Separation costs include severance pay and any other separation allowances the departed salesperson may receive.

Recruiting and training costs. These costs have already been discussed. Since the departed salesperson must be replaced, his or her replacement must be recruited and trained.

Territory costs. When one salesperson leaves, his or her level of sales productivity is not instantly matched even when a replacement is made immediately. Thus, there are opportunity losses that may be involved. If a replacement cannot be made immediately, the territory is vacant, which implies even more opportunity losses.

Differential operating costs. When a salesperson is replaced, there may be changes in costs due to compensation differences and/or increased managerial supervision. For example, a sales manager may have to devote much more time to the new salesperson than would have been the case with the departed salesperson.

As can be seen by the above, the costs involved in turnover can be significant. One estimate is that the costs to replace a lost salesperson can range from $25,000 to $75,000 per person.[46] These figures appear to reflect out-of-pocket costs and not opportunity losses so total costs may be even higher.

Equally important is the rate of turnover—the rate at which salespeople leave the salesforce. If costs are high and the turnover rate is also high, the problem is much more serious than if the rate is low. Given the importance of the turnover rate, a discussion is in order. Figures differ appreciably regarding the turnover rate in business sales forces. Table 15.8 illustrates annual turnover rates as found in research by Cahners Publishing Company. As the table shows, there are variances among industries with an overall average of 8.6 percent per year. A similar study conducted by McGraw-Hill Research department found an aver-

TABLE 15.8 **Average Annual Turnover Rates of Business Salespeople in Selected Industries**

Industry	Average Annual Turnover Rate
Electronics and computer manufacturing	9.6%
Nonmanufacturing/services	10.3%
Foodservice	5.8%
Building and construction	10.8%
Manufacturing	6.8%
Industry average	8.6%

Source: Reprinted by permission from Cahners Publishing Company, *Cahners Advertising Research Report,* No. 550.7 (Newton, MA: Cahners Publishing Company, 1989).

age U.S. turnover rate of 9.4 percent.[47] The range in this study varied from a low of 5.0 percent in transportation equipment to a high of 22.6 percent in business services. Other studies show the rate to be much higher. A study of 500 U.S. and Canadian sales managers and salespeople found an average turnover rate of 27 percent.[48] In still another study, Dartnell Corporation determined the overall rate to be 17.3 percent.[49] As can be seen, there is not much agreement on what the actual rate may be. However, all the studies indicate that turnover in sales forces in business marketing is a major problem and a costly one.

In summary, sales force turnover is important and costly in a number of ways. First, recruiting and training costs are never truly recouped when salespeople leave a job position. In the previous case of pharmaceutical salespeople ($50,200 to train), about 12 percent of the salespeople were either terminated or quit. A high turnover rate only compounds recruiting and training costs. In addition, turnover affects sales in the field in that those leaving must be replaced. When this situation occurs, the replacements typically are not immediately effective, which means sales and their accompanying profits may be lost until the new salespeople become productive. Reducing the turnover rate is a managerial responsibility that may place great emphasis on more effective selection of salespeople by sales managers. Despite the enormity of the salesforce turnover problem, relatively little research has attempted to uncover its antecedents and consequents.[50] In addition, despite the high costs few organizations seem to have developed systematic procedures and policies for keeping salesforce turnover under control.[51]

SALES MANAGEMENT IN BUSINESS MARKETING

The use of salespeople in the promotional mix requires the management of those salespeople. In business marketing, this function belongs to **sales management,** which must manage the outside sales force. The executive in charge of this area is the sales manager, who normally answers to the marketing manager. A highly complex area, sales management involves many tasks. For example, the sales manager is usually responsible for developing a sales plan consistent with the overall marketing plan. Within this plan, sales objectives, forecasts, and budgets are determined. The sales manager is also responsible for organizing the sales force, which includes defining territories and establishing quotas for field sales representatives, along with developing necessary sales support systems such as inside sales. In addition, sales management includes writing job descriptions and job analyses for field salespeople as well as recruiting, hiring, training, evaluating, and terminating those same people. Sales managers also are typically involved in developing compensation plans, promoting and reassigning field salespersons, and appointing regional and/or district sales managers if needed.

These tasks indicate that sales management is a rather specific area and is not to be confused with marketing management. The marketing manager is responsible for the company's entire marketing program, whereas the sales manager is responsible for just one part of that program—the personal sales aspects. Viewed in another manner, the sales manager reports to the marketing manager, as do the product managers, advertising managers, marketing research managers, sales promotion managers, and other such functional marketing officers.

As has been stated numerous times throughout this text, personal contact is of great importance in business marketing, which of course implies a great emphasis on personal selling. This emphasis in turn places equally great importance on the sales management function. The preceding section listed some of the sales manager's tasks. In this text, neither time nor space permits an in-depth analysis of each. They are covered in great depth in most sales management texts, and reference can be made to these texts if more information is desired. However, it is worthwhile to discuss the following tasks, which are considered critical to effective sales management in business markets: (1) selection of business salespersons, (2) time management of salespersons, and (3) compensation of salespersons. These are areas in which evidence indicates that business sales managers need to improve.

Selection of Business Salespersons

Finding applicants who will turn out to be successful salespersons is a real problem in business marketing. As has been shown, the selling job calls for professionals who possess technical and sales capabilities in addition to other important personal characteristics. It is difficult to find individuals who have both the technical ability and the desire to sell. Poor selection increases turnover, which in turn increases the cost of personal selling.

When salespersons are hired and either quit or are fired before becoming productive, the cost of selling rises. Better than one-half of business salesperson turnover is accounted for by those who are released because they cannot produce in the market, and another 30 percent are released because they have bad habits or are unreliable, lazy, or insubordinate.[52] To quote Herbert M. Greenberg of Personality Dynamics, "More than one-half of the people now occupying sales positions shouldn't be. They are not suited for careers in sales. One of four people walking out in the streets has a selling aptitude superior to more than 50 percent of the people now selling for a living."[53] Certainly, it can be argued that most of these people never should have been hired, which indicates poor selection by business sales managers. Add to this argument the contention that 75 percent to 80 percent of all sales are accounted for by 20 percent to 25 percent of the salespeople, and the poor selection accusation is reinforced.[54]

A major problem in the selection of business salespeople lies in the development of appropriate criteria. What characteristics make a good business salesperson? Many sales managers apparently do not know. Determining those characteristics necessary for effective selling is difficult, and agreement is rarely found. For example, a study of top-ranking sales executives found that they considered the following characteristics important in a salesperson: (1) enthusiasm, (2) well organized, (3) ambition, (4) highly persuasive, (5) previous sales experience,

(6) high verbal skill, (7) high previous recommendations, (8) willingness to follow instructions, and (9) sociability.[55] Different characteristics emerge when purchasing professionals were asked what qualities they believed made a good salesperson. Table 15.9 shows the results of a survey of professional buyers. These studies both relate to field salespeople and point out the problem: Determining specific characteristics to use in recruiting and selection is a difficult task at best.

Another factor in selection involves inside salespeople. Different characteristics are generally desired in these types than in field salespersons. One source claims the most important assets for an inside salesperson are (1) personality—a good, positive attitude and interpersonal skills, pleasant telephone voice and manner; (2) technical competence—ability to bring relevant expertise to bear on the customer's special problems; (3) customer service orientation—willingness to provide service above and beyond order taking; (4) sales initiative—ability and willingness to sell products, even in the face of customer resistance; and (5) efficiency—good work habits and self-management ability, an organized approach to duties.[56] These results show that selection criteria differ between inside and field salespeople and among types of field salespeople. Characteristics desired in a sales engineer or resident salesperson will probably differ from those desired in a supplies salesperson. Because of this problem, job descriptions are often so loosely written that they are useless in screening applicants.

Many sales managers are uncertain of the path to follow in building their sales forces. Because they cannot find a sufficient number of candidates who possess both technical and selling capabilities, they face a dilemma. Should they hire technically oriented individuals such as engineers and teach them to sell, or should they recruit people who want to sell and teach them the technical aspects of field selling?

There is a lot of controversy among sales managers over which approach is best, and the uncertainty in the minds of many sales managers undoubtedly con-

TABLE 15.9 **Qualities Seen as Most Important in a Sales Representative by Organizational Buyers and Buying Influences**

Quality	Percent Seeing this Quality as Important
Knowledge of his or her product line	92%
Thoroughness and follow-through	83%
Ability to apply products to buyers' needs	62%
Willingness to go to bat for the buyer within the salesperson's firm	58%
Market knowledge	44%
Knowledge of the buyer's business or product line	42%

Source: Reprinted by permission from Cahners Publishing Company, *Cahners Advertising Research Report,* No. 550.8A (Newton, MA: Cahners Publishing Company, 1989).

tributes to salesperson turnover. There appears to be a trend toward recruiting applicants with the desire to sell and then training them technically—the logic being that technical skills can be learned but that selling ability is inborn. Some authorities in this area believe that certain characteristics compose a "sales personality," and selection of salespersons should focus primarily on those characteristics, as they are much less able to be developed on the job.[57] In simple terms, the feeling is that if applicants are hired who want to sell, turnover will be reduced.

Although there is no universal agreement as to what personal selling traits must be, the following are typical of those that comprise the sales personality: (1) energy, (2) aggressiveness, (3) creativity, (4) drive, (5) ability to communicate, (6) sensitivity, (7) tendency to plan, (8) realistic thinking, (9) initiative, and (10) self-discipline.[58] Applicants are then screened by a battery of tests that indicate the presence or absence of the desired characteristics. The more of these traits an individual possesses, the more likely that it is that the person has the disposition to sell and thus is less likely to quit or be fired.

Conversely, such characteristics as the following are considered detrimental to effective field selling and thus are to be avoided if possible: (1) a record of job-hopping, (2) recent business failure, (3) marital difficulties, (4) untidy appearance, (5) emotional instability, (6) excessive indebtedness, (7) too high previous earnings, (8) too low previous earnings, (9) unexplained gaps in employment record, and (10) poor credit rating.[59] Applicants are screened in terms of these factors, and the more of these factors found in an individual, the more prone he or she may be to turnover.

Implied in this belief is that candidates ranking high on the positive factors and low on the negative ones will want to sell and will possess the emotional characteristics necessary to sell effectively. Those applicants with reverse rankings are more likely to find selling unproductive, unfulfilling, discouraging, and generally distasteful. The latter are, of course, the kind who contribute to high turnover—the kind who were never psychologically adjusted to the selling task.

Factors such as these should only be used as guidelines and not as hard-and-fast criteria. Nevertheless, more tests are being used to select salespeople. A typical test costs the manager as little as $80 to $150 and can offer valuable insight into a sales candidate.[60] Such tests have their limitations and must be used with caution. Some of the more common criticisms leveled at these tests are that (1) applicants can rig answers, (2) the tests can show interest in sales but cannot show ability, (3) the tests usually favor group conformity rather than individual creativity, and (4) the tests tend to isolate on individual factors and not the whole person.[61] There is logic in test use, and the increased usage of such tests bears out this point. If a candidate with high positive rankings can be taught such things as product knowledge, shop experience, and how to locate the key buying influences, it seems logical to conclude that he or she could become a productive salesperson and thus reduce costs affiliated with the turnover problem. Certainly, the present business salesperson turnover rate suggests the need for selection criteria such as those just described.

Time Management of Business Salespersons

Another area of business sales management worthy of attention is the time management of business salespersons. As stated earlier, McGraw-Hill Research Department has found that the average business salesperson spends only 25 percent of his or her time actually selling and 25 percent traveling and waiting for interviews. A study by the Sales Executive Club of New York found that only 20 percent of a salesperson's time is spent selling to customers and/or prospects.[62] Another study revealed that 65 percent of all sales calls are made on the wrong people.[63] Data such as these imply that many field salespeople do not manage their time effectively. Often, they do not have the ability to do so, or they lack the interest. It is often argued that such behavior is caused by ineffective sales management, which in turn contributes to the high cost of personal selling. One source states, "Rising costs . . . can be blamed in no small way on the fact that many sales managers manage salesmen almost as if time did not equal money."[64]

In other words, many sales managers are not managing their field salespeople effectively. They are allowing them to spend too much time traveling and waiting and not enough time actually selling. At a time when the cost of a business sales call is rising out of proportion to the cost of living, this allowance amounts to an intolerable situation for many business marketing companies. The point is that the cost of a business sales call may be made acceptable if more sales calls can be achieved in the field. More sales calls can be achieved through salespeople spending more time in selling and less time in other activities, especially traveling and waiting in offices. The key to accomplishing this task is to impress on the salespeople the need for better time management and to have the sales manager show them how such management can be accomplished. These are not simple tasks, because business salespeople, just like most salespeople, are an independent group and not always easy to control.

One approach that has been used with some success is for the sales manager to impress on the salespeople how valuable their time is to themselves. Most business salespeople are not impressed by data such as the McGraw-Hill figures, which relate to the rising costs of a sales call to their companies. They believe that controlling these costs is the sales manager's problem, not theirs, but they are impressed when it comes to the value of their own time. To illustrate, McGraw-Hill Research estimates that the average business salesperson works 240 days per year for a total of 2,117 hours. If only 25 percent of the time is spent in actual selling, this person has only 529 hours per year to actually sell. If the salesperson's desired annual income is $65,000, selling time is worth $122.87 per hour to that salesperson. Waiting in an office for an hour or driving around needlessly for an hour costs that person $122.87 in lost earnings. As shown in Table 15.10, as the desired income goes up, so does the value of the salesperson's time. A salesperson who aspires to earn $75,000 per year can see that his or her time is worth over $140 per hour. This argument has a sobering effect on field salespeople and can contribute to improved time management by field salespeople. To use this technique, an individual sales manager should substitute company figures for the McGraw-Hill figures, but that step is easily accomplished.

TABLE 15.10   Value of an Hour's Time to a Salesperson

Salesperson's Desired Annual Income	Value of 1 Hour of Salesperson's Time
$25,000	$ 47.26
35,000	66.16
45,000	85.07
55,000	103.97
65,000	122.87
75,000	141.78
85,000	160.68
95,000	179.58

Another approach has been for sales managers to instruct field salespersons on ways to manage their time better through sales seminars, training programs, and other similar functions. The following tips were suggested by a Sales Executive Forum conducted by *Industrial Marketing* magazine for helping salespersons use their time in the field more effectively.[65]

1. Prearrange appointments by phone.

2. Once appointments are made, keep them and be punctual.

3. Know the convenient calling hours of all customers and get there during those hours.

4. Make a schedule of calls in advance and plan itineraries to travel systematically and not haphazardly to those calls.

5. Organize travel so that a maximum number of calls can be made with a minimum amount of travel.

6. Know who is going to be seen at each customer plant and have something specific to accomplish on each call—stop the casual visits.

7. Learn to get as much information as possible from receptionists regarding waiting time, interest level, and so on.

8. Eliminate calls on marginal accounts that require inordinate time, travel, and effort.

Yet another approach is to use the computer's capabilities to help the salesperson use field time more effectively. An example is a computer-based system used by Pennwalt Chemical Corporation in Philadelphia. In this system, the salesperson feeds the computer data on each of his or her accounts, such as the number of calls made in the current three-month period, the number of expected calls in the upcoming three-month period, average time per call, expected annual sales, minimum and maximum sales calls that can be made, expected sales for each account, and a sales adjustment factor based on the account's impact on profitability due to purchased products or commissions. With such data, the computer is then programmed to fit sales response curves through expected sales volumes of different call frequencies. It then prints optimum call policies that are designed to maximize sales, profits, or commissions.[66] This approach allows the salesperson to contribute to time management, and it concomitantly relieves the salesperson of the time needed to calculate such data himself or herself.

Evidence suggests that many salespeople do not manage time effectively on their own. For example, a ten-day study of calls by fifty-nine salespeople on a business found that only eight called before 10:00 A.M. and only eleven called between 10:00 A.M. and 11:30 A.M. The bulk called between 12:45 P.M. and 3:00 P.M.; all had to wait to see the buyer, and all had to shorten their sales presentations because others were waiting. These events occurred despite the fact that the company's hours were from 7:30 A.M. to 5:30 P.M.[67] Unless motivated by their sales managers, many business salespeople do not think about time management.

Fuel shortages in the 1970s caused by the energy crunch forced many business sales managers and their marketing managers to look more closely at call frequencies and routing of their field salespeople. Waiting in line for an hour to buy five gallons of gas (the maximum permitted by many service stations) cut deeply into salesperson productivity and shook up many lethargic sales managers. Many managers pressured their salespeople to plan calls more effectively, drive less, and use the phone and public transportation more. This advice may have always made good marketing sense, but it took a crisis to force many sales managers and field salespeople to realize it. On the other hand, once salespeople are inclined to think about the management of their time, they can work toward increasing their efficiency. A good example can be found in the case of a plastics industry salesperson who monitored his own activities and broke them down into "productive and nonproductive selling activities." Through such a job activities analysis, the salesperson found three aspects that provided him with more selling time: (1) secretaries in the sales department could handle his paperwork and other correspondence; (2) he could phone in his orders, customer service requests, and other routine information instead of returning to the office at 4:30 P.M. each day; and (3) he could limit his waiting time to fifteen minutes on calls that could be handled easily on callbacks.[68] These rather minor adjustments allowed this salesperson to spend more time in selling activities and increased sales productivity.

Compensation of Business Salespersons

Another important aspect of business sales management is the **compensation** of salespersons, since the methods of compensation used may serve to motivate or discourage sales effort. In fact, the previously cited study of 500 U.S. and Canadian sales managers and salespeople found inadequate compensation to be one of the major reasons accounting for turnover.[69] Given the turnover problem, the increased costs of recruiting and training, and the rising cost of sales calls, the manager must compensate his or her sales force members so as to bring about a high degree of sales productivity to offset these costs. The marketing manager and the sales manager must develop a compensation program that encourages the type of sales effort consistent with overall marketing strategy and objectives. This undertaking is much more difficult than it appears.

In developing a sound field sales compensation program, a number of factors must be considered. An effective program must compensate the salesperson for all required activities. If salespeople are required to provide feedback or aftersale service calls, a straight commission plan will not compensate them for those activities. Any well-implemented compensation plan should be such that it attracts new sales personnel as well as retains high-producing salespeople. In addition, it should both provide incentives for selling and still motivate the salesperson to serve the customer's interests. For example, straight salary has been used effectively with sales engineers who may perceive commissions as negative rather than positive. In such cases, the straight salary actually provides incentive for both selling and serving customer needs. A good compensation plan should be flexible enough to adapt to changing market conditions and be within the company's ability to pay. Finally, compensation plans should distinguish between high- and low-profit products and markets. A plan that rewards salespeople the same regardless of profit is not well designed.

Table 15.11 illustrates forms of compensation programs found in both the consumer and business markets. A straight salary plan means that the salesperson is paid a fixed salary regardless of the volume of sales made. A draw against commission plan means that the salesperson is paid a commission on sales made but can draw against future commissions to be earned. A salary plus commission plan means that the salesperson is compensated by a combination of salary and commission based on sales. A salary plus individual bonus plan means that the salesperson receives a salary plus an annual or semiannual bonus based on his or her individual sales performance. A salary plus group bonus plan takes place when the bonus is based not on individual performance but rather on the performance of a group in which the salesperson is a member. For example,

TABLE 15.11   **Sales Compensation Plans in Business Markets**

	Percent of Companies Using Each Type of Plan		
Type of Plan	Consumer Products	Business Products	Other Commerce/ Industry
Straight salary	12.4%	14.2%	27.4%
Draw against commission	5.1	6.5	8.4
Salary plus commission	21.2	32.5	25.9
Salary plus individual bonus	46.0	33.4	25.9
Salary plus group bonus	4.4	2.0	1.5
Salary plus commission plus bonus	10.9	11.4	10.9
Total	100.0	100.0	100.0

Source: Sales Personnel Report, 1984/1985, 29th ed.: Executive Compensation Service, a subsidiary of The Wyatt Company, Two Executive Drive, Fort Lee, NJ 07024.

a salesperson working out of a district or regional sales office may receive a bonus at year end based on the performance of his or her district or region. Finally, a salary plus commission plus bonus plan combines these three compensation methods together in some manner. The salesperson receives a salary plus commission on sales plus either a group or individual bonus or both.

Table 15.11 shows that the most widely used plans in business markets are (1) salary plus individual bonus, (2) salary plus commission, and (3) straight salary. With so many types of business salespeople, no single compensation plan has universal application. Currently, the use of straight salary has been decreasing, and the use of salary plus commission plus bonus has been increasing. In addition, there have been movements toward more incentive than salary in the incentive/salary mix of compensation plans.

The business marketing manager and the sales manager must select that plan or combination of plans that best accomplishes desired objectives. Each type has its advantages and disadvantages that must be carefully considered. Each type is also appropriate for different market conditions, which the manager must understand if an optimum compensation plan is to be developed. Table 15.12 illustrates the basic advantages and disadvantages of each type and describes typical situations in which each is appropriate. This analysis provides a

---

TABLE 15.12 **Analysis of Sales Compensation Plans Used in Business Marketing**

Type of Plan	Major Advantages	Major Disadvantages	Situations Where Most Effective
Straight salary	Encourages salesperson to be concerned with more than immediate sale; encourages service, technical assistance, feedback, maintenance selling; high service to sales potential; easy to budget and administer; provides incentive for sales trainees	Provides little incentive for additional sales efforts; salesperson may adjust effort to salary received; salary not tied to sales productivity or profitability; performance difficult to determine	Team-selling situations; where service and technical assistance are required; where feedback by sales personnel is important; where maintenance selling is needed; where sales take a long time to complete; with sales trainees and inside salespeople
Straight commission/ draw against commission	Provides great incentive to sell; high income potential for experienced sales personnel; good motivator for experienced sales personnel; easy to administer; selling costs directly related to commission paid; draw provides some security	No incentive to provide service, technical assistance, or feedback; little financial security for salesperson; commission sometimes seen as penalty and not reward; has limitations with seasonal products	High volume, rapid turnover, quickly sold products where technical assistance, service, or feedback not required; sales force must be experienced

TABLE 15.12   (Continued)

Type of Plan	Major Advantages	Major Disadvantages	Situations Where Most Effective
Salary plus commission	Provides incentive to sell in addition to providing security; regularly paid commissions can be related to specific sales to provide motivation over salary; salary provides bottom for income but leaves top open for salesperson; relatively easy to administer; a combination plan that can be tailored to most business selling situations; more flexible than either straight salary or straight commission	Balance between salary and commission critical; if salary too high, commission incentive drops; if commission side too high, security of salary drops; plan does not provide the security of straight salary or the incentive of straight commission	Where market requires sale, service, feedback, or technical assistance, but potential exists in new customers and incentive needed to motivate salesperson to do both; where neither straight salary nor straight commission is appropriate
Salary plus individual bonus	Encourages attention to service, technical assistance, and feedback, but can motivate salesperson toward performance of other tasks for which bonus will be paid based on individual performance; bonus can be tied to sale of various products to various markets; provides financial security of salary plus incentive to bonus-related tasks	Bonus may be seen as part of salary over time; bonus may be taken for granted as opposed to something that must be earned; long time between sale and bonus payment may make for poor sales motivation	Similar to straight salary situations except that bonus may provide incentives to push certain products to certain markets; useful where much negotiation is needed and sales take long time to materialize
Salary plus group bonus	Similar to salary plus individual bonus but provides incentive for increased group sales performance; good motivator for sales by office, district, region	Similar to salary plus individual bonus, but group bonus may discourage individual performance; high, low, and average salespeople may all receive same group bonus	Similar to salary plus individual bonus but appropriate where incentive needed to push sales by office, district, or region as opposed to individual salesperson
Salary plus commission plus individual or group bonus	Combines the security of salary with the incentive advantages of both commission and bonus; provides incentive for sales, technical assistance, service, or feedback, but also permits stressing of certain tasks such as pushing certain products to certain markets	Often quite complicated; hard to administer and hard for salespeople to understand; balance between salary, commission, and bonus quite delicate, and three elements could be counterproductive if ratio not proper	Similar to salary plus commission situations but where other tasks are also desired and can be accomplished by paying bonus for them

useful framework for determining the type or types of plans to be used. For example, a business cleaning supplies marketer whose market includes all types of manufacturers who continually buy such supplies in volume may find a straight commission or a commission with draw most appropriate. Little service or technical assistance is required, and the salespeople have a steady flow of sales and are assured a good income. Conversely, a manufacturer of sophisticated and expensive equipment that takes months to sell cannot use such a plan. Since presale and postsale service and technical assistance are required and closing a sale can take up to a year, a straight salary or salary plus bonus may be much more effective.

An individual company is not restricted to a single plan. One plan may be used for sales trainees, another used for experienced field salespersons, and still another for inside salespersons. Whatever arrangement is used, the total compensation package must accomplish the desired objectives.

There are few hard-and-fast rules—compensation plans must be tailored to market conditions, company objectives, and salesperson interests. The manager must understand what options are available and when each makes the most sense if a sound program is to be developed.

In summary, direct selling by company sales personnel is an expensive channel of distribution that is becoming more expensive every year. Since it is a necessity for many business marketing managers, the manager must look for ways to lower this cost. Three areas of opportunity for doing so are in the selection of business salespeople, more effective compensation for salespeople, and more effective time management of these salespeople.

CHAPTER SUMMARY

Once target markets have been defined, products and/or services developed to meet needs in those markets, and channels determined and implemented, the marketing manager must address the promotional area of marketing. In business markets, the promotional mix typically involves some combination of personal selling, advertising, sales promotion, and publicity and public relations. The purpose of this mix is to communicate effectively and efficiently with buying influences in the target markets.

This chapter has addressed the first component of the promotional mix—the area of personal selling. In business marketing, personal selling is a very important element. Three aspects of personal selling were addressed. First, the chapter examined types of salespeople found

in business marketing and reviewed situations where each is most appropriate. In addition, areas of personal selling other than field salespeople were analyzed with emphasis on inside salespeople, national account salespeople, and telemarketing. Trends taking place in contemporary selling in business marketing were also examined. A profile of the average business salesperson was developed to provide a better understanding of the characteristics particular to this type of salesperson.

The chapter then focused on the costs involved in personal selling. In particular, an examination was made of the costs involved in making a sales call in business marketing. Reasons why these costs are increasing were given and situations affecting these same costs were also reviewed. Costs of recruiting and training new salespeople were also developed. Finally, costs involved in salesperson turnover were examined for their impact on marketing management in business markets.

The chapter then included a discussion of the area of sales management in business marketing with particular emphasis on selection of salespeople, time management of field sales-people, and development of compensation programs. These three areas of sales management are of particular relevance to business marketing given the costs and turnover problems inherent in business markets. The following chapter builds on this chapter by integrating advertising and sales promotion into the personal selling area of business marketing.

KEY TERMS

business supplies salesperson
compensation
executive salesperson
inside salesperson
missionary salesperson
national account
personal selling

promotional strategy
sales engineer
sales management
sales team
selling costs
telemarketing
turnover

QUESTIONS

1. The high costs of personal selling have forced business sales and marketing managers to seek ways of controlling those costs without impairing sales productivity. Explain how the use of inside salespeople and/or telemarketing could accomplish these ends.

2. Partner relationships between suppliers and customers have become commonplace in business marketing in recent years and have had effects on personal selling. Explain how personal selling differs between customers and prospects in relationship and transaction markets.

3. Because of the high costs associated with company salespeople, many business marketing managers have considered the use of distributors, manufacturers' reps, or both as substitutes for their company salespeople. Explain the pros and cons of such changes.

4. Turnover of salespeople is a major problem in business marketing because of the costs associated and the rate of turnover. What costs are involved and how are they compounded by the turnover rate?

5. Some marketing managers believe that time management is the responsibility of the individual field salesperson and not of the sales manager. What is wrong with this position?

6. Explain why there is a trend toward the use of more national accounts in business marketing. Why is the concept of the national account increasing in use and popularity? And, what are the implications if national accounts are used in channels where industrial distributors or manufacturers' representatives are used?

7. Sales teams are becoming more popular in business marketing for a number of reasons. Explain what is meant by a "sales team" and relate who might be involved in such a team. Why are teams becoming so popular in business marketing?

8. Selection of business salespeople is a major area of responsibility for sales managers in business marketing. Poor selection can result in higher

turnover, lower productivity, and higher costs, yet selection of productive salespeople is an elusive task. Explain why this is true.

9. Selection criteria may differ appreciably depending on the type of salesperson involved. Discuss the criteria you believe would be most important in recruiting the following types of salespeople: (a) sales engineer, (b) inside salesperson, (c) resident salesperson, and (d) national accounts salesperson.

10. Since personal selling is considered but one element in the promotional mix, why should personal selling not be viewed as an entity in and of itself? How do nonpersonal promotional efforts in advertising, sales promotion, and publicity and public relations affect decisions made in the personal selling area?

NOTES

1. *Marketing Definitions: A Glossary of Marketing Terms* (Chicago: American Marketing Association, 1960).
2. Ibid.
3. Ibid.
4. *The Mathematics of Selling* (New York: McGraw-Hill Research Department, 1973), 17.
5. George C. Webster, Speech before the Southwestern Bell Telephone Company, October 12, 1978.
6. Ibid.
7. Interview with Edward Brady, general manager of Ducommun Metals & Supply Company, San Diego, CA, October 10, 1972.
8. "The Pro in Professional Selling," *Industrial Distribution* 74 (February 1984): 43.
9. Robert C. Patchen, "What Drives the Salesman, or . . . the Many Sides of Motivation," *Industrial Distribution* 64 (June 1974): 62.
10. Robert J. Zimmer and Paul S. Hugstad, "A Contingency Approach to Specializing an Industrial Sales Force," *Journal of Personal Selling & Sales Management* 1 (Spring–Summer 1981): 34.
11. See "48 Ways to Use Inside Salespeople," *Agency Sales Magazine* 13 (February 1983): 26–29.
12. *Laboratory of Advertising Performance Report*, No. 8013.9 (New York: McGraw-Hill Research Department, 1988).
13. Kate Bertrand, "Manufacturers 'Rethink' Distribution Channels," *Business Marketing* 72 (February 1987): 42.
14. Roy Voorhees and John Coppett, "Telemarketing in Distribution Channels," *Industrial Marketing Management* 12 (1983): 105.
15. Eddy Christman, "Telemarketing Services Eye Business Market," *Business Marketing* 69 (June 1983): 22.
16. Ibid.
17. "Telemarketing: The Cost Factor," *Sales & Marketing Management* 132 (June 4, 1984): 52–53.
18. Richard L. Bencin, "How to Start a Business-to-Business Telemarketing Program," *Marketing News* 18 (March 16, 1984): 8.
19. Voorhees and Coppett, op. cit., 106.
20. "Industrial Newsletter," *Sales & Marketing Management* 131 (November 14, 1983): 32.
21. Norman Weiner, "Software Unlocks the PC's Power," *Sales & Marketing Management* 132 (March 12, 1984): 55.
22. The editors of *Industrial Distributor News*, "Women in Industrial Sales: Just the Beginning," *Salesman '75* (Philadelphia: Ames Publishing Company, 1969), 18.
23. Douglas L. Fugate, Philip J. Decker, and Joyce J. Brewer, "Women in Professional Selling: A Human Resource Management Perspective," *Journal of Personal Selling & Sales Management* 8 (November 1988): 33.
24. "Trainees Get Pay Jumps," *Industrial Marketing* 67 (February 1982): 43.
25. _____, "Women in Sales: Percentages by Industry," *Sales & Marketing Management* 138 (February 26, 1990): 81.
26. John E. Swan, David R. Rink, G. E. Kiser, and

Warren G. Martin, "Industrial Buyer Image of the Saleswoman," *Journal of Marketing* 48 (Winter 1984): 114.

27. "Marketers Cater to National Accounts," *Business Marketing* 74 (May 1989): 37.

28. "House Accounts Survey: The Good News . . . The Bad News," *Agency Sales Magazine* 19 (November 1989): 35.

29. Zimmer and Hugstad, op. cit., 27.

30. "Up from Low Tech," *Sales & Marketing Management* 132 (February 6, 1984): 24–25.

31. "Getting Your Money's Worth from Your Salesmen," *Industry Week* 123 (February 19, 1979): 104.

32. Philip Mahar, "Sales Call Cost Rises 15% to $205, LAP Says," *Business Marketing* 69 (July 1984): 12.

33. "Sales Call Statistics and Operating Expenses," *Sales & Marketing Management* 138 (February 26, 1990): 79.

34. "Turnover Rates in Selected Industries," *Sales & Marketing Management* 138 (February 26, 1990): 78.

35. "Average Cost of Sales Training Per Salesperson," *Sales & Marketing Management* 132 (February 20, 1984): 72.

36. *Cahners Advertising Research Report* No. 542.1F (Newton, MA: Cahners Publishing Company, 1989).

37. See *Laboratory of Advertising Performance Report,* Nos. 8013.9 and 8052.3 (New York: McGraw-Hill Research Department, 1988, 1986).

38. *Trade Show Bureau Research Report Study Number 18* (New Canaan, CT: Trade Show Bureau, 1983).

39. Patchen, op. cit.

40. "Average Cost of Sales Training Per Salesperson," op. cit., 49.

41. *Laboratory of Advertising Performance Report,* No. 8014.7 (New York: McGraw-Hill Research Department, 1986).

42. "How Selling Costs Will Grow," *Sales & Marketing Management* 123 (December 10, 1979): 41.

43. Douglas J. Dalrymple, *Sales Management: Concepts and Cases,* 2d ed. (New York: John Wiley & Sons, 1985), 57.

44. Rene Y. Darmon, "Identifying Sources of Turnover Costs: A Segmentational Approach," *Journal of Marketing* 54 (April 1990): 47–48.

45. Ibid.

46. Edward F. Fern, Ramon A. Avila, and Dhruv Grewal, "Salesforce Turnover: Those Who Left and Those Who Stayed," *Industrial Marketing Management* 18 (1989): 1.

47. *Laboratory of Advertising Performance Report,* No. 8054.1 (New York: McGraw-Hill Research Department, 1985).

48. Kate Bertrand, "Is Sales Turnover Inevitable?" *Business Marketing* 44 (November 1989): 26.

49. "Turnover Rates in Selected Industries," op. cit.

50. Fern, Avila, and Grewal, op. cit.

51. Darmon, op. cit., 46.

52. Ronald Johnson, "Hiring Techniques for Salesmen," *Industrial Marketing* 50 (October 1965): 70–71.

53. "Professionalizing the Salesman," *Industrial Distribution* 69 (September 1979): 47.

54. William J. Tobin, "How to Find More Time to Sell in 1983," *Agency Sales Magazine* 13 (January 1983): 21.

55. Stan Moss, "What Sales Executives Look for in New Salespeople," *Sales & Marketing Management* 121 (March 1978): 47.

56. "The Pro in Professional Selling," *Industrial Distribution* 74 (February 1984): 53.

57. Jesse E. Nirenberg, "What 10 Qualities Make a Top-Notch Salesman?" *Industrial Marketing* 49 (May 1964): 84.

58. Ibid.

59. Henry Bernstein, "How to Recruit Good Salesmen," *Industrial Marketing* 50 (October 1965): 72.

60. *Laboratory of Advertising Performance Report,* No. 8054.1, op. cit.

61. "Professionalizing the Salesman," op. cit., 48.

62. Tobin, op. cit., 20.

63. Ibid., 21.

64. "Industrial Selling: Now It's $60 a Call," *Sales Management* 110 (January 8, 1974): 4.

65. "Teaching Time Management to Industrial Salesmen," *Industrial Marketing* 50 (April 1965): 131.

66. "Putting More Profit in a Salesman's Time," *Sales Management* 105 (November 10, 1970): 19.

67. See Miriam Blauvelt, "Four-Day Weeks and Five-Hour Days," *Sales & Marketing Management* 132 (February 20, 1984): 18–21.

68. Tobin, op. cit.

69. Bertrand, "Is Sales Turnover Inevitable?" op. cit.

SUGGESTED ADDITIONAL READINGS

Anderson, Erin. *The Salesperson as Outside Agent or Employee: A Transaction Cost Analysis.* Cambridge, MA: Marketing Science Institute, 1984.

Becherer, Richard C., Fred W. Morgan, and Lawrence M. Richard. "The Job Characteristics of Industrial Salespersons: Relationships to Motivation and Satisfaction." *Journal of Marketing* 46 (Fall 1982): 125–132.

Collins, Robert H. "Salesforce Support System: Potential Applications to Increase Productivity." *Journal of the Academy of Marketing Science* 15 (Summer 1987): 49–54.

Coughlan, Anne T., and Subrata K. Sen. *Sales Force Compensation: Insights from Management.* Cambridge, MA: Marketing Science Institute, 1986.

Cron, William J. "Industrial Salesperson Development: A Career Perspective." *Journal of Marketing* 48 (Fall 1984): 41–52.

Darmon, Rene. "Identifying Sources of Turnover Costs: A Segmental Approach." *Journal of Marketing* 54 (April 1990): 45–56.

Fern, Edward F., Ramon A. Avila, and Dhruv Grewal. "Salesforce Turnover: Those Who Left and Those Who Stayed." *Industrial Marketing Management* 18 (1989): 1–9.

Forrester, William R., Jr., and William B. Locander. "Effects of Sales Presentation Topic on Cognitive Responses in Industrial Buying Groups." *Journal of the Academy of Marketing Science* 17 (Fall 1989): 305–313.

Fugate, Douglas L., Philip J. Decker, and Joyce J. Brewer. "Women in Professional Selling: A Human Resource Management Perspective." *Journal of Personal Selling & Sales Management* 8 (November 1988): 33–41.

Futtrell, Charles M., and A. Parasuraman. "The Relationship of Satisfaction and Performance to Salesforce Turnover." *Journal of Marketing* 48 (Fall 1984): 33–40.

Jackson, Donald W., Janet E. Keith, and Richard K. Burdick. "The Relative Importance of Various Promotional Elements in Different Industrial Purchase Situations." *Journal of Advertising* 16 (1987): 25–33.

Johnston, Wesley J. "Industrial Sales Force Selection: Current Knowledge and Needed Research." *Journal of Personal Selling & Sales Management* 1 (Spring 1981): 49–57.

Leigh, Thomas W., and Patrick F. McGraw. "Mapping the Procedural Knowledge of Industrial Sales Personnel: A Script-Theoretic Investigation." *Journal of Marketing* 53 (January 1989): 16–34.

Moncrief, William C., III. "Selling Activity and Sales Position Taxonomies for Industrial Salesforces." *Journal of Marketing Research* 23 (August 1986): 261–270.

———. "Ten Key Activities of Industrial Salespeople." *Industrial Marketing Management* 15 (1986): 309–317.

Moore, James R., Donald W. Eckrich, and Lorry Carlson. "A Hierarchy of Industrial Selling Competencies." *Journal of Marketing Education* (Spring 1986): 79–88.

Parasuraman, A., and Charles M. Futtrell. "Demographics, Job Satisfaction, Propensity to Leave of Industrial Salesmen." *Journal of Business Research* 11 (Summer 1983): 33–48.

Shapiro, Benson P., and Rowland T. Moriarty. *Organizing the National Account Force.* Cambridge, MA: Marketing Science Institute, 1984.

Swan, John E., David R. Rink, G. E. Kiser, and Warren S. Martin. "Industrial Buyer Image of the Saleswoman." *Journal of Marketing* 48 (Winter 1984): 110–116.

16

Promotional Strategy in Business Marketing— Advertising and Sales Promotion

•••

The previous chapter introduced the concept that an effective promotional strategy in business marketing requires the integration of personal selling, advertising, sales promotion, and publicity and public relations. That chapter also emphasized the important role of personal selling in the promotional mixes of business marketing firms. While few would deny that personal selling is often the dominant component in the promotional mix in business marketing, they would also agree that advertising, sales promotion, and publicity and public relations also play important roles. Proper use of these nonpersonal areas of the promotional mix can often increase a salesperson's effectiveness. In business marketing, advertising, sales promotion, and publicity and public relations are typically viewed as support activities for personal selling. This chapter will develop the integration of these areas of promotion with personal selling in order to create an effective and efficient promotional strategy. Advertising, sales promotion, and to a lesser extent publicity and public relations will each be discussed so that their full effects on the overall promotional mix may be better understood.

ADVERTISING IN BUSINESS MARKETING

In a general sense, advertising is advertising whether it is in consumer markets or business markets. It is basically a communication process that, like all communication processes, aims to reach and influence people with its message. The type of influence may be emotional or cognitive. Viewed in this context, the general objective of advertising is to cause a change in a target market—a change in awareness, level of knowledge, attitude, or whatever. This kind of desired change is positive, but advertising is also used to maintain levels of awareness and knowledge. In this sense, advertising's objective is to prevent a negative change.

Successful Advertising and Sales Promotion in Business Marketing

In the mid-1980s, PPG Industries, Inc., of Pittsburgh, Pennsylvania, developed an energy-efficient coated glass for the construction industry. While the product had definite advantages over existing glass products, PPG had difficulties because business customers were not convinced that their customers would use such a product. Thus, PPG developed an advertising campaign to attract both end users and business customers to the use of the new product.

To reach end users, PPG ran advertisements in consumer magazines such as *Reader's Digest* and *Better Homes & Gardens*. These ads described the new product's benefits and encouraged readers to check out the new product at their local distributors. At the same time, PPG provided point-of-purchase (POP) materials to their distributors so that when the end users went to the distributors, they would see the same material and graphics in the POP materials that they had seen in the ads. Thus, the POP materials reinforced the message carried in the advertisements.

At the same time, the company advertised in trade journals to reach manufacturers, builders, and remodelers. The ads mentioned PPG's promotional efforts aimed at end users so these business customers would realize that PPG was also attempting to stimulate business for them. Those ads also encouraged builders and remodelers to contact PPG distributors for additional information. In addition, PPG also used direct mail to contact the manufacturers, builders, and remodelers. Direct mail ads aimed at manufac-

turers promoted product benefits while those directed toward builders and remodelers stressed the value-added aspect of the PPG windows for their customers—the end users. PPG also developed videotapes to promote the product to builders, and the builders then used the same tapes to sell to their customers.

All of this was intended to stimulate derived demand for PPG distributors and business customers such as manufacturers, builders, and remodelers. The purpose of the campaign was to educate end users through print advertising and at the same time develop product awareness among manufacturers, distributors, builders, and remodelers through a combination of trade journal and direct mail advertising. The campaign was so successful in creating awareness and interest that PPG was able to switch its ad focus entirely. The company's current advertising objective is to generate inquiries for its manufacturing customers—it dropped the original trade journal and direct mail ads aimed at these customers. It did, however, continue to advertise to end users in the consumer magazines and to builders and remodelers in trade journals.

PPG's campaign shows how both advertising in various media and sales promotion can be used in conjunction to stimulate both direct demand from manufacturers, distributors, builders, and remodelers and derived demand from end users in the market.

Source: Adapted from "OEM Product: Awareness with a Media Blend," *Business Marketing* 75 (April 1990): 41.

In understanding advertising in business marketing, it is important to recall that business customers and prospects are organizations, as was developed in Chapter 1. This being the case, **advertising** in business markets involves ads developed for and directed toward buyers and buying influences in private commercial, governmental, institutional, and reseller organizations. In most cases, business ads are not directed toward ultimate consumers and, as will be seen, ad media in business markets reflect this. There are situations where business marketers design ads to influence final consumers but these are often designed to stimulate derived demand. In this chapter, the primary focus will be placed on advertising to organizational customers and prospects.

Advertising is characterized by its nonpersonal mass appeal. It is at the opposite end of the communication spectrum from personal selling, which is usually aimed at the individual. As such, these promotional components should not compete but should work in tandem. Collectively, they can provide a more effective promotional mix, which is imperative in business markets. Based on the cost of communicating with a customer or prospect, advertising is much cheaper than personal selling, and as such, it can perform certain tasks much more economically than company salespeople can. On the other hand, as has been shown, business marketing frequently requires personal contact if sales are to be consummated. Organizational buyers and buying influences rarely buy goods and services initially through advertising alone.[1] Thus, advertising can perform some promotion tasks better than the salesperson can, whereas the salesperson can outperform advertising on other tasks. This situation almost naturally leads to a blending of the two components, although some business marketing managers may fail to realize this point. For example, it is still quite common to find sales managers and advertising managers quarreling over budgets, assignments, and status to the detriment of the overall company.

The business sales manager who fails to realize that advertising can make salespeople more effective does the company a great injustice and possible harm, as does the advertising manager who believes advertising is so influential that it can do all things. The marketing manager's job—to blend the two together for optimum productivity out of each—is emphasized in the following quotation:

> A new breed of industrial marketers is winning ball games by using advertising to relieve the salesman of as much of his communication job as it can. . . . The secret of efficient and profitable communication is to use cheap multiple communications to do as much of the job as they can do, and to use expensive individual communication only to the extent you must. The result is lower communication cost per sale or higher sales per dollar of communication costs.[2]

Advertising's Roles in Business Marketing

Business advertising's roles differ from the roles played in the consumer market. Consumer marketing managers are often able to use advertising alone to bring a prospective customer all the way from awareness to the closing of the sale and to keep that customer sold. In most cases, business advertisements cannot do so.

Product complexities and buyer expectations require personal contact, which alters advertising's role in business markets. The following describe some of the major roles advertising plays in business marketing.

To Create a Favorable Climate for Personal Sales   One of the major roles played by advertising in business marketing is to lay a foundation before the salesperson's call. The best way to illustrate this concept is with a picture. The McGraw-Hill "man-in-chair" advertisement shown in Figure 16.1 is considered a business marketing classic. The moral of the advertisement is straightforward and simple: No salesperson should have to take time out of a sales call to answer questions such as the purchasing agent in the advertisement is asking. Advertising should have answered these questions before the salesperson's arrival.

Advertising is most capable of providing general information on the company and its products, and it should be used for such purposes. The role of business advertising has always been primarily supportive, and perhaps it always will be. It provides an entry for the salesperson and reinforces the sales presentation after the fact.[3] In view of the high cost of a business sales call, it does not make good marketing sense to use the highest-cost communication medium to answer questions that can be answered by lower-cost advertising. In addition, the salesperson is often more successful when advertising has created a more favorable selling environment. One study of business salespeople found that 59 percent could recall situations in which their company's advertising contributed valuable sales help in a selling situation.[4]

To Reach Inaccessible Buying Influences   Often, buying influences are inaccessible to company field salespeople. One estimate is that the average business salesperson contacts only three out of every ten buying influences that should be reached.[5] Buying influences may refuse to see salespeople for various reasons, although they may exert considerable influence on products being purchased by their companies from various suppliers. These people, however, may read trade publication journals and general business publications, and thus they may be reached through advertising. Business advertising often fulfills a role of reaching such buying influences.

To Reach Unknown Buying Influences   Sometimes field salespeople do not know all of their buying influences. This case is often true with new salespeople or new customers, but it can even be true with experienced salespeople when customer corporate reorganizations and the like have shuffled buying influences. Because the buying influences often read trade publications, it is possible to communicate with them through advertising. A study conducted by U.S. Steel on one of its customers, the Harnischfeger Corporation of Milwaukee, found that advertising located prospects the salespeople did not know.[6]

To Generate Leads for Salespeople   A major role of advertising in business markets is to generate leads that may be passed on to field salespeople for follow-up. Advertisements placed in trade publications or sent via direct mail

FIGURE 16.1   McGraw-Hill's "Man-in-Chair" Advertisement

Source: Photograph courtesy of McGraw-Hill Research Department.

typically offer opportunities for the viewer to respond in some manner. These responses may be in the form of a request for additional information or asking that a salesperson call. These leads are then sent to the appropriate field salesperson after they are qualified as true leads and not simply casual responses. When the leads are qualified as sound, the salesperson is able to spend time contacting live prospects as opposed to cold calls. A study of 2,500 business-to-business salespeople revealed that more than 85 percent received such leads in one year, and 80 percent claimed their companies had programs to follow up on such inquiries.[7]

To Supplement Field Sales Communication   Chapter 15 noted that the average business salesperson only visits a buying influence about 2.8 times per year. Salespeople typically cannot see their customers and prospects as much as they would like, which creates an opportunity for advertising to provide communication between the sales calls. A McGraw-Hill Research Department study found that 90.3 percent of buying influences surveyed had not been contacted by a company salesperson in the past two months in situations in which the respondents were aware of advertisements by that same company.[8] The survey's findings are representative of what typically occurs in business marketing, and it illustrates the opportunity for the effective use of advertising.

To Inform Channel Intermediaries   Advertising can also be used by business marketers to communicate with present and prospective channel intermediaries such as distributors and manufacturers' representatives. These ads may take the form of introducing new products, convincing the intermediary to carry the marketing firm's product line, and so forth. Such ads may take different forms and use different media depending on whether present or prospective intermediaries are involved. For example, ads may be placed in trade journals to reach prospective intermediaries or they may be sent via direct mail. Figure 16.2 provides an example of such advertising as carried out by PPG Industries, Inc.

To Stimulate Derived Demand   Because of the volatility of derived demand in business marketing, some business marketing managers use advertising to stimulate demand for their customers' products, thus bolstering direct business demand. Examples can be found in beer and soft drink industries, in which glass, steel, and aluminum manufacturers advertise in the consumer market to persuade ultimate consumers to purchase drinks in steel cans rather than aluminum or glass bottles by using such arguments as quick chill properties, weight differences, and recycling possibilities. Boeing has also used television advertising to inform consumers of the merits of air travel, thus stimulating the demand for that mode of travel, which in turn affects the airlines' demands for new aircraft.

To Project a Favorable Corporate Image   Business marketing companies may use advertising to project a favorable image to the public. Generally, the company wishes to communicate its concerns or records of achievement on social and environmental issues. In this way, it can position itself favorably in the minds of consumers, organizational buyers, and other buying influences. This image is important because most companies cannot chance being labeled socially undesirable or uncaring. Buyers and buying influences in business markets do consider the images of competing suppliers when making purchasing decisions, especially when factors such as price, service, technical assistance, and delivery are relatively equal for all suppliers.

Examples of this type of advertising often differ in theme and media selection. Sprayon Products, a division of the Sherwin-Williams Company, markets industrial aerosols and was greatly influenced by the public concern expressed over the effects of aerosols on the ozone layer. In its trade publication ads, Sprayon promoted the idea that its industrial aerosol products were not harmful to the ozone and provided high-performance finishes, lubricants, coatings, and cleaners. Perkin-Elmer developed a television advertising campaign positioning the company as "a company that can help man see into the cosmos and solve critical problems in business and laboratories on earth."[9] Perkin-Elmer is a high-tech company that produces such products as a NASA space telescope, the 32-bit superminicomputer, and an entire line of analytical instruments.

To Provide the Most Economical Promotional Mix   Advertising plays an important role in business marketing because it can reduce promotional costs, often without any detrimental effects. Typically, the proper combination of advertising and personal selling can be more effective than the use of either alone. A classic example may help make the desired point. U.S. Steel was interested in advertising's ability to perform a role in the market as an indirect salesperson. Through arrangements with one of its customers, the Harnischfeger Corporation of Milwaukee, U.S. Steel studied the roles of its salespeople and advertising in marketing to Harnischfeger. U.S. Steel found that its salespeople could not reach all of the appropriate Harnischfeger buying influences, nor could they call often enough. Thus, U.S. Steel concluded that advertising seemed likely to carry the bulk of the contact work. In its 1962 study, which is considered a business marketing classic, U.S. Steel estimated that at least 850 advertising calls were completed stemming from advertising in business publications, for a total cost of $350.00, or about 15.1 cents per call.[10] At that time (1961), McGraw-Hill Research Department's cost of a business sales call was $30.35. In 1969, a follow-up U.S. Steel/Harnischfeger study was conducted, and it found that the cost of a completed advertising call had dropped to 14.2 cents per call, at which time the McGraw-Hill Research Department estimated the cost of a business sales call to be $49.30.[11]

These data may be updated using research conducted by Cahners Publishing Company. In 1988, Cahners estimated the cost of a business sales call to be $240.00. The cost of reaching a prospect with a one-page, four-color, six-time ad in a trade publication was determined to be 26 cents.[12] From these data, it should not be concluded that an advertising call accomplishes the same things as a sales call. Rather, the point is that if advertising can be used effectively in the

FIGURE 16.2   PPG Industries Ad Aimed at Channel Intermediaries

FIGURE 16.2 continued

WHY IT'S TWICE AS SMART FOR YOU TO SELL THE INTELLIGENT WINDOW.

It's a matter of profit. Windows with *Sungate®* coated glass by PPG give your customers the value *they* want. And they give you the selling edge *you* want.

VALUE WITH CURB APPEAL.

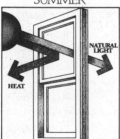

The Intelligent Window can tell the difference between light and heat. Using *Sungate* coated glass, it lets in sunlight. But it keeps inside heat – the heat consumers pay for – from escaping. That means big energy savings. But it's just the beginning.

The Intelligent Window also offers curb appeal. *Sungate* coated glass isn't reflective glass. It admits 90% as much light as an ordinary insulated window. You can't see the difference.

A SELLING EDGE FOR YOU.

The Intelligent Window also offers other valuable selling benefits. With *Sungate* coated glass, your customers' curtains and carpets are less likely to fade. Their houses will be more comfortable, too. *Sungate* coated glass helps eliminate cold downdrafts near windows.

And, there is a whole family of *Sungate* coated glass products to meet specific needs. For example, a bronze style helps

Sunbelt homeowners solve the problem of solar heat gain during air-conditioning months. Yet it still provides insulation values when the weather is cold.

Don't forget: *Sungate* coated glass is made by PPG, a name you know for glass quality and advanced technology.

THE PRODUCT
Sungate coated glass features a low-emissivity, high-transmittance coating. This means that the coating transmits visible light from outdoors, yet it will reflect rather than emit much of the indoor energy. Of the total energy spectrum emitted by the sun, about three percent is ultraviolet, 44 percent is visible and 53 percent is infrared. Carpeting, furniture and draperies absorb solar energy, then re-radiate it as long-wave infrared energy. The coating on *Sungate* keeps the heat inside, by reflecting much of this long-wave infrared energy back into the room, so heat is retained, not lost through the glass.

THE NUMBERS				
	Relative Heat Gain	U-Value	Heat Gain Reduction*	Heat Loss Reduction*
Sungate 100 glass	167	.35	22%	70%
Sungate 100 bronze glass	119	.35	44%	70%

Data for calculating U-value and relative heat gain based on ASHRAE Standards. ASHRAE Handbook 1981 Fundamentals. Sungate construction: 2 lites ⅛″ float glass with ⅜″ air space.
* Compared to ⅛″ clear float glass.

AND THEN IT GIVES YOU MORE.

Promotion. PPG's consumer advertising is telling the *Sungate* coated glass story in major consumer magazines. *Sungate* coated glass is a registered trademark: a mark consumers will recognize, appreciate for the added value it means, and ask for.

The Intelligent Window. It's the window made from *Sungate* coated glass. And it can give you the selling edge you need for better profits. For a comprehensive brochure, plus a list of the sash and door manufacturers who use *Sungate* coated glass, drop us a postcard at the address below. Or ask your sash and door supplier about The Intelligent Window: The one with *Sungate* coated glass from PPG.

Sungate Coated Glass
Builder Marketing B115
PPG Industries, Inc.
One PPG Place
Pittsburgh, PA 15272

Source: Photograph courtesy of PPG Industries, Inc., Glass Group.

awareness and interest stages, the overall cost of promotion can be lowered with no adverse effects. This point applies to more than just advertising per se, and it is addressed again later in the chapter. For example, advertising, trade shows, catalogs, inside sales, and telemarketing can complement each other. As such, they can increase sales effectiveness while reducing overall promotion costs.

This discussion shows that advertising can play a number of roles in the marketing of business goods and services. It should be noted, however, that many of these roles are support roles. Properly used, advertising can greatly increase the effectiveness of personal selling in business markets in many ways. While it may at times be used by some business marketing firms to directly influence sales, this is not usually considered its major role in business marketing.

The Effectiveness of Business Advertising

There is some controversy among business marketers as regards the effectiveness of business advertising. Some business marketing managers believe that business advertising can be very productive and at relatively little cost. Others, however, are just plain skeptical and feel that measuring advertising effectiveness is elusive. But there have been many studies conducted on the effectiveness of the advertising of business goods and services. Arthur D. Little, Inc., discovered over 1,100 separate studies pertaining to the effectiveness of advertising in business markets.[13] Over the years, these studies have provided empirical evidence to support the contention that advertising can be a valuable business marketing tool if used properly. Table 16.1 summarizes the findings of some of the major studies.

MEDIA IN BUSINESS ADVERTISING

Almost all types of advertising media have been used at one time or another by business advertisers, but three types appear to have the widest application: (1) space advertising in specialized business or trade publications, (2) direct mail, and (3) industrial directories. Table 16.2 illustrates media use in business markets based on a study of members of the Business/Professional Advertising Association. The table is read as follows. Of those surveyed, 95 percent use trade journal publications as a business **advertising medium.** Expenditures on this medium account for 31 percent of the total promotional budget (advertising and sales promotion). Of the promotional budget, 55 percent is spent for advertising media, and 40 percent is spent for sales promotion media. Thus, 56.4 percent of all advertising media expenditures are used for trade publications. Use of the other media is computed similarly.

The percentages in the table account for pure advertising expenditures and do not include spending for trade shows, catalogs, dealer and distributor materials, or publicity and public relations. All of these except for publicity and public relations are regarded as sales promotion rather than advertising, and they are covered later in this chapter. Newspapers, radio, and television advertising

TABLE 16.1   Major Studies Conducted on the Effectiveness of Advertising in Business Marketing

Who Conducted the Study	Major Findings
U.S. Steel/Harnischfeger	Business advertising can effectively reach buying influences not normally reached by sales representatives
John Morrill	Business advertising, by supplementing personal sales efforts, reduces the cost per sales call
Modern Medicine magazine	Business advertising improves the reader's familiarity with and perception of the product, and ultimately helps increase sales
Allis Chalmers	Reduced business advertising results in lower levels of name and product awareness in business markets
American Metal Market	Advertising of specific business products or services increases the share of potential buyers who will consider the product or service
Production Magazine	Business advertising can reach buyers and buying influences that sales representatives either cannot find or do not have time to cover
McGraw-Hill Research Department	Frequent advertising in trade publications increases sales and profitability of portable safety products and commercial transportation products
Cahners Publishing Company and the Strategic Planning Institute	Increased advertising and promotion leads to increased brand awareness, higher perceived product quality, increased market share, and increased return on investment
Advertising Research Foundation and the Association of Business Publishers	Markets exposed to greater amounts of trade publication advertising for two business products purchased more of those products than markets receiving less advertising
Association of Business Publishers	Aggressive business advertising increases brand awareness, which leads to increased market share, which in turn leads to increased profits

TABLE 16.2   Advertising Media Use in Business Marketing

Advertising Medium	Percent Using This Medium	Percent of Total Promotional Budget	Percent of Advertising Media Expenditures
Trade journal publications	95%	31%	56.4%
Direct mail	75%	10%	18.2%
Industrial directories	33%	2%	3.6%
General business publications	19%	4%	7.3%
General magazines	8%	1%	1.8%
Newspapers	12%	2%	3.6%
Radio	6%	*	*
Television	6%	1%	1.8%
Outdoor	3%	*	*
Telemarketing	13%	1%	1.8%
All other	21%	3%	5.5%
Total		55%	100.0%

Source: Adapted by permission from *1990 B/PAA Salary/Job/Budget Profile Study* (Edison, NJ: Business/Professional Advertising Association, 1990), 10.

Note: Breakdown excludes expenditures for production and research.

Note: * Denotes less than .5 percent.

forms are not widely used in business markets even though they may be appropriate media for performing a number of advertising's roles in business marketing.

A similar pattern may be seen in the results of a study conducted by *Business Marketing* magazine and the Association of Business Publishers. This study analyzed how much the nation's business marketers spent in a year's time in major media.[14] The results showed that 31.5 percent of all business advertising media budgets was spent on advertising in trade publications, 31.4 percent on direct mail advertising, and 18.3 percent on advertising in various types of directories. Thus, over 80 percent of business advertising media budgets on a national basis was spent in these three media. Eleven percent was spent in various types of consumer publications, 3.5 percent in radio, 3.1 percent in television, and 1.3 percent in outdoor advertising media of different sorts. These two studies are quite consistent and show clearly that the bulk of business advertising is carried by three media. Thus, a brief examination of each is in order.

Trade Publications Advertising

Space advertising loosely defines all advertising placed in (1) general magazines such as *Newsweek, Time,* and *U.S. News & World Report;* (2) general business publications such as *Fortune, Business Week,* and the *Wall Street Journal;* and (3) trade journal publications such as *Purchasing Magazine, Chemical Week, Industrial Distribution,* and the *Journal of the American Oil Chemists Society.* Space advertising can range from broad corporate advertisements in the general magazines read by many businesspeople to specific and highly technical product advertisements in specialized trade journals read only by highly trained and technically competent specialists.

From a business marketing manager's perspective, the value of trade, general business, or general magazine publications depends on the ability of the individual publication to reach desired buying influences. Properly selected, space advertising can accomplish this task with an appropriate message for each. In this area, the manager can call on rating services that provide data on various publications such as circulation and readership broken down by four-digit SIC numbers and by title and function of readers. Probably the best-known rating service is Standard Rate and Data Service's Business Publication Section (BPS), which provides such information on over 4,000 publications. In addition, the individual publications often provide such information in terms of circulation by SIC designation, plant size and location, and percent of subscribers by name and title. Many publications provide on request data that give insight into advertising readership, reader preferences in comparison to those for competing publications, and comparative cost information. Any business marketing manager or advertising manager who is serious about space advertising should obtain such data before placing advertisements in space media.

As both of the previously cited studies show, **trade publications,** also called **trade journals,** constitute the most widely used type of space advertising. Therefore, discussion here will center on the use of trade publications rather than on general magazines.

Types of Trade Publications   There are many trade publications available to the business advertiser. As stated earlier, Standard Rate and Data provides information on over 4,000 separate publications. These trade journals may be classified in the following ways:

1. Some may be considered as *vertical,* which means that they are designed to be read by people within a specific industry. Some examples are *Steel, Iron Age,* and *Chemical Week.*

2. Some are considered to be *horizontal,* meaning that they are more job- or occupation-related and may be read by readers in a wide variety of industries. A good example is *Purchasing Magazine,* which is read by purchasing professionals in many industries.

3. Some trade publications are *national* in scope while others are *regional* in their coverage.

4. Some are circulated *free* to their readers while others are paid for by the readers. In the case of the free journals, the cost to produce and distribute them is borne by advertisers.

As can be seen, the business advertiser has options in trade journal use. He or she may select a regional vertical publication or a national vertical publication depending upon the market to be reached. Figure 16.3 provides some examples of trade journals used in business marketing.

Selecting Trade Publications   In selecting particular trade publications in which to advertise, the marketing manager and the advertising manager should be guided by three general factors: (1) reaching as many people as possible in those organizations in the defined target markets, (2) reaching as many buying influences as possible within those same organizations, and (3) accomplishing both of these at the most reasonable cost. More specifically, the manager will use such criteria as the match of the trade publication to buying influences in the target markets, circulation, frequency of publication, editorial climate, and cost per thousand (CPM). Table 16.3 shows the responses of a large sample of trade publications advertisers when asked what criteria were most important to them in selecting specific trade journals. As can be seen, match with target market buying influences and circulation were major considerations.

A study conducted by Cahners Publishing Company across seven different markets provides information on the determination of the number of publications to employ. Using the top trade publication in the field, 83 percent of target market customers were reached. Using the top two publications, reach increased to 88 percent. When the top three were used, reach increased to 91 percent. It increased to 93 percent with the top four publications, and remained the same (93 percent) when the top five publications were used. These figures are averages taken from the seven markets. Actual reach figures for the markets ranged from 71 percent to 92 percent, and reach for the combination of five publications ranged from 84 percent to 99 percent.[15] Assuming similar media costs for each publication, the advertiser would find that advertising in the five publications

FIGURE 16.3 Examples of Trade Journals in Business Markets

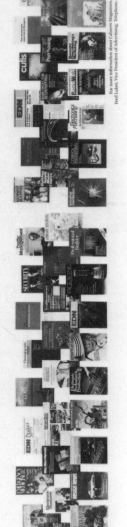

Cahners Means Business in Business Magazines

There are over 50 Cahners magazines and no two of them are alike. Each one is carefully designed to serve the needs of readers and advertisers in one well-defined market or industry. But all Cahners magazines share these important characteristics and qualities: A commitment to editorial integrity and excellence; circulation standards that assure you of reaching the most important buyers and specifiers in your market; and a record of service and performance that has made Cahners the adver-

tising leader in the field of specialized business magazines. It all begins with the 2,000 Cahners magazine division employees. They are highly trained specialists in business journalism, the graphic arts, and in marketing, and they share the Cahners company-wide commitment to publish the best magazines in their field — most informative, most readable, most useful. *Cahners Means Business.* That's why we're the first choice of American Business in Specialized Business Magazines.

Cahners Publishing Company
A Division of Reed Publishing USA

275 Washington Street · Newton, MA 02150-1630 · 617/964-3030

For more information about Cahners Magazines, contact: Fred Lubet, Vice President of Advertising, Telephone: 312/635-8800

Source: Photograph courtesy of Cahners Publishing Company.

TABLE 16.3   Criteria Seen as Most Important by Business Advertisers When Selecting Trade Journal Publications in Which to Advertise

Criterion	Percentage of Industrial Advertisers Citing This Criterion as Important
Quality of circulation	71%
Coverage of buyers/specifiers	69
Editorial quality	63
Inquiry production	42
Readership documentation	34
Advertising agency recommendation	32
Marketing support	26
Reputation	21
Previous experience	19
Advertising leadership	10

Source: Reprinted by permission from Cahners Publishing Company, *Cahners Advertising Research Report*, No. 501.1 (Newton, MA: Cahners Publishing Company, 1984).

would increase reach by 10 percent but at five times the cost. This figure implies that advertising in all trade journals appropriate for specific buying influences may not be cost effective. The manager must trade off increases in reach or market penetration against cost in arriving at the optimum number of trade journals for each type of buying influence.

The process of selecting trade publications for advertising may be seen in Figure 16.4. This process attempts to match a specific trade publication to the buying influence to be reached, and as can be seen, the process addresses that match. A couple of points might be addressed here. First, step 5 involves determining which publications best match target market buying influences. Here, the manager must first determine the type of publication he or she wishes to use. Should it be horizontal or vertical? National or regional? After that determination has been made, the specific media vehicle or trade publication should be chosen. Which specific publication or publications will be used? This is covered in steps 6 and 7. As the figure shows, this decision is based on such factors as cost, circulation, percent of market coverage, editorial content, and article value. Cost often implies the use of the CPM (cost per thousand) criterion. This can be illustrated with the use of an example. Assume that the manager is considering two trade publications—A and B. A full-page ad in publication A costs $6,150 and circulation is determined to be 2,000 target market buying influences. The same ad in publication B costs $4,450 and its circulation is 1,000 buying influences. Publication A's CPM is $3.08 while that for publication B is $4.45. Use of this criterion permits the manager to evaluate the two publications in terms of a common denominator, the cost of reaching 1,000 prospects or customers.

Another useful tool that may be used in the selection process is what is

FIGURE 16.4   **Process for Selecting Trade Publications in Business Marketing**

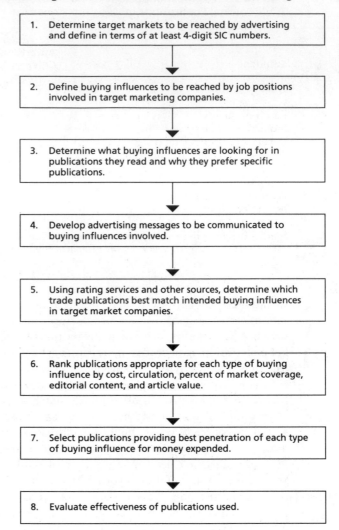

1. Determine target markets to be reached by advertising and define in terms of at least 4-digit SIC numbers.

2. Define buying influences to be reached by job positions involved in target marketing companies.

3. Determine what buying influences are looking for in publications they read and why they prefer specific publications.

4. Develop advertising messages to be communicated to buying influences involved.

5. Using rating services and other sources, determine which trade publications best match intended buying influences in target market companies.

6. Rank publications appropriate for each type of buying influence by cost, circulation, percent of market coverage, editorial content, and article value.

7. Select publications providing best penetration of each type of buying influence for money expended.

8. Evaluate effectiveness of publications used.

called the weighted number of exposures. This is computed in the following manner: [16]

$$WE = R + F + I$$

where

WE = weighted number of exposures
R = number of different people exposed at least once in the time period

F = number of times the person is exposed—frequency of ad runs
I = impact or qualitative value of the exposure in the medium

Again using trade publications A and B, the use of this tool may be illustrated. Publication A reaches 2,000 buying influences. If twelve ads are run in a year and the manager subjectively gives publication A a value of 1 for impact, its weighted exposure figure is 2,400. Publication B reaches 1,000 buying influences. If the same twelve ads are used but the manager rates the impact here at 1.5, its weighted exposure figure is 3,000. This tool is very subjective as can be seen by the impact ratings. The manager may believe that publication B is perceived as a higher quality journal by recipients, has better editorial content or better articles, and thus publication B is rated higher than publication A. Space does not permit an exhaustive discussion of all the methods that might be used to select among specific trade journals but these two examples illustrate the point being made.

Cost of Trade Publications Advertising Trade journal advertising is a relatively low-cost form of advertising compared with other forms. In addition, its cost is considerably lower than costs associated with both personal selling and sales promotion. Earlier in this chapter, it was pointed out that Cahners Publishing Company found the cost of a one-page, four-color, six-time ad in a trade publication to be 26 cents in terms of reaching a prospect. This can be compared with Cahners' estimate of $240.00 for the cost of a personal sales call.[17]

Another way of looking at the cost of trade publication advertising is to compare it with advertising in general business publications. Table 16.4 illustrates cost comparisons between general business publications and trade publications. Note that it costs almost ten times as much to run the same advertisement in a general business publication as it does to run it in a typical trade

---

TABLE 16.4 **Pertinent Data on Business Trade Journal Advertisements Classified by Advertisement Size**

Ad Size	Average Cost of an Ad in a Trade Journal	Average Number of Inquiries Generated	Average Cost Per Inquiry	Average Cost to Reach a Recipient	Average Cost of an Ad in a General Business Publication
1 Page	$5,147	76	$67.73	$.064	$48,232
⅔ Page	3,970	68	58.38	.049	35,823
½ Page	3,047	56	54.41	.038	28,950
⅓ Page	2,131	47	45.34	.027	18,949
¼ Page	1,693	52	32.56	.021	N/A

Source: Reprinted by permission from Cahners Publishing Company, *Cahners Advertising Research Report*, Nos. 250.1A, 250.2A, 541.1A (Newton, MA: Cahners Publishing Company, 1988, 1989).

Note: N/A = not available.

journal. The table also shows that the average cost of an inquiry through trade journals is quite low compared with alternatives such as a personal sales call.

Other Characteristics of Trade Publication Advertising   There are other characteristics of trade publication advertising that contribute to its wide use as a business advertising medium. Trade journal advertisements have credibility with organizational buyers and buying influences. Purchasing agents, plant engineers, production supervisors, department heads, and others look to trade publications for information and assistance. One study found that trade journal ads represented the single source used most often by buying influences to find information about new products and suppliers.[18] Therefore, trade journal advertising can often reach buying influences inaccessible to or unknown by field sales personnel.

Cahners Publishing Company has undertaken considerable research into the characteristics of readers of business trade publications. Table 16.5 lists

---

TABLE 16.5   **Characteristics of Readers of Business Trade Publications**

What is the demographic profile of the average reader of business trade publications?	The average reader is 43.5 years of age; 65% have a college degree or better; may be male or female; experienced with over 11 years with present company and 14 years of industry experience; and earns an average of $47,000 annually.
Do readers truly "read" trade publications?	92% read them occasionally (about 1 out of every 4 issues), but 80% read them regularly (about 3 out of every 4 issues). Each issue is read through or looked at more than twice by a reader.
Are readers of trade publications buying influences?	Approximately 9 of 10 are actively involved in purchases for their company; and 9 of 10 purchasing influences read business trade publications.
How much time do readers spend in reading trade publications?	Average readership for business trade publications is 2 hours and 22 minutes per week; almost 65% read such publications at least 1 hour per week.
Do readers have supervisory responsibilities?	80% are in professional or managerial positions and have responsibility for supervising staff; 25% supervise 25 or more employees; 41% supervise between 1 and 10 employees; and 21% have no responsibility for supervising staff.
Do readers attend professional meetings and seminars?	87% attend seminars or industry shows.
Do readers influence company purchases?	90% of buying influences read specialized business trade publications serving their industries.
Do readers read the ads to the same degree they read feature editorials?	2 out of 3 readers read the ads as much as they read editorial content; only 10% do not read the ads on any regular basis.

Source: Reprinted by permission from various *Cahners Advertising Research Reports* (Newton, MA: Cahners Publishing Company, 1983–1990).

some of these characteristics. Analysis of this table reveals that readers of trade journal publications are important people in the business marketplace—they have considerable job experience, have supervisory responsibilities, are well educated, and are well paid. The table also shows that these people read trade journals regularly, and they read them in depth. All of this information also helps to explain why trade journals are a prime medium in business advertising.

Another factor that influences the effectiveness of advertising in trade publications is that the journals are typically passed on by the initial recipient to others within his or her organization. Figure 16.5 shows what happens to trade journals after they are read by the initial receiver. As can be seen, only 15 percent discard them after reading. Twenty-three percent pass them on directly to someone else, while another 32 percent either save them or put them in the firm library so others may also use them. This study suggests that trade publications have lasting value and readership is not restricted to the initial recipient.

All this discussion helps to explain the popularity of trade journal advertising in business marketing. In summary, trade publication advertising is relatively cheap, highly focused in many instances, well read, credible, and lasting. Compared to other forms of advertising, these are highly desirable characteristics and help explain the wide use of this medium.

The manager also must realize that trade publication advertising has definite disadvantages. One big disadvantage is that advertisements compete in the same issue with competitors' advertisements. The reader's attention is divided among

FIGURE 16.5   **What Happens to Trade Journals After They Are Read?**

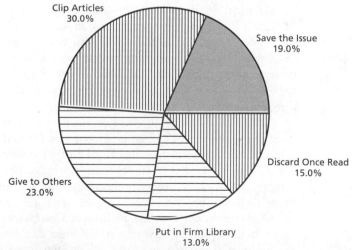

Source: Reprinted by permission from Cahners Publishing Company, *Cahners Advertising Research Report,* No. 412.2A (Newton, MA: Cahners Publishing Company, 1990).

competitive advertisements. Quantity and quality of circulation are often troublesome. Some journals have large circulations but are distributed free, which may mean that they are not well read by all subscribers. In addition, different publications, even in the same general area, are perceived differently in the marketplace. What appear to be basically similar trade journals often are seen as being quite different by buying influences in prospective customer companies. Therefore, advertisements placed in one journal may have a different market impact than those placed in another. Most of the disadvantages of trade publication advertising, however, are involved with choosing among alternative journals rather than with deciding whether or not to use this particular medium.

However, most business marketing and advertising managers appear to believe that the medium's positive attributes overshadow its negative ones. This is apparent when viewing the statistics on its use in business markets. To quote a communications director at Eaton Corporation's Truck Components Division, "Trade magazines are probably the most cost-effective way to reach customers—provided they are well targeted."[19] This quotation summarizes the feelings about this medium by many business marketers.

Direct Mail Advertising

As Table 16.2 illustrates, **direct mail** is the second most used business advertising medium. *Direct mail* is defined as any printed or processed form directed to selected individuals by controlled distribution. There are three basic types of direct mail: (1) direct mail advertising, which is basically the same as other advertising except that it uses the direct mail medium—the advertising copy may be identical to that used in space advertising; (2) direct mail sales promotion, which tries to get the respondent to react in some manner, such as to obtain leads for salespeople, open the door for salespeople, or get the respondent to identify himself or herself by offering further information; and (3) direct mail selling, in which the sender actually tries to sell by mail with no personal selling involved. This third type is not as common in business markets as the first two types, but it can be used effectively with established customers who know and trust the advertiser. In this discussion, no differences between the three types are emphasized; they are all treated as direct mail advertising.

Direct mail can be an effective business advertising medium when prospective buying influences can be identified and located by name. It is an extremely selective and flexible medium. Unlike other media, almost any format or approach can be used with direct mail. Business marketing companies have used direct mail to send brochures, catalog sheets, letters, bulletins, folders, sales manuals, price lists, and even samples (see Figure 16.6).

A survey by the Cahners Publishing Company provides insight into the way direct mail is used to advertise to business customers and prospects. Based on the findings of this survey, Cahners estimates that 90 percent of all direct mail programs in business marketing are designed to stimulate action in some man-

FIGURE 16.6   Types of Direct Mail Used in Business Marketing

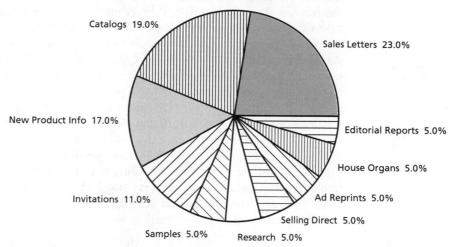

Catalogs 19.0%

Sales Letters 23.0%

New Product Info 17.0%

Editorial Reports 5.0%

House Organs 5.0%

Ad Reprints 5.0%

Invitations 11.0%

Selling Direct 5.0%

Samples 5.0%   Research 5.0%

Source: Reprinted by permission from Cahners Publishing Company, *Cahners Advertising Research Report*, No. 560.1 (Newton, MA: Cahners Publishing Company, 1984).

ner. Sales letters, catalogs, and new product mailings composed 59 percent of all such programs. In addition, the study shows how flexible this medium is—direct mail may be used for many different communication purposes and in many different ways.

Direct mail can also be the most personal of all media. It can be sent to the prospect by name and company position, and confidential information can be communicated. Direct mail also can be timed more precisely than other media, as it is not restricted to publication dates of journals, and the delivery date can be timed to mail deliveries. In a sense, there is less competition with direct mail—there are no competitive advertisements or any journal articles or editorials to distract the reader.

There are, however, definite disadvantages to using direct mail. If prospects cannot be pinpointed, direct mail can be wasteful and expensive. "Nothing wastes money and time faster than an untargeted direct-mail marketing campaign."[20] Direct mail is also more expensive than is commonly realized. More than postage is involved, and costs can vary considerably depending on the content of the direct mail piece. For example, if the direct mail program involves dictated personal letters, the cost of a direct mail call is close to the cost of a business letter. The Dartnell Institute of Financial Research estimated this cost to be $7.60 in 1984, compared with $5.59 in 1979.[21] Assuming such a campaign is directed toward 5,000 prospects, the cost approximates $28,000, which is expensive for a one-time endeavor. It is even more expensive if many of the 5,000 are not true prospects. Actual costs can be higher or lower. For example, direct mailing a computerized letter costs less, whereas direct mailing a catalog costs much more. As a general rule, a direct mail call costs much less than a personal sales call but more than a trade publication advertising call.

Costs may vary appreciably from company to company but direct mail advertising is generally more expensive than trade publication advertising. Eaton Corporation's Truck Components Division estimated that it cost about 15 cents to reach a prospect in a trade journal and about $1.00 to reach the same prospect via direct mail.[22] As postage rates continue to rise, so will the cost of using this medium in business advertising. One point needs to be made here. Given that direct mail's CPM is higher than trade publication advertising's CPM, that difference can be offset if the quality of the direct mail recipient is higher. In other words, if everyone on the mailing list for a direct mail ad campaign is a known buying influence (which may not be true for everyone on the journal's circulation list), then the higher cost may well be justified. This brings about a need to discuss the subject of mailing lists.

The Mailing List Whether or not direct mail can be used effectively in business markets depends a great deal on the adequacy of the business marketing manager's **mailing list.** A mailing list is simply a list of prospects to whom the advertisements are directed. In business marketing, the prospects should be the buying influences in organizations that use or can use the company's products or services. If the advertisements can be mailed directly to the appropriate buying influences by name and position, direct mail can be an effective medium in terms of reaching the defined market.

Three factors are required to compile an effective business marketing mailing list: (1) prospect firms must be identified by SIC number and be specifically located, (2) buying influences must be identified for the marketing manager's products or services involved, and (3) buying influences should be identified by name and position. Most business marketing managers who use the direct mail medium are able to meet these requirements—over time, they have compiled customer and prospect mailing lists of key buying influences in organizations in their target markets.

There are two ways to compile a mailing list. The first way, although not necessarily the best, is to build a list from within the company. After target markets are defined and buying influences determined by position, the marketing manager makes a concentrated effort to find the names of the individuals filling those positions in each customer firm. This task can be accomplished through salespeople in the field, distributors, representatives, personal contacts, and other such sources. Names can be obtained from trade show leads and requests for additional information from space media advertisements. Names can also be found through the use of state industrial directories and other private sources, such as the directories detailed in Chapter 8. The approach here is to build a mailing list without going outside the company to purchase it. This approach takes time, effort, and constant attention to upgrade it, but it is often used effectively. This method usually is not the quickest way to build a mailing list, and it is normally considered inappropriate if the marketing manager wants such a list in a hurry.

The second method, which again is not necessarily the best, is to purchase the mailing list from outside the company. Mailing lists can be purchased from companies specializing in lists, such as R. L. Polk & Company, National Business Lists, Hitchcock Business Lists, Burnett, Thomas Publishing Company's List Services, and the Marketing Services Division of Dun & Bradstreet. Polk's prospect list contains about 117,000 executives in the country's top 22,000 companies, with an average of five officers in each company. The files of National Business Lists contain more than 4 million businesses, institutions, and professional firms, all classified by four-digit SIC numbers. Thomas Publishing Company's "Industrial Buying Influence" list contains about 295,000 key decision makers by name and title.

Using such outside sources to build a mailing list can be quick and relatively inexpensive if markets are previously defined in specific terms. Such lists, however, may not be precise enough for some managers in terms of required customer types or buying influences. The purchased mailing lists may not contain the names of the required buying influences. For the marketing manager requiring such a list in a hurry, purchasing a list from an outside source is probably the best course of action, provided the required buying influences are included. To purchase a list without such information, no matter how low the price, makes little marketing sense. Naturally, both methods of compiling a list can be used in conjunction to build a single mailing list.

Direct mail advertising is not a substitute for trade publication advertising, nor should the use of one preclude the use of the other. When properly used, direct mail and trade publication advertising can complement one another. An example took place with a California company that advertised in twenty business publications and accompanied its advertisements with reader action cards. The advertisements were general in that they related to the nature of the product rather than to its application to specific industries. The action cards produced 12,000 inquiries, which were then followed up with a direct mail campaign providing more specific industry data. The end result was that company sales doubled.[23]

Like trade publication advertising, direct mail can help reduce overall promotional costs and should be viewed from this perspective. A survey by the National Sales Executive Club showed that when direct mail preceded the salesperson's call, thirty-eight orders were averaged per 100 sales calls. This figure can be compared with eight orders per 100 calls when no promotion preceded the salesperson's arrival. In addition, the survey disclosed that sales calls combined with subsequent mailouts cost 25 percent less than calls made without such help.[24]

Despite all the advantages of direct mail, it is questionable whether business marketing and advertising managers use direct mail to full advantage. A study by *Industrial Marketing* magazine reported that less than one-half of business marketers using direct mail set any goals or objectives for their campaigns.[25]

Industrial Directory Advertising

As Table 16.2 illustrates, the third medium of consequence in business advertising is **industrial directories,** which are also called buyer's guides. Advertising in directories accounts for about 4 percent of business advertising budgets. In a sense, this figure is misleading, because some marketing managers and their advertising managers use them extensively and swear by their effectiveness, implying that although their overall usage may be relatively low, they account for a big part of the advertising budgets of some companies.

The idea of advertising in industrial directories seems inconsistent to many marketing managers and advertising managers. Basically, an industrial directory lists supply sources for various products and is intended for use as a buying guide in industry. If a purchasing agent or plant engineer wishes to purchase a certain product, he or she may refer to a directory to find out who can supply such a product. Thus, all appropriate suppliers generally are listed whether or not they advertise in the directory. Many advertisers believe that this type of advertising implies duplication, if they advertise in the same directory in which they are listed. This conclusion may not be valid, however, because the buyer using the directory may be looking for information that is not in the listing. If the needed information is in the advertisement, it can well influence the decision to pick a source of supply.

Research has shown that directories are used by buyers and buying influences. Two classic studies on the use of directories were conducted in 1949 and 1969. In both studies, industry plant and engineering people were asked the question "How did you first learn of the company whose product you sought?" In both studies, the most frequently mentioned source was industrial directories, which was cited by 23 percent of the respondents.[26] More recently, a study of purchasing agents in Fortune 500 companies found 98 percent claim to prefer a well-known directory, the *Thomas Register,* as their primary source of locating suppliers. In Fortune 1000 companies, 80 percent of engineers prefer the *Thomas Register* as their primary source.[27] Studies such as these indicate that directories are a good medium for creating awareness and stimulating interest.

Table 16.6 illustrates some characteristics of industrial directory advertising as revealed by research conducted by Cahners Publishing Company. These data show clearly that directories are used by buyers and buying influences in business markets and that they are kept for reference purposes. Other studies have found that 97 percent of all organizational purchases are initiated by the buyer, not by the seller, and 90 percent of all buyers require printed information before they buy or specify to buy.[28] Adding all these findings together, it can easily be seen that directory advertising could produce results for the business marketer.

Probably the best-known and most comprehensive of all directories is the

TABLE 16.6   Data Relating to the Use of Industrial Directories in Business Markets

How often are directories consulted by buyers or buying influences?	Average is 2.7 times per month; 80.3% refer to a directory 1–3 times per month; 14.5% refer 4–6 times; and 5.2% refer over 6 times per month
How long are directories saved?	9 out of 10 are kept a year or longer; 43% keep them for a year; and 48% keep them longer
How many people in an organization use the directories?	4 people, other than the primary recipient, refer to directories
Are advertisements in directories read by buyers and buying influences?	72% refer to the advertisements in the directories
What actions are taken after referring to a directory?	58% phone or write the manufacturer when they find something of interest in the directory; 50% send in the reader service cards in the directory

Source: Reprinted by permission from Cahners Publishing Company, *Cahners Advertising Research Report,* Nos. 450.1A, 450.2, 450.3, 450.4 (Newton, MA: Cahners Publishing Company, 1980–1985).

Thomas Register, an eleven-volume directory that is published annually. The research department of the Thomas Publishing Company estimates that over 165,000 sets of its *Thomas Register* are in use in the United States, and over 30,000 are in key buying locations overseas. An average of twelve or more people use each set in the United States, and about nine people use each overseas edition.[29] In addition, there is also a *Thomas Register Catalog File,* called *Thomcat,* which accompanies the register. *Thomcat* is a three-volume set consisting of manufacturers' catalogs bound together in alphabetical order and cross-referenced within the product volumes of the register itself. Other well-known directories include the *Conover-Mast Purchasing Directory,* the *Standard and Poor's Register,* the *Million Dollar Directory,* the *Middle Market Directory,* *MacRae's Blue Book,* and the *U.S. Industrial Directory.* Because these directories all contain advertising space, they are an appropriate business advertising medium.

There are advantages and disadvantages to advertising in industrial directories. Directories are good in that they are used as reference materials by buyers and buying influences. Thus, although a direct mail piece or a specific issue of a trade publication may be thrown out, industrial directories are kept for reference even after new issues are published. It is commonplace for previous editions to be passed on to others. Advertisements in directories are more permanent. Moreover, as the previously quoted Conover-Mast study showed, buyers do refer to directories when making decisions. Directories are a highly credible medium—to many in business markets, the directory is the basic buying tool. In addition, advertisements in directories are often good complements for company catalogs, as is shown later in this chapter.

On the other hand, to advertise in directories is expensive and can mean duplication, since the company is listed anyway. Because directories also include competitors, advertising readership is often fractionalized, which can be a disadvantage. In addition, directories are expensive, and many organizations do not purchase them for this reason. Finally, directory advertising may be more of a shotgun approach than is advertising by direct mail or in trade journals. It may not be able to match the advertising message with the defined buying influence as can direct mail and trade journal advertising.

Other Business Advertising Media

As has been developed, the bulk of business advertising is carried by trade publication, direct mail, and directory media. Other media are used, however, as Table 16.2 illustrates, but they are not used to any great extent by most business marketing companies. It may be worthwhile, however, to briefly discuss the use of some of these other media.

Before discussing these other media, it should be recalled that business advertising is directed toward buyers and buying influences in organizational markets. Thus, the use of major consumer advertising media, such as television and radio, is seen by many business marketers as inefficient.[30] In many instances, these media are just too costly and too broadly focused to be of much value in reaching segmented business markets. Where these media are used, the purpose is often to stimulate derived demand in customers' markets or to create and maintain an image. As Table 16.2 shows, there is still limited use of television so that medium is used by some business marketers. An interesting example of the use of television can be seen in the case of Intel Corporation. This company sponsored an eleven-part series on the public broadcasting service (PBS) called "Struggle for Democracy."[31] In this instance, research showed that 28 percent of PBS viewers purchase microcomputers for their companies and thus the television medium matched well with its company markets. For most business advertisers, television has two major drawbacks—expense and wasted viewership.[32] The same arguments appear to apply to radio, newspapers, consumer magazines, outdoor, and in many cases, general business publications. The latter may often be appropriate when buying influences are at the high corporate level but it may also be quite inappropriate when they are better reached with trade publications. In summary, business advertising must be designed to reach particular types of people in their organizations and this is best accomplished through the use of trade publications, direct mail, and directories.

BUSINESS ADVERTISING MESSAGES

In addition to selecting media, the business advertiser must decide on the **advertising message** or messages to be used in company advertisements. The basis for the message or theme should be the buying influence that the advertisement is supposed to reach. As has been discussed, buying influences are interested in different things—their problems differ, and so do their responsibilities. Thus, they look for different things in their advertisements, even though they are all being exposed to the same product or service.

To illustrate, assume that a user customer is considering the purchase of forging machines for use in its production process. The key buying influences are found to be the purchasing agent, the comptroller, the vice president of production, and the production supervisor. Although each is considering the purchase of the same product (the forging machines), each is looking for something different. The purchasing agent may be concerned with price, ability of the supplier to deliver on time, freight rates, FOB points, the supplier's reputation, other companies the supplier now sells these products to, and so on. The comptroller may be interested in price, financing arrangements available, the payback period of the investment, the return on investment from the machines, and the like. The vice president of production may be looking for information on technical assistance offered, service requirements, ability of the supplier to deliver on time, ability of the new machines to be integrated into the present production process, employee training or retraining required, and so forth. The production supervisor may well be interested in such factors as ease of operation of the machines, number of persons required to operate them, training or retraining required, and so on.

The point is clear: Although they are looking at the same product, all four buying influences have different wants, needs, expectations, and desires. If the advertisements used by the marketing manager or advertising manager do not relate to the interests of the particular buying influence, there is no real communication, and therefore, no real advertising. In this example, an advertisement aimed at the purchasing agent stressing training or retraining requirements may have little meaning if he or she is seeking other information to make their decisions.

The example reinforces the point made repeatedly throughout this text: Buying influences must be identified for effective business marketing to occur. Advertising effectively in business markets requires media that reach the specified buying influences and advertisements placed in those media that communicate information relevant to the interests of those buying influences.

Corporate Versus Product Advertising

An age-old controversy in business marketing regards advertising themes or messages. The controversy centers around whether advertisements should stress the company or its products or services. Proponents of **corporate advertising** claim that to sell business products or services, it is first necessary to create a favorable corporate image. Their reasoning is that organizational buyers and buying influences are persuaded in their purchasing by corporate image and reputation. Advertisements following this approach stress such aspects as company awareness, company reputation, educating or informing about subjects important to the company's future, and stating a company's position or record on important social or environmental issues. Proponents of **product advertising** argue that such advertising leads to product or service adoption and use, which in time achieves the desired company image. Advertisements following this approach may stress product specifications, quality and uniformity, durability, ease of installation, cost of installation, and economy in operation. Given the right buying influences and proper advertisement execution, both approaches appear to work, which is the basis of the controversy. There is, of course, nothing to imply that advertising copy must be exclusively corporate or product in its thrust, as both may be involved at the same time.

This area has been researched extensively. Studies indicate that business advertisers use more product-oriented than corporate-oriented advertisements. A study conducted by *Industrial Marketing* magazine found that although 50 percent of business advertisers surveyed ran corporate advertising programs, these accounted for only 37 percent of advertising budgets.[33] These findings are consistent with those of previous surveys. The implication is that most business marketing managers prefer to stress product attributes in their advertisements as opposed to company image. To quote one authority: "Readers of business publications seek information that will help them do their jobs and are not interested in ads that consist mostly of expressions of the advertiser's self-esteem."[34]

Both corporate and product advertising can make contributions to an effective ad campaign when properly used. Product advertising helps buyers and prospects to evaluate products by informing, persuading, and reminding them about a product or service, with the intent of ultimately making a sale.[35] But, corporate advertising can also help a business marketing company achieve desired objectives. Corporate advertising is useful for informing the public of company goals, policies, and standards, and it can also be used to build a favorable image for the company. In addition, corporate ads can help build a positive feeling for the company in the minds of employees and investors.[36]

Whether the advertising message is corporate or product oriented and comparative is interesting, but it may be immaterial to the practicing marketing manager. If buyers and buying influences are seeking product knowledge, then product-oriented advertisements should be used. If the buying influences are impressed by the corporate images of suppliers, then corporate advertising themes should be employed. Advertising is a form of communication, and as such, it must relate to the interests of those being reached.

Are Business Advertising Messages Effective?

The effectiveness of themes or messages used in business advertising has been the subject of considerable criticism. Critics claim that business advertising messages lack appeal in terms of what buying influences are seeking and that they focus more on what creators of the ads think is important. When this situation occurs, of course, the communicability of the advertisements may be questioned.

There is evidence that the critics are often correct. Table 16.7 illustrates the results of a study in which groups involved in the advertising process were requested to rank the importance of twenty-four different ad themes. It is worth-

TABLE 16.7 Ranking of Business Advertising Themes by Various Groups Involved in the Advertising Process

Advertising Theme	Advertising Agencies	Engineers	Purchasing Agents	Advertising Managers	Top Management	Sales Representatives	Industrial Distributors
Product advantages	1	5	8	1	1	1	1
Product specifications	9	1	5	3	4	2	6
Savings in time/money	2	13	7	4	3	6	3
Availability/delivery	7	7	1	7	6	8	4
Product photos	5	6	14	2	5	3	5
Reliability/quality	3	11	3	10	5	9	8
Performance data	8	3	11	8	7	4	10
Price	18	2	2	9	12	10	13
Application engineering services	11	10	9	5	9	13	17
Application notes	12	12	16	6	8	7	11
Ease of installation/operation	4	18	18	12	10	11	7
List of reps/distributors	17	14	4	18	24	5	2
Mil specs	13	16	13	17	19	12	9
Product limitations	24	4	6	14	11	23	15
Custom product availability	15	15	12	11	18	14	18
Environmental characteristics	21	8	17	13	13	19	12
Repair/service warranties	16	17	10	15	20	22	24
Case histories	10	21	22	16	15	16	19
Testimonials	6	24	24	19	15	15	21
Product safety	14	19	15	20	23	18	16
Product schematics	22	9	19	21	22	20	22
Defects in competitive products	23	20	23	24	14	24	24
Listing of other products	20	22	21	23	17	21	20
R & D capabilities	19	23	20	22	21	17	23

Source: Reprinted with permission from *Mainly Marketing*, January 1984. Copyright © 1983 by Schoonmaker Associates, P.O. Drawer M, Coram, NY 11727.

while to compare the rankings of advertising agencies, which create the ad messages, and the rankings of engineers and purchasing agents, who are the intended audience for the ads. If advertising themes are ranked similarly by creators and viewers, then it can be argued that the messages are meaningful and relevant to customers. In this case, however, the rank correlation coefficient between agencies and engineers is .13. Similarly, between agencies and purchasing agents, the coefficient is .26. These figures indicate a lack of significant statistical correlation between creators and their intended audience. This fact can be seen by looking at the ranks in the table. The ad agencies believed a copy theme extolling product advantages to be the most important, but this aspect was ranked fifth by the engineers and eighth by the purchasing agents.

Another study surveyed 400 consulting engineers, architects, electrical contractors, and nonresidential building contractors and forty-eight advertisers to those markets. The survey measured both groups' assessments of the importance of fourteen advertising messages. The study revealed that there were statistically significant differences between the two groups on nine of the factors. For example, all buyer groups rated testimonials from buyers and specifiers as negatively influential, and yet the advertisers considered this type of appeal a strong one.[37] Both of these studies indicate that business advertisers may not always be using ad themes or messages that are important to their customers.

There are reasons to explain these situations. In many business marketing companies, advertisers are not completely brought into the marketing process but rather are expected to develop ads after everything else has been decided. In addition, there often may be a lack of communication between advertising and other marketing areas of responsibility. Ads may be developed without major input from the market, and agencies may be relied on as the experts in the writing of ad copy. When these situations occur, ad messages often fail to communicate with the intended buying influences. This case does not have to be true. Exhibit 16.1 provides a good example of a business marketing company developing ads based on customer research. By using marketing research, Loctite Corporation was able to create ad copy based on the behavior of their primary buying influences.

SALES PROMOTION IN BUSINESS MARKETING

In many business marketing firms, little difference is made between advertising and sales promotion. Often, the two areas are handled as one—there is a single budget out of which allocations to both areas are made, and one manager is responsible for both areas. In other companies, advertising and sales promotion are separate departments; each has its own department head who reports directly to the marketing manager. In this section, **sales promotion** includes the nonpersonal areas of promotion other than advertising.

Table 16.8 illustrates sales promotion media use in business markets based on the previously discussed study conducted by the Business/Professional Ad-

EXHIBIT 16.1   Matching Business Advertising Themes with the Needs of Buying Influences

Loctite Corporation is a manufacturer of industrial sealants and adhesives. In the company's target markets, key buying influences are seen as mechanical engineers. The company found that these engineers often are not comfortable with the idea of using adhesives in lieu of fasteners in their design, production, and maintenance work. Using an outside research agency to conduct in-depth interviews with a sample of design, maintenance, and production engineers, Loctite discovered some contrasting views.

Design engineers were risk avoiders even though they considered themselves innovators, futuristic types, and problem solvers. Despite such views of themselves, they felt pressured to be right and were fearful of wrong decisions. They did not respond to advertising appeals to be innovative, and they did not like being told they had a problem. They saw a risk of failure in being innovative and believed a problem implied they had made a mistake. They liked to see charts, diagrams, and graphs used in advertisements. In its advertising themes to these design engineers, Loctite used tables, pictures, and cutaway diagrams to explain specifically how a particular product worked.

Maintenance engineers, on the other hand, considered themselves unsung company heroes. They perceived themselves as the fixers who kept things running with creative, expedient solutions to maintenance, repair, and overhaul problems. They were uncomfortable with sophisticated Madison Avenue advertising styles and preferred photos to diagrams or graphs explaining performance abstractions. In advertising to maintenance engineers, Loctite used photos extolling the merits of pipe sealants used to lock threaded pipes together compared with the more common use of tape. Advertisements tried to overcome fears that the sealant would permanently lock the pieces together and to show that the sealant would not leak, as would tape.

Production engineers were found to feel the pressures for performance, to be "today-oriented," and concerned about making mistakes that would have large financial repercussions for the company or their jobs. Advertising copy to these buying influences stressed the avoidance of risk in the use of sealants and adhesives.

Loctite attempted to use psychographic research on its key buying influences to understand them better and to permit advertising copy to match their needs.

Source: Adapted from Bob Donath, "What Loctite Learned with Psychological Insights," *Business Marketing* 69 (July 1984): 100–134.

vertising Association. Since most business marketing firms use catalogs, trade shows, dealer and distributor materials, and specialty advertising, a discussion of each may be useful. Because slides, movies, and videotapes are basically sales support tools, there is no need to examine them in detail. House organs also are excepted, since they are not often considered to be marketing tools.

Catalogs

As Table 16.8 shows, business marketing firms spend more on **catalogs** (about 40 percent of sales promotional budgets) than on any other single sales promotional medium. It has been estimated that U.S. business marketing firms spend

TABLE 16.8   Sales Promotion Media Use in Business Marketing

Medium	Percent Using This Medium	Percent of Total Promotional Budget	Percent of Sales Promotion Media Expenditures
Trade shows/exhibits	84%	14%	35.0%
Catalogs	65%	16%	40.0%
Slides and movies	34%	2%	5.0%
Specialty advertising	30%	1%	2.5%
Dealer/distributor aids	28%	2%	5.0%
Internal house organs	23%	2%	5.0%
External house organs	21%	1%	2.5%
Videotapes	34%	2%	5.0%
Total		40%	100.0%

Source: Adapted by permission from *1990 B/PAA Salary/Job/Budget Profile Study* (Edison, NJ: Business/Professional Advertising Association, 1990), 10.

Note: Breakdown excludes expenditures for production and research.

in excess of $25 million annually on catalogs. Catalogs are a vitally important communications vehicle for the business marketer. Without a catalog, customers may not be able to find the company's products. With a poorly prepared catalog, customers may select products from a competitor.[38] For business marketing managers, the question is neither the appropriateness nor the place of the catalog in the selling process; the major question concerns its makeup and effectiveness on sales.[39]

Broadly defined, a catalog is "complete or comprehensive printed information about a product, designed for demonstration and/or reference work."[40] The catalog is unique in that it is a reference form of promotion. Buyers and buying influences in industry keep catalogs in their organizations, and when purchasing opportunities arise, they refer to their catalogs for comparisons of specifications, prices, terms, and so on to screen potential suppliers in this manner. The manufacturer of business products or services whose catalog is not available to the purchaser may not even be considered. Sometimes referred to as the "silent salesperson," the catalog is a natural complement to the personal sales call—it is there for reference before the salesperson arrives, and it can be referred to after the sales call is completed.

Effective use of the catalog depends on how well it is prepared, how well it is distributed, and the use the sales force makes of it. A poorly prepared or incomplete catalog soon loses credibility regardless of how well it is distributed to those who would use it. Table 16.9 illustrates some tips for developing more effective copy in catalogs. On the other hand, even a perfectly organized catalog is of little practical value if it never reaches those buying influences who make the decision. Moreover, if the salespeople are not properly trained to use the catalog in the field, effective integration of personal selling and sales promotion

TABLE 16.9   Catalog Promotional Message Varies with the Type of Product Being Marketed

Type of Product	Role of the Catalog	Promotional Message
High-priced, infrequently purchased products	Catalog is the first step to a sale	Concentrate on technical details; show how product works with pictures and diagrams; facts should be supported with tabular or graphic material where possible
Components, replacement equipment, supplies	Catalog helps close the sale and make ordering easy	Provide specific details on what is available; provide completed data on sizes, differences between models, and special features; illustrations are important
Products for in-plant and/or OEM applications	Catalog must provide performance and application data to create interest in knowing more	Provide info on physical and chemical properties, specifications, and performance properties; provide information on supplier's quality control, capacity, and reliability
Custom fabrication and special services	Catalog must inform prospect of services and facilities available	Provide information about size, track record, and previous clients if possible; assure prospect that quality, performance, and dependability are appropriate; show examples of work and photographs of facilities and personnel

Source: Adapted from *How to Prepare and Distribute Your Catalog* (New York: Thomas Register of American Manufacturers, 1990), 5–6.

in the overall promotional mix cannot occur. In regard to preparing the catalog, the Thomas Publishing Company of New York, publisher of the previously discussed *Thomas Register* and *Thomcat,* has a suggested format for organizing the catalog that is reproduced in Exhibit 16.2. Adherence to such a format can aid greatly in effectively using the catalog as a promotional tool.

Distributing the catalog is a problem for the business marketing manager. Catalogs are a relatively high-priced promotional medium, and their cost appreciates rapidly when ineffectively distributed. Overdistribution increases out-of-pocket costs of production and distribution, whereas underdistribution brings about opportunity losses because the catalogs do not reach the key buying influences, who then specify competitive products. A business marketing manager who is contemplating the use of catalogs in the promotional mix should specifically delineate customer firms by SIC and precisely define key buying influences. As has been the theme throughout this text, these factors should be known prior to producing the catalog. If the required distribution is too broad and too expensive, another medium should be considered.

Four general methods of distribution may be used collectively or individually according to overall marketing and promotional objectives: (1) catalogs can be mailed to the buying influences; (2) space ads and direct mail can be used to get prospects to request catalogs—this method often turns up unknown buying influences and can easily be used in conjunction with mail distribution;

(3) salespeople can distribute catalogs to the buying influences; and (4) catalogs can be distributed in a prefiled catalog, which is a bound volume of many manufacturers' catalogs (for example, *Thomcat*). Generally, combinations of these four methods provide the most effective distribution.

EXHIBIT 16.2   **Organization of the Catalog**

Here are ten steps to a well-organized catalog:

1. Decide which products will be included and which will not. Discovering too late that a product must be added or deleted can wreck an otherwise well-planned catalog.

2. If possible, group products into "families." This can make it far easier for the buyer to use your catalog and may stimulate the sale of accessories or other related products.

3. Make a folder for each product or group of products. Put all relevant material inside it: previous catalogs, technical bulletins, engineering reports, sales literature, photos, illustrations, testimonials, competitive literature, etc.

4. Review the folders for completeness. You'll immediately spot gaps: missing data, needed photos, etc.

5. Take steps to obtain what's missing. Determine what and who is slowing down the process. Apply firm management pressure to correct the situation.

6. Make a rough outline of contents. This is the skeletal framework of the finished job and will help you in budgeting, scheduling, and layout. Here are the key elements involved:
   a. The cover
   b. The index (table of contents)
   c. General company background—history, policies, etc. (if needed)
   d. Product pages
   e. Service pages (including locations, how to get more information, etc.)
   The form a catalog takes depends on the product or service being offered.

7. Determine exact format: color, size, binding, etc. At this point you can get preliminary printing bids to help finalize budgets.

8. Make an organized layout. A layout is a graphic representation of your catalog's contents. Yours will, of course, be very rough. But you'll find it essential in determining number of pages, places for pictures, etc. This will then be turned over to a professional layout artist.

9. Plan and write the copy. Or, if someone is doing it for you, make sure the writer understands the objectives of the catalog as well as you do.

10. Set up a timetable for completion. Make sure you know exactly when each step must be completed: writing, photography, retouching, finished art, binding, delivery of envelopes, distribution.

Source: Reprinted by permission from *How to Make Your Catalog Work Harder* (New York: Thomas Publishing Company, 1987), 12.

The major points to remember with catalog promotion is that it is constantly in-house with the customer and that buying influences use catalogs as references much as they use industrial directories. A study conducted by the Thomas Publishing Company found that 51 percent of organizational buyers surveyed used buying guides and catalogs as their principal source of new suppliers, and 75 percent of engineers used buying guides and catalogs for specifying and buying information.[41] If these buying influences do not have the manufacturer's catalog, sales can be lost without the marketing manager even realizing it.

There are problems with catalog promotion that should be discussed. While there seems to be little doubt that catalogs are seen as useful by organizational buyers and buying influences, studies have shown that their use is not always efficient on the part of either the customer or the supplier. For example, one study found that just eight weeks after a typical catalog is received, there is only a 20 percent likelihood that the recipient can find it.[42] Another survey disclosed that while 98 percent of 1,500 product specifiers believed catalogs to be important in their work, only 27 percent could quickly find a catalog if they needed it.[43] These data indicate that customers are sometimes not very well organized in their storage and use of catalogs. In addition, it has been estimated that over 40 percent of all catalogs sent out by suppliers arrive too late to be considered in the purchase decision.[44] As with all other types of promotion in business marketing, catalogs are not perfect and the marketing manager must take steps to ensure against loss, late deliveries, etc.

Changes are occurring in the catalog's role in business promotion. Because of the high cost of personal selling, some companies have used their catalogs to replace their sales representatives. This trend has been mainly with low dollar volume, relatively simple, off-the-shelf type products. For example, a number of traditional industrial distributors now sell 100 percent through catalogs. Where they once used field salespeople to call on customers, they now use their catalogs and telemarketing personnel to accomplish the same thing. Their approach is to stress quality, reliability, and speed through catalog promotion and back it up with efficient handling of orders by their telemarketing personnel.[45] Another interesting change involves computerized catalogs. The marketer's catalog can be displayed by phone hookup on the customer's cathode ray tube (CRT) screen, and the computer can even place orders by phone.[46] This approach permits instant updating of information, prices, and delivery information, and eases ordering, which is advantageous to buyer and seller. Catalog promotion is also becoming increasingly more popular in global marketing. Firms such as Unisys Corporation, Hewlett–Packard, and Olivetti have found catalogs to have wide application in reaching global markets. The Unisys approach is to develop a core range of equipment that it then supplements with specific products developed for each market. To quote a Unisys spokesperson, "A catalog is like a shop window enabling us to target a range of products at specific markets within Europe."[47]

In summary, the catalog is a very useful sales promotional medium. With exceptions, its real value appears to be as a sales aid for field salespeople, and it should be viewed in this manner. The business marketing manager should bear in mind that the basic purpose of a catalog is to make products easy to locate by customers and prospects.[48]

Trade Shows

As Table 16.8 illustrates, **trade shows** are a common form of business sales promotion. Trade shows are about the oldest form of promotion, and their origin can be traced to medieval times, when artisans exhibited their wares at fairs. In a general sense, today's trade show is still a business fair, complete in many instances with all the characteristics of any fair. Trade shows have a basic characteristic different from all other forms of business promotion—they bring the customer to the company rather than vice versa, which results in a concentration of customers that may not be achieved in any other manner. Often, an industry's trade shows assemble the bulk of buyers and buying influences under one roof for the express purpose of shopping. Trade show promotion has concentrated power unequaled by other forms of promotion used in business marketing.

Trade shows are big business in both the domestic and international scenes. It is estimated that U.S. businesses alone invest in excess of $9 billion annually in this medium.[49] Most industries hold trade shows annually, inviting companies in that industry to open a booth and display products and services to interested industry members.[50] Often, trade associations in those industries organize and manage these shows. *Successful Meetings* magazine surveyed 11,748 American trade associations and found 95.2 percent conducted annual conventions.[51] Such trade shows can be national or regional in scope, but they all basically perform the same marketing functions.

Probably more than 11,000 business trade shows of one type or another take place in the United States in a given year. These events may range in size from ten exhibit booths to hundreds of displays covering 100,000 square feet.[52] Trade shows are big business, and they are growing. To quote the Trade Show Bureau's managing director, "Trade shows are growing in size and attendance because they offer the most cost-effective way of reaching potential customers."[53]

Despite the impressive size and growth of this medium, trade show promotion is not universally accepted by business marketing managers. Some place great emphasis on trade show promotion, and others place little and sometimes no emphasis on them. Some business marketers are skeptical about the use of trade show promotion. One stated, "Trade shows are terribly expensive and of limited value for the business you do versus the dollars spent."[54] Another stated, "Everything nowadays is done for the show management, not the exhibitors. The only other ones to get anything out of trade shows are the hotels and the prostitutes."[55] On the other hand, trade show promotion has its strong advocates among marketing managers. To quote a Burroughs Corporation spokesman, "It's a service we must provide our current customers. If we're not in a show, they notice more than if we are. They'll want to know why. And in our absence, they'll be exposed to competitors."[56] Such diverse opinions about the same promotional medium appear to stem from the approach taken by individual managers. Skeptics fear the unknown effectiveness and relative high cost of trade shows. In addition, they often do not have an organized approach to measure trade show effectiveness. Advocates appear to be more organized. Velsicol Chemicals, for example, traced sales ninety days following a show and found the increase in new sales paid for the trade show expense.[57] Given the level of misunderstanding that exists, we will discuss the value of trade show promotion.

The Value of Trade Show Promotion   Perhaps the best way to understand the role the trade show plays in business promotion is to look at some examples of how it is used. Honeywell used trade shows with the following objectives in mind: (1) meeting potential customers, (2) accumulating a mailing list, (3) introducing new products, (4) discovering new applications for existing products, (5) demonstrating nonportable equipment, (6) hiring new personnel, and (7) establishing new representatives and dealers.[58] Philip S. Hunt Chemical's trade show objectives are (1) to teach salespeople special trade show techniques, (2) to increase trade show selling skills, (3) to teach salespeople to target specific markets at shows, (4) to teach salespeople follow-up techniques, (5) to increase morale and motivation, and (6) to coordinate all activities before, during, and after the show.[59] Table 16.10 provides a summary of why business marketing firms exhibit at trade shows based on data collected by the Trade Show Bureau. These examples show the flexibility of this medium. It is highly unlikely that any other single form of promotion can be used to accomplish such objectives effectively

TABLE 16.10   Reasons Why Business Marketing Firms Exhibit at Trade Shows

Reason	Percentage of Exhibiting Firms Citing This Reason
To generate leads/inquiries	87%
To introduce a new product or service	61
Because competitors are exhibiting	28
To recruit dealers or distributors	20
To support a sponsoring association	12
To write orders on the exhibit floor	11
To maintain seniority in selecting space at a trade show	9
To maintain company image/exposure	7
To recruit sales personnel and representatives	6
All other reasons	2

Source: Reprinted by permission from *Trade Show Bureau Research Report,* Study No. 19 (New Canaan, CT: Trade Show Bureau, June 1983).

and economically. Exhibit 16.3 shows how Apple Computer used trade show promotion.

Another way to look at the value of trade show promotion is to compare trade show leads with leads obtained from other forms of promotion. Westinghouse found that some 7,000 sales leads were uncovered annually. Of the 7,000, 50 percent (3,500) came from publicity, 35 percent (2,450) came from advertising, and 15 percent (1,050) came from trade shows. Actual sales converted from these leads, however, tell a different story. Of the 3,500 leads uncovered by publicity, 10 percent (350) were converted to actual sales. Of the 2,450 uncovered by advertising, 50 percent (1,225) were converted to sales. Of the 1,050 trade show leads, 80 percent (840) were converted to sales.[60] These figures show that although trade shows uncovered the fewest number of sales leads, they were the best leads in terms of conversion to actual sales, which may be the real test for the effectiveness of a promotional medium.

Probably the major reason for this result is that good trade shows draw few casual visitors; thus, sales leads come largely from buying influences who are truly interested. Data compiled by the Trade Show Bureau reveal visitors attend trade shows for five basic reasons: (1) 50 percent attend to see new products and developments, (2) 15 percent attend because they have an interest in the subject area of the show, (3) 10 percent attend to see a specific product or company, (4) 9 percent do so to attend technical/educational sessions at the show, and (5) 7 percent attend to obtain technical or product information.[61] New products

---

EXHIBIT 16.3   **Trade Show Promotion in Business Markets**

Apple Computer, Inc., of Cupertino, California, entered the 1989 Seybold Computer Publishing Conference & Exposition in San Francisco with a 2,500 square foot island exhibit. This conference was one of the premier executive forums in desktop publishing and afforded Apple a chance to promote its desktop products.

In entering the show, Apple determined three objectives: (1) to position Apple as the leading computer vendor for people communicating ideas in powerful and effective ways, (2) to position Apple as a visionary of future communicating experiences, and (3) to reinforce Apple's commitment to providing customers with a range of powerful personal computing products.

To achieve these objectives, the company stressed the features and quality of its products under the theme "Freedom of Expression." The company was able to show, at both its booth and its press briefings, how its products, technologies, and third parties combine to provide customers with powerful and creative ways to express their ideas and information. This particular exhibit was judged by Exhibit Surveys, Inc., as the second most remembered exhibit in 1989 at trade shows of 100,000 square feet or less.

Source: Adapted from Richard K. Swandby, Ian K. Sequeira, and Janet H. Goldsmith, "1989's Most Memorable Exhibits," *Business Marketing* 75 (September 1990):63.

and technical information are the major reasons for attendance. This type of technical interest may be more predominant in trade show attendees than in readers of business advertisements and publicity releases.

One other way to view trade show promotion is in its cost and effectiveness. It is an expensive promotional medium, and may exceed $50,000 for participation in each show.[62] At the same time, the cost of making a face-to-face contact at a trade show is considerably less than the cost of a personal sales call. This relationship is illustrated in Figure 16.7. These differences may be even more meaningful regarding the cost of closing a sale. In Chapter 15, it was shown that McGraw-Hill's Research Department determined 4.3 calls were required to close a business sale. The Trade Show Bureau's research shows that less than one call (0.8 call) was necessary to close a sale initiated by a trade show contact.[63] This finding implies that trade show contacts cost less than sales call contacts and that they take much less follow-up effort to consummate the sale. Carried to its conclusion, it appears that, compared with field selling, trade show promotion can be cost effective. Treating the two as pure substitutes is probably

FIGURE 16.7   **Cost of Making a Face-to-Face Contact at a Trade Show Compared to the Cost of a Personal Sales Call in Business Marketing**

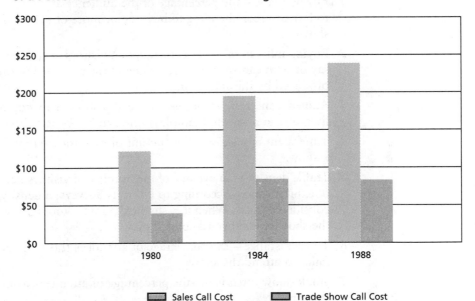

Source: Reprinted by permission from Cahners Publishing Company, *Cahners Advertising Research Report,* No. 542.1F (Newton, MA: Cahners Publishing Company, 1989); and from the Trade Show Bureau, *Trade Show Bureau Research Report,* No. SM/20 (Denver, CO: Trade Show Bureau, 1991).

not realistic, but cost-effective comparisons have managerial validity when the usefulness of trade show promotion is being evaluated.

Trade show promotion also permits the business marketer to contact buying influences that have not been reached by salespeople in the field. Research conducted by the Trade Show Bureau found that of qualified buyers who stopped at a booth, over 80 percent had not been visited by the exhibiting company's salesperson in the preceding twelve months. This figure was fairly consistent across many industries for many types of products, which again indicates that salespeople cannot reach all buying influences and that additional communication support is needed.

Selection of Trade Shows For the business marketing manager, choosing trade shows to enter is much like choosing trade journals in which to advertise. There are many trade shows, even within specific industries, and entering all of them would be expensive and wasteful. Therefore, the manager must determine some means of selecting those shows to enter.

The key to selection depends on which factors make a good trade show for a particular business marketing manager. Exhibits Surveys, an organization that specializes in trade show evaluations, specifies the following indicators as the best for measuring trade show activity and audience quality: [64]

1. Buying plans—the percentage of the audience at a trade show planning to buy or recommending to buy one or more of the products seen at a show.

2. Buying influences—that percentage of visitors at a show who have a final say or who can specify or recommend the purchase of the type of products produced by the exhibitor.

3. Audience interest—that percentage at a show who stop to talk or get literature at a selected sample of the exhibitors at a show.

4. Time spent at a show—the amount of time the average visitor spends at a show.

5. Traffic density—an average of the number of visitors per 100 square feet of exhibit space. According to Exhibits Surveys, a density factor of 4.0 is considered ideal: When it is smaller, traffic is too light, when it is higher, the show tends toward congestion.

6. Travel distance—the percentage of attendees traveling more than 400 miles to attend the show.

7. Single-show attendees—the percentage of attendees who attend only one show per year.

Using these criteria, Exhibits Surveys samples trade shows across the United States. Its 1989 surveys provide insight to what these criteria look like on a nationwide basis. The company sampled fifty-seven major exhibitions and found the following information: (1) 84 percent of all attendees were buying influences, (2) 61 percent planned to buy or recommend to buy products seen at a show, (3) average audience interest factor was 48 percent, (4) the average attendee spent 7.3 hours at a show, (5) average traffic density was 3.2, (6) 44 percent of all attendees traveled more than 400 miles, and (7) 52 percent were single-show attendees.[65] These are averages for all shows and can vary appreciably from show to show. For example, 94 percent of attendees of the Pittsburgh Analytical Chemistry Conference, held in Atlanta, were found to be buying influences. Similarly, 91 percent of attendees at the PGA Merchandise Show, held in Orlando, Florida, expressed buying plans.

What these factors mean to the business marketing manager is easy to see. When prospective trade shows are reviewed in terms of these factors, those with the highest percentage of buying plans, the greatest number of buying influences, the highest audience interest factors, the most time spent at the show, the highest percentage of attendees traveling over 400 miles, the highest percentage of single-show attendees, and a density factor close to 4.0 are the most appropriate candidates. Information regarding trade shows can be obtained from such organizations as Exhibits Surveys, the Audit Bureau of Circulation, and the Trade Show Bureau. The Trade Show Bureau, in conjunction with *Tradeshow Week* magazine, publishes the *Tradeshow Week Data Book,* which is an annual statistical directory for more than 5,000 U.S. trade shows. This source provides information on individual shows such as projected number of attendees, analysis of types of exhibitors and products, and analysis of types and qualifications of attendees. With such information readily available, marketing managers can get the most for every dollar spent on trade show promotion.

Expectations are that trade show promotion will continue to prosper in business marketing. Experts believe the formation of the European Community's single market in 1992 will increase the number of European companies exhibiting in the United States. In addition, more U.S. business marketing companies will exhibit in European trade shows.[66] All this strongly suggests that trade show promotion is a viable business marketing tool that will continue to be used.

Dealer and Distributor Materials

Approximately 5 percent of business sales promotion budgets go toward dealer and distributor materials that manufacturers provide to their channel intermediaries to help them promote effectively in their local markets. Typical of such materials are point-of-purchase (POP) displays for dealer showrooms, technical bulletins, dealer sales kits, specialty advertising items such as calendars and business gifts, direct mail stuffers, price lists, and other similar pieces of promotion. For any manufacturers that use distributors and/or manufacturers' representatives in the channel of distribution, this form of promotion is virtually a necessity if any degree of control is to be exercised over local promotion at the channel intermediary level.

Specialty Advertising

Specialty advertising is also used by a number of business marketing firms. *Specialty advertising* is defined as "that advertising and sales promotion medium which utilizes useful articles to carry the advertiser's name, address, and advertising message to his target audience."[67] Specialty advertising items are distributed without cost or obligation to the prospect. Typical specialty advertising items are calendars, business gifts, and advertising specialties such as ballpoint pens, cigarette lighters, memo pads, notebooks, and other useful products. Advocates of this medium claim it builds goodwill, and it ultimately contributes to a prospect's preference for the advertiser.[68] Critics claim these specialties are useful at early stages of the purchase decision but doubt their effectiveness in generating new sales. "Nobody is going to buy a $50,000 piece of equipment just because somebody gave them a key chain."[69] Despite mixed feelings, specialty advertising is a commonly used business sales promotional medium, and most users integrate it with other forms of promotion. Figure 16.8 provides an example of the use of specialty advertising in business marketing and shows that this imaginative medium can be integrated into the overall promotional strategy, adding to its effectiveness.

PUBLICITY AND PUBLIC RELATIONS IN BUSINESS MARKETING

The previously cited study by the Business/Professional Advertising Association revealed that business marketers spend only about 5 percent of their promotional budgets on publicity. This can be compared with 55 percent spent on advertising and 40 percent on sales promotion. Thus **publicity** and **public relations** appear to play lesser roles in the marketing of business goods and services.

In many companies, publicity and public relations are lumped together and assumed to be the same, even though there are technical differences. These differences were explained in the preceding chapter. Regardless, this type of promotion can be productive for the marketing manager who believes in the corporate promotion approach. Publicity and public relations have been widely used by some business marketing companies to create a favorable public image in reaction to charges by environmentalists. As well, this type of promotion has been used to help create a more favorable climate for the company's salespeople.

A point of clarification should be made here. While it is true that publicity is not paid for by the sponsor (the business marketing firm), that does not mean that the marketer does not spend time and resources in attempting to influence coverage by the media. The marketing manager must recognize that publicity can be bad as well as good and that bad publicity harms marketing efforts. For examples, there have been news releases criticizing some business marketing firms for harming the environment, cheating the federal government, etc. Obviously, such stories are harmful and the manager should work diligently to get

Campaign improves advertiser's image

Menasha Corporation - Neenah Container Plant

Neenah, Wisconsin

Industrial/Agricultural Promotion - Budget Category L

OBJECTIVE: To secure new accounts and provide a focused presentation for salespeople.

STRATEGY & EXECUTION: To open new doors for its sales people, the corrugated container company embarked upon a six-month campaign targeted to 100 marketing managers and purchasing agents of firms it was not doing business with. The campaign was prefaced by a blind survey that revealed that buyers of corrugate ranked Menasha no higher than sixth in any one category among eight suppliers. Each month of the promotion offered two related specialties, the first being mailed and the second hand-delivered by an account manager. The first-month items, a coaster tile and a coffee mug, were imprinted with the campaign theme, "Our promise...as good as gold," and were personalized with the recipient's name. In subsequent months, recipients were issued additional personalized specialties including a pen with red and black refills (copy: "A corporation's bottom line can take one of two colors — red or black. Proper packaging can indeed enhance your bottom line").

RESULTS: A post-promotion survey showed notable improvement, with Menasha ranking no lower than third in any category. The company was said to have made sales to 21 of the 100 propects and to have developed a business relationship of quoting and sampling with 70% of the targeted group.

Source: Reprinted by permission of the *Specialty Advertising Association International.*

positive publicity from the press and avoid situations where negative publicity could possibly ensue. This requires effort and thus publicity should not simply be viewed as a free form of promotion.

BUSINESS ADVERTISING AND SALES PROMOTION BUDGETS

Despite the importance of advertising and sales promotion to most business marketing firms, the budgets for these activities are small when compared to consumer marketing companies. One study of 519 business marketing firms that ranged in size from under $10 million to over $500 million in sales revealed that 49 percent spent less than $100,000 annually for advertising and sales promotion activities.[70] Studies conducted by the American Marketing Association found that on average, business marketing budgets are only about one-fifth the size of their consumer marketing counterparts.[71]

In addition, business marketers typically allocate the largest proportion of promotion budgets to sales, which leaves much less for advertising, sales promotion, and publicity. Studies conducted by McGraw-Hill Research Department found that business marketing firms spend .7 percent of sales in advertising, 1.0 percent of sales in sales promotion, and 5.9 percent of sales in direct sales expenses.[72]

All this does not mean that advertising and sales promotion are viewed as unimportant by business marketing managers. Rather, it probably indicates that lower-cost media are available in business marketing that still provide excellent nonpersonal communication with buyers and buying influences in target market organizations.

It is also common for business marketing companies to view advertising and sales promotion collectively in terms of budgeting. Since both are seen as forms of sales support activities, they are perceived as similar enough to include in the same budget. Methods used to determine promotional budgets in business markets appear to differ based on studies conducted. For example, a study of U.S. advertising executives in sixty-four of the top 100 national business advertisers found five methods used: (1) 74 percent used an objective-and-task approach, (2) 33 percent used a what-could-be-afforded approach, (3) 23 percent used a percentage of the previous year's sales, (4) 21 percent matched competitors' budgets, and (5) 16 percent used a percentage of anticipated sales.[73] Percentages added up to more than 100 percent because some respondents used more than one method.

A similar study of 560 British business marketing companies found seven methods used in the following way: (1) 54 percent used a what-could-be-afforded method, (2) 40 percent used an objective-and-task method, (3) 33 percent used a percentage of anticipated sales, (4) 7 percent experimented in setting their budgets, (5) 6 percent used a "desired-share-of-voice" approach, (6) 5 percent accepted the budget proposed by their advertising agency, and (7) 4 percent matched the competition.[74] Collectively, these two studies summarize the methods used by business marketers to budget advertising and sales promotional activities. The methods used most widely are (in order) objective and task, percentage of sales, what can be afforded, and matching competition.

EVALUATING THE EFFECTIVENESS OF ADVERTISING AND SALES PROMOTION

There are indications that business marketers are not often as sophisticated in evaluating the effectiveness of their advertising and sales promotion as their consumer marketing counterparts are. There are a number of reasons for this situation. First, business marketing firms are not as research-oriented as consumer firms are. Second, smaller advertising and sales promotion budgets may attract less attention in terms of evaluation efforts. Third, business advertisers may not be as sophisticated as their consumer marketing peers in terms of knowledge of methods to evaluate effectiveness. However, the reasons do not mean that effectiveness is not measured at all. A study of readers of *Business Marketing* magazine found that lead or inquiry generation is the number one evaluation criterion for promotional activities.[75] Of those surveyed, 85 percent used the number of qualified inquiries to evaluate the effectiveness of trade publications, direct mail, directories, trade shows, and catalogs. Forty-five percent used total inquiries, whether qualified or not, as a measure. Some respondents used both, which only reinforces the concept that advertising and sales promotion are seen as sales support activities in business marketing.

Figure 16.9 provides an example of measuring the effectiveness of specific ads by researching trade publications readers. In this case, the reader is given a list of advertisements that ran in a specific issue and requested to indicate if he or she: (1) remembers seeing the ad, (2) remembers reading the ad, and (3) read more than half of the ad. In this manner, the impact of particular trade journal ads may be measured. Since measuring ad effectiveness basically involves marketing research, this was covered in Chapter 11 and will not be developed here.

OVERALL BUSINESS PROMOTIONAL STRATEGY

In the final analysis, the business marketing manager's task is to integrate personal selling, advertising, and sales promotion so that the total promotional mix communicates effectively with buyers and buying influences in the target markets. This integration is necessary whether customers are private commercial, institutional, reseller, or governmental and whether they are domestic or global. One method of accomplishing this goal is to examine the various promotional media as they relate to tasks in the business promotional process. Table 16.11 illustrates this approach. Specific promotional tasks are defined, and the manager then attempts to achieve those tasks through the optimum combination of media. In this manner, promotional effectiveness can be increased, and the over-

FIGURE 16.9   Measuring the Effectiveness of Trade Publication Advertisements in Business Markets

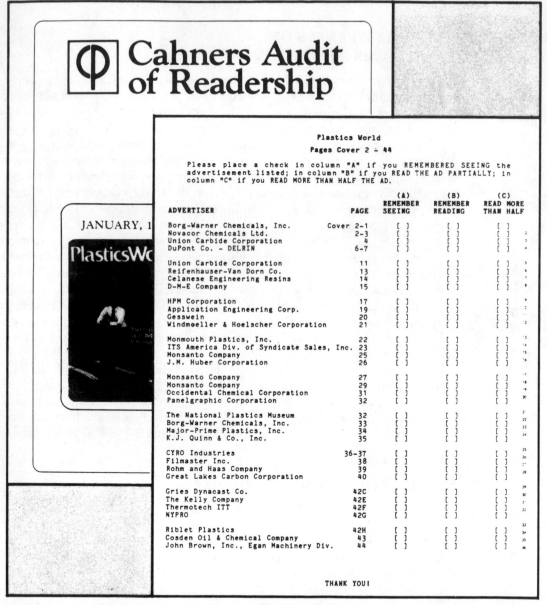

Source: Used by permission from *Cahners Research Services* (Newton, MA: Cahners Publishing Company, 1986), 12.

TABLE 16.11   Media Most Appropriate for Accomplishing Tasks in the Promotion Process in Business Marketing

Tasks in the Promotion Process	To Accomplish This Task Employ This Medium or These Media	
	New Customers	Existing Customers
Making contact	Trade publications, general publications, trade shows, direct mail, industrial directories	Inside salesperson, telemarketing, catalogs, direct mail, specialty advertising
Arousing interest	Trade publications, general publications, trade shows, direct mail, industrial directories	Inside salesperson, telemarketing, catalogs, direct mail, specialty advertising
Creating preference	Field salesperson, direct mail, trade shows, industrial directories, telemarketing	Field salesperson, inside salesperson, direct mail, catalogs, telemarketing
Making specific proposals	Field salesperson	Field salesperson, inside salesperson, telemarketing
Closing the order	Field salesperson	Field salesperson, inside salesperson, telemarketing
Keeping customers sold	Field salesperson, inside salesperson, telemarketing, direct mail, specialty advertising	Field salesperson, inside salesperson, telemarketing, direct mail, specialty advertising

Source: Tasks in the industrial promotion process reprinted by permission of McGraw-Hill Research Department.

all cost of promotion decreased. When these tasks are accomplished, the marketing manager has been successful in the formulation of promotional strategy.

CHAPTER SUMMARY

This chapter and Chapter 15 have described the promotional strategy areas of business marketing. This chapter focused on the advertising and sales promotional areas of the promotional mix. In many business markets, these areas primarily support personal selling, as discussed in Chapter 15.

Both advertising and sales promotion, if properly designed and executed, can lead to more effective and efficient selling by field salespeople, which in turn may reduce the overall cost of promotion. Advertising's many roles were examined, and studies were cited to show that advertising has proven itself to be an effective part of business marketing. Media used in business marketing were examined with particular attention paid to trade publications, direct mail, and directories. The concept of advertising messages or appeals was developed with emphasis placed on corporate versus product themes. Evidence was presented to indicate that a problem may exist in business markets when advertisers do not understand the buying influences they are trying to reach.

Sales promotion, catalogs, and trade shows were examined in detail as these apply to pro-

motion in business marketing. Other promotional areas such as publicity, public relations, dealer and distributor materials, and specialty advertising were also described.

Methods of determining advertising and sales promotion budgets were analyzed, and the evaluation of these forms of promotion was discussed. The chapter concluded with a section on how all promotional activities (personal selling, advertising, and sales promotion) are integrated into the total promotion process. Overall, the chapter developed the concept that nonpersonal promotional activities are important and that they contribute to more effective and efficient field selling in terms of generation of inquiries and lower costs.

KEY TERMS

advertising
advertising medium
advertising message
catalog
corporate advertising
direct mail
industrial directory
mailing list

product advertising
public relations
publicity
sales promotion
specialty advertising
trade publication journal
trade show

QUESTIONS

1. In business marketing, advertising and sales promotion activities are often considered to be support activities. Explain what this means and then relate why advertising and sales promotion would play such a role.

2. Explain how multiple buying influences complicate the job of the business advertising manager in both selecting media and developing advertising copy.

3. The catalog is a commonly used sales promotion medium in business marketing and is sometimes referred to as the "silent salesperson." Explain what this means and then relate how

catalogs can increase the effectiveness of field salespeople.

4. What do you see as the similarities and differences between a personal sales call and a face-to-face contact with a prospect at a trade show? Why should they be viewed as complements in the promotional mix and not as substitutes for each other?

5. Many business marketing managers believe that advertising and sales promotion activities can decrease the overall cost of selling and yet increase sales productivity at the same time. Do you believe this is true? Explain your answer.

6. For the business marketing manager, a major task is to coordinate personal selling, advertising, and sales promotion into a total promotional mix that communicates both effectively and efficiently with target market customers. Provide an example to show how all three can be coordinated to produce an effective and efficient mix.

7. In business advertising, both trade journal and direct mail are said to be "pinpoint" media. Explain what this means and then relate why these media may not be as effective in consumer marketing as they are in business marketing.

8. While television is used on occasion in business markets, the medium is not that popular in business marketing. Why is this so? Do you think this will change in the future?

9. Direct mail advertising is claimed to be the most flexible of all business advertising media. What is meant by this statement? How might the marketing manager use this flexibility to advantage?

10. What do you see as the differences and similarities between a personal sales call and an advertising call in business marketing? Why should they be viewed as complements to each other and not as substitutes?

NOTES

1. Richard E. Plank and Linda L. Fernandes, "More Industrial Does Not Mean More Consumer-Type Promotion," *Marketing News* 18 (April 3, 1984): 10.

2. Irwin W. Tyson, speech given before the Fourteenth Biennial Ohio Valley Industrial Advertising Conference, May 9, 1972.

3. Plank and Fernandes, op. cit.

4. John Couretas, "Study to Measure Ad's Effect on Sales Force," *Business Marketing* 69 (May 1984): 34.

5. "The Short Reach of Salespeople," *Sales & Marketing Management* 133 (July 2, 1984): 34.

6. Sim A. Kolliner, "Measuring Industrial Advertising," *Journal of Marketing* 29 (October 1965): 53.

7. "Salespeople Find Advertising Works," *Sales & Marketing Management* 137 (January 1987): 22.

8. *Laboratory of Advertising Performance Report,* No. 1029.3 (New York: McGraw-Hill Research Department, 1987).

9. "High-Tech Firm Starts TV Ads," *Business Marketing* 69 (May 1984): 14.

10. Kolliner, op. cit.

11. *Summary of a New Report on Advertising Effectiveness* (New York: American Business Press, 1975).

12. *Cahners Advertising Research Report,* No. 542.1F (Newton, MA: Cahners Publishing Company, 1989).

13. *Summary of a New Report on Advertising Effectiveness,* op. cit.

14. Tom Eisenhart, "What's Right, What's Wrong with Each Medium," *Business Marketing* 75 (April 1990): 40–47.

15. *Cahners Advertising Research Report,* No. 441.1 (Newton, MA: Cahners Publishing Company, 1978).

16. Philip Kotler, *Marketing Management,* 2d ed. (Englewood Cliffs, NJ: Prentice-Hall, Inc., 1980), 510.

17. *Cahners Advertising Research Report,* No. 542.1F, op. cit.

18. *Ads for Chemicals Pay Off in Sales When They Run in Chemical & Engineering News* (Northfield, IL: *Chemical & Engineering News,* 1978).

19. Eisenhart, op. cit., 40.

20. *Direct Mail Marketing Guide* (New York: Dun & Bradstreet, 1978), 1.

21. Lloyd Shearer, "New High for Business Letter," *Parade* (January 1, 1984): 9.

22. Eisenhart, op. cit., 40.

23. "Ads, Direct Mail Double Sales for Biomation," *Industrial Marketing* 58 (September 1973): 10.

24. George C. McNutt, *Business/Industrial Marketing and Communications: Key to More Productive Selling* (Chicago: Crain Books, 1978), 37.

25. "Industrial Marketing Survey: Business/Industrial Direct Response Promotion," *Industrial Marketing* 67 (August 1982): 75.

26. See *How to Increase Your Sales Through Industrial Directory Advertising* (Greenwich, CT: Conover-Mast Purchasing Directory Research Department, 1969), 2–3.

27. See "Reaching All the Industrial Prospects," *ZIP Target Marketing* (April 1984), a promotional piece of the Thomas Publishing Company.

28. *How to Prepare and Distribute Your Catalog* (New York: Thomas Register of American Manufacturers, 1990), 15.

29. "*IM*'s Survey of Corporate Advertising," *Industrial Marketing* 67 (February 1982): 12.

30. Tom Eisenhart, "Business Marketers Turning to Public TV," *Business Marketing* 75 (October 1990): 14.

31. Ibid.

32. Eisenhart, "What's Right, What's Wrong With Each Medium," op. cit., 46.

33. "*IM*'s Survey of Corporate Advertising," op. cit.

34. "Progress in a Primitive Art—Industrial Advertising," *Industrial Marketing* 66 (May 1981): 81.

35. *Laboratory of Advertising Performance Report*, No. 3248.3 (New York: McGraw-Hill Research Department, 1987).

36. Ibid.

37. See Gordon McAleer, *How Customers of Industrial Products Rate Advertising Appeals* (Princeton, NJ: Center for Marketing Communications, 1974).

38. Janet Zaleski, "Make Your Product Catalogue User-Friendly," *Sales & Marketing Management* 133 (September 10, 1984): 85.

39. George M. Zinkhan and Lauren A. Vachris, "The Impact of Selling Aids on New Prospects," *Industrial Marketing Management* 13 (1984): 189.

40. *How to Build and Distribute Your Next Catalog* (New York: Thomas Publishing Company, 1970), 3.

41. *The Bible of Industry* (New York: Thomas Publishing Company, 1979), 3.

42. *How to Prepare and Distribute Your Catalog* (New York: Thomas Register of American Manufacturers, 1990), 16.

43. *Cahners Advertising Research Report*, No. 140.2A (Newton, MA: Cahners Publishing Company, 1986).

44. *How to Prepare and Distribute Your Catalog*, op. cit.

45. "Catalog Selling Is on a Roll," *Industrial Distribution* 77 (July 1988): 7.

46. *How to Prepare and Distribute Your Catalog*, op. cit.

47. Sean Milmo, "Cross-Border Campaigns Use Catalogs to Market Computers," *Business Marketing* 74 (December 1989): 22.

48. *How to Build and Distribute Your Next Catalog*, op. cit.

49. Robert J. Francisco, "Face Up to Winning Exhibit Design," *Business Marketing* 73 (March 1988): 82.

50. Joseph A. Bellizzi and Delilah J. Lipps, "Managerial Guidelines for Trade Show Effectiveness," *Industrial Marketing Management* 13 (1984): 49.

51. "Exhibits/Trade Shows," *Successful Meetings* 32 (February 1983): 26.

52. "Trade Shows," *Agency Sales Magazine* 11 (October 1981): 4.

53. Thomas V. Bonoma, "Get More Out of Your Trade Shows," *Harvard Business Review* 61 (January–February 1983): 75.

54. Ibid.

55. Allan Konopacki, "The Different Sell at Trade Shows," *Sales & Marketing Management* 132 (September 1983): 72.

56. "Show and Tell Thieves at Industry Trade Shows," *In Focus* 2 (1984): 3.

57. Konopacki, op. cit.

58. "Honeywell Divisions Cut National Shows," *Industrial Marketing* 52 (August 1967): 52–55.

59. "Hunt Chemicals Changes Its Trade Show Formula," *Sales & Marketing Management* 133 (February 6, 1984): 8.

60. "What Happens to Trade Show Leads," *Sales Management* 99 (July 15, 1967): 85–89.

61. *Trade Show Bureau Research Report*, Study No. 3 (New Canaan, CT: Trade Show Bureau, 1979).

62. A. J. Faria and J. R. Dickinson, "Behind the Push to Exhibit at Trade Shows," *Business Marketing* 70 (August 1985): 100.

63. See Richard K. Swandby and Jonathan Cox, "Trade Show Trends: Business Up and Growing," *Business Marketing* 69 (May 1984): 78–84.

64. Richard K. Swandby, Jonathan M. Cox, and

Ian K. Sequeira, "Trade Show Indicators," *Business Marketing* 75 (May 1990): 52.

65. See Richard K. Swandby, Jonathan M. Cox, and Ian K. Sequeira, "Trade Shows Poised for 1990s Growth," *Business Marketing* 75 (May 1990): 46–52.

66. Swandby, Cox, and Sequeira, "Trade Show Indicators," op. cit.

67. "The Specialty Advertising Association Very Important Professor Program," *Linage* 22 (Spring 1970): 24.

68. Richard G. Ebel, "Specialty Advertising: 9½ Ways to Use a Powerful Marketing Tool," *Industrial Marketing* 67 (February 1982): 80.

69. Daniel B. Cartledge, "Trade Shows: Specialties on Parade," *Impact* (Fall 1987): 53.

70. "Highlights of *Sales & Marketing Management's* Survey on Industrial Advertising," *Sales & Marketing Management* 130 (June 8, 1981): 53.

71. Peter Finch, "Survey: '86 Ad/Promotion Budgets to Climb 10%," *Business Marketing* 71 (January 1986): 22.

72. *Laboratory of Advertising Report,* No. 8015.8 (New York: McGraw-Hill Research Department, 1985).

73. See Vincent J. Blasko and Charles H. Patti, "The Advertising Budgeting Practices of Industrial Advertisers," *Journal of Marketing* 48 (Fall 1984): 104–110.

74. See James E. Lynch and Graham J. Hooley, "Advertising Budgeting Practices of Industrial Advertisers," *Industrial Marketing Management* 16 (1987): 63–69.

75. Hugh Farrell, "Are Business and Consumer Advertising Different Breeds?" *Business Marketing* 71 (February 1986): 64–72.

SUGGESTED ADDITIONAL READINGS

Balasubramanian, Siva K., and V. Kumar. "Analyzing Variations in Advertising and Promotional Expenditures: Key Correlates in Consumer, Industrial and Service Markets." *Journal of Marketing* 54 (April 1990): 57–68.

Bellizzi, Joseph A., and Delilah J. Lipps. "Managerial Guidelines for Trade Show Effectiveness." *Industrial Marketing Management* 13 (1984): 49–52.

Blasko, Vincent J., and Charles H. Patti. "The Advertising Budgeting Practices of Industrial Marketers." *Journal of Marketing* 48 (Fall 1984): 104–110.

Bonoma, Thomas V. "Get More Out of Your Trade Shows." *Harvard Business Review* 61 (January–February 1983): 75–83.

Clark, Gary L., Peter F. Kaminski, and Gene Brown. "The Readability of Advertisements and Articles in Trade Journals." *Industrial Marketing Management* 19 (1990): 251–260.

Eisenhart, Tom. "What's Right, What's Wrong with Each Medium." *Business Marketing* 75 (April 1990): 40–47.

Grass, Robert C. "Response Latency in Industrial Advertising Research." *Journal of Advertising Research* 20 (December 1980): 63–65.

Hanssens, Dominique M., and Barton A. Weitz. "The Effectiveness of Industrial Print Advertisements Across Product Categories." *Journal of Marketing Research* 17 (August 1980): 294–306.

How to Prepare and Distribute Your Catalog (New York: Thomas Register of American Manufacturers, 1990).

Jackson, Donald W., Janet E. Keith, and Richard K. Burdick. "The Relative Importance of Various Promotional Elements in Different Industrial Purchase Situations." *Journal of Advertising* 16 (1987): 25–33.

Kerin, Roger A., and William L. Cron. "Assessing Trade Show Functions and Performance: An Exploratory Study." *Journal of Marketing* 51 (July 1987): 87–94.

Lynch, James E., and Graham J. Hooley. "Advertising Budgeting Practices of Industrial Advertisers." *Industrial Marketing Management* 16 (1987): 63–69.

O'Keefe, Philip. "Get Discovered with Directories." *Business Marketing* 72 (June 1987): 130–137.

Solely, Lawrence C. "Copy Length and Industrial Advertising Readership." *Industrial Marketing Management* 15 (1986): 245–251.

Swandby, Richard K., Jonathan M. Cox, and Ian K.

Sequeira. "Trade Shows Poised for 1990s Growth." *Business Marketing* 75 (May 1990): 46–52.

The *"How To" Book on Industrial Advertising.* Cleveland: *New Equipment Digest* Magazine, 1986.

Williams, Jerome D. "Industrial Publicity: One of the Best Promotional Tools." *Industrial Marketing Management* 12 (1983): 207–211.

Zinkhan, George M. "Rating Industrial Advertisements." *Industrial Marketing Management* 13 (1984): 43–48.

ʾ17ʾ

Pricing Strategy
in Business Marketing

● ●

Thus far, discussion has focused on the product, distribution, and promotional elements of the marketing mix. At this point, pricing must be integrated into the mix. This does not mean that pricing takes place only after target markets have been defined, buying influences determined, and substrategies developed for products and services, distribution, and promotion. To proceed through all of these activities and then determine price can lead to marketing disaster. Pricing should be considered when the product or service is in the screening stage and new product or service ideas whose costs are predicted to exceed possible market prices should be screened out. In fact, many business marketers consider the product and pricing areas to be so interrelated as to view them almost as one activity. Nevertheless, in a text such as this, discussing pricing strategy makes better sense after the other mix elements have been developed than before because many of those elements affect pricing decisions.

The importance of pricing in business marketing should not be underestimated. Depending on the particular product or service involved, however, its importance may vary considerably. For example, price is often extremely critical in the marketing of commodity type products where often the only differentiating factor is the price. Similarly, price is also crucial in competitive bidding situations where slight differences in price can directly cause success or failure. On the other hand, price may be much less important to some organizational buyers than product quality, service, ability to deliver on time, technical assistance, and sales competence. For example, it makes little sense for a buyer in a manufacturing company to buy lower-priced products if the supplier cannot deliver the right quantity on time. Thus, the basic role of pricing in the marketing mix is often subject to many constraints and its importance may change appreciably from marketer to marketer.

At the same time, there is considerable evidence to support the contention

593

An Example of the Importance of Price in Business Marketing

In many instances, price can be a very important component in the business marketing mix. An example of this took place in the late 1980s when Shell Oil Company invited bids to build what at that time was to be the world's largest oil platform. Named "Bullwinkle," the platform was to be constructed in the Gulf of Mexico. The platform would be taller than the Sears Tower in Chicago and would weigh four times more than the Brooklyn Bridge.

When Shell extended invitations to bid, the feeling in the oil platform construction industry was that one of the larger industry leaders would get the contract. A number of reasons accounted for this belief. First, industry leaders had had no competition in the gulf for over thirty years—they had been awarded every previous contract. Second, the industry leaders had existing strong relationships with Shell and management believed these would play a major factor. These leaders in fact promoted their years of faithful service to Shell and one company even offered to build the platform without making any profit. Thus, industry consensus was that even though it was to be a bid job, one of the leaders would surely win the contract.

What happened was totally unexpected. Shell Oil awarded the contract to Gulf Marine Fabricators, a small firm that had only been in existence a few months. Gulf Marine was the low bidder and based on that was awarded the contract despite its lack of contacts and the relationships of the industry leaders. Gulf Marine was able to outbid its far larger competitors by capitalizing on its much lower cost structure. For example, it used already fabricated steel from Japan, assembled the platform on leased land, and launched it into the gulf on a Dutch-manufactured barge. This approach permitted a small company like Gulf Marine to qualify for such a large project and thus the company became a legitimate competitor. Industry leaders in the oil field platform industry had failed to recognize this. Their cost structures were appreciably higher than Gulf Marine's and as a result, they were unable to compete on price and lost the contract to a relative upstart. Their costs were higher because of poor planning and far too optimistic forecasts of their markets—they had simply become too fat while the market had changed toward a more economic approach to the building of platforms.

Thus, with a far smaller organization and much leaner cost structure, Gulf Marine was able to outsmart its larger competitors and in this way become the low bidder on the project. As can be seen, price played a vital role in this situation and better cost controls permitted a smaller company to win the contract and break the hold of the industry leaders.

Source: Adapted from Thomas Petzinger, Jr., "Upstart's Winning Bid for Offshore Platform Stuns Its Older Rivals," *Wall Street Journal,* November 20, 1985, 1, 25.

that business marketers do not give pricing the attention it deserves despite rapidly changing costs, recession, shortages of materials, increasing competition, etc. Pricing is said to be the least rational of all mix decisions made in business marketing.[1] It has been stated that there may be more "hunch" in pricing than in all other areas of the business marketing mix. Whether these statements are true or not is open to conjecture but they do suggest that pricing may not command the attention that is paid to the other areas of the mix. Thus, there is a need to examine pricing in more detail since this element is both an important part of the mix and perhaps not as well understood as it should be.

This chapter concludes the discussion of the business marketing mix and focuses on pricing to organizational customers and prospects. These organizations may be private commercial, reseller, institutional, or governmental. There are often differences based on the type of market involved and these will be examined. Factors that influence business pricing decisions are analyzed in detail and the concept of list and net prices is examined. Various pricing methods found in business marketing are also developed including target return pricing, bidding, negotiated pricing, and leasing.

WHAT IS PRICE?

Price is a relatively simple term, but its full interpretation is not simple. Some business marketers price goods and services by taking the costs involved in producing and distributing those goods and services and then adding a desired markup. Yet, this result is too simplified to express price. From a marketing perspective, what is lacking is that value to the customer is completely overlooked. Regardless of the costs involved or the desired margin, customers will buy or not buy based on the value to them of the product or service involved. Pricing on a "cost-plus" basis lacks reality, and it does not take into account the following:[2]

- Market conditions
- Excess production capacity
- Competitive prices
- Available substitutes and their prices
- Product differences
- Phase of the product life cycle
- Growth rate of the market
- Whether other prices are rising, stable, or falling
- Market share
- The market's ability to buy
- The market's expectations about prices
- Competitors' typical responses to price
- Industry changes

In this text, price is defined as the monetary figure assigned to a product or service that (1) covers the costs of producing and marketing, (2) returns an adequate profit to the seller and meets pricing objectives, (3) matches the value perceived by buyers, and (4) permits the seller to compete in the marketplace. **Pricing** is thus the process of determining the proper monetary figure.

PRICING IN BUSINESS MARKETS

The role of price in business marketing is basically similar to the role price plays in consumer marketing, although there are some distinct, important differences. For example, many organizational buyers rate price as a much less important buying consideration than certainty of delivery, quality of the products, service provisions by the manufacturer, and technical assistance. For these buyers, it makes little sense to buy lower-priced products if the suppliers cannot deliver on time and in the quantity required or if their product quality is lower. With a production process, these factors add to cost rather than save money for these customers. To illustrate, if a buyer switches suppliers to purchase OEM component parts at a lower price, what has been saved if the new vendor cannot deliver on time and the production line comes to a halt? Similarly, if the buyer switches to a new user product supplier because of lower price only to find the latter's service is poor and down time is increased, what has the buyer gained from the lower price?

Another factor that affects the role of price for some business marketing managers is the bidding process. This area is covered in detail later in this chapter, but it deserves some mention here. In bidding situations, because all bidders must conform to specifications, price may be the deciding factor in a sale. Million-dollar orders can be lost because of $50 differences in bids. The bidding process puts tremendous pressure on some marketing managers and their pricing analysts. The bidding process has brought about the use of bidding models and other sophisticated approaches to the pricing of business products and services.

An additional factor involved with the pricing of business products and services is negotiation. Many products and services are marketed at a price agreed on by both buyer and seller through mutual negotiation. To understand better how this process works, assume that a purchasing director wishes to purchase a line of OEM products. He or she then contacts appropriate suppliers to bid on the components. Requests for proposals (RFPs) are sent to the suppliers. These RFPs request unit prices by size and in various quantities in accordance with bid specifications. The quotations that come back will almost always vary by unit price and overall price. The buyer can then bargain with suppliers for a better price. Such negotiation is very common in business marketing, even in bidding situations.

Derived demand also affects pricing's role in business marketing. For example, the manufacturer of a consumer good such as an automobile will only purchase component parts such as batteries and tires when there is a demand for its product. Thus, when auto sales drop off, as they did in 1974–1975, 1979–

1980, and again in 1991, the demand for auto OEM component parts also drops off, regardless of price. In other words, derived demand makes price less influential than it might otherwise be. An OEM customer may purchase no more when prices are dropped than it otherwise would when demand for its final products drops off. Thus, the industry price elasticity of demand is relatively inelastic, but the demand for the product of each supplier in that industry may be relatively elastic, as the negotiation process indicates.

Still another factor involved in business pricing is that prices charged and prices actually paid may be quite different. Sticker prices and actual prices paid are generally the same in the consumer market, whereas it is often impossible to determine the actual price paid in business markets. To illustrate, many business marketing managers begin with list prices, which are those prices actually printed on their price lists. Yet, none of their customers may pay those list prices. Net prices, or prices actually paid, are determined from list prices minus such factors as cash discounts, trade and quantity discounts, sales rebates, and geographic freight differences. Determining who paid what for what is almost impossible, and actual prices paid are often a mystery. Of course, buyers and sellers know the actual price, but such secrets are often jealously guarded. As has been said, "Owing to hidden discounts and concessions, a company's quoted prices are often very different from the prices that it actually gets."[3] In other words, there are often two prices in business markets—quoted prices and actual prices—and both must be considered!

Table 17.1 summarizes some differences between pricing practices in the consumer and business markets. Although pricing plays basically the same role in the two markets, there are meaningful differences in actual practice.

CONSIDERATIONS IN PRICING BUSINESS GOODS AND SERVICES

In setting realistic prices in the marketplace, the business marketing manager and others involved in pricing often find their decisions influenced by six major considerations: (1) value to the customer or prospect, (2) competition, (3) cost considerations, (4) company pricing objectives, (5) company top management, and (6) government. Prices set without adequate consideration of each of these factors can be unrealistic and detrimental to the company's success. Therefore, a careful look at each factor is in order.

Value to the Customer or Prospect

A major consideration in business pricing concerns the customer's or prospect's perceived value of the product or service involved. Organizational buyers and buying influences will not pay a price that they believe exceeds the product's or service's value. The perceived customer value thus places a ceiling on the range of prices that may be considered. This value can change from product to product and even from customer to customer when the same product is involved. In at-

TABLE 17.1   Comparison of Pricing Strategy Factors in the Consumer and Business Markets

Factor	Consumer Markets	Business Markets
Importance of pricing strategy in marketing mix	Often a major factor; price is often a prime determinant of customer demand	In bidding situations, pricing is of critical importance; also very important in commodity products; in other situations, price may be less important than service, delivery, and technical assistance
Elasticity of demand	Industry demand may be elastic or inelastic depending on nature of product; same may be true of company demand	Industry demand often inelastic because of derived demand; company demand may be elastic or inelastic depending on competitive offerings
Competitive bidding	Not commonly found in consumer marketing (auctions are an exception)	Common in business markets; a large percentage of business sales involve various forms of competitive bidding
Negotiated pricing	Occurs at times with large consumer purchases such as cars and houses; often not available with most consumer products	Very common in business marketing, even when bidding occurs; almost always in situations involving major purchases and contracts
List and net prices	In most consumer product purchases, customer pays the list (sticker) price	List and net prices are used in almost all areas of business marketing; customer rarely pays the list price
Discounts	Discounts are sometimes given for cash purchases, but other types of discounts are rarely used	Discounts such as for quantity of goods purchased, type of customer, and credit worthiness are commonplace
Financing assistance provided by marketer	Often found in consumer markets in form of company credit cards, layaways, and other such short-term arrangements	Equally common in business marketing, but may take form of leasing and other forms of longer-term arrangements
Partnering relationships between marketer and customer	Not common in consumer marketing; price often determined on a transaction-by-transaction basis	Quite common in business marketing; involves price being determined on a long-run basis

tempting to gauge **value to the customer,** the marketing manager should understand that this value does not equate only to price. A common fallacy associated with business pricing is the belief that buyers act solely to minimize the price paid.[4] The highest price a customer will pay has been described as perceived benefits minus costs other than price.[5] A customer's perceived value has been defined by the following equation:

perceived value = perceived benefits/price

where

$$price = \text{purchase price} + \text{acquisition costs} + \text{transportation} + \text{installation} + \text{order handling} + \text{risk of failure}$$
$$\text{perceived benefits} = \text{benefits determined by physical attributes, service attributes, and technical support}$$

In determining whether or not a price is acceptable, the organizational buyer or buying influence may look at value in the following ways: (1) economic or cost value, (2) exchange or negotiated value, (3) aesthetic value, and (4) relative or competitive value.[6] These values are not mutually exclusive, and they often occur at the same time in a single buyer's evaluation. A look at each may be helpful.

Economic or Cost Value The economic value of a particular product to a buyer typically is based on such factors as (1) purchase price, (2) any additional postpurchase costs such as retraining of employees or installation modifications, and (3) the product's ability to enhance profits. An example is helpful.[7] Assume a potential manufacturing customer now uses a piece of light machinery costing $1,000. Present employee training and startup costs total $300, and all other postpurchase costs add up to another $400. The total economic cost of this machine to that customer is now $1,700. If a competitor develops a new product, how would its economic value to the customer be judged? The newly developed machine has an advantage over the old one in that it can produce a better finish, which allows the buying company to raise the price of its product by $100. Employee training on the new machine will be only $200, and other postpurchase costs will be reduced to $300. The marketing manager of the new replacement product knows his or her product is superior, but he or she still needs to assess the customer's perceived value before establishing price. In the case of the new product, its economic value can be computed as $1,300:

$1,700.00 total cost of customer's present machine
+ 100.00 incremental cost increase

$1,800.00
− 200.00 training costs
− 300.00 additional postpurchase costs

$1,300.00 new total economic value

This type of approach to understanding the customer's economic value is useful in that it forces the marketer to see the buyer's position. This empathy, in turn, is necessary if price is to be accepted, and it should be applied before making a major commitment to any product.[8]

Exchange or Negotiated Value The organizational buyer may also perceive an exchange or negotiated value. An exchange value is common in business marketing and occurs when the customer perceives a certain value of a product based on a position of strength or weakness in the negotiation process. For example, a buyer may purchase from two suppliers. By playing one against the other, a more favorable price may be obtained. In such a case, perceived value may be based more on what the buyer feels that he or she can negotiate rather than on strict economic value. Negotiation is developed in more detail later in this chapter.

Aesthetic Value   Contrary to popular belief, many business products and services have aesthetic value. Aesthetic value occurs when one product, service, or supplier is seen as more attractive than others. For example, a buyer may wish to buy from innovative suppliers who are considered industry leaders. When this situation occurs, the buyer may subconsciously place a higher aesthetic value on one company's products than on competitors' products, even though all may meet specifications.

Relative or Comparative Value   Organizational buyers often determine a product's value by comparing it with others. Such factors as quality, service, technical assistance, physical distribution service, warranties, and sales assistance may affect the perceived value of one product over another. These factors explain why buyers are sometimes willing to pay more for one product than for another, even when they are technically the same. For example, certainty of delivery may provide the buyer with a higher perceived value of one product versus another.

Determining the value of a product or service to a business customer is complex and arduous, as this discussion has pointed out. Nevertheless, it must be done, since the buyer will make the purchase decision on this basis. Customer value is a basic and necessary element in business pricing, and prices should be based on the value of a product to the customer—a concept marketing people understand.[9] A good example can be seen in IBM's adoption of "value-based" pricing for its software products, in which the price an organization pays for a software program depends on the size of its computer. Prices rise as the size of the computer increases. Previously, IBM charged the same price for identical programs regardless of the computer on which they ran.[10]

It is often argued that an emphasis on price as a reflection of customer value will allow for greater flexibility in pricing.[11] This is logical in that customers will ultimately accept or reject a particular product or service based on an evaluation of its price against their value estimate. Pricing without good insight to customer value would seem to be flawed. Most business marketers understand the importance of customer value in effective pricing but there is evidence to suggest that many business marketing companies do not address the subject in a systematic, strategic fashion.[12] A study of business marketing firms in Florida revealed that the two major ways of estimating customer value were by managerial judgment and informal customer feedback.[13]

A number of reasons account for the lack of use of customer value in determining prices in business markets. First, it is a difficult process, as can be seen in the example developed earlier, and it gets even more difficult when multiple markets are involved. Second, there is a lack of tools or models that can be used to determine customer value. The most basic economic concept for understanding customer price behavior is elasticity of demand, but this is not sufficient when variables other than price become involved. Third, studies have shown that business marketers tend to place more emphasis on costs and profit objectives than on customer value when setting prices.[14] Thus, while it is generally acknowledged that customer value is one of the most important considerations in pricing business goods and services, there is little evidence to conclude that it is being used with very much effectiveness. There are, however, exceptions, as can be seen in the previously cited IBM software products example, and advantages exist for those marketers who are able to determine such values.

Competition

Of the six considerations affecting pricing, competition may command the most attention by business marketing firms. One study found that pricers of business goods rated aspects of competitive-level pricing above all other factors. Competitive-level pricing such as matching or beating competitors was seen as the single most important factor in pricing.[15] A study of the pricing practices of sixty-seven Canadian business marketing firms found that even when prices were determined systematically, they were then adjusted to match those of competitors. If competitive prices could not be matched, the products were not marketed.[16] This behavior appears to be quite common in business marketing: For one reason or another, the pricer accepts a price set by competition. The pricing decision maker then adjusts to that price by trying to obtain a desired profit margin by bringing down costs within the competitive price constraint. This process probably occurs because of the previously discussed difficulty in determining customer value and the assumption that competitive prices reflect this demand.

Competition plays a large role when a business marketing manager contemplates price increases or decreases. Competitors will then react to such moves, and their anticipated reactions affect the value of the decision. For example, if the manager increases the price of a product and the competition does not follow, the product may be priced out of the market. On the other hand, if price is decreased and competitors follow suit, a price war takes place. Price wars in business marketing benefit nobody in most cases. Because industry demand for many goods and services is inelastic due to derived demand, market shares do not increase, and profits suffer. Thus, threats of competitive reactions keep prices stable in many business markets. Since no company gains by price changes in such situations, the emphasis often shifts to nonprice competition.

The exception to this situation occurs when the marketing manager initiating the price increase works for the company that is the industry price leader. Price leaders are quite common in business markets. The paper industry provides a good example. In this industry, there are several price leaders, because different companies have strong commitments to different types of paper. To illustrate, Abitibi-Price is a price leader in newsprint, St. Regis is a price leader in linerboard, and Great Northern is a price leader in uncoated groundwood papers. Successful price leaders in the paper industry tend to share the following characteristics:[17]

1. A large productive capacity
2. A large market share
3. A strong commitment to particular types of paper
4. New, cost-efficient mills

5. Strong distribution systems

6. Good customer relations

7. An effective market information system

8. Sensitivity to the price and profit needs of the rest of the industry

9. A good sense of timing

10. Sound management organization for pricing

11. Effective product-line financial controls

12. An awareness of the legal issues involved

Contrary to popular belief, the largest firm in the industry is not automatically the price leader, although it can be. Furthermore, the company that is the price leader for one product in an industry is not necessarily the price leader for other products in that industry. Being a price leader is dependent on competitors' willingness to follow. Three factors appear to be necessary for a company to be accepted as a price leader in the case of a price increase. First, the industry must believe that the demand for the product is such that a price increase will not reduce the total size of the market for that product. Second, all major suppliers in the industry must share this belief. Third, the industry must feel that the price increase is for the good of the entire industry and not just for the good of the company initiating the price increase. If these factors are absent, the company initiating the price increase will find itself with a price greater than prices of competitors that did not follow. Many business marketing managers have been in this situation. Obviously, the phenomenon causes great risk if the manager's firm is not the price leader.

The use of price decreases as a business marketing tool makes sense only when product or service demand is relatively elastic, overall revenues will be increased, and competitors will not automatically follow and even undercut. Thus, because of competition, price decreases are very risky, and they should not be attempted unless the manager is reasonably certain that competition cannot or will not retaliate and that demand is relatively elastic.

Price decreases sometimes can be employed to the marketer's benefit, as when the cost structures of competitors are known to be higher and when those competitors cannot match price decreases because of adverse effects on their desired profit margins. When competitors are operating at a high percentage of production capacity and have ample backlogs of orders, they may not retaliate because they do not need the additional business at that particular time. If competitors cannot match a price decrease until they retool or retrain employees and so forth, it may mean increased sales to the marketing manager. Small companies can often use price decreases against their larger competitors, because the latter will not retaliate for fear that reacting will trigger an industrywide price war. Large companies sometimes will not react to price decreases because of fear of antitrust or other governmental intervention, which enables smaller competitors to use price decreases to advantage.

Use of examples such as these is dangerous, as miscalculations can have dire effects on marketing strategy. They are provided only to show the importance of competition in business pricing decisions. Any pricing decision made without assessing competitive reaction is probably incomplete and can lead to marketing failure. The marketing manager must obtain information on every major competitor and its pricing behavior before making any pricing decisions. Only when this task is accomplished can the manager reasonably expect price increases or decreases to result in success. Of course, such information may be incorporated into the company's marketing information system, so that a continuous flow of such data is available.

Competition plays a restrictive role in the pricing of business goods and services. Pricing above competitive levels is difficult unless the product or service involved can be differentiated enough to increase its value to the customer. Because of specifications, such differentiation is often not easy to accomplish. Within the confines of perceived customer value, competition thus further restricts the range of prices that the marketing manager can consider. A price that is consistent with a buyer's value but is above competitors' prices may be detrimental to the rest of the marketing mix.

Exhibit 17.1 provides an example of the importance of competition in pricing in business markets. In this situation, while the product had distinct advantages over competing products, the key to success lay in pricing it in a very competitive manner since competition was seen as more important than the increased value to the customer. But penetration pricing like this is not necessarily the rule. For example, EDS won a long-term contract with a Japanese firm on the basis of EDS's technological expertise, not low price.

EXHIBIT 17.1 The Importance of Competitor Price in the Marketing of Commodity Products in Business Markets

---

A good example of the importance of competitor price in business marketing may be seen when Eastman Kodak Company developed teflon-coated floppy computer diskettes. Traditional diskettes could be damaged by spills, fingerprints, smudges, etc., but the new teflon-coated product was not affected by such mishaps because the teflon coating allowed such stains, smudges, etc., to be simply wiped off the diskette. In introducing the product, Kodak officials termed it "the most exciting floppy disk innovation in the past decade."

The teflon-coated diskette enjoyed a distinct benefit over its traditional competitors because its teflon coating was almost like an "insurance policy" against the data loss that was possible with existing diskettes. Despite this advantage, the key factor in the product's success was seen to be in its pricing. To quote one market analyst, "The key to the new disk's success in the highly competitive floppy disk market will be its price." Many thought success would be dependent on how close Kodak priced the diskettes to existing competitive products. It was felt that if the new product could be price competitive, it could gain a significant share of the market. Based on this thinking, Kodak entered the market with a price about 15 percent higher than the price of its own traditional diskette.

Source: Adapted from "Price Could Be Sticking Point on Teflon Disks, Analysts Say," *San Diego Union,* October 11, 1987, D1.

Costs

Customer value typically sets the upper limit on the price the business marketing manager can charge, and cost considerations normally determine the lower limit. To price without considering cost makes little sense, and few business pricers do so. On the contrary, too many managers use cost almost exclusively as the basis of their prices. The fixed and variable costs of producing and marketing the product or service are determined, and then a desired profit margin is tacked on for the final selling price. Basically, this type of pricing amounts to complete emphasis on the company's supply curve and almost no emphasis on the demand curve.

An estimated one-fourth of U.S. business marketing firms use some form of a "cost-plus" approach to pricing.[18] The previously cited survey of the pricing practices of Canadian business marketing companies showed that 52 percent used a cost-plus system.[19] Cost-plus pricing appears to be widely used by those companies that do little research on their pricing. Studies have shown that many firms employ cost-plus pricing based on past cost data and future cost estimates plus a recognized profit margin that remains stable over time. This profit margin is considered normal for those operations. In addition, many business marketing companies marketing to governmental and institutional customers have used forms of cost-plus pricing such as cost plus fixed fee, cost-incentive contracts, cost plus incentive fee, cost plus award fee, cost only, and cost-sharing contracts. When prices are set under these constraints, cost is the basic element in the prices charged.

The point is not that the business marketing manager should price using the cost-plus method but rather that cost must be incorporated into the final price with other elements such as customer value and competition. The most common method for achieving this integration is by **break-even analysis.** In simple terms, break-even analysis tells the manager how many units must be sold at a given price to break even or to cover total costs. Break-even analysis provides a useful tool for gauging the relative feasibility of various prices.

Break-even analysis is a common financial tool and does not require an indepth discussion in this text. To employ this concept, the marketing manager must know the fixed and variable costs involved with the production and marketing of a single product or service and also the price under consideration. To illustrate, assume the manager of a company marketing an OEM component part wishes to price a product at $25.95. Given fixed costs of $400,000 and variable costs of $7.85 per unit, how many units must be sold to break even? The answer is 22,099 units, which is computed as follows:

$$\$25.95x = \$400,000 + \$7.85x$$
$$\$18.10x = \$400,000$$
$$x = 22,099 \text{ units}$$

Table 17.2 shows break-even analysis applied to a range of six possible prices. As the table illustrates, if the manager considers dropping the $25.95

TABLE 17.2   Price and Cost Relationships

	Price					
	1	2	3	4	5	6
Unit selling price	$ 19.95	$ 21.95	$ 23.95	$ 25.95	$ 27.95	$ 29.95
Unit variable cost	7.85	7.85	7.85	7.85	7.85	7.85
Unit contribution	12.10	14.10	16.10	18.10	20.10	22.10
Estimated sales	30,000	27,500	25,000	22,500	20,000	18,000
Revenue	598,500	603,625	598,750	583,875	559,000	539,100
Fixed costs	400,000	400,000	400,000	400,000	400,000	400,000
Variable costs	235,500	215,875	196,250	176,625	157,000	141,300
Profit (loss)	(37,000)	(12,250)	2,500	7,250	2,000	(2,200)
Break-even (units)	33,058	28,369	24,845	22,099	19,900	18,100

price to $23.95, then 24,845 units must be sold to break even. The value of this type of analysis may be realized when the units required to break even at each price are compared with the units that are estimated to be purchased at that price. This concept is also illustrated in Table 17.2. For example, at the $19.95 price, customers are expected to purchase 30,000 units. To break even at this price, however, 33,058 units must be sold. If the $19.95 price is used, a loss of $37,000 will occur. Analysis of the table reveals that estimated unit sales exceed the break-even point only at $23.95, $25.95, and $27.95. In terms of profitability, the optimum price is $25.95. This discussion emphasizes the importance of cost in business pricing. Pricing without correct cost considerations can be a major error. Pricing solely on the basis of cost, however, makes just as little marketing sense. Proper pricing involves the integration of cost with the other factors discussed in this section.

A concept that deserves mention at this point is that of **life cycle costing.** This is a method of calculating costs over the life span of the product.[20] For example, assume that the business marketer is attempting to price the OEM component illustrated in Table 17.2. Assume also that this component is expected to have a five-year life. What effects will this five-year period have on fixed and variable costs? Will the fixed cost remain at $400,000 and the variable cost at $7.85 per unit for all five years? Or will those costs grow at some rate over time? To illustrate, what if electricity costs are expected to escalate at a rate of 8 percent per year? Life cycle costing reflects rising costs of labor, materials, etc., over the expected life span of the product. While life cycle costing complicates the task of determining true costs, it can be seen also that the concept more realistically reflects true costs.

Table 17.3 illustrates cost changes over the five-year period based on expected increases in costs of 5 percent per year. As can be seen, the product could not be priced at $25.95 over the five-year life cycle due to the expected increase in costs. Thus, while the $25.95 price was seen as the most optimum in Table 17.2, it can now be seen that this would not be feasible if the product had a

---

TABLE 17.3   Life Cycle Costs in Business Marketing

Year	Estimated Sales	Sales	Fixed Costs	Variable Costs	Total Costs	Profit (Loss)
1	22,500	$583,875	$400,000	$176,625	$576,625	$ 7,250
2	22,500	583,875	420,000	185,400	605,400	(21,525)
3	22,500	583,875	441,000	194,625	635,625	(51,750)
4	22,500	583,875	463,050	204,525	667,575	(83,700)
5	22,500	583,875	486,203	214,650	700,853	(116,978)

Note: Based on a unit sales price of $25.95, a unit variable cost of $7.85, and fixed costs of $400,000 in the first year subject to a 5% increase in costs each year.

projected five-year life span. This subject of life cycle costing will again be addressed when the concept of target return pricing is addressed. At this point, all that is necessary is to recognize that costs will change over the life cycle of a product or service and this must be addressed in the pricing decision.

A good example of what can happen when costs are not fully understood occurred when an industry leader watched a small competitor cut steadily into its business with lower prices. Analysis of competitive products revealed that material content, quality, performance characteristics, and presumably costs were essentially the same. Completely overlooking its bloated overhead costs, management concluded that its cost structure and that of the smaller competitor were the same and that the smaller firm was simply willing to operate at little or no profit. Following this line of thinking, management felt that time would work in its favor and would lead the smaller competitor to financial problems. This situation didn't happen, however, and the competitor flourished at the leader's expense, primarily because its overhead costs were considerably lower and it was able to generate high profit margins with the lower prices.[21] Such an example aptly illustrates the point that business pricers must stay current on cost if effective pricing is to take place.

Another point should be made regarding cost in business pricing. When a business marketing firm's costs are higher than those of competitors, pricing competitively becomes difficult, which often negatively affects sales and profits. A good example can be seen in the case of manufacturers of electronic subassemblies. The cost to manufacture and assemble these products in the United States was $140. However, the cost to assemble the U.S. components in Mexico was $91, and the cost to assemble them in Taiwan with U.S. and Asian components was $85. These figures included costs of components (both U.S. and Asian), labor, transportation, and tariffs.[22] For a U.S. manufacturer to use cost-plus pricing in this case could result in a large decrease in market share.

Some business marketers use market segmentation to adapt to cost constraints. For example, Chandler & Farquar Company, Inc., of Boston bases its pricing on cost plus margin but actively seeks out small and mid-size customers who will pay that margin. The company has larger customers, but they pressure the company for lower margins. Therefore, Chandler & Farquar protects itself with customers who accept the margin objectives. The problem with such an approach is that the firm is vulnerable to competitors who offer lower prices.[23]

Company Pricing Objectives

The marketing manager's pricing decisions should be in accordance with company pricing objectives, which typically are derived from overall corporate and marketing objectives and may differ from company to company. U.S. companies commonly use the following five pricing objectives, which apply to business marketing firms as well as to consumer marketing organizations: (1) pricing to achieve a target return on investment, (2) stabilization of price or margin, (3) pricing to maintain or improve market position, (4) pricing to meet or follow competition, and (5) pricing related to product differentiation. A brief discussion of each is worthwhile.

Target Return Pricing **Target return pricing** means that the manager views the pricing of a product as a capital investment project. Investment in the product is determined and its anticipated life cycle is estimated. Sales and profit at various possible prices over the life cycle are investigated to determine which prices, if any, will yield the desired return on investment. This type of pricing objective is common in business markets. In the paper industry, for example, companies that use this approach start with a rate of return they consider satisfactory. They then set a price that allows them to earn that return when their plant utilization is at some standard rate, typically around 90 percent. This industry often defines *return on investment* as the ratio of income to total operating assets.[24] Because of the prominence of this form of pricing, it is developed in detail later in the chapter. An example of target return pricing may be seen in the case of Alcoa, which once had a principal pricing objective of 10 percent return on investment after taxes.[25]

Pricing to Stabilize Price or Margin While price stabilization and margin stabilization are often listed together, they are not technically the same thing. An objective to stabilize price means that the business marketer attempts to keep prices stable in the marketplace and to compete on nonprice considerations. An example of this might be Kennecott, whose principal pricing objective at one time was "stabilization of prices."[26] Stabilization of margin is basically a cost-plus approach whereby the marketer attempts to maintain the same margin regardless of changes in cost.

Market Share Pricing With a **market share pricing** objective, the manager uses price to increase, maintain, or even decrease market share. A company wishing to increase its market share may use penetration pricing to accomplish this end while a firm trying to maintain its market share may use a skimming pricing approach. An example of this can be seen in the case of American Can, whose principal pricing objective at one time was stated as "maintenance of market share."[27]

Competitive Pricing **Competitive pricing** objectives occur when a company wishes to determine its prices by following or beating competitors' prices. This practice is often exemplified in situations in which "follow the leader" pricing takes place. An example of this was National Steel, whose principal pricing objective at one time was stated as "matching the market price follower."[28] What this implied was that National Steel would increase its price, not when the price leader raised price, but after others in the industry followed the leader.

Pricing Related to Product Differentiation   Some companies base their pricing objectives on a desire to differentiate the product or service under consideration. High-quality products are thus priced in a premium manner, and products that cannot be differentiated by price may reflect prices closer to those of competitors. A good example of this can be seen in Exhibit 17.1 where Eastman Kodak priced its teflon-coated diskettes at a 15 percent premium because it felt the product was better than competitive offerings.

Studies that have been conducted into the pricing of business marketing firms indicate that the most common of these objectives are target return pricing and variations of cost-plus objectives.[29]

Company pricing objectives such as these affect actual pricing decisions. For example, at one time U.S. Steel's primary price objective was to attain an 8 percent return on investment after taxes. Its secondary objectives were stable price, stable margin, and to maintain a market share of 30 percent. At this same time, National Steel had a primary objective of matching the market price follower and a secondary objective to increase market share.[30] Thus, the prices set by these two competitors differed, even when identical products were involved. Such differences were not caused by product or customer differences but by differing pricing objectives. The pricing decision of the manager or the pricing analyst should integrate these objectives into customer value, competitive, and cost considerations.

Company Top Management

Top management in many business marketing companies exerts great influence over prices attached to their products. Although the actual pricing decisions often are made in the sales or marketing department, these prices are commonly reviewed in some manner by company top management. The previously cited Canadian survey of sixty-seven companies revealed that the sales or marketing department was responsible for making the pricing decision in 52 percent of those firms, the finance department made the pricing decision in 26 percent of the firms, and the production department made the decision in 19 percent of the firms. All sixty-seven firms confirmed that pricing decisions were reviewed by senior management, and 84 percent of the companies cited a committee decision in such reviews. Moreover, 70 percent claimed that established prices could only be changed by those people who had initially set them.[31] Although this sample is admittedly small, it appears typical of the behavior in many business marketing firms.

Price is important, and it is something that everyone relates to; thus, top managements tend to become involved in pricing decisions, whereas they may never affect marketing decisions regarding channels, sales promotion, and so on. Therefore, pricing decisions are often affected by top management preferences, desires, expectations, and whims, which the business marketing manager must be able to anticipate and react to if his or her own pricing convictions differ.

Government

Government at all levels, but especially at the federal level, may have considerable influence on the pricing practices of business marketing managers. This area is quite complex and cannot be covered in full in a text of this size; however, some of the major considerations are addressed. Basically, government can affect a business marketing company's pricing in the following ways: (1) through taxes, which can directly and indirectly affect the price being charged; (2) through legislation or threat of legislation; (3) through sales of stockpiled strategic materials such as copper, aluminum, and zinc; (4) as a customer (and usually a large one); and (5) through the threat of reduced or curtailed purchases if a price increase by a supplier is enacted. Development of some of these factors may be helpful for better understanding the role government plays in pricing in business markets.

The federal government has stockpiled strategic materials at 130 locations across the country for use as emergency reserves in case of war. Some ninety-one materials are stockpiled, primarily in the Midwest. These stockpiles have been maintained in various sizes and composition since officially established in 1946. The bulk of stockpiled materials is made up of aluminum, metallurgical-grade bauxite, metallurgical-grade chromite, cobalt, industrial diamond bort and stones, lead, magnesium, metallurgical-grade manganese, molybdenum, quartz crystals, tin, tungsten, and zinc. Other stockpiled materials include copper, fibers, mica, cadmium, beryl, castor oil, fluorite, iodine, jewel bearings, mercury, platinum, rubber, silicon carbide, silver, titanium, vanadium, and tannin. Although the original idea was to use such materials in case of war, they were used during the Nixon administration to alleviate shortages in the economy and to fight inflation. When the reserves are sold into the marketplace, supply is increased, and prices are driven downward. This type of behavior can affect the pricer of products similar to the stockpiled products. The government does not actually have to sell its reserves to bring about the desired change; sometimes the threat to do so is enough to influence a company not to increase prices.

As a customer, government also affects prices of some business goods and services. It does so directly with such contracts as cost plus fixed fee, in which it dictates the price that will be charged. Government also can indirectly affect prices of some goods in business markets. For example, a firm selling the same product to both commercial or institutional customers and large government buying organizations such as the General Services Administration (GSA) may find that the large governmental purchases allow the firm to take advantage of economies of scale and produce all items at a lower unit cost. Such governmental purchases, in turn, permit the company to charge lower prices to its other customers. In addition, when government is a customer, it can react to price increases by threatening to stop its purchasing from the supplier enacting the increase. Obviously, this threat has a definite influence on the pricing decision involved.

One of the main influences of government on pricing lies in the area of legislation. Again, this area is complex, but the following are major areas of federal pricing legislation that affect every business marketing manager.

Sections 1 and 2 of the Sherman Antitrust Act forbid agreements among suppliers to fix prices in their industry, and violations carry a fine, imprisonment, or both, as well as triple damages to parties injured by the violation. In 1974, Congress amended the Sherman Act to make criminal violations a felony. This amendment increased the maximum penalty for an individual up to a fine of $100,000 or up to three years in prison, or both.[32] Perhaps the best-remembered example of price fixing occurred in 1961, when charges were brought against twenty-nine firms in the electrical equipment industry. These firms were fined a total of $2 million. In addition, seven senior-level executives received jail sentences, and twenty-four others received suspended sentences. More recently, price fixing charges were brought against seven defendants in the paper label industry. In this case, the judge sentenced executives to give speeches before civic groups on the wrongs of price fixing.

Not all charges end up in convictions. The government dropped charges when it found that four companies under investigation in the iron ore and steel industries controlled a much smaller share of the iron ore pellet market than suspected.[33] Still, price fixing does not appear to be unusual in business markets, and the government is constantly looking for and finding instances of bid rigging or of competing companies that agree to set minimum prices.

Section 2 of the Clayton Antitrust Act and the Robinson-Patman amendment to the Clayton Act are also very important to the business marketing manager in that they prohibit price discrimination among similar buyers of identical products. Sections 2(a) through 2(f) of the Robinson-Patman Act (as it is more commonly called) specifically relate to different prices and price concessions offered to customers, distributors, and manufacturers' representatives. Because business marketing uses discounts, rebates, commissions, and so on in arriving at net prices from list prices, the marketing manager must be aware of these laws and how they restrict pricing decisions.

The Borah-Van Nuys amendment is now Section 3 of the Robinson-Patman Act, and it specifically prohibits general price discriminations, geographic price discriminations, and the use of unreasonably low prices to drive out competition. Some states also have laws that prohibit conspiring to fix prices, such as California's Cartwright Act. All told, there is no doubt that government influences the pricing decisions of many business marketing managers. The astute manager must know and understand these laws.

Summary of Business Pricing Considerations

Prices in business marketing often seem to be compromises between what the customer will pay, what competition will allow, what costs will permit, what is consistent with company pricing objectives, what top management will agree to, and what government will allow. The task of the business marketing manager and those responsible for pricing is somehow to integrate all of these constraints into a base price for every product or service involved.

There is concern over how well this integration is being performed in business markets. Many business marketing companies rarely have attempted pricing that is not based mainly on cost. Only recently have some firms recognized that the old ways of pricing should be analyzed and probably changed.[34] To quote another authority:

> I would argue that the place where American marketers are the weakest is in the developing of good pricing procedures because they haven't institutionalized a very tight process to make such decisions. Companies fail because they lack a systematic approach to pricing.[35]

More specifically, ineffective pricing decisions occur because companies lack reliable data regarding (1) customer value, (2) competitive actions and reactions, and (3) appropriate costs, or they do not fully integrate pricing into the total marketing mix. When any combination of these elements is lacking, the pricing decision is incomplete.

Effective pricing requires sound accounting, financial, and market data as well as information on competitors' actual and expected prices, cost structures, and capacity utilization. In addition, the manager must possess insight into buyers' reactions to price and a sound understanding of the company's own corporate objectives. Underlying all of these factors should be a consistent marketing strategy that includes price.[36]

Discussion so far has focused on some of the more generalized aspects of pricing in business markets. It is now time to discuss areas of particular relevance to business marketing that pertain to pricing. In this regard, attention will now be focused on six areas of particular importance. These are: (1) techniques used in pricing in business markets, (2) list and net prices, (3) bidding, (4) negotiated pricing, (5) leasing, and (6) new developments in pricing in business marketing with particular attention to partnering relationships and JIT.

PRICING TECHNIQUES USED IN BUSINESS MARKETS

Business marketing pricers, just as their consumer counterparts, use a number of techniques in pricing business goods and services. A look at some of the more widely accepted techniques is in order.

Break-Even Analysis

Using break-even analysis as a pricing technique is not restricted to business marketing. It is also used by many consumer marketing firms. However, since it does have applications to business markets, it should be discussed here in at least a cursory manner. An easy way to illustrate its use is to refer back to Table 17.2 where the business marketer is considering six possible prices for his or her product. Given prices ranging from $19.95 to $29.95 per unit, a unit variable cost of $7.85, fixed costs of $400,000, and forecasted sales for each price, the manager can now compute the break-even point in units for each price. As the table shows, at $19.95 the firm would have to sell 33,058 units to break even, but the firm's demand analysis shows that only 30,000 units can be expected to be sold at this price. Thus, the firm cannot expect to sell enough units to break even indicating that the $19.95 price is not feasible. The same is true for the $21.95 and $29.95 prices, leaving only three prices—$23.95, $25.95, and $27.95—where demand exceeds the break-even point. Of these three, the table shows that the highest profits are at the $25.95 price and this is where the price would be set. As can be seen, the break-even technique is useful in selecting among possible prices and provides a good tool for integrating cost and demand in the pricing decision.

An important point should be made here. This analysis is based on estimates of demand and cost. For example, the firm expects to sell 30,000 units at the $19.95 price. What if demand is underestimated and the firm can actually sell 60,000 units? The same applies to both fixed and variable costs. What if either or both of these increase or decrease unexpectedly? In other words, break-even analysis as a pricing technique is only as good as the data on which it is based. Another factor to be considered is that these same data may in some cases be influenced by the marketing manager. For example, might not a sales or advertising campaign increase demand to over 30,000 units? If so, what would be the effects of such a campaign on variable costs? Such actions would dictate a recalculation of the break-even point, but the same principles are still involved. For most business marketers, the break-even technique is relatively simple to understand and easy to use, which accounts for its wide usage in business marketing.

Learning or Experience Curves

A related technique is that of the **learning or experience curve.** This concept holds that production costs decline as output rises, not so much because of economies of scale but because workers and machines "learn" with time and "experience" how to produce more efficiently. The result is a lower unit variable cost figure per item produced. One estimate is that every time experience is doubled (as measured by cumulative volume) costs go down 20 percent to 30 percent.[37] But such reductions are not automatic, nor are they necessarily similar from one situation to another. It is a logical concept, however, in that cost reductions would occur when engineering and production become more efficient with experience. Thus, the experience or learning curve applies to a lowering of the unit variable cost figure and thus directly affects pricing.

To see how this technique works, refer again to Table 17.2. There it can be seen what happens when the unit variable cost is $7.85. Assume now that, because of the experience curve, this cost can be lowered to $6.85. Table 17.4 shows the effects of this reduced unit variable cost figure when all else remains the same.

TABLE 17.4   Price and Cost Relationships Using the Learning or Experience Curve

	Price					
	1	2	3	4	5	6
Unit selling price	$ 19.95	$ 21.95	$ 23.95	$ 25.95	$ 27.95	$ 29.95
Unit variable cost	6.85	6.85	6.85	6.85	6.85	6.85
Unit contribution	13.10	15.10	17.10	19.10	21.10	23.10
Estimated sales	30,000	27,500	25,000	22,500	20,000	18,000
Revenue	598,500	603,625	598,750	583,875	559,000	539,100
Fixed costs	400,000	400,000	400,000	400,000	400,000	400,000
Variable costs	205,500	188,375	171,250	154,125	137,000	123,300
Profit (loss)	(7,000)	15,250	27,500	29,750	22,000	15,800
Break-even (units)	30,534	26,490	23,392	20,942	18,957	17,316

The impact of this variable cost reduction is impressive: At the $25.95 price, profit increases from $7,250 to $29,750. The marketing manager may now maintain the $25.95 price and assume the additional profit, or the manager may consider dropping the price and passing some or all of the savings on to customers. For example, if the price is dropped as low as $21.95, profit is still doubled—from $7,250 to $15,250. If the $23.95 price is adopted, profit is $27,500. The decision as to which price to use depends on competitive prices and allegiances to customers. The $25.95 price may be retained if customers do not react negatively and if competitors are unable to make inroads. If, however, the lower price offers the company a distinct competitive advantage and a more favorable image with customers, that option may be selected. There is always the danger that predicted cost reductions may not take place, and the manager must be aware of this possibility. On the other hand, maintaining a high price even when costs decrease is dangerous in that it invites competitors to offer lower prices. Moving down the experience curve can maintain market share and profit and preempt competitors.[38]

Target Return Pricing Techniques

As stated earlier in this chapter, target return pricing is common in business marketing. One estimate is that over one-half of all U.S. business marketing firms use some form of target return pricing. Target return pricing occurs when a company develops a set of product or service prices designed to provide a predetermined return on capital employed in the production and distribution of whatever goods or services are involved.[39] Some firms use target return pricing to price single products in a single year; others use it for longer-run purposes. Some apply it to single products or services while others apply it to all their products and services. Some companies use the concept in a very rigid manner and others use it as a benchmark for their pricing. Regardless of the manner in which it is used, it can be seen that target return pricing is widely used in business marketing and thus deserves attention here.

Controversy exists over this approach to pricing because of the many different techniques marketers use to compute target market returns. There are probably as many methods used to calculate return figures as there are firms using this approach. For example, some companies price to achieve a desired return on investment (ROI), whereas others do so to attain a predetermined return on assets (ROA). Many different computational techniques are used, as there is no single accepted definition of what constitutes return on investment. The following is one approach:[40]

$$\text{Selling price} = DVC + \frac{F}{X} + \frac{rK}{X}$$

where

DVC = direct unit variable costs
F = fixed cost

X = standard unit volume
r = desired return rate
K = capital (total operating assets)

Assume the marketing manager wishes a 15 percent return and determines that (1) direct unit variable costs are $10.00, (2) fixed costs are $100,000, (3) total operating assets are $200,000, and (4) volume is 1,000 units. Given these factors, what price will provide the desired 15 percent return? By plugging these figures into the formula, a $140.00 price can be determined:

$$\text{Selling price} = \$10.00 + \frac{\$100,000}{1,000} + \frac{0.15 \times \$200,000}{1,000} = \$140.00$$

Simplified approaches such as this formula are common, but they fail to consider the time value of money. For example, suppose a firm expects to sell 1,000 units over a five-year period. It is theoretically incorrect to assume that the value to the marketing firm of units sold at $140.00 in the fifth year is the same as that received in the first year. The time value of money should be considered in any returns computations. The most accepted method for accomplishing this task involves discounting annual profits to their present value and dividing that figure by the initial investment. This approach can be adapted to the pricing of business products when ROI, for example, is desired for benchmark purposes. Evidence indicates that many marketing managers in business markets use ROI as a screening device for pricing.[41] Thus, these managers establish an acceptable return figure and then determine whether or not various prices attached to products or product lines will achieve that desired return. If so, the price is accepted, and the product is marketed. If not and costs cannot be adjusted downward, the product may be dropped, since no price will help achieve the desired return. This practice is what is meant by benchmark return pricing.

An example is useful in explaining this concept. Assume the marketing manager is considering the introduction of a new product. The initial investment in production and marketing is determined to be $220,000, and the equipment involved is expected to have a salvage value of $10,000 at the end of an expected ten-year life cycle. Fixed costs are estimated at $10,000 per year, and unit variable costs are projected to be $100.00. The manager desires a 12 percent return after taxes, which are expected to be in the 34 percent bracket. Unit sales are forecasted over the ten-year period as shown in Table 17.5, based on a $950.00 selling price. Should the manager market the product at the $950.00 price?

Table 17.5 shows the computations that would be involved to answer the question. If the manager's facts and forecasted data are correct, the decision should be made to price the product at $950.00 per unit. At this price, the present value of future benefits exceeds the initial investment—therefore, the 12 percent return objective is realized. If the present value figure were less than $220,000 and no other price were feasible, the decision might have been to drop the product.

Earlier in this chapter, the topic of life cycle costing was discussed. Now it

TABLE 17.5   Target Return Pricing Technique Computations

Year	Number of Units Demanded	Gross Sales	Fixed Costs	Variable Costs	Total Costs	Gross Profits	Tax Adjustment 1 − 0.34	After-Tax Profits	Present Value at 12%	Discounted Profits
1	52	$ 49,400	$10,000	$ 5,200	$15,200	$ 34,200	0.66	$22,572	0.89	$ 20,089
2	65	61,750	10,000	6,500	16,500	45,250	0.66	29,865	0.80	23,892
3	80	76,000	10,000	8,000	18,000	58,000	0.66	38,280	0.71	27,179
4	109	103,550	10,000	10,900	20,900	82,650	0.66	54,549	0.64	34,911
5	131	124,450	10,000	13,100	23,100	101,350	0.66	66,891	0.57	38,128
6	136	129,200	10,000	13,600	23,600	105,600	0.66	69,696	0.51	35,545
7	101	95,950	10,000	10,100	20,100	75,850	0.66	50,061	0.45	22,527
8	62	58,900	10,000	6,200	16,200	42,700	0.66	28,182	0.40	11,273
9	46	43,700	10,000	4,600	14,600	29,100	0.66	19,206	0.36	6,914
10	21	19,950	10,000	2,100	12,100	7,850	0.66	5,181	0.32	1,658

Total present value of anticipated profits from sales 222,116

Present value of salvage ($10,000 × 0.32) 3,200

Total present value of anticipated profits from sales plus salvage 225,316

can be tied into the target return pricing technique. Referring back to Table 17.5, what would happen if fixed and variable costs were expected to escalate at a rate of 1 percent per year? Or 3 percent or 5 percent per year? If such escalations take place, would the price of $950.00 still achieve the desired 12 percent return on investment? Table 17.6 shows the effects of the three possible cost increases on the total present value of anticipated profits from sales plus salvage. Given the initial investment of $220,000, the table shows that the $950.00 price still achieves the ROI objective even if costs increase by 1 percent per year. But the same is not the case with the 3 percent and 5 percent annual increases. If a 3 percent annual increase is expected, the present value of $217,522 is less than the initial investment and thus the product should not be priced at $950.00 per unit. Life cycle costing is easily integrated into this target return pricing technique as the latter contains all the information required.[42]

It is also possible to work the learning or experience curve into this technique. For example, if the marketer knew that every time experience was doubled variable costs would decrease by a certain percent, that too could be integrated. And, of course, both an escalation rate and a learning curve could take place at the same time. Regardless, the technique would work in the same basic manner.

An example of the use of target return pricing in the paper industry aids in understanding this approach. Companies that use target return pricing start with a rate of return on investment that they deem satisfactory. They then set a price that allows them to earn that return when their plant utilization is at some "standard" rate, typically a little over 90 percent. *Return on investment* usually is defined as the ratio of income to total operating assets and usually has an inflation premium built into it.[43]

TABLE 17.6   **Target Return Pricing Technique Using Life Cycle Costing**

Year	Discounted Profits with a 1% Expected Annual Increase in Costs	Discounted Profits with a 3% Expected Annual Increase in Costs	Discounted Profits with a 5% Expected Annual Increase in Costs
1	$ 20,089	$ 20,089	$ 20,089
2	23,841	23,631	23,456
3	27,010	26,665	26,314
4	34,645	34,093	33,520
5	37,778	37,037	36,255
6	35,144	34,280	33,350
7	22,165	21,369	20,497
8	10,968	10,290	9,532
9	6,630	5,989	5,283
10	1,420	879	249
Salvage	3,200	3,200	3,200
Total	$222,890	$217,522	$211,745

Target return pricing is quite common in business marketing for a number of reasons. First, it allows the marketing manager to use the principles of capital budgeting in the pricing of products, so that new products or services are treated as investments rather than expenses. The manager can thus treat new and existing offerings just as he or she would any other capital investment in which capital funds are expended. Target return pricing also enables managers to compare performances of products and services by giving them all a common denominator—a required target return figure. As can be seen in the example, target return pricing is not easy to implement, and its use can be risky if costs are not accurate or if demand schedules are unreliable. Properly used, however, such a technique can prevent product losses through poor pricing. In fact, target return pricing may be the most feasible technique for a price leader to use.

Business marketing managers use several approaches to selecting the target return figures in their objectives including (1) deciding what seems to be fair or accepted in their industry, (2) wanting a better return than has been achieved in the past, (3) establishing what they believe they can get in the long run, (4) basing the figure on their cost of capital, and (5) using a particular return figure that will stabilize industry prices. Regardless of the method used, target return pricing is common in business markets and should be understood by the marketing manager.

LIST AND NET PRICES IN BUSINESS MARKETS

Business marketing firms often use a list and net price concept in their pricing. The **list price** is the figure specified on the company's price list; the **net price** is the figure actually paid by the customer. The difference between these two prices generally is caused by various **discounts**. Discounts from the list price are common in business markets; such discounting from the list price creates the net price. The concept is often misunderstood, but it does make sense. The business marketing manager prints up a single price list for all of his or her company's products. This price list is then distributed to all customers and prospects regardless of their type or classification. A discount system is then established whereby each customer type or classification is given certain discounts off that list for the net price to be charged. In most cases, no one pays the list price.

The advantage to the manufacturer is that a single list price sheet is printed up—any price changes are accomplished by adjusting the discount system. Thus, costs of printing and reprinting price lists are eliminated. This savings is a considerable one for firms that produce multiple product lines, especially when production and marketing costs are changing rapidly, in turn causing price changes. In addition, the list price concept allows competitors to hide their actual prices, at least to a degree. Knowledge of discounts and net prices is guarded jealously, and although they can be found out, it is often with much effort. Thus, although the list price and net price concept does not appear to make much sense, it is logical, and its application to the pricing of many business products and services is widespread. A more complete listing of the types of discounts used follows.

Cash Discounts

Cash discounts are those given to encourage rapid payment by customers and to allow quicker cash flow for the marketing manager's firm. Typical of such discounts are $2/10;n/30$, whereby the customer deducts 2 percent if it pays within ten days of invoice and the full amount if it takes longer. Although these discounts are often stated contractual terms between buyers and sellers, they are flagrantly abused and tolerated. If a large customer takes the 2 percent discount but does not pay for sixty days, the seller may do nothing. On the other hand, a new customer may not be permitted such a privilege. Cash discounts are widely used in business markets to (1) encourage prompt payment, (2) reduce credit risks and the cost of collecting overdue accounts, and (3) follow industry practices.[44]

It is important that the marketing manager watch cash discounts carefully, because they can detrimentally affect profits if abused. For example, if viewed by the month, the 2 percent discount in the $2/10;n/30$ seems harmless when customers are claiming the discount without earning it. But when compiled over a year's time, a considerable amount of money is involved.[45] Another potential problem is the tendency to extend the terms to aid sales. To illustrate, changing the terms to $2/10;n/60$ may be attractive to more customers, but it constitutes a cost that must be recognized if enough customers take the sixty days to pay.

Trade Discounts

Trade discounts, sometimes called functional discounts, are those given to different classifications of customers and/or channel intermediaries according to their trade or functions performed. For example, an industrial equipment manufacturer sells through distributors into the commercial market and directly to OEM customers and to government. Three types of distributors are used: (1) a Class A distributor, who, by contract, purchases equipment from the manufacturer to display on the showroom floor as a promotional device; (2) a Class B distributor, who is also authorized to sell the manufacturer's products, but who does not agree to floor-display equipment; and (3) overseas distributors, who operate in foreign countries. The following shows the trade discounts allowed to each type of customer off the basic list price:

Class B distributor	Class A distributor	Overseas distributor	Original equipment manufacturer	Government
25%	25% + 5%	25% + 5% + 5%	25% + 5% + 5%	25% + 5% + 5%

The use of trade discounts must be carefully watched, as different discounts given to basically the same types of customers can amount to violation of the

Robinson-Patman Act and are tantamount to price discrimination. In this case, the discounts are legal because the customers are not the same—flooring and overseas price requirements permit additional 5 percent discounts to some distributors, and OEM and government customers are not the same. In addition, the discount system is an incentive to distributors to floor-display equipment and for large OEMs and government to buy directly from the manufacturer, providing the discounts are competitive.

Quantity Discounts

Quantity discounts are those given for the amount or quantity of goods purchased, either on individual orders or purchases over a longer period such as one year. The objective of such a discount is to encourage customers to buy in large volumes. Typically, such discounts accelerate as the volume increases; for example, no discounts are given if under twenty-five units are purchased, 2 percent if between twenty-six and fifty units are bought, 4 percent if from fifty-one to 100 units are purchased, and so on. Quantity discounts are not in violation of the Robinson-Patman Act as long as they are available to any and all customers. Of course, quantity discounts in the long run permit the same types of customers to pay different prices depending on the volume purchased.

The most common form of quantity discount is a direct price discount, which may either be a reduction in the invoiced price or a rebate at the end of an agreed time period.[46] Rebates are covered in the following section, since they are variations of the standard quantity discount. Quantity discounts can also take nonprice forms such as when suppliers absorb certain costs, reduce delivery charges, provide free goods, or guarantee prices. There are some good reasons to use nonprice quantity discounts. For example, a marketer offering a 10 percent cash discount when ten units are purchased might consider instead offering one free unit when ten are purchased. If manufacturing costs are 40 percent of the selling price, the customer is still receiving a 10 percent discount, but it costs the manufacturer only 4 percent.[47]

Quantity discounts, although offered to all customers, may still be in violation of the Robinson-Patman Act if the discount granted cannot be proved to be equal to or less than the savings gained by doing business on the increased quantity. In such violations, both buyer and seller can be charged; anyone can report the suspected violation, and the government can then assume the case against both parties.

Rebates

Rebates are a special kind of quantity discount and are quite common in some industries. The basic difference between a rebate system and a longer time period quantity discount is the time when the buyer actually receives the discount. In the latter case, discounts are given off list price on invoices. In the rebate system, the buyer receives an actual cash rebate at the end of the designated period that is based on sales volume during that period. Rebates encourage customers to concentrate their purchases with a single supplier.[48] A typical rebate system may work as follows. If a customer purchases less than $10,000 in equipment per year, it receives no rebate; if it purchases between $10,000 and $25,000, it may receive a 2 percent cash rebate; if it buys from $25,000 to $50,000 of equipment, the rebate may be 4 percent; if it buys from $50,000 to $100,000, the rebate may be 6 percent; and so on. The rebate is a cash incentive for encouraging larger purchasers and is not in violation of the Robinson-Patman Act as long as all customers are able to participate in it. Rebates encourage some strange pricing on the part of channel intermediaries, as in the case of a New York distributor of commercial kitchen equipment who sold equipment at cost and made a profit on the rebate. Again, rebate systems indirectly affect the actual price paid by customers from the published list price.

FOB Considerations

FOB points can also affect the prices paid by organizational customers. For example, if a manufacturer ships goods on an FOB origin, also called an FOB freight collect basis, the customer pays a net price plus whatever freight is involved. Thus, the farther away a customer is from the manufacturer's factory, the higher the freight charges, and the actual price paid, including freight, may differ from customer to customer. Many business marketing firms ship by this basis, because it relieves the manufacturer from handling transportation problems that may occur and the same net return applies to every sale regardless of the customer's location.

Goods also are commonly shipped on a delivered, or FOB destination, basis. This system is basically a freight prepaid method of shipment. Typically, such an approach involves a subsidy by customers located near the shipping point to customers in the outer extremities of the company's marketing area. The closer customers are compelled to pay a "phantom freight" charge, which means they pay more than the marketing company actually spends to ship the goods. The more distant customers are involved in what is called "freight absorption," which means they actually pay less freight than the seller incurs in shipping the goods. In summary, the manufacturer recoups losses in freight absorption through the profits gained in phantom freight. Manufacturers establish multiple zone pricing systems to accommodate this approach. Many business marketing companies use this method of pricing because it permits them to be price competitive in more distant markets and simplifies final prices to customers, since everyone in the same pricing zone pays the same freight. The Federal Trade Commission and the federal courts have tested this system and found it to be legal unless it involves conspiracy among competitors.[49] These examples of FOB origin and destination pricing illustrate clearly how freight considerations can affect a customer's final price for a product.

A business marketing company typically sets forth such pricing specifics in a statement of pricing policy that is communicated to all present and prospective customers. This statement eliminates any confusion over prices charged and explains to customers how final prices are determined. Exhibit 17.2 illustrates a

EXHIBIT 17.2   Typical Statement of Pricing Policy in Business Marketing

HAAS ENGINEERING, INC.
12011 Industry Court
San Diego, California 92110 USA
TELEPHONE (619) 265-0000 * TELEX 123456

PRICE LIST

Model No.	Price	Model No.	Price	Model No.	Price
1101	$150	3301	$ 995	5501	$5,785
1102	195	3302	820	5502	5,885
1103	705	3303	975	5503	3,380
1104	95	3304	1,885	5504	3,380
1105	395	3305	1,795	5505	3,380
2201	195	4401	1,700	6601	2,990
2202	515	4402	1,700	6602	2,120
2203	315	4403	3,720	6603	5,585
2204	535	4404	3,435	6604	4,195
2205	449	4405	2,775	6605	5,785

QUANTITY DISCOUNTS

1–4 units: list price   5–9: less 5%   10–24: less 10%

TRADE DISCOUNTS

Class B Distributor	Class A Distributor	Overseas Distributor	Original Equipment Manufacturer	Government
25%	25% + 5%	25% + 5% + 5%	25% + 5% + 5%	25% + 5% + 5%

OTHER PRICE CONSIDERATIONS

- All prices subject to change without notice.
- U.S. terms are net 30 days from invoice date on approved credit. A 1½% service charge per month will be assessed on past due balances. FOB San Diego, California, plant. COD if credit not arranged in advance.
- Shipments will be made freight collect after receipt of purchase order in writing at plant in San Diego, California.
- Claims for shortages must be filed within ten (10) days after receipt of shipment.
- Delivery to carrier constitutes delivery to purchaser.
- Claims for merchandise damaged in transit must be filed with carrier within ten (10) days after receipt of merchandise.
- Minimum billing 50.00 U.S. dollars.

LEASING PLAN

Many models may be leased if available. Lease rates are fifteen percent (15%) of list price per month or five percent (5%) per day with a minimum of $350.00 per order. Eighty percent (80%) of lease rate may be applied toward purchase. Please contact Haas Customer Service Department for further details.

RETURN AND REPLACEMENT POLICY

Merchandise may not be returned without written authorization and shipment must be made freight prepaid. Where factory defects are found in current merchandise, then following the authorized return of merchandise, Haas Engineering will make replacement without charge if claim is justified. Return shipment will be made freight prepaid. In addition, credit will be issued to cover the incoming freight cost incurred on returned shipment of defective merchandise. Authorized returns of saleable merchandise, other than shipments made in error, will be subject to a 20% restocking charge.

hypothetical policy statement that was developed using a number of actual policy statements. Notice that this statement covers discounts, FOB points, missing or damaged goods problems, charges for late payments, leasing particulars, and returns and replacement policies. With such a statement, it is easy to determine net prices for any type of customers.

Assume that Haas Engineering, Inc., receives orders for the same products from two different distributors: Amos Distributors, Inc., and the Minchen Distribution Company. Amos has agreed to display Haas equipment on its display floor and thus is accorded Class A status. Minchen is a Class B status distributor. The two distributors are ordering the same products but not in the same quantities. Table 17.7 shows the computations involved in determining the price to be charged to each distributor. In addition to the net prices shown, freight charges and credit problems can cause additional differences. For example, both shipments are FOB origin, which means that freight charges are higher for the distributor most distant from the plant. Also, if Amos were to pay after thirty-five days, it would incur a penalty of 1½ percent of its past due balance, which would add an additional $135.96 to its final price.

TABLE 17.7   Application of Discounts in Pricing in Business Markets

Amos Distributors, Inc. Status: Class A		Minchen Distribution Company Status: Class B	
Order			
5 #1105 @ $ 395.00 =	$ 1,975.00	3 #1105 @ $ 395.00 =	$1,185.00
15 #2205 @ $ 449.00 =	6,735.00	2 #2205 @ $ 449.00 =	898.00
1 #6605 @ $5785.00 =	5,785.00	1 #6605 @ $5785.00 =	5,785.00
Total order	$14,495.00	Total order	$7,868.00
Quantity Discounts			
21 units purchased		6 units purchased	
Total order amount	$14,495.00	Total order amount	$7,868.00
Less: 10% discount	1,449.50	Less: 5% discount	393.40
	$13,045.50		$7,474.60
Trade Discounts			
Total order amount	$13,045.50	Total order amount	$7,474.60
Less: 25% + 5%	3,750.59	Less: 25%	1,868.65
	$ 9,294.91		$5,605.95
Cash Discounts			
Terms: net 30 days		Terms: net 30 days	
Net price if invoice paid within 30 days exclusive of freight charges and any late payment penalties:		Net price if invoice paid within 30 day period exclusive of freight charges and any late payment penalties:	
	$ 9,294.91		$5,605.95

This simple example shows the merits of list and net pricing as it is used in business marketing. Different classifications of customers are offered different net prices because of a discount system based on one list price. The example also shows the complexities of pricing under such a system.

BIDDING IN BUSINESS MARKETS

Many business marketing transactions are conducted through the inquiry/bid system, also called the **bidding** process. In this process, a purchasing agent in a company desiring to buy certain products and services may send requests for proposals (RFPs), also called requests for quotations (RFQs) or invitations to bid, to those companies believed capable of producing the product involved. Sometimes the RFPs are sent only to selected firms on the buyer's bid list. At other times open bidding is encouraged whereby any supplier is free to bid. Figure 17.1 shows a typical invitation to bid. In this case, it was published in a newspaper and any interested bidders were encouraged to submit bids. In bidding, the emphasis is placed on price—the RFP gives all the necessary data regarding the requirements of the prospective buyer, including the product's specifications, terms, and conditions of the bid. Bids may cover individual products or lines of products, and they may be for a single sale or for term contracts for a longer period. Many buyers use the bidding system because they feel that it enables them to obtain the most reasonable price in the purchase of required goods and/or services. In accordance with the conditions of the RFP, suppliers must submit bids to the prospective purchaser, stipulating their prices. The bids are then analyzed by the buyer, and a choice is made on the basis of price in awarding the sales contract.

Nevertheless, the lowest bidder does not necessarily get the contract, as some companies and many governmental and institutional customers award contracts on the basis of what is commonly referred to as the "lowest responsible bidder." This term is subject to interpretation by the individual purchaser, but basically it includes an assessment of the bidder's ability to deliver as promised, production capabilities, and past record. A study of 112 bid purchases, ranging in price from a low of $52 to a high of $775,000, revealed that the purchase was made from the lowest bidder 59 percent of the time. In this study, two major reasons were given for not buying from the lowest bidder: (1) the low bidder's product did not meet the required specifications; and (2) the low bidder's product was not interchangeable with existing equipment in the buyer's company.[50] In other instances, the purchaser does not automatically buy at the bid price submitted by the winning bidder but negotiates further on the actual price. In this type of situation, the bidding process is used to decide with whom to negotiate. In any case, because everything else must conform to the specifications in the RFP, price may become a critical factor, and it sometimes becomes the sole deciding factor in the award of a contract.

The following criteria must be present for the bidding process to occur:

FIGURE 17.1   Example of an Invitation to Bid in Business Marketing

---

NOTICE TO BIDDERS
IFB 1-91-95

Notice is hereby given that sealed bids will be received by the North San Diego County Transit District in the office of the Contract Specialist, 311 South Tremont, Oceanside, CA 92054 up to 2:00 p.m. on March 20, 1991 for:

> Purchase, Delivery, Installation and Testing of an Automatic Vehicle Washer System and Disassembly and Removal of the Existing Washer System.

Bids are required for the entire work described in the specifications. The bids will be opened and read aloud at the time and place listed above. A report of the names of all bidders and the amount of each bid will be made to the North San Diego County Transit Development Board (the governing Board of the District) at the first regularly scheduled meeting following opening of the bids. The award of a contract will be made by the Board on the basis of the lowest, responsive and responsible bid complying with all of the provisions of the specifications.

The award of the contract is subject to a financial assistance contract between the Board and the U.S. Department of Transportation. Any name appearing on the Comptroller General's list of the ineligible contractors for federally financed or assisted contracts is not an eligible bidder.

Contractor will be required to comply with all applicable Equal Employment Opportunity laws and regulations. The North San Diego County Transit District hereby notifies all bidders that it will affirmatively ensure that in any contract entered into pursuant to this advertisement, disadvantaged business enterprises will be afforded full opportunity to submit bids in response to this invitation and will not be discriminated against on the grounds of race, color, sex or national origin in consideration for an award.

Bids shall be submitted on the proposal forms furnished by the District and enclosed in a sealed envelope addressed to the Contract Specialist with the title of the work, IFB number, and the name and business address of the bidder clearly marked on the cover.

A pre-bid conference is scheduled for Tuesday, March 5, 1991 at 10:00 a.m. at the North County Transit District Escondido Facility at 755 Norlak, Escondido, CA 92025. All prospective bidders are encouraged to attend. The District reserves the right to reject any and all bids or to waive any errors or discrepancies.

Bids documents and specifications are available at 303 Via Del Norte, Oceanside 92054 or by calling (619) 967-2829 between the hours of 8:00 a.m. and 5:00 p.m.

> Richard L. Fifer, Executive Director
> North County Transit District

2/20 (040167)

Source: Reprinted by permission of North County Transit District, Oceanside, CA.

1. The item in question must be capable of being defined specifically so that both buyer and seller are clear on what is involved.

2. There must be enough sellers to allow for bids to compete.

3. The sellers must want the job and be willing to bid competitively.

4. The product's dollar value must be large enough to support the costs to both buyer and seller.

5. Sufficient time must be available for the bidding process to take place.

The bidding process presents an interesting problem for the business marketing manager and the pricing analyst. For companies pricing in this manner, decisions as to how many jobs to bid on and how many jobs to win depend entirely on the pricing mechanism used. In business markets, there are three major approaches to the bidding process.[51] The first may be called the adaptive approach, and it involves the bidder adapting to or reacting to the market. The bid price is based on capacity and the workload situation, which means higher bids when capacity is high and lower bids when work is needed. Users of this approach view each bid opportunity by itself, and the objective is to win as many jobs as possible within capacity constraints. The second approach is the strategic approach, which is somewhat similar to the adaptive approach but looks at the bidding strategy as more of a continuous process. Bid opportunities are viewed in terms of the value of the job and how well the particular job would fit in with longer-run objectives and the strategic market plan. The third approach is the quantitative approach, which focuses on mathematical data such as past winning bid prices, cost, and the probability of winning bids. Users of this approach often employ quantitative bidding models that are used to determine prices in competitive bidding situations.

The Probability Bidding Model

Perhaps the most common of all quantitative approaches to bidding is the probability model. All probabilistic bidding models are based on three criteria: (1) the size of the bid in terms of its dollar value, (2) the probability that the bid will be accepted, and (3) the profit to be expected if the bid is accepted. From a number of possible bid prices, the optimum bid is the one that will return the highest expected profit. The following conceptual formula has been used to express this optimum bid: [52]

$$E(X) = P(X)Z(X)$$

where

X = the dollar amount of the bid
$Z(X)$ = expected profit if the bid is accepted
$P(X)$ = probability of the bid at this price being accepted
$E(X)$ = expected profit of a bid at this price

The formula tells the pricing analyst that the best bid price to submit is the one that offers the highest overall profitability. Use of this formula represents the genesis of the bidding model. The model is a tool that aids the pricing analyst in determining what price should be attached to the bid.

An example is useful in showing how a business marketer may use such a model in determining a bid price. Assume the manufacturer of a piece of heavy equipment must submit a bid in response to an RFP. This bid will be in competition with those of several other manufacturers and the contract will be offered to the lowest bidder, since all are considered qualified and responsible suppliers. The manufacturer's total cost of producing this piece of equipment is $500,000, which represents the lowest possible bid price, since a sale below this price will result in a loss. The higher the bid, the more profitable it will be, but the chances of submitting the lowest of all competing bids are reduced. The marketing manager and/or the pricing analyst must now find a balance between profit on the bid and the probability of winning the contract.

The problem now is to develop some method for determining the probability of various bid prices winning the bid. This procedure may be difficult if the manufacturer is new in this market or has not faced these competitors previously. In such cases, since little data exists, a subjective assessment is probably used based on experience, feel of the market, competitive analysis, and similar factors. However, if the manufacturer has been in this market against these competitors previously and has developed a distribution of past winning bids, a more objective approach may be used. Figure 17.2 illustrates how winning bids might be analyzed. Here, the manufacturer has plotted the distribution of the last 120 winning bids. This analysis reveals that winning bids over time have ranged from

FIGURE 17.2   **Analysis of the Distribution of Past Winning Bids**

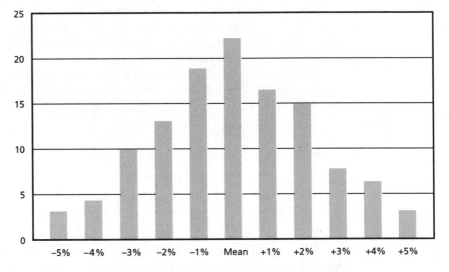

Source: Adapted from Arleigh W. Walker, "How to Price Industrial Products," *Harvard Business Review* 45 (September–October 1967): 127–132.

a low of 5 percent below the mean of all the winning bids to a high of 5 percent above the mean. The figure also shows how many bids were awarded at each price. For example, the winning bid was at the mean price twenty-two times, at 1 percent above the mean seventeen times, etc. Based on this analysis, the manufacturer is now in the position to make some determination of the probability of winning a bid at various prices.

Regardless of approach, assume the manager and/or analyst has determined a range of possible bid prices and their probability of being accepted (Figure 17.3). The figure is read in the following manner. If the marketing manager were to submit a bid of $450,000, he or she believes it would have a 100 percent chance of winning the bid. Similarly, a bid of $475,000 is seen as having a 95 percent chance. Such bids have a high probability of being accepted, but neither would be submitted because they are both below the cost to produce the equipment. Figure 17.3 illustrates the manager's assessment of bids from $450,000 to $700,000 and their probabilities of winning the bid.

FIGURE 17.3   **Probability of Each Bid Price Winning the Bid**

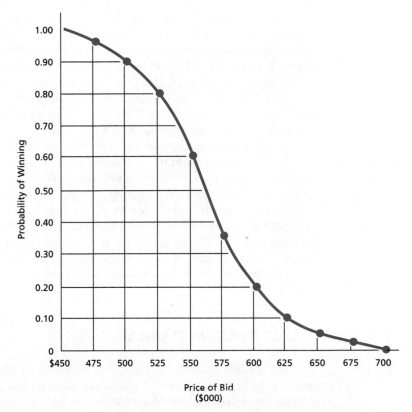

TABLE 17.8   Computation of Expected Profit in a Probability Bidding Model

Possible Bid Price	Cost	Cumulative Probability of Winning with This Bid Price	Profit If This Bid Price Wins	Expected Profit or Loss
$450,000	$500,000	1.00	−$ 50,000	−$50,000
475,000	500,000	0.95	− 25,000	− 23,750
500,000	500,000	0.90	0	0
525,000	500,000	0.80	25,000	20,000
545,000*	500,000	0.64	45,000	28,800
550,000	500,000	0.60	50,000	30,000
555,000*	500,000	0.54	55,000	29,700
575,000	500,000	0.35	75,000	26,250
600,000	500,000	0.20	100,000	20,000
625,000	500,000	0.10	125,000	12,500
650,000	500,000	0.05	150,000	7,500
675,000	500,000	0.02	175,000	3,500
700,000	500,000	0.00	200,000	0

Note: *Data for these possible bid prices estimated from Figure 17.3.

With these data and the $500,000 cost figure, the manager is now in a position to compute an optimum bid price. Table 17.8 illustrates the expected profit (or loss) for each possible bid price. As can be seen, the expected profit increases up to a bid price of $550,000. At that point, the expected profit then decreases, indicating that a bid of $550,000 is the optimum price. Confirmation of the bid price of $550,000 may be obtained by computing the expected profits of bids of $545,000 and $555,000. Based on this analysis, the manager should submit a bid of $550,000 in response to the RFP.

Use of such a bidding model is dependent on cost figures and a realistic evaluation of the probability of any bid price winning the contract. Thus, the model is no substitute for pricing decision making. Rather, the model is a tool for facilitating such decision making. In truth, a bidding model is only as good as the person using it. It does, however, eliminate a lot of guesswork from a difficult business marketing decision. The model used in this discussion is probably the most basic of all bidding models. It is beyond the scope of this text to analyze this area in more detail. If more insight into this bidding subject is desired, reference may be made to many excellent articles that relate specifically to bidding models.[53]

NEGOTIATED PRICING IN BUSINESS MARKETS

As the preceding section described, not all prices in business marketing are the result of the bidding process. It is also common to find prices arrived at through the process of negotiation. *Negotiation* is defined as "the process of working out a procurement and sales program together, to the point of reaching a mutually satisfactory agreement."[54] Negotiation in business markets typically occurs in more complex buying situations in which buyer and seller both make a number of proposals and counterproposals before a price is agreed on. In addition to price, other factors commonly involved include service, technical assistance, delivery, product characteristics, and quality.

In **negotiated pricing,** the buyer is a representative of the buying center and must try to satisfy the demands and expectations of that buying center. On the other hand, the sales representative must reconcile the demands and expectations of various individuals within the selling firm. These role requirements often bring about inflexibility in negotiating behavior and may cause negotiations to deteriorate into a win–lose encounter.[55] When this situation occurs, a less than amiable relationship often ensues as one party may feel put upon by the other. From a marketing perspective, intelligent negotiating cannot permit this to happen. Both buyer and seller should believe that their respective companies have gained through the negotiation process if a harmonious relationship is to continue.

Negotiated pricing is popular in business marketing for a number of reasons, including the following:

1. The bidding process works well only when product specifications are airtight—when the buyer knows exactly what is wanted. In purchases of sophisticated business products and services, this is often not the case. Negotiation permits buyer and seller to work out an arrangement that is not possible using the bidding process.

2. Many organizational buyers and buying influences believe that negotiated prices come closer to the "right" price than straightforward bid prices. Therefore, many buyers prefer negotiated prices to bid prices.

3. Sellers often prefer to negotiate rather than be tied to hard quotation prices because of the uncertainties involved with new products and/or when little manufacturing experience is available.

4. Many buyers prefer to negotiate, because with good negotiating tactics, they can get concessions from suppliers who really want the business.

5. Negotiation is also found in instances in which a buyer requests bids but then finds none of them to be satisfactory. None may meet requirements, and the buyer may want to negotiate for these.

6. Many sellers prefer to negotiate price rather than be tied to a fixed bid price because of inflation, rising costs, and shortages of materials. This behavior is especially true with longer-term contracts, such as take place with partner relationships.

7. It is common to find negotiation taking place between the buyer and the winning bidder even when the bidding process is used.

Determining what proportion of sales are negotiated rather than bid is virtually impossible, but the business marketing manager can expect to negotiate often. There are almost always chances to negotiate, even for basic commodities. Buyers pride themselves on their negotiating prowess, and the marketing manager must be prepared for some shrewd bargaining tactics when price is to be negotiated. Many buyers utilize some interesting tactics in negotiating prices with business field salespeople and marketing managers. For example, the following tactical rules have been suggested to buyers: (1) negotiate only on your home ground according to your arrangements, (2) let the supplier do most of the talking, (3) do not fumble over facts and figures when you talk, (4) do not get emotional, (5) permit the supplier to retreat gracefully on a point, (6) avoid premature showdowns, and (7) satisfy the emotional needs of the people you are negotiating with.[56]

A company that purchases goods and services has an obvious profit motive in developing buyers who are skilled in negotiation.[57] Buyers who effectively use negotiation tactics similar to those previously discussed can often gain an advantage over salespeople, especially when the latter are not well versed in negotiating. For business marketers, an understanding of organizational buyers' negotiation behavior should assist in developing effective sales strategies.[58] The business marketing manager must recognize the demands of the negotiation process on personal selling and make certain that company salespeople are trained in this important area.

LEASING IN BUSINESS MARKETS

Another area that deserves some mention is **leasing** in business markets. Leasing of capital equipment by organizational customers, as opposed to purchasing capital equipment, is a trend that has gained great momentum in the past several years. According to the American Machine Tool Distributors' Association, leasing of equipment is becoming an increasingly important marketing tool.[59] Thus, any company that markets user type products should consider the option of leasing rather than selling. The argument is made that any good product that can be sold can also be leased. This statement appears to be true. The following are types of products that have been or are being leased to organizational customers: printing presses, metal-fabricating equipment, forklift trucks, oil well meter equipment, machine tools, dairy equipment, compressors, warehouse machinery, tallow-rendering equipment, kelp-drying ovens, cargo-handling equipment, earth-moving equipment, and airliners. A good example may be seen in American Airlines' decision to lease, rather than buy, forty new jetliners worth $2.5 billion. Leasing arrangements were made with Boeing and Airbus Industrie, which allowed American Airlines to return the planes on short notice, thus minimizing the risk to the airline.[60]

For the business marketing manager in any company marketing such goods, leasing can be an alternative to selling those products to potential customers. Leasing may also allow the company to penetrate markets that may otherwise not exist for that company's products if it had to sell them outright. For example, the purchase of $100,000 of office equipment can be prohibitive for a small, financially constrained business. However, if this same equipment can be leased by that business for $29,280 per year over a five-year period, that business may become a viable marketing prospect. Simply stated, leasing may allow the prospect to acquire something desired, and it allows payment over a longer period of time, thus expanding the market. Viewed in this manner, leasing broadens a company's product and service offerings and expands its opportunity for profit.[61]

The magnitude of business leasing is difficult to determine, but most estimates indicate that it is large and growing even larger. An estimated 20 percent of all capital expenditures are financed through leases of various types.[62] The annual rate of growth in leasing has been estimated at approximately 16 percent annually, which can be compared to a 6 percent annual increase in purchases of similar products.[63] Tight money has greatly contributed to this growth, as financially strapped organizational customers have turned to leases, rentals, and other such financing approaches rather than outright purchase. All indications are that business leasing will continue to grow and should be viewed as a marketing tool by the business marketing manager.

Advantages and Disadvantages of Leasing

The marketing manager must understand that leasing has benefits and disadvantages when viewed from the customer's perspective. On the benefit side, leasing can provide customers with up to 100 percent financing in some instances. Leasing can also help the customer obtain more favorable cash flows, and it can conserve the customer's working capital, giving that customer more flexibility. Since leasing is basically an alternative to borrowing, the well-financed customer may find that the cost of leasing is less than the cost of borrowing the equivalent amount of money. Leasing can often help the customer protect itself against loss from product obsolescence, and many organizational customers prefer to lease heavy equipment for just this reason. In addition, it is argued that if a lease is properly constructed, it provides a method of financing equipment without showing debt on the lessee's balance sheet, thus giving the customer a more favorable financial picture. This advantage has been tempered by the passage of Standard 13 by the Financial Accounting Standards Board. Standard 13 requires that any lease that meets any of the following criteria be capitalized and appear in the lessee's balance sheet: (1) if the lease transfers ownership to the lessee at the end of the lease, (2) if the lease contains a bargain purchase option, (3) if the lease term is equal to 75 percent or more of the estimated economic life of the leased product, (4) if the present value of the minimum lease payments equals or exceeds 90 percent of the fair value of the leased product.[64] These rules apply to the majority of financial leases in business markets. When such leases must appear as assets and liabilities on the customer's balance sheet, they do not provide the hidden financial advantage described here. In summary, the customer gains from leasing because it avoids the cash purchase price, avoids the interest and operating expenses, and takes advantage of the tax shield provided by lease payments. These are general advantages that may or may not apply to specific lease agreements.

Leasing equipment also has disadvantages. In the long run, leasing usually requires a greater outlay of capital than debt financing does. Thus, the customer may pay more for the same equipment. In addition, although the customer may view lease payments as operating expenses, they are fixed payments that must be met. Some customers also take great pride in owning their businesses, including their plant and equipment. Such customers do not see leasing as advantageous. Finally, lease agreements can be hazardous if the customer is not careful. This case is especially true if the equipment leased is subject to rapid obsolescence, as the customer can be tied to a lease agreement whose duration exceeds the useful life of the equipment. Again, these are general disadvantages that may or may not apply to specific lease agreements.

A study of executives in 191 U.S. business marketing firms found that six factors affected their decision to lease rather than buy: [65]

1. Leasing provides 100 percent deductibility of costs.

2. Leasing does not dilute ownership or control.

3. Leasing allows for piecemeal financing of small acquisitions.

4. The after-tax cost of leasing is less than the after-tax cost of equity.

5. Leasing allows for the pass-through of the investment tax credit to companies with low or heavily sheltered earnings (no longer possible under revised tax laws).

6. Lease payments provide a greater tax shield than depreciation or interest.

The business marketing manager can lease equipment using four possible methods. First, the manager's company itself can lease to the customer. In this case, the company must carry the financing and work out the lease arrangements itself, which is a form of pricing. Second, many large companies are forming credit subsidiaries to provide such leasing for their customers. Such companies as International Harvester, John Deere, Itek, Gould, Borg-Warner, Allis Chalmers, and General Electric are all using this concept to lease business products. This approach is becoming popular because it permits the company to tap an additional profit center and still provide needed service to customers. As well, this method allows the manufacturer to defer taxes through the use of installment sales treatment for tax reporting, while still being able to record a 100 percent sale for financial bookkeeping purposes. Third, many financial institutions such as banks are involved in the leasing of equipment to organizational customers. The marketing manager can lease the company's equipment through such a bank leasing arrangement by negotiating with the bank involved. Fourth, some companies specialize in the business leasing market, such as CIT Financial, Commercial Credit, General Finance Corporation, U.S. Leasing, and U.S. Industrial Tools. The marketing manager can lease the company's equipment through such organizations to its customers.

Although there are many types of business leases, they are usually one of two basic types: (1) the financial lease and (2) the operating or service lease. The financial lease is a purely financial mechanism that is typically long or intermediate term and fully amortized over the term of the lease. The operating or service lease is usually short term, not fully amortized, and can be canceled. The primary purpose of the service lease is to provide the customer with equipment that is only needed for short periods. Typically, the lessor or marketer provides maintenance, service, and other provisions, which is why it is called a service lease. Since leasing permits considerable flexibility and leasing plans normally are developed to the specific demands of the markets involved, many variations of these basic types commonly occur.

An Example of a Typical Business Leasing Arrangement

Understanding how a business leasing arrangement works may best be seen through a scenario. A customer is interested in acquiring a piece of equipment priced at $100,000. The marketing company offers the prospect two options: (1) outright purchase at $100,000, or (2) a five-year equipment lease at $29,280 per year. In either case the lessee (the customer) will own the equipment at the end of the five years with a tax basis of $10,000. The lessee's tax rate is 28 percent, and its desired return on investment on capital funds is 15 percent. The method of depreciation for tax purposes is straight line to a 10 percent scrap value. Tables 17.9 and 17.10 illustrate the two options. Note that the customer pays more for the equipment by leasing ($29,280 × 5 = $146,400) than by purchasing outright ($100,000). But because of tax considerations, leasing actually saves the customer $4,611, or 4.6 percent. In addition, the customer can more easily pay the $29,280 annually than the total $100,000. In this case, leasing offers the customer a lower price and an easier payment schedule. For the marketing company (the lessor), the lease payments plus depreciation make the lease profitable despite interest-carrying charges over the five years. Thus, a leasing arrangement such as this one offers advantages to both the marketing company and the customer, which accounts for the popularity of this type of financing.

TABLE 17.9   **Cost to the Customer to Purchase the Equipment**

Year	Purchase Price	Depreciation after Tax (28%)	Present Value at 15%	Cost
0	$100,000			$100,000
1		(5,040)	.928	(4,672)
2		(5,040)	.800	(4,032)
3		(5,040)	.689	(3,473)
4		(5,040)	.593	(2,989)
5		(5,040)	.511	(2,575)
Total cost				$ 82,254

Source: Adapted from materials provided by Capital Equipment Leasing, San Diego, CA.

TABLE 17.10   Cost to the Customer to Lease the Equipment

Year	Annual Payment	Payment after Tax (28%)	Present Value at 15%	Cost
1	$29,280	$21,082	.928	$19,564
2	29,280	21,082	.800	16,866
3	29,280	21,082	.689	14,525
4	29,280	21,082	.593	12,502
5	29,280	21,082	.511	10,773
Residual	10,000	7,200	.474	3,413
Total cost				$77,643

Source: Adapted from materials provided by Capital Equipment Leasing, San Diego, CA.

The important marketing point is that leasing provides a pricing alternative. To quote a spokesperson for a machine tool manufacturer: "We look upon it (leasing) as a marketing tool, it is that extra thing that salespeople will utilize."[66]

RELATIONSHIP MARKETING AND PRICING

Throughout this text, the subject of partnering relationships and alliances between suppliers and customers has been discussed as it applies to various areas of the marketing mix. Its impact on pricing should now be discussed. Relationship marketing involves long-term contractual relationships between the marketing firm and its customers. Also inherent in the concept is that fewer suppliers are used and that product and service quality becomes extremely important. These conditions may somewhat affect the role of pricing as compared to that in transaction marketing. For example, in a single transaction, pricing may follow quite closely what has been discussed in this chapter. Each purchase involves its own pricing decision and thus price could change considerably from purchase to purchase depending on trade, quantity, and other discounts. This will not work in a partnering relationship where pricing will have to be based on many purchases over time.

Based on this premise, differences may be determined between pricing in single-transaction versus relationship purchases. Some of the factors that will influence pricing are:

1. Longer-term relationships usually involve more stable prices.
2. Product quality and delivery capabilities may be more important than price.
3. Pricing is based on long-term contractual arrangements.
4. Competition is reduced since fewer suppliers will be used.
5. While the actual price may be less important, the total costs of purchases become very important.

6. Demand is also more stable and may be easier to determine since requirements are provided ahead of time by the customer.

Factors such as these affect pricing in business markets to a considerable degree. Since demand will be longer-term and more predictable, lower prices will probably occur. Given the stable pricing required in the relationship, price is also unlikely to undergo significant fluctuations. Thus, it is quite likely the business marketing firm may employ a penetration pricing policy and emphasize price stabilization as one of its objectives. To do anything else could well affect the sole sourcing position that exists in relationship marketing. To illustrate, if the customer reduced suppliers to enter into a long-term relationship with a particular supplier, that decision would be seriously reconsidered if prices were seen as high and price fluctuations occurred. Thus, pricing has to meet the customer's perceived values and must be stable to keep the relationship operating.

At the same time, however, the business marketer still has costs to cover and pricing objectives to achieve, which complicates the issue. Lowering price to create or maintain the relationship makes little sense if that price results in losses. Since the relationships are typically on longer-run bases, life cycle costing and the use of the learning or experience curve become more important in truly understanding costs. Thus, it can be seen that even in relationship marketing, the points covered in this chapter still apply. They just need to be adapted to the requirements of the individual relationship.

Pricing in Just-in-Time (JIT) Situations

A particular type of relationship pricing situation occurs when the business marketing firm is involved with JIT customers. This subject has also been covered in detail in previous chapters but now needs to be examined for its pricing implications. It should be recalled that under the JIT concept, the customer no longer retains any inventory but rather relies on suppliers to deliver needed quantities of parts or materials at the exact times required and in the exact amounts. For the customer, adoption of this concept results in lower costs. Major cost advantages to the customer include: [67]

1. Lower inventory carrying costs.
2. Reduced warehousing and storage handling costs.
3. Quicker detection of defects because of smaller and more frequent shipments.
4. Less need for inspection due to closer relations with the supplier and the smaller shipments.
5. Faster response to engineering changes, again due to the closer relationship with the supplier.

All of these cost savings are realized because the customer can now keep its materials and parts inventories at the lowest level at which operations can be maintained. These savings can be considerable. To illustrate, at one time a typical U.S. auto manufacturer, using the EOQ concept, carried $775 in inventory for each car built. This can be compared to $150 in inventory by the typical Japanese auto manufacturer buying under the JIT concept. In essence, the Japanese manufacturer needed less plant and warehouse space and less money to finance its goods-in-process inventories. A U.S. assembly plant with a capacity of 1,000 cars per day required 2,000,000 square feet where a comparable Japanese manufacturer needed 1,500,000 square feet. Because of the JIT concept, the Japanese were able to obtain higher-quality output at lower cost.[68]

For the business marketer, the cost savings for the customer will usually involve increased costs for the supplier. If the marketer now has to maintain the inventory safety stocks for the customer, this typically involves increased distribution costs in inventory and warehousing. In addition, JIT customers require more frequent and smaller shipments, which might also increase cost. In other words, it can hardly be business as usual in pricing for the business marketer when a customer switches to JIT. The increased costs must be considered in the pricing equation. At the same time, demand is more stable and more long term, which can actually lower costs of production. As a general rule, however, it is probably safe to say that costs for the marketer usually increase with JIT customers. Thus, it can be seen why one authority states that pricing in JIT situations is "more complex."[69]

The increased costs now borne by the business marketer become important in pricing. What is equally important is value to the customer, and price may be less important than the total costs to the customer in making the transaction. To illustrate, the customer may be quite willing to accept a 5 percent increase in price if this increase in turn causes a 10 percent decrease in inventory carrying costs, etc. In other words, pricing now becomes part of a much bigger picture and pricing decisions require the integration of many factors other than those involved in more standard transactions. As with other types of partnering relationships, pricing is somewhat different but still involves the basic considerations developed in this chapter.

CHAPTER SUMMARY

Pricing is the fourth but not necessarily last major substrategy in overall marketing strategy. This chapter focused specifically on pricing and how pricing decisions are made in business marketing. Pricing decisions should be integrated with decisions regarding products and services, channels, personal selling, and advertising. Pricing should be considered simultaneously with all other functional marketing decisions and is not simply adding a margin to costs.

The chapter examined the roles that pric-ing plays in overall business marketing strategy. Factors that influence business pricing decisions were reviewed, and emphasis was placed on customer value, competition, cost, pricing objectives, top management, and governmental constraints. The chapter stressed the need for integration of all these factors if effective pricing is to be achieved.

List and net prices were also analyzed, and different types of discounts and price concessions were examined to determine situations in which they are appropriate. The concept of target return pricing, which is heavily used in business markets, was examined in terms of its marketing implications and its actual applications.

The chapter looked at the concept of bidding, which is also common in business marketing. Criteria necessary for bidding were reviewed, and bidding models were discussed as regards their contribution to more effective pricing. Since not all business pricing involves bidding, the topic of negotiated pricing was also explored. The chapter then looked at leasing in terms of pricing and marketing implications.

Finally, the subject of relationship marketing was discussed as it relates to pricing in business markets. Factors inherent in long-run partnering relationships were examined for their

effects on pricing decisions. Then, the concept of just-in-time purchasing was analyzed for its pricing implications with particular attention being paid to increased costs to the business marketer.

This chapter has discussed the factors that impact business pricing decisions and outlined what types of pricing decisions must be made. In addition, ways of implementing those decisions were included. In final analysis, it should be recognized that price does not typically play the dominant role it often does in consumer marketing. Organizational customers will pay higher prices if assured of high product quality, product reliability, and certainty of delivery. These customers normally will not accept less, even if the price is lower.

KEY TERMS

bidding
break-even analysis
competitive pricing
discount
learning experience curve
leasing
life cycle costing
list price

market share pricing
negotiated pricing
net price
price
pricing
target return pricing
value to the customer

QUESTIONS

1. You are the marketing manager in a business marketing firm and your CEO makes the following statement: "Pricing is the least important marketing decision area and I can't see the justification for any sizable budget to spend on it." How would you respond to this statement?

2. You are the pricing analyst for a business marketing company contemplating the introduction of a new product. Fixed costs are estimated to be $50,000 and variable costs are projected to be $1.00 per unit. You are considering pricing the new product at $1.25 per unit. How many units will you have to sell to break even?

3. Many marketing managers may not realize that discount systems must be properly administered to be cost effective. This situation is certainly true of cash discounts. Assume a marketing manager sells on a $2/10; n/30$ basis and annual sales are $5 million. If 30 percent of the customers taking the 2 percent discount do not pay within the ten days, what is the annual cost to the marketing firm?

4. The XYZ Steel Company estimates fixed costs to be 15.4 percent of total costs when the plant operates at 100 percent capacity. At 50 percent capacity, 26 percent of total costs are fixed, and

at 10 percent capacity, 57.2 percent of total costs would be fixed. It is also determined that variable cost per unit produced is $55.73, which is constant between 18 percent and 90 percent capacity. The company is now producing 1,000 units, which is 50 percent of capacity. What price would the company have to charge for the product to break even?

5. Why should the business marketing manager look at leasing as a viable option to selling outright? What are the pricing implications involved in the decision to lease products to customers as opposed to selling them to the same customers?

6. The pricing manager of the Capital Chemical Company, a small subcontractor, explains his company's pricing policy as follows. He takes the variable costs, including labor, of producing the products. To that cost he adds a "flexible margin" to arrive at the selling price. If business is slow and capacity is low, he lowers the margin; if business is good and capacity is high, he raises the margin. Comment on this pricing policy.

7. A U.S. manufacturer faces a market with demand conditions such that the manufacturer has excess capacity for a period of time. Its product has variable unit costs of $7.85 and under normal conditions bears a full cost of $12.10. During this low demand period, the company is approached by a global prospective customer that wishes to purchase a large quantity of products and offers to pay $11.00 per unit. Since the firm has capacity, it can produce the required number of products for the overseas customer and still supply its existing customers. Should it accept the new order at the $11.00 price?

8. A manufacturer of electronic component parts sold 500,000 units at a price of $1.39 each in year 1. In year 2, it reduced the price to $1.36 and sold 550,000. In year 3, price was again dropped to $1.33 and sales increased to 580,000. Finally, the firm drops price again in year 4 and sales increase to 600,000 units. Compute the historical price elasticity of demand for this product.

9. In business markets, prices are either bid, negotiated, or both. Explain what this means and then explain when bidding makes the best sense, when negotiated pricing makes the best sense, and when a combination of the two makes the best sense.

10. The marketing manager of the Amalgamated Fastener Company prices the company's products by taking the fixed and variable costs of producing and marketing the product and adding on a desired markup of 20 percent. What do you see as the strong and weak points of this pricing approach?

NOTES

1. Arleigh W. Walker, "How to Price Industrial Products," *Harvard Business Review* 45 (September–October 1967), in *HBR Reprints,* No. 4041 (1980): 38.

2. Seymour E. Haymann, "Consider Other Factors and Cost When Pricing Industrial Products," *Marketing News* 13 (April 4, 1980): 11.

3. Gilbert Burck, "The Myths and Realities of Corporate Pricing," *Fortune* 85 (April 1972): 88.

4. Kent B. Monroe, "Pricing New Industrial Products," in *Product Line Strategies,* Report No. 816, edited by Earl L. Bailey (New York: The Conference Board, 1982), 68.

5. Barbara B. Jackson, "Manage Risk in Industrial Pricing," *Harvard Business Review* 58 (July–August 1980): 122.

6. Ibid.

7. Adapted from Ross B. Elliott, "Pricing Process for New Industrial Products Can Be More of a Science Than It Usually Is," *Marketing News* 15 (April 16, 1982): 12.

8. Ibid.

9. Diane L. Kastiel, "Firms Grope for Solution in Price Struggle," *Business Marketing* 72 (January 1987): 21.

10. Ibid.

11. Michael H. Morris and Mary L. Joyce, "How Marketers Evaluate Price Sensitivity," *Industrial Marketing Management* 17 (1988): 169.

12. Ibid., 175.

13. Ibid., 173.

14. Ibid., 175.

15. Jon G. Udell, *Successful Marketing Strategies* (Madison, WI: Mimir Publishers, 1972), 109.

16. Isaiah A. Litvak, James A. Johnson, and Peter M. Banting, "Industrial Pricing—Art or Science?" *Business Quarterly* (Autumn 1967): 41.

17. Stuart U. Rich, "Price Leadership in the Paper Industry," *Industrial Marketing Management* 12 (1983): 103.

18. Udell, op. cit.

19. Litvak, Johnson, and Banting, op. cit.

20. See Robert J. Brown, "A New Marketing Tool: Life-Cycle Costing," *Industrial Marketing Management* 8 (1979): 109–113.

21. B. Charles Ames, "In Tough Times, Profitable Industrial Pricing Demands Policy Plus Enforcer," *Marketing News* 13 (April 4, 1980): 1.

22. "Comparing Electronic Sub-Assembly Costs," *San Diego Union*, March 22, 1987, C7.

23. George M. Fodor, "Orchestrating a Pricing Strategy," *Industrial Distribution* 77 (August 1987): 31.

24. Rich, op. cit., 101.

25. See Robert F. Lanzillotti, "Pricing Objectives in Large Companies," *American Economic Review* 48 (December 1958): 921–940.

26. Ibid.

27. Ibid.

28. Ibid.

29. Morris and Joyce, op. cit.

30. Lanzillotti, op. cit.

31. Litvak, Johnson, and Banting, op. cit., 42.

32. Bruce A. Jacobs, "Price Fixing: Is It Worth the Risk?" *Industry Week* 202 (August 24, 1981): 44.

33. Ibid., 46.

34. Monroe, op. cit., 67.

35. Brian S. Moskal, "Pricing: New Forces Prompt New Philosophies," *Industry Week* 199 (December 11, 1978): 49.

36. Monroe, op. cit., 72.

37. Elliott, op. cit.

38. Ibid.

39. Lanzillotti, op. cit.

40. Monroe, op. cit., 179.

41. For more details, see Moskal, op. cit., 48–55; "Flexible Pricing," *Business Week* 2513 (December 12, 1978): 78–88; and Benson P. Shapiro and Barbara B. Jackson, "Industrial Pricing to Meet Customer Needs," *Harvard Business Review* 56 (November–December 1978): 119–127.

42. Brown, op. cit.

43. Jacobs, op. cit., 46.

44. Kent B. Monroe, *Pricing: Making Profitable Decisions* (New York: McGraw-Hill, 1979): 179.

45. Stewart A. Washburn, "Is 'Policy' Eroding Your Prices and Profits?" *Business Marketing* 70 (December 1985): 94.

46. George S. Day and Adrian B. Ryans, "Using Price Discounts for a Competitive Advantage," *Industrial Marketing Management* 17 (1988): 6.

47. Washburn, op. cit.

48. Day and Ryans, op. cit., 4.

49. See James C. Johnson, "How Competitive Is Delivered Pricing?" *Journal of Purchasing and Materials Management* 12 (Summer 1976): 26–51.

50. J. Patrick Kelly and James W. Coaker, "The Importance of Price as a Choice Criterion for Industrial Purchasing Decisions," *Industrial Marketing Management* 5 (1976): 285.

51. Paul D. Boughton, "The Competitive Bidding Process: Beyond Probability Models," *Industrial Marketing Management* 16 (1987): 88.

52. Lee J. Lamar and Donald W. Dobler, *Purchasing and Materials Management: Text and Cases* (New York: McGraw-Hill, 1965), 97.

53. See Wayne J. Morse, "Probabilistic Bidding Models: A Synthesis," *Business Horizons* 28 (April 1975): 67–74; Franz Edelman, "Art & Science of Competitive Bidding," *Harvard Business Review* 43 (July 1965): 53–66.

54. Stuart F. Henritz and Paul V. Ferrell, *Purchasing Principles and Applications* (Englewood Cliffs, NJ: Prentice-Hall, 1965), 148.

55. Stephen W. Clopton, "Seller and Buying Firm Factors Affecting Industrial Buyers' Negotiation Behavior and Outcomes," *Journal of Marketing Research* 21 (February 1984): 39.

56. Henritz and Ferrell, op. cit.

57. Clopton, op. cit.

58. Ibid.

59. "Leasing a New Marketing Tool, Says AMTDA," *Industrial Distribution* 76 (January 1986): 12.

60. "American to Rent 40 Jetliners," *San Diego Union*, March 4, 1987, F1.

61. Paul F. Anderson and William Lazer, "Industrial Lease Marketing," *Journal of Marketing* 42 (January 1978): 72.

62. M. Bruce McAdam, "Equipment Leasing: An Integral Part of Financial Services," *Business Economics* (July 1988): 45.

63. See Frost & Sullivan, *Equipment Leasing Market,* Report No. 382 (New York: Frost & Sullivan, 1976); Brian S. Moskal, "Equipment Leasing: A Recession Option," *Industry Week* 202 (September 3, 1979): 94.

64. Paul F. Anderson, "Account Changes Should Benefit Equipment Lease Marketer," *Marketing News* 9 (December 17, 1976): 6.

65. Paul F. Anderson, "Industrial Equipment Leasing Offers Economic and Competitive Edge," *Marketing News* 13 (April 4, 1980): 20.

66. "Better Than No Sale at All," *Sales & Marketing Management* 122 (April 4, 1983): 138.

67. Thomas J. Peters and Robert H. Waterman, *In Search of Excellence: Lessons from America's Best* (New York: Harper & Row, 1982), 161.

68. William F. Schoell, *Marketing,* 2d ed. (Boston: Allyn and Bacon, 1985), 439.

69. Michael H. Morris, *Industrial and Organizational Marketing* (Columbus, OH: Merrill Publishing Company, 1988), 68.

SUGGESTED ADDITIONAL READINGS

Alberts, William W. "The Experience Curve Doctrine Reconsidered." *Journal of Marketing* 53 (July 1989): 36–49.

Anderson, Paul F., and Monroe Bird. "Marketing to the Industrial Lease Buyer." *Industrial Marketing Management* 9 (1980): 111–116.

Boughton, Paul D. "The Competitive Bidding Process: Beyond Probability Models." *Industrial Marketing Management* 16 (1987): 87–94.

Day, George S., and Adrian B. Ryans. "Use Price Discounts for a Competitive Advantage." *Industrial Marketing Management* 17 (1988): 1–14.

Forbis, John L., and Nitan T. Mehta. "Value-Based Strategies for Industrial Pricing." *Business Horizons* 24 (May–June 1981): 32–42.

Friedmann, Roberto, and Warren A. French. "Pricing Augmented Commercial Services." *Journal of Product Innovation Management* 4 (1987): 33–42.

Jackson, Barbara B. "Industrial Pricing to Meet Customer Needs." *Harvard Business Review* 56 (November–December 1978): 119–127.

———. "Manage Risk in Industrial Pricing." *Harvard Business Review* 58 (July–August 1980): 122.

Kijewski, Valerie, and Eunsang Yoon. "Market-Based Pricing: Beyond Price-Performance Curves." *Industrial Marketing Management* 19 (1990): 11–19.

Lamm, David V., and Lawrence C. Vose. "Seller Pricing Strategies: A Buyer's Perspective." *Journal of Purchasing and Materials Management* 24 (Fall 1988): 9–13.

Monroe, Kent B. "Pricing New Industrial Products." In *Product Line Strategies,* Report No. 816. Edited by Earl L. Bailey. New York: The Conference Board, 1982, 101–104.

Morris, Michael H., and Mary L. Joyce. "How Marketers Evaluate Price Sensitivity." *Industrial Marketing Management* 17 (1988): 169–176.

Morse, Wayne J. "Probabilistic Bidding Models: A Synthesis." *Business Horizons* 28 (April 1975): 67–74.

Ross, Elliot B. "Making Money with Proactive Pricing." *Harvard Business Review* 62 (November–December 1984): 145–155.

Shipley, David, and Elizabeth Bourdon. "Distributor Pricing in Very Competitive Markets." *Industrial Marketing Management* 19 (1990): 215–224.

Simon, Hermann. *Price Management.* New York: Elsevier Science Publishing Company, Inc., 1989.

Tellis, Gerald J. "Beyond the Many Faces of Price: An Integration of Pricing Strategies." *Journal of Marketing* 50 (October 1986): 146–160.

Teplitz, Charles J. "Negotiating Quantity Discounts Using a 'Learning Curve Style' Analysis." *Journal of Purchasing and Materials Management* 24 (Summer 1988): 33–40.

Walker, Arleigh W. "How to Price Industrial Products." *Harvard Business Review* 45 (September–October 1967): 125–132.

Washburn, Stewart A. "Establishing Strategy and Determining Costs in the Pricing Decision." *Business Marketing* 70 (July 1985): 64–78.

———. "Understanding Competitive Price Changes." *Business Marketing* 70 (December 1985): 92–97.

Wilcox, James B., Roy D. Howell, Paul Kuzdrall, and Robert Britney. "Price Quantity Discounts: Some Implications for Buyers and Sellers." *Journal of Marketing* 51 (July 1987): 60–70.

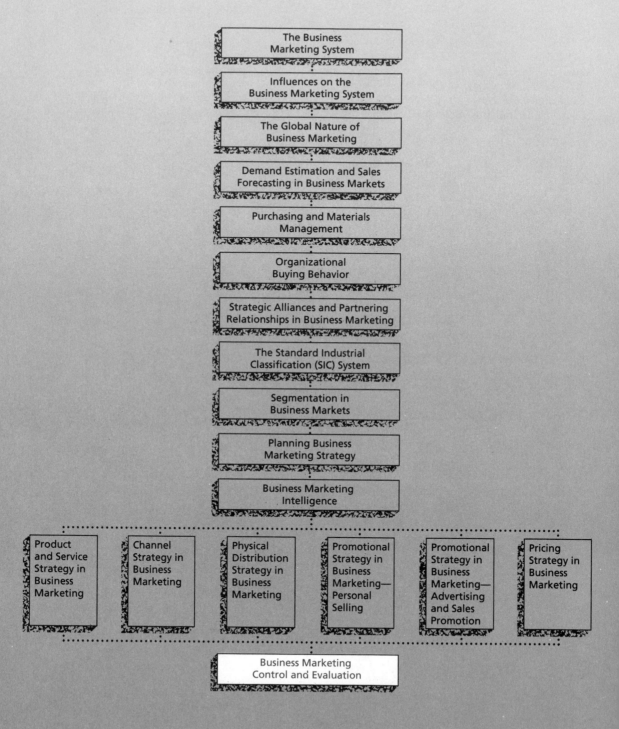

Business Marketing Performance: Control and Evaluation

'18'

Business Marketing Control and Evaluation

•••

As has been developed throughout the text, business marketing planning and strategy formulation is a complex undertaking that requires coordinating many activities and people. The marketing plan integrates all these activities over time and delegates responsibilities for these activities. However, these statements do not mean to imply that all activities are performed adequately or on time. The marketing manager must determine which elements in the overall marketing plan have been effectively conceived and implemented and which have not. For example, an advertising campaign to stimulate interest in a new product may be successful when it is solid in concept and properly implemented. If either or both facets are not achieved, that campaign may be a failure. If that happens, the new product itself may fail. Monitoring the activities and personnel involved in the overall marketing plan constitutes the area of marketing control and evaluation, which is a fundamental responsibility of the marketing manager.

This chapter focuses on control and evaluation of those marketing strategies and programs that have been developed in the overall marketing plan. This area may best be seen by looking at Figure 18.1, which depicts the marketing planning process used by a large chemical firm. Step 6 illustrates a measurement, control, and review procedure that follows the preceding steps in which strategies and tactics are outlined. The process represented in the figure is typical of what exists in business markets. Without control and evaluation procedures, the business marketing manager cannot take corrective actions when needed. This chapter emphasizes the importance of control and evaluation in the marketing planning process and develops an understanding of both concepts as they apply to business marketing. The chapter describes levels of marketing to be controlled and evaluated. Useful mechanisms for controlling and evaluating business marketing management actions are also illustrated and explored.

Controlling and Evaluating Marketing and Promotional Efforts in Business Marketing

Business marketing companies cannot simply develop and implement marketing and promotional efforts and then forget about them. Controlling and evaluating these efforts is as important as implementing them in the first place if shortcomings are to be discovered, addressed, and corrected. Thus, controlling and evaluating marketing efforts is standard practice in business marketing.

A good example of this took place with the Federal-Mogul Corporation of Detroit, Michigan. This company produced an industrial product line that it wished to reposition in the minds of design engineers in the OEM market from a primarily price differentiated commodity product. To accomplish this goal, Federal-Mogul initiated an intensified advertising and sales promotional campaign to increase brand awareness and sales in the target market. At the same time, management wanted to closely monitor changes in the market brought about by the increased promotion expenditures. Controlling and evaluating the new campaign was important in that it provided the company with information regarding the impact of the new efforts.

At the time of initiation of the campaign, the company spent .6 percent of sales in advertising and enjoyed a 10 percent brand awareness in the target market. These figures provided the basis for both control and evaluation. In the first year of the campaign, advertising as a percent of sales was increased from .6 percent to 1.5 percent. As a result, brand awareness increased from 10 percent to 40 percent. In the second year, Federal-Mogul reduced advertising as a percent of sales to 1.2 percent with the result being that awareness dropped to 36 percent and sales also declined. In the next year, advertising as a percent of sales then was increased from 1.2 percent to 1.6 percent and awareness increased to 46 percent and sales grew. Over the entire project, the percent of sales spent in advertising increased from .6 percent to 1.6 percent with the result that awareness rose from 10 percent to 40 percent while sales and profit contribution increased by 52 percent.

Through careful control and evaluation, Federal-Mogul was able to determine the relationships between percent of sales spent in advertising and brand awareness in the market. The company also discovered how gains in awareness and market share were subject to declines when the program efforts were reduced or cut significantly.

Source: Adapted by permission from Cahners Publishing Company, *Cahners Advertising Research Report*, No. 3000.2 (Newton, MA: Cahners Publishing Company, 1988).

FIGURE 18.1   **The Marketing Planning Process of a Large Chemical Corporation**

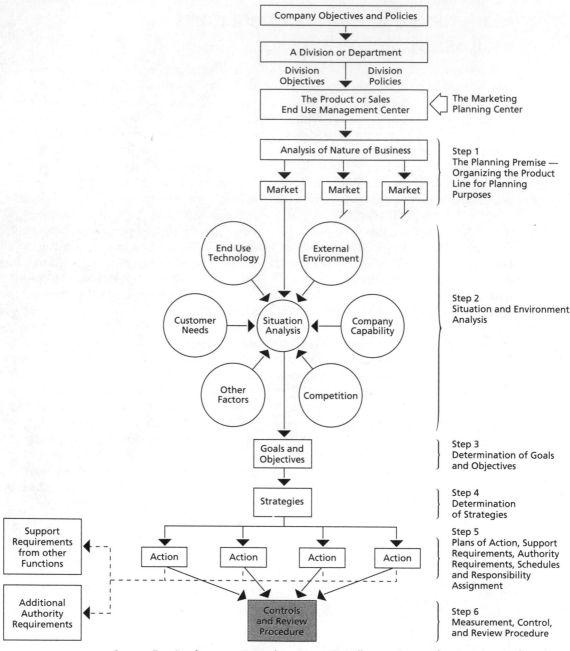

Source: Reprinted per permission from Ernest C. Miller, *Marketing Planning: Approaches of Selected Companies,* Research Study No. 81 (New York: American Management Association, Inc., 1967), 60. Copyright © James O. Rice Associates, Inc.

CONTROL AND EVALUATION DEFINED

The terms *control* and *evaluation* are sometimes used synonymously; however, they are different enough from a managerial perspective that their individual meanings should be clarified. **Control** implies keeping on track or on target and typically takes place while activities or programs are in progress. Individual managers, such as product or sales managers, are informed when meaningful deviations from objectives are observed. For example, a product manager may have an objective of achieving a 15 percent share of a particular market at the end of a specified period, such as five years. Control would involve monitoring progress toward that specific objective. **Evaluation** is more diagnostic in nature and is concerned with reviewing results to determine how well or poorly objectives are being achieved. Evaluation is aimed at explaining differences that are observed in the control process.

An example may better explain these differences. When Canon U.S.A. introduced its model NP-200 desktop plain paper copier, its objective was to increase its 2½ percent share of the convenience segment of the plain paper copier market to 10 percent within a five-year period.[1] Canon management's control process would be concerned with monitoring progress from 2½ percent to 10 percent during the five-year period to ensure that the objective was realistic and that marketing activities were contributing toward achieving the objective. Evaluation, on the other hand, would be involved in determining reasons for variations between actual and forecasted sales. If the market share increased by only ½ percent over the first three years, why is performance lagging behind objectives? This lag may be due to poor product or service performance, ineffective communication, improper channels, changing customer needs, improper market selection, or a competitor's strategy. Canon's evaluation process would attempt to pinpoint reasons for the variations that have been observed so that corrective actions could be taken.

In actual practice, control and evaluation usually are considered a single, interrelated process of detecting, assessing, and correcting differences between desired and actual performances in various marketing activities. From here on, control and evaluation are considered as a single process.

LEVELS OF MARKETING CONTROL AND EVALUATION ACTIVITY

The interrelated process of control and evaluation can be applied to several levels of marketing activity. These **control levels** can range from a company's overall marketing strategy or plan to individual managers of marketing functions such as advertising, sales, or marketing research. They may also include the actions of outside organizations. Figure 18.2 depicts the various levels of marketing control and evaluation that may be found in business marketing firms. Not

FIGURE 18.2 Levels of Marketing Control and Evaluation

all companies use all six levels, but a discussion of each is appropriate, since all may be involved at one time or another.

Level 1: Control and Evaluation of Overall Marketing Planning and Strategy

Chapter 10 explained that the overall marketing strategy or marketing plan is a business marketing company's basic approach to its marketplace. Overall marketing strategy involves identifying market opportunities, selecting the most profitable markets, and determining how the company should serve these selected markets in a manner most consistent with company objectives. As Chapter 10 detailed, strategy development is the most basic marketing activity. All other marketing decisions, programs, and tactics must be consistent with this overall strategy. Therefore, control and evaluation of the overall marketing strategy chosen by a business marketing company is a logical management function.

The control and evaluation of the overall marketing strategy or plan should answer three basic questions:

1. Is the marketing strategy being carried out at all?
2. If it is being carried out, how well is it being implemented?
3. Is the strategy that is being implemented really the most effective in terms of changing competitive and market conditions?

These considerations are of more than passing interest—they are essential to any realistic control and evaluation of a business marketing manager's overall strategy. A look at each is constructive.

Is the Marketing Strategy Being Carried Out at All?   The marketing manager cannot assume that his or her strategy is being carried out simply because it has been developed. The following quotation illustrates what often happens in this regard:

> All too often, the end-product of present-day strategic planning activities is a strategic plan—period. Nothing really new happens as a result of the plan, except that everyone gets a warm glow of security and satisfaction now that the uncertainty of the future has been contained.[2]

Many reasons account for this lack of implementation: The strategy may be neither clear nor easily understood; the manager may not have communicated it well to subordinates who are expected to implement it; responsibilities for various activities were never properly delegated; subordinates may not have had any input into the strategy and thus resent it being impressed on them. The business marketing manager must be aware of any such problems in his or her control and evaluation process. In addition, budgets, progress reports, tactical programs, and other such devices should be used to provide clear evidence that the overall marketing strategy is or is not being implemented.

How Well Is the Strategy Being Implemented?   If the manager determines that the strategy is being used, the next logical control and evaluation concern is establishing how well it is being implemented. The manager must ascertain the degree of implementation as well as coordination among the various marketing activities. For example, the manager may find that the company is attempting to follow his or her plan carefully, but disagreements among product managers, advertising managers, and sales managers as to how to best communicate with customers in the marketplace are causing problems with actual implementation.

Is the Strategy as Effective as It Should Be in Light of Changing Conditions?   This concern differs from the first two in that the manager now must address the problem of how relevant the strategy is in view of changes in suppliers, customers, and competitors. Many changes occur between the time a strategy is developed and when it is implemented, which may render a strategy out of date and useless. Changes in strategy elements such as products, channels, advertising, sales, and prices may be necessary to update a strategy and restore its relevance and effectiveness.

Overall strategy control and evaluation is one of the business marketing manager's prime responsibilities. Although it is true that many managers delegate control and evaluation tasks to staff assistants, the ultimate responsibility rests directly with the marketing manager.

Level 2: Control and Evaluation of Profit Centers or Business Unit Strategy

Chapter 10 discussed strategic planning and its ramifications for marketing planning and strategy formulation. The Boston Consulting Group (BCG) recommended that multiproduct, multimarket companies create "business units" or "profit centers" and then develop separate strategies for each as if they were unrelated entities. The composite strategies would then be compiled into an overall strategy, but each would be evaluated independently of each other. Since each business unit would have its own portfolio of products and/or services, it would be controlled and evaluated on this basis. The reader may wish to refer to Figure 10.6 that depicts the BCG growth–share matrix, which is a useful technique for controlling and evaluating business units.

This type of control and evaluation has become common as business firms adopt strategic planning and focus more on business units or profit centers than on individual products. In a sense, this level of control and evaluation is similar to that involved with specific programs, and many of the points that relate to program control and evaluation are appropriate here.

Level 3: Control and Evaluation of Specific Marketing Programs

Within an overall marketing strategy and within business unit strategies, it is common to find programs developed to carry out those strategies. A marketing program is a detailed, time-phased action sequence intended to guide and coordinate marketing activities to meet market needs and reach marketing objectives most effectively. In its most basic form, the marketing program outlines specific functions or tasks to be performed, specifies time frames for performance, allocates budget for each activity, and assigns responsibility for performance.[3] Program evaluation involves viewing the components of the individual program as a system rather than as a collection of unrelated parts. All elements should be considered in an interrelated, synergistic fashion. If one element changes (for example, price is increased due to rising costs), the effects will be felt by other elements (for example, product quality and specifications, channels, distribution, advertising, and sales) as well as by the total program. Individual program control and evaluation should take place within this perspective.

A business marketing company may employ a number of programs simultaneously within the same overall marketing strategy. Canon U.S.A., for example, developed a marketing program specifically for its new NP-200 desktop copier. At the same time, it employed other programs specifically for other products in its copier line. These programs collectively composed the overall strategy, but they must be controlled and evaluated individually to gain each program's proper perspective.

Program control and evaluation requires the marketing manager to devote attention to several major concerns:

1. How well does each program coincide with the company's overall strategy? Are some programs out of step with overall strategy? Are some programs inconsistent with one another or even mutually exclusive?

2. How effectively are resources being allocated to the various programs? Should some programs receive more attention and resources? Should others receive less? Is the funding adequate to ensure the success of each program?

3. How effective and efficient is the marketing mix in each program? If each program is viewed as a system, the marketing mix of each program should be reviewed in terms of cost and effectiveness.

Program control and evaluation may or may not be the business marketing manager's *direct* responsibility, but it is always his or her *ultimate* responsibility. To illustrate, when a company uses product managers, market managers, or program managers, those individuals typically are responsible for controlling and evaluating their own programs. These people often, however, are also responsible to the marketing manager. Thus, the latter is ultimately held responsible by top management for individual program successes and failures. In addition, the responsibility for controlling and evaluating the overall mix of individual programs is almost always given to the marketing manager.

Level 4: Control and Evaluation of Marketing Functions

Within overall strategy, business unit strategies, and specific programs, marketing activities or functions are carried out by departments such as sales, advertising, and marketing research. How well each functional department performs is what is involved in control and evaluation at this level. Here, strategy changes to tactics. In product strategy, for example, attention focuses on specifications, grades and models, service, and warranties; in advertising, the focus is on evaluating copy and media; and in sales, it is the number of calls, orders, and average order size obtained by sales force members.

Table 18.1 illustrates an approach used to evaluate an advertising campaign for a particular business product. Individual advertisements and media are evaluated according to cost and leads generated. Note that the cost of a lead varies from a high of $11.68 for a direct mail advertisement to a low of $2.20 for a trade journal advertisement. Note also that some advertisements generate more

TABLE 18.1   Advertising Analysis Report

Medium Description	Advertising Cost	Circulation	Number of Leads Generated	Leads as a Percentage of Circulation	Percentage of Total Leads	Cost per Lead	Percentage of Leads Qualified for Sales Follow-Up	Percentage of Qualified Leads Converted into Sales
Advertisement 1								
Industrial directory 1992	$1,500	10,000	236	2.4%	12.6%	$ 6.36	44%	27%
Advertisement 2								
Direct mail 1/92	2,300	1,000	197	19.7	10.5	11.68	17	67
Advertisement 3								
Direct mail 3/92	2,300	1,000	277	27.7	14.7	8.30	23	64
Advertisement 4								
Trade journal A 5/92	1,250	2,500	406	16.2	21.6	3.08	31	24
Advertisement 5								
Trade journal B 7/92	750	2,000	341	17.1	18.1	2.20	41	19
Advertisement 6								
Trade journal C 9/92	900	2,400	278	11.6	14.8	3.24	21	6
Advertisement 7								
Trade journal A 11/92	1,250	2,500	144	6.0	7.7	8.68	32	26
Total	$10,250		1,879		100.0%	$ 5.46		

qualified leads than others, and the percentage of leads turned into actual sales varies significantly. Data such as these provide input that the advertising manager and the marketing manager can use to control and evaluate past advertising and thereby improve future advertising campaigns. For example, the relatively poor response generated by advertisement 7, which ran in trade journal A in November, indicates that year-end advertisements are not as effective as advertisements placed at other times of the year. Similarly, direct mail advertisements, although expensive, seem to generate the highest percentages of qualified sales leads into actual sales.

Control and evaluation of specific marketing functions typically requires standards peculiar to the particular function involved. Advertising is not evaluated according to the same standards as those used in distribution or pricing. Usually, functional standards are stated in terms of overall marketing goals, such as market share or sales volume growth, or in terms of more intermediate goals, such as awareness and knowledge of product features among target market customers.

An example may help make the desired product. Clark Equipment, a manufacturer of truck equipment, used a specialty advertising, direct mail campaign to identify buying influences that could recommend Clark's transmissions to truck buyers. Initially, golf shirts with Clark's logo were mailed to 750 truck dealers with three response cards that the recipient was to pass along to his or her salespeople. These salespeople composed the audience that Clark really wanted to reach. The salespeople who completed the cards also received golf shirts. The names of those who filled out the cards were then compiled on a mailing list, and those people received a three-ring binder with information sheets covering Clark transmission features. Finally, a third mailing explained to these people that Clark had established a direct phone line to its new information center through which any questions about Clark's five-speed transmission sales or service would be answered. In this case, Clark Equipment evaluated the campaign on the basis of additions to its mailing list brought on by the campaign itself. Since the company's mailing list grew 400 percent, from 750 to 3,000 entries, Clark Equipment management judged the campaign a success.[4]

This example illustrates a major problem with control and evaluation of particular marketing functions—there are often no universal standards to employ. Standards often must be tailor-made to the particular function involved and its intended objectives. Each function should have a specific purpose and should be evaluated in relation to that purpose. For example, advertising's purpose might be to create awareness or generate leads. Sales's purpose might be to convert the leads into actual sales. Physical distribution's purpose might be to deliver on-time to the newly converted sales prospects. This illustrates the point being made—each function plays its own role in the overall mix but each has somewhat different objectives against which its performance should be judged.

Another problem with functional control and evaluation lies in the interdependence among functional elements, which often makes it difficult to assign problem symptoms to the proper function. To illustrate, if a company introduced a totally new product and achieved only a 2 percent market share in two years, company management might consider that product a poor performer and recommend that it be dropped. However, other functional areas such as poor advertising, ineffective sales effort, improper channels, poor physical distribution, or ineffective pricing could well have contributed to the product's demise. Isolation of the real functional cause or causes is difficult because of the interdependence factor. For this reason, many marketing managers argue that functional areas should be evaluated collectively and not separately. This thinking has helped foster the use of marketing audits, which are discussed later in this chapter.

Level 5: Control and Evaluation of the Marketing Organization's Individual Personnel

Individual members of the company's marketing organization typically are assigned responsibilities that are expected to contribute to the achievement of functional or program objectives. Individuals ranging from advertising managers, product managers, and sales managers down to field sales personnel usually are subject to some form of control and evaluation.

There are basic reasons for control and evaluation of individual efforts. A major reason is to identify areas in which performance may be improved. Another reason is to provide information regarding personnel decisions such as promotion, salary adjustments, and even termination. The point is that although many business marketing managers do not like to apply control and evaluation to subordinates, it is necessary for numerous reasons.

Standards for assessing individual performance are often derived from the person's present job description (what he or she is expected to do) and from the job description of the next highest job to which the person may be promoted. Three types of standards are commonly used: [5]

1. *Hard standards,* which refer to precise numbers such as sales volume quotas or contributions to profit.

2. *Soft standards,* which involve factors such as personality, character, initiative, judgment, and organizing ability.

3. *Task-specific standards,* which are directly related to short-term problems or projects. For example, a field sales representative may be expected to set up twenty-five new industrial distributors within one year for a new product. Such task-specific standards may be both "hard" and "soft," but they are tied directly to defined projects rather than overall performance.

Level 6: Control and Evaluation of Outside Marketing Organizations

Since many business marketing managers make use of outside organizations, control and evaluation of these organizations is a necessity. Typical of these are manufacturers' representatives, industrial distributors, sales agents, common carriers, public warehouses, computer service organizations, and advertising agencies. They all perform different functions, and thus they must be evaluated according to different standards. For example, the Jordan Valve Company is a big user of manufacturers' representatives. The company evaluates its representatives on the basis of three criteria: (1) their selling and technical competence, (2) their ability to conduct a reputable, profitable, and enduring business, and (3) their personal and character traits, such as good health, lack of distracting personal problems, honesty, openness, ability to work with others, reliability, and integrity.[6] These standards would not be appropriate for evaluating an industrial distributor or an advertising agency, where vastly different functions are performed. The amount of this type of control and evaluation is directly proportionate to the number of outside organizations used. Companies that are heavy users of representatives, distributors, or both will spend considerable time evaluating their performance.

MECHANISMS FOR MARKETING CONTROL AND EVALUATION

The following sections summarize some of the major **control and evaluation mechanisms** that the business marketing manager can use in the control and evaluation of strategies, profit centers, programs, functions, personnel, and outside organizations. Sources of information are referenced in each section, so that the reader can find additional information on each topic.

Schedules and Control Charts

Many business marketers use **control charts** to schedule key events and map out dates of completion. Both Chapters 10 and 12 described the use of PERT charts and critical path analysis to plan events. This chapter examines these tools for their control and evaluation contributions.

A control chart is used for repetitive activities to detect when an activity deviates from its standards significantly enough to be investigated.[7] Figure 18.3 illustrates a critical path control chart used in the introduction of a new industrial product. Note that each activity is (1) assigned a time frame and (2) assigned to a function such as marketing, engineering, or manufacturing. Using such a chart, the marketing manager can compare actual completion times with expected completion times and determine areas in which variation is significant. In addition, where significant variance does occur, it can be traced back to a specific area of responsibility.

Schedules and control charts are useful for controlling functional activities and, when tied to responsibility centers, they can also be used to evaluate personnel. They are also useful in monitoring overall marketing plans and programs in which many separate activities must be coordinated for optimum impact. Finally, control charts can be used with quantitative standards to provide quantifiable performance standards.

FIGURE 18.3   **Critical Path Method Graph for a Business Product Introduction**

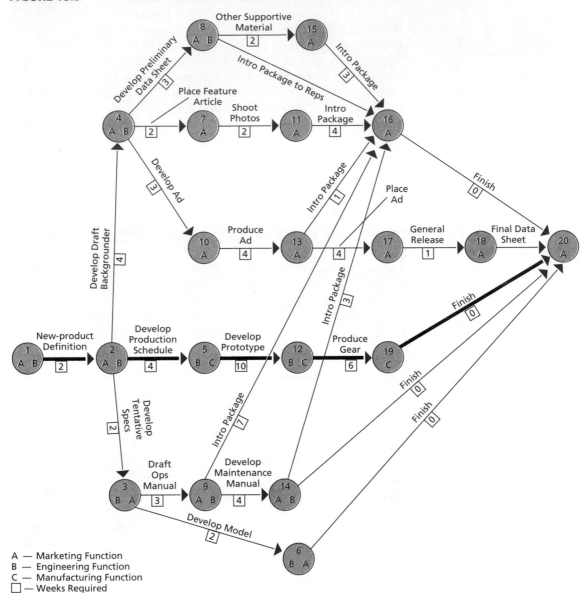

A — Marketing Function
B — Engineering Function
C — Manufacturing Function
☐ — Weeks Required
Note: The description of the activity is on the arrow to the
left of the circle. The critical path is the dark line.

Source: Reprinted by permission from G. A. Marken, "New Product Introduction Schedule Yields Fantastic Results," *Marketing News* (April 15, 1974): 4. Published by the American Marketing Association.

Reports

Another common control and evaluation technique is the report. Like other organizations, business marketing companies use various reports to communicate progress and results among employees. The following types of reports are most common.

Progress Reports   Progress reports are usually short, descriptive reports prepared at dates of important events by managers responsible for completing the activities involved. They are a widely used means of controlling scheduled events and are often used in conjunction with PERT charts or other scheduling devices.

Activity Reports   Managers typically use **activity reports** to evaluate activities performed by subordinates. Perhaps the best known activity report is the field salesperson's call report, which outlines such factors as number of calls made, length of sales call, amount of travel, and person seen. From these reports, comparisons can be made with other salespeople for control and evaluation purposes.

Exhibit 18.1 provides an example of a typical call report. Such reports, when required of and provided by all field sales personnel, give the sales manager both quantitative and qualitative information that can be used for more effective control and evaluation of such field salespeople. The daily call report has been described as the one report universally viewed as a control device by sales managers.[8]

Informational Reports   Informational reports are basically what the term implies—they are reports submitted by subordinates to inform their superiors of the status of various activities or circumstances. A common example is when field sales representatives are required to report on developments in their market areas.

The business marketing manager must be careful in the use of reports for control and evaluation purposes. Report gathering often becomes an obsession, and its value is diminished by the bulk of paperwork involved. Many business marketing companies have incorporated their report-gathering activities into their marketing information systems to facilitate more effective report processing and to reduce paperwork.

Budgets

Budgets that are developed as parts of the planning process are also useful control and evaluation tools. As a marketing manager accounts for the various activities that will compose the overall strategy, he or she also must provide funding for those activities. This funding will become the marketing **budget.** As the activities are performed, their actual costs may be compared with budgeted figures for control purposes. A typical budget may be the one-year budget, in which annual costs for each category are often subdivided by quarters, months, or even weeks for control purposes. Each category's budget level may then become a

EXHIBIT 18.1   Example of a Salesperson's Call Report

Salesperson Name & Number _____

Territory Number _____

Date _____

Company _____

Address _____

Person(s) Contacted _____

_____

_____

Reason for Sales Call: Result of Sales Call:

[ ] First Call/Prospecting   _____

[ ] Follow-up of Advertising Lead   _____

[ ] Customer Request for Information   _____

[ ] Sales Presentation   _____

[ ] Proposal/Cost Analysis   _____

[ ] Close Sale   _____

[ ] Follow-up of Previous Sale   _____

[ ] Service Call   _____

Next Action and Call Back Date:

_____

_____

Additional Comments:

_____

_____

Source: Adapted from Hal Fahner, "Call Reports That Tell It All," *Sales & Marketing Management* 123 (November 12, 1984): 50–52.

standard similar to that used in a control chart. As the manager compares actual expenditures with budgeted figures, variances between the two may be seen.

Table 18.2 illustrates how a marketing budget can be used for control purposes. Note that the total $10,000,000 marketing budget is broken down initially into two parts: $8,500,000 of the total budget is allocated to achieving sales of $40,000,000 to existing customers; the remaining $1,500,000 is allocated to achieving sales of $10,000,000 by adding seventy-five new customers.

TABLE 18.2   Budgeting the Marketing Program

A. Marketing Objectives and Strategy Statement: Achieve sales forecast objectives through sales of existing product line to new and present customers.
1. Sell $40,000,000 value to existing customers—strategic rating 85%.
2. Add 75 new customers who will purchase $10,000,000 value—strategic rating 15%.

B. Marketing Program Budget: $10,000,000

Objectives and Tasks	Task and Value % and $	Organization Resource					
		Personal Selling	Advertising	Sales Promotion	Physical Distribution	Marketing Research	Sales Administration
1. SELL TO EXISTING CUSTOMERS	$8,500,000						
a. Sell new products	15% $1.3*	75% $.98	18% $.23		3% $.04	2% $.02	2% $.02
b. Increase sales of existing products	40% $3.4	79% $2.7	15% $.51		2% $.07	1% $.03	3% $.10
c. Set up 5,000 displays	30% $2.6	10% $.26	20% $.52	64% $1.9	1% $.03	3% $.08	2% $.05
d. Train personnel	5% $.43	95% $.41					5% $.02
e. Increase consumer brand awareness to ___%	10% $.85		85% $.73	15% $.13			
2. ADD NEW CUSTOMERS	$1,500,000						
a. Make 1,200 prospect calls	50% $.75	90% $.68		2% $.015	3% $.023	2% $.015	3% $.023
b. Acquire new leads	10% $.15		90% $.135			10% $.015	
c. Create 200,000 brand impressions	15% $.225		75% $.169		25% $.056		
d. Create 300 trade impressions	25% $.375	40% $.150	44% $.165	7% $.026		8% $.030	1% $.004

Source: Reprinted by permission from Martin R. Schlissel and Joseph A. Giacalone, "Budgeting the Strategic Marketing Plan," *Managerial Planning* 30 (January/February 1982):28.

Note: * All dollar figures should be read in millions of dollars.

These allocations are then further refined by marketing task involved and marketing mix components. For example, of the $1,300,000 allocated to selling new products to existing customers, $980,000 will be given to personal selling and $230,000 to advertising. With this type of budget, the manager can look at sales results and determine if budgets have been adequate or overestimated. To illustrate, if sales to new customers do not reach the desired $10,000,000, it may be because the $169,000 spent in advertising was not sufficient to create 200,000 brand impressions.

Budget control is most appropriate for levels of marketing activity that involve functions and individuals. At these levels, costs are best isolated and traced to persons responsible. Where variances are observed, they can often be identified quickly and remedied at these levels.

In another type of budget control, the marketing manager may compare his or her actual and budgeted functional expenses with industry standards. For example, suppose the advertising budget of a chemical producer amounts to 1.5 percent of sales. Is the company spending too much, too little, or about the right amount? Similarly, suppose sales force selling expenses are 2.5 percent of sales. Is this figure too high, too low, or about right? Comparisons with industry standards are sometimes useful in control and evaluation. Tables 18.3 through 18.9 illustrate average percentages of sales for various industries spent on such marketing-related activities as research and development (R & D), physical distribution, advertising, sales force expenses, and marketing research. Figures such as these provide additional budget standards with which to compare.

TABLE 18.3 Percentage of Sales Spent in Research and Development in Selected Business Markets

Industry	Total R & D Expenditures as a Percentage of Sales
Iron and steel	1.5%
Nonferrous metals	.8%
Electrical equipment	7.1%
Machinery	5.6%
Aerospace	16.0%
Fabricated metal products	.5%
Instruments	8.7%
Stone, clay, and glass	.8%
Chemicals	4.7%
Paper	.8%
Rubber	1.3%
Petroleum	1.6%
Food	.3%
Textiles	.3%
All manufacturing	3.2%

Source: Reprinted by permission from the 33rd Annual DRI/McGraw-Hill Survey of Research & Development Expenditures, 1988–90.

TABLE 18.4   Percentage of Sales Spent in Physical Distribution Activities in Business Markets

Physical Distribution Activity	Activity Expenditures as a Percentage of Sales
Inbound transportation:	
Common carrier	1.5%
Private carrier	1.0%
Outbound transportation:	
Common carrier	2.8%
Private carrier	2.0%
Administration	1.0%
Receiving and shipping	1.0%
Packaging	1.0%
Order processing	1.0%
Warehousing:	
In plant	1.2%
Field—private	1.0%
Field—public	1.0%
Inventory carrying cost	2.0%
Interest	3.0%
Taxes, insurance, etc.	1.3%
Total	20.8%

Source: Reprinted by permission from Bernard J. LaLonde, Martha C. Cooper, and Thomas G. Noordewier, *Customer Service: A Management Perspective* (Oak Brook, IL: Council of Logistics Management, 1988), Question III.B.2.

TABLE 18.5   Percentage of Sales Spent in Marketing* in Selected Business Markets

Industry	Marketing Expenditures as a Percentage of Sales
Furniture and fixtures	7.9%
Chemicals and allied products	9.0%
Fabricated metal products	7.4%
Machinery, except electrical	9.6%
Electronic computing equipment	15.2%
Electrical and electronic equipment	8.7%
Transportation equipment	4.7%
Instruments and related products	13.6%
All reporting industries	8.9%

Source: Reprinted by permission from *Laboratory of Advertising Performance Report,* No. 8015.6 (New York: McGraw-Hill Research Department, 1985).

Note: * Marketing costs include marketing communications, direct selling, marketing support, and marketing research expenses.

TABLE 18.6   Percentage of Sales Spent in Advertising in Selected Business Markets

Industry	Print Advertising Expenditures as a Percentage of Sales
Furniture and fixtures	0.4%
Chemicals and allied products	0.6%
Fabricated metal products	0.4%
Machinery, except electrical	0.7%
Electronic computing equipment	1.1%
Electrical and electronic equipment	0.8%
Transportation equipment	0.3%
Instruments and related products	1.1%
All reporting industries	0.6%

Industry	Direct Mail Advertising Expenditures as a Percentage of Sales
Furniture and fixtures	0.1%
Chemicals and allied products	0.2%
Fabricated metal products	0.1%
Machinery, except electrical	0.1%
Electronic computing equipment	0.1%
Electrical and electronic equipment	0.1%
Transportation equipment	0.1%
Instruments and related products	0.2%
All reporting industries	0.1%

Source: Reprinted by permission from *Laboratory of Advertising Performance Report,* No. 8015.8 (New York: McGraw-Hill Research Department, 1985).

TABLE 18.7   Percentage of Sales Spent in Sales Promotion* in Selected Business Markets

Industry	Sales Promotion Expenditures as a Percentage of Sales
Furniture and fixtures	1.0%
Chemicals and allied products	1.0%
Fabricated metal products	0.6%
Machinery, except electrical	0.9%
Electronic computing equipment	1.7%
Electrical and electronic equipment	1.0%
Transportation equipment	0.8%
Instruments and related products	1.5%
All reporting industries	1.0%

Source: Reprinted by permission from *Laboratory of Advertising Performance Report,* No. 8015.8 (New York: McGraw-Hill Research Department, 1985).

Note: *Sales promotion costs include exhibits and trade shows, catalogs and directories, literature, dealer and distributor aids, publicity, and public relations.

TABLE 18.8 Percentage of Sales Spent in Direct Selling Expenses*
in Selected Business Markets

Industry	Direct Selling Expenditures as a Percentage of Sales
Furniture and fixtures	5.4%
Chemicals and allied products	4.8%
Fabricated metal products	5.6%
Machinery, except electrical	6.4%
Electronic computing equipment	8.0%
Electrical and electronic equipment	5.7%
Transportation equipment	2.9%
Instruments and related products	9.5%
All reporting industries	5.9%

Source: Reprinted by permission from *Laboratory of Advertising Performance Report,*
No. 8015.8 (New York: McGraw-Hill Research Department, 1985).

Note: * Direct selling expenses include salaries, bonuses, commissions, travel and entertainment,
and telemarketing costs.

TABLE 18.9 Percentage of Sales Spent in Market Research* in Selected Business Markets

Industry	Market Research Expenditures as a Percentage of Sales
Furniture and fixtures	0.03%
Chemicals and allied products	1.1%
Fabricated metal products	0.1%
Machinery, except electrical	0.4%
Electronic computing equipment	1.2%
Electrical and electronic equipment	0.2%
Transportation equipment	0.3%
Instruments and related products	0.2%
All reporting industries	0.3%

Source: Reprinted by permission from *Laboratory of Advertising Performance Report,*
No. 8015.8 (New York: McGraw-Hill Research Department, 1985).

Note: * Market research costs include salaries, direct expenses, administrative overhead, interviewing, and computer-related expenses.

The marketing manager must be careful in the use of such budgeting considerations in control and evaluation. Many managers use budget figures as in-
flexible, absolute standards, which may not be valid when the market environment is rapidly changing. Therefore, flexible budgeting is often employed. This
form of budgeting provides for changes in costs associated with changes in sales
revenues and market opportunities. Stated simply, flexible budgeting allows for
greater expenditures in variable cost categories (such as advertising, sales, and

distribution) when sales volumes exceed expectations or market opportunities are expanding. When opportunity exists, increased spending in promotion, R & D, and distribution may be needed to capitalize on the potential rather than basing budgeted amounts on a percentage of the previous year's sales. Unfortunately, the latter method of budgeting is still common in business marketing.

Using industry budget standards as a control and evaluation mechanism is not without risk. Take, for example, the chemical industry averages discussed previously. Before the marketing manager uses 1.5 percent of sales as an advertising budget standard, he or she should recognize that (1) these figures change over time, (2) they change according to the size of company involved, and (3) they may differ for various types of chemical industries. Despite shortcomings such as these, the use of budgets as control and evaluation tools is commonplace in business markets.[9]

Sales and Cost Analyses

Sales analysis and **cost analysis** are used to discover weaknesses or unexpected patterns in marketing results. Typically, overall company sales may be subdivided according to product type, customer type, geographic area, or some other similar classification. Each classification then is analyzed in terms of its sales and cost considerations. Table 18.10 illustrates a sales and cost analysis based on types of product in the product mix. The value of this approach is that although overall sales volume and revenue may be acceptable, the performance of individual products or markets may not be nearly as acceptable. Some breakdown, however, is required to discover this point. For example, products A, B, C, and H are good performers, but products D, E, F, G, and I are losing money. This true picture would have been overlooked if the manager had been satisfied with overall results and had not analyzed the contribution of individual products. Sales and cost analyses aid the manager in deciding which areas should receive marketing attention and which are functioning properly.

Cost analysis is often difficult—much more so than sales analysis—because many costs are not chargeable to individual categories. This practice is particularly true of many overhead costs. For example, how much of a sales manager's salary should be charged against each product? Some form of allocation system must be used to employ cost analyses effectively. Many patterns are used, and business marketing companies vary appreciably in the format of their marketing costs analyses treatments.[10] Regardless of the difficulties involved, many business marketing managers see cost analysis as a necessary element in control and evaluation.

Variance Analysis

Variance analysis, which is an extension of sales and cost analysis, is the process of identifying those factors that cause differences between actual costs or sales and targeted costs or sales. Here, the manager compares such specific factors as quantity sold, price per unit, profit contribution, and market share to find areas

TABLE 18.10 Sales and Cost Analysis by Product Type

Product	Unit Sales	Percent of Total Number of Sales	Total Sales Revenue	Percent of Total Sales Revenue	Direct Costs	Allocated Indirect Costs	Total Costs	Percent of Total Costs	Pretax Profits
A	5,620	11.9%	$1,138,594	18.4%	$ 549,935	$ 214,371	$ 764,306	13.4%	$374,288
B	4,747	10.1	319,998	5.2	111,551	168,328	279,879	4.9	40,119
C	9,328	19.8	1,325,880	21.4	895,056	330,732	1,225,788	21.5	100,092
D	13,816	29.4	288,829	4.7	110,508	180,671	291,179	5.1	-2,350
E	141	0.3	92,578	1.5	31,032	138,006	169,038	3.0	-76,460
F	5,302	11.3	198,623	3.2	65,916	169,197	235,113	4.1	-36,490
G	6,431	13.7	495,674	8.0	203,504	307,736	511,240	9.0	-15,566
H	1,402	3.0	2,231,155	36.0	1,334,405	668,035	2,002,440	35.1	228,715
I	281	0.6	101,095	1.6	83,953	135,661	219,614	3.9	-118,519
Total product line	47,068	100.0%	$6,192,426	100.0%	$3,385,860	$2,312,737	$5,698,597	100.0%	$493,829

where large variances exist. These areas are then analyzed further to determine the reasons for such divergence, so that action may be taken to correct these variances in the future.[11]

Figure 18.4 illustrates a conceptual model that could be used to conduct

FIGURE 18.4   **Conceptual Model of Variance Analysis Used for Control and Evaluation Purposes in Business Markets**

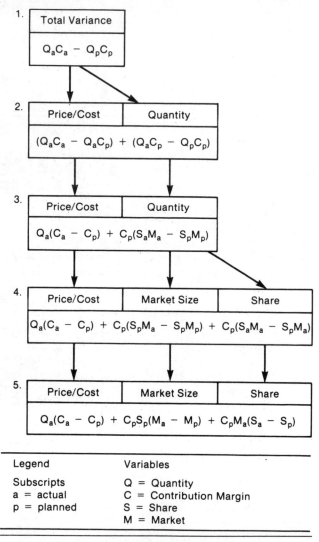

1. Total Variance
$$Q_aC_a - Q_pC_p$$

2.

Price/Cost	Quantity

$$(Q_aC_a - Q_aC_p) + (Q_aC_p - Q_pC_p)$$

3.

Price/Cost	Quantity

$$Q_a(C_a - C_p) + C_p(S_aM_a - S_pM_p)$$

4.

Price/Cost	Market Size	Share

$$Q_a(C_a - C_p) + C_p(S_pM_a - S_pM_p) + C_p(S_aM_a - S_pM_a)$$

5.

Price/Cost	Market Size	Share

$$Q_a(C_a - C_p) + C_pS_p(M_a - M_p) + C_pM_a(S_a - S_p)$$

Legend   Variables

Subscripts Q = Quantity
a = actual C = Contribution Margin
p = planned S = Share
        M = Market

Source: Reproduced by permission of the American Marketing Association from James M. Hulbert and Norman E. Toy, "A Strategic Framework for Marketing Control," *Journal of Marketing* 41 (April 1977): 19.

variance analysis. This model examines such marketing variables as quantity, margin contribution, share, and market in terms of planned and actual performances. The intent is to determine why actual performance deviates from planned performance in terms of each of the variables involved. While conceptual in nature, the figure illustrates a logical approach to the use of variance analysis as a control and evaluation mechanism.

Exhibit 18.2 illustrates an approach to variance analysis applied to trade show promotion. By comparing current budgeted and actual expenses, the marketing manager can pinpoint those activities that contribute to any significant variance. For example, if total actual expenses exceed total budgeted expenses, the cause may lie in the underestimation of support services expenses or entertainment expenses. Specific causes of the variance can be isolated and addressed.

EXHIBIT 18.2	Control and Evaluation of Trade Show Expenses

EXHIBITORS' BUDGET

A comprehensive show budget that leaves little chance for surprises or unforeseen expenses is especially important these days, as exhibit costs continue to rise.

Martha Krafton, director of conventions for the National Office Products Association, designed this sample, which we think is quite comprehensive (although you might want to add under "Personal Expenses" your booth personnel's salaries during the show). It's a sample to tailor to your own special needs.

You can use it to figure costs per show, and annual costs for multiple-show participation. To do the latter, fill out a budget sheet for each show, combine the expenditures in each category, and transfer these totals to a separate budget sheet. If you are using the same exhibit booth for all of your shows, be sure to amortize your booth construction costs.

As a rule of thumb, says Krafton, total exhibit costs per show should be approximately six times the exhibit-space rental fees. But use this only as a rough computation. Remember, developing a comprehensive budget is the first step toward tracking the cost effectiveness of show participation. A budget analysis combined with a measurement of the visitors you reached will tell you whether it cost you $10 or $100 per booth visitor.

	Last Year's Actual Expenses	Current Year's Budget	Current Year's Actual Expenses
Space rental	$_____	$_____	$_____
Booth construction			
Design	$_____	$_____	$_____
Construction materials	$_____	$_____	$_____
Construction labor	$_____	$_____	$_____
Booth rental	$_____	$_____	$_____
Refurbishing used booth	$_____	$_____	$_____
Booth purchase	$_____	$_____	$_____
Total booth construction expenses	$_____	$_____	$_____

continues

EXHIBIT 18.2   continued

	Last Year's Actual Expenses	Current Year's Budget	Current Year's Actual Expenses
Shipping and storage expenses			
Booth freight	$_____	$_____	$_____
Product freight	$_____	$_____	$_____
Drayage	$_____	$_____	$_____
Storage of booth until next show	$_____	$_____	$_____
Total shipping and storage expenses	$_____	$_____	$_____
Support service expenses			
Carpenter labor	$_____	$_____	$_____
Cleaning services	$_____	$_____	$_____
Electrical labor	$_____	$_____	$_____
Booth security	$_____	$_____	$_____
Insurance	$_____	$_____	$_____
Florist	$_____	$_____	$_____
Furniture, equipment, decoration rentals	$_____	$_____	$_____
Signs	$_____	$_____	$_____
Carpeting	$_____	$_____	$_____
Photographer	$_____	$_____	$_____
Telephone	$_____	$_____	$_____
Model and talent agency	$_____	$_____	$_____
Audio/visual	$_____	$_____	$_____
Total support service expenses	$_____	$_____	$_____
Personal expenses			
Convention registration	$_____	$_____	$_____
Hotel or housing	$_____	$_____	$_____
Food and beverage	$_____	$_____	$_____
Transportation	$_____	$_____	$_____
Total personal expenses	$_____	$_____	$_____
Advertising and promotion expenses			
Preshow invitations	$_____	$_____	$_____
Advertising in convention guide	$_____	$_____	$_____
Advertising in other trade publications	$_____	$_____	$_____
Show promotions and give-aways	$_____	$_____	$_____
Postshow thank you's	$_____	$_____	$_____
Mass mailing on show specials	$_____	$_____	$_____
Hand-out literature	$_____	$_____	$_____
Press kits and conference	$_____	$_____	$_____
Total advertising and promotion expenses	$_____	$_____	$_____
Entertainment expenses			
Hospitality suite	$_____	$_____	$_____
Special meetings and meal functions	$_____	$_____	$_____
Catering services	$_____	$_____	$_____
Total entertainment expenses	$_____	$_____	$_____
Total show expenses	$_____	$_____	$_____

Source: Reprinted with permission from *Successful Meetings* magazine. Copyright © 1984, Bill Communications, Inc.

By conducting variance analysis in this manner, the manager is in a better position to develop more realistic trade show promotion in the future.

Performance Appraisals

In many business marketing companies, the performance of individual marketing personnel is appraised annually by one or more superiors.[12] Typically, a marketing manager must appraise performance of subordinates such as product managers, the sales manager, the advertising manager, and the marketing research manager. Those managers in turn must evaluate the performances of their staff employees. Many approaches are used in **performance appraisal,** but the following three are the most popular.

Rating Systems   Rating systems use predetermined scales that define employee and job characteristics. For example, a superior may rate a product manager on his or her planning ability on a five-point scale, where 1 is poor and 5 is excellent. Any number of factors may be rated, the composite of which forms the employee's evaluation. A major problem with the rating system is the subjectivity of the person doing the rating. Many companies use two or more raters to offset the subjectivity. Other firms use so-called behaviorally anchored rating scales in which scale positions are described in terms of actual job activities or behavior determined to be specific to the position being rated. Although there are problems with rating systems, they are used often in evaluating the performance of business marketing personnel.

Open-Ended Evaluations   Another form of individual performance appraisal is the open-ended evaluation, in which supervisors are required to submit written evaluations in terms of such factors as "willingness to make decisions" or "need for specific instruction." This method is often well suited to situations in which job functions are newly developed or rapidly changing or in which specific criteria for performance are not easily determined. Two major problems, however, may be involved: (1) considerable rater time is required, and (2) much depends on the rater's writing skills—a rater who writes poorly can unknowingly jeopardize a subordinate's appraisal.

Management by Objectives   Still another common performance evaluation tool is management by objectives, or MBO. In the MBO process, the employee and the supervisor jointly agree on the employee's goals for the period involved. This method provides the employee with input into the establishment of his or her goals, which in turn provides motivation in that the employee was at least partially responsible for setting them. With such a process, no two employees are evaluated by the same set of criteria; thus, the MBO approach is the most individualized of the three methods discussed here. This individualized approach requires considerable planning and time on the part of the supervisor. A study of the use of MBO in marketing organizations found the following:

The success stories associated with MBO revolve around an appreciation of formal training, top management commitment, evaluation, modification, patience, and reinforcement. On the other hand, many of the failures can be attributed to the assumptions that MBO is simplistic and easy to implement, nothing more than participative management, and requires only minimal attention for participants.[13]

Marketing Audits

The most comprehensive control and evaluation process in marketing is the **marketing audit.** The *marketing audit* is defined as a "comprehensive, systematic, independent, and periodic examination of a company's, or a business unit's, activities with a view to determining problem areas and opportunities and recommending a plan of action to improve the company's marketing performance."[14] *Systematic* implies a logical framework to guide the audit; *comprehensive* means that all factors that influence marketing performance are considered; and *independent* indicates that the audit is to be carried out objectively by people who do not have a vested interest in its outcome.

Marketing audits are complex and costly, and they constitute a major undertaking. The overall audit is often broken down into subaudits such as (1) a marketing environment audit, (2) a marketing strategy audit, (3) a marketing organization audit, (4) a marketing systems audit, (5) a marketing productivity audit, and (6) a marketing function audit.[15] Thus, the contents of a firm's overall marketing audit often parallel the contents of its marketing plan. This parallelism is logical in that the audit is considered to be the control element in the marketing plan.

Because marketing audits are so all-inclusive and comprehensive, neither time nor space permits an in-depth coverage of this subject in this text. This discussion is not intended to provide a detailed explanation of what a marketing audit involves but rather to point out its use in performing control and evaluation tasks in business marketing.

Business marketers' use of audits is difficult to determine. One study of marketing executives (both consumer and business) found that 28 percent of their companies had completed at least one marketing audit.[16] Another study of company auditing departments revealed that 53 percent of the firms surveyed had carried out some form of audit of their marketing operations.[17] The conclusion: Although marketing audits are the most comprehensive of all control and evaluation tools, their use is tempered by their complexity and high cost of implementation.

Other Control and Evaluation Mechanisms

The reader will recall that Profit Impact of Marketing Strategies (PIMS) and the Boston Consulting Group (BCG) were discussed in Chapter 10 as planning and strategy formulation tools. Both also have application as control and evaluation tools and are reviewed here from that perspective.[18] In addition, the ADVISOR studies from the Massachusetts Institute of Technology are discussed.

Profit Impact of Marketing Strategies Since the PIMS materials have already been discussed in detail, there is no need to develop them here. Instead, we examine their control and evaluation usefulness. Some of the PIMS materials provide useful standards for evaluating performance based on company market share. Figure 18.5 illustrates relationships found by PIMS research between return on investment (ROI) and market share, pricing of products, R & D expen-

FIGURE 18.5 Selected Control and Evaluation Standards from PIMS Findings

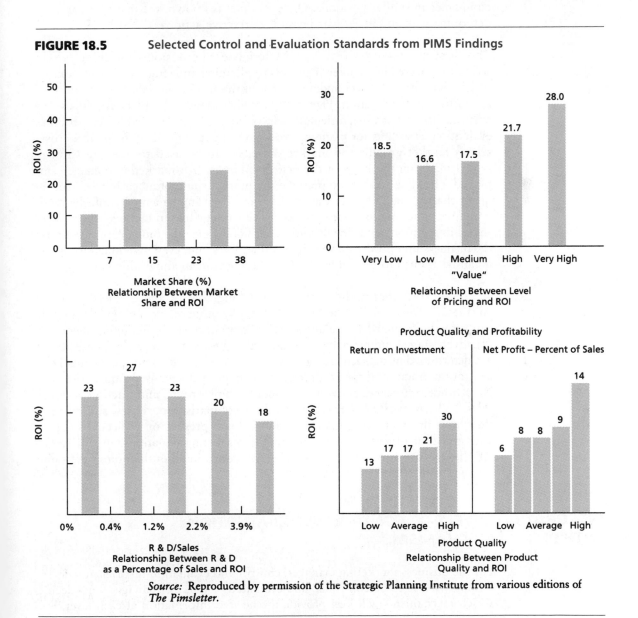

Source: Reproduced by permission of the Strategic Planning Institute from various editions of *The Pimsletter.*

ditures as a percentage of sales, and product quality. These findings provide additional standards against which to judge marketing performance. Comparisons with the PIMS data must be made carefully, but they can be useful and may have profound control and evaluation implications. To illustrate, if a business marketing manager discovered that his or her company was spending over 4 percent on R & D but was achieving only an 8 percent ROI, comparison with the PIMS findings would indicate that the company was not performing as well as other companies in similar positions. Once this fact is known, the manager can then determine why and investigate possible corrective actions.

The Boston Consulting Group   Materials of the Boston Consulting Group were also covered in Chapter 10 as aids to planning and strategy formulation. As is the case with the PIMS findings, some of the BCG materials have application to control and evaluation. Figure 10.6, which depicts the BCG growth–share matrix, shows that this particular form of analysis can be used for control and evaluation as well as for planning. For example, inasmuch as the matrix cross-relates market growth and market share, it can be used to evaluate strategy moves made on the basis of the matrix findings. If a marketing manager employed a holding strategy to preserve the market share of a "cash cow," subsequent matrix analysis after the strategy had been implemented could be compared with the original matrix to see if the strategy had in fact held the market share. In addition, since the BCG concept fits the overall company product mix, the business unit product portfolio, product lines, and even individual products, it can be applied to several levels of marketing control and evaluation.

ADVISOR   Another useful business marketing control and evaluation tool is ADVISOR. Developed at the Massachusetts Institute of Technology, ADVISOR can provide the marketing manager with three norms: (1) marketing spending, (2) advertising spending, and (3) the advertising to marketing ratio. These norms are determined using such criteria as sales, number of customers, customer concentration, fraction of special orders, stage in life cycle, plans, product complexity, attitude differences between customers and prospects, and fraction of direct sales.[19] The ADVISOR norms are useful for comparison purposes, and through their use, the marketing manager can evaluate present or projected budgets with those of other companies in similar marketing situations. In this sense, ADVISOR can contribute to more effective control and evaluation in the same manner as the PIMS program does.

INTEGRATING LEVELS OF CONTROL AND EVALUATION WITH PROPER MECHANISMS

For the business marketing manager, control and evaluation involves first determining what is to be controlled and evaluated. Then, the manager must decide which mechanisms will best provide the needed information at each level. For

TABLE 18.11   Relating Control and Evaluation Mechanisms to Levels of Marketing Control and Evaluation Activities

Levels of Marketing Control and Evaluation	Schedules and Control Charts	Reports	Budgets	Sales and Cost Analyses	Variance Analysis	Performance Appraisals	Marketing Audit
Overall marketing	X		X	X	X		X
Profit centers, SBUs	X	X	X	X	X		
Specific marketing programs	X	X	X	X	X		
Marketing functions	X	X	X	X	X		
Marketing personnel	X	X				X	
Outside marketing organizations	X	X		X	X	X	

example, the manager may wish to control and evaluate his or her company's overall marketing performance. To do this, the manager may then elect to use a marketing audit, or he or she might consider using a PERT chart, sales or cost analysis, or variance analysis. But it is highly unlikely that the same mechanisms would be employed if the manager wanted to assess the performance of middle-level marketing managers such as product, distribution, advertising, or sales managers. Here, the manager might elect to use performance appraisals, budgets, or activity, progress, or informational reports. Table 18.11 illustrates the applicability of the previously discussed mechanisms to each level of control and evaluation activity. Thus, it can be seen that control and evaluation is not truly a precise science. Rather, it appears to be the manner in which the manager uses the proper mechanism to get the most information for decisions to be made at each level. There is no single best way to perform control and evaluation activities in business marketing. Much depends on managerial preferences, the information available, and what specific performances are to be measured.

CHAPTER SUMMARY

Marketing performance must be evaluated in light of objectives to be achieved, acceptable standards of performance, opportunities for improvement, variances in actual and forecasted performances, and redirected marketing efforts required. Marketing plans are complex. They include many diverse activities as well as many different people who are involved in designing and carrying out those activities. Thus, control and evaluation is a very necessary part of overall marketing planning and strategy development. Typically, control and evaluation take place at different levels. These levels are defined in terms of the overall marketing planning and strategy level, profit center or business unit level, specific programs level, marketing tactical or functional level, individual marketing personnel level, and outside organization level. This chapter focused on control and evaluation as it relates to all six of these levels.

In addition, tools and mechanisms were examined that are typically used for control and evaluation purposes in business markets. These included discussion of schedules and control charts, reports, budgets, sales and cost analyses, variance analysis, performance appraisals, and

marketing audits. Examples of each were provided so that their application could be more easily understood.

This chapter discussed the complexity, costliness, and time-consuming nature of control and evaluation. At the same time, however, the chapter emphasized the necessity of control and evaluation for effective marketing planning and strategy development.

KEY TERMS

activity report
budget
control
control and evaluation mechanism
control chart
control level
cost analysis

evaluation
informational report
marketing audit
performance appraisal
progress report
sales analysis
variance analysis

QUESTIONS

1. What do you see as the major differences between control and evaluation in business marketing? Is it possible for the business marketing manager to combine the two into a single element so as to simplify the control and evaluation task?

2. You are the marketing manager of the ABC Company. Your firm uses five product managers to oversee the marketing of five separate product lines that are sold into five distinct markets. If you wished to evaluate these five managers, which mechanisms would you use? Explain why each would be used.

3. Interdependence of the marketing activities makes it difficult to control and evaluate functional elements in business marketing. What does this statement mean and why is it basically true? Provide examples.

4. Explain how a PERT chart can be both a marketing planning tool and a control and evaluation tool. How can the business marketing manager use this same tool for two entirely different purposes?

5. Why should the business marketing manager view control and evaluation as an integral part of the marketing planning and strategy process and not as an independent activity?

6. John Smith is the marketing manager for a business marketing firm that uses manufacturers' representatives rather than company salespeople to sell its products and services. The company, however, has no programs to evaluate the performance of these independent reps. When you ask Mr. Smith why he does not make any attempts to evaluate their performance, he states, "Why should I have to evaluate them when they are paid only on commission from what they sell? I retain only qualified reps and I trust them to do what they are supposed to do—sell our products and services without being badgered by me." Comment on his stand on this issue.

7. What does the marketing manager gain by looking at control and evaluation in terms of several levels? Why not simply combine all these levels into a comprehensive, single-level control and evaluation process?

8. You are the advertising manager for a business marketing firm that is experiencing trouble with a newly introduced product that is not gaining anticipated market acceptance. The product was expected to attain a 5 percent market share by year's end but only achieved a 1 percent share. You are called in by your marketing manager, who wants you to explain why your department failed to meet its objective—the 5 percent share of the market. What will you tell your marketing manager?

9. Explain how the overall marketing budget can be used by the business marketing manager for control and evaluation purposes. Why does it make good marketing sense to use the budget for such purposes?

10. Explain the differences between sales and cost analyses and variance analysis as mechanisms to be used in the control and evaluation process. Then explain why variance analysis may be more beneficial than sales and cost analyses in control and evaluation in business markets.

NOTES

1. "Copier Grabs 60% of Budget," *Industrial Marketing* 65 (March 1980): 28.
2. Louis V. Gerstener, Jr., "Can Strategic Planning Pay Off?" *Business Horizons* 15 (December 1972): 7.
3. Robert W. Haas and Thomas R. Wotruba, *Marketing Management: Concepts, Practice and Cases* (Plano, TX: Business Publications, 1983), 342.
4. "Right People Reached Through Specialty Promo," *Specialty Advertising Report* 15 (4th Quarter 1979): 3.
5. David S. Hopkins, *Marketing Performance Evaluation* (New York: The Conference Board, 1979), 7–8.
6. "What Manufacturers Want from Their Representatives," *The Agent and Representative* 22 (March 1970): 6.
7. Burton D. Seeley, "Interpretation of Sales Data for Action," *Akron Business and Economic Review* 3 (Spring 1972): 35–42.
8. Hal Fahner, "Call Reports That Tell It All," *Sales & Marketing Management* 123 (November 12, 1984): 50.
9. For more information on industrial marketing budgets, see *Survey of Selling Costs,* published annually as a special issue of *Sales & Marketing Management,* and McGraw-Hill Research Department's *Laboratory of Advertising Reports* covering advertising expenditures and budgets.
10. For a further understanding of cost analysis and the approaches that are used, see Charles H. Sevin, "Marketing Profits from Financial Analyses," *Financial Executive* 34 (May 1966): 22–

30; Leland L. Beik and S. L. Busby, "Profitability Analysis by Market Segments," *Journal of Marketing* 37 (July 1973): 48–53; Frank H. Mossman, Paul M. Fischer, and W. J. E. Crissy, "New Approaches to Analyzing Marketing Profitability," *Journal of Marketing* 38 (April 1974): 43–48; and Patrick M. Dunne and H. I. Wolk, "Marketing Cost Analysis: A Modularized Contribution Approach," *Journal of Marketing* 41 (July 1977): 83–94.
11. For a further understanding of variance analysis, see L. Gayle Rayburn, "Accounting Tools in the Analysis and Control of Marketing Performance," *Industrial Marketing Management* 6 (1977): 180.
12. Hopkins, op. cit.
13. Michael J. Etzel and J. M. Ivancevich, "Management by Objectives in Marketing Philosophy, Process, and Problems," *Journal of Marketing* 38 (October 1974): 55.
14. Philip Kotler, *Principles of Marketing* (Englewood Cliffs, NJ: Prentice-Hall, 1980), 124.
15. Ibid., 126–129.
16. Louis M. Capella and W. S. Sekely, "The Marketing Audit: Methods, Problems, and Perspectives," *Akron Business and Economic Review* 9 (Fall 1979): 37.
17. Paul Macchiaverina, *Internal Auditing,* Report No. 748 (New York: The Conference Board, 1978), 39.
18. For a further understanding of PIMS and BCG, see Ben M. Enis, "GE, PIMS, BCG, and the PLC," *Business* 30 (May–June 1980): 10–18.
19. See Gary L. Lilien, "Keeping Up with the Mar-

keting Joneses," *Industrial Marketing* 65 (March 1980): 76–84; and Gary L. Lilien and David Weinstein, "An International Compari-

son of the Determinants of Industrial Marketing Expenses," *Journal of Marketing* 48 (Winter 1984): 46–53.

SUGGESTED ADDITIONAL READINGS

Blasko, Vincent J., and Charles H. Patti. "The Advertising Budgeting Practices of Industrial Marketers." *Journal of Marketing* 48 (Fall 1984): 104–110.

Buzby, Stephen L., and L. E. Heitger. "Profit Oriented Reporting for Marketing Decision Makers." *MSU Business Topics* 24 (Summer 1976): 60–68.

Buzzell, Robert D., and Paul W. Farris. *Industrial Marketing Costs: An Analysis of Variations in Manufacturers' Expenditures*. Cambridge, MA: Marketing Science Institute, December 1976.

Christopher, William F. "Marketing Achievement Reporting: A Profitability Approach." *Industrial Marketing Management* 6 (1977): 149–162.

Feder, Richard A. "How to Measure Marketing Performance." *Harvard Business Review* 43 (May–June 1965): 132–142.

Galper, Morton. *Communications Spending Decisions for Industrial Products: A Literature Review*. Cambridge, MA: Marketing Science Institute, October 1979.

Hulbert, James M., and Norman E. Toy. "A Strategic Framework for Marketing Control." *Journal of Marketing* 41 (April 1977): 12–20.

Jackson, Donald W., Lonnie L. Ostrom, and Kenneth R. Evans. "Measures Used to Evaluate Industrial Marketing Activities." *Industrial Marketing Management* 11 (1982): 269–274.

Kijewski, Valerie. *Advertising and Promotion: How Much Should You Spend?* Cambridge, MA: Strategic Planning Institute, 1983.

Kirpalani, V. H., and Stanley J. Shapiro. "Financial Dimensions of Marketing Management." *Journal of Marketing* 37 (July 1973): 40–42.

Lambert, Douglas M., and Jay U. Sterling. "What Types of Profitability Reports Do Marketing Managers Receive?" *Industrial Marketing Management* 16 (1987): 295–303.

Lilien, Gary L., and David Weinstein. "An International Comparison of the Determinants of Industrial Marketing Expenditures." *Journal of Marketing* 48 (Winter 1984): 46–53.

Lusch, Robert F., and William F. Bentz. "A Marketing–Accounting Framework for Controlling Product Profitability." *Management Accounting* (January 1980): 17–25.

Morgan, Dana Smith, and Fred W. Morgan. "Marketing Cost Controls: A Survey of Industry Practices." *Industrial Marketing Management* 9 (1980): 217–221.

Mossman, Frank H., Paul M. Fischer, and W. J. E. Crissy. *Financial Dimensions of Marketing Management*. New York: Wiley, 1978.

Mossman, Frank H., and Malcolm E. Worrell, Jr. "Analytical Methods of Measuring Marketing Profitability: A Matrix Approach." *MSU Business Topics* 14 (Autumn 1966): 25–45.

Shank, John K., and Neil C. Churchill. "Variance Analysis: A Management Oriented Approach." *Accounting Review* 52 (October 1977): 950–957.

Shapiro, Stanley J., and V. H. Kirpalani. *Marketing Effectiveness: Insights from Accounting and Finance*. Boston: Allyn and Bacon, Inc., 1984.

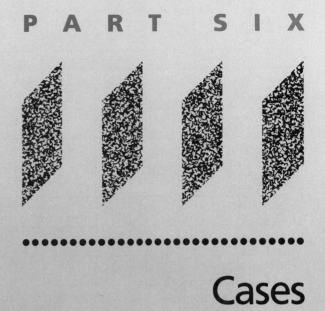

PART SIX

Cases

Case	Name	Product/Service/Industry	Competitive Analysis	Market Measurement	Buyer Behavior	Market Segmentation	Marketing Organization	Marketing Strategy	Marketing Research	Product/Service	Channels of Distribution	Physical Distribution	Personal Selling	Sales Management	Advertising and Sales Promotion	Pricing	Marketing Control and Evaluation
1	City of Brookings	Communications Equipment	X		O								X			X	
2	Electrotech, Inc.	Component Parts	X		O	X		O	X	X		X	X	X		X	X
3	Carolina Jam & Jelly (A)	Food Processing			O	X			X	X							X
4	Carolina Jam and Jelly (B)	Food Processing	X		O				X	X							X
5	Autoscrap Disposal, Inc.	Scrap Metal	X	O						X						X	
6	Atlas Power Tools	Portable Power Tools		X	X			X	O	X							X
7	Milford Glove Company	Industrial Work Gloves	X	O	X	X		O	O		X	X				X	X
8	DOW–IRMA	Industrial Roofing	X	X	X			O		O	O		O	O		O	
9	Gypsum Wallboard Corporation	Wallboard	X					O		O							X
10	Great Lakes Building Products Company	Building Materials		X	X			O		O							
11	Medical Electronic Instruments	Medical Electronic Equipment						X		O							
12	Fairchild Lubricants, Inc.	Cleaning and Lubricants Equipment & Supplies			X				X		O		X			X	
13	Bay City Steam Fittings, Inc.	Thermostatic Steam Traps	X			X		X			O					X	
14	ABC Computer Corporation	Computers			X	X		X			O						
15	MPM Corporation	Testing Equipment		X			O				O		O				X
16	Prime Plastics, Inc.	Industrial Plastics				X	X			X			O				X
17	Southwest Paper, Inc.	Printing Paper		X				X			X		O	O			X
18	Royal Corporation	Copiers			X								O	O			X
19	The D. F. Hardware Company	Hand and Power Tools		X		X							O	O			
20	General Supply Company	Printing Inks and Solvents			O		O							O			X
21	Bolter Turbines, Inc.	Gas Compressors								X				O		X	
22	Wind Technology	Wind Profiling Radar Systems	X	X		X								X	O		
23	Geodesic Domes, Inc.	Domed Warehouses	X		X			X							O		
24	Veber Chemical Corporation	Chemical Resins	X										X	X		O	X
25	Superior Equipment Company	Materials Handling Equipment	X	X					X				X	X		O	X

City of Brookings

Marketing to the Local Government Market

BACKGROUND

Brookings, California, a suburb of a major city in northern California, has a population of over 100,000. The city has been incorporated for over ten years and has grown substantially during the 1980s. City management has evolved in a smooth fashion during this time, and its departmentalization is typical of most cities of its size. The local government of Brookings is much like that found in other towns of the same size in the state.

It has come to the attention of Lars Bloomquist, the city's street maintenance supervisor, that to keep in contact with an ever-increasing field staff, an updated communications system is needed. The present system cannot adequately serve the communication needs of his growing department. Simply stated, Bloomquist needs a system that enables him to contact all field staff as well as provides a way for field staff to contact the department office if the need arises. The present system does not have this capability.

Bloomquist's department includes sixty field maintenance operators, all of whom need their own communications devices. In addition, twenty-three vehicles in the city's maintenance fleet require installation of two-way radios. Some type of base station is also needed.

The design of a two-way communications system is a highly sophisticated and complex task. The two-way communications industry is extremely competitive, and there are many suppliers from which to choose.

Lars Bloomquist has requested a meeting with Milo Bates, the city communications officer. He wants to discuss with Bates the needs of the street mainte-

Case contributed by Steven Turtletaub, Graduate Assistant, San Diego State University.

nance department. After extensive discussion, Bates, who is presently bogged down in the development of the communication system for the city's department of emergency services, agrees that something must be done to enhance the adequacy of the maintenance system.

The system presently used by the maintenance department is an older Mason Electronics system that the city had purchased years before from the neighboring suburb of Clayton. The transaction took place when Clayton purchased a new system and sold the old one to Brookings. The system was adequate at the time, but with Brookings's rapid growth, the city had simply outgrown it. Before working for the city of Brookings, Bates had worked for Mason Electronics, and he still has a number of contacts in that firm. He suggests to Bloomquist that they contact Mason and conduct some fact finding before proceeding. Bates considers telephoning Rodney Slinger, his former boss at Mason. He tells Bloomquist that Slinger, who has been promoted to Mason's senior sales engineer, is likely to be willing to meet with them.

Before meeting with Slinger, Bloomquist and Bates meet and develop a list of questions that they want to have answered. They hope that Slinger's answers to these questions will aid them in their decisions. Some of the major questions are as follows:

1. Can the city keep the equipment now in service and simply add on to the existing system?

2. If adding on is possible, what will be the cost to bring the system up to the city's requirements?

3. What are the expansion possibilities of any such add-on system?

4. How long will it take to build an add-on system once a contract is awarded?

5. If adding on is not feasible, what is the cost of a new system to meet the city's needs?

6. What are the expansion possibilities of any new system?

7. What lead time is involved with a new system?

8. What, if any, personnel requirements are required by either system?

9. If additional personnel are needed, what salary requirements may be involved?

10. Will training programs be involved with either system?

With the development of these questions, Bates telephones Slinger to arrange a meeting.

THE TELEPHONE CALL

Milo Bates places a call to Rodney Slinger at Mason Electronics.

"Hello Rod, this is Milo Bates."

"Hello Milo, how is life in the municipal sector treating you?"

"Well Rod, it is never boring. The reason I am calling you is that our maintenance department is considering an overhaul of their two-way system. I would like your input, if that is possible. Please understand that we are just in the initial stages—all we are doing right now is fact finding."

"That sounds good. Let's meet for lunch if you would like." As he spoke, Rod Slinger was calling up the city of Brookings's listing on his computer database. "Is Lars Bloomquist still with the department?"

"Yes he is."

"Good. I think it would be a good idea for him to be at the meeting. Would next Wednesday at 11:30 be good for the two of you?"

"It is fine with me, but I will have to check with Bloomquist and get back to you."

"OK Milo, I'll talk to you soon. Take care."

"Good-bye."

Milo hangs up the phone and calls Lars Bloomquist to set up the appointment.

THE LUNCHEON MEETING

At the Wednesday meeting, it becomes apparent to Lars Bloomquist that there is no feasible way for Mason Electronics to expand the current system. Slinger states that the cost of expanding is so close to the cost of buying a totally new system that there is little justification to updating the old one. By the end of the meeting, Lars Bloomquist is ready to begin preparing a proposal for a new communications system.

THE DELAY

Three weeks pass since the fact-finding luncheon with Slinger, and no real progress takes place on the development of a proposal despite Bloomquist's good intentions. Bates has been very involved in a battle between the emergency services department and city hall in regard to updating the communications system for fire and paramedic units. Thus, he has not had time for the maintenance department's problems. Bloomquist too has been busy. Severe winter storms have kept him occupied, even though the lack of an adequate communications system consistently hampers road repairs. When Slinger telephones Bloomquist to inquire about progress of the proposal, he is told that the project has been put on the back burner due to more pressing concerns.

With the delay, Lars Bloomquist feels continually frustrated with his inadequate communications system. Two months after the luncheon meeting, he still, however, has not begun to work on the proposal. He decides to call Rodney Slinger.

"Hello Rod. I have been unable to put much thought into development of a system proposal. As you know, this has been an unusually bad winter, and Bates has been embroiled in the emergency services confrontation. We still really do need a new system—it would make my job and everybody else's jobs much easier. We would get roads repaired quicker, and the whole city would benefit."

"I would like to help in any way I can," said Slinger as he listened intently.

Bloomquist continued, "I think you understand our needs. What I would like you to do is write up a complete proposal, specifications, personnel requirements, arguments for a new rather than an add-on system, growth potential, etc."

"Do you also want cost estimates?" Slinger asked.

"Yes, but you need to understand that this will go out to bid."

"Of course. I can begin work on the proposal right away and should have it ready for you in a couple of weeks."

"Thanks Rod, I will look for it. Take care of yourself."

"Good-bye Lars, I will be in touch."

With that, Slinger goes to work on the proposal.

Within two weeks, Bloomquist receives Slinger's finished proposal. This proposal sets specifications around a patented two-way communications system belonging to Mason Electronics. The cost of the equipment alone is $46,000, with an additional $5,000 for installation and training. Bloomquist then submits the proposal to the city's purchasing department for action. He hopes his proposal will start the wheels turning that will provide his department with its badly needed communications system.

A PROBLEM ARISES

Gail Fenster is the purchasing officer for the City of Brookings. On receiving her copy of the proposal, she is taken by surprise, since the proposal is the first she has heard of the entire situation. After reading the plan thoroughly, she calls Mason Electronics to get more information about the system. One week later, she sends Milo Bates and Lars Bloomquist copies of the interoffice memorandum shown in Exhibit 1.

Two weeks later, Fenster, Bates, and Bloomquist meet in regard to Slinger's proposal. The main problem discussed at the meeting is that although Mason Electronics has always provided the city with quality equipment, the specifications in the proposal are drawn so tightly around the Mason system that competitive bids will be difficult to obtain. There are a number of locally owned communications companies that Fenster believes should have the opportunity to submit bids on the system. She feels strongly about supporting local businesses whenever possible. In addition, she claims that Mason bids in the past have been much higher than those of many other competitors.

City regulations require that competitive bids be obtained on any product or service involving over $500. In addition, on items costing over $10,000, formal bidding must take place.

There is general agreement among the three that something has to be done to alleviate the maintenance department's communications problem. They also agree that due to increasing workloads, neither Milo Bates nor Lars Bloomquist has the time to develop a detailed request for proposal. Although Lars knows

EXHIBIT 1   Memo from Fenster to Bates and Bloomquist

CITY OF BROOKINGS
Purchasing Department

TO: Milo Bates, Communications Officer
        Lars Bloomquist, Street Maintenance Supervisor
FROM: Gail Fenster, Purchasing Officer
DATE: February 1, 1989

PURCHASING PROCEDURES

The primary function of the Purchasing Department is to assist the City departments in securing supplies, services, and equipment necessary to carry out their duties at the most economical cost.

The staff of the Purchasing Department acts as a liaison between the departments and the vendors and contractors serving them. The duties and responsibilities of the Purchasing Department are carried out in accordance with the legal requirements established in the Brookings Municipal Code and by the general laws of the State of California.

It is my belief that the Maintenance Department has circumvented specific purchasing procedures, believing such avoidance of procedures would facilitate the implementation of a badly needed communications system.

Gentlemen, there are inherent problems with the proposal that has been submitted for the communications system. I suggest a meeting between the Purchasing Officer, Communications Officer, and Street Maintenance Supervisor. Specific problems regarding the ethicality and practicality, along with purchasing procedures, will be the topic of discussion at the meeting.

I suggest you review pages 1–18 of the City purchasing manual and sections 3.28.001–3.28.180 of the Brookings Municipal Code prior to the meeting.

Gail Fenster
Purchasing Officer

---

what his department needs, he does not have the time to research alternatives to the Mason system or to write up the specifications. The following conversation takes place. "Although cost is always a factor," Fenster states, "I feel that if Lars can write up the specific needs of his department, a consultant may be very valuable in this situation." (Gail Fenster does not like having to hire consultants, but she feels it is justified in this case.) "Do you agree, Milo?"

Bates responds, "A consultant seems to be the quickest way for us to develop an unbiased request for proposal (RFP). I have an excellent list of communications consultants."

"I have an outline," says Bloomquist. "I can have a description of the department's needs to Gail by the end of next week."

"Good," responds Fenster, "you give me your description, and I will put together an RFP for the consultant. Milo, I would appreciate a copy of your list of consultants. That will make my job a lot easier. I have another meeting to go to now. Thanks for your time this morning."

Gail Fenster leaves the room.

"Well Lars, it's in the works. Hopefully, you will have your system in four or five months."

"Great! Just in time for next winter," chuckles Lars.

THE RFP IS SENT TO THE CONSULTANTS

Gail Fenster's proposal is twenty-five pages in length and is mailed to all thirty consultants on Bates's list. The RFP describes the city's purchasing procedures and the general needs of the street maintenance department. In addition, respondents are asked to include (1) prior history of dealing with similar systems and in what capacity they served, (2) sample plans and specifications, (3) a time schedule, (4) costs, (5) a list of employees who will be involved in the project and their backgrounds, and (6) a brochure or written description of the firm giving pertinent information, especially financial. A cost summary sheet is included with the proposal. Respondents are to use this sheet to total all costs. A thirty-day time period is set for responses.

Of the thirty consultants on Bates's list, seven respond within the thirty-day time period. Five of the seven arrive on the last day via overnight mail. The proposals are opened, and proposed consulting fees are read in public from the prepared summary sheets. The purchasing department's secretary keeps track of the bids on a bid summary sheet. Three of the consultants are present at the bid reading and take notes. The bids range in price from $7,000 to $28,000. Total time elapsed in the reading of the bids is seven minutes. After reading the final bid, Gail Fenster states:

"The choice of consultant will be based on qualifications, past performance, and cost of service. The city has a standard consultant agreement that we will use when the selected consultant is hired. We will review all of these proposals and have a decision two weeks from today. Thank you all for attending."

A CONSULTANT IS SELECTED

Thirty-five days following the bid opening, the field of seven consultants is narrowed to just two. These finalists are requested to make presentations to the city council. Both Bates and Bloomquist attend the presentations. Two weeks following these presentations, the consulting project is awarded to the consulting division of Amos & Fitch, Inc. This firm has a large division dedicated to consulting for a number of California municipal governments. The contract is awarded for $16,000.

Reporting to Fenster and Bates, the consultant's staff assigned to this project will spend the next sixty days interviewing field and supervisory staff. Interviews at the communications centers of neighboring communities will be carried out to establish a degree of compatibility with their communications systems. In addition, consultant staff will investigate the market and find a range of products, companies, and services from which to choose. The staff will then write a request for proposal, which will be mailed to potential suppliers of the communications system. A bid list of potential suppliers will be obtained from the city's purchasing department, and it will be incorporated into the consultant's own bid list. Notices inviting bids will be placed in local newspapers and journals fifteen days prior to the formal bid opening.

As stated earlier, the solicitation of competitive bids in the selection process is required by city charter. Since any system purchased will cost over $10,000, the city council has the authority to execute the bid award.

THE BIDDING PROCESS TAKES PLACE

The Amos & Fitch consulting team prepares an eighty-five page RFP that is mailed to twenty-five communications companies qualifying under the conditions developed by the consulting firm. Respondents are given sixty days to present their proposals. At that time, all proposals will be opened, and the bid prices will be read publicly.

Twelve of the twenty-five companies respond with proposals. Only four of them send representatives to the bid opening. Of these four firms, three are from companies based in Brookings. The other is headquartered in the neighboring city of Amherst. Bid prices range from $29,000 to $67,000. These prices include installation and training. Amos & Fitch's consulting team will then take thirty to forty-five days to evaluate the proposals, at which time their selection will be presented to the city council for final approval.

By now, almost one year has passed since Bloomquist and Bates first discussed the overhaul of the street maintenance department's communications system. The Brookings City Council awards the contract to Brookings Communications, a locally owned dealer of Standard Communications equipment. The contract price is $31,000. The system will be compatible with the communications system of two nearby suburbs, so that in case of emergency, the three cities can pool their resources. In addition, system expansion is available at a fraction of the cost of any of the other systems considered. Brookings Communications will order the equipment and begin work installing the system.

FINAL COMMENTS

Lars Bloomquist stands outside his second-floor office looking out over the mountains to the east. An early winter storm is threatening. Brookings Communications has begun work installing two-way radios in vehicles as planned. The base station, however, will not arrive for another week. Milo Bates is discussing something with the installation supervisor down in the parking lot. Lars turns to watch them. As he puts his hand out over the railing to catch the first few rain drops, Milo Bates turns his head toward the mountains and then up to Lars.

"Maybe we should requisition some umbrellas for the work crews," Milo calls up to Lars.

"Don't you have a friend at K Mart who could write up specs for us?" Lars calls back.

"Do you think it is necessary? They say next winter is going to be a dry one," Milo counters.

DISCUSSION QUESTIONS

1. Compare the purchasing practices of Brookings with those found in private firms. Can you identify similarities and differences?

2. Analyze the buying influences involved in this case. What role does each play in this purchasing situation? Which of the buying influences do you consider to be key buying influences? Explain.

3. The city saved only a few thousand dollars by not using the Mason Electronics system that it could have purchased a year earlier. What do you think the city gained and lost by taking the time to go through such a long and complicated process?

4. If you were Rodney Slinger at Mason Electronics, what would you do if you found out that the contract was awarded to Brookings Communications?

5. In terms of specific points, what has this case taught you about marketing to local government customers?

Electrotech, Inc.

Adapting to Changing Customer Requirements

BACKGROUND

Jim Mills and Bill Thompson have just returned from an all-day session with Bob Watson, director of procurement for one of their larger accounts. The customer, a manufacturer of major appliances, is located in central Michigan. Bob had called the meeting to discuss problems Electrotech had encountered over the past several months in meeting the customer's quality and delivery requirements.

Jim Mills is the director of marketing and Bill Thompson is the central region sales manager for Electrotech. Jean Brady, the account representative, accompanied them on the visit. She had been unable to meet with Jim and Bill as they reviewed the visit because she had immediately returned to her office to expedite replacement units for two shipments, totalling 20,000 units, that were rejected by the customer the day before due to quality problems. She was also expediting an order to this account that was three days late.

Jim had called Bill into his office to review the highlights of the customer meeting, which hadn't been a pleasant one. The relationship between the two companies had historically been a solid one. Electrotech had often been favored over their major three competitors due to their lower prices, but during the past eighteen months the relationship had deteriorated severely.

The recent meeting with Bob Watson had focused on his increasing expectations of Electrotech and other suppliers as the customer's competitive environment became more intense. He explained that his company had launched a program to become a leader in the industry with a three-pronged focus on quality, cost, and delivery. His company had initiated a total quality program commit-

Case contributed by Charles O'Neal, Professor of Marketing, University of Evansville. Copyright © 1990 by Charles O'Neal.

ting all organizational units—product design, process engineering, materials management, manufacturing, distribution, marketing, and the support units—to the program. Each unit was to cooperate fully with the other units as they worked as cross-functional teams to develop an integrated customer-oriented product development/delivery system. Key elements of this program were just-in-time (JIT) and early supplier involvement (ESI) programs. Bob Watson had expressed his concern about Electrotech's quality and delivery performance level, especially in view of the need for progressively higher quality and more rigorous delivery requirements. Bob had emphasized this as the direction of his entire industry.

THE COMPANY

Electrotech is a medium-sized producer of electrical motors with annual sales volume in the $80 million to $100 million range. While it is currently developing a line of motors for the computer industry, its primary market is the major household appliance industry—refrigerators, washers, dryers, and dishwashers. It has chosen to market its products through its own sales force, which consists of twenty field sales (account) representatives divided into three regions across the nation. The central region accounts for about 60 percent of the total volume due to the concentration of the appliance industry in the midwest.

Electrotech was formed in 1928 and has achieved steady sales and profit growth. However, profits have declined in the past couple of years due to more competitive pricing and the cost of scrapping and reprocessing a greater proportion of products because of more stringent quality demands by several of their customers. The primary emphasis in both the production and marketing of its product has been low cost–low price. It has been able to achieve relatively low costs due to its early entry in the market and the relatively steep experience curve it has enjoyed with its product. The narrow product line and its industry focus have been significant factors in holding costs at a low level. Much of its R & D investment has been aimed at keeping down manufacturing costs. As a result, it is one of the lowest cost producers in the industry.

A marketing strategy it has found effective in the past has been to bid on high-volume procurements that extend over a year or more for a single product model. This allows long production runs of a single model, thus minimizing the cost of model changeovers and the overhead costs per unit produced. These products are placed in factory inventory and shipped as requested by the customer.

THE COMPETITION

Electrotech faces a variety of competitors. There are numerous local and regional competitors that, like Electrotech, manufacture a narrow line of specialty products that are designed for one or very few industry applications. Most of the local manufacturers do not have the resources to compete for the higher-volume business at larger manufacturers. On the other hand, some of the regional producers are its toughest competitors because of their low overhead costs and proximity to their customers.

The competitors that pose the greatest threat to Electrotech are the larger, diversified, and often vertically integrated companies. These companies often produce a wide range of motors as well as complementary products and may use large quantities of their own component products. They tend to be more sophisticated in planning with customer intelligence systems and have excellent R & D facilities and manufacturing and logistics systems. These companies are also beginning to introduce JIT and ESI programs into their final equipment manufacturing operations.

THE MARKET ENVIRONMENT

The major household appliance market is a relatively stable one. Much of the demand (up to 75 percent of some mature products) consists of replacement purchases. The segment of the market of interest to Electrotech is very concentrated and also very large, as shown in Exhibit 1. Total volume of these four products is approximately 20 million units. The share of industry by manufacturer and total volume are illustrative of a typical recent year.

The major appliance industry is very mature and very competitive. While Pacific Rim producers have totally dominated the microwave oven market, their encroachment on the four major appliance markets in Exhibit 1 has been much more gradual. European-based Electrolux has become a major factor since its acquisition of White Consolidated Industries, a major producer of private-branded products.

Cost pressures stemming from stable demand and intense competition have caused the major manufacturers to move to product design and operational strategies that will result in higher-quality and lower-cost products and the additional capability of introducing new products more quickly. Significant quality- and cost-responsive technologies producers are beginning to implement JIT and ESI systems.

THE JIT/ESI INDUSTRY MOVEMENT

JIT, a Japanese innovation pioneered by Toyota, was introduced into the U.S. by the automotive industry in the early 1980s. The stimulus for its adoption was the significant impact Japanese automobile producers were having on the U.S. automotive industry. Japanese cars were perceived by consumers as having substantially higher quality with prices below comparable U.S. models, and the market share held by U.S. manufactures rapidly began to erode.

JIT, broadly defined, is a business philosophy that focuses on waste elimination in all elements of an organization's systems, as well as in its organizational exchange systems. This includes waste in time, space, materials, human effort,

EXHIBIT 1 Major Appliance Industry: Selected Products

Product	Manufacturer		Share	Total Volume (million units)
Refrigerators	GE		30%	6.5
	Whirlpool		25	
	WCI (Electrolux)		20	
	Admiral (Maytag)		15	
	Amana (Raytheon)		5	
	Others		5	
		Total	100%	
Dishwashers	GE		40%	4.0
	D & M		20	
	Whirlpool		20	
	Maytag		5	
	WCI		5	
	Hobart/Emerson		5	
	Others		5	
		Total	100%	
Washers	Whirlpool		50%	6.0
	Maytag		15	
	GE		15	
	WCI		10	
	Others		10	
		Total	100%	
Electric Dryers	Whirlpool		55%	3.0
	GE		15	
	Maytag		10	
	WCI		10	
	Norge (Maytag)		5	
	Others		5	
		Total	100%	

and any activities involved in the product transformation and exchange process. The strategy resulting from the application of JIT includes a program of continuous improvement with the objective of providing perfect-quality products in exact quantities at the precise time needed by the customer, and at minimum total cost. Two additional points should be emphasized: the "customer" includes internal customers as well as the external customers; and the JIT system requires a commitment by the adopter to a total quality control process (TQC) with total people involvement (TPI).

It is obvious that JIT has a very ambitious objective and it requires a totally different mindset than traditional operational processes. It is controlled by a market-driven "customer pull" rather than the traditional producer push. All upstream (supplier) processes are synchronized with customer demand. The potential of the JIT/TQC/TPI process is tremendous. Adopters have been able to move from quality levels measured in the traditional parts-per-hundred acceptable quality level (AQL), to measurement in parts-per-million (PPM) defective.

Surprisingly the emphasis on preventive quality measures (doing things right the first time), rather than the traditional corrective approach through inspection of the finished product with much scrap and rework, has resulted in dramatic reductions in product costs.

The ESI approach is a companion to JIT. It brings key suppliers into the product/service planning stage very early during the product concept-development phase. This allows the manufacturer to take advantage of the supplier's expertise in product design, materials selection, processing techniques, etc. The supplier becomes an extension of the producer, and partnerships are often formed. This long-term relationship fosters an atmosphere of openness and trust, which allows them to work closely together to find optimal ways of meeting the needs of the final customer.

Many industrial firms, including the major appliance industry, are beginning to realize the critical importance of their materials suppliers. Recent studies have revealed that, across all U.S. manufacturing industries, externally sourced materials account for over 50 percent of the total product cost. Of course, the quality and cycle time of manufacturers are substantially influenced by external suppliers.

The JIT and ESI programs of manufacturers have caused them to become much more selective in choosing materials suppliers. As a result, they are reducing their supplier bases. These reductions frequently reach 50 percent and in some instances 80 percent to 90 percent.

The reason for the supplier reduction is two-fold: (1) to choose only those suppliers that have the capability of meeting the more rigorous demands, and (2) to reduce the number of suppliers for a single commodity (e.g., motors) to a very select few (often, only one) with which long-term partnership agreements can be negotiated.

The adoption of JIT and ESI, along with their much more demanding and precise requirements, brings additional functional representatives into the manufacturer's buying center. In addition to purchasing, which has traditionally been a major influence, significant influences often include: (1) design engineering, with a major role in working with technology capabilities in the design and development of new products; (2) materials management, with key responsibility for the inbound logistics activities, requiring materials to arrive in exact quantities and in relatively narrow time windows; (3) operations management, with their greater concern for the quality and ease (cost) of using incoming materials in the manufacturing operations; and (4) quality assurance, with a major stake in assuring that the incoming materials are "perfect" and suitable for use.

In many JIT arrangements, manufacturers are increasingly placing the responsibility for the quality of incoming materials fully on the supplier (referred to as "quality at the source"). This removes the need for incoming inspection, yet assures that incoming materials conform to the manufacturer's requirements.

ELECTROTECH'S CHALLENGE

Jim and Bill, along with Jean Brady, had been taken on a plant tour by Bob Watson during their recent visit. They were astounded by what they observed. The factory was spotless and the emphasis on quality was obvious. The aisles were clear, uncluttered by work-in-process (WIP) inventory. The only WIP inventory were very small lots being actively used at each work station.

The production facilities were arranged in U-shaped cells (referred to as group technology) with each cell producing a specific family of product models. The workers in each cell were formed into teams headed by team leaders. Each worker and the team leader could, and often did, perform the task of each other worker. This provided much flexibility and gave each worker a sense of doing the total job.

Bob Watson took great pride in the tremendous strides his company had made in model changeover times—a very important factor given the increased number of models they were providing to customers. They had already reduced set-up times for most processes by at least 80 percent and had a goal of having all set-up times reduced to twenty minutes or less within the next year. Some of these set-up times had formerly taken from four to six hours, which had been considered a "given" by the process engineering and operations staff. The reduced set-up times allowed the company to mix models on the same production line, that is, produce a family of models that conformed to the mix desired by the customer.

Bob Watson's company was already arranging with a few major product suppliers (compressors, for instance) to produce and ship "in sequence" so that the supplier's product could be delivered directly to the point of assembly, with quality assured. This would result in major reductions in materials rehandling, transportation, storage, and inspection costs. Their plan was to gradually bring additional key components, including electric motors, into this program.

Jim and Bill grew increasingly concerned as they reflected on this visit. They were at a loss to understand why Jean Brady had not been aware of many of these customer developments. Of course, much of her time was spent calling on smaller accounts and prospects across her territory, and most of her remaining time had been spent checking, tracing, and expediting orders and shipments to try to meet her other larger accounts' more demanding requirements. She had also been on the phone frequently with Electrotech's pricing specialist to try to get more competitive price schedules. Her primary customer contacts at Bob Watson's company were Ed Field, senior buyer for electrical components, David McCray, incoming materials receiving specialist, and Betty Bevins, materials quality supervisor. Electrotech was being required to make more frequent shipments of smaller lots of motors, and the expediting problem caused by delivery delays and defective products was consuming most of Jean's attention. Jim realized that Electrotech would have to make some major changes if it was to keep Bob Watson's company as a customer. Moreover, other major customers might also be moving in the same direction. He began to see the problem as extending beyond the marketing function but he realized that his responsibility was directing marketing and sales, the primary link with customer. Another puzzling question, "What about our other major accounts?" Are they also shifting to the JIT-ESI approach? He decided that he had no time to waste if Electrotech was going to hold its position as a primary supplier to the major appliance industry.

Key questions he knew he must find answers to quickly included: "What strategy must we employ to remain an effective supplier?" "Who must become involved, and in what way?" "What is my role?"

DISCUSSION QUESTIONS

1. What strategy should Electrotech employ to remain an effective supplier to Bob Watson's company?

2. Who must become involved in Electrotech's new strategy? Who else in the company, besides marketing personnel, should be included in this strategy? Why should these others be involved?

3. What do you see as Jim Mills's role in any changing strategy?

4. What do you believe will happen in this case if Electrotech continues its present marketing strategy? Explain your answer.

Carolina Jam & Jelly (A)

....

Conducting Value Analysis

INTRODUCTION

Tracy Lowe is the purchasing agent for Carolina Jam & Jelly, Inc., and she has a real problem facing her. Al Perkins, the plant manager of the Hickory plant, called Tracy on the phone to tell her that he was getting sick and tired of fooling with his old Acme 407 jar finish machine (the machine that puts the top on a filled jar and attaches the label to #4 size jelly jars). He says that the machine breaks down from time to time and the repair and maintenance costs are eating him alive. Besides, he just thinks he would like to have a new machine, and so do his equipment operators.

Al pointed out that Appalachian Equipment makes a fine piece of equipment that can do the job—in fact, Carolina Jam & Jelly's South Carolina peach plant has one. Furthermore, Al says he has already talked to the Appalachian sales rep and has worked with the rep and the plant engineers to develop a complete set of specs. He has put the specs in the mail to Tracy along with a request that Tracy conduct a thorough value analysis comparing the alternatives of keeping the old Acme machine versus buying the new Appalachian machine. If the value analysis works out favorably, he wants Tracy to buy him the new machine since he thinks he can set aside about $85,000 in his budget for new equipment for the next fiscal year starting in January.

The next day, Tracy received the specs, formulated a request for quotation for the new machine, and sent it out to the Appalachian sales rep, Jim Roberts. Then she began to try to get some information that might help her do a value analysis.

Case contributed by Ronald H. King and W. E. Patton III, Professors of Marketing, Appalachian State University.

THE ACME MACHINE

First, Tracy called the plant engineer to discuss the costs involved in getting the new machine on line. He estimated that it would cost $10,000 to yank out the old machine, install new footings and mountings, and make other physical alterations. It would cost another $1,000 for new electrical wiring, hook-ups, etc. Tracy asked him for some figures on operating costs, but he referred her to the plant controller.

The plant controller provided Tracy with some data on labor, material, and power costs per hour of operation of the Acme machine, along with information on interest, insurance, and other such costs. He also was able to provide Tracy with some estimates for the next year's operation. According to the controller, labor costs will amount to $8 per hour for every hour the Acme is in operation. Materials costs for the Acme (oil, lubricants, rags, etc.) should be $2 per hour, and power costs should also be about $2 per hour. He pointed out that these were his best estimates for the hourly costs for next year (1992). He estimated insurance, interest, etc., would be only $300 for the Acme for the entire year of 1992.

He warned that although these estimates were probably solid for next year, some costs would increase after that. He pointed out that hourly labor rates and the cost of power were both expected to increase at a rate of 5 percent per year over the next five years or so. The interest, insurance, etc., should remain stable for several years. He had a real question about the materials costs and noted that the amount of oil and lubricants charged to the Acme machine were increasing rapidly, and his best guess was that these costs would increase at a rate of 20 percent per year as the machine got older.

When Tracy asked about maintenance and repair costs, he suggested that she really should visit with the maintenance shop, since they had the records for the Acme machine. She went down to the shop floor to the maintenance shop and found the maintenance supervisor who suggested that Tracy also get the machine operator to help get some figures together.

Tracy's discussion with these "front-line troops" gave her a feel for what was going wrong with the Acme. The operator pointed out that the number of jars the machine could handle per hour was dropping at a steady rate of 10 percent per year. Several years ago, the Acme could handle 1,500 jars per hour, but the quota agreed on for 1992 was only 1,000 per hour and would drop 10 percent per year of operation.

The maintenance supervisor pointed out that not only was the machine processing fewer jars per hour, it was messing up jar tops and labels more often and costing more to maintain and repair. He estimated that regular routine maintenance and repair next year would cost $4 per hour of operation and would increase by 20 percent each year. He said that Tracy would have to go see the quality control people to find out what was happening with reject rates.

Before Tracy left, the plant engineer came in and asked the maintenance supervisor if he had given her the figures they had worked up on the problems of the failing throw-jig idler arm on the Acme. The maintenance supervisor slapped his head, swore, and pulled some papers out of his desk. It appears that all the jar finish machines have a problem with throw-jig idler arms—they carry great stress and can break right in the middle of processing, causing a real mess.

Sometimes, the arm simply broke, stopped the machine, and had to be replaced—with an estimated repair cost of $500 for 1992. Other times, though, the arm would flail into other parts of the machine causing extensive damage. If the damage was heavy, costs for repair in 1992 would be $4,000. If damage was moderate, the 1992 cost of repair would be $2,000, and even if such damage was light, the cost would be $1,000.

When Tracy asked how often this throw-jig idler arm failed, the maintenance supervisor and the plant engineer both smiled broadly and brought out the results of a study they had done to help estimate the probability of various types of damage, and the probability of failure of the throw-jig idler arm. They showed her the table in Exhibit 1.

They pointed out that not only were the probabilities of failure and damage expected to grow over the next five years, but the costs of the failure and damages were also expected to grow at a rate of 5 percent per year after 1992. Then they told Tracy that if she *really* wanted to get some insight into what was happening with the Acme 407, she should go talk to quality control and see what information they had.

Tracy's visit with quality control was revealing. The quality control people had nothing nice to say about the Acme (or jar finishing machines in general). They pointed out that last year about one out of every twelve jars that came through the Acme was messed up by the machine somehow. Either the jar top was bent, the label was torn, or the jar even broken, so that the jar was rejected and had to be completely removed from normal shipments. The QC people estimated that the rejects were not cheap—each jar rejected will cost Carolina Jam & Jelly 20 cents in 1992 and the cost of each rejected unit will increase at 5 percent per year thereafter along with most other costs.

EXHIBIT 1   **Probabilities of Acme Throw-Jig Idler Arm (TJIA) Failure and Associated Outcomes**

	Year				
	1992	1993	1994	1995	1996
Probability that TJIA will fail	.7	.8	.9	1.0	1.0
If TJIA fails, probability that it will damage other components	.6	.7	.8	.9	1.0
If TJIA fails and other damage is done:					
Probability of heavy damage	.2	.3	.4	.5	.6
Probability of medium damage	.5	.5	.5	.5	.5
Probability of light damage	.3	.2	.1	.0	.0

They also pointed out that the rejection rate for the Acme was increasing rapidly. They expect to reject one in every ten jars that come through the Acme in 1992, and it will get worse every year thereafter. They expect the rate to increase by two percentage points every year (from 10 percent in 1992 to 12 percent in 1993 to 14 percent in 1994, and so on) until the machine completely dies.

By this time, Tracy was beginning to see why Al Perkins wanted a new machine! The old Acme was obviously a very costly enterprise, and although the machine had several more years of life (the plant engineer actually joked that the Acme would still be running the day he died), it was getting more costly to support each year.

THE APPALACHIAN MACHINE

After gathering the data on the old Acme, Tracy began gathering some similar information on the new Appalachian machine. The first thing she did was to call the South Carolina plant manager to get some operating data on the Appalachian machine down there. The plant manager was happy to provide as much information on past history and her estimates for the future as possible. A summary of what she told Tracy is shown in Exhibit 2.

EXHIBIT 2	Operating Estimates for the Appalachian Jar Finishing Machine if Bought New January 1, 1992: First Year of Operation
Expected number of jars processed per hour	2000
Operating costs per hour of operation:	
Labor	$8
Materials (oil, etc.)	$1
Power	$5
Regular maintenance and repair cost per hour of operation	$2
Rejection rate	1%
Cost per rejection	.20
Probability of throw-jig idler arm failure	.1
Probability of failure damaging other components	.6
If TJIA fails and damages other components:	
Probability of light damage	.5
Probability of moderate damage	.3
Probability of heavy damage	.2
Cost of TJIA failure:	
With no other damage	$ 800
With light damage to other comp.	2000
With medium damage to other comp.	4000
With heavy damage to other comp.	8000

These figures were quite encouraging: The Appalachian was obviously faster, more efficient, and cheaper to operate than the old Acme (with a few exceptions) but the major repair costs, though not very likely to occur, were quite high since the Appalachian is a newer, more complex piece of equipment.

In addition, the South Carolina plant manager indicated that while all of these figures were solid, Tracy should expect hourly labor, materials, power, and maintenance costs to increase at a rate of 5 percent per year after 1992, as would the unit cost per rejection and the costs of repairs resulting from TJIA failure. She also pointed out that the reject rate was expected to increase by only one percentage point per year, so that the reject rate for 1993 would be 2 percent, 3 percent for 1994, and so on.

About this time, Tracy decided that it was time to talk to Jim Roberts, the Appalachian Equipment rep, so she called him and invited him to come make a presentation when he brought the price quotation Tracy had requested. Jim showed up right on time, along with a sales engineer and a marketing support rep, and they made a very nice presentation, complete with a video of the Appalachian Jar Finisher in action.

Although Tracy nodded off a bit during the jar finisher action scenes, she got the main thrust of what was going on. The Appalachian machine did seem to be just about what the doctor ordered—new, efficient, computerized, digital displays, and lots of bells and whistles. Jim, like any good salesperson, held the price until last. He dramatically pulled an envelope from his coat pocket and presented Tracy with the "quote" she had requested. The amount made Tracy take a deep breath: $72,000—just to put tops and labels on jelly jars!

Jim pointed out that the price included delivery to the plant in Hickory, but not the costs of installation or training the machine operator. Tracy had forgotten that last item, but Jim and the marketing support rep assured her that Appalachian could provide the training, which should take about thirty hours. Appalachian would charge $17 per hour, and Carolina Jam & Jelly would have to pay the operator $8 per hour while training.

Tracy asked Jim and his cohorts to review the figures she had received from the South Carolina plant and they all agreed that they looked like they were "in the ball park." Jim asked Tracy when she would like delivery, but Tracy smiled and told him that she would get back to him. Jim assured her that she could have delivery by January 1, 1992, but urged her to move quickly.

After they left, Tracy called the controller at the Hickory plant who indicated that the quoted figures matched what they expected and fit within the budget proposal for 1992 if they decided to buy the Appalachian. He also provided Tracy with an estimate that the cost of interest, insurance, etc., on the new machine should run $4,000 per year for the next five years or so.

Finally, Tracy dropped in to see Carolina Jam & Jelly's vice president for marketing to get some estimated sales forecasts for the type of product processed through the Acme jar finisher. The V.P. was interested in the project, and she asked Tracy to tell Jim hello for her, since she had been Jim's sales manager at another firm several years ago.

The marketing vice president gave Tracy figures that showed that sales of jams and jellies in the #4 size jelly jar were expected to be 2 million jars in 1992, and 25 percent of these would be the grape jelly processed in Hickory on the Acme machine. She further estimated that unit sales of this SKU would grow at a rate of 5 percent per year. She warned Tracy, however, that the latest strategic plan included solid plans to drop the #4 size jelly jar at the end of 1995. The #4 size would be replaced by a #18 jar that, although it looked larger than a #4, was actually one-quarter ounce smaller. They would be in full production of the #4 until December 31, 1995, but would drop it with the introduction of the new jar.

This latest revelation sent Tracy back to her office to search for just a bit more information. She talked to a friend in the used equipment business and found out that the old Acme had virtually no resale value, but a four-year old Appalachian would go for $5,000. Tracy also called the plant engineer who informed her that neither the Acme nor the Appalachian could handle anything other than a #4 jelly jar.

▶ THE PROBLEM

Tracy is running out of time. Al wants to know something soon. If Tracy wants the new machine by January 1992, she has to get to work. She needs to do a complete value analysis and decide whether to recommend that Al go for the new machine or stay with the old Acme.

▶ ASSIGNMENT

Put yourself in Tracy Lowe's shoes. Go through all of the information available and conduct a thorough value analysis. Then:

1. Write a memo to Al, giving your recommendation. Include exhibits, etc., so Al will be able to see exactly how you came to your decision. In analyzing and presenting your cost figures, be sure to group them according to initial purchase, installation costs, operating costs, etc., so they are easy to understand. Make sure you tell Al exactly what you suggest and why.

2. Be prepared to make a formal presentation to Al and to the V.P. for operations (who is Tracy's and Al's boss) to explain your suggestion in detail.

Carolina Jam & Jelly (B)

···

Conducting Vendor Analysis

INTRODUCTION

As was explained in the Carolina Jam & Jelly (A) case, Tracy Lowe is the purchasing agent for Carolina Jam & Jelly, Inc., a large fruit processor and manufacturer of fruit jam and jelly with headquarters in Charlotte, North Carolina. Tracy is currently faced with the task of evaluating four vendors who are currently supplying Carolina Jam & Jelly with tops and lids for jelly jars. Although the firm is currently buying tops and lids from all four vendors, management has decided to reduce the number of vendors, and ideally would use only one vendor in the future.

The blanket contract for #4 jar lids will be expiring soon, and Tracy has asked the four current suppliers to submit bids. The firms were asked to submit a per-gross, FOB plant, freight-prepaid quotation for 500,000 #4 lids to be delivered during the next year. A blanket purchase order would be issued to the successful bidder, and each Carolina Jam & Jelly plant would place orders under this purchase order as lids were required during the year.

Tracy and her department, working with the other departments in the firm, have developed a rating system similar to that used in many other industries. Under this system, a vendor earns points depending on its past performance in nine different areas. These points are summed to give a score that can be used to compare vendors in overall performance and can also be used to adjust bid prices for comparison purposes. The system developed by Carolina Jam & Jelly is shown in Exhibit 1.

Case contributed by Ronald H. King and W. E. Patton III, Professors of Marketing, Appalachian State University.

EXHIBIT 1	Carolina Jam & Jelly Vendor Analysis Cost Ratio Rating System

Product Class: Component Parts: Jar Tops

Quality (defect rate)		Delivery		Expediting (number of contacts required during order cycle)	
>5%	1.75	>2 weeks late	+.15	>2 contacts	+.03
5%	1.40	1–2 weeks late	+.07	2 contacts	+.01
4%	1.25	0–1 week late	+.01	1 contact	.0
3%	1.10	0–1 week early	−.01	0 contacts and	
2%	1.05	1–2 weeks early	+.02	supplies status info	−.04
<2%	1.00	>2 weeks early	+.05		

Response to Order Routine (i.e., order acknowledgment, invoicing, documentation)		Technical Cooperation		Facilities (capacity, dependability of equipment, technology, etc.)	
Outstanding	−.005	Outstanding	−.005	Outstanding	−.005
Satisfactory	.0	Satisfactory	.0	Satisfactory	.0
Unsatisfactory	+.01	Unsatisfactory	+.05	Unsatisfactory	+.05

Financial Status (key ratio index)		Value of Sales Calls		Our Business as a Proportion of Vendor's Total Output	
>120	−.02	Regular, helpful, informative	−.01	>50%	+.05
110–120	−.01	Regular only	.0	25–50%	−.01
100–109	0	Helpful but irregular	+.005	10–25%	0
<100	+.02	Very infrequent	+.01	0–10%	+.01

Instructions: Rate each vendor on each item and sum the points. This becomes the vendor's cost ratio score. To determine an adjusted bid, multiply the cost ratio score by the amount bid.

Each vendor would be judged along each performance dimension, points would be assigned along each dimension, and then the points would be summed for a total performance score. For example, assume that a company had a defect rate of 4 percent, delivery was typically four days late, one contact per order was required for expediting, the order routine response and technical cooperation were both satisfactory, facilities were outstanding, the financial status as indicated by a key ratio index was 95, the sales calls were helpful but irregular, and Carolina Jam & Jelly's business amounted to 30 percent of the vendor's total output. In this case the vendor would earn a total score of 1.27 (1.25 + .01 + 0 + 0 + 0 − .005 + .02 + .005 − .01).

Note that better performance generates lower scores, reflecting the fact that good vendor performance should save money for Carolina Jam & Jelly and thus lower overall costs. Conversely, poorer vendor performance would increase costs for Carolina Jam & Jelly. The points given in each category were developed through an extensive study of the relationship between vendor performance and costs within Carolina Jam & Jelly and the magnitude of each reflects average cost and performance changes over the past four years.

The points system was also constructed so that the total score earned by each vendor could be used to adjust a vendor's bid price to reflect differences in performance-related costs. For example if vendor X bid $5 and earned a total of 1.20 points, the adjusted bid would be $5 × 1.2 or $6. Conversely, another vendor who bid $6 and earned a total point score of .90 would have an adjusted bid of $6 × .9 or $5.40 and might get the bid even though the actual raw bid was higher. The cost ratio rating system allows for the explicit recognition that the raw bid figure is not the only cost involved in a procurement action.

Tracy Lowe has just received the last of the quotations or bids from the four vendors on the bid list. Before opening the bids, Tracy quickly reviewed the previous performance of the vendors over the past year (a summary of this review is shown in Exhibit 2). After reviewing the performance summary, Tracy examined

---

EXHIBIT 2   Information on Current Vendors of #4 Jar Tops

---

1. *Ajax Corporation:* Carolina Jam & Jelly's (CJJ) business accounts for 15% of Ajax output. Ajax is in good financial condition (a key ratio index of 110) and has satisfactory facilities. The quality of Ajax lids is good, with a defect rate of only 2%. They typically deliver four days before the due date, their response to order routine is satisfactory, and they typically require one expediting contract per order cycle. Their technical cooperation has been outstanding, and the sales rep calls regularly and is helpful and informative.

2. *Baker Lid Company:* CJJ's business accounts for 22% of Baker's output. Baker is in satisfactory financial condition (index = 105) and has satisfactory facilities. The quality of Baker's lids is outstanding, with a defect rate of only 1%, but their delivery is a bit slow—they usually run four days late. Their response to our order routine is satisfactory, but their expediting leaves a bit to be desired since we usually have to contact them twice for expediting during an order cycle. Their technical cooperation is satisfactory and although their sales rep calls regularly, he is not particularly helpful or informative.

3. *Charles Closure Company:* CJJ's business accounts for 26% of Charles's total output. Charles is in excellent financial condition (a ratio index of 125) and they have outstanding modern facilities. The quality of Charles's lids is not the strongest, resulting in a defect rate of 3%. Their delivery times are right on the button, usually a day early, and their expediting system is outstanding—we never have to contact them and they automatically provide us with regular status reports on shipments and delivery. Their response to our order routine and their technical cooperation are both outstanding. Their sales rep calls regularly and is helpful and informative.

4. *Dogg Top Co.:* CJJ's business accounts for only 5% of Dogg's output. Dogg is in somewhat shaky financial condition (index = 94), but their facilities are satisfactory. The defect rate of their lids is really pretty bad: 4% of them are defective. Their delivery is very slow (typically 10 days to 2 weeks late), we generally have to make three expediting calls in an order cycle, and their response to our order routine has been unsatisfactory in that they rarely acknowledge orders, only provide four copies of an invoice, etc. Their technical cooperation is limited and unsatisfactory, and their sales rep calls infrequently and is not particularly helpful or informative.

the bids from the four vendors. All bids were for 500,000 #4 lids, FOB plant, freight prepaid, and all allowed order-at-will by each plant in the Carolina system. The amounts bid were as follows:

Vendor	Bid (per gross)
Ajax Corp.	$2.88
Baker Lid Co.	$2.85
Charles Closure Co.	$2.90
Dogg Top Co.	$2.04

Tracy had expected the bids to be pretty close, and she was startled by the very low bid by the Dogg Top Company. She was very glad that she had developed the vendor rating system to help her evaluate these bids.

DISCUSSION QUESTIONS

1. If Tracy must purchase all of the #4 jar lids from one vendor, which vendor should she select? Why?

2. If Tracy (and Carolina Jam & Jelly's management) decided to use two suppliers, and if Tracy thought she could negotiate with one of the firms *not* selected in question 1 above, which firm should she negotiate with and what new bid price would be required from this firm to be comparable to the one selected in question 1? Explain.

3. If Dogg Top Co. had bid $1.85 per gross instead of $2.04 (and the other three had bid as indicated earlier), what vendor should Tracy select? Why?

4. What suggestions would you make for improving Carolina Jam & Jelly's vendor rating system?

Autoscrap Disposal, Inc.

••

Measuring Market and Sales Potentials

BACKGROUND

Autoscrap Disposal, Inc., is a shredder of scrap steel from automobile wrecks and junks. Located in a major metropolitan area on the west coast, Autoscrap owns and operates one of the largest shredders in the country. The company's shredder processes 100 tons of scrap per hour or 800 tons per working shift, which averages to 200,000 tons per year.

Autoscrap's shredder is one of approximately ninety operating in the United States. Costs of such shredders range from $400,000 to $4 million, and these machines can process from 25,000 to 250,000 tons of scrap per year. Autoscrap estimates the replacement of its shredder at $2.2 million.

The primary source of scrap is automobile wrecks and junks. Of the approximately 8 million autos scrapped in the United States annually, it is estimated that the shredder industry processes 7 million into recycled steel. The remaining 1 million hulks join the approximately 20 million others resting somewhere in the nation's junkyards.

The average Detroit-made car provides approximately $56 of marketable ferrous and nonferrous scrap metal. Processing costs, however, are high. Autoscrap estimates $50 of processing cost to yield the scrap-market price of $56. On a national basis, 40 million tons of steel is recycled from scrap out of a total U.S. steel output of 190 million tons.

Case reprinted by permission from Robert W. Haas and Thomas R. Wotruba, *Marketing Management: Concepts, Practice and Cases* (Plano, TX: Business Publications, Inc., 1983).

Based on studies compiled by the U.S. Bureau of Mines, scrapped autos are transported to the nation's shredders the following distances.

Distance (miles)	Percent of auto hulks collected
0–9	8%
10–24	14
25–49	49
50–99	14
100–199	10
200–299	4
300+	1

Since it operates its own fleet of trucks, Autoscrap estimates that hulks collected as far away as 250 miles are profitable.

The company is located in a very auto-intensive part of the country and management feels virtually assured of a continuous supply of scrap metal. In 1972, an estimated 8 million autos were scrapped in the United States. The company estimates that about 7.5 percent of 600,000 hulks are available annually in the ten-county area that falls within the 250-mile limit. In addition, it provides the only scrapping facility in the major metropolitan area and has no local competition. From an ecological perspective, the company provides a valuable service (eliminating junked autos) and has a good public image in the community.

The year is early 1972, and the company sells its entire scrap output to the Japanese steel industry. Autoscrap sells to the Japanese through a sales agent, and the company has no sales force of its own. The company does little or no advertising or sales promotion. Since the company is located on the coast and only ten miles from a major port, scrap shipments require no distribution facilities away from the shredding site.

THE PROBLEM

The price paid by the Japanese for scrap steel has been dropping steadily. As a result, profits are being depressed. This alarmed Autoscrap's top management. The company president, Ralph Ferrara, is convinced the company must seek out alternative markets if Autoscrap is to continue as a profitable business. He gives the problem a considerable amount of thought and believes the best solution lies in processing the scrap steel in some manner rather than just selling it. He is particularly intrigued by the idea that Autoscrap purchase an electric so-called mini-steel mill. A minimill is one that employs electric heat and operates at under 400,000 tons per year capacity. Ferrara envisions use of the minimill in conjunction with the shredder to make Autoscrap basically a steel producer.

In addition, Ferrara would like to purchase a metal-forming machine that could take the output of the minimill and process a variety of bar forms. The particular machine Ferrara saw is capable of producing: (1) concrete reinforcing bars of various sizes, (2) one-inch angle iron bar, (3) one-inch square bar, or (4) two-inch flat bar. In his research, Ferrara discovered that the major products of the nation's minimills are steel bars used to reinforce concrete construction. The cost to Autoscrap to acquire the minimill and the accompanying bar-making machinery is approximately $18 million.

Ferrara called in the company marketing director, Henry Roller, and explained the situation with the declining Japanese scrap prices. He also advised him of the company's interest in the minimill operation and reinforcing bar manufacturing. Roller agrees that such a change might be best for Autoscrap Disposal, Inc.

The problem faced by Autoscrap is the $18 million investment requirement. The company would have to borrow funds. In initial talks with possible investors, Ferrara realized that a considerable amount of interest exists, but all want to see a very detailed analysis of the market potential and company potential for output. Ferrara concluded that this means an in-depth study of bar demand, and he instructed Roller to determine the market potential and to assess Autoscrap's possible market share. The two agreed that the primary market area to consider is the immediate county in which Autoscrap is located (La Mirage County) and the two largest surrounding counties (Estrada County and Bayside County). Population in this three-county market is as follows:

County	Previous year's population	Current year's population
Estrada	1,522,000	1,573,000
Bayside	7,030,000	7,050,000
La Mirage	1,416,000	1,461,000

THE PRODUCT

Although the bar-forming machinery is capable of producing four distinctly different bar forms, Ferrara believes the greatest potential lies in producing steel reinforcing bars used in concrete construction. Exhibit 1 illustrates examples of such reinforcing bar, which is commonly called *rebar*. Rebar is produced and marketed in standard bar size designations, which are shown in Exhibit 1. Autoscrap's bar-making machinery will be capable of producing sizes 3 through 11. Ferrara does not believe that measurement of the demand for each size is necessary for the investors' purposes and thus is interested in the measurement of the three-county market for all sizes of rebar as a single product category. Roller's task is to determine this measurement.

EXHIBIT 1   Rebar Producers and Sizes

30 NORTHERN STEEL, INCORPORATED	**37** POLLAK STEEL COMPANY
31 NORTHWEST STEEL ROLLING MILLS, INC.	**37** POLLAK STEEL COMPANY
32 NORTHWESTERN STEEL & WIRE CO.	**38** REPUBLIC STEEL CORPORATION
33 OREGON STEEL MILLS	**39** ROANOKE ELECTRIC STEEL CORP.
34 OWEN ELECTRIC STEEL COMPANY	**40** ROBLIN STEEL COMPANY Bars #4, #5, #6 only. Type not designated.
35 PACIFIC STATES STEEL CORPORATION	**41** SCHINDLER BROS. STEEL CO.
36 PHOENIX MANUFACTURING CO.	**42** SOULE' STEEL COMPANY
36 PHOENIX MANUFACTURING CO.	**43** SOUTHERN ELECTRIC STEEL CO. DIVISION OF THE CECO CORPORATION

continues

EXHIBIT 1 continued

ASTM Standard Reinforcing Bars

Bar Size Designation	Weight (Pounds Per Foot)	Nominal Dimensions—Round Sections		
		Diameter (Inches)	Cross Sectional Area (Sq. Inches)	Perimeter (Inches)
3	.376	.375	.11	1.178
4	.668	.500	.20	1.571
5	1.043	.625	.31	1.963
6	1.502	.750	.44	2.356
7	2.044	.875	.60	2.749
8	2.670	1.000	.79	3.142
9	3.400	1.128	1.00	3.544
10	4.303	1.270	1.27	3.990
11	5.313	1.410	1.56	4.430
14	7.65	1.693	2.25	5.32
18	13.60	2.257	4.00	7.09

Note: Sizes 14 and 18 are large bars generally not carried in regular stock. These sizes available only by arrangement.

THE MINI-STEEL INDUSTRY

The use of electric steel mills has been increasing. In 1972, there were forty-three such mills in the United States with a combined raw-steelmaking capacity of 6.5 million tons. Most of these mills were relatively new—thirty of them were built since the late 1950s. The forty-three plants were located throughout the country with the exceptions of the west central and Rocky Mountain areas. Most of the mills produce mainly from scrap, as Autoscrap intends to do, and their primary products are types of bar used in construction. There are no other mini-steel manufacturers in La Mirage County, but there are some in the three-county area. These are discussed in the section on competition.

THE MARKET

Roller's initial research indicated there are three major components of demand for reinforcing steel bar. More than 90 percent of all reinforcing steel (80 percent of all reinforcing steel is in bar form) is used in: (1) residential construction—single-unit, two-unit, and multiunit residential housing; (2) nonresidential construction—industrial buildings, office buildings, service stations, stores, buildings for religious, educational, and amusement purposes, hospitals, garages, and other types; and (3) engineering construction contracts—highways, bridges, sewers, waterworks, storm drains, dam and flood control projects, harbors, wharves, docks, military, and other heavy construction projects.

In his research in a local university library, Roller found that data on such types of construction for the previous year are readily available from the: (1) U.S. Department of Commerce *Construction Reports;* (2) U.S. Department of Commerce *Construction Review;* and (3) F. W. Dodge *Daily Construction Reports.* The data are shown for the three counties in the following table.

Previous Year's Three-County Construction Figures ($000)

	Estrada County	Bayside County	La Mirage County
Residential: *			
Single unit	$186,157	$203,695	$190,646
Two unit	4,788	8,317	10,206
Multiunit	174,083	541,897	124,834
Nonresidential: †			
Industrial buildings	49,800	83,600	16,800
Office buildings	29,200	252,800	22,400
Service stations	1,300	12,300	2,300
Stores	38,300	128,100	33,800
Religious buildings	3,100	9,400	2,900
Educational buildings	2,300	16,400	1,400
Hospitals	17,900	62,300	7,300
Amusement buildings	6,200	12,000	3,200
Residential garages	6,600	7,500	1,900
All other nonresidential buildings	27,600	100,600	29,200
Engineering construction contracts: ‡			
Highways and bridges	21,765	97,842	59,859
Sewers, waterworks, and storm drains	18,075	103,303	34,416
Dams and flood control projects	2,430	23,345	11,774
Habors, wharves, docks	0	8,963	3,356
Military	1,696	1,743	2,001
Miscellaneous	7,837	46,932	7,250

* U.S. Department of Commerce, *Construction Reports.*
† U.S. Department of Commerce, *Construction Review.*
‡ F. W. Dodge, *Daily Construction Reports.*

Roller's library research uncovered two other interesting points in regard to reinforcing steel demand. First, he found an article titled "Estimating Demand for Fabricated Structural Steel," published in the December 1956 issue of the *Construction Review.* In this article, the author had used regression analysis to produce the following market measurement equation:

$$X_1 = 1532.87 + 0.23523X_2 + 1.00204X_3 + 0.04064X_4$$

where

X_1 = Shipments of structural steel in thousands of tons
X_2 = New industrial building construction ($ millions)
X_3 = New warehouse and office building construction ($ millions)
X_4 = New highway construction ($ millions)

Roller realized that the regression equation was more than fifteen years old but wondered if it could be updated.

In addition, he found other articles in the *Construction Review* that imply relationships between various types of construction and rebar demand. For example, one article claimed that $2.70 of reinforcing steel is used for every $1,000 of residential construction. Similarly, in school construction, the value of reinforcing steel is 5.7 percent of the total materials cost, which in turn averages about 55 percent of the total construction cost. And, about $14.60 of reinforcing steel is used for every $1,000 of hospital construction. Roller believed information such as this was useful but he was unsure of how to use it and its currency. In addition, he was unable to find such relationships for all types of construction.

COMPETITION

From discussions with some of the many contractors in the area, Roller concluded that major competition will come from five steel producers, only two of which are located in the three-county area. The other three are located over 400 miles from the general-market area. The largest perceived competitor is located outside the state at least 400 miles from the three-county market. Four of the five competitors operate mini-steel facilities. In the cases of all five competitors, reinforcing steel is one of many steel products and not the company's sole product as with Autoscrap.

Competition from imported rebar is not considered a major factor. Based on information from the Iron and Steel Institute, Roller discovered that 19,587 tons of rebar came through West Coast ports in the previous year, but none of it entered the port of the metropolitan area where the company is located. Imported rebar came from Mexican and Japanese steelmakers.

MARKET STRUCTURE

Reinforcing steel is typically marketed to contractor customers through reinforcing steel distributors. The distributors perform many functions other than merely supplying reinforcing steel. They also provide: (1) reinforcing steel estimating, (2) detailing, (3) fabricating, (4) installation, (5) reinforcing steel placing, and (6) consultation and technical assistance. If Autoscrap enters this market, it must arrange with such a distributor. Fortunately, the company has contacts with a number of distributors.

EXHIBIT 2   Shipments of Reinforcing Bars by Market Classifications in the United States, 1970

Market Classification	Net Tons
1. Net shipments for conversion, further processing, or resale	5,010
2. Steel service centers and distributors	562,643
3. Construction, including maintenance	2,043,104
4. Contractors' products	10,457
5. Rail transportation	977
6. Oil and gas drilling	22
7. Mining, quarrying, and lumbering	3,129
8. Agriculture	746
9. Machinery, industrial equipment, and tools	53
10. Other domestic and commercial equipment	19
11. Ordnance and other military	210
12. Export	84,395
13. Nonclassifiable shipments	2,180,574
Total shipments	4,891,339

Source: 1970 Annual Statistical Report, American Iron and Steel Institute, p. 28.

EXHIBIT 3   Net Shipments of Reinforcing Bars in the United States, 1961–1971
(net tons in 000s)

Shipments		Shipments	
1971	4,521	1965	3,150
1970	4,891	1964	3,229
1969	3,658	1963	2,683
1968	3,241	1962	2,389
1967	3,249	1961	2,442
1966	3,276		

Source: Annual Statistical Report, American Iron and Steel Institute.

EXHIBIT 4   Values of Selected New Construction Put in Place in the United States, 1961–1971
(millions of current dollars)

Year	Industrial Buildings	Highways	Religious Buildings	Educational Buildings	Sewer Systems	Office Buildings	Hospital Buildings	Residential Buildings
1961	2,780	5,854	1,003	3,661	914	2,398	1,140	21,680
1962	2,842	6,365	1,036	3,631	1,072	2,610	1,267	24,292
1963	2,906	7,084	1,007	3,726	1,190	2,534	1,510	25,843
1964	3,565	7,133	992	4,541	1,325	2,738	1,760	30,526
1965	4,179	7,550	1,201	5,071	1,195	3,059	1,914	30,235
1966	4,793	8,405	1,145	6,320	1,300	3,338	1,934	28,611
1967	5,407	8,591	1,063	7,036	1,058	3,638	1,969	28,737
1968	6,021	9,321	1,079	7,208	1,551	3,938	2,277	34,172
1969	6,783	9,252	989	6,947	1,342	4,770	2,970	37,214
1970	6,538	9,986	929	6,534	1,543	4,949	3,367	35,863
1971	5,423	10,658	813	6,555	1,829	5,896	3,847	48,514

Source: Developed from various editions of *Construction Review.*

Fourteen distributors operate in the three-county area. Nine operate exclusively in Bayside County; one operates exclusively in Estrada County; two operate exclusively in La Mirage County. The remaining two operate in all three counties.

In talking to some of the distributors, Roller made some important observations: (1) they are unaware of where their rebar is actually used. Since it is bought by contractors who build both in and out of the three-county area, the distributors do not know where the rebar ends up. Nor do they care; (2) distributor loyalty to steel producers is fleeting. Once product specifications are met, distributors are motivated primarily by turnover and margin; (3) Autoscrap's product line will be competitive; and (4) Autoscrap's close physical proximity will be an advantage.

PRICING

Autoscrap intends to price the rebar at $115 per ton for rebar sizes 3 through 11. This is considerably less than competing prices. All five competitors priced at $127 per ton plus freight. The largest competitor in the area (who ships rebar in from over 400 miles away) charges $9 per ton for a delivered price of $136 per ton. Autoscrap's financial department advised Ferrara that it expects the cost to produce a ton of steel to be between $90 and $92 per ton. Given these costs and a selling price of $115 per ton, the company would operate at a 20 percent profit margin. For example, if Autoscrap could realize gross sales of $20 million, total profit would be $4 million.

BUDGET

Ferrara informed Roller that while the project is important to the company, only limited funds are available. Roller is budgeted $2,000 for the development of a measurement of the rebar market in the three counties.

At this point, Roller must develop an estimate of the market potential for reinforcing bar in the three-county market. In addition, he must attempt to project Autoscrap's possible share of this market. Once the project is completed, Ferrara will use the findings to approach prospective lenders. Advise Mr. Roller of the market potential and the company's demand.

DISCUSSION QUESTIONS

1. Determine the market potential for reinforcing bar in the three-county market.

2. Determine the sales potential for Autoscrap Disposal, Inc., in the three-county market.

Atlas Power Tools

•••

Interpreting Research Results

COMPANY BACKGROUND

Atlas Power Tools is a large midwestern manufacturer of electric-powered portable tools and a major supplier in the electric portable tool industry. Well established, the company has been in its present location for over thirty years and has developed a good reputation in the industry. Atlas Power Tools serves the entire United States providing electric-powered hand tools for ultimate consumers and industrial types of customers.

Product Mix

The company manufactures seven basic products, all of which are electrically powered and available in either 115 or 230 volts. Although there are several models of each type of product, the basic product line consists of (1) hammer drills, (2) hand drills, (3) sanders and grinders, (4) saws, (5) electric screwdrivers (fasteners), (6) magnetic drill presses, and (7) electric impact wrenches.

Markets Served

Atlas Power Tools distributes its line of products nationally to five basic markets: industrial, construction, government, institutional, and consumer.

The Industrial Market Atlas markets its tools into the industrial market—plants and factories that purchase hand-powered tools as light equipment to be used primarily for production or maintenance applications. The company's customers in this market are almost exclusively manufacturers in SIC codes 20–39, and Atlas focuses its major attention in these SIC designations. In terms of sales

715

volume, the industrial market is the largest of the five markets served. Products typically are marketed by direct sales to larger customers in this market and through a network of industrial distributors to medium-size and smaller customers.

The Construction Market   Atlas tools are also aggressively marketed into the construction industry and are purchased by builders and contractors. These customers purchase tools from building supply houses, electrical, plumbing, and hardware distributors, and wholesalers. In terms of sales revenue, the construction market is the second largest of the company's five markets.

The Government Market   The company also markets its products to governmental customers at all levels. Large governmental customers such as the General Services Administration, the Defense Supply Agency, and state governments typically are served by direct sales. Smaller local and county markets are served through hardware wholesalers, hardware distributors, and even retailers. The governmental market is the third largest in terms of sales volume, but it is considerably smaller than the construction and industrial markets.

The Institutional Market   Atlas tools are also sold to institutional customers such as trade and vocational schools. Sales to such customers are relatively small, exceeding only sales to the ultimate consumer market. This market is served exclusively by hardware distributors and wholesalers, and no direct company sales effort is involved in contacting the customers in this market.

The Consumer Market   Atlas tools are marketed into the ultimate consumer market and are purchased by homeowners from various retail outlets. The products are sold mainly through retail hardware stores and discount houses. Although consumer market sales are sizeable, this market is the smallest of the five served by the company.

The company markets the same basic seven products into all five markets with some minor variations. These occur because of slightly differing specifications peculiar to customers in the different markets. For the most part, however, the total market for the company's line of products is horizontal.

Marketing Organization

Exhibit 1 illustrates the marketing organization used by Atlas Power Tools to market its line of seven products into five distinct markets. As the exhibit shows, the company uses a combination of functional and market approaches in its organization. Five market managers are responsible for developing marketing programs for each of the five markets. Atlas believes this type of specialization is required because of differences in the buying behavior of customers in each of the markets. Functional managers in advertising, marketing research, sales, sales promotion, and distribution then work with the five market managers in for-

EXHIBIT 1   Marketing Organization of Atlas Power Tools

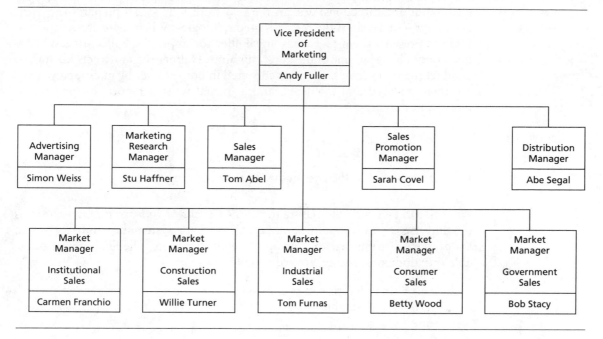

mulating and implementing individual market programs and strategies. The entire marketing department is headed by a vice president of marketing, Andy Fuller, who reports to Atlas's chief executive officer.

THE SITUATION

Andy Fuller has some reservations about the company's performance in the industrial market, although sales in this market exceed those in any of the other four markets. He wonders just where the company stands and how it compares with competitors.

Fuller meets with Tom Furnas, the market manager for industrial sales, and Fuller explains his concerns. The two men agree that Atlas needs more information before any specific strategies can be determined. Furnas suggests that two marketing research studies be considered. One study would survey industrial users of hand power tools in SICs 20–39, and the other would survey distributors who stock and handle such tools. In both studies, Furnas is seeking data that will show how Atlas and Atlas tools are perceived in relation to competitors' tools. Fuller agrees with Furnas and tells him to work out the particulars with Stu Haffner, the company's marketing research manager. The two men meet, and Furnas explains to Haffner what he is looking for. Haffner, using Furnas's input and directions, designs the two studies. His staff prepares the questionnaires and develops the research methodologies. When these are completed, Haffner presents them to Furnas and Fuller for approval. Fuller suggests only one minor change in one of the questionnaires. Haffner then instructs his staff to conduct the two surveys. Data are collected in both studies by mail survey. They are then analyzed and tabulated, and a formal written report is submitted to Fuller and Furnas.

Survey Methodologies

Data are collected in the two studies in the following manner.

The Distributor Survey   Using the *1989 Census of Industrial Distributors* as the universe, 1,013 company names are drawn on a systematic *n*th basis from a list of those distributors stocking portable electric tools. The final sample of usable questionnaires is then arrived at as follows:

1,013	total questionnaires mailed
−17	undeliverable
996	total effective mailing
342	total returns
−37	unusable returns
305	total usable returns

Haffner's survey results are drawn from these 305 returned questionnaires.

The User Customer Survey   Using the *1989 Survey of Industrial Purchasing Power,* the *Standard & Poor's Register,* Dun & Bradstreet's *Million Dollar Directory,* and *Middle Market Directory,* Haffner develops a list of user customers in SIC codes 20–39. From this list, he selects 1,000 companies on an *n*th name selection basis, matching the sample number in each two-digit SIC category so that it is proportionate to the actual number of companies in that category. In this way, Haffner attempts to ensure that firms selected do not all come from the same industry or even a few concentrated industries. The final sample is then determined as follows:

1,000	total questionnaires mailed
347	total returns
−11	unusable returns
336	total usable returns

Haffner draws his user survey results on the basis of these 336 completed returned questionnaires.

Survey Results Both studies reveal that Atlas Power Tools is one of six major suppliers of electric portable power tools to the industrial market, although a number of other suppliers are also active in this market. The results of both surveys show Atlas's position in relation to its five major competitors and an "all others" category. The two studies disclose many points of interest, but major findings can be seen in Exhibits 2–7. Exhibits 2 and 3 illustrate the major findings of the distributor study; Exhibits 4–7 show the major findings of the user customer survey.

EXHIBIT 2   Percentage of Distributors Stocking Portable Electrical Power Tools of Major Manufacturers ($n = 305$)

Manufacturer	Percentage of Distributors Stocking Tools of This Manufacturer
Atlas Power Tools	44.6
Competitor A	47.5
Competitor B	24.6
Competitor C	31.8
Competitor D	20.0
Competitor E	10.8
All others	13.5

Note: Total exceeds 100 percent because many distributors stock more than one manufacturer's tools.

EXHIBIT 3   Rankings of Manufacturers of Electrical Power Tools by Distributors Based on Selected Factors ($n = 305$)

Manufacturer	Product Quality	Product Innovation	Broad Selection	Product Availability	Delivery	Marketing Support	Service	Price	Overall Ranking
Atlas Power Tools	1st	2nd	3rd	6th	6th	2nd	1st	2nd	2nd
Competitor A	2nd (tie)	1st	1st	1st	1st	1st	2nd	1st	1st
Competitor B	4th	5th	4th	2nd	2nd	4th	3rd	4th (tie)	4th
Competitor C	2nd (tie)	3rd	2nd	4th (tie)	5th	3rd	4th	3rd	3rd
Competitor D	6th	6th	5th	3rd	3rd	6th	5th	4th (tie)	5th
Competitor E	5th	4th	6th	4th (tie)	4th	5th	6th	6th	6th

EXHIBIT 4 Sources of Supply Used by Manufacturers in Buying Electric Portable Power Tools

Source	Size of Plant by Number of Employees (%)					
	Total Respondents (n = 285)	Under 100 (n = 58)	100–249 (n = 62)	250–999 (n = 98)	1,000 or More (n = 52)	Employee Size Not Known (n = 15)
Direct from manufacturers	22	17	11	22	37	4
From distributors						
Automobile	5	3	3	7	2	20
Hardware	20	19	24	17	21	13
Sheet metal	1	5	2	0	0	0
Building supply	3	5	2	1	6	0
Industrial	71	64	73	79	64	73
Tool supply	45	48	26	51	46	60
Electrical	14	17	21	7	15	13
Plumbing	3	3	6	1	4	0
Welding	7	14	5	6	6	7
From catalogs	0.4	2	0	0	0	0
From local retailers	0.7	0	0	1	2	0

Note: Totals will exceed 100 percent because many manufacturers purchase from multiple sources. The *n* of 285 is due to 51 respondents not answering the question.

EXHIBIT 5 Departments of Primary Buying Influences Based on Size of User Customer Company (Number of Employees)

Primary Buying Influences Department	Size of Plant by Number of Employees (%)				
	Under 100 (n = 61)	100–249 (n = 64)	250–999 (n = 111)	1,000 or More (n = 75)	Employee Size Not Known (n = 25)
Top management	21	12	2	1	0
Plant management	21	11	5	3	0
Manufacturing/production	10	16	17	13	8
Plant engineering/maintenance	43	61	73	81	32
All others*	5	0	3	0	0
Unknown	0	0	0	3	60

Note: * Includes tool room manager, plant engineer, master mechanic, shop superintendent, and environmental engineer.

EXHIBIT 6 User Industries Purchasing Preferences: Manufacturer's Brands Most Often Purchased by Type of Electrical Product (SICs 20–39; n = 336)

Manufacturer's Brand Most Often Purchased	Hammer Drills (%) (n = 168)	Hand Drills (%) (n = 351)	Sanders/ Grinders (%) (n = 264)	Saws (%) (n = 268)	Screwdrivers (%) (n = 69)	Magnetic Drill Presses (%) (n = 79)	Electric Impact Wrenches (%) (n = 106)
Atlas Power Tools	18	9	9	8	7	16	7
Competitor A	32	49	41	33	33	42	28
Competitor B	22	17	16	30	9	0	9
Competitor C	5	7	8	8	0	8	6
Competitor D	1	2	2	2	7	0	1
Competitor E	1	1	3	2	1	0	1
All others*	21	15	21	17	43	34	48

Note: This table is interpreted as follows: of 336 companies surveyed, 168 purchased hammer drills. Of these 168, 18 percent purchased an Atlas hammer drill most often.

* All others comprised the following number of manufacturer's brands: hammer drills, 16 other manufacturers; hand drills, 10; sanders/grinders, 13; saws, 19; screwdrivers, 15; magnetic drill presses, 13; and impact wrenches, 11. None of the others had a significant share of any product market.

EXHIBIT 7 Buying Influences' Personal Preferences for Manufacturer's Brands of Electric Portable Power Tools (SICs 20–39; n = 336)

Manufacturer's Brand Most Preferred by Buying Influences	Number Citing This Manufacturer's Brand as First Choice	Number Citing This Manufacturer's Brand as Second Choice	Number Citing This Manufacturer's Brand as Third Choice	Total Number Citing This Manufacturer's Brand
Atlas Power Tools	28	17	12	57
Competitor A	109	42	9	160
Competitor B	36	33	14	83
Competitor C	11	7	3	21
Competitor D	4	3	0	7
Competitor E	3	2	1	6
All others (14 other manufacturers)	17	19	16	52

Note: Total responses exceed 336 because some buying influences checked all three choices.

THE PROBLEM

With the results of both surveys in his possession, Furnas must now (1) analyze and interpret both surveys carefully and draw conclusions and (2) present strategy recommendations for Fuller's consideration.

Advise Tom Furnas. Refer also to Discussion Questions on page 722.

DISCUSSION QUESTIONS

1. How do you evaluate the research methods used by Haffner? How do these methods affect Furnas's interpretation of the data?
2. What do you see as Atlas Tools' major strengths and weaknesses in its industrial market in terms of both distributors and users?
3. What do you see as the major strengths and weaknesses of Atlas's major competitors in the industrial market in terms of both distributors and users?
4. How do you reconcile differences between the attitudes and opinions of distributors as opposed to those of users?
5. What do you see as the major problems faced by Atlas Tools, based on the findings of the two surveys?
6. What opportunities for marketing strategy or substrategies do you see as a result of both studies?

CASE 7

Milford Glove Company

Interpreting Marketing Research Findings

Ken Jones has a strategy meeting this afternoon at 3:15 P.M. with the executive committee to discuss Milford's marketing strategy for 1988. Ken has just received the initial data from the consultant's market research study, which was initiated to improve forecasting and better understand the buying process. Ken was on his third cup of coffee this morning as he looked through the ten tables he had just received from the researcher.

BACKGROUND

Milford Glove Company is a major manufacturer of industrial gloves. Milford sells its gloves to distributors, who sell to companies that provide their employees with gloves. These companies represent a variety of industries and consequently the gloves have different applications. The four general applications include: general purpose (GP), chemical resistant (CR), temperature protection (TP), and product protection (PP).

Milford Glove Company prepared numerous internal reports on its glove sales and had previously employed consultants to analyze certain aspects of the sales. Unfortunately this previous research did not help Milford to accurately forecast its sales. Milford wanted to establish a system by which to improve sales forecasting. While forecasting was a primary objective, Milford also wanted to improve its understanding of the customer's buying process.

Case contributed by Hubert D. Hennessey, Associate Professor of Marketing, Babson College. Copyright © 1987 by Hubert D. Hennessey.

SITUATION

The work glove industry is a mature industry that is experiencing little or no growth. Milford marketing efforts over the past few years have put an emphasis on new product development, heavy sales effort to the top 400 distributors (Milford sells to 1,700 distributors), and exhibiting at major end user trade shows. Traditionally, Milford's gloves are priced 5 percent to 10 percent over competitive gloves based on their high quality. In 1986 Milford began to offer a 10 percent to 15 percent discount to distributors who purchased in large quantities. Milford has a high brand awareness. Studies by magazine publishers indicate that 80 percent of the distributors and 60 percent of the end users are aware of Milford.

METHODOLOGY

In order to meet Milford's objectives, an outside consultant was hired to conduct an extensive study using internal and external sources. The following is a list of sources employed:

> Milford personnel
>
> Industry associations
>
> Government statistics
>
> Survey of end users
>
> Survey of distributors

The information gathered from the latter two sources provided the major source of input to fulfill the objectives.

Through use of a telephone survey, 669 end users were contacted. Of these, 393 interviews were completed; 256 companies were not eligible since they did not provide gloves; and twenty companies refused to participate. The sample selection process for the end user survey follows:

1. Milford decides on SICs for the appropriate industries.

2. Names of companies are purchased from commercial mailing lists (information provided: respondent's name, plant location, plant size and telephone number).

3. Companies are randomly selected (every nth name) within each SIC code of locations with fifty or more employees.

4. Quotas are set for each industry group to obtain a minimum number of interviews per group.

5. Sample (Exhibit 1) shows final breakdown. The survey was conducted with the safety engineer, plant manager, or production manager, or purchasing agent.

6. Brand/product awareness data are weighted by plant size so that the responses of the larger plants carried more weight.

EXHIBIT 1   Number of End User Contacts

Industry Group	SIC	Companies Not Supplying Gloves	Companies Supplying Gloves
Mining, oil, gas	11–13	33	19
Contractors	15–17	26	10
Food	20	15	37
Lumber, wood, paper	24–27	20	35
Chemicals	28	12	35
Petrochemicals, coal	29	7	14
Rubber, plastic, glass	30–32	20	38
Primary metals	33	4	24
Fabricated metals	34	17	32
Nonelectric machinery	35	12	26
Semiconductors	36–74	12	17
Electrical, except semiconductors	36	32	41
Transportation	37	19	28
Utilities	44–49	27	37
Total		256	393

Source: End user survey, January 1987.

Three questionnaires were used—one for distributors, one introductory questionnaire for all end users, then a detailed questionnaire by tape of application. Therefore, each end user was asked detailed questions about only his application (GP, CR, TP, or PP).

The survey of distributors included eighty-five interviews—sixty-three with Milford distributors and twenty-two with non-Milford distributors. The Milford distributors were randomly selected from the list provided by company. Only distributors with Milford purchases of $75,000 or more were used. The non-Milford distributors were randomly selected from a compiled list supplied by the end user respondents and the Milford regional sales managers.

RESULTS

Approximately 200 tables were generated from both sets of surveys. The tables were condensed in order to summarize the results.

Forecasting

Exhibit 2 provides the number of gloves broken down by application for each industry. Exhibit 3 gives the end users perception of whether their respective industries will increase their glove usage, while Exhibit 4 provides the distributors' perception of the growth of these industries.

EXHIBIT 2   Number of Gloves Used by Industry, 1986 (000 Dozen)[1]

	General Purpose	Chemical Resistant	Temperature Protection	Product Protection	Total
Mining	3,462	1,404	386	0	5,252
Contractors	2,298	1,840	1,107	0	5,245
Food	15,964	2,578	2,921	7,787	29,250
Lumber	20,490	5,311	6,297	5,008	37,106
Chemicals	6,010	1,197	1,869	5,980	15,056
Petroleum	1,078	1,147	1,058	230	3,513
Rubber, glass, plastic	8,707	1,856	1,882	7,286	19,731
Primary metals	7,098	451	1,164	5,166	13,879
Fabricated	6,814	2,835	626	6,742	17,017
Nonelectric	28,146	1,754	4,190	9,116	43,206
Semiconductors	300	1,081	115	1,546	3,042
Electric	17,460	2,110	5,816	6,218	31,604
Transportation	16,788	1,731	1,038	33,692	53,249
Utilities	5,031	4,467	1,704	28,083	39,285
Total	139,646	29,762	30,173	116,854	316,435

Note: [1]The 1986 glove consumption by industry was estimated as follows:

Total 1986 employment by industry
× % of employees working in plants who provide gloves
× % of employees in the plant who use gloves for that application
× number of gloves per year/per employee
= average number of gloves used for that application in that industry provided by the plant.

Source: End user survey, January 1987.

EXHIBIT 3   End Users Expected 1986 Change over 1985

	Increasing		Decreasing			Total Effect
	%[1]*	Average %[‡] Increase	%[2]*	Average %[‡] Decrease	% No Change	Weighted % Net Change
Mining	20	51	1	25	79	10
Contractors	27	26	4	54	69	7
Food	10	22	10	28	80	0
Wood, paper	53	11	1	30	46	5.8
Chemicals	8	10	0	0	92	0
Petrochemical	26	36	0	0	74	9.4
Rubber, glass	35	36	2	15	63	12.6
Primary metals	13	10	0	0	87	0
Fabricated metals	9	16	83	25	8	(19.3)
Nonelectric mach.	34	15	3	26	63	5
Semiconductors	72	14	0	0	28	10
Electric mach.	67	7	0	20	33	4.7
Transportation	48	11	40	4	12	3.7
Utilities	2	100	33	6	65	0

Notes: [1]This column equals the % of end users in each industry who thought their use of gloves would increase in 1986 over 1985.

[2]This column is the % of end users who expect a decrease.

* Based on question "Do you anticipate the number of gloves used in your plant next year to be equal to, greater than, or less than the number used last year?"

[‡]Based on question "What % (increase/decrease) do you anticipate?"

Source: End user survey, January 1987.

EXHIBIT 4   Industries Reported by Distributors to Have the Greatest Increase/Decrease in 1986 (% of Respondents)

	Milford Distributors		Non-Milford Distributors		Total	
	Increase*	Decrease‡	Increase*	Decrease‡	Increase	Decrease
Mining	1.6	1.6	0	0	1.2	1.2
Construction	4.8	9.5	13.6	9.1	7.1	9.4
Food	14.3	4.8	4.5	4.5	11.8	3.7
Lumber, wood	6.3	1.6	4.5	0	5.9	1.2
Chemical	9.5	3.2	9.1	0	9.4	2.4
Petroleum	4.9	0	0	4.5	3.5	1.2
Rubber	1.6	0	0	0	1.2	0
Stone, glass, clay	0	1.6	0	4.5	0	2.4
Primary metals	11.1	7.9	0	9.1	8.2	8.2
Fabricated metals	3.2	4.8	4.5	0	3.5	3.5
Nonelectric machinery	1.6	4.8	9.1	0	3.5	3.5
Electric machinery and semiconductors	14.3	3.2	22.7	0	16.5	2.4
Transportation equipment	6.3	4.8	9.1	0	7.1	3.5
Medical	0	1.6	4.5	0	1.2	1.2
None	12.7	12.7	13.6	12.9	12.9	13.6

Notes: *Based on question "Over the next year which industry will show the greatest increase in glove usage?"
‡Based on question "Over the next year which industry will show the greatest decrease in glove usage?"
Source: Distributor survey, January 1987.

Buying Process

The buying process involves several factors. The following exhibits reflect particular decisions Milford has to make in terms of an overall marketing strategy.

1. Choosing a manufacturer
   End user perspectives: Exhibit 5 provides a summary of factors important in choosing a particular manufacturer.
   Distributor perspectives: Exhibit 6 provides a set of factors that Milford felt was important in determining why they carry a particular manufacturer's glove.

2. Rating of suppliers
   How Milford ranked in terms of the important characteristics is depicted from both end user and distributor perspectives. Exhibit 7 provides the end users' point of view, while Exhibit 8 illustrates Milford's standing in terms of its major competitors from a distributor's perspective.

3. Choosing a distributor
   Exhibit 9 depicts how distributors are chosen by end users, and Exhibit 10 provides a summary of the number of distributors end users employ.

EXHIBIT 5   **End User Factors of Greatest Influence on the Choice of Manufacturer (% of Users)**

	Use Milford Most Often		Aware Nonusers[1]	
	Brand Buyers[2]	Generic Buyers[3]	Brand Buyers[2]	Generic Buyers[3]
Glove price	23.0	90.7	67.5	94.7
Glove quality	45.5	88.7	50.9	67.4
Employee preference	70.1	2.8	.6	11.2
Specification for glove	4.9	28.3	23.1	10.7
Preference of purchasing	50.7	3.6	5.3	0
Preference of other key people	58.7	0	0	0
Distributor recommendation	0	32.4	46.2	2.7
Delivery	2.4	8.5	13.6	3.7
Past experience manufacturing	2.4	26.7	1.9	.5
Manufacturer reputation	1.3	2.0	45.6	0

Notes: Based on question "In the purchase process for (application) gloves, what factors seem to have the greatest influence on which manufacturer's glove is used?"

[1] These purchasers are aware of Milford but do not use their gloves.

[2] These purchasers purchased gloves by name of manufacturer.

[3] These purchasers purchased gloves only by material, i.e., cotton, leather, synthetic, asbestos.

Source: End user survey, January 1987.

EXHIBIT 6   **Distributor Factors Influencing the Decision to Carry a Manufacturer (% of Respondents)**

	Milford Distributors	Non-Milford Distributors	Total
Quality	82.8	68.2	77.6
Price	69.0	63.6	70.6
Delivery/availability	31.0	31.8	30.6
Service	24.1	13.6	23.5
Requested by customers	20.7	22.7	21.2

Note: *Based on question "What factors influence your decision to carry a particular glove manufacturer? Are there any other factors?" (Unaided)

Source: Distributor survey, January 1987.

| **EXHIBIT 7** | **End User Ratings* of Milford (by Application)** | | | | |

	General Purpose	Chemical Resistant	Temperature Protection	Product Protection	Total
Excellent quality	4.24	4.24	4.98	4.11	4.32
Good delivery	4.69	4.13	4.78	4.17	4.27
Good tech. support	4.38	4.11	4.72	4.06	4.19
Lot consistency	4.92	4.67	4.92	4.12	4.65
Low purchase price	4.25	2.62	1.68	4.17	2.70
Wide range	4.67	4.45	5.0	4.01	4.48
Innovative company	3.88	4.18	5.0	4.07	4.26
Good cost/wear rating	4.42	4.10	4.91	3.28	4.13
Good sales rep.	4.58	4.11	4.83	4.10	4.22

Notes: Ratings based on a scale of 1–5, in which 1 = disagree strongly, and 5 = agree strongly.

* Based on question "I'd like you to rate several manufacturers of gloves on a number of characteristics. Please rate these companies on a scale from 1 to 5 where 5 means you strongly agree and 1 means you strongly disagree for the following items." (Milford was used as if it had awareness.)

Source: End user survey, January 1987.

| **EXHIBIT 8** | **Distributor Ratings of Manufacturers‡ (Mean)** | | | | | |

Characteristics (Descending Order)	Importance* of Character- istics	Milford	Boss	Husky	Wilson	Leader
Quality	4.72	4.82	4.36	4.25	4.40	Milford
Delivery	4.66	3.98	4.36	3.50	3.93	Boss
Good customer service	4.52	4.41	4.36	4.00	4.20	Milford
Prices	4.39	4.08	4.42	3.56	3.87	Boss
Broad product line	4.08	4.61	3.97	3.63	3.73	Milford
Good credit/freight	3.99	4.13	4.15	3.75	4.40	Wilson
Effective sales	3.84	4.20	3.39	3.31	2.87	Milford
Quality sales literature	3.73	4.56	3.97	4.25	4.13	Milford
Good advertising	3.66	4.39	3.61	3.69	3.80	Milford
Manufacturing requested	3.65	4.32	3.67	3.50	3.00	Milford
Sales leads	3.35	3.42	2.70	3.19	2.13	Milford
Base	85	70	35	22	16	

Notes: * Based on question "I'm going to read you a list of characteristics of glove manufacturers that you may find important when deciding which manufacturer's gloves to carry. Please use a scale from 0 to 5 to indicate how important each item is in choosing a manufacturer. A 5 means extremely important, a 0 means not important at all."

‡ Based on question "I'd like you to rate several manufacturers of gloves on the same characteristics. (Three leading manufacturers' distributors carried.) Please rate these companies on a scale of 1 to 5, with 5 being extremely important and 1 being not important at all."

Source: Distributor survey, January 1987.

EXHIBIT 9 Why Distributor Is Used Most Often by End Users (% of Respondents)

	Aware of Milford		By Purchase Behavior		
	User	Nonuser	Brand Buyer	Generic Buyer	Total
Conveniently located	30.2	29.1	29.6	39.8	36.0
Serviced long time	57.8	11.2	42.7	23.5	30.4
Carry brands needed	41.5	45.5	27.7	25.8	26.8
Reputation outstanding	43.9	31.8	43.8	4.3	18.9
Price	12.0	17.0	5.8	22.2	16.3
Provides other products	45.5	23.2	40.1	2.5	16.2
Other factors	.1	0	.5	23.3	14.9
Delivery	1.9	.3	9.4	.3	3.6
Reliability/service	.5	20.9	.9	4.5	3.2
Specialist in gloves	2.3	8.9	4.8	1.9	3.1
Quality	1.9	.8	.9	1.9	1.5

Note: Based on question "Why do you use (name of distributor previously given) most often?" (Unaided)
Source: End user survey, January 1987.

EXHIBIT 10 End User Purchasing System Used Most Often (% of Users)

	Aware of Milford		By Purchase Behavior		
	User	Nonuser	Brand	Generic	Total
Number of different distributors	63.9	14.9	47.5	48.8	48.1
One distributor at all times	8.7	45.3	28.2	19.8	23.1
One distributor most of the time but occasionally others	14.9	38.7	10.3	19.2	15.9
Purchase direct	.2	1.1	5.1	10.8	8.6

Note: Based on question "When buying gloves do you use . . . (read list)?"
Source: End user survey, January 1987.

Ken wondered if he could use the data collected for some of the following reasons:

1. Improvement of sales forecasting.
2. Changes in Milford's advertising to end users and distributors. Currently Milford's advertising emphasizes glove quality.
3. Changes in Milford's sales effort that would convince distributors to promote Milford's gloves over other gloves the distributor carries.
4. Any other changes that would increase Milford's sales.

DOW—IRMA

....

Marketing Program for a New Roofing System

In late 1970, marketing executives at The Dow Chemical Company were wrestling with their marketing efforts for an entirely new concept in building roofs on industrial and commercial buildings. The market was not a new one for Dow (their STYROFOAM * brand plastic foam had been sold uneconomically in the roofing market for some six years), but it was a terribly difficult one. Whatever marketing efforts they decided on would have to be consistent with a complex array of contractors, roof-installers, architects, etc., each of whom had a set of attitudes on industrial roofing that differed significantly from the others.

THE COMPANY

The Dow Chemical Company is a world leader in the manufacture and sale of chemicals, metals, plastic materials and products, pharmaceuticals, ag-chemicals, and consumer products. Located in Midland, Michigan, it had sales of over $2 billion, had plants all over the world, employed over 40,000 people, and engaged in a complete variety of marketing activities (through many different divisions) from the use of industrial distribution to sell basic chemicals to television advertising of Saran-Wrap brand plastic film and Dowgard * coolant antifreeze.

One major Dow department is Functional Products and Systems. This department includes groups handling heat transfer, ion exchange resins, and con-

* Trademark of the Dow Chemical Company.
Case contributed by the Graduate School of Business Administration, the University of Michigan. This case was prepared by C. Merle Crawford with the research assistance of Kenneth A. Epstein. Copyright © 1976 by the Division of Research, the University of Michigan.

struction materials. People in the construction group work on end-use applications, one of which is roofing. The people in the roofing area are then responsible for the IRMA (Insulated Roof Membrane Assembly) system.

THE ROOFING MARKET

Although there are many types of roofs in the world, the IRMA system concerns only the insulated industrial roof found in developed nations where heating or air conditioning are essential and costly.

Roof Systems

Insulated roofs are those roofs that include a structural decking surface (for example, wood, steel, concrete), above which is located some sort of waterproofing (usually the distillate of coal called coal tar pitch or the residue of petroleum called asphalt) and some type of material that reduces the transfer of heat or cold from the interior of the building to the exterior or vice versa. The use of insulation inside the building underneath the roof deck (for example, batting) is not relevant here because it is not part of the roof structure per se. It is an indirect competitor, of course.

Three basic types of insulated roofs exist in Europe and North America. The materials used in the three systems are basically the same. The first type, the *conventional* insulated roof system, includes a structural roof deck (for example, wood), on top of which is attached insulation. This insulation is then covered with a waterproofing layer made from a plurality of sheets of roofing felt. The felts are attached to the insulation by the use of a bituminous product, such as coal tar pitch or asphalt. These felts are usually organic, nonwoven fabrics made by combining felted paper and shredded wood fiber (or used newspaper), and then this combination is saturated with either asphalt or coal tar pitch. The plurality of roofing felts are placed together with a bituminous adhesive. Thus, four plies of roofing felt have four layers of adhesive. The bituminous adhesive between layers does the bulk of the waterproofing. The nonwoven sheets are used to distribute stresses in the roof system and stop liquid from entering the building. The plurality of felts and adhesive are called a built-up roof (BUR) membrane.

The order in which the insulation and BUR membrane was applied to the roof deck had remained the same for forty-five years. However, this order had been reversed in some roofs in the past six years. The built-up roof membrane was being placed directly onto the roof deck and insulation then placed on top of the built-up roof instead of underneath it. This type of roof is called the insulated roof membrane assembly (IRMA), the inverted roof assembly, the upside-down roof, and skeptically, the wrong-side-up roof.

The third type of roof system employed the principles of the conventional roof system and was called the sprayed-in-place roof. In this system the insulation was sprayed onto the roof. The waterproofing layer was then sprayed or brushed onto the foam. This waterproofing layer was usually a liquid material that cured when exposed to moisture into a rubbery sheet-like membrane.

The Dow Chemical Company's Involvement in Roofing Market

The Dow Chemical Company, with respect to the roofing area, manufactured only plastic insulation. These insulations were prefabricated into rectangular boardstock of two-foot width, four-foot length, and variable thicknesses necessary to meet the customers' desired insulating requirements. Dow did not produce bituminous products, roofing felts, or roofing decks, nor did Dow produce formulated spray-in-place insulations or liquid waterproofing membranes.

Dow had been the sole producer of extruded polystyrene foam (which it sold [sells] under the trademark STYROFOAM®) for over twenty years. Expanded polystyrene foam (also called beadboard) was produced by Dow, BASF Wyandotte, and many other manufacturers. Fabricators could buy molding equipment and expandable polystyrene beads and make their own beadboards. Polyurethane insulation was also produced by Dow and by many other chemical companies in Europe and North America.

Other rigid, prefabricated insulations available were cellular glass, preformed fiberglass board, wood-fiber board, perlite aggregate board, and corkboard, none of which were produced by Dow.

The Buying Process

In all industrial buying situations there are many variations on the common theme, and roofing is no exception. But, generally speaking, the participants and their roles in the purchase of insulated industrial roofs are as follows.

Participants On new construction or total roof replacements, the owners of the building play no essential role. They hire architects (or occasionally have their own architectural staffs) and give them certain guiding parameters—site, height, size, purpose, operating conditions. The architect then develops the design and material specifications for the roof. Even subsequent management reviews rarely concern the roof itself unless there is a question of overall building shape or a necessity to reduce costs.

Besides the owner and the architect, a third party is the general contractor. He too has little knowledge regarding roofing and little influence on design or materials. He turns these matters over to the fourth party—the roofing subcontractor, whose people actually build the roof.

The subcontractor influences the architect directly (when consulted) and indirectly through feedback on the ease and success of the architect's plans. He is the only party to influence the architect significantly. (In fact, on roof repair and some total replacements, there may not even be an architect.)

The fifth party is the local or regional distributor of the materials used and, except for a few areas around the country, he too has no influence on design or materials.

Other parties are tangential and operate only in highly specialized ways. Government inspectors, for example, are not influential, although their laws sometimes are. Utilities occasionally offer technical help. Manufacturers (like Dow) provide technical information about their products, but the architects are too knowledgeable for consumer-type promotion to be effective. Consultants play a very minor role, as do educators.

Attitudes   Some new products quickly win widespread acceptance, but generally speaking architects are very conservative on roofing decisions.

Experimentation and innovation on roofing are not really in the architect's best interest. Experimentation is usually expensive, since worker unfamiliarity slows installation. Moreover, an architectural firm's reputation can be seriously damaged if roof failure on a public or major private building is traced to such experimentation. Finally, since most roofs are flat and few people see them or are interested in their technical design, innovation and experimentation in roofing products and design usually do not enhance a building's beauty or advance an architect's reputation.

Furthermore, innovation requires complete understanding of technical information, something that few have. Few receive proper academic training in roofing, and those who do rarely keep their knowledge current—there is no generally accepted authority or text.

Additionally, experimentation requires a trust in manufacturers' products, which architects do not have. Unfavorable past experiences with new products from even such companies as Dow, Owens-Corning, Armstrong, and Reynolds have resulted in a deep-seated distrust of new products and the firms producing them. Architects question laboratory research results (including accelerated tests) because some past tests did not correctly identify product deficiencies or simulate the realities of application. This distrust, coupled with the architectural firm's lack of facilities to test new products, has led architects to require extensive field test results before they will accept a new product. In fact, they insist that five years of field tests are necessary.

As a result of this conservatism, no major changes in roofing products or designs had occurred in the previous twenty-five years. Four-ply pitch or asphalt membranes maintained their market dominance, and basic designs had become formulas or recipes to the persons developing specifications.

A few new products had gained acceptance, however, based on various appeals. Products such as single-ply and spray-on membranes allowed the architect new design freedom. Four-ply roofs could not be applied to a complicated form, and architects' desire to design roofs with unusual configurations outweighed their conservative tendencies, thus motivating them to experiment with these new products.

Another reason new products gained acceptance was the growing concern among architects regarding bond responsibility disputes. Moreover, they had to build roofs that would withstand increasing amounts of foot traffic.

In fact, more architects were coming to realize that today's roof products and basic designs were not satisfying their requirements. A growing need for better products was being expressed, but it was still not the architect's nature to be an experimenter. He wanted new products, but without any risk to himself.

Subcontractors were even more rigid and resistant to change than architects. Unlike architects, they believed the four-ply roof was perfect, for example, and therefore were not actively seeking a substitute for it.

Subcontractors' conservatism was based primarily on roofing labor conditions. New products often require extensive applicator retraining, and since retraining reduces an applicator's productive time, it reduces subcontractor's income. Furthermore, worker reeducation is an arduous task; roofing workers are not receptive to change and have difficulty understanding complicated applications.

Most new products do not offer subcontractors "defense in depth" against applicator errors. The standard four-ply roof provided insurance against roof failures traceable to careless workmanship (it was almost foolproof) and, therefore, it reduced their liability.

Subcontractors also equated new products with increased callbacks. Some products had been introduced prematurely in the past and unanticipated repairs and adjustments occurred. These callbacks, because they split the roofer's work force and could not be scheduled, caused subcontractor resistance to any new product.

Finally, in the early stages of a new product introduction, the manufacturer lacks field experience in application and consequently tends to underestimate application costs. If the roofer relies on the manufacturer's projections, his profit is reduced; yet he hasn't had the experience to make his own estimates.

Subcontractors believe that many roof failures resulting from product failure or design weakness are mistakenly blamed on them. The subcontractor does not want to risk using new products if his reputation as a skilled applicator could be endangered by product or design deficiencies.

Likewise subcontractors have known manufacturers to remove a new product from the marketplace if it doesn't sell well, thereby forcing them to make roof repairs without proper materials.

At the same time, some factors tend to mitigate subcontractor conservatism. Subcontractors, for example, have not actually blocked introduction of new roofing products or designs, since they are rarely asked for advice during the specification writing stage, and once the bid is won, only minor changes are permitted. Most roofers bid for every job for which they can compete, and their strongest urge is to keep the work force busy even if it requires using new materials or design.

New products can actually appeal to roofers. They can help increase profits if the percentage of labor to in-place cost is low. Reduced labor input means more jobs can be completed with the same size work force or the same number of jobs with a smaller force. It also means that profits are affected less by wage increases. Profits are improved, since the accuracy of bids is improved, material costs being more predictable than labor costs. Finally, return on investment could be increased, since most of the newer products required a smaller equipment investment than the four-ply roof.

Dow's View of the Market

The nonresidential roofing market had several characteristics that made it an unattractive marketing opportunity for Dow. Two of these—widespread inertia and labor conditions—have been discussed in the preceding section. A third was Dow's image.

Dow was considered a newcomer to roofing, and moreover, a newcomer that did not understand the market. Architects and roofing contractors pointed to STYROFOAM* brand plastic foam, a roofing product marketed many years before a need was established, and SARALOY* flashing. Comments from architects and roofing contractors regarding Dow's sales force ranged from "unexceptional" to "technically incompetent in roofing," though it was apparent that these customers did not distinguish between salesmen employed by Dow and those employed by Dow's distributors.

These three undesirable characteristics were somewhat offset by several other factors. Nonresidential roofing was a large market, totaling perhaps $640,000,000 in the United States alone.

Dow also noted that firms competing for this market did not do so effectively. Manufacturers had a strong production orientation and failed to base their plans on market needs. Lack of marketing skill was demonstrated by their weak sales efforts and limited services.

Finally, the roofing market was plagued with poor workmanship, poor quality of materials, and high liability. Fifteen percent of all roofs failed within five years. The average life of roofs that are not failing is accepted to be 20 years.

There is an implied liability for the performance of any roofing system on any building, and this implied liability covers all damages and repairs if such problems occur. In other words, if a roof leaks or has to be replaced within five to ten years, the owner of the building first tries to negotiate a financial settlement with the people who were involved in the roof's initial construction—the architect, the roofing contractor, the felt manufacturer, the insulation manufacturer, and the roof deck manufacturer. If no satisfactory settlement is obtained, the owner sues all of them. Unless there is an obvious culprit (which is unusual) the cost is split among the defendants. The roofer pays by supplying the labor, the architect pays some money and services, the manufacturers supply the materials and the rest of the money.

* Trademark of the Dow Chemical Company.

THE DOW CONCEPT: IRMA

IRMA is partly product and partly system, and traces its existence to an almost accidental beginning. Dow had originally marketed a new rigid plastic foam in 1948 under the trademark STYROFOAM. It was not used for roofing or so promoted, but a Dow engineer used it that way in 1953 when a Dow building needed a special repair job. Later, in 1958, another repair was required and the engineer used the same solution. On the basis of these successful roofing installations, Dow applied for and obtained patents covering the IRMA system.

By this time, some roofers were using STYROFOAM brand plastic foam and the company even recommended it. Then in 1964 a special STYROFOAM RM was introduced, but it never caught on.

By 1970, under company pressure to fish or cut bait, the roofing group had developed that engineer's earlier idea to the point where they felt they had a marketable system.

IRMA (standing for Insulated Roof Membrane Assembly) was a patented system that reversed the usual application of roofing materials. The built-up roof membrane was placed directly on the deck, and then the insulation was placed above the membrane. By placing the membrane under the insulation, the IRMA system eliminated the major causes for premature built-up roof failures. The insulation: (1) had enough strength to protect the roof membrane from physical damage (workers and tools); (2) protected the roof membrane from ultraviolet degradation; and (3) protected the membrane from temperature extremes. The advantages of the IRMA system were that: (1) the vapor barrier was always in correct location; (2) the system used only standard materials and roofing practices; (3) the system protected the membrane from severe temperature extremes; (4) it minimized maintenance; and (5) the system extended the construction season.

The ideal insulation properties for any roofing system are: (1) ultraviolet stability; (2) nonbuoyancy; (3) noncombustibility; (4) dimension stability; (5) water impermeability; (6) freeze/thaw resistance; and (7) high compressive strength. No insulation meets all seven properties; however, STYROFOAM RM brand plastic foam met requirements 4 through 7 and stone placed on top of the STYROFOAM provided properties 1 through 3.

The IRMA system was expected to perform much better than the conventional roof system, and the patent allows Dow to control the installation of the system. Even though Dow did not make any of the roof materials other than insulation, the system allowed Dow to assure a good job because the insulation took most of the abuse in a properly installed roof.

Marketing Research

The Construction Materials Marketing Department had conducted several market studies that provided the information about market participants discussed earlier. These same studies yielded several conclusions about the typical roof installation procedures with which IRMA would compete: (1) The workmanship of roofing crews was the worst of all the construction trades. The inclement weather further devalued the quality obtainable. (2) The materials used in roofs, such as bitumen and felts, had no production specifications at all and varied from job to job. (3) No special instructions or supervision had been provided to the roofers for the proper application of STYROFOAM brand insulation. Since STYROFOAM brand insulation will melt above 200°F and bitumen is applied on top of the insulation at about 200°F, problems frequently developed. (4) Owners and general contractors were apathetic. These people wanted the roof on first, and fast—so all the other trades could work. Thus, the jobs were rushed and quality fell. (5) Competition among the suppliers and the applicators was so intense that products were introduced with very little research and development and with poor quality because the low prices obtained for them wouldn't permit otherwise.

PRESENT SITUATION

Dow management was convinced that the IRMA system, using inverted application and proper directions for STYROFOAM brand insulation, could be successful. J. P. Sheehan, the researcher who conducted most of the market studies for this development, was now roofing marketing manager and was responsible for developing a strategy for marketing IRMA. He was given great latitude, even to being told that he could create his own full-time field marketing organization if he wanted to. Price, distribution, and promotion were all at issue, but before getting into too many details, Mr. Sheehan wanted to develop an overall marketing strategy. He was especially concerned about the makeup of market participants and their attitudes, as well as the oftentimes rather poor result of their efforts. He knew that IRMA would be unique and risky, but he also deeply believed it would work.

Gypsum Wallboard Corporation
···

Analysis of a Product Failure

BACKGROUND

In January 1992, Warren Farmingham, a thirty-year-old product manager of gypsum wallboard for Gypsum Wallboard Corporation (GWC), is pondering his next strategy recommendation. Applying the methodology that he has learned as part of his M.B.A. studies, as well as his previous experience with a large consumer packaged goods company, Farmingham begins with a situation analysis.

SITUATION ANALYSIS

GWC is a manufacturer with nationwide sales of close to $1 billion annually. It is one of the leading suppliers of gypsum wallboard (SIC 327512) for the construction industry.

Wallboard Manufacturers

In the classroom, Farmingham would have described wallboard manufacturers as a homogeneous oligopoly. Annual industry sales are about 20 billion square feet. As of 1992, the wallboard industry is comprised of a dozen or so domestic manufacturers with virtually identical product lines, prices, promotion tactics, and distribution methods. Among the leaders are such giants as Celotex Corporation, USG Corporation, Weyerhaeuser Company, National Gypsum Company, Georgia-Pacific Corporation, and other conglomerates. In recent years,

Case contributed by Harold W. Fox, former Professor of Marketing, Pan American University and currently a leader of business seminars.

however, smaller firms such as Republic Gypsum Company and American Gypsum Company have captured viable market shares in their respective regions.

Small companies can compete in a region because in the wallboard industry the critical marketing factor is distribution—product availability and low-cost transportation. The high cost of freight relative to product value protects the manufacturers from overseas competition.

As noted, the marketing mixes of the oligopolistic rivals are quite similar. This close equivalence stems in part from the conservative culture prevalent among members of this basic industry. More fundamentally, the wallboard industry's standard marketing mix has been shaped over time in response to the structure of the market.

Market Structure

Final buyers of gypsum wallboard are builders. Construction is America's largest industry, and it is characterized by ease of entry and difficulty of survival, severe instability, and powerful craft unions buttressed by local building codes. Resistance to change is inherent.

Thus, in contrast to just a few producers, there are many end buyers, in size from small to large. Typically, these OEMs operate on minimum or inadequate capital. In fact, many builders incorporate each construction project separately, so that if one goes awry, they can put it into bankruptcy, yet continue their other operations without disruption.

Lack of capital often forces builders into a just-in-time buying mode. (Before this term became fashionable, they were said to buy "hand-to-mouth.") Moreover, builders do not purchase just one type of construction input by itself. Many thousands of different types of light equipment, consumable supplies, component parts, raw materials, and processed materials are used in or incorporated into the construction of a building. Each item is purchased in small quantities. Some are needed simultaneously; others are needed sequentially. Delays are exorbitantly expensive. All together, these financial and operating realities force buyers to rely on a central source. Similar to a consumer's one-stop shopping, a builder buys assortments.

Marketing Mix

The logical way to distribute wallboard is for the few large producers to ship their output first in carload quantities to industrial distributors that specialize in construction materials. Then, these distributors disperse the wallboard to lumberyards and other resellers that are located conveniently to the builders. These local outlets sell many types of construction needs in small quantities as desired by their customers, the builders. Final buyers can combine the different kinds of construction inputs that are stocked by an outlet into whatever unique assortment they require.

This manner of distribution dictates the commodity status of gypsum wallboard. Builders cannot afford to wait for some distinctive type of drywall to become available. They buy *interchangeable* pieces, whatever their supplier happens to have in stock. Therefore, inventory at each local outlet is critical!

Moreover, the distributors and local outlets have reasons of their own to insist on standard wallboards. Substitutability among suppliers allows the intermediaries to operate on low inventories. Most important to them, substitutability strengthens the intermediaries' bargaining power. By pitting each vendor against its competitors, the intermediaries can extract various concessions.

Among the oligopolists, nonprice competition is fierce. But traditionally, prices of their commodity products are alike. (In fact, four gypsum producers were convicted of price fixing in 1975.) During building booms prices of drywall skyrocket, and prices plunge when construction activity slumps.

In the promotion mix of wallboard manufacturers, personal selling predominates. The main selling effort consists of pushing the factories' output onto the industrial distributors (which, in turn, unload their purchases on their customers). Large manufacturers augment the distributors' efforts by having missionary sales personnel and architect service representatives ask builders and influencers to specify particular brands. But since competing products and prices are identical, brand preference is virtually nonexistent.

Neither has a modest advertising effort succeeded in developing brand preference. The functions of wallboard manufacturers' advertising in industrial publications are (1) to generate leads, (2) to disseminate the vendor's name among members of various buying centers, (3) to nurture good relations with publishers and gain favorable publicity, (4) to assist the sales force, and (5) to give the sponsor's executives some feelings of prestige and reassurance. These manufacturers usually do not try to measure advertising effectiveness.

Most wallboard manufacturers make liberal use of sales promotion methods. These include sales force incentives, special programs for distribution, and participation in trade shows.

BUILDERS' COMPLAINT

The previous mentioned elements have comprised the large wallboard manufacturers' marketing mix for as long as anybody can remember. Therefore, any changes Farmingham recommends are invariably turned down. "This is the way things have always been done around here," said the executive vice president, who has been with the company for forty-one years. The director of sales is more explicit, although not more helpful: "Whatever works for consumer packaged goods does not apply to the industrial field."

Although Farmingham respects the judgment of these experienced executives, he feels that a long-standing builders' complaint should no longer be ignored. At trade shows and other meetings with end buyers, Farmingham has heard the same criticism over and over: There is an unsightly gap wherever the edges of two sheets of wallboard are joined. In most cases, builders are able to cover up this flaw. But frequently, the juncture buckles, especially when the temperature changes. Complaints from the building buyer and costly repairs then follow. Builders are fond of saying, "Whoever eliminates that gap will make millions."

Gypsum wallboard executives have also heard this complaint many times. Their usual response is to affirm their concern for the builders and to lament that this problem cannot be remedied. In fact, nobody has ever tried.

But this conventional wisdom does not deter Warren Farmingham. He begins to tinker with the production equipment at night and on weekends. Before long, he overcomes the deficiency (the gap). Only minor modifications of the equipment are needed to produce a smooth juncture.

Elated by his discovery, Farmingham proceeds cautiously and without attracting internal attention. He subjects a run of the modified drywall to various tests, all of which have favorable results. For example, Underwriters' Laboratories certifies that the new product gives as much fire protection as the old. Farmingham also sounds out union leaders, who voice no objection, and his own company's house counsel advises him that building codes pose no difficulty.

Farmingham's greatest fear is that his superior will veto commercialization. Fortunately for Farmingham, the director of sales is preoccupied with vacation plans. Without carefully reading the memo, he approves Farmingham's recommendation that vaguely delineates a slightly changed marketing strategy.

PUSH STRATEGY

Farmingham's marketing strategy leaves most of the traditional elements intact. The only changes are the improved product and related promotional efforts. The formal objectives are to switch immediately all GWC customers to the improved product and to increase market share by converting as many of the competitors' customers as possible. Intermediaries and builders are notified that, effective next month, the old wallboard will be discontinued. On all orders, the new version will be shipped without delay. Thus, the manufacturer is able to retain economies of scale.

Promotional Mix

Farmingham explains the campaign at a national sales meeting. His detailed indoctrination program includes displays of the old and the new product to dramatize the improvement. Design engineers explain the technical change and interpret the test results.

All of this information is incorporated into trade advertising and publicity releases. Also, the displays of old and new products are exhibited at various trade shows. Later, after product introduction, Farmingham invites satisfied builders to regional sales meetings where they endorse the innovation.

At the national sales meeting, Farmingham announces higher sales force quotas to meet the goal of increased market share. The company also sponsors a nationwide contest with desirable prizes. No other programming changes are contemplated; pricing and placement are to continue as before.

Other Mix Elements

The centerpiece of the promotional campaign is, of course, the product innovation trademarked "Smooth Wall." Penetration pricing (same amounts as for the conventional version) is used. The new product is available in large quantities and it is easy to copy. Moreover, the builders are very price-sensitive, and Farmingham does not want anything to interfere with his quest for enlarged market share. Distribution practices remain the same as before.

Early Success

From the beginning, response to the new product is overwhelmingly favorable— far beyond Farmingham's hopes and quotas. Indeed, at GWC headquarters, bitter rivalries erupt among production and sales executives as each claims credit for the innovation and its huge success. Builders, at last, have the product for which they have been clamoring.

The company has the field to itself, as competitors have no product to counter GWC's thrust. In desperation, competitors spread false rumors and employ other scare tactics to fend off the "Smooth Wall" innovation. Even though these rumors are without foundation, the disparagements do cause damage to the marketing campaign.

Subsequent Failure

Soon enough, however, some evidence emerges that supports the rumors. Apparently, the inexperienced Farmingham has not realized that the new wallboard is unsuitable for steel stud buildings—a tiny part of the market. Had he known, he could have simply forfeited this negligible segment by means of warning labels and other informative devices. Instead, his ignorance gives competitors the factual ammunition they need to denigrate the innovation.

Other Problems

However serious, lack of fitness for a small market segment and amplification of this deficiency by rival salespeople turn out to be the least of the new product's problems. Farmingham is surprised to learn that equal price from the manufacturer does not mean equal cost to buyers. At construction sites, the "Smooth Wall" slabs are more difficult to handle and align. Hangers and tapers, needing extra processing time, demand higher compensation per unit to maintain the same hourly income that they had negotiated for conventional wallboard. Relative to the total cost of a building, the required pay increase is small, but none of the many parties involved in a construction project is prepared to absorb it. With his background in consumer packaged goods, Farmingham had visualized the benefits of convenience and savings in finished products, but he had neglected to simulate the processing cycle.

Yet another unexpected blow is the antipathy toward "Smooth Wall" by many builders. They applaud the concept, but they decline to assume the risks of using an unproved innovation. If the new product turns out to be unsatisfactory—as competitors' salespeople have charged—small builders cannot afford to reconstruct their houses. The more open-minded ones wait for the experience of early adopters.

But the biggest obstacle, which really aborts the introductory period, emanates from the resellers. Soon the new product is out of stock, and it remains unavailable to final buyers. After first enthusiastically welcoming the innovation, distributors refuse to reorder. Why? "Smooth Wall" has the same price and allows the same margins as conventional wallboard, but it causes an escalation of administrative expenses. Because conventional and differentiated wallboards cannot be mixed on a job, intermediaries must double their inventories, segregate them, and maintain detailed records. (As long as all makes were interchangeable, different brands were commingled and visual control sufficed.) Lack of substitutability also deprives the distributors of the leverage to play each vendor against the others and to force special favors from them. (This motive is not openly admitted, of course.) All these problems provide enough gossip to rationalize a drop decision by distributors as a protection of their customers' interests.

What to Do?

Meanwhile, at GWC headquarters, executives distance themselves from association with the new product. They heap blame on Farmingham, citing his lack of experience in industrial marketing and the campaign's shortcomings. Trying to be more constructive, Farmingham is racking his brains to extricate his company (and himself) from this fiasco.

DISCUSSION QUESTIONS

1. What basic marketing precept is violated by Farmingham's marketing objectives and execution? Name some supposedly sophisticated marketers of consumer goods that have made the same mistake—with similarly disastrous results.

2. What pricing options does GWC now have for "Smooth Wall"? In particular, should GWC reduce its price? Justify your answer.

3. Besides riskiness of an unproved innovation, what causes delays in the acceptance of an available new product such as "Smooth Wall"?

4. What alternative to the failed push strategy can Farmingham propose? Why? Explain systematically.

5. What results do you anticipate from the new strategy you have proposed in Question 4?

Great Lakes Building Products Company

Introducing a New Product

BACKGROUND

Great Lakes Building Products Company is located in Joliet, Illinois, a city known for its industrial development and high business and work ethics. Great Lakes has been a producer of innovative building materials for over thirty-five years. From its experience, Great Lakes has developed a high level of knowledge of the home-building industry. Its potential markets include the colder midwestern region consisting of the states of Michigan, Ohio, Indiana, Illinois, Wisconsin, Iowa, and Minnesota. Great Lakes Building Products Company has been able to meet and surpass its major competitors in the areas of product innovation, quality, delivery, and service, which constitutes its primary competitive advantage. The building products industry has been characterized in recent years as a high-tech, highly innovative industry. The industry has been motivated to accept the innovation of new materials, products, and building methods that result in the improvement of energy efficiency, labor saving, and cost-efficient building products, which has resulted in a higher quality of life for the home purchaser.

Great Lakes Building Products Company is recognized by architects, developers, contractors, and competitors as a leader in the development of new innovative building products. During its early years, the company pioneered the development of both hard and soft copper potable (drinkable) water lines to replace the older iron pipes. With the advent of plastics, Great Lakes pioneered the replacement of lead-jointed copper water lines and cast iron sewage pipes with its unique "snap-together" plastic piping systems. These innovations were widely

Case contributed by G. Dean Kortge and Patrick A. Okonkwo, Associate Professors of Marketing, Central Michigan University.

accepted by the building industry because they provide better-quality products while reducing the installation labor costs.

In an effort to take further advantage of its knowledge and skills in the manufacturing of plastic building products, Great Lakes Building Products Company developed a triple-glass, thermopane, wood-core, plastic-coated, double-hung window. Its ability to adapt plastics to home-building products also led to the development of a plastic-sided, urethane-foamed-core exterior door that could be stained or painted to look like real wood. The company subsequently developed a plastic interior door and mouldings that could also be stained or painted to look like real wood and to match Early American, Modern, Spanish, and similar decor. At one time, Great Lakes had developed a wood-like plastic siding for homes but had abandoned this project late in its development cycle. A marketing research study had shown that several major vendors had already captured a large share of this market, which had reached the latter portion of the growth stage of the product life cycle.

Great Lakes Building Products Company recently developed a plastic foam insulation material that could be attached to the exterior walls and ceilings of new or existing homes. When covered with plywood, siding, or concrete mortar, this insulation provided additional insulating R value to reduce heating and/or air conditioning power requirements and costs. Sales of this product have not reached Great Lakes's projected forecast level. Several competitors had also introduced similar insulation materials into the market. Moreover, the consumer adoption rate of these materials had been slow to develop, which had vastly limited industry sales.

PRESENT OPPORTUNITY

Great Lakes Building Products Company is considering the possible opportunity for the development of an innovative stress-skin type building material called "Total-Wall." The concept of the Total-Wall is to construct a layer of insulating foam sandwiched between ¾-inch plywood on the exterior side and ½-inch drywall material or plywood on the interior side of the wall. The purpose of the Total-Wall is to construct homes that can be superinsulated with wall R values of 20 to 30 and ceiling R values of 40 to 60. Such superinsulation can significantly reduce the costs of the homeowner's heating needs in the winter and the air conditioning power requirements during the summer.

The Total-Wall would be produced in modules of varying thicknesses of from two to twelve inches of foam (R-5 per inch), from eight to twelve feet in height, and in varying lengths up to sixty feet. The modules would be able to be cut to any desired length on the job with an ordinary electric-powered circular hand saw. The corners, tops, and bottoms of the Total-Wall could be butt, angle, or tongue-and-groove jointed and foam-sealed to eliminate air penetration. Openings for doors, windows, etc., could also be made with the same hand saw or with a heavy-duty extended-bit router. Door and window frames could be mounted in these openings and foam-sealed to eliminate all air leakage.

Specifications for building products are usually determined by the designing architect, subdivision developer, building contractor, or at the request of the homeowner. The final decision is usually made by the homeowner when contracting to build to his or her own requirements, or by the subdivision developer when building a "speculation" home. The promotion of the Total-Wall would require promoting the benefits of this product to the architect, developer, contractor, and homeowner. The sales and delivery of the product would be direct to the building contractor who would purchase and install the wall in accordance with the architect's drawings and specifications, and the developer's and homeowner's decision. The average home built in Great Lakes's marketing area contains approximately 1,500 to 2,200 square feet. The average cost of conventional home construction in this region runs $50 per square foot of floor space. The additional cost of the Total-Wall panel will add 22 cents per square foot of wall and roof space per inch of foam, plus 63 cents per square foot of wall and roof space for plywood and drywall. A Total-Wall panel 3½ inches thick, eight feet wide, and thirty feet in length will cost $336 ($0.22 × 3½ = $0.77 + $0.63 = $1.40 per square foot × 8 × 30). This cost would consist of 60 percent materials, 10 percent profit for Great Lakes, 10 percent transportation to the job site, 15 percent installation, and 5 percent profit for the contractor.

The Total-Wall (stress-skin) type of construction is generally limited to three types of construction systems. The first type is the "post-and-beam" timber-framed home. Large posts and beams are pegged together using mortice and tenon fittings and the Total-Wall is fastened to the outside of the wooden framework. The Total-Wall would form both the inside (drywall) and the outside (plywood) walls (see Exhibit 1). The electrical wiring is pulled through a tunnel that opens in the length of the Total-Wall, and electrical boxes and fixtures are recessed into the wall. An alternative approach is to surface-mount the wiring, boxes, and fixtures on the face of the wall.

Second, the normal 2 × 4 stud wall is constructed and recessed to allow the Total-Wall to be fastened to the outside of the studs forming mainly the outside (plywood) wall (see Exhibit 2). Electrical wiring (and plumbing runs), boxes, and fixtures are mounted within the stud wall in a normal fashion. Fiberglass insulation batts (R-3 per inch) are installed inside, or loose fiberglass or cellulose is blown into the stud openings.

Third, a conventional log house is constructed with the Total-Wall being fastened to the inside of the log walls forming mainly the inside (drywall or plywood) wall (see Exhibit 3). The electrical wiring is installed along the depressions of the logs and pulled through holes in the Total-Wall as it is installed. The wiring boxes and fixtures are recessed into or surface-mounted on the Total-Wall.

Three types of roofs may also be utilized with the stress-skin construction approach. First, a normal 1-in-4 slope with a two-foot overhang prebuilt truss is installed and the ceiling and roof are attached to the truss joist and rafters. Fiber-

EXHIBIT 1   Post-and-Beam Application

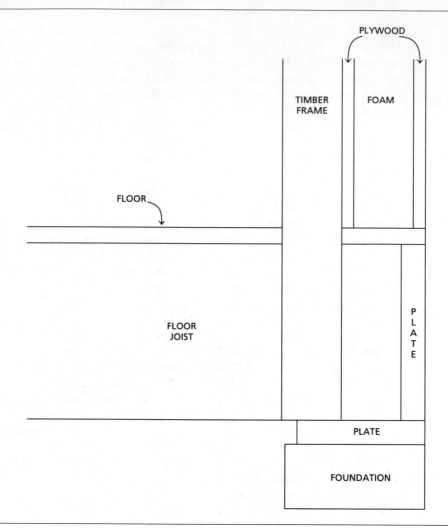

glass batts are installed, or loose fiberglass or cellulose insulation (R-3 per inch) is blown into the space between the joist and rafters. A second variation to the normal truss is to install a high-energy truss (an additional $50 per truss), which has a twelve-inch offset between the ceiling joist and the roof rafters. This allows for extra amounts of fiberglass or cellulose insulation to be installed between the joist and rafters. The third alternative is to utilize the post-and-beam timber-framed, log, or truss type of construction and to install the Total-Wall panels on the roof rafters.

EXHIBIT 2   Stud Wall Application

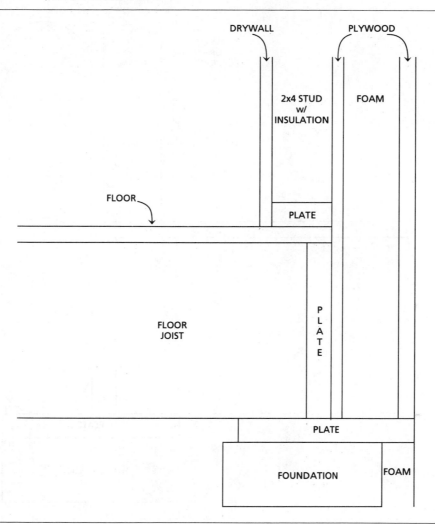

EXISTING SITUATION

Anthony Cox, Manager of Product Development, Margot Railsback, Chief Engineer, Michael Curtis, Production Supervisor, Patrick Lee, Marketing Manager, Diane Griswold, Interior Designer, and Gary Dean, Product Manager, all agreed that such a "Total-Wall" concept, if properly developed and marketed, could revolutionize the home-building industry. They felt that Great Lakes, as the leader and innovator of the product, would capture a large and profitable mar-

EXHIBIT 3 Log Wall Application

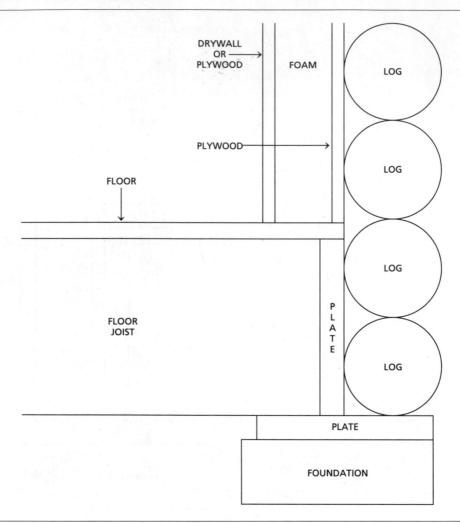

ket share. This share would be achieved before competitors could develop their own product and construct the required manufacturing facilities to enter this market. Jeffrey Keith, owner of Great Lakes Building Products Company, was reluctant to enter this new product market because of the company's recent bad experience with the foam insulation material product.

Anthothy Cox and Margot Railsback felt that the Total-Wall product must first be fully developed so that market testing, facilities design, production methods and costs, etc., could be fully and accurately identified and determined. Michael Curtis and Patrick Lee believed that no additional funds should be invested into new product development until the business aspects such as costs, facilities, ROI, etc., and a marketing strategy, including test marketing, sales forecasts, target markets, etc., could first be developed. A third group consisting of Diane Griswold, Gary Dean, and Jeffrey Keith felt that the new product development process should continue simultaneously with the marketing strategy development process. Each group expressed the financial gamble that Great Lakes would be facing and their desire to not commit additional funds to the development of a new innovative product until the risk of product failure in the marketplace could be reduced to a minimum.

TOTAL-WALL SALES FORECAST

	Market share	Market potential
1991	10%	$ 5,000,000
1992	12%	8,000,000
1993	16%	12,000,000
1994	20%	17,000,000
1995	23%	25,000,000

The executives and managers of Great Lakes Building Products Company are now facing the problem of how they might best assure themselves that future funds spent on the development of the Total-Wall product may be spent effectively. The development costs should be restricted until a suitable new product development process and a marketing strategy development process can be formulated that will reduce the rate of product failure in the marketplace.

Jeffrey Keith, the company's owner, assigned Anthony Cox the task of formulating a new product development process. He assigned Patrick Lee the task of formulating an appropriate marketing strategy development process. Mr. Keith insisted that they "coordinate their efforts to formulate a detailed new product/marketing strategy development process that would guarantee the successful introduction and adoption of the Total-Wall concept to our product line." They agreed to turn the entire project over to Gary Dean, product manager, to study the alternatives and to devise a new product development/marketing strategy development process and implementation program.

THE CHALLENGE

Place yourself in Mr. Dean's role and position and simultaneously develop a new product development process and a marketing strategy development process as demanded by Mr. Keith, including which alternative(s) you would recommend and how you propose to implement these strategies.

Medical Electronic Instruments

···

Preparing a PERT Chart

In April 1992, Fred Young, product manager for nondestructive testing products, was considering the problem of releasing a new piece of nondestructive test equipment to the field sales and service organization of Medtronics.

Medtronics is a manufacturer of a wide variety of medical electronic equipment used in industry, hospitals, and large clinics. Sales for 1991 exceeded $10 million, and at least a 20 percent increase was expected for 1992. The corporate headquarters and major manufacturing facility was located in Minneapolis.

Fred had recently received his M.B.A. degree in marketing from the University of Minnesota. He felt that he could apply the techniques of operations research to his problem, particularly network planning.

The product to be released was a highly technical product that would be different in many ways from those the sales force currently handled. In order to make a major impact on the industry, Fred had decided to introduce the product at a major trade show, the National Convention of the American Society of Nondestructive Testing, to be held Aug. 1–5 at San Diego. The product would be released to the national sales force immediately following the show.

There were many things to get done before this trade show. Fred was able to group these activities into nine major categories.

A. *Provide product training to the field sales force.* This activity included both lectures and hands-on equipment training in the use of the product. It would take approximately five days to train the sales force.

B. *Provide product training to the service force.* While it was essential for the sales force to possess product knowledge, a completely different training

Case contributed by Robert H. Collins, Ph.D., Hilton Distinguished Professor of Marketing, and Chairman, Department of Marketing, University of Nevada, Las Vegas.

program had to be developed to teach the service force how to maintain the product. This training would also take about five days.

C. *Preparation of service kits.* Each serviceperson must have a tool kit to service the new product, and be trained in its use. It would take about a day and a half to prepare these kits.

D. *Preparation of sales aids.* Each salesperson would receive a sales manual, plus assorted flip-charts, literature, product mock-ups, and visual aids to assist in communicating with the customer. Sales aids must be prepared prior to the sales training program, and preparation would take about seven and a half days.

E. *Preparation of warranty and service contracts.* As more industrial customers show reluctance to provide their own service, warranty and service contracts have become more important as competitive product features. Hence, the sales force and the servicepeople must be aware of them. It will take about five days to draw up these contracts.

F. *Designate factory support teams.* Factory support teams act as a backup to the field sales and service force. It will take about half a day to select these personnel.

G. *Preparation of instruction manuals.* Proper operation and maintenance by the customer is a major factor in ensuring product satisfaction, reducing warranty costs, and creating an overall favorable image for the manufacturer. Preparation will take about twenty-five days.

H. *Prerelease promotion.* Prior to the actual release of the product, promotion must be directed at potential customers. A combination of direct mail and trade advertising is used to create interest in the product and announce Medical Electronic Instruments' attendance at the ASNDT trade show. It will take approximately five days to prepare this promotion.

I. *Preparation for the trade show.* It will take about six days to construct an effective exhibit.

Fred felt that a PERT chart would be of assistance in scheduling the many activities required to release his new product to the sales force. Therefore, he summarized these activities and completion times in the following chart (Exhibit 1).

DISCUSSION QUESTIONS

1. Draw a project network (PERT chart) that depicts the logical sequence of events required to introduce Fred's new product.

2. What is the critical path, and how many days will he need to complete the project?

3. What is the near critical path? What is the probability that the near critical path will become critical? What are the consequences of a shift from the critical path to the near critical path?

EXHIBIT 1   **Chart of Activities and Their Completion Times**

Activity	Predecessors	a	m	b
Train sales force (A)	D, E, G	4.5	5	6
Train service force (B)	C, E, G	4.5	5	6.75
Prepare service kits (C)	None	1	1.5	2
Prepare sales aids (D)	F	5	7.5	10
Prepare warranty/service contracts (E)	None	4.5	5	6.25
Designate factory support (F)	None	0.25	0.5	1
Instruction manuals (G)	None	20	25	35
Prerelease promotion (H)	D	4.5	5	6
Prepare for trade show (I)	E, G, H	5	6	9
Attend trade show (J)	A, I	5	5	5

Notes: a: Most optimistic completion time.
m: Most likely completion time.
b: Most pessimistic completion time.

Fairchild Lubricants, Inc.

··

Selecting Industrial Distributors

BACKGROUND

Fairchild Lubricants, Inc., located in Racine, Wisconsin, is a nationally known supplier of cleaning and lubricant products and equipment. The company has for sixty years produced and marketed a broad line of products that includes tank degreasers, strippers, lubricants, and hand-care products. Its customers are primarily industrial and transportation users of these types of industrial products. Fairchild has never served the household market and has no intention now of entering that market.

Sales in 1991 are $25 million, with 75 percent of sales being made by company field sales representatives. The remaining 25 percent of sales are made through industrial distributors. The company recently completed a two-year study that revealed that Fairchild's freight and personal selling costs were rising far out of proportion to all other company costs. Based on this study, company management has decided to expand sales through distributors in an attempt to lower both freight and selling costs. Therefore, a number of company field sales representatives will be replaced by distributors.

The termination of field sales representatives and their replacement with industrial distributors is somewhat bothersome to company management, but the step is seen as a necessary move. In addition to lowering freight and sales costs, it is estimated that distributors can help attract customers that the sales reps have been unable to reach. Management estimates that distributors can expand the industrial and transportation sales potential to ten times that of last year's sales. The company feels this potential can be realized if sales through distributors are increased from the present 25 percent of sales to 50 percent. Product lines average approximately 25 percent gross profit margins, and Fairchild products appear to be widely accepted in the marketplace. The company is well established and has a sound reputation that has been built up over the years. Management believes that these traits will attract good distributors and that a network of distributors will not be difficult to develop.

THE PROBLEM

Mac Ghormley is the national sales manager of Fairchild Lubricants. His office is located in the company headquarters building in Racine. Ghormley has been in charge of Fairchild's field sales representatives for the past nine years and is seen by top management as the most logical member of management to supervise the potential distributor network. He will have the responsibility of establishing a total distributor network as well as screening and selecting individual distributors and then managing the network. Ghormley has mixed emotions about the added responsibility. On one hand, he has worked with the field sales representatives long enough to know many of them personally. Replacing some of these people with distributors will be difficult and stressful. On the other hand, he has also seen the rising sales and transportation costs and knows something has to be done. He sees the replacement of some field sales representatives with distributors as a necessity if these costs are to be controlled effectively.

The first sales territory Ghormley wants to address is the Pacific northwest (Oregon and Washington). Since he has been sales manager, this territory has been a thorn in his side and a disappointment. Ghormley feels that the company sales representative covering this territory, Mitch Greenwood, has not been doing an acceptable job. Although Greenwood has always met sales quotas, he is difficult to manage and sometimes quite unwilling to take orders from Ghormley. Greenwood is also overbearing and abrasive, and Ghormley has never personally liked the man. Thus, he sees the company's decision to move to distributors as an opportunity to get rid of Greenwood once and for all. He selects the Pacific northwest territory as a test case for replacing field representatives with distributors. He does not, however, intend to notify Greenwood of his dismissal until he has found a suitable distributor to cover the area. Once that task is accomplished, Ghormley plans to terminate Greenwood's employment with Fairchild Lubricants. His problem is finding a distributor to replace Mitch Greenwood.

DETERMINING DISTRIBUTOR SELECTION CRITERIA

One of the first tasks Ghormley undertakes is to determine the criteria to be used in the distributor selection process. He knows that distributors may be selected based on any number of factors, but he also knows that any selection process cannot use every conceivable factor that may be involved. Therefore, he decides on five criteria to be used in evaluating and selecting prospective distributors. These are (1) sales capabilities—the size and experience of a distributor's field and inside sales force; (2) interest—the level of interest expressed by a distributor's management in carrying Fairchild products; (3) product line compatibility—the compatibility of a distributor's present product lines with Fairchild products; (4) service capabilities—the distributor's service facilities and experience of its service personnel to handle Fairchild products; and (5) warehousing and delivery capabilities—the size of the distributor's warehouse, inventory levels, number of branch sites, and transportation abilities. After considerable thought, Ghormley is convinced that these five factors are the most important. He will use these criteria in selecting among prospective distributors.

Ghormley acknowledges that these five criteria are not equal in importance and should not be weighted the same in any selection process. Since the distributors are to replace existing company field sales representatives, he believes strongly that any prospective distributor must be able to provide outstanding sales coverage. At the same time, he believes that the product lines of a prospective distributor must complement and help sell Fairchild products. He is also concerned that any prospective distributor be able to provide adequate service to Fairchild customers and possess ample warehouse space and equipment. Finally, he believes the interest level expressed by the distributor's management in carrying Fairchild's products should be considered. Based on these feelings, Ghormley weights these five criteria as shown in Exhibit 1.

Ghormley feels this weighting scheme adequately represents his objectives in replacing company field sales representatives with industrial distributors. He plans to evaluate all prospective distributors on the basis of these five criteria and then select the single distributor for each territory that best meets his criteria. He intends to test this selection process on the Pacific northwest territory.

DETERMINING POSSIBLE DISTRIBUTORS

At this point, Ghormley faces the task of finding potential distributors for the Pacific northwest territory. Knowing that in the past, Fairchild's products have been purchased by many types of industrial and transportation users, Ghormley decides that general line distributors make the most logical prospects. Thus, he rules out specialist distributors from further consideration. Using the *Directory of Industrial Distributors,* Ghormley finds twenty-one general line distributors that can possibly carry Fairchild products in the Pacific northwest. By careful

---

EXHIBIT 1 **Weighting of Criteria for Prospective Distributors**

Rating Criterion	Relative Weight in the Selection Process
Sales capabilities	35%
Product line compatibility	25%
Service capabilities	15%
Warehousing and delivery capabilities	15%
Interest in carrying Fairchild products	10%

analysis of information provided in the directory, Ghormley is able to determine that many of these distributors are not acceptable. In his estimation, some are simply too small to cover the territory. Others appear to lack sufficient numbers of salespeople. Still others do not possess sufficient warehouse space to retain Ghormley's interest. After this screening, Ghormley is left with five distributors that he believes can adequately cover the territory for Fairchild if they had the interest to do so. He realizes now that he cannot judge these five distributors without visiting them personally for a more detailed investigation of their facilities, personnel, and interest level. The five distributors are shown in Exhibit 2.

GHORMLEY MAKES A TRIP TO THE PACIFIC NORTHWEST TERRITORY

Ghormley decides to fly to the Pacific northwest and spend a week with the prospective distributor candidates. Since only five prospects are involved, he believes he can spend approximately one day with each and come away with a reasonably good assessment of their respective strengths and weaknesses. From information in the *Directory of Industrial Distributors,* Ghormley obtains the names of the general managers and their phone numbers. He then calls each of them, introduces himself, and explains his reason for calling. He explains to each manager that Fairchild is considering his or her company for an exclusive distributorship in Oregon and Washington and states that he would like to visit, talk to personnel, and tour the facilities. All five general managers are aware of the Fairchild line, and all five express an interest in at least talking to Ghormley. After some scheduling difficulties are ironed out, he is able to find a week in which all five general managers are available. Appointments are made by phone, and Ghormley makes his travel plans. He will fly first to Seattle, visiting the Pacific Distributing Company on the first day. Remaining in Seattle on the second day, he will see the Ames & Hobart Company. On the morning of the third day, he will rent a car and drive to Tacoma to spend a day each with Northwest Distributors and Devon Distributing Company. On the evening of the fourth day, he

EXHIBIT 2	Prospective Distributors for Pacific Northwest Territory		

Distributor	Main Office Location	Number of Branches	Branch Locations
Pacific Distributing Company	Seattle, WA	2	Portland, OR Everett, WA
Northwest Distributors, Inc.	Tacoma, WA	0	N/A
Ames & Hobart Company	Seattle, WA	1	Spokane, WA
Devon Distributing Company	Tacoma, WA	2	Portland, OR Seattle, WA
Shasta Distributors, Inc.	Portland, OR	2	Seattle, WA Spokane, WA

plans to fly to Portland, and spend the final day with Shasta Distributors. He will then return to Racine.

Typically, his visits take place as follows. He first meets with the respective distributor's general manager and management team. They discuss topics such as the distributor's interest in carrying Fairchild products, suppliers of other products in the distributor's line, territories covered, inventory levels, methods of payment, and other factors. He then interviews the distributor's sales manager, and later the service manager. When possible, he talks to field sales personnel. The interviews usually end with a tour of both warehouse and service facilities. The days are full, and Ghormley is convinced he knows each distributor's total operation much better than before. He is pleased with the reception at every distributor and is gratified to hear that all five general managers think highly of the Fairchild line. All five also appear to be impressed by the fact that he is visiting them personally. His trip convinces him of two things. First, it appears that industrial distributors are interested and can be used to replace some field sales representatives. Second, any selection process must include such personal visits.

GHORMLEY DRAWS HIS IMPRESSIONS OF THE VISITED DISTRIBUTORS

On his return to Racine, Ghormley reviews his notes and summarizes his impressions of each of the five distributors based on his observations and other materials he has brought back. He attempts to focus these impressions principally on the five selection criteria he has chosen. He realizes, however, that other points may creep in. He summarizes his impressions as follows.

Pacific Distributing Company

Main office in Seattle, with branch offices in Portland, Oregon, and Everett, Washington. Seattle warehouse has 15,000 square feet of space, and Portland and Everett warehouses have 10,000 square feet of space each. Inventory records in all three warehouses are totally computerized, and combined average monthly inventory in all three warehouses is $500,000. The company has eight outside field salespeople and five inside salespeople working out of the three offices. Salespeople appear to be very experienced, and there has been very little sales turnover in the past five years. Interviews with field salespeople leave the impression that they are aggressive, competent, and fairly satisfied. They have no real dissatisfactions with the company's compensation plan. Fairchild products fit in well with the existing product lines, although some product lines are good and others are not. Service personnel appear competent, and service equipment is modern and in good shape. Service space is quite limited in all three sites. The general manager expresses real interest in handling Fairchild products and seems fairly willing to follow Fairchild policies and directions. No problems with inventory level requirements as long as they are "reasonable."

Northwest Distributors, Inc.

Only one office in Tacoma and one warehouse of 10,000 square feet at that location. Inventory records are not totally computerized as yet, and average monthly inventory is estimated at $250,000. Company has three outside salespeople and three inside salespeople, all working out of the Tacoma office. Sales turnover has been a problem. Interviewed salespeople seem aggressive but also appear to lack experience. Product line is "average," but the company does have a gap that Fairchild products can easily fill. Service staff is small, and there is a relatively small service area. Service equipment is not the most modern, and some appears run down. General manager seems only moderately interested. He appears to have some other options and seems more interested in them than in Fairchild. He also balks at some of Fairchild's inventory level requirements.

Ames & Hobart Company

Main office is in Seattle with one branch in Spokane. Each location has a 10,000 square foot warehouse and a totally computerized inventory system. Average monthly inventory is valued at $400,000. There are two outside salespersons and two inside salespersons working out of each office. There has been some turnover in the past, but interviewed salespeople appear experienced. Compensation plan is about average. Product line is uneven, with some excellent lines and some rather poor lines. However, Fairchild products appear to fit well into the total line. Service staff, equipment, and space are about average. Distributor seems interested in carrying Fairchild products, but it also insists on carrying competitive products as well. General manager expresses some concerns regarding Fairchild's inventory level requirements.

Devon Distributing Company

Main office is in Tacoma with two offices in Seattle and Portland. In Tacoma, there is 18,000 square feet of warehouse space, and 10,000 square feet in both the Seattle and Portland branch locations. Inventory system is totally computerized throughout the three locations, and average monthly inventory in all three is about $480,000. Working out of the three locations are ten outside salespeople and three inside salespeople. Salespeople have been with the company a long time, and turnover has been very low. Interviewed salespeople appear very experienced, dedicated, and well prepared. All are satisfied with the company's compensation plan. Good products in their existing line, and Fairchild products provide a very good fit with other lines. Fairchild would be replacing a competitor's line that has not done well for Devon. Service staff appears good, but equipment not the most modern, and service area space is only average. General manager likes our products and will carry our lines, but he insists on carrying competitive lines if occasion presents itself. He also wants a consignment deal for carrying our inventory.

Shasta Distributors, Inc.

Main office is in Portland with branch locations in Seattle and Spokane. There are 16,000 square feet of warehouse space at main office, 12,000 square feet in Spokane, and 9,000 square feet in Seattle. Company has a totally computerized inventory system integrated throughout the three offices, and combined average monthly inventory is about $495,000. In the three locations, there are six outside salespeople and four inside salespeople. Salespeople appear competent, experienced, and dedicated, but they have many gripes about the company's compensation plan. There is a good fit between Fairchild products and distributor's present line. Our products complement many others in their present line. Their line includes a number of good lines but also a couple of weak ones. Good modern service facilities with ample space at all three locations. Interviewed service personnel appear very experienced and competent, and other suppliers recommend their service capabilities. The interest level is there, and general manager likes Fairchild's reputation, but he indicates that he will probably ignore our directions if they are not in his company's best interests. He also expresses some concerns about our inventory level requirements.

To help determine an overall or composite rating of each of the prospective distributors, Ghormley develops the rating form shown in Exhibit 3. He wants

---

EXHIBIT 3	Distributor Rating Form

DISTRIBUTOR _____

Rating Criteria	Rating Scale				
1. Sales capabilities—size and experience of field and inside sales force	1	2	3	4	5
	Low				High
2. Interest—level of interest of distributor in carrying the manufacturer's products	1	2	3	4	5
	Low				High
3. Product line compatibility—compatibility of distributor's present product line with the manufacturer's products	1	2	3	4	5
	Low				High
4. Service capabilities—service facilities and experience of service personnel to handle the manufacturer's products	1	2	3	4	5
	Low				High
5. Warehousing and delivery capabilities—size of warehouse, inventory levels, and transportation abilities	1	2	3	4	5
	Low				High

ADDITIONAL COMMENTS:

to transcribe his impressions and notes onto a rating form for each distributor, so that he may better summarize his evaluations. He also believes that by completing such a rating form for each distributor, he can facilitate his decision to select one of the five to cover exclusively the Pacific northwest territory of Oregon and Washington.

Recommend to Ghormley which one of the five distributors he should appoint to cover this territory.

DISCUSSION QUESTIONS

1. If Ghormley decides to use a selective rather than an exclusive distributor system in Oregon and Washington and wants three distributors to cover the territory, which three do you recommend?

2. Assume Ghormley changes his mind and now perceives service as the most important criterion in selecting distributors. He reweights the criteria as follows: sales capabilities, 25 percent; interest level, 10 percent; product line compati-

bility, 25 percent; service capabilities, 35 percent; and warehousing and delivery capabilities, 5 percent. Now, which distributor do you recommend to cover the territory if Ghormley still wants an exclusive distributorship arrangement?

3. If none of the five selected distributors will agree to carry the Fairchild line in the Pacific Northwest territory, what do you think Ghormley should do?

Bay City Steam Fittings, Inc.

Losing Control of the Channel of Distribution

THE BEGINNING

Bay City Steam Fittings, Inc., of Bay City, Michigan, was founded by Jerry Ball in the spring of 1970. Jerry had previously been a sales engineer with Toledo Forging Company but had left that firm when his father died, leaving him a sizeable inheritance. Jerry had then taken a year to develop and patent a new type of thermostatic steam trap that would have broad application in a variety of types of industrial steam systems. With his own funds and a small loan from a group of investors, Jerry was able to lease a small casting, forging, machining, and assembly facility in his home town of Bay City, Michigan, and was ready to begin production of his newly patented steam trap by April of 1970.

Prior to starting production, Jerry had visited with key people at the larger manufacturing facilities with extensive steam systems and with utility companies in the Great Lakes region. The engineers and purchasing people at these firms were quite receptive, and by April, ten of these firms had given Jerry orders for a sufficient number of traps for Jerry to begin production. Once production began, Jerry began to call on major industrial distributors in the region, and six of these agreed to stock the Bay City trap. By the end of 1970, Jerry had secured enough business so that he could project a break-even year for 1971.

The year 1971 turned out to be better than break-even. The Bay City steam trap found a strong acceptance in the marketplace and positive word-of-mouth about Bay City's quality, durability, and dependability spread quickly. Several of the buyers suggested that Jerry add a line of strainers and relief valves, and Jerry

Case contributed by Ronald H. King and W. E. Patton III, Professors of Marketing, Appalachian State University.

began manufacturing and selling these in late 1971. By mid-1972, Bay City had outgrown its original facilities, and in early 1973 Bay City Steam Fittings moved into a larger plant in the new industrial park outside of Bay City.

EARLY GROWTH

As the production facilities expanded, Jerry Ball found that it was becoming impossible for him to maintain contact with customers and oversee the operation of the entire firm, so in March 1973 Jerry hired Arlen Frost as a sales rep. Arlen had a degree in business from the University of Michigan, had served in Viet Nam, and had a year of experience on the road selling for a major industrial distributor. Arlen began to rapidly expand the number of major distributors carrying Bay City's steam fittings throughout the midwest, while Jerry added a few more major end user accounts (the large manufacturing firms and utility companies).

Each man negotiated prices individually with buyers, and the prices and other terms-of-sale conditions varied from buyer to buyer. This allowed Bay City to meet any competition and adjust quickly to a changing, growing market, but by 1975 the number of customers had grown so large that pricing problems began to emerge. It was becoming difficult to keep up with who paid what for which fittings, and some of the distributors began to get together and discover that some paid more than others without apparent justification. After several complaints, Arlen suggested to Jerry that they establish a more formal, stable pricing policy.

The policy that Jerry and Arlen developed was quite simple. Bay City established a list price for each unit in Bay City's product line that was slightly higher than the price a mid-sized end user might be expected to pay. Distributors were then offered a discount of 25 percent from the list price, but prices to the larger end user accounts would continue to be based on Jerry's negotiations with those buyers. All purchases would be shipped FOB origin, freight prepaid and added. As part of the pricing package, Bay City developed a list of its large key end user accounts and notified the distributors that these would be "house accounts" for Bay City and thus off-limits to the distributors.

This pricing package seemed to clear up what little conflict had existed with the distributors, and soon Arlen had established distribution through industrial distributors in most of the major markets in the midwest. By 1977, Bay City had added additional lines of steam valves and the list of individual stock keeping units (SKUs) expanded to over fifty. Arlen and Jerry had also decided that Bay City needed another sales rep to keep up with the demand, so they hired Bill Jennings who took over sales in the eastern and southern parts of the midwest. By the end of 1977, Jennings had expanded sales so that Bay City was now selling to industrial distributors as far east as Pittsburgh and as far south as Louisville, Kentucky. Arlen took on the title of sales manager but continued to maintain responsibility for sales in the upper midwest and Great Lakes region.

MAJOR EXPANSION

In early 1978, Arlen and Jerry attended an industrial trade show in New York and met Saul Cohen, an established manufacturers' representative who handled a full line of steam fittings in the northeastern part of the country. Saul showed some interest in taking Bay City on as a principal because of Jerry's patented steam trap and because of Bay City's growing reputation as a major vendor of quality steam fittings. Arlen and Jerry were impressed by Saul's enthusiasm, and after checking him out carefully through friends in the industry, Arlen sat down with Saul and hammered out an agency agreement.

Saul Cohen would have responsibility for representing Bay City to industrial distributors and end users in eastern New York, eastern Pennsylvania, and all of New England. List prices, discounts and shipping terms would be the same as for all of Bay City's customers: Distributors would get a 25 percent discount from list, prices to major end users would be negotiated with Arlen's approval, and all shipments would be FOB origin, freight prepaid and added. Saul would be paid a 10 percent commission on all sales and would agree to adhere to Bay City's pricing schedule and territorial limitations. The impact of the agreement was immediate and impressive: By the end of 1979, sales of Bay City's fittings through Saul Cohen amounted to over $750,000.

Although the additional volume generated by Cohen was substantial, this volume was nearly matched when Arlen hired another company sales rep, Hugh Long, in 1980. Despite the strong recession in 1980, Bay City continued to grow in sales volume by expanding slowly into new territories. By the end of 1982, Arlen Frost was handling the distributors along the Chicago–Cleveland axis and the Michigan peninsula, while Bill Jennings took over the northern midwest and Hugh Long assumed responsibility for the "frontier"—the southern part of the midwest. Long developed strong sales to several industrial distributors in Kentucky and Virginia, and even established a "beachhead" across the Mississippi River by setting up an industrial distributor in St. Louis.

In 1983, the economy began a strong recovery, and Bay City's sales volume grew sharply. Bay City added several new lines of Ys, nipples, pumps, and retrofit kits and became established as a major vendor for a full line of steam fittings. The company moved into newer, larger facilities in Bay City to handle the new product lines. At the same time, sales manager Arlen Frost began to study the possibility of expanding the company's sales force to keep up with the increasing demand.

Three factors had caused Arlen to consider this expansion. First, there appeared to be a strong potential for growth in the "frontier"—Kentucky, Virginia, and even Tennessee and North Carolina were becoming very attractive markets. Second, Saul Cohen was not keeping up with the growing market in New England—Cohen's sales volume had not grown substantially since 1980. Finally, there was a strong indication that Bay City was stretching its sales force too thin—it was becoming difficult to call on all of the growing number of smaller and middle-sized industrial distributors who were now expressing interest in Bay City fittings.

RESTRUCTURING FOR THE 1980s

Arlen spent nearly three months studying the situation, visiting industrial distributors, talking to his own sales reps, and even consulting with Saul Cohen and other independent manufacturers' representatives. By September 1983, Arlen had realized that the problem was more than a sales force problem but was also a channels of distribution and pricing problem. After considering several alternatives, Arlen developed the proposal outlined in Exhibit 1, and he presented the proposal to Jerry Ball in early October. A key element of this proposal was the classification of distributors as Class A and Class B dealers as defined in Exhibit 1. After being assured that Bay City's current distributors would be happy with

---

EXHIBIT 1   **Proposed Bay City Fittings Sales, Distribution, and Pricing Policy, October 1983**

---

1. Bay City Fittings will sell direct to major key end user accounts and to major industrial distributors, as identified in a list to be developed by Bay City and updated quarterly. The end users on the list will be called "key accounts" and the major industrial distributors will be called "Class A dealers."

2. The Class A dealers will have responsibility for stocking a full line of Bay City fittings at appropriate stocking levels, and will sell to smaller distributors (to be called "Class B dealers") in their markets as well as to non-key account end users in their markets. Bay City agrees to avoid selling to Class B dealers or non-key account end users in the markets of Class A dealers. Areas of market responsibility for each Class A dealer will be established by Bay City Fittings in consultation with the Class A dealer involved, and the Class A dealers will agree to market Bay City fittings aggressively to customers in their respective areas of market responsibility.

3. Class B dealers will have no stocking or market responsibilities but will develop appropriate relationships with Class A dealers to ensure adequate representation in the market.

4. Independent manufacturers' representatives will no longer be utilized. The agreement with Saul Cohen will not be renewed for 1984.

5. The Bay City sales force will be responsible for calling on all key accounts and Class A dealers. The sales force will have six sales representatives. One of these will be designated as a key account rep and will have responsibility for selling to all major end user accounts designated as key accounts and developing new prospects to become key accounts. The other five representatives will sell to Class A dealers and will be assigned to territories that will cover the area east of the Mississippi River and as far south as Tennessee and North Carolina. The sales force will expand as market conditions demand. Total sales force expenses are expected to be within 4 percent to 5 percent of sales.

6. A new pricing policy will go into force that recognizes: (1) the new role of Class A dealers, (2) that there can be a considerable difference in volume of purchases among these dealers, and (3) that Class A dealers should be encouraged to generate larger volumes and to order in larger quantities where possible.

EXHIBIT 1 continued

7. The new pricing policy will be as follows:
   a. Bay City Fittings will establish and publish an appropriate list price for each SKU in the product line. The list prices will be established to represent a price that would be appropriate for most end users to expect to pay and would be competitive in the end user marketplace.
   b. A trade discount structure of 20/10 will be adopted. Class B dealers would be entitled to a 20 percent discount from list. Class A dealers would get an additional 10 percent discount from list. For example, SKU 4267109 lists for $100. Class B dealers would pay $80 for this item ($100 − $20 = $80). Class A dealers would pay $72 for the item ($80 − $8 = $72). Thus, Class A dealers would earn a 10 percent margin on items sold to Class B dealers. They would earn a 28 percent margin on items sold at list to end users.
   c. Prices to key accounts will continue to be on an individually negotiated or bid basis.
   d. Cumulative quantity discounts will be offered to customers whose purchases for a given calendar year exceed certain levels. The discount level achieved will apply to total calendar year sales and only the highest level achieved applies. The quantity discount for the calendar year will be paid in the form of a rebate to be paid by the end of January of the following year. Calendar year purchase requirements and discount levels are as follows:

Calendar Year Purchase Requirement (if purchases exceed this amount)	Discount Level (The buyer will receive a rebate of this percentage of total sales)
$100,000	1%
$200,000	2%
$300,000	3%
$400,000	4%
$500,000 and up	5%

Thus, a Class A dealer who purchases $250,000 in a year would receive a rebate check of $5,000 in January of the following year. This rebate plan is quite forward-looking in that only 40 percent of Bay City's current accounts would qualify for the 1 percent level or above, and only 5 percent would currently qualify for the 2 percent level. The above structure allows for growth in volume in the future.

   e. With the exception of shipments with a net invoice value of over $30,000 per shipment, all shipments will continue to be shipped FOB origin, freight prepaid and added. Orders with a net invoice value of over $30,000 will be shipped FOB destination, freight prepaid. It is hoped that his policy will encourage larger orders and shipments and thus save Bay City the handling and billing costs associated with small orders.
   f. Payment terms are net thirty with a 1-1/2 percent service charge per month on past-due balances. Terms are COD for accounts sixty days or more past due.

8. Bay City's lawyer will develop a contract reflecting the above terms for execution with the Class A dealers. The contract will be for an indefinite term with provisions for cancellation by either party with thirty days' notice. The contract would stipulate that list prices, discount levels, and other terms of sale could be modified by Bay City Fittings with ten days' notice.

the new structure, Jerry enthusiastically endorsed the proposal and told Arlen to put the plan into effect—under his new title: Arlen Frost, vice president for sales.

By the end of 1984, Arlen had implemented the plan. The industrial distributors were generally enthusiastic and agreed to the terms of the proposal with only minor disagreements with Class A dealers over definitions of market areas and what constituted appropriate stocking levels. The dealers were impressed with Bay City's sense of fair play and cooperation, and particularly liked Bay City's promise to refrain from selling direct to their potential customers.

While getting the dealers signed up was time consuming, Arlen found that the toughest part of the implementation was expanding the sales force. Good reps were hard to find and hire, the compensation plan had to be revised, and there were some squabbles over territory assignment. Bill Jennings became the key account sales rep and Hugh Long became a "frontier" specialist with responsibility for southern Indiana, southern Illinois, Kentucky, Tennessee, Virginia, and North Carolina. The four new reps were assigned territories in the western midwest, Great Lakes region, New England, and central Atlantic.

The plan worked well and provided for orderly expansion. A solid network of industrial distributors was developed throughout Bay City's coverage area, even down through Tennessee and North Carolina. By the end of 1987, Bay City was selling to approximately 120 Class A dealers and to forty key accounts. The Class A dealers served nearly 1,800 Class B dealers and 6,000 end user accounts. Class B dealers, in turn, were serving over 50,000 small end user accounts, from Maine to Memphis. Bay City was generating sales volume of nearly $16 million, with 90 percent of sales going to Class A dealers and 10 percent to end users. The business seemed quite stable, growing in a controlled manner and generating a solid bottom line profit.

LOOKING SOUTH

By mid-1988 Arlen Frost was beginning to tire of stability. He had been accustomed to the fast growth of the 1970s and early 1980s, and he missed the excitement of new ventures. About this time, Arlen read several articles about the boom in the Sun Belt, and particularly about the growth in manufacturing in the south. "If there is that much growth in manufacturing," he thought, "that must mean more and bigger factories, which means more steam pipes and systems, and more demand for steam traps, valves, and fittings." Arlen decided to investigate.

Arlen flew to Nashville where he met Hugh Long, and the two of them headed south. Their first stop was a major industrial distributor who served the thriving area of Huntsville, Alabama. The owner of the firm was willing to spend over an hour with Arlen and Hugh, describing his business and the industry in north Alabama in detail. Arlen and Hugh quickly realized that the industrial distributors in north Alabama were similar to the Class A and Class B dealers in Bay City's current coverage area, with one large exception. The Class A dealers tended to buy many of their lines from industrial wholesalers rather than directly from the manufacturer.

The Huntsville distributor explained that he purchased about 85 percent of his MRO items from Jackson Supply Company, a large industrial "super-distributor" in Atlanta. The distributor explained that Jackson provided quicker and better service than most manufacturers could at virtually the same price that the manufacturer would charge. The distributor pointed out that Atlanta was a lot closer than most industrial manufacturers (who tended to be located in the north), both geographically and culturally. It was clear that the Huntsville distributor was very pleased with his relationship with Jackson, and the loyalty would be difficult to shake. The distributor did indicate, however, that he would be very interested in stocking Bay City items if he could buy them through Jackson Supply.

THE GEORGIA CONNECTION

Arlen and Hugh encountered the Jackson Supply Company again in Birmingham. The industrial distributor they visited there was actually owned by Jackson Supply Company and was physically housed in Jackson Supply's large regional warehouse in southern Birmingham. The manager of the Birmingham operation gave Arlen and Hugh a tour of the facilities, explaining that Jackson operated similar warehouse/sales branch facilities in Columbia, South Carolina, and Jacksonville, Florida, in addition to a huge facility just outside Atlanta, Georgia. All of the facilities utilized state-of-the-art materials handling equipment, inventory control systems, and order processing systems, and the firm owned its own fleet of trucks for delivery throughout the southeast.

After the visit with the Jackson distributor in Birmingham, Arlen sent Hugh back to Nashville and then flew to Atlanta. He was able to set up an appointment with Jackson Supply's steam parts buyer for the next afternoon and he planned the meeting to be one of information gathering rather than a sales call. The Jackson Supply buyer was quite helpful in answering Arlen's questions and even provided him with a professionally prepared vendor's information kit, which contained a complete financial report, a description of the firm's distributor network, details on sales volume by product type, and other such information.

Arlen was amazed. He had never heard of the firm, and yet it generated sales of over $200 million per year (including nearly $5 million in steam system items) in the coverage area of Alabama, Mississippi, Georgia, South Carolina, and Florida. Jackson Supply had developed a network of Class A dealers and end users that was similar in structure to that of Bay City's, with the exception that Jackson actually owned or held part interest in ten of the Class A dealers in the south, including those housed at Jackson's warehouses. The thing that most impressed Arlen, however, was the high degree of professionalism of everyone he had met—they were all enthusiastic go-getters who seemed to be on top of everything.

Near the end of the visit, the steam parts buyer brought Arlen into the office of Emmett Jackson, the founder and CEO of Jackson Supply. Arlen was introduced to the CEO and his son, Emmett, Jr. (who had just received his MBA from the University of Georgia), and found them both to be bright, energetic, and very friendly people. Arlen was quite surprised when the senior Jackson said that he was familiar with Bay City fittings and had been impressed with their reputation for quality and durability. He would certainly be open to a proposal from Bay City, since there had been a few problems with their current vendor of steam traps and fittings. The CEO suggested that Arlen and the steam parts buyer see if they could come up with something.

They could "come up with something," and they did in a surprisingly short time. The tentative agreement reached was quite similar to the agreement Bay City had reached with its Class A dealers to the north, with the exception of the inclusion of a new level of trade discount for Jackson Supply. Jackson Supply would agree to aggressively market Bay City's product lines to Class A dealers and end users throughout Jackson Supply's coverage area and agreed to stock the full line of Bay City items in appropriate quantities in all of its warehouses. Furthermore, Jackson Supply guaranteed to purchase a minimum of $2 million (net) in Bay City items per calendar year.

In return, Bay City would agree not to sell directly to Class A or Class B dealers or to end users (other than those identified as key accounts) in Jackson's market area. After some negotiation, a trade discount structure of 20/10/10 was agreed on, with the discounts to be applied to Bay City's standard published list prices. Under this plan, Jackson would pay $64.80 for an item that listed for $100, and would be expected to resell it to Class A dealers for $72. Bay City and Jackson also would agree to the quantity discount and shipping terms implemented by Bay City in 1984, with the additional agreement that Jackson could request shipment direct to its regional warehouses or "captive" Class A dealers, if desired.

Prior to signing any formal agreement, Arlen presented the proposed new distribution and pricing structure to Jerry Ball for approval (see Exhibit 2). Jerry was a bit concerned at giving control of such a large area of the south to an independent wholesale distributor and giving up an additional 10 percent in margin to Jackson in the discount structure. Arlen pointed out that the discount structure was similar to that offered by Jackson's other vendors, and furthermore, Jackson had such a stranglehold on the south that it would be difficult to penetrate the deep south without using them. Finally, Arlen pointed out that they would not have to expand Bay City's sales force with the attendant costs and headaches, and that using Jackson Supply would greatly simplify shipping and reduce the amount of inventory Bay City would normally have to carry to facilitate such an expansion.

Jerry finally gave his blessing to the agreement, and a formal contract with Jackson Supply was signed in October 1988. The contract was for an indefinite term, cancelable by either party with thirty days' notice, but the parties also agreed to review the terms of the contract annually to determine if any revisions were needed. Bay City shipped its first truckload of fittings to Jackson in November, and by the end of December 1988 the Jackson warehouses were fully stocked with the full line of Bay City Fittings steam system parts.

EXHIBIT 2   **New Channel and Pricing Structure: 1989**

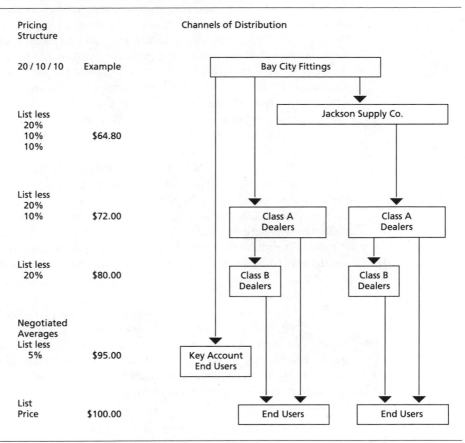

Pricing Structure		Channels of Distribution
20 / 10 / 10	Example	Bay City Fittings → Jackson Supply Co.
List less 20% 10% 10%	$64.80	
List less 20% 10%	$72.00	Class A Dealers Class A Dealers
List less 20%	$80.00	Class B Dealers Class B Dealers
Negotiated Averages List less 5%	$95.00	Key Account End Users
List Price	$100.00	End Users End Users

CLOSING THE 1980s ON THE UPSWING

By far the biggest year in Bay City Fittings' history was 1989. Sales in its traditional coverage area (the midwest, northeast, and south through Tennessee and North Carolina) were almost $18 million despite an economy that was beginning to show some signs of softness. The brightest spot in the firm's performance for 1989, however, was the volume generated by Jackson Supply in the deep south. Jackson had purchased just over $3 million in Bay City merchandise over the course of the year, with increases in volume each month. Bay City was now generating total sales of $21 million, with almost 15 percent of that coming from Jackson Supply.

The people at Jackson Supply were also quite pleased with the venture with Bay City. Although the sales of Bay City merchandise amounted to less than 2 percent of Jackson's volume, the quality of the products and the dependability of Bay City's deliveries had made the venture virtually trouble-free. Jackson had been so satisfied that they had included the Bay City items in one of their quarterly direct mail pieces and featured the Bay City thermostatic steam trap on the cover of the semiannual Jackson catalog published in June.

At Emmett Jackson's invitation, Jerry Ball and Arlen Frost flew to Atlanta in early January 1990 to review the previous year and to plan for the future. The meeting at Jackson headquarters was most pleasant for everyone since everyone seemed to be happy with 1989's performance, all were optimistic about 1990, and it appeared that no adjustments in the contract were needed for the next year. The meeting ended with a presentation by Emmett Jackson, Jr. (the CEO's son), who had been named Jackson Supply's Vice President for Marketing in late 1989.

Emmett, Jr. (called "Stoney" by his dad, a truncation of Emmett, Jr.'s nickname—Stonewall) presented a well-developed, professionally prepared view of the year ahead for Jackson Supply and its vendors. He pointed out that the economy throughout the nation would be flat at best for 1990, but the chance for a recession was minimal until 1991 at the earliest. He made a strong case, however, for the fact that any growth in sales volume for an industrial supplies marketer would have to be the result of aggressive marketing rather than economic growth. Any dollars in growth would have to come either from expansion into new markets or from competitors.

Stoney Jackson gave few specifics for Jackson's plans for 1990, but he closed the meeting with a spirited claim that Jackson Supply could be counted on to mount an extremely aggressive sales and marketing plan for 1990, and he could promise that sales of Bay City items through Jackson would increase by 25 percent in 1990. Despite the fact that they had snickered a bit at Emmett, Jr.'s nickname, Jerry and Arlen were very impressed and returned to Bay City with a very positive feeling about 1990.

◢ JACKSON'S ATTACK

The positive feeling did not last long. In March 1990, Arlen received a frantic call from Hugh Long in Nashville. At first Arlen thought Hugh was drunk—he was babbling about an "invasion" and "double cross" and used a large amount of profanity. Arlen finally calmed Hugh and as Hugh began to explain what he was calling about, Arlen began to understand why Hugh was so upset.

It seems that Hugh had just discovered that Jackson Supply had recently purchased controlling interest in the two largest Class A dealers in Tennessee and North Carolina—the Nashville dealer and the Raleigh dealer. Furthermore, the manager of the Nashville dealer had told Hugh that Jackson Supply was planning on expanding into Tennessee, North Carolina, and even into Tidewater, Virginia, by mid-year, and planned on establishing a regional warehouse in at least one of the states.

Arlen could hardly believe what he was hearing and wanted to check things out on his own. He first called Jackson Supply in Atlanta, but both Jacksons were out of town. Arlen then flew to Nashville and visited the Class A dealer there to verify Hugh's story. It turned out to be correct and was only the tip of the iceberg. Arlen called on three Class A dealers in middle Tennessee and all three apologetically told Arlen the same story: a sales rep from Jackson Supply had called on them and had offered their full lines (including Bay City Fittings) at competitive prices and with free delivery on any size order.

The dealers pointed out that their orders from Bay City were always too small to get the freight paid by Bay City, and Jackson Supply could not only provide free delivery, they could actually deliver more quickly since they ran their own trucks up from Birmingham. Finally, the dealers pointed out that they could vastly simplify their ordering by buying a wide variety of merchandise from one source rather than from many different vendors. They were fond of Hugh and Arlen, but all three dealers said they planned to buy their lines of steam system parts from Jackson Supply rather than direct from Bay City, and they suspected most other Class A dealers and some of the major end users would do likewise.

Arlen kept his laptop computer busy on the flight back to Atlanta. The Class A dealers' decisions to buy from Jackson Supply were built on sound economics, and certainly the business would be profitable for Jackson Supply. Everything was very rational, but there was a very large problem for Bay City— they stood to lose as many as twenty Class A dealers and five key accounts to Jackson Supply. By Arlen's calculations, the lost sales volume to these accounts could amount to nearly $3 million annually, half of Hugh Long's total sales!

THE STONEWALL AND RETREAT

Arlen reported to Jerry immediately upon his return to Bay City, and Jerry's response was an explosive "They can't do that! That wasn't part of our agreement! That's *our* territory!" He picked up the phone, called Jackson Supply, and reached Stoney Jackson. Jerry pointed out in no uncertain terms that he didn't like Jackson straying out of the deep south and "bootlegging" in Tennessee and North Carolina, and he wanted Jackson to retreat.

Stoney responded that he could certainly understand Jerry's initial response to Jackson's move north, but this was part of Jackson's aggressive marketing and expansion plans that he had mentioned back in January. Furthermore, he was expanding all of Jackson Supply's business into new territories, not just the Bay City lines, and Bay City was a fairly small portion of Jackson's volume. Stoney suggested that if Jerry really strongly objected to Jackson Supply selling the Bay City items in Tennessee and North Carolina, they could simply cancel the contract with Jackson—the whole contract. Jackson Supply would find another vendor to take Bay City's place in Jackson's catalogs throughout the deep south.

Jerry took a deep breath. Jackson Supply's business could well exceed $4 million in 1990, and it was business that Bay City might not be able to pick up through any other channel of distribution. Before Jerry could speak, Stoney said, "Jerry, don't worry. Think about this. You will still be selling Bay City steam parts in Tennessee, North Carolina, or wherever we sell them; we'll just be doing the hard work. Sure, your sales rep in Nashville may not sell a Bay City steam trap—but you will be selling it to us instead. You are still getting the business without having the burden. And I'll promise you a ton of business—we'll sell more of your merchandise than your sales force ever could."

Jerry recognized that Jackson was not going to back down, and he feared losing the Jackson account altogether, so he ended the conversation by telling Stoney that while he did not like what was happening, he hoped that everything would turn out well for both parties if they continued to work together. When he hung up the phone, Jerry turned to Arlen and shook his head, "We'll just have to adjust to it," he said.

Adjusting wasn't easy. Arlen was faced with the problem of completely restructuring the sales force to cope with the loss of direct sales in Tennessee and North Carolina. Neither of the possible ways of doing it was pleasant: Arlen could either keep all of the current reps and reassign them to new, smaller territories, or he could lay off a rep and reassign the remainder to newly structured territories. He was sure that the business would continue to grow somehow, so he decided to keep all of the reps and reassign them. None of the reps was happy with the reassignment, and all of them grumbled about lower earnings, changed customers, and anything else they could think of.

By August, it was clear that Jackson's move north was having an impact, but the impact was not exactly what Jerry and Arlen had expected it to be. Arlen prepared a set of sales and margin figures showing Bay City's performance for 1989, the projections Bay City had made in early 1990 prior to Jackson's change in tactics, and a set of projections for 1990 based on actual performance through July (see Exhibit 3).

Jerry scanned the figures, but his eyes moved quickly to the "bottom line" figures—the contribution margin figure in this instance. He was not at all pleased with what he saw. "We're going to be way under projection—and even under last year! What gives?" he asked, looking at Arlen.

Arlen pointed out first of all that unit volume (as measured by sales at list) was holding up to 1989 figures but was well under the original projections. Jackson Supply was moving more merchandise than originally projected, but the original projections had not taken Jackson's move north into account. The problem appeared to be that Bay City's lost sales in Tennessee and Kentucky were not being made up by Jackson Supply. Arlen had originally thought that the flat economy might have caused a decrease in sales volume, but a check of shipments to Bay City's current Class A dealers and key accounts indicated that their purchases were within two percentage points of the original 1990 projections. The problem, then, appeared to be in the south.

Jerry Ball called Stoney Jackson to discuss the matter, but Stoney was aggressively defensive. He blustered that business was tough to get—anyone who read the *Wall Street Journal* knew that. Furthermore, Stoney said that he couldn't

EXHIBIT 3   Bay City Fittings Sales and Profit Figures: Actual 1989 and 1990 Projections

1989 Actual Performance by Customer Type and Total (figures in $000)

	To Class A Dealers	To Key Accounts	To Jackson Supply	Total
Volume at list price	$22,501	$2,001	$4,816	$29,318
Sales	16,201	1,900	3,121	21,222
Gross margin	4,950	900	713	6,563
Less volume rebate	(243)	(10)	(156)	(409)
Free freight exp.	(104)	(7)	(36)	(147)
Contribution margin	4,603	884	521	6,008

1990 Initial Projections* by Customer Type and Total (figures in $000)

	To Class A Dealers	To Key Accounts	To Jackson Supply	Total
Volume at list price	$23,611	$2,105	$6,173	$31,889
Sales	17,000	2,000	4,000	23,000
Gross margin	5,194	947	914	7,055
Less volume rebate	(255)	(10)	(200)	(465)
Free freight exp.	(105)	(8)	(40)	(153)
Contribution margin	4,834	929	674	6,437

* Projections made in January prior to Jackson Supply's move north.

1990 Revised Projections‡ by Customer Type and Total (figures in $000)

	To Class A Dealers	To Key Accounts	To Jackson Supply	Total
Volume at list price	$18,631	$1,814	$9,418	$29,862
Sales	13,414	1,723	6,103	21,240
Gross margin	4,099	816	1,394	6,309
Less volume rebate	(201)	(9)	(305)	(515)
Free freight exp.	(92)	(6)	(55)	(153)
Contribution margin	3,806	802	1,034	5,641

‡ Revised, based on actual 1990 performance through July 1990.

believe Jerry was calling to complain. "Look at your own numbers," Stoney said, "We're going to buy twice as much from you this year than last. Look, if you don't want our business, say so and I'll get another vendor. In the meantime, we have some aggressive marketing plans for the last quarter and I'll ensure that they include Bay City steam parts as a prominent feature. We'll move some brass for you."

Again, Jerry could find no argument to present to Stoney that would not risk losing the Jackson Supply account. After the call, he called in his top executives and presented Arlen's figures to them. He asked them to take measures to cut costs to try to make up for the potential loss of nearly $800,000 in contribution margin from the original projections even if it meant laying off people. "A fine thing," Jerry thought, "I try to expand my business and end up having to lay people off."

▶ JACKSON'S FLANKING MANEUVER

Bay City Fitting's problems with Jackson Supply were just beginning. In mid-October 1990, Arlen received another hysterical call from Hugh Long, who was now the Bay City sales rep for Kentucky, Virginia, West Virginia, and Maryland. Hugh had just received a royal chewing out by the owner of a large Class A account in Louisville. The owner waved an eight-page direct mail flyer in Hugh's face and shouted that he just couldn't continue to do business with Bay City unless Hugh did something about what was going on.

Hugh had grabbed the direct mail piece out of the owner's hands and was horrified at what he saw. On the cover was a picture of Bay City's best-selling line—the patented thermostatic steam trap—with a headline underneath that screamed "30% off of List Price on America's Finest!" The copy offered a 30 percent discount from list price on any Bay City steam parts, and even gave three examples showing the list price and the discount price. There was also an 800 number to call and a promise of next-day shipment out of Nashville or Richmond, FOB origin, freight prepaid and added. The remainder of the mini-catalog included another page with a complete listing of Bay City Fittings product lines with list prices and discount prices along with six pages of illustrations and listings for the lines of a dozen or so other major manufacturers with a similar cut-price offering. The mailer was from Jackson Supply Company, and it had been sent to every Class A dealer, every Class B dealer, and even to small and middle-sized end users throughout Hugh's territory.

The Louisville dealer told Hugh that Jackson was also calling potential accounts on the phone offering the "direct marketing" service, quicker delivery, as well as the discount prices. The tactic had obviously been effective, since most of the Louisville dealer's Class B accounts in southern Kentucky had made at least one purchase from Jackson. The Class B dealers had offered to continue to buy from Louisville if Louisville could meet Jackson Supply's price, but the Louisville dealer pointed out that under the 20/10 discount structure he did not even get a full 30 percent discount from Bay City. In fact, the Class A dealer in Louisville could now actually buy an item from Jackson Supply for less than he could buy it direct from Bay City Fittings—the only problem was that he couldn't sell it at a profit.

Arlen told Hugh to settle down, that he'd check into what was going on and come up with something. After hanging up, Arlen rushed to Jerry Ball's office to give him the news. His mind was spinning as he tried to understand what was happening, what it could mean to Bay City Fittings, and what could be done about it.

Jerry greeted Arlen at the office door with a stunned look on his face. He had just gotten angry phone calls from Class A dealers in Richmond, Baltimore, and Norfolk, and a particularly nasty call from a major key account in Washington, D.C., had really rattled him. Every one of the calls was about Jackson Supply's new telemarketing/direct mail campaign. The Class A dealers were upset at being undercut by an outside "bootlegger" who could sell Bay City merchandise to their customers for less than they paid Bay City for the items. The major key account was upset because he felt Bay City had been overcharging him and he would henceforth buy from Jackson Supply who not only would sell for less but would also give quicker delivery.

"How can they do that?" exclaimed Jerry. "I think I know *why* they're doing it, but *how* can they do it?"

Arlen responded with an example, using the pricing structure of the steam trap Jackson had featured on the front page of the mailer. The steam trap listed for $500 and would be sold for that figure to most end user accounts (except key accounts, who might pay as little as $450 in a negotiated deal). Under the current trade discount structure, Class B dealers bought the trap from Class A dealers for $400 ($500 less 20 percent). Class A dealers, in turn, bought the traps from Bay City for $360 ($400 less 10 percent).

In the case of traps sold through Jackson Supply, Jackson received an additional 10 percent trade discount, so that Jackson Supply paid only $324 for the traps purchased from Bay City. Furthermore, Jackson Supply also earned the full 5 percent quantity rebate (something few of Bay City's other accounts could do) and always ordered in sufficient quantities to earn the freight-paid shipping. Thus, a Bay City steam trap that listed for $500 would cost Jackson Supply only $307.80, delivered to Nashville, or Richmond—or wherever Jackson Supply had a major warehouse facility. Jackson could sell the trap for list less 30 percent (or $350) and still earn a gross margin of $42.20 per trap, which translated to a margin of about 12 percent of sales.

Jackson Supply could indeed undercut even Bay City itself and still earn a reasonable margin. Direct mail and telemarketing costs could be spread over several product lines so the marginal cost for any given line would be negligible. Furthermore, Jackson's warehouse facilities in Nashville and Richmond were much closer to customers in the direct marketing target area than was Bay City's facility in Michigan, so Jackson could deliver more quickly and at lower freight cost.

Jerry and Arlen agreed that although Jackson's direct marketing approach made economic sense to Jackson Supply—and to the Class B dealers and end users in the target area who would probably now buy from Jackson—the approach would cause a complete disruption to Bay City's dealer network in the area. It would be quite likely that Bay City would lose at least twenty-five Class A dealers in the area, and Class A dealers averaged buying $135,000 per year in Bay City items. And the danger existed that Jackson might even penetrate even further north. It became obvious that Bay City had to put a stop to Jackson Supply's latest tactic.

A FAILING DEFENSE

Once again Jerry Ball found himself talking to Stoney Jackson about Jackson Supply's invasion of Bay City's market area. Jerry demanded that Jackson stop this bootlegging and return to selling Bay City's steam parts in the part of the country they had originally agreed on. Furthermore, Jerry demanded that Jackson Supply immediately stop the price cutting and adhere to the discount structure they had agreed on.

Stoney was silent for a moment and then responded icily: "Jerry, I buy merchandise from Bay City and I take title to it. I can sell it wherever I wish, to whomever I wish, at whatever price I wish. Don't you forget that. The only way you can stop me is to not sell me the merchandise in the first place, and for a variety of reasons, I don't think you'll stop selling to me."

Before Jerry could respond, Stoney continued, "Jerry, you've got to change with the times. Telemarketing and direct mail are the modern, cost-effective way of reaching large numbers of smaller customers, and this direct marketing approach will continue to be a part of our aggressive marketing plan if this trial run in Kentucky, Tennessee, and the coast works as well as it looks like it will. In fact, we're hoping to give it a try in Arkansas, Louisiana, and Missouri after the first of the year. And remember, every Bay City fitting we sell, we buy from you—you aren't losing any volume, and if we expand west, you'll gain right along with us. Give it some thought after you've settled down, and let me know what you want to do." And Stoney hung up.

Jerry slumped in his chair. How in the world had he gotten into this mess? A simple agreement with some hospitable southern gentlemen had turned into a nightmare. What seemed like an easy, painless way of expanding into the south through Jackson Supply had turned into a situation in which many of Bay City's customers were very angry, Jackson Supply could well control half of Bay City's volume by 1991, and there seemed to be nothing Bay City could do to get control.

RETREAT, SURRENDER, OR COUNTERATTACK?

Jerry looked up and stared at Arlen across the desk. "Arlen," he said, "you're the one who got us into this mess. If you hadn't cooked up that deal with Jackson, this would never have happened. You got us into it—you get us out! I want you to develop a set of alternatives for us to consider, and I want your recommended course of action. And, I want it tomorrow. Get on it *now!*"

DISCUSSION QUESTIONS

1. Exactly what is Bay City's problem? What caused the problem to develop? What could Bay City have done to avoid the problem in the first place?

2. What should Bay City do now? What alternatives should Arlen develop? Which should he recommend? Why?

ABC Computer Corporation

Marketing and Distribution to Governments

BACKGROUND

ABC Computer Corporation was founded in the early 1970s in the belief that there was a large potential market for easy-to-use personal computers. The target markets for the products were the home consumer and small to large commercial accounts. One of the underlying tenets for success was to build a strong and independent dealer organization for distribution and service of the products.

ABC, a West Coast company, contacted existing local dealers of similar products throughout the United States to promote the addition of ABC products to their product lines. ABC promised quality products, good delivery times, and both support and independence to the dealers. There were neither quotas, minimum order quantities, nor target customer groups required of the dealers. In other words, the dealers could continue "business as usual" with the advantage of new products as a potential to increase sales. At the same time, ABC provided training, product information, and service incentives.

As sales increased, ABC gained a reputation for quality, easy-to-use products in the home consumer and industrial markets. ABC dealers experienced increased sales and consistent support from ABC without interference in the dealers' independence. As time passed, more and more dealers were willing to add ABC products to their lines, and ABC achieved its objective of building a strong and independent dealer organization for distribution and service of its products.

Case contributed by Carla S. Lallatin, Lallatin & Associates, Rego Park, NY.

DEALER EXPERIENCE WITH THE PUBLIC SECTOR

Dealers for ABC products were able to establish unit prices based on their costs and the condition of their local markets. Most dealers for ABC products concentrated on the home consumer and industrial markets. However, some discovered opportunities in the public sector—specifically, in their own state and local governments.

In marketing to this segment, dealers quickly discovered significant differences between public and industrial accounts. Beyond a specific dollar amount (usually established by state or local law and called a "bid limit"), purchases in the public sector had to be advertised and open to competition (frequently through competitive sealed bidding) from all suppliers of the same or similar products. For this legal requirement to be waived, the purchaser had to "prove" that the required product was the only product capable of producing the necessary results and was available from only one source. This type of purchase is called a sole source or proprietary purchase, and it normally requires several approvals beyond the end user.

When an end user is making a purchase beyond this specific bid limit, he or she notifies the central purchasing office to make the purchase to ensure that all legal requirements for acquisitions are met. In the case of data processing products, governments frequently have a central data processing agency that must approve acquisitions beyond a specific dollar amount before the purchasing office can issue a competitive bid.

Below the bid limit or specific dollar amount, the processes and approvals required for acquisitions are significantly reduced. Often, the end user is authorized to make the purchase directly, merely notifying the central purchasing and data processing agencies of his or her activities.

In the 1970s, personal computers were used only to a limited degree by governments. At that time, orientation was still toward large mainframes. Therefore, neither central purchasing nor data processing offices were equipped to handle end user requests for personal computers. The tendency by these offices was to disregard them as insignificant and infrequent.

Dealers interested in the public sector found that marketing efforts to the end user had the highest payoff. Marketing efforts to the central purchasing and data processing offices had little or no payoff, as these efforts were largely ignored. In marketing to the end user, dealers looked for the following:

1. Daily activities that could be supported easily by personal computers and existing software;

2. Planned purchases that required neither competitive sealed bids nor additional approvals;

3. End users disillusioned by their experience with mainframes and/or their central data processing facility.

When dealers discovered end users meeting these parameters, they sent product literature, met with the end user, explained their products in terms of end user solutions, and usually made a sale with a minimum of bureaucratic red tape. These dealers found that activities in one government were the same or similar to activities in other governments, so they were able to leverage what they discovered in one location to market and sell to others.

A GROWING CONCERN TO GOVERNMENTS

By the late 1970s and early 1980s, central purchasing and data processing agencies were concerned about the large number of purchases of personal computers. End users were buying more and more personal computers, as they discovered they could automate their daily activities and eliminate interference from their central data processing facility. In other words, they could control their own environment and activities and not rely on central data processing's understanding (or misunderstanding) of their requirements.

As the concern of central purchasing and data processing offices increased, these agencies began to take steps to align the processes and approvals used in the acquisition of personal computers with the processes and approvals required in other acquisitions. Central purchasing began to develop specifications to use in the competitive bidding of personal computers. Data processing assisted in this effort and required that annual contracts for personal computers be established for use by all end users, since most were buying at least some personal computers.

As this transition occurred, dealers found they had to expand their marketing efforts to include the central purchasing and data processing offices. The marketing efforts to central purchasing consisted mainly of increasing product awareness, ensuring that specifications were not written to exclude their products, and ensuring that they (the dealers) were notified of all intended purchases. To data processing offices, marketing efforts increased product awareness, described end user support, and explained interface (or lack thereof) with the central facility. Although there were more processes, approvals, and paperwork involved with these central offices, dealers found their increased marketing efforts paid off in opportunities for larger sales. These dealers were successful in competing on competitive sealed bids, and ABC products, in particular, were synonymous with the dealer in the government's mind.

ABC'S NEW GOVERNMENT DIVISION

Having firmly established itself in the home consumer and industrial markets and observing the increased use of personal computers in the public sector, ABC Computer Corporation decided to establish a government division in the mid-1980s. Within this division were twelve regional offices scattered throughout the United States. These offices reported directly to headquarters, and they were assigned specific states as sales territories (Exhibit 1).

EXHIBIT 1   ABC Government Division's Regional Offices

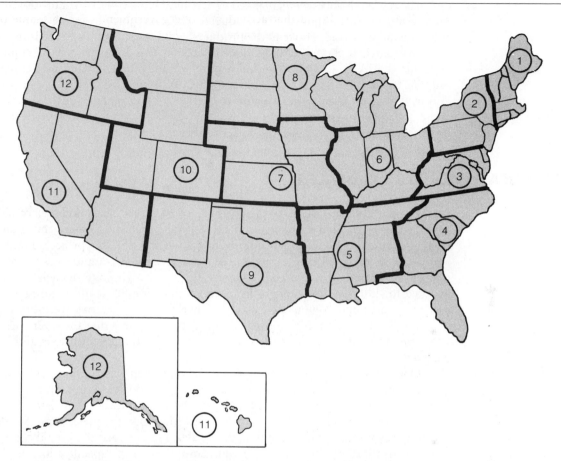

1. **New England Regional Office**—Boston, MA; Maine, New Hampshire, Vermont, Massachusetts, Rhode Island

2. **Northeastern Regional Office**—Newark, NJ; New York, New Jersey, Connecticut, Pennsylvania

3. **Midatlantic Regional Office**—Washington, DC; Delaware, Maryland, West Virginia, Virginia, District of Columbia

4. **Southeastern Regional Office**—Atlanta, GA; Florida, Georgia, North Carolina, South Carolina

5. **Southern Regional Office**—Little Rock, AR; Arkansas, Louisiana, Mississippi, Alabama, Tennessee

6. **Great Lakes Regional Office**—Chicago, IL; Illinois, Indiana, Michigan, Ohio, Kentucky

7. **Midwestern Regional Office**—Kansas City, MO; Missouri, Kansas, Nebraska, Iowa

8. **Northern Regional Office**—St. Paul, MN; Wisconsin, Minnesota, North Dakota, South Dakota

9. **Southwestern Regional Office**—Dallas, TX; Texas, Oklahoma, New Mexico

10. **Rocky Mountain Regional Office**—Denver, CO; Colorado, Wyoming, Montana, Utah

11. **Western Regional Office**—Los Angeles, CA; California, Nevada, Arizona, Hawaii

12. **Northwestern Regional Office**—Seattle, WA; Washington, Oregon, Idaho, Alaska

The regional offices were assigned to market, bid, and sell direct to state and local governments. Shipments of products would be direct from the manufacturer. Installation and service of the products would be through a local dealer of the government's choosing. Bid prices would be based on the federal supply schedule that ABC Corporation had negotiated with the U.S. General Services Administration. Although ABC Computer Corporation advised its dealers of this new division, it made no attempt to curtail or coordinate its dealers' activities in the government markets. This decision was based on the success ABC had experienced through its policy of dealer independence.

MANUFACTURER VERSUS DEALER

In the mid-1980s, a southeastern state was reviewing its past purchases of personal computers. Don Frankel, from the central purchasing office, and Elaine Shaw, from central data processing, were responsible for this project. Frankel and Shaw determined that annual purchases of personal computers warranted the establishment of an annual contract for use by all state agencies. They worked together to develop specifications so that Frankel could competitively bid out a personal computers contract. Once the specifications were drafted, they notified all suppliers of record and potential suppliers that they were holding a prebid conference for review and comment on the specifications and bid package.

One of the suppliers that Frankel and Shaw notified was Southeastern Computers. This local computer equipment and supply dealer represented several different brands of personal computers. In the past, Southeastern had sold a number of ABC products to the state. Richard Manning, the president of Southeastern, was interested in continuing these sales. He attended the prebid conference to ensure that ABC products would comply with the specifications in the upcoming bid.

In the meantime, Bob Hutchinson, the manager of the ABC Southeastern Regional Office, had sent product literature to the appropriate state offices and had requested placement on the bid list. He did not meet with state personnel, nor did he make any attempt to explain to the state the new ABC Corporate Government Division or its relationship with dealers. In lieu of attending the prebid conference, he requested a copy of the specifications, and in reviewing them, he determined that he could supply ABC products.

When the state issued the bid for personal computers, it required the bidder to supply products in accordance with the specifications and to describe specifically how installation and service would be handled. Richard Manning submitted a bid for ABC products and described Southeastern Computers' installation and service procedures. Manning based his bid prices on his costs plus a low profit margin. Bob Hutchinson also submitted a bid for ABC products and stated that installation and service would be handled by a local dealer of the state's choice. He based his prices on ABC's federal supply schedule.

In reviewing and evaluating the bids received, Don Frankel determined that Richard Manning (Southeastern Computers) had complied in all ways with the requirements of the bid package and had submitted the lowest product price. Further, he determined that Bob Hutchinson (ABC Computer Southeastern Regional Office) did not comply with all requirements of the bid package in that installation and service were not specifically described. Frankel notified all bidders of the intent to award the contract to Southeastern Computers.

When Bob Hutchinson received this notice, he protested the award. He claimed that ABC Computer complied with the requirements of the bid in that they would provide installation and service through the dealer of the state's choice. The state explained that providing service through a dealer was acceptable but that ABC had to select the dealer, since an arbitrary selection by the state would be unfair to competing dealers—and probably illegal. Further, Hutchinson stated that Southeastern Computers would be unable to perform under the requirements of the contract, as it had neither the resources to supply the anticipated product quantities nor the necessary installation and service requirements. The state explained that the products bid by both ABC Computer Corporation and Southeastern Computers were identical and that both companies had signed a legal document stating their ability to perform in accordance with the contract. The state raised the question as to why the manufacturer was competing against one of its dealers. Nonetheless, the state overruled Hutchinson's protest and awarded the bid to Southeastern Computers.

DISCUSSION QUESTIONS

1. How did ABC Computer Corporation get into its present situation?
2. Was the buyer's behavior predictable? Why or why not?
3. Develop recommendations for future actions for ABC Computer Corporation. Include opportunities for marketing strategies and short- and long-range marketing opportunities. As well, include a definition and development of channels of distribution. Consider the impact of federal, state, and other laws and regulations on your recommended actions.

MPM Corporation

Company Salespeople or Manufacturers' Representatives?

BACKGROUND

James Dunfee is the director of marketing for the MPM Corporation, a manufacturer of electrical testing equipment. Located in central Missouri, the company had been started in the early 1960s by Milo Mapes. Mapes was an electrical engineer who had worked in the R & D departments of several large manufacturers of electrical testing equipment. He had started the business in 1962, and with his many contacts, had built a fairly successful business. By the mid-1970s, Mapes found that he did not possess the time, interest, or expertise necessary to handle both the production and marketing sides of MPM. He hired James Dunfee to manage the firm's sales and marketing activities. Mapes continued to head the engineering and production responsibilities at MPM and gave Dunfee free rein in running the firm's marketing and sales programs.

James Dunfee had an excellent background in industrial marketing. In 1960, he graduated from Rensselaer Polytechnic Institute in upstate New York with a degree in electrical engineering. On graduation from college, he accepted a position in engineering sales with a large national producer of testing equipment. He performed well in that company's extensive in-house training program and then was assigned to field sales in the northern Michigan area. There, his sales performance was remarkable, and he was seen as a rising star in the company. In the mid-1970s, he met Milo Mapes at a national trade show in Chicago, and Mapes invited him to join MPM as the company's director of marketing. Mapes was so impressed with the young man that he created the position specifically for Dunfee. Dunfee was enthusiastic with the opportunity afforded him by Mapes, and he accepted Mapes's offer in April 1975.

The company's success is attributable to a small bench-testing apparatus called Testor. Although there are a number of variations of Testor, their specifications are similar, and all perform basically the same testing functions. The product possesses some advantages over those of competitors, and MPM has carved a good niche in the market. Testor is purchased by machine shops of all sizes and has a relatively horizontal demand. Sales of the product were reasonably good right from the start, although the recessions in the mid- and late 1970s did depress sales during those periods.

MPM CORPORATION'S FIELD SALES FORCE

In taking over MPM's sales force, Dunfee inherited five full-time salespeople in the field sales staff. These five people had been personally hired and trained by Mapes and covered sales territories in New England, the middle Atlantic states, the east north central states, the south Atlantic states, and the Pacific coast. These territories are shown in Exhibit 1. Back in 1980, Dunfee had seriously con-

---

EXHIBIT 1   **Sales Territories of the MPM Corporation**

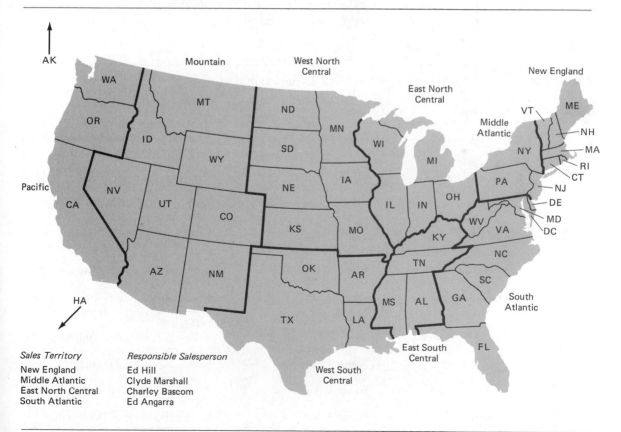

Sales Territory	Responsible Salesperson
New England	Ed Hill
Middle Atlantic	Clyde Marshall
East North Central	Charley Bascom
South Atlantic	Ed Angarra

---

sidered replacing some of his field salespeople with manufacturers' representatives. At that time, he had been especially concerned about sales in the south Atlantic and east north central areas and thought that replacing company salespeople with manufacturers' representatives might be more profitable. He abandoned the idea when the economy began to turn upward in the early 1980s. As the company grew, however, he added more salespeople, and by early 1985, MPM had ten full-time salespeople in its field sales force. Exhibit 2 shows these salespeople, their territories, and the states covered in each.

CONSIDERATION OF MANUFACTURERS' REPRESENTATIVES

In January 1989, Dunfee again begins to consider the possible merits of switching all or some of the territories to manufacturers' representatives. He has always been a little uncomfortable about a company of MPM's size having full-time company salespeople in territories that do not appear to justify their continued use. Dunfee knows that the marketing of Testor requires extensive personal contact, as the apparatus is fairly complicated and a considerable amount of educational selling is required. The market is characterized by non-price competition and by buyers who place great importance on the personal

EXHIBIT 2	Sales Territories of the MPM Corporation		
Territory	Salesperson	Area	States Covered
1	Ed Hill	New England	Connecticut, Massachusetts, Maine, New Hampshire, Vermont, Rhode Island
2	Clyde Marshall	Middle Atlantic	Delaware, New Jersey, New York, Pennsylvania
3	Charley Bascom	East North Central	Illinois, Indiana, Michigan, Ohio, Wisconsin
4	Ed Angarra	South Atlantic	Florida, Georgia, Maryland, North Carolina, South Carolina, Virginia, West Virginia
5	Iris Dunn	East South Central	Alabama, Kentucky, Mississippi, Tennessee
6	Frank Hoopes	West North Central	Iowa, Kansas, Minnesota, Missouri, Nebraska, North Dakota, South Dakota
7	Kyle Whitmarsh	West South Central	Arkansas, Louisiana, Oklahoma, Texas
8	Russ Warner	North Mountain	Idaho, Montana, Nevada, Wyoming
9	Carl Meyer	South Mountain	Arizona, Colorado, New Mexico, Utah
10	Winifred Fowler	Pacific Coast	California, Oregon, Washington

contact by highly qualified salespeople and the personal touch they can provide. For this reason, Dunfee has concluded that some type of personal selling is imperative if Testor is to continue as a marketable product.

The company does some trade journal advertising and a little direct mail advertising, and it occasionally participates in regional trade shows. These efforts support and supplement the company's field sales, and Dunfee does not consider either advertising or trade show promotion as substitutes for the higher-cost personal selling efforts. He firmly believes that manufacturers' representatives, if properly selected, can provide the type of personal contact required. He is convinced that these manufacturers' representatives can be used effectively in some, if not all, of the ten territories, and he sets about investigating the possibility.

ANALYSIS OF SALES FORCE COSTS

Dunfee first analyzes direct selling costs paid by the company to its field salespeople. Each salesperson receives a fixed monthly salary plus a 5 percent commission on sales made in his or her territory. In addition, each receives monthly allowances of $1,400 for travel, lodging, meals, and entertainment purposes. Exhibit 3 shows the results of his analysis as applied to each of the company's ten sales territories.

Next, Dunfee reviews his past sales records and computes average monthly sales figures for each of his ten salespeople in their respective territories. These results are shown in Exhibit 4. For example, Ed Hill in New England averages 75 Testor sales per month, and Winifred Fowler in the Pacific coast area averages 175.

Dunfee next estimates sales for each territory by replacement manufacturers' representatives. These estimates are also shown in Exhibit 4. Based

EXHIBIT 3	**Present Compensation Plan of MPM Salespersons**			
Territory	Salesperson	Present Monthly Salary	Present Monthly Allowances	Sales Commission Rate
1	Ed Hill	$2,795	$1,400	5%
2	Clyde Marshall	3,000	1,400	5%
3	Charley Bascom	2,400	1,400	5%
4	Ed Angarra	2,000	1,400	5%
5	Iris Dunn	2,200	1,400	5%
6	Frank Hoopes	2,395%	1,400	5%
7	Kyle Whitmarsh	2,895%	1,400	5%
8	Russ Warner	2,400	1,400	5%
9	Carl Meyer	2,595%	1,400	5%
10	Winifred Fowler	3,000	1,400	5%

EXHIBIT 4   Present Sales by MPM Salespersons and Anticipated Sales by Replacement Manufacturers' Representatives

Territory	Area	Average Number of Monthly Sales by Present Salesperson	Percentage of Present Monthly Sales Anticipated by Replacement Manufacturers' Representatives
1	New England	75	45%
2	Middle Atlantic	125	55%
3	East North Central	72	75%
4	South Atlantic	60	45%
5	East South Central	92	60%
6	West North Central	47	45%
7	West South Central	135	75%
8	North Mountain	35	40%
9	South Mountain	65	80%
10	Pacific Coast	175	60%

on interviews with prospective representative firms and analysis of company records, Dunfee concludes that any replacement representative probably will only sell 45 percent of what Ed Hill has been selling because the representatives either cannot or will not give undivided attention to selling Testor, as the present company salespeople are doing. Despite this shortcoming, he still thinks the move can reduce the high selling costs and result in higher profits. His investigation also reveals that an 8 percent commission is standard for manufacturers' representatives in this industry, with payment being made after MPM receives its payment from the customer. His conversations with representatives lead him to conclude that many of them are enthusiastic and willing to carry Testor. Therefore, Dunfee does not believe that finding replacement manufacturers' representatives will be a major problem in any of the ten territories.

PRICE AND COST CONSIDERATIONS

Testor currently sells for a net price of $695 FOB delivered, which means that MPM pays the freight to transport the product to the customer's job site. The freight charge currently averages $35 per unit delivered. Inasmuch as this FOB-delivered policy is reflective of common industry practice, Dunfee feels that any move to a FOB factory shipment basis will result in lost sales, as buyers probably will switch before paying the additional freight. In addition, there is relatively little price cutting in the market, and Dunfee does not feel that a price change in either direction will benefit sales or profits. He also wants to avoid competing with larger competitors on the basis of price if at all possible. MPM's total cost to manufacture Testor is $555 per unit produced.

Dunfee believes that each of the present salespeople is competent, experienced, and covers his or her territory in a conscientious manner. He does not feel that replacing any of them with other company salespersons will solve the problem of high selling costs. In addition, he does not see that much untapped potential in any of the present sales territories. He interprets these beliefs to mean that the solution to the rising sales costs does not mean replacing existing salespeople with new company salespeople; therefore, he is leaning toward their replacement with manufacturers' representatives.

THE PROBLEM

Dunfee's problem is determining whether representatives can or should be substituted for company salespeople, given the 8 percent commission rate. He is primarily concerned with increased sales profitability in the ten territories and is uncertain whether he should replace all the present salespeople with representatives, replace only some of them, or replace none of them.

Advise Mr. Dunfee, using the 8 percent commission rate.

DISCUSSION QUESTIONS

1. Dunfee finds that he must pay the representatives a 9 percent commission. How does this change affect your decision made on the basis of the 8 percent commission?
2. If Dunfee can get by with paying a 7 percent commission, how does this change affect the decision you made at an 8 percent commission?

3. How may Dunfee change the existing company salesperson compensation plan in an attempt to reduce sales costs and improve sales profitability?
4. What do you think Dunfee may be overlooking in viewing such a possible change primarily from a short-run profitability perspective?

Prime Plastics, Inc.

···

Implementing a Telemarketing Program

BACKGROUND

In May 1982, Hank Naulty, president of Prime Plastics, Inc., was trying to decide what action to take with regard to the company's telemarketing program. This program had been initiated early in 1982 in an effort to halt the erosion of sales and profits that Prime Plastics had been experiencing.

Prime Plastics, Inc., was a full-service distributor of plastic materials for industrial use. Its product line included a wide variety of plastic sheet, rod, and tube. These items were sold either by the pound or by the sheet. The majority of sales consisted of standard items custom cut to customer specifications. These items were sold (1) to manufacturers of consumer products (i.e., coffee mugs), (2) to manufacturers of industrial products (i.e., computer circuits, machine parts), and (3) directly to end users for windows and storm doors.

In 1982, total U.S. manufacturers' shipments of plastics of all types were estimated at over $3 billion annually, of which about 50 percent was sheet, rod, and tube. Direct factory sales to very large users accounted for about 50 percent of the market. The remaining 50 percent went through distributors, of which 10 percent was in the geographic area served by Prime.

The U.S. plastics industry operates on a multistage basis, as shown in Exhibit 1. In the first stage, petrochemicals and other raw materials are processed into resins from which plastic products can be made. Resins are made in large,

Case contributed by Larry Isaacson, Professor, Babson College, Linda Block, Associate Professor, Bentley College, and Hubert D. Hennessey, Associate Professor, Babson College, based on a student report by Edward Block, Sharon Mills, Tim McMahon, and Rafi Rosenthalis. Copyright © 1983 by Hubert D. Hennessey.

EXHIBIT 1   Prime Plastics, Inc.: Channels of Distribution for Plastics

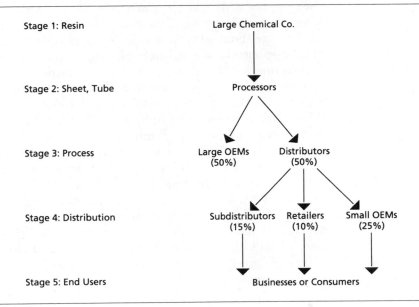

integrated plants by major chemical producers such as Dupont and Monsanto. These resins are then processed into standard-size plastic sheet and tube by many smaller companies. Some are subsidiaries of large corporations, but most are independents. All processors generally produce products that meet industry standards. Prime Plastics buys from more than thirty processors. Only a very small share of the business is for specialized products for which there were only a few suppliers.

The industry includes fewer than ten large national distributors, but there are more than 1,000 regional and local distributors, of which about 100 serve the Chicago market. Of these, about fifteen stock standard phenolic items, but only four carry full lines of these products. These four account for about 60 percent of the business. Phenolics are a specialty plastic with unique properties of water acid resistance. Mr. Naulty believes that his firm is the third largest phenolics dealer in the area, but the first two firms, Acme and Supreme, had phenolic sales of about $1.8 million and $1.2 million respectively. These two firms are among the top five plastics distributors in the area, and both had their own field sales forces. Acme, a leading local firm, had total sales of $7 million in 1981 and a field force of eight salespeople. Its pretax profits were about $300,000. Supreme, with total sales of $5 million, had a field sales force of seven salespeople. Supreme is a branch of a large national distributor. Hank Naulty estimated its profits at about $200,000.

THE DISTRIBUTOR MARKET

There are few barriers to entry in the distributor market and little or no product differentiation. This stage of the market is very price competitive, and gross margins average about 40 percent of sales to end users. Most customers call two or three distributors for bids before placing orders. Therefore, price, service, and delivery time are key factors in gaining a competitive edge. Each distributor tries to specialize in serving certain types of customers. Instead of carrying large, high-cost inventories of all products, most distributors specialize in certain items. They buy these items in bulk and then sell part of the inventory to other distributors who specialize in other products but want to meet the low volume needs of some of their customers for products outside their normal inventories.

Prime specializes in phenolics, which accounts for about 10 percent of the dollar volume of all sheet rod and tube sales in the United States. Phenolics provide higher than average contribution margins because they are more difficult than most plastics to cut or shape to precision standards. Because they are so difficult to work, Mr. Naulty refers to them as "the dirty side of the plastics business." About 30 percent of Prime's sales are made to other distributors at a 35 percent gross margin on sales. Phenolics make up almost all of these distributor sources.

PRIME PLASTICS CHANGES ITS STRATEGY

The national economic slowdown that began in 1979 had adversely affected Prime, as it had other companies in the plastics industry. Increasing competition has been further eroding profit margins. Mr. Naulty believes that the only way the company can return to profitability is to change its strategy. For the past several years, Naulty has been directing the company toward greater specialization in phenolics, his highest-margin items. Despite this concentration, however, profits have continued to decline and Naulty is looking for new ways to increase profits.

In addition to carrying a full line of phenolic products, Naulty maintains a relatively large inventory of other standard plastic items. This inventory is much larger than is common in the industry and includes polyolefins, polyvinylchloride, Delvin, Teflon, and nylon.

In early 1982, about 65 percent of Prime Plastics' sales and one-third of its inventories were phenolics. Until early 1982, Prime Plastics' sales of non-phenolics had been over 50 percent of its business. After receiving a study from his accountant showing that sales of nonphenolic items barely covered their variable cost, Mr. Naulty had decided to stop quoting uneconomically low prices on these items. When Naulty decided to raise minimum margins on nonphenolic items, sales of these items fell nearly 50 percent. As a result, the cost of handling these items also increased and contribution from them remained essentially zero.

Prime Plastics' inventory of nonphenolic items had also been inflated by Mr.

Naulty's decision, over the 1978–1981 period, to keep profits up by buying all products in lots large enough to qualify for maximum discounts. He estimated that this practice had increased Prime Plastics' gross margin by about 3 percent of sales over this period. About 50 percent of the nonphenolic inventory consisted of items for which Prime Plastics was currently experiencing no significant demand. Mr. Naulty recently had been contacted by a distributor who had offered to buy $130,000 book value of this slow-moving inventory for $100,000 cash. Naulty intended to accept this offer, as the cash would provide the means to reinvigorate his business.

PRIME'S ORGANIZATION AND COMPANY HISTORY

Prime Plastics' entire operation is located in a pre–World War II, three-story warehouse building in Chicago. The first floor of the building is divided between 4,000 square feet of office space and a 2,200-square-foot warehouse and cutting area. The two upper floors are rented out as office space. Income from this space offsets the taxes and some other out-of-pocket costs of the space occupied by the company. The company's work force consists of eighteen people, in addition to Naulty. There are three telemarketing representatives, two customer service representatives (CSRs), five clerical/bookkeeping employees, and eight warehouse/shipping employees.

Prime was established in 1957 by Hank's father, Bill Naulty. The U.S. government had a huge surplus of plastics after the Korean War, and Bill seized the opportunity to capitalize on the excess plastic. Over the course of several years, he bought large quantities of this surplus from the government for about 10 cents on the dollar and resold it at excellent markups. By the time this opportunity had ended, he had established a good reputation and a large customer base.

By 1972, Bill Naulty had developed this plastics distributorship into a profitable operation with annual sales of $650,000 and profits of $65,000. Tragedy struck in December 1972, as a storm ravaged Prime Plastics' Chicago warehouse and destroyed the business. Faced with the task of rebuilding, Bill Naulty decided to retire. He turned the limited remaining assets of the business over to his son, Hank, a 1970 graduate of a leading business school. He also loaned Hank the $200,000 fire insurance proceeds. Hank Naulty used these assets to repair the building, replace some of the ruined inventory, and attempt to recapture Prime Plastics' former customers.

Sales for 1973 were just $400,000; but in 1974, sales skyrocketed to $1.4 million as plastics prices nearly quadrupled during the Arab oil embargo. Profits rose to $400,000 in 1974 as low-cost inventory was sold off at high prices. When petrochemical prices stabilized somewhat, sales for the company fell off to about the $1,000,000 level in 1975. Profits fell to $100,000 in 1975 and have been declining ever since. Exhibits 2 through 4 show excerpts from 1978–1981 profit and loss statements, balance sheets, and an analysis of 1982 expenses. Mr. Naulty believes that other companies in the industry are experiencing similar

EXHIBIT 2   Prime Plastics, Inc.: Profit and Loss Statements ($000)

	1978	1979	1980	1981	1982 (Projected)
Sales	$1,300	$1,450	$1,420	$1,600	$1,200
Cost of goods sold	(910)	(1,085)	(1,095)	(1,275)	(958)
Gross margin	$ 390	$ 365	$ 325	$ 325	$ 242
Operating expenses*	(240)	(260)	(280)	(300)	(282)
Mr. Naulty's salary	(80)	(60)	(40)	(25)	(25)
Profit before taxes	70	45	5	—	(65)
Taxes	(10)	(5)	—	—	15
Profit after taxes	$ 60	$ 40	$ 5	$ —	$ (50)
Dividends paid to Hank Naulty	$ 30	$ 20	$ 20	$ 10	$ —
Price index for prime products (1973 = 100)	80	84	88	92	90

Note: All figures have been rounded off.

* Net of rental income from office space in company building.

EXHIBIT 3   Prime Plastics, Inc.: Balance Sheet (12/31) ($000)

	1978	1979	1980	1981	1982 (Projected)
Assets					
Cash	$ 15	$ 5	$ 5	$ 5	$ 5
Accounts receivable	240	210	210	220	250
Inventory	200	300	310	350	390
Plant and equipment*	140	200	220	240	250
Other	20	20	20	25	25
Total	$615	$735	$765	$840	$920
Liabilities					
Accounts payable	$180	$270	$290	$360	$450
Notes payable†	210	180	165	160	180
Other current debt	30	40	50	80	110
Long-term mortgage debt‡	60	90	120	110	100
Equity	135	155	140	130	80
Total	$615	$735	$765	$840	$920

Notes: * Net of depreciation.

† Principally to Bill Naulty.

‡ Of which $50,000 was guaranteed by Bill Naulty.

EXHIBIT 4   **Prime Plastics, Inc.: Operating Cost, Monthly Average, 1982**

Personnel		
Warehouse/shipping (8)	$6,000	
Clerical/bookkeeping (5)	4,000	
Customer service (2)	1,800	
Telemarketing (3)	2,000	
Subtotal		$13,800
Space and Equipment		
Mortgage	$ 800	
Insurance/utilities	2,000	
Equipment rental/repair	400	
Depreciation	1,000	
Subtotal		$ 4,200
Other		
Freight in and out	$1,300	
Telephone/postage	2,000	
Interest	1,200	
Telemarketing consultant	1,000	
Subtotal		$ 5,500
Total		$23,500

pressures, and he estimates that more than 30 percent of the plastics distributors active in 1974 had left the business or failed by 1982.

PRIME'S PRESENT SALES STRATEGY

Until late 1981, Naulty used a single field salesperson to call on existing accounts, open new accounts, and take field orders. Most orders were taken over the telephone by the customer service representatives (CSRs). While Naulty would have preferred to have enough field salespeople to call on the firm's 5,000-plus prospects in the midwest market, he did not believe they could generate enough volume to make such an approach viable. Naulty himself occasionally spoke by phone with a few larger accounts, but he generally concentrated his efforts on home office administration and he approved all significant price reductions quoted to customers. In making pricing decisions, both the CSRs and Naulty used a weekly computer report that showed inventory on hand for each of the 2,000 stock keeping units (SKUs) in Prime Plastics' inventory. This report showed the average unit price at which this inventory had been purchased. Suppliers' recent price lists also were available, and Naulty and the CSRs knew they could call suppliers for up-to-date quotes on items not in stock or to help price large orders. Price lists became outdated quickly when oversupply or under-supply caused rapid fluctuations in the prices of plastic products. Such fluctuations had been common since 1973.

In late 1981, Naulty was approached by Peter Marksman, a telemarketing consultant. Marksman suggested that telephone selling might well be a more cost effective way to gain new accounts and renew old ones than were expensive field sales calls. He spent several weeks studying Prime Plastics' sales and marketing records and determined that, of the 5,000 potential customers the company had identified in the midwest, Prime Plastics had at some time received orders from 2,110. Of these, 171 (37%) had placed orders with Prime Plastics in the second half of 1981, an additional 648 (31%) had purchased in 1980 or the first half of 1981, and 691 (32%) had not purchased within the past two years.

An estimated 30 percent of Prime Plastics' business had come from thirty distributors. Fifty large, nondistributor accounts represented 20 percent of sales, and 50 percent of sales came from more than 690 nondistributor accounts. Of the nondistributor accounts, 50 percent came from manufacturers and 20 percent from plastic retailers, hardware stores, and building supply retailers.

Based on these findings, Marksman recommended that Prime should

Hire three home office telemarketers and fire the field salesperson.

Commence an awareness campaign.

Activate a "customer service" approach that would better meet customer needs for quick quotes and on-time shipments.

Evaluate customer segments for potential.

Prepare and introduce measurement standards and controls to monitor the telemarketing activity.

Base telemarketer compensation on customer retention and reactivation.

PRIME'S NEW TELEMARKETING PROGRAM

Naulty was impressed with this proposal and retained Marksman to implement it. For some time he had been unconvinced of the value of Prime's field sales effort. Three telemarketers were hired, none of whom had had prior experience either in plastics or telemarketing. They therefore received one day of introductory training from Marksman in telemarketing techniques and two days of training in plastics and plastic pricing procedures. They were to implement the new account program outlined in Exhibit 5. They were also to follow up on requests for quotes that had come into the customer service representatives but had not turned into sales, and to develop and carry out an account reactivation program.

By early May, two of the original three telemarketers had quit. Only one had been replaced and trained, but another was being sought. Every two months Marksman reported the program's progress to Naulty. Data from Marksman's report on March and April activity are shown as Exhibit 6. The telemarketers worked thirty-five hours per week and were paid a base salary of $600 per

EXHIBIT 5   Prime Plastics, Inc.: New Account Program for Telemarketers

- Within five (5) work days after acquisition, mail a thank you note for your business letter.
  Attempt to remit directly to decision maker.
  Allow a degree of continuity and general goodwill.
  Use a basic form letter.
  All new accounts will be noted on new accounts list for subsequent follow-up, until the list is automated.
- Thirty (30) days from point of acquisition, conduct telemarketing campaign.
  Reintroduce company.
  Inquire about our service and so on.
  Inquire about new quotes.
  Thank them for being a Prime customer.
- Sixty (60) days from point of acquisition, mail a special customer offer.
  Introduce offer.
  Inquire for business.
- Place in normal call pattern.

EXHIBIT 6   Prime Plastics, Inc.: Telemarketing Group Call Analysis, March–April 1982

Tele-marketer	Completed Calls	No. of Days Worked	Average No. of Calls/Day	No. of Quotes	% of Quotes to Calls	Dollar Sales ($000)	No. of Orders	% of Orders to Calls	Average Order	Average Sales per Day	Average No. of Orders/ Day
Frank	639	36	17.8	65	10%	$ 6.2	26	4%	$238	$172	0.7
Cathy	1,307	44	30.0	80	6	5.5	40	3	138	125	0.9
Total	1,946	80	24.3	145	7	11.7	66	3.3	177	146	0.8

month each. In addition, they could earn commissions computed on a sliding scale basis, as follows:

Monthly orders taken	Commission
$0–$5,000	0
$5,000–$10,000	3%
Over $10,000	5%

Marksman was also asked to evaluate CSR activity. The CSRs received incoming requests for information and quotes. In many instances, they gave quotes on the spot, using standard or minimum markups over costs. Most quotes tended to be at the minimum. Special orders and requests for discounts were referred to Mr. Naulty, and the CSRs then telephoned accounts with the quotes. Exhibit 7 is Marksman's summary of March 1982 CSR activity. Mr. Naulty estimated that about one incoming call in five resulted in an order and that the Prime Plastics' average order size was about $300. Only about one order in 100 was from a customer not sold to in the past six months.

Marksman developed the order process flow found in Exhibit 8. Orders were filled out on the sales sheet, also designed by Marksman, shown in Exhibit

---

EXHIBIT 7   Prime Plastics, Inc.: Customer Service Group Inbound Call Analysis, March 1982

CSR	No. of Calls	No. of Days Worked	Average Number of Calls		Est. Min. per Call	Est. Phone Hours/ Day	% of Day
			Per Day	Per Week			
John	588	15	39	196	4	2.6	33%
Al	526	20	26	132	4	1.8	23
Sue	416	15	28	139	4	1.8	23
Total	1,530	50	30.6	153	4	2.04	26

EXHIBIT 8   Prime Plastics, Inc.: Telemarketing Order Flow Procedures

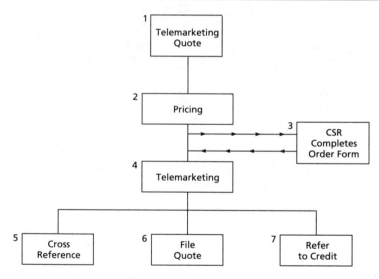

1–2   Telemarketers currently refer quotes to appropriate person for pricing and maintain a copy for follow-up. When returned, customer is contacted with quote and order is closed, or the customer is placed in follow-up cycle. If an order is placed, Step 3 is followed.

3–4   Customer service representative completes order and refers directly back to telemarketing with all appropriate materials.

5–7   Telemarketers cross-reference order form to original quote. They then file quote and refer completed order form to credit.

9. Exhibit 10 depicts the process flow used on call-back orders, and the accompanying script is shown in Exhibit 11. Marksman also developed a script, shown in Exhibit 12, that the telemarketers used to call inactive accounts or new or potential customers. This script offered a special discount to the prospective clients to encourage them to try Prime.

Although the telemarketing system has been in place for less than three months, Hank Naulty is anxious to determine whether it is likely to be successful. To date, total sales have continued to decline and margins are smaller than ever. Naulty must make an immediate change if this approach is not working, as losses are mounting and cash is running out.

Advise Hank Naulty.

EXHIBIT 9   Prime Plastics, Inc.: Telemarketing Sales Sheet

Ship to: _____   Date: _____

Company name: _____

Address: _____

City: _____   State: _____   Zip: _____

Telephone: (_____) _____   SIC: _____   TM: _____

Contact: _____

Last product purchased: _____   1st active date: _____

Date last purchased: _____ $ _____

Product Number	Description	Qty.	Price

Special instructions: _____
_____
_____
_____
_____
_____
_____

EXHIBIT 10

Prime Plastics, Inc.: Follow-Up Quote Procedure for Customer Service
Representatives. Objective: To Call Back Quoted Jobs and Obtain Orders
or Initiate Future Order Activity

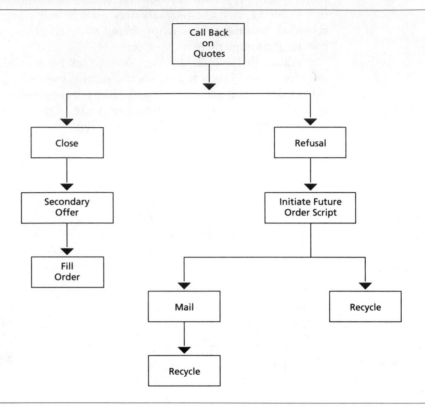

EXHIBIT 11   Prime Plastics, Inc.: Future Order Script for Customer Service Representatives

Good _____, this is _____, from Prime Plastics in Chicago.
May I speak with (name) please?
(Name), (your name) from Prime Plastics in Chicago.
I'm calling regarding that quote we gave you (time period, i.e., last week) on (material).
    Response: Not needed: Price
                            Competition
(Name), could you tell us why you didn't purchase from Prime?
    Response: Price
Overall, (name), we are one of the more competitive firms in the area in (material). We
hope that you'll give us another opportunity to quote on a job in the future.
    Objections
Is there a good time I could call you back on a quote?
    Response
Fine, we believe we are competitive. We'll call you in (approximate time period). In the
meantime, as specials become available we'll give you a call. . . . And keep you in our
brochure mailings! Thanks again for your time.

EXHIBIT 12   **Prime Plastics, Inc.: Telemarketer Special Pricing Script**

Good _____ , this is _____ from Prime Plastics in Chicago. May I speak with the purchasing manager please! (obtain name)

(Name), (your name) of Prime Plastics in Chicago. We're calling shops in the (city) area today to introduce Prime Plastics Company. Are you familiar with our company?

      (Yes) . . .   As you know . . .

      (No)

We're distributors of most of the major brands of plastics in sheet, rod, and tube! . . . And we have one of the largest inventories in the midwest as well as being one of the major manufacturers of phenolic rod! . . . And again our primary purpose in calling is to introduce Prime Plastics and . . . to offer our introductory special on G-10.

      (Objections)

With your first order, we'll take 10 percent off the purchase price!

      (Close)

      (Objections)

Fine, (name), we would like you to keep Prime Plastics in mind when you need G-10 or any other laminates. We can generally ship within twenty-four hours! And we carry most major brands. . . . For example, nylon, which we can offer on our 10 percent off special!

Fine, at least you're aware! As part of our continuing service to you we'll call from time to time with our specials. . . . When would be the best time to check back with you? . . . Also, periodically we send out our brochures. . . . Would you like to be included in our mailing? (confirm contact name & address)

Again, (name), thanks for your time and remember Prime Plastics of Chicago on your next order!

Southwest Paper, Inc.

···

Conflict Between Field and Inside Salespeople

BACKGROUND

Southwest Paper, Inc., is a regional distributor of paper products based in Dallas, Texas. The company sells the paper used in magazines, catalogs, and brochures to publishers and printers. With sales growing at approximately 14 percent over the past three years, 1990 showed revenues at an all-time high.

The future was not always so promising for Southwest. Just five years earlier, the firm was on the verge of bankruptcy. Southwest Paper employed four field sales representatives who covered the states of Texas, Oklahoma, Louisiana, Arkansas, Kansas, Missouri, Iowa, Nebraska, Colorado, and Tennessee. Because of such expansive sales territories, travel and selling expenses were growing out of control.

Southwest's sales manager, Charlie Duncan, summed up the problem succinctly when he stated, "With our target market concentrated on large printing firms, the territories we must cover are vast because these firms are spread so far apart geographically. We must find a method to maintain our relationships with customers and prospects, but we must also keep our costs under control."

A DIRECT MARKETING PROGRAM IS INITIATED

Charlie Duncan was a member of the North Texas Direct Marketing Association so he logically turned first to them for some possible solutions to his problem. The Direct Marketing Association studied the company's situation and recom-

Case contributed by John Macfie, San Diego State University.

mended the purchase of a computer system and the use of direct mail to inform customers and prospects of new product offerings, promotion and pricing specials, technical information from trade publications, and any other information that might have marketing value. Duncan thought that these recommendations had merit as sales-support tools and so he moved to implement the Direct Marketing Association's recommendations.

EVALUATION OF THE DIRECT MARKETING PROGRAM

Duncan gave the program time to develop and after the first year, he believed he had sufficient sales information to review the program. Analysis revealed that sales for the year were flat for the most part. Where there were slight increases, they were offset by the higher costs brought on by the direct mail program. A survey showed that customers did find the new program useful and they seemed to especially appreciate the technical articles and product updates. However, the program failed to bring in any new business, which was disappointing to Duncan since that was a basic objective of the direct mail campaign. Duncan was now more puzzled than ever and requested a meeting with the company president, Gary White.

THE PRESENT SALES SITUATION

The present four field sales representatives were in the field four days each week. They spent the other day in the office setting up appointments, doing general telephone maintenance work, and completing their paperwork. This mix of four days in the field and one in the office worked well thanks to Southwest's Customer Service Representatives, Bill Reed and Joan Ryan. When the sales reps were in the field, Reed and Ryan were able to handle inquiries, take orders, give price quotes, check inventory, mail samples, and perform other such duties. Duncan expressed his concerns about the failure of the direct mail program and asked White for possible suggestions.

White did have some ideas that might be considered in any revision of the current sales program. The two customer service representatives were doing a very good job. Both were professional, handled each call with care, and took great pride in their work. But White had also noticed that both had considerable spare time on their hands as they waited for their phones to ring. White wondered whether these two could be converted in some manner to inside salespeople. Duncan concurred and the two arranged to have a sales meeting that would include the customer service representatives as well as the field sales representatives.

THE MEETING TAKES PLACE

President White began the meeting by informing everyone that he thought they were all doing excellent jobs. He went on to explain, however, that the company was facing high travel and expense costs and desperately needed to increase sales quickly by attracting new customers. Everyone in the room understood the problem but there were concerns expressed. Paul Adams, who was the most experienced and productive field sales representative, stated, "We understand the situation you are in, but we (the field sales reps) are spread thin enough as it is. I have little time to call on new prospects because I am so busy just maintaining business with existing customers." White agreed with Adams, and thought this was exactly why his idea might help everyone out.

White then praised Reed and Ryan again for their outstanding jobs. He then asked them to estimate how many hours in a typical day they would consider "down time" with little or nothing to do. Reed and Ryan conferred briefly and then Ryan responded, "It depends on how busy things are, but at least three to four hours a day could be used to perform additional tasks if this is needed." Based on this response, White thought both Reed and Ryan might take additional steps to help the field sales reps. For example, they could try to contact prospective customers and set up appointments for the field reps. They could also recontact past customers who no longer did business with Paper Source. White thought the two customer service representatives could easily make such outbound calls during their downtime hours.

Everyone at the meeting thought the idea had merit and was worth a try, but there were still concerns. Adams argued, "I have no problem with them calling accounts that I have been unable to open, but I don't want anyone calling my good customers. I have worked hard to build up those relationships and don't want to jeopardize them." White could see this as a legitimate concern and assured him that this would not happen as his purpose was to get new customers. Existing customers would continue to be served in the same manner as before with the customer service representatives providing only their traditional support role.

Following the meeting, the field sales representatives made up lists of accounts for the inside salespeople to contact. They also provided names of customers who were not to be contacted per the agreement with White. Reed and Ryan were to begin making outbound calls and would be expected to try to complete from thirty-five to forty calls per day. With these guidelines, the inside sales program was initiated.

RESULTS OF THE INSIDE SALES PROGRAM

Two weeks passed and analysis revealed very positive results. The field sales reps had appointments with prospects that they had never before been able to make. More impressively, Reed and Ryan generated orders just by discussing the company's product line with prospects. This surprised both White and Duncan because the purpose of the calls had been simply to develop interest with the hope of possibly setting up appointments. In fact, inside sales generated a $60,000 order for four truckloads of paper, which was considered large by any company standards. Credit for this particular order went to Paul Adams since the customer was in his sales territory, even though Adams had never had any previous contact with that customer. In regard to this order, the field reps joked that it was due more to luck than to selling ability. They insinuated that Ryan had been lucky enough to call at a time when the prospect was in a real bind and that was the only reason the sale was made. There may have been some truth to this, but the sale was part of a pattern that was beginning to emerge—inside sales could sell Southwest Paper products!

Months passed and the inside sales concept kept gaining momentum. Appointments set up for the field reps saved time and also helped bring in new accounts. In addition, there were instances where inside sales efforts directly created new accounts. All field reps reached their quotas for two quarters in a row, something that had never happened before on any consistent basis. Reed and Ryan were both awarded raises in salary to $24,000 and given small bonuses based on the performance of the field sales representatives. When a field sales rep reached quota, Reed and Ryan shared in the benefits. Another six months passed and each field sales rep again achieved above-quota sales.

THE SALES FORCE IS REORGANIZED

White was pleased with the increased performance, but felt that the sales force could become even more efficient. Analysis revealed that the majority of sales came from the Texas, Oklahoma, Louisiana, and Arkansas territories. He and Duncan again called a meeting with the four field sales reps and the two inside salespeople. He presented his findings to them and expressed his opinion that greater sales concentration in these four states could increase revenues even more. He recommended that the four field sales reps exclusively cover this four-state area, and that the other six states be sold via inside sales. Exhibit 1 outlines his proposal. Paul Adams was assigned to cover the state of Texas, Leo Horne was to cover Oklahoma, Bob Kaminski was assigned Louisiana, and Bill Bishop would cover Arkansas. Bill Reed was assigned coverage of Colorado, Kansas, and Missouri, while Joan Ryan was to cover accounts in Nebraska, Iowa, and Tennessee.

Adams objected to such a reorganization and said, "It seems like my 'reward' for having produced more is a smaller territory and fewer accounts." The other field sales reps felt basically the same and saw such a reorganization as penalizing them. White sympathized with their position but reasoned that Adams could sell more if he were able to concentrate more locally, and he could even make more money this way. The field reps were skeptical but saw the logic in this position—White's point did make some sense.

EXHIBIT 1   White's Proposed New Sales Force Reorganization and Revised Sales
                    Territories

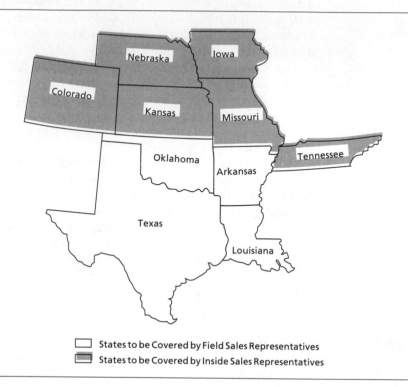

☐ States to be Covered by Field Sales Representatives
▨ States to be Covered by Inside Sales Representatives

The four target states were divided among the four field reps, as described above, based on potential sales volumes. All attempts were made to keep field reps in areas where they had previously established relationships. Each rep was given a monthly salary of $4,000; a travel and entertainment allowance of $1,500 per month; and a 5 percent bonus on all sales exceeding a sales quota of $75,000 per month.

Reed and Ryan were then to split up the remaining six states as previously described, which was also based on sales potentials. Again, all efforts were made to maintain existing relationships. Both were given a salary of $2,000 per month, which was to cover both their jobs as inside salespeople and as customer service representatives. They would spend approximately half of their time on each function. Each was also given a sales quota of $50,000 per month and a 2 percent bonus on all sales exceeding this quota figure. In addition, each was given a $500 per month travel allowance in order to visit key accounts and maintain relationships. Both Reed and Ryan were happy with the new arrangement as they now had full account responsibility, quotas to work toward, and an opportunity to prove themselves on their own. Neither saw any major conflict in being a sales rep half of the time and a customer service rep the other half. In fact, both saw the servicing of field rep accounts as a welcome change to break the monotony of inside selling.

RESULTS OF THE REORGANIZED SALES FORCE

Review of the reorganized sales force's performance took place after a six-month trial. This review showed that Southwest Paper reached record sales levels while sales costs dropped dramatically with the concentration on more local markets by the field sales reps. Each field sales rep had achieved higher sales in the smaller territories. In addition, both Reed and Ryan exceeded their quotas. White felt like a genius as he reviewed the figures shown in Exhibit 2. He instructed Duncan to post the figures for all to see and to congratulate everyone for jobs well done.

EXHIBIT 2 **First and Second Quarter 1990 Sales Performances Under the Newly Reorganized Sales Force**

Field Sales Representatives	Territory	1st Quarter Sales	2nd Quarter Sales
Adams	Texas	$450,000	$510,000
Horne	Oklahoma	380,000	415,000
Kaminski	Louisiana	285,000	310,000
Bishop	Arkansas	230,000	295,000

Inside Sales Representatives	Territory	1st Quarter Sales	2nd Quarter Sales
Reed	Colorado, Kansas, and Missouri	$305,000	$330,000
Ryan	Nebraska, Iowa, and Tennessee	315,000	325,000
Total company sales		$1,965,000	$2,185,000

A MAJOR PROBLEM ARISES

In informing everyone about the increases in sales performances, both White and Duncan expected they would increase morale and stimulate the salespeople to even higher performances. But this is not what happened. Both Reed and Ryan were upset. As inside sales reps, their salaries were only half those paid to the field sales reps; their bonuses for exceeding sales quotas were much less; and their travel and entertainment allowances were only one-third those given to the field salespeople. Looking at the sales data, they could see that each of them had outperformed the lower two field reps (Kaminski and Bishop) even though the latter had also met their quotas. Furthermore, Reed and Ryan had achieved these performances by working their accounts only four hours per day—the other four hours were spent in servicing the accounts of the field sales reps. In addition, the inside salespeople felt they had a tougher selling job in that their more distant territories required longer delivery times. In short, both felt they were being treated like "second-class sales citizens" despite the fact that they were producing more than two of the field reps. They wanted equal pay for equal work and protested vociferously to both Duncan and White. In their collective opinion, the new sales figures proved that they were not "second-class sales citizens" and they demanded a more equitable compensation system—one that would reward sales productivity on a basis equal to that now provided to the field sales representatives.

Because of all this controversy, Duncan decided to conduct some secondary research on the ten-state market area. He felt he needed more information before any decision was made regarding the complaints of the two inside salespeople. Exhibits 3, 4, and 5 were developed using the latest data from the *U.S. Census of Manufactures*. He sent these exhibits to Gary White and recommended that they meet as soon as possible.

DISCUSSION QUESTIONS

1. What particular events occurred that explain the problem described at the end of the case? How might White and Duncan have prevented the crisis that has occurred?

2. If you were Duncan or White, how would you handle the complaints by Reed and Ryan and their request for such large compensation increases?

3. Based on the case data, how would you evaluate White's reorganization of the sales force? Would you continue it or would you recommend another reorganization? If another, outline your program.

4. Evaluate the mix of field sales reps and inside sales reps as designed by White. Do you feel this mix is the most efficient and effective? If yes, why? If not, what would you change?

5. Write job descriptions and job analyses for both the field sales representatives and the inside sales reps under White's present program. If you recommended a revision in question 3, show how these descriptions and analyses would change.

EXHIBIT 3   Data on Commercial Printing Establishments (SIC 2752) in the Ten State Market Area

State	1987						1982		
	Total No. of Establishments	No. With 20+ Employees	No. of Employees (1000)	Value Added by Manufacturing ($ million)	Cost of Materials ($ million)	Value of Shipments ($ million)	New Capital Expenditures ($ million)	No. of Employees (1000)	Value Added by Manufacturing ($ million)
Arkansas	141	21	2.1	$ 85.4	$ 81.0	$ 165.6	$21.7	1.6	$ 47.7
Colorado	506	56	5.2	216.7	184.5	401.6	16.0	3.5	115.6
Iowa	271	53	4.0	156.0	128.4	283.5	NA	4.6	146.0
Kansas	247	46	3.7	168.3	224.3	396.8	NA	3.7	117.7
Louisiana	269	28	2.7	96.8	86.6	183.0	5.1	2.3	68.0
Missouri	562	94	8.7	388.7	315.4	702.0	26.1	7.1	244.4
Nebraska	161	34	3.2	114.5	115.6	229.6	NA	2.5	74.5
Oklahoma	295	26	2.8	117.9	119.7	237.6	16.0	2.1	64.7
Tennessee	451	74	7.5	312.8	312.8	530.8	37.9	5.2	152.9
Texas	1,669	207	19.9	828.7	828.7	1,507.0	51.4	16.2	544.0

Source: U.S. Census of Manufactures.

EXHIBIT 4 Additional Data on Types of Commercial Printing Establishments (SIC 2752) in the Ten-State Market Area ($ million)

State	SIC 27521		SIC 27523		SIC 27525	
	1987	1982	1987	1982	1987	1982
Arkansas	NA	NA	NA	NA	33.9	11.0
Colorado	32.0	14.2	66.5	8.5	99.3	38.0
Iowa	62.5	74.2	27.7	23.9	115.7	45.5
Kansas	29.6	19.1	14.2	17.0	206.7	50.0
Louisiana	3.0	2.4	NA	NA	57.9	34.7
Missouri	50.5	55.6	82.0	65.4	251.7	112.5
Nebraska	NA	NA	20.8	10.2	42.9	38.3
Oklahoma	39.8	28.1	7.6	3.5	102.8	13.3
Tennessee	112.3	78.2	41.2	11.6	131.3	62.3
Texas	176.1	79.3	86.9	82.6	424.6	211.7

SIC 27521—Magazine and periodical printers
SIC 27523—Catalog and directory printers
SIC 27525—Advertising and brochure printers

NA indicates data not disclosed because sales were under $2 million or because data would disclose individual companies.

Source: U.S. Census of Manufactures.

EXHIBIT 5 Additional Data on Types of Commercial Printing Establishments in the Total United States in 1987

	Number of Establishments	Value of Shipments ($ million)
SIC 2752—Commercial printers	24,980	$32,698.2
SIC 27521—Magazine printers	451	3,725.3
SIC 27523—Catalog printers	290	2,538.3
SIC 27525—Advertising and brochure printers	2,499	10,742.5

Source: U.S. Census of Manufactures.

CASE **18**

Royal Corporation

. . . .

Evaluating the Performance of a Business Salesperson

As Mary Jones, a third-year sales representative for the Royal Corporation, reviewed her call plans for tomorrow, she thought about her sales strategy. It was only July 1983 but Jones was already well on her way toward completing her best year financially with the company. In 1982, she had sold the largest dollar volume of copies of any sales representative in the northeast and was the tenth most successful rep in the country.

But Jones was not looking forward to her scheduled activities for the next day. In spite of her excellent sales ability, she had not been able to sell the Royal Corporate Copy Center (CCC). This innovative program was highly touted by Royal upper management. Jones was one of the few sales reps in her office who had not sold a CCC in 1982. Although Jones had an excellent working relationship with her sales manager, Tom Stein, she was experiencing a lot of pressure from him of late because he could not understand her inability to sell CCCs. Jones had therefore promised herself to concentrate her efforts on selling the CCC even if it meant sacrificing sales of other products.

Jones had five appointments for the day—9 A.M., Acme Computers; 9:45 A.M., Bickford Publishing; 11:45 A.M., ABC Electronics; 12:30 P.M., CG Advertising; and 2:00 P.M., General Hospital. At Acme, Bickford, and ABC, Jones would develop CCC prospects. She was in various states of information gathering and proposal preparation for each of the accounts. At CG, Jones planned to present examples of work performed by a model 750 color copier. At General Hospital, she would present her final proposal for CCC adoption. Although the focus of her day would be on CCCs, she still needed to call and visit other accounts that she was developing.

Case contributed by Hubert D. Hennessey, Associate Professor, Babson College, and Barbara Kalunian. Copyright © 1983 by Hubert D. Hennessey. Names and locations have been disguised. Reproduced by permission.

ROYAL INTRODUCES THE CCC CONCEPT

In 1980, Royal had introduced its Corporate Copy Center facilities management program (CCC). Under this concept, Royal offered to equip, staff, operate, and manage a reproduction operation for its clients on the clients' premises. After analyzing the needs of the client, Royal selected and installed the appropriate equipment and provided fully trained, Royal-employed operators. The CCC equipment also permits microfilming, sorting, collating, binding, covering, and color copying, in addition to high-volume copying. The major benefits of the program include reproduction contracted for at a specified price, guaranteed output, tailor-made capabilities, and qualified operators.

As she pulled into the Acme Computers parking lot, she noticed that an unexpected traffic jam had made her ten minutes late for the 9:00 A.M. appointment. This made her uncomfortable, as she valued her time and assumed that her clients appreciated promptness. Jones had acquired the Acme Computers account the previous summer and had dealt personally with Betty White, director of printing services, ever since. She had approached White six months earlier with the idea of purchasing a CCC, but had not pursued the matter further until now because Betty had seemed very unreceptive. For today's call, Jones had worked several hours preparing a detailed study of Acme's present reproduction costs. She was determined to make her efforts pay off.

Jones gave her card to the new receptionist, who buzzed White's office and told her that Jones was waiting. A few minutes later, Betty appeared and led Jones to a corner of the lobby. They always met in the lobby, a situation that Jones found frustrating but it was apparently company policy.

"Good morning, Betty, it's good to see you again. Since I saw you last, I've put together the complete analysis on the CCC that I promised. I know you'll be excited by what you see. As you are aware, the concept of a CCC is not that unusual anymore. You may recall from the first presentation that I prepared for you, the CCC can be a tremendous time and money saver. Could you take a few moments to review the calculations that I have prepared exclusively for Acme Computers?" Betty flipped through the various pages of exhibits that Jones had prepared, but it was obvious that she had little interest in the proposal. "As you can see," Jones continued, "the savings are really significant after the first two years."

"Yes, but the program is more expensive the first two years. But what's worse is that there will be an outsider here doing our printing. I can't say that's an idea I could ever be comfortable with."

Jones realized that she had completely lost the possibility of White's support, but she continued.

"Betty, let me highlight some of the other features and benefits that might interest Acme."

"I'm sorry, Mary, but I have a 10 o'clock meeting that I really must prepare for. I can't discuss this matter further today."

"Betty, will you be able to go over these figures in more depth a little later?"

"Why don't you leave them with me. I'll look at them when I get the chance," White replied.

Jones left the proposal with White hoping that she would give it serious consideration, but as she pulled out of the driveway she could not help but feel that the day had gotten off to a poor start.

The Royal Corporation established the Royal Reproduction Center (RRC) division in 1956. With fifty-one offices located in twenty-four states in the United States, the RRC specializes in high-quality quick-turnaround copying, duplicating, and printing on a service basis. In addition to routine reproduction jobs, the RRC is capable of filling various specialized requests including duplicating engineering documents and computer reports, microfilming, color copying, and producing overhead transparencies. In addition, the RRC sales representatives sell the Royal 750 color copier (the only piece of hardware sold through the RRC) and the Royal Corporate Copy Center program (CCC). Although the RRC accepts orders from "walk-ins," the majority of the orders are generated by the field representatives who handle certain named accounts that are broken down by geographic territory.

At 9:45 A.M., Jones stopped at Bickford Publishing for her second sales call of the day. She waited in the lobby while Joe Smith, director of corporate services, was paged. Bickford Publishing was one of Jones's best accounts. Last year her commission from sales to Bickford totaled 10 percent of her pay. But her relationship with Joe Smith always seemed to be on unstable ground. She was not sure why, but she had always felt that Smith harbored resentment toward her. However, she decided not to dwell on the matter as long as a steady stream of large orders kept coming in. Jones had been calling on Bickford ever since Tim McCarthy, the sales representative before her, had been transferred. Competition among the RRC sales reps for the Bickford account had been keen, but Stein had decided that Jones's performance warranted a crack at the account, and she had proven that she deserved it by increasing sales 40 percent within six months.

"Good morning, Miss Jones, how are you today?" Smith greeted her. He always referred to her formally as Miss Jones.

"I'm fine, Mr. Smith," Jones replied. "Thank you for seeing me today. I needed to drop by and give you some additional information on the CCC idea that I reviewed with you earlier."

"Miss Jones, to be perfectly honest with you, I reviewed the information that you left with me, and although I think that your CCC is a very nice idea, I really don't believe it is something that Bickford would be interested in at this particular point in time."

"But Mr. Smith, I didn't even give you any of the particulars. I have a whole set of calculations here indicating that the CCC could save Bickford a considerable amount of time, effort, and money over the next few years."

"I don't mean to be rude, Miss Jones, but I am in a hurry, I really don't care to continue this conversation."

"Before you go, do you think that it might be possible to arrange to present this proposal to Mr. Perry (Tony Perry, V.P. corporate facilities, Joe Smith's immediate supervisor) in the near future? I'm sure that he would be interested in seeing it. We had discussed this idea in passing earlier, and he seemed to feel that it warranted serious consideration."

"Maybe we can talk about that the next time you are here. I'll call you if I need to have something printed. Now I really must go."

As Jones returned to her car, she decided that, in spite of what Smith had told her about waiting until next time, she should move ahead to contact Perry directly. He had seemed genuinely interested in hearing more about the CCC when she had spoken to him earlier, even though she had mentioned it only briefly. She decided that she would return to the office and send Perry a letter requesting an appointment to speak with him.

Although Jones was not yet aware of it, Joe Smith had returned to his desk and immediately began drafting the following memo to be sent to Tony Perry:

To: Tony Perry, V.P. Corporate Facilities
From: Joe Smith, Corporate Services
Re: Royal CCC

Tony:

I spoke at length with Mary Jones of Royal this morning. She presented me with her proposal for the adoption of the CCC program at Bickford Publishing. After reviewing the proposal in detail, I have determined that the program: a) is not cost effective, b) has many problem areas that need ironing out, c) is inappropriate for our company at this time.

Therefore, in light of the above, my opinion is that this matter does not warrant any serious consideration or further discussion at this point in time.

ROYAL 750 COLOR COPIER

The Royal 750 color copier made its debut in 1973 and was originally sold by color copier specialists in the equipment division of Royal. But sales representatives did not want to sell the color copier exclusively and sales managers did not want to manage the color copier specialists. Therefore, the 750 was not a particularly successful product. In 1979, the sales responsibility for the color copier was transferred to the RRC division. Since the RRC sales representatives were already taking orders from customers needing the services of a color copier, it was felt that the reps would be in an advantageous position to determine when current customer requirements would justify the purchase of a 750.

Jones arrived back at her office at 10:45. She checked her mailbox for messages, grabbed a cup of coffee, and returned to her desk to draft the letter to Tony Perry. After making several phone calls setting up appointments for the next week and checking on client satisfaction with some jobs that had been delivered today, she gathered up the materials she needed for her afternoon sales calls. Finishing her coffee, she noticed the poster announcing a trip for members of the "President's Club." To become a member, a sales representative had to meet 100 percent of his or her sales budget, sell a 750 color copier, sell a CCC program, and sell a short-term rental. Jones believed that making budget would be difficult but attainable, even though her superior performance in 1982 led to a budget increase of 20 percent for 1983. She had already sold a color copier and a short-term rental. Therefore, the main thing standing in her way of making the President's Club was the sale of a CCC. Not selling a CCC this year would have even more serious ramifications, she thought. Until recently, Jones had considered herself the prime candidate for the expected opening for a senior sales representative in her office. But Michael Gould, a sales rep who also had three years' experience, was enjoying an excellent year. He had sold two color copiers and had just closed a deal on a CCC to a large semiconductor manufacturing firm. Normally everyone in the office celebrated the sale of a CCC. As a fellow sales rep was often heard saying, "it takes the heat off of all of us for a while." Jones, however, found it difficult to celebrate Gould's sale, for not only was he the office "golden boy" but now, in her opinion, he was also the prime candidate for the senior sales rep position. Gould's sale also left Jones as one of the few reps in the office without the sale of a CCC to his or her credit. "It is pretty difficult to get a viable CCC lead," Jones thought, "but I've had one or two this year that should have been closed." Neither the long discussions with her sales manager nor the numerous in-service training sessions and discussions on how to sell the CCC had helped. "I've just got to sell one of these soon," Jones resolved.

On her way out, she glanced at the clock. It was 11:33. She had just enough time to make her 11:45 appointment with Sam Lawless, operations manager at ABC Electronics. This was Jones's first appointment at ABC and she was excited about getting a foot in the door there. A friend of hers was an account assistant at ABC. She had informed Jones that the company spent more than $15,000 a month on printing services and that they might consider a CCC proposal. Jones knew who the competition was, and although their prices were lower on low-volume orders, Royal could meet or beat their prices for the kind of volume of work for which ABC was contracting. But Jones wasn't enthusiastic about garnering the account for reproduction work. She believed she could sell ABC a CCC.

Jones's friend had mentioned management dissatisfaction with the subcontracting of so much printing. Also, there had been complaints regarding the quality of work. Investment in an in-house print shop had been discussed. Jones had assessed ABC's situation and had noticed a strong parallel with the situation of Star Electronics, a multidivision electronics manufacturing firm that had been sold CCCs for each of their four locations in the area. That sale, which occurred over a year ago, was vital in legitimatizing the CCC with potential customers in the northeast. Jones hoped to sell ABC on the same premise that Fred Myers had sold Star Electronics. Myers had been extremely helpful in reviewing his sales plan with Jones and had given her ideas on points he felt had been instrumental in closing the Star deal. She felt well prepared for this call.

Jones had waited four months to get an appointment with Lawless. He had a reputation for disliking to speak with salespeople, but Jones's friend had passed along to him some CCC literature and he had seemed interested. Finally, after months of being unable to reach him by telephone or get a response by mail, she had phoned two weeks ago and he had consented to see her. Today she planned to concentrate on how adoption of the CCC program might solve ABC's current reproduction problems. She also planned to ask Lawless to provide her with the necessary information to produce a convincing proposal in favor of CCC. Jones pulled into a visitor parking space and grabbed her briefcase. "This could end up being the one," she thought as she headed for the reception area.

Jones removed a business card from her wallet and handed it to the receptionist. "Mary Jones to see Sam Lawless. I have an appointment," Jones announced.

"I'm sorry," the receptionist replied, "Mr. Lawless is no longer with the company."

Jones tried not to lose her composure. "But I had an appointment to see him today. When did he leave?"

"Last Friday was Mr. Lawless's last day. Mr. Bates is now operations manager."

"May I see Mr. Bates, please?" Jones inquired, knowing in advance the response.

"Mr. Bates does not see salespeople. He sees no one without an appointment."

"Could you tell him that I had an appointment to see Mr. Lawless? Perhaps he would consider seeing me."

"I can't call him, but I'll leave him a note with your card. Perhaps you can contact him later."

"Thank you, I will." Jones turned and left ABC, obviously shaken. "Back to square one," she thought as she headed back to her car. It was 12:05 P.M.

Jones headed for her next stop, CG Advertising, still upset from the episode at ABC. But she had long since discovered that no successful salesperson can dwell on disappointments. "It interferes with your whole attitude," she reminded herself. Jones arrived at the office park where CG was located. She was on time for her 12:30 appointment.

CG was a large, full-service agency. Jones's color copy orders from CG had been increasing at a rapid rate for the past six months and she had no reason to believe that their needs would decrease in the near future. Therefore she believed the time was ripe to present a case for the purchase of a 750 color copier. Jones had been dealing primarily with Jim Stevens, head of creative services. They had a good working relationship, even though on certain occasions Jones had found him to be unusually demanding about quality. But she figured that characteristic seemed to be common in many creative people. She had decided to use his obsession with perfection to work to her advantage.

Jones also knew that money was only a secondary consideration as far as Stevens was concerned. He had seemingly gotten his way on purchases in several other instances, so she planned her approach to him. Jones had outlined a proposal that she was now ready to present to Jim.

"Good morning, Jim, how's the advertising business?"

"It's going pretty well for us here, how's things with you?"

"Great, Jim," Jones lied, "I have an interesting idea to discuss with you. I've been thinking that CG has been ordering large quantities of color copies. I know that you use them in the presentations of advertising and marketing plans to clients. I also know that you like to experiment with several different concepts before actually deciding on a final idea. Even though we have exceptionally short turn-around time, it occurred to me that nothing would suit your needs more efficiently and effectively than the presence of one of our Royal 750 color copiers right here in your production room. That way, each time you consider a revision one of your artists will be able to compose a rough, and you can run a quick copy and decide virtually immediately if that is the direction in which you want to go, with no need to slow down the creative process at all."

"Well, I don't know; our current situation seems to be working out rather well. I really don't see any reason to change it."

"I'm not sure that you're fully aware of all the things that the 750 color copier is capable of doing," Jones pressed on. "One of the technicians and I have been experimenting with the 750. Even I have discovered some new and interesting capabilities to be applied in your field, Jim. Let me show you some of them."

She reached into her art portfolio and produced a wide variety of samples to show Stevens. "You know that the color copier is great for enlarging and reducing as well as straight duplicating. But look at the different effects we got by experimenting with various sizes and colors. Don't you think that this is an interesting effect?"

"Yes, it really is," Stevens said, loosening up slightly.

"But wait," Jones added, "I really have the ultimate to show you." Jones produced a sheet on which she had constructed a collage from various slides that Stevens had given her for enlarging.

"Those are my slides! Hey, that's great."

"Do you think that a potential client might be impressed by something like this? And the best part is you can whip something like this up in a matter of minutes, if the copier is at your disposal."

"Hey, that's a great idea, Mary, I'd love to be able to fool around with one of those machines. I bet I'd be able to do some really inventive proposals with it."

"I'm sure you would, Jim."

"Do you have a few minutes right now? I'd like to bounce this idea off Bill Jackson, head of purchasing, and see how quickly we can get one in here."

Jones and Stevens went down to Jackson's office. Before they even spoke, Jones felt that this deal was closed. Jim Stevens always got his own way. Besides, she believed she knew what approach to use with Bill Jackson. She had dealt with him on several other occasions. Jackson had failed to approve a purchase for her the prior fall on the basis that the purchase could not be justified. He was right on that account. Their present 600 model was handling their reproduction needs sufficiently, but you can't blame a person for trying, she thought. Besides, she hadn't had Stevens in her corner for that one. This was going to be different.

"How's it going, Bill? You've met Mary Jones before haven't you?"

"Yes, I remember Miss Jones. She's been to see me several times, always trying to sell me something we don't need," he said cynically.

"Well, this time I do have something you need and not only will this purchase save time, but it will save money, too. Let me show you some figures I've worked out regarding how much you can save by purchasing the 750 color copier." Jones showed Jackson that, at their current rate of increased orders of color copies, the 750 would pay for itself in three years. She also stressed the efficiency and ease of operation. But she knew that Jackson was really only interested in the bottom line.

"Well, I must admit, Miss Jones, it does appear to be a cost-effective purchase."

Stevens volunteered, "Not only that, but we can now get our artwork immediately, too. This purchase will make everyone happy."

Jones believed she had the order. "I'll begin the paperwork as soon as I return to the office. May I come by next week to complete the deal?"

"Well, let me see what needs to be done on this end, but I don't foresee a problem," Jackson replied.

"There won't be any problem," Stevens assured Jones.

"Fine, then. I'll call Jim the first of next week to set up an appointment for delivery."

Jones returned to her car at 1:00. She felt much better having closed the sale on the 750. She had planned enough time to stop for lunch.

During lunch, Jones thought about her time at Royal. She enjoyed her job as a whole. If it weren't for the pressure she was feeling to sell the Corporate Copy Center program, everything would be just about perfect. Jones had been a straight "A" student in college where she had majored in marketing. As far back as she could remember, she had always wanted to work in sales. Her father had started out in sales, and enjoyed a very successful and profitable career. He had advanced to sales manager and sales director for a highly successful Fortune 500 company and was proud that his daughter had chosen to pursue a career in sales. Often they would get together, and he would offer suggestions that had proven effective for him when he had worked in the field. When Jones's college placement office had announced that a Royal collegiate recruiter was visiting the campus, Jones had immediately signed up for an interview. She knew several recent graduates who had obtained positions with Royal and were very happy there. They were also doing well financially. She was excited at the idea of working for an industry giant. When she was invited for a second interview, she was ecstatic. Several days later, she received a phone call offering her a position at the regional office and she accepted immediately. Jones attended various pretraining workshops for six weeks at her regional office preparing her for her two-week intensive training period at the Royal Training Headquarters. Her training consisted of product training and sales training. She had excelled there, and graduated from that course at the head of her class and from that point on everything continued smoothly . . . until this problem with selling the CCC.

After a quick sandwich and coffee, Jones left the restaurant at 1:30. She allowed extra time before her 2:00 appointment at General Hospital, located just four blocks from the office, to stop into the office first, check for messages, and check in with her sales manager. She informed Tom Stein that she considered the sale of a 750 to CG almost certain.

"That's great, Mary. I never doubted your ability to sell the color copiers, or repro for that matter. But what are we going to do about our other problem?"

"Tom, I've been following CCC leads all morning. To tell you the truth, I don't feel as though I've made any progress at all. As a matter of fact, I've lost some ground." Jones went on to explain the situation that had developed at ABC Electronics, and how she felt when she learned that Sam Lawless was no longer with the company. "I was pretty excited about that prospect, Tom. The news was a little tough to take."

"That's okay. We'll just concentrate on his replacement, now. It might be a setback, but the company's still there and they still have the same printing needs and problems. Besides, you're going to make your final presentation to General Hospital this afternoon, and you really did your homework for that one." Stein had worked extensively with Jones on the proposal from start to finish. They both knew that it was her best opportunity of the year to sell a CCC.

"I'm leaving right now. Wish me luck."

He did. She filled her briefcase with her personals and CCC demonstration kit that she planned to use for the actual presentation and headed toward the parking lot.

Jones's appointment was with Harry Jameson of General Hospital. As she approached his office, his receptionist announced her. Jameson appeared and led her to the board room for their meeting. Jones was surprised to find three other individuals seated around the table. She was introduced to Bob Goldstein, V.P. of operations, Martha Chambers, director of accounting, and Dr. J. P. Dunwitty, chairman of the board. Jameson explained that whenever an expenditure of this magnitude was being considered, the hospital's executive committee had to make a joint recommendation.

Jones set up her demonstration at the head of the table so that it was easily viewed by everyone and began her proposal. She presented charts outlining the merits of the CCC and also the financial calculations that she had generated based on the information supplied to her by Jameson.

Forty minutes later, Jones finished her presentation and began fielding questions. The usual concerns were voiced regarding hiring an "outsider" to work within the hospital. But the major concern seemed to revolve around the loss of employment on the part of two present printing press operators. One, John Brown, had been a faithful employee for more than five years. He was married and had a child. There had never been a complaint about John personally, or with regard to the quality or quantity of his work. The second operator was Peter Dunwitty, a recent graduate of a nearby vocational school and nephew of Dr. Dunwitty. Although he had only been employed by the hospital for three months, there was no question about his ability and performance.

In response to this concern, Jones emphasized that the new equipment was more efficient, but different, and did not require the skills of experienced printers like Brown and Dunwitty. She knew, however, that this was always the one point about the adoption of a CCC program that even she had the most difficulty justifying. She suddenly felt rather ill.

"Well, Miss Jones, if you'll excuse us for a few minutes, we'd like to reach a decision on this matter," said Jameson.

"There's no need to decide right at this point. You all have copies of my proposal. If you'd like to take a few days to review the figures, I'd be happy to come by then," said Jones, in a last-ditch attempt to gain some additional time.

"I think that we'd like to meet in private for a few minutes right now, if you don't mind," interjected Dunwitty.

"No, that's fine," Jones said as she left the room for the lobby. She sat in a waiting room and drank a cup of coffee. She lit a cigarette, a habit she seldom engaged in. Five minutes later, the board members called her back in.

"This CCC idea is really sound, Miss Jones," Jameson began. "However, here at General Hospital, we have a very strong commitment to our employees. There really seems to be no good reason to put two fine young men out of work. Yes, I realize that from the figures that you've presented to us, you've indicated a savings of approximately $30,000 over three years. But I would have to question some of the calculations. Under the circumstances, we feel that maintaining sound employee relations has more merit than switching to an unproven program right now. Therefore, we've decided against purchasing a CCC."

Jones was disappointed, but she had been in this situation often enough not to show it. "I'm sorry to hear that, Mr. Jameson. I thought that I had presented a very good argument for participation in the CCC program. Do you think that if your current operators decided to leave, you might consider CCC again before you filled their positions?"

"I can't make a commitment to that right now. But feel free to stay in touch," Jameson countered.

"I'll still be coming in on a regular basis to meet all your needs for other work not capable of being performed in your print shop," Jones replied.

"Then you'll be the first to know if that situation arises," said Jameson.

"Thank you all for your time. I hope that I was of assistance even though you decided against purchase. If I may be of help at any point in time, don't hesitate to call," Jones remarked as she headed for the door.

Now, totally disappointed, Jones regretted having scheduled another appointment for that afternoon. She would have liked to call it a day. But she knew she had an opportunity to pick up some repro work and develop a new account. So she knew she couldn't cancel.

Jones stopped by to see Paul Blake, head of staff training at Pierson's, a large department store with locations throughout the state. Jones had made a cold call one afternoon the previous week and had obtained a sizeable printing order. Now she wanted to see whether Blake was satisfied with the job, which had been delivered earlier in the day. She also wanted to speak to him about some of the other services available at the RRC. Jones was about to reach into her briefcase for her card to offer to the receptionist when she was startled by a "Hello, Mary" coming from behind her.

"Hello, Paul," Jones responded, surprised and pleased that he had remembered her name. "How are you today?"

"Great! I have to tell you, that report that you printed for us is far superior to the work that we have been receiving from some of our other suppliers. I've got another piece that will be ready to go out in about an hour. Can you have someone come by and pick it up then?"

"I'll do better than that. I'll pick it up myself," Jones replied.

"See you then," he responded as he turned and headed back toward his office.

"I'm glad I decided to stop by after all," Jones thought as she pressed the elevator button. She wondered how she could best use the next hour to help salvage the day. When the elevator door opened, out stepped Kevin Fitzgerald, operations manager for Pierson's. Jones had met him several weeks earlier when she had spoken with Ann Leibman, a sales rep for Royal Equipment Division. Leibman had been very close to closing a deal that would involve selling Pierson several "casual" copying machines that they were planning to locate in various offices to use for quick copying. Leibman informed Jones that Tom Stein had presented a CCC proposal to Pierson's six months earlier but the plan was flatly refused. Fitzgerald, she explained, had been sincerely interested in the idea, but the plan involved a larger initial expenditure than Pierson's was willing to make. Now, Leibman explained, there would be a much larger savings involved, since the "casual" machines would not be needed if a CCC were involved. Jones had suggested to Fitzgerald that the CCC proposal be reworked to include the new machines so that a current assessment could be made. He had once again appeared genuinely interested and suggested that Jones retrieve the necessary figures from Jerry Query, head of purchasing. Jones had not yet done so. She had phoned Query several times, but he had never responded to her messages.

"Nice to see you again, Mr. Fitzgerald. Ann Leibman introduced us. I'm Mary Jones from Royal."

"Yes, I remember. Have you spoken with Mr. Query yet?"

"I'm on my way to see him right now," Jones said as she thought this would be the perfect way to use the hour.

"Fine, get in touch with me when you have the new calculations."

Jones entered the elevator that Fitzgerald had been holding for her as they spoke. She returned to the first floor and consulted the directory. Purchasing was on the third floor. As she walked off the elevator on the third floor, the first thing that she saw was a sign that said, "Salespeople seen by appointment only. Tuesdays and Thursdays, 10 A.M.–12 Noon."

"I'm really out of luck," Jones thought, "not only do I not have an appointment, but today's Wednesday. But I'll give it my best shot as long as I'm here."

Jones walked over to the receptionist who was talking to herself as she searched through a large pile of papers on her desk. Although Jones knew she was aware of her presence, the receptionist continued to avoid her.

"This could be a hopeless case," Jones thought. Just then the receptionist looked up and acknowledged her.

"Good afternoon. I'm Mary Jones from Royal. I was just speaking to Mr. Fitzgerald who suggested that I see Mr. Query. I'm not selling anything. I just need to get some figures from him."

"Just a minute," the receptionist replied as she walked toward an office with Query's name on the door.

"Maybe this is not going to be so bad after all," Jones thought.

"Mr. Query will see you for a minute," the receptionist announced as she returned to her desk.

Jones walked into Query's plushly furnished office. Query was an imposing figure at 6′4″, nearly 300 pounds, and bald. Jones extended her hand, which Query grasped firmly. "What brings you here to see me?" Query inquired.

Jones explained her conversations with Ann Leibman and Kevin Fitzgerald. As she was about to ask her initial series of questions, Query interrupted. "Miss

Jones, I frankly don't know what the hell you are doing here!" Query exclaimed. "We settled this issue over six months ago, and now you're bringing it up again. I really don't understand. You people came in with a proposal that was going to cost us more money than we were spending. We know what we're doing. No one is going to come in here and tell us our business."

"Mr. Query," Jones began, trying to remain composed, "the calculations that you were presented with were based on the equipment that Pierson's was using six months ago. Now that you are contemplating additional purchases, I mentioned to Mr. Fitzgerald that a new comparison should be made. He instructed me to speak with you in order to obtain the information needed to prepare a thorough proposal," Jones tried to explain.

"Fitzgerald! What on earth does Fitzgerald have to do with this? This is none of his damn business. He sat at the same table as I six months ago when we arrived at a decision. Why doesn't he keep his nose out of affairs that don't concern him. We didn't want this program six months ago, and we don't want it now!" Query shouted.

"I'm only trying to do my job, Mr. Query. I was not part of the team that presented the proposal six months ago. But from all the information that is available now, I still feel that a CCC would save you money here at Pierson's."

"Don't you understand, Miss Jones? We don't want any outsiders here. You have no control over people that don't work for you. Nothing gets approved around here unless it has my signature on it. That's control. Now I really see no need to waste any more of my time or yours."

"I appreciate your frankness," Jones responded, struggling to find something positive to say.

"Well, that's the kind of man I am, direct and to the point."

"You can say that again," Jones thought. She said, "One other thing before I go, Mr. Query. I was noticing the color copies on your desk."

"Yes, I like to send color copies of jobs when getting production estimates. For example, these are of the bogs that we will be using during our fall promotion. I have received several compliments from suppliers who think that by viewing color copies they get a real feel for what I need."

"Well, it just so happens that my division of Royal sells color copiers. At some time it may be more efficient for you to consider purchase. Let me leave you some literature on the 750 copier, which you can review at your leisure."

Jones removed a brochure from her briefcase. She attached one of her business cards to it and handed it to Query. As she shook his hand and left the office, Jones noted that she had half an hour before the project of Blake's would be ready for pick-up. She entered the donut shop across the street and as she waited for her coffee, she reviewed her day's activities. She was enthusiastic about the impending color copier sale at CG Advertising, and about the new repro business that she had acquired at Pierson's. But the rest of the day had been discouraging. Not only had she been "shot down" repeatedly, but she'd now have to work extra hard for several days to ensure that she would make 100 percent of budget for the month. "Trying to sell the CCC is even harder than I thought it was," Jones thought.

DISCUSSION QUESTIONS

1. What three products/services are sold by the RRC? Who is the decision maker for each of these products/services?
2. What are the benefits to the user of each of these three products/services?
3. Examine Mary Jones's efforts at Acme Computers, Bickford Publishing, and General Hospital. What are the similarities among these situations?
4. Should Mary Jones directly contact Tom Perry of Bickford Publishing? Why or why not?
5. What could Mary Jones have done differently to sell the CCC to General Hospital?
6. What actions should Tom Stein (Jones's sales manager) take regarding Mary Jones?

The D. F. Hardware Company

....

Determining Sales Territories and Quotas

BACKGROUND

The D. F. Hardware Company was a hardware wholesaler/distributor located in Cleveland, Ohio. The company handled hardware products for a number of manufacturers, selling primarily to retail hardware stores in the greater Cleveland area. Sales were made by a company salesperson, Ted Tyler, who called on the local retailers. D. F. Hardware trucks later delivered the purchased products to these retailers. Tyler reported to Matt Simmons, the company's general manager, who also acted in the capacity of D. F. Hardware's sales manager. With only one salesperson, this position did not occupy much of Simmons's time.

One of D. F. Hardware's most valued suppliers was the Livingston Tool Corporation, a large manufacturer of hand and power tools. Livingston Tool sold its products in many markets, one of which was retail hardware stores such as were handled by D. F. Hardware. In this particular market, Livingston Tool used selective distributors, since most of the stores were small and widely distributed. D. F. Hardware had functioned as a distributor for Livingston Tool for a number of years in the Cleveland marketplace. The association between the two companies was very amiable—D. F. Hardware valued the Livingston Tool distributorship and its line of high-quality products, and Livingston Tool was pleased with D. F. Hardware's performance in the marketplace.

In April 1978, Cecil Andrews, the national sales manager of Livingston Tool, approached Simmons with an interesting offer. Livingston Tool was revising its policy on its distributor network. Instead of using several distributors to cover a market area, Livingston Tool was consolidating and attempting to cover

Adapted from U.S. Department of Commerce, *Measuring Markets* (Washington, DC: U.S. Government Printing Office, 1966), 60–63.

the same area with an exclusive distributorship. In Ohio, for example, Livingston Tool had been using distributors in Columbus, Toledo, Cincinnati, and Steubenville in addition to D. F. Hardware in Cleveland. Andrews wanted to replace the five with a single distributor that would be granted the exclusive right to sell Livingston Tool products in Ohio. He offered the exclusive Ohio distributorship to Simmons and D. F. Hardware.

THE PROBLEM

The Livingston Tool offer was an exciting one for Matt Simmons. As was stated, D. F. Hardware had been pleased with the Cleveland area distributorship, and the thought of having this position for all of Ohio really excited Simmons. The Livingston Tool product line was high-quality, profitable, and fast-moving, and Simmons saw it as a major profit maker for D. F. Hardware.

As inviting as the Livingston Tool offer was, Simmons knew its acceptance would involve profound change for his company. The new franchise would necessitate an expansion of D. F. Hardware's sales force with the establishment of sales territories and sales quotas in the entire Ohio market area. Ted Tyler could continue to sell to the Cleveland area, but he could not be expected to cover the entire state. In addition, Simmons knew that an acceptance of the Livingston Tool offer would involve changes in his company's physical distribution network, inventory policy, credit policies, and other such related areas.

Simmons found none of these changes formidable enough to warrant the rejection of the Livingston Tool offer. The prospect of having the profitable Livingston Tool franchise for all of Ohio seemed to overshadow any possible obstacles. In addition, he felt that such a move would be the first his company might make in regard to increasing its market penetration and its size. He envisioned that D. F. Hardware would someday be a large regional distributor and that this move was but the forerunner of several similar ones. After weighing all the pros and cons, Simmons accepted Andrews's offer as Livingston Tool's exclusive distributor in Ohio. Andrews then informed the other four Ohio distributors (in Columbus, Toledo, Cincinnati, and Steubenville) of Livingston Tool's decision and told them that as of June 1, 1978, D. F. Hardware would serve as its exclusive Ohio distributor. After signing the contract, Simmons felt that his first task was to develop sales territories and quotas and determine how many salespersons the company would need to adequately serve the newly enlarged market area.

MARKET CHARACTERISTICS

Not long after the contract was signed, Simmons met with Andrews. This meeting was set up so that Andrews could provide Simmons with market characteristics and other information that would help D. F. Hardware in its new territories.

In addition, the meeting was intended to establish the sales volume performance that Livingston Tool expected from D. F. Hardware in Ohio for the coming year. More specifically, Andrews informed Simmons of the following:

1. D. F. Hardware was to sell Livingston Tool products *only* to retail hardware stores in the Ohio area. Although Livingston Tool products were distributed through other retail outlets such as discount houses, department stores, and farm equipment dealers, the company used other channels to reach these types of customers. Livingston Tool wanted its distributor to cover the retail hardware store marketplace only.

2. Total U.S. shipments by hand and power tool manufacturers such as Livingston Tool had been $2,196.6 million in the previous year, according to data generated by the *Survey of Industrial Purchasing Power*. In that same year, Livingston Tool's shipments amounted to $140.6 million, or 6.4 percent of total shipments. Andrews thought that this 6.4 percent market share estimate was appropriate for the state of Ohio.

3. Andrews estimated that 21.8 percent of hardware store retail sales were accounted for by products similar to those manufactured by Livingston Tool, based on analyses his company had conducted over time. This percentage would give Simmons a good idea of the size of the Ohio retail sales market for the types of products D. F. Hardware would distribute.

4. Andrews expected sales of Livingston Tool products in Ohio to increase by 3.75 percent over the previous year because of increased sales effort due primarily to consolidation of distributors and D. F. Hardware's expected increased sales performance. Livingston Tool would provide D. F. Hardware with sales materials and would participate in cooperative advertising with the distributor to assist in reaching this 3.75 percent objective.

5. Andrews had determined that a typical distributor salesperson could average about five sales calls per day, or approximately 1,250 calls in a 250-day work year, based on past experience with other successful distributors across the country. He believed these figures to be appropriate for Ohio but cautioned Simmons to make certain that sales territories were drawn on the basis of both the number of calls to be made and an equal distribution of the total company's sales quota. If these points were not adequately considered, salesperson dissatisfaction would occur and problems would develop. Simmons understood and agreed.

6. Andrews also had determined that a distributor salesperson should call at least once every month on the larger retail accounts (twenty or more employees) and at least once every three months on the smaller ones (fewer than twenty employees). He recommended that this procedure would be a good rule of thumb for Simmons to follow, at least initially, in setting up his sales force.

Simmons found the meeting with Andrews to be quite helpful. After their meeting, Simmons began to outline the approach he would use to develop sales territories and quotas and then to determine the optimum number of salespeople for D. F. Hardware to employ. He immediately recognized the need for pertinent data on his Ohio marketplace. The next morning, he visited the library of the local state university to seek out the data he required. Using such sources as the U.S. Department of Commerce's *County Business Patterns* and the *Census of Retail Trade,* he developed Exhibits 1, 2, and 3. He also located a map of Ohio that outlined all standard metropolitan statistical areas (SMSAs) and showed their relationships to all other Ohio counties. This map is shown in Exhibit 4. Since these data were published in the previous year, 1977, Simmons believed they were reliable enough to use in any calculations he might want to make. From these sources, he estimated that there were more than 1,000 hardware retail stores in his new market area with total estimated retail sales exceeding $240 million. With these data, Simmons believed he had sufficient information to determine sales territories and appropriate quotas and to decide on the optimum number of salespeople to employ.

Advise Matt Simmons.

EXHIBIT 1   Estimated Total Retail Sales by Hardware Stores SIC 5251 in Ohio by SMSA

SMSA	Estimated Total Retail Sales ($000)	Number of Establishments
Akron	$ 11,797	59
Canton	13,837	49
Cincinnati	31,635	133
Cleveland	39,901	191
Columbus	23,595	93
Dayton	20,139	79
Hamilton–Middletown	4,510	19
Huntington–Ashland	10,037	41
Lima	7,808	36
Lorain–Elyria	6,555	27
Mansfield	2,695	14
Parkersburg–Marietta	2,310	17
Springfield	3,843	16
Steubenville–Weirton	5,300	15
Toledo	16,963	84
Wheeling, W. Va.–Ohio	3,531	21
Youngstown–Warren	14,837	40
Total	$219,293	934

Source: U.S. Census of Retail Trade, 1977.

EXHIBIT 2

Estimated Total Retail Sales by Hardware Stores SIC 5251 in Ohio by Counties Not Included in SMSA Classifications

County	Estimated Total Retail Sales ($000)	Number of Establishments
Ashtabula	$ 3,456	17
Columbiana	5,437	18
Erie	D	5
Hancock	1,383	13
Huron	2,157	12
Licking	D	9
Marion	1,601	11
Muskingum	910	8
Ross	D	5
Sandusky	D	6
Scioto	D	6
Seneca	2,186	4
Tuscarawas	D	10
Wayne	4,839	17
Total	$21,969	141

Note: D indicates counties in which retail sales were withheld to avoid disclosing data for individual companies.

Source: U.S. Census of Retail Trade, 1977.

EXHIBIT 3

Number of Hardware Stores SIC 5251 by Size in Each SMSA and Other Counties in Ohio

SMSA	Outlets with Fewer Than 20 Employees	Outlets with More Than 20 Employees
Akron	58	1
Canton	45	4
Cincinnati	133	0
Cleveland	186	5
Columbus	88	5
Dayton	75	4
Hamilton–Middletown	18	1
Huntington–Ashland	41	0
Lima	36	0
Lorain–Elyria	26	1
Mansfield	14	0
Parkersburg–Marietta	17	0
Springfield	15	1
Steubenville–Weirton	14	1
Toledo	83	1
Wheeling	21	0
Youngstown–Warren	34	6

continues

EXHIBIT 3 continued

SMSA	Outlets with Fewer Than 20 Employees	Outlets with More Than 20 Employees
Other Counties Outside SMSAs		
Ashtabula	16	1
Columbiana	18	0
Erie	5	0
Hancock	13	0
Huron	12	0
Licking	9	0
Marion	11	0
Muskingum	8	0
Ross	5	0
Sandusky	6	0
Scioto	6	0
Seneca	3	1
Tuscarawas	10	0
Wayne	16	1

Note: None of the remaining counties show retail hardware outlets.

Source: Adapted from *Census of Retail Trade, 1977,* and *County Business Patterns, 1977.*

DISCUSSION QUESTIONS

1. Based on Andrews's ratios and percentages, estimate the sale potential for D. F. Hardware for 1979. (Be sure to include Andrews's 3.75 percent expected increase in your calculations.)

2. Assuming that Andrews's customer call frequencies are valid and that a salesperson should be able to make five calls per day, determine an optimum number of salespeople for Simmons to employ in Ohio.

3. Using Exhibit 4 as a guide, determine the sales territories Simmons should use in most effectively covering the Ohio market area.

4. Determine sales quota figures for each of your defined territories.

EXHIBIT 4   Standard Metropolitan Statistical Areas for Ohio

OHIO

LEGEND

⊙ Places of 100,000 or more inhabitants
● Places of 50,000 to 100,000 inhabitants
□ Central cities if SMSA's with fewer than 50,000 inhabitants
○ Places of 25,000 to 50,000 inhabitants outside SMSA's

Standard Metropolitan
Statistical Areas (SMSA's)

SCALE
0   10   20   30   40   50 MILES

**U.S. Department of Commerce
BUREAU OF THE CENSUS**

General Supply Company

··

Organizing a Sales Force

General Supply Company is a large distributor of ink and solvents that are used in the printing industry and for office use in mimeographing and duplicating. The company depends heavily on its sales force to provide its customers with technical information, training, problem solving, and a lot of plain, old-fashioned "hand-holding" and "showing the flag"—just being there when needed. The sales force is obviously also responsible for selling General Supply's merchandise to its customers through direct sales activity.

The firm is nationwide in scope and has been in business for over fifty years. The firm's sales have grown rapidly over the past ten years, and sales for next year are expected to exceed $150,000,000. General Supply's headquarters and main distribution center are in Chicago, but the firm also has distribution centers in St. Louis, Newark, Boston, Richmond, New Orleans, Atlanta, Denver, and Sacramento.

Vance Metzgar has just been selected for promotion from his position as the western North Carolina sales representative for General Supply Company to a position in sales management for General Supply. He is to spend two weeks in the headquarters office in Chicago to train for the new job prior to being assigned to the district for which he will be the new district sales manager.

Upon Vance's arrival in Chicago, Al Swanson, the national sales manager, tells Vance that he has a chore he wants done, and he wants Vance to do it in addition to his management training duties: He wants Vance to determine the number of sales reps the firm should have for each region of the country, for each of the product groups, and the total number of sales reps the firm should have.

Case contributed by Ronald H. King and W. E. Patton III, Professors of Marketing, Appalachian State University.

He also wants a detailed organizational chart that will show him how the marketing department of General Supply should be organized. Swanson wants a detailed chart for the whole marketing department, but suggests that Vance pay particular attention to the sales force and be sure to show enough detail so that Swanson will know where and how every salesperson fits into the organization. He also wants a brief explanation of why the structure suggested is the best.

Vance immediately begins to gather information, and comes up with the following information.

General Supply distributes two very distinct product groups to distinct customer types, as shown in Exhibit 1.

The market can be divided into four geographical regions, each with its own idiosyncrasies, as shown in Exhibit 2.

Each of these regions can be divided into as many as (but no more than) four reasonably similar but distinct geographic districts if necessary.

A study of the corporate policy manual reveals that the following functions or responsibilities are assigned to a vice president for marketing:

- Personal selling
- Advertising
- Sales promotion
- Publicity
- Sales planning
- Sales analysis

- Marketing research
- Sales training
- Sales supervision
- Pricing strategy
- Sales forecasting
- Customer relations

- Distribution, including warehousing, transportation, inventory control, etc.
- Product/brand management

EXHIBIT 1   **Product Groups and Customer Types**

Product Group	Customer Types	% of Total Sales
Industrial printing inks and solvents	Class A: Large, multipurpose, full-service printing firms. Annual sales volume potential of over $20,000.	14.9%
	Class B: Medium-sized, limited-service printing firms. Annual sales volume potential of $10,000 to $19,999.	11.5%
	Class C: Small "Mom and Pop" printers. Annual sales volume potential of less than $10,000.	10.9%
Packaged inks for mimeographs and duplicating	Class D: Large to medium-sized office supply dealers that operate "storefront" operations and sell directly to end users (offices, businesses, individuals, etc). Annual sales volume potential of $10,000 to $19,999.	25.1%
	Class E: Large office supply wholesalers that operate warehouses that sell to small office supply dealers. Annual sales volume potential of over $75,000 per year.	37.6%

EXHIBIT 2	Regional Sales Distribution	
Region	**% of National Sales**	
Northeast	26.8%	
Midwest	32.1%	
Southern	22.4%	
Western	18.7%	

The sales force for General Supply is responsible for calling on and selling to all of the customer types indicated in Exhibit 1. Each customer type is a bit different from the others, but Classes A, B, and C are somewhat similar in that all are printing operations and have similar needs. The sales reps who call on these printers are usually well educated and must have extensive knowledge of the printing industry, printing technology, and other technical knowledge. These classes require fairly frequent calls, and the batting average for these accounts is typically less than .500, indicating that many calls are for hand-holding, servicing, and showing the flag. Gross margins on sales of industrial inks and solvents typically run about 40 percent of sales, and sales reps who sell these lines are paid a straight commission of 8 percent of sales. The reps for this line typically work fifty weeks a year and fifty-five hours per week. The reps, on average, earn about $45,000 per year.

Class D and E customers are not printers, but instead are merchants. Sales reps who call on Class D customers are typically less well educated and must have a knowledge of the office supply business, particularly at the store level, and those who call on Class E customers should have this plus an understanding of the volume wholesale business. Class D accounts require fairly infrequent contact, and Class E accounts require fairly frequent contact, but the batting average for both classes is above .500. Gross margins on the sales of mimeo and duplicating ink are considerably lower than for industrial inks and solvents, and the reps who sell the mimeo and duplicating ink are paid a salary plus an individual incentive and bonus based on performance. These reps also work fifty weeks per year, but usually only work fifty-two hours per week. The reps average about $35,000 per year in earnings.

Regardless of the class of customer involved, the General Supply sales reps operate largely on their own, do their own call planning, etc., but the field sales managers must exercise some supervision and other management activity involved in operating the sales force. Experience has shown that the span of control for first-level field sales managers should be no less than eight and no more than ten.

District-level (first-level) field sales force managers typically earn about $60,000 per year in salary and incentive. Regional-level sales managers typically earn about $90,000 per year. Product/brand managers usually earn about $60,000 per year. The national sales manager typically earns about $150,000 per year in salary and incentive. The firm wishes to keep its total cost for line sales managers within 1 percent of sales.

A search through sales reports in the home office revealed the information shown in Exhibits 3–6.

The figures in Exhibits 3–6 have remained quite stable over the past several years, and are expected to remain at current levels for some time.

Using the information you have, prepare the report to the National Sales Manager. Remember, he wants to see:

1. How many sales representatives the firm should have for each region, for each product group, and in total (he would probably like to see how the figures were developed).

2. A complete, detailed organization chart for the marketing department, with particular attention to the sales force. Be sure to show how the sales reps fit within the organization. Briefly explain why this structure is suggested.

EXHIBIT 3   **Number of Active Accounts**

Product Type	Customer Type	Region				Total
		NE	MW	S	W	
Inks and	A	318	257	139	183	897
solvents	B	358	330	279	183	1150
	C	794	733	920	825	3272
Mimeo and	D	910	751	520	318	2499
duplicating ink	E	202	376	260	238	1076
Total		2582	2447	2118	1747	8894

EXHIBIT 4   **Required Call Frequency (Number of Times per Month a Customer Must Be Called On)**

Product Type	Customer Type	Region				Total
		NE	MW	S	W	
Inks and	A	3	3	3	3	12.00
solvents	B	3	3	3	3	12.00
	C	1.5	1.5	1.25	1	5.25
Mimeo and	D	2	2	2	2	8.00
duplicating ink	E	1.5	1.5	1	1	5.00
Total		11.00	11.0	10.25	10.00	42.25

EXHIBIT 5   Amount of Time (in Minutes) Required for Face-to-Face Contact and Contact-Related Paperwork

Product Type	Customer Type	Region				Total
		NE	MW	S	W	
Inks and	A	75	75	75	75	300
solvents	B	75	75	75	75	300
	C	75	75	75	75	300
Mimeo and	D	45	45	45	45	180
duplicating ink	E	90	90	90	90	360
Total		360	360	360	360	1440

EXHIBIT 6   Time Allocation (Percent of a Sales Rep's Time Typically Spent in Each Activity)

Product Type	Region				Total
	NE	MW	S	W	
Selling Inks and Solvents:					
Face-to-face contact*	65%	60%	57%	50%	58%
Travel	25%	30%	33%	40%	32%
Paperwork‡	10%	10%	10%	10%	10%
Total	100%	100%	100%	100%	100%
Selling Mimeo and Duplicating Ink					
Face-to-face contact*	70%	65%	60%	55%	62%
Travel	20%	25%	30%	35%	28%
Paperwork‡	10%	10%	10%	10%	10%
Total	100%	100%	100%	100%	100%

* Face-to-face contact includes all activities involved in calling on the customer: selling, hand-holding, contact-related paperwork, record updates, etc.

‡ Paperwork time includes completing daily and weekly reports and planning next week's schedule.

Bolter Turbines, Inc.

···

Negotiation Simulation

Negotiation is the most frequent means of resolving conflicts between organizations, particularly in industrial marketing, when "big ticket" or high-technology products are involved. Nevertheless, principles of effective negotiation and negotiation skills are seldom part of the curriculum in business schools. The Bolter Turbines, Inc. (BTI) negotiation simulation has been developed specifically to provide a context for experiential learning and practical discussion of business negotiations. Through the simulation and associated debriefing, case participants are familiarized with the complex bargaining issues, strategies, and pressures that typify relationships between industrial firms.

BACKGROUND

Maverick Natural Gas, Inc., is in the process of building an offshore natural gas production platform in the Gulf of Mexico. The platform has been designed and scheduled for construction by PARTEX and Associates Company, a specialist in the construction of offshore oil and gas platforms. Gas compressors, such as Bolter's model JR2000, are an integral part of the production platform and are used to withdraw gas from the wells and move it through underwater pipelines to distribution facilities ashore. At the request of Maverick Natural Gas, Bolter Turbines has submitted the price quotation shown in Exhibit 1. A meeting has been scheduled as a result of this quotation, and Bolter's sales team and Maverick's purchasing team hope to find an agreement acceptable to both companies.

John L. Graham, "Bolter Turbines, Inc. Negotiation Simulation," *Journal of Marketing Education* (Spring 1984): 28–36. Reprinted by permission of the publisher, Business Research Division, University of Colorado at Boulder.

EXHIBIT 1   Bolter Turbines Price Quotation for Maverick Gas

BOLTER TURBINES, INC.
PRICE QUOTATION

For: Maverick Gas, Inc.   Installation: Offshore
       7 Euwing Avenue   Production
       Dallas, Texas   Platform #6
                                                                    Gulf of Mexico

Model JR2000 Natural Gas Compressor Set	$2,500,000
Product Options:	
Custom-built marine shelter	400,000
Recuperator	500,000
Salt spray air filters	100,000
Service Contract (2 years normal maintenance, parts, and labor)	150,000
Total price	$3,650,000

STANDARD TERMS AND CONDITIONS

Delivery	6 months
Penalty for late delivery	$10,000/month
Cancellation charges (if client cancels order)	10% of contract price
Warranty (for defective machinery)	parts, one year
Terms of payment	COD
Inflation escalator*	15% per year

*In the event that delivery is delayed by client, the quoted price will be increased at a rate of 15% per year, computed on a monthly basis.

THE NEGOTIATION SIMULATION

The negotiation simulation in this case calls for six participants, although your instructor may elect to use a different number. There are three members of the Bolter Turbines, Inc., selling team: (1) a sales representative, (2) a sales manager, and (3) an applications engineer. There are also three members of Maverick's purchasing team: (1) a purchasing agent, (2) a production engineer, and (3) a consulting design engineer. Each of the six participants has an individual role to play in this negotiation process. Your instructor will provide the details of each role and further instructions. These details and instructions provide directions useful to case participants. Using these details and instructions, the two teams are to negotiate an agreement that both are willing to accept. Exhibit 2 provides a contract that is to be completed and signed by representatives of both the Bolter and Maverick groups as a result of the negotiation.

EXHIBIT 2	**The Bolter/Maverick Contract**

FINAL CONTRACT TERMS

JR2000 Compressor Set
   Product Options (circle those selected)
      Shelter
      Recuperator
      Filter

TOTAL PRICE $ _____

Service Contract (list conditions)

_____

_____

PRICE $ _____

Terms and Conditions   _____
Delivery   _____
Penalty   _____
Cancellation Charges   _____
Terms of Payment   _____

                                                                          _____
Inflation Escalator   _____
Warranty   parts _____ labor _____ years _____
Arbitration Clause   yes _____ no _____

Signatures:

_____   _____
Maverick Representative   Bolter Representative

PURPOSE OF THE CASE

The importance of negotiation in industrial marketing has already been discussed. One of the best ways to teach the principles of effective marketing negotiations is through experiential learning and role playing. The Bolter Turbines, Inc., case is intended to serve as (1) an opportunity for students to participate in a realistic industrial marketing negotiation and (2) a context for discussing the various negotiation strategies and tactics appropriate for industrial marketers.

Wind Technology

···

Selecting the Appropriate Promotional Mix

Kevin Cage, general manager of Wind Technology, sat in his office on a Friday afternoon watching the snow fall outside his window. It was January 1991 and he knew that during the month ahead he would have to make some difficult decisions regarding the future of his firm. The market for the wind profiling radar systems that his company designed had been developing at a much slower rate than he had anticipated.

WIND TECHNOLOGY

During Wind Technology's ten-year history the company had produced a variety of weather-related radar and instrumentation. In 1986, the company condensed its product mix to include only wind profiling radar systems. Commonly referred to as wind profilers, these products measure wind and atmospheric turbulence for weather forecasting, detection of wind direction at NASA launch sites, and other meteorological applications (i.e., at universities and other scientific monitoring stations). Kevin had felt that this consolidation would position the company as a leader in what he anticipated to be a high-growth market with little competition.

Wind Technology's advantages over Unisys, the only other key player in the wind profiling market, included the following: (1) The company adhered strin-

Case contributed by Jakki Mohr, Assistant Professor of Marketing, University of Colorado, and Ken Manning, Doctoral Candidate, University of South Carolina. © 1990 by Jakki Mohr.

gently to specifications and quality production. (2) Wind Technology had the technical expertise to provide full system integration. This allowed customers to order either basic components or a full system including software support. (3) Wind Technology's staff of meteorologists and atmospheric scientists provided the customer with sophisticated support including operation and maintenance training and field assistance. (4) Finally, Wind Technology had devoted all of its resources to its wind profiling business. Kevin believed that the market would perceive this as an advantage over a large conglomerate like Unisys.

Wind Technology customized each product for individual customers as the need arose; the total system could cost a customer from $400,000 to $5 million. Various governmental entities such as the Department of Defense, NASA, and state universities had consistently accounted for about 90 percent of Wind Technology's sales. In lieu of a field sales force, Wind Technology relied on top management and a team of engineers to call on prospective and current customers. Approximately $105,000 of its annual salaries was charged to a direct selling expense.

THE PROBLEM

The consolidation strategy that the company had undertaken in 1986 was partly due to the company having been purchased by Vaitra, a high-technology European firm. Wind Technology's ability to focus on the wind profiling business had been made possible by Vaitra's financial support. However, since 1986 Wind Technology had shown little commercial success, and due to low sales levels the company was experiencing severe cash flow problems. Kevin knew that Wind Technology could not continue to meet payroll much longer. Also, he had been informed that Vaitra was not willing to continue to pour more money into Wind Technology. Kevin estimated that he had nine to twelve months (until the end of 1991) in which to implement a new strategy with the potential to improve the company's cash flow. The new strategy was necessary to enable Wind Technology to survive until the wind profiler market matured. Kevin and other industry experts anticipated that it would be two years until the wind profiling market achieved the high growth levels that the company had initially anticipated.

One survival strategy that Kevin had in mind was to spin off and market component parts used in making wind profilers. Initial research indicated that, of all the wind profiling system's component parts, the high-voltage power supply (HVPS) had the greatest potential for commercial success. Furthermore, Kevin's staff on the HVPS product had demonstrated knowledge of the market. Kevin felt that by marketing the HVPS, Wind Technology could reap incremental revenues with very little addition to fixed costs. (Variable costs would include the costs of making and marketing the HVPS. The accounting department had estimated that production costs would run approximately 70 percent of the selling price and that 10 percent of other expenses, such as top management direct selling expenses, should be charged to the HVPS.)

HIGH-VOLTAGE POWER SUPPLIES

For a vast number of consumer and industrial products that require electricity, the available voltage level must be transformed to different levels and types of output. The three primary types of power supplies are linears, switchers, and converters. Each type manipulates electrical current in terms of the type of current (AC or DC) and/or the level of output (voltage). Some HVPS manufacturers focus on producing a standardized line of power supplies, while others specialize in customizing power supplies to the user's specifications.

High-voltage power supplies vary significantly in size and level of output. Small power supplies with relatively low levels of output (under 3 kV*) are used in communications equipment. Medium-sized power supplies that produce an output between 3 kV and 10 kV are used in a wide range of products including radars and lasers. Power supplies that produce output greater than 10 kV are used in a variety of applications, such as high-powered X rays and plasma etching systems.

BACKGROUND ON WIND TECHNOLOGY'S HVPS

One of Wind Technology's corporate strategies was to control the critical technology (major component parts) of its wind profiling products. Management felt that this control was important since the company was part of a high-technology industry in which confidentiality and innovation were crucial to each competitor's success. This strategy also gave Wind Technology a differential advantage over its major competitors, all of whom depended on a variety of manufacturers for component parts. Wind Technology had successfully developed almost all of the major component parts and the software for the wind profiler, yet the development of the power supply had been problematic.

To adhere to the policy of controlling critical technology in product design (rather than purchasing an HVPS from an outside supplier), Wind Technology management had hired Anne Ladwig and her staff of HVPS technicians to develop a power supply for the company's wind profiling systems. Within six months of joining Wind Technology, Anne and her staff had completed development of a versatile power supply that could be adapted for use with a wide variety of equipment. Some of the company's wind profiling systems required up to ten power supplies, each modified slightly to carry out its role in the system.

* kV (kilovolt) = 1,000 volts.

Kevin Cage had delegated the responsibility of investigating the sales potential of the company's HVPS to Anne Ladwig since she was very familiar with the technical aspects of the product and had received formal business training while pursuing an MBA. Anne had determined that Wind Technology's HVPS could be modified to produce levels of output between 3 kV and 10 kV. Thus, it seemed natural that if the product was brought to market, Wind Technology should focus on applications in this range of output. Wind Technology did not have the production capabilities to compete in the high-volume, low-voltage segment of the market, nor did the company have the resources and technical expertise to compete in the high-output (10 kV +) segment.

◢ THE POTENTIAL CUSTOMER

Power supplies in the 3 kV to 10 kV range could be used to conduct research, to produce other products, or as a component in other products such as lasers. Thus, potential customers could include research labs, large end users, OEMs, or distributors. Research labs each used an average of three power supplies. Other types of customers ordered a widely varying quantity of power supplies.

HVPS users were demanding increasing levels of reliability, quality, customization, and system integration. *System integration* refers to the degree that other parts of a system are dependent on the HVPS for proper functioning and the extent to which these parts are combined into a single unit or piece of machinery.

Anne had considered entering several HVPS market segments in which Wind Technology could reasonably compete. She had estimated the domestic market potential of these segments at $237 million. To evaluate these segments, Anne had compiled growth forecasts for the year ahead and had evaluated each segment in terms of the anticipated level of customization and system integration demanded by the market. Anne felt that the level of synergy between Wind Technology and the various segments was also an important consideration in the selection of a target market. Exhibit 1 summarizes this information. Anne believed that if the product was produced, Wind Technology's interests would be best served by selecting only one target market on which to initially concentrate.

◢ COMPETITION

Anne had contacted five HVPS manufacturers in order to gather competitive information. She found that the manufacturers varied significantly in terms of size and marketing strategy (see Exhibit 2). Each listed a price in the $5,500 to $6,500 range on power supplies with the same features and output levels as the HVPS that had been developed for Wind Technology. After she spoke with these firms, Anne had the feeling that Wind Technology could offer the HVPS market

EXHIBIT 1   HVPS Market Segments in the 3 kV–10 kV Range

Application	Forecasted Annual Growth (%)	Level of Customization/ Level of System Integration*	Synergy Rating[†]	% of $237 Million Power Supply Market[‡]
General/university laboratory	5.40%	Medium/Medium	3	8%
Lasers	11.00%	Low/Medium	4	10%
Medical equipment	10.00%	Medium/Medium	3	5%
Microwave	12.00%	Medium/High	4	7%
Power modulators	3.00%	Low/Low	4	25%
Radar systems	11.70%	Low/Medium	5	12%
Semiconductor	10.10%	Low/Low	3	23%
X-ray systems	8.60%	Medium/High	3	10%

*The level of customization and system integration that is generally in demand within each of the applications is defined as low, medium, or high.

[†]Synergy ratings are based on a scale of 1 to 5; 1 is equivalent to a very low level of synergy and 5 is equivalent to a very high level of synergy. These subjective ratings are based on the amount of similarities between the wind profiling industry and each application.

[‡]Percentages total 100% of the $237 million market in which Wind Technology anticipated it could compete.

Note: This list of applications is not all-inclusive.

EXHIBIT 2   Competitor Profile (3 kV–10 kV Range)

Company	Gamma	Glassman	Kaiser	Maxwell*	Spellman
Approximate annual sales	$2 Million	$7.5 Million	$3 Million		$7 Million
Market share	1.00%	3.00%	1.50%		2.90%
Price[†]	$5,830	$5,590	$6,210	$5000–$6000	$6,360
Delivery	12 weeks	10 weeks	10 weeks	8 weeks	12 weeks
Product customization	No	Medium	Low	Medium	Low
System integration experience	Low	Low	Low	Medium	Low
Customer targets	General labs	Laser	Laser	Radar	Capacitors
	Space	Medical	Medical	Power Modulator	General labs
	University labs	X-ray	Microwave	X-ray	Microwave
			Semiconductor	Medical equipment	X-ray

* Maxwell was in the final stages of product development and stated that the product would be available in the spring. Maxwell anticipated that the product would sell in the $5000–$6000 range.

[†]Price quoted for an HVPS with the same specifications as the "standard" model developed by Wind Technology.

superior levels of quality, reliability, technical expertise, and customer support. She optimistically believed that a one-half percent market objective could be achieved the first year.

PROMOTION

If Wind Technology entered the HVPS market, it would require a hard-hitting, thorough promotional campaign to reach the selected target market. Three factors made the selection of elements in the promotion mix especially important to Wind Technology: (1) Wind Technology's poor cash flow, (2) the lack of a well-developed marketing department, and (3) the need to generate incremental revenue from sales of the HVPS at a minimum cost. In fact, a rule of thumb used by Wind Technology was that all marketing expenditures should be about 9 percent to 10 percent of sales. Kevin and Anne were contemplating the use of the following elements.

Collateral Material

Sales literature, brochures, and data sheets are necessary in communicating the product benefits and features to potential customers. These materials are designed to be mailed to customers as part of direct mail campaigns or in response to customer requests, given away at trade shows, and left behind after sales presentations.

Because no one in Wind Technology was an experienced copywriter, Anne and Kevin considered hiring a marketing communications agency to write the copy and to design the layout of the brochures. This agency would also complete the graphics (photographs and artwork) for the collateral material. The cost for 5,000 pieces (including the 10 percent markup for the agency) was estimated to be $5.50 each.

Public Relations

Kevin and Anne realized that one very cost-efficient tool of promotion is publicity. They contemplated sending out new product announcements to a variety of trade journals whose readers were part of Wind Technology's new target market. By using this tool, interested readers could call or write to Wind Technology and the company could then send the prospective customers collateral material. The drawback of relying too heavily on this element was very obvious to Kevin and Anne—the editors of the trade journals could choose not to print Wind Technology's product announcements if its new product was not deemed "newsworthy."

The cost of using this tool would include the time necessary to write the press release and the expense of mailing the release to the editors. Direct costs were estimated by Wind Technology to be $500.

Direct Mail

Kevin and Anne were also contemplating a direct mail campaign. The major expenditure for this option would be buying a list of prospects to whom the collateral material would be mailed. Such lists usually cost around $5,000, depending on the number of names and the list quality. Other costs would include postage and the materials mailed. These costs were estimated to be $7,500 for a mailing of 1,500.

Trade Shows

The electronics industry had several annual trade shows. Wind Technology, if it chose to exhibit at one of these trade shows, would incur the cost of a booth, the space at the show, and the travel and incidental costs of the people attending the show to staff the booth. Kevin and Anne estimated these costs at approximately $50,000 for the exhibit, space, and materials and $50,000 for a staff of five people to attend.

Trade Journal Advertising

Kevin and Anne also contemplated running a series of ads in trade journals. Several journals that they considered are listed in Exhibit 3, along with circulation, readership, and cost information for each.

EXHIBIT 3   Trade Publications

Trade Publication	Editorial	Cost per Color Insertion (1 Page)	Circulation
Electrical Manufacturing	For purchasers and users of power supplies, transformers, and other electrical products.	$4,077	35,168 nonpaid
Electronic Component News	For electronics OEMs. Products addressed include workstations, power sources, chips, etc.	$6,395	110,151 nonpaid
Electronic Manufacturing News	For OEMs providing manufacturing and contracting of components, circuits, and systems.	$5,075	25,000 nonpaid
Design News	For design OEMs covering components, systems, and materials.	$8,120	170,033 nonpaid
Weatherwise	For meteorologists covering imaging, radar, etc.	$1,040	10,186 paid

Note: This is a partial list of applicable trade publications. Standard Rate and Data Service lists other possible publications.

Personal Selling

Telemarketing (Inbound/Inside Sales) * Kevin and Anne also considered hiring a technical salesperson to respond to HVPS product inquiries generated by product announcements, direct mail, and advertising. This person's responsibilities would include answering phone calls, prospecting, sending out collateral material, and following up with potential customers. The salary and benefits for one individual would be about $50,000.

Field Sales The closing of sales for the HVPS might require some personal selling at the customer's location, especially if Wind Technology pursued the customized option. Kevin and Anne realized that this tool would potentially provide them with the most incremental revenue, but it also had the potential to be the most costly. Issues such as how many salespeople to hire, where to position them in the field (geographically), etc., were major concerns. Salary plus expenses and benefits for an outside salesperson were estimated to be about $80,000.

DECISIONS

As Kevin sat in his office and perused the various facts and figures available to him, he knew that he would have to make some decisions quickly. He sensed that the decision about whether to proceed with the HVPS spin-off was risky, but he also felt that to do nothing to improve the cash flow situation of the firm was equally risky. Kevin also knew that, if he decided to proceed with the HVPS, there were a number of segments in that market in which Wind Technology could position its HVPS. He mulled over which segment appeared to be a good fit for Wind Technology's abilities (given Anne's recommendation that a choice of one segment would be best). Finally, Kevin was concerned that if they entered the HVPS market, promotion for their product would be costly, further exacerbating the cash flow situation. He knew that promotion would be necessary, but the exact mix of elements would have to be designed with financial constraints in mind.

DISCUSSION QUESTIONS

1. Should Wind Technology compete in the HVPS market?
2. Which segments should the company target?

How should the company and its product be positioned?
3. What promotion strategy should be pursued?

---

* "Inbound" refers to calls that potential customers make to Wind Technology, rather than "outbound," in which Wind Technology calls potential customers (i.e., solicits sales).

Geodesic Domes, Inc.

··

Developing an Advertising Strategy

BACKGROUND

Geodesic Domes, Inc., is a major producer of wooden domed homes in the western part of the United States. The company is headquartered in Spokane, Washington, and has been one of the leaders in fostering the domed concept in the residential market. Started in the 1960s, Geodesic Domes, Inc., has designed and built thousands of homes in the U.S. and around the world. Domed houses have proven popular to many homeowners for a number of reasons. A domed home is 30 percent to 50 percent less costly to heat or cool than is a conventional rectangular home of comparable size. The dome concept provides both simplicity and strength, and domed houses can be constructed more quickly than conventional homes can be built. Geodesic Domes, Inc., has been successful in the production of such homes, and management plans to continue to concentrate in the household market.

By August 1988, the company has realized considerable success in the residential market, although top management is concerned about having such a narrow focus. In recent top-level meetings, company president Todd Wathan has stressed the importance of seeking out new markets in which the company can make use of its dome construction technology. One problem, however, is that Geodesic Domes, Inc., has focused almost entirely on the residential building market. Its contacts with architects, contractors, and so on are almost all in residential construction. Any move into new markets may involve considerable research before decisions can be made. Wathan wants to diversify, but he does not want to see the company extend into markets that it does not understand or in which it cannot compete effectively. Thus, Wathan directs vice president of marketing Dick Heath to research other potential markets for domed construction applications. Heath is told to conduct whatever research is needed and to report to Wathan in about a month with his findings and possible recommendations.

THE DOMED CONSTRUCTION CONCEPT

Domed construction is not new in the United States. Many examples exist, perhaps most notably the Astrodome in Houston, Texas, and the Silverdome in Pontiac, Michigan. These examples are of very large domed buildings, but domes of all sizes can be found across the country. In fact, the first domes were relatively small vacation and retirement homes.

The geodesic dome concept is generally attributed to the genius of Buckminster Fuller, who in the 1920s realized that the triangle was the strongest and simplest geometric shape in nature. The geodesic dome was the result of his research. The triangle is the basic element in geodesic construction. A domed building has no load-bearing interior walls, as triangular panels set into a spherical shape are self-supporting. Exhibit 1 illustrates a basic, one-quarter sphere, low-profile dome roof. As can be seen, the building is composed of forty-five triangular panels in a spherical configuration. Triangles placed in this manner are self-supporting, leaving the entire inside of the building free from posts, supports, walls, and so forth.

EXHIBIT 1   One-Quarter Sphere, Low-Profile Dome Roof

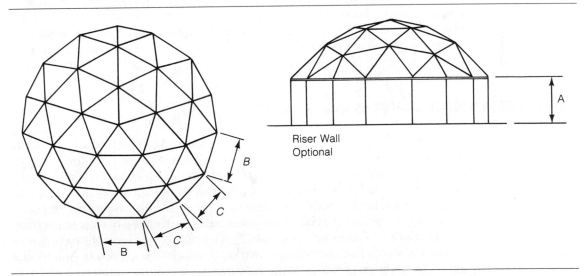

Riser Wall
Optional

THE INITIAL INVESTIGATION

Dick Heath realizes that Wathan's concerns are legitimate and that focusing only on the residential market has obvious shortcomings. At the same time, he also knows that Geodesic Domes, Inc., is virtually unknown outside the residential market. In addition, the company lacks personnel who are knowledgeable in other possible markets. He finds himself in a quandary: He feels he must make recommendations to Wathan in a relatively short period of time, and yet he lacks insight into other potential markets. He reads through a number of architectural journals and finds that geodesic systems have many applications. For example, he finds that domes have been used at times for fire stations, airplane hangars, medical offices, restaurants, banks, exhibition halls, schools, churches, warehouses, and gymnasiums. To Heath, it becomes clear that the company has been overlooking commercial applications for the dome concept.

Although realizing that the geodesic dome has many possible markets, Heath is apprehensive about recommending a move into sophisticated commercial applications. He reasons that the company has a better chance of success if it limits expansion into simpler applications. If it can do that, it can later expand into more esoteric uses for the dome. Heath also feels that the initial expansion should be made in a geographically concentrated area, so that better control can be exerted. In short, he knows he has to make some recommendation for expansion, but he wishes that expansion to be of a conservative nature. His initial research leads him to believe that warehouse construction provides the simplest application of the geodesic system. Few frills are required, and the company's expertise in dome construction can easily be adapted to this type of building. Thus, Heath wants to focus initially on the potential in the warehouse construction market. In addition, he decides that southern California offers the greatest potential in the western part of the United States for a controlled market approach. Specifically, he wishes to concentrate efforts in the heavily populated southern California counties of Los Angeles, Orange, Riverside, and San Diego.

THE WAREHOUSE MARKET IS INVESTIGATED

Ann Tanaka is a market analyst in Heath's marketing department at Geodesic Domes, Inc. She is generally the one who is requested to collect information or conduct research efforts when such are required. Heath believes Ann to be the best researcher in his department, and he decides to assign her to investigate the warehouse market in southern California. Specifically, he assigns her responsibility for (1) assessing the size of the warehouse construction market in the four-county southern California area and (2) determining the decision-making process in the warehouse construction market. Basically, Heath wants Ann to find out if the market is of sufficient size to warrant the company's interests and then to develop an understanding of what Geodesic Domes, Inc., might face if it entered that market. Ann Tanaka is asked to report back as soon as she has substantive information.

POTENTIAL OF THE WAREHOUSE MARKET

Ann Tanaka begins her research by investigating construction industry sources in a major university library. First, she finds that warehouse construction figures are not reported in a single category. Warehouse construction is included in the category "Other Commercial Construction." Also included in this category are grain elevators, shopping centers, parking garages, banks, fast-food restaurants, and gas stations. She discovers, however, that about one-quarter of all construction in this category is attributable to warehouses; about one-half is accounted for by shopping centers. Exhibit 2 shows "Other Commercial Construction" figures for the United States over a ten-year period. Since one-quarter of the category relates to warehouses, Tanaka concludes that the market is both large and growing.

Further library research shows that warehouse construction is on the rise. Inventory levels are increasing because of (1) growing retail sales, (2) slightly lower interest rates, (3) increasing imports, and (4) larger stocks of agricultural products. Warehouse users across the United States are expanding their demand, leading to continued interest by investors. However, Tanaka also learns that long-term demand for warehouses may be tempered by the increased use of computerized inventory control systems. Although these trends are national in scope, Tanaka reasons that they also probably apply to the southern California area. All evidence indicates that the warehouse market is a viable one for Geodesic Domes, Inc.

Exhibit 3 shows the results of Ann's research regarding construction in the

EXHIBIT 2	Value of "Other Commercial Construction" Put in Place in the United States Between 1977 and 1987

Year	$ Billions*
1977	$15.1
1982	14.2
1983	14.5
1984	20.4
1985	25.2
1986	25.2
1987	24.7

Note: * In 1982 dollars.

Source: "Construction Outlook for 1987," *Construction Review* 32 (November–December, 1986): 2.

EXHIBIT 3   Total Private Construction Authorized by Building Permit for Southern California for 1986 ($ millions)

Type	Anaheim, Santa Ana (PMSA)	Los Angeles, Long Beach (PMSA)	Riverside, San Bernardino (PMSA)	San Diego (MSA)
Industrial buildings	$178.7	$543.5	$260.3	$103.2
Other nonresidential buildings	78.7	222.6	45.2	42.1

Note: MSA = selected metropolitan statistical area; PMSA = primary metropolitan statistical area.
Source: Construction Review 33 (March–April 1987):47–52.

four-county southern California area. She assumes that the "Other Nonresidential Construction" category is the same as "Other Commercial Construction" and concludes that about one-quarter of the latter category applies to warehouses. Thus, her research shows that warehouse construction in the four-county area was approximately $58 million in 1986.

Reporting back to Dick Heath, Ann Tanaka shows him the results of her research. Both agree that the figures support Heath's idea of focusing on warehouse construction in the four-county southern California market area. Heath thanks Ann Tanaka for her materials and instructs her to investigate the decision-making process in the warehouse construction market.

THE DECISION-MAKING PROCESS IN WAREHOUSE CONSTRUCTION

Ann Tanaka meets with a number of contractors she knows to determine how warehouse construction takes place and who is likely to be involved. Through these conversations, she is able to piece together a reasonable understanding of the typical process.

Usually, many contractors are involved. There is always a general contractor, who is the overall supervisor and who generally selects subcontractors. Typical subcontractors include (1) a cement contractor, who pours the pad on which the building sets; (2) a plumbing contractor; (3) an electrical contractor; (4) a masonry contractor if block walls are involved; (5) carpenters; (6) a roofing contractor; (7) an insulation contractor; (8) an HVAC (heating, venting, and air conditioning) contractor; (9) a drywall or plastering contractor; and (10) a sprinkler system contractor. Even the simple application of warehouse construction may involve a number of contractors. However, Tanaka learns that although many subcontractors may be involved, it is the general contractor who is the most important from a marketing perspective.

The general contractor usually is not involved in the early stages. More typically, an owner decides he or she needs a warehouse and determines any general requirements. At this point, the owner usually contacts a commercial architect. The architect may then hire an engineer to help determine the specifications based on the owner's needs. The architect generally takes the project through the planning and permit stages. When the architect has determined the specifications, the project may be put out to bid, at which time general contractors submit their bids. The decision as to which general contractor to select is made by the architect, although in some cases the owner may well be involved.

Others may also be involved. County or city planning boards often must be consulted for their approval. Building inspectors are involved in all stages of construction. In many municipalities, the fire department must approve the sprinkler systems of commercial buildings. In addition, some industrial parks have their own planning commissions that may rule on style of construction to ensure uniformity throughout such parks.

Ann Tanaka's research thus indicates that a number of buying influences are involved in warehouse construction. Although the process is quite different from that found in residential construction, she does not feel it to be a prohibitive factor that should discourage Geodesic Domes, Inc., from seriously considering the warehouse market. She expresses this opinion to Heath.

PROS AND CONS OF THE DOMED CONCEPT IN WAREHOUSES

Armed with Tanaka's information, Heath proceeds to put together the analysis and recommendation he wants to make to Todd Wathan. Although he agrees with Tanaka that the warehouse construction market appears to be a likely candidate, he still wishes to build a case to show that the domed concept will be acceptable in this market. Without such evidence, Heath does not believe he can assess the true potential of the new market.

Heath concludes that a geodesic warehouse can have a number of advantages over more conventional rectangular warehouses. These advantages are (1) no interior posts or supports, leaving more room to store inventory; (2) shorter construction time, as a dome exterior can be put up in two days—saving owners both time and money; (3) a dome warehouse can be cheaper to heat and cool; (4) a dome warehouse costs about $6.00 less per square foot to build than a conventional warehouse; (5) a dome warehouse uses about 40 percent to 50 percent less lumber in the roof than a conventional warehouse; (6) since the dome design is standard, the owner can save on architectural and engineering fees; and (7) a dome warehouse can be aesthetically attractive if correctly constructed and landscaped—thus bringing more recognition to the building. In summary, Heath believes a dome warehouse can be cheaper for a warehouse owner to build because of reduced costs of labor, materials, and financing. In addition, Heath discovers that there are only about five major dome producers in the country, and that none are currently concentrating on warehouse construction.

At the same time, Heath recognizes that some distinct disadvantages must be overcome. These are (1) if there are height restrictions involved, the dome concept may not permit warehouses of larger size—height limits of thirty-two feet are common, and over that variances must be obtained; (2) extremely large warehouses cannot be made of wood but must use aluminum, and these domes are about five times more expensive to build than those made of wood; (3) a dome warehouse can be an inefficient use of some lots—placing a round warehouse on a square lot can waste valuable land; (4) the somewhat revolutionary design may discourage the number of general contractors willing to bid and thus increase price; (5) domed warehouses may not be permitted by codes and restrictions in some areas; (6) some owners may view domes as not conveying the proper image for warehouses; and (7) the spherical interior of a domed warehouse may not be appropriate for inventory storage of some materials—square or rectangular containers fit better in a conventional warehouse. With reflection, it is obvious to Heath that some real disadvantages do exist.

A DECISION IS MADE

At this point, Dick Heath feels he is ready to meet with Todd Wathan. Based on the market information provided by Ann Tanaka and his own assessments, he feels the company should attempt to penetrate the warehouse market in the southern California area. Although somewhat apprehensive, he believes this approach to diversification is the safest and yet still offers considerable promise. He schedules a meeting with Wathan and presents his findings and recommendations. Wathan is impressed by the detail of Heath's presentation, and he basically agrees with Heath's recommendations. At this point, the decision is made to enter the warehouse market on the limited basis outlined by Heath. Since Geodesic Domes, Inc., is not well known in the commercial construction market, Wathan and Heath agree that the first step is to create awareness of the firm in the warehouse construction market. Until this task is accomplished, very little can take place. As vice president of marketing, Dick Heath is given the responsibility for developing an advertising strategy to favorably position Geodesic Domes, Inc., as a provider of warehouse construction in the southern California market.

Assist Dick Heath in the development of an appropriate and effective advertising strategy.

DISCUSSION QUESTIONS

1. Who do you see as the key buying influences in the warehouse construction market? What factors do you believe each of the key buying influences will be looking for in an ad?
2. What advertising objectives do you recommend to Heath before actual advertising strategy is developed?
3. What specific media recommendations do you make to Heath to reach those key buying influ-

ences involved? Justify your selection of specific media chosen.
4. Develop an actual print advertisement that you think can be used by Geodesic Domes, Inc., to create awareness of the firm as a reputable supplier of warehouses. Make sure your ad positions the domed concept as a viable substitution for conventional warehouses.

Veber Chemical Corporation

....

Pricing to Discourage Competition

COMPANY HISTORY

The Veber Corporation is a small, privately held chemical company located on Long Island, New York. Veber was founded in 1939 by Heinrich Veber, who started up a company to manufacture polyvinyl compounds for the manufacture of phonograph records. The company had grown over the years by diversifying into other chemical resins and no longer manufactured vinyl compounds or vinyl resins.

In 1963, Veber Chemical Corporation was sold to a much larger chemical company, Booker Chemical Company. Mr. Veber retired a year later and in that same year, Booker Chemical was acquired by one of the world's largest chemical companies, AmChem. Since Booker was so preoccupied with its integration into the AmChem organization, Veber was really not of much interest to Booker management. Veber was run as a separate Booker division within the huge AmChem umbrella and remained fairly autonomous.

Veber management became frustrated dealing with the Booker and AmChem bureaucracy and their lack of interest in the Veber business. Booker and AmChem treated Veber as a cash cow, or perhaps a cash calf, for at $45 million a year in sales in 1988 it was considered an insignificant part of the AmChem and Booker portfolios. It was considered nearly impossible for Veber to get funding from Booker or AmChem for capital improvements or for research and development on new products.

In 1988, Booker put Veber up for sale. Veber's management team at this time consisted of four individuals: Joe O'Malley, General Manager; Tony De-

Case contributed by Linda Rochford, Assistant Professor of Marketing, San Diego State University.

Dominici, Manufacturing Manager; Tony Zoratti, Marketing Manager; and Lou Forelli, the R & D Manager. Recognizing that a potential acquisition could mean dramatic change, the management began to investigate the companies that had expressed an interest in buying the company. The team came to the conclusion that acquisition by another large chemical company would not correct many of the problems that Veber was experiencing as a part of Booker and AmChem. Veber management decided to go to AmChem with an offer to buy the business.

By late 1989, the Veber management team succeeded in purchasing Veber in a leveraged buyout. The four principals had equal shares in the business and all had assumed significant personal financial risk as a result of the purchase. O'Malley became president while each of the others became vice president of his respective functional area. After almost twenty-six years, Veber was an independent company once again.

The buyout meant some pressure for the firm from a financial standpoint but it had given the organization much more flexibility in pursuing opportunities. Booker and AmChem had considered Veber's markets small and had not been committed to developing the business. Veber's management now felt that they had the control to develop the company to its full potential.

VEBER'S PRODUCTS

Veber had two main product lines. Veber manufactured polyester resins and urethane coatings. Veber polyesters were used primarily by customers for such applications as polyurethane coatings, elastomers, fiber (spandex fibers), and flexible and rigid foam. Veber also used its own polyester resins to produce its "Veber-a-thane" specialty urethane coatings. In this respect, Veber competed with some potential polyester customers that might use polyester to produce their own urethane coatings. The bulk of Veber's business, more than 80 percent of sales, was in polyesters.

Veber was considered a consistent, high-quality, and reliable manufacturer by customers and competitors. Veber had one manufacturing plant, located at the same site as the corporate offices and labs. The manufacturing facility, by industry standards, was considered small-scale. This meant that it was difficult for Veber to compete on price for large-volume business since it might take Veber two or three batches over several days to produce what could be manufactured by a larger supplier with a single large "kettle." On the other hand, Veber could be competitive when it came to specialty business that involved smaller volumes. Larger manufacturers often did not have the smaller kettles to efficiently meet these needs, and would have to manufacture the product from a lab or pilot plant facility at a substantial cost.

Most of Veber's specialty business was not particularly price-sensitive. Quality and batch-to-batch consistency were critical. Veber's product quality and consistency were considered excellent by its customers. Veber could often produce to tighter product specifications than any of its competitors. In fact, Veber was often the sole-source supplier for many applications requiring extremely tight product specifications because other manufacturers could not consistently meet customer specifications.

VEBER SALES AND MARKETING ORGANIZATION

Inside sales support consisted of Bertha Gordon, who followed up with established customers on shipping dates and requirements. Bertha also called for reorders, handled sample requests, and maintained close relationships with customers. Bertha had been with Veber for almost twenty years, having worked her way up from file clerk to one of Veber's best marketing assets. Bertha was known to have sent two dozen New York bagels to a customer in the southeast and an extra dozen for the truck driver. She would send Halloween treats to a purchasing agent's children. In short, she genuinely cared about the customers, both as business for Veber and as individuals. She was a unique company resource.

While Veber's customer service and manufacturing control were a plus, the sales group had been decimated. Two salespeople left the company when the buyout was announced, leaving Zoratti, the vice president of marketing and co-owner, and one veteran salesperson, Bob Sheeley, to cover the market. It later became apparent that the two former salespeople had been doctoring their call reports and many Veber customers had not seen a salesperson for as long as two and a half years. The damage to Veber in the marketplace had been minimized somewhat through Bertha's inside sales and service efforts but many customers still felt neglected.

Tony Zoratti hired two experienced salespeople shortly after the buyout in 1989. Kirsten Andersen was hired to cover the midwest territory and Don Compton was hired to cover the northeast. Sheeley covered the southeast and south. A small two-person rep company covered the west coast. Most of Veber's customers were located on the east coast. The geographic concentration of customers meant that Compton had the smallest geographic territory while Andersen had the largest.

Each salesperson was responsible for calling on accounts within his or her territory. If an account had locations outside a given salesperson's territory, it would be called on by the salesperson responsible for that area. However, credit for sales went to the salesperson calling on the headquarters of a given account. The territories were fairly well balanced with comparable numbers of headquarters accounts for each salesperson. For example, Bob was credited with sales from headquarters accounts in his territory and Kirsten called on Bob's accounts that had manufacturing facilities in her territory. Kirsten received credit for sales from headquarters accounts in her territory and Bob would call on the manufacturing facilities in his territory. This reciprocal arrangement meant that there was an incentive for all of the salespeople to cooperate and support one another. Occasionally, the headquarters salesperson would accompany the plant salesperson to the manufacturing facility to keep up to date and to facilitate communication.

RESEARCH AND DEVELOPMENT TEAM

Veber did not have the resources to support a significant research and development department. There were two technical group leaders, John McLaughlin, Group Leader for polyester research and development, and Ross Phillips, Group Leader for urethane coating research and development. Both John and Ross reported to Lou Forelli, vice president of R & D and one of the co-owners. Three additional chemists and two technicians worked for the R & D group, the majority in the polyester group.

The emphasis in the R & D department had been more on development than on research. This was partly due to historical neglect and lack of funding for Veber's research efforts by Booker and AmChem. It was also partially a reflection of Lou Forelli's personality. Lou loved to meet with customers and was always eager to get the technical people going on tailoring special products for a particular customer's needs. Usually these products just involved "tweaking" existing products. Unfortunately, it also meant that there were literally hundreds of Veber products, many only marginally different in chemical composition or performance. Tony Zoratti, often frustrated by R & D's proliferation of the product line, would jokingly refer to Lou Forelli as the "best salesperson in the company. He'll make anything for anyone."

THE URETHANE MARKET

Most of Veber's urethane business was with small-volume urethane coatings users in the northeast. Approximately 20 percent of Veber's sales came from its urethane business.

Veber-a-thane coatings were primarily low-solids, solvent-based materials. The Environmental Protection Agency (EPA) and Occupational Safety and Health Administration (OSHA) had been and were continuing to place restrictions on coatings users so that they would use high-solids or water-based coatings to reduce environmental impact. Veber did not have an extensive product line of coatings to address these market needs. For this reason, Zoratti did not consider urethane coatings to be a growth market for Veber. He also felt it was not worthwhile to develop the technology for such coatings because of the potential for competition with some very good polyester customers. In addition, the Veber-a-thane products generated only modest, stable volumes and profit margins.

The exception was urethane latices. Urethane latices were produced from a polymerization emulsion technology and, as a water-based system, did not suffer from the same environmental problems as the other Veber-a-thane coatings. Under Booker, Veber had undertaken a modest development effort to manufacture urethane latices. However, because of Booker's general unwillingness to invest in Veber, Booker required Veber to price their latex products to recover all investment in the project within three years.

THE MARKET FOR VEBER-A-THANE LATICES

The largest known market for the Veber latex product line, and the primary objective of the original project, had been the fiberglass market. There were four domestic manufacturers of fiberglass in the United States. Urethane latex was a crucial material in the manufacture of fiberglass. The latex was used to coat the drawn glass to increase its strength and resilience. These characteristics were particularly important in reinforced fiberglass applications such as automotive body panels. Furthermore, latex was the highest-priced raw material used in the manufacture of fiberglass.

All fiberglass manufacturers were very concerned about the quality, consistency, and price of latex. Because many of the fiberglass manufacturers' customers used fiberglass in automotive or other high-impact or critical applications, any change in raw materials, suppliers, or specifications necessitated notification, testing, evaluation, and requalification to assure the consistency of the fiberglass customer's product. This meant that in addition to evaluation by the fiberglass manufacturer the fiberglass customers often had to incur substantial and significant expense and time requalifying their reinforced fiberglass products. In some automotive applications, for example, the testing and evaluation can cost as much as $100,000 per product to conduct smoke and burn, impact, aging, and stress tests, among others, and take up to six months.

Because there were so few customers, and the total market was currently no more than 5 million pounds per year, Zoratti felt that Veber had to have at least two of the customers in the market to make it in the business. In 1990, Veber had the two largest fiberglass manufacturers in the market, TRG and American FiberGlass, and was aggressively pursuing the other two manufacturers who were evaluating various samples of Veber-a-thane latices.

THE CUSTOMERS

TRG Corporation. TRG Corporation was a large multinational corporation with multiple industrial and chemical operations. The headquarters and research facilities were located in St. Louis. While the company had manufacturing facilities throughout the United States and globally, there were two plants (one located in Texas and one in North Carolina) that were being served by Veber.

Veber started selling urethane latex to TRG approximately three years prior to the management buyout. TRG was the first Veber customer for latex and the largest manufacturer of fiberglass in the United States. In addition to manufacturing fiberglass and glass products, TRG was a well-diversified chemical company with separate divisions manufacturing paint, coatings, and raw materials to supply various divisions within the company. Kirsten called on the headquarters and research facilities in St Louis while Bob called on the manufacturing plants in Texas and North Carolina.

The North Carolina plant was currently buying 40,000 to 50,000 pounds of Veber-a-thane 710 per month in bulk. It was expected that this volume would grow to at least 80,000 pounds per month. The Texas plant was not currently buying but was thought to have a potential of about half that of the North Carolina facility.

American FiberGlass. American was headquartered in a suburb of Detroit with research and development located west of Detroit in Ann Arbor, Michigan. American was not as large as TRG in the fiberglass market nor was it as diversified and large in absolute terms as TRG. American's business was primarily fiberglass. American's manufacturing facility was located in South Carolina.

American was currently buying about 40,000 pounds of Veber-a-thane 720 per month in bulk. American was expected to purchase at least 60,000 pounds per month. Veber-a-thane 730 was being evaluated for possible use in new fiberglass applications with no current estimates of potential volume available at present.

PRICING

As a result of Booker's payback requirement, Veber-a-thane latex products were a fairly expensive component in the manufacture of fiberglass. Exhibit 1 lists the prices for the products purchased by American and TRG. Kirsten Andersen, primarily responsible for latex sales due to the fact that all customers were headquartered in her territory, had the highest profit accounts within Veber. While most of Veber's products had gross profit margins of about 30 percent, latex gross profit margins were more than 60 percent. Exhibit 2 lists the costs for producing and marketing the Veber-a-thane latex products.

EXHIBIT 1   **Veber-a-thane Price List**

	0–29 Drums	30–59 Drums	60+ Drums	Bulk
Veber-a-thane 710	$3.50	$3.45	$3.40	$3.30
Veber-a-thane 720	$3.50	$3.45	$3.40	$3.30
Veber-a-thane 730	$3.55	$3.50	$3.45	$3.35

All prices per pound. One drum approximately equal to 500 pounds. All prices FOB Hempstead, NY.

EXHIBIT 2	**Veber-a-thane Costs at Current Volumes**
Raw material costs	$1.15/lb.
Manufacturing costs	$ .10/lb.
Marketing costs	$ .20/lb.
Overhead costs	$ .10/lb.
Total costs	$1.55/lb.

Raw material costs for 710 and 720 are identical. 730 material costs are 4 cents per pound higher.

Raw material costs do not reflect potential economies for larger volumes.

COMPETITION

Veber's primary competitor in both the polyester and urethane coatings product lines was Sysco Chemical Corporation. Sysco was based in the Chicago area and was easily five to ten times as large as Veber in terms of sales. Sysco was just getting started in the fiberglass market and had begun sampling fiberglass customers with their urethane latices. Sysco was a well-established polyester and urethane manufacturer, but was just beginning to market urethane latices to the fiberglass market. Sysco pricing reflected this fact. Prices for Sysco products were roughly 5 cents per pound less than comparable Veber products (with the exception of bulk prices) to give it additional leverage in entering the market (see Exhibit 3).

The U.S. subsidiaries of several European chemical companies also had the potential to serve the market but it seemed unlikely that they would do so considering the market size and the inability of the small number of domestic customers to support several suppliers. Hence, Veber was faced with only one direct competitor in the market.

At least one of the fiberglass manufacturers had been "burned" in the past by having a single source of supply for latex. Prior to Veber's entry into the market, there had been only one, German-owned, supplier of latex for this market. When ASF ChemWerk decided to exit the market shortly after Veber introduced its first latex, at least one major fiberglass manufacturer was unprepared to switch its process over to a new latex supplier. A three-year supply of latex was purchased from ASF ChemWerk to tide the company over the transition period. However, the fiberglass manufacturer purchasing agent failed to consider that the latex shelf-life was no more than eighteen months, resulting in hundreds of thousands of pounds of unusable ASF latex as well as the necessity to quickly qualify a new supplier.

Perhaps a more serious threat to Veber's market than Sysco or the European chemical companies was that Veber's fiberglass customers, especially TRG, could attempt to manufacture the latex themselves. TRG's manufacturing costs would most likely be very close to Veber's costs in the long run, but perhaps higher than Veber initially. The volumes involved were much smaller than what

EXHIBIT 3   Sysco Price List

	0–29 Drums	30–59 Drums	60+ Drums	Bulk
Syscothane L1011	$3.45	$3.40	$3.35	$3.30
Syscothane L1012	$3.45	$3.40	$3.35	$3.30

All prices per pound. All prices FOB Chicago, IL.

Syscothane L1011 comparable to Veber-a-thane 710.

Syscothane L1012 comparable to Veber-a-thane 720. Sysco has no comparable product to Veber-a-thane 730.

was considered economic quantities for the TRG coatings and resins division. Initially, TRG would probably have to produce in a pilot plant facility at much higher manufacturing costs. Of course, TRG could decide to purchase and install a small-scale kettle. This would probably cost at least $110,000 but would reduce manufacturing costs close to those for Veber. Overhead costs would be substantially higher, possibly as much as twice to three times as high as Veber. Although marketing costs would be zero, there would be a transfer cost added to provide a profit for the coatings and resins division to produce the latex for the fiberglass division.

STRATEGY FOR THE LATEX MARKET

In September, the marketing manager, Tony Zoratti, called Kirsten Andersen into his office to discuss the urethane market for fiberglass. The following conversation ensued.

Tony: "I'm very concerned about the urethane fiberglass business. As you know, Kirsten, your accounts in this market are the highest profit margin business in the company. It's good business and we need to keep it going. I feel we are in danger of losing TRG, one of our key accounts, and the largest urethane fiberglass account in the country."

Kirsten: "I know that the TRG technical people in the lab have been evaluating the Sysco product but that product doesn't seem to offer any advantage compared with our product. The Sysco product is experimental and hasn't been produced in quantity yet, as far as I know."

Tony: "I don't think we want to give TRG an excuse to evaluate the Sysco product any further. TRG could analyze our latex, if they haven't already, and easily manufacture it themselves. I think we should cut the price on our Veber-a-thane latices for fiberglass applications."

Kirsten: "Tony, I haven't heard anything about a TRG product developed internally. Where are you getting this information?"

Tony: "From my discussions with Bob I get the impression that TRG's manufacturing people are under a lot of pressure to reduce consumption and waste of our material. I have an uneasy feeling about TRG. I've been in this business for a long time and sometimes you just get a 'feeling' that you need to act on something."

Kirsten: "If we drop the price, how are we going to explain this to TRG and our other customers? Won't TRG suspect that we've been price gouging if the price is dropped dramatically? Worse yet, what if lowering the price doesn't deter TRG and our other customers from evaluating competitive products?"

Tony: "I'm afraid that if we don't take some action now to solidify our position with TRG and our other customers, we will lose share. We can't afford to serve this market without having TRG. There are too few customers. We can't afford to lose any of them."

DISCUSSION QUESTIONS

1. Should Veber drop its price of urethane latex to TRG? If not, why not? If so, what price should be charged?
2. If prices are dropped for TRG, how will this affect pricing to all other customers?
3. If you were a marketing manager at Sysco, what sort of response would you recommend if Veber decides to leave prices at current levels? What would your recommendation be if Veber decides to lower its price?
4. Assume that Veber decides to lower its prices. Put yourself in the place of Kirsten Andersen and outline your sales presentation plan for approaching TRG to announce the lower prices.

Superior Equipment Company

Preparing a Bid Price

As industrial equipment sales manager for Superior Equipment Company of Charlotte, North Carolina, Al Hardy is responsible for the sales of a broad line of industrial materials handling equipment in North and South Carolina. Superior Equipment is a franchised dealer for lines of forklift trucks, front-end loaders, motorized carts, and other self-propelled equipment. In addition to equipment sales, Superior also provides repair parts and service for industrial equipment. Approximately 40 percent of Al's sales volume comes from the sale of the Superlift line of forklift trucks, which are used in the textile, furniture manufacturing, wholesale and retail trade, and in building materials industries.

MEETING WITH THE FIELD SALESPERSON

On January 3, 1988, Al Hardy meets with Gus Jennings, the Superior Equipment salesman for western North Carolina, to discuss sales plans for the first quarter. During the conversation, Gus reveals that he has been working hard on a potentially lucrative new account in the furniture industry in his territory. He mentions that Al should be receiving a bid request from them in the next few days.

The new firm is Eon Furniture of Morganton, North Carolina, a manufacturer of mid-priced modern and traditional case goods and upholstered furniture. The firm was formed by several former executives of Drexton Furniture of Hickory, North Carolina. In fact, Eon's new purchasing agent, Joe Balognetta, was the purchasing agent at Drexton. Eon Furniture is completing

Case contributed by Ronald H. King and W. E. Patton III, Professors of Marketing, Appalachian State University.

construction of a new plant in Morganton, and it expects to begin limited manufacturing operations by late spring. Eon would need at least four forklift trucks by the end of March, and it could be expected to buy at least twenty forklift trucks by the end of the summer.

Gus mentions that he sold quite a bit of equipment to Drexton Furniture when Joe Balognetta was purchasing agent there. Gus also tells Al that when he visited with Joe at Eon just before Christmas, Joe told him that he hoped to continue the good relationship with Superior now that he was with Eon. At that time, Gus and Joe discussed Eon's needs, and Gus said that he felt that Superior's equipment could closely match what Eon would be requiring. Joe Balognetta had given Gus his assurance that Superior would be asked to bid on the equipment, and he also indicated that he would be getting bids only from Superior and two of Superior's major competitors, Excell Industrial Distributors of Asheville, North Carolina, and Star, Inc., of Greensboro, North Carolina.

Gus closes the meeting with Al by acknowledging that pricing in such bid situations is the sales manager's responsibility, but he makes a strong plea for Al to "get his pencil sharp" and submit a very competitive price when responding to Eon's upcoming bid request. Gus also points out that although Joe Balognetta is a very price-conscious buyer, he is a very loyal one. If Superior wants to have a chance at future Eon business, it is critical to get a foot in the door on this initial bid. Al responds that he will take Gus's comments into consideration when formulating the bid and that he will keep Gus posted as matters develop.

THE BID REQUEST IS RECEIVED

On January 10, Al Hardy receives the bid request from Eon Furniture (Exhibit 1) and begins the job of formulating the bid. After reading the specifications in the bid request, Al's immediate reaction is that either of two Superior models (the Superlift 950 or the Superlift 1100) may fit Eon's requirements, but he still must study the specifications in detail to be sure. He also needs to know which of the competition's models may match the specifications.

From past experience, Al knows that Excell's Hightopper I and Hightopper II models as well as Star's Liftstar GT and XL models are the closest fit to the specifications. Al then asks the office manager to prepare (1) a detailed listing of standard and optional equipment available on these competitors' models and (2) a summary of the last twenty bids and their results for situations in which Superior had bid similarly equipped Superlift 950s and 1100s to the furniture industry in North Carolina. The resulting equipment specification comparison is shown in Exhibit 2 and the bid history is shown in Exhibit 3.

After reviewing the equipment specification comparison, Al Hardy realizes that he can meet Eon's specifications by adding some optional equipment to his Superlift 1100. He can also come close to meeting the specs with an option-loaded Superlift 950. Al carefully compares the competitors' specifications to see

EXHIBIT 1	Bid Request from Eon Furniture

Eon Furniture
70 Hwy 70 E
Morganton, North Carolina 28655

January 7, 1988

Superior Equipment Company
116 Trade Street
Charlotte, North Carolina

Gentlemen:

Please quote us a firm price, delivery, and terms for the following equipment:

    4 each   1988 model electric forklift trucks

        Specifications:
          20-hp motor
          1,000-lb. minimum lift-load capacity
          8-ft. lift height
          Adjustable 3-ft. forks
          Solid rubber tires
          Power steering
          Full-width, foam-padded seat
          Load lights
          Safety equipment to meet OSHA standards
          Maximum 4-ft. wheelbase, 5-ft. overall length (excluding forks),
            minimum 14″ ground clearance

Bids will be opened in our corporate offices in Morganton at 10:00 A.M. on February 11, 1988. Purchase orders will be issued by February 25, 1988. We retain the right to accept or reject any or all bids.

Please submit your bid in a sealed envelope marked "Forklift Truck Bid, 2/11/88." Your prompt reply will be appreciated.

Sincerely,

Joseph R. Balognetta
Purchasing Agent

which of their models best fit Eon's requirements. Finally, he carefully analyzes the bid history in an attempt to determine a pattern in the bidding and the awarding of previous bids.

Al's initial reaction to his examination of the bid history is that the low bidder was awarded the bid in a majority of the cases, but it also appears that few bids were awarded to suppliers who bid equipment that did not meet the buyers' specifications. Also, Al identifies bid numbers 4, 8, and 15 as bids to Drexton Furniture while Joe Balognetta was purchasing agent there, and bid numbers 2, 9, and 19 as bids to Bromont Furniture, one of Eon's direct competitors in the Morganton area. Again, it appears that the bidding was quite competitive, with low bidders being favored substantially as long as they met the buyers' specifications.

THE CONFLICT ARISES

As Al continues to review the bid history, he is troubled by the apparent importance of being the low bidder. Recently, Superior's general manager had told Al in no uncertain terms that he needed to improve his gross margin performance. The general manager had pointed out that Al's gross margin had fallen a full percentage point below the target gross margin of 20 percent of sales. The general manager suggested that Al takes steps to boost the unit margins. At the same time, however, the general manager had complimented Al on his market share performance and urged him to continue to build the share through aggressive bidding.

Gus Jennings's earlier comments also disturbed Al somewhat. He knew that Gus was right about the importance of getting Eon's initial order. If Superior lost this order for four units, it might also lose the entire account, which would play havoc with Superior's market share performance. Finally, Al was a bit worried about a trade journal article he had read concerning violations of the Robinson-Patman Act in industrial sales, especially since he had recently bid to at least one of Eon's direct competitors.

PREPARING THE BID

With these thoughts in mind, Al Hardy reaches for his Superlift Price List (Exhibit 4) and a clean sheet of paper. Before making any calculations, however, Al knows he must first devise a strategy that will include which unit Superior will bid (the Superlift 950 or the Superlift 1100), the optional equipment to include in the bid, and the actual price to bid. This strategy depends on Al's objectives, his estimate of which units the competition may be expected to bid, the price the competition may bid, and Al's assessment of the odds of getting the bid for each of the possible alternative bid strategies available.

EXHIBIT 2   Forklift Truck Equipment Specification Comparison

| | Supplier and Model | | | | | |
| Equipment/ Specification Characteristic | Superior Equipment Company Charlotte, NC | | Excell Industrial Distributors Asheville, NC | | Star, Inc. Greensboro, NC | |
	Superlift 950	Superlift 1100	Hightopper I	Hightopper II	Liftstar GT	Liftstar XL
Wheelbase	48"	48"	47"	49"	48"	48"
Overall length (excluding forks)	60"	60"	60"	63"	60"	60"
Ground clearance	14"	14"	12"	14"	14"	15"
Weight	2,100 lbs.	2,500 lbs.	2,000 lbs.	2,200 lbs.	2,100 lbs.	2,500 lbs.
Engine size	18 hp. std., 22 hp. optional	22 hp. std., 26 hp. optional	16 hp. std., 18 hp. optional	19 hp. std., no optional engine	20 hp. std., 24 hp. optional	25 hp. std., 28 hp. optional
Lift height	90"	96"	88"	96"	96"	102"
Lift capacity	950 lbs.	1,100 lbs.	900 lbs.	1,050 lbs.	1,000 lbs.	1,200 lbs.
Forks	36" adjustable	36" adjustable	34" fixed	34" adjustable	36" adjustable	36" adjustable
Tires	Rubber balloon std., solid rubber opt.	Solid rubber std.	Synthetic balloon std., solid synthetic opt.	Solid synthetic std.	Solid rubber std.	Solid rubber std.

Seat	24" cotton pad std., full-width foam opt.	Full-width cotton std., full-width foam opt.	24" metal std., 24" foam opt.	26" cotton std., 26" foam opt.	Full-width foam std.	Full-width foam std.
Finish	Four-coat acrylic	Four-coat acrylic	Two-coat enamel	Two-coat enamel	Three-coat acrylic	Four-coat acrylic
OSHA requirements	Meets	Exceeds	Meets	Meets	Meets	Exceeds
Warranty	12 months, parts and labor	12 months, parts and labor	12 months, parts, 6 months labor	12 months, parts, 6 months labor	12 months, parts and labor	12 months, parts and labor
Seat belts	Standard	Standard	N/A	N/A	Optional	Standard
Tool kit	Standard	Standard	N/A	N/A	Optional	Standard
HD elect. system	Optional	Optional	N/A	Optional	Optional	Standard
Power steering	Optional	Optional	N/A	Optional	Standard	Standard
Load lights	Optional	Optional	Optional	Optional	Standard	Standard
2-way radio	Optional	Optional	Optional	Optional	Optional	Standard
Extended lift ht.	N/A	Optional	N/A	N/A	102" optional	N/A
HD front safety shield	N/A	Optional	N/A	N/A	Standard	Standard

Note: All equipment shown as standard is included in unit base price. Equipment shown as optional is optional at extra cost. N/A indicates not available.

EXHIBIT 3   Bid History: Last 20 Similar Situation Bids

Bid #	Superior Bid Model	Meet Specs?	Price	Excell Bid Model	Meet Specs?	Price	Star Bid Model	Meet Specs?	Price	Buyer Awarded Bid To:
1	SL950	No	$29,000	Hightopper I	No	$28,500	Liftstar GT	Yes	$31,100	Excell
2	SL1100	Yes	31,500	Hightopper II	Yes	30,900	Liftstar GT	No	31,200	Excell
3	SL1100	Yes	31,800	Hightopper II	No	29,800	Liftstar XL	Yes	32,900	Excell
4	SL950	Yes	29,500	Hightopper II	Yes	29,800	Liftstar GT	Yes	31,100	Superior
5	SL1100	Yes	31,750	Hightopper II	No	30,900	Liftstar GT	Yes	31,950	Superior
6	SL1100	Yes	31,100	Hightopper II	Yes	30,700	Liftstar GT	No	30,400	Star
7	SL950	No	28,600	Hightopper I	No	28,750	Liftstar GT	Yes	31,100	Superior
8	SL1100	Yes	30,300	Hightopper II	Yes	30,400	Liftstar XL	Yes	33,700	Superior
9	SL1100	Yes	31,400	Hightopper II	Yes	29,750	Liftstar GT	Yes	31,100	Excell
10	SL950	No	30,100	Hightopper I	No	28,900	Liftstar GT	Yes	30,900	Star
11	SL1100	Yes	31,900	Hightopper II	Yes	30,900	Liftstar XL	Yes	33,200	Superior
12	SL950	Yes	29,200	Hightopper I	Yes	28,750	Liftstar GT	Yes	30,400	Excell
13	SL1100	Yes	31,100	Hightopper II	Yes	31,000	Liftstar GT	Yes	30,900	Star
14	SL950	Yes	29,900	Hightopper II	Yes	30,100	Liftstar GT	Yes	31,100	Superior
15	SL1100	Yes	31,100	Hightopper II	No	30,200	Liftstar GT	Yes	30,900	Star
16	SL1100	No	30,500	Hightopper II	Yes	30,700	Liftstar XL	Yes	32,800	Excell
17	SL1100	Yes	30,600	Hightopper II	Yes	30,900	Liftstar GT	Yes	31,950	Superior
18	SL1100	Yes	31,100	Hightopper II	Yes	30,700	Liftstar GT	Yes	30,400	Star
19	SL950	Yes	29,500	Hightopper I	Yes	28,400	Liftstar GT	Yes	30,800	Excell
20	SL1100	Yes	30,800	Hightopper II	Yes	30,900	Liftstar GT	Yes	31,100	Star

Note: All bid prices adjusted to FOB destination basis.

EXHIBIT 4   Price List for Superior Equipment Company 1988 Model Forklift Trucks

Item	Dealer Net (Cost to Superior, Delivered in Charlotte, NC)	List Price
Superlift 950 (SL950) with all standard equipment, FOB Charlotte, NC	$22,190	$29,587
Optional equipment for SL950:		
Solid rubber tires	800	1,100
Foam-padded F/W seat	120	160
22-horsepower engine	1,200	1,600
Heavy-duty electrical system	500	675
Power steering	1,100	1,475
Load lights	150	200
Two-way radio	380	510
Superlift 1100 (SL1100) with all standard equipment, FOB Charlotte, NC	25,027	33,370
Optional equipment for SL1100:		
Foam-padded F/W seat	100	135
26-horsepower engine	1,600	2,135
Heavy-duty electrical system	600	800
Power steering	1,200	1,600
Load lights	150	200
Two-way radio	380	510
102″ extended load height	600	800
HD front safety shield	210	280

Note: Estimated freight/delivery charges for delivery to Morganton, NC, are $180 per unit for SL950s and $200 per unit for SL1100s.

DISCUSSION QUESTIONS

1. Using the data available, develop a bid strategy for Al Hardy and Superior Equipment Company. Include an analysis of the bid history, the possible and probable bids of competitors, the alternative approaches available to Superior, and the model, equipment, and price that Al Hardy should bid. Explain in detail why you chose your strategy.

2. Prepare a bid letter to Eon Furniture in response to the bid request.

Glossary

● ●

acquisition   Situation where one business marketing firm acquires another for the purpose of entering a new market, strengthening its position in an existing market, or diversifying

activity report   Report used by marketing manager to evaluate activities performed by subordinates

advertising   Any paid form of nonpersonal presentation and promotion of ideas, goods, or services by an identified sponsor

advertising medium   Means of conveying advertising to target market business customers and prospects such as trade journals, direct mail, directories, and the like

advertising message   Theme or appeal in an advertisement

alliance linkage   Factors that hold strategic alliances together such as those of a technical, logistical, informational, social, economic, or legal nature

backorder   Situation in which only part of a shipment is made at time of purchase order (the remainder is "backordered")

basic screening   Objective and orderly assessment of new product or service ideas so as not to discard good ideas or spend inordinate amounts of time, effort, and money on ideas with little chance of commercial success

benefit segmentation   Segmentation of business markets based on similar benefits of a product or service as perceived by customers and prospects

bidding   Process in which an organization sends requests to prospective suppliers to provide bids, either sealed or open, on requested products or services

break-even analysis   Determining what volume of sales would have to take place at a given price for a product or service to break even given fixed and variable costs

budget   Plan for coordinating business marketing income and expenses that may be used for control purposes

business/commercial organization   Private business or commercial organization that buys goods and services to use either directly or indirectly in the operation of business

business marketing   The marketing of goods and services to organizational customers and prospects as opposed to marketing to individuals and households

business marketing management   The analysis, planning, implementation, and control of programs designed to create, build, and maintain mutually beneficial exchanges and relationships with target markets for the purpose of achieving organizational objectives

business marketing system   Total marketing system composed of producers of business goods and services, suppliers to these producers, customers for business goods and services, and channels linking producers and customers

business network   Situation where a buyer and its suppliers are tied together electronically so as to increase communication and facilitate more effective buying and marketing

business product   Product or good marketed to and used by organizational customers and prospects (as opposed to individuals and households), such as heavy and light equipment, supplies, component parts, and raw and processed materials

business service   Service used by organizational customers and prospects (as opposed to individuals and households), such as transportation services, consulting services, maintenance services, etc.

business supplies salesperson   Salesperson in business marketing who sells relatively standardized products and services such as component parts, supplies, and so forth

business-to-business marketing   Synonymous term for business marketing

buygrid analytical framework   Model of the organizational buying process that illustrates a typology of buying situations

buying center   People in a buying organization who interact at a particular stage of the buying process are considered to comprise a buying center

buying influence   People in a buying organization who in one way or another actually influence what is or is not purchased

buying motivation   Purchasing motives of buying influences involved in the buying process of an organization

buying process segmentation   Segmentation of business markets based on similar buying processes of customers and prospects

catalog   Complete or comprehensive printed information about a product, designed for demonstration and/or as a reference work

Census of Manufactures   Census published by the U.S. Department of Commerce providing detailed information on all U.S. manufacturing

channel control   Ability of one channel member to influence the marketing behavior of other channel members; also called *channel power*

channel intermediary   Organization operating in channel of distribution in business marketing such as an industrial distributor or a manufacturers' representative

channel of distribution   Group of interrelated intermediaries directing products or services to customers; also called *marketing channel*

channel strategy   Process of determining channel objectives, choosing channel arrangements to be used, deciding to use or not use intermediaries, determining types and numbers of intermediaries, and implementing tactical programs

chief marketing officer   Person in the organization responsible for the overall marketing process taking place in an effective and economical manner; may hold title of vice president of marketing, marketing director, or marketing manager

combination house distributor   Type of industrial distributor that carries consumer products as well as business products; a combination of distributor and wholesaler

commission   Remittance paid to a manufacturers' representative or company salesperson for the sale of a business product or service

compensation   Remuneration paid to business salespeople for sales; may be in form of salary, commission, bonus, or combination

competitive force   Force affecting the business marketing system brought about by a company's competitors such as the introduction of a new product or service

competitive pricing   Pricing determined by following or beating prices of competitors

control   Monitoring of a plan, such as a marketing or product plan, to determine if it is on track in terms of achieving objectives

control and evaluation mechanism   Tool used by marketing manager in control and evaluation of strategies, programs, or products, such as a report, schedule, budget, and the like

control chart   Chart used for repetitive marketing activities to detect when an activity deviates from its standards to the point where it requires investigation

control level   Different levels of marketing activity are subject to different control levels, such as control of overall marketing, of specific programs, or of marketing subordinates

corporate advertising   Advertising that stresses the company doing the advertising rather than the product or service involved

correlation and regression technique   Statistical technique used to determine the degree of relationship between a dependent variable and one or more independent variables

cost analysis   Analysis of marketing costs to determine which areas are functioning properly and which require attention

cross distribution   Alliance between a business marketing firm and a distribution intermediary such as a common carrier, public warehouse, and the like

cross licensing   Agreement whereby a business marketing firm gives another company the right to produce or market its product or service

customized product/service   Business product or service produced to the exact specifications of an organizational customer or prospect

database source   Private company providing database services on a fee basis particular to business markets such as Dun & Bradstreet

data collection   Step in the marketing research process that involves collecting primary or secondary data

decider   A buying influence who actually says yes or no to a contemplated purchase

demographic segmentation   Segmentation of business markets based on such demographic characteristics as sales volume, number of employees, SIC code, value added, value of shipments, and the like

derived demand   A business customer's demand for goods and services is derived from the demand of its customers for the products or services it produces

direct channel   Channel of distribution containing no independent intermediaries; direct from producer to customer

direct derivation technique   Statistical technique used to determine demand for business products and services by computing the amount of a product or service used directly or indirectly in the production of another product or service

direct mail   Printed or processed form directed to selected individuals by controlled distribution

discount   Reduction made from regular or list price for different classes of buyers or purchases, such as a quantity discount or a trade discount

diversification strategy   A strategy that emphasizes the marketing of new products and services into new markets

domestic market   A market within a particular country, such as the U.S. market as opposed to a global or multinational market

ecological force   Force affecting the business marketing system brought about by concerns about the natural environment such as air, water, and solid waste pollution, effects on the ozone layer, concerns about diminishing natural resources, and the like

economic force   Force affecting the business marketing system brought about by changes in the national and/or world economy such as recession, inflation, unemployment, and the like

economic order quantity (EOQ)   Purchasing concept that balances the cost of inventory against the cost of ordering to determine the most optimum purchase order size

electronic data interchange (EDI)   Electronic transmission of data between buyer and seller in the purchasing of goods and services in business markets

environmental force Any force affecting the business marketing manager that is not controllable by that manager and that is of an economic, technological, political and/or legal, competitive, global, or ecological nature

European Economic Community (EEC) Alliance of twelve European countries to form an economic community to better compete in world markets; composed of Belgium, Denmark, France, Germany, Greece, Ireland, Italy, Luxembourg, the Netherlands, Portugal, Spain, and the United Kingdom

evaluation Diagnostic activities concerned with reviewing results of a plan, such as a marketing or product plan, to determine how well or how poorly objectives are being achieved

executive salesperson Salesperson in business marketing who sells business products and services to executives of organizational customers and prospects

export A business product or service marketed to foreign countries

external marketing intelligence Useful marketing information obtained from sources outside the marketing company

facilitating force Any force affecting the business marketing manager brought about by organizations that are not directly involved in the business marketing system but that become involved in some capacity, such as financial institutions, public warehouses, and the like

field test Operation of a business product under actual conditions to test product performance and customer reactions before commercialization

focus group A small panel of people who spend a few hours with a skilled interviewer to discuss a product, service, organization, or some other marketing entity

foreign trade organization (FTO) Organization formerly used by Eastern European countries to buy business goods and services for organizational customers on a centralized basis; organizational customers can now purchase themselves

gatekeeper A buying influence who controls information and/or access to decision makers

generalist distributor Industrial distributor that stocks a wide variety of business products and has no area of specialization

geographic demand Demand based on the geographic location of business customers and prospects

geographic segmentation Segmentation of business markets based on geographic characteristics such as region of the country, state, county, ZIP code, census tract, or region of the world

global competition Competition faced by U.S. business marketing firms that is multinational in nature; competition from Asian, European, North American business marketing companies

global force Force affecting the business marketing system brought about by multinational changes of an economic, technological, political and/or legal, competitive, global, or ecological nature

global market A market for a business product or service that is multinational or global, as opposed to domestic, in nature

global marketing Marketing on a multinational or global basis as opposed to domestic marketing

global marketing strategy Marketing strategy designed to attract and retain organizational customers in multinational or global markets as opposed to domestic markets

global partner Situation where a business marketing company forms a partnership with a company or companies in another country for the purpose of being more competitive worldwide

governmental organization Federal, state, or local organization buying business goods and services to use either directly or indirectly in its operation

idea generation Process of generating a steady and reliable flow of new product or service ideas to be considered for possible adoption

import A business product or service purchased by a domestic organizational customer from a foreign source

indirect channel Channel of distribution containing independent intermediaries such as industrial distributors or manufacturers' representatives

industrial directory Directory used in business marketing as a reference for organizational buyers, such as the *Thomas Register*; also called *buyer's guide*

industrial distributor Channel intermediary that is independently owned and managed and that buys, stocks, and sells business products and services

industrial marketing Traditional term for business marketing but today seen as outdated because of its emphasis primarily on manufacturing customers and prospects

informational report Report submitted by subordinate to marketing manager to inform on the status of an activity or circumstance

initiator A buying influence who first recognizes or anticipates a problem that may be solved by buying a product or service

input–output Concept based on the premise that the sales or outputs of one industry are the purchases or inputs of other industries

inside salesperson Salesperson in business marketing who sells via telephone as opposed to field selling

institutional organization Organizational customer or prospect that is not truly of a private commercial or governmental nature, such as a church, some schools and colleges, some hospitals, and other such nonprofit organizations, buying business goods and services to use directly or indirectly in its operation

internal marketing intelligence Useful marketing information obtained from sources within the marketing company such as from purchasing, production, accounting, and the like

international trading company Channel intermediary that buys from many manufacturers, consolidates the products, and then distributes them to global markets

inventory control Physical distribution activity that involves the determination of inventory sizes in warehouses to provide customers with what is needed at the time it is needed and in the right quantity

inventory management Efforts by buying organizations to reduce warehouse inventory levels, to better estimate production needs, and to increase the frequencies of deliveries

joint demand Situation where the demand for one business product or service depends on it being used in conjunction with another business product or service

joint venture Interorganizational agreements between business marketing firms, both domestic and global, to share costs and expertise, facilitate distribution, and decrease competition

judgmental technique Technique used to determine demand for business products and services based on the premise that various groups of people possess sufficient knowledge so that a composite of their views provides an estimate of demand

just-in-time (JIT) Purchasing concept where the customer expects the supplier to deliver the exact quantity of goods needed at the precise time needed

key buying influence A buying influence who for one reason or another is able to sway other buying influences to his or her way of thinking

learning/experience curve Concept that holds that production costs decline as output rises because workers and machines learn with time and experience to produce more efficiently

leasing Concept of leasing or renting business products to organizational customers as opposed to selling them the same products

legal/political force Force affecting the business marketing system brought about by legal or political changes such as legislation, regulations, court rulings, and the like

licensing Agreement whereby a business marketing company gives the right to produce its product to other companies, which may be domestic or global in nature

life cycle costing Method of calculating costs over the life span of a business product or service to reflect changes in fixed and variable costs over time

list price Price printed on the marketing company's price list

macro level force Force other than a competitive force that affects the environment of a business marketing company as well as the business marketing system

macrosegmentation Segmentation between or among organizations such as geographic location or number of employees

mailing list List of prospects to whom business advertisements will be sent via direct mail

mailing list company Private company providing mailing lists and other related information relative to business markets on a fee basis

make-or-buy Situation where the buying organization has the ability to make the required products in-house or to purchase them from outside sources

manufacturers' representative Channel intermediary that is independently owned and operated and represents one or more manufacturers on a commission basis; also called *manufacturers' agent* or *agency*

market development strategy A strategy that emphasizes the marketing of existing products or services into new markets

market forecast Estimate of the sales of a product or service that all firms in an industry expect in a specified period of time under all the firms' respective marketing plans

marketing audit Comprehensive, systematic, independent, and periodic examination of a company's marketing performance to determine problems and opportunities, followed by recommendations for improvement

marketing information system (MIS) A continuous information-gathering system that provides information for a company's formal marketing plan and becomes an integral part of the firm's overall marketing strategy

marketing intelligence Any useful information that may be used by the marketing manager to enhance the competitive position of his or her company

marketing mix The combination of the four major components of marketing (product, distribution, promotion, and price) used as decision variables

marketing plan The central written instrument that directs and controls all marketing effort

marketing planning   The process of analyzing marketing opportunities, researching and selecting target markets, designing marketing strategies, planning marketing programs, and controlling the marketing effort

marketing objective   A goal to be achieved by a marketing strategy and marketing plan

marketing research   The systematic gathering, recording, and analyzing of data about problems relating to the marketing of goods and services

marketing research department   That department in a business marketing firm responsible for undertaking marketing research activities for that firm

marketing researcher   A person educated in and technically competent in the areas of marketing research who conducts research activities for the marketing firm

marketing research process   The process of conducting marketing research; process that involves the steps of defining the research problem, developing the hypothesis, collecting the data, interpreting the findings, and reporting the research findings

market penetration strategy   A strategy that emphasizes the marketing of existing products or services into existing markets

market potential   Maximum sales of a product or service that all firms in an industry expect in a specified period of time under all the firms' respective marketing plans

market segmentation   The process of breaking down a total heterogeneous market into more manageable homogeneous parts or segments

market segmentation approach   Approach used to segment business markets such as the two-stage process of macrosegmentation and microsegmentation

market segmentation base   Criterion used to segment business markets, such as segmenting on the basis of geographic, demographic, organizational purchasing, buyer personal, or supplier/customer characteristics

market segmentation process   The process used to segment business markets

market share pricing   Pricing to maintain, increase, or decrease a specified market share

materials handling   Physical distribution activity that involves the physical movement of inventory in warehouses or elsewhere in the physical distribution system

materials management   Functional area that combines purchasing, transportation, inventory control, receiving, and, in some cases, production control

materials requirements planning (MRP)   Concept where the purchasing firm estimates future sales, schedules its production based on these estimates, and then orders required products or services compatible with the production schedule to better control inventory levels

measurement technique   Technique used in marketing research to measure results such as semantic differential, Likert scaling, multidimensional scaling, and the like

merger   Absorption by one business marketing company of one or more other companies

microsegmentation   Segmenting within the organization as opposed to segmenting between organizations

missionary salesperson   Salesperson in business marketing who works with customers and channel intermediaries in a consulting or advisory capacity to indirectly increase sales

multiple buying influences   Situation where more than one person influences the purchasing of a product or service in an organization

national account   Large influential customer that is sold direct by a national account manager as opposed to a field salesperson; also called *house account* or *major account*

negotiated pricing Process where price is determined by buyer and seller working out a mutually acceptable agreement on the price of a business product or service

negotiation Process of purchasing goods and services where buyer and seller confer to arrive at a purchasing agreement acceptable to both

nested segmentation Segmentation approach that examines five criteria in a nested manner: demographics, operating variables, customer purchasing approaches, situational factors, and personal characteristics

net price Price determined by subtracting appropriate discounts from list price

new product/service Product or service being marketed for the first time to present customers or prospects who are also buying for the first time

new product/service planning process Process of developing a new product or service that begins with an idea generation stage and culminates with a commercialization stage

nondisclosure rule Rule that bars information on government SIC sources that could disclose the identity of a specific company

North America Free Trade Pact Pact that would eliminate barriers to the flow of goods and services between Canada, Mexico, and the United States

open marketing system Viewing the business marketing firm as a set of interdependent parts or subsystems that interact with other organizations in the business marketing system and are influenced by forces in the environment

opportunistic alliance Alliance formed when two business marketing firms see an opportunity to gain an immediate, though perhaps temporary, competitive advantage through their joint efforts

order cycle time Time between the placing of an order by a customer and delivery to that customer

order processing Physical distribution activity that involves collecting, checking, and transmitting sales order information

organizational buying behavior Study of the purchasing of products and services by organizations that has resulted in the development of a number of models

organizational buying process The relatively standardized process that describes how organizations purchase needed products and/or services

original equipment manufacturer (OEM) An organizational customer or prospect that buys a business good or service to incorporate into the product or service it sells to its customers

outside research organization Private company conducting marketing research activities on a fee basis for a business marketing company

partnering relationship Situation where a business marketing company forms a partnership with a competitor, customer, supplier, or channel intermediary

partnership status Purchasing situation in business markets where buyer and seller form a partnership agreement as opposed to buying on a transaction-to-transaction basis

performance appraisal Appraisal of the performance of marketing personnel by one or more superiors, such as a marketing manager appraising the performance of a product manager

personal selling Oral presentation in a conversation with one or more prospective purchasers for the purpose of making sales

physical distribution All activities involved in the physical movement of business products to organizational customers

physical distribution costs Costs involved in physical distribution activities, such as transportation, warehousing, inventory carrying costs, and the like

physical distribution management The management of the physical distribution function in business marketing which includes decisions made in transportation, field warehousing, inventory control, materials handling, protective packaging, and order processing

physical distribution process Process of physically moving goods to a customer that begins when the order is placed and concludes when ordered products are delivered

price Value of a business product or service expressed in monetary terms and acceptable to both buyer and seller

pricing Process of determining the price of a business product or service in a target market

primary data Data observed or recorded directly from respondents in the marketing research process

private business directory Directory published by a private company that provides SIC-based information on individual firms, such as *Standard & Poor's Register of Corporations*

product Everything that is considered inclusive of the satisfactions and utilities that the buyer obtains in the purchase; something that provides want-satisfying utility

product advertising Advertising that stresses the product involved rather than the company doing the advertising

product demand Demand based on the characteristics of the particular product or service involved

product development strategy A strategy that emphasizes the marketing of new products or services in existing markets

product failure A product or service that fails to achieve company objectives and is thus removed from the market

product feature segmentation Segmentation of business markets based on the features or attributes of the product or service involved

product management Management of the product and service components of the marketing mix

product planning Planning of activities required to develop and maintain the product and service components of the marketing mix

product strategy Process of determining product or service product policies, establishing objectives, determining types of products or services to be marketed, and establishing tactical programs to implement the strategy

product support Services that accompany a business product, such as warranties, service contracts, spare parts, replacement parts, instructions, and the like

progress report Short descriptive report prepared at dates of important events by marketing personnel responsible for completing an activity

promotional strategy Process of integrating personal selling, advertising, and sales promotion into one overall promotion package that is then integrated into the total marketing strategy

protective packaging Physical distribution activity that involves providing protection to business products during storage and transportation

publicity Anything that appears in print or broadcast media about a company

public relations   Activities designed to create goodwill among a company's publics, which may include employees, customers, unions, governmental agencies, communities, and other such entities

purchaser   A buying influence who processes the paperwork and places the order

purchasing   The process by which organizations buy required products and services

purchasing department   The department in an organization with the primary responsibility for buying required products and services

purchasing professional   Term given to anyone in the buying organization with primary responsibility for purchasing required products and services; may hold such titles as buyer, purchasing agent, purchasing manager, procurement manager, materials management manager, and the like

purchasing strategy   Strategy employed by an organization in its buying of required products or services, such as assured supply, cost reduction, supply support, environmental changes, and competitive edge strategies

quality partner   Term applied to the highest level of partner in alliances in business markets

research and development consortium   Alliance formed by two or more business marketing firms to join together to conduct research and development activities at the industry level

research hypothesis   Step in the marketing research process that is either a reasonable guess or an assumption about the problem defined; the research findings are then used to accept or reject the hypothesis

reseller organization   An organization that buys a business good or service solely for the purpose of resale, such as a retailer, a wholesaler, or a distributor

sales analysis   Analysis of sales to determine which areas are functioning properly and which require attention

sales engineer   Salesperson in business marketing who sells highly technical products and services to technically oriented buying influences; may often be an engineer who sells

sales forecast   Estimate of the sales of a product or service that an individual firm expects in a specified period of time under a given marketing plan

sales management   Management of the outside or field sales force

sales potential   Maximum sales of a product or service available to an individual firm within a specified period of time

sales promotion   Short-term incentives to encourage the purchase or sale of a business product or service

sales team   Selling in business marketing by a team of company personnel as opposed to a single salesperson; often used to counter committee buying by organizational customers

secondary data   Data compiled inside or outside the organization for purposes other than for current research but that are applicable to the research problem

selling costs   Costs involved in the personal selling area of business marketing; includes compensation, travel, entertainment, training, recruiting, and the like

service   Application of human and/or mechanical efforts to organizational customers or prospects, such as consulting, computer, and financial services

service alliance   Alliance formed when two or more business marketing firms with a similar need join together to create a new entity to fill the common need

situation analysis A sound analysis of the present marketing situation, both internal and external, that becomes the first step in the marketing planning process

specialist distributor Industrial distributor specializing in business products where one product category, such as cutting tools or fasteners, accounts for 50 percent or more of sales

specialty advertising Advertising and sales promotion medium that utilizes useful articles, such as calendars, specialties, and business gifts, to carry the advertiser's name, address, and advertising message to the target market audience

specifications Detailed, precise presentation of those characteristics desired in a particular business product or service

stakeholder alliance Alliance formed between two or more business marketing firms involved at different stages of the value-creation chain, such as between a manufacturer and customer, supplier, channel intermediary, or the like

Standard Industrial Classification (SIC) code Numerical code assigned to an industry or product under the Standard Industrial Classification system

Standard Industrial Classification expansion Expansion of the basic four-digit SIC code by many of the private sources to five-, six-, seven-, and eight-digit codes

Standard Industrial Classification Manual Manual published by the Office of Management and Budget that provides the basic four-digit SIC codes

Standard Industrial Classification (SIC) system A uniform numbering system for classifying establishments in the United States according to their economic activity; developed by the Office of Management and Budget

standardized product/service Business product or service produced to general specifications acceptable to many different organizational customers or prospects

state/county business directory Industrial directory published within an individual state or county providing information on organizations within that state or county, such as the *New Jersey Directory of Manufacturers*

stocking representative Manufacturers' representative that stocks inventory for its principal and ships from that inventory

stockout No shipment is made at the time of purchase order because of lack of ordered items in inventory

strategic alliance Cooperative interorganizational agreement between business marketing firms of a strategic or long-term rather than a short-term transactional nature

strategic alliance control Control mechanism necessary for an interorganizational relationship to succeed over time

strategic global alliance Partnership between a U.S. business marketing company and a company in another country to jointly market goods and services

strategic marketing planning The managerial process of developing and maintaining a strategic fit between the organization and its marketing opportunities

strategy An organized statement of broad tasks and/or areas of activity necessary to achieve an objective

substitute product Product that is seen by a business customer or prospect as a substitute for another product even though it does not meet the same specifications, such as substituting asphalt for concrete in paving a highway

survey technique Technique used to determine demand for business products or services based on answers supplied by respondents to some form of questionnaire

tactical action program A program designed to contain all the individual activities necessary to put a strategy into action

target market   An aggregate of organizations that presently purchase or potentially can purchase a product or service for direct or indirect use in their operations; characterized by a need for the product or service, the ability to purchase, the willingness to purchase, and the authority to buy

target return pricing   Pricing determined by finding the price that will yield a desired rate of return on investment; employed to produce and distribute the product or service involved

technological force   Force affecting the business marketing system brought about by technological changes, such as advances in electronics, robotics, and material sciences

telemarketing   Marketing communication that uses telecommunication technology and trained personnel to conduct planned marketing activities, such as selling, directed at targeted organizational customers and prospects

total integrated system of physical distribution   Perspective of viewing the physical distribution areas, such as warehousing and transportation, not as separate activities but as interrelated in a total integrated system

trade publication   Specialized publication used in business marketing to communicate with target market buying influences; may be industry related or job/occupation related; also called *trade journal*

trade show   Show, exposition, convention, or mart that permits business marketing firms to exhibit products and services to potential buyers

transportation   Physical distribution activity that involves the selection of modes of transportation to be used in shipping products to organizational customers

trend analysis technique   Statistical technique used to determine demand for business products or services that examines historical data to detect trends and patterns that may then be projected into the future

turnover   Term used to refer to salespeople either leaving an employer of their accord or being terminated for lack of productivity or some other reason

user   A buying influence who ultimately uses the product or service purchased

value analysis   Analysis performed by a purchasing organization to compare the function performed by a purchased item with its cost to find a lower-cost alternative

value to the customer   Perceived value of a business product or service to a customer or prospect that includes perceived benefits compared to price

variance analysis   Process of identifying those factors that cause differences between actual costs or sales and targeted costs or sales

vendor analysis   Analysis performed by a purchasing organization to evaluate performances of its suppliers

volatility of derived demand   Situation where slight changes in the demand for consumer goods and services bring about large fluctuations in the demand for the business products and services required to produce the consumer goods and services

warehousing   Physical distribution activity that involves determining to use field warehouses, deciding where to locate those warehouses, and deciding on the size of the warehouses

Author Index

Subject Index